American Government and Politics Today

Lessons 1-60 Microsoft Word 2003

Texas Edition

SCHMIDT/SHELLEY/BARDES/MAXWELL

Australia • Brazil • Japan • Korea • Mexico • Singapore • Spain • United Kingdom • United States

CENGAGE
Learning™

American Government and Politics Today
Texas Edition
13th Edition

Vanhuss / Forde / Woo / Hefferin

Executive Editor:
Michele Baird

Maureen Staudt

Michael Stranz

Project Development Editor:
Linda de Stefano

Senior Marketing Coordinators:
Sara Mercurio

Lindsay Shapiro

Production/Manufacturing Manager:
Donna M. Brown

PreMedia Services Supervisor:
Rebecca A. Walker

Rights & Permissions Specialist:
Kalina Hintz

Cover Image:
Getty Images*

For product information and technology assistance, contact us at
Cengage Learning Customer & Sales Support, 1-800-354-9706
For permission to use material from this text or product,
submit all requests online at **cengage.com/permissions**
Further permissions questions can be emailed to
permissionrequest@cengage.com

ISBN-13: 978-0-495-45866-1

ISBN-10: 0-495-45866-X

Cengage Learning
5191 Natorp Boulevard
Mason, Ohio 45040
USA

Cengage Learning is a leading provider of customized learning solutions with office locations around the globe, including Singapore, the United Kingdom, Australia, Mexico, Brazil, and Japan. Locate your local office at:
international.cengage.com/region

Cengage Learning products are represented in Canada by Nelson Education, Ltd.

For your lifelong learning solutions, visit **custom.cengage.com**

Visit our corporate website at **cengage.com**

Printed in the United States of America

Contents in Brief

Contents

CHAPTER 3 | Federalism 77

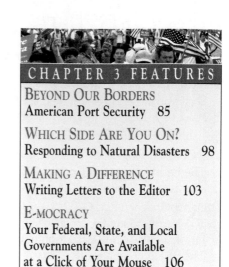

PART TWO
CIVIL RIGHTS AND CIVIL LIBERTIES

CHAPTER 4 | Civil Liberties 107

CHAPTER 4 FEATURES

CHAPTER 5 | Civil Rights 145

PART THREE
PEOPLE AND POLITICS

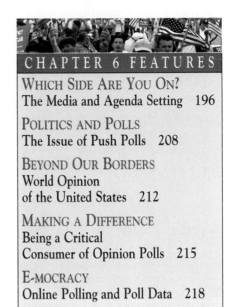

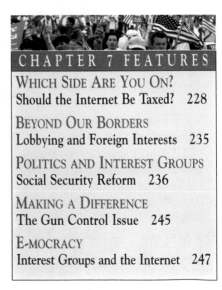

CHAPTER 8 | Political Parties 249

CHAPTER 8 FEATURES

CHAPTER 9 | Campaigns, Nominations, and Elections 285

CHAPTER 9 FEATURES

PART FOUR
POLITICAL INSTITUTIONS

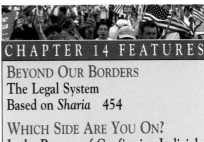

KEY TERMS ■ CHAPTER SUMMARY ■ SELECTED PRINT AND MEDIA RESOURCES

PART FIVE
PUBLIC POLICY

CHAPTER 15 | Domestic Policy   481

CHAPTER 15 FEATURES

CHAPTER 16 | Economic Policy 515

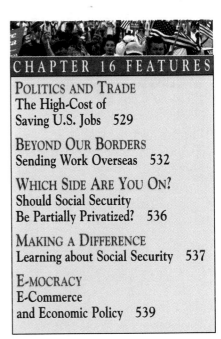

CHAPTER 17 | Foreign Policy 541

PART SIX
TEXAS POLITICS

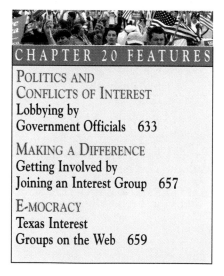

CHAPTER 21 | Political Parties in Texas 661

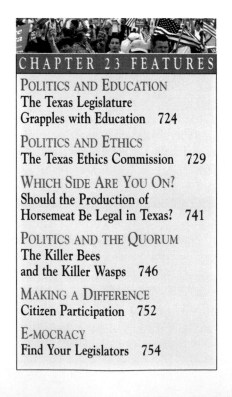

CHAPTER 24 | The Texas Executive Branch 755

CHAPTER 24 FEATURES

BEYOND OUR BORDERS
Should Texas Recognize Identity
Cards Issued by Mexico? 764

POLITICS AND INTEREST GROUPS
Governor Perry and the
Enterprise Fund: Boon to
Texas or Corporate Welfare? 769

POLITICS AND
GUBERNATORIAL INFLUENCE
Regulating the
Insurance Industry 770

POLITICS AND
ADMINISTRATIVE LAW
The Department of Agriculture
and the Pesticide Issue 775

MAKING A DIFFERENCE
Become a Smart Consumer
of State Services 784

E-MOCRACY
Contacting the Governor 786

CHAPTER 25 | The Texas Judiciary, Law, and Due Process 787

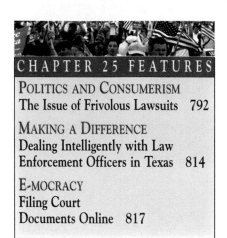

CHAPTER 25 FEATURES

POLITICS AND CONSUMERISM
The Issue of Frivolous Lawsuits 792

MAKING A DIFFERENCE
Dealing Intelligently with Law
Enforcement Officers in Texas 814

E-MOCRACY
Filing Court
Documents Online 817

We are pleased to present the 2007–2008 Texas edition of *American Government and Politics Today*. This text, which is a comprehensive survey of American and Texas politics, uses the theme of participation to actively engage students in the course and in the American political system. As with our other books, this Texas edition of *American Government and Politics Today* contains some of the most current revisions available for the American government course. Many of these changes were made necessary by the ongoing war on terrorism both at home and abroad, the continuing nation-building effort in Iraq, and the increasingly tense and partisan nature of the domestic political landscape.

Many events have affected the course of American politics and the shape of our nation's government since the last edition of this text. Hurricane Katrina spread misery throughout the Gulf Coast, and tens of thousands of Americans displaced by the catastrophic storm have yet to return home. The government's role in such disasters has been debated and scrutinized ever since. Americans witnessed a storm of a different kind when interest groups and politicians clashed over the future of the United States Supreme Court. When the dust settled, the Court had two new members, Chief Justice John Roberts, Jr., and Justice Samuel Alito. Only time will tell how their appointments will affect the nation's highest court. Matters abroad have been no less tempestuous, as the occupation and rebuilding effort in Iraq continues and the United States continues its global effort to combat terrorism. The recent conflict in Lebanon between Israel and the militant Islamic group Hezbollah, along with Iran's defiant stance on its nuclear enrichment aims, has threatened to widen the conflict in the Middle East. The old Chinese curse "May you live in interesting times" certainly seems apt at the present.

The changes we have made to this edition, however, are not limited to bringing the text up to date. We have also made major revisions based on the latest research. Finally, pedagogy in the profession has evolved over time, and this edition represents our latest and best approach to introducing American government and politics to today's students.

2006 Election Results Included and Analyzed

Our experience has been that students respond to up-to-date information about political events. Consequently, we have included the results of the November 2006 elections, which gave control over both chambers of Congress to the Democrats. We also analyze how these results will affect our political processes at the national, state, and local levels. While we have updated all of the text to be consistent with these results, in particular we have added throughout the text numerous special subsections dedicated to the elections.

The Texas Chapters

The Texas chapters cover major historical, demographic, political, and cultural trends. They also explain the background, the institutions, the "rules of the game," and the political players in Texas. We give special attention to interest groups throughout. We highlight similarities and differences between the Texas government and the governments of other states and of the nation.

New Chapter on Texas Public Policy

Chapter 26, titled Texas Public Policy, is new to this 2007–2008 Texas edition of *American Government and Politics Today*. This chapter features an in-depth explanation of how the state's budgeting process works—from the various sources of revenue to how the state decides to budget and spend these funds. To illustrate how the budgetary process influences the day-to-day life of every Texan, we focus on how public policy affects education, health and human services, and transportation in the state. Specifically, we discuss the problems plaguing public school financing, the pros and cons of public-assistance programs, and the heavy burden that automobiles and road construction impose on the budget.

The Interactive Focus of This Text

Whether the topic is voter participation, terrorism, or the problems that face the president, we constantly strive to involve the student reader in the analysis. We make sure that the reader comes to understand that politics is not an abstract process but a very human enterprise. We emphasize how different outcomes can affect students' civil rights and liberties, employment opportunities, and economic welfare.

Throughout the text, we encourage the reader to think critically. Almost all of the features end with questions designed to pique the student's interest. A feature titled *Which Side Are You On?* challenges the reader to find a connection between controversial issues facing the nation and the reader's personal positions on these issues. In this edition, we have also added a new feature, titled *Beyond Our Borders*, to encourage students to think globally. We further encourage interaction with the political system by ending each chapter with a feature titled *Making a Difference*, which shows students not only what they can do to become politically involved but why they should care enough to do so. Online exercises (to be discussed shortly) that conclude each chapter show students how to access and analyze political information.

The Most Complete Web Connection

We continue to make sure that our text leads the industry in its integration with the Web. For this edition, you will find the following Web-based resources:

■ **ThomsonNOW**—At www.thomsonedu.com/thomsonnow to access sign-in for those who purchased a book with ThomsonNOW or the chance to purchase access. ThomsonNOW will generate a personalized study plan for students and direct them to the appropriate premium resources, including an integrated online e-book, interactive Simulations, Video Case Studies, MicroCase exercises, and Timelines. Adopting instructors will be given password-protected access to management tools so that they can assign and supervise their students' use of ThomsonNOW if they wish to do so.

■ **Companion Web site for the Texas edition of *American Government and Politics Today***—At www.thomsonedu.com/politicalscience/schmidt, students will find free and open access to Learning Objectives, Quizzes, Chapter Glossaries, Flash Cards, Crossword Puzzles, and Internet activities. Adopting instructors will receive password-protected access to an electronic version of the *Instructor's Manual* and Microsoft® PowerPoint® lecture presentations.

■ **Turnitin®**—This proven online plagiarism-prevention software promotes fairness in the classroom by helping students learn to cite sources correctly and allowing instructors to check for originality before reading and grading papers. Turnitin quickly checks student papers against billions of pages of Internet content, millions of published works, and millions of student papers and within seconds generates a comprehensive originality report. A booklet, *How to Avoid Plagiarism Using Turnitin*, is also available; ask your Thomson representative for details.

■ **WebTutor™ on WebCT or Blackboard**—Deliver your course online! We can build a WebCT or Blackboard course for you with our content. Ask your local sales representative for details of this program.

Special Pedagogy and Features

The 2007–2008 Texas edition of *American Government and Politics Today* contains many pedagogical aids and high-interest features to assist both students and instructors. The following list summarizes the special elements that can be found in each chapter:

■ *What If . . .*—A chapter-opening feature that discusses a hypothetical situation.

■ *Beyond Our Borders*—A new feature appearing in each chapter that discusses a topic such as globalization, the war on terrorism, immigration, or comparative government that is relevant to the chapter. This feature replaces the *Global View* and *America's Security* features that appeared in previous editions.

■ *Margin Definitions*—For all important terms.

■ *Did You Know . . . ?*—Margin features presenting various facts and figures that add interest to the learning process.

■ *Which Side Are You On?*—A feature designed to elicit student responses to controversial issues.

■ *Politics and . . .*—A feature that examines the influence of politics on a variety of issues. Several of these features focus on the theme of *Politics and Diversity*. Others address topics such as *Politics and Elections* or *Politics and the Presidency*.

■ *Making a Difference*—A chapter-ending feature that gives the student some specific reasons why he or she should care about the topics covered in the chapter and provides ways in which she or he can become actively involved in American politics.

■ *Key Terms*—A chapter-ending list, with page numbers, of all terms in the chapter that were **boldfaced** and defined in the margins.

■ *Chapter Summary*—A point-by-point summary of the chapter text.

■ *Selected Print and Media Resources*—An annotated list of suggested scholarly readings as well as popular books and films relevant to chapter topics.

■ *E-mocracy*—A feature that discusses politics and the Internet and suggests Web sites and Internet activities related to the chapter's topics.

Appendices

Because we know that this book serves as a reference, we have included important documents for the student of American government to have close at hand. A fully annotated copy of the U.S. Constitution appears at the end of Chapter 2, as an appendix to that chapter. In addition, we have included the following appendices:

■ The Declaration of Independence

■ How to Read Case Citations and Find Court Decisions

■ *Federalist Papers* Nos. 10, 51, and 78

■ Justices of the United States Supreme Court since 1900

■ Party Control of Congress since 1900

■ Spanish Equivalents for Important Terms in American Government

Useful material is also located immediately inside the front and back covers of this text. Inside the front cover, you will find a simple reference map of the United States, plus a cartogram that distorts the size of the various states to indicate their relative weight in the electoral college. Inside the back cover, you will find a list of Texas governors and a timeline of the six flags of Texas.

A Comprehensive Supplements Package

We are proud to be the authors of a text that has the most comprehensive, accessible, and fully integrated supplements package on the market. Together, the text and the supplements listed below constitute a total learning/teaching package for you and your students. For further information on any of these supplements, contact your Wadsworth, Thomson Higher Education sales representative.

Supplements for Instructors

- **Multimedia Manager with Instructor Resources CD-ROM: A Microsoft PowerPoint Tool**—This one-stop lecture and class preparation tool makes it easy for you to assemble, edit, publish, and present custom lectures for your course, using Microsoft PowerPoint. The Multimedia Manager lets you bring together text-specific lecture outlines and art from Wadsworth texts, along with video clips from our ABC Video selections. In addition, you can add your own materials—culminating in a powerful, personalized, media-enhanced presentation. The CD also contains the **Instructor's Manual, Test Bank in Microsoft Word format and ExamView® computerized testing, a Resource Integration Guide,** the Video Case Studies **Instructor's Manual,** and **electronic transparencies,** including tables, charts, and graphs.

- **ThomsonNOW**—At **www.thomsonedu.com/thomsonnow,** adopting instructors will be given password-protected access to management tools so that they can assign and supervise their students' use of ThomsonNOW if they wish to do so.

- **Companion Web site for the Texas edition of** *American Government and Politics Today*—At **www.thomsonedu.com/politicalscience/schmidt,** adopting instructors will receive password-protected access to an electronic version of the *Instructor's Manual* and Microsoft PowerPoint lecture presentations.

- **Turnitin**—This proven online plagiarism-prevention software promotes fairness in the classroom by helping students learn to cite sources correctly and allowing instructors to check for originality before reading and grading papers. Turnitin quickly checks student papers against billions of pages of Internet content, millions of published works, and millions of student papers and within seconds generates a comprehensive originality report. A booklet, *How to Avoid Plagiarism Using Turnitin,* is also available; ask your Thomson representative for details.

- **Political Theatre DVD**—Video and audio clips drawn from key political events from the last seventy-five years: presidential speeches, campaign ads, debates, news reports, national convention coverage, demonstrations, speeches by civil rights leaders, and more.

- **New: Texas Political Theatre DVD/VHS**—Drawn from key Texas political events, this video that is available in VHS or DVD format is compiled from speeches by famous Texans as well as clips from debates, news reports, and campaign ads.

- **JoinIn on TurningPoint for Political Theatre**—For even more interaction, combine **Political Theatre** with the innovative teaching tool of a classroom response system through JoinIn. Poll your students with questions we have created for you or create your own. Built within the Microsoft PowerPoint software, it's easy to integrate into your current lectures, in conjunction with the "clicker" hardware of your choice.

- **ABC News Videos for American Government**—A collection of three- to six-minute video clips on relevant political issues. They serve as great lecture or discussion launchers and are available on VHS or DVD.

- **Video Case Studies for American Government**—Free to adopters, this award-winning video contains twelve case studies on the debates on recent policy issues, such as affirmative action. Each case ends with questions designed to spark classroom discussion.

- **Wadsworth Political Science Video Library**—So many exciting new videos . . . so many great ways to enrich your lectures and spark discussion of the material in this text. Your Wadsworth/Thomson representative will be happy to provide details on our video policy by adoption size.

- **WebTutor**—Rich with content for your American government course, this Web-based teaching and learning tool includes course management, study/ mastery, and communication aids. Use WebTutor to provide virtual office hours, post your syllabus, and track student progress with the program's quizzing material. For students, WebTutor offers real-time access to interactive online tutorials and simulations, practice quizzes, and Web links—all correlated to *American Government and Politics Today*. Available in WebCT and Blackboard.

- **Building Democracy: Readings in American Government**—This extraordinary collection provides access to more than 500 readings to create the ideal supplement for any American government course. Thomson Custom Solutions' intuitive **TextChoice** Web site at **www.textchoice.com/democracy** allows you to quickly browse the collection, preview selections, arrange your table of contents, and create a custom cover that will include your own course information. Or if you prefer, your local Thomson representative will be happy to guide you through the process.

Supplements for Students

- **ThomsonNOW**—At **www.thomsonedu.com/thomsonnow** to access sign-in for those who purchased a book with ThomsonNOW or the chance to purchase access. ThomsonNOW will generate a personalized study plan for students and direct them to the appropriate premium resources, including an integrated online e-book, interactive Simulations, Video Case Studies, MicroCase exercises, and Timelines.

- *The Handbook of Selected Court Cases*—Includes more than thirty United States Supreme Court cases.

- *The Handbook of Selected Legislation and Other Documents*—Features excerpts from twelve laws passed by the U.S. Congress that have had a significant impact on American politics.

- **Companion Web site for the Texas edition of** *American Government and Politics Today*—At **www.thomsonedu.com/politicalscience/schmidt,** students will find free and open access to Learning Objectives, Quizzes, Chapter Glossaries, Flash Cards, Crossword Puzzles, and Internet activities.

- **WebTutor on WebCT or Blackboard**—A content-rich, easy-to-use, Web-based study aid for students that includes presentations of concepts, Flash Cards with audio clips, Web links, tutorials, discussion questions, and more.

- *Election 2006: An American Government Supplement*—By John A. Clark and Brian Schaffner. The use of real examples in this election booklet, which addresses both the 2006 congressional and gubernatorial races, makes the concepts covered come alive for students.

- *Regime Change: Origins, Execution, and Aftermath of the Iraq War,* **Second Edition**—By David Kinsella. Provides an overview of the recent war with Iraq, including its origins, the political and legal debate over regime change, the conduct of the war, and the challenges of postwar stabilization and reconstruction.

- *9/11: Aftershocks of the Attack*—By Jeremy Meyer. Focuses on how the American political system is responding to the challenges posed by the 9/11 attacks.

- *Battle Supreme: The Confirmation of Chief Justice John Roberts and the Future of the Supreme Court*—By David W. Neubauer and Stephen S. Meinhold. An inside look at the United States Supreme Court nomination process examining the confrontation over the replacements of Justice Sandra Day O'Connor and Chief Justice William Rehnquist, which involved every aspect of the American political system.

■ *American Government: Using MicroCase ExplorIt,* **Ninth Edition**—By Barbara Norrander. Windows-compatible package that includes access to MicroCase datasets and workbook. Students make their own decisions about the issues as they analyze and interpret current NES and GSS data.

■ *Classics in American Government,* **Third Edition**—By Jay M. Shafritz and Lee S. Weinberg. A collection of many of the most important readings in American government.

■ *Current Perspectives: Readings from InfoTrac College Edition: American Government*—Includes sixteen articles on issues in American politics, covering a range of topics from political theory to political socialization—giving students a comprehensive introduction to American government.

■ *Thinking Globally, Acting Locally*—By John Soares. Designed to help students get involved and become active citizens. Topics include tips for writing letters to the editor, volunteering, changing laws, and registering to vote.

For Users of the Previous Edition

As usual, we thank you for your past support of our work. We have made numerous changes to this text for the 2007–2008 Texas edition, many of which we list below. We have rewritten much of the text, added numerous new features, and updated the book to reflect the results of the 2006 elections.

New *What If* . . . Features

■ "What If . . . Citizens Were Required to Vote?" (Chapter 1)
■ "What If . . . *Roe v. Wade* Were Overturned?" (Chapter 2)
■ "What If . . . The Government Monitored All E-Mail?" (Chapter 4)
■ "What If . . . Illegal Immigrants Were Granted Citizenship?" (Chapter 5)
■ "What If . . . Students Were Required to Pass a National Civics Exam?" (Chapter 6)
■ "What If . . . Parties Were Supported Solely by Public Funding?" (Chapter 8)
■ "What If . . . Spending Limits Were Placed on Campaigns?" (Chapter 9)
■ "What If . . . The Media Had to Reveal All Their Sources?" (Chapter 10)
■ "What If . . . Nonpartisan Panels Drew Congressional Districts?" (Chapter 11)
■ "What If . . . Supreme Court Justices Had Term Limits?" (Chapter 14)
■ "What If . . . We Had Universal Health Care?" (Chapter 15)
■ "What If . . . The Federal Government Were Required to Balance Its Budget?" (Chapter 16)
■ "What If . . . All American Troops Were Restricted to U.S. Soil?" (Chapter 17)
■ "What If . . . Texas Adopted a School Voucher Plan?" (Chapter 26)

Significant Changes within Chapters

Each chapter contains new features, updated facts and tabular data, and whenever feasible, the most current information available on the problems facing the nation. In addition, significant changes have been made to the chapters listed below:

■ Chapter 1 (The Democratic Republic)—Issues related to the USA Patriot Act and the National Security Agency's domestic spying program have been added to the discussion of liberty versus order in American government. The material related to Hispanic Americans has been updated and enhanced.

- Chapter 3 (Federalism)—A discussion of the Katrina disaster is used to illustrate how responsibilities are divided between the federal and state governments. More emphasis has been placed on the coercive measures that the federal government employs in a cooperative federalism model.

- Chapter 4 (Civil Liberties)—The renewal of the USA Patriot Act receives significant attention. A discussion of intelligent design and the controversies surrounding it has been added. The chapter has also been updated throughout to highlight recent Supreme Court decisions related to our civil liberties.

- Chapter 5 (Civil Rights)—More attention has been given to Hispanic Americans, and a new section on immigration has been added. The discussion of same-sex marriages has been updated to include the granting of marriage rights in Massachusetts as well as the numerous ballot measures in other states designed to block same-sex couples from marrying.

- Chapter 6 (Public Opinion and Political Socialization)—The section on models of political socialization has been almost completely rewritten. New examples have been used to illustrate how political events influence socialization. The material related to religion has been significantly reworked to focus on the influence of evangelical groups.

- Chapter 7 (Interest Groups)—The numerous recent lobbying scandals are discussed, and special attention is given to the proliferation of lobbyists in Washington and the K Street Project.

- Chapter 10 (The Media and Cyberpolitics)—Greater coverage and emphasis have been given to electronic media and the challenges the Internet poses to traditional media. The emergence of Web logs (blogs) receives special attention and is discussed at length.

- Chapter 11 (The Congress)—The chapter has received significant updating, including an enhanced section relating to redistricting and gerrymandering as well as greater coverage of filibustering and pork-barrel spending.

- Chapter 12 (The President)—A new section about the president's power to persuade has been added. Executive privilege receives greater scrutiny in the text, as does the extent of presidential powers during the war on terrorism.

- Chapter 14 (The Courts)—Recent changes in the United States Supreme Court's composition are discussed, as is the nature of partisanship within the federal judiciary. The most up-to-date information regarding the new "Roberts Court" is also included.

Acknowledgments for the First Texas Edition

The following reviewers contributed greatly to the state chapters featured in the first Texas edition of *American Government and Politics Today*.

Juliet Alfaro
San Antonio College, Texas

Evelyn Ballard
Houston Community College, Texas

Dewey Clayton
University of Louisville, Kentucky

William De Soto
Texas State University,
San Marcos, Texas

Don Thomas Dugi
Transylvania University, Louisville, Kentucky

Christopher W. Hammons
Houston Baptist University, Texas

Jesse Horton
San Antonio College, Texas

Frank Jones
Del Mar College, Corpus Christi, Texas

Jeffrey L. Prewitt
Brewton-Parker College, Mt. Vernon, Georgia

Gregory Schaller
Villanova University, Villanova, Pennsylvania;
and St. Joseph's University, Philadelphia

Charles R. Shedlak
Ivy Tech State College, South Bend, Indiana

Robert E. Sterken, Jr.
University of Texas, Tyler

Ronald W. Vardy
University of Houston, Texas

Acknowledgments for the Second Texas Edition

Additionally, the following reviewers have offered helpful comments and instructions pertaining to the Texas chapters contained within this 2007–2008 Texas edition of *American Government and Politics Today*.

Robert Ballinger
South Texas College

JoAnn DiGeorgio-Lutz
Texas A&M University, Commerce

Gary D. McEhany
Southwestern Assemblies of God University

John Robey
University of Texas, Brownsville

H. Ibrahim Salih
Texas Wesleyan University

Albert C. Waite
Central Texas College

Van A. Wigginton
San Jacinto College

In preparing this Texas edition of *American Government and Politics Today*, we were the beneficiaries of the expert guidance of a skilled and dedicated team of publishers and editors. We would like, first of all, to thank Susan Badger, the CEO of Thomson Learning Higher Education Group, for the support she has shown for this project. We have benefited greatly from the supervision and encouragement given by Carolyn Merrill, executive editor, and Clark Baxter, the publisher. Catherine Wein, our developmental editor, also deserves our thanks for her efforts in coordinating reviews and in many other aspects of project development. We are also indebted to editorial assistant Patrick Rheaume for his contributions to this project.

We are grateful to Bill Stryker, our production manager, for a remarkable design and for making it possible to get the text out on time. We also thank Anne Sheroff, who worked on graphics issues. In addition, our gratitude goes to all of those who worked on the various supplements offered with this text, especially supplements coordinator Rebecca Green, and to Inna Fedoseyeva, who coordinates the Web site. We would also like to thank Janise Fry, marketing manager, for her tremendous efforts in marketing the text. Additionally, we are also indebted to the staff at Parkwood Composition. Their ability to generate the pages for this text quickly and accurately made it possible for us to meet our ambitious printing schedule.

Many other people helped during the research and editorial stages of this edition. Paul Bartels skillfully coordinated the authors' efforts and provided editorial and research assistance from the outset of this project to the end. We also wish to thank Greg Scott for his help in providing the 2006 election updates. Copyediting by Mary Berry and Pat Lewis, as well as the proofreading of Judy Kiviat and Suzie Franklin DeFazio contributed greatly to the book. We also thank Vickie Reierson and Roxie Lee for their proofreading and other assistance, which helped us to meet our printing schedule, and Sue Jasin of K&M Consulting for her contributions to the smooth running of the project.

Any errors remain our own. We welcome comments from instructors and students alike. Suggestions that we have received in the past have helped us to improve this text and to adapt it to the changing needs of instructors and students.

Steffen Schmidt   Mack Shelley   Barbara Bardes
William Earl Maxwell   Ernest Crain

About the Authors

Steffen W. Schmidt

Steffen W. Schmidt is a professor of political science at Iowa State University. He grew up in Colombia, South America, and studied in Colombia, Switzerland, and France. He obtained his Ph.D. from Columbia University, New York, in public law and government.

Schmidt has published six books and more than 150 journal articles. He is also the recipient of numerous prestigious teaching prizes, including the Amoco Award for Lifetime Career Achievement in Teaching and the Teacher of the Year award. He is a pioneer in the use of Web-based and real-time video courses and is a member of the American Political Science Association's section on computers and multimedia. He is on the editorial board of the *Political Science Educator* and is the technology and teaching editor of the *Journal of Political Science Education*.

Schmidt has a political talk show on WOI radio, where he is known as Dr. Politics, streaming live once a week at **www.woi.org**. The show has been broadcast live from various U.S. and international venues. He is a frequent political commentator for *CNN en Español* and the British Broadcasting Corporation.

Schmidt likes to snow ski, ride hunter jumper horses, race sailboats, and scuba dive.

Mack C. Shelley II

Mack C. Shelley II is professor of political science, professor of statistics, and director of the Research Institute for Studies in Education at Iowa State University. After receiving his bachelor's degree from American University in Washington, D.C., he completed graduate studies at the University of Wisconsin at Madison, where he received a master's degree in economics and a Ph.D. in political science. He taught for two years at Mississippi State University before arriving at Iowa State in 1979.

Shelley has published numerous articles, books, and monographs on public policy. From 1993 to 2002, he served as elected coeditor of the *Policy Studies Journal*. His published books include *The Permanent Majority: The Conservative Coalition in the United States Congress; Biotechnology and the Research Enterprise* (with William F. Woodman and Brian J. Reichel); *American Public Policy: The Contemporary Agenda* (with Steven G. Koven and Bert E. Swanson); and *Redefining Family Policy: Implications for the 21st Century* (with Joyce M. Mercier and Steven Garasky). Other recent work has focused on electronic government and the "digital divide," learning communities, how to improve student life (especially in residence halls), and public health.

His leisure time includes traveling, working with students, and playing with the family dog and three cats.

Barbara A. Bardes

Barbara A. Bardes is a professor of political science at the University of Cincinnati. She received her bachelor of arts degree and master of arts degree from Kent State University. After completing her Ph.D. at the University of Cincinnati, she held faculty positions at Mississippi State University and Loyola University in Chicago. She returned to the University of Cincinnati as dean of one of its colleges. She has also worked as a political consultant and directed polling for a research center.

Bardes has written articles on public opinion and foreign policy, and on women and politics. She has authored *Thinking about Public Policy; Declarations of Independence: Women and Political Power in Nineteenth-Century American Fiction;* and *Public Opinion: Measuring the American Mind* (with Robert W. Oldendick). Her current research interests include public opinion on terrorism and homeland security and media effects in elections.

Bardes's home is located in a very small hamlet in Kentucky called Rabbit Hash, famous for its 150-year-old general store. Her hobbies include traveling, gardening, needlework, and antique collecting.

William Earl Maxwell

William Earl Maxwell is a professor emeritus at San Antonio College, where he has taught courses in U.S. and Texas government since 1971. San Antonio College is a teaching institution, and throughout his career Maxwell has focused on innovative teaching techniques and improving the teaching and learning environments for the students at the college. As a part of that effort, in 1975 Maxwell co-authored *Understanding Texas Politics*, his first text on Texas government. In the years that followed, he has co-authored such texts as *Politics in Texas* (1975) and *The Challenge of Texas Politics: Text with Readings* (1980).

Maxwell performed his undergraduate and graduate work at Sam Houston State University. His home town is Lovelady in East Texas, although he has lived in San Antonio since 1971. Maxwell enjoys fishing, chess, Frog Juice, and mystery movies. Currently, he roots for his grandson's Little League baseball team and his granddaughter's soccer team. Maxwell also enthusiastically follows the St. Louis Cardinals—a lifelong infatuation.

Ernest Crain

Ernest Crain has been in the political science department at San Antonio College for thirty-five years. He received his B.A. and M.A. degrees from the University of Texas in Austin. His specializations are political party competition, comparative state politics, and Texas public policy.

Crain has co-authored *Understanding Texas Politics; Politics in Texas; The Challenge of Texas Politics: Text with Readings;* and four editions of *Introduction to Texas Politics.* He has also developed instructional material for Clifton McCleskey's *The Government and Politics of Texas.*

Crain's pastimes include world travel, art collecting (especially original Van Goghs, works by impressionists and post-impressionists, and primitive oils and sketches), gourmet meals, numismatics, philatelics, and rockhounding. He is fond of serious drama and enjoys going to New York for first-run theatrical performances.

Other Members of the Texas Team

Edwin S. Davis is a professor of political science and criminal justice at Sam Houston State University. He is the author of *Public Policy: The Basics*, Third Edition and was the founding editor of the *Texas Journal of Political Studies*. His most recent article, "Examining School Experiences of Youthful Offenders," appeared in the *Journal of At-Risk Behavior*, Winter 2006. Davis received a Ph.D. from Texas Tech University.

Elizabeth N. Flores is a professor of political science at Del Mar College in Corpus Christi. She received her M.A. degree from the University of Michigan. Flores has served as a director of the Corpus Christi Regional Transit Authority, written on politics for the Corpus Christi *Caller-Times*, and co-hosted a public affairs show on PBS.

Joseph Ignagni is a professor of political science at the University of Texas at Arlington, where he has received four teaching awards and served as an associate dean. Ignagni received a Ph.D. from Michigan State University. He has published articles in the *American Journal of Political Science, Political Research Quarterly, American Politics Quarterly,* and *Judicature.*

Cynthia Opheim is a professor of political science at Texas State University–San Marcos. Opheim received a Ph.D. from the University of Texas at Austin. She has published in the *Legislative Studies Quarterly, State and Local Government Review,* and *Public Administration Review.* She co-authored *State and Local Politics: The Individual and the Governments.* In 2003, she became president of the Southwestern Political Science Association (SWPSA).

Christopher Wlezien is a professor of political science at Temple University in Philadelphia and received a Ph.D. from the University of Iowa. Wlezien has published in the *American Journal of Political Science, British Journal of Political Science, Journal of Politics, Political Analysis,* and *Public Opinion Quarterly.* He is coeditor of the *Journal of Elections, Public Opinion and Parties* and has edited *The Future of Election Studies* and *Britain Votes.* In 2004, he became president of the SWPSA.

1 | The Democratic Republic

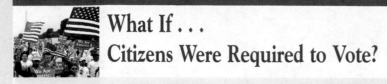

What If . . .
Citizens Were Required to Vote?

BACKGROUND

The United States is a democratic republic, or a *representative democracy.* In a representative democracy, the people elect representatives to make the laws. Governors and presidents are elected to carry out these laws.

Clearly, a representative democracy relies on a politically informed and active citizenry to elect leaders. Yet the United States has a notoriously low rate of voter turnout in elections when compared to other Western democracies. Low voter turnout translates into elected officials who merely represent the interests of the majority of those citizens who actually cast ballots. Often, this result can have a negative social or economic impact on nonvoters.

WHAT IF CITIZENS WERE REQUIRED TO VOTE?

If all eligible Americans were required to vote, elected representatives would reflect the views of a majority of the entire voting-age population. Passive consent of the nonvoters aside, today's politicians frequently ascend to their positions with the support of only a relatively small minority of citizens. In the past one hundred years, voter turnout for national elections has rarely exceeded 60 percent of registered voters, and turnout has even dipped below 40 percent on occasion during nonpresidential-election years. The result is that many elected politicians receive votes from less than one-fourth of the nation's voting-age population. Thus, these representatives do not necessarily reflect the desires and beliefs of a majority of citizens.

Consider the election of George W. Bush in 2004. In that election, Bush garnered roughly 51 percent of the total popular vote. When voter turnout is considered, however, Bush was elected by only 27.6 percent of the voting-age population. Given that 72.4 percent of age-eligible voters did *not* cast a ballot for him in 2004, Bush's postelection claim to have earned "a mandate from the people" seemed overstated.

The question is, would full voter participation have changed the outcome of the 2004 elections—or any elections? It is nearly impossible to say one way or the other. Mandatory voting could, however, have effects on policy decisions.

EFFECTS ON POLICY DECISIONS

If citizens were required to vote, elected officials would have to consider all of their constituents when making policy decisions. In a representative democracy, the nonvoters, or groups of nonvoters, can be adversely affected by policy decisions. For example, Congress authorized significant cuts to federal student loan programs in 2006. This action was doubtless made easier because turnout among younger Americans is relatively low. If students tended to vote in greater numbers, members of Congress standing for reelection might have opposed these cuts, knowing that the youth vote mattered.

Certainly, the clout of older Americans, who turn out to vote in high numbers, is evident in policy choices. President Bush's push for partial privatization of Social Security lost momentum when older Americans and related interest groups mobilized in opposition to his proposal. Members of Congress knew that going on record in favor of a plan that was unpopular among older Americans would potentially ruin their chances of reelection.

POSSIBLE OBJECTIONS

Of course, optimism over mandatory voting must be tempered by some of the unintended consequences that might result. First of all, requiring every citizen to vote would undoubtedly increase the number of uninformed voters. Indeed, a common complaint in our existing system is that voters do not adequately follow politics or know individual candidates' stances on important issues. Requiring uninterested or uninformed citizens to vote against their will could lead to undesirable results.

Many of those who drafted the Constitution feared what they termed "the passions of the masses." The founders did not necessarily think that all Americans were capable of voting intelligently. Opponents of mandatory voting could argue that the Constitution's silence on the issue of full voter participation reflects the founders' distrust of mass participation in government.

Even if mandatory voting passed constitutional muster, there would still be a problem with enforcement. How would the government ensure that every American had cast his or her ballot? Voting might become akin to paying taxes, with audits to assure that citizens were meeting their legal obligations.

FOR CRITICAL ANALYSIS

1. Do you agree with the concept that every American should be required to cast a ballot? Why or why not?
2. If citizens were required to vote, should they also be required to be well informed on the candidates and the issues? Explain your answer.

Politics, for many people, is the "great game"—better than soccer, better than chess. Scores may only be tallied every two years, at elections, but the play continues at all times. The game, furthermore, is played for high stakes. Politics can affect what you have in your purse or wallet. It can determine what you can legally do in your spare time. In worst-case circumstances, it can even threaten your life. Few topics are so entertaining—and so important.

Given the importance of political decisions, should all citizens be required to vote? We examined this question in the *What If . . .* feature that opened this chapter. Although voting is extremely important, it is only one of the ways that citizens can exercise their political influence. Americans can also join a political organization or interest group, stage a protest, or donate funds to a political campaign or cause. There are countless ways to become involved. Informed participation begins with knowledge, however, and this text aims to provide you with a strong foundation in American government and politics. We hope that this book helps introduce you to a lifetime of political awareness and activity.

Politics and Government

What is politics? **Politics** can be understood as the process of resolving conflicts and deciding, as political scientist Harold Lasswell put it, "who gets what, when, and how."[1] More specifically, politics is the struggle over power or influence within organizations or informal groups that can grant or withhold benefits or privileges.

We can identify many such groups and organizations. In families, all members may meet together to decide on values, priorities, and actions. Wherever there is a community that makes decisions through formal or informal rules, politics exists. For example, when a church decides to construct a new building or hire a new minister, the decision may be made politically. Politics can be found in schools, social groups, and any other organized collection of people. Of all of the organizations that are controlled by political activity, however, the most important is the government.

What is the government? Certainly, it is an **institution**—that is, an ongoing organization with a life separate from the lives of the individuals who are part of it at any given moment in time. The **government** can be defined as an institution in which decisions are made that resolve conflicts or allocate benefits and privileges. The government is also the *preeminent* institution within society. It is unique because it has the ultimate authority for making decisions and establishing political values.

| Politics
The struggle over power or influence within organizations or informal groups that can grant or withhold benefits or privileges.

| Institution
An ongoing organization that performs certain functions for society.

| Government
The institution in which decisions are made that resolve conflicts or allocate benefits and privileges. It is unique because it has the ultimate authority within society.

Why Is Government Necessary?

Perhaps the best way to assess the need for government is to examine circumstances in which government, as we normally understand it, does not exist. What happens when multiple groups compete with each other for power within a society? There are places around the world where such circumstances exist. A current example is the African nation of Somalia. Since 1991, Somalia has not had a central government. Mogadishu, the capital, is divided among several warlords, each of whom controls a bloc of neighborhoods. When Somali warlords compete for the control of a particular locality, the result is war, widespread devastation, and famine. In general, multiple armed forces compete by fighting, and the absence of a unified government is equivalent to civil war.

The Need for Security

As the example of Somalia shows, one of the original purposes of government is the maintenance of security, or **order**. By keeping the peace, the government protects the people from violence at the hands of private or foreign armies. It dispenses

| Order
A state of peace and security. Maintaining order by protecting members of society from violence and criminal activity is the oldest purpose of government.

---

[1] Harold Lasswell, *Politics: Who Gets What, When, and How* (New York: McGraw-Hill, 1936).

justice and protects the people against the violence of criminals. If order is not present, it is not possible to provide any of the other benefits that people expect from government.

Consider the situation in Iraq. In March and April 2003, U.S. and British coalition forces invaded that nation, which was governed by the dictator Saddam Hussein. The relatively small number of coalition troops had little trouble in defeating their military opponents, but they experienced serious difficulties in establishing order within Iraq when the war was over.

Once it became clear that Saddam Hussein was no longer in control of the country, widespread looting broke out. Ordinary citizens entered government buildings and made off with the furniture. Looters stole crucial supplies from hospitals, making it difficult to treat Iraqis injured during the war. Thieves stripped the copper from electrical power lines, which made it impossible to quickly restore electrical power. In various localities, demonstrators confronted coalition troops, often with fatal results. Clearly, a degree of security and order would have to be restored before it would be possible to begin the reconstruction of Iraqi society. Order is a political value that we will return to later in this chapter.

Limiting Government Power

Order cannot be the only important political value. Under Saddam Hussein, Iraq certainly experienced a kind of order. For many unfortunate Iraqi citizens, that order took the form of the "peace of the grave"—large numbers of people were killed by Saddam Hussein's security forces, sometimes for trivial reasons. Protection from the violence of domestic criminals or foreign armies is not enough. Citizens also need protection from abuses of power by the government.

U.S. President George W. Bush and British Prime Minister Tony Blair argued—mistakenly, as it turned out—that Saddam Hussein possessed weapons of mass destruction. Eliminating those weapons was a principal goal of the war. A second major goal, however, was to promote stability in the greater Middle East by freeing the Iraqi people from a despotic regime. Eliminating Saddam Hussein would not be enough to guarantee the freedom of the Iraqi people. Iraqis are divided among themselves by religion, ethnicity, and language. How could each of the various groups that make up Iraq

Members of Iraq's new national unity government meet for the first time. In the front row are representatives from each of the three major Iraqi factions—the Sunnis, the Shiites, and the Kurds. One of the major issues facing these Iraqi politicians is security and order. What other reasons can you think of that make government necessary? (AP Photo/Khalid Mohammed)

be prevented from oppressing the others? To protect the liberties of the Iraqi people, it would be necessary to limit the powers of the new Iraqi government.

Liberty—the greatest freedom of the individual consistent with the freedom of other individuals—is a second major political value, along with order. Liberty is a value that may be promoted by government, but it can also be invoked *against* government. We will further discuss this value later in this chapter.

Authority and Legitimacy

Every government must have **authority**—that is, the right and power to enforce its decisions. Ultimately, the government's authority rests on its control of the armed forces and the police. Virtually no one in the United States, however, bases his or her day-to-day activities on fear of the government's enforcement powers. Most people, most of the time, obey the law because this is what they have always done. Also, if they did not obey the law, they would face the disapproval of friends and family. Consider an example: Do you avoid injuring your friends or stealing their possessions because you are afraid of the police—or because if you did these things, you would no longer have friends?

Under normal circumstances, the government's authority has broad popular support. People accept the government's right to establish rules and laws. When authority is broadly accepted, we say that it has **legitimacy.** Authority without legitimacy is a recipe for trouble. Iraq can again serve as an example. Although many Iraqis were happy to see the end of Saddam Hussein's regime, they were also not pleased that their nation was occupied by foreign troops. Many Iraqis, especially in districts inhabited by Sunni Arabs (the former politically dominant group in Iraq), did not accept the legitimacy of the U.S.-led Coalition Provisional Authority (CPA). Terrorists and other groups hostile to the CPA could organize attacks on coalition troops or the new Iraqi police, knowing that their neighbors would not report their activities. A perceived precondition of making progress toward a fully peaceful country was that the CPA yield its authority to a government chosen by the Iraqis themselves—a government with substantial legitimacy, rather than one imposed by outside forces.

Democracy and Other Forms of Government

There are a variety of different types of government, which can be classified according to which person or group of people controls society through the government.

Types of Government

At one extreme is a society governed by a **totalitarian regime.** In such a political system, a small group of leaders or a single individual—a dictator—makes all political decisions for the society. Every aspect of political, social, and economic life is controlled by the government. The power of the ruler is total (thus, the term *totalitarianism*).

A second type of system is authoritarian government. **Authoritarianism** differs from totalitarianism in that only the government itself is fully controlled by the ruler. Social and economic institutions exist that are not under the government's control.

Many of our terms for describing the distribution of political power are derived from the ancient Greeks, who were the first Western people to study politics systematically. One form of rule by the few was known as **aristocracy**, literally meaning "rule by the best." In practice, this meant rule by leading members of wealthy families.

The Greek term for rule by the people was **democracy.** Within the limits of their culture, some of the Greek city-states operated as democracies. Today, in much of the world, the people will not grant legitimacy to a government unless it is based on democracy.

Liberty
The greatest freedom of individuals that is consistent with the freedom of other individuals in the society.

Authority
The right and power of a government or other entity to enforce its decisions and compel obedience.

Legitimacy
Popular acceptance of the right and power of a government or other entity to exercise authority.

Totalitarian Regime
A form of government that controls all aspects of the political and social life of a nation.

Authoritarianism
A type of regime in which only the government itself is fully controlled by the ruler. Social and economic institutions exist that are not under the government's control.

Aristocracy
Rule by the "best"; in reality, rule by an upper class.

Democracy
A system of government in which political authority is vested in the people. Derived from the Greek words *demos* ("the people") and *kratos* ("authority").

Direct Democracy as a Model

The system of government in the ancient Greek city-state of Athens is usually considered the purest model of **direct democracy** because the citizens of that community debated and voted directly on all laws, even those put forward by the ruling council of the city. The most important feature of Athenian democracy was that the **legislature** was composed of all of the citizens. Women, foreigners, and slaves, however, were excluded because they were not citizens. This form of government required a high level of participation from every citizen; that participation was seen as benefiting the individual and the city-state. The Athenians believed that although a high level of participation might lead to instability in government, citizens, if informed about the issues, could be trusted to make wise decisions.

Direct Democracy Today.　Direct democracy has also been practiced in Switzerland and, in the United States, in New England town meetings. At New England town meetings, which can include all of the voters who live in the town, important decisions—such as levying taxes, hiring city officials, and deciding local ordinances—are made by majority vote. Some states provide a modern adaptation of direct democracy for their citizens; representative democracy is supplemented by the **initiative** or the **referendum**—processes by which the people may vote directly on laws or constitutional amendments. The **recall** process, which is available in many states, allows the people to vote to remove an official from state office.

Teledemocracy.　Today, because of the Internet, Americans have more access to political information than ever before. Voters can now go online to examine the record of any candidate for any office. Constituents can badger their congressional representatives and state legislators by sending them e-mail. Individuals can easily and relatively inexpensively form political interest groups using the Internet. They can even contribute to a particular politician's campaign through the Internet. Therefore, to some extent, we are gradually progressing toward a type of teledemocracy in which citizens and their political representatives communicate with each other easily and frequently online. In 2000, Colorado offered its citizens the opportunity of voting online.[2]

[2]Since then, other jurisdictions have offered online voting.

This town meeting in Vermont allows every citizen of the town to vote directly and in person for elected officials, for proposed policies, and, in some cases, for the town budget. To be effective, such a form of direct democracy requires that the citizens stay informed about local politics, attend town meetings, and devote time to discussion and decision making. Why might citizens be willing to spend the time necessary to attend town meetings? (AP Photo/Toby Talbot)

The Dangers of Direct Democracy

Although they were aware of the Athenian model, the framers of the U.S. Constitution were opposed to such a system. They regarded democracy as a dangerous idea that could lead to instability. Nevertheless, in the 1700s and 1800s, the idea of government based on the **consent of the people** gained increasing popularity. Such a government was the main aspiration of the American Revolution, the French Revolution in 1789, and many subsequent revolutions. At the time of the American Revolution, however, the masses were still considered to be too uneducated to govern themselves, too prone to the influence of demagogues (political leaders who manipulate popular prejudices), and too likely to subordinate minority rights to the tyranny of the majority.

James Madison defended the new scheme of government set forth in the U.S. Constitution, while warning of the problems inherent in a "pure democracy":

This campaign worker in Chicago is helping a recent immigrant register to vote. If this person ends up voting in the next election, is he participating in a direct or a representative democracy? (AP Photo/Nam Y. Huh)

> A common passion or interest will, in almost every case, be felt by a majority of the whole . . . and there is nothing to check the inducements to sacrifice the weaker party or an obnoxious individual. Hence it is that such democracies have ever been spectacles of turbulence and contention, and have ever been found incompatible with personal security or the rights of property; and have in general been as short in their lives as they have been violent in their deaths.[3]

Like other politicians of his time, Madison feared that pure, or direct, democracy would deteriorate into mob rule. What would keep the majority of the people, if given direct decision-making power, from abusing the rights of minority groups?

A Democratic Republic

The framers of the U.S. Constitution chose to craft a **republic,** meaning a government in which sovereign power rests with the people, rather than with a king or monarch. A republic is based on **popular sovereignty.** To Americans of the 1700s, the idea of a republic also meant a government based on common beliefs and virtues that would be fostered within small communities. The rulers were to be amateurs—good citizens who would take turns representing their fellow citizens.

The U.S. Constitution created a form of republican government that we now call a **democratic republic.** The people hold the ultimate power over the government through the election process, but all policy decisions are made by elected officials. For the founders, even this distance between the people and the government was not sufficient. The Constitution made sure that the Senate and the president would be selected by political elites rather than by the people, although later changes to the Constitution allowed the voters to elect members of the Senate directly.

Despite these limits, the new American system was unique in the amount of power it granted to the ordinary citizen. Over the course of the following two centuries, democratic values became more and more popular, at first in the West and then throughout the rest of the world. The spread of democratic principles gave rise to another name for our system of government—**representative democracy.** The term *representative democracy* has almost the same meaning as *democratic republic*, with one exception. In a republic, not only are the people sovereign, but there is no king. What if a nation develops into a democracy, but preserves the monarchy as a largely ceremonial institution? This is exactly what happened in Britain. Not surprisingly, the

| Consent of the People
The idea that governments and laws derive their legitimacy from the consent of the governed.

| Republic
A form of government in which sovereignty rests with the people, as opposed to a king or monarch.

| Popular Sovereignty
The concept that ultimate political authority is based on the will of the people.

| Democratic Republic
A republic in which representatives elected by the people make and enforce laws and policies.

| Representative Democracy
A form of government in which representatives elected by the people make and enforce laws and policies; may retain the monarchy in a ceremonial role.

---

[3]James Madison, in Alexander Hamilton, James Madison, and John Jay, *The Federalist Papers*, No. 10 (New York: Mentor Books, 1964), p. 81. See Appendix C of this textbook.

| Universal Suffrage
The right of all adults to vote for their representatives.

| Majority
More than 50 percent.

| Majority Rule
A basic principle of democracy asserting that the greatest number of citizens in any political unit should select officials and determine policies.

| Limited Government
The principle that the powers of government should be limited, usually by institutional checks.

| Majoritarianism
A political theory holding that in a democracy, the government ought to do what the majority of the people want.

| Elite Theory
A perspective holding that society is ruled by a small number of people who exercise power to further their self-interest.

British found the term *democratic republic* to be unacceptable, and they described their system as a representative democracy instead.

Principles of Democratic Government.   All representative democracies rest on the rule of the people as expressed through the election of government officials. In the 1790s in the United States, only free white males were able to vote, and in some states they had to be property owners as well. Women did not receive the right to vote in national elections in the United States until 1920, and the right to vote was not secured in all states by African Americans until the 1960s. Today, **universal suffrage** is the rule.

Because everyone's vote counts equally, the only way to make fair decisions is by some form of **majority** will. But to ensure that **majority rule** does not become oppressive, modern democracies also provide guarantees of minority rights. If political minorities were not protected, the majority might violate the fundamental rights of members of certain groups, especially groups that are unpopular or that differ from the majority population, such as racial minorities.

To guarantee the continued existence of a representative democracy, there must be free, competitive elections. Thus, the opposition always has the opportunity to win elective office. For such elections to be totally open, freedom of the press and speech must be preserved so that opposition candidates may present their criticisms of the government.

Constitutional Democracy.   Yet another key feature of Western representative democracy is that it is based on the principle of **limited government.** Not only is the government dependent on popular sovereignty, but the powers of the government are also clearly limited, either through a written document or through widely shared beliefs. The U.S. Constitution sets down the fundamental structure of the government and the limits to its activities. Such limits are intended to prevent political decisions based on the whims or ambitions of individuals in government rather than on constitutional principles.

| What Kind of Democracy Do We Have?

Political scientists have developed a number of theories about American democracy, including *majoritarian* theory, *elite* theory, and theories of *pluralism*. Advocates of these theories use them to describe American democracy either as it actually is or as they believe it should be.

Democracy for Everyone

Many people believe that in a democracy, the government ought to do what the majority of the people want. This simple proposition is the heart of majoritarian theory. As a theory of what democracy should be like, **majoritarianism** is popular among both political scientists and ordinary citizens. Many scholars, however, consider majoritarianism to be a surprisingly poor description of how U.S. democracy actually works. In particular, they point to the low level of turnout for elections. Polling data have shown that many Americans are neither particularly interested in politics nor well informed. Few are able to name the persons running for Congress in their districts, and even fewer can discuss the candidates' positions.

Democracy for the Few

If ordinary citizens are not really making policy decisions with their votes, who is? One answer suggests that elites really govern the United States. American government, in other words, is a sham democracy. **Elite theory** is usually used simply to describe the American system. Few people today believe it is a good idea for the country to be run by a privileged minority. In the past, however, many people believed that it was appropriate for the country to be run by an elite. Consider the words of Alexander Hamilton, one of the framers of the Constitution:

> All communities divide themselves into the few and the many. The first are the rich and the wellborn, the other the mass of the people. . . . The people are turbulent and changing; they seldom judge or determine right. Give therefore to the first class a distinct, permanent share in the government. They will check the unsteadiness of the second, and as they cannot receive any advantage by a change, they therefore will ever maintain good government.[4]

Some versions of elite theory posit a small, cohesive, elite class that makes almost all the important decisions for the nation,[5] whereas others suggest that voters choose among competing elites. New members of the elite are recruited through the educational system so that the brightest children of the masses allegedly have the opportunity to join the elite stratum.

Democracy for Groups

A different school of thought holds that our form of democracy is based on group interests. Even if the average citizen cannot keep up with political issues or cast a deciding vote in any election, the individual's interests will be protected by groups that represent her or him.

Theorists who subscribe to **pluralism** see politics as a struggle among groups to gain benefits for their members. Given the structures of the American political system, group conflicts tend to be settled by compromise and accommodation. Because there are a multitude of interests, no one group can dominate the political process. Furthermore, because most individuals have more than one interest, conflict among groups need not divide the nation into hostile camps.

Many political scientists believe that pluralism works very well as a descriptive theory. As a theory of how democracy *should* function, however, pluralism has problems. Poor citizens are rarely represented by interest groups. At the same time, rich citizens are often overrepresented. As political scientist E. E. Schattschneider observed, "The flaw in the pluralist heaven is that the heavenly chorus sings with a strong upper-class accent."[6] There are also serious doubts as to whether group decision making always reflects the best interests of the nation.

Indeed, critics see a danger that groups may become so powerful that all policies become compromises crafted to satisfy the interests of the largest groups. The interests of the public as a whole, then, are not considered. Critics of pluralism have suggested that a democratic system can be virtually paralyzed by the struggle among interest groups. We will discuss interest groups at greater length in Chapter 7.

Some scholars argue that none of these three theories—majoritarianism, elite theory, or pluralism—fully describes the workings of American democracy. These experts say that each theory captures a part of the true reality but that we need all three theories to gain a full understanding of American politics.

Fundamental Values

The writers of the American Constitution believed that the structures they had created would provide for both democracy and a stable political system. They also believed that the nation would be sustained by its **political culture**—a concept

[4]Alexander Hamilton, "Speech in the Constitutional Convention on a Plan of Government," in *Writings*, ed. Joanne B. Freeman (New York: Library of America, 2001).
[5]Michael Parenti, *Democracy for the Few*, 7th ed. (Belmont, Calif.: Wadsworth Publishing, 2002).
[6]E. E. Schattschneider, *The Semi-Sovereign People* (Hinsdale, Ill.: The Dryden Press, 1975; originally published in 1960).

DID YOU KNOW . . .
That there are over 500,000 elected officials in the United States, which is more than all the bank tellers in the country?

Pluralism
A theory that views politics as a conflict among interest groups. Political decision making is characterized by bargaining and compromise.

Political Culture
The collection of beliefs and attitudes toward government and the political process held by a community or nation.

defined as a patterned set of ideas, values, and ways of thinking about government and politics.

Political Socialization

There is considerable consensus among American citizens about certain concepts basic to the U.S. political system. Given that the vast majority of Americans are descendants of immigrants having diverse cultural and political backgrounds, how can we account for this consensus? Primarily, it is the result of **political socialization**—the process by which beliefs and values are transmitted to new immigrants and to our children. The nation depends on several different agents to transmit the precepts of our national culture.

The most obvious source of political socialization is the family. Parents teach their children about the value of participating in the political system through their example and through their approval. One of the primary functions of the public education system in the United States is to teach the values of the political culture to students through history courses, discussions of political issues, and the rituals of pledging allegiance to the flag and celebrating national holidays.

The most fundamental concepts of the American political culture are those of the **dominant culture.** The dominant culture in the United States has its roots in Western European civilization. From that civilization, American politics has inherited a bias toward individualism, private property, and Judeo-Christian ethics. Other cultural heritages honor community or family over individualism and sometimes place far less emphasis on materialism. Additionally, changes in our own society have led to the erosion of some values, such as the sanctity of the family structure, and the acceptance of others, such as women's pursuit of careers in the workplace.

Liberty versus Order

In the United States, our civil liberties include religious freedom—both the right to practice whatever religion one chooses and freedom from any state-imposed religion. Our civil liberties also include freedom of speech—the right to express our opinions freely on all matters, including government actions. Freedom of speech is perhaps one of our most prized liberties, because a democracy could not endure

| Political Socialization
The process through which individuals learn a set of political attitudes and form opinions about social issues. The family and the educational system are two of the most important forces in the political socialization process.

| Dominant Culture
The values, customs, and language established by the group or groups that traditionally have controlled politics and government in a society.

Each year thousands of immigrants are sworn in as new U.S. citizens. The U.S. Constitution, in Article I, Section 8, declares that Congress shall have the power to "establish a uniform Rule of Naturalization." Naturalization is the process by which individuals become U.S. citizens. Are the values that immigrants bring with them from their homelands likely to influence the values of their new country? (Joseph Sohm/Corbis)

without it. These and many other basic guarantees of liberty are found in the Bill of Rights, the first ten amendments to the Constitution.

Liberty, however, is not the only value widely held by Americans. A substantial portion of the American electorate believes that certain kinds of liberty threaten the traditional social order. The right to privacy is a particularly controversial liberty. The United States Supreme Court has held that the right to privacy can be derived from other rights that are explicitly stated in the Bill of Rights. The Supreme Court has also held that under the right to privacy, the government cannot ban either abortion[7] or private homosexual behavior by consenting adults.[8] Cultural conservatives believe that such rights threaten the sanctity of the family and the general cultural commitment to moral behavior. Of course, more liberal Americans disagree with this conservative point of view.

Security is another issue. When Americans feel particularly fearful or vulnerable, the government has emphasized national security over civil liberties. Following the terrorist attacks on the World Trade Center and the Pentagon on September 11, 2001, Congress passed legislation designed to provide greater security at the expense of some civil liberties. In particular, the USA Patriot Act gave law enforcement and intelligence-gathering agencies greater latitude to search out and investigate suspected terrorists. Many Americans objected to the Patriot Act, pointing out that it compromised numerous civil liberties, such as protection from unreasonable searches and seizures. When the news broke in December 2005 that the National Security Agency (NSA) had been engaging in warrantless secret surveillance, many wondered if civil liberties had been eroded too far in the name of national security. The NSA spying issue is discussed further in this chapter's *Which Side Are You On?* feature on the following page.

Equality versus Liberty

The Declaration of Independence states, "All men are created equal." The proper meaning of equality, however, has been disputed by Americans since the Revolution.[9] Much of American history—and indeed, world history—is the story of how the value of **equality** has been extended and elaborated.

First, the right to vote was granted to all adult white males regardless of whether they owned property. The Civil War resulted in the end of slavery and established that, in principle at least, all citizens were equal before the law. The civil rights movement of the 1950s and 1960s sought to make that promise of equality a reality for African Americans. Other movements have sought equality for other racial and ethnic groups, for women, for persons with disabilities, and for gay men and lesbians. We discuss these movements in Chapter 5.

To promote equality, it is often necessary to place limits on the desire by some to treat people unequally. In this sense, equality and liberty are conflicting values. Today, the denial of equal treatment to members of a particular race has very few defenders. Yet as recently as sixty years ago, such denial was a cultural norm.

Economic Equality. Equal treatment regardless of race, religion, gender, and other characteristics is a popular value today. Equal opportunity for individuals to develop their talents and skills is another value with substantial support. Equality of economic status, however, is a controversial value.

For much of history, few people even contemplated the idea that the government could do something about the division of society between rich and poor. Most

A high point of the civil rights movement of the 1950s and 1960s was the March on Washington on August 8, 1963, led by Martin Luther King, Jr. Nearly 250,000 people participated in the event. The following year, Congress passed the Civil Rights Act of 1964, one of the most important civil rights acts in the nation's history. Why does the mandate of equal treatment for all groups of Americans sometimes come into conflict with the concept of liberty? (Library of Congress)

Equality
As a political value, the idea that all people are of equal worth.

---

[7]*Roe v. Wade*, 410 U.S. 113 (1973).
[8]*Lawrence v. Texas*, 539 U.S. 558 (2003).
[9]Gary B. Nash, *The Unknown American Revolution: The Unruly Birth of Democracy and the Struggle to Create America* (New York: Viking, 2005); and Alfred F. Young, ed., *Beyond the American Revolution: Explorations in the History of American Radicalism* (DeKalb, Ill.: Northern Illinois University Press, 1993).

WHICH SIDE ARE YOU ON? | Domestic Surveillance

In December 2005, government sources leaked to the press that President George W. Bush had authorized the National Security Agency (NSA) to secretly intercept calls between potential terrorist suspects overseas and Americans inside the United States. The spying was occurring without the court-approved warrants that are ordinarily required for domestic surveillance. The Bush administration claimed that the surveillance was being conducted as part of the government's efforts to combat terrorism. Under the eavesdropping program, NSA agents were listening to inbound and outbound international phone calls between individuals suspected of terrorist involvement. Many members of Congress and civil liberties advocates, however, quickly denounced the president's actions as unconstitutional.

SPYING IS NECESSARY TO COMBAT TERROR

Proponents of domestic spying argue that the president must exercise broad powers to thwart the efforts of terrorists. Defenders of the program also say that it is a vital tool that could save millions of lives. The United States is at war, they claim, and measures that would be unnecessary in times of peace must be used to protect the nation. And when the enemy relies on secrecy, the government must combat that shroud of secrecy with its own covert actions.

Ordinary Americans have nothing to fear from such surveillance, supporters claim. Individuals without terrorist ties will not be targeted by the NSA. After all, the government has no interest in what kind of pizza ordinary citizens are ordering for

Members of the audience, some wearing black hoods, stand up and turn their backs on Attorney General Alberto Gonzales as he speaks at Georgetown University Law School in January 2006. Is warrantless surveillance critical to prevent another terrorist attack within the United States, as Gonzales has asserted? Why or why not? (AP Photo/Charles Dharapak)

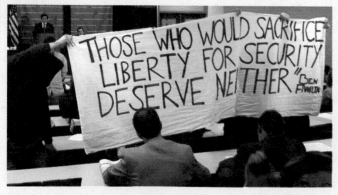

dinner or what time they plan to meet at the neighborhood park. Only phone conversations potentially related to terrorist activity are targeted. Indeed, Bush has offered assurances that the program includes internal safeguards to protect the civil liberties of innocent Americans.

SPYING WITHOUT A WARRANT IS UNCONSTITUTIONAL

Opponents of the NSA's domestic surveillance program claim that it is illegal and unconstitutional. Congress did not specifically authorize such a measure. Indeed, most members of Congress were not aware that the program existed. Even the controversial USA Patriot Act contains no provision that allows government agents to conduct wiretapping and other forms of spying without a judge-approved warrant. The Bush administration ignored the proper checks and balances of the U.S. government in executing its surveillance program.

Critics of the surveillance program also point out that the NSA is supposed to engage solely in international intelligence gathering. Thus, by authorizing spying on domestic individuals, the president has instructed the NSA to act outside its jurisdiction and organizational mission.

The Bush administration has said that innocent Americans are not being targeted. Some Americans are skeptical, however, because there have been reports in the media that the Bush administration has sought information about individuals with ties to the American Civil Liberties Union, Greenpeace, and various groups opposed to the war in Iraq. Some Americans argue that Bush has often attempted to squelch any kind of dissent to his policies and actions and that loyal Americans who do not agree with him may be subject to unwarranted spying and government intrusion into their private affairs.

WHAT'S YOUR POSITION?

How comfortable are you with the NSA's current domestic spying program? Do you feel that it could include adequate safeguards for Americans who are not linked to terrorist organizations? Explain.

GOING ONLINE

To learn more about the National Security Agency, including its history, visit **www.nsa.gov**.

people assumed that such an effort was either impossible or undesirable. This assumption began to lose its force in the 1800s. As a result of the growing wealth of the Western world and a visible increase in the ability of government to take on large projects, some people began to advocate the value of universal equality, or *egalitarianism*. Some radicals dreamed of a revolutionary transformation of society that would establish an egalitarian system—that is, a system in which wealth and power would be redistributed on a more equal basis.

Many others rejected this vision but still came to endorse the values of eliminating poverty and at least reducing the degree of economic inequality in society. Antipoverty advocates believed then and believe now that such a program could alleviate much suffering. In addition, they believed that reducing economic inequality would promote fairness and enhance the moral tone of society generally.

Property Rights and Capitalism. The value of reducing economic inequality is in conflict with the right to **property.** This is because reducing economic inequality typically involves the transfer of property (usually in the form of money) from some people to others. For many people, liberty and property are closely entwined. A capitalist system is based on private property rights. Under **capitalism,** property consists not only of personal possessions but also of wealth-creating assets, such as farms and factories. The investor-owned corporation is in many ways the preeminent capitalist institution. The funds invested by the owners of a corporation are known as *capital*—hence, the very name of the system. Capitalism is also typically characterized by considerable freedom to make binding contracts and by relatively unconstrained markets for goods, services, and investments.

Property—especially wealth-creating property—can be seen as giving its owner political power and the liberty to do whatever he or she wants. At the same time, the ownership of property immediately creates inequality in society. The desire to own property, however, is so widespread among all classes of Americans that egalitarian movements have had a difficult time securing a wide following here.

A conflict between property rights and commercial development came before the United States Supreme Court in the 2005 case of *Kelo v. City of New London*.[10]

---

[10]545 U.S. 469 (2005).

Property
Anything that is or may be subject to ownership. As conceived by the political philosopher John Locke, the right to property is a natural right superior to human law (laws made by government).

Capitalism
An economic system characterized by the private ownership of wealth-creating assets, free markets, and freedom of contract.

This house in Weare, New Hampshire, belongs to United States Supreme Court justice David Souter. The man in front, Logan Darrow Clements, led a signature drive for a ballot initiative that would have asked the town of Weare to seize Souter's land for the purpose of building a hotel. Clements and others were annoyed at the Supreme Court's 2005 decision to allow the city of New London, Connecticut, to seize private land in order to allow private developers to build an office park and expensive apartments. How does this issue relate to the concept of eminent domain? (AP Photo/Jim Cole)

Many residents of New Orleans had to flee to higher ground when a levee broke during Hurricane Katrina. The flooding destroyed large sections of that city and left many of its residents without shelter. Critics of local and state governments and, more important, of the federal government claimed that not enough was done quickly enough to help those who were adversely affected by the flooding. How might all levels of government have done a better job in the wake of this major natural disaster? (Marty Bahamonde/FEMA)

| Eminent Domain
A power set forth in the Fifth Amendment to the U.S. Constitution that allows government to take private property for public use under the condition that just compensation is offered to the landowner.

| Ideology
A comprehensive set of beliefs about the nature of people and about the role of an institution or government.

The case arose when the city of New London, Connecticut, attempted to seize property from numerous homeowners through the power of **eminent domain**, which allows government to take private land for *public use* in return for *just compensation*. Some homeowners resisted because they did not want to move, regardless of the compensation being offered by the city. They also objected because the city planned to turn the land over to private developers who wished to build an office park and expensive condominiums. The homeowners claimed that such a transfer did not constitute a public use. The Supreme Court disagreed, stating that the economic stimulation and increased tax revenues that the city would gain by the transfer of ownership fulfilled the public use requirement for eminent domain takings. The Court's decision caused an immediate uproar across the nation. The widespread disapproval compelled many state and local governments to pass laws against the kind of takings at issue in the *Kelo* case.

Tensions over Big Government

To many Americans, the *Kelo* case exemplified their objections to "big government" overreaching its power. Tensions over the size and scope of government have always plagued Americans. American citizens often express contradictory opinions on the size of government and the role that it should play in their lives. Those who complain about the amount of taxes that they pay each year may also despair over the lack of funds for more teachers in the local schools. Individuals who fear future terrorist attacks may react with outrage at the thought of a government official snooping through their e-mail correspondence.

When Hurricane Katrina ripped through the Gulf Coast region in 2005, the federal government received much of the blame for the extent of the devastation that occurred. Thousands of poor people were left in the city of New Orleans to weather the storm and its aftermath. When the city's levee system failed to keep floodwaters out, homes, jobs, and even lives were lost. Most Americans were quick to argue that the government should have been better prepared for the storm and that government officials should have ensured that everyone was properly evacuated. And many people believed that it was the government's responsibility to clean up the devastation and care for those displaced by the hurricane. Such a level of involvement requires tremendous government power, funds, and resources, however. Clearly, in the case of Katrina, for many, big government seemed necessary and even desirable.

Yet Americans value limited government when it comes to their private lives and civil liberties. Consider the recent objections to domestic surveillance that many individuals have expressed. Opponents of the Bush administration's national security policies have argued that government needs to be restrained and that its powers to invade citizens' private lives should be very limited. As you read in the *Which Side Are You On?* feature on page 12, many citizens have contended that the government has used the war on terrorism to become too powerful. Implicit in that contention is a call for smaller, more limited government.

| Political Ideologies

A political **ideology** is a closely linked set of beliefs about politics. Political ideologies offer their adherents well-organized theories that propose goals for the society and the means by which those goals can be achieved. At the core of every political ideology is a set of guiding values. The two ideologies most commonly referred to in discussions of American politics are *liberalism* and *conservatism*.

Liberalism versus Conservatism

The set of beliefs called **conservatism** includes a limited role for the government in helping individuals. Conservatism also includes support for traditional values. These values usually include a strong sense of patriotism. Conservatives believe that the private sector probably can outperform the government in almost any activity. Believing that the individual is primarily responsible for his or her own well-being, conservatives typically oppose government programs to redistribute income or change the status of individuals.

The set of beliefs called **liberalism** includes advocacy of government action to improve the welfare of individuals, support for civil rights, and tolerance for social change. American liberals believe that government should take positive action to reduce poverty, to redistribute income from wealthier classes to poorer ones, and to regulate the economy. Liberals are often seen as an influential force within the Democratic Party, and conservatives are often regarded as the most influential force in the Republican Party.

The Traditional Political Spectrum

A traditional method of comparing political ideologies is to array them on a continuum from left to right, based primarily on how much power the government should exercise to promote economic equality. Table 1–1 shows how ideologies can be arrayed in a traditional political spectrum. In addition to liberalism and conservatism, the table includes the ideologies of socialism and libertarianism.

Socialism falls on the left side of the spectrum. Socialists play a minor role in the American political arena, although socialist parties and movements have been important in other countries around the world. In the past, socialists typically advocated replacing investor ownership of major businesses with either government ownership or ownership by employee cooperatives. Socialists believed that such steps would break the power of the very rich and lead to an egalitarian society. In more recent times, socialists in Western Europe have advocated more limited programs that redistribute income.

On the right side of the spectrum is **libertarianism**, a philosophy of skepticism toward most government activities. Libertarians strongly support property rights and typically oppose regulation of the economy and redistribution of income. Libertarians support *laissez-faire* capitalism. (*Laissez faire* is French for "let it be.") Libertarians also tend to oppose government attempts to regulate personal behavior and promote moral values.

"Classical" Liberalism

The word *liberal* has an odd history. It comes from the same root as *liberty*, and originally it simply meant "free." In that broad sense, the United States as a whole is a liberal country, and all popular American ideologies are variants of liberalism. In a

"*You'll be happy to know, Father, he's not a Liberal, Moderate or Conservative. Jason's a nothing.*"

Conservatism
A set of beliefs that includes a limited role for the national government in helping individuals, support for traditional values and lifestyles, and a cautious response to change.

Liberalism
A set of beliefs that includes the advocacy of positive government action to improve the welfare of individuals, support for civil rights, and tolerance for political and social change.

Socialism
A political ideology based on strong support for economic and social equality. Socialists traditionally envisioned a society in which major businesses were taken over by the government or by employee cooperatives.

Libertarianism
A political ideology based on skepticism or opposition toward almost all government activities.

TABLE 1–1 | THE TRADITIONAL POLITICAL SPECTRUM

	SOCIALISM	LIBERALISM	CONSERVATISM	LIBERTARIANISM
How much power should the government have over the economy?	Active government control of major economic sectors.	Positive government action in the economy.	Positive government action to support capitalism.	Almost no regulation of the economy.
What should the government promote?	Economic equality, community.	Economic security, equal opportunity, social liberty.	Economic liberty, morality, social order.	Total economic and social liberty.

more restricted definition, a *liberal* was a person who believed in limited government and who opposed religion in politics. A hundred years ago, liberalism referred to a philosophy that in some ways resembled modern-day libertarianism. For that reason, many libertarians today refer to themselves as *classical liberals*.

How did the meaning of the word *liberal* change? In the 1800s, the Democratic Party was seen as the more liberal of the two parties. The Democrats of that time stood for limited government and opposition to moralism in politics. Democrats opposed Republican projects such as building roads, freeing the slaves, and prohibiting the sale of alcoholic beverages. Beginning with Democratic president Woodrow Wilson (1913–1921), however, the party's economic policies began to change. By the time of President Franklin Delano Roosevelt (1933–1945), the Democrats stood for positive government action to help the economy. Although Roosevelt stood for new policies, he kept the old language—as Democrats had long done, he called himself a liberal. We will discuss the history of the two parties in greater detail in Chapter 8.

Outside the United States and Canada, the meaning of the word *liberal* never changed. For this reason, you might hear a left-of-center European denounce U.S. president Ronald Reagan (1981–1989) or British prime minister Margaret Thatcher (1979–1990) for their "liberalism." What is meant, of course, is that these two leaders were enthusiastic advocates of *laissez-faire* capitalism.

Problems with the Traditional Political Spectrum

Many political scientists believe that the traditional left-to-right spectrum does not reflect the complexities of today's political ideologies. Take the example of libertarians. In Table 1–1 on page 15, libertarians are placed to the right of conservatives. If the only question is how much power the government should have over the economy, this is where they belong. Libertarians, however, advocate the most complete possible freedom in social matters. They oppose government action to promote traditional moral values, although such action is often favored by other groups on the political right. Libertarians' strong support for civil liberties seems to align them more closely with modern liberals than with conservatives.

Liberalism is often described as an ideology that supports "big government." If the objective is to promote equality, the description has some validity. In the moral sphere, however, conservatives tend to support more government regulation of social values and moral decisions than do liberals. Thus, conservatives tend to oppose gay rights legislation and propose stronger curbs on pornography. Liberals usually show greater tolerance for alternative lifestyle choices and oppose government attempts to regulate personal behavior and morals.

A Four-Cornered Ideological Grid

For a more sophisticated breakdown of American popular ideologies, many scholars use a four-cornered grid, as shown in Figure 1–1. The grid provides four possible ideologies. Each quadrant contains a substantial portion of the American electorate. Individual voters may fall anywhere on the grid, depending on the strength of their beliefs about economic and cultural issues.

Note that there is no generally accepted term for persons in the lower-left position, which we have labeled "economic liberals, cultural conservatives." Some scholars have used terms such as *populist* to describe this point of view, but such terms can be misleading.

Individuals who are economic liberals and cultural conservatives tend to support government action both to promote the values of economic equality and fairness

FIGURE 1–1 | A FOUR-CORNERED IDEOLOGICAL GRID

In this grid, the colored squares represent four different political ideologies. The vertical choices range from cultural order to cultural liberty. The horizontal choices range from economic equality to economic liberty.

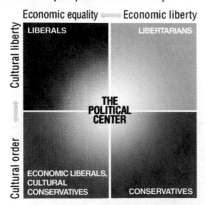

and to defend traditional values such as the family and marriage. These individuals may describe themselves as conservative or moderate. They may be Democrats due to their support of economic liberalism, or they may vote for a Republican candidate due to their conservative values.

Libertarian, as a position on our four-way grid, does not refer to the small Libertarian Party, which has only a minor role in the American political arena. Rather, libertarians more typically support the Republican Party. They are more likely than conservatives to vote for a compatible Democrat, however.

Classifying the Voters. If the traditional political spectrum held, most voters would fall into the liberal or conservative quarters of our ideological grid. Actually, there are a substantial number of voters in each quadrant. Asking whether the government should guarantee everyone a job, for example, divides the electorate roughly in half on the economic dimension. Certain questions about abortion also divide the electorate roughly in half on the social dimension. Knowing how a voter answered one of these questions, however, does not tell us how he or she answered the other one. Many people would give a "liberal" answer to the jobs question but a "conservative" answer to the abortion question; also, many people would give a "conservative" answer to the jobs question and a "liberal" answer on abortion.

Conservative Popularity. Even though all four ideologies are popular, it does not follow that the various labels we have used in the four-cornered grid are equally favored. Voters are much more likely to describe themselves as conservative than as liberal. There are a variety of reasons for this, but one is that *liberal* has come to imply "radical" to many people, whereas *conservative* often implies "moderate." Because most Americans value moderation, the conservative label has an advantage, and few politicians today willingly describe themselves as liberal. The designation *libertarian* has an even more radical flavor than *liberal*, and the number of voters with obvious libertarian tendencies far exceeds the number who are willing to adopt the label. We will look further at popular ideologies in Chapter 6.

Other Ideologies

Two other important ideologies fit poorly into the traditional political spectrum. These are communism and fascism. Neither ideology has had a significant following in the United States. Their impact on Europe and Asia, however, determined the course of twentieth-century history.

The first communists were a radical faction that broke away from the socialist movement. Traditionally, socialists had always considered themselves to be democrats. The communists, however, believed that they could abolish capitalism and institute socialism through a severe partisan dictatorship. The Soviet Union, founded by Russian Communists after World War I (1914–1918), succeeded in establishing government control of farms, factories, and businesses of all kinds and in replacing the market system with central planning. Under Joseph Stalin (1924–1953), the Soviet Union also developed into a brutal totalitarian regime.

The most famous example of fascism was Nazi Germany (1933–1945). As with communism, the success of fascism depended on a large body of disciplined followers and a populist appeal. Fascism, however, championed elitism rather than egalitarianism. It was strongly influenced by Charles Darwin's concept of "the survival of the fittest." It valued action over rational deliberation and explicitly rejected liberal individualism—it exalted the national collective, united behind an absolute ruler. Fascism appealed to patriotism or nationalism, but it shaped these common sentiments into virulent racism.

DID YOU KNOW . . .

That Russia is expected to lose 30 million people by 2050 and will have a population of only 118 million, compared to the predicted 420 million for the United States?

Communism
A revolutionary variant of socialism that favors a partisan (and often totalitarian) dictatorship, government control of all enterprises, and the replacement of free markets by central planning.

Fascism
A twentieth-century ideology—often totalitarian—that exalts the national collective behind an absolute ruler. Fascism rejects liberal individualism, values action over rational deliberation, and glorifies war.

The al Qaeda terrorist group frequently uses the Internet to broadcast messages from Osama bin Laden. On the particular day that this Web site was shown, it contained an audiotape in which bin Laden claimed that none of the prisoners held in Guantánamo Bay, Cuba, by the American government had anything to do with al Qaeda operations. Is it possible to label bin Laden as the "chief" or "leader" of the al Qaeda movement? (AP Photo/IntelCenter)

Ideology in the Islamic World

The terrorists who attacked the World Trade Center and the Pentagon on September 11, 2001, were ideologically motivated. These terrorists were members of the al Qaeda[11] network led by Osama bin Laden. Al Qaeda's ideology is based on a radical and fundamentalist interpretation of Islam, an interpretation sometimes called *Islamism*. Al Qaeda rejects all Western democratic values and calls for the establishment of a worldwide Islamic political order (the *caliphate*). Al Qaeda's Islamist allies in Afghanistan—the Taliban—were, in fact, able to impose an Islamist government until they were brought down by a U.S.-led invasion and internal opponents supported by Western nations.

Saddam Hussein's Baath Party in Iraq also gained power as an authoritarian movement. One of the many surprises faced by the U.S.-led coalition after it took control of Iraq was the durability of the Baath Party.[12] Unlike the Iraqi army, the Baath Party did not dissolve on Hussein's defeat but continued to try to hold power. Baathists played a prominent role in the subsequent terrorist attacks on coalition troops. The Baath Party gained strength from the fact that it is ideologically based and was not created for the sole purpose of supporting Hussein.

The Baath Party was founded by Syrian ideologue Michel Aflaq. Although Baathists are often referred to as Arab nationalists, Baath ideology goes beyond pan-Arab nationalism and actually views the Arabs as a kind of master race. Baathism glorifies constant struggle and is relatively nonreligious. The ideological similarity between Baathism and fascism is quite striking. Hussein also borrowed organizational techniques from Stalin's Communist Party and openly cited the Soviet leader as a role model.

Even before the Second Gulf War in 2003, Baathism had limited appeal in the Arab world. Radical Islamism is a more attractive and widespread ideology. The United States may be responding to Islamist movements for many years to come.

The Changing Face of America

The face of America is changing as its citizens age, become more diverse, and generate new needs for laws and policies. Long a nation of growth, the United States has also become a middle-aged nation with a low birthrate and an increasing number of older citizens who want services from the government. Both the aging of the population and its changing ethnic composition will have significant political consequences.

The Aging of America

Like other economically advanced countries, the United States has in recent decades experienced falling birthrates and an increase in the number of older citizens. The "aging of America" is a weaker phenomenon than in many other wealthy countries, however. Today, the median age of the population is 35.5 in the United States and 38.2 in Europe. By 2050, the median age in the United States is expected to rise slightly to 36.2. In Europe, it is expected to reach 52.7.

---

[11]*Al Qaeda*, sometimes transliterated as *al Qaida* or *al-Qa'idah*, is Arabic for "the base."
[12]*Baath* is Arabic for "renaissance."

Although the United States is aging, it is not aging quickly enough to halt the growth of its population. One reason for this is immigration. Of course, new immigrants add directly to the population of the country. In addition, however, a great many new immigrants are of exactly the right age to become mothers and fathers.

Figure 1–2 shows the predicted change in the proportion of the retirement-age population in the United States over the next half-century. By 2025, that proportion is expected to be about one and a half times what it is today. As a result, the government will be under pressure to revise the Social Security system. A larger portion of each worker's wages will have to go toward taxes to support benefits for the retired population—or else the benefits may be reduced.

The larger number of older persons will also strain health-care budgets. Not only do older persons require more medical care, but we can expect that advances in medical science will cause the demand for medical services to rise in future years.

Our Growing Population

The United States differs from most economically advanced nations in the growth of its population. In 2050, there are expected to be about 420 million Americans, up from 300 million today.

The End of the Population Explosion.   In recent decades, population growth rates have been falling throughout the world. The great population explosion of the late twentieth century is reaching its end—the world's population, currently about 6.5 billion, is expected to stabilize at perhaps 9 billion by 2050. While growth rates remain high in many African and Muslim nations, most economically advanced nations will have smaller populations in 2050 than they do today.[13] The United States will continue to grow during these years, however. For that reason, the portion of the world's population living in the United States in 2050 will be close to what it is today.

U.S. Fertility Rates.   Today, the United States has a fertility rate of 2.1 children per woman. The *fertility rate* measures the average number of children that a group of women are expected to have over the course of a lifetime. A fertility rate of 2.1 happens to be equal to the "long-term replacement rate." In other words, if a nation maintains a fertility rate of 2.1 over a long period of time, the population of that nation will eventually stabilize—it will neither grow nor shrink.

A fertility rate of 2.1 does not mean that the population of the United States has already stopped growing, however. If—as is true of the United States—a country has been growing in the past, it may take a long time for the population to stabilize. Because of past growth, the median age of the population is younger than it would otherwise be. This means that there are more potential mothers and fathers. Only after its residents age will the population of a country stabilize.

Ethnic Change

As a result of differences in fertility rates and immigration, the ethnic character of the United States is also changing. Non-Hispanic white Americans have a fertility rate of just over 1.8. African Americans have a fertility rate of 2.1. Hispanic Americans, however, have a current fertility rate of almost 3.0. (The fertility rate in Mexico is only 2.5.) Figure 1–3 on the following page shows the projected changes in the U.S. ethnic distribution in future years.

A large share of all new immigrants are Hispanic, which also serves to increase the Hispanic proportion of the U.S. population. A **Hispanic** is someone who can

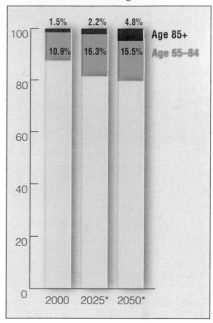

FIGURE 1–2 | THE AGING OF AMERICA
The figures show that the portion of the population over age sixty-five will increase during the next half-century. Growth in the proportion of the elderly will slow by 2050 due to the effects of immigration.

*Data for 2025 and 2050 are projections.
Source: U.S. Bureau of the Census.

| Hispanic
Someone who can claim a heritage from a Spanish-speaking country (other than Spain). The term is used only in the United States or other countries that receive immigrants—Spanish-speaking persons living in Spanish-speaking countries do not normally apply the term to themselves.

---

[13]Exceptions include countries with large immigrant populations, such as Canada and Australia; also, Britain and France are expected to post modest population gains.

FIGURE 1–3 | DISTRIBUTION OF THE U.S. POPULATION BY RACE AND HISPANIC ORIGIN, 1980 TO 2075

By about 2060, minorities will constitute a majority of the U.S. population.

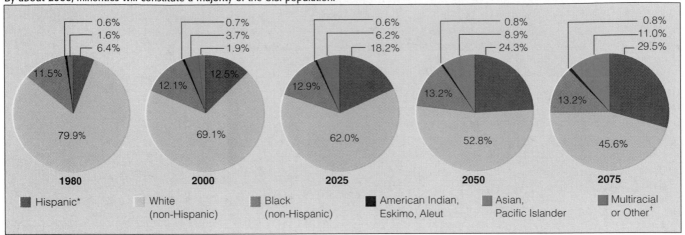

Data for 2025, 2050, and 2075 are projections.

*Persons of Hispanic origin can be of any race.

†The "multiracial or other" category in 2000 is not an official census category but represents all non-Hispanics who chose either "some other race" or two or more races in the 2000 census.

Source: U.S. Bureau of the Census.

claim a heritage from a Spanish-speaking country (other than Spain). Table 1–2 shows the places of origin for immigrants entering the United States in 2004. By 2015, they will no longer be the majority in Texas. Immigration can be a politically tense subject, especially in states bordering Mexico. For a look at one dimension of the illegal immigration issue, see this chapter's *Beyond Our Borders* feature.

TABLE 1–2 | PLACES OF ORIGIN OF IMMIGRANTS INTO THE UNITED STATES, 2004

REGION OR COUNTRY	NUMBER	PERCENT
Mexico	173,664	18.4
El Salvador	29,285	3.1
Cuba	15,385	1.6
Dominican Republic	30,049	3.2
Haiti	13,502	1.4
Canada	22,437	2.4
Jamaica	13,565	1.4
Other North America	40,406	4.3
Colombia	17,887	1.9
Other South America	51,290	5.4
India	65,472	6.9
China	45,942	4.9
Philippines	54,632	5.8
Vietnam	30,064	3.2
Korea	19,441	2.1
Iran	5,898	0.6
Other Asia	83,040	8.8
Europe	130,151	13.8
Africa	62,510	6.6
Oceania	6,929	0.7
Unknown	24,592	2.6
TOTAL	946,141	100.0*

*Numbers do not add up exactly to 100 percent due to rounding off.

Source: Bureau of Citizenship and Immigration Services.

BEYOND OUR BORDERS | Mexico's Pamphlet for Migrants

Immigration is a sensitive topic for many Americans. According to government statistics, roughly 350,000 individuals enter the United States illegally each year. The majority of these immigrants enter the United States by way of Mexico.

Illegal immigrants often rely heavily on government social services and aid, thus placing an additional strain on taxpayers in some communities, particularly in states bordering Mexico. Not surprisingly, many Americans became enraged when news broke that the Mexican government had been publishing a pamphlet that gives advice to prospective migrants wishing to enter the United States illegally. Entitled *The Guide for the Mexican Migrant,* the thirty-two-page pamphlet uses a comic book format to explain to Mexicans what they should and should not do to cross the border safely.

SAFETY A SERIOUS CONCERN

The Mexican Foreign Ministry has defended its decision to publish the guide, saying that it had no intention of encouraging or promoting illegal immigration to the United States. Rather, safety was the primary concern. The Foreign Ministry estimates that more than three hundred Mexicans die each year while attempting to cross the border. The journey to the

The cover of *The Guide for the Mexican Migrant,* taken from the official Web site maintained by the Mexican government.

United States often involves a long and difficult trek across desert terrain. Snakes and dehydration pose significant hazards, as do river crossings. The guide attempts to offer practical advice about these dangers.

Numerous illegal immigrants residing in the United States have called the pamphlet useless, though. Individuals who have made the trek say that common sense, proper supplies, and a trustworthy *coyote* (smuggler) are far more helpful in ensuring safe passage than the Mexican government's publication. Some liken the pamphlet to Mexico's attempt to create desert survival kits, nicknamed "Happy Meals," which were laughed out of existence in 2001.

SOME AMERICANS OUTRAGED

The pamphlet seemed to make a greater impression on Americans than on the Mexican migrants it was intended to help. Proponents of stricter enforcement of immigration laws denounced the guide as a thinly veiled endorsement of illegal immigration by the Mexican government. Many argue that the guide reflects the Mexican government's interest in maintaining the status quo on immigration. After all, claim these critics, Mexicans living in the United States send roughly $15 billion per year back to family members in Mexico. This amount represents a significant portion of Mexico's foreign income, exceeded only by the $16 billion in annual revenue Mexico generates from oil exports.

The controversy over the pamphlet may broaden. The Mexican government recently suspended plans to distribute maps of the border region to prospective migrants. U.S. Department of Homeland Security secretary Michael Chertoff said that the United States opposed any such plan "in the strongest terms." Mexican officials claim that increased diplomatic pressure from the United States was not the reason they abandoned their plans to distribute the map. Instead, the Mexican officials feared that American anti-immigrant groups, such as the so-called Minutemen, would use the maps to discover where migrants were likely to gather.

FOR CRITICAL ANALYSIS

Few deny that illegal immigrants constitute an increasingly important segment of the American economy. Entire industries, such as construction and agriculture, rely heavily on the labor of both legal and illegal immigrants. As it formulates immigration policy, how should the U.S. government balance these contributions with the stresses that immigrants place on social services?

POLITICS AND DIVERSITY | The Problem of Racial Classifications

Today, the lines separating racial groups are becoming increasingly blurred, in part because of marriage between men and women of different races. Illegal in sixteen states until a 1967 ruling by the United States Supreme Court,* interracial marriage has become more common in recent decades. When Oprah Winfrey asked golfer Tiger Woods about his ethnicity, Woods said he was not a black but a "Cablinasian"—a combination of Caucasian, black, Indian, and Asian.

WHAT ARE THE NUMBERS?

Interracial marriage is especially common among races with relatively small populations. For example, about 43 percent of married non-Hispanic Native American women have spouses of a different category. "Out-marriage" by African Americans is less common—only 4 percent of African American women are married to men of a different race. In contrast, 22 percent of Asian American women are married outside the Asian American category, and 18 percent of Hispanic women are married to non-Hispanic men.

These figures are for all marriages, and they include older married persons who found their mates at a time when interracial marriage was often unacceptable. Younger people are more likely to intermarry. New immigrants, however, are less likely to intermarry than native-born citizens, and so our growing immigrant population also holds down the total number of interracial marriages.

A POLITICAL ISSUE

The U.S. government uses racial classifications to determine who is eligible for certain benefits, notably protections against

*Loving v. Virginia, 388 U.S. 1 (1967).

discrimination. Yet how can these classifications be applied to the millions of Americans with mixed backgrounds? Before the 2000 census, the U.S. Congress debated which questions should appear on the census forms. A group of multiracial activists campaigned for a "multiracial" option on the census and received support from the Republican leadership.

This proposal was opposed, however, by established civil rights organizations. The problem was not just that a multiracial option might reduce the official number of African Americans and therefore reduce black political influence. Some opponents of the classification argued that multiracialism did not really exist. Traditionally, a person with any identifiable African ancestry has been considered black in the United States. In effect, the multiracial activists and the African American leadership were at odds over deeply held but conflicting definitions of identity.

In the end, the multiracial option was not created. Census respondents were allowed to check more than one racial box, however, and 2.4 percent of all respondents did so. Some activists have since argued that the government should not collect information on racial identity at all. An initiative to prevent the state of California from collecting such data was placed on the ballot in 2003 but was voted down by large margins.

FOR CRITICAL ANALYSIS

Some people have suggested that, partly due to intermarriage, Americans will eventually begin to see groups such as Japanese Americans and Chinese Americans as essentially "white." What impact would this have on African Americans?

The number of persons who identify themselves as "multiracial" is also growing due to interracial marriages. Those who consider themselves as multiracial may have one parent of Chinese descent and another of Mexican descent, for example. What might be the consequences of a large multiracial population? We look at that question in this chapter's *Politics and Diversity* feature above.

Why the Term *Hispanic?*

To the U.S. Census Bureau, *Hispanics* are those who identify themselves by that term. Hispanics can be of any race. Hispanics can be new immigrants or the descendants of families that have lived in the United States for centuries.

Hispanics may come from any of about twenty primarily Spanish-speaking countries,[14] and they differ among themselves in many ways. Hispanic Americans, as a result, are a highly diverse population. The three largest Hispanic groups are Mexican

---

[14]According to the census definition, "Hispanic" includes the relatively small number of Americans whose ancestors came directly from Spain itself. Few of these people are likely to check the "Hispanic" box on a census form, however.

Mexican Americans at 58.5 percent of all Hispanics; Puerto Ricans (all of whom are U.S. citizens) at 9.6 percent of the total; and Cuban Americans at 3.5 percent.

The term *Hispanic* itself, although used by the government, is not popular among all Hispanic Americans. Some prefer the term *Latino*. Most prefer a name that identifies their heritage more specifically—many Mexican Americans would rather be called Latino than Hispanic. Some Mexican Americans prefer the term *Chicano*, which, to many, means "neither from here, nor from there" in reference to the United States and Mexico. Chicanos strongly dislike being classified as Hispanics and view their ethnicity in overtly political terms as a struggle to maintain ethnic pride in the face of Anglo-American cultural domination.

The diversity among Hispanic Americans results in differing political behavior. The majority of Hispanic Americans vote Democratic. In 2004, they backed Democratic presidential candidate John Kerry over Republican George W. Bush by 53 to 44 percent. Cuban Americans, however, are usually Republican. Most Cuban Americans left Cuba because of Fidel Castro's Communist regime, and their strong anticommunism translates into conservative politics.

This is a typical street scene in Queens, New York. Within the New York City region, there are over two million Hispanics. There are also numerous Spanish-language television stations and a number of Spanish-language daily newspapers. How might different Hispanic groups in different geographic areas have varying political views? (AP Photo/Tina Fineberg)

The Hispanic Vote in the 2006 Elections

In 2000, Bush received 34 percent of the Hispanic vote. By 2004, that number exceeded 44 percent. In 2006, in contrast, surveys consistently showed that Hispanics favored Democratic candidates over Republicans by 73 percent to 26 percent. Since his days as Texas governor, Bush had envisioned creating a stronger long-term Republican coalition by adding Hispanics. Indeed, Hispanic voters responded favorably in the past to Bush's campaign appeals based on religious and family values, and patriotism. So what went wrong? In a word: immigration. While Bush favored an amnesty approach to illegal immigrants coupled with a guest worker program and the possibility of citizenship, most Republican members of Congress took a hard line against immigration. Consequently, Hispanics viewed Democrats as better able to handle immigration issues than Republicans. Barring an unexpected shift in immigration sentiment among Republicans, the Hispanic vote in 2008 will again favor Democratic candidates.

Other Trends

Various other social trends reveal changes that are under way in American society. Among the most important shifts has been the increasing number of women participating in the labor force. In 1960, only 36 percent of women over the age of sixteen were working outside the home or actively seeking work. By the time of the 2000 census, that number had risen to 58 percent.[15] An interesting point is that during the same years, labor force participation by men actually dropped. In 1960, the participation rate was 80 percent. By 2000, it was 71 percent. Likely causes of this decline include more years spent in higher education and earlier retirement.

Americans today are better educated than in the past. In 1960, only two-fifths of the population over the age of twenty-five had graduated from high school. By 2000, about four-fifths of all adults were high school graduates. In 1960, only 8 percent of Americans had a college degree. Today, one-fourth have a degree.

Abortion is a major political and social issue. Abortion rates rose sharply after abortion was legalized in 1973 but have declined since. The rate of divorce, another social indicator, rose from 2.5 divorces a year for every 1,000 people in 1965 to 4.8 in 1975. Over the last ten years the rate has begun to drop, and by 2006 it was at 4.2 divorces for every 1,000 people. The abortion and divorce rates parallel a large number of other indicators of social trouble, such as the murder rate—years of increases were followed by significant declines over the last decade.

---

[15]Though it is now several years old, the 2000 census is still the most accurate source for many kinds of data and will remain valuable until the next census is taken in 2010.

MAKING A DIFFERENCE | Seeing Democracy in Action

One way to begin to understand the American political system is to observe a legislative body in action. There are thousands of elected legislatures in the United States at all levels of government. You might choose to visit a city council, a school board, a township board of trustees, a state legislature, or the U.S. Congress.

Why Should You Care?

State and local legislative bodies can have a direct impact on your life. For example, local councils or commissions typically oversee the police, and the behavior of the police is a matter of interest even if you live on-campus. If you live off-campus, local authorities are responsible for an even greater number of issues that affect you directly. Are there items that the Sanitation Department refuses to pick up? You might be able to change its policies by lobbying your councilperson.

Even if there are no local issues that concern you, there are still benefits to be gained from observing a local legislative session. You may discover that local government works rather differently than you expected. You might learn, for example, that the representatives of your political party do not serve your interests as well as you thought—or that the other party is much more sensible than you had presumed.

What Can You Do?

To find out when and where local legislative bodies meet, look up the number of the city hall or county building in the telephone directory, and call the clerk of the council. In many communities, city council meetings and county board meetings can be seen on public access TV channels. Many cities and almost all state governments have Internet Web sites.

Before attending a business session of the legislature, try to find out how the members are elected. Are the members chosen by the "at-large" method of election, so that each member represents the whole community, or are they chosen by specific geographic districts or wards? Is there a chairperson or official leader who controls the meetings? What are the responsibilities of this legislature?

When you visit the legislature, keep in mind the theory of representative democracy. The legislators or council members are elected to represent their constituents (those who live in their geographic area). Observe how often the members refer to their constituents or to the special needs of their community or electoral district. Listen for sources of conflict within a community. If there is a debate, for example, over a zoning proposal that involves the issue of land use, try to figure out why some members oppose the proposal.

If you want to follow up on your visit, try to get a brief interview with one of the members of the council or board. In general, legislators are very willing to talk to students, particularly students who also are voters. Ask the member how he or she sees the job of representative. How can the wishes of constituents be identified? How does the representative balance the needs of the ward or district with the good of the entire community? You can write to many legislators via e-mail. You might ask how much e-mail they receive and who actually answers it.

Key Terms

aristocracy 5

authoritarianism 5

authority 5

capitalism 13

communism 17

consent of the people 7

conservatism 15

democracy 5

democratic republic 7

direct democracy 6

dominant culture 10

elite theory 8

eminent domain 14

equality 11

fascism 17

government 3

Hispanic 19

ideology 14

initiative 6

institution 3

legislature 6

legitimacy 5

liberalism 15

libertarianism 15

liberty 5

limited government 8

majoritarianism 8

majority 8

majority rule 8

order 3

pluralism 9

political culture 9

political socialization 10

politics 3

popular sovereignty 7

property 13

recall 6

referendum 6

representative democracy 7

republic 7

socialism 15

totalitarian regime 5

universal suffrage 8

Chapter Summary

1 Politics is the process by which people decide which members of society get certain benefits or privileges and which members do not. It is the struggle over power or influence within institutions and organizations that can grant benefits or privileges. Government is the institution within which decisions are made that resolve conflicts or allocate benefits and privileges. It is unique because it has the ultimate authority within society.

2 Two fundamental political values are order, which includes security against violence, and liberty, the greatest freedom of the individual consistent with the freedom of other individuals. Liberty can be both promoted by government and invoked against government. To be effective, government authority must be backed by legitimacy.

3 In a direct democracy, such as ancient Athens, the people themselves make the important political decisions. The United States is a representative democracy, where the people elect representatives to make the decisions.

4 Theories of American democracy include majoritarianism, in which the government does what the majority wants; elite theory, in which the real power lies with one or more elites; and pluralist theory, in which organized interest groups contest for power.

5 Fundamental American values include liberty, order, equality, and property. Not all of these values are fully compatible. The value of order often competes with civil liberties, and economic equality competes with property rights.

6 Popular political ideologies can be arrayed from left (liberal) to right (conservative). We can also analyze economic liberalism and conservatism separately from cultural liberalism and conservatism.

7 The face of America is changing as the population ages and becomes more ethnically diverse. Other changes—including the growing number of women in the workforce and higher levels of education—are also altering the face of the nation.

Selected Print and Media Resources

SUGGESTED READINGS

Harrison, Lawrence E., and Samuel P. Huntington, eds. *Culture Matters: How Values Shape Human Progress*. New York: Basic Books, 2001. Each of the essays included in this book gives insight into an important question: How and why do some cultures do a better job of creating freedom, prosperity, and justice than others?

Lasswell, Harold. *Politics: Who Gets What, When and How*. New York: McGraw-Hill, 1936. This classic work defines the nature of politics.

Levy, Bernard-Henri. *American Vertigo: Traveling America in the Footsteps of Tocqueville*. New York: Random House, 2006. The author, a French journalist and philosopher, seeks to explore the question of what it means to be an American today. Just as Alexis de Tocqueville did in the 1820s, Levy provides a foreigner's description of American culture and life.

Ngai, Mae M. *Impossible Subjects: Illegal Aliens and the Making of Modern America*. Princeton, N.J.: Princeton University Press, 2005. This study explains why and how illegal immigration became the central problem in U.S. immigration policy. Ngai delves into the complex subjects of citizenship, race, and state authority.

Tocqueville, Alexis de. *Democracy in America*. Edited by Phillips Bradley. New York: Vintage Books, 1945. Life in the United States is described by a French writer who traveled through the nation in the 1820s.

MEDIA RESOURCES

All Things Considered—A daily broadcast of National Public Radio that provides extensive coverage of political, economic, and social news stories.

The Conservatives—A program that shows the rise of the conservative movement in America from the 1940s, through the presidential candidacy of Barry Goldwater, to the presidency of Ronald Reagan. In addition to Goldwater and Reagan, leaders interviewed include William F. Buckley, Jr., Norman Podhoretz, and Milton Friedman.

Liberalism vs. Conservatism—A 2001 film from Teacher's Video that focuses on two contrasting views of the role of government in society.

Mr. Smith Goes to Washington—A classic movie, produced in 1939, starring Jimmy Stewart as the honest citizen who goes to Congress trying to represent his fellow citizens. The movie dramatizes the clash between representing principles and representing corrupt interests.

The Values Issue and American Politics: Values Matter Most—Ben Wattenberg travels around the country in this 1995 program speaking to a broad range of ordinary Americans. He examines what he calls the "values issue"—the issues of crime, welfare, race, discipline, drugs, and prayer in the schools. Wattenberg believes that candidates who can best address these issues will win elections.

E·MOCRACY | Connecting to American Government and Politics

The Web has become a virtual library, a telephone directory, a contact source, and a vehicle to improve your understanding of American government and politics today. To help you become familiar with Web resources, we conclude each chapter in this book with an *E-mocracy* feature. The *Logging On* section in each of these features includes Internet addresses, or uniform resource locators (URLs), that will take you to Web sites focusing on topics or issues discussed in the chapter. Realize that Web sites come and go continually, so some of the Web sites that we include in the *Logging On* section may not exist by the time you read this book.

Each *E-mocracy* feature also includes an InfoTrac Internet activity. These activities are designed to lead you to Web sites that you can explore to learn more about an important political issue.

A word of caution about Internet use: Many students surf the Web for political resources. When doing so, you need to remember to approach these sources with care. For one thing, you should be very careful when giving out information about yourself. You also need to use good judgment because the reliability or intent of any given Web site is often unknown. Some sites are more concerned with accuracy than others, and some sites are updated to include current information while others are not.

| Logging On

We have a powerful and interesting Web site for the textbook, which you can access through the Wadsworth American Government Resource Center. Go to

www.politicalscience.wadsworth.com/ amgov

You may also want to visit the home page of Dr. Politics—offered by Steffen Schmidt, one of the authors of this book—for some interesting ideas and activities relating to American government and politics. Go to

www.public.iastate.edu/~sws/ homepage.html

Information about the rules and requirements for immigration and citizenship can be found at the Web site of the U.S. Citizenship and Immigration Services:

www.uscis.gov/graphics/index.htm

For a basic "front door" to almost all U.S. government Web sites, click onto the very useful site maintained by the University of Michigan:

www.lib.umich.edu/govdocs/ govweb.html

For access to federal government offices and agencies, go to the U.S. government's official Web site at

www.firstgov.gov

To learn about the activities of one of the nation's oldest liberal political organizations, go to the Web site of the Americans for Democratic Action (ADA) at the following URL:

www.adaction.org

You can find a wealth of information about the changing face of America at the Web site of the Bureau of the Census:

www.census.gov

| Online Review

At **www.politicalscience.wadsworth.com/ schmidt12**, you will find a free Study Guide to this book. For each chapter, there are two online quizzes to help you master the material.

• The PoliPrep Self-Study Assessment provides a pretest for each major section of the chapter. PoliPrep then generates a customized study plan. After you complete the study plan, a posttest evaluates your progress.

• The Tutorial Quiz for each chapter provides questions on the chapter contents, including the features. The questions are organized to match the major sections of the chapter.

2 | The Constitution

What If . . .
Roe v. Wade Were Overturned?

BACKGROUND

The U.S. Constitution is the supreme law of the land, taking precedence over any state or local laws. As you will read in this chapter, there are a number of methods for changing the Constitution. One such method is *judicial review,* the power of the United States Supreme Court or other courts to declare unconstitutional laws and other acts of government. Supreme Court cases are often hotly contested because of the powerful role judicial review plays in shaping the laws that all Americans must follow.

The decision in the 1973 case *Roe v. Wade* is one of the most contentious ever handed down by the Supreme Court. In the *Roe* case, the Court declared that a woman has a constitutionally protected right to privacy when consulting her physician about an abortion. Therefore, said the Court, the states cannot restrict a woman's access to abortion during the first three months of pregnancy. More than thirty years later, however, the debate over the legality of abortion still rages in the United States.

WHAT IF *ROE V. WADE* WERE OVERTURNED?

If the Supreme Court overturned *Roe v. Wade,* the authority to regulate abortion would fall again to the states. Prior to the *Roe* case, each state exercised the authority to decide whether abortion would be legal within its borders. Laws regarding abortion usually emanated from the state legislatures. Some critics of *Roe's* constitutional merits have argued that allowing the Supreme Court to proclaim (or deny) the uniform legality of abortion is undemocratic because the justices are not elected officials. In contrast, if state legislatures regained the power to create abortion policy, the resulting laws would reflect the majority opinion of each state's voters. Legislators would have to respect popular sentiment on the issue or risk losing their next reelection bids.

If *Roe* were overturned, states would thus decide under which circumstances abortion would be legal, if at all. States in which abortion rights are considered vital would continue to place very few restrictions on women seeking to terminate their pregnancies. Other states whose residents favor greater restrictions on abortion might allow the procedure only in instances of rape or incest, or if the mother's health would be put at risk by her giving birth. Still others might ban abortions altogether.

THE POSSIBILITY OF STATE BANS ON ABORTION

Given the support of at least limited abortion rights among Americans, women's access to abortion would be unlikely to change drastically if the *Roe* case were overturned. Indeed, simply overturning the *Roe* case would not make abortion illegal overnight. In many states, abortion rights are very popular. A legislature in one of these states would not seriously consider a measure to ban abortion or even further restrict access to it. Such an attempt would be an act of political futility—if not stupidity.

Even if conservative states such as Mississippi, Kentucky, and the Dakotas were to outlaw abortions, women living in those states would not face a markedly changed reality. In each of these states, 98 percent of the counties do not have an abortion clinic. Many women desiring the procedure already have to travel long distances. If abortion were banned, these women could still cross state lines to obtain an abortion. In the unlikely case that twenty-one of the most conservative states banned abortion, only 170 providers would be affected—less than 10 percent of the national total.

A CHALLENGE AWAITS IN SOUTH DAKOTA

Undoubtedly feeling optimism over President George W. Bush's recent conservative Supreme Court appointments—John Roberts and Samuel Alito—South Dakota's legislature passed a law in February 2006 banning abortion. By any standards, the new law is unconstitutional given the existing precedent of the *Roe v. Wade* decision. Planned Parenthood, which operates the only abortion clinic in South Dakota, announced plans to sue the state over the new law.

Many observers have indicated that South Dakota's law is aimed at forcing the Supreme Court to revisit the *Roe* decision. The law's supporters undoubtedly hope that the newly constituted Court will overturn *Roe.* Much is at stake in this clash over abortion rights, and considerable amounts of funds and energy are likely to be expended by both sides in what may be a prolonged legal contest. Already, private donors have pledged funds to help the South Dakota state government in its pending legal battle with Planned Parenthood.

FOR CRITICAL ANALYSIS

1. Why do you think that abortion remains a contentious topic more than thirty years after the *Roe v. Wade* decision? Should the *Roe* decision be revisited? Why or why not?
2. How significant a role should the courts play in deciding constitutional questions about abortion? Do you feel that individual states should have a say in the legality of abortion within their own borders? Why or why not?

We the People of the United States, in Order to form a more perfect Union, establish Justice, insure domestic Tranquility, provide for the common defence, promote the general Welfare, and secure the Blessings of Liberty to ourselves and our Posterity, do ordain and establish this Constitution for the United States of America.

Every schoolchild in America has at one time or another been exposed to these famous words from the Preamble to the U.S. Constitution. The document itself is remarkable. The U.S. Constitution, compared with others in the fifty states and in the world, is relatively short. Because amending it is difficult, it also has relatively few amendments. The Constitution has remained largely intact for over two hundred years. To a great extent, this is because the principles set forth in the Constitution are sufficiently broad that they can be adapted to meet the needs of a changing society. (Sometimes questions arise over the extent to which and how the Constitution should be adapted, as you read in this chapter's *What If . . .* feature.)

How and why the U.S. Constitution was created is a story that has been told and retold. It is worth repeating, because knowing the historical and political context in which this country's governmental machinery was formed is essential to understanding American government and politics today. The Constitution did not result just from creative thinking. Many of its provisions were grounded in the political philosophy of the time. The delegates to the Constitutional Convention in 1787 brought with them two important sets of influences: their political culture and their political experience. In the years between the first settlements in the New World and the writing of the Constitution, Americans had developed a political philosophy about how people should be governed and had tried out several forms of government. These experiences gave the founders the tools with which they constructed the Constitution.

> **DID YOU KNOW . . .**
> That the first English claim to territory in North America was made by John Cabot, on behalf of King Henry VII, on June 24, 1497?

The Colonial Background

In 1607, the English government sent a group of farmers to establish a trading post, Jamestown, in what is now Virginia. The Virginia Company of London was the first to establish a permanent English colony in the Americas. The king of England gave the backers of this colony a charter granting them "full power and authority" to make laws "for the good and welfare" of the settlement. The colonists at Jamestown instituted a **representative assembly,** setting a precedent in government that was to be observed in later colonial adventures.

Jamestown was not an immediate success. Of the 105 men who landed, 67 died within the first year. But 800 new arrivals in 1609 added to their numbers. By the spring of the next year, frontier hazards had cut their numbers to 60. Of the 6,000 people who left England for Virginia between 1607 and 1623, 4,800 perished. This period is sometimes referred to as the "starving time for Virginia." Climatological researchers suggest that this "starving time" may have been brought about by a severe drought in the Jamestown area, which lasted from 1607 to 1612.

Representative Assembly
A legislature composed of individuals who represent the population.

Separatists, the *Mayflower,* and the Compact

The first New England colony was established in 1620. A group of mostly extreme Separatists, who wished to break with the Church of England, came over on the ship *Mayflower* to the New World, landing at Plymouth (Massachusetts). Before going onshore, the adult males—women were not considered to have any political status—drew up the Mayflower Compact, which was signed by forty-one of the forty-four men aboard the ship on November 21, 1620. The reason for the compact was obvious. This group was outside the jurisdiction of the Virginia Company of London, which had chartered its settlement in Virginia, not Massachusetts. The Separatist leaders feared that some of the *Mayflower* passengers might conclude that they were no longer under

The signing of the compact aboard the *Mayflower.* In 1620, the Mayflower Compact was signed by almost all of the men aboard the ship *Mayflower,* just before disembarking at Plymouth, Massachusetts. It stated, "We . . . covenant and combine ourselves togeather into a civil body politick . . . ; and by vertue hearof to enacte, constitute, and frame such just and equal laws . . . as shall be thought [necessary] for the generall good of the Colonie." (Library of Congress)

any obligations of civil obedience. Therefore, some form of public authority was imperative. As William Bradford (one of the Separatist leaders) recalled in his accounts, there were "discontented and mutinous speeches that some of the strangers amongst them had let fall from them in the ship; That when they came a shore they would use their owne libertie; for none had power to command them."[1]

The compact was not a constitution. It was a political statement in which the signers agreed to create and submit to the authority of a government, pending the receipt of a royal charter. The Mayflower Compact's historical and political significance is twofold: it depended on the consent of the affected individuals, and it served as a prototype for similar compacts in American history. According to Samuel Eliot Morison, the compact proved the determination of the English immigrants to live under the rule of law, based on the *consent of the people.*[2]

More Colonies, More Government

Another outpost in New England was set up by the Massachusetts Bay Colony in 1630. Then followed Rhode Island, Connecticut, New Hampshire, and others. By 1732, the last of the thirteen colonies, Georgia, was established. During the colonial period, Americans developed a concept of limited government, which followed from the establishment of the first colonies under Crown charters. Theoretically, London governed the colonies. In practice, owing partly to the colonies' distance from London, the colonists exercised a large measure of self-government. The colonists were able to make their own laws, as in the Fundamental Orders of Connecticut in 1639. The Massachusetts Body of Liberties in 1641 supported the protection of individual rights and was made a part of colonial law. In 1682, the Pennsylvania Frame of Government was passed. Along with the Pennsylvania Charter of Privileges of 1701, it foreshadowed our modern Constitution and Bill of Rights. All of this legislation enabled the colonists to acquire crucial political experience. After independence was declared in 1776, the states quickly set up their own new constitutions.

[1]John Camp, *Out of the Wilderness: The Emergence of an American Identity in Colonial New England* (Middleton, Conn.: Wesleyan University Press, 1990).
[2]See Morison's "The Mayflower Compact" in Daniel J. Boorstin, ed., *An American Primer* (Chicago: University of Chicago Press, 1966), p. 18.

British Restrictions and Colonial Grievances

The conflict between Britain and the American colonies, which ultimately led to the Revolutionary War, began in the 1760s when the British government decided to raise revenues by imposing taxes on the American colonies. Policy advisers to Britain's young King George III, who ascended the throne in 1760, decided that it was only logical to require the American colonists to help pay the costs of Britain's defending them during the French and Indian War (1756–1763). The colonists, who had grown accustomed to a large degree of self-government and independence from the British Crown, viewed the matter differently.

In 1764, the British Parliament passed the Sugar Act. Many colonists were unwilling to pay the tax imposed by the act. Further regulatory legislation was to come. In 1765, Parliament passed the Stamp Act, providing for internal taxation—or, as the colonists' Stamp Act Congress, assembled in 1765, called it, "taxation without representation." The colonists boycotted the purchase of English commodities in return. The success of the boycott (the Stamp Act was repealed a year later) generated a feeling of unity within the colonies. The British, however, continued to try to raise revenues in the colonies. When Parliament passed duties on glass, lead, paint, and other items in 1767, the colonists again boycotted British goods. The colonists' fury over taxation climaxed in the Boston Tea Party: colonists dressed as Mohawk Indians dumped close to 350 chests of British tea into Boston Harbor as a gesture of tax protest. In retaliation, Parliament passed the Coercive Acts (the "Intolerable Acts") in 1774, which closed Boston Harbor and placed the government of Massachusetts under direct British control. The colonists were outraged—and they responded.

The Colonial Response: The Continental Congresses

New York, Pennsylvania, and Rhode Island proposed the convening of a colonial congress. The Massachusetts House of Representatives requested that all colonies hold conventions to select delegates to be sent to Philadelphia for such a congress.

The First Continental Congress

The First Continental Congress was held at Carpenter's Hall on September 5, 1774. It was a gathering of delegates from twelve of the thirteen colonies (delegates from Georgia did not attend until 1775). At that meeting, there was little talk of independence. The Congress passed a resolution requesting that the colonies send a petition to King George III expressing their grievances. Resolutions were also passed requiring that the colonies raise their own troops and boycott British trade. The British government condemned the Congress's actions, treating them as open acts of rebellion.

The delegates to the First Continental Congress declared that in every county and city, a committee was to be formed whose mission was to spy on the conduct of friends and neighbors and to report to the press any violators of the trade ban. The formation of these committees was an act of cooperation among the colonies, which represented a step toward the creation of a national government.

The Second Continental Congress

By the time the Second Continental Congress met in May 1775 (this time all of the colonies were represented), fighting already had broken out between the British and the colonists. One of the main actions of the Second Congress was to establish an army. It did this by declaring the militia that had gathered around Boston an army and

King George III (1738–1820) was king of Great Britain and Ireland from 1760 until his death on January 29, 1820. Under George III, the British Parliament attempted to tax the American colonies. Ultimately, the colonies, exasperated at repeated attempts at taxation, proclaimed their independence on July 4, 1776. (National Portrait Gallery)

naming George Washington as commander in chief. The participants in that Congress still attempted to reach a peaceful settlement with the British Parliament. One declaration of the Congress stated explicitly that "we have not raised armies with ambitious designs of separating from Great Britain, and establishing independent states." But by the beginning of 1776, military encounters had become increasingly frequent.

Public debate was acrimonious. Then Thomas Paine's *Common Sense* appeared in Philadelphia bookstores. The pamphlet was a colonial best seller. (To do relatively as well today, a book would have to sell between nine and eleven million copies in its first year of publication.) Many agreed that Paine did make common sense when he argued that

> a government of our own is our natural right: and when a man seriously reflects on the precariousness [instability, unpredictability] of human affairs, he will become convinced, that it is infinitely wiser and safer, to form a constitution of our own in a cool and deliberate manner, while we have it in our power, than to trust such an interesting event to time and chance.[3]

Students of Paine's pamphlet point out that his arguments were not new—they were common in tavern debates throughout the land. Rather, it was the near poetry of his words—which were at the same time as plain as the alphabet—that struck his readers.

Declaring Independence

On April 6, 1776, the Second Continental Congress voted for free trade at all American ports with all countries except Britain. This act could be interpreted as an implicit declaration of independence. The next month, the Congress suggested that each of the colonies establish state governments unconnected to Britain. Finally, in July, the colonists declared their independence from Britain.

The Resolution of Independence

On July 2, the Resolution of Independence was adopted by the Second Continental Congress:

> RESOLVED, That these United Colonies are, and of right ought to be free and independent States, that they are absolved from allegiance to the British Crown, and that all political connection between them and the state of Great Britain is, and ought to be, totally dissolved.

The actual Resolution of Independence was not legally significant. On the one hand, it was not judicially enforceable, for it established no legal rights or duties. On the other hand, the colonies were already, in their own judgment, self-governing and independent of Britain. Rather, the Resolution of Independence and the subsequent Declaration of Independence were necessary to establish the legitimacy of the new nation in the eyes of foreign governments, as well as in the eyes of the colonists themselves. What the new nation needed most were supplies for its armies and a commitment of foreign military aid. Unless it appeared to the world as a political entity separate and independent from Britain, no foreign government would enter into a contract with its leaders.

July 4, 1776—The Declaration of Independence

By June 1776, Thomas Jefferson already was writing drafts of the Declaration of Independence in the second-floor parlor of a bricklayer's house in Philadelphia. On adoption of the Resolution of Independence, Jefferson argued that a declaration

Drawing by Handelsman; © 1970 The New Yorker Magazine, Inc.

"You know, the idea of taxation with representation doesn't appeal to me very much either."

[3]*The Political Writings of Thomas Paine*, Vol. 1 (Boston: J. P. Mendum Investigator Office, 1870), p. 46.

clearly putting forth the causes that compelled the colonies to separate from Britain was necessary. The Second Congress assigned the task to him, and he completed his work on the declaration, which enumerated the colonists' major grievances against Britain. Some of his work was amended to gain unanimous acceptance (for example, his condemnation of the slave trade was eliminated to satisfy Georgia and North Carolina), but the bulk of it was passed intact on July 4, 1776. On July 19, the modified draft became "the unanimous declaration of the thirteen United States of America." On August 2, it was signed by the members of the Second Continental Congress.

Universal Truths. The Declaration of Independence has become one of the world's most famous and significant documents. The words opening the second paragraph of the Declaration are known most widely:

> We hold these Truths to be self-evident, that all Men are created equal, that they are endowed by their Creator with certain unalienable Rights, that among these are Life, Liberty, and the Pursuit of Happiness—That to secure these Rights, Governments are instituted among Men, deriving their just Powers from the Consent of the Governed, that whenever any Form of Government becomes destructive of these Ends, it is the Right of the People to alter or abolish it, and to institute new Government.

Natural Rights and a Social Contract. The assumption that people have **natural rights** ("unalienable Rights"), including the rights to "Life, Liberty, and the Pursuit of Happiness," was a revolutionary concept at that time. Its use by Jefferson reveals the influence of the English philosopher John Locke (1632–1704), whose writings were familiar to educated American colonists, including Jefferson.[4] In his *Two Treatises on Government,* published in 1690, Locke had argued that all people possess certain natural rights, including the rights to life, liberty, and property, and that the primary purpose of government was to protect these rights. Furthermore, government was established by the people through a **social contract**—an agreement among the people to form a government and abide by its rules. As you read earlier, such contracts, or compacts, were not new to Americans. The Mayflower Compact was the first of

| **Natural Rights**
Rights held to be inherent in natural law, not dependent on governments. John Locke stated that natural law, being superior to human law, specifies certain rights of "life, liberty, and property." These rights, altered to become "life, liberty, and the pursuit of happiness," are asserted in the Declaration of Independence.

| **Social Contract**
A voluntary agreement among individuals to secure their rights and welfare by creating a government and abiding by its rules.

---

[4]Not all scholars believe that Jefferson was truly influenced by Locke. For example, Jay Fliegelman states that "Jefferson's fascination with Homer, Ossian, Patrick Henry, and the violin is of greater significance than his indebtedness to Locke." Jay Fliegelman, *Declaring Independence: Jefferson, Natural Language, and the Culture of Performance* (Palo Alto, Calif.: Stanford University Press, 1993).

Members of the Second Continental Congress adopted the Declaration of Independence on July 4, 1776. Minor changes were made in the document in the following two weeks. On July 19, the modified draft became the "unanimous declaration of the thirteen United States of America." On August 2, the members of the Second Continental Congress signed it. The first official printed version carried only the signatures of the Congress's president, John Hancock, and its secretary, Charles Thompson. (Painting by John Trumbull, 1819, Library of Congress)

several documents that established governments or governing rules based on the consent of the governed. In citing the "pursuit of happiness" instead of "property" as a right, Jefferson clearly meant to go beyond Locke's thinking.

After setting forth these basic principles of government, the Declaration of Independence goes on to justify the colonists' revolt against Britain. Much of the remainder of the document is a list of what "He" (King George III) had done to deprive the colonists of their rights. (See Appendix A at the end of this book for the complete text of the Declaration of Independence.)

Once it had fulfilled its purpose of legitimating the American Revolution, the Declaration of Independence was all but forgotten for many years. According to scholar Pauline Maier, the Declaration did not become enshrined as what she calls "American Scripture" until the 1800s.[5]

The Rise of Republicanism

Although the colonists had formally declared independence from Britain, the fight to gain actual independence continued for five more years—until the British general Cornwallis surrendered at Yorktown in 1781. In 1783, after Britain formally recognized the independent status of the United States in the Treaty of Paris, Washington disbanded the army. During these years of military struggles, the states faced the additional challenge of creating a system of self-government for an independent United States.

Some colonists had demanded that independence be preceded by the formation of a strong central government. But others, who called themselves Republicans, were against a strong central government. They opposed monarchy, executive authority, and virtually any form of restraint on the power of local groups.

From 1776 to 1780, all of the states adopted written constitutions. Eleven of the constitutions were completely new. Two of them—those of Connecticut and Rhode Island—were old royal charters with minor modifications. Republican sentiment led to increased power for the legislatures. In Pennsylvania and Georgia, **unicameral** (one-body) **legislatures** were unchecked by executive or judicial authority. Basically, the Republicans attempted to maintain the politics of 1776. In almost all states, the legislature was predominant.

| Unicameral Legislature
A legislature with only one legislative chamber, as opposed to a bicameral (two-chamber) legislature, such as the U.S. Congress. Today, Nebraska is the only state in the Union with a unicameral legislature.

| Confederation
A political system in which states or regional governments retain ultimate authority except for those powers they expressly delegate to a central government. A voluntary association of independent states, in which the member states agree to limited restraints on their freedom of action.

| State
A group of people occupying a specific area and organized under one government; may be either a nation or a subunit of a nation.

| The Articles of Confederation: The First Form of Government

The fear of a powerful central government led to the passage of the Articles of Confederation, which created a weak central government. The term **confederation** is important; it means a voluntary association of *independent* **states,** in which the member states agree to only limited restraints on their freedom of action. As a result, confederations seldom have an effective executive authority.

In June 1776, the Second Continental Congress began the process of drafting what would become the Articles of Confederation. The final form of the Articles was achieved by November 15, 1777. It was not until March 1, 1781, however, that the last state, Maryland, agreed to ratify what was called the Articles of Confederation and Perpetual Union. Well before the final ratification of the Articles, however, many of them were implemented: the Continental Congress and the thirteen states conducted American military, economic, and political affairs according to the standards and the form specified by the Articles.[6]

[5]See Pauline Maier, *American Scripture: Making the Declaration of Independence* (New York: Knopf, 1997).
[6]Robert W. Hoffert, *A Politics of Tensions: The Articles of Confederation and American Political Ideas* (Niwot, Colo.: University Press of Colorado, 1992).

Under the Articles, the thirteen original colonies, now states, established on March 1, 1781, a government of the states—the Congress of the Confederation. The Congress was a unicameral assembly of so-called ambassadors from each state, with each state possessing a single vote. Each year, the Congress would choose one of its members as its president (that is, presiding officer), but the Articles did not provide for a president of the United States.

The Congress was authorized in Article X to appoint an executive committee of the states "to execute in the recess of Congress, such of the powers of Congress as the United States, in Congress assembled, by the consent of nine [of the thirteen] states, shall from time to time think expedient to vest with them." The Congress was also allowed to appoint other committees and civil officers necessary for managing the general affairs of the United States. In addition, the Congress could regulate foreign affairs and establish coinage and weights and measures. But it lacked an independent source of revenue and the necessary executive machinery to enforce its decisions throughout the land. Article II of the Articles of Confederation guaranteed that each state would retain its sovereignty. Figure 2–1 illustrates the structure of the government under the Articles of Confederation; Table 2–1 summarizes the powers—and the lack of powers—of Congress under the Articles of Confederation.

Accomplishments under the Articles

The new government had some accomplishments during its eight years of existence under the Articles of Confederation. Certain states' claims to western lands were settled. Maryland had objected to the claims of the Carolinas, Connecticut, Georgia, Massachusetts, New York, and Virginia. It was only after these states consented to give up their land claims to the United States as a whole that Maryland signed the Articles of Confederation. Another accomplishment under the Articles was the passage of the Northwest Ordinance of 1787, which established a basic pattern of government for new territories north of the Ohio River. All in all, the Articles represented the first real pooling of resources by the American states.

FIGURE 2–1 | THE CONFEDERAL GOVERNMENT STRUCTURE UNDER THE ARTICLES OF CONFEDERATION

Congress
Congress had one house. Each state had two to seven members, but only one vote. The exercise of most powers required approval of at least nine states. Amendments to the Articles required the consent of all the states.

Committee of the States
A committee of representatives from all the states was empowered to act in the name of Congress between sessions.

Officers
Congress appointed officers to do some of the executive work.

The States

TABLE 2–1 | POWERS OF THE CONGRESS OF THE CONFEDERATION

CONGRESS HAD POWER TO	CONGRESS LACKED POWER TO
• Declare war and make peace. • Enter into treaties and alliances. • Establish and control armed forces. • Requisition men and revenues from states. • Regulate coinage. • Borrow funds and issue bills of credit. • Fix uniform standards of weight and measurement. • Create admiralty courts. • Create a postal system. • Regulate Indian affairs. • Guarantee citizens of each state the rights and privileges of citizens in the several states when in another state. • Adjudicate disputes between states on state petition.	• Provide for effective treaty-making power and control foreign relations; it could not compel states to respect treaties. • Compel states to meet military quotas; it could not draft soldiers. • Regulate interstate and foreign commerce; it left each state free to set up its own tariff system. • Collect taxes directly from the people; it had to rely on states to collect and forward taxes. • Compel states to pay their share of government costs. • Provide and maintain a sound monetary system or issue paper money; this was left up to the states, and monies in circulation differed tremendously in value.

Weaknesses of the Articles

In spite of these accomplishments, the Articles of Confederation had many defects. Although Congress had the legal right to declare war and to conduct foreign policy, it did not have the right to demand revenues from the states. It could only ask for them. Additionally, the actions of Congress required the consent of nine states. Any amendments to the Articles required the unanimous consent of the Congress and confirmation by every state legislature. Furthermore, the Articles did not create a national system of courts.

Basically, the functioning of the government under the Articles depended on the goodwill of the states. Article III of the Articles simply established a "league of friendship" among the states—no national government was intended.

Probably the most fundamental weakness of the Articles, and the most basic cause of their eventual replacement by the Constitution, was the lack of power to raise funds for the militia. The Articles contained no language giving Congress coercive power to raise revenues (by levying taxes) to provide adequate support for the military forces controlled by Congress. When states refused to send revenues to support the government (not one state met the financial requests made by Congress under the Articles), Congress resorted to selling off western lands to speculators or issuing bonds that sold for less than their face value. Due to a lack of resources, the Continental Congress was forced to disband the army, even in the face of serious Spanish and British military threats.

Shays' Rebellion and the Need for Revision of the Articles

Because of the weaknesses of the Articles of Confederation, the central government could do little to maintain peace and order in the new nation. The states bickered among themselves and increasingly taxed each other's goods. At times they prevented trade altogether. By 1784, the country faced a serious economic depression. Banks were calling in old loans and refusing to give new ones. People who could not pay their debts were often thrown into prison.

By 1786, in Concord, Massachusetts, the scene of one of the first battles of the Revolution, there were three times as many people in prison for debt as there were for all other crimes combined. In Worcester County, Massachusetts, the ratio was even higher—twenty to one. Most of the prisoners were small farmers who could not pay their debts because of the disorganized state of the economy.

In August 1786, mobs of musket-bearing farmers led by former revolutionary captain Daniel Shays seized county courthouses and disrupted the trials of debtors in Springfield, Massachusetts. Shays and his men then launched an attack on the federal arsenal at Springfield, but they were repulsed. Shays' Rebellion demonstrated that the central government could not protect the citizenry from armed rebellion or provide adequately for the public welfare. The rebellion spurred the nation's political leaders to action. As John Jay wrote to Thomas Jefferson,

> Changes are Necessary, but what they ought to be, what they will be, and how and when to be produced, are arduous Questions. I feel for the Cause of Liberty . . . . If it should not take Root in this Soil[,] Little Pains will be taken to cultivate it in any other.[7]

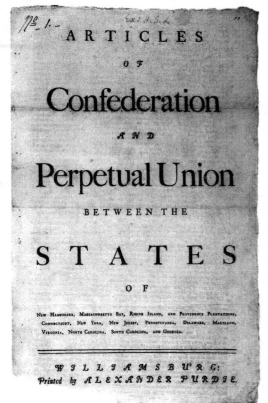

The title page from an early printing of the Articles of Confederation. (Library of Congress)

---

[7]Excerpt from a letter from John Jay to Thomas Jefferson written in October 1786, as reproduced in Winthrop D. Jordan *et al.*, *The United States*, combined ed., 6th ed. (Englewood Cliffs, N.J.: Prentice Hall, 1987), p. 135.

Drafting the Constitution

The Virginia legislature called for a meeting of all the states to be held at Annapolis, Maryland, on September 11, 1786—ostensibly to discuss commercial problems only. It was evident to those in attendance (including Alexander Hamilton and James Madison) that the national government had serious weaknesses that had to be addressed if it were to survive. Among the important problems to be solved were the relationship between the states and the central government, the powers of the national legislature, the need for executive leadership, and the establishment of policies for economic stability.

The result of this meeting was a petition to the Continental Congress for a general convention to meet in Philadelphia in May 1787 "to consider the exigencies of the union." Congress approved the convention in February 1787. When those who favored a weak central government realized that the Philadelphia meeting would in fact take place, they endorsed the convention. They made sure, however, that the convention would be summoned "for the sole and express purpose of revising the Articles of Confederation." Those in favor of a stronger national government had different ideas.

The designated date for the opening of the convention at Philadelphia, now known as the Constitutional Convention, was May 14, 1787. Because few of the delegates had actually arrived in Philadelphia by that time, however, the convention was not formally opened in the East Room of the Pennsylvania State House until May 25.[8] Fifty-five of the seventy-four delegates chosen for the convention actually attended. (Of those fifty-five, only about forty played active roles at the convention.) Rhode Island was the only state that refused to send delegates.

Who Were the Delegates?

Who were the fifty-five delegates to the Constitutional Convention? They certainly did not represent a cross section of American society in the 1700s. Indeed, most were members of the upper class. Consider the following facts:

1. Thirty-three were members of the legal profession.
2. Three were physicians.
3. Almost 50 percent were college graduates.
4. Seven were former chief executives of their respective states.
5. Six were owners of large plantations.
6. Eight were important businesspersons.

They were also relatively young by today's standards: James Madison was thirty-six, Alexander Hamilton was only thirty-two, and Jonathan Dayton of New Jersey was twenty-six. The venerable Benjamin Franklin, however, was eighty-one and had to be carried in on a portable chair borne by four prisoners from a local jail. Not counting Franklin, the average age was just over forty-two.

The Working Environment

The conditions under which the delegates worked for 115 days were far from ideal and were made even worse by the necessity of maintaining total secrecy. The framers of the Constitution believed that if public debate took place on particular positions, delegates would have a more difficult time compromising or backing down to reach agreement. Consequently, the windows were usually shut in the East

| DID YOU KNOW . . .
That the 1776 constitution of New Jersey granted the vote to "all free inhabitants," including women, but the large number of women who turned out to vote resulted in male protests and a new law limiting the right to vote to "free white male citizens"?

---

[8]The State House was later named Independence Hall. This was the same room in which the Declaration of Independence had been signed eleven years earlier.

Room of the State House. Summer quickly arrived, and the air became heavy, humid, and hot by noon of each day. Also, when the windows were open, flies swarmed into the room. The delegates did, however, have a nearby tavern and inn to which they retired each evening. The Indian Queen became the informal headquarters of the delegates.

Factions among the Delegates

We know much about the proceedings at the convention because James Madison kept a daily, detailed personal journal. A majority of the delegates were strong nationalists—they wanted a central government with real power, unlike the central government under the Articles of Confederation. George Washington and Benjamin Franklin preferred limited national authority based on a separation of powers. They were apparently willing to accept any type of national government, however, as long as the other delegates approved it. A few advocates of a strong central government, led by Gouverneur Morris of Pennsylvania and John Rutledge of South Carolina, distrusted the ability of the common people to engage in self-government.

Among the nationalists, several went so far as to support monarchy. This group included Alexander Hamilton, who was chiefly responsible for the Annapolis Convention's call for the Constitutional Convention. In a long speech on June 18, he presented his views: "I have no scruple in declaring . . . that the British government is the best in the world and that I doubt much whether anything short of it will do in America."

Another important group of nationalists were of a more democratic stripe. Led by James Madison of Virginia and James Wilson of Pennsylvania, these democratic nationalists wanted a central government founded on popular support.

Still another faction consisted of nationalists who were less democratic in nature and who would support a central government only if it was founded on very narrowly defined republican principles. This group was made up of a relatively small number of delegates, including Edmund Randolph and George Mason of Virginia, Elbridge Gerry of Massachusetts, and Luther Martin and John Francis Mercer of Maryland.

Many of the other delegates from Connecticut, Delaware, Maryland, New Hampshire, and New Jersey were concerned about only one thing—claims to western lands. As long as those lands became the common property of all of the states, they were willing to support a central government.

Finally, there was a group of delegates who were totally against a national authority. Two of the three delegates from New York quit the convention when they saw the nationalist direction of its proceedings.

Politicking and Compromises

The debates at the convention started on the first day. James Madison had spent months reviewing European political theory. When his Virginia delegation arrived ahead of most of the others, it got to work immediately. By the time George Washington opened the convention, Governor Edmund Randolph of Virginia was prepared to present fifteen resolutions. In retrospect, this was a masterful stroke on the part of the Virginia delegation. It set the agenda for the remainder of the convention—even though, in principle, the delegates had been sent to Philadelphia for the sole purpose of amending the Articles of Confederation. They had not been sent to write a new constitution.

The Virginia Plan. Randolph's fifteen resolutions proposed an entirely new national government under a constitution. It was, however, a plan that favored the large states, including Virginia. Basically, it called for the following:

Elbridge Gerry (1744–1814), from Massachusetts, was a patriot during the Revolution. He was a signatory of the Declaration of Independence and later became governor of Massachusetts (1810–1812). He became James Madison's new vice president when Madison was reelected in December 1812. (Library of Congress)

1. A **bicameral** (two-chamber) **legislature,** with the lower chamber chosen by the people and the smaller upper chamber chosen by the lower chamber from nominees selected by state legislatures. The number of representatives would be proportional to a state's population, thus favoring the large states. The legislature could void any state laws.

2. The creation of an unspecified national executive, elected by the legislature.

3. The creation of a national judiciary, appointed by the legislature.

It did not take long for the smaller states to realize they would fare poorly under the Virginia plan, which would enable Virginia, Massachusetts, and Pennsylvania to form a majority in the national legislature. The debate on the plan dragged on for a number of weeks. It was time for the small states to come up with their own plan.

The New Jersey Plan. On June 15, lawyer William Paterson of New Jersey offered an alternative plan. After all, argued Paterson, under the Articles of Confederation all states had equality; therefore, the convention had no power to change this arrangement. He proposed the following:

1. The fundamental principle of the Articles of Confederation—one state, one vote—would be retained.

2. Congress would be able to regulate trade and impose taxes.

3. All acts of Congress would be the supreme law of the land.

4. Several people would be elected by Congress to form an executive office.

5. The executive office would appoint a Supreme Court.

Basically, the New Jersey plan was simply an amendment of the Articles of Confederation. Its only notable feature was its reference to the **supremacy doctrine,** which was later included in the Constitution.

The "Great Compromise." The delegates were at an impasse. Most wanted a strong national government and were unwilling even to consider the New Jersey plan. But when the Virginia plan was brought up again, the small states threatened to leave. It was not until July 16 that the **Great Compromise** was achieved. Roger Sherman of Connecticut proposed the following:

1. A bicameral legislature in which the lower chamber, the House of Representatives, would be apportioned according to the number of free inhabitants in each state, plus three-fifths of the slaves.

| **Bicameral Legislature**
A legislature made up of two parts, called chambers. The U.S. Congress, composed of the House of Representatives and the Senate, is a bicameral legislature.

| **Supremacy Doctrine**
A doctrine that asserts the priority of national law over state laws. This principle is rooted in Article VI of the Constitution, which provides that the Constitution, the laws passed by the national government under its constitutional powers, and all treaties constitute the supreme law of the land.

| **Great Compromise**
The compromise between the New Jersey and Virginia plans that created one chamber of the Congress based on population and one chamber representing each state equally; also called the Connecticut Compromise.

George Washington presided over the Constitutional Convention of 1787. Although the convention was supposed to have started on May 14, 1787, few of the delegates had actually arrived in Philadelphia by that date. The convention formally opened in the East Room of the Pennsylvania State House (later named Independence Hall) on May 25. Only Rhode Island did not send any delegates. (Corbis)

2. An upper chamber, the Senate, which would have two members from each state elected by the state legislatures.

This plan, also called the Connecticut Compromise because of the role of the Connecticut delegates in the proposal, broke the deadlock. It did exact a political price, however, because it permitted each state to have equal representation in the Senate. Having two senators represent each state in effect diluted the voting power of citizens living in more heavily populated states and gave the smaller states disproportionate political powers. But the Connecticut Compromise resolved the large-state/small-state controversy. In addition, the Senate acted as part of a checks-and-balances system against the House, which many feared would be dominated by, and responsive to, the masses.

The Three-Fifths Compromise.   The Great Compromise also settled another major issue—how to deal with slaves in the representational scheme. Slavery was still legal in many northern states, but it was concentrated in the South. Many delegates were opposed to slavery and wanted it banned entirely in the United States. Charles Pinckney of South Carolina led strong southern opposition to a ban on slavery. Furthermore, the South wanted slaves to be counted along with free persons in determining representation in Congress. Delegates from the northern states objected. Sherman's three-fifths proposal was a compromise between northerners who did not want the slaves counted at all and southerners who wanted them counted in the same way as free whites. Actually, Sherman's Connecticut plan spoke of three-fifths of "all other persons" (and that is the language of the Constitution itself). It is not hard to figure out, though, who those other persons were.

The three-fifths compromise illustrates the power of the southern states at the convention.[9] The three-fifths rule meant that the House of Representatives and the electoral college would be apportioned in part on the basis of *property*—specifically, property in slaves. Modern commentators have referred to the three-fifths rule as valuing African Americans only three-fifths as much as whites. Actually, the additional southern representatives elected because of the three-fifths rule did not represent the slaves at all. Rather, these extra representatives were a gift to the slave owners—the additional representatives enhanced the power of the South in Congress.

The three-fifths compromise did not completely settle the slavery issue. There was also the question of the slave trade. Eventually, the delegates agreed that Congress could not ban the importation of slaves until after 1808. The compromise meant that the matter of slavery itself was never addressed directly. The South won twenty years of unrestricted slave trade and a requirement that escaped slaves in free states be returned to their owners in slave states. Could the authors of the Constitution have done more to address the issue of slavery? See this chapter's *Politics and Diversity* feature for a further discussion of this question.

Other Issues.   The South also worried that the northern majority in Congress would pass legislation unfavorable to its economic interests. Because the South depended on agricultural exports, it feared the imposition of export taxes. In return for acceding to the northern demand that Congress be able to regulate commerce among the states and with other nations, the South obtained a promise that export taxes would not be imposed. As a result, the United States is among the few countries that do not tax their exports.

There were other disagreements. The delegates could not decide whether to establish only a Supreme Court or to create lower courts as well. They deferred the issue by mandating a Supreme Court and allowing Congress to establish lower courts. They also disagreed over whether the president or the Senate would choose the Supreme

---

[9]See Garry Wills, *"Negro President": Jefferson and the Slave Power* (New York: Houghton Mifflin, 2003).

POLITICS AND DIVERSITY | Could the Founders Have Banned Slavery Outright?

One of the most hotly debated issues at the Constitutional Convention concerned slavery. As we discussed elsewhere, the three-fifths compromise was the result of that debate. There was also another compromise: the importation of slaves would not be banned until after 1808. The debate over slavery—or, more specifically, over how the founders dealt with it—continues to this day. Some contend that those delegates who opposed slavery should have made greater efforts to ban it completely.*

DID THE FOUNDERS HAVE NO OTHER CHOICE?

Some historians argue that the founders had no choice. The South was an important part of the economy, and the southern states had over 600,000 slaves. Major leaders from Virginia, such as George Washington, had serious doubts about slavery. It appears, however, that the delegates from North Carolina, South Carolina, and Georgia would never have agreed to the Constitution if slavery had been threatened—meaning that these states would not have remained part of the Union. The founders believed, as James Madison said, "Great as the evil is, a dismemberment of the Union would be worse . . . . If those states should disunite from the other states, . . . they might solicit and obtain aid from foreign powers."† Benjamin Franklin, then president of the Pennsylvania Society for the Abolition of

Slavery, also feared that without a slavery compromise, delegates from the South would abandon the convention.

CRITICS ARGUE THAT ETHICS SHOULD HAVE PREVAILED

Critics of the founders' actions nonetheless believe that any compromise on slavery implicitly acknowledged the validity of the institution. According to these critics, the delegates who opposed slavery had a moral obligation to make greater efforts to ban it. Many of the delegates' contemporaries considered the compromise to be a "betrayal" of the Declaration of Independence's principle of equality among all men.

FOR CRITICAL ANALYSIS

Do you think that antislavery delegates to the convention could have obtained a better result if they had taken a stronger stand? If Georgia and the Carolinas had stayed out of the Union, what would subsequent American history have been like? Would the eventual freedom of the slaves have been advanced—or delayed?

*See Paul Finkelman's criticism of the founders' actions on the slavery issue in *Slavery and the Founders: Race and Liberty in the Age of Jefferson,* 2d ed. (Armonk, N.Y.: M. E. Sharpe, 2001).

†Speech before the Virginia ratifying convention on June 17, 1788, as cited in Bruno Leone, ed., *The Creation of the Constitution* (San Diego: Greenhaven Press, 1995), p. 159.

Court justices. A compromise was reached with the agreement that the president would nominate the justices and the Senate would confirm the nominations.

These compromises, as well as others, resulted from the recognition that if one group of states refused to ratify the Constitution, it was doomed.

Working toward Final Agreement

The Connecticut Compromise was reached by mid-July. The make-up of the executive branch and the judiciary, however, was left unsettled. The remaining work of the convention was turned over to a five-man Committee of Detail, which presented a rough draft of the Constitution on August 6. It made the executive and judicial branches subordinate to the legislative branch.

| Separation of Powers
The principle of dividing governmental powers among different branches of government.

| Madisonian Model
A structure of government proposed by James Madison in which the powers of the government are separated into three branches: executive, legislative, and judicial.

| Checks and Balances
A major principle of the American system of government whereby each branch of the government can check the actions of the others.

James Madison (1751–1836) earned the title "master builder of the Constitution" because of his persuasive logic during the Constitutional Convention. His contributions to the *Federalist Papers* showed him to be a brilliant political thinker and writer. (Library of Congress)

The Madisonian Model—Separation of Powers.   The major issue of **separation of powers** had not yet been resolved. The delegates were concerned with structuring the government to prevent the imposition of tyranny—either by the majority or by a minority. It was Madison who proposed a governmental scheme—sometimes called the **Madisonian model**—to achieve this: the executive, legislative, and judicial powers of government were to be separated so that no one branch had enough power to dominate the others. The separation of powers was by function, as well as by personnel, with Congress passing laws, the president enforcing and administering laws, and the courts interpreting laws in individual circumstances.

Each of the three branches of government would be independent of the others, but they would have to cooperate to govern. According to Madison, in *Federalist Paper* No. 51 (see Appendix C), "the great security against a gradual concentration of the several powers in the same department consists in giving to those who administer each department the necessary constitutional means and personal motives to resist encroachments of the others."

The Madisonian Model—Checks and Balances.   The "constitutional means" Madison referred to is a system of **checks and balances** through which each branch of the government can check the actions of the others. For example, Congress can enact laws, but the president has veto power over congressional acts. The Supreme Court has the power to declare acts of Congress and of the executive unconstitutional, but the president appoints the justices of the Supreme Court, with the advice and consent of the Senate. (The Supreme Court's power to declare acts unconstitutional was not mentioned in the Constitution, although arguably the framers assumed that the Court would have this power—see the discussion of judicial review later in this chapter.) Figure 2–2 outlines these checks and balances.

Madison's ideas of separation of powers and checks and balances were not new. Indeed, the influential French political thinker Baron de Montesquieu (1689–1755) had explored these concepts in his book *The Spirit of the Laws*, published in 1748. Montesquieu not only discussed the "three sorts of powers" (executive, legislative, and judicial) that were necessarily exercised by any government but also gave examples of how, in some nations, certain checks on these powers had arisen and had been effective in preventing tyranny.

In the years since the Constitution was ratified, the checks and balances built into it have evolved into a sometimes complex give-and-take among the branches of government. Generally, for nearly every check that one branch has over another, the branch that has been checked has found a way of getting around it. For example, suppose that the president checks Congress by vetoing a bill. Congress can override the presidential veto by a two-thirds vote. Additionally, Congress holds the "power of the purse." If it disagrees with a program endorsed by the executive branch, it can simply refuse to appropriate the funds necessary to operate that program. Similarly, the president can impose a countercheck on Congress if the Senate refuses to confirm a presidential appointment, such as a judicial appointment. The president can simply wait until Congress is in recess and then make what is called a "recess appointment," which does not require the Senate's approval.

The Executive.   Some delegates favored a plural executive made up of representatives from the various regions. This was abandoned in favor of a single chief executive. Some argued that Congress should choose the executive. To make the presidency completely independent of the proposed Congress, however, an **electoral college** was adopted. To be sure, the electoral college created a cumbersome presidential election process (see Chapter 9). The process even made it possible for a candidate who came in second in the popular vote to become president by being the top vote getter in the electoral college, which happened in 2000. The electoral college insulated the president, however, from direct popular control. The seven-year single term that some of the delegates had proposed was replaced by a four-year term and the possibility of reelection.

| **Electoral College**
A group of persons called *electors* selected by the voters in each state and the District of Columbia (D.C.); this group officially elects the president and vice president of the United States. The number of electors in each state is equal to the number of each state's representatives in both chambers of Congress. The Twenty-third Amendment to the Constitution grants D.C. as many electors as the state with the smallest population.

| The Final Document

On September 17, 1787, the Constitution was approved by thirty-nine delegates. Of the fifty-five who had attended originally, only forty-two remained. Three delegates refused to sign the Constitution. Others disapproved of at least parts of it but signed anyway to begin the ratification debate.

The Constitution that was to be ratified established the following fundamental principles:

1. Popular sovereignty, or control by the people.
2. A republican government in which the people choose representatives to make decisions for them.

FIGURE 2–2 | CHECKS AND BALANCES

The major checks and balances among the three branches are illustrated here. The U.S. Constitution does not mention some of these checks, such as judicial review—the power of the courts to declare federal or state acts unconstitutional—and the president's ability to refuse to enforce judicial decisions or congressional legislation. Checks and balances can be thought of as a confrontation of powers or responsibilities. Each branch checks the action of another; two branches in conflict have powers that can result in balances or stalemates, requiring one branch to give in or both to reach a compromise.

The Supreme Court can declare presidential actions unconstitutional.

The Supreme Court can declare congressional laws unconstitutional.

The president nominates federal judges; the president can refuse to enforce the Court's decisions; the president grants pardons.

THE JUDICIARY

Congress can rewrite legislation to circumvent the Court's decisions; the Senate confirms federal judges; Congress determines the number of judges.

The president proposes laws and can veto congressional legislation; the president makes treaties, executive agreements, and executive orders; the president can refuse, and has refused, to enforce congressional legislation; the president can call special sessions of Congress.

THE PRESIDENCY

Congress makes legislation and can override a presidential veto of its legislation; Congress can impeach and remove a president; the Senate must confirm presidential appointments and consent to the president's treaties based on a two-thirds concurrence; Congress has the power of the purse and provides funds for the president's programs.

THE CONGRESS

3. Limited government with written laws, in contrast to the powerful British government against which the colonists had rebelled.

4. Separation of powers, with checks and balances among branches to prevent any one branch from gaining too much power.

5. A federal system that allows for states' rights, because the states feared too much centralized control.

You will read about federalism in detail in Chapter 3. Suffice it to say here that in the **federal system** established by the founders, sovereign powers—ruling powers—are divided between the states and the national government. The Constitution expressly granted certain powers to the national government. For example, the national government was given the power to regulate commerce among the states. The Constitution also declared that the president is the nation's chief executive and the commander in chief of the armed forces. Additionally, the Constitution made it clear that laws made by the national government take priority over conflicting state laws. At the same time, the Constitution provided for extensive states' rights, including the right to control commerce within state borders and to exercise those governing powers that were not delegated to the national government.

The federal system created by the founders was a novel form of government at that time—no other country in the world had such a system. It was invented by the founders as a compromise solution to the controversy over whether the states or the central government should have ultimate sovereignty. As you will read in Chapter 3, the debate over where the line should be drawn between states' rights and the powers of the national government has characterized American politics ever since. The founders did not go into detail about where this line should be drawn, thus leaving it up to scholars and court judges to divine the founders' intentions.

Federal System
A system of government in which power is divided between a central government and regional, or subdivisional, governments. Each level must have some domain in which its policies are dominant and some genuine political or constitutional guarantee of its authority.

Ratification
Formal approval.

Federalist
The name given to one who was in favor of the adoption of the U.S. Constitution and the creation of a federal union with a strong central government.

Anti-Federalist
An individual who opposed the ratification of the new Constitution in 1787. The Anti-Federalists were opposed to a strong central government.

The Difficult Road to Ratification

The founders knew that **ratification** of the Constitution was far from certain. Indeed, because it was almost guaranteed that many state legislatures would not ratify it, the delegates agreed that each state should hold a special convention. Elected delegates to these conventions would discuss and vote on the Constitution. Further departing from the Articles of Confederation, the delegates agreed that as soon as nine states (rather than all thirteen) approved the Constitution, it would take effect, and Congress could begin to organize the new government.

The Federalists Push for Ratification

The two opposing forces in the battle over ratification were the Federalists and the Anti-Federalists. The **Federalists**—those in favor of a strong central government and the new Constitution—had an advantage over their opponents, called the **Anti-Federalists,** who wanted to prevent the Constitution as drafted from being ratified. In the first place, the Federalists had assumed a positive name, leaving their opposition the negative label of *Anti*-Federalist.[10] More important, the Federalists

[10] There is some irony here. At the Constitutional Convention, those opposed to a strong central government pushed for a federal system because such a system would allow the states to retain some of their sovereign rights (see Chapter 3). The label *Anti-Federalists* thus contradicted their essential views.

had attended the Constitutional Convention and knew of all the deliberations that had taken place. Their opponents had no such knowledge, because those deliberations had not been open to the public. Thus, the Anti-Federalists were at a disadvantage in terms of information about the document. The Federalists also had time, power, and money on their side. Communications were slow. Those who had access to the best communications were Federalists—mostly wealthy bankers, lawyers, plantation owners, and merchants living in urban areas, where communications were better. The Federalist campaign was organized relatively quickly and effectively to elect Federalists as delegates to the state ratifying conventions.

The Anti-Federalists, however, had at least one strong point in their favor: they stood for the status quo. In general, the greater burden is always placed on those advocating change.

The *Federalist Papers.* In New York, opponents of the Constitution were quick to attack it. Alexander Hamilton answered their attacks in newspaper columns over the signature "Caesar." When the Caesar letters had little effect, Hamilton switched to the pseudonym Publius and secured two collaborators—John Jay and James Madison. In a very short time, those three political figures wrote a series of eighty-five essays in defense of the Constitution and of a republican form of government.

These widely read essays, called the *Federalist Papers,* appeared in New York newspapers from October 1787 to August 1788 and were reprinted in the newspapers of other states. Although we do not know for certain who wrote every one, it is apparent that Hamilton was responsible for about two-thirds of the essays. These included the most important ones interpreting the Constitution, explaining the various powers of the three branches, and presenting a theory of *judicial review*—to be discussed later in this chapter. Madison's *Federalist Paper* No. 10 (see Appendix C), however, is considered a classic in political theory; it deals with the nature of groups—or factions, as he called them. In spite of the rapidity with which the *Federalist Papers* were written, they are considered by many to be perhaps the best example of political theorizing ever produced in the United States.[11]

The Anti-Federalist Response. The Anti-Federalists used such pseudonyms as Montezuma and Philadelphiensis in their replies. Many of their attacks on the Constitution were also brilliant. The Anti-Federalists claimed that the Constitution was written by aristocrats and would lead to aristocratic tyranny. More important, the Anti-Federalists believed that the Constitution would create an overbearing and overburdening central government hostile to personal liberty. (The Constitution said nothing about freedom of the press, freedom of religion, or any other individual liberty.) They wanted to include a list of guaranteed liberties, or a bill of rights. Finally, the Anti-Federalists decried the weakened power of the states.

The Anti-Federalists cannot be dismissed as unpatriotic extremists. They included such patriots as Patrick Henry and Samuel Adams. They were arguing what had been the most prevalent contemporary opinion. This view derived from the French political philosopher Montesquieu, who, as mentioned earlier, was an influential political theorist at that time. Montesquieu believed that liberty was safe only in relatively small societies governed by direct democracy or by a large legislature with small districts. The Madisonian view favoring a large republic, particularly expressed in *Federalist Papers* No. 10 and No. 51 (see Appendix C), was actually the more *un*popular view at the time. Madison was probably convincing because citizens were already persuaded that a strong national government was necessary to combat

---

[11]Some scholars believe that the *Federalist Papers* played only a minor role in securing ratification of the Constitution. Even if this is true, they still have lasting value as an authoritative explanation of the Constitution.

foreign enemies and to prevent domestic insurrections. Still, some researchers believe it was mainly the bitter experiences with the Articles of Confederation, rather than Madison's arguments, that persuaded the state conventions to ratify the Constitution.[12]

The March to the Finish

The struggle for ratification continued. Strong majorities were procured in Delaware, Pennsylvania, New Jersey, Georgia, and Connecticut. After a bitter struggle in Massachusetts, that state ratified the Constitution by a narrow margin on February 6, 1788. By the spring, Maryland and South Carolina had ratified by sizable majorities. Then on June 21 of that year, New Hampshire became the ninth state to ratify the Constitution. Although the Constitution was formally in effect, this meant little without Virginia and New York—the latter did not ratify for another month (see Table 2–2).

Did the Majority of Americans Support the Constitution?

In 1913, historian Charles Beard published *An Economic Interpretation of the Constitution of the United States*.[13] This book launched a debate that has continued ever since—the debate over whether the Constitution was supported by a majority of Americans.

Beard's Thesis.   Beard's central thesis was that the Constitution had been produced primarily by wealthy property owners who desired a stronger government able to protect their property rights. Beard also claimed that the Constitution had been imposed by undemocratic methods to prevent democratic majorities from exercising real power. He pointed out that there was never any popular vote on whether to hold a constitutional convention in the first place.

---

[12]Of particular interest is the view of the Anti-Federalist position contained in Herbert J. Storing, *What the Anti-Federalists Were For* (Chicago: University of Chicago Press, 1981). Storing also edited seven volumes of the Anti-Federalist writings, *The Complete Anti-Federalist* (Chicago: University of Chicago Press, 1981). See also Josephine F. Pacheco, *Antifederalism: The Legacy of George Mason* (Fairfax, Va.: George Mason University Press, 1992).

[13]Charles A. Beard, *An Economic Interpretation of the Constitution of the United States* (New York: Macmillan, 1913; New York: Free Press, 1986).

TABLE 2–2 | RATIFICATION OF THE CONSTITUTION

State	Date	Vote For–Against
Delaware	Dec. 7, 1787	30–0
Pennsylvania	Dec. 12, 1787	43–23
New Jersey	Dec. 18, 1787	38–0
Georgia	Jan. 2, 1788	26–0
Connecticut	Jan. 9, 1788	128–40
Massachusetts	Feb. 6, 1788	187–168
Maryland	Apr. 28, 1788	63–11
South Carolina	May 23, 1788	149–73
New Hampshire	June 21, 1788	57–46
Virginia	June 25, 1788	89–79
New York	July 26, 1788	30–27
North Carolina	Nov. 21, 1789*	194–77
Rhode Island	May 29, 1790	34–32

*Ratification was originally defeated on August 4, 1788, by a vote of 84–184.

Furthermore, even if such a vote had been taken, state laws generally restricted voting rights to property-owning white males, meaning that most people in the country (white males without property, women, Native Americans, and slaves) were not eligible to vote. Finally, Beard pointed out that even the word *democracy* was distasteful to the founders. The term was often used by conservatives to smear their opponents.

State Ratifying Conventions.   As for the various state ratifying conventions, the delegates had been selected by only 150,000 of the approximately four million citizens. That does not seem very democratic—at least not by today's standards. Some historians have suggested that if a Gallup poll could have been taken at that time, the Anti-Federalists would probably have outnumbered the Federalists.[14]

Certainly, some of the delegates to state ratifying conventions from poor, agrarian areas feared that an elite group of Federalists would run the country just as oppressively as the British had governed the colonies. Amos Singletary, a delegate to the Massachusetts ratifying convention, contended that those who urged the adoption of the Constitution "expect to get all the power and all the money into their own hands, and then they will swallow up all us little folks . . . just as the whale swallowed Jonah."[15] Others who were similarly situated, though, felt differently. Jonathan Smith, who was also a delegate to the Massachusetts ratifying convention, regarded a strong national government as a "cure for disorder"—referring to the disorder caused by the rebellion of Daniel Shays and his followers.[16]

Support Was Probably Widespread.   Much has also been made of the various machinations used by the Federalists to ensure the Constitution's ratification (and they did resort to a variety of devious tactics, including purchasing at least one printing press to prevent the publication of Anti-Federalist sentiments). Yet the perception that a strong central government was necessary to keep order and protect the public welfare appears to have been fairly pervasive among all classes—rich and poor alike.

Further, although the need for strong government was a major argument in favor of adopting the Constitution, even the Federalists sought to craft a limited government. Compared with constitutions adopted by other nations in later years, the U.S. Constitution, through its checks and balances, favors limited government over "energetic" government to a marked degree.

| The Bill of Rights

The U.S. Constitution would not have been ratified in several important states if the Federalists had not assured the states that amendments to the Constitution would be passed to protect individual liberties against incursions by the national government. Many of the recommendations of the state ratifying conventions included specific rights that were considered later by James Madison as he labored to draft what became the Bill of Rights.

A "Bill of Limits"

Although called the Bill of Rights, essentially the first ten amendments to the Constitution were a "bill of limits," because the amendments limited the powers of the national government over the rights and liberties of individuals.

---

[14]Jim Powell, "James Madison—Checks and Balances to Limit Government Power," *The Freeman,* March 1996, p. 178.
[15]As quoted in Bruno Leone, ed., *The Creation of the Constitution* (San Diego: Greenhaven Press, 1995), p. 215.
[16]*Ibid.,* p. 217.

Ironically, a year earlier Madison had told Jefferson, "I have never thought the omission [of the Bill of Rights] a material defect" of the Constitution. But Jefferson's enthusiasm for a bill of rights apparently influenced Madison, as did his desire to gain popular support for his election to Congress. Madison promised in his campaign letter to voters that, once elected, he would force Congress to "prepare and recommend to the states for ratification, the most satisfactory provisions for all essential rights."

Madison had to cull through more than two hundred state recommendations.[17] It was no small task, and in retrospect he chose remarkably well. One of the rights appropriate for constitutional protection that he left out was equal protection under the laws—but that was not commonly regarded as a basic right at that time. Not until 1868 did the states ratify an amendment guaranteeing that no state shall deny equal protection to any person. (The Supreme Court has since applied this guarantee to certain actions of the federal government as well.)

The final number of amendments that Madison and a specially appointed committee came up with was seventeen. Congress tightened the language somewhat and eliminated five of the amendments. Of the remaining twelve, two—dealing with the apportionment of representatives and the compensation of the members of Congress—were not ratified immediately by the states. Eventually, Supreme Court decisions led to reform of the apportionment process. The amendment on the compensation of members of Congress was ratified 203 years later—in 1992!

No Explicit Limits on State Government Powers

On December 15, 1791, the national Bill of Rights was adopted when Virginia agreed to ratify the ten amendments. On ratification, the Bill of Rights became part of the U.S. Constitution. The basic structure of American government had already been established. Now the fundamental rights and liberties of individuals were protected, at least in theory, at the national level. The proposed amendment that Madison characterized as "the most valuable amendment in the whole lot"—which would have prohibited the states from infringing on the freedoms of conscience, press, and jury trial—had been eliminated by the Senate. Thus, the Bill of Rights as adopted did not limit state power, and individual citizens had to rely on the guarantees contained in a particular state constitution or state bill of rights. The country had to wait until the violence of the Civil War before significant limitations on state power in the form of the Fourteenth Amendment became part of the national Constitution.

Altering the Constitution: The Formal Amendment Process

The U.S. Constitution consists of 7,000 words. It is shorter than any state constitution except that of Vermont, which has 6,880 words. One of the reasons the federal Constitution is short is that the founders intended it to be only a framework for the new government, to be interpreted by succeeding generations. One of the reasons it has remained short is that the formal amending procedure does not allow for changes to be made easily. Article V of the Constitution outlines the ways in which amendments may be proposed and ratified (see Figure 2–3).

Two formal methods of proposing an amendment to the Constitution are available: (1) a two-thirds vote in each chamber of Congress or (2) a national convention that is called by Congress at the request of two-thirds of the state legislatures (the second method has never been used).

[17]For details on these recommendations, including their sources, see Leonard W. Levy, *Origins of the Bill of Rights* (New Haven, Conn.: Yale University Press, 1999).

FIGURE 2–3 | THE FORMAL CONSTITUTIONAL AMENDING PROCEDURE

There are two ways of proposing amendments to the U.S. Constitution and two ways of ratifying proposed amendments. Among the four possibilities, the usual route has been proposal by Congress and ratification by state legislatures.

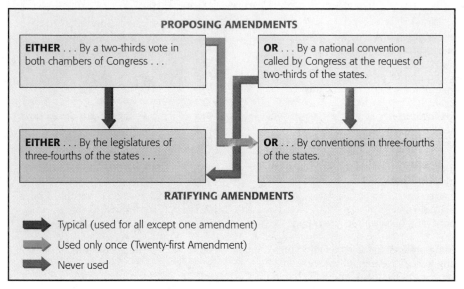

Ratification can occur by one of two methods: (1) by a positive vote in three-fourths of the legislatures of the various states or (2) by special conventions called in the states and a positive vote in three-fourths of them. The second method has been used only once, to repeal Prohibition (the ban on the production and sale of alcoholic beverages). That situation was exceptional because it involved an amendment (the Twenty-first) to repeal an amendment (the Eighteenth, which had created Prohibition). State conventions were necessary for repeal of the Eighteenth Amendment because the "pro-dry" legislatures in the most conservative states would never have passed the repeal. (Note that Congress determines the method of ratification to be used by all states for each proposed constitutional amendment.)

Many Amendments Proposed, Few Accepted

Congress has considered more than eleven thousand amendments to the Constitution. Many proposed amendments have been advanced to address highly specific problems. An argument against such "narrow" amendments has been that amendments ought to embody broad principles, in the way that the existing Constitution does. For that reason, many people have opposed such narrow amendments as one to protect the American flag.

Only thirty-three amendments have been submitted to the states after having been approved by the required two-thirds vote in each chamber of Congress, and only twenty-seven have been ratified—see Table 2–3 on the following page. (The full, annotated text of the U.S. Constitution, including its amendments, is presented in a special appendix at the end of this chapter.) It should be clear that the amendment process is much more difficult than a graphic depiction such as Figure 2–3 can indicate. Because of competing social and economic interests, the requirement that two-thirds of both the House and Senate approve the amendments is difficult to achieve. Thirty-four senators, representing only seventeen sparsely populated states, could block any amendment. For example, the Republican-controlled House approved the Balanced Budget Amendment within the first one hundred days of the 104th Congress in 1995, but it was defeated in the Senate by one vote.

TABLE 2–3 | AMENDMENTS TO THE CONSTITUTION

Amendment	Subject	Year Adopted	Time Required for Ratification
1st–10th	The Bill of Rights	1791	2 years, 2 months, 20 days
11th	Immunity of states from certain suits	1795	11 months, 3 days
12th	Changes in electoral college procedure	1804	6 months, 3 days
13th	Prohibition of slavery	1865	10 months, 3 days
14th	Citizenship, due process, and equal protection	1868	2 years, 26 days
15th	No denial of vote because of race, color, or previous condition of servitude	1870	11 months, 8 days
16th	Power of Congress to tax income	1913	3 years, 6 months, 22 days
17th	Direct election of U.S. senators	1913	10 months, 26 days
18th	National (liquor) prohibition	1919	1 year, 29 days
19th	Women's right to vote	1920	1 year, 2 months, 14 days
20th	Change of dates for congressional and presidential terms	1933	10 months, 21 days
21st	Repeal of the Eighteenth Amendment	1933	9 months, 15 days
22d	Limit on presidential tenure	1951	3 years, 11 months, 3 days
23d	District of Columbia electoral vote	1961	9 months, 13 days
24th	Prohibition of tax payment as a qualification to vote in federal elections	1964	1 year, 4 months, 9 days
25th	Procedures for determining presidential disability and presidential succession and for filling a vice-presidential vacancy	1967	1 year, 7 months, 4 days
26th	Prohibition of setting minimum voting age above eighteen in any election	1971	3 months, 7 days
27th	Prohibition of Congress's voting itself a raise that takes effect before the next election	1992	203 years

After approval by Congress, the process becomes even more arduous. Three-fourths of the state legislatures must approve the amendment. Only those amendments that have wide popular support across parties and in all regions of the country are likely to be approved.

Why was the amendment process made so difficult? The framers feared that a simple amendment process could lead to a tyranny of the majority, which could pass amendments to oppress disfavored individuals and groups. The cumbersome amendment process does not seem to stem the number of amendments that are proposed each year in Congress, however, particularly in recent years.

Limits on Ratification

A reading of Article V of the Constitution reveals that the framers of the Constitution specified no time limit on the ratification process. The Supreme Court has held that Congress can specify a time for ratification as long as it is "reasonable." Since 1919, most proposed amendments have included a requirement that ratification be obtained within seven years. This was the case with the proposed Equal Rights Amendment, which sought to guarantee equal rights for women. When three-fourths of the states had not ratified in the allotted seven years, however, Congress extended the limit by an additional three years and three months. That extension expired on June 30, 1982, and the amendment still had not been ratified. Another proposed amendment, which would have guaranteed congressional representation to the District of Columbia, fell far short of the thirty-eight state ratifications needed before its August 22, 1985, deadline.

On May 7, 1992, Michigan became the thirty-eighth state to ratify the Twenty-seventh Amendment (on congressional compensation)—one of the two "lost" amendments of the twelve that originally were sent to the states in 1789. Because most of the amendments proposed in recent years have been given a time limit of only seven years by Congress, it was questionable for a time whether the amend-

Demonstrators opposing a constitutional amendment defining marriage as between a man and a woman gather in front of the Capitol in the summer of 2006. Whom do these demonstrators hope to influence? (AP Photo/Dennis Cook)

ment would take effect even if the necessary number of states ratified it. Is 203 years too long a lapse of time between the proposal and the final ratification of an amendment? It apparently was not, because the amendment was certified as legitimate by archivist Don Wilson of the National Archives on May 18, 1992.

The National Convention Provision

The Constitution provides that a national convention requested by the legislatures of two-thirds of the states can propose a constitutional amendment. Congress has received approximately 400 convention applications since the Constitution was ratified; every state has applied at least once. Fewer than 20 applications were submitted during the Constitution's first hundred years, but more than 150 have been filed in the last two decades. No national convention has been held since 1787, and many national political and judicial leaders are uneasy about the prospect of convening a body that conceivably could do as the Constitutional Convention did—create a new form of government. The state legislative bodies that originate national convention applications, however, do not appear to be uncomfortable with such a constitutional modification process; more than 230 state constitutional conventions have been held.

Informal Methods of Constitutional Change

Formal amendments are one way of changing our Constitution, and, as is obvious from their small number, they have been resorted to infrequently. If we discount the first ten amendments (the Bill of Rights), which were adopted soon after the ratification of the Constitution, there have been only seventeen formal alterations of the Constitution in the more than two hundred years of its existence.

But looking at the sparse number of formal constitutional amendments gives us an incomplete view of constitutional change. The brevity and ambiguity of the original document have permitted great alterations in the Constitution by way of varying interpretations over time. As the United States grew, both in population and territory, new social and political realities emerged. Congress, presidents, and the courts found it necessary to interpret the Constitution's provisions in light of these new realities. The Constitution has proved to be a remarkably flexible document, adapting itself time and again to new events and concerns.

Congressional Legislation

The Constitution gives Congress broad powers to carry out its duties as the nation's legislative body. For example, Article I, Section 8, of the Constitution gives Congress the power to regulate foreign and interstate commerce. Although there is no clear definition of foreign commerce or interstate commerce in the Constitution, Congress has cited the *commerce clause* as the basis for passing thousands of laws that have defined the meaning of foreign and interstate commerce.

Similarly, Article III, Section 1, states that the national judiciary shall consist of one supreme court and "such inferior courts, as Congress may from time to time ordain and establish." Through a series of acts, Congress has used this broad provision to establish the federal court system of today.

In addition, Congress has frequently delegated to federal agencies the legislative power to write regulations. These regulations become law unless challenged in the court system. Nowhere does the Constitution outline this delegation of legislative authority.

Presidential Actions

Even though the Constitution does not expressly authorize the president to propose bills or even budgets to Congress,[18] presidents since the time of Woodrow Wilson (who served as president from 1913 to 1921) have proposed hundreds of bills to Congress each year. Presidents have also relied on their Article II authority as commander in chief of the nation's armed forces to send American troops abroad into combat, although the Constitution provides that Congress has the power to declare war.

The president's powers in wartime have waxed and waned through the course of American history. President George W. Bush significantly expanded presidential power in the wake of the terrorist attacks of 2001. Until then, there had been a period of decline in the latitude given to presidents since the Vietnam War ended in 1975.

Presidents have also conducted foreign affairs by the use of **executive agreements,** which are legally binding documents made between the president and a foreign head of state. The Constitution does not mention such agreements.

| **Executive Agreement**
An international agreement between chiefs of state that does not require legislative approval.

Judicial Review

Another way of changing the Constitution—or of making it more flexible—is through the power of judicial review. **Judicial review** refers to the power of U.S. courts to examine the constitutionality of actions undertaken by the legislative and executive branches of government. A state court, for example, may rule that a statute enacted by the state legislature is unconstitutional. Federal courts (and ultimately, the United States Supreme Court) may rule unconstitutional not only acts of Congress and decisions of the national executive branch but also state statutes, state executive actions, and even provisions of state constitutions.

| **Judicial Review**
The power of the Supreme Court and other courts to declare unconstitutional federal or state laws and other acts of government.

Not a Novel Concept. The Constitution does not specifically mention the power of judicial review. Those in attendance at the Constitutional Convention, however,

---

[18]Note, though, that the Constitution, in Article II, Section 3, does state that the president "shall from time to time . . . recommend to [Congress's] consideration such measures as he shall judge necessary and expedient." Some scholars interpret this phrase to mean that the president has the constitutional authority to propose bills and budgets to Congress for consideration.

probably expected that the courts would have some authority to review the legality of acts by the executive and legislative branches, because, under the common law tradition inherited from England, courts exercised this authority. Indeed, Alexander Hamilton, in *Federalist Paper* No. 78 (see Appendix C), explicitly outlined the concept of judicial review. Whether the power of judicial review can be justified constitutionally is a question that has been subject to some debate, particularly in recent years. For now, suffice it to say that in 1803, the Supreme Court claimed this power for itself in *Marbury v. Madison*,[19] in which the Court ruled that a particular provision of an act of Congress was unconstitutional.

Allows Court to Adapt the Constitution.   Through the process of judicial review, the Supreme Court adapts the Constitution to modern situations. Electronic technology, for example, did not exist when the Constitution was ratified. Nonetheless, the Supreme Court has used the Fourth Amendment guarantees against unreasonable searches and seizures to place limits on the use of wiretapping and other electronic eavesdropping methods by government officials. The Court has needed to decide whether antiterrorism laws passed by Congress or state legislatures, or declared by the president, violate the Fourth Amendment or other constitutional provisions. Additionally, the Supreme Court has changed its interpretation of the Constitution in accordance with changing values. It ruled in 1896 that "separate-but-equal" public facilities for African Americans were constitutional; but by 1954 the times had changed, and the Supreme Court reversed that decision.[20] Woodrow Wilson summarized the Supreme Court's work when he described it as "a constitutional convention in continuous session." Basically, the law is what the Supreme Court says it is at any given time. In saying what the law is, the Supreme Court sometimes consults the laws of other countries, as this chapter's *Beyond Our Borders* feature on the following page describes.

The United States Supreme Court in 2006, including the two newest members—Chief Justice John Roberts, Jr. (seated in the middle), and Justice Samuel Alito, Jr., standing on the far right. Justice John Paul Stevens, seated second from the left, is the longest-sitting member, having been nominated by President Gerald Ford and confirmed by the Senate in 1975. What role does the Supreme Court play in the American political system? (AP Photo/J. Scott Applewhite)

---

[19]5 U.S. 137 (1803). See Chapter 14 for a further discussion of the *Marbury v. Madison* case.
[20]*Brown v. Board of Education of Topeka*, 347 U.S. 483 (1954).

BEYOND OUR BORDERS | Foreign Law and Judicial Review

As you have read, judicial review is one of the ways in which the Constitution can be changed. Consequently, the federal courts have become battlegrounds for many heated issues, ranging from gay and lesbian rights to the war on terrorism. The United States Supreme Court's decisions on contentious issues inevitably raise objections from one side or the other. In addition, the way in which Supreme Court justices arrive at their decisions is coming under ever-increasing scrutiny. Recently, consideration of foreign law in Supreme Court rulings has opened debate on the relationship of the Constitution and the laws of other nations.

RECENT APPLICATIONS OF FOREIGN LAW

The majority of the sitting justices on the Supreme Court have cited international law in their decisions at one time or another. Even Justice Antonin Scalia, an outspoken critic of the practice, referred to foreign law in an assisted-suicide case.* As Justice Stephen Breyer points out, the Supreme Court increasingly must deal with international problems, from global antitrust disputes to terrorism. "Those are the cases we're getting," Breyer stated. "And that reflects the truth about the world." Indeed, ignoring the global community is a difficult prospect considering the broad movements toward greater international interdependence.

Yet foreign law has also been cited or discussed in cases that did not have international parties or ramifications. In *Roper v. Simmons,* the Court ruled that the death penalty was "cruel and unusual punishment" when applied to offenders who were juveniles when they committed their crimes. Justice Anthony Kennedy, writing the Court's majority opinion, noted that the United States was "alone in a world that has turned its face against the juvenile death penalty."† The *Roper* decision followed an earlier case, *Atkins v. Virginia,* which barred the execution of mentally handicapped convicts.‡ The Court's majority in *Atkins* noted that "within the world community"

such executions are "overwhelmingly disapproved." International law also entered into the decision in *Lawrence v. Texas,* which struck down state antisodomy laws.§ The majority opinion observed that the European Court of Human Rights had affirmed the right of homosexual adults to engage in sexual conduct.

OBJECTIONS TO THE PRACTICE

The use of international law has met with criticism, however. Justice Scalia has spoken out against the practice on numerous occasions. He has argued that citing foreign law when writing opinions can be problematic because it is taken out of its natural context and is used only selectively. Chief Justice John Roberts has called the use of foreign law undemocratic. "If we're relying on a German judge about what our Constitution means, no president accountable to the people appointed that judge and no Senate accountable to the people confirmed that judge," Roberts argued. "And yet, he's playing a role in shaping the law that binds the people in this country."

Members of Congress have also attacked the use of foreign law. In 2005, Representative Tom Feeney (R., Fla.) sponsored a bill that would declare "inappropriate judicial reliance" on foreign sources of law to be a threat to "the sovereignty of the United States, the separation of powers, and the president's and the Senate's treaty-making authority." Although Feeney's bill had seventy-three co-sponsors in 2005, neither it nor any similar measure has gained traction in either the House or the Senate.

FOR CRITICAL ANALYSIS

How could consulting international law prove to be helpful in deciding contentious issues that come before the courts? How might the practice prove dangerous to the primacy of the U.S. Constitution?

*Washington v. Glucksberg, 521 U.S. 702 (1997).
†543 U.S. 551 (2005).
‡536 U.S. 304 (2002).

§539 U.S. 558 (2003).

Interpretation, Custom, and Usage

The Constitution has also been changed through interpretation by both Congress and the president. Originally, the president had a staff consisting of personal secretaries and a few others. Today, because Congress delegates specific tasks to the president and the chief executive assumes political leadership, the executive office staff alone has increased to several thousand persons. The executive branch provides legislative leadership far beyond the expectations of the founders.

Changes in the ways of doing political business have also altered the Constitution. The Constitution does not mention political parties, yet these informal, "extraconstitutional" organizations make the nominations for offices, run the campaigns, organize the members of Congress, and in fact change the election system from time to time. The emergence and evolution of the party system, for example, have changed the way the president is elected. The Constitution calls for the electoral college to choose the president. Today, the people vote for electors who are pledged to the candidate of their party, effectively choosing the president themselves. Perhaps most striking, the Constitution has been adapted from serving the needs of a small, rural republic to providing a framework of government for an industrial giant with vast geographic, natural, and human resources.

MAKING A DIFFERENCE | How Can You Affect the U.S. Constitution?

The U.S. Constitution is an enduring document that has survived more than two hundred years of turbulent history. It is also a changing document, however. Twenty-seven amendments have been added to the original Constitution. How can you, as an individual, actively influence constitutional amendments?

Why Should You Care?

The laws of the nation have a direct impact on your life, and none more so than the Constitution—the supreme law of the land. The most important issues in society are often settled by the Constitution. For example, for the first seventy-five years of the republic, the Constitution implicitly protected the institution of slavery. If the Constitution had never been changed through the amendment process, slavery might still be legal today.

Since the passage of the Fourteenth Amendment in 1868, the Constitution has defined who is a citizen and who is entitled to the protections the Constitution provides. Constitutional provisions define our liberties. The First Amendment protects our freedom of speech more thoroughly than do the laws of many other nations. Few other countries have constitutional provisions governing the right to own firearms (the Second Amendment).

All of these are among the most fundamental issues we face.

What Can You Do?

Consider how one person decided to affect the Constitution. Shirley Breeze, head of the Missouri Women's Network, decided to bring the Equal Rights Amendment (ERA) back to life after its "death" in 1982. She spearheaded a movement that has gained significant support. Today, bills to ratify the ERA have been introduced not only in Missouri but also in other states that did not ratify it earlier, including Illinois, Oklahoma, and Virginia.

At the time of this writing, national coalitions of interest groups are supporting or opposing a number of proposed amendments. One hotly debated proposed amendment concerns abortion. If you are interested in this issue and would like to make a difference, you can contact one of several groups.

An organization whose primary goal is to secure the passage of the Human Life Amendment is

American Life League
P.O. Box 1350
Stafford, VA 22555
540-659-4171
www.all.org

The Human Life Amendment would recognize in law the "personhood" of the unborn, secure human rights protections for an unborn child from the time of fertilization, and prohibit abortion under any circumstances.

A political action and information organization working on behalf of "pro-choice" issues—that is, the right of women to have control over reproduction—is

NARAL Pro-Choice America (formerly the National Abortion and Reproductive Rights Action League)
1156 15th St., Suite 700
Washington, DC 20005
202-973-3000
www.naral.org

There is also another way that you can affect the Constitution—by protecting your existing rights and liberties under it. In the wake of the 9/11 attacks, a number of new laws have been enacted that many believe go too far in curbing our constitutional rights. If you agree and want to join with others who are concerned about this issue, a good starting point is the Web site of the American Civil Liberties Union (ACLU) at **www.aclu.org**.

Key Terms

Anti-Federalist 44	executive agreement 52	Madisonian model 42	social contract 33
bicameral legislature 39	federal system 44	natural rights 33	state 34
checks and balances 42	Federalist 44	ratification 44	supremacy doctrine 39
confederation 34	Great Compromise 39	representative assembly 29	unicameral legislature 34
electoral college 43	judicial review 52	separation of powers 42	

Chapter Summary

1 The first permanent English colonies were established at Jamestown in 1607 and Plymouth in 1620. The Mayflower Compact created the first formal government for the British colonists. By the mid-1700s, other British colonies had been established along the Atlantic seaboard from Georgia to Maine.

2 In 1763, the British tried to impose a series of taxes and legislative acts on their increasingly independent-minded colonies. The colonists responded with boycotts of British products and protests. Representatives of the colonies formed the First Continental Congress in 1774. The delegates sent a petition to the British king expressing their grievances. The Second Continental Congress established an army in 1775 to defend the colonists against attacks by British soldiers.

3 On July 4, 1776, the Second Continental Congress approved the Declaration of Independence. Perhaps the most revolutionary aspects of the Declaration were its assumptions that people have natural rights to life, liberty, and the pursuit of happiness; that governments derive their power from the consent of the governed; and that people have a right to overthrow oppressive governments. During the Revolutionary War, the colonies adopted written constitutions that severely curtailed the power of executives, thus giving their legislatures predominant powers. By the end of the Revolutionary War, the states had signed the Articles of Confederation, creating a weak central government with few powers. The Articles proved to be unworkable because the national government had no way to ensure compliance by the states with such measures as securing tax revenues.

4 General dissatisfaction with the Articles of Confederation prompted the call for a convention at Philadelphia in 1787. Although the delegates ostensibly convened to amend the Articles, the discussions soon focused on creating a constitution for a new form of government. The Virginia plan and the New Jersey plan did not garner widespread support. A compromise offered by Connecticut helped to break the large-state/small-state disputes dividing the delegates. The final version of the Constitution provided for the separation of powers, checks and balances, and a federal form of government.

5 Fears of a strong central government prompted the addition of the Bill of Rights to the Constitution. The Bill of Rights secured for Americans a wide variety of freedoms, including the freedoms of religion, speech, and assembly. It was initially applied only to the federal government, but amendments to the Constitution following the Civil War made it clear that the Bill of Rights would apply to the states as well.

6 An amendment to the Constitution may be proposed either by a two-thirds vote in each house of Congress or by a national convention called by Congress at the request of two-thirds of the state legislatures. Ratification can occur either by a positive vote in three-fourths of the legislatures of the various states or by special conventions called in the states for the specific purpose of ratifying the proposed amendment and a positive vote in three-fourths of these state conventions. Informal methods of constitutional change include congressional legislation, presidential actions, judicial review, and changing interpretations of the Constitution.

Selected Print and Media Resources

SUGGESTED READINGS

Bailyn, Bernard. *To Begin the World Anew: The Genius and Ambiguities of the American Founders*. New York: Knopf, 2003. In a series of essays, a two-time Pulitzer Prize–winning historian discusses the themes of order and liberty in the *Federalist Papers* and the advantages of the founders' provincialism.

Breyer, Stephen G. *Active Liberty: Interpreting Our Democratic Constitution*. New York: Knopf, 2005. Supreme Court justice Stephen Breyer offers his thoughts on the Constitution as a living document. He argues that the genius of the Constitution rests in the adaptability of its great principles to cope with current problems.

Dahl, Robert A. *How Democratic Is the American Constitution?* New Haven, Conn.: Yale University Press, 2002. This book compares the U.S. Constitution with the constitutions of other democratic countries in the world.

Hamilton, Alexander, *et al. The Federalist: The Famous Papers on the Principles of American Government*. Benjamin F. Wright, ed. New York: Friedman/Fairfax Publishing, 2002. This is an updated version of the papers written by Alexander Hamilton, James Madison, and John Jay, and published in the *New York Packet*, in support of the ratification of the Constitution.

MEDIA RESOURCES

In the Beginning—A 1987 Bill Moyers program that features discussions with three prominent historians about the roots of the Constitution and its impact on our society.

John Locke—A 1994 video exploring the character and principal views of John Locke.

Thomas Jefferson—A 1996 documentary by acclaimed director Ken Burns. The film covers Jefferson's entire life, including his writing of the Declaration of Independence, his presidency, and his later years in Virginia. Historians and writers interviewed include Daniel Boorstin, Garry Wills, Gore Vidal, and John Hope Franklin.

E·MOCRACY | The Internet and Our Constitution

Today, you can find online many important documents from the founding period, including descriptions of events leading up to the American Revolution, the Articles of Confederation, notes on the Constitutional Convention, the Federalists' writings, and the Anti-Federalists' responses.

You are able to access the Internet and explore a variety of opinions on every topic imaginable because you enjoy the freedoms—including freedom of speech—guaranteed by our Constitution. Even today, more than two hundred years after the U.S. Bill of Rights was ratified, citizens in some countries do not enjoy the right to free speech. Nor can they surf the Web freely, as U.S. citizens do.

For example, the Chinese government employs a number of methods to control Internet use. One method is to use filtering software to block electronic pathways to objectionable sites, including the sites of Western news organizations. Another technique is to prohibit Internet users from sending or discussing information that has not been publicly released by the government. Still another practice is to monitor the online activities of Internet users. None of these methods is foolproof, however. Indeed, some observers claim that the

Internet, by exposing citizens in politically oppressive nations to a variety of views on politics and culture, will eventually transform those nations.

We should note that such restrictions also can exist in the United States. For example, there have been persistent efforts by Congress and many courts to limit access to Web sites deemed pornographic. Free speech advocates have attacked these restrictions as unconstitutional, as you will read in Chapter 4.

Logging On

For U.S. founding documents, including the Declaration of Independence, scanned originals of the U.S. Constitution, and the *Federalist Papers*, go to Emory University School of Law's Web site at

www.law.emory.edu/erd/ docs/federalist

The University of Oklahoma Law Center has a number of U.S. historical documents online, including many of those discussed in this chapter. Go to

www.law.ou.edu/hist

The National Constitution Center provides information on the Constitution

—including its history, current debates over constitutional provisions, and news articles—at the following site:

www.constitutioncenter.org

To look at state constitutions, go to

www.findlaw.com/casecode/ state.html

Online Review

At **www.politicalscience.wadsworth.com/ schmidt12**, you will find a free Study Guide to this book. For each chapter, there are two online quizzes to help you master the material.

- The PoliPrep Self-Study Assessment provides a pretest for each major section of the chapter. PoliPrep then generates a customized study plan. After you complete the study plan, a posttest evaluates your progress.
- The Tutorial Quiz for each chapter provides questions on the chapter contents, including the features. The questions are organized to match the major sections of the chapter.

The Constitution of the United States*

The Preamble

We the People of the United States, in Order to form a more perfect Union, establish Justice, insure domestic Tranquility, provide for the common defence, promote the general Welfare, and secure the Blessings of Liberty to ourselves and our Posterity, do ordain and establish this Constitution for the United States of America.

The Preamble declares that "We the People" are the authority for the Constitution (unlike the Articles of Confederation, which derived their authority from the states). The Preamble also sets out the purposes of the Constitution.

ARTICLE I. | (Legislative Branch)

The first part of the Constitution, Article I, deals with the organization and powers of the lawmaking branch of the national government, the Congress.

Section 1. Legislative Powers
All legislative Powers herein granted shall be vested in a Congress of the United States, which shall consist of a Senate and House of Representatives.

Section 2. House of Representatives
Clause 1: Composition and Election of Members. The House of Representatives shall be composed of Members chosen every second Year by the People of the several States, and the Electors in each State shall have the Qualifications requisite for Electors of the most numerous Branch of the State Legislature.

Each state has the power to decide who may vote for members of Congress. Within each state, those who may vote for state legislators may also vote for members of the House of Representatives (and, under the Seventeenth Amendment, for U.S. senators).

When the Constitution was written, nearly all states limited voting rights to white male property owners or taxpayers at least twenty-one years old. Subsequent amendments granted voting power to African American men, all women, and everyone at least eighteen years old.

Clause 2: Qualifications. No Person shall be a Representative who shall not have attained to the Age of twenty five Years, and been seven Years a Citizen of the United States, and who shall not, when elected, be an Inhabitant of that State in which he shall be chosen.

Each member of the House must be at least twenty-five years old, a citizen of the United States for at least seven years, and a resident of the state in which she or he is elected.

Clause 3: Apportionment of Representatives and Direct Taxes. Representatives [and direct Taxes][1] shall be apportioned among the several States which may be included within this Union, according to their respective Numbers [which shall be determined by adding to the whole Number of free Persons, including those bound to Service for a Term of Years, and excluding Indians not taxed, three fifths of all other Persons].[2] The actual Enumeration shall be made within three Years after the first Meeting of the Congress of the United States, and within every subsequent Term of ten Years, in such Manner as they shall by Law direct. The Number of Representatives shall not exceed one for every thirty Thousand, but each State shall have at Least one Representative; and until such enumeration shall be made, the State of New Hampshire shall be entitled to chuse three, Massachusetts eight, Rhode Island and Providence Plantations one, Connecticut five, New York six, New Jersey four, Pennsylvania eight, Delaware one, Maryland six, Virginia ten, North Carolina five, South Carolina five, and Georgia three.

A state's representation in the House is based on the size of its population. Population is counted in each decade's census, after which Congress reapportions House seats. Since early in the twentieth century, the number of seats has been limited to 435.

---

*The spelling, capitalization, and punctuation of the original have been retained here. Brackets indicate passages that have been altered by amendments to the Constitution. We have added article titles (in parentheses), section titles, and clause designations. We have also inserted annotations in blue italic type.

---

[1]Modified by the Sixteenth Amendment.
[2]Modified by the Fourteenth Amendment.

Clause 4: Vacancies. When vacancies happen in the Representation from any State, the Executive Authority thereof shall issue Writs of Election to fill such Vacancies.

The "Executive Authority" is the state's governor. When a vacancy occurs in the House, the governor calls a special election to fill it.

Clause 5: Officers and Impeachment. The House of Representatives shall chuse their Speaker and other Officers; and shall have the sole Power of Impeachment.

The power to impeach is the power to accuse. In this case, it is the power to accuse members of the executive or judicial branch of wrongdoing or abuse of power. Once a bill of impeachment is issued, the Senate holds the trial.

Section 3. The Senate

Clause 1: Term and Number of Members.   The Senate of the United States shall be composed of two Senators from each State [chosen by the Legislature thereof],[3] for six Years; and each Senator shall have one Vote.

Every state has two senators, each of whom serves for six years and has one vote in the upper chamber. Since the Seventeenth Amendment in 1913, all senators have been elected directly by voters of the state during the regular election.

Clause 2: Classification of Senators.   Immediately after they shall be assembled in Consequence of the first Election, they shall be divided as equally as may be into three Classes. The Seats of the Senators of the first Class shall be vacated at the Expiration of the second Year, of the second Class at the Expiration of the fourth Year, and of the third Class at the Expiration of the sixth Year, so that one third may be chosen every second Year; [and if Vacancies happen by Resignation, or otherwise, during the Recess of the Legislature of any State, the Executive thereof may make temporary Appointments until the next Meeting of the Legislature, which shall then fill such Vacancies].[4]

One-third of the Senate's seats are open to election every two years (in contrast, all members of the House are elected simultaneously).

Clause 3: Qualifications.   No Person shall be a Senator who shall not have attained to the Age of thirty Years, and been nine Years a Citizen of the United States, and who shall not, when elected, be an Inhabitant of that State for which he shall be chosen.

Every senator must be at least thirty years old, a citizen of the United States for a minimum of nine years, and a resident of the state in which he or she is elected.

[3]Repealed by the Seventeenth Amendment.
[4]Modified by the Seventeenth Amendment.

Clause 4: The Role of the Vice President.   The Vice President of the United States shall be President of the Senate, but shall have no Vote, unless they be equally divided.

The vice president presides over meetings of the Senate but cannot vote unless there is a tie. The Constitution gives no other official duties to the vice president.

Clause 5: Other Officers.   The Senate shall chuse their other Officers, and also a President pro tempore, in the Absence of the Vice President, or when he shall exercise the Office of President of the United States.

The Senate votes for one of its members to preside when the vice president is absent. This person is usually called the president pro tempore because of the temporary nature of the position.

Clause 6: Impeachment Trials.   The Senate shall have the sole Power to try all Impeachments. When sitting for that Purpose, they shall be on Oath or Affirmation. When the President of the United States is tried, the Chief Justice shall preside: And no Person shall be convicted without the Concurrence of two thirds of the Members present.

The Senate conducts trials of officials that the House impeaches. The Senate sits as a jury, with the vice president presiding if the president is not on trial.

Clause 7: Penalties for Conviction.   Judgment in Cases of Impeachment shall not extend further than to removal from Office, and disqualification to hold and enjoy any Office of honor, Trust, or Profit under the United States: but the Party convicted shall nevertheless be liable and subject to Indictment, Trial, Judgment, and Punishment, according to Law.

On conviction of impeachment charges, the Senate can only force an official to leave office and prevent him or her from holding another office in the federal government. The individual, however, can still be tried in a regular court.

Section 4. Congressional Elections: Times, Manner, and Places

Clause 1: Elections.   The Times, Places and Manner of holding Elections for Senators and Representatives, shall be prescribed in each State by the Legislature thereof; but the Congress may at any time by Law make or alter such Regulations, except as to the Places of chusing Senators.

Congress set the Tuesday after the first Monday in November in even-numbered years as the date for congressional elections. In states with more than one seat in the House, Congress requires that representatives be elected from districts within each state. Under the Seventeenth Amendment, senators are elected at the same places as other officials.

Clause 2: Sessions of Congress. [The Congress shall assemble at least once in every Year, and such Meeting shall be on the first Monday in December, unless they shall by Law appoint a different Day.]⁵

Congress has to meet every year at least once. The regular session now begins at noon on January 3 of each year, subsequent to the Twentieth Amendment, unless Congress passes a law to fix a different date. Congress stays in session until its members vote to adjourn. Additionally, the president may call a special session.

Section 5. Powers and Duties of the Houses

Clause 1: Admitting Members and Quorum. Each House shall be the Judge of the Elections, Returns, and Qualifications of its own Members, and a Majority of each shall constitute a Quorum to do Business; but a smaller Number may adjourn from day to day, and may be authorized to compel the Attendance of absent Members, in such Manner, and under such Penalties as each House may provide.

Each chamber may exclude or refuse to seat a member-elect.

The quorum rule requires that 218 members of the House and 51 members of the Senate be present to conduct business. This rule normally is not enforced in the handling of routine matters.

Clause 2: Rules and Discipline of Members. Each House may determine the Rules of its Proceedings, punish its Members for disorderly Behaviour, and, with the Concurrence of two thirds, expel a Member.

The House and the Senate may adopt their own rules to guide their proceedings. Each may also discipline its members for conduct that is deemed unacceptable. No member may be expelled without a two-thirds majority vote in favor of expulsion.

Clause 3: Keeping a Record. Each House shall keep a Journal of its Proceedings, and from time to time publish the same, excepting such Parts as may in their Judgment require Secrecy; and the Yeas and Nays of the Members of either House on any question shall, at the Desire of one fifth of those Present, be entered on the Journal.

The journals of the two chambers are published at the end of each session of Congress.

Clause 4: Adjournment. Neither House, during the Session of Congress, shall, without the Consent of the other, adjourn for more than three days, nor to any other Place than that in which the two Houses shall be sitting.

Congress has the power to determine when and where to meet, provided, however, that both chambers meet in the same city.

Neither chamber may recess for more than three days without the consent of the other.

Section 6. Rights of Members

Clause 1: Compensation and Privileges. The Senators and Representatives shall receive a Compensation for their services, to be ascertained by Law, and paid out of the Treasury of the United States. They shall in all Cases, except Treason, Felony and Breach of the Peace, be privileged from Arrest during their Attendance at the Session of their respective Houses, and in going to and returning from the same; and for any Speech or Debate in either House, they shall not be questioned in any other Place.

Congressional salaries are to be paid by the U.S. Treasury rather than by the members' respective states. The original salaries were $6 per day; in 1857 they were $3,000 per year. Both representatives and senators were paid $165,200 in 2006.

Treason is defined in Article III, Section 3. A felony is any serious crime. A breach of the peace is any indictable offense less than treason or a felony. Members cannot be arrested for things they say during speeches and debates in Congress. This immunity applies to the Capitol Building itself and not to their private lives.

Clause 2: Restrictions. No Senator or Representative shall, during the Time for which he was elected, be appointed to any civil Office under the Authority of the United States, which shall have been created, or the Emoluments whereof shall have been encreased during such time; and no Person holding any Office under the United States, shall be a Member of either House during his Continuance in Office.

During the term for which a member was elected, he or she cannot concurrently accept another federal government position.

Section 7. Legislative Powers: Bills and Resolutions

Clause 1: Revenue Bills. All Bills for raising Revenue shall originate in the House of Representatives; but the Senate may propose or concur with Amendments as on other Bills.

All tax and appropriation bills for raising money have to originate in the House of Representatives. The Senate, though, often amends such bills and may even substitute an entirely different bill.

Clause 2: The Presidential Veto. Every Bill which shall have passed the House of Representatives and the Senate, shall, before it becomes a Law, be presented to the President of the United States; If he approve he shall sign it, but if not he shall return it, with his Objections to the House in which it shall have originated, who shall enter the Objections at large on their Journal, and proceed to reconsider it. If after such Reconsideration two thirds of that House shall agree to pass the Bill, it shall be sent together with the Objections, to the other House, by which it shall likewise be reconsidered, and if approved by two thirds of that House, it shall become a Law. But

---

⁵Changed by the Twentieth Amendment.

in all such Cases the Votes of both Houses shall be determined by Yeas and Nays, and the Names of the Persons voting for and against the Bill shall be entered on the Journal of each House respectively. If any Bill shall not be returned by the President within ten Days (Sundays excepted) after it shall have been presented to him, the Same shall be a Law, in like Manner as if he had signed it, unless the Congress by their Adjournment prevent its Return in which Case it shall not be a Law.

When Congress sends the president a bill, he or she can sign it (in which case it becomes law) or send it back to the chamber in which it originated. If it is sent back, a two-thirds majority of each chamber must pass it again for it to become law. If the president neither signs it nor sends it back within ten days, it becomes law anyway, unless Congress adjourns in the meantime.

Clause 3: Actions on Other Matters. Every Order, Resolution, or Vote to which the Concurrence of the Senate and House of Representatives may be necessary (except on a question of Adjournment) shall be presented to the President of the United States; and before the Same shall take Effect, shall be approved by him, or being disapproved by him, shall be repassed by two thirds of the Senate and House of Representatives, according to the Rules and Limitations prescribed in the Case of a Bill.

The president must have the opportunity to either sign or veto everything that Congress passes, except votes to adjourn and resolutions not having the force of law.

Section 8. The Powers of Congress

Clause 1: Taxing. The Congress shall have Power to lay and collect Taxes, Duties, Imposts and Excises, to pay the Debts and provide for the common Defence and general Welfare of the United States; but all Duties, Imposts and Excises shall be uniform throughout the United States;

Duties are taxes on imports and exports. Impost is a generic term for tax. Excises are taxes on the manufacture, sale, or use of goods.

Clause 2: Borrowing. To borrow Money on the credit of the United States;

Congress has the power to borrow money, which is normally carried out through the sale of U.S. treasury bonds on which interest is paid. Note that the Constitution places no limit on the amount of government borrowing.

Clause 3: Regulation of Commerce. To regulate Commerce with foreign Nations, and among the several States, and with the Indian Tribes;

This is the commerce clause, which gives to Congress the power to regulate interstate and foreign trade. Much of the activity of Congress is based on this clause.

Clause 4: Naturalization and Bankruptcy. To establish an uniform Rule of Naturalization, and uniform Laws on the subject of Bankruptcies throughout the United States;

Only Congress may determine how aliens can become citizens of the United States. Congress may make laws with respect to bankruptcy.

Clause 5: Money and Standards. To coin Money, regulate the Value thereof, and of foreign Coin, and fix the Standard of Weights and Measures;

Congress mints coins and prints and circulates paper money. Congress can establish uniform measures of time, distance, weight, and so on. In 1838, Congress adopted the English system of weights and measurements as our national standard.

Clause 6: Punishing Counterfeiters. To provide for the Punishment of counterfeiting the Securities and current Coin of the United States;

Congress has the power to punish those who copy American money and pass it off as real. Currently, the fine is up to $5,000 and/or imprisonment for up to fifteen years.

Clause 7: Roads and Post Offices. To establish Post Offices and post Roads;

Post roads include all routes over which mail is carried—highways, railways, waterways, and airways.

Clause 8: Patents and Copyrights. To promote the Progress of Science and useful Arts, by securing for limited Times to Authors and Inventors the exclusive Right to their respective Writings and Discoveries;

Authors' and composers' works are protected by copyrights established by copyright law, which currently is the Copyright Act of 1976, as amended. Copyrights are valid for the life of the author or composer plus seventy years. Inventors' works are protected by patents, which vary in length of protection from fourteen to twenty years. A patent gives a person the exclusive right to control the manufacture or sale of her or his invention.

Clause 9: Lower Courts. To constitute Tribunals inferior to the supreme Court;

Congress has the authority to set up all federal courts, except the Supreme Court, and to decide what cases those courts will hear.

Clause 10: Punishment for Piracy. To define and punish Piracies and Felonies committed on the high Seas, and Offences against the Law of Nations;

Congress has the authority to prohibit the commission of certain acts outside U.S. territory and to punish certain violations of international law.

Clause 11: Declaration of War. To declare War, grant Letters of Marque and Reprisal, and make Rules concerning Captures on Land and Water;

Only Congress can declare war, although the president, as commander in chief, can make war without Congress's formal declaration. Letters of marque and reprisal authorized private parties to capture and destroy enemy ships in wartime. Since the middle of the nineteenth century, international law has prohibited letters of marque and reprisal, and the United States has honored the ban.

Clause 12: The Army. To raise and support Armies, but no Appropriation of Money to that Use shall be for a longer Term than two Years;

Congress has the power to create an army; the money used to pay for it must be appropriated for no more than two-year intervals. This latter restriction gives ultimate control of the army to civilians.

Clause 13: Creation of a Navy. To provide and maintain a Navy;

This clause allows for the maintenance of a navy. In 1947, Congress created the U.S. Air Force.

Clause 14: Regulation of the Armed Forces. To make Rules for the Government and Regulation of the land and naval Forces;

Congress sets the rules for the military mainly by way of the Uniform Code of Military Justice, which was enacted in 1950 by Congress.

Clause 15: The Militia. To provide for calling forth the Militia to execute the Laws of the Union, suppress Insurrections and repel Invasions;

The militia is known today as the National Guard. Both Congress and the president have the authority to call the National Guard into federal service.

Clause 16: How the Militia Is Organized. To provide for organizing, arming, and disciplining the Militia, and for governing such Part of them as may be employed in the Service of the United States, reserving to the States respectively, the Appointment of the Officers, and the Authority of training the Militia according to the discipline prescribed by Congress;

This clause gives Congress the power to "federalize" state militia (National Guard). When called into such service, the National Guard is subject to the same rules that Congress has set forth for the regular armed services.

Clause 17: Creation of the District of Columbia. To exercise exclusive Legislation in all Cases whatsoever, over such District (not exceeding ten Miles square) as may, by Cession of particular States, and the Acceptance of Congress, become the Seat of the Government of the United States, and to exercise like Authority over all Places purchased by the Consent of the Legislature of the State in which the Same shall be, for the Erection of Forts, Magazines, Arsenals, dock-Yards, and other needful Buildings;—And

Congress established the District of Columbia as the national capital in 1791. Virginia and Maryland had granted land for the District, but Virginia's grant was returned because it was believed it would not be needed. Today, the District covers sixty-nine square miles.

Clause 18: The Elastic Clause. To make all Laws which shall be necessary and proper for carrying into Execution the foregoing Powers, and all other Powers vested by this Constitution in the Government of the United States, or in any Department or Officer thereof.

This clause—the necessary and proper *clause,* or the elastic clause—*grants no specific powers, and thus it can be stretched to fit different circumstances. It has allowed Congress to adapt the government to changing needs and times.*

Section 9. The Powers Denied to Congress

Clause 1: Question of Slavery. The Migration or Importation of such Persons as any of the States now existing shall think proper to admit, shall not be prohibited by the Congress prior to the Year one thousand eight hundred and eight, but a Tax or duty may be imposed on such Importation, not exceeding ten dollars for each Person.

"Persons" referred to slaves. Congress outlawed the slave trade in 1808.

Clause 2: Habeas Corpus. The privilege of the Writ of Habeas Corpus shall not be suspended, unless when in Cases of Rebellion or Invasion the public Safety may require it.

A writ of habeas corpus is a court order directing a sheriff or other public officer who is detaining another person to "produce the body" of the detainee so the court can assess the legality of the detention.

Clause 3: Special Bills. No Bill of Attainder or ex post facto Law shall be passed.

A bill of attainder is a law that inflicts punishment without a trial. An ex post facto law is a law that inflicts punishment for an act that was not illegal when it was committed.

Clause 4: Direct Taxes. [No Capitation, or other direct, Tax shall be laid, unless in Proportion to the Census or Enumeration herein before directed to be taken.]⁶

---

⁶Modified by the Sixteenth Amendment.

A capitation *is a tax on a person. A direct tax is a tax paid directly to the government, such as a property tax. This clause was intended to prevent Congress from levying a tax on slaves per person and thereby taxing slavery out of existence.*

Clause 5: Export Taxes. No Tax or Duty shall be laid on Articles exported from any State.

Congress may not tax any goods sold from one state to another or from one state to a foreign country. (Congress does have the power to tax goods that are bought from other countries, however.)

Clause 6: Interstate Commerce. No Preference shall be given by any Regulation of Commerce or Revenue to the Ports of one State over those of another: nor shall Vessels bound to, or from, one State, be obliged to enter, clear, or pay Duties in another.

Congress may not treat different ports within the United States differently in terms of taxing and commerce powers. Congress may not give one state's port a legal advantage over the ports of another state.

Clause 7: Treasury Withdrawals. No Money shall be drawn from the Treasury, but in Consequence of Appropriations made by Law; and a regular Statement and Account of the Receipts and Expenditures of all public Money shall be published from time to time.

Federal funds can be spent only as Congress authorizes. This is a significant check on the president's power.

Clause 8: Titles of Nobility. No Title of Nobility shall be granted by the United States: And no Person holding any Office of Profit or Trust under them, shall, without the Consent of the Congress, accept of any present, Emolument, Office, or Title, of any kind whatever, from any King, Prince, or foreign State.

No person in the United States may hold a title of nobility, such as duke or duchess. This clause also discourages bribery of American officials by foreign governments.

Section 10. Those Powers Denied to the States

Clause 1: Treaties and Coinage. No State shall enter into any Treaty, Alliance, or Confederation; grant Letters of Marque and Reprisal; coin Money; emit Bills of Credit; make any Thing but gold and silver Coin a Tender in Payment of Debts; pass any Bill of Attainder, ex post facto Law, or Law impairing the Obligation of Contracts, or grant any Title of Nobility.

Prohibiting state laws "impairing the Obligation of Contracts" was intended to protect creditors. (Shays' Rebellion—an attempt to prevent courts from giving effect to creditors' legal actions against debtors—occurred only one year before the Constitution was written.)

Clause 2: Duties and Imposts. No State shall, without the Consent of the Congress, lay any Imposts or Duties on Imports or Exports, except what may be absolutely necessary for executing its inspection Laws; and the net Produce of all Duties and Imposts, laid by any State on Imports or Exports, shall be for the Use of the Treasury of the United States; and all such Laws shall be subject to the Revision and Controul of the Congress.

Only Congress can tax imports. Further, the states cannot tax exports.

Clause 3: War. No State shall, without the Consent of Congress, lay any Duty of Tonnage, keep Troops, or Ships of War in time of Peace, enter into any Agreement or Compact with another State, or with a foreign Power or engage in War, unless actually invaded, or in such imminent Danger as will not admit of delay.

A duty of tonnage is a tax on ships according to their cargo capacity. No states may tax ships according to their cargo unless Congress agrees. Additionally, this clause forbids any state to keep troops or warships during peacetime or to make a compact with another state or foreign nation unless Congress so agrees. A state, in contrast, can maintain a militia, but its use has to be limited to disorders that occur within the state—unless, of course, the militia is called into federal service.

ARTICLE II. | (Executive Branch)

Section 1. The Nature and Scope of Presidential Power

Clause 1: Four-Year Term. The executive Power shall be vested in a President of the United States of America. He shall hold his Office during the Term of four Years, and, together with the Vice President, chosen for the same Term, be elected, as follows.

The president has the power to carry out laws made by Congress, called the executive power. He or she serves in office for a four-year term after election. The Twenty-second Amendment limits the number of times a person may be elected president.

Clause 2: Choosing Electors from Each State. Each State shall appoint, in such Manner as the Legislature thereof may direct, a Number of Electors, equal to the whole Number of Senators and Representatives to which the State may be entitled in the Congress; but no Senator or Representative, or Person holding an Office of Trust or Profit under the United States, shall be appointed an Elector.

The "Electors" are known more commonly as the "electoral college." The president is elected by electors—that is, representatives chosen by the people—rather than by the people directly.

Clause 3: *The Former System of Elections.* [The Electors shall meet in their respective States, and vote by Ballot for two Persons, of whom one at least shall not be an Inhabitant of the same State with themselves. And they shall make a List of all the Persons voted for, and of the Number of Votes for each; which List they shall sign and certify, and transmit sealed to the Seat of the Government of the United States, directed to the President of the Senate. The President of the Senate shall, in the Presence of the Senate and House of Representatives, open all the Certificates, and the Votes shall then be counted. The Person having the greatest Number of Votes shall be the President, if such Number be a Majority of the whole Number of Electors appointed; and if there be more than one who have such Majority, and have an equal Number of Votes, then the House of Representatives shall immediately chuse by Ballot one of them for President; and if no Person have a Majority, then from the five highest on the List the said House shall in like Manner chuse the President. But in chusing the President, the Votes shall be taken by States, the Representation from each State having one Vote; A quorum for this Purpose shall consist of a Member or Members from two thirds of the States, and a Majority of all the States shall be necessary to a Choice. In every Case, after the Choice of the President, the Person having the greater Number of Votes of the Electors shall be the Vice President. But if there should remain two or more who have equal Votes, the Senate shall chuse from them by Ballot the Vice President.][7]

The original method of selecting the president and vice president was replaced by the Twelfth Amendment. Apparently, the framers did not anticipate the rise of political parties and the development of primaries and conventions.

Clause 4: *The Time of Elections.* The Congress may determine the Time of chusing the Electors, and the Day on which they shall give their Votes; which Day shall be the same throughout the United States.

Congress set the Tuesday after the first Monday in November every fourth year as the date for choosing electors. The electors cast their votes on the Monday after the second Wednesday in December of that year.

Clause 5: *Qualifications for President.* No person except a natural born Citizen, or a Citizen of the United States, at the time of the Adoption of this Constitution, shall be eligible to the Office of President; neither shall any Person be eligible to that Office who shall not have attained to the Age of thirty five Years, and been fourteen Years a Resident within the United States.

The president must be a natural-born citizen, be at least thirty-five years of age when taking office, and have been a resident within the United States for at least fourteen years.

Clause 6: *Succession of the Vice President.* [In Case of the Removal of the President from Office, or of his Death, Resignation or Inability to discharge the Powers and Duties of the said Office, the same shall devolve on the Vice President, and the Congress may by Law provide for the Case of Removal, Death, Resignation or Inability, both of the President and Vice President, declaring what Officer shall then act as President, and such Officer shall act accordingly, until the Disability be removed, or a President shall be elected.][8]

This section provided for the method by which the vice president was to succeed to the presidency, but its wording is ambiguous. It was replaced by the Twenty-fifth Amendment.

Clause 7: *The President's Salary.* The President shall, at stated Times, receive for his Services, a Compensation, which shall neither be encreased nor diminished during the Period for which he shall have been elected, and he shall not receive within that Period any other Emolument from the United States, or any of them.

The president maintains the same salary during each four-year term. Moreover, she or he may not receive additional cash payments from the government. Originally set at $25,000 per year, the salary is currently $400,000 a year plus a $50,000 non-taxable expense account.

Clause 8: *The Oath of Office.* Before he enter on the Execution of his Office, he shall take the following Oath or Affirmation: "I do solemnly swear (or affirm) that I will faithfully execute the Office of President of the United States, and will to the best of my Ability, preserve, protect and defend the Constitution of the United States."

The president is "sworn in" prior to beginning the duties of the office. The taking of the oath of office occurs on January 20, following the November election. The ceremony is called the inauguration. The oath of office is administered by the chief justice of the United States Supreme Court.

Section 2. *Powers of the President*
Clause 1: *Commander in Chief.* The President shall be Commander in Chief of the Army and Navy of the United

---

[7]Changed by the Twelfth Amendment.

[8]Modified by the Twenty-fifth Amendment.

States, and of the Militia of the several States, when called into the actual Service of the United States; he may require the Opinion, in writing, of the principal Officer in each of the executive Departments, upon any Subject relating to the Duties of their respective Offices, and he shall have Power to grant Reprieves and Pardons for Offences against the United States, except in Cases of Impeachment.

The armed forces are placed under civilian control because the president is a civilian but still commander in chief of the military. The president may ask for the help of the head of each of the executive departments (thereby creating the cabinet). The cabinet members are chosen by the president with the consent of the Senate, but they can be removed without Senate approval.

The president's clemency powers extend only to federal cases. In those cases, he or she may grant a full or conditional pardon, or reduce a prison term or fine.

Clause 2: Treaties and Appointment. He shall have Power, by and with the Advice and Consent of the Senate, to make Treaties, provided two thirds of the Senators present concur; and he shall nominate, and by and with the Advice and Consent of the Senate, shall appoint Ambassadors, other public Ministers and Consuls, Judges of the supreme Court, and all other Officers of the United States, whose Appointments are not herein otherwise provided for, and which shall be established by Law; but the Congress may by Law vest the Appointment of such inferior Officers, as they think proper, in the President alone, in the Courts of Law, or in the Heads of Departments.

Many of the major powers of the president are identified in this clause, including the power to make treaties with foreign governments (with the approval of the Senate by a two-thirds vote) and the power to appoint ambassadors, Supreme Court justices, and other government officials. Most such appointments require Senate approval.

Clause 3: Vacancies. The President shall have Power to fill up all Vacancies that may happen during the Recess of the Senate, by granting Commissions which shall expire at the end of their next Session.

The president has the power to appoint temporary officials to fill vacant federal offices without Senate approval if the Congress is not in session. Such appointments expire automatically at the end of Congress's next term.

Section 3. Duties of the President

He shall from time to time give to the Congress Information of the State of the Union, and recommend to their Consideration such Measures as he shall judge necessary and expedient; he may, on extraordinary Occasions, convene both Houses, or either of them, and in Case of Disagreement between them, with Respect to the Time of Adjournment, he may adjourn

them to such Time as he shall think proper; he shall receive Ambassadors and other public Ministers; he shall take Care that the Laws be faithfully executed, and shall Commission all the Officers of the United States.

Annually, the president reports on the state of the union to Congress, recommends legislative measures, and proposes a federal budget. The State of the Union speech is a statement not only to Congress but also to the American people. After it is given, the president proposes a federal budget and presents an economic report. At any time, the president may send special messages to Congress while it is in session. The president has the power to call special sessions, to adjourn Congress when its two chambers do not agree on when to adjourn, to receive diplomatic representatives of other governments, and to ensure the proper execution of all federal laws. The president further has the ability to empower federal officers to hold their positions and to perform their duties.

Section 4. Impeachment

The President, Vice President and all civil Officers of the United States, shall be removed from Office on Impeachment for, and Conviction of, Treason, Bribery, or other high Crimes and Misdemeanors.

Treason denotes giving aid to the nation's enemies. The phrase high crimes and misdemeanors *is usually considered to mean serious abuses of political power. In either case, the president or vice president may be accused by the House (called an* impeachment*) and then removed from office if convicted by the Senate. (Note that impeachment does not mean removal but rather refers to an accusation of treason or high crimes and misdemeanors.)*

ARTICLE III. | (Judicial Branch)

Section 1. Judicial Powers, Courts, and Judges

The judicial Power of the United States, shall be vested in one supreme Court, and in such inferior Courts as the Congress may from time to time ordain and establish. The Judges, both of the supreme and inferior Courts, shall hold their Offices during good Behaviour, and shall, at stated Times, receive for their Services a Compensation, which shall not be diminished during their Continuance in Office.

The Supreme Court is vested with judicial power, as are the lower federal courts that Congress creates. Federal judges serve in their offices for life unless they are impeached and convicted by Congress. The payment of federal judges may not be reduced during their time in office.

Section 2. Jurisdiction

Clause 1: Cases under Federal Jurisdiction. The judicial Power shall extend to all Cases, in Law and Equity, arising under this Constitution, the Laws of the United States, and Treaties made, or which shall be made, under their

Authority;—to all Cases affecting Ambassadors, other public Ministers and Consuls;—to all Cases of admiralty and maritime Jurisdiction;—to Controversies to which the United States shall be a Party;—to Controversies between two or more States; [—between a State and Citizens of another State;—][9] between Citizens of different States;—between Citizens of the same State claiming Lands under Grants of different States, [and between a State, or the Citizens thereof, and foreign States, Citizens or Subjects.][10]

The federal courts take on cases that concern the meaning of the U.S. Constitution, all federal laws, and treaties. They also can take on cases involving citizens of different states and citizens of foreign nations.

Clause 2: Cases for the Supreme Court. In all Cases affecting Ambassadors, other public Ministers and Consuls, and those in which a State shall be a Party, the supreme Court shall have original Jurisdiction. In all the other Cases before mentioned, the supreme Court shall have appellate Jurisdiction, both as to Law and Fact, with such Exceptions, and under such Regulations as the Congress shall make.

In a limited number of situations, the Supreme Court acts as a trial court and has original jurisdiction. These cases involve a representative from another country or involve a state. In all other situations, the cases must first be tried in the lower courts and then can be appealed to the Supreme Court. Congress may, however, make exceptions. Today, the Supreme Court acts as a trial court of first instance on rare occasions.

Clause 3: The Conduct of Trials. The Trial of all Crimes, except in Cases of Impeachment, shall be by Jury; and such Trial shall be held in the State where the said Crimes shall have been committed; but when not committed within any State, the Trial shall be at such Place or Places as the Congress may by Law have directed.

Any person accused of a federal crime is granted the right to a trial by jury in a federal court in that state in which the crime was committed. Trials of impeachment are an exception.

Section 3. Treason
Clause 1: The Definition of Treason. Treason against the United States, shall consist only in levying War against them, or, in adhering to their Enemies, giving them Aid and Comfort. No Person shall be convicted of Treason unless on the Testimony of two Witnesses to the same overt Act, or on Confession in open Court.

Treason is the making of war against the United States or giving aid to its enemies.

Clause 2: Punishment. The Congress shall have Power to declare the Punishment of Treason, but no Attainder of Treason shall work Corruption of Blood, or Forfeiture except during the Life of the Person attainted.

Congress has provided that the punishment for treason ranges from a minimum of five years in prison and/or a $10,000 fine to a maximum of death. "No Attainder of Treason shall work Corruption of Blood" prohibits punishment of the traitor's heirs.

ARTICLE IV. | (Relations among the States)

Section 1. Full Faith and Credit
Full Faith and Credit shall be given in each State to the public Acts, Records, and judicial Proceedings of every other State. And the Congress may by general Laws prescribe the Manner in which such Acts, Records and Proceedings shall be proved, and the Effect thereof.

All states are required to respect one another's laws, records, and lawful decisions. There are exceptions, however. A state does not have to enforce another state's criminal code. Nor does it have to recognize another state's grant of a divorce if the person obtaining the divorce did not establish legal residence in the state in which it was given.

Section 2. Treatment of Citizens
Clause 1: Privileges and Immunities. The Citizens of each State shall be entitled to all Privileges and Immunities of Citizens in the several States.

A citizen of a state has the same rights and privileges as the citizens of another state in which he or she happens to be.

Clause 2: Extradition. A Person charged in any State with Treason, Felony, or other Crime, who shall flee from Justice, and be found in another State, shall on Demand of the executive Authority of the State from which he fled, be delivered up, to be removed to the State having Jurisdiction of the Crime.

Any person accused of a crime who flees to another state must be returned to the state in which the crime occurred.

Clause 3: Fugitive Slaves. [No Person held to Service or Labour in one State, under the Laws thereof, escaping into another, shall, in Consequence of any Law or Regulation therein, be discharged from such Service or Labour, but shall be delivered up on Claim of the Party to whom such Service or Labour may be due.][11]

This clause was struck down by the Thirteenth Amendment, which abolished slavery in 1865.

---

[9]Modified by the Eleventh Amendment.
[10]Modified by the Eleventh Amendment.

[11]Repealed by the Thirteenth Amendment.

Section 3. Admission of States

Clause 1: The Process.   New States may be admitted by the Congress into this Union; but no new State shall be formed or erected within the Jurisdiction of any other State; nor any State be formed by the Junction of two or more States, or Parts of States, without the Consent of the Legislatures of the States concerned as well as of the Congress.

Only Congress has the power to admit new states to the union. No state may be created by taking territory from an existing state unless the state's legislature so consents.

Clause 2: Public Land.   The Congress shall have Power to dispose of and make all needful Rules and Regulations respecting the Territory or other Property belonging to the United States; and nothing in this Constitution shall be so construed as to Prejudice any Claims of the United States, or of any particular State.

The federal government has the exclusive right to administer federal government public lands.

Section 4. Republican Form of Government

The United States shall guarantee to every State in this Union a Republican Form of Government, and shall protect each of them against Invasion; and on Application of the Legislature, or of the Executive (when the Legislature cannot be convened) against domestic Violence.

Each state is promised a republican form of government—that is, one in which the people elect their representatives. The federal government is bound to protect states against any attack by foreigners or during times of trouble within a state.

ARTICLE V. | (Methods of Amendment)

The Congress, whenever two thirds of both Houses shall deem it necessary, shall propose Amendments to this Constitution, or on the Application of the Legislatures of two thirds of the several States, shall call a Convention for proposing Amendments, which, in either Case, shall be valid to all Intents and Purposes, as Part of this Constitution, when ratified by the Legislatures of three fourths of the several States, or by Conventions in three fourths thereof, as the one or the other Mode of Ratification may be proposed by the Congress; Provided that no Amendment which may be made prior to the Year One thousand eight hundred and eight shall in any Manner affect the first and fourth Clauses in the Ninth Section of the First Article; and that no State, without its Consent, shall be deprived of its equal Suffrage in the Senate.

Amendments may be proposed in either of two ways: a two-thirds vote of each chamber (Congress) or at the request of two-thirds of the states. Ratification of amendments may be carried out in two ways: by the legislatures of three-fourths of the states or by the voters in three-fourths of the states. No state may be denied equal representation in the Senate.

ARTICLE VI. | (National Supremacy)

Clause 1: Existing Obligations.   All Debts contracted and Engagements entered into, before the Adoption of this Constitution shall be as valid against the United States under this Constitution, as under the Confederation.

During the Revolutionary War and the years of the Confederation, Congress borrowed large sums. This clause pledged that the new federal government would assume those financial obligations.

Clause 2: Supreme Law of the Land.   This Constitution, and the Laws of the United States which shall be made in Pursuance thereof; and all Treaties made, or which shall be made, under the Authority of the United States, shall be the supreme Law of the Land; and the Judges in every State shall be bound thereby, any Thing in the Constitution or Laws of any State to the Contrary notwithstanding.

This is typically called the supremacy clause; *it declares that federal law takes precedence over all forms of state law. No government at the local or state level may make or enforce any law that conflicts with any provision of the Constitution, acts of Congress, treaties, or other rules and regulations issued by the president and his or her subordinates in the executive branch of the federal government.*

Clause 3: Oath of Office.   The Senators and Representatives before mentioned, and the Members of the several State Legislatures, and all executive and judicial Officers, both of the United States and of the several States, shall be bound by Oath or Affirmation, to support this Constitution; but no religious Test shall ever be required as a Qualification to any Office or public Trust under the United States.

Every federal and state official must take an oath of office promising to support the U.S. Constitution. Religion may not be used as a qualification to serve in any federal office.

ARTICLE VII. | (Ratification)

The Ratification of the Conventions of nine States shall be sufficient for the Establishment of this Constitution between the States so ratifying the Same.

Nine states were required to ratify the Constitution. Delaware was the first and New Hampshire the ninth.

Done in Convention by the Unanimous Consent of the States present the Seventeenth Day of September in the Year of our Lord one thousand seven hundred and Eighty seven and of the Independence of the United States of America the Twelfth. In witness whereof we have hereunto subscribed our Names,

> Go. WASHINGTON
> Presid't.
> and deputy from Virginia

Attest William Jackson Secretary

DELAWARE	{	Geo. Read
		Gunning Bedford jun
		John Dickinson
		Richard Bassett
		Jaco. Broom

MARYLAND	{	James McHenry
		Dan of St. Thos. Jenifer
		Danl. Carroll

VIRGINIA	{	John Blair
		James Madison Jr.

NORTH CAROLINA	{	Wm. Blount
		Richd. Dobbs Spaight
		Hu. Williamson

SOUTH CAROLINA	{	J. Rutledge
		Charles Cotesworth Pinckney
		Charles Pinckney
		Pierce Butler

GEORGIA	{	William Few
		Abr. Baldwin

NEW HAMPSHIRE	{	John Langdon
		Nicholas Gilman

MASSACHUSETTS	{	Nathaniel Gorham
		Rufus King

CONNECTICUT	{	Wm. Saml. Johnson
		Roger Sherman

NEW YORK	{	Alexander Hamilton

NEW JERSEY	{	Wh. Livingston
		David Brearley
		Wm. Paterson
		Jona. Dayton

PENNSYLVANIA	{	B. Franklin
		Thomas Mifflin
		Robt. Morris
		Geo. Clymer
		Thos. FitzSimons
		Jared Ingersoll
		James Wilson
		Gouv. Morris

AMENDMENTS TO THE CONSTITUTION OF THE UNITED STATES (The Bill of Rights)[12]

Articles in addition to, and amendment of, the Constitution of the United States of America, proposed by Congress and ratified by the Legislatures of the several states, pursuant to the Fifth Article of the original Constitution.

AMENDMENT I. | (Religion, Speech, Assembly, and Petition)

Congress shall make no law respecting an establishment of religion, or prohibiting the free exercise thereof; or abridging the freedom of speech, or of the press; or the right of the people peaceably to assemble, and to petition the Government for a redress of grievances.

Congress may not create an official church or enact laws limiting the freedom of religion, speech, the press, assembly, and petition. These guarantees, like the others in the Bill of Rights (the first ten amendments), are not absolute—each may be exercised only with regard to the rights of other persons.

AMENDMENT II. | (Militia and the Right to Bear Arms)

A well regulated Militia, being necessary to the security of a free State, the right of the people to keep and bear Arms, shall not be infringed.

To protect itself, each state has the right to maintain a volunteer armed force. States and the federal government regulate the possession and use of firearms by individuals.

AMENDMENT III. | (The Quartering of Soldiers)

No Soldier shall, in time of peace be quartered in any house, without the consent of the Owner, nor in time of war, but in a manner to be prescribed by law.

Before the Revolutionary War, it had been common British practice to quarter soldiers in colonists' homes. Military troops do not have the power to take over private houses during peacetime.

[12]On September 25, 1789, Congress transmitted to the state legislatures twelve proposed amendments, two of which, having to do with congressional representation and congressional pay, were not adopted. The remaining ten amendments became the Bill of Rights. In 1992, the amendment concerning congressional pay was adopted as the Twenty-seventh Amendment.

AMENDMENT IV. | (Searches and Seizures)

The right of the people to be secure in their persons, houses, papers, and effects, against unreasonable searches and seizures, shall not be violated, and no Warrants shall issue, but upon probable cause, supported by Oath or affirmation, and particularly describing the place to be searched, and the persons or things to be seized.

Here the word warrant *means "justification" and refers to a document issued by a magistrate or judge indicating the name, address, and possible offense committed. Anyone asking for the warrant, such as a police officer, must be able to convince the magistrate or judge that an offense probably has been committed.*

AMENDMENT V. | (Grand Juries, Self-Incrimination, Double Jeopardy, Due Process, and Eminent Domain)

No person shall be held to answer for a capital, or otherwise infamous crime, unless on a presentment or indictment of a Grand Jury, except in cases arising in the land or naval forces, or in the Militia, when in actual service in time of War or public danger; nor shall any person be subject for the same offence to be twice put in jeopardy of life or limb; nor shall be compelled in any criminal case to be a witness against himself, nor be deprived of life, liberty, or property, without due process of law; nor shall private property be taken for public use, without just compensation.

There are two types of juries. A grand jury considers physical evidence and the testimony of witnesses and decides whether there is sufficient reason to bring a case to trial. A petit jury hears the case at trial and decides it. "For the same offence to be twice put in jeopardy of life or limb" means to be tried twice for the same crime. A person may not be tried for the same crime twice or forced to give evidence against herself or himself. No person's right to life, liberty, or property may be taken away except by lawful means, called the due process of law. Private property taken for use in public purposes must be paid for by the government.

AMENDMENT VI. | (Criminal Court Procedures)

In all criminal prosecutions, the accused shall enjoy the right to a speedy and public trial, by an impartial jury of the State and district wherein the crime shall have been committed, which district shall have been previously ascertained by law, and to be informed of the nature and cause of the accusation; to be confronted with the witnesses against him; to have compulsory process for obtaining witnesses in his favor, and to have the Assistance of Counsel for his defence.

Any person accused of a crime has the right to a fair and public trial by a jury in the state in which the crime took place. The charges against that person must be indicated. Any accused person has the right to a lawyer to defend him or her and to question those who testify against him or her, as well as the right to call people to speak in his or her favor at trial.

AMENDMENT VII. | (Trial by Jury in Civil Cases)

In Suits at common law, where the value in controversy shall exceed twenty dollars, the right of trial by jury shall be preserved, and no fact tried by jury, shall be otherwise re-examined in any Court of the United States, than according to the rules of the common law.

A jury trial may be requested by either party in a dispute in any case involving more than $20. If both parties agree to a trial by a judge without a jury, the right to a jury trial may be put aside.

AMENDMENT VIII. | (Bail, Cruel and Unusual Punishment)

Excessive bail shall not be required, nor excessive fines imposed, nor cruel and unusual punishments inflicted.

Bail is that amount of money that a person accused of a crime may be required to deposit with the court as a guaranty that she or he will appear in court when requested. The amount of bail required or the fine imposed as punishment for a crime must be reasonable compared with the seriousness of the crime involved. Any punishment judged to be too harsh or too severe for a crime shall be prohibited.

AMENDMENT IX. | (The Rights Retained by the People)

The enumeration in the Constitution, of certain rights, shall not be construed to deny or disparage others retained by the people.

Many civil rights that are not explicitly enumerated in the Constitution are still held by the people.

AMENDMENT X. | (Reserved Powers of the States)

The powers not delegated to the United States by the Constitution, nor prohibited by it to the States, are reserved to the States respectively, or to the people.

Those powers not delegated by the Constitution to the federal government or expressly denied to the states belong to the states and to the people. This amendment in essence allows the states to pass laws under their "police powers."

AMENDMENT XI. | (Ratified on February 7, 1795— Suits against States)

The Judicial power of the United States shall not be construed to extend to any suit in law or equity, commenced or prosecuted against one of the United States by Citizens of another State, or by Citizens or Subjects of any Foreign State.

This amendment has been interpreted to mean that a state cannot be sued in federal court by one of its own citizens, by a citizen of another state, or by a foreign country.

AMENDMENT XII. | (Ratified on June 15, 1804— Election of the President)

The Electors shall meet in their respective states, and vote by ballot for President and Vice-President, one of whom, at least, shall not be an inhabitant of the same State with themselves; they shall name in their ballots the person voted for as President, and in distinct ballots the person voted for as Vice-President, and they shall make distinct lists of all persons voted for as President, and of all persons voted for as Vice-President, and of the number of votes for each, which lists they shall sign and certify, and transmit sealed to the seat of the government of the United States, directed to the President of the Senate;—The President of the Senate shall, in the presence of the Senate and House of Representatives, open all the certificates and the votes shall then be counted;—The person having the greatest number of votes for President, shall be the President, if such number be a majority of the whole number of Electors appointed; and if no person have such majority, then from the persons having the highest numbers not exceeding three on the list of those voted for as President, the House of Representatives shall choose immediately, by ballot, the President. But in choosing the President, the votes shall be taken by States, the representation from each State having one vote; a quorum for this purpose shall consist of a member or members from two-thirds of the States, and a majority of all States shall be necessary to a choice. [And if the House of Representatives shall not choose a President whenever the right of choice shall devolve upon them, before the fourth day of March next following, then the Vice-President shall act as President, as in the case of the death or other constitutional disability of the President.][13]—The person having the greatest number of votes as Vice-President, shall be the Vice-President, if such number be a majority of the whole number of Electors appointed, and if no person have a majority, then from the

---

[13]Changed by the Twentieth Amendment.

two highest numbers on the list, the Senate shall choose the Vice-President; a quorum for the purpose shall consist of two-thirds of the whole number of Senators, and a majority of the whole number shall be necessary to a choice. But no person constitutionally ineligible to the office of President shall be eligible to that of Vice-President of the United States.

The original procedure set out for the election of president and vice president in Article II, Section 1, resulted in a tie in 1800 between Thomas Jefferson and Aaron Burr. It was not until the next year that the House of Representatives chose Jefferson to be president. This amendment changed the procedure by providing for separate ballots for president and vice president.

AMENDMENT XIII. | (Ratified on December 6, 1865— Prohibition of Slavery)

Section 1.
Neither slavery nor involuntary servitude, except as a punishment for crime whereof the party shall have been duly convicted, shall exist within the United States, or any place subject to their jurisdiction.

Some slaves had been freed during the Civil War. This amendment freed the others and abolished slavery.

Section 2.
Congress shall have power to enforce this article by appropriate legislation.

AMENDMENT XIV. | (Ratified on July 9, 1868— Citizenship, Due Process, and Equal Protection of the Laws)

Section 1.
All persons born or naturalized in the United States, and subject to the jurisdiction thereof, are citizens of the United States and of the State wherein they reside. No State shall make or enforce any law which shall abridge the privileges or immunities of citizens of the United States; nor shall any State deprive any person of life, liberty, or property, without due process of law; nor deny to any person within its jurisdiction the equal protection of the laws.

Under this provision, states cannot make or enforce laws that take away rights given to all citizens by the federal government. States cannot act unfairly or arbitrarily toward, or discriminate against, any person.

Section 2.
Representatives shall be apportioned among the several States according to their respective numbers, counting the whole number of persons in each State, excluding Indians not taxed. But when the right to vote at any election for the choice of electors for President and Vice President of the United States, Representatives in Congress, the Executive and Judicial officers of a State, or the members of the Legislature thereof, is denied to any of the male inhabitants of such State, being [twenty-one][14] years of age, and citizens of the United States, or in any way abridged, except for participation in rebellion, or other crime, the basis of representation therein shall be reduced in the proportion which the number of such male citizens shall bear to the whole number of male citizens twenty-one years of age in such State.

Section 3.
No person shall be a Senator or Representative in Congress, or elector of President and Vice President, or hold any office, civil or military, under the United States, or under any State, who having previously taken an oath, as a member of Congress, or as an officer of the United States, or as a member of any State legislature, or as an executive or judicial officer of any State, to support the Constitution of the United States, shall have engaged in insurrection or rebellion against the same, or given aid or comfort to the enemies thereof. But Congress may by a vote of two-thirds of each House, remove such disability.

This provision forbade former state or federal government officials who had acted in support of the Confederacy during the Civil War to hold office again. It limited the president's power to pardon those persons. Congress removed this "disability" in 1898.

Section 4.
The validity of the public debt of the United States, authorized by law, including debts incurred for payment of pensions and bounties for services in suppressing insurrection or rebellion, shall not be questioned. But neither the United States nor any State shall assume or pay any debt or obligation incurred in aid of insurrection or rebellion against the United States, or any claim for the loss or emancipation of any slave, but all such debts, obligations and claims shall be held illegal and void.

Section 5.
The Congress shall have power to enforce, by appropriate legislation, the provisions of this article.

[14]Changed by the Twenty-sixth Amendment.

AMENDMENT XV. | (Ratified on February 3, 1870— The Right to Vote)

Section 1.

The right of citizens of the United States to vote shall not be denied or abridged by the United States or by any State on account of race, color, or previous condition of servitude.

No citizen can be refused the right to vote simply because of race or color or because that person was once a slave.

Section 2.

The Congress shall have power to enforce this article by appropriate legislation.

AMENDMENT XVI. | (Ratified on February 3, 1913— Income Taxes)

The Congress shall have power to lay and collect taxes on incomes, from whatever source derived, without apportionment among the several States, and without regard to any census or enumeration.

This amendment allows Congress to tax income without sharing the revenue so obtained with the states according to their population.

AMENDMENT XVII. | (Ratified on April 8, 1913— The Popular Election of Senators)

Section 1.

The Senate of the United States shall be composed of two Senators from each State, elected by the people thereof, for six years; and each Senator shall have one vote. The electors in each State shall have the qualifications requisite for electors of the most numerous branch of the State legislatures.

Section 2.

When vacancies happen in the representation of any State in the Senate, the executive authority of such State shall issue writs of election to fill such vacancies: *Provided,* That the legislature of any State may empower the executive thereof to make temporary appointments until the people fill the vacancies by election as the legislature may direct.

Section 3.

This amendment shall not be so construed as to affect the election or term of any Senator chosen before it becomes valid as part of the Constitution.

This amendment modified portions of Article I, Section 3, that related to election of senators. Senators are now elected by the voters in each state directly. When a vacancy occurs, either the state may fill the vacancy by a special election, or the governor of the state involved may appoint someone to fill the seat until the next election.

AMENDMENT XVIII. | (Ratified on January 16, 1919— Prohibition)

Section 1.

After one year from the ratification of this article the manufacture, sale, or transportation of intoxicating liquors within, the importation thereof into, or the exportation thereof from the United States and all territory subject to the jurisdiction thereof for beverage purposes is hereby prohibited.

Section 2.

The Congress and the several States shall have concurrent power to enforce this article by appropriate legislation.

Section 3.

This article shall be inoperative unless it shall have been ratified as an amendment to the Constitution by the legislatures of the several States, as provided in the Constitution, within seven years from the date of the submission hereof to the States by the Congress.[15]

This amendment made it illegal to manufacture, sell, and transport alcoholic beverages in the United States. It was repealed by the Twenty-first Amendment.

AMENDMENT XIX. | (Ratified on August 18, 1920— Women's Right to Vote)

Section 1.

The right of citizens of the United States to vote shall not be denied or abridged by the United States or by any State on account of sex.

Section 2.

Congress shall have power to enforce this article by appropriate legislation.

Women were given the right to vote by this amendment, and Congress was given the power to enforce this right.

---

[15]The Eighteenth Amendment was repealed by the Twenty-first Amendment.

AMENDMENT XX. | (Ratified on January 23, 1933— The Lame Duck Amendment)

Section 1.

The terms of the President and Vice President shall end at noon on the 20th day of January, and the terms of Senators and Representatives at noon on the 3d day of January, of the years in which such terms would have ended if this article had not been ratified; and the terms of their successors shall then begin.

This amendment modified Article I, Section 4, Clause 2, and other provisions relating to the president in the Twelfth Amendment. The taking of the oath of office was moved from March 4 to January 20.

Section 2.

The Congress shall assemble at least once in every year, and such meeting shall begin at noon on the 3d day of January, unless they shall by law appoint a different day.

Congress changed the beginning of its term to January 3. The reason the Twentieth Amendment is called the Lame Duck Amendment is that it shortens the time between when a member of Congress is defeated for reelection and when he or she leaves office.

Section 3.

If, at the time fixed for the beginning of the term of the President, the President elect shall have died, the Vice President elect shall become President. If a President shall not have been chosen before the time fixed for the beginning of his term, or if the President elect shall have failed to qualify, then the Vice President elect shall act as President until a President shall have qualified; and the Congress may by law provide for the case wherein neither a President elect nor a Vice President elect shall have qualified, declaring who shall then act as President, or the manner in which one who is to act shall be selected, and such person shall act accordingly until a President or Vice President shall have qualified.

This part of the amendment deals with problem areas left ambiguous by Article II and the Twelfth Amendment. If the president dies before January 20 or fails to qualify for office, the presidency is to be filled as described in this section.

Section 4.

The Congress may by law provide for the case of the death of any of the persons from whom the House of Representatives may choose a President whenever the rights of choice shall have devolved upon them, and for the case of the death of any of the persons from whom the Senate may choose a Vice President whenever the right of choice shall have devolved upon them.

Congress has never created legislation pursuant to this section.

Section 5.

Sections 1 and 2 shall take effect on the 15th day of October following the ratification of this article.

Section 6.

This article shall be inoperative unless it shall have been ratified as an amendment to the Constitution by the legislatures of three-fourths of the several States within seven years from the date of its submission.

AMENDMENT XXI. | (Ratified on December 5, 1933— The Repeal of Prohibition)

Section 1.

The eighteenth article of amendment to the Constitution of the United States is hereby repealed.

Section 2.

The transportation or importation into any State, Territory, or possession of the United States for delivery or use therein of intoxicating liquors, in violation of the laws thereof, is hereby prohibited.

Section 3.

This article shall be inoperative unless it shall have been ratified as an amendment to the Constitution by conventions in the several States, as provided in the Constitution, within seven years from the date of the submission hereof to the States by the Congress.

The amendment repealed the Eighteenth Amendment but did not make alcoholic beverages legal everywhere. Rather, they remained illegal in any state that so designated them. Many such "dry" states existed for a number of years after 1933. Today, there are still "dry" counties within the United States, in which the sale of alcoholic beverages is illegal.

AMENDMENT XXII. | (Ratified on February 27, 1951— Limitation of Presidential Terms)

Section 1.

No person shall be elected to the office of the President more than twice, and no person who has held the office of President, or acted as President, for more than two years of a term to which some other person was elected President shall be elected to the office of President more than once. But this Article shall not apply to any person holding the office of President when this Article was proposed by the Congress, and shall not prevent any person who may be holding the office of President, or acting as President, during the term within which this Article becomes operative from holding the office of President or acting as President during the remainder of such term.

Section 2.

This article shall be inoperative unless it shall have been ratified as an amendment to the Constitution by the legislatures of three-fourths of the several States within seven years from the date of its submission to the States by the Congress.

No president may serve more than two elected terms. If, however, a president has succeeded to the office after the halfway point of a term in which another president was originally elected, then that president may serve for more than eight years, but not to exceed ten years.

AMENDMENT XXIII. | (Ratified on March 29, 1961— Presidential Electors for the District of Columbia)

Section 1.

The District constituting the seat of Government of the United States shall appoint in such manner as the Congress may direct:

A number of electors of President and Vice President equal to the whole number of Senators and Representatives in Congress to which the District would be entitled if it were a State, but in no event more than the least populous State; they shall be in addition to those appointed by the States, but they shall be considered, for the purposes of the election of President and Vice President, to be electors appointed by a State; and they shall meet in the District and perform such duties as provided by the twelfth article of amendment.

Section 2.

The Congress shall have power to enforce this article by appropriate legislation.

Citizens living in the District of Columbia have the right to vote in elections for president and vice president. The District of Columbia has three presidential electors, whereas before this amendment it had none.

AMENDMENT XXIV. | (Ratified on January 23, 1964— The Anti–Poll Tax Amendment)

Section 1.

The right of citizens of the United States to vote in any primary or other election for President or Vice President, for electors for President or Vice President, or for Senator or Representative in Congress, shall not be denied or abridged by the United States, or any State by reason of failure to pay any poll tax or other tax.

Section 2.

The Congress shall have power to enforce this article by appropriate legislation.

No government shall require a person to pay a poll tax to vote in any federal election.

AMENDMENT XXV. | (Ratified on February 10, 1967— Presidential Disability and Vice Presidential Vacancies)

Section 1.

In case of the removal of the President from office or of his death or resignation, the Vice President shall become President.

Whenever a president dies or resigns from office, the vice president becomes president.

Section 2.

Whenever there is a vacancy in the office of the Vice President, the President shall nominate a Vice President who shall take office upon confirmation by a majority vote of both Houses of Congress.

Whenever the office of the vice presidency becomes vacant, the president may appoint someone to fill this office, provided Congress consents.

Section 3.

Whenever the President transmits to the President pro tempore of the Senate and the Speaker of the House of Representatives his written declaration that he is unable to discharge the powers and duties of his office, and until he transmits to them a written declaration to the contrary, such powers and duties shall be discharged by the Vice President as Acting President.

Whenever the president believes she or he is unable to carry out the duties of the office, she or he shall so indicate to Congress in writing. The vice president then acts as president until the president declares that she or he is again able to carry out the duties of the office.

Section 4.

Whenever the Vice President and a majority of either the principal officers of the executive departments or of such other body as Congress may by law provide, transmit to the President pro tempore of the Senate and the Speaker of the House of Representatives their written declaration that the President is unable to discharge the powers and duties of his office, the Vice President shall immediately assume the powers and duties of the office as Acting President.

Thereafter, when the President transmits to the President pro tempore of the Senate and the Speaker of the House of Representatives his written declaration that no inability exists, he shall resume the powers and duties of his office unless the Vice President and a majority of either the principal officers of the executive department or of such other body as Congress may by law provide, transmit within four days to the President pro tempore of the Senate and the Speaker of the House of Representatives their written declaration that the President is unable to discharge the powers and duties of his office. Thereupon Congress shall decide the issue, assembling within forty-eight hours for that purpose if not in session. If the Congress, within twenty-one days after receipt of the latter written declaration, or, if Congress is not in session, within twenty-one days after Congress is required to assemble, determines by two-thirds vote of both Houses that the President is unable to discharge the powers and duties of his office, the Vice President shall continue to discharge the same as Acting President; otherwise, the President shall resume the powers and duties of his office.

Whenever the vice president and a majority of the members of the cabinet believe that the president cannot carry out her or his duties, they shall so indicate in writing to Congress. The vice president shall then act as president. When the president believes that she or he is able to carry out her or his duties again, she or he shall so indicate to the Congress. However, if the vice president and a majority of the cabinet do not agree, Congress must decide by a two-thirds vote within three weeks who shall act as president.

AMENDMENT XXVI. | (Ratified on July 1, 1971— The Eighteen-Year-Old Vote)

Section 1.
The right of citizens of the United States, who are eighteen years of age or older, to vote shall not be denied or abridged by the United States or by any State on account of age.

No one over eighteen years of age can be denied the right to vote in federal or state elections by virtue of age.

Section 2.
The Congress shall have power to enforce this article by appropriate legislation.

AMENDMENT XXVII. | (Ratified on May 7, 1992— Congressional Pay)

No law, varying the compensation for the services of the Senators and Representatives, shall take effect, until an election of representatives shall have intervened.

This amendment allows the voters to have some control over increases in salaries for congressional members. Originally submitted to the states for ratification in 1789, it was not ratified until 203 years later, in 1992.

3 | Federalism

What If . . .
One State's Same-Sex Marriages Had to Be Recognized Nationwide?

BACKGROUND

As you will learn in this chapter, the Constitution requires that each state give full faith and credit to every other state's public acts. If a man and woman are married under the laws of Nevada, the other forty-nine states must recognize that marriage. But what if one state recognizes same-sex marriages? Does that mean that all other states must recognize such marriages and give each partner the benefits accorded to partners in opposite-sex marriages?

In 1996, Congress attempted to prevent such a result through the Defense of Marriage Act, which allows state governments to ignore same-sex marriages performed in other states. But what would happen if the United States Supreme Court ruled that the Defense of Marriage Act is unconstitutional? If this happened, then all of the state laws that refuse to recognize same-sex marriages performed in another state would be unconstitutional as well, because the U.S. Constitution is the supreme law of the land.

WHAT IF ONE STATE'S SAME-SEX MARRIAGES HAD TO BE RECOGNIZED NATIONWIDE?

If same-sex marriages were allowed, then same-sex relationships would be much more conspicuous. Marriage is an issue in many contexts—from registering at a hotel to applying for a line of credit. Hotel clerks or bankers who would prefer not to deal with same-sex couples would be forced to confront the reality of these relationships.

What about federal benefits? The national government has traditionally left marriage to the states. In the past, the Internal Revenue Service, the Social Security Administration, and other federal agencies recognized marriages when, and only when, the states recognized them. With the Defense of Marriage Act, the national government established its own definition of marriage for the first time. Under the act, no matter what the states do, federal agencies cannot recognize same-sex marriages. If the Defense of Marriage Act were declared unconstitutional, however, the federal government might again have to accept all state-defined marriages, and a same-sex marriage in a state that allowed such unions would entitle the couple to federal benefits.

ENFORCING THE LAW

A majority of the American electorate is opposed to marriages that unite two lesbians or two gay men. In some parts of the country, such opposition may be overwhelming. By 2006, either by statute or by constitutional amendment, forty-four states had adopted laws banning same-sex marriages.

If same-sex marriages were legal nationwide, officials in conservative states might refuse to recognize such marriages, regardless of the law. It could take a long campaign of lawsuits to enforce widespread compliance.

Advocates of same-sex marriage have challenged the legal process. In February 2004, San Francisco began issuing marriage licenses to same-sex couples even though the marriages were against California law. By March, officials in other jurisdictions had begun to copy San Francisco. In effect, these officials—and the people they married—were engaging in acts of civil disobedience on behalf of same-sex marriage.

HOW IT COULD HAPPEN

Two things must happen for nationwide recognition of same-sex marriages. One is that the Defense of Marriage Act be ruled unconstitutional. It is open to question whether the Supreme Court would actually issue such a ruling. The other requirement, however—legalization of same-sex marriage by one or more states—is in place already. In November 2003, the Massachusetts Supreme Judicial Court ruled that same-sex couples have a right to civil marriage under the Massachusetts state constitution.* The court also ruled that civil unions would not suffice. *Civil unions* are legally recognized partnerships that provide some or all of the state benefits provided to married couples. As of 2006, Vermont and Connecticut are the only states with laws that recognize civil unions for same-sex couples.

FOR CRITICAL ANALYSIS

1. President George W. Bush has endorsed an amendment to the U.S. Constitution to ban same-sex marriage. What difficulties do the advocates of this amendment face in getting it adopted?
2. What impact would widespread same-sex marriage have on American culture generally?

Goodridge v. Department of Public Health, 798 N.E.2d 941 (Mass. 2003). The Massachusetts Supreme Judicial Court reaffirmed its ruling in February 2004.

In the United States, rights and powers are reserved to the states by the Tenth Amendment. It may appear that since September 11, 2001, the federal government, sometimes called the national or central government, predominates. Nevertheless, that might be a temporary exaggeration, for there are 87,900 separate governmental units in this nation, as you can see in Table 3–1.

Visitors from France or Spain are often awestruck by the complexity of our system of government. Consider that a criminal action can be defined by state law, by national law, or by both. Thus, a criminal suspect can be prosecuted in the state court system or in the federal court system (or both). Often, economic regulation over exactly the same matter exists at the local level, the state level, and the national level—generating multiple forms to be completed, multiple procedures to be followed, and multiple laws to be obeyed. Many programs are funded by the national government but administered by state and local governments.

Relations between central governments and local units are structured in various ways. *Federalism* is one of these ways. Understanding federalism and how it differs from other forms of government is important in understanding the American political system. Indeed, many political issues today, including the same-sex marriage issue discussed in this chapter's opening *What If . . .* feature, would be substantially different if we did not have a federal form of government in which governmental authority is divided between the central government and various subunits.

Three Systems of Government

There are nearly two hundred independent nations in the world today. Each of these nations has its own system of government. Generally, though, we can describe how nations structure relations between central governments and local units in terms of three models: (1) the unitary system, (2) the confederal system, and (3) the federal system. The most popular, both historically and today, is the unitary system.

A Unitary System

A **unitary system** of government is the easiest to define. Unitary systems allow ultimate governmental authority to rest in the hands of the national, or central, government. Consider a typical unitary system—France. There are regions, departments,

TABLE 3–1 | GOVERNMENTAL UNITS IN THE UNITED STATES

With almost 88,000 separate governmental units in the United States today, it is no wonder that intergovernmental relations in the United States are so complicated. Actually, the number of school districts has decreased over time, but the number of special districts created for single purposes, such as flood control, has increased from only about 8,000 during World War II to over 35,000 today.

Federal government	**1**
State governments	**50**
Local governments	**87,849**
Counties	3,034
Municipalities	19,431
(mainly cities or towns)	
Townships	16,506
(less extensive powers)	
Special districts	35,356
(water, sewer, and so on)	
School districts	13,522
TOTAL	**87,900**

Source: U.S. Census Bureau.

| Unitary System
A centralized governmental system in which local or subdivisional governments exercise only those powers given to them by the central government.

Massachusetts was the first state to recognize same-sex marriages in 2004. These demonstrators are celebrating the one-year anniversary of this event in front of the State House in Boston. Why wouldn't individual states be able to pass such laws if the United States had a unitary system of government? (AP Photo/Elise Amendola)

| Confederal System
A system consisting of a league of independent states, each having essentially sovereign powers. The central government created by such a league has only limited powers over the states.

and municipalities (communes) in France. The regions, departments, and communes have elected and appointed officials. So far, the French system appears to be very similar to the U.S. system, but the similarity is only superficial. Under the unitary French system, the decisions of the lower levels of government can be overruled by the national government. The national government also can cut off the funding of many local government activities. Moreover, in a unitary system such as that in France, all questions of education, police, the use of land, and welfare are handled by the national government. Britain, Egypt, Ghana, Israel, Japan, the Philippines, and Sweden—in fact, most countries today—have unitary systems of government.[1]

A Confederal System

You were introduced to the elements of a **confederal system** of government in Chapter 2, when we examined the Articles of Confederation. A *confederation* is the opposite of a unitary governing system. It is a league of independent states in which a central government or administration handles only those matters of common concern expressly delegated to it by the member states. The central government has no ability to make laws directly applicable to member states unless the members explicitly support such laws. The United States under the Articles of Confederation was a confederal system.

Few, if any, confederations of this kind exist. One possible exception is the European Union, a league of countries that is developing unifying institutions, such as a common currency. Nations have also formed organizations with one another for limited purposes, such as military or peacekeeping cooperation. Examples are the North Atlantic Treaty Organization and the United Nations. These organizations, however, are not true confederations.

A Federal System

The federal system lies between the unitary and confederal forms of government. As mentioned in Chapter 2, in a *federal system*, authority is divided, usually by a written constitution, between a central government and regional, or subdivisional, governments (often called *constituent governments*). The central government and the constituent governments both act directly on the people through laws and through the actions of elected and appointed governmental officials. Within each government's sphere of authority, each is supreme, in theory. Thus, a federal system differs sharply from a unitary one in which the central government is supreme and the constituent governments derive their authority from it. Australia, Brazil, Canada, Germany, India, and Mexico are other examples of nations with federal systems. See Figure 3–1 for a comparison of the three systems.

| Why Federalism?

Why did the United States develop in a federal direction? We look here at that question, as well as at some of the arguments for and against a federal form of government.

A Practical Solution

As you saw in Chapter 2, the historical basis of our federal system was laid down in Philadelphia at the Constitutional Convention, where advocates of a strong national government opposed states' rights advocates. This dichotomy continued

---

[1]Recent legislation has altered somewhat the unitary character of the French political system. In Britain, the unitary nature of the government has been modified by the creation of the Scottish Parliament.

through to the ratifying conventions in the several states. The resulting federal system was a compromise. The supporters of the new Constitution were political pragmatists—they realized that without a federal arrangement, the new Constitution would not be ratified. The appeal of federalism was that it retained state traditions and local power while establishing a strong national government capable of handling common problems.

Even if the colonial leaders had agreed on the desirability of a unitary system, size and regional isolation would have made such a system difficult operationally. At the time of the Constitutional Convention, the thirteen colonies taken together were much larger geographically than England or France. Slow travel and communication, combined with geographic spread, contributed to the isolation of many regions within the colonies. It could take several weeks for all of the colonies to be informed about a particular political decision.

Other Arguments for Federalism

The arguments for federalism in the United States and elsewhere involve a complex set of factors, some of which we have already noted. First, for big countries, such as the United States, India, and Canada, federalism allows many functions to be "farmed out" by the central government to the states or provinces. The lower levels of government that accept these responsibilities thereby can become the focus of political dissatisfaction rather than the national authorities. Second, even with modern transportation and communications systems, the large area or population of some nations makes it impractical to locate all political authority in one place. Finally, federalism brings government closer to the people. It allows more direct access to, and influence on, government agencies and policies, rather than leaving the population restive and dissatisfied with a remote, faceless, all-powerful central authority.

Benefits for the United States.   In the United States, federalism historically has yielded many benefits. State governments long have been a training ground for future national leaders. Many presidents made their political mark as state governors. The

> **| DID YOU KNOW . . .**
>
> That under Article I, Section 10, of the Constitution, no state is allowed to enter into any treaty, alliance, or confederation?

FIGURE 3–1 | THE FLOW OF POWER IN THREE SYSTEMS OF GOVERNMENT

In a unitary system, power flows from the central government to the local and state governments. In a confederal system, power flows in the opposite direction—from the state governments to the central government. In a federal system, the flow of power, in principle, goes both ways.

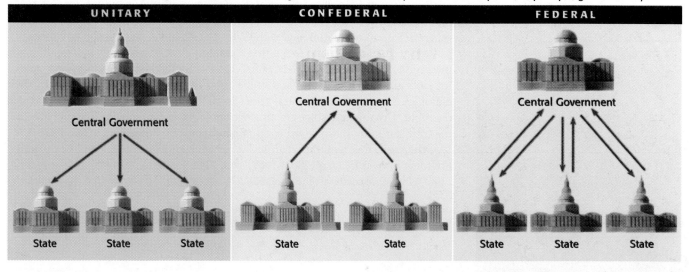

states themselves have been testing grounds for new government initiatives. As United States Supreme Court justice Louis Brandeis once observed:

> It is one of the happy incidents of the federal system that a single courageous state may, if its citizens choose, serve as a laboratory and try novel social and economic experiments without risk to the rest of the country.[2]

Examples of programs pioneered at the state level include unemployment compensation, which began in Wisconsin, and air-pollution control, which was initiated in California. Today, states are experimenting with policies ranging from education reforms, to health insurance for all residents, to homeland security defense strategies. Since the passage of the 1996 welfare reform legislation—which gave more control over welfare programs to state governments—states also have been experimenting with different methods of delivering welfare assistance.

Allowance for Many Political Subcultures.   The American way of life always has been characterized by a number of political subcultures, which divide along the lines of race and ethnic origin, region, wealth, education, and, more recently, degree of religious fundamentalism and sexual preference. The existence of diverse political subcultures would appear to be incompatible with a political authority concentrated solely in a central government. Had the United States developed into a unitary system, various political subcultures certainly would have been less able to influence government behavior than they have been, and continue to be, in our federal system.

Political scientist Daniel Elazar has claimed that one of federalism's greatest virtues is that it encourages the development of distinct political subcultures. These political subcultures reflect differing needs and desires for government, which vary from region to region. Federalism, he argues, allows for "a unique combination of governmental strength, political flexibility, and individual liberty."[3] Indeed, the existence of political subcultures allows a wider variety of factions to influence government. As a result, political subcultures have proved instrumental in driving reform even at the national level.

Arguments against Federalism

Not everyone thinks federalism is such a good idea. Some see it as a way for powerful state and local interests to block progress and impede national plans. Smaller political units are more likely to be dominated by a single political group, and the dominant groups in some cities and states have resisted implementing equal rights for minority groups. (This was essentially the argument that James Madison put forth in *Federalist Paper* No. 10, which you can read in Appendix C of this text.) Some argue, however, that the dominant factions in other states have been more progressive than the national government in many areas, such as the environment.

Critics of federalism also argue that too many Americans suffer as a result of the inequalities across the states. Individual states differ markedly in educational spending and achievement, crime and crime prevention, and even the safety of their buildings. Not surprisingly, these critics argue for increased federal legislation and oversight. This might involve creating national educational standards, national building code standards, national expenditure minimums for crime control, and so on.

Others see dangers in the expansion of national powers at the expense of the states. President Ronald Reagan (1981–1989) said, "The Founding Fathers saw the federalist system as constructed something like a masonry wall. The States are the bricks, the

Air pollution in Los Angeles, California. In our federal system of government, states have often been the testing grounds for programs later adopted by the federal government for nationwide implementation. Air-pollution control, for example, was initiated in California to cope with the threatening conditions produced by a large population in a relatively enclosed valley. (AP Photo/Jerome T. Nakagawa)

[2]*New State Ice Co. v. Liebmann*, 285 U.S. 262 (1932).
[3]Daniel Elazar, *American Federalism: A View from the States*, 2d ed. (New York: Crowell, 1972).

national government is the mortar. . . . Unfortunately, over the years, many people have increasingly come to believe that Washington is the whole wall."[4]

The Constitutional Basis for American Federalism

The term *federal system* cannot be found in the U.S. Constitution. Nor is it possible to find a systematic division of governmental authority between the national and state governments in that document. Rather, the Constitution sets out different types of powers. These powers can be classified as (1) the powers of the national government, (2) the powers of the states, and (3) prohibited powers. The Constitution also makes it clear that if a state or local law conflicts with a national law, the national law will prevail.

Powers of the National Government

The powers delegated to the national government include both expressed and implied powers, as well as the special category of inherent powers. Most of the powers expressly delegated to the national government are found in Article I, Section 8, of the Constitution. These enumerated powers include coining money, setting standards for weights and measures, making uniform naturalization laws, admitting new states, establishing post offices, and declaring war. Another important enumerated power is the power to regulate commerce among the states—a topic we deal with later in this chapter.

Enumerated Powers
Powers specifically granted to the national government by the Constitution. The first seventeen clauses of Article I, Section 8, specify most of the enumerated powers of the national government.

The Necessary and Proper Clause. The implied powers of the national government are also based on Article I, Section 8, which states that Congress shall have the power

> [t]o make all Laws which shall be necessary and proper for carrying into Execution the foregoing Powers, and all other Powers vested by this Constitution in the Government of the United States, or in any Department or Officer thereof.

This clause is sometimes called the elastic clause, or the necessary and proper clause, because it provides flexibility to the U.S. constitutional system. It gives Congress all of those powers that can be reasonably inferred but that are not expressly stated in the brief wording of the Constitution. The clause was first used in the Supreme Court decision of *McCulloch v. Maryland*[5] (discussed later in this chapter) to develop the concept of implied powers. Through this concept, the national government has succeeded in strengthening the scope of its authority to meet the numerous problems that the framers of the Constitution did not, and could not, anticipate.

Elastic Clause, or
Necessary and Proper Clause
The clause in Article I, Section 8, that grants Congress the power to do whatever is necessary to execute its specifically delegated powers.

Inherent Powers. A special category of national powers that is not implied by the necessary and proper clause consists of what have been labeled the inherent powers of the national government. These powers derive from the fact that the United States is a sovereign power among nations, and so its national government must be the only government that deals with other nations. Under international law, it is assumed that all nation-states, regardless of their size or power, have an *inherent* right to ensure their own survival. To do this, each nation must have the ability to act in its own interest among and with the community of nations—by, for instance, making treaties, waging

---

[4]Text of the address by the president to the National Conference of State Legislatures, Atlanta, Georgia (Washington, D.C.: The White House, Office of the Press Secretary, July 30, 1981), as quoted in Edward Millican, *One United People: The Federalist Papers and the National Idea* (Lexington, Ky.: The University Press of Kentucky, 1990).
[5]4 Wheaton 316 (1819).

war, seeking trade, and acquiring territory. In 2006, many Americans were outraged to learn that the federal government had considered allowing a Middle East–based company to take over the contracts for operating several American ports. Such an action would have been an exercise of the federal government's inherent powers. To learn more about this issue, see this chapter's *Beyond Our Borders* feature.

Note that no specific clause in the Constitution says anything about the acquisition of additional land. Nonetheless, through the federal government's inherent powers, we made the Louisiana Purchase in 1803 and then went on to acquire Florida, Texas, Oregon, Alaska, Hawaii, and other lands. The United States grew from a mere thirteen states to fifty states, plus several "territories."

The national government has these inherent powers whether or not they have been enumerated in the Constitution. Some constitutional scholars categorize inherent powers as a third type of power, completely distinct from the delegated powers (both expressed and implied) of the national government.

Powers of the State Governments

The Tenth Amendment states that the powers not delegated to the United States by the Constitution, nor prohibited by it to the states, are reserved to the states, or to the people. These are the reserved powers that the national government cannot deny to the states. Because these powers are not expressly listed—and because they are not limited to powers that are expressly listed—there is sometimes a question as to whether a certain power is delegated to the national government or reserved to the states. State powers have been held to include each state's right to regulate commerce within its borders and to provide for a state militia. States also have the reserved power to make laws on all matters not prohibited to the states by the U.S. Constitution or state constitutions and not expressly, or by implication, delegated to the national government. Furthermore, the states have **police power**—the authority to legislate for the protection of the health, morals, safety, and welfare of the people. Their police power enables states to pass laws governing such activities as crimes, marriage, contracts, education, intrastate transportation, and land use.

| **Police Power**
The authority to legislate for the protection of the health, morals, safety, and welfare of the people. In the United States, most police power is reserved to the states.

The ambiguity of the Tenth Amendment has allowed the reserved powers of the states to be defined differently at different times in our history. When there is widespread support for increased regulation by the national government, the Tenth Amendment tends to recede into the background. When the tide turns the other way (in favor of states' rights), the Tenth Amendment is resurrected to justify arguments supporting increased states' rights.

Concurrent Powers

| **Concurrent Powers**
Powers held jointly by the national and state governments.

In certain areas, the states share **concurrent powers** with the national government. Most concurrent powers are not specifically listed in the Constitution; they are only implied. An example of a concurrent power is the power to tax. The types of taxation are divided between the levels of government. For example, states may not levy a tariff (a set of taxes on imported goods); only the national government may do this. Neither government may tax the facilities of the other. If the state governments did not have the power to tax, they would not be able to function other than on a ceremonial basis. Other concurrent powers include the power to borrow funds, to establish courts, and to charter banks and corporations. To a limited extent, the national government exercises police power, and to the extent that it does, police power is also a concurrent power. Concurrent powers exercised by the states are normally limited to the geographic area of each state and to those functions *not* granted by the Constitution exclusively to the national government (such as the coinage of money and the negotiation of treaties).

BEYOND OUR BORDERS | American Port Security

In February 2006, news broke that the U.S. government had tentatively agreed to allow the ownership of the operations at six U.S. ports to be transferred to a Middle Eastern company, Dubai Ports World (DPW). With memories of the September 11, 2001, terrorist attacks still fresh in the minds of many Americans, public sentiment regarding the proposed deal was overwhelmingly critical. The deal eventually fell through, much to the relief of residents in the port cities who feared that President George W. Bush and other federal officials had not given adequate consideration to their local security concerns.

FOREIGN CORPORATIONS AND AMERICAN PORTS

During the debate over DPW's proposed takeover of these port operations, the public learned that many American ports already were overseen by foreign corporations. DPW actually was buying out a British company's stake in the American ports. The lack of objection to the British company's previous ownership of the ports likely stemmed from Great Britain's alliance with the United States in the war in Iraq.

In contrast to the British company, which is privately owned, DPW is based in the United Arab Emirates (UAE) and is under the control of the UAE government. Although the UAE is regarded as a U.S. ally in the war on terrorism, the UAE purportedly had links in the past to the Taliban regime in Afghanistan and Middle Eastern terrorist groups such as al Qaeda. Despite these concerns, Bush voiced his support of the DPW takeover, citing the need to maintain and encourage relations between the UAE and the United States.

Currently, port operations contracts are administered by the Committee on Foreign Investment, an interagency body directed by the secretary of the treasury. Bush and some members of Congress want to continue this arrangement, arguing that foreign investment in the United States is a natural consequence of economic globalization. To discourage such investment, they claim, would send the wrong message to foreign corporations seeking to do business in the United States.

LOCAL FEARS AND NATIONAL SECURITY INTERESTS

Citizens across America, and especially those residing in major port cities, were shaken by the proposed DPW takeover. Most terrorism experts have concluded that the likeliest method of smuggling a weapon of mass destruction into the United States would be through a port. Though nearly 95 percent of all goods entering the United States arrive by sea, only 6 percent of incoming cargo is inspected for security threats. Federal customs officials carry out such inspections.

Ultimate responsibility for port security technically falls on the U.S. Coast Guard, which is a part of the Department of Homeland Security. In practice, though, the Coast Guard mostly just establishes the regulations under which port companies operate. The companies are responsible for actually hiring the security officers who guard cargo and oversee the unloading process.

Many Americans have criticized the practice of allowing any foreign corporations to play such a vital role. Strangely, nobody had protested when a Middle Eastern company took over numerous stevedore (ship-unloading) contracts just a few years before the DPW incident. Very likely, this is because until the attempted DPW transfer, these activities were not widely publicized. Still, constituents' concerns over DPW led numerous members of Congress from both parties to denounce the idea of a Middle Eastern company overseeing American ports. A number of bills requiring American ownership of port operations have since been proposed in Congress. Ultimately, DPW did not take over ownership of any U.S. port operations.

FOR CRITICAL ANALYSIS

The debate over port security revealed tensions between federal policymaking and local security interests. In your opinion, would it be better if port security contracts were awarded by the national government or by state and local governments? Explain.

Prohibited Powers

The Constitution prohibits or denies a number of powers to the national government. For example, the national government expressly has been denied the power to impose taxes on goods sold to other countries (exports). Moreover, any power not granted expressly or implicitly to the federal government by the Constitution is prohibited to it. For example, the national government cannot create a national divorce law system. The states are also denied certain powers. For example, no state is allowed to enter into a treaty on its own with another country.

| Supremacy Clause
The constitutional provision that makes the Constitution and federal laws superior to all conflicting state and local laws.

The Supremacy Clause

The supremacy of the national constitution over subnational laws and actions is established in the **supremacy clause** of the Constitution. The supremacy clause (Article VI, Clause 2) states the following:

> This Constitution, and the Laws of the United States which shall be made in Pursuance thereof; and all Treaties made . . . under the Authority of the United States, shall be the supreme Law of the Land; and the Judges in every State shall be bound thereby, any Thing in the Constitution or Laws of any State to the Contrary notwithstanding.

In other words, states cannot use their reserved or concurrent powers to thwart national policies. All national and state officers, including judges, must be bound by oath to support the Constitution. Hence, any legitimate exercise of national governmental power supersedes any conflicting state action.[6] Of course, deciding whether a conflict actually exists is a judicial matter, as you will see when we discuss the case of *McCulloch v. Maryland*.

National government legislation in a concurrent area is said to *preempt* (take precedence over) conflicting state or local laws or regulations in that area. One of the ways in which the national government has extended its powers, particularly during the twentieth century, is through the preemption of state and local laws by national legislation. In the first decade of the twentieth century, fewer than 20 national laws preempted laws and regulations issued by state and local governments. By the beginning of the twenty-first century, the number had risen to nearly 120.

Some political scientists believe that national supremacy is critical for the longevity and smooth functioning of a federal system. Nonetheless, the application of this principle has been a continuous source of conflict. Indeed, as you will see, the most extreme example of this conflict was the Civil War.

Vertical Checks and Balances

Recall from Chapter 2 that one of the concerns of the founders was to prevent the national government from becoming too powerful. For that reason, they divided the government into three branches—legislative, executive, and judicial. They also created a system of checks and balances that allowed each branch to check the actions of the others. The federal form of government created by the founders also involves checks and balances. These are sometimes called *vertical checks and balances* because they involve relationships between the states and the national government. They can be contrasted with *horizontal checks and balances*, in which the branches of government that are on the same level—either state or national—can check one other.

For example, the reserved powers of the states act as a check on the national government. Additionally, the states' interests are represented in the national legislature (Congress), and the citizens of the various states determine who will head the executive branch (the presidency). The founders also made it impossible for the central government to change the Constitution without the states' consent, as you read in Chapter 2. Finally, national programs and policies are administered by the states, which gives the states considerable control over the ultimate shape of those programs and policies.

The national government, in turn, can check state policies by exercising its constitutional powers under the clauses just discussed, as well as under the commerce clause (to be examined later). Furthermore, the national government can influence state policies indirectly through federal grants, as you will learn later in this chapter.

---

[6]An example of this is President Dwight Eisenhower's disciplining of Arkansas governor Orval Faubus in 1957 by federalizing the National Guard to enforce the court-ordered desegregation of Little Rock High School.

Interstate Relations

So far we have examined only the relationship between central and state governmental units. The states, however, have constant commercial, social, and other dealings among themselves. The national Constitution imposes certain "rules of the road" on interstate relations. These rules have had the effect of preventing any one state from setting itself apart from the other states. The three most important clauses governing interstate relations in the Constitution, all taken from the Articles of Confederation, require each state to do the following:

1. Give full faith and credit to every other state's public acts, records, and judicial proceedings (Article IV, Section 1).
2. Extend to every other state's citizens the privileges and immunities of its own citizens (Article IV, Section 2).
3. Agree to return persons who are fleeing from justice in another state back to their home state when requested to do so (Article IV, Section 2).

Following these constitutional mandates is not always easy for the states. For example, one question that has arisen in recent years is whether states will be constitutionally obligated to recognize same-sex marriages performed in other states, as you read in the chapter-opening *What If . . .* feature.

Additionally, states may enter into agreements called **interstate compacts**—if consented to by Congress. In reality, congressional consent is necessary only if such a compact increases the power of the contracting states relative to other states (or to the national government). Typical examples of interstate compacts are the establishment of the Port Authority of New York and New Jersey by an interstate compact between those two states in 1921 and the regulation of the production of crude oil and natural gas by the Interstate Oil and Gas Compact of 1935.

Defining Constitutional Powers—The Early Years

Recall from Chapter 2 that constitutional language, to be effective and to endure, must have some degree of ambiguity. Certainly, the powers delegated to the national government and the powers reserved to the states contain elements of ambiguity, thus leaving the door open for different interpretations of federalism. Disputes over the boundaries of national versus state powers have characterized this nation from the beginning. In the early 1800s, the most significant disputes arose over differing interpretations of the implied powers of the national government under the necessary and proper clause and over the respective powers of the national government and the states to regulate commerce.

Although political bodies at all levels of government play important roles in the process of settling such disputes, ultimately it is the Supreme Court that casts the final vote. As might be expected, the character of the referee will have an impact on the ultimate outcome of any dispute. From 1801 to 1835, the Supreme Court was headed by Chief Justice John Marshall, a Federalist who advocated a strong central government. We look here at two cases decided by the Marshall Court: *McCulloch v. Maryland*[7] and *Gibbons v. Ogden*.[8] Both cases are considered milestones in the movement toward national government supremacy.

McCulloch v. Maryland (1819)

The U.S. Constitution says nothing about establishing a national bank. Nonetheless, at different times Congress chartered two banks—the First and Second Banks of the

Interstate compacts have long been used as a way to address issues that affect more than one state. An interstate compact between New York and New Jersey in 1921 created the Port Authority of New York and New Jersey to develop and maintain harbor facilities in that area, including the Port Authority Bus Terminal shown here. Today, there are over two hundred interstate compacts. (Robert Brenner/PhotoEdit)

Interstate Compact
An agreement between two or more states. Agreements on minor matters are made without congressional consent, but any compact that tends to increase the power of the contracting states relative to other states or relative to the national government generally requires the consent of Congress. Such compacts serve as a means by which states can solve regional problems.

[7] 4 Wheaton 316 (1819).
[8] 9 Wheaton 1 (1824).

John Marshall (1755–1835) was the fourth chief justice of the Supreme Court. When Marshall took over, the Court had little power and almost no influence over the other two branches of government. Some scholars have declared that Marshall is the true architect of the American constitutional system, because he single-handedly gave new power to the Constitution. What consequences might have followed if Marshall had taken a more restrictive view of the national government's powers? (Library of Congress)

| Commerce Clause
The section of the Constitution in which Congress is given the power to regulate trade among the states and with foreign countries.

United States—and provided part of their initial capital; thus, they were national banks. The government of Maryland imposed a tax on the Second Bank's Baltimore branch in an attempt to put that branch out of business. The branch's cashier, James William McCulloch, refused to pay the Maryland tax. When Maryland took McCulloch to its state court, the state of Maryland won. The national government appealed the case to the Supreme Court.

One of the issues before the Court was whether the national government had the implied power, under the necessary and proper clause, to charter a bank and contribute capital to it. The other important question before the Court was the following: If the bank was constitutional, could a state tax it? In other words, was a state action that conflicted with a national government action invalid under the supremacy clause?

Chief Justice Marshall held that if establishing such a national bank aided the national government in the exercise of its designated powers, then the authority to set up such a bank could be implied. Having established this doctrine of implied powers, Marshall then answered the other important question before the Court and established the doctrine of national supremacy. Marshall ruled that no state could use its taxing power to tax an arm of the national government. If it could, "the declaration that the Constitution . . . shall be the supreme law of the land, is [an] empty and unmeaning [statement]."

Marshall's decision enabled the national government to grow and to meet problems that the Constitution's framers were unable to foresee. Today, practically every expressed power of the national government has been expanded in one way or another by use of the necessary and proper clause.

Gibbons v. Ogden (1824)

One of the most important parts of the Constitution included in Article I, Section 8, is the so-called **commerce clause,** in which Congress is given the power "[t]o regulate Commerce with foreign Nations, and among the several States, and with the Indian Tribes." The meaning of this clause was at issue in *Gibbons v. Ogden*.

The Background of the Case. Robert Fulton and Robert Livingston secured a monopoly on steam navigation on the waters in New York State from the New York legislature in 1803. They licensed Aaron Ogden to operate steam-powered ferryboats between New York and New Jersey. Thomas Gibbons, who had obtained a license from the U.S. government to operate boats in interstate waters, decided to compete with Ogden, but he did so without New York's permission. Ogden sued Gibbons. The New York state courts prohibited Gibbons from operating in New York waters. Gibbons appealed to the Supreme Court.

There were actually several issues before the Court in this case. The first issue was how the term *commerce* should be defined. New York's highest court had defined the term narrowly to mean only the shipment of goods, or the interchange of commodities, *not* navigation or the transport of people. The second issue was whether the national government's power to regulate interstate commerce extended to commerce within a state (*intra*state commerce) or was limited strictly to commerce among the states (*inter*state commerce). The third issue was whether the power to regulate interstate commerce was a concurrent power (as the New York court had concluded) or an exclusive national power.

Marshall's Ruling. Marshall defined *commerce* as all commercial intercourse—all business dealings—including navigation and the transport of people. Marshall also held that the commerce power of the national government could be exercised in state jurisdictions, even though it cannot reach *solely* intrastate commerce. Finally, Marshall emphasized that the power to regulate interstate commerce was an *exclusive* national power. Marshall held that because Gibbons was duly authorized by the national government to navigate in interstate waters, he could not be prohibited from doing so by a state court.

Marshall's expansive interpretation of the commerce clause in *Gibbons v. Ogden* allowed the national government to exercise increasing authority over all areas of economic affairs throughout the land. Congress did not immediately exploit this broad grant of power. In the 1930s and subsequent decades, however, the commerce clause became the primary constitutional basis for national government regulation—as you will read later in this chapter.

States' Rights and the Resort to Civil War

The controversy over slavery that led to the Civil War took the form of a dispute over national government supremacy versus the rights of the separate states. Essentially, the Civil War brought to an ultimate and violent climax the ideological debate that had been outlined by the Federalist and Anti-Federalist parties even before the Constitution was ratified.

The Shift Back to States' Rights

As we have seen, while John Marshall was chief justice of the Supreme Court, he did much to increase the power of the national government and to reduce that of the states. During the Jacksonian era (1829–1837), however, a shift back to states' rights began. The question of the regulation of commerce became one of the major issues in federal-state relations. When Congress passed a tariff in 1828, the state of South Carolina unsuccessfully attempted to nullify the tariff (render it void), claiming that in cases of conflict between a state and the national government, the state should have the ultimate authority over its citizens.

Over the next three decades, the North and South became even more sharply divided—over tariffs that mostly benefited northern industries and over the slavery issue. On December 20, 1860, South Carolina formally repealed its ratification of the Constitution and withdrew from the Union. On February 4, 1861, representatives from six southern states met at Montgomery, Alabama, to form a new government called the Confederate States of America.

A Currier & Ives print depicting the siege and capture of Vicksburg, Mississippi, on July 4, 1863. How did the Civil War change attitudes toward the government in the South and in the North? (Library of Congress)

War and the Growth of the National Government

The ultimate defeat of the South in 1865 permanently ended any idea that a state could successfully claim the right to secede, or withdraw, from the Union. Ironically, the Civil War—brought about in large part because of the South's desire for increased states' rights—resulted in the opposite: an increase in the political power of the national government.

The War Effort. Thousands of new employees were hired to run the Union war effort and to deal with the social and economic problems that had to be handled in the aftermath of war. A billion-dollar ($1.3 billion, which is over $11.9 billion in today's dollars) national government budget was passed for the first time in 1865 to cover the increased government expenditures. The first (temporary) income tax was imposed on citizens to help pay for the war. This tax and the increased national government spending were precursors to the expanded future role of the national government in the American federal system. Civil liberties were curtailed in the Union and in the Confederacy in the name of the wartime emergency. The distribution of pensions and widows' benefits also boosted the national government's social role. Many scholars contend that the North's victory set the nation on the path to a modern industrial economy and society.

The Civil War Amendments. The expansion of the national government's authority during the Civil War was reflected in the passage of the Civil War amendments to the Constitution. Before the war, it was a bedrock constitutional principle that the national government should not interfere with slavery in the states. The Thirteenth Amendment, ratified in 1865, did more than interfere with slavery—it abolished the institution altogether. By abolishing slavery, the amendment also in effect abolished the rule by which three-fifths of the slaves were counted when apportioning seats in the House of Representatives (see Chapter 2). African Americans were now counted in full.

The central image of this print by Thomas Kelly, published in 1870, depicts a parade celebrating the ratification of the 15th Amendment. The surrounding portraits and vignettes illustrate African American life and the rights granted by the Amendment. The key to the illustrations in the lower margin reads as follows:

1. Reading Emancipation Proclamation.
2. Life, Liberty, and Independence.
3. We Unite the bonds of Fellowship.
4. Our Charter of Rights the Holy Scriptures.
5. Education will prove the Equality the Races.
6. Liberty Protects the Mariage Alter [sic].
7. Celebration of Fifteenth Amendment May 19, 1870.
8. The Ballot Box is open to us.
9. Our representative Sits in the National Legislature.
10. The Holy Ordinances of Religion are free.
11. Freedom unites the Family Circle.
12. We will protect our Country as it defends our Rights.
13. We till our own Fields.
14. The Right of Citizens of the U.S. to vote shall not be denied or abridged by the U.S. or any State on account of Race Color or Condition of Servitude 15th Amendment. (Library of Congress)

The Fourteenth Amendment (1868) defined who was a citizen of each state. It sought to guarantee equal rights under state law, stating that

[no] State [shall] deprive any person of life, liberty, or property, without due process of law; nor deny to any person within its jurisdiction the equal protection of the laws.

In time, the courts interpreted these words to mean that the national Bill of Rights applied to state governments, a development that we will examine in Chapter 4. The Fourteenth Amendment also confirmed the abolition of the three-fifths rule. Finally, the Fifteenth Amendment (1870) gave African Americans the right to vote in all elections, including state elections—although a century would pass before that right was enforced.

The Continuing Dispute over the Division of Power

Although the outcome of the Civil War firmly established the supremacy of the national government and put to rest the idea that a state could secede from the Union, the war by no means ended the debate over the division of powers between the national government and the states. The debate over the division of powers in our federal system can be viewed as progressing through at least two general stages since the Civil War: dual federalism and cooperative federalism.

Dual Federalism and the Retreat of National Authority

During the decades following the Civil War, the prevailing model was what political scientists have called **dual federalism**—a doctrine that emphasizes a distinction between federal and state spheres of government authority. Various images have been used to describe different configurations of federalism over time. Dual federalism is commonly depicted as a layer cake, because the state governments and the national government are viewed as separate entities, like separate layers in a cake. The national government is the top layer of the cake; the state government is the bottom layer. Nevertheless, the two layers are physically separate. They do not mix. For the most part, advocates of dual federalism believed that the state and national governments should not exercise authority in the same areas.

A Return to Normal Conditions. The doctrine of dual federalism represented a revival of states' rights following the expansion of national authority during the Civil War. Dual federalism, after all, was a fairly accurate model of the prewar consensus on state-national relations. For many people, it therefore represented a return to normal. The national income tax, used to fund the war effort and the reconstruction of the South, was ended in 1872. The most significant step to reverse the wartime expansion of national power took place in 1877, when President Rutherford B. Hayes withdrew the last federal troops from the South. This meant that the national government was no longer in a position to regulate state actions that affected African Americans. While the black population was now free, it was again subject to the authority of southern whites.

The Role of the Supreme Court. The Civil War crisis drastically reduced the influence of the United States Supreme Court. In the prewar *Dred Scott* decision,[9] the Court had attempted to abolish the power of the national government to restrict slavery in the territories. In so doing, the Court placed itself on the losing side of the impending conflict. After the war, Congress took the unprecedented step of exempting the entire process of southern reconstruction from judicial review. The Court had little choice but to acquiesce.

> **Dual Federalism**
> A system in which the states and the national government each remain supreme within their own spheres. The doctrine looks on nation and state as co-equal sovereign powers. Neither the state government nor the national government should interfere in the other's sphere.

---

[9]*Dred Scott v. Sanford*, 19 Howard 393 (1857).

This photograph shows teenagers and young boys leaving a coal mine near Fairmont, West Virginia. In the 1800s, even very young children worked in coal mines. Today, national child-labor laws prohibit employers from hiring young workers for dangerous occupations. Why do you think the parents of these youths and children allowed them to work at such dangerous jobs? If no child-labor laws existed today, would a large percentage of children still be working in dangerous occupations? Why or why not? (Lewis Hine/Library of Congress)

In time, the Supreme Court reestablished itself as the legitimate constitutional umpire. Its decisions tended to support dual federalism, defend states' rights, and limit the powers of the national government. In 1895, for example, the Court ruled that a national income tax was unconstitutional.[10] In subsequent years, the Court gradually backed away from this decision and eventually might have overturned it. In 1913, however, the Sixteenth Amendment explicitly authorized a national income tax.

For the Court, dual federalism meant that the national government could intervene in state activities through grants and subsidies, but for the most part, it was barred from regulating matters that the Court considered to be purely local. The Court generally limited the exercise of police power to the states. For example, in 1918, the Court ruled that a 1916 national law banning child labor was unconstitutional because it attempted to regulate a local problem.[11] In effect, the Court placed severe limits on the ability of Congress to legislate under the commerce clause of the Constitution.

The New Deal and Cooperative Federalism

The doctrine of dual federalism receded into the background in the 1930s as the nation attempted to deal with the Great Depression. Franklin D. Roosevelt was inaugurated on March 4, 1933, as the thirty-second president of the United States. In the previous year, nearly 1,500 banks had failed (and 4,000 more would fail in 1933). Thirty-two thousand businesses had closed down, and almost one-fourth of the labor force was unemployed. The public expected the national government to do something about the disastrous state of the economy. But for the first three years of the Great Depression (1930–1932), the national government did very little.

---

[10]*Pollock v. Farmers' Loan & Trust Co.*, 157 U.S. 429 (1895); *Pollock v. Farmers' Loan & Trust Co.*, 158 U.S. 601 (1895).

[11]*Hammer v. Dagenhart*, 247 U.S. 251 (1918). This decision was overruled in *United States v. Darby*, 312 U.S. 100 (1940).

President Franklin Delano Roosevelt (1933–1945). Roosevelt's national approach to addressing the effects of the Great Depression was overwhelmingly popular, although many of his specific initiatives were controversial. How did the Great Depression change the political beliefs of many ordinary Americans? (Bettmann/Corbis)

The "New Deal."   President Herbert Hoover (1929–1933) clung to the doctrine of dual federalism and insisted that unemployment and poverty were local issues. The states, not the national government, had the sole responsibility for combating the effects of unemployment and providing relief to the poor. Roosevelt, however, did not feel bound by this doctrine, and his new Democratic administration energetically intervened in the economy. Roosevelt's "New Deal" included large-scale emergency antipoverty programs. In addition, the New Deal introduced major new laws regulating economic activity, such as the National Industrial Recovery Act of 1933, which established the National Recovery Administration (NRA). The NRA, initially the centerpiece of the New Deal, provided codes for every industry to restrict competition and regulate labor relations.

The End of Dual Federalism.   Roosevelt's expansion of national authority was challenged by the Supreme Court, which continued to adhere to the doctrine of dual federalism. In 1935, the Court ruled that the NRA program was unconstitutional.[12] The NRA had turned out to be largely unworkable and was unpopular. The Court, however, rejected the program on the ground that it regulated intrastate, not interstate, commerce. This position appeared to rule out any alternative recovery plans that might be better designed. Subsequently, the Court struck down the Agricultural Adjustment Act, the Bituminous Coal Act, a railroad retirement plan, legislation to protect farm mortgages, and a municipal bankruptcy act.

In 1937, Roosevelt proposed legislation that would allow him to add up to six new justices to the Supreme Court. Presumably, the new justices would be more friendly to the exercise of national power than the existing members were. Roosevelt's move was widely seen as an assault on the Constitution. Congressional Democrats refused to support the measure, and it failed. Nevertheless, the "court-packing scheme" had its intended effect. Although the membership of the Court did not change, after 1937 the Court ceased its attempts to limit the national government's powers under

---

[12]*Schechter Poultry Corp. v. United States*, 295 U.S. 495 (1935).

the commerce clause. For the next half-century, the commerce clause would provide Congress with an unlimited justification for regulating the economic life of the country.

Cooperative Federalism.   Some political scientists have described the era since 1937 as characterized by **cooperative federalism,** in which the states and the national government cooperate in solving complex common problems. Roosevelt's New Deal programs, for example, often involved joint action between the national government and the states. The pattern of national-state relationships during these years gave rise to a new metaphor for federalism—that of a marble cake. Unlike a layer cake, in a marble cake the two types of cake are intermingled, and any bite contains cake of both flavors.

As an example of how national and state governments work together under the cooperative federalism model, consider Aid to Families with Dependent Children (AFDC), a welfare program that was established during the New Deal. (In 1996, AFDC was replaced by Temporary Assistance to Needy Families—TANF.) Under the AFDC program, the national government provided most of the funding, but state governments established benefit levels and eligibility requirements for recipients. Local welfare offices were staffed by state, not national, employees. In return for national funding, the states had to conform to a series of regulations on how the program was to be carried out. These regulations tended to become more elaborate over time.

The 1960s and 1970s were a time of even greater expansion of the national government's role in domestic policy. The evolving pattern of national-state-local government relationships during the 1960s and 1970s gave rise to yet another metaphor—**picket-fence federalism,** a concept devised by political scientist Terry Sanford. The horizontal boards in the fence represent the different levels of government (national, state, and local), while the vertical pickets represent the various programs and policies in which each level of government is involved. Officials at each level of government work together to promote and develop the policy represented by each picket.

Methods of Implementing Cooperative Federalism

Even before the Constitution was adopted, the national government gave grants to the states in the form of land to finance education. The national government also provided land grants for canals, railroads, and roads. In the twentieth century, federal grants increased significantly, especially during Roosevelt's administration during the Great Depression and again during the 1960s, when the dollar amount of grants quadrupled. These funds were used for improvements in education, pollution control, recreation, and highways. With this increase in grants, however, came a bewildering number of restrictions and regulations.

Categorical Grants.   By 1985, **categorical grants** amounted to more than $100 billion a year. They were spread out across four hundred separate programs, but the largest five accounted for over 50 percent of the revenues spent. These five programs involved Medicaid (health care for the poor), highway construction, unemployment benefits, housing assistance, and welfare programs to assist mothers with dependent children and people with disabilities. For fiscal year 2006, the national government gave an estimated $225 billion to the states through federal grants. The shift toward a greater role for the central government in the United States can be seen clearly in Figure 3–2, which shows the increase in central government spending as a percentage of total government spending.

Before the 1960s, most categorical grants by the national government were *formula grants*. These grants take their name from the method used to allocate

| Cooperative Federalism
The theory that the states and the national government should cooperate in solving problems.

| Picket-Fence Federalism
A model of federalism in which specific programs and policies (depicted as vertical pickets in a picket fence) involve all levels of government—national, state, and local (depicted by the horizontal boards in a picket fence).

| Categorical Grants
Federal grants to states or local governments that are for specific programs or projects.

funds. They fund state programs using a formula based on such variables as the state's needs, population, or willingness to come up with matching funds. Beginning in the 1960s, the national government began increasingly to offer *program grants*. This funding requires states to apply for grants for specific programs. The applications are evaluated by the national government, and the applications may compete with one another. Program grants give the national government a much greater degree of control over state activities than formula grants.

Why have federal grants to the states increased so much? One reason is that Congress has decided to offload some programs to the states and provide a major part of the funding for them. Also, Congress continues to use grants to persuade states and cities to operate programs devised by the federal government. Finally, states often are happy to apply for grants because they are relatively "free," requiring only that the state match a small portion of each grant. States can still face criticism for accepting the grants because their matching funds may be diverted from other state projects.

Feeling the Pressure—The Strings Attached to Federal Grants. No dollars sent to the states are completely free of "strings," however; all funds come with requirements that must be met by the states. Often, through the use of grants, the national government has been able to exercise substantial control over matters that traditionally have been under the purview of state governments. When the federal government gives federal funds for highway improvements, for example, it may condition the funds on the state's cooperation with a federal policy. This is exactly what the federal government did in the 1980s and 1990s to force the states to raise their minimum drinking age to twenty-one.

Such carrot-and-stick tactics have been used as a form of coercion in recent years as well. In 2002, for example, President George W. Bush signed the No Child Left Behind (NCLB) Act into law. Under NCLB, Bush promised billions of dollars to the states to bolster their education budgets. The funds would only be delivered, however, if states agreed to hold schools accountable to new federal achievement benchmarks on standardized tests designed by the federal government. Education traditionally had been under state control, and the conditions for receiving NCLB funds effectively stripped the states of some autonomy in creating standards for public schools.

FIGURE 3–2 | THE SHIFT TOWARD CENTRAL GOVERNMENT SPENDING

Before the Great Depression, local governments accounted for 60 percent of all government spending, with the federal government accounting for only 17 percent. By 2007, federal government spending was almost two-thirds of the total.

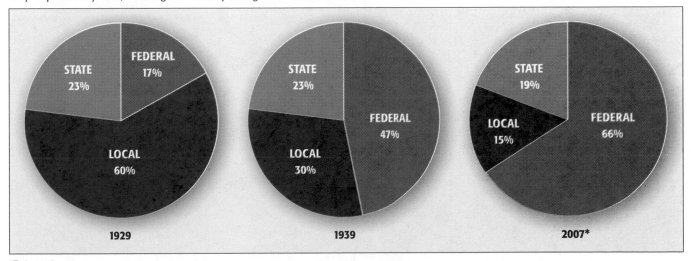

*Estimated.
Sources: U.S. Department of Commerce, Bureau of the Census, and Bureau of Economic Analysis; Congressional Budget Office.

That part of the $4.2 million federal block grants received by four Native American tribes since 1997 has gone toward the building of "smoke shops"— stores that sell discounted cigarettes and pipe tobacco?

Block Grants
Federal programs that provide funds to state and local governments for general functional areas, such as criminal justice or mental-health programs.

Federal Mandate
A requirement in federal legislation that forces states and municipalities to comply with certain rules.

Under the No Child Left Behind Act, a school that is rated "in need of improvement" over a period of five years must be "restructured." Presumably, this could mean closing the school, as suggested by the cartoonist. The No Child Left Behind Act imposes certain federal mandates on the states in return for funding by the national government. In what way might this act represent a shift away from the federal system?

Block Grants.   Block grants lessen the restrictions on federal grants given to state and local governments by grouping a number of categorical grants under one broad heading. Governors and mayors generally prefer block grants because such grants give the states more flexibility in how the money is spent.

One major set of block grants provides aid to state welfare programs. The Personal Responsibility and Work Opportunity Reconciliation Act of 1996 ended the AFDC program. The TANF program that replaced AFDC provided a welfare block grant to each state. Each grant has an annual cap. According to some, this is one of the most successful block grant programs. Although state governments prefer block grants, Congress generally favors categorical grants because the expenditures can be targeted according to congressional priorities.

Federal Mandates.   For years, the federal government has passed legislation requiring that states improve environmental conditions and the civil rights of certain groups. Since the 1970s, the national government has enacted literally hundreds of federal mandates requiring the states to take some action in areas ranging from the way voters are registered, to ocean-dumping restrictions, to the education of persons with disabilities. The Unfunded Mandates Reform Act of 1995 requires the Congressional Budget Office to identify mandates that cost state and local governments more than $50 million to implement. Nonetheless, the federal government routinely continues to pass mandates for state and local governments that cost more than that to implement.

For example, the estimated total cost of complying with federal mandates concerning water purity, over just a four-year period, is in the vicinity of $29 billion. In all, the estimated cost of federal mandates to the states in the early 2000s was more than $70 billion annually. One way in which the national government has moderated the burden of federal mandates is by granting *waivers*, which allow individual states to try out innovative approaches to carrying out the mandates. For example, Oregon received a waiver to experiment with a new method of rationing health-care services under the federally mandated Medicaid program.

The Politics of Federalism

As we have observed, the allocation of powers between the national and state governments continues to be a major issue. In 2005, the devastation caused by Hurricane Katrina unleashed a heated debate about federalism, as Americans disagreed on which level of government should be held accountable for inadequate preparations and the failures in providing aid afterward. For more on this debate, see this chapter's *Which Side Are You On?* feature on the next page.

What Has National Authority Accomplished?

Why is it that conservatives have favored the states and liberals have favored the national government? One answer is that throughout American history, the expansion of national authority typically has been an engine of social change. Far more than the states, the national government has been willing to alter the status quo. The expansion of national authority during the Civil War freed the slaves—a major social revolution. During the New Deal, the expansion of national authority meant unprecedented levels of government intervention in the economy. In both the Civil War and New Deal eras, support for states' rights was a method of opposing these changes and supporting the status quo.

Some scholars believe that this equation was also a subtext in the Supreme Court's defense of states' rights between the Civil War and 1937. These scholars argue that the Supreme Court, in those years, came increasingly under the influence of *laissez-faire* economics—a belief that any government intervention in the economy was improper. When the Court struck down national legislation against child labor, for example, it was not acting only in defense of the states; an underlying motivation was the Court's belief that laws banning child labor were wrong no matter which level of government implemented them.

Civil Rights and the War on Poverty. A final example of the use of national power to change society was the presidency of Lyndon B. Johnson (1963–1969). Johnson oversaw the greatest expansion of national authority since the New Deal. Under Johnson, a series of civil rights acts forced the states to grant African Americans equal treatment under the law. Crucially, these acts included the abolition of all measures designed to prevent African Americans from voting. Johnson's Great Society and War on Poverty programs resulted in major increases in spending by the national government. As before, states' rights were invoked to support the status quo—states' rights meant no action on civil rights and no increase in antipoverty spending.

Why Should the States Favor the Status Quo? When state governments have authority in a particular field, there may be great variations from state to state in how the issues are handled. Inevitably, some states will be more conservative than others. Therefore, bringing national authority to bear on a particular issue may have the effect of imposing national standards on states that, for whatever reason, have not adopted such standards. One example is the voting rights legislation passed under President Johnson. By the 1960s, there was a national consensus that all citizens, regardless of race, should have the right to vote. A majority of the white electorate in certain states, however, did not share this view. National legislation was necessary to impose the national consensus on the recalcitrant states.

Another factor that may make the states more receptive to limited government, especially on economic issues, is competition among the states. It is widely believed that major corporations are more likely to establish new operations in states with a "favorable business climate." Such a climate may mean low taxes and therefore relatively more limited social services. If states compete with one another to offer the

President Lyndon B. Johnson's Great Society and War on Poverty were among programs that asserted the most national authority since the New Deal. The top photo shows Johnson shaking the hand of one of the residents of Appalachia during his Poverty Tour in 1964. The photo on the bottom shows Johnson signing the Poverty Bill (also known as the Economic Opportunity Act) on August 20, 1964, while press and supporters of the bill look on. (LBJ Library/Cecil Stoughton)

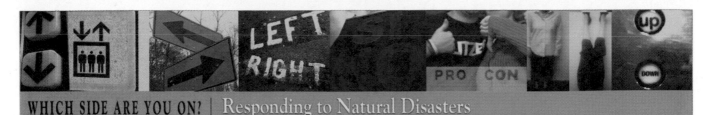

WHICH SIDE ARE YOU ON? | Responding to Natural Disasters

When Hurricane Katrina hit the Gulf Coast on August 29–31, 2005, it instantly became one of the most destructive natural disasters in the history of the United States. Some 1,300 people died as a result of the storm, while property damage totaled tens of billions of dollars. The government's failures before and after Katrina set off a heated debate. Some contended that the federal government should bear most of the blame for the suffering in Louisiana and other Gulf states because the government failed to render effective aid in a timely fashion. Others claimed that most of the problems were a result of poor planning and coordination at the state and local levels.

RESPONSIBILITY FALLS ON FEMA AND THE FEDS

Many Americans felt that the federal government's response to Katrina was woefully inadequate. Much of their criticism centered on the failures of the Federal Emergency Management Agency (FEMA) in the aftermath of Katrina. FEMA, the government agency responsible for coordinating disaster preparedness and relief efforts, was disorganized and slow to respond in the days following the storm. On their arrival in the Gulf Coast, FEMA officials often acted counterproductively—on some occasions denying the delivery of storm aid that their agency had not authorized. Indeed, thousands of New Orleans residents spent days stranded in hazardous flood conditions without adequate food, water, and shelter before FEMA officials finally provided aid and arranged transportation to safe locations.

Many critics of the federal government's handling of Katrina pointed out that FEMA's director, Michael Brown, had no disaster management experience before being appointed by President George W. Bush. Indeed, Brown was a political appointee, earning the directorship because of his work for Bush as a loyal campaign organizer, not because of his training or experience in emergency management operations. Katrina exposed the risks involved in awarding such an important federal government position to an unqualified individual.

STATE AND LOCAL OFFICIALS WERE INCOMPETENT AND ILL PREPARED

Other Americans claimed that state and local politicians deserved more of the blame for the Katrina failures. These officials, including Louisiana governor Kathleen Blanco and New Orleans mayor Ray Nagin, were not adequately prepared for the storm. Local officials knew the region and its residents best, yet they failed to make proper provisions for evacuating vulnerable residents. People without cars, nursing home residents, and hospital patients were left behind to weather the storm.

In 2005, the head of the Department of Homeland Security, Michael Chertoff (right), and Undersecretary of FEMA, Michael Brown (center), met with the mayor of New Orleans, Ray Nagin, in the aftermath of Hurricane Katrina. Each of the officials were criticized as ineffective. (Jocelyn Augustino/FEMA)

Local officials also failed to keep order when looting and violence broke out in New Orleans in the storm's aftermath. Investigations into local law enforcement failures and misconduct are ongoing. Moreover, communications breakdowns often delayed the delivery of aid to storm victims. Indeed, Blanco and Nagin, their critics argue, engaged in petty and costly power struggles with federal officials following the storm.

WHAT'S YOUR POSITION?

Which level of government should carry most of the blame for the inadequate preparations before Hurricane Katrina hit the Gulf states and the lack of immediate and effective relief efforts afterward? Generally, which level of government should have the greatest responsibility for disaster preparedness and response? Why?

GOING ONLINE

Hurricane Katrina devastated not only New Orleans but also numerous other communities along the Gulf Coast. To read ongoing coverage about Katrina recovery in South Mississippi, check out the Web site of the Biloxi Sun Herald at **www.sunherald.com/mld/sunherald/news/ special_packages/hurricane_katrina.**

best business climate, the competition may force down taxes all around. Competition of this type also may dissuade states from implementing environmental regulations that restrict certain business activities. Those who deplore the effect of such competition often refer to it as a "race to the bottom." National legislation, in contrast, is not constrained by interstate competition.

A final factor that may encourage the states to favor the status quo is the relative power of local economic interests. A large corporation in a small state, for example, may have a substantial amount of political influence. Such a corporation, which has experienced success within the existing economic framework, may be opposed to any changes to that framework. These local economic interests may have less influence at the national level. This observation echoes James Madison's point in *Federalist Paper* No. 10 (see Appendix C of this text). Madison argued that a large federal republic would be less subject to the danger of "factions" than a small state.

Federalism Becomes a Republican Issue

In the years after 1968, the **devolution** of power from the national government to the states became a major ideological theme for the Republican Party. This devolution of power is commonly referred to as "federalism." This is a relatively new meaning for the word *federalism*, which traditionally was used to describe the American system generally, regardless of where the line between national and state power was to be drawn. Advocates of federalism today, however, have in mind a much stronger role for the states.

Devolution
The transfer of powers from a national or central government to a state or local government.

The "New Federalism."   The architects of Lyndon Johnson's War on Poverty were reluctant to let state governments have a role in the new programs. This reluctance was a response to the resistance of many southern states to African American civil rights. The Johnson administration did not trust the states to administer antipoverty programs in an impartial and efficient manner.

Republican president Richard Nixon (1969–1974), who succeeded Johnson in office, saw political opportunity in the Democrats' suspicion of state governments. Nixon advocated what he called a "New Federalism" that would devolve authority from the national government to the states. In part, the New Federalism involved the conversion of categorical grants into block grants, thereby giving state governments greater flexibility in spending. A second part of Nixon's New Federalism was *revenue sharing*. Under the revenue-sharing plan, the national government provided direct, unconditional financial support to state and local governments.

Nixon was able to obtain only a limited number of block grants from Congress. The block grants he did obtain, plus revenue sharing, substantially increased financial support to state governments. Republican president Ronald Reagan was also a strong advocate of federalism, but some of his policies withdrew certain financial support from the states. Reagan was more successful than Nixon in obtaining block grants, but Reagan's block grants, unlike Nixon's, were less generous to the states than the categorical grants they replaced. Under Reagan, revenue sharing was eliminated.

Federalism in the Twenty-First Century.   Today, federalism (in the sense of limited national authority) continues to be an important element in conservative ideology. At this point, however, it is not clear whether competing theories of federalism truly divide the Republicans from the Democrats in practice. Consider that under Democratic president Bill Clinton (1993–2001), Congress replaced AFDC, a categorical welfare program, with the TANF block grants. This change was part of the Welfare Reform Act of 1996, which was perhaps the most significant domestic policy initiative of Clinton's administration. In contrast, a major domestic initiative of Republican president George W. Bush was increased federal funding and control of education—long a preserve of state and local governments.

President Clinton prepares to sign the Welfare Reform Act of 1996, overhauling America's welfare system and replacing Aid to Families with Dependent Children (AFDC)—a categorical program—with TANF, a block grant program that transfers control from the federal government to state governments. How can you explain this given the traditional divide between the Democrats and the Republicans in setting the theoretical limits of national authority? (AP Photo/J. Scott Applewhite)

Also, in some circumstances, liberals today may benefit from states' rights. One example is the issue of same-sex marriages, which we examined in the chapter-opening *What If . . .* feature. A minority of the states are much more receptive than the rest of the nation to same-sex marriages or to "civil unions" for gay male or lesbian partners. Liberals who favor such marriages or civil unions therefore have an incentive to oppose national legislation or an amendment to the national Constitution on this topic.

Federalism and the Supreme Court Today

The United States Supreme Court, which normally has the final say on constitutional issues, necessarily plays a significant role in determining the line between federal and state powers. Consider the decisions rendered by Chief Justice John Marshall in the cases discussed earlier in this chapter. Since the 1930s, Marshall's broad interpretation of the commerce clause has made it possible for the national government to justify its regulation of virtually any activity, even when an activity would appear to be purely local in character.

Since the 1990s, however, the Supreme Court has been reining in somewhat the national government's powers under the commerce clause. The Court also has given increased emphasis to state powers under the Tenth and Eleventh Amendments to the Constitution. At the same time, other recent rulings have sent contradictory messages with regard to states' rights and the federal government's power.

Reining in the Commerce Power

In a widely publicized 1995 case, *United States v. Lopez,*[13] the Supreme Court held that Congress had exceeded its constitutional authority under the commerce clause when it passed the Gun-Free School Zones Act in 1990. The Court stated that the

---

[13]514 U.S. 549 (1995).

act, which banned the possession of guns within one thousand feet of any school, was unconstitutional because it attempted to regulate an area that had "nothing to do with commerce, or any sort of economic enterprise." This marked the first time in sixty years that the Supreme Court had placed a limit on the national government's authority under the commerce clause.

In 2000, in *United States v. Morrison*,[14] the Court held that Congress had overreached its authority under the commerce clause when it passed the Violence against Women Act in 1994. The Court invalidated a key section of the act that provided a federal remedy for gender-motivated violence, such as rape. The Court noted that in enacting this law, Congress had extensively documented that violence against women had an adverse "aggregate" effect on interstate commerce: it deterred potential victims from traveling, from engaging in employment, and from transacting business in interstate commerce. It also diminished national productivity and increased medical and other costs. Nonetheless, the Court held that evidence of an aggregate effect on commerce was not enough to justify national regulation of noneconomic, violent criminal conduct.

State Sovereignty and the Eleventh Amendment

In recent years, the Supreme Court has issued a series of decisions that bolstered the authority of state governments under the Eleventh Amendment to the Constitution. As interpreted by the Court, that amendment in most circumstances precludes lawsuits against state governments for violations of rights established by federal laws unless the states consent to be sued. For example, in a 1999 case, *Alden v. Maine*,[15] the Court held that Maine state employees could not sue the state for violating the overtime pay requirements of a federal act. According to the Court, state immunity from such lawsuits "is a fundamental aspect of the sovereignty which [the states] enjoyed before the ratification of the Constitution, and which they retain today."

In 2000, in *Kimel v. Florida Board of Regents*,[16] the Court held that the Eleventh Amendment precluded employees of a state university from suing the state to enforce a federal statute prohibiting age-based discrimination. In 2003, however, in *Nevada v. Hibbs*,[17] the Court ruled that state employers must abide by the federal Family and Medical Leave Act (FMLA). The reasoning was that the FMLA seeks to outlaw gender bias, and government actions that may discriminate on the basis of gender must receive a "heightened review status" compared with actions that may discriminate on the basis of age or disability. Also, in 2004 the Court ruled that the Eleventh Amendment could not shield states from suits by individuals with disabilities who had been denied access to courtrooms located on the upper floors of buildings.[18]

Tenth Amendment Issues

The Tenth Amendment states: "The powers not delegated to the United States by the Constitution, nor prohibited by it to the States, are reserved to the States respectively, or to the people." In 1992, the Court held that requirements imposed on the state of New York under a federal act regulating low-level radioactive waste were inconsistent with the Tenth Amendment and thus unconstitutional. According to

---

[14]529 U.S. 598 (2000).
[15]527 U.S. 706 (1999).
[16]528 U.S. 62 (2000).
[17]538 U.S. 721 (2003).
[18]*Tennessee v. Lane*, 541 U.S. 509 (2004).

In 2005, these people waited at the steps of the United States Supreme Court building because they wished to be the first to find out about the Court's decision in the government's appeal against Oregon's "death with dignity" law. The Court decided against the federal government and in favor of Oregon. Why would the federal government go to court in an attempt to prevent legally assisted suicide in one state? (AP Photo/Charles Dharapak)

the Court, the act's "take title" provision, which required states to accept ownership of waste or regulate waste following Congress's instructions, exceeded the enumerated powers of Congress. Although Congress can regulate the handling of such waste, "it may not conscript state governments as its agents" in an attempt to enforce a program of federal regulation.[19]

In 1997, the Court revisited this Tenth Amendment issue. In *Printz v. United States*,[20] the Court struck down the provisions of the federal Brady Handgun Violence Prevention Act of 1993 that required state employees to check the backgrounds of prospective handgun purchasers. Said the Court:

> [T]he federal government may neither issue directives requiring the States to address particular problems, nor command the States' officers, or those of their political subdivisions, to administer or enforce a federal regulatory program.

Other Federalism Cases

In recent years, the Supreme Court has sent mixed messages in federalism cases. At times the court has favored states' rights, while on other occasions it has backed the federal government's position.

There has been a general drift toward favoring the states in cases involving federalism issues. Despite this trend, the Supreme Court argued in 2005 that the federal government's power to seize and destroy illegal drugs trumped California's law legalizing the use of marijuana for medical treatment.[21] Yet, less than a year later, the Court favored states' rights in another case rife with federalism issues, *Gonzales v. Oregon*.[22] After a lengthy legal battle, the Court upheld Oregon's controversial "death with dignity" law, which allows patients with terminal illnesses to choose to end their lives early and thus alleviate suffering.

---

[19]*New York v. United States*, 505 U.S. 144 (1992).
[20]521 U.S. 898 (1997).
[21]*Gonzales v. Raich*, 545 U.S. 1 (2005).
[22]126 S.Ct. 904 (2006).

As you read in Chapter 1, the decision handed down in *Kelo v. City of New London*[23] created an uproar among property rights advocates. Many state and local governments proposed legislation that would bar the taking of private land unaffected by blight if it would be transferred to a private developer. Steps taken by the states to combat *Kelo* gained so much political traction that the U.S. Congress is considering legislation that would forbid such takings nationwide.

---

[23]545 U.S. 469 (2005).

MAKING A DIFFERENCE | Writing Letters to the Editor

The federal system encourages debate over whether a particular issue should be a national, state, or local question. Also, because many questions are, in fact, state or local ones, it is easier for you to make a significant contribution to the discussion on these issues. Even in the largest states, there are many fewer people to persuade than in the nation as a whole. Attempts to influence your fellow citizens, by letters to the editor or other methods, can therefore be more effective.

Why Should You Care?

In this chapter, we have described a variety of issues arising from our federal system that may concern you directly. While the national government provides aid to educational programs, education is still primarily a state and local responsibility. The total amount of money spent on education is determined by state and local governments. Therefore, you can address this issue at the state or local level. Welfare payments and sentences for crimes are also set at the state level. Gambling laws are another state responsibility. Do you enjoy gambling—or do you believe that the effects of gambling make it a social disaster?

State law—or state negotiations with American Indian tribes—determines the availability of gambling.

The question of which level of government should handle an issue also may affect you directly. Are you concerned with current state laws regarding same-sex marriage and civil unions? Or, do you believe that Congress needs to create a uniform national policy either in favor of or against such unions? Either way, in any state that seeks to permit same-sex marriage, the question of national versus state authority will determine the outcome of the debate.

What Can You Do?

One of the best ways to make your point on these or other issues is by writing an effective letter to the editor of your local newspaper (or even to a national newspaper such as the *New York Times*). First, you should familiarize yourself with the kinds of letters that are accepted by the newspapers to which you want to write. Then follow these rules for writing an effective letter.

1. Use a computer, and double-space the lines. If possible, use a spelling checker and grammar checker.

2. Your lead topic sentence should be short, to the point, and powerful.

3. Keep your thoughts on target—choose only one topic to discuss in your letter. Make sure it is newsworthy and timely.

4. Make sure your letter is concise; never let your letter exceed a page and a half in length (double-spaced).

5. If you know that facts were misstated or left out in current news stories about your topic, supply the facts. The public wants to know.

6. Don't be afraid to express moral judgments. You can go a long way by appealing to the readers' sense of justice.

7. Personalize the letter by bringing in your own experiences, if possible.

8. Sign your letter, and give your address (including your e-mail address, if you have one) and your telephone number.

9. Send your letter to the editorial office of the newspaper or magazine of your choice. Virtually all publications now have e-mail addresses and home pages on the Web. The Web sites usually give information on where you can send mail.

Key Terms

Chapter Summary

1 There are three basic models for ordering relations between central governments and local units: (a) a unitary system (in which ultimate power is held by the national government), (b) a confederal system (in which ultimate power is retained by the states), and (c) a federal system (in which governmental powers are divided between the national government and the states). A major reason for the creation of a federal system in the United States is that it reflected a compromise between the views of the Federalists (who wanted a strong national government) and those of the Anti-Federalists (who wanted the states to retain their sovereignty).

2 The Constitution expressly delegated certain powers to the national government in Article I, Section 8. In addition to these expressed powers, the national government has implied and inherent powers. Implied powers are those that are reasonably necessary to carry out the powers expressly delegated to the national government. Inherent powers are those held by the national government by virtue of its being a sovereign state with the right to preserve itself.

3 The Tenth Amendment to the Constitution states that powers not delegated to the United States by the Constitution, nor prohibited by it to the states, are reserved to the states, or to the people. In certain areas, the Constitution provides for concurrent powers, such as the power to tax, which are powers that are held jointly by the national and state governments. The Constitution also denies certain powers to both the national government and the states.

4 The supremacy clause of the Constitution states that the Constitution, congressional laws, and national treaties are the supreme law of the land. States cannot use their reserved or concurrent powers to override national policies. "Vertical" checks and balances allow the states to influence the national government and vice versa.

5 The three most important clauses in the Constitution on interstate relations require that (a) each state give full faith and credit to every other state's public acts, records, and judi-

cial proceedings; (b) each state extend to every other state's citizens the privileges and immunities of its own citizens; and (c) each state agree to return persons who are fleeing from justice back to their home state when requested to do so.

6 Two landmark Supreme Court cases expanded the constitutional powers of the national government. Chief Justice John Marshall's expansive interpretation of the necessary and proper clause of the Constitution in *McCulloch v. Maryland* (1819) enhanced the implied power of the national government. Marshall's broad interpretation of the commerce clause in *Gibbons v. Ogden* (1824) further extended the constitutional regulatory powers of the national government.

7 The controversy over slavery that led to the Civil War took the form of a fight over national government supremacy versus the rights of the separate states. Ultimately, the effect of the South's desire for increased states' rights and the subsequent Civil War was an increase in the political power of the national government.

8 Since the Civil War, federalism has evolved through at least two general phases: dual federalism and cooperative federalism. In dual federalism, each of the states and the federal government remain supreme within their own spheres. The era since the Great Depression has sometimes been labeled one of cooperative federalism, in which states and the national government cooperate in solving complex common problems.

9 Categorical grants from the federal government to state governments help finance many projects, such as Medicaid, highway construction, unemployment benefits, and welfare programs. By attaching special conditions to the receipt of federal grants, the national government can effect policy changes in areas typically governed by the states. Block grants, which group a number of categorical grants together, usually have fewer strings attached, thus giving state and local governments more flexibility in using funds. Federal mandates—laws requiring states to implement certain policies, such as policies to protect the environment—have generated controversy because of their cost.

10 Traditionally, conservatives have favored states' rights, and liberals have favored national authority. In part, this is because the national government has historically been an engine of change, while state governments have been more content with the status quo. States have also been reluctant to increase social spending because of a fear that the resulting taxes could interfere with a "favorable business climate" and discourage new business enterprises.

11 Resistance to African American civil rights by the southern states prejudiced many people against states' rights in the 1960s. Renamed "federalism," the states' rights cause received Republican support in the 1970s and 1980s.

Republican presidents Richard Nixon and Ronald Reagan sought to return power to the states through block grants and other programs. Under Republican president George W. Bush, however, the national government has gained power relative to that of the states.

12 The United States Supreme Court plays a significant role in determining the line between state and federal powers. Since the 1990s, the Court has been reining in somewhat the national government's powers under the commerce clause and has given increased emphasis to state powers under the Tenth and Eleventh Amendments to the Constitution.

| Selected Print and Media Resources

SUGGESTED READINGS

Hamilton, Alexander, *et al. The Federalist: The Famous Papers on the Principles of American Government.* Benjamin F. Wright, ed. New York: Friedman/Fairfax Publishing, 2002. These essays remain an authoritative exposition of the founders' views on federalism.

Karmis, Dimitrios, and Wayne Norman, eds. *Theories of Federalism: A Reader.* New York: Palgrave MacMillan, 2005. This reader brings together the most significant writings on federalism from the late eighteenth century to the present.

Manna, Paul. *School's In: Federalism and the National Education Agenda.* Washington, D.C.: Georgetown University Press, 2006. The author examines the changing relationship between the federal government and the states with regard to our public education system.

Nagel, Robert F. *The Implosion of American Federalism.* New York: Oxford University Press, 2002. The author contends that despite the states' rights trend of recent years, which has been given force by the Supreme Court in several of its decisions, the nation faces the danger of increasingly centralized power.

MEDIA RESOURCES

Can the States Do It Better?—A 1996 film in which various experts discuss how much power the national government should have. The film uses documentary footage and other resources to illustrate this debate.

City of Hope—A 1991 movie by John Sayles. The film is a story of life, work, race, and politics in a modern New Jersey city. An African American alderman is one of the several major characters.

The Civil War—The PBS documentary series that made director Ken Burns famous. *The Civil War*, first shown in 1990, marked a revolution in documentary technique. Photographs, letters, eyewitness memoirs, and music are used to bring the war to life. The DVD version was released in 2002.

McCulloch v. Maryland and *Gibbons v. Ogden*—These programs are part of the series *Equal Justice under Law: Landmark Cases in Supreme Court History.* They provide more details on cases that defined our federal system.

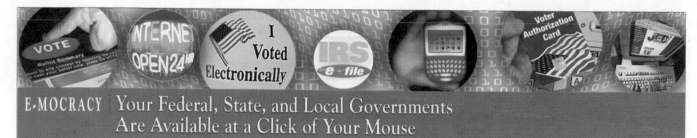

E·MOCRACY | Your Federal, State, and Local Governments Are Available at a Click of Your Mouse

Although online voting remains rare, your access to federal, state, and local government offices has improved dramatically since the Internet entered just about everybody's life. The number of government services available online is growing rapidly. Some researchers now talk about *e-government*. Instead of waiting in line to renew car registrations, residents of Scottsdale, Arizona, can renew online. In Colorado, heating and air-conditioning contractors can obtain permits from a Web site run by NetClerk, Inc. In many jurisdictions, all parking tickets can be handled with a credit card and a computer connected to the Internet.

At most colleges, it is now possible to apply online for financial aid. The federal government allows online applications for Social Security benefits and strongly encourages taxpayers to file their income tax returns electronically. Many citizens have found that e-government programs such as these make interactions with the government much simpler. It is no longer necessary to wait in line or to put up with the "bureaucratic shuffle."

| Logging On

You can learn how some communities have benefited from implementing online government through EzGov, Inc., by reading some of the comments at EzGov's Web site. Go to

www.ezgov.com/customers

Federalism is an important aspect of our democracy. To learn more about the establishment of our federal form of government and about current issues relating to federalism, visit the Web sites listed in the remainder of this section.

To learn the founders' views on federalism, you can access the *Federalist Papers* online at

www.law.emory.edu/erd/docs/federalist

The following site has links to U.S. state constitutions, the *Federalist Papers*, and international federations, such as the European Union:

www.constitution.org/cs_feder.htm

The Council of State Governments is a good source for information on state responses to federalism issues. Go to

www.csg.org

Another good source of information on issues facing state governments and federal-state relations is the National Governors Association's Web site at

www.nga.org

You can find a directory of numerous federalism links at

www.gmu.edu

The Brookings Institution's policy analyses and recommendations on a variety of issues, including federalism, can be accessed at

www.brook.edu

For a libertarian approach to issues relating to federalism, go to the Cato Institute's Web page at

www.cato.org

| Online Review

At **www.politicalscience.wadsworth.com/schmidt12**, you will find a free Study Guide to this book. For each chapter, there are two online quizzes to help you master the material.

• The PoliPrep Self-Study Assessment provides a pretest for each major section of the chapter. PoliPrep then generates a customized study plan. After you complete the study plan, a posttest evaluates your progress.

• The Tutorial Quiz for each chapter provides questions on the chapter contents, including the features. The questions are organized to match the major sections of the chapter.

4 | Civil Liberties

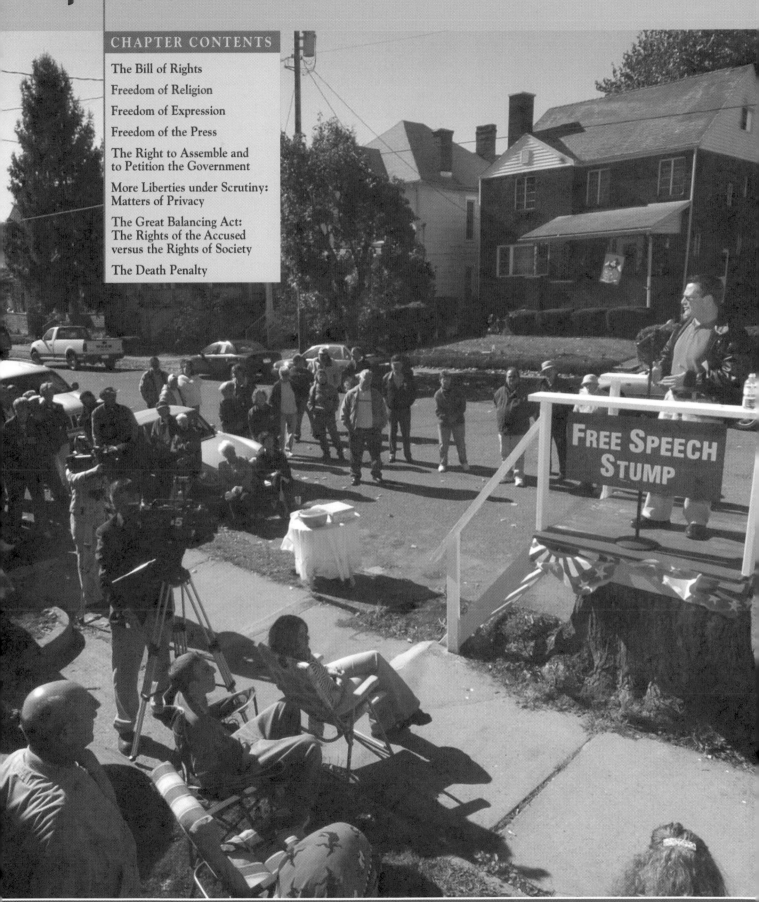

What If . . .
The Government Monitored All E-mail?

BACKGROUND

Shortly after the terrorist attacks of September 11, 2001, the U.S. government passed the USA Patriot Act. Designed to help law enforcement and intelligence-gathering agencies combat terrorism threats, the Patriot Act raised serious *civil liberties* concerns. Civil liberties typically involve restraints on the government's actions against individuals. Critics of the Patriot Act believe that it endangers numerous constitutionally protected freedoms that all Americans enjoy.

As you read in Chapter 1, the National Security Agency (NSA) secretly eavesdropped on international phone conversations without warrants. President George W. Bush was quick to defend the NSA's actions as vital to the nation's security, claiming that the eavesdropping program was legal under provisions of the Patriot Act. Many Americans, however, have questioned the constitutionality of such spying and have wondered what other measures the government may take in the name of national security.

WHAT IF THE GOVERNMENT MONITORED ALL E-MAIL?

If the government filtered all e-mail, Americans would experience the kind of invasion of privacy that is commonplace in nations such as China. Software that can track Internet activity, such as spyware and keystroke-capturing programs, has been in existence for quite some time. The use of such programs is typically associated with criminal activities such as identity theft and cyberstalking. The government could easily employ variations of these types of software to monitor individuals' e-mail and Internet activity.

There is already precedent for using electronic monitoring programs in the United States. Numerous U.S. corporations have implemented electronic surveillance programs to monitor their employees' e-mail and Web use. In a number of instances, the information gleaned from such practices has resulted in employees being terminated or having criminal charges brought against them.

Such electronic monitoring would also represent a serious threat to freedom of speech. Americans would be less likely to express themselves candidly or research topics that might cast suspicion on them. Web logs ("blogs"), especially those with political content, would undoubtedly suffer. The Internet has become an important marketplace of ideas and information, and any threat to freedom of expression would likely curtail its growth, scope, and diversity of content.

THE USA PATRIOT ACT

When the NSA's spying activity leaked to the press, many Americans became concerned that the government was dangerously infringing on citizens' privacy. After all, if the government were secretly eavesdropping on phone conversations, what would stop it from expanding its efforts to other modes of communication?

Some civil liberties advocates are concerned that legislation such as the Patriot Act may be used abusively to justify electronic monitoring beyond the scope of the "war on terrorism." Certainly, e-mail and Internet surveillance would be a powerful tool in tracking down terrorists and squelching terror plots. Yet there are still concerns about the possible abuse of such a powerful tool. Various reports have surfaced regarding government investigations into mainstream activist organizations such as the American Civil Liberties Union and Greenpeace.

CHINA'S ELECTRONIC SURVEILLANCE

The Chinese government has imposed a draconian level of electronic surveillance. Although the U.S. government is highly unlikely to take such extensive and abusive measures, the Chinese example is interesting nonetheless.

In China, the government employs more than 30,000 individuals to monitor Internet traffic of all forms. E-mail and blogs are censored and scrutinized. Many words, including *freedom,* are blocked out by software and government employees. In addition, most Internet users are forced to log in and register through a government program so that their activities can be tracked and subjected to surveillance. Privacy on the Internet is almost completely nonexistent. Interestingly, much of the software used by China was developed by U.S. and other Western companies.

FOR CRITICAL ANALYSIS

1. Would you use the Internet any differently if you thought that the government might be monitoring your e-mail and Internet activity? Explain.
2. Your college or university owns the rights over all e-mail activity you engage in through the school's e-mail server. Would a government-owned e-mail server be any more or less invasive of your privacy? Why or why not?

"The land of the free." When asked what makes the United States distinctive, Americans commonly say that it is a free country. Americans have long believed that limits on the power of government are an essential part of what makes this country free. The first ten amendments to the U.S. Constitution—the Bill of Rights—place such limits on the national government. Of these amendments, none is more famous than the First Amendment, which guarantees freedom of religion, speech, the press, and other rights.

Most other democratic nations have laws to protect these and other **civil liberties,** but none of the laws is quite like the First Amendment. Take the issue of "hate speech." What if someone makes statements that stir up hatred toward a particular race or other group of people? In Germany, where memories of Nazi anti-Semitism remain alive, such speech is unquestionably illegal. In the United States, the issue is not so clear. The courts have often extended constitutional protection to this kind of speech.

In this chapter, we describe the civil liberties provided by the Bill of Rights and some of the controversies that surround them. We look first at the First Amendment liberties and at the right to privacy, which we touched on in the *What If . . .* feature that opened this chapter. We also examine the rights of defendants in criminal cases.

| **DID YOU KNOW . . .**

That one of the proposed initial constitutional amendments—"No State shall infringe the equal rights of conscience, nor the freedom of speech, nor of the press, nor of the right of trial by jury in criminal cases"—was never sent to the states for approval because the states' rights advocates in the First Congress defeated this proposal?

| Civil Liberties
Those personal freedoms that are protected for all individuals. Civil liberties typically involve restraining the government's actions against individuals.

| The Bill of Rights

As you read through this chapter, bear in mind that the Bill of Rights, like the rest of the Constitution, is relatively brief. The framers set forth broad guidelines, leaving it up to the courts to interpret these constitutional mandates and apply them to specific situations. Thus, judicial interpretations shape the true nature of the civil liberties and rights that we possess. Because judicial interpretations change over time, so do our liberties and rights. As you will read in the following pages, there have been many

These employees of the National Security Agency (NSA) are working at the Threat Operations Center in Fort Meade, Maryland. This supersecret intelligence operation is heavily guarded. The NSA has admitted that it has engaged in domestic surveillance. Why did many commentators criticize these actions? (AP Photo/Evan Vucci)

conflicts over the meaning of such simple phrases as *freedom of religion* and *freedom of the press*. To understand what freedoms we actually have, we need to examine how the courts—and particularly the United States Supreme Court—have resolved some of those conflicts. One important conflict was over the issue of whether the Bill of Rights in the federal Constitution limited the powers of state governments as well as those of the national government.

Extending the Bill of Rights to State Governments

Many citizens do not realize that, as originally intended, the Bill of Rights limited only the powers of the national government. At the time the Bill of Rights was ratified, there was little concern over the potential of state governments to curb civil liberties. For one thing, state governments were closer to home and easier to control. For another, most state constitutions already had bills of rights. Rather, the fear was of the potential tyranny of the national government. The Bill of Rights begins with the words, "Congress shall make no law . . . ." It says nothing about *states* making laws that might abridge citizens' civil liberties. In 1833, in *Barron v. Baltimore*,[1] the United States Supreme Court held that the Bill of Rights did not apply to state laws.

We mentioned that most states had bills of rights. These bills of rights were similar to the national one, but there were some differences. Furthermore, each state's judicial system interpreted the rights differently. Citizens in different states, therefore, effectively had different sets of civil rights. It was not until after the Fourteenth Amendment was ratified in 1868 that civil liberties guaranteed by the national Constitution began to be applied to the states. Section 1 of that amendment provides, in part, as follows:

> No State shall . . . deprive any person of life, liberty, or property, without due process of law.

Incorporation of the Fourteenth Amendment

There was no question that the Fourteenth Amendment applied to state governments. For decades, however, the courts were reluctant to define the liberties spelled out in the national Bill of Rights as constituting "due process of law," which was protected under the Fourteenth Amendment. Not until 1925, in *Gitlow v. New York*,[2] did the United States Supreme Court hold that the Fourteenth Amendment protected the freedom of speech guaranteed by the First Amendment to the Constitution.

Only gradually, and never completely, did the Supreme Court accept the **incorporation theory**—the view that most of the protections of the Bill of Rights are incorporated into the Fourteenth Amendment's protection against state government actions. Table 4–1 shows the rights that the Court has incorporated into the Fourteenth Amendment and the case in which it first applied each protection. As you can see in that table, in the fifteen years following the *Gitlow* decision, the Supreme Court incorporated into the Fourteenth Amendment the other basic freedoms (of the press, assembly, the right to petition, and religion) guaranteed by the First Amendment. These and the later Supreme Court decisions listed in Table 4–1 have bound the fifty states to accept for their citizens most of the rights and freedoms that are set forth in the U.S. Bill of Rights. We now look at some of those rights and freedoms, beginning with the freedom of religion.

| Incorporation Theory
The view that most of the protections of the Bill of Rights apply to state governments through the Fourteenth Amendment's due process clause.

---

[1]7 Peters 243 (1833).
[2]268 U.S. 652 (1925).

TABLE 4–1 | INCORPORATING THE BILL OF RIGHTS INTO THE FOURTEENTH AMENDMENT

YEAR	ISSUE	AMENDMENT INVOLVED	COURT CASE
1925	Freedom of speech	I	*Gitlow v. New York*, 268 U.S. 652.
1931	Freedom of the press	I	*Near v. Minnesota*, 283 U.S. 697.
1932	Right to a lawyer in capital punishment cases	VI	*Powell v. Alabama*, 287 U.S. 45.
1937	Freedom of assembly and right to petition	I	*De Jonge v. Oregon*, 299 U.S. 353.
1940	Freedom of religion	I	*Cantwell v. Connecticut*, 310 U.S. 296.
1947	Separation of church and state	I	*Everson v. Board of Education*, 330 U.S. 1.
1948	Right to a public trial	VI	*In re Oliver*, 333 U.S. 257.
1949	No unreasonable searches and seizures	IV	*Wolf v. Colorado*, 338 U.S. 25.
1961	Exclusionary rule	IV	*Mapp v. Ohio*, 367 U.S. 643.
1962	No cruel and unusual punishment	VIII	*Robinson v. California*, 370 U.S. 660.
1963	Right to a lawyer in all criminal felony cases	VI	*Gideon v. Wainwright*, 372 U.S. 335.
1964	No compulsory self-incrimination	V	*Malloy v. Hogan*, 378 U.S. 1.
1965	Right to privacy	I, III, IV, V, IX	*Griswold v. Connecticut*, 381 U.S. 479.
1966	Right to an impartial jury	VI	*Parker v. Gladden*, 385 U.S. 363.
1967	Right to a speedy trial	VI	*Klopfer v. North Carolina*, 386 U.S. 213.
1969	No double jeopardy	V	*Benton v. Maryland*, 395 U.S. 784.

Freedom of Religion

In the United States, freedom of religion consists of two main principles as they are presented in the First Amendment. The *establishment clause* prohibits the establishment of a church that is officially supported by the national government, thus guaranteeing a division between church and state. The *free exercise clause* constrains the national government from prohibiting individuals from practicing the religion of their choice. These two precepts can inherently be in tension with one another, however. For example, would prohibiting a group of students from holding prayer meetings in a public school classroom infringe on the students' right to free exercise of religion? Or would allowing the meetings amount to unconstitutional government support for religion? You will read about a number of difficult freedom of religion issues in the following discussion.

The Separation of Church and State— The Establishment Clause

The First Amendment to the Constitution states, in part, that "Congress shall make no law respecting an establishment of religion." In the words of Thomas Jefferson, the **establishment clause** was designed to create a "wall of separation of Church and State." Perhaps Jefferson was thinking about the religious intolerance that characterized the first colonies. Many of the American colonies were founded by groups that were in pursuit of religious freedom. Nonetheless, the early colonists were quite intolerant of religious beliefs that did not conform to those held by the majority of citizens within their own communities. Jefferson undoubtedly was also aware that state churches (denominations) were the rule; among the original thirteen American colonies, nine had *official* churches.

| Establishment Clause
The part of the First Amendment prohibiting the establishment of a church officially supported by the national government. It is applied to questions of state and local government aid to religious organizations and schools, the legality of allowing or requiring school prayers, and the teaching of evolution versus intelligent design.

This woodcut from 1871 shows a woman who symbolizes justice standing at the door of a building that represents government. Soldiers block the steps to members of different religions. What principle outlined in the Bill of Rights was the originator of this engraving trying to demonstrate? (Library of Congress)

CHURCH AND STATE—NO UNION UPON ANY TERMS.

As interpreted by the United States Supreme Court, the establishment clause in the First Amendment means at least the following:

Neither a state nor the federal government can set up a church. Neither can pass laws which aid one religion, aid all religions, or prefer one religion over another. Neither can force nor influence a person to go to or to remain away from church against his will or force him to profess a belief or disbelief in any religion. No person can be punished for entertaining or professing religious beliefs or disbeliefs, for church attendance or nonattendance. No tax in any amount, large or small, can be levied to support any religious activities or institutions, whatever they may be called, or whatever form they may adopt to teach or practice religion. Neither a state nor the federal government can, openly or secretly, participate in the affairs of any religious organizations or groups and vice versa.[3]

The establishment clause covers all conflicts about such matters as the legality of state and local government aid to religious organizations and schools, allowing or requiring school prayers, the teaching of evolution versus intelligent design, the posting of the Ten Commandments in schools or public places, and discrimination against religious groups in publicly operated institutions. The establishment clause's mandate that government can neither promote nor discriminate against religious beliefs raises particularly knotty questions at times.

Aid to Church-Related Schools. Throughout the United States, all property owners except religious, educational, fraternal, literary, scientific, and similar nonprofit institutions must pay property taxes. A large part of the proceeds of such taxes goes to support public schools. But not all children attend public schools. Fully 12 percent of school-aged children attend private schools, of which 85 percent have religious affiliations. Many cases have reached the United States Supreme Court; the Court has tried to draw a fine line between permissible public aid to students in church-related schools and impermissible public aid to religion. These issues have arisen most often at the elementary and secondary levels.

---

[3]*Everson v. Board of Education*, 330 U.S. 1 (1947).

In 1971, in *Lemon v. Kurtzman*,[4] the Court ruled that direct state aid could not be used to subsidize religious instruction. The Court in the *Lemon* case gave its most general statement on the constitutionality of government aid to religious schools, stating that the aid had to be secular (nonreligious) in aim, that it could not have the primary effect of advancing or inhibiting religion, and that the government must avoid "an excessive government entanglement with religion." All laws under the establishment clause are now subject to the three-part *Lemon* test. How the test is applied, however, has varied over the years.

In a number of cases, the Supreme Court has held that state programs helping church-related schools are unconstitutional. The Court also has denied state reimbursements to religious schools for field trips and for developing achievement tests. In a series of other cases, however, the Supreme Court has allowed states to use tax funds for lunches, textbooks, diagnostic services for speech and hearing problems, standardized tests, computers, and transportation for students attending church-operated elementary and secondary schools.

A Change in the Court's Position.   Generally, today's Supreme Court has shown a greater willingness to allow the use of public funds for programs in religious schools than was true at times in the past. Consider that in 1985, in *Aguilar v. Felton*,[5] the Supreme Court ruled that state programs providing special educational services for disadvantaged students attending religious schools violated the establishment clause. In 1997, however, when the Supreme Court revisited this decision, the Court reversed its position. In *Agostini v. Felton*,[6] the Court held that *Aguilar* was "no longer good law." What had happened between 1985 and 1997 to cause the Court to change its mind? Justice Sandra Day O'Connor answered this question in the *Agostini* opinion: what had changed since *Aguilar*, she stated, was "our understanding" of the establishment clause. Between 1985 and 1997, the Court's make-up had changed significantly. In fact, six of the nine justices who participated in the 1997 decision were appointed after the 1985 *Aguilar* decision.

School Vouchers.   Questions about the use of public funds for church-related schools are likely to continue as state legislators search for new ways to improve the educational system in this country. An issue that has come to the forefront in recent years is school vouchers. In a voucher system, educational vouchers (state-issued credits) can be used to "purchase" education at any school, public or private.

School districts in Florida, Ohio, and Wisconsin have all been experimenting with voucher systems. In 2000, the courts reviewed a case involving Ohio's voucher program. Under that program, some $10 million in public funds is spent annually to send 4,300 Cleveland students to fifty-one private schools, all but five of which are Catholic schools. The case presented a straightforward constitutional question: Is it a violation of the principle of separation of church and state for public tax money to be used to pay for religious education?

In 2002, the Supreme Court held that the Cleveland voucher program was constitutional.[7] The Court concluded, by a five-to-four vote, that Cleveland's use of taxpayer-paid school vouchers to send children to private schools was constitutional even though more than 95 percent of the students use the vouchers to attend Catholic or other religious schools. The Court's majority reasoned that the program did not unconstitutionally entangle church and state, because families theoretically could use the vouchers for their children to attend religious schools, secular private

| DID YOU KNOW . . .
That on the eve of the American Revolution, fewer than 20 percent of American adults adhered to a church in any significant way, compared with the 60 percent that do so today?

[4]403 U.S. 602 (1971).
[5]473 U.S. 402 (1985).
[6]521 U.S. 203 (1997).
[7]*Zelman v. Simmons-Harris*, 536 U.S. 639 (2002).

academies, suburban public schools, or charter schools, even though few public schools had agreed to accept vouchers. The Court's decision raised a further question that will need to be decided—whether religious and private schools that accept government vouchers must comply with disability and civil rights laws, as public schools are required to do.

Despite the United States Supreme Court's decision upholding the Cleveland voucher program, in 2006 the Florida Supreme Court declared Florida's voucher program unconstitutional. The Florida court held that the Florida state constitution bars public funding from being diverted to private schools that are not subject to the uniformity requirements of the state's public school system. The decision could have national implications if other states mount similar challenges to voucher programs. It remains to be seen whether the United States Supreme Court will review the Florida ruling.

The Issue of School Prayer—*Engel v. Vitale.* Do the states have the right to promote religion in general, without making any attempt to establish a particular religion? That is the question raised by school prayer and was the precise issue presented in 1962 in *Engel v. Vitale*,[8] the so-called Regents' Prayer case in New York. The State Board of Regents of New York had suggested that a prayer be spoken aloud in the public schools at the beginning of each day. The recommended prayer was as follows:

> Almighty God, we acknowledge our dependence upon Thee,
> And we beg Thy blessings upon us, our parents, our teachers, and our Country.

Such a prayer was implemented in many New York public schools.

The parents of a number of students challenged the action of the regents, maintaining that it violated the establishment clause of the First Amendment. At trial, the parents lost. The Supreme Court, however, ruled that the regents' action was unconstitutional because "the constitutional prohibition against laws respecting an establishment of a religion must mean at least that in this country it is no part of the business of government to compose official prayers for any group of the American people to recite as part of a religious program carried on by any government." The Court's conclusion was based in part on the "historical fact that governmentally established religions and religious persecutions go hand in hand." In *Abington School District v. Schempp*,[9] the Supreme Court outlawed officially sponsored daily readings of the Bible and recitation of the Lord's Prayer in public schools.

The Debate over School Prayer Continues. Although the Supreme Court has ruled repeatedly against officially sponsored prayer and Bible-reading sessions in public schools, other means for bringing some form of religious expression into public education have been attempted. In 1983, the Tennessee legislature passed a bill requiring public school classes to begin each day with a minute of silence. Alabama had a similar law. In 1985, in *Wallace v. Jaffree*,[10] the Supreme Court struck down as unconstitutional the Alabama law authorizing one minute of silence for prayer or meditation in all public schools. Applying the three-part *Lemon* test, the Court concluded that the law violated the establishment clause because it was "an endorsement of religion lacking any clearly secular purpose."

Children pray outside a Texas school. Officially organized prayer in public schools is in violation of Supreme Court rulings based on the First Amendment. If the Court were to hold that officially sponsored prayer in the schools did not violate the Constitution, what consequences might follow? (AP Photo/*The Lufkin News*/Joel Andrews)

---

[8]370 U.S. 421 (1962).
[9]374 U.S. 203 (1963).
[10]472 U.S. 38 (1985).

Since then, the lower courts have interpreted the Supreme Court's decision to mean that states can require a moment of silence in the schools as long as they make it clear that the purpose of the law is secular, not religious.

Prayer outside the Classroom.   The courts have also dealt with cases involving prayer in public schools outside the classroom, particularly prayer during graduation ceremonies. In 1992, in *Lee v. Weisman*,[11] the United States Supreme Court held that it was unconstitutional for a school to invite a rabbi to deliver a nonsectarian prayer at graduation. The Court said nothing about *students* organizing and leading prayers at graduation ceremonies and other school events, however, and these issues continue to come before the courts. A particularly contentious question in the last few years has been the constitutionality of student-initiated prayers before sporting events, such as football games. In 2000, the Supreme Court held that while school prayer at graduation did not violate the establishment clause, students could not use a school's public-address system to lead prayers at sporting events.[12]

In spite of the Court's ruling, students in a number of schools in Texas continue to pray over public-address systems at sporting events. In other areas, the Court's ruling is skirted by avoiding the use of the public-address system. For example, in a school in North Carolina, a pregame prayer was broadcast over a local radio station and heard by fans who took radios to the game for that purpose.

The Ten Commandments.   A related church-state issue is whether the Ten Commandments may be displayed in public schools—or on any public property. In recent years, a number of states have considered legislation that would allow or even require schools to post the Ten Commandments in school buildings. Supporters of the "Hang Ten" movement claim that schoolchildren are not being taught the fundamental religious and family values that frame the American way of life. They argue further that the Ten Commandments are more than just religious documents. The commandments are also secular in nature because they constitute a part of the official and permanent history of American government.

Opponents of such laws claim that they are an unconstitutional government entanglement with the religious life of citizens. Still, various Ten Commandments installations have been found to be constitutional. For example, the Supreme Court ruled in 2005 that a granite monument on the grounds of the Texas state capitol that contained the commandments was constitutional because the monument as a whole was secular in nature.[13] In another 2005 ruling, however, the Court ordered that displays of the Ten Commandments in front of two Kentucky county courthouses had to be removed because they were overtly religious.[14]

The Ten Commandments controversy took an odd twist in 2003 when, in the middle of the night, former Alabama chief justice Roy Moore installed a two and a half ton granite monument featuring the commandments in the rotunda of the state courthouse. When Moore refused to obey a federal judge's order to remove the monument, the Alabama Court of the Judiciary was forced to expel him from the judicial bench. The monument was wheeled away to a storage room.

Forbidding the Teaching of Evolution.   For many decades, certain religious groups, particularly in southern states, have opposed the teaching of evolution in the schools. To these groups, evolutionary theory directly counters their religious belief that human beings did not evolve but were created fully formed, as described in the biblical story of the creation. State and local attempts to forbid the teaching of evolution, however, have not passed constitutional muster in the eyes of the United States Supreme Court. For example, in 1968 the Supreme Court held, in *Epperson v.*

[11]505 U.S. 577 (1992).
[12]*Santa Fe Independent School District v. Doe*, 530 U.S. 290 (2000).
[13]*Van Orden v. Perry*, 125 S.Ct. 2854 (2005).
[14]*McCreary County v. American Civil Liberties Union*, 125 S.Ct. 2722 (2005).

Are the Ten Commandments so secular in nature that they constitute part of the history of American government? Or, are the Ten Commandments so overtly religious in nature that they cannot be displayed in or around any government building? (AP Photo/Harry Cabluck)

Arkansas,[15] that an Arkansas law prohibiting the teaching of evolution violated the establishment clause, because it imposed religious beliefs on students. The Louisiana legislature passed a law requiring the teaching of the biblical story of the creation alongside the teaching of evolution. In 1987, in *Edwards v. Aguillard,*[16] the Supreme Court declared that this law was unconstitutional, in part because it had as its primary purpose the promotion of a particular religious belief.

Nonetheless, state and local groups around the country, particularly in the so-called Bible Belt, continue their efforts against the teaching of evolution. The Cobb County school system in Georgia attempted to include a disclaimer in its biology textbooks that proclaims, "Evolution is a theory, not a fact, regarding the origin of living things." A federal judge later ruled that the disclaimer stickers must be removed. Other school districts have considered teaching "intelligent design" as an alternative explanation of the origin of life. Proponents of intelligent design contend that evolutionary theory has "gaps" that can be explained only by the existence of an intelligent creative force (God). To read more about the intelligent design controversy, see this chapter's *Which Side Are You On?* feature. Many critics of intelligent design argue that it is merely a repackaged version of creationism.

Religious Speech.   Another controversy in the area of church-state relations concerns religious speech in public schools or universities. For example, in *Rosenberger v. University of Virginia,*[17] the issue was whether the University of Virginia violated the establishment clause when it refused to fund a Christian group's newsletter but granted funds to more than one hundred other student organizations. The Supreme Court ruled that the university's policy unconstitutionally discriminated against religious speech. The Court pointed out that the funds came from student fees, not general taxes, and was used for the "neutral" payment of bills for student groups.

Later, the Supreme Court reviewed a case involving a similar claim of discrimination against a religious group, the Good News Club. The club offers religious instruction to young schoolchildren. The club sued the school board of a public school in Milford, New York, when the board refused to allow the club to meet on school property after the school day ended. The club argued that the school board's refusal to allow the club to meet on school property, when other groups—such as

[15]393 U.S. 97 (1968).
[16]482 U.S. 578 (1987).
[17]515 U.S. 819 (1995).

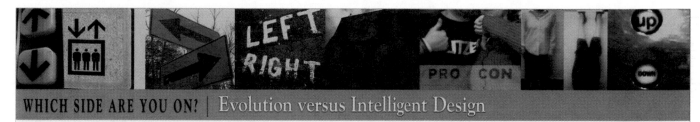

WHICH SIDE ARE YOU ON? | Evolution versus Intelligent Design

More than eighty years have passed since the infamous Scopes "monkey trial," in which a Tennessee biology teacher was taken to court for teaching Darwin's theory of evolution. Today, evolution is the most commonly accepted theory of the origins of biological life. The debate over evolution has yet to subside, though. Some public school districts have attempted to require textbooks to include disclaimers stating that evolution is merely a theory, one of many. Others have offered an alternative to the theory of evolution—*intelligent design.*

INTELLIGENT DESIGN FILLS IN THE GAPS

Those who support intelligent design contend that numerous "holes" or "gaps" exist in the theory of evolution. As a result of these gaps in the evidence, Darwin's overarching arguments regarding natural selection and succession supposedly break down. Proponents of intelligent design claim that only the existence of an intelligent creative force (God) can explain such voids in the evidence supporting evolutionary theory. Some scientists and philosophers of science have flocked to certain institutes that are dedicated to studying the origins of life and that forward the notion of intelligent design.

Proponents of intelligent design see no problem with teaching the theory in public schools. They argue that intelligent design is science, not religion. Therefore, teaching it would not breach the separation of church and state. Indeed, intelligent design endorses no specific religious doctrine and makes no attempt to provide scientific evidence for religious creation narratives. Thus, according to its adherents, intelligent design is an alternative scientific viewpoint that is worthy of being taught alongside evolutionary theory and would enrich scientific discussion regarding the origins of life.

EVOLUTIONARY THEORY IS ACCEPTED BY THE SCIENTIFIC COMMUNITY

Virtually all members of the scientific community have backed the importance of the theory of evolution for decades. A proverbial mountain of scientific evidence supports its validity. Evolutionary theory itself provides the backbone of modern biological thought. If there were truly inexplicable "holes" in the theory of evolution, then more scientists would have attempted to rework the theory or to offer a new theory altogether. In fact, scientists have already discredited some of the alleged gaps claimed by intelligent design proponents. Indeed, it is the very nature of the scientific profession to question and test all theories. The fact remains that evolution has withstood the trials of the scientific method as well as the test of time.

Critics of intelligent design have pointed out that many of its proponents have a religious agenda. Conservative evangelical Christians have often been the driving force behind efforts to teach intelligent design alongside evolution. The same religious groups also once backed creationism, a discredited theory that attempted to provide scientific evidence for the Bible's creation narrative. Furthermore, say the critics, intelligent design is not even a theory in the scientific sense of the word, as its claims cannot be disproved by examining real-world data. Therefore, intelligent design is a belief system. They insist that such religious agendas have no place in the public school system, where a firm separation between church and state must be respected.

WHAT'S YOUR POSITION?

How should public schools evaluate intelligent design? Is there an argument for teaching it alongside evolutionary theory in the public schools? Why or why not?

GOING ONLINE

One source of information on intelligent design is the Discovery Institute's Web site, **www.discovery.org**. The Discovery Institute is perhaps the most influential scientific think tank dedicated to furthering intelligent design.

the Girl Scouts and the 4-H Club—were permitted to do so, amounted to discrimination on the basis of religion. Ultimately, the Supreme Court agreed, ruling in *Good News Club v. Milford Central School*[18] that the Milford school board's decision violated the establishment clause.

The Free Exercise Clause

The First Amendment constrains Congress from prohibiting the free exercise of religion. Does this **free exercise clause** mean that no type of religious practice can be prohibited or restricted by government? Certainly, a person can hold any religious

| **Free Exercise Clause**
The provision of the First Amendment guaranteeing the free exercise of religion.

---

[18]533 U.S. 98 (2001).

belief that he or she wants, or a person can have no religious belief. When, however, religious *practices* work against public policy and the public welfare, the government can act. For example, regardless of a child's or parent's religious beliefs, the government can require certain types of vaccinations. Additionally, public school students can be required to study from textbooks chosen by school authorities.

The extent to which government can regulate religious practices has always been a subject of controversy. For example, in 1990, in *Oregon v. Smith*,[19] the United States Supreme Court ruled that the state of Oregon could deny unemployment benefits to two drug counselors who had been fired for using peyote, an illegal drug, in their religious services. The counselors had argued that using peyote was part of the practice of a Native American religion. Many criticized the decision as going too far in the direction of regulating religious practices.

The Religious Freedom Restoration Act.   In 1993, Congress responded to the public's criticism by passing the Religious Freedom Restoration Act (RFRA). One of the specific purposes of the act was to overturn the Supreme Court's decision in *Oregon v. Smith*. The act required national, state, and local governments to "accommodate religious conduct" unless the government could show that there was a *compelling* reason not to do so. Moreover, if the government did regulate a religious practice, it had to use the least restrictive means possible.

Some people believed that the RFRA went too far in the other direction—it accommodated practices that were contrary to the public policies of state governments. Proponents of states' rights complained that the act intruded into an area traditionally governed by state laws, not by the national government. In 1997, in *City of Boerne v. Flores*,[20] the Supreme Court agreed and held that Congress had exceeded its constitutional authority when it passed the RFRA. According to the Court, the act's "sweeping coverage ensures its intrusion at every level of government, displacing laws and prohibiting official actions of almost every description and regardless of subject matter."

Free Exercise in the Public Schools.   The courts have repeatedly held that U.S. governments at all levels must remain neutral on issues of religion. In the *Good News Club* decision discussed on page 116, the Supreme Court ruled that "state power is no more to be used to handicap religions than it is to favor them." Nevertheless, by overturning the RFRA, the Court cleared the way for public schools to set regulations that, while ostensibly neutral, effectively limited religious expression by students. An example is a rule banning hats, which has been instituted by many schools as a way of discouraging the display of gang insignia. This rule has also been interpreted as barring yarmulkes, the small caps worn by strictly observant Jewish boys and men.

The national government found a new way to ensure that public schools do not excessively restrict religion. To receive funds under the No Child Left Behind Act of 2002, schools must certify in writing that they do not ban prayer or other expressions of religion as long as they are made in a constitutionally appropriate manner.

Freedom of Expression

Perhaps the most frequently invoked freedom that Americans have is the right to free speech and a free press without government interference. Each of us has the right to have our say, and all of us have the right to hear what others say. For the

---

[19]494 U.S. 872 (1990).
[20]521 U.S. 507 (1997).

most part, Americans can criticize public officials and their actions without fear of reprisal by any branch of government.

No Prior Restraint

Restraining an activity before that activity has actually occurred is called **prior restraint.** When expression is involved, prior restraint means censorship, as opposed to subsequent punishment. Prior restraint of expression would require, for example, that a permit be obtained before a speech could be made, a newspaper published, or a movie or TV show exhibited. Most, if not all, Supreme Court justices have been very critical of any governmental action that imposes prior restraint on expression. The Court clearly displayed this attitude in *Nebraska Press Association v. Stuart*,[21] a case decided in 1976:

> A prior restraint on expression comes to this Court with a "heavy presumption" against its constitutionality. . . . The government thus carries a heavy burden of showing justification for the enforcement of such a restraint.

One of the most famous cases concerning prior restraint was *New York Times v. United States*[22] in 1971, the so-called Pentagon Papers case. The *Times* and the *Washington Post* were about to publish the Pentagon Papers, an elaborate secret history of the U.S. government's involvement in the Vietnam War (1964–1975). The secret documents had been obtained illegally by a disillusioned former Pentagon official. The government wanted a court order to bar publication of the documents, arguing that national security was threatened and that the documents had been stolen. The newspapers argued that the public had a right to know the information contained in the papers and that the press had the right to inform the public. The Supreme Court ruled six to three in favor of the newspapers' right to publish the information. This case affirmed the no-prior-restraint doctrine.

The Protection of Symbolic Speech

Not all expression is in words or in writing. Articles of clothing, gestures, movements, and other forms of expressive conduct are considered **symbolic speech.** Such speech is given substantial protection today by our courts. For example, in a landmark decision issued in 1969, *Tinker v. Des Moines School District*,[23] the United States Supreme Court held that the wearing of black armbands by students in protest against the Vietnam War was a form of speech protected by the First Amendment. The case arose after a school administrator in Des Moines, Iowa, issued a regulation prohibiting students in the Des Moines School District from wearing the armbands. The Supreme Court reasoned that the school district was unable to show that the wearing of the armbands had disrupted normal school activities. Furthermore, the school district's policy was discriminatory, as it banned only certain forms of symbolic speech (the black armbands) and not others (such as lapel crosses and fraternity rings).

In 1989, in *Texas v. Johnson*,[24] the Supreme Court ruled that state laws that prohibited the burning of the American flag as part of a peaceful protest also violated the freedom of expression protected by the First Amendment. Congress responded by passing the Flag Protection Act of 1989, which was ruled unconstitutional by the Supreme Court in June 1990.[25] Congress and President George H. W. Bush immediately

Prior Restraint
Restraining an action before the activity has actually occurred. When expression is involved, this means censorship.

Symbolic Speech
Nonverbal expression of beliefs, which is given substantial protection by the courts.

---

[21]427 U.S. 539 (1976). See also *Near v. Minnesota*, 283 U.S. 697 (1931).
[22]403 U.S. 713 (1971).
[23]393 U.S. 503 (1969).
[24]488 U.S. 884 (1989).
[25]*United States v. Eichman*, 496 U.S. 310 (1990).

A man, center left, tries to stop the burning of the American flag near the Washington Monument. The protesters he opposes are burning an American flag as a symbolic expression of their opposition to government policy. Would a constitutional amendment to prohibit such actions place unacceptable limitations on their symbolic speech or would it give appropriate and necessary protection to the very symbol of the nation? (AP Photo/Evan Vucci)

pledged to work for a constitutional amendment to "protect our flag"—an effort that has yet to be successful.

In 2003, however, the Supreme Court held that a Virginia statute prohibiting the burning of a cross with "an intent to intimidate" did not violate the First Amendment. The Court concluded that a burning cross is an instrument of racial terror so threatening that it overshadows free speech concerns.[26]

The Protection of Commercial Speech

| **Commercial Speech**
Advertising statements, which increasingly have been given First Amendment protection.

Commercial speech usually is defined as advertising statements. Can advertisers use their First Amendment rights to prevent restrictions on the content of commercial advertising? Until the 1970s, the Supreme Court held that such speech was not protected at all by the First Amendment. By the mid-1970s, however, more and more commercial speech had been brought under First Amendment protection. According to Justice Harry A. Blackmun, "Advertising, however tasteless and excessive it sometimes may seem, is nonetheless dissemination of information as to who is producing and selling what product for what reason and at what price."[27] Nevertheless, the Supreme Court will consider a restriction on commercial speech valid as long as it (1) seeks to implement a substantial government interest, (2) directly advances that interest, and (3) goes no further than necessary to accomplish its objective. In particular, a business engaging in commercial speech can be subject to liability for factual inaccuracies in ways that do not apply to noncommercial speech.

Permitted Restrictions on Expression

At various times, restrictions on expression have been permitted. A description of several such restrictions follows.

Clear and Present Danger.   When a person's remarks create a clear and present danger to the peace or public order, they can be curtailed constitutionally. Justice

---

[26]*Virginia v. Black*, 538 U.S. 343 (2003).
[27]*Virginia State Board of Pharmacy v. Virginia Citizens Consumer Council, Inc.*, 425 U.S. 748 (1976).

Oliver Wendell Holmes used this reasoning in 1919 when examining the case of a socialist who had been convicted for violating the Espionage Act by distributing a leaflet that opposed the military draft. Holmes stated:

> The question in every case is whether the words are used in such circumstances and are of such a nature as to create a *clear and present danger* that they will bring about the substantive evils that Congress has a right to prevent. It is a question of proximity and degree.[28] [Emphasis added.]

According to the **clear and present danger test,** then, expression may be restricted if evidence exists that such expression would cause a condition, actual or imminent, that Congress has the power to prevent. Commenting on this test, Justice Louis D. Brandeis in 1920 said, "Correctly applied, it will reserve the right of free speech . . . from suppression by tyrannists, well-meaning majorities, and from abuse by irresponsible, fanatical minorities."[29]

Clear and Present Danger Test
The test proposed by Justice Oliver Wendell Holmes for determining when government may restrict free speech. Restrictions are permissible, he argued, only when speech creates a *clear and present danger* to the public order.

Modifications to the Clear and Present Danger Rule.   Since the clear and present danger rule was first enunciated, the United States Supreme Court has modified it. In *Gitlow v. New York*,[30] the Court introduced the *bad-tendency rule*. According to this rule, speech or other First Amendment freedoms may be curtailed if there is a possibility that such expression might lead to some "evil." In the *Gitlow* case, a member of a left-wing group was convicted of violating New York State's criminal anarchy statute when he published and distributed a pamphlet urging the violent overthrow of the U.S. government. In its majority opinion, the Supreme Court held that although the First Amendment afforded protection against state incursions on freedom of expression, Gitlow could be punished legally in this particular instance because his expression would tend to bring about evils that the state had a right to prevent.

The Supreme Court again modified the clear and present danger test in a 1951 case, *Dennis v. United States*.[31] At the time, there was considerable tension between the United States and the Soviet Union, a Communist-ruled country that included Russia and several other modern-day nations. Twelve members of the American Communist Party were convicted of violating a statute that made it a crime to conspire to teach, advocate, or organize the violent overthrow of any government in the United States. The Supreme Court affirmed the convictions, significantly modifying the clear and present danger test in the process. The Court applied a *grave and probable danger rule*. Under this rule, "the gravity of the 'evil' discounted by its improbability justifies such invasion of free speech as is necessary to avoid the danger." This rule gave much less protection to free speech than did the clear and present danger test.

Some claim that the United States did not achieve true freedom of political speech until 1969. In that year, in *Brandenburg v. Ohio*,[32] the Supreme Court overturned the conviction of a Ku Klux Klan leader for violating a state statute. The statute prohibited anyone from advocating "the duty, necessity, or propriety of sabotage, violence, or unlawful methods of terrorism as a means of accomplishing industrial or political reform." The Court held that the guarantee of free speech does not permit a state "to forbid or proscribe advocacy of the use of force or of law violation except where such advocacy is directed to inciting or producing imminent lawless actions and is likely to incite or produce such action." The incitement test enunciated by the Court in this case is a difficult one for prosecutors to meet. As a

---

[28]*Schenck v. United States*, 249 U.S. 47 (1919).
[29]*Schaefer v. United States*, 251 U.S. 466 (1920).
[30]268 U.S. 652 (1925).
[31]341 U.S. 494 (1951).
[32]395 U.S. 444 (1969).

result, the Court's decision significantly broadened the protection given to advocacy speech.

Unprotected Speech: Obscenity

A large number of state and federal statutes make it a crime to disseminate obscene materials. Generally, the courts have not been willing to extend constitutional protections of free speech to what they consider obscene materials. But what is obscenity? Justice Potter Stewart once stated, in *Jacobellis v. Ohio*,[33] a 1964 case, that even though he could not define *obscenity*, "I know it when I see it." The problem, of course, is that even if it were agreed on, the definition of *obscenity* changes with the times. Victorians deeply disapproved of the "loose" morals of the Elizabethan Age. The works of Mark Twain and Edgar Rice Burroughs at times have been considered obscene (after all, Tarzan and Jane were not legally wedded).

Definitional Problems. The Supreme Court has grappled from time to time with the difficulty of specifying an operationally effective definition of *obscenity*. In 1973, in *Miller v. California*,[34] Chief Justice Warren Burger created a formal list of requirements that must be met for material to be legally obscene. Material is obscene if (1) the average person finds that it violates contemporary community standards; (2) the work taken as a whole appeals to a prurient interest in sex; (3) the work shows patently offensive sexual conduct; and (4) the work lacks serious redeeming literary, artistic, political, or scientific merit. The problem, of course, is that one person's prurient interest is another person's medical interest or artistic pleasure. The Court went on to state that the definition of *prurient interest* would be determined by the community's standards. The Court avoided presenting a definition of *obscenity*, leaving this determination to local and state authorities. Consequently, the *Miller* case has been applied in a widely inconsistent manner.

Protecting Children. The Supreme Court has upheld state laws making it illegal to sell materials showing sexual performances by minors. In 1990, in *Osborne v. Ohio*,[35] the Court ruled that states can outlaw the possession of child pornography in the home. The Court reasoned that the ban on private possession is justified because owning the material perpetuates commercial demand for it and for the exploitation of the children involved. At the federal level, the Child Protection Act of 1984 made it a crime to receive knowingly through the mails sexually explicit depictions of children.

Pornography on the Internet. A significant problem facing Americans and their lawmakers today is how to control obscenity and child pornography that are disseminated by way of the Internet. In 1996, Congress first attempted to protect minors from pornographic materials on the Internet by passing the Communications Decency Act (CDA). The act made it a crime to make available to minors online any "obscene or indecent" message that "depicts or describes, in terms patently offensive as measured by contemporary community standards, sexual or excretory activities or organs." The act was immediately challenged in court as an unconstitutional infringement on free speech. The Supreme Court held that the act imposed unconstitutional restraints on free speech and was therefore invalid.[36] In the eyes of the Court, the terms *indecent* and *patently offensive* covered large amounts of nonpornographic material with serious educational or other value.

---

[33]378 U.S. 184 (1964).
[34]413 U.S. 5 (1973).
[35]495 U.S. 103 (1990).
[36]*Reno v. American Civil Liberties Union*, 521 U.S. 844 (1997).

Later attempts by Congress to curb pornography on the Internet also encountered stumbling blocks. For example, the Child Online Protection Act (COPA) of 1998 banned the distribution of material "harmful to minors" without an age-verification system to separate adult and minor users. In 2002, the Supreme Court upheld a lower court injunction suspending the COPA, and in 2004 the Court again upheld the suspension of the law on the ground that it was probably unconstitutional.[37] In 2000, Congress enacted the Children's Internet Protection Act (CIPA), which requires public schools and libraries to install filtering software to prevent children from viewing Web sites with "adult" content.

Children use computers at a Boston public library. Under the Children's Internet Protection Act (CIPA), public schools and libraries must install filtering software on their computers to prevent children from viewing pornographic material. What problems might the CIPA pose for adult library patrons? (AP Photo/Chitose Suzuki)

Should "Virtual" Pornography Be Deemed a Crime?   In 2001, the Supreme Court agreed to review a case challenging the constitutionality of another federal act attempting to protect minors in the online environment—the Child Pornography Prevention Act (CPPA) of 1996. This act made it illegal to distribute or possess computer-generated images that appear to depict minors engaging in lewd and lascivious behavior. At issue was whether digital child pornography should be considered a crime even though it uses only digitally rendered images and no actual children are involved.

The Supreme Court, noting that virtual child pornography is not the same as child pornography, held that the CPPA's ban on virtual child pornography restrained a substantial amount of lawful speech.[38] The Court stated, "The statute proscribes the visual depiction of an idea—that of teenagers engaging in sexual activity—that is a fact of modern society and has been a theme in art and literature throughout the ages." The Court concluded that the act was overbroad and thus unconstitutional.

Unprotected Speech: Slander

Can you say anything you want about someone else? Not really. Individuals are protected from **defamation of character,** which is defined as wrongfully hurting a person's good reputation. The law imposes a general duty on all persons to refrain from making false, defamatory statements about others. Breaching this duty orally is the wrongdoing called *slander.* Breaching it in writing is the wrongdoing called *libel,* which we discuss later. The government itself does not bring charges of slander or libel. Rather, the defamed person may bring a civil suit for damages.

Legally, **slander** is the public uttering of a false statement that harms the good reputation of another. Slanderous public uttering means that the defamatory statements are made to, or within the hearing of, persons other than the defamed party. If one person calls another dishonest, manipulative, and incompetent to his or her face when no one else is around, that does not constitute slander. The message is

Defamation of Character
Wrongfully hurting a person's good reputation. The law imposes a general duty on all persons to refrain from making false, defamatory statements about others.

Slander
The public uttering of a false statement that harms the good reputation of another. The statement must be made to, or within the hearing of, persons other than the defamed party.

---

[37]*Ashcroft v. American Civil Liberties Union,* 542 U.S. 656 (2004).
[38]*Ashcroft v. Free Speech Coalition,* 535 U.S. 234 (2002).

not communicated to a third party. If, however, a third party accidentally overhears defamatory statements, the courts have generally held that this constitutes a public uttering and therefore slander, which is prohibited.

Campus Speech

In recent years, students have been facing free speech challenges on campuses. One issue has to do with whether a student should have to subsidize, through student activity fees, organizations that promote causes that the student finds objectionable.

Student Activity Fees.   In 2000, this question came before the United States Supreme Court in a case brought by several University of Wisconsin students. The students argued that their mandatory student activity fees—which helped to fund liberal causes with which they disagreed, including gay rights—violated their First Amendment rights of free speech, free association, and free exercise of religion. They contended that they should have the right to choose whether to fund organizations that promoted political and ideological views that were offensive to their personal beliefs. To the surprise of many, the Supreme Court rejected the students' claim and ruled in favor of the university. The Court stated that "the university may determine that its mission is well served if students have the means to engage in dynamic discussions of philosophical, religious, scientific, social, and political subjects in their extracurricular life. If the university reaches this conclusion, it is entitled to impose a mandatory fee to sustain an open dialogue to these ends."[39]

Campus Speech and Behavior Codes.   Another free speech issue is the legitimacy of campus speech and behavior codes. Some state universities have established codes that challenge the boundaries of the protection of free speech provided by the First Amendment. These codes are designed to prohibit so-called hate speech—abusive speech attacking persons on the basis of their ethnicity, race, or other criteria. For example, a University of Michigan code banned "any behavior, verbal or physical, that stigmatizes or victimizes an individual on the basis of race, ethnicity, religion, sex, sexual orientation, creed, national origin, ancestry, age, marital status, handicap" or Vietnam-veteran status. A federal court found that the code violated students' First Amendment rights.[40]

Although the courts generally have held, as in the University of Michigan case, that campus speech codes are unconstitutional restrictions on the right to free speech, such codes continue to exist. Whether hostile speech should be banned on high school campuses has also become an issue. In view of school shootings and other violent behavior in the schools, school officials have become concerned about speech that consists of veiled threats or that could lead to violence. Some schools have even prohibited students from wearing clothing, such as T-shirts bearing verbal messages (such as sexist or racist comments) or symbolic messages (such as the Confederate flag), that might generate "ill will or hatred."

Defenders of campus speech codes argue that they are necessary not only to prevent violence but also to promote equality among different cultural, ethnic, and racial groups on campus and greater sensitivity to the needs and feelings of others. In recent years, law schools even attempted to bar military recruiters from their campuses. The law schools argued that the military's policy toward homosexuals was discriminatory and should not be tolerated on a college campus. To read more about this issue, see this chapter's *Politics and Diversity* feature.

---

[39]*Board of Regents of the University of Wisconsin System v. Southworth*, 529 U.S. 217 (2000).
[40]*Doe v. University of Michigan*, 721 F.Supp. 852 (1989).

POLITICS AND DIVERSITY | Military Recruiters' Access on Campus

As you read in this chapter, colleges and universities have taken significant steps to curb discrimination. Many of their policies have incited serious debate. One such instance captured national attention when law schools took a stand against the U.S. military over perceived discrimination against gay men and lesbians.

"DON'T ASK, DON'T TELL"

In 1993, Congress passed the "don't ask, don't tell" policy concerning homosexuals in the military. The policy basically requires any member of the armed forces to be discharged if he or she admits to being homosexual or having engaged in homosexual acts. "Don't ask, don't tell" was strongly opposed by many U.S. law schools. These schools had policies barring campus access to any potential employer that failed to conform to their antidiscrimination codes. Consequently, numerous law schools began denying military recruiters access to school-sponsored career fairs.

THE SOLOMON AMENDMENT

Obviously, barring military recruiters from campus did not sit well with many government officials. In response, Congress passed the Solomon Amendment, which required all colleges and universities receiving federal funds to open their campuses to military recruiters. Unless the recruiters were granted the same access as any other company or prospective employer, federal funding would be forfeited.

Later, Congress agreed to continue providing financial aid funds, such as Stafford loans, to students at the affected schools. That concession was tempered by subsequent legislation that required federal grants to be revoked from the *entire* university if one of its subdivisions (such as the law school) ran afoul of the Solomon Amendment.

RUMSFELD V. FAIR

In 2003, the law schools and numerous concerned faculty members formed Forum for Academic and Institutional Rights (FAIR) and filed a suit in federal court. The law schools claimed that the Solomon Amendment violated their rights to free speech and freedom of association. The United States Supreme Court disagreed. In March 2006 the Court handed down a unanimous eight-to-zero decision holding the Solomon Amendment constitutional.* Chief Justice John Roberts noted in his opinion that the amendment does not infringe in any way on an institution's freedom of speech. Roberts also held that Congress could even directly force schools to allow recruiting through the "raise and support Armies" clause of the Constitution.

FOR CRITICAL ANALYSIS

What other options might be available to students and faculty who consider military recruiters' presence on campus to be a breach of the school's antidiscrimination code?

*Rumsfeld v. Forum for Academic and Institutional Rights, Inc., 126 S.Ct. 1297 (2006).

Hate Speech on the Internet

Extreme hate speech appears on the Internet, including racist materials and denials of the Holocaust (the murder of millions of Jews by the Nazis during World War II). Can the federal government restrict this type of speech? Should it? Content restrictions can be difficult to enforce. Even if Congress succeeded in passing a law prohibiting particular speech on the Internet, an army of "Internet watchers" would be needed to enforce it. Also, what if other countries attempt to impose their laws that restrict speech on U.S. Web sites? This is not a theoretical issue. In 2000, a French court found Yahoo in violation of French laws banning the display of Nazi memorabilia. In 2001, however, a U.S. district court held that this ruling could not be enforced against Yahoo in the United States.[41]

---

[41]*Yahoo!, Inc. v. La Ligue Contre le Racisme et l'Antisemitisme,* 169 F.Supp.2d 1181 (N.D.Cal. 2001).

Freedom of the Press

Freedom of the press can be regarded as a special instance of freedom of speech. Of course, at the time of the framing of the Constitution, the press meant only newspapers, magazines, and books. As technology has modified the ways in which we disseminate information, the laws touching on freedom of the press have been modified. What can and cannot be printed still occupies an important place in constitutional law, however. (To see how freedom of the press is viewed elsewhere in the world, see this chapter's *Beyond Our Borders* feature.)

Defamation in Writing

Libel
A written defamation of a person's character, reputation, business, or property rights.

Libel is defamation in writing (or in pictures, signs, films, or any other communication that has the potentially harmful qualities of written or printed words). As with slander, libel occurs only if the defamatory statements are observed by a third party. If one person writes a private letter to another wrongfully accusing him or her of embezzling funds, that does not constitute libel. It is interesting that the courts have generally held that dictating a letter to a secretary constitutes communication of the letter's contents to a third party, and therefore, if defamation has occurred, the wrongdoer can be sued.

A 1964 case, *New York Times Co. v. Sullivan*,[42] explored an important question regarding libelous statements made about public officials. The Supreme Court held that only when a statement against a public official was made with **actual malice**—that is, with either knowledge of its falsity or a reckless disregard of the truth—could damages be obtained.

Actual Malice
Either knowledge of a defamatory statement's falsity or a reckless disregard for the truth.

Public Figure
A public official, movie star, or other person known to the public because of his or her position or activities.

The standard set by the Court in the *New York Times* case has since been applied to **public figures** generally. Public figures include not only public officials but also public employees who exercise substantial governmental power and any persons who are generally in the public limelight. Statements made about public figures, especially when they are made through a public medium, usually are related to matters of general public interest; they are made about people who substantially affect all of us. Furthermore, public figures generally have some access to a public medium for answering disparaging falsehoods about themselves, whereas private individuals do not. For these reasons, public figures have a greater burden of proof (they must prove that the statements were made with actual malice) in defamation cases than do private individuals.

A Free Press versus a Fair Trial: Gag Orders

Another major issue relating to freedom of the press concerns media coverage of criminal trials. The Sixth Amendment to the Constitution guarantees the right of criminal suspects to a fair trial. In other words, the accused have rights. The First Amendment guarantees freedom of the press. What if the two rights appear to be in conflict? Which one prevails?

Gag Order
An order issued by a judge restricting the publication of news about a trial or a pretrial hearing to protect the accused's right to a fair trial.

Jurors certainly may be influenced by reading news stories about the trial in which they are participating. In the 1970s, judges increasingly issued **gag orders,** which restricted the publication of news about a trial in progress or even a pretrial hearing. In a landmark 1976 case, *Nebraska Press Association v. Stuart*,[43] the Supreme Court unanimously ruled that a Nebraska judge's gag order had violated the First Amendment's guarantee of freedom of the press. Chief Justice Warren

---

[42]376 U.S. 254 (1964).
[43]427 U.S. 539 (1976).

BEYOND OUR BORDERS | An Uproar over Cartoons

An international imbroglio erupted when a Danish newspaper printed cartoon images deemed offensive by many Muslims. The cartoons, many of which depicted the Prophet Muhammad unfavorably and linked the Islamic faith to international terrorism, enraged Muslims all over the globe. When newspapers in some other European countries reprinted the offensive cartoons, riots broke out, European embassies were attacked, and already tense relations between Muslims and Westerners degraded. The dispute over the cartoons opened an international debate about freedom of expression.

THE FREEDOM TO OFFEND?

Without question, the caricatures of Muhammad were offensive. In the Islamic faith, creating any kind of image of the Prophet or Allah (God) is strictly forbidden. Thus, the offensive nature of the cartoons merely added further insult to an already taboo portrayal. Moreover, many Muslims living in Europe perceived the cartoons as yet another example of racial and religious discrimination.

In contrast, many Westerners saw the publication of the cartoons as a freedom of expression issue. Nonetheless, a majority of Westerners viewed the cartoons as offensive and unnecessarily inflammatory. The European newspaper editors argued that they had every right to publish the images, even as they apologized for offending the Muslim community. The editors felt that freedom of expression should not be restrained, regardless of the reaction it may cause. French and German newspapers insisted that democratic freedoms include the "right to blasphemy."

REVEALING DEEPER TENSIONS AND DIFFERENCES

The cartoon dispute also revealed a deeper cultural rift between many Muslims and Westerners. Significant numbers of Muslims living in Europe and North America have been revolted by what they consider to be overly "liberal" attitudes toward personal freedom, individualism, sex, family structure, and religion. For their part, many Westerners have been critical of what they perceive as Muslims' religious fundamentalism and immigrant Muslims' unwillingness to assimilate culturally and politically to their new surroundings.

Most Westerners were shocked at the reaction spurred by the cartoons. The violent attacks on European and American embassies in the Middle East and other Muslim areas were perhaps the most bewildering. In Gaza, for example, gunmen appeared at the offices of the European Union, firing automatic weapons and threatening further violence unless the offending nations apologized for the cartoons.

U.S. MEDIA AND THE CARTOONS

Most U.S. media sources decided not to reprint the offending cartoons. Some outlets, such as NBC News, chose to offer links to the images via their Web sites. Nonetheless, the cartoons were a hot topic on television news channels and in newspaper editorial sections across the country. Some defended the cartoons as free speech, while others focused on the need to be more respectful of sensitive religious and cultural topics. Columnist Kathleen Parker summed up the difficulty of reconciling Western notions of free expression with the fundamentalist reactions of some Muslims: "Until Muslim nations and peoples get the idea that free expression means freedom to offend as well as the necessary correlative—to be offended—we have a problem."

FOR CRITICAL ANALYSIS

Some commentators spoke of the need to find a "balance" between freedom of expression and respect for religious beliefs. Do you believe that such a balance can be found? Is it desirable to restrict freedom of expression in some instances? Explain.

Burger indicated that even pervasive adverse pretrial publicity did not necessarily lead to an unfair trial and that prior restraints on publication were not justified. Some justices even went so far as to suggest that gag orders are never justified.

In spite of the *Nebraska Press Association* ruling, the Court has upheld certain types of gag orders. In *Gannett Co. v. De Pasquale*[44] in 1979, for example, the highest court held that if a judge found a reasonable probability that news publicity would harm a defendant's right to a fair trial, the court could impose a gag rule: "Members of the public have no constitutional right under the Sixth and Fourteenth Amendments to attend criminal trials."

---

[44]443 U.S. 368 (1979).

Radio "shock jock" Howard Stern offended the sensibilities of the Federal Communications Commission (FCC). That regulatory body fined Stern's radio station owner hundreds of thousands of dollars for Stern's purportedly obscene outbursts on radio in 1992 and again in 2004. The extent to which the FCC can regulate speech over the air involves the First Amendment. But the current FCC regulation does not apply to pay-for-service satellite radio, pay-for-service cable TV, or satellite TV. To take advantage of this, in December of 2005 Stern took his show to satellite radio, thus, for now, evading FCC regulation. Why is it that what is permissible and acceptable on radio and TV today probably would have been considered obscene three decades ago? (Bill Swersey/Getty Images)

The *Nebraska* and *Gannett* cases, however, involved pretrial hearings. Could a judge impose a gag order on an entire trial, including pretrial hearings? In 1980, in *Richmond Newspapers, Inc. v. Virginia*,[45] the Court ruled that actual trials must be open to the public except under unusual circumstances.

Films, Radio, and TV

As we have noted, only in a few cases has the Supreme Court upheld prior restraint of published materials. The Court's reluctance to accept prior restraint is less evident with respect to motion pictures. In the first half of the twentieth century, films were routinely submitted to local censorship boards. In 1968, the Supreme Court ruled that a film can be banned only under a law that provides for a prompt hearing at which the film is shown to be obscene. Today, few local censorship boards exist. Instead, the film industry regulates itself primarily through the industry's rating system.

Radio and television broadcasting has the least First Amendment protection. Broadcasting initially received less protection than the printed media because, at that time, the number of airwave frequencies was limited. In 1934, the national government established the Federal Communications Commission (FCC) to regulate electromagnetic wave frequencies. No one has a right to use the airwaves without a license granted by the FCC. The FCC grants licenses for limited periods and imposes a variety of regulations on broadcasting. For example, the FCC can impose sanctions on radio or TV stations that broadcast "filthy words," even if the words are not legally obscene.

The Right to Assemble and to Petition the Government

The First Amendment prohibits Congress from making any law that abridges "the right of the people peaceably to assemble, and to petition the Government for a redress of grievances." Inherent in such a right is the ability of private citizens to

---

[45]448 U.S. 555 (1980).

communicate their ideas on public issues to government officials, as well as to other individuals. The Supreme Court has often put this freedom on a par with freedom of speech and freedom of the press. Nonetheless, it has allowed municipalities to require permits for parades, sound trucks, and demonstrations so that public officials can control traffic or prevent demonstrations from turning into riots.

The freedom to demonstrate became a major issue in 1977 when the American Nazi Party sought to march through Skokie, Illinois, a largely Jewish suburb where many Holocaust survivors resided. The American Civil Liberties Union defended the Nazis' right to march (in spite of its opposition to the Nazi philosophy). The Supreme Court let stand a lower court's ruling that the city of Skokie had violated the Nazis' First Amendment guarantees by denying them a permit to march.[46]

Street Gangs

An issue that has surfaced in recent years is whether communities can prevent gang members from gathering together on the streets without violating their right of assembly or associated rights. Although some actions taken by cities to prevent gang members from gathering together or "loitering" in public places have passed constitutional muster, others have not. For example, in a 1997 case, the California Supreme Court upheld a lower court's order preventing gang members from appearing in public together.[47] In 1999, however, the United States Supreme Court held that Chicago's "antiloitering" ordinance violated the constitutional right to due process of law because, among other things, it left too much power to the police to determine what constituted "loitering."[48]

---

[46]*Smith v. Collin*, 439 U.S. 916 (1978).
[47]*Gallo v. Acuna*, 14 Cal.4th 1090 (1997).
[48]*City of Chicago v. Morales*, 527 U.S. 41 (1999).

These protestors are going to a rally for immigration rights that was held in Washington, D.C., in the spring of 2006. At the time, dozens of other marches occurred in an action touted as "a campaign for immigrants' dignity" because Congress was considering a new immigration bill. The House version of that bill would have negatively impacted millions of illegal immigrants in the United States. Does the constitutional right to petition the government extend to those who do not have legal resident status in this country? (AP Photo/Evan Vucci)

Online Assembly

A question for Americans today is whether individuals should have the right to "assemble" online for the purpose of advocating violence against certain groups (such as physicians who perform abortions) or advocating values that are opposed to our democracy (such as terrorism). While some online advocacy groups promote interests consistent with American political values, other groups have as their goal the destruction of those values. Whether First Amendment freedoms should be sacrificed (by the government's monitoring of Internet communications, for example) in the interests of national security is a question that will no doubt be debated for some time to come, as was discussed in this chapter's opening *What If . . .* feature.

More Liberties under Scrutiny: Matters of Privacy

No explicit reference is made anywhere in the Constitution to a person's right to privacy. Until the second half of the 1990s, the courts did not take a very positive approach toward the right to privacy. For example, during Prohibition, suspected bootleggers' telephones were tapped routinely, and the information obtained was used as a legal basis for prosecution. In *Olmstead v. United States*[49] in 1928, the Supreme Court upheld such an invasion of privacy. Justice Louis Brandeis, a champion of personal freedoms, strongly dissented from the majority decision in this case. He argued that the framers of the Constitution gave every citizen the right to be left alone. He called such a right "the most comprehensive of rights and the right most valued by civilized men."

In the 1960s, the highest court began to modify the majority view. In 1965, in *Griswold v. Connecticut*,[50] the Supreme Court overturned a Connecticut law that effectively prohibited the use of contraceptives, holding that the law violated the right to privacy. Justice William O. Douglas formulated a unique way of reading this right into the Bill of Rights. He claimed that the First, Third, Fourth, Fifth, and Ninth Amendments created "penumbras [shadows], formed by emanations [things sent out from] from those guarantees that help give them life and substance," and he went on to describe zones of privacy that are guaranteed by these rights. When we read the Ninth Amendment, we can see the foundation for his reasoning: "The enumeration in the Constitution, of certain rights, shall not be construed to deny or disparage [belittle] others retained by the people." In other words, just because the Constitution, including its amendments, does not specifically talk about the right to privacy does not mean that this right is denied to the people.

Some of today's most controversial issues relate to privacy rights. One issue involves the erosion of privacy rights in an information age, as computers make it easier to compile and distribute personal information. Other issues concern abortion and the "right to die." Since the terrorist attacks of September 11, 2001, Americans have faced another crucial question regarding privacy rights: To what extent should Americans sacrifice privacy rights in the interests of national security?

Privacy Rights in an Information Age

An important privacy issue, created in part by new technology, is the amassing of information on individuals by government agencies and private businesses, such as marketing firms. Personal information on the average American citizen is filed away

---

[49]277 U.S. 438 (1928). This decision was overruled later in *Katz v. United States*, 389 U.S. 347 (1967).
[50]381 U.S. 479 (1965).

in dozens of agencies—such as the Social Security Administration and the Internal Revenue Service. Because of the threat of indiscriminate use of private information by unauthorized individuals, Congress passed the Privacy Act in 1974. This was the first law regulating the use of federal government information about private individuals. Under the Privacy Act, every citizen has the right to obtain copies of personal records collected by federal agencies and to correct inaccuracies in such records.

The ease with which personal information can be obtained by using the Internet for marketing and other purposes has led to unique privacy issues. Some fear that privacy rights in personal information may soon be a thing of the past. Whether privacy rights can survive in an information age is a question that Americans and their leaders continue to confront.

Privacy Rights and Abortion

Historically, abortion was not a criminal offense before the "quickening" of the fetus (the first movement of the fetus in the uterus, usually between the sixteenth and eighteenth weeks of pregnancy). During the last half of the nineteenth century, however, state laws became more severe. By 1973, performing an abortion at any time during pregnancy was a criminal offense in a majority of the states.

Roe v. Wade. In 1973, in *Roe v. Wade*,[51] the United States Supreme Court accepted the argument that the laws against abortion violated "Jane Roe's" right to privacy under the Constitution. The Court held that during the first trimester (three months) of pregnancy, abortion was an issue solely between a woman and her physician. The state could not limit abortions except to require that they be performed by licensed physicians. During the second trimester, to protect the health of the mother, the state was allowed to specify the conditions under which an abortion could be performed. During the final trimester, the state could regulate or even outlaw abortions except when necessary to preserve the life or health of the mother.

---

[51]410 U.S. 113 (1973). Jane Roe was not the real name of the woman in this case. It is a common legal pseudonym used to protect a person's privacy.

On the thirty-third anniversary of *Roe v. Wade*, opposing sides on the abortion issue argued with each other in front of the United States Supreme Court building in Washington, D.C. What was the major argument against laws prohibiting abortion that the Court used in the *Roe* case?
(AP Photo/Pablo Martinez Monsivais)

After *Roe*, the Supreme Court issued decisions in a number of cases defining and redefining the boundaries of state regulation of abortion. During the 1980s, the Court twice struck down laws that required a woman who wished to have an abortion to undergo counseling designed to discourage abortions. In the late 1980s and early 1990s, however, the Court took a more conservative approach. For example, in *Webster v. Reproductive Health Services*[52] in 1989, the Court upheld a Missouri statute that, among other things, banned the use of public hospitals or other taxpayer-supported facilities for performing abortions. And, in *Planned Parenthood v. Casey*[53] in 1992, the Court upheld a Pennsylvania law that required preabortion counseling, a waiting period of twenty-four hours, and, for girls under the age of eighteen, parental or judicial permission. As a result, abortions are now more difficult to obtain in some states than others.

The Controversy Continues.   Abortion continues to be a divisive issue. Right-to-life forces continue to push for laws banning abortion, to endorse political candidates who support their views, and to organize protests. Because of several episodes of violence attending protests at abortion clinics, in 1994 Congress passed the Freedom of Access to Clinic Entrances Act. The act prohibits protesters from blocking entrances to such clinics. The Supreme Court ruled in 1993 that such protesters can be prosecuted under laws governing racketeering, and in 1998 a federal court in Illinois convicted right-to-life protesters under these laws. In 1997, the Supreme Court upheld the constitutionality of prohibiting protesters from entering a fifteen-foot "buffer zone" around abortion clinics and from giving unwanted counseling to those entering the clinics.[54] In 2006, however, the Supreme Court unanimously reversed its earlier decision that antiabortion protesters could be prosecuted under laws governing racketeering.[55]

In a 2000 decision, the Court upheld a Colorado law requiring demonstrators to stay at least eight feet away from people entering and leaving clinics unless people consented to be approached. The Court concluded that the law's restrictions on speech-related conduct did not violate the free speech rights of abortion protesters.[56]

Demonstrators hold up signs as they protest South Dakota's new abortion ban outside the federal court building in downtown Sioux Falls, South Dakota in March 2006. (AP Photo/Nati Harnik)

In the same year, the Supreme Court again addressed the abortion issue directly when it reviewed a Nebraska law banning "partial-birth" abortions. Similar laws had been passed by at least twenty-seven states. A partial-birth abortion, which physicians call intact dilation and extraction, is a procedure that can be used during the second trimester of pregnancy. Abortion rights advocates claim that in limited circumstances the procedure is the safest way to perform an abortion, and that the government should never outlaw specific medical procedures. Opponents argue that the procedure has no medical merit and that it ends the life of a fetus that might be able to live outside the womb. The Supreme Court invalidated the Nebraska law on the grounds that, as written, the law could be used to ban other abortion procedures and it contained no provisions for protecting the health of the pregnant woman.[57] In 2003, legislation similar to the Nebraska statute was passed by the U.S. Congress and signed into law by president George W. Bush. It was immediately challenged in court.

In a move that will likely set off another long legal battle, in 2006 the South Dakota legislature passed a law that banned almost all forms of abortion in the state. The bill's supporters hope that it will eventually force the United States Supreme Court to reconsider *Roe v. Wade*. Opponents of the bill have already filed suit.

---

[52]492 U.S. 490 (1989).
[53]505 U.S. 833 (1992).
[54]*Schenck v. ProChoice Network*, 519 U.S. 357 (1997).
[55]*Scheidler v. National Organization for Women*, 126 S.Ct. 1264 (2006).
[56]*Hill v. Colorado*, 530 U.S. 703 (2000).
[57]*Stenberg v. Carhart*, 530 U.S. 914 (2000).

Privacy Rights and the "Right to Die"

A 1976 case involving Karen Ann Quinlan was one of the first publicized right-to-die cases.[58] The parents of Quinlan, a young woman who had been in a coma for nearly a year and who had been kept alive during that time by a respirator, wanted her respirator removed. In 1976, the New Jersey Supreme Court ruled that the right to privacy includes the right of a patient to refuse treatment and that patients unable to speak can exercise that right through a family member or guardian. In 1990, the Supreme Court took up the issue. In *Cruzan v. Director, Missouri Department of Health,*[59] the Court stated that a patient's life-sustaining treatment can be withdrawn at the request of a family member only if there is "clear and convincing evidence" that the patient did not want such treatment.

What If There Is No Living Will?   Since the 1976 *Quinlan* decision, most states have enacted laws permitting people to designate their wishes concerning life-sustaining procedures in "living wills" or durable health-care powers of attorney. These laws and the Supreme Court's *Cruzan* decision have resolved the right-to-die controversy for situations in which the patient has drafted a living will. Disputes are still possible if there is no living will. An example is the case of Terri Schiavo. The husband of the Florida woman, who had been in a persistent vegetative state for over a decade, sought to have her feeding tube removed on the basis of oral statements that she would not want her life prolonged in such circumstances. Schiavo's parents fought this move in court but lost on the ground that a spouse, not a parent, is the appropriate legal guardian for a married person. Although the Florida legislature passed a law allowing Governor Jeb Bush to overrule the courts, the state Supreme Court held that the law violated the state constitution.[60]

The case escalated into a national drama in March 2005 when the U.S. Congress intervened and passed a law allowing Schiavo's case to be heard in the federal court system. The federal courts, however, essentially agreed with the Florida state courts' findings and refused to order the reconnection of the feeding tube, which had been disconnected a few days earlier. After twice appealing to the United States Supreme Court without success, the parents gave up hope, and Schiavo died shortly thereafter.

Physician-Assisted Suicide.   In the 1990s, another issue surfaced: Do privacy rights include the right of terminally ill people to end their lives through physician-assisted suicide? Until 1996, the courts consistently upheld state laws that prohibited this practice, either through specific statutes or under their general homicide statutes. In 1996, after two federal appellate courts ruled that state laws banning assisted suicide (in Washington and New York) were unconstitutional, the issue reached the United States Supreme Court. In 1997, in *Washington v. Glucksberg,*[61] the Court stated, clearly and categorically, that the liberty interest protected by the Constitution does not include a right to commit suicide, with or without assistance. In effect, the Supreme Court left the decision in the hands of the states. Since then, assisted suicide has been allowed in only one state—Oregon. In 2006, the Supreme Court upheld Oregon's physician-assisted suicide law against a challenge from the Bush administration.[62]

In 2006, the United States Supreme Court upheld Oregon's position on its physician-assisted suicide law. In this photo, Scott Rice, whose wife used Oregon's law to end her life, shows an artist's sketch of the Court's proceedings. How can the right to privacy be used by proponents of Oregon's death with dignity act? (AP Photo/Don Ryan)

---

[58]*In re Quinlan,* 70 N.J. 10 (1976).
[59]497 U.S. 261 (1990).
[60]*Bush v. Schiavo,* 885 So.2d 321 (Fla. 2004).
[61]521 U.S. 702 (1997).
[62]*Gonzales v. Oregon,* 126 S.Ct. 904 (2006).

Privacy Rights versus Security Issues

As former Supreme Court justice Thurgood Marshall once said, "Grave threats to liberty often come in times of urgency, when constitutional rights seem too extravagant to endure." Not surprisingly, antiterrorist legislation since the attacks on September 11, 2001, has eroded certain basic rights, in particular the Fourth Amendment protections against unreasonable searches and seizures. Current legislation allows the government to conduct "roving" wiretaps.

Previously, roving wiretaps could only be requested for persons suspected of one of a small number of serious crimes. Now if persons are suspected of planning a terrorist attack, they can be monitored no matter what form of electronic communication they use. Such roving wiretaps contravene the Supreme Court's interpretation of the Fourth Amendment, which requires a judicial warrant to describe the *place* to be searched, not just the person. One of the goals of the framers was to avoid *general* searches. Further, once a judge approves an application for a roving wiretap, when, how, and where the monitoring occurs will be left to the discretion of law enforcement agents. Supporters of these new procedures say that they allow agents to monitor individuals as they move about the nation. Previously, a warrant issued in one federal district might not be valid in another.

Moreover, President George W. Bush approved a plan by the National Security Agency to eavesdrop on telephone calls between individuals overseas and those in the United States if one party was a terrorist suspect. This plan was carried out without warrants because the administration claimed that speed was more important. Critics called for immediate termination of such eavesdropping.

The USA Patriot Act.   Much of the government's failure to anticipate the attacks of September 11, 2001, has been attributed to a lack of cooperation among government agencies. At that time, barriers prevented information sharing between the law enforcement and intelligence arms of the government. A major objective of the USA Patriot Act was to lift those barriers. Lawmakers claimed that the Patriot Act would improve lines of communication between agencies such as the Federal Bureau of Investigation (FBI) and the Central Intelligence Agency (CIA), thereby allowing the government to better anticipate terrorist plots. With improved communication, various agencies could more effectively coordinate their efforts in combating terrorism.

In addition, the Patriot Act eased restrictions on the government's ability to investigate and arrest suspected terrorists. Because of the secretive nature of terrorist groups, supporters of the Patriot Act argue that the government must have greater latitude in pursuing leads on potential terrorist activity. The act authorizes law enforcement officials to secretly search a suspected terrorist's home. It also allows the government to monitor a suspect's Internet activities, phone conversations, financial records, and book purchases. For the first time in American history, the government can even open a suspect's mail. Although a number of these search and surveillance tactics have long been a part of criminal investigations, the Patriot Act expanded their scope and streamlined the process of obtaining warrants to use them.

Civil Liberties Concerns.   Proponents of the Patriot Act insist that ordinary, law-abiding citizens have nothing to fear from the government's increased search and surveillance powers. Groups such as the American Civil Liberties Union (ACLU) have objected to the Patriot Act, however, arguing that it poses a grave threat to constitutionally guaranteed rights and liberties. Under the Patriot Act, FBI agents are required to certify the need for search warrants to the court, but the court cannot, in fact, reject the request for a warrant. In addition, an individual or financial institution that is served with such a warrant cannot speak about the government's investigation to anyone. Thus, many argue that this provision of the Patriot Act contradicts the First Amendment by making free speech a crime. Finally, if the gov-

The American Civil Liberties Union (ACLU) has consistently opposed the Patriot Act as an unconstitutional violation of a citizen's right to privacy. These information sheets were passed out to both the Republican and Democratic delegates at the national conventions in 2004. What argument does the federal government use to support the Patriot Act? (Courtesy of **www.aclu.org**)

ernment decides to take a suspected terrorist into custody, the suspect can be summarily denied bail—a breach of the Eighth Amendment.

Opponents of the Patriot Act fear that these expanded powers of investigation might be used to silence government critics or to threaten members of interest groups who oppose government polices today or in the future. Congress debated all of these issues in 2005 and then renewed most of the provisions of the act in 2006.

The Great Balancing Act: The Rights of the Accused versus the Rights of Society

The United States has one of the highest murder rates in the industrialized world. It is not surprising, therefore, that many citizens have extremely strong opinions about the rights of those accused of violent crimes. When an accused person, especially one who has confessed to some criminal act, is set free because of an apparent legal "technicality," many people believe that the rights of the accused are being given more weight than the rights of society and of potential or actual victims. Why, then, give criminal suspects rights? The answer is partly to avoid convicting innocent people, but mostly because all criminal suspects have the right to due process of law and fair treatment.

The courts and the police must constantly engage in a balancing act of competing rights. At the basis of all discussions about the appropriate balance is, of course, the U.S. Bill of Rights. The Fourth, Fifth, Sixth, and Eighth Amendments deal specifically with the rights of criminal defendants. (You will learn about some of your rights under the Fourth Amendment in the *Making a Difference* feature at the end of this chapter.)

Rights of the Accused

The basic rights of criminal defendants are outlined next. When appropriate, the specific constitutional provision or amendment on which a right is based is also given.

Limits on the Conduct of Police Officers and Prosecutors
- No unreasonable or unwarranted searches and seizures (Amend. IV).
- No arrest except on probable cause (Amend. IV).
- No coerced confessions or illegal interrogation (Amend. V).
- No entrapment.
- On questioning, a suspect must be informed of her or his rights.

Defendant's Pretrial Rights
- **Writ of *habeas corpus*** (Article I, Section 9).
- Prompt **arraignment** (Amend. VI).
- Legal counsel (Amend. VI).
- Reasonable bail (Amend. VIII).
- To be informed of charges (Amend. VI).
- To remain silent (Amend. V).

Trial Rights
- Speedy and public trial before a jury (Amend. VI).
- Impartial jury selected from a cross section of the community (Amend. VI).
- Trial atmosphere free of prejudice, fear, and outside interference.
- No compulsory self-incrimination (Amend. V).
- Adequate counsel (Amend. VI).
- No cruel and unusual punishment (Amend. VIII).
- Appeal of convictions.
- No double jeopardy (Amend. V).

Extending the Rights of the Accused

During the 1960s, the Supreme Court, under Chief Justice Earl Warren, significantly expanded the rights of accused persons. In *Gideon v. Wainwright*,[63] a case decided in 1963, the Court held that if a person is accused of a felony and cannot afford an attorney, an attorney must be made available to the accused person at the government's expense. Although the Sixth Amendment to the Constitution provides for the right to counsel, the Supreme Court had established a precedent twenty-one years earlier in *Betts v. Brady*,[64] when it held that only criminal defendants in capital (death penalty) cases automatically had a right to legal counsel.

Miranda v. Arizona. In 1966, the Court issued its decision in *Miranda v. Arizona*.[65] The case involved Ernesto Miranda, who was arrested and charged with the kidnapping and rape of a young woman. After two hours of questioning, Miranda confessed and was later convicted. Miranda's lawyer appealed his conviction, arguing that the police had never informed Miranda that he had a right to remain silent and a right to be represented by counsel. The Court, in ruling in Miranda's favor, enunciated the *Miranda* rights that are now familiar to virtually all Americans:

> Prior to any questioning, the person must be warned that he has a right to remain silent, that any statement he does make may be used against him, and that he has a right to the presence of an attorney, either retained or appointed.

Two years after the Supreme Court's *Miranda* decision, Congress passed the Omnibus Crime Control and Safe Streets Act of 1968. Section 3501 of the act re-

| Writ of *Habeas Corpus*
Habeas corpus means, literally, "you have the body." A writ of *habeas corpus* is an order that requires jailers to bring a prisoner before a court or judge and explain why the person is being held.

| Arraignment
The first act in a criminal proceeding, in which the defendant is brought before a court to hear the charges against him or her and enter a plea of guilty or not guilty.

---

[63]372 U.S. 335 (1963).
[64]316 U.S. 455 (1942).
[65]384 U.S. 436 (1966).

This man is being read his *Miranda* rights by the arresting officer. Suspects often waive, or forgo, their *Miranda* rights. Why might arrested persons choose not to exercise these rights? (Elana Rooraid/PhotoEdit)

instated a rule that had been in effect for 180 years before *Miranda*—that statements by defendants can be used against them if the statements were voluntarily made. The Justice Department immediately disavowed Section 3501 as unconstitutional and has continued to hold this position. As a result, Section 3501, although it was never repealed, has never been enforced. In 2000, in a surprise move, a federal appellate court held that the all-but-forgotten provision was enforceable, but the Supreme Court held that the *Miranda* warnings were constitutionally based and could not be overruled by a legislative act.[66]

Exceptions to the *Miranda* Rule.   As part of a continuing attempt to balance the rights of accused persons against the rights of society, the Supreme Court has made a number of exceptions to the *Miranda* rule. In 1984, for example, the Court recognized a "public-safety" exception to the rule. The need to protect the public warranted the admissibility of statements made by the defendant (in this case, indicating where he had placed a gun) as evidence in a trial, even though the defendant had not been informed of his *Miranda* rights.

In 1985, the Court further held that a confession need not be excluded even though the police failed to inform a suspect in custody that his attorney had tried to reach him by telephone. In an important 1991 decision, the Court stated that a suspect's conviction will not be automatically overturned if the suspect was coerced into making a confession. If the other evidence admitted at trial is strong enough to justify the conviction without the confession, then the fact that the confession was obtained illegally in effect can be ignored. In yet another case, in 1994, the Supreme Court ruled that suspects must unequivocally and assertively state their right to counsel in order to stop police questioning. Saying, "Maybe I should talk to a lawyer" during an interrogation after being taken into custody is not enough. The Court held that police officers are not required to decipher the suspect's intentions in such situations.

---

[66]*Dickerson v. United States*, 530 U.S. 428 (2000).

| **Exclusionary Rule**
A policy forbidding the admission at trial of illegally seized evidence.

Video Recording of Interrogations.   In view of the numerous exceptions, there are no guarantees that the *Miranda* rule will survive indefinitely. Increasingly, though, law enforcement personnel are using digital cameras to record interrogations. According to some scholars, the recording of *all* custodial interrogations would satisfy the Fifth Amendment's prohibition against coercion and in the process render the *Miranda* warnings unnecessary. Others argue, however, that recorded interrogations can be misleading.

The Exclusionary Rule

At least since 1914, judicial policy has prohibited the admission of illegally seized evidence at trials in federal courts. This is the so-called **exclusionary rule.** Improperly obtained evidence, no matter how telling, cannot be used by prosecutors. This includes evidence obtained by police in violation of a suspect's *Miranda* rights or of the Fourth Amendment. The Fourth Amendment protects against unreasonable searches and seizures and provides that a judge may issue a search warrant to a police officer only on *probable cause* (a demonstration of facts that permit a reasonable belief that a crime has been committed). The question that must be determined by the courts is what constitutes an "unreasonable" search and seizure.

The reasoning behind the exclusionary rule is that it forces police officers to gather evidence properly, in which case their due diligence will be rewarded by a conviction. Nevertheless, the exclusionary rule has always had critics who argue that it permits guilty persons to be freed because of innocent errors.

This rule was first extended to state court proceedings in a 1961 United States Supreme Court decision, *Mapp v. Ohio.*[67] In this case, the Court overturned the conviction of Dollree Mapp for the possession of obscene materials. Police found pornographic books in her apartment after searching it without a search warrant and despite her refusal to let them in.

Over the last several decades, the Supreme Court has diminished the scope of the exclusionary rule by creating some exceptions to its applicability. For example, in 1984 the Court held that illegally obtained evidence could be admitted at trial if law enforcement personnel could prove that they would have obtained the evidence legally anyway. In another case decided in the same year, the Court held that a police officer who used a technically incorrect search warrant form to obtain evidence had acted in good faith and therefore the evidence was admissible at trial. The Court thus created the "good faith" exception to the exclusionary rule.

| The Death Penalty

Capital punishment remains one of the most debated aspects of our criminal justice system. Those in favor of the death penalty maintain that it serves as a deterrent to serious crime and satisfies society's need for justice and fair play. Those opposed to the death penalty do not believe it has any deterrent value and hold that it constitutes a barbaric act in an otherwise civilized society.

Cruel and Unusual Punishment?

The Eighth Amendment prohibits cruel and unusual punishment. Throughout history, "cruel and unusual" referred to punishments that were more serious than the crimes—the phrase referred to torture and to executions that prolonged the agony of dying. The Supreme Court never interpreted "cruel and unusual" to prohibit all forms of capital punishment in all circumstances. Indeed, a number of states had imposed the death penalty for a variety of crimes and allowed juries to decide when

---

[67]367 U.S. 643 (1961).

A death penalty opponent at a rally in California. The rally took place at the capitol building in Sacramento. A major death penalty issue is whether the penalty has a deterrent effect. Why might the death penalty have such an effect—and why might it not? (AP Photo/Rich Pedroncelli)

the condemned could be sentenced to death. Many believed, however, and in 1972 the Supreme Court agreed, in *Furman v. Georgia*,[68] that the imposition of the death penalty was random and arbitrary.

The Supreme Court's 1972 decision stated that the death penalty, as then applied, violated the Eighth and Fourteenth Amendments. The Court ruled that capital punishment is not necessarily cruel and unusual if the criminal has killed or attempted to kill someone. In its opinion, the Court invited the states to enact more precise laws so that the death penalty would be applied more consistently. By 1976, twenty-five states had adopted a two-stage, or *bifurcated*, procedure for capital cases. In the first stage, a jury determines the guilt or innocence of the defendant for a crime that has been determined by statute to be punishable by death. If the defendant is found guilty, the jury reconvenes in the second stage and considers all relevant evidence to decide whether the death sentence is, in fact, warranted.

In *Gregg v. Georgia*,[69] the Supreme Court ruled in favor of Georgia's bifurcated process, holding that the state's legislative guidelines had removed the ability of a jury to "wantonly and freakishly impose the death penalty." The Court upheld similar procedures in Texas and Florida, establishing a "road map" for all states to follow that would assure them protection from lawsuits based on Eighth Amendment grounds. On January 17, 1977, Gary Mark Gilmore became the first American to be executed (by Utah) under the new laws.

The Death Penalty Today

Today, thirty-eight states (see Figure 4–1 on the following page) and the federal government have capital punishment laws based on the guidelines established by the *Gregg* case. State governments are responsible for almost all executions in this country. The executions of Timothy McVeigh and Juan Raul Garza in 2001 marked the first death sentences carried out by the federal government since 1963. At this time, there are about 3,700 prisoners on death row across the nation.

---

[68]408 U.S. 238 (1972).
[69]428 U.S. 153 (1976).

The number of executions per year reached a high in 1998 at ninety-eight and then began to fall. Some believe that the declining number of executions reflects the waning support among Americans for the imposition of the death penalty. In 1994, polls indicated that 80 percent of Americans supported the death penalty. Recent polls, however, suggest that this number has dropped to between 50 and 60 percent, depending on the poll.

The number of executions may decline even further due to the Supreme Court's 2002 ruling in *Ring v. Arizona*.[70] The Court held that only juries, not judges, could impose the death penalty, thus invalidating the laws of five states that allowed judges to make this decision. The ruling meant that the death sentences of 168 death row inmates would have to be reconsidered by the relevant courts. The sentences of many of these inmates have been commuted to life in prison.

Time Limits for Death Row Appeals

In 1996, Congress passed the Anti-Terrorism and Effective Death Penalty Act. The law limits access to the federal courts for all defendants convicted in state courts. It also imposes a severe time limit on death row appeals. The law requires federal judges to hear these appeals and issue their opinions within a specified time period. Many are concerned that the shortened appeals process increases the possibility that innocent persons may be put to death. Recently, DNA testing has shown that some innocent people may have been convicted unjustly of murder. Since 1973, more than one hundred prisoners have been freed from death row after new evidence suggested that they were convicted wrongfully. On average, it takes about seven years to exonerate someone on death row. Currently, however, the time between conviction and execution has been shortened from an average of ten to twelve years to an average of six to eight years.

[70]536 U.S. 548 (2002).

FIGURE 4–1 | THE STATES AND THE DEATH PENALTY: EXECUTIONS SINCE 1976 AND THE DEATH ROW POPULATION

Today, as shown in this figure, thirty-eight states and the federal government have laws permitting capital punishment. On June 24, 2004, the New York Court of Appeals (that state's highest court) ruled that New York's death penalty law violated the state constitution. On December 17, 2004, Kansas's death penalty statute was declared unconstitutional. Also, New Hampshire has a death penalty statute, but that state has not sentenced any defendants to death since 1972. Connecticut, Kansas, New Jersey, and South Dakota have inmates on death row, but none of these states has actually executed anyone since 1972.

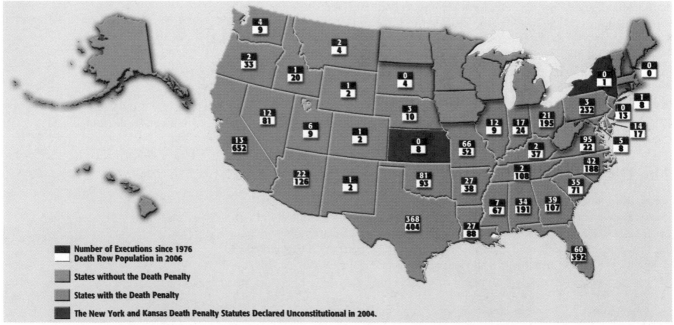

Sources: U.S. Department of Justice, Office of Justice Programs, Bureau of Justice Statistics; and **www.deathpenaltyinfo.org**.

MAKING A DIFFERENCE | Your Civil Liberties: Searches and Seizures

Our civil liberties include numerous provisions, many of them listed in the Bill of Rights, that protect persons who are suspected of criminal activity. Among these are limits on how the police—as agents of the government—can conduct searches and seizures.

Why Should You Care?

You may be the most law-abiding person in the world, but that will not guarantee that you will never be stopped, arrested, or searched by the police. Sooner or later, the great majority of all citizens will have some kind of interaction with the police. People who do not understand their rights or how to behave toward law enforcement officers can find themselves in serious trouble. The words of advice in this feature actually provide you with key survival skills for life in the modern world.

What Can You Do?

How should you behave if you are stopped by police officers? Your civil liberties protect you from having to provide information other than your name and address. Normally, even if you have not been placed under arrest, the officers have the right to frisk you for weapons, and you must let them proceed. The officers cannot, however, check your person or your clothing further if, in their judgment, no weaponlike object is produced.

The officers may search you only if they have a search warrant or probable cause to believe that a search will likely produce incriminating evidence. What if the officers do not have probable cause or a warrant? Physically resisting their attempt to search you can lead to disastrous results. It is best simply to refuse orally to give permission for the search, preferably in the presence of a witness. Being polite is better than acting out of anger and making the officers irritable. It is usually advisable to limit what you say to the officers. If you are arrested, it is best to keep quiet until you can speak with a lawyer.

If you are in your car and are stopped by the police, the same fundamental rules apply. Always be ready to show your driver's license and car registration. You may be asked to get out of the car. The officers may use a flashlight to peer inside if it is too dark to see otherwise. None of this constitutes a search. A true search requires either a warrant or probable cause. No officer has the legal right to search your car simply to find out if you may have committed a crime. Police officers can conduct searches that are incident to lawful arrests, however.

If you are in your home and a police officer with a search warrant appears, you can ask to examine the warrant before granting entry. A warrant that is correctly made out will state the place or persons to be searched, the object sought, and the date of the warrant (which should be no more than ten days old); and it will bear the signature of a judge or magistrate. If the warrant is in order, you need not make any statement. If you believe the warrant to be invalid, or if no warrant is produced, you should make it clear orally that you have not consented to the search, preferably in the presence of a witness. If the search later is proved to be unlawful, normally any evidence obtained cannot be used in court.

Officers who attempt to enter your home without a search warrant can do so only if they are pursuing a suspected felon into the house. Rarely is it advisable to give permission for a warrantless search. You, as the resident, must be the one to give permission if any evidence obtained is to be considered legal. The landlord, manager, or head of a college dormitory cannot give legal permission. A roommate, however, can give permission for a search of his or her room, which may allow the police to search areas where you have belongings.

If you are a guest in a place that is being legally searched, you may be legally searched as well. But unless you have been placed under arrest, you cannot be compelled to go to the police station or get into a squad car.

If you would like to find out more about your rights and obligations under the laws of searches and seizures, you might wish to contact the following organization:

American Civil Liberties Union
125 Broad St., 18th Floor
New York, NY 10004
212-549-2500
www.aclu.org

Key Terms

actual malice 126	**commercial speech** 120	**gag order** 126	**slander** 123
arraignment 136	**defamation of character** 123	**incorporation theory** 110	**symbolic speech** 119
civil liberties 109	**establishment clause** 111	**libel** 126	**writ of *habeas corpus*** 136
clear and present danger test 121	**exclusionary rule** 138	**prior restraint** 119	
	free exercise clause 117	**public figure** 126	

Chapter Summary

1 Originally, the Bill of Rights limited only the power of the national government, not that of the states. Gradually and selectively, however, the Supreme Court accepted the incorporation theory, under which no state can violate most provisions of the Bill of Rights.

2 The First Amendment protects against government interference with freedom of religion by requiring a separation of church and state (under the establishment clause) and by guaranteeing the free exercise of religion. Controversial issues that arise under the establishment clause include the following: aid to church-related schools, school prayer, the teaching of evolution versus intelligent design, school vouchers, the posting of the Ten Commandments in public places, and discrimination against religious speech. The government can interfere with the free exercise of religion only when religious practices work against public policy or the public welfare.

3 The First Amendment protects against government interference with freedom of speech, which includes symbolic speech (expressive conduct). The Supreme Court has been especially critical of government actions that impose prior restraint on expression. Commercial speech (advertising) by businesses has received limited First Amendment protection. Restrictions on expression are permitted when the expression creates a clear and present danger to the peace or public order. Speech that has not received First Amendment protection includes expression judged to be obscene or slanderous.

4 The First Amendment protects against government interference with the freedom of the press, which can be regarded as a special instance of freedom of speech. Speech by the press that does not receive protection includes libelous statements. Publication of news about a criminal trial may be restricted by a gag order in some circumstances.

5 The First Amendment protects the right to assemble peaceably and to petition the government. Permits may be required for parades, sound trucks, and demonstrations to maintain the public order, and a permit may be denied to protect the public safety.

6 Under the Ninth Amendment, rights not specifically mentioned in the Constitution are not necessarily denied to the people. Among these unspecified rights protected by the courts is a right to privacy, which has been inferred from the First, Third, Fourth, Fifth, and Ninth Amendments. A major privacy issue today is how best to protect privacy rights in cyberspace. Whether an individual's privacy rights include a right to an abortion or a "right to die" continues to provoke controversy. Another major challenge concerns the extent to which Americans must forfeit privacy rights to control terrorism.

7 The Constitution includes protections for the rights of persons accused of crimes. Under the Fourth Amendment, no one may be subject to an unreasonable search or seizure or be arrested except on probable cause. Under the Fifth Amendment, an accused person has the right to remain silent. Under the Sixth Amendment, an accused person must be informed of the reason for his or her arrest. The accused also has the right to adequate counsel, even if he or she cannot afford an attorney, and the right to a prompt arraignment and a speedy and public trial before an impartial jury selected from a cross section of the community.

8 In *Miranda v. Arizona* (1966), the Supreme Court held that criminal suspects, before interrogation by law enforcement personnel, must be informed of certain constitutional rights, including the right to remain silent and the right to be represented by counsel.

9 The exclusionary rule forbids the admission in court of illegally seized evidence. There is a "good faith exception" to the exclusionary rule: illegally seized evidence need not be thrown out owing to, for example, a technical defect in a search warrant. Under the Eighth Amendment, cruel and unusual punishment is prohibited. Whether the death penalty is cruel and unusual punishment continues to be debated.

Selected Print and Media Resources

SUGGESTED READINGS

Ackerman, Bruce. *Before the Next Attack: Preserving Civil Liberties in an Age of Terrorism*. New Haven, Conn.: Yale University Press, 2006. The author advocates creating an "emergency constitution" with specific time limits that would give the government enhanced national security powers in times of crisis. He argues that such a solution would better protect civil liberties during normal circumstances.

Behe, Michael. *Darwin's Black Box: The Biochemical Challenge to Evolution*. New York: Simon and Schuster, 2006. Considered a seminal work in the intelligent design movement, Behe's book has been updated to include further evidence for his claims that evolution does not fully explain the origins of life.

Epps, Garrett. *To an Unknown God: Religious Freedom on Trial*. New York: St. Martin's Press, 2001. The author chronicles the journey through the courts of *Oregon v. Smith* (discussed earlier in this chapter), a case concerning religious practices decided by the Supreme Court in 1990. The author regards this case as one of the Supreme Court's most momentous decisions on religious freedom in the last fifty years.

Lewis, Anthony. *Gideon's Trumpet*. New York: Vintage, 1964. This classic work discusses the background and facts of *Gideon v. Wainwright*, the 1963 Supreme Court case in which the Court held that the state must make an attorney available for any person accused of a felony who cannot afford a lawyer.

MEDIA RESOURCES

The Abortion War: Thirty Years after Roe v. Wade—An ABC News program released in 2003 that examines the abortion issue.

The Chamber—A movie, based on John Grisham's novel by the same name, about a young lawyer who defends a man (his grandfather) who has been sentenced to death and faces imminent execution.

Execution at Midnight—A video presenting the arguments and evidence on both sides of the controversial death penalty issue.

Gideon's Trumpet—An excellent 1980 movie about the *Gideon v. Wainwright* case. Henry Fonda plays the role of the convicted petty thief Clarence Earl Gideon.

May It Please the Court: The First Amendment—A set of audiocassette recordings and written transcripts of the oral arguments made before the Supreme Court in sixteen key First Amendment cases. Participants in the recording include nationally known attorneys and several Supreme Court justices.

The People versus Larry Flynt—An R-rated 1996 film that clearly articulates the conflict between freedom of the press and how a community defines pornography.

Skokie: Rights or Wrong?—A documentary by Sheila Chamovitz. The film documents the legal and moral crisis created when American Nazis attempted to demonstrate in Skokie, Illinois, a predominantly Jewish suburb that was home to many concentration camp survivors.

E·MOCRACY | Understanding Your Civil Liberties

Today, the online world offers opportunities for Americans to easily access information concerning the nature of their civil liberties, how they originated, and how they may be threatened by various government actions. Several of the Web sites in the *Logging On* section of Chapter 2 present documents that set forth and explain the civil liberties guaranteed by the Constitution. In the *Logging On* section that follows, we list other Web sites you can visit to gain insights into the nature of these liberties.

| Logging On

The American Civil Liberties Union (ACLU), the nation's leading civil liberties organization, provides an extensive array of information and links concerning civil rights issues at

www.aclu.org

The Liberty Counsel describes itself as "a nonprofit religious civil liberties education and legal defense organization established to preserve religious freedom." The URL for its Web site is

www.lc.org

Summaries and the full text of Supreme Court decisions concerning constitutional law, plus a virtual tour of the Supreme Court, are available at

www.oyez.org/oyez/frontpage

If you want to read historic Supreme Court decisions, you can search for them at

supct.law.cornell.edu/ supct/search/index.html

The Center for Democracy and Technology (CDT) focuses on how developments in communications technology are affecting the constitutional liberties of Americans. You can access the CDT's site at

www.cdt.org

The American Library Association's Web site provides information on free speech issues, especially issues of free speech on the Internet. Go to

www.ala.org

You can find current information on Internet privacy issues at the Electronic Privacy Information Center's Web site.

Go to

www.epic.org/privacy

For the history of flag protection and the First Amendment, as well as the status of the proposed flag amendment in Congress, go to

www.freedomforum.org/ packages/first/Flag/timeline.htm

| Online Review

At **www.politicalscience.wadsworth.com/ schmidt12**, you will find a free Study Guide to this book. For each chapter, there are two online quizzes to help you master the material.

• The PoliPrep Self-Study Assessment provides a pretest for each major section of the chapter. PoliPrep then generates a customized study plan. After you complete the study plan, a posttest evaluates your progress.

• The Tutorial Quiz for each chapter provides questions on the chapter contents, including the features. The questions are organized to match the major sections of the chapter.

Civil Rights

... UNTIL JUSTICE ROLLS DOWN LIKE WATERS AND RIGHTEOUSNESS LIKE A MIGHTY STREAM

REV. JAMES REEB MARCH N... BEATEN TO DEATH... MA...

STATE TROOPERS BEAT BACK... EDMUND PETTUS BRIDGE SELMA A...

JIMMIE LEE JACKSON CIVIL RIGHTS MARCH KILLED BY STATE TROOPER...

LT. COL. LEMUEL PENN NORTH CO... WHILE DRIVING

11 · MAR · 1965

7 · MAR · 1965

26 · FEB · 1965

What If . . .
Illegal Immigrants Were Granted Citizenship?

BACKGROUND

By most estimates, there are roughly twelve million illegal immigrants living in the United States. The majority of the illegal immigrants came to the United States from Latin American countries, with more than half coming from Mexico alone. In 2006, many illegal immigrants and their advocates took to the streets to protest pending immigration legislation. Those who chose to join the protests and marches voiced one overriding common request: the desire to obtain U.S. citizenship.

WHAT IF ILLEGAL IMMIGRANTS WERE GRANTED CITIZENSHIP?

Granting citizenship to every illegal immigrant now residing in the United States would have significant repercussions. The illegal immigrants' sheer numbers would command attention from both political parties. The already important "Hispanic vote" would take on even greater significance.

A massive grant of citizenship would make employment and income tax practices (or lack thereof) associated with illegal immigrants more transparent. Finally, by granting citizenship to those who had entered the country illegally, the United States would likely face a tide of new immigrants.

INCREASED POLITICAL CLOUT FOR THE HISPANIC COMMUNITY

In recent years, Hispanics have begun to reverse their reputation for being politically inactive or disinterested. Voter participation within the Hispanic community has increased. Hispanics have become more politically active and outspoken. Indeed, such developments are reflected in the growing number of individuals of Hispanic descent holding public office as mayors of major cities, governors, and members of Congress.

That granting citizenship to illegal immigrants is even a topic of discussion represents a significant turn of events for Hispanic Americans. Factions within both major parties have proposed different measures that would lead to citizenship for illegals. Political interest groups have formed to champion immigrant rights. Some broader-based groups have advocated on behalf of both legal and illegal immigrants of Hispanic origin.

EMPLOYMENT AND TAXES

Most illegal immigrants come to the United States to work. Many illegal immigrants send part of their earnings in America back to relatives in their home countries. The wages sent home to family members by individuals working in the United States (both legally and illegally) are the second-largest source of foreign income in Mexico.

The Internal Revenue Service has had difficulty collecting taxes on the wages that illegal immigrants earn, however. Some employers who knowingly hire illegal immigrants simply pay those workers "under the table" to avoid a paper trail. Often, the arrangement is a cash transaction, which is difficult to track. If all illegal immigrants were granted citizenship, most employers would no longer be able to engage in such tax-evasion schemes.

Employers sometimes take advantage of illegal immigrants by refusing to pay them for work or changing the terms of work agreements. Other employers use illegal immigrants as employees because they often accept lower wages than American citizens would. Some employers break the law by hiring illegal immigrants to get around paying state or federal minimum wages. If citizenship were granted to illegal immigrants, employers would have to reconsider their practices. Moreover, as wages were properly reported, tax revenues would increase. Employers, however, might eliminate some jobs if they were forced to pay higher wages.

U.S. IMMIGRATION POLICY

Obviously, illegal immigrants violate U.S. immigration laws. Anyone seeking to enter the United States legally faces a lengthy application process and annual quota limitations that depend on national origin. Enforcement of immigration law has always been difficult. Record numbers of illegal immigrants continue to enter the United States despite increased efforts to control the borders.

Granting citizenship to all illegal immigrants now residing in the United States could be considered unfair to all those who are waiting for legal entry. It would be difficult for the United States to justify keeping its borders closed if citizenship were granted to those already within its borders illegally.

FOR CRITICAL ANALYSIS

1. Some politicians have advocated a "gradual" process for granting citizenship to illegal immigrants. Do you think that a gradual process would be more appropriate than an automatic grant of citizenship? Or do you oppose any proposal—gradual or immediate—to offer citizenship to illegal immigrants? Explain your position.
2. Do you think immigration would significantly increase if the United States unveiled some type of policy to grant citizenship to illegal immigrants? Why or why not?

In spite of the words set forth in the Declaration of Independence that "all Men are created equal," the concept of equal treatment under the law was a distant dream in those years. In fact, the majority of the population had few rights. As you learned in Chapter 2, the framers of the Constitution permitted slavery to continue. Slaves thus were excluded from the political process. Women also were excluded for the most part, as were Native Americans, African Americans who were not slaves, and even white men who did not own property. In reality, it has taken this nation more than two hundred years to approach even a semblance of equality among all Americans. Today, in contrast, we have numerous civil rights. Some people claim that we have too many rights and that the expansion of civil rights has circumvented reasonable approaches to handling social problems.

Equality is at the heart of the concept of civil rights. Generally, the term **civil rights** refers to the rights of all Americans to equal treatment under the law, as provided for by the Fourteenth Amendment to the Constitution. Although the terms *civil rights* and *civil liberties* are sometimes used interchangeably, scholars make a distinction between the two. As you learned in Chapter 4, civil liberties are basically *limitations* on government; they specify what the government *cannot* do. Civil rights, in contrast, specify what the government *must* do—to ensure equal protection and freedom from discrimination.

Essentially, the history of civil rights in America is the story of the struggle of various groups to be free from discriminatory treatment. In this chapter, we first look at two movements that had significant consequences for the history of civil rights in America: the civil rights movement of the 1950s and 1960s and the women's movement, which began in the mid-1800s and continues today. Each of these movements resulted in legislation that secured important basic rights for all Americans—the right to vote and the right to equal protection under the laws. We then explore a question with serious implications for today's voters and policymakers: What should the government's responsibility be when equal protection under the law is not enough to ensure truly equal opportunities for Americans?

As you read in the chapter-opening *What If . . .* feature, the Hispanic American population has grown rapidly over the past two decades. With that growth has come challenges, for both the Hispanic community and American society as a whole. In this chapter, we look at some of the issues related to Hispanic Americans and immigration. Note that most minorities in this nation have suffered—and some continue to suffer—from discrimination. Native Americans, Asian Americans, Arab Americans from Middle Eastern countries, and persons from India all have had to struggle for equal treatment, as have people from various island nations and other countries. The fact that these groups are not singled out for special attention in the following pages should not be construed to mean that their struggle for equality is any less significant than the struggles of those groups that we do discuss.

African Americans and the Consequences of Slavery in the United States

Before 1863, the Constitution protected slavery and made equality impossible in the sense in which we use the word today. African American leader Frederick Douglass pointed out that "Liberty and Slavery—opposite as Heaven and Hell—are both in the Constitution." As Abraham Lincoln stated sarcastically, "All men are created equal, except Negroes."

The constitutionality of slavery was confirmed just a few years before the outbreak of the Civil War in the famous *Dred Scott v. Sanford*[1] case of 1857. The Supreme Court held that slaves were not citizens of the United States, nor were

[1] 19 Howard 393 (1857).

| Civil Rights
Generally, all rights rooted in the Fourteenth Amendment's guarantee of equal protection under the law.

This is a portrait of Dred Scott (1795–1858), an American slave who was born in Virginia and who later moved with his owner to Illinois, where slavery was illegal. He was the nominal plaintiff in a test case that sought to obtain his freedom on the ground that he lived in the free state of Illinois. Although the United States Supreme Court ruled against him, he was soon emancipated and became a hotel porter in St. Louis. (Missouri Historical Society)

they entitled to the rights and privileges of citizenship. The Court also ruled that
the Missouri Compromise, which banned slavery in the territories north of 36°30'
latitude (the southern border of Missouri), was unconstitutional. The *Dred Scott*
decision had grave consequences. Most observers contend that the ruling contributed to making the Civil War inevitable.

Ending Servitude

With the emancipation of the slaves by President Lincoln's Emancipation
Proclamation in 1863 and the passage of the Thirteenth, Fourteenth, and Fifteenth
Amendments during the Reconstruction period following the Civil War, constitu-
tional inequality was ended.

The Thirteenth Amendment (1865) states that neither slavery nor involuntary
servitude shall exist within the United States. The Fourteenth Amendment (1868)
tells us that *all* persons born or naturalized in the United States are citizens of the
United States. It states, furthermore, that "[n]o State shall make or enforce any law
which shall abridge the privileges or immunities of citizens of the United States; nor
shall any State deprive any person of life, liberty, or property, without due process
of law; nor deny to any person within its jurisdiction the equal protection of the
laws." Note the use of the terms *citizen* and *person* in this amendment. *Citizens* have
political rights, such as the right to vote and run for political office. Citizens also
have certain privileges or immunities (see Chapter 4). All *persons*, however, including noncitizen immigrants, have a right to due process of law and equal protection
under the law.

The Fifteenth Amendment (1870) reads as follows: "The right of citizens of the
United States to vote shall not be denied or abridged by the United States or by any
State on account of race, color, or previous condition of servitude."

The Civil Rights Acts of 1865 to 1875

From 1865 to 1875, Congress passed a series of civil rights acts that were aimed at
enforcing these amendments. The Civil Rights Act of 1866 extended citizenship to
anyone born in the United States and gave African Americans full equality before

Abraham Lincoln reads the Emancipation
Proclamation on July 22, 1862. The
Emancipation Proclamation did not abolish
slavery (that was done by the Thirteenth
Amendment, in 1865), but it ensured that
slavery would be abolished if and when the
North won the Civil War. After the Battle of
Antietam on September 17, 1862, Lincoln
publicly announced the Emancipation
Proclamation and declared that all slaves
residing in states that were still in rebellion
against the United States on January 1,
1863, would be freed once those states
came under the military control of the
Union Army. (Library of Congress)

the law. The act further authorized the president to enforce the law with national armed forces. The Enforcement Act of 1870 set out specific criminal sanctions for interfering with the right to vote as protected by the Fifteenth Amendment and by the Civil Rights Act of 1866. Equally important was the Civil Rights Act of 1872, known as the Anti–Ku Klux Klan Act. This act made it a federal crime for anyone to use law or custom to deprive an individual of rights, privileges, and immunities secured by the Constitution or by any federal law. The Second Civil Rights Act, passed in 1875, declared that everyone is entitled to full and equal enjoyment of public accommodations, theaters, and other places of public amusement, and it imposed penalties for violators.

The Ineffectiveness of the Civil Rights Laws

The Reconstruction statutes, or civil rights acts, ultimately did little to secure equality for African Americans. Both the *Civil Rights Cases* and the case of *Plessy v. Ferguson* (discussed below) effectively nullified these acts. Additionally, various barriers were erected that prevented African Americans from exercising their right to vote.

The *Civil Rights Cases*. The Supreme Court invalidated the 1875 Civil Rights Act when it held, in the *Civil Rights Cases*[2] of 1883, that the enforcement clause of the Fourteenth Amendment (which states that "[n]o State shall make or enforce any law which shall abridge the privileges or immunities of citizens") was limited to correcting actions by states in their *official* acts; thus, the discriminatory acts of *private* citizens were not illegal. ("Individual invasion of individual rights is not the subject matter of the Amendment.") The 1883 Supreme Court decision met with widespread approval throughout most of the United States.

Twenty years after the Civil War, the white majority was all too willing to forget about the three Civil War amendments and the civil rights legislation of the 1860s and 1870s. The other civil rights laws that the Court did not specifically invalidate became dead letters in the statute books, although they were never repealed by Congress. At the same time, many former proslavery secessionists had regained political power in the southern states.

Plessy v. Ferguson: Separate but Equal. A key decision during this period concerned Homer Plessy, a Louisiana resident who was one-eighth African American. In 1892, he boarded a train in New Orleans. The conductor made him leave the car, which was restricted to whites, and directed him to a car for nonwhites. At that time, Louisiana had a statute providing for separate railway cars for whites and African Americans.

Plessy went to court, claiming that such a statute was contrary to the Fourteenth Amendment's equal protection clause. In 1896, the United States Supreme Court rejected Plessy's contention. The Court concluded that the Fourteenth Amendment "could not have been intended to abolish distinctions based upon color, or to enforce social . . . equality." The Court stated that segregation alone did not violate the Constitution: "Laws permitting, and even requiring, their separation in places where they are liable to be brought into contact do not necessarily imply the inferiority of either race to the other."[3] So was born the **separate-but-equal doctrine**.

Plessy v. Ferguson became the judicial cornerstone of racial discrimination throughout the United States. Even though *Plessy* upheld segregated facilities in railway cars only, it was assumed that the Supreme Court was upholding segregation everywhere as long as the separate facilities were equal. The result was a system of

Separate-but-Equal Doctrine
The doctrine holding that separate-but-equal facilities do not violate the equal protection clause.

---

[2]109 U.S. 3 (1883).
[3]*Plessy v. Ferguson*, 163 U.S. 537 (1896).

| DID YOU KNOW . . .

That the original Constitution failed to describe the status of *citizen* or how this status could be acquired?

| **White Primary**
A state primary election that restricts voting to whites only; outlawed by the Supreme Court in 1944.

| **Grandfather Clause**
A device used by southern states to disenfranchise African Americans. It restricted voting to those whose grandfathers had voted before 1867.

| **Poll Tax**
A special tax that must be paid as a qualification for voting. The Twenty-fourth Amendment to the Constitution outlawed the poll tax in national elections, and in 1966 the Supreme Court declared it unconstitutional in all elections.

| **Literacy Test**
A test administered as a precondition for voting, often used to prevent African Americans from exercising their right to vote.

racial segregation, particularly in the South—supported by laws collectively known as Jim Crow laws—that required separate drinking fountains; separate seats in theaters, restaurants, and hotels; separate public toilets; and separate waiting rooms for the two races. "Separate" was indeed the rule, but "equal" was never enforced, nor was it a reality.

Voting Barriers. The brief enfranchisement of African Americans ended after 1877, when the federal troops that occupied the South during the Reconstruction era were withdrawn. Southern politicians regained control of state governments and, using everything except race as a formal criterion, passed laws that effectively deprived African Americans of the right to vote. By using the ruse that political parties were private bodies, the Democratic Party was allowed to keep black voters from its primaries. The **white primary** was upheld by the Supreme Court until 1944 when, in *Smith v. Allwright*,[4] the Court ruled it a violation of the Fifteenth Amendment.

Another barrier to African American voting was the **grandfather clause,** which restricted voting to those who could prove that their grandfathers had voted before 1867. **Poll taxes** required the payment of a fee to vote; thus, poor African Americans—as well as poor whites—who could not afford to pay the tax were excluded from voting. Not until the Twenty-fourth Amendment to the Constitution was ratified in 1964 was the poll tax eliminated as a precondition to voting. **Literacy tests** were also used to deny the vote to African Americans. Such tests asked potential voters to read, recite, or interpret complicated texts, such as a section of the state constitution, to the satisfaction of local registrars—who were, of course, never satisfied with the responses of African Americans.

Extralegal Methods of Enforcing White Supremacy. The second-class status of African Americans was also a matter of social custom, especially in the South. In their interactions with southern whites, African Americans were expected to observe an informal but detailed code of behavior that confirmed their inferiority. The most serious violation of the informal code was "familiarity" toward a white woman by an African American man or boy. The code was backed up by the com-

---

[4]321 U.S. 649 (1944).

Jim Crow laws required the segregation of the races, particularly in public facilities such as this theater. The name "Jim Crow," which came from a vaudeville character of the 1800s, was applied to laws and practices that enforced segregation. Facilities provided to African Americans under segregation were almost always inferior to the ones provided to whites. What factors may have led to this kind of discrimination? (Library of Congress)

mon practice of *lynching*—mob action to murder an accused individual, usually by hanging and sometimes accompanied by torture. Lynching was a common response to an accusation of "familiarity." Of course, lynching was illegal, but southern authorities rarely prosecuted these cases, and white juries would not convict.

African Americans outside the South were subject to a second kind of violence—race riots. In the early twentieth century, race riots were typically initiated by whites. Frequently, the riots were caused by competition for employment. For example, there were a number of serious riots during World War II (1939–1945), when labor shortages forced northern employers to hire more black workers.

The End of the Separate-but-Equal Doctrine

A successful attack on the separate-but-equal doctrine began with a series of lawsuits in the 1930s that sought to admit African Americans to state professional schools. By 1950, the Supreme Court had ruled that African Americans who were admitted to a state university could not be assigned to separate sections of classrooms, libraries, and cafeterias.

In 1951, Oliver Brown decided that his eight-year-old daughter, Linda Carol Brown, should not have to go to an all-nonwhite elementary school twenty-one blocks from her home, when there was a white school only seven blocks away. The National Association for the Advancement of Colored People (NAACP), formed in 1909, decided to support Oliver Brown. The outcome would have a monumental impact on American society.

Brown v. Board of Education of Topeka.   The 1954 unanimous decision of the United States Supreme Court in *Brown v. Board of Education of Topeka*[5] established that segregation of races in the public schools violates the equal protection clause of the Fourteenth Amendment. Chief Justice Earl Warren said that separation implied inferiority, whereas the majority opinion in *Plessy v. Ferguson* had said the opposite.

"With All Deliberate Speed."   The following year, in *Brown v. Board of Education*[6] (sometimes called the second *Brown* decision), the Court declared that the lower courts needed to ensure that African Americans would be admitted to schools on a nondiscriminatory basis "with all deliberate speed." The district courts were to consider devices in their desegregation orders that might include "the school transportation system, personnel, [and] revision of school districts and attendance areas into compact units to achieve a system of determining admission to the public schools on a nonracial basis."

Reactions to School Integration

The white South did not let the Supreme Court ruling go unchallenged. Governor Orval Faubus of Arkansas used the state's National Guard to block the integration of Central High School in Little Rock in September 1957. The federal court demanded that the troops be withdrawn. Finally, President Dwight Eisenhower had to federalize the Arkansas National Guard and send in

[5]347 U.S. 483 (1954).
[6]349 U.S. 294 (1955).

In September 1957, Governor Orval Faubus of Arkansas shows a photograph of federal troops implementing integration in Little Rock Central High School. Faubus accused the federal government of using "police state" methods. Such public school integration was the result of which Supreme Court decision? (Bettmann/Corbis)

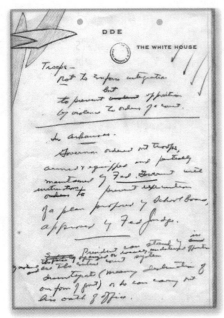

This note handwritten by President Eisenhower in September 1957 indicated that the president simply wished to enforce the law handed down by the Supreme Court in its *Brown* decision, not to enforce the ideology of integration *per se.* (Dwight D. Eisenhower Library)

| *De Facto* Segregation
Racial segregation that occurs because of past social and economic conditions and residential racial patterns.

| *De Jure* Segregation
Racial segregation that occurs because of laws or administrative decisions by public agencies.

| Busing
In the context of civil rights, the transportation of public school students from areas where they live to schools in other areas to eliminate school segregation based on residential patterns.

the Army's 101st Airborne Division to quell the violence. Central High became integrated.

The universities in the South, however, remained segregated. When James Meredith, an African American student, attempted to enroll at the University of Mississippi in Oxford in 1962, violence flared there, as it had in Little Rock. The white riot at Oxford was so intense that President John Kennedy was forced to send in 30,000 U.S. combat troops, a larger force than the one then stationed in Korea. There were 375 military and civilian injuries, many from gunfire, and two bystanders were killed. Ultimately, peace was restored, and Meredith began attending classes.[7]

An Integrationist Attempt at a Cure: Busing

In most parts of the United States, residential concentrations by race have made it difficult to achieve racial balance in schools. Although it is true that a number of school boards in northern districts created segregated schools by drawing school district lines arbitrarily, the residential concentration of African Americans and other minorities in well-defined geographic locations has contributed to the difficulty of achieving racial balance. This concentration results in *de facto* **segregation**, as distinct from *de jure* **segregation**, which results from laws or administrative decisions.

Court-Ordered Busing. The obvious solution to both *de facto* and *de jure* segregation seemed to be transporting some African American schoolchildren to white schools and some white schoolchildren to African American schools. Increasingly, the courts ordered school districts to engage in such **busing** across neighborhoods. Busing led to violence in some northern cities, such as in south Boston, where African American students were bused into blue-collar Irish Catholic neighborhoods. Indeed, busing was unpopular with many groups. In the mid-1970s, almost 50 percent of African Americans interviewed were opposed to busing, and approximately three-fourths of the whites interviewed held the same opinion. Nonetheless, through the next decade, the Supreme Court fairly consistently upheld busing plans in the cases it decided.

The End of Integration? During the 1980s and the early 1990s, the Supreme Court tended to back away from its earlier commitment to busing and other methods of desegregation. By the late 1990s and early 2000s, the federal courts were increasingly unwilling to uphold race-conscious policies designed to further school integration and diversity—outcomes that are not mandated by the Constitution. For example, in 2001, a federal appellate court held that the Charlotte-Mecklenburg school district in North Carolina had achieved the goal of integration,[8] meaning that race-based admission quotas could no longer be imposed constitutionally.

The Resurgence of Minority Schools. Today, schools around the country are becoming segregated again, in large part because of *de facto* segregation. The rapid decline in the relative proportion of whites who live in large cities and high minority birthrates have increased the minority presence in those urban areas. Today, one out of every three African American and Hispanic students goes to a school with more than 90 percent minority enrollment. In the largest U.S. cities, fifteen out of sixteen African American and Hispanic students go to schools with almost no non-Hispanic whites.

---

[7]William Doyle, *An American Insurrection: James Meredith and the Battle of Oxford, Mississippi, 1962* (New York: Anchor, 2003).
[8]*Belk v. Charlotte-Mecklenburg Board of Education,* 269 F.3d 305 (4th Cir. 2001).

Generally, Americans are now taking another look at what desegregation means. The attempt to integrate the schools, particularly through busing, has largely failed to improve educational resources and achievement for African American children. The goal of racially balanced schools envisioned in the 1954 *Brown v. Board of Education of Topeka* decision is giving way to the goal of better education for children, even if that means educating them in schools in which students are of the same race or in which race is not considered.

The Civil Rights Movement

The *Brown* decision applied only to public schools. Not much else in the structure of existing segregation was affected. In December 1955, a forty-three-year-old African American woman, Rosa Parks, boarded a public bus in Montgomery, Alabama. When the bus became crowded and several white people stepped aboard, Parks was asked to move to the rear of the bus (the "colored" section). She refused, was arrested, and was fined $10; but that was not the end of the matter. For an entire year, African Americans boycotted the Montgomery bus line. The protest was headed by a twenty-seven-year-old Baptist minister, Dr. Martin Luther King, Jr. During the protest period, he went to jail, and his house was bombed. In the face of overwhelming odds, King won. In 1956, a federal district court issued an injunction prohibiting the segregation of buses in Montgomery. The era of civil rights protests had begun.

King's Philosophy of Nonviolence

The following year, in 1957, King formed the Southern Christian Leadership Conference (SCLC). King advocated nonviolent **civil disobedience** as a means to achieve racial justice. King's philosophy of civil disobedience was influenced, in part, by the life and teachings of Mahatma Gandhi (1869–1948). Gandhi had led resistance to the British colonial system in India from 1919 to 1947. He used tactics such as demonstrations and marches, as well as nonviolent, public disobedience to unjust laws. King's followers successfully used these methods to gain wider public acceptance of their cause.

| **DID YOU KNOW . . .**

That during the Mississippi Summer Project in 1964, organized by students to register African American voters, 1,000 students and voters were arrested, 80 were beaten, 35 were shot, and 6 were murdered; 30 buildings were bombed; and 25 churches were burned?

| Civil Disobedience
A nonviolent, public refusal to obey allegedly unjust laws.

More than 30,000 visitors filed past the casket of Rosa Parks in the U.S. Capitol Rotunda in 2005. Parks became the first woman to lay in honor in the Rotunda. Born in Alabama, Rosa Parks was active in the Montgomery Voters' League and the NAACP (National Association for the Advancement of Colored People) League Council. After the successful boycott of the Montgomery bus system, which was sparked by her actions, she was fired from her job and subsequently moved to Detroit. Can actions by an ordinary person change history? Why or why not? (AP Photo/Susan Walsh)

Dr. Martin Luther King, Jr., acknowledges the crowd at the August 1963 March on Washington for Jobs and Freedom. Nearly a quarter-million African Americans and sympathetic whites participated in the march. The march is best remembered for King's eloquent "I Have a Dream" speech and the assembled multitude singing "We Shall Overcome," the anthem of the civil rights movement. (AP Photo)

Nonviolent Demonstrations. For the next decade, African Americans and sympathetic whites engaged in sit-ins, freedom rides, and freedom marches. In the beginning, such demonstrations were often met with violence, and the contrasting image of nonviolent African Americans and violent, hostile whites created strong public support for the civil rights movement. When African Americans in Greensboro, North Carolina, were refused service at a Woolworth's lunch counter, they organized a sit-in that was aided day after day by sympathetic whites and other African Americans. Enraged customers threw ketchup on the protesters. Some spat in their faces. The sit-in movement continued to grow, however. Within six months of the first sit-in at the Greensboro Woolworth's, hundreds of lunch counters throughout the South were serving African Americans.

The sit-in technique also was successfully used to integrate interstate buses and their terminals, as well as railroads engaged in interstate transportation. Although buses and railroads engaged in interstate transportation were prohibited by law from segregating African Americans from whites, they stopped doing so only after the sit-in protests.

Marches and Demonstrations. One of the most famous of the violence-plagued protests occurred in Birmingham, Alabama, in 1963, when Police Commissioner Eugene "Bull" Connor unleashed police dogs and used electric cattle prods against the protesters. People throughout the country viewed the event on television with indignation and horror. King himself was thrown in jail. The media coverage of the Birmingham protest and the violent response by the city government played a key role in the process of ending Jim Crow in the United States. The ultimate result was the most important civil rights act in the nation's history, the Civil Rights Act of 1964 (to be discussed shortly).

In August 1963, African American leaders A. Philip Randolph and Bayard Rustin organized a massive March on Washington for Jobs and Freedom. Before nearly a quarter-million white and African American spectators and millions watching on television, King told the world his dream: "I have a dream that my four little children will one day live in a nation where they will not be judged by the color of their skin but by the content of their character."

Another Approach—Black Power

Not all African Americans agreed with King's philosophy of nonviolence or with the idea that King's strong Christian background should represent the core spirituality of African Americans. Black Muslims and other African American separatists advocated a more militant stance and argued that desegregation should not result in cultural assimilation. During the 1950s and 1960s, when King was spearheading nonviolent protests and demonstrations to achieve civil rights for African Americans, black power leaders insisted that African Americans should "fight back" instead of turning the other cheek. Indeed, some would argue that without the fear generated by black militants, a "moderate" such as King would not have garnered such widespread support from white America.

Malcolm Little (who became Malcolm X when he joined the Black Muslims in 1952) and other leaders in the black power movement believed that African Americans fell into two groups: the "Uncle Toms," who peaceably accommodated the white establishment, and the "New Negroes," who took pride in their color and culture and who preferred and demanded racial separation as well as power. Malcolm X was assassinated in 1965, but he became an important reference point for a new generation of African Americans and a symbol of African American identity.

Malcolm X, shown here in March 1964 along with Martin Luther King, Jr., opposed the philosophy of nonviolence espoused by Dr. King, and he urged African Americans to "fight back" against white supremacy. Some people have argued that such a militant approach is almost always counterproductive. Others believe that a militant alternative may have made King's peaceful appeal more attractive. Is either of these arguments persuasive? Why or why not? (Library of Congress)

The Climax of the Civil Rights Movement

Police-dog attacks, cattle prods, high-pressure water hoses, beatings, bombings, the March on Washington, and black militancy—all of these events and developments led to an environment in which Congress felt compelled to act on behalf of African Americans. The second era of civil rights acts, sometimes referred to as the second Reconstruction period, was under way.

Civil Rights Legislation

As the civil rights movement mounted in intensity, equality before the law came to be "an idea whose time has come," in the words of then Republican Senate Minority Leader Everett Dirksen.

The Civil Rights Act of 1964. The Civil Rights Act of 1964, the most far-reaching bill on civil rights in modern times, forbade discrimination on the basis of race, color, religion, gender, and national origin. The major provisions of the act were as follows:

1. It outlawed arbitrary discrimination in voter registration.
2. It barred discrimination in public accommodations, such as hotels and restaurants, whose operations affect interstate commerce.
3. It authorized the federal government to sue to desegregate public schools and facilities.
4. It expanded the power of the Civil Rights Commission and extended its life.
5. It provided for the withholding of federal funds from programs administered in a discriminatory manner.
6. It established the right to equality of opportunity in employment.

Title VII of the Civil Rights Act of 1964 is the cornerstone of employment-discrimination law. It prohibits discrimination in employment based on race, color,

President Lyndon Johnson shakes hands with civil rights leader Martin Luther King, Jr., during the signing of the Civil Rights Act of 1964. Some of the objectives of the act, such as equal voting rights, proved to be easier to obtain than others (for example, desegregated schools). Why would some goals of the act be more difficult to reach? (Bettmann/Corbis)

religion, gender, or national origin. Under Title VII, executive orders were issued that banned employment discrimination by firms that received any federal funding. The 1964 Civil Rights Act created a five-member commission, the Equal Employment Opportunity Commission (EEOC), to administer Title VII.

The EEOC can issue interpretive guidelines and regulations, but these do not have the force of law. Rather, they give notice of the commission's enforcement policy. The EEOC also has investigatory powers. It has broad authority to require the production of documentary evidence, to hold hearings, and to **subpoena** and examine witnesses under oath.

Subpoena
A legal writ requiring a person's appearance in court to give testimony.

The Voting Rights Act of 1965. As late as 1960, only 29.1 percent of African Americans of voting age were registered in the southern states, in stark contrast to 61.1 percent of whites. The Voting Rights Act of 1965 addressed this issue. The act had two major provisions. The first one outlawed discriminatory voter-registration tests. The second authorized federal registration of voters and federally administered voting procedures in any political subdivision or state that discriminated electorally against a particular group. In part, the act provided that certain political subdivisions could not change their voting procedures and election laws without federal approval. The act targeted counties, mostly in the South, in which less than 50 percent of the eligible population was registered to vote. Federal voter registrars were sent to these areas to register African Americans who had been kept from voting by local registrars. Within one week after the act was passed, forty-five federal examiners were sent to the South. A massive voter-registration drive covered the country.

Urban Riots. Even as the civil rights movement was experiencing its greatest victories, a series of riots swept through African American inner-city neighborhoods.

These urban riots were different in character from the race riots described earlier in this chapter. The riots in the first half of the twentieth century were street battles between whites and blacks. The urban riots of the late 1960s and early 1970s, however, were not directed against individual whites—in some instances, whites actually participated in small numbers. The riots were primarily civil insurrections, although these disorders were accompanied by large-scale looting of stores. Inhabitants of the affected neighborhoods attributed the riots to racial discrimination.[9] The riots dissipated much of the goodwill toward the civil rights movement that had been built up earlier in the decade among northern whites. Together with widespread student demonstrations against the Vietnam War (1964–1975), the riots pushed many Americans toward conservatism.

The Civil Rights Act of 1968 and Other Housing Reform Legislation.   Martin Luther King, Jr., was assassinated on April 4, 1968. Despite King's message of peace, his death was followed by the most widespread rioting to date. Nine days after King's death, President Johnson signed the Civil Rights Act of 1968, which forbade discrimination in most housing and provided penalties for those attempting to interfere with individual civil rights (giving protection to civil rights workers, among others). Subsequent legislation added enforcement provisions to the federal government's rules against discriminatory mortgage-lending practices. Today, all lenders must report to the federal government the race, gender, and income of all mortgage-loan seekers, along with the final decision on their loan applications.

Consequences of Civil Rights Legislation

As a result of the Voting Rights Act of 1965 and its amendments, and the large-scale voter-registration drives in the South, the number of African Americans registered to vote climbed dramatically. By 1980, 55.8 percent of African Americans of voting age in the South were registered. In recent elections, the percentage of

> **DID YOU KNOW . . .**
> That after the assassination of Martin Luther King, Jr., riots took place in over 100 cities, 75,000 troops and members of the National Guard were mobilized, 27,000 African Americans were jailed, and 39 African Americans were killed?

---

[9] Angus Campbell and Howard Schuman, *ICPSR 3500: Racial Attitudes in Fifteen American Cities, 1968* (Ann Arbor: Inter-University Consortium for Political and Social Research, 1997). Campbell and Schuman's survey documents both white participation and the attitudes of the inhabitants of affected neighborhoods. This survey is available online at **www.grinnell.edu/academic/data/sociology/minorityresearch/raceatt1968**.

When civil rights leader Dr. Martin Luther King, Jr., was assassinated in Memphis, Tennessee, on April 4, 1968, rioting broke out throughout the United States. This photo shows the result of such rioting in Washington, D.C., the following day. Why do we read less about civil rights leaders today than Americans did in the 1960s? (AP Photo)

voting-age African Americans who have registered to vote has been just slightly less than the percentage of voting-age whites who have done so. Some of the provisions in the Voting Rights Act of 1965 were due to "sunset" (expire) in 2007. In July 2006, President George W. Bush signed a twenty-five-year extension of these provisions following heated congressional debate.

Political Participation by African Americans.   Today, there are more than 8,500 African American elected officials in the United States. The movement of African American citizens into high elected office has been sure, if exceedingly slow. Notably, recent polling data show that most Americans do not consider race a significant factor in choosing a president. In 1958, when the Gallup poll first asked whether respondents would be willing to vote for an African American as president, only 38 percent of the public said yes. By 2005, this number had reached 92 percent. This high figure may have been attained, at least in part, because of the emergence of several African Americans who are widely considered to be of presidential caliber. They include Colin Powell, formerly chair of the Joint Chiefs of Staff and later secretary of state under President George W. Bush, and the current secretary of state, Condoleezza Rice, who has been championed by some Republicans as a possible successor to Bush. On the Democratic side, Illinois senator Barack Obama is widely considered a rising star who may be a presidential contender in the future.

Political Participation by Other Minorities.   As mentioned earlier, the civil rights movement focused primarily on the rights of African Americans. Yet the legislation resulting from the movement has ultimately benefited virtually all minority groups. The Civil Rights Act of 1964, for example, prohibits discrimination against any person because of race, color, or national origin. Subsequent amendments to the Voting Rights Act of 1965 extended its protections to other minorities, including Hispanic Americans, Asian Americans, Native Americans, and Native Alaskans. To further protect the voting rights of minorities, the law now provides that states must make bilingual ballots available in counties where 5 percent or more of the population speaks a language other than English.

The political participation of other minority groups in the United States has also been increasing. Hispanics are gaining political power in several states. Even though political participation by minorities has increased dramatically since the 1960s, the

Things have changed in the span of years since a 1958 poll, when only 38 percent of Americans said they would be willing to vote for an African American candidate for president; now 92 percent say they are willing to do so. To what degree can this public acceptance of African Americans be attributed to the high-profile participation in public life of exceptionally accomplished individuals such as Illinois senator Barack Obama (left), Secretary of State Condoleezza Rice (center), and former Secretary of State Colin Powell? (Photos Courtesy of Senator Barack Obama and the U.S. Department of State)

number of political offices held by members of minority groups remains dispropor-tionately low compared with their numbers in the overall population. This will likely change in the future due to the continued influx of immigrants, particularly from Mexico. Collectively, Hispanics, African Americans, Native Americans, and Asian Americans are now a majority of the populations in California, Hawaii, and New Mexico. It is estimated that by 2015 minority populations will collectively out-number whites in Texas as well. The impact of immigration will be discussed in more detail later in the chapter.

Lingering Social and Economic Disparities.   According to Joyce Ladner of the Brookings Institution, one of the difficulties with the race-based civil rights agenda of the 1950s and 1960s is that it did not envision remedies for cross-racial problems. How, for example, should the nation address problems, such as poverty and urban violence, that affect underclasses in all racial groups? In 1967, when Martin Luther King, Jr., proposed a Poor People's Campaign, he recognized that a civil rights coali-tion based entirely on race would not be sufficient to address the problem of poverty among whites as well as blacks. During his 1984 and 1988 presidential campaigns, African American leader Jesse Jackson also acknowledged the inadequacy of a race-based model of civil rights when he attempted to form a "Rainbow Coalition" of minorities, women, and other underrepresented groups, including the poor.[10]

Some, including many liberals, contend that government intervention is nec-essary to eliminate the social and economic disparities that persist within the American population. Others, including a number of conservatives, believe that the most effective means of addressing these issues is through coalitions of govern-ment groups, private businesses, community-based groups, and individuals. Indeed, a number of civil rights activists currently are pursuing the latter strategy.

Finally, even today, race consciousness continues to divide African Americans and white Americans. Whether we are talking about college attendance, media stereotyping, racial profiling, or academic achievement, the black experience is dif-ferent from the white one. As a result, African Americans view the nation and many specific issues differently than their white counterparts do.[11] In survey after survey, when blacks are asked whether they have achieved racial equality, few believe that they have. In contrast, whites are five times more likely than blacks to believe that racial equality has been achieved.[12] In spite of the civil rights move-ment and civil rights legislation, African Americans continue to feel a sense of injustice in matters of race, and this feeling is often not apparent to, or appreciated by, the majority of white America.

Women's Struggle for Equal Rights

Like African Americans and other minorities, women also have had to struggle for equality. During the first phase of this struggle, the primary goal of women was to obtain the right to vote. Some women had hoped that the founders would provide such a right in the Constitution. The Constitution did not include a provision guar-anteeing women the right to vote, but neither did it deny to women—or to any oth-ers—this right. Rather, the founders left it up to the states to decide such issues, and, as mentioned earlier, by and large, the states limited the franchise to adult white males who owned property.

---

[10]Joyce A. Ladner, "A New Civil Rights Agenda," *The Brookings Review*, Vol. 18, No. 2 (Spring 2000), pp. 26–28.
[11]Lawrence D. Bobo *et al.*, "Through the Eyes of Black America," *Public Perspective*, May/June 2001, p. 13.
[12]*Ibid.*, p. 15, Figure 2.

Elizabeth Cady Stanton (1815–1902), left, was a social reformer and a women's suffrage leader. At her wedding to Henry B. Stanton in 1840, she insisted on dropping the word *obey* from the marriage vows. She wrote *The History of Women's Suffrage*, which was published in 1886.

Susan B. Anthony (1820–1906), a leader of the women's suffrage movement, was also active in the antialcohol and antislavery movements. In 1869, with Elizabeth Cady Stanton, she founded the National Woman Suffrage Association. In 1888, she organized the International Council of Women and, in 1904, the International Women's Suffrage Alliance, in Berlin. (Library of Congress)

| Suffrage
The right to vote; the franchise.

Early Women's Political Movements

The first political cause in which women became actively engaged was the movement to abolish slavery. Yet even male abolitionists felt that women should not take an active role on the subject in public. When the World Antislavery Convention was held in London in 1840, women delegates were barred from active participation. Partly in response to this rebuff, two American delegates, Lucretia Mott and Elizabeth Cady Stanton, returned from that meeting with plans to work for women's rights in the United States.

In 1848, Mott and Stanton organized the first women's rights convention in Seneca Falls, New York. The three hundred people who attended approved a Declaration of Sentiments: "We hold these truths to be self-evident: that all men *and women* are created equal." In the following twelve years, groups that supported women's rights held seven conventions in different cities in the Midwest and East. With the outbreak of the Civil War, however, advocates of women's rights were urged to put their support behind the war effort, and most agreed.

Women's Suffrage Associations

Susan B. Anthony and Elizabeth Cady Stanton formed the National Woman Suffrage Association in 1869. In their view, women's **suffrage** was a means to achieve major improvements in the economic and social situation of women in the United States. In other words, the vote was to be used to seek broader goals. Nowadays, we commonly see the women's rights movement as a liberal cause, but many of the broader goals of the suffrage advocates would not be regarded as liberal today. An example was the prohibition of alcoholic beverages, which received widespread support among women in general and women's rights activists in particular. It should be noted that many women considered prohibition to be a method of combating domestic violence.

Unlike Anthony and Stanton, Lucy Stone, a key founder of the rival American Woman Suffrage Association, believed that the vote was the only major issue. Members of the American Woman Suffrage Association traveled to each state; addressed state legislatures; and wrote, published, and argued their convictions. They achieved only limited success. In 1880, the two organizations joined forces. The resulting National American Woman Suffrage Association had only one goal—the enfranchisement of women—but it made little progress.

The Congressional Union, founded in the early 1900s by Alice Paul, rejected the state-by-state approach. Instead, the Union adopted a national strategy of obtaining an amendment to the U.S. Constitution. The Union also employed militant tactics. It sponsored large-scale marches and civil disobedience—which resulted in hunger strikes, arrests, and jailings. Finally, in 1920, the Nineteenth Amendment was passed: "The right of citizens of the United States to vote shall not be denied or abridged by the United States or by any State on account of sex." (Today, the word *gender* is typically used instead of *sex*.) Although it may seem that the United States was slow to give women the vote, it was really not too far behind the rest of the world (see Table 5–1). For more on women's rights around the world, see this chapter's *Beyond Our Borders* feature.

TABLE 5–1 | YEARS, BY COUNTRY, IN WHICH WOMEN GAINED THE RIGHT TO VOTE

1893: New Zealand	1919: Germany	1945: Italy	1953: Mexico
1902: Australia	1920: United States	1945: Japan	1956: Egypt
1913: Norway	1930: South Africa	1947: Argentina	1963: Kenya
1918: Britain	1932: Brazil	1950: India	1971: Switzerland
1918: Canada	1944: France	1952: Greece	1984: Yemen

Source: Center for the American Woman and Politics.

BEYOND OUR BORDERS | The Struggle for Women's Rights around the World

Although in the last several decades women's rights have emerged as a global issue, progress has been slow. The struggle for women's rights in countries where cultural or legal practices perpetuate the inequality of women is especially difficult.

THE PROBLEM OF VIOLENCE

Most people consider the right to be free from violence as one of the most basic human rights. Women's rights advocates point out that this right is threatened in societies that do not accept the premise that men and women are equal. Some parts of India, for example, implicitly tolerate the practice of dowry killing. (A *dowry* is a sum of money given to a husband by the bride's family.) In a number of cases, husbands, dissatisfied with the size of dowries, have killed their wives in order to remarry for a "better deal"—a crime that is rarely prosecuted.

THE SITUATION IN AFGHANISTAN

In 2001, a startling documentary, "Behind the Veil," was aired repeatedly on CNN. A courageous female reporter had secretly filmed Afghan women being beaten in the streets, killed in public for trivial offenses, and generally subjugated in extreme ways. For the first time ever, women's rights became a major issue in our foreign policy. Americans learned that Afghan girls were barred from schools, and by law women were not allowed to work. Women who had lost their husbands during Afghanistan's civil wars were forced into begging and prostitution. Women had no access to medical care. Any woman found with an unrelated man could be executed by stoning, and many were.

NATION BUILDING AND WOMEN'S RIGHTS

After the collapse of the Taliban regime, the United States and its allies were able to influence the status of Afghan women. The draft constitution of Afghanistan, adopted in January 2004, gave women equality before the law and 20 percent of the seats in the National Assembly. Much of the country remained outside the control of the national government, however. Women continued to face daunting abuse, including arson

Iraqi girls wait for the start of class at the Eastern Secondary School in Baghdad. The role of women in the new Iraq remains uncertain. What negative consequences could result if discriminatory laws forced Iraqi women—among the region's most educated—to retreat to their homes? (AP Photo/Alexander Zemlianichenko)

attacks on girls' schools, forced marriages, and imposition of the all-covering burka garment.

Women in Iraq have enjoyed greater equality than in most Arab nations. In line with the secular ideology of the Baath Party, Saddam Hussein's government tended to treat men and women alike. A problem for the U.S.-led Coalition Provisional Authority (CPA) that governed Iraq until June 2004 was ensuring that women did not lose ground under the new regime. Some members of the Iraqi Governing Council, for example, advocated traditional Islamic laws that would have deprived women of equal rights. Women's organizations campaigned against these provisions, and they were vetoed by the CPA. The interim Iraqi constitution, adopted in March 2004, allotted 25 percent of the seats in the parliament to women.

FOR CRITICAL ANALYSIS

Is it fair or appropriate for one country to judge the cultural practices of another? Why or why not?

The Modern Women's Movement

Historian Nancy Cott contends that the word *feminism* first began to be used around 1910. At that time, **feminism** meant, as it does today, political, social, and economic equality for women—a radical notion that gained little support among members of the suffrage movement.

After gaining the right to vote in 1920, women engaged in little independent political activity until the 1960s. The civil rights movement of that decade resulted

Feminism
The movement that supports political, economic, and social equality for women.

in a growing awareness of rights for all groups, including women. Increased participation in the workforce gave many women greater self-confidence. Additionally, the publication of Betty Friedan's *The Feminine Mystique* in 1963 focused national attention on the unequal status of women in American life.

In 1966, Friedan and others who were dissatisfied with existing women's organizations, and especially with the failure of the Equal Employment Opportunity Commission to address discrimination against women, formed the National Organization for Women (NOW). Many observers consider the founding of NOW to be the beginning of the modern women's movement—the feminist movement. NOW immediately adopted a blanket resolution designed "to bring women into full participation in the mainstream of American society *now*, exercising all the privileges and responsibilities thereof in truly equal partnership with men."

Feminism gained additional impetus from young women who entered politics to support the civil rights movement or to oppose the Vietnam War. Many of them found that despite the egalitarian principles of these movements, women remained in second-class positions. These young women sought their own movement. In the late 1960s, "women's liberation" organizations began to spring up on college campuses. Women also began organizing independent "consciousness-raising groups" in which they discussed how gender issues affected their lives. The new women's movement experienced explosive growth, and by 1970 it had emerged as a major social force.

Who are the feminists today? It is difficult to measure the support for feminism at present because the word means different things to different people. When the dictionary definition of *feminist*—"someone who supports political, economic, and social equality for women"—was read to respondents in a survey, 67 percent labeled themselves as feminists.[13] In the absence of such prompting, however, the term *feminist* (like the term *liberal*) implies radicalism to many people, who therefore shy away from it.

The Equal Rights Amendment.   The initial focus of the modern women's movement was not on expanding the political rights of women. Rather, leaders of NOW and other liberal women's rights advocates sought to eradicate gender inequality

[13]Nancy E. McGlen and Karen O'Connor, *Women, Politics, and American Society*, 4th ed. (Upper Saddle River, N.J.: Prentice Hall, 2004).

In November 1977, more than 20,000 people gathered in Houston, Texas, to celebrate International Women's Year. This was the first and only national women's conference sponsored by the federal government. Among the many prominent women's rights advocates at this conference were Bella Abzug, second from the left (wearing a scarf) and Betty Friedan, on the right (wearing a red coat). Would the federal government sponsor such a conference today? Why or why not? (Time Life Pictures/ Getty Images/Steve Northup)

through a constitutional amendment. The proposed Equal Rights Amendment (ERA), which was first introduced in Congress in 1923 by leaders of the National Women's Party (a successor to the Congressional Union), states as follows: "Equality of rights under the law shall not be denied or abridged by the United States or by any state on account of sex." For years the amendment was not even given a hearing in Congress, but finally it was approved by both chambers and sent to the state legislatures for ratification in 1972.

As was noted in Chapter 2, any constitutional amendment must be ratified by the legislatures (or conventions) in three-fourths of the states before it can become law. Since the early 1900s, most proposed amendments have required that ratification occur within seven years of Congress's adoption of the amendment. The necessary thirty-eight states failed to ratify the ERA within the seven-year period specified by Congress, even though it was supported by numerous national party platforms, six presidents, and both chambers of Congress. To date, efforts to re-introduce the amendment have not succeeded.

During the national debate over the ratification of the ERA, a women's counter-movement emerged. Many women perceived the goals pursued by NOW and other liberal women's organizations as a threat to their way of life. At the head of the countermovement was Republican Phyllis Schlafly and her conservative organization, Eagle Forum. Eagle Forum's "Stop ERA" campaign found significant support among fundamentalist religious groups and various other conservative organizations. The campaign was effective in blocking the ratification of the ERA.

Additional Women's Issues. While NOW concentrated on the ERA, a large number of other women's groups, many of them entirely local, addressed a spectrum of added issues. One of these was the issue of *domestic violence*—that is, assaults within the family. Typically, this meant husbands or boyfriends assaulting their wives or girlfriends. During the 1970s, feminists across the country began opening *battered women's shelters* to house victims of abuse.

Abortion soon emerged as a key concern. Virtually the entire organized women's movement united behind the "freedom-of-choice" position, at the cost of alienating potential women's rights supporters who favored the "right-to-life" position instead. Because abortion was a national issue, the campaign was led by national organizations such as NARAL Pro-Choice America, formerly the National Abortion and

> **| DID YOU KNOW . . .**
> That in 1922, at age eighty-seven, Rebecca Latimer Felton was the first and oldest woman to serve in the U.S. Senate—although she was appointed as a token gesture and was allowed to serve only one day?

In 1977, protesters holding signs against the Equal Rights Amendment gathered outside the White House. Why were some women against this constitutional amendment? (Library of Congress)

| Gender Discrimination
Any practice, policy, or procedure that denies equality of treatment to an individual or to a group because of gender.

Shown here is Sergeant Leigh Ann Hester of the 617th Military Police Company. She received a Silver Star, making her the first female soldier serving in Operation Iraqi Freedom to receive such an award. As team leader and vehicle commander, Hester helped thwart an insurgent attack against a coalition convoy. What reasoning was previously used for preventing female soldiers from being put into combat situations in military engagements? (Spc. Jeremy D. Crisp/U.S. Army)

Reproductive Rights Action League. (For information about organizations on both sides of this debate, see the *Making a Difference* feature in Chapter 2.)

Another issue—pornography—tended to divide the women's movement rather than unite it. While a majority of feminists found pornography demeaning to women, many were also strong supporters of free speech. Others, notably activists Andrea Dworkin and Catharine Mackinnon, believed that pornography was so central to the subjugation of women that First Amendment protections should not apply. In some ways, the campaign against pornography was reminiscent of the "social control" tendencies of the suffrage movement that had been expressed in such issues as prohibition.

Challenging Gender Discrimination in the Courts.   When the ERA failed to be ratified, women's rights organizations began a campaign to win more limited national and state laws that would guarantee the equality of women. This more limited campaign met with much success. Women's rights organizations also challenged discriminatory statutes and policies in the federal courts, contending that **gender discrimination** violated the Fourteenth Amendment's equal protection clause. Since the 1970s, the Supreme Court has tended to scrutinize gender classifications closely and has invalidated a number of such statutes and policies. For example, in 1977 the Court held that police and firefighting units cannot establish arbitrary rules, such as height and weight requirements, that tend to keep women from joining those occupations.[14] In 1983, the Court ruled that life insurance companies cannot charge different rates for women and men.[15]

A question that the Court has not ruled on is whether women should be allowed to participate in military combat. Generally, the Supreme Court has left this decision up to Congress and the Department of Defense. Recently, women have been allowed to serve as combat pilots and on naval warships. To date, however, they have not been allowed to join infantry direct-combat units, although they are now permitted to serve in combat-support units. In 1996, the Supreme Court held that the state-financed Virginia Military Institute's policy of accepting only males violated the equal protection clause.[16]

Expanding Women's Political Opportunities.   Following the failure of the ERA, in addition to fighting discrimination in the courts, the women's movement began to work for increased representation in government. Several women's political organizations that are active today concentrate their efforts on getting women elected to political offices. These organizations include the National Women's Political Caucus, the Coalition for Women's Appointments, the Feminist Majority Foundation, and the National Education for Women's Leadership (the NEW Leadership).

Women in Politics Today

The efforts of women's rights advocates have helped to increase the number of women holding political offices at all levels of government.

Women in Congress.   Although a men's club atmosphere still prevails in Congress, the number of women holding congressional seats has increased significantly in recent years. Elections during the 1990s brought more women to Congress than

[14]*Dothard v. Rawlinson*, 433 U.S. 321 (1977).
[15]*Arizona v. Norris*, 463 U.S. 1073 (1983).
[16]*United States v. Virginia*, 518 U.S. 515 (1996).

All of the fourteen women senators from the 109th Congress are shown here. What obstacles have women faced in their attempts to reach the highest political ranks in America? (AP Photo)

either the Senate or the House had seen before. In 2001, for the first time, a woman was elected to a leadership post in Congress. Nancy Pelosi of California was elected as the Democrats' minority whip in the U.S. House of Representatives. In 2002, she became minority leader.

Women in Congress after the 2006 Elections.   The big news about women in Congress was, of course, that Nancy Pelosi would become the first woman Speaker of the House in the history of the United States. In all, 151 women ran for Congress in 2006. Seventy of the 139 women who ran for seats in the House of Representatives won their races. Eight of the 12 women who ran for seats in the Senate won. The Senate now includes 16 women, up from 14 in the 109th Congress—and an all-time record.

Women in the Executive and Judicial Branches.   Although no woman has yet been nominated for president by a major political party, in 1984 a woman, Geraldine Ferraro, became the Democratic nominee for vice president. Another woman, Elizabeth Dole, made a serious run for the Republican presidential nomination in the 2000 campaigns. A recent Gallup poll found that 92 percent of Americans said that they would vote for a qualified woman for president if she were nominated by their party.

Increasing numbers of women are also being appointed to cabinet posts. President Bill Clinton (1993–2001) appointed four women to his cabinet, more than any previous president. Madeleine Albright was appointed to the important post of secretary of state. President George W. Bush also appointed several women to cabinet positions, including Condoleezza Rice as his secretary of state in 2005, and a number of other women to various federal offices.

Increasing numbers of women are sitting on federal judicial benches as well. President Ronald Reagan (1981–1989) was credited with a historic first when he appointed Sandra Day O'Connor to the Supreme Court in 1981. President Clinton appointed a second woman, Ruth Bader Ginsburg, to the Court. O'Connor retired from the Court in 2006. President Bush initially nominated another woman, Harriet Miers, to take her place on the bench. Miers, however, later withdrew her nomination.

Continuing Disproportionate Leadership.   For all their achievements in the political arena, the number of women holding political offices remains disproportionately low compared with their participation as voters. In recent elections, the turnout of female voters nationally has been slightly higher than that of male voters.

Gender-Based Discrimination in the Workplace

Traditional cultural beliefs concerning the proper role of women in society continue to be evident not only in the political arena but also in the workplace. Since the 1960s, however, women have gained substantial protection against discrimination through laws mandating equal employment opportunities and equal pay.

Title VII of the Civil Rights Act of 1964

Title VII of the Civil Rights Act of 1964 prohibits gender discrimination in employment and has been used to strike down employment policies that discriminate against employees on the basis of gender. Even so-called protective policies have been held to violate Title VII if they have a discriminatory effect. In 1991, for example, the Supreme Court held that a fetal protection policy established by Johnson Controls, Inc., the country's largest producer of automobile batteries, violated Title VII. The policy required all women of childbearing age working in jobs that entailed periodic exposure to lead or other hazardous materials to prove that they were infertile or to transfer to other positions. Women who agreed to transfer often had to accept cuts in pay and reduced job responsibilities. The Court concluded that women who are "as capable of doing their jobs as their male counterparts may not be forced to choose between having a child and having a job."[17]

In 1978, Congress amended Title VII to expand the definition of gender discrimination to include discrimination based on pregnancy. Women affected by pregnancy, childbirth, or related medical conditions must be treated—for all employment-related purposes, including the receipt of benefits under employee benefit programs—the same as other persons not so affected but similar in ability to work.

Sexual Harassment

| Sexual Harassment
Unwanted physical or verbal conduct or abuse of a sexual nature that interferes with a recipient's job performance, creates a hostile work environment, or carries with it an implicit or explicit threat of adverse employment consequences.

The Supreme Court has also held that Title VII's prohibition of gender-based discrimination extends to **sexual harassment** in the workplace. Sexual harassment occurs when job opportunities, promotions, salary increases, and the like are given in return for sexual favors. A special form of sexual harassment, called hostile-environment harassment, occurs when an employee is subjected to sexual conduct or comments that interfere with the employee's job performance or are so pervasive or severe as to create an intimidating, hostile, or offensive environment.

In two 1998 cases, the Supreme Court clarified the responsibilities of employers in preventing sexual harassment. In *Faragher v. City of Boca Raton*, the question was the following: Should an employer be held liable for a supervisor's sexual harassment of an employee even though the employer was unaware of the harassment? The Court ruled that the employer in this case was liable but stated that the employer might have avoided such liability if it had taken reasonable care to prevent harassing behavior—which the employer had not done. In the second case, *Burlington Industries v. Ellerth*, the Court similarly held that an employer was liable for sexual harassment caused by a supervisor's actions even though the employee had suffered no tangible job consequences as a result of those actions. Again, the Court emphasized that a key factor in holding the employer liable was whether the

---

[17]*United Automobile Workers v. Johnson Controls, Inc.*, 499 U.S. 187 (1991).

employer had exercised reasonable care to prevent and promptly correct any sexually harassing behavior.[18]

In another 1998 case, *Oncale v. Sundowner Offshore Services, Inc.*,[19] the Supreme Court addressed a further issue: Should Title VII protection be extended to cover situations in which individuals are harassed by members of the same gender? The Court answered this question in the affirmative.

Wage Discrimination

By 2010, women will constitute a majority of U.S. workers. Although Title VII and other legislation since the 1960s have mandated equal employment opportunities for men and women, women continue to earn less, on average, than men do.

The Equal Pay Act of 1963.   The issue of wage discrimination was first addressed during World War II (1939–1945), when the War Labor Board issued an "equal pay for women" policy. In implementing the policy, the board often evaluated jobs for their comparability and required equal pay for comparable jobs. The board's authority ended with the war. Although it was supported by the next three presidential administrations, the Equal Pay Act was not enacted until 1963 as an amendment to the Fair Labor Standards Act of 1938.

Basically, the Equal Pay Act requires employers to provide equal pay for substantially equal work. In other words, males cannot legally be paid more than females who perform essentially the same job. The Equal Pay Act did not address the fact that certain types of jobs traditionally held by women pay lower wages than the jobs usually held by men. For example, more women than men are salesclerks and nurses, whereas more men than women are construction workers and truck drivers. Even if all clerks performing substantially similar jobs for a company earned the same salaries, they typically would still be earning less than the company's truck drivers.

---

[18]524 U.S. 725 (1998); and 524 U.S. 742 (1998).
[19]523 U.S. 75 (1998).

President John Kennedy is shown here passing out pens he used to sign a bill to provide equal pay for women on June 10, 1963. Do you think that this federal law has been effective in equalizing the pay of men and women in the United States? Why or why not? (AP Photo/Harvey Georges)

When Congress passed the Equal Pay Act in 1963, a woman, on average, made 59 cents for every dollar earned by a man. Figures recently released by the U.S. Department of Labor suggest that women now earn 76 cents for every dollar that men earn. In some areas, the wage gap is widening. According to the results of a General Accounting Office survey reported in 2002, female managers in ten industries made less money relative to male managers in 2000 than they did in 1995. In the entertainment industry, for example, in 2000 female managers earned 62 cents for every dollar earned by male managers—down from 83 cents in 1995.[20]

The Glass Ceiling.   Although greater numbers of women are holding jobs in professions or business enterprises that were once dominated by men, few women hold top positions in their firms. Less than 12 percent of the Fortune 500 companies in the United States—the nation's leading corporations—have a woman as one of their five highest-paid executives. In all, according to Census Bureau statistics, men still hold 93 percent of the top corporate management positions in this country. Because the barriers faced by women in the corporate world are subtle and not easily pinpointed, they have been referred to as the "glass ceiling."

Over the last decade, women have been breaking through the glass ceiling in far greater numbers than before. Alternatively, some corporations have offered a "mommy track" to high-achieving women. The mommy track allows a woman more time to pursue a family life but usually rules out promotion to top jobs. The mommy track therefore tends to reinforce the glass ceiling.

Immigration, Hispanics, and Civil Rights

Time and again, this nation has been challenged and changed—and culturally enriched—by immigrant groups. All of these immigrants have faced the challenges involved in living in a new and different political and cultural environment. Most of them have had to overcome language barriers, and many have had to deal with discrimination in one form or another because of their color, their inability to speak English fluently, or their customs. The civil rights legislation passed during and since the 1960s has done much to counter the effects of prejudice against immigrant groups by ensuring that they obtain equal rights under the law.

One of the questions facing Americans and their political leaders today concerns the effect of immigration on American politics and government. This is especially true with regard to the Hispanic American community. With the influx of individuals from Latin American countries growing exponentially, issues related to immigration and Hispanic Americans will continue to gain greater attention in years to come.

The Continued Influx of Immigrants

Today, immigration rates are the highest they have been since their peak in the early twentieth century. Every year, about one million people immigrate to this country, and those who were born on foreign soil now constitute more than 10 percent of the U.S. population—twice the percentage of thirty years ago.

Since 1977, more than 80 percent of immigrants have come from Latin America or Asia. Hispanics are now overtaking African Americans as the nation's largest minority. If current immigration rates continue, by the year 2050 minority groups collectively will constitute the "majority" of Americans. If Hispanics, African Americans, and perhaps Asians were to form coalitions, they could increase their

---

[20]The results of this survey are online at **www.gao.gov/audit.htm**. To view a copy of the results, enter "GAO-02-156" in the search box. In 2004, the name of this agency was changed to the "Government Accountability Office."

political strength dramatically and would have the numerical strength to make significant changes. According to Ben Wattenberg of the American Enterprise Institute, in the future the "old guard" white majority will no longer dominate American politics.

Illegal Immigration

As you read in the chapter-opening *What If . . .* feature, illegal immigration has become a significant national issue. Latin Americans, and especially those migrating from Mexico, constitute the majority of people entering the United States illegally. In southwestern states bordering Mexico, Hispanic populations have exploded largely because of the ever-increasing influx of illegal immigrants. The immigrants typically come to the United States to work, and their labor tends to be in high demand. The most recent housing boom across the nation, for example, was partially fueled by the steady stream of illegal immigrants seeking jobs.

One civil rights question that has often surfaced is whether the government should provide services to those who enter the country illegally. At one point, a bill that would criminalize assisting illegal immigrants circulated in the House of Representatives. This bill and similar measures at the state level have come in response to residents of southwestern states who have complained about the need to shore up border control. These citizens perceive illegal immigrants as a burden on government-provided social services and the health-care industry. Some schools have become crowded with the children of illegal immigrants. Often these children require greater attention because of their inability to speak English. Moreover, hospitals and health-care providers in many communities have been overwhelmed because a significant proportion of illegal immigrants do not have any type of health insurance.

These illegal Mexican migrant workers have been placed in a holding facility before they are returned to Mexico. What arguments are used to justify such actions by the United States Border Patrol? (Gerald L. Nino/ U.S. Department of Homeland Security)

Citizenship.   Illegal immigrants are not without advocates, however. Members of Congress from both parties have proposed legislation that would either immediately or gradually extend citizenship to illegal immigrants now residing in the United States. Although not all Americans agree that citizenship should be extended to illegal immigrants, the greater Hispanic community in the United States has taken up the cause. Numerous protests and marches calling for citizenship occurred in 2006, with more than one million individuals participating in demonstrations on May 1, 2006, alone. To be sure, the citizenship question will be an important political topic for the foreseeable future.

Border Crime.   Crime is another concern related to illegal immigration and border control. Smugglers who help illegal immigrants cross the border are quite common in border towns. Although some smugglers simply collect a fee, others take advantage of the situation. Many individuals attempting to enter the United States illegally are swindled or physically harmed by criminals. Indeed, many Mexican women trying to enter the United States have been raped and sexually abused by smugglers. Some of these women have said that such abuse is the price of a better life on the American side of the border. Drugs have also been a significant problem along the U.S.-Mexican border. In 2005, federal agents discovered an extensive underground tunnel that was being used as a pipeline for a lucrative drug-trafficking scheme. The governors of Arizona and New Mexico had to declare a state of emergency in 2005 because of border control problems.

Bilingual Education

The continuous influx of immigrants into this country presents another ongoing challenge—how to overcome language barriers. About half of the states have responded to this challenge by passing "English-only" laws, making English the official language of those states. Language issues have been particularly difficult for the schools. Throughout our history, educators have been faced with the question of how best to educate children who do not speak English or do not speak it very well.

During the 1950s, increased immigration from Mexico and Latin American countries caused many educators to be concerned about the language problems fac-

Children are taught in Spanish and English at the J. F. Oyster Bilingual Elementary School in Washington, D.C. Proponents of bilingual education argue that such instruction helps students acquire English more quickly than English-only programs and builds greater literacy in both the first language and in English. Evidence in California seems to point in the other direction, however. After that state's bilingual program was terminated, achievement in formerly bilingual schools actually improved. Why might this have occurred? (AP Photo/Evan Vucci)

ing these immigrants. Spanish had effectively become America's second language, yet local school districts in some parts of the Southwest prohibited children from speaking Spanish, even on school playgrounds. In the 1960s, bilingual education programs began to be implemented as a solution to the language problems facing immigrants.

Accommodating Diversity with Bilingual Education. Bilingual education programs teach children in their native language while also teaching them English. To some extent, today's bilingual education programs are the result of the government policies favoring multiculturalism that grew out of the civil rights movement. Multiculturalism involves the belief that the government should accommodate the needs of different cultural groups and should protect and encourage ethnic and cultural differences.

Children attending classes taught in English were frequently encouraged by their teachers as well as their parents to speak English as much as possible, both at school and at home. Children who did so felt distanced from their grandparents and family members who spoke no English and, as a result, felt cut off from their ethnic backgrounds. Bilingual education was premised on the hope that, over time, Hispanic children would become truly bilingual without having to sacrifice their close family relationships and cultural heritage.

Congress authorized bilingual education programs in 1968 when it passed the Bilingual Education Act, which was intended primarily to help Hispanic children learn English. In a 1974 case, *Lau v. Nichols*,[21] the Supreme Court bolstered the claim that children have a right to bilingual education. In that case, the Court ordered a California school district to provide special programs for Chinese students with language difficulties if a substantial number of these children attended school in the district. Today, most bilingual education programs are for Hispanic American children, particularly in areas of the country, such as California and Texas, where there are large numbers of Hispanic residents.

Controversy over Bilingual Education. The bilingual programs established in the 1960s and subsequently have increasingly come under attack. Indeed, in 1998 California residents passed a ballot initiative that called for the end of bilingual education programs in that state. The law allowed schools to implement "English-immersion" programs instead. In these programs, students are given intensive instruction in English for a limited period of time and then placed in regular classrooms.

The law was immediately challenged in court on the ground that it unconstitutionally discriminated against non-English-speaking groups. A federal district court, however, concluded that the new law did not violate the equal protection clause and allowed the law to stand, thus ending bilingual education efforts in California.

Affirmative Action

As noted earlier in this chapter, the Civil Rights Act of 1964 prohibited discrimination against any person on the basis of race, color, national origin, religion, or gender. The act also established the right to equal opportunity in employment. A basic problem remained, however: minority groups and women, because of past discrimination, often lacked the education and skills to compete effectively in the marketplace. In 1965, the federal government attempted to remedy this problem by implementing the concept of affirmative action. **Affirmative action** policies attempt to "level the playing field" by giving special preferences in educational

| **Affirmative Action**
A policy in educational admissions or job hiring that gives special attention or compensatory treatment to traditionally disadvantaged groups in an effort to overcome present effects of past discrimination.

---

[21]414 U.S. 563 (1974).

admissions and employment decisions to groups that have been discriminated against in the past.

In 1965, President Lyndon Johnson ordered that affirmative action policies be undertaken to remedy the effects of past discrimination. All government agencies, including those of state and local governments, were required to implement such policies. Additionally, affirmative action requirements were imposed on companies that sell goods or services to the federal government and on institutions that receive federal funds. Affirmative action policies were also required whenever an employer had been ordered to develop such a plan by a court or by the Equal Employment Opportunity Commission because of evidence of past discrimination. Finally, labor unions that had been found to discriminate against women or minorities in the past were required to establish and follow affirmative action plans.

Affirmative action programs have been controversial because they allegedly result in discrimination against majority groups, such as white males (or discrimination against other minority groups that may not be given preferential treatment under a particular affirmative action program). At issue in the current debate over affirmative action programs is whether such programs, because of their discriminatory nature, violate the equal protection clause of the Fourteenth Amendment to the Constitution.

The *Bakke* Case

The first Supreme Court case addressing the constitutionality of affirmative action plans examined a program implemented by the University of California at Davis. Allan Bakke, a white student who had been turned down for medical school at the Davis campus, discovered that his academic record was better than those of some of the minority applicants who had been admitted to the program. He sued the University of California regents, alleging **reverse discrimination.** The UC-Davis Medical School had held sixteen places out of one hundred for educationally "disadvantaged students" each year, and the administrators at that campus admitted to using race as a criterion for admission for these particular minority slots. At trial in 1974, Bakke said that his exclusion from medical school violated his rights under the Fourteenth Amendment's provision for equal protection of the laws. The trial court agreed. On appeal, the California Supreme Court agreed also. Finally, the regents of the university appealed to the United States Supreme Court.

In 1978, the Supreme Court handed down its decision in *Regents of the University of California v. Bakke.*[22] The Court did not rule against affirmative action programs. Rather, it held that Bakke must be admitted to the UC-Davis Medical School because its admissions policy had used race as the sole criterion for the sixteen "minority" positions. Justice Lewis Powell, speaking for the Court, indicated that while race can be considered "as a factor" among others in admissions (and presumably hiring) decisions, race cannot be the sole factor. So affirmative action programs, but not specific quota systems, were upheld as constitutional.

Further Limits on Affirmative Action

A number of cases decided during the 1980s and 1990s placed further limits on affirmative action programs. In a landmark decision in 1995, *Adarand Constructors, Inc. v. Peña,*[23] the Supreme Court held that any federal, state, or local affirmative action program that uses racial or ethnic classifications as the basis for making decisions is subject to "strict scrutiny" by the courts. Under a strict-scrutiny analysis, to be constitutional, a discriminatory law or action must be narrowly tailored to meet a *compelling* government interest. In effect, the Court's opinion in *Adarand* means that

Reverse Discrimination

Reverse Discrimination
The charge that an affirmative action program discriminates against those who do not have minority status.

---

[22]438 U.S. 265 (1978).
[23]515 U.S. 200 (1995).

an affirmative action program cannot make use of quotas or preferences for unqualified persons, and once the program has succeeded in achieving that compelling government interest, the program must be changed or dropped.

In 1996, a federal appellate court went even further. In *Hopwood v. State of Texas*,[24] two white law school applicants sued the University of Texas School of Law in Austin, alleging that they had been denied admission because of the school's affirmative action program. The program allowed admissions officials to take race and other factors into consideration. The federal appellate court held that the program violated the equal protection clause because it discriminated in favor of minority applicants. Significantly, the court directly challenged the *Bakke* decision by stating that the use of race even as a means of achieving diversity on college campuses "undercuts the Fourteenth Amendment."

In 2003, however, in two cases involving the University of Michigan, the Supreme Court indicated that limited affirmative action programs continue to be acceptable and that diversity is a legitimate goal. The Court struck down the affirmative action plan used for undergraduate admissions at the university, which automatically awarded a substantial number of points to applicants based on minority status.[25] At the same time, it approved the admissions plan used by the law school, which took race into consideration as part of a complete examination of each applicant's background.[26]

State Ballot Initiatives

A ballot initiative passed by California voters in 1996 amended that state's constitution to end all state-sponsored affirmative action programs. The law was challenged immediately in court by civil rights groups and others. These groups claimed that the law violated the Fourteenth Amendment by denying racial minorities and women the equal protection of the laws. In 1997, however, a federal appellate court upheld the constitutionality of the amendment. Thus, affirmative action is now illegal in California in all state-sponsored institutions, including state agencies and educational institutions. In 1998, Washington voters also approved a law banning affirmative action in that state.

Special Protection for Older Americans

Americans are getting older. In colonial times, about half the population was under the age of sixteen. In 2000, fewer than one in four Americans was under the age of sixteen. Today, about 38 million Americans (nearly 13 percent of the population) are aged sixty-five or older. By the year 2025, this figure is projected to reach about 70 million. By 2050, the portion of the population over age sixty-five will have almost doubled from the current figure.

Older citizens face a variety of difficulties unique to their group. One problem that seems to endure, despite government legislation designed to prevent it, is age discrimination in employment.

Age Discrimination in Employment

Age discrimination is potentially the most widespread form of discrimination, because anyone—regardless of race, color, national origin, or gender—could be a victim at some point in life. The unstated policies of some companies not to hire or

On the University of Michigan campus, students react to a federal appeals court decision in 2002 to uphold the use of race in admissions to the university's law school. The two students in the back are supporting affirmative action. The student in the front is opposing it. (AP Photo/Danny Moloshok)

---

[24]84 F.3d 720 (5th Cir. 1996).
[25]*Gratz v. Bollinger*, 539 U.S. 244 (2003).
[26]*Grutter v. Bollinger*, 539 U.S. 306 (2003).

to demote or dismiss people they feel are "too old" have made it difficult for some older workers to succeed in their jobs or continue with their careers. Additionally, older workers have fallen victim at times to cost-cutting efforts by employers. To reduce operational costs, companies may replace older, higher-salaried workers with younger, lower-salaried workers.

The Age Discrimination in Employment Act of 1967

In an attempt to protect older employees from such discriminatory practices, Congress passed the Age Discrimination in Employment Act (ADEA) in 1967. The act, which applies to employers, employment agencies, and labor organizations and covers individuals over the age of forty, prohibits discrimination against individuals on the basis of age unless age is shown to be a bona fide occupational qualification reasonably necessary to the normal operation of the particular business.

To succeed in a suit for age discrimination, an employee must prove that the employer's action, such as a decision to fire the employee, was motivated, at least in part, by age bias. Even if an older worker is replaced by a younger worker falling under the protection of the ADEA—that is, by a younger worker who is also over the age of forty—the older worker is entitled to bring a suit under the ADEA.[27] As discussed in Chapter 3 in the context of federalism, in 2000 the Supreme Court limited the applicability of the ADEA in its decision in *Kimel v. Florida Board of Regents*.[28] The Court held that the sovereign immunity granted to the states by the Eleventh Amendment to the Constitution precluded suits against a state by private parties alleging violations of the ADEA. Victims of age discrimination can bring actions under state statutes, however, and most states have laws protecting their citizens from age discrimination.

Mandatory Retirement
Forced retirement when a person reaches a certain age.

The ADEA, as initially passed, did not address one of the major problems facing older workers—**mandatory retirement** rules, which require employees to retire when they reach a certain age. Mandatory retirement rules often mean that competent, well-trained employees who want to continue working are unable to do so. In 1978, in an amendment to the ADEA, Congress prohibited mandatory retirement rules for most employees under the age of seventy. In 1986, Congress outlawed mandatory retirement rules entirely for all but a few selected occupations, such as firefighting.

Securing Rights for Persons with Disabilities

Like older Americans, persons with disabilities did not fall under the protective umbrella of the Civil Rights Act of 1964. In 1973, however, Congress passed the Rehabilitation Act, which prohibited discrimination against persons with disabilities in programs receiving federal aid. A 1978 amendment to the act established the Architectural and Transportation Barriers Compliance Board. Regulations for ramps, elevators, and the like in all federal buildings were implemented. Congress passed the Education for All Handicapped Children Act in 1975. It guarantees that all children with disabilities will receive an "appropriate" education. The most significant federal legislation to protect the rights of persons with disabilities, however, is the Americans with Disabilities Act (ADA), which Congress passed in 1990.

The Americans with Disabilities Act of 1990

The ADA requires that all public buildings and public services be accessible to persons with disabilities. The act also mandates that employers must reasonably

---

[27]*O'Connor v. Consolidated Coin Caterers Corp.*, 517 U.S. 308 (1996).
[28]528 U.S. 62 (2000).

accommodate the needs of workers or potential workers with disabilities. Physical access means ramps; handrails; wheelchair-accessible restrooms, counters, drinking fountains, telephones, and doorways; and easily accessible mass transit. In addition, other steps must be taken to comply with the act. Car rental companies must provide cars with hand controls for disabled drivers. Telephone companies are required to have operators to pass on messages from speech-impaired persons who use telephones with keyboards.

The ADA requires employers to "reasonably accommodate" the needs of persons with disabilities unless to do so would cause the employer to suffer an "undue hardship." The ADA defines persons with disabilities as persons who have physical or mental impairments that "substantially limit" their everyday activities. Health conditions that have been considered disabilities under federal law include blindness, alcoholism, heart disease, cancer, muscular dystrophy, cerebral palsy, paraplegia, diabetes, acquired immune deficiency syndrome (AIDS), and infection with the human immunodeficiency virus (HIV) that causes AIDS.

The ADA does not require that *unqualified* applicants with disabilities be hired or retained. If a job applicant or an employee with a disability, with reasonable accommodation, can perform essential job functions, however, then the employer must make the accommodation. Required accommodations may include installing ramps for a wheelchair, establishing more flexible working hours, creating or modifying job assignments, and creating or improving training materials and procedures.

Limiting the Scope and Applicability of the ADA

Beginning in 1999, the Supreme Court has issued a series of decisions that effectively limit the scope of the ADA. In 1999, for example, the Court held in *Sutton v. United Airlines, Inc.*[29] that a condition (in this case, severe nearsightedness) that can be corrected with medication or a corrective device (in this case, eyeglasses) is not considered a disability under the ADA. In other words, the determination of whether a person is substantially limited in a major life activity is based on how the person functions when taking medication or using corrective devices, not on how the person functions without these measures. Since then, the courts have held that plaintiffs with bipolar disorder, epilepsy, diabetes, and other conditions do not fall under the ADA's protections if the conditions can be corrected with medication or corrective devices—even though the plaintiffs contended that they were discriminated against because of their conditions.

In a 2002 decision, the Court held that carpal tunnel syndrome did not constitute a disability under the ADA. The Court stated that although an employee with carpal tunnel syndrome could not perform the manual tasks associated with her job, the injury did not constitute a disability under the ADA because it did not "substantially limit" the major life activity of performing manual tasks.[30]

The Supreme Court has also limited the applicability of the ADA by holding that lawsuits under the ADA cannot be brought against state government employers.[31] In a 2001 case, the Court concluded—as it did with the ADEA, as mentioned earlier—that states, as sovereigns, are immune from lawsuits brought against them by private parties under the federal ADA.

A man and a woman communicate in sign language at work. Sign language is not a method of representing English but is an entirely unique language system. Despite the fact that it is not English, could sign language be exempted from the effects of "English-only" laws that have been adopted in some jurisdictions? Why or why not? (Michael Newman/PhotoEdit)

---

[29]527 U.S. 471 (1999).
[30]*Toyota Manufacturing, Kentucky, Inc. v. Williams*, 534 U.S. 184 (2002).
[31]*Board of Trustees of the University of Alabama v. Garrett*, 531 U.S. 356 (2001).

The Rights and Status of Gay Males and Lesbians

On June 27, 1969, patrons of the Stonewall Inn, a New York City bar popular with gay men and lesbians, responded to a police raid by throwing beer cans and bottles because they were angry at what they felt was unrelenting police harassment. In the ensuing riot, which lasted two nights, hundreds of gay men and lesbians fought with police. Before Stonewall, the stigma attached to homosexuality and the resulting fear of exposure had tended to keep most gay men and lesbians quiescent. In the months immediately after Stonewall, however, "gay power" graffiti began to appear in New York City. The Gay Liberation Front and the Gay Activist Alliance were formed, and similar groups sprang up in other parts of the country. Thus, Stonewall has been called "the shot heard round the homosexual world."

Growth in the Gay Male and Lesbian Rights Movement

The Stonewall incident marked the beginning of the movement for gay and lesbian rights. Since then, gay men and lesbians have formed thousands of organizations to exert pressure on legislatures, the media, schools, churches, and other organizations to recognize their right to equal treatment.

To a great extent, lesbian and gay groups have succeeded in changing public opinion—and state and local laws—relating to their status and rights. Nevertheless, they continue to struggle against age-old biases against homosexuality, often rooted in deeply held religious beliefs, and the rights of gay men and lesbians remain an extremely divisive issue in American society. These attitudes were clearly illustrated in a widely publicized case involving the Boy Scouts of America. The case arose after a Boy Scout troop in New Jersey refused to allow gay activist James Dale to be a Scout leader. In 2000, the case came before the Supreme Court, which held that, as a private organization, the Boy Scouts had the right to determine the requirements for becoming a Scout leader.[32]

---

[32]*Boy Scouts of America v. Dale*, 530 U.S. 640 (2000).

James Dale, center, was not allowed to be a Boy Scout leader because he is gay. Although a New Jersey state appeals court ruled that the Boy Scouts of America's ban on admitting gay individuals violated New Jersey's laws against discrimination, the United States Supreme Court held that the Boy Scouts, as a private organization, had the right to bar gay men from becoming Scout leaders. Had the Boy Scouts been receiving partial government funding, do you think the Court would have ruled the same way? (AP Photo/Stuart Ramson)

State and Local Laws Targeting Gay Men and Lesbians

Before the Stonewall incident, forty-nine states had sodomy laws that made various kinds of sexual acts, including homosexual acts, illegal (Illinois, which had repealed its sodomy law in 1962, was the only exception). During the 1970s and 1980s, more than half of these laws were either repealed or struck down by the courts.

The trend toward repealing state antigay laws was suspended in 1986 with the Supreme Court's decision in *Bowers v. Hardwick*.[33] In that case, the Court upheld, by a five-to-four vote, a Georgia law that made homosexual conduct between two adults a crime. In 2003, the Court reversed its earlier position on sodomy with its decision in *Lawrence v. Texas*.[34] In this case, the Court held that laws against sodomy violate the due process clause of the Fourteenth Amendment. The Court stated: "The liberty protected by the Constitution allows homosexual persons the right to choose to enter upon relationships in the confines of their homes and their own private lives and still retain their dignity as free persons." The result of *Lawrence v. Texas* was to invalidate all remaining sodomy laws throughout the country.

Today, twelve states[35] and more than 230 cities and counties have special laws protecting lesbians and gay men against discrimination in employment, housing, public accommodations, and credit. At one point, Colorado adopted a constitutional amendment to invalidate all state and local laws protecting homosexuals from discrimination. Ultimately, however, the Supreme Court, in *Romer v. Evans*,[36] invalidated the amendment, ruling that it violated the equal protection clause of the U.S. Constitution because it denied to homosexuals in Colorado—but to no other Colorado residents— "the right to seek specific protection of the law." Several laws at the national level have also been changed over the past two decades. Among other things, the government has lifted a ban on hiring gay men and lesbians and voided a 1952 law prohibiting gay men and lesbians from immigrating to the United States.

The Gay Community and Politics

Politicians at the national level have not overlooked the potential significance of homosexual issues in American politics. While conservative politicians generally have been critical of efforts to secure gay and lesbian rights, liberals, by and large, have been speaking out for gay rights in the last twenty-five years. In 1980, the Democratic platform included a gay plank for the first time.

President Bill Clinton long embraced much of the gay rights agenda and became the first sitting president to address a gay rights organization. In 1997, in a speech intentionally reminiscent of Harry Truman's 1947 speech to an African American civil rights group, Clinton pledged his support for equal rights for gay and lesbian Americans at a fund-raiser sponsored by the Human Rights Campaign Fund. In 2000, George W. Bush became the first Republican presidential candidate to meet with a large group of openly gay leaders to discuss their issues. Although Bush asserted that he would continue to oppose gay marriage and adoption, he also said that being openly gay would not disqualify a person from serving in a prominent position in his administration.

To date, eleven openly gay men and lesbians have been elected to the House of Representatives, but none has succeeded yet in gaining a seat in the Senate. Gay rights groups continue to work for increased political representation in Congress, however.

DID YOU KNOW . . .

That in October 1999, Scouts Canada, the Canadian equivalent of the Boy Scouts of America, officially approved North America's first gay Scout troop?

---

[33]478 U.S. 186 (1986).

[34]539 U.S. 558 (2003).

[35]California, Connecticut, Hawaii, Maryland, Massachusetts, Minnesota, Nevada, New Hampshire, New Jersey, Rhode Island, Vermont, and Wisconsin. Maine also had a law protecting gay and lesbian rights until February 1998, when the law was repealed in a referendum.

[36]517 U.S. 620 (1996).

Gay Men and Lesbians in the Military

The U.S. Department of Defense traditionally has viewed homosexuality as incompatible with military service. Supporters of gay and lesbian rights have attacked this policy in recent years, and in 1993 the policy was modified. In that year, President Clinton announced that a new policy, generally characterized as "don't ask, don't tell," would be in effect. Enlistees would not be asked about their sexual orientation, and gay men and lesbians would be allowed to serve in the military so long as they did not declare that they were gay or lesbian or commit homosexual acts. Military officials endorsed the new policy, after opposing it initially, but supporters of gay rights were not enthusiastic. Clinton had promised during his presidential campaign to repeal outright the long-standing ban.

Several gay men and lesbians who have been discharged from military service have protested their discharges by bringing suit against the Defense Department. Often at issue in these cases are the constitutional rights to free speech, privacy, and the equal protection of the laws. A widely publicized 1998 case involved the Navy's dismissal of a naval officer, Timothy McVeigh,[37] on the ground that he had entered "gay" on a profile page for his account with America Online (AOL). Naval officers claimed that this amounted to a public declaration of McVeigh's gay status and thus justified his discharge. McVeigh argued that it was not a public declaration. Furthermore, contended McVeigh, the Navy had violated a 1986 federal privacy law governing electronic communications by obtaining information from AOL without a warrant or a court order. In 1998, a federal court judge agreed and ordered the Navy to reinstate McVeigh.[38]

---

[37]This is not the Timothy McVeigh who was convicted for the 1995 bombing of the Alfred P. Murrah Federal Building in Oklahoma City.

[38]*McVeigh v. Cohen*, 983 F.Supp. 215 (D.C. 1998).

Not all gays and lesbians and their supporters were in favor of the Pentagon's "Don't ask, don't tell" policy. On Veteran's Day 2005, these gay veterans and activists held a parade and memorial service to honor the contributions of gays and lesbians in the military. (AP Photo/Paul Sakuma)

Same-Sex Marriages

Perhaps one of the most sensitive political issues with respect to the rights of gay and lesbian couples is whether they should be allowed to marry, just as heterosexual couples are.

Defense of Marriage Act. The controversy over this issue was fueled in 1993 when the Hawaii Supreme Court ruled that denying marriage licenses to gay couples might violate the equal protection clause of the Hawaii constitution.[39] In the wake of this event, other states began to worry about whether they might have to treat gay men or lesbians who were legally married in another state as married couples in their state as well. Opponents of gay rights pushed for state laws banning same-sex marriages, and a number of states enacted such laws. At the federal level, Congress passed the Defense of Marriage Act of 1996, which bans federal recognition of lesbian and gay couples and allows state governments to ignore same-sex marriages performed in other states.

Citizens calling for a ballot measure to prohibit legal recognition of same-sex marriages demonstrate their cause near the Minnesota Senate chamber in 2006, in St. Paul. Numerous states have voted on similar measures in recent years. Should the issue of gay marriage be left for the states to decide? (AP Photo/Jim Mone)

The controversy over gay marriages was fueled again by developments in the state of Vermont. In 1999, the Vermont Supreme Court ruled that gay couples are entitled to the same benefits of marriage as opposite-sex couples.[40] Subsequently, in April 2000, the Vermont legislature passed a law permitting gay and lesbian couples to form "civil unions." The law entitled partners forming civil unions to receive some three hundred state benefits available to married couples, including the rights to inherit a partner's property and to decide on medical treatment for an incapacitated partner. It did not, however, entitle those partners to receive any benefits allowed to married couples under federal law, such as spousal Social Security benefits. In 2005, Connecticut became the second state to adopt civil unions. Some felt that the Vermont and Connecticut legislatures did not go far enough—they should have allowed full legal marriage rights to same-sex couples.

State Recognition of Gay Marriages. Massachusetts was the first state to recognize gay marriage. In November 2003, the Massachusetts Supreme Judicial Court ruled that same-sex couples have a right to civil marriage under the Massachusetts state constitution.[41] The court also ruled that civil unions would not suffice. In 2005, the Massachusetts legislature voted down a proposed ballot initiative that would have amended the state constitution to explicitly state that marriage could only be between one man and one woman (but would have extended civil union status to same-sex couples). Also in 2005, the California state legislature attempted to legalize gay marriage. Since then, the highest courts in several states, including New York and Washington State, have upheld bans on gay marriages. Same-sex marriage is currently accepted nationwide in Belgium, Canada, the Netherlands, South Africa, and Spain.

---

[39]*Baehr v. Lewin*, 852 P.2d 44 (Hawaii 1993).
[40]*Baker v. Vermont*, 744 A.2d 864 (Vt. 1999).
[41]*Goodridge v. Department of Public Health*, 798 N.E.2d 941 (Mass. 2003).

Child Custody and Adoption

Gay men and lesbians have also faced difficulties in obtaining child-custody and adoption rights. Courts around the country, when deciding which of two parents should have custody, have wrestled with how much weight, if any, should be given to a parent's sexual orientation. For some time, the courts were split fairly evenly on this issue. In about half the states, courts held that a parent's sexual orientation should not be a significant factor in determining child custody. Courts in other states, however, tended to give more weight to sexual orientation. In one case, a court even went so far as to award custody to a father because the child's mother was a lesbian, even though the father had served eight years in prison for killing his first wife. Today, however, courts in the majority of states no longer deny custody or visitation rights to persons solely on the basis of their sexual orientation.

The last decade has also seen a sharp climb in the number of gay men and lesbians who are adopting children. To date, twenty-two states have allowed lesbians and gay men to adopt children through state-operated or private adoption agencies.

| The Rights and Status of Juveniles

Approximately 76 million Americans—almost 30 percent of the total population—are under twenty-one years of age. The definition of *children* ranges from persons under age sixteen to persons under age twenty-one. However defined, children in the United States have fewer rights and protections than any other major group in society.

The reason for this lack of rights is the common presumption of society and its lawmakers that children basically are protected by their parents. This is not to say that children are the exclusive property of the parents. Rather, an overwhelming case in favor of *not* allowing parents to control the actions of their children must be presented before children can be given authorization to act without parental consent (or before the state can be given authorization to act on children's behalf without regard to their parents' wishes).

Supreme Court decisions affecting children's rights began a process of slow evolution with *Brown v. Board of Education of Topeka*, the landmark civil rights case of 1954 discussed earlier in this chapter. In *Brown*, the Court granted children the status of rights-bearing persons. In 1967, in *In re Gault*,[42] the Court expressly held that children have a constitutional right to be represented by counsel at the government's expense in a criminal action. Five years later, the Court acknowledged that "children are 'persons' within the meaning of the Bill of Rights. We have held so over and over again."[43] In 1976, the Court recognized a girl's right to have an abortion without consulting her parents.[44] (More recently, however, the Court has allowed state laws to dictate whether the child must obtain consent.)

Voting Rights and the Young

The Twenty-sixth Amendment to the Constitution, ratified on July 1, 1971, reads as follows:

> The right of citizens of the United States, who are eighteen years of age or older, to vote shall not be denied or abridged by the United States or by any State on account of age.

Before this amendment was ratified, the age at which citizens could vote was twenty-one in most states. Why did the Twenty-sixth Amendment specify age eigh-

---

[42]387 U.S. 1 (1967).
[43]*Wisconsin v. Yoder*, 406 U.S. 205 (1972).
[44]*Planned Parenthood of Central Missouri v. Danforth*, 428 U.S. 52 (1976).

A teacher gathers voter-registration forms from graduating seniors in Verona, Wisconsin. Do you think these students will actually vote, or do you think they will stay away from the polls like many of their peers? (Obviously, registering to vote is not equivalent to actually voting.) (AP Photo/Andy Manis)

teen? Why not seventeen or sixteen? And why did it take until 1971 to allow those between the ages of eighteen and twenty-one to vote? One of the arguments used for granting suffrage to eighteen-year-olds was that, because they could be drafted to fight in the country's wars, they had a stake in public policy. At the time, the example of the Vietnam War (1964–1975) was paramount.

Have eighteen- to twenty-year-olds used their right to vote? Yes and no. In 1972, immediately after the passage of the Twenty-sixth Amendment, 58 percent of eighteen- to twenty-year-olds were registered to vote, and 48.4 percent reported that they had voted. But by the 2004 presidential elections, of the 11.5 million U.S. residents in the eighteen-to-twenty age bracket, 50.7 percent were registered, and 41 percent reported that they had voted. Subsequent elections have shown similar results. In contrast, voter turnout among Americans aged sixty-five or older is very high, usually between 60 and 70 percent.

The Rights of Children in Civil and Criminal Proceedings

Children today have limited rights in civil and criminal proceedings in our judicial system. Different procedural rules and judicial safeguards apply under civil and criminal laws. **Civil law** relates in part to contracts among private individuals or companies. **Criminal law** relates to crimes against society that are defined by society acting through its legislatures.

Civil Rights of Juveniles.   The civil rights of children are defined exclusively by state law with respect to private contract negotiations, rights, and remedies. The legal definition of **majority** varies from eighteen to twenty-one years of age, depending on the state. As a rule, an individual who is legally a minor cannot be held responsible for contracts that he or she forms with others. In most states, only contracts entered into for so-called **necessaries** (things necessary for subsistence, as determined by the courts) can be enforced against minors. Also, when minors engage in negligent behavior, typically their parents are liable. If, for example, a minor destroys a neighbor's fence, the neighbor may bring suit against the child's parent but not against the child.

Civil Law
The law regulating conduct between private persons over noncriminal matters. Under civil law, the government provides the forum for the settlement of disputes between private parties in such matters as contracts, domestic relations, and business interactions.

Criminal Law
The law that defines crimes and provides punishment for violations. In criminal cases, the government is the prosecutor because crimes are violations of the public order.

Majority
Full age; the age at which a person is entitled by law to the right to manage her or his own affairs and to the full enjoyment of civil rights.

Necessaries
In contract law, necessaries include whatever is reasonably necessary for suitable subsistence as measured by age, state, condition in life, and so on.

Civil law also encompasses the area of child custody. Child-custody rulings traditionally have given little weight to the wishes of the child. Courts have maintained the right to act on behalf of the child's "best interests" but have sometimes been constrained from doing so by the "greater" rights possessed by adults. For instance, a widely publicized Michigan Supreme Court ruling awarded legal custody of a two-and-a-half-year-old Michigan resident to an Iowa couple, the child's biological parents. A Michigan couple, who had cared for the child since shortly after her birth and who had petitioned to adopt the child, lost out in the custody battle. The court said that the law had allowed it to consider only the parents' rights and not the child's best interests.

Children's rights and their ability to articulate their rights for themselves in custody matters were strengthened, however, by several well-publicized rulings involving older children. In one case, for example, an eleven-year-old Florida boy filed suit in his own name, assisted by his own privately retained legal counsel, to terminate his relationship with his biological parents and to have the court affirm his right to be adopted by foster parents. The court granted his request, although it did not agree procedurally with the method by which the boy initiated the suit.[45] The news media characterized the case as the first instance in which a minor child had "divorced" himself from his parents.

Criminal Rights of Juveniles. One of the main requirements for an act to be criminal is intent. The law has given children certain defenses against criminal prosecution because of their presumed inability to have criminal intent. Under the **common law,** children up to seven years of age were considered incapable of committing a crime because they did not have the moral sense to understand that they were doing wrong. Children between the ages of seven and fourteen were also presumed to be incapable of committing a crime, but this presumption could be challenged by showing that the child understood the wrongful nature of the act. Today, states vary in their approaches. Most states retain the common law approach, although age limits vary from state to state. Other states have simply set a minimum age for criminal responsibility.

| Common Law
Judge-made law that originated in England from decisions shaped according to prevailing customs. Decisions were applied to similar situations and thus gradually became common to the nation.

---

[45]*Kingsley v. Kingsley*, 623 So.2d 780 (Fla.App. 1993).

Police restrain a teenager. Had this youth engaged in a criminal act, does his age determine whether he is responsible? (AP Photo/Mary Altaffer)

All states have juvenile court systems that handle children below the age of criminal responsibility who commit delinquent acts. The aim of juvenile courts is allegedly to reform rather than to punish. In states that retain the common law approach, children who are above the minimum age but are still juveniles can be turned over to the criminal courts if the juvenile court determines that they should be treated as adults. Children sent to juvenile court still do not have the right to trial by jury or to post bail. Also, in most states parents can commit their minor children to state mental institutions without allowing the child a hearing.

Although minors do not usually have the full rights of adults in criminal proceedings, they have certain advantages. In felony, manslaughter, murder, armed robbery, and assault cases, traditionally juveniles were not tried as adults. They were often sentenced to probation or "reform" school for a relatively short term regardless of the seriousness of their crimes. Today, however, most states allow juveniles to be tried as adults (often at the discretion of the judge) for certain crimes, such as murder. When they are tried as adults, they are given due process of law and tried for the crime, rather than being given the paternalistic treatment reserved for the juvenile delinquent. Juveniles who are tried as adults may also face adult penalties. These used to include the death penalty. In 2005, however, the Supreme Court ruled that executing persons who were under the age of eighteen when they committed their crimes would constitute cruel and unusual punishment. The Court opined that sixteen- and seventeen-year-olds do not have a fully developed sense of right and wrong, nor do they necessarily understand the full gravity of their misdeeds.[46]

Approaches to Dealing with Crime by Juveniles.   What to do about crime committed by juveniles is a pressing problem for today's political leaders. One approach to the problem is to treat juveniles as adults, which more and more judges seem to be doing. There appears to be widespread public support for this approach, as well as for lowering the age at which juveniles should receive adult treatment in criminal

---

[46]*Roper v. Simmons*, 543 U.S. 551 (2005).

A thirteen-year-old boy is led out of a courthouse in Washington State following a court appearance. The boy was accused of fatally shooting a neighbor and wounding the man's wife. He was convicted and received a sentence of fifty-eight years. What are the best ways of handling very young persons who commit violent felonies? (AP Photo/Jeremiah Coughlan/*The Columbian*)

proceedings. Polling data show that two-thirds of U.S. adults think that juveniles under the age of thirteen who commit murder should be tried as adults. Another method is to hold parents responsible for the crimes of their minor children (a minority of the states do so under so-called parental-responsibility laws). These are contradictory approaches, to be sure. Yet they perhaps reflect the divided opinion in our society concerning the rights of children versus the rights of parents.

In the wake of crimes committed in the schools, many districts have implemented what are called *zero-tolerance policies*. These policies have become controversial in recent years because, according to some, they are enforced without regard to the particular circumstances surrounding an incident. Should they be modified or revoked? See this chapter's *Which Side Are You On?* feature for a discussion of this issue.

WHICH SIDE ARE YOU ON? | Zero-Tolerance Policies

Because of fears of violence among America's youth, both in and out of school, a large number of school districts have implemented zero-tolerance rules.

Under zero-tolerance rules, students have faced mandatory expulsion for threats of violence, disobedience, defiance of authority, disruptive behavior, profanity, and possession of drugs or alcohol. Obviously, enforcement varies from school district to school district.

The federal government estimates that almost 100,000 students are expelled under zero-tolerance rules each year. In the Chicago public schools alone, about 2,500 students are expelled each year and another 13,000 are suspended.

ZERO-TOLERANCE POLICIES SEND A CLEAR MESSAGE

Supporters of zero-tolerance policies say that they send a clear message that certain behavior will not be tolerated in school. These people argue that the impartiality of these policies is their greatest strength. Zero tolerance can eliminate discrimination, because school administrators cannot be more lenient toward a white student from a middle-class background than a poor, minority student who breaks the same rule.

Former American Federation of Teachers president Sandra Feldman recalls a tough high school in the Bronx. The discipline code was not consistently enforced, and students wandered into class whenever they felt like it. A new principal worked out a plan. When the bell rang, teachers would shut their doors, and students who were in the hall would be sent to detention. On the first day, despite warnings, dozens of students were shut out of class. In a few weeks, however, lateness was no longer a problem, and the whole atmosphere of the school changed.

ZERO-TOLERANCE POLICIES SOMETIMES LEAD TO THE ABSURD

Opponents of zero tolerance point out that many students have been suspended for trivial actions. A Massachusetts girl

was expelled for bringing a plastic knife with her lunch. A Pennsylvania boy was suspended for having a soft plastic toy axe as part of his Halloween firefighter costume. Two Chicago eighth graders were arrested for bringing bags of colored powder to school. The bags contained Kool-Aid. Only after the children's attorneys forced the authorities to test the substance were the charges dropped.

Benjamin Ratner, an eighth grader at a middle school in Virginia, took a knife away from a schoolmate who said she was considering suicide. He was suspended for four months because he was caught holding the knife. The school has a zero-tolerance policy.

Given these examples, why do zero-tolerance policies remain popular among school administrators? "I think it has more to do with the fear of lawsuits than anything else," says Rutgers University psychology professor Maurice Elias. "On a deeper level, I think it bespeaks adults trying to stake their moral authority when there are really many shades of gray."

WHAT'S YOUR POSITION?

School-ground killings make the news, but they constitute less than 0.6 percent of all youth homicides. Do these statistics justify the loosening of zero-tolerance policies? Why or why not?

GOING ONLINE

To learn about the problems that can occur if schools do not have strong discipline policies, see the Web site of the American Federation of Teachers. Articles on discipline are at **www.aft.org/topics/discipline/index.htm**. For a more critical approach to the topic, see the Web site of the New York University Child Study Center at **www.aboutourkids.org/aboutour/articles/zerotolerance.html**. For a look at the effect of zero-tolerance policies on special education students, see **www.wrightslaw.com/info/discipl.index.htm**.

MAKING A DIFFERENCE | Dealing with Discrimination

Anyone applying for a job may be subjected to a variety of possibly discriminatory practices based on race, color, gender, religion, age, sexual preference, or disability. There may be tests, some of which could have a discriminatory effect. At both the state and federal levels, the government continues to examine the fairness and validity of criteria used in screening job applicants, and as a result, there are ways of addressing the problem of discrimination.

Why Should You Care?

Some people may think that discrimination is only a problem for members of racial or ethnic minorities. Actually, almost everyone can be affected. Consider that in some instances, white men have actually experienced "reverse discrimination"—and have obtained redress for it. Also, discrimination against women is common, and women constitute half the population. Even if you are male, you probably have female friends whose well-being is of interest to you. Therefore, the knowledge of how to proceed when you suspect discrimination is another useful tool to have when living in the modern world.

What Can You Do?

If you believe that you have been discriminated against by a potential employer, consider the following steps:

1. Evaluate your own capabilities, and determine if you are truly qualified for the position.
2. Analyze the reasons why you were turned down. Would others agree with you that you have been the object of discrimination, or would they uphold the employer's claim?
3. If you still believe that you have been treated unfairly, you have recourse to several agencies and services.

You should first speak to the personnel director of the company and explain politely that you believe you have not been evaluated adequately. If asked, explain your concerns clearly. If necessary, go into explicit detail, and indicate that you may have been discriminated against.

If a second evaluation is not forthcoming, contact your local state employment agency. If you still do not obtain adequate help, contact one or more of the following state agencies, usually listed in your telephone directory under "State Government."

1. If a government entity is involved, a state ombudsperson or citizen aide may be available to mediate.
2. You can contact the state civil rights commission, which at least will give you advice even if it does not wish to take up your case.
3. The state attorney general's office normally has a division dealing with discrimination and civil rights.
4. There may be a special commission or department specifically set up to help you, such as a women's status commission or a commission on Hispanics or Asian Americans. If you are a woman or a member of such a minority group, contact these commissions.

Finally, at the national level, you can contact:
American Civil Liberties Union
125 Broad St.
New York, NY. 10004-2400
212-549-2500
www.aclu.org

You can also contact the most appropriate federal agency:
Equal Employment Opportunity Commission
1801 L St. NW
Washington, DC 20507
202-663-4900
www.eeoc.gov

Key Terms

affirmative action 171

busing 152

civil disobedience 153

civil law 181

civil rights 147

common law 182

criminal law 181

de facto segregation 152

de jure segregation 152

feminism 161

gender discrimination 164

grandfather clause 150

literacy test 150

majority 181

mandatory retirement 174

necessaries 181

poll tax 150

reverse discrimination 172

separate-but-equal doctrine 149

sexual harassment 166

subpoena 156

suffrage 160

white primary 150

Chapter Summary

1 The civil rights movement started with the struggle by African Americans for equality. Before the Civil War, most African Americans were slaves, and slavery was protected by the Constitution and the Supreme Court. Constitutional amendments after the Civil War legally ended slavery, and African Americans gained citizenship, the right to vote, and other rights through legislation. This legal protection was largely a dead letter by the 1880s, however, and politically and socially African American inequality continued.

2 Legal segregation was declared unconstitutional by the Supreme Court in *Brown v. Board of Education of Topeka* (1954), in which the Court stated that separation implied inferiority. In *Brown v. Board of Education* (1955), the Supreme Court ordered federal courts to ensure that public schools were desegregated "with all deliberate speed." Also in 1955, the modern civil rights movement began with a boycott of segregated public transportation in Montgomery, Alabama. Of particular impact was the Civil Rights Act of 1964. The act bans discrimination on the basis of race, color, religion, gender, or national origin in employment and public accommodations. The act created the Equal Employment Opportunity Commission to administer the legislation's provisions.

3 The Voting Rights Act of 1965 outlawed discriminatory voter-registration tests and authorized federal registration of persons and federally administered procedures in any state or political subdivision evidencing electoral discrimination or low registration rates. The Voting Rights Act and other protective legislation passed during and since the 1960s apply not only to African Americans but to other ethnic groups as well. Minorities have been increasingly represented in national and state politics, although they have yet to gain representation proportionate to their numbers in the U.S. population. Lingering social and economic disparities have led to a new civil rights agenda—one focusing less on racial differences and more on economic differences.

4 In the early history of the United States, women were considered citizens, but by and large they had no political rights. After the first women's rights convention in 1848, the women's movement gained momentum. Not until 1920, when the Nineteenth Amendment was ratified, did women finally obtain the right to vote. The modern women's movement began in the 1960s in the wake of the civil rights and anti–Vietnam War movements. The National Organization for Women (NOW) was formed in 1966 to bring about complete equality for women in all walks of life. Efforts to secure the ratification of the Equal Rights Amendment failed, but the women's movement has been successful in obtaining new laws, changes in social customs, and increased political representation of women.

5 Although women have found it difficult to gain positions of political leadership, their numbers in Congress and in other government bodies increased significantly in the 1990s and early 2000s. Women continue to struggle against gender discrimination in employment. Federal government efforts to eliminate gender discrimination in the workplace include Title VII of the Civil Rights Act of 1964, which prohibits, among other things, gender-based discrimination, including sexual harassment on the job. Wage discrimination also continues to be a problem for women, as does the "glass ceiling" that prevents them from rising to the top of business or professional firms.

6 America has always been a land of immigrants and will continue to be so. Today, more than one million immigrants enter the United States each year, and more than 10 percent of the U.S. population consists of foreign-born persons. In particular, the Hispanic American community in the United States has experienced explosive growth. In recent years, illegal immigration has surfaced as a significant national issue. Indeed, one of the pressing concerns facing today's politicians is whether U.S. immigration policy should be reformed.

7 Affirmative action programs have been controversial because they can lead to reverse discrimination against majority groups or even other minority groups. Supreme Court decisions have limited affirmative action programs, and voters in California and Washington passed initiatives banning state-sponsored affirmative action in those states. Two Supreme Court decisions in cases brought against the University of Michigan have confirmed the principle that limited affirmative action programs are constitutional.

8 Problems associated with aging and retirement are becoming increasingly important as the number of older persons in the United States increases. The Age Discrimination in Employment Act of 1967 prohibited job-related discrimination against individuals who are over forty years old on the basis of age, unless age is shown to be a bona fide occupational qualification reasonably necessary to the normal operation of the business. Amendments to the act prohibit mandatory retirement except in a few selected professions.

9 The Rehabilitation Act of 1973 prohibited discrimination against persons with disabilities in programs receiving federal aid. Regulations implementing the act provide for ramps, elevators, and the like in federal buildings. The Education for All Handicapped Children Act (1975) provides that children with disabilities should receive an "appropriate" education. The Americans with Disabilities Act of 1990 prohibits job discrimination against persons with physical and mental disabilities, requiring that positive steps be taken to comply with the act. The act also requires expanded access to public facilities, including transportation, and to services offered by such private concerns as car rental and telephone companies.

10 Gay and lesbian rights groups, which first began to form in 1969, now number in the thousands. These groups work to promote laws protecting gay men and lesbians from discrimination and to repeal antigay laws. After 1969, sodomy laws that criminalized specific sexual practices were repealed or struck down by the courts in all but eighteen states, and in 2003 a Supreme Court decision effectively invalidated all remaining sodomy laws nationwide. Twelve states and more than 230 cities and counties now have laws prohibiting discrimination based on sexual orientation. Gay men and lesbians are no longer barred from federal employment or from immigrating to this country. Since 1980, liberal Democrats at the national level have supported gay and lesbian rights and

sought electoral support from these groups. The military's "don't ask, don't tell" policy has fueled extensive controversy, as have same-sex marriages and child-custody issues.

11 Although children form a large group of Americans, they have the fewest rights and protections, in part because it is commonly presumed that parents protect their children. The Twenty-sixth Amendment grants the right to vote to those aged eighteen or older. In most states, only contracts entered into for necessaries can be enforced against minors. When minors engage in negligent acts, their parents may be held liable. Minors have some defense against criminal prosecution because of their presumed inability to have criminal intent below certain ages. For those under the age of criminal responsibility, there are state juvenile courts. When minors are tried as adults, they are entitled to the procedural protections afforded to adults and are sometimes subject to adult penalties.

|Selected Print and Media Resources

SUGGESTED READINGS

Anderson, Terry H. *The Pursuit of Fairness: A History of Affirmative Action.* New York: Oxford University Press, 2004. Anderson offers an evenhanded history of affirmative action. His account extends from the administrations of Franklin D. Roosevelt and Harry Truman in the 1940s to the 2003 University of Michigan cases that have established the current constitutional parameters of affirmative action policies.

Friedan, Betty. *The Feminine Mystique.* New York: W. W. Norton & Co., 2001. Friedan's work is the feminist classic that helped launch the modern women's movement in the United States. This edition contains an up-to-date introduction by columnist Anna Quindlen.

Moats, David. *Civil Wars: A Battle for Gay Marriage.* New York: Harcourt, 2004. Moats, a Pulitzer Prize–winning Vermont journalist, chronicles the battle over same-sex marriage in Vermont. The result was a law legalizing civil unions.

Ngai, Mae M. *Impossible Subjects: Illegal Aliens and the Making of Modern America.* Princeton, N.J.: Princeton University Press, 2005. The author explains why and how illegal immigration became the central problem in U.S. immigration policy.

Roberts, Gene, and Hank Kilbanoff. *The Race Beat: The Press, Civil Rights Struggle, and the Awakening of a Nation.* New York: Knopf, 2006. The authors recount the story of how the press finally recognized the civil rights struggle in the 1950s and 1960s. This book describes the awakening of the public to America's race problems.

Woodward, C. Vann. *The Strange Career of Jim Crow.* New York: Oxford University Press, 1957. This is the classic study of how segregation was created in the southern states.

MEDIA RESOURCES

Beyond the Glass Ceiling—A CNN-produced program showing the difficulties women face in trying to rise to the top in corporate America.

G.I. Jane—A 1997 film about a woman who is out to prove that she can survive Navy SEAL training that is so rigorous that many (60 percent) of the men do not make it.

I Have a Dream—A film on Martin Luther King, Jr., focusing on the 1963 March on Washington and King's "I Have a Dream" speech, which some consider to be one of the greatest speeches of all time.

Malcolm X—A 1992 film, directed by Spike Lee and starring Denzel Washington, that depicts the life of the controversial "black power" leader Malcolm X. Malcolm X, who was assassinated on February 21, 1965, clearly had a different vision from that of Martin Luther King, Jr., regarding how to achieve civil rights, respect, and equality for black Americans.

Separate but Equal—A video focusing on Thurgood Marshall, the African American lawyer (and later Supreme Court justice) who took the struggle for equal rights to the Supreme Court, and on the rise and demise of segregation in America.

Shot by a Kid—A film documenting the relationship among children, guns, and violence in four major U.S. cities.

E·MOCRACY | Civil Rights Information Online

Today, thanks to the Internet, information on civil rights issues is literally at your fingertips. By simply accessing the American Civil Liberties Union's Web site (the URL for this organization is given below, in the *Logging On* section), you can learn about the major civil rights issues facing Americans today. A host of other Web sites offer data on the extent to which groups discussed in this chapter are protected under state and federal laws. You can also find numerous advocacy sites that indicate what you can do to help promote the rights of a certain group.

Logging On

For information on, and arguments in support of, affirmative action and the rights of the groups discussed in this chapter, a good source is the American Civil Liberties Union's Web site. Go to

www.aclu.org

The National Organization for Women (NOW) offers online information and updates on the status of women's rights, including affirmative action cases involving women. Go to

www.now.org

An excellent source of information on issues facing African Americans is the Web site of the National Association for the Advancement of Colored People at

www.naacp.org

You can find information on the Americans with Disabilities Act (ADA) of 1990, including the act's text, at

www.jan.wvu.edu/links/ adalinks.htm

You can access the Web site of the Human Rights Campaign Fund, the nation's largest gay and lesbian political organization, at

www.hrc.org

If you are interested in children's rights and welfare, a good starting place is the Web site of the Child Welfare Institute. Go to

www.gocwi.org

Online Review

At **www.politicalscience.wadsworth.com/ schmidt12**, you will find a free Study Guide to this book. For each chapter, there are two online quizzes to help you master the material.

• The PoliPrep Self-Study Assessment provides a pretest for each major section of the chapter. PoliPrep then generates a customized study plan. After you complete the study plan, a posttest evaluates your progress.

• The Tutorial Quiz for each chapter provides questions on the chapter contents, including the features. The questions are organized to match the major sections of the chapter.

6 | Public Opinion and Political Socialization

What If . . .
Students Were Required to Pass a National Civics Exam?

BACKGROUND

In this chapter, you will read about the various ways in which Americans are politically socialized. Certainly, the nation's public schools play an important role in the political socialization process. A solid civic education ensures that citizens have a basic grasp on how their government is structured and functions. It also serves as a foundation for lifelong democratic participation.

As Thomas Jefferson once noted, "If a nation expects to be both ignorant and free, in a state of civilization, it expects what never was and never will be." In a democratic republic such as the United States, a well-informed, politically active citizenry is necessary for good government. Yet, by most quantitative accounts, young Americans are not particularly well versed in how the United States government works.

WHAT IF STUDENTS WERE REQUIRED TO PASS A NATIONAL CIVICS EXAM?

Younger Americans would be forced to become more cognizant of the structure and function of government if they were required to pass a national civics exam to graduate from high school.

A deeper knowledge of government would make younger Americans more conscientious voters, better consumers of the news, and more capable of understanding political issues facing the nation. Given that the voting age is eighteen years old in the United States, an examination during the student's senior year would seem logical.

Voter-participation rates among younger Americans could increase significantly if a national civics exam were implemented. After taking the necessary steps to pass the exam, students would be more likely to have confidence in their ability to make wise decisions at the polls.

Passing a national civics examination as a criterion for graduation from high school would also most likely change the amount of coverage American government receives in school curricula. Most states require only a semester-long course in civics or government. Indeed, many political scientists have called the current standards unacceptable. A national test would force schools to bolster their current offerings.

THE CHALLENGE OF INCREASED INSTRUCTION

One challenge that more in-depth American government instruction would present is the problem of who will teach the courses. Most states currently use a broad-based "social studies" certification for those who teach civics or government courses. These teachers are often also responsible for teaching history, global studies, economics, and other social science courses. Some teachers may have had little to no political science coursework in college, while others had either a major or extensive coursework. This lack of uniformity in the level of educational background among teachers can present significant hurdles to successfully implementing a more extensive American government curriculum.

Some schools might be forced to hire additional teachers with a background in political science and American government. With many schools nationwide facing budget problems, any hiring to augment civics instruction might force cutbacks in other academic departments.

THE NAEP AND PAST NATIONAL CIVICS EXAMS

The National Assessment of Educational Progress (NAEP), also known as "The Nation's Report Card," covers a variety of subject areas and has been administered periodically since 1969. The NAEP last offered its civics exam in 1998. The results reflected a startling lack of understanding regarding basic concepts related to American government among high school seniors. Only 30 percent of those tested showed proficiency in civics knowledge, while 35 percent could not even demonstrate the most basic levels of understanding.

Indeed, only 9 percent of students could list two ways in which a democratic society benefits from the active participation of its citizens.

The NAEP civics exam will be administered again in the near future as part of President Bush's No Child Left Behind act, which attempts to make schools more accountable for student achievement. Any federally mandated examination that carries consequences for schools and students would likely have a host of critics. Education has traditionally been regulated by state governments, and any attempt to create a national policy will rankle some.

FOR CRITICAL ANALYSIS

1. How significant an impact would a national civics exam have on younger Americans' voter participation? What other factors beside lack of knowledge might keep them away from the polls?
2. Why might state governments react negatively toward further federal intrusions into education policy?

In a democracy, the ability of the people to freely express their opinions is fundamental. Americans can express their opinions in many ways. They can write letters to newspapers. They can organize politically. They can vote. They can respond to opinion polls. Public opinion clearly plays an important role in our political system, just as it does in any democracy.

President George W. Bush found out how important public opinion can be when he announced plans to reform Social Security. In his first major speech following his reelection in 2004, the president proclaimed that reforming Social Security would be his top priority. He then delivered sixty speeches in sixty days around the nation to build support for his reform program, which included voluntary private accounts for younger Americans. The president, fresh from his reelection, sought help from the Republican majority in Congress. By early summer in 2005, however, the initiative had stalled. Rather than increasing, public opinion in favor of reform had declined. Few members of Congress came forward to help the president because they too saw the lack of public support for the proposed changes. By 2006, the movement to reform the pension system had failed. Indeed, Bush's approval ratings had fallen to less than 40 percent, and his influence on Congress and the nation seemed to be declining.

There is no doubt that public opinion can be powerful. Political scientists often point to two presidential decisions to illustrate this power. In 1968, President Lyndon Johnson decided not to run for reelection because of the intense and negative public reaction to the war in Vietnam. In 1974, President Richard Nixon resigned in the wake of a scandal when it was obvious that public opinion no longer supported him. The extent to which public opinion affects policymaking is not always so clear, however. For example, suppose that public opinion strongly supports a certain policy. If political leaders adopt that position, is it because they are responding to public opinion or to their own views on the issue? In addition, to some extent, political leaders themselves can shape public opinion. For these and other reasons, scholars must deal with many uncertainties when analyzing the impact of public opinion on policymaking.

President Lyndon B. Johnson addresses the nation from the Oval Office in 1968, announcing a halt to the bombing in Vietnam and his intention not to run for reelection. How much did public opinion have to do with his decision? (Yoichi R. Okamoto/LBJ Presidential Library)

Defining Public Opinion

There is no single public opinion, because there are many different "publics." In a nation of almost 300 million people, there may be innumerable gradations of opinion on an issue. What we do is describe the distribution of opinions among the members of the public about a particular question. Thus, we define **public opinion** as the aggregate of individual attitudes or beliefs shared by some portion of the adult population.

Typically, public opinion is distributed among several different positions, and the distribution of opinion can tell us how divided the public is on an issue and whether compromise is possible. When a large proportion of the American public appears to express the same view on an issue, we say that a **consensus** exists, at least at the moment the poll was taken. Figure 6–1 shows a pattern of opinion that might be called consensual. Issues on which the public holds widely differing attitudes result in **divisive opinion** (see Figure 6–2). Sometimes, a poll shows a distribution of opinion indicating that most Americans either have no information about the issue or are not interested enough in the issue to formulate a position. Politicians may believe that the public's lack of knowledge about an issue gives them more room to maneuver, or they may be wary of taking any action for fear that opinion will crystallize after a crisis.

An interesting question arises as to when private opinion becomes public opinion. Everyone probably has a private opinion about the competence of the president, as well as private opinions about more personal concerns, such as the state of a neighbor's lawn. We say that private opinion becomes public opinion when the opinion is publicly expressed and concerns public issues. When someone's private opinion becomes so strong that the individual is willing to go to the polls to vote for or against a candidate or an issue—or is willing to participate in a demonstration, discuss the issue at work, speak out on television or radio, or participate in the political process in any one of a dozen other ways—then the opinion becomes public opinion.

Public Opinion
The aggregate of individual attitudes or beliefs shared by some portion of the adult population.

Consensus
General agreement among the citizenry on an issue.

Divisive Opinion
Public opinion that is polarized between two quite different positions.

FIGURE 6–1 | CONSENSUS OPINION

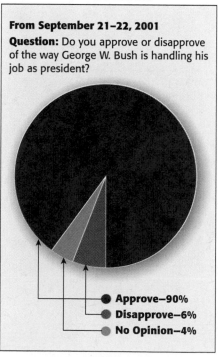

From September 21–22, 2001
Question: Do you approve or disapprove of the way George W. Bush is handling his job as president?

● Approve—90%
● Disapprove—6%
● No Opinion—4%

Source: Gallup Poll, September 21–22, 2001.

FIGURE 6–2 | DIVISIVE OPINION

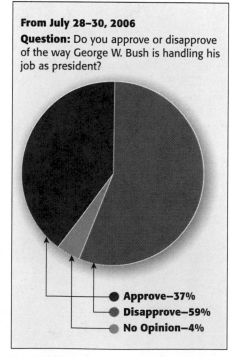

From July 28–30, 2006
Question: Do you approve or disapprove of the way George W. Bush is handling his job as president?

● Approve—37%
● Disapprove—59%
● No Opinion—4%

Source: Gallup Poll, August 15, 2006.

How Public Opinion Is Formed: Political Socialization

Most Americans are willing to express opinions on political issues when asked. How do people acquire these opinions and attitudes? Typically, views that are expressed as political opinions are acquired through the process of **political socialization.** By this we mean that people acquire their political attitudes, often including their party identification, through relationships with their families, friends, and co-workers.

| Political Socialization
The process by which people acquire political beliefs and attitudes.

Models of Political Socialization

The most important early sources of political socialization are found in the family and the schools. Individuals' basic political orientations are formed in the family if the family members hold strong views. When the adults in a family view politics as relatively unimportant and describe themselves as independent voters or disaffected from the political system, children receive very little socialization.

In the last few decades, more and more sources of information about politics have become available to all Americans and especially to young people. Although their basic outlook on the political system may be formed by early family influences, young people are now exposed to many other sources of information about issues and values. Scholars believe that this greater access to information may explain why young Americans are more liberal than their parents on many social issues.

The Family and the Social Environment

Not only do our parents' political attitudes and actions affect our opinions, but the family also links us to other factors that affect opinion, such as race, social class, educational environment, and religious beliefs. How do parents transmit their political attitudes to their offspring?

Studies suggest that the influence of parents is due to two factors: communication and receptivity. Parents communicate their feelings and preferences to children constantly. Because children have such a strong need for parental approval, they are very receptive to their parents' views. Children are less likely to influence their parents, because parents expect deference from their children.[1]

Nevertheless, other studies show that if children are exposed to political ideas at school and in the media, they will share these ideas with their parents, giving the parents what some scholars call a "second chance" at political socialization. Children can also expose their parents to new media, such as the Internet.[2]

Education as a Source of Political Socialization.   From the early days of the republic, schools were perceived to be important transmitters of political information and attitudes. Children in the primary grades learn about their country mostly in patriotic ways. They learn about the Pilgrims, the flag, and some of the nation's presidents. They also learn to celebrate national holidays. Later, in the middle grades, children learn more historical facts and come to understand the structure of government and the functions of the president, judges, and Congress. By high school, students have a more complex understanding of the political system, may identify with a political party, and may take positions on issues.

[1]Barbara A. Bardes and Robert W. Oldendick, *Public Opinion: Measuring the American Mind*, 3rd ed. (Belmont, Calif.: Wadsworth Publishing Co., 2006), p. 73.
[2]For a pioneering study in this area, see Michael McDevitt and Steven H. Chaffee, "Second Chance Political Socialization: 'Trickle-up' Effects of Children on Parents," in Thomas J. Johnson *et al.*, eds., *Engaging the Public: How Government and the Media Can Reinvigorate American Democracy* (Lanham, Md.: Rowman & Littlefield Publishers, 1998), pp. 57–66.

An eight-year-old boy looks at a map of Europe under the gaze of his mother. Parents constantly communicate with their children on a variety of matters that influence their views on the world. How might parents pass on political beliefs without even realizing that they are doing so? (Tannen Maury/Landov)

Generally, education is closely linked to political participation. The more education a person receives, the more likely that person will be interested in politics, be confident in his or her ability to understand political issues, and be an active participant in the political process. Public opinion polls, however, suggest that even well-educated younger Americans are not strongly interested in politics.[3]

Peers and Peer Group Influence.   Once a child enters school, the child's friends become an important influence on behavior and attitudes. For children and for adults, friendships and associations in **peer groups** affect political attitudes. We must, however, separate the effects of peer group pressure on opinions and attitudes in general from the effects of peer group pressure on political opinions. For the most part, associations among peers are nonpolitical. Political attitudes are more likely to be shaped by peer groups when the peer groups are involved directly in political activities.

Individuals who join interest groups based on ethnic identity may find, for example, a common political bond through working for the group's civil liberties and rights. African American activist groups may consist of individuals who join together to support government programs that will aid the African American population. Members of a labor union may be strongly influenced to support certain pro-labor candidates.

Opinion Leaders' Influence.   We are all influenced by those with whom we are closely associated or whom we hold in high regard—friends at school, family members and other relatives, and teachers. In a sense, these people are **opinion leaders,**

| Peer Group
A group consisting of members sharing common social characteristics. These groups play an important part in the socialization process, helping to shape attitudes and beliefs.

| Opinion Leader
One who is able to influence the opinions of others because of position, expertise, or personality.

[3]Jane Eisner, *Taking Back the Vote: Getting American Youth Involved in Our Democracy* (Boston: Beacon Press, 2004).

but on an *informal* level; that is, their influence on our political views is not necessarily intentional or deliberate. We are also influenced by *formal* opinion leaders, such as presidents, lobbyists, congresspersons, news commentators, and religious leaders, who have as part of their jobs the task of swaying people's views. Their interest lies in defining the political agenda in such a way that discussions about policy options will take place on their terms.

The Impact of the Media

Clearly, the media—newspapers, television, radio, and Internet sources—strongly influence public opinion. This is because the media inform the public about the issues and events of our times and thus have an agenda setting effect. In other words, to borrow from Bernard Cohen's classic statement about the media and public opinion, the media may not be successful in telling people what to think, but they are "stunningly successful in telling their audience what to think about."[4] For competing views on the media's role in agenda setting, see this chapter's *Which Side Are You On?* feature on the following page.

Today, many contend that the media's influence on public opinion has grown to equal that of the family. For example, in her analysis of the role played by the media in American politics,[5] media scholar Doris A. Graber points out that high school students, when asked where they obtain the information on which they base their attitudes, mention the mass media far more than they mention their families, friends, and teachers. This trend, combined with the increasing popularity of such information sources as talk shows and the Internet, may significantly alter the nature of the media's influence on public debate in the future. The media's influence will be discussed in more detail in Chapter 10.

---

[4]*The Press and Foreign Policy* (Princeton, N.J.: Princeton University Press, 1963), p. 81.
[5]See Doris A. Graber, *Mass Media and American Politics*, 7th ed. (Chicago: University of Chicago Press, 2005).

| DID YOU KNOW . . .
That CNN reaches more than 1.5 billion people in over 212 countries?

| Media
The channels of mass communication.

| Agenda Setting
Determining which public-policy questions will be debated or considered.

A young mother in Vermilion, Ohio, tries to watch President George W. Bush's televised State of the Union address while her children play nearby. People are no longer limited to viewing news produced by the three major networks, as they were years ago. Could the multiplicity of news outlets today limit the ability of the media to affect people's political opinions? Why or why not? (AP Photo/John Kuntz/*The Plain Dealer*)

WHICH SIDE ARE YOU ON? | The Media and Agenda Setting

The media clearly have a significant impact on the way that Americans think about politics. As you have read in this chapter, the media play a considerable role in *agenda setting*—determining which public-policy issues will be debated or considered. Traditional outlets such as television, radio, and the daily newspaper have long influenced what information reaches the public and how that information is packaged. Some Americans criticize the media, claiming that the media impose their own political agenda on the public. Others disagree, arguing that the rise of the "new" media of the Internet such as Web logs, or blogs, has provided a wider selection of viewpoints in the information marketplace.

THE MEDIA IMPOSE AN AGENDA

Some Americans believe that the media dictate what information the public receives. Certain media critics argue that the public does not have access to a full spectrum of information about issues and events related to American politics and government. The media, these critics claim, serve as information sifters, deciding which stories are discussed and which are ignored. Some Americans even argue that the growth of media monopolies in recent years has created a collusive environment in which corporate interests dictate which information will be disseminated to Americans.

Indeed, sometimes financial motivations do influence the information that is disseminated to the public. For example, a media outlet might ignore a potential news story that reflects poorly on a corporation that buys significant advertising from that particular outlet. More often, though, media outlets decide what topics to cover based on their entertainment or ratings value. In other words, media outlets devote the most attention to stories that will attract the widest possible audience. Some argue that such decision criteria lead to a "dumbing down" of the news provided to the public. Other times, content deci-

sions may be related to the political bias or slant of the media outlet itself. Critics argue that some media outlets even cater specifically to one political ideology or party affiliation.

THE MEDIA ARE TOO BROAD FOR A SPECIFIC AGENDA

Others disagree with the notion that the media impose an agenda on the American people. Pointing to the information revolution of the Internet, many argue that anyone can pursue her or his own personal information-gathering agenda. Rather than being forced to sit through a predetermined set of stories on the nightly news, Americans can now surf countless Web sites, blogs, and chat rooms dedicated to political events and issues. If anyone deems one source to be biased or questionable, numerous other sites and sources are at the user's fingertips.

Obviously, most Americans still utilize traditional news sources. As more and more homes have Internet access, however, an ever-increasing portion of the American public has a wide variety of media outlets available. The sheer number of potential sources for information makes it nearly impossible for a concerted agenda to be foisted on the public as a whole.

WHAT'S YOUR POSITION?

In what ways, if at all, do you think the media have an agenda that determines what issues and events are discussed? Why would the media have such an agenda in the first place?

GOING ONLINE

The Pew Research Center for the People and the Press, at **www.people-press.org**, offers polls and commentary regarding public opinion about the media.

The Influence of Political Events

Generally, older Americans tend to be somewhat more conservative than younger Americans, particularly on social issues and, to some extent, on economic issues. This effect is known as the **lifestyle effect.** It probably occurs because older adults are concerned about their own economic situations and are likely to retain the social values that they learned at a younger age. Young people, especially today, are more liberal than their grandparents on social issues such as the rights of gay men and lesbians and racial and gender equality. Nevertheless, a more important factor than a person's age is the impact of important political events that shape the political attitudes of an entire generation. When events produce such a long-lasting result, we refer to it as a **generational effect** (also called the *cohort effect*).

Voters who grew up in the 1930s during the Great Depression were likely to form lifelong attachments to the Democratic Party, the party of Franklin D. Roosevelt.

| Lifestyle Effect
The phenomenon of certain attitudes occurring at certain chronological ages.

| Generational Effect
A long-lasting effect of the events of a particular time on the political opinions of those who came of political age at that time.

In the 1960s and 1970s, the war in Vietnam and the **Watergate break-in** and the subsequent presidential cover-up fostered widespread cynicism toward government. There is evidence that the years of economic prosperity under President Ronald Reagan during the 1980s led many young people to identify with the Republican Party. It is less clear whether more recent presidents—including Democrat Bill Clinton (1993–2001) and Republican George W. Bush—have been able to affect the party identification of young voters.

| Watergate Break-In
The 1972 illegal entry into the Democratic National Committee offices by participants in President Richard Nixon's reelection campaign.

Political Preferences and Voting Behavior

Various socioeconomic and demographic factors appear to influence political preferences. These factors include education, income and **socioeconomic status,** religion, race, gender, geographic region, and similar traits. People who share the same religion, occupation, or any other demographic trait are likely to influence one another and may also have common political concerns that follow from the common characteristic. Other factors, such as party identification, perception of the candidates, and issue preferences, are closely connected to the electoral process itself. Table 6–1 illustrates the impact of some of these variables on voting behavior.

| Socioeconomic Status
The value assigned to a person due to occupation or income. An upper-class person, for example, has high socioeconomic status.

TABLE 6–1 | VOTES BY GROUPS IN PRESIDENTIAL ELECTIONS, 1988–2004 (IN PERCENTAGES)

	1988		1992			1996		2000		2004	
	DUKAKIS (DEM.)	BUSH (REP.)	CLINTON (DEM.)	BUSH (REP.)	PEROT (REF.)	CLINTON (DEM.)	DOLE (REP.)	GORE (DEM.)	BUSH (REP.)	KERRY (DEM.)	BUSH (REP.)
Total vote	45	53	43	38	19	49	41	48	48	48	51
Gender											
Men	41	57	41	38	21	43	44	42	53	44	55
Women	49	50	46	37	17	54	38	54	43	51	48
Race											
White	40	59	39	41	20	43	46	42	54	41	58
Black	86	12	82	11	7	84	12	90	8	88	11
Hispanic	69	30	62	25	14	72	21	67	31	54	44
Educational Attainment											
Not a high school graduate	56	43	55	28	17	59	28	59	39	50	50
High school graduate	49	50	43	36	20	51	35	48	49	47	52
College graduate	37	62	40	41	19	44	46	45	51	46	52
Postgraduate education	48	50	49	36	15	52	40	52	44	54	45
Religion											
White Protestant	33	66	33	46	21	36	53	34	63	32	68
Catholic	47	52	44	36	20	53	37	49	47	47	52
Jewish	64	35	78	12	10	78	16	79	19	75	24
White fundamentalist	18	81	23	61	15	NA	NA	NA	NA	21	79
Union Status											
Union household	57	42	55	24	21	59	30	59	37	59	40
Family Income											
Under $15,000	62	37	59	23	18	59	28	57	37	63	37
$15,000–29,000	50	49	45	35	20	53	36	54	41	57	41
$30,000–49,000	44	56	41	38	21	48	40	49	48	50	49
Over $50,000	42	56	40	42	18	44	48	45	52	43	56
Size of Place											
Population over 500,000	62	37	58	28	13	68	25	71	26	60	40
Population 50,000 to 500,000	52	47	50	33	16	50	39	57	40	50	50
Population 10,000 to 50,000	38	61	39	42	20	48	41	38	59	48	51
Rural	44	55	39	40	20	44	46	37	59	39	60

NA = Not asked.
Sources: *The New York Times;* Voter News Service; and CBS News.

Demographic Influences

Demographic influences reflect the individual's personal background and place in society. Some factors have to do with the family into which a person was born: race and (for most people) religion. Others may be the result of choices made throughout an individual's life: place of residence, educational achievement, and profession.

It is also clear that many of these factors are interrelated. People who have more education are likely to have higher incomes and to hold professional jobs. Similarly, children born into wealthier families are far more likely to complete college than children from poor families. Many other interrelationships are not so immediately obvious; for example, many people might not guess that 88 percent of African Americans report that religion is very important in their lives, compared with only 57 percent of whites.[6]

Education.   In the past, having a college education tended to be associated with voting for Republicans. In recent years, however, this correlation has become weaker. In particular, individuals with a postgraduate education—more than a bachelor's degree—have become increasingly Democratic. Also, a higher percentage of voters with only a high school education voted Republican in 2000 and 2004, compared with the pattern in previous elections, in which that group of voters tended to favor Democrats.

Many people with postgraduate degrees are professionals, such as physicians, attorneys, and college instructors. Typically, a postgraduate degree is an occupational requirement for professionals. Despite the recent popularity of the master of business administration (MBA) degree, businesspersons are more likely to have only a bachelor's degree. They are also much more likely to vote Republican.

The Influence of Economic Status.   Family income is a strong predictor of economic liberalism or conservatism. Those with low incomes tend to favor government action to benefit the poor or to promote economic equality. Those with high incomes tend to oppose government intervention in the economy or to support it only when it benefits business. On economic issues, therefore, the traditional economic spectrum described in Chapter 1 on page 15 is a useful tool. The rich tend toward the right; the poor tend toward the left.

If we examine cultural as well as economic issues, however, the four-cornered ideological grid discussed in Chapter 1 on page 16 becomes important. It happens that upper-class voters are more likely to endorse cultural liberalism, and lower-class individuals are more likely to favor cultural conservatism. Support for the right to have an abortion, for example, rises with income. It follows that libertarians—those who oppose government action on both economic and social issues—are concentrated among the wealthier members of the population. (Libertarians constitute the upper-right-hand corner of the grid in Figure 1–1 in Chapter 1.) Those who favor government action both to promote traditional moral values and to promote economic equality—economic liberals, cultural conservatives—are concentrated among groups that are less well off. (This group fills up the lower-left-hand corner of the grid.)

Economic Status and Voting Behavior.   Normally, the higher a person's income, the more likely the person will be to vote Republican. Manual laborers, factory workers, and especially union members are more likely to vote Democratic (see Table 6–2). If socioeconomic status is measured by profession, then traditionally those of higher socioeconomic status—professionals and businesspersons, as well as white-collar workers—have tended to vote Republican.

---

[6]The Gallup Poll, "A Look at Americans and Religion Today," March 23, 2004.

There are no hard-and-fast rules, however. Some very poor individuals are devoted Republicans, just as some extremely wealthy people support the Democratic Party. Indeed, recent research indicates that a realignment is occurring among those of higher economic status: as just mentioned, professionals now tend to vote Democratic, while small-business owners, managers, and corporate executives tend to vote Republican.[7]

Religious Influence: Denomination. Traditionally, scholars have examined the impact of religion on political attitudes by dividing the population into such categories as Protestant, Catholic, and Jewish. In recent decades, however, such a breakdown has become less valuable as a means of predicting someone's political preferences. It is true that in the past, Jewish voters were notably more liberal than members of other groups, on both economic and cultural issues, and they continue to be more liberal today. Persons reporting no religion are very liberal on social issues but have mixed economic views. Northern Protestants and Catholics, however, do not differ that greatly from each other, and neither do southern Protestants and Catholics. This represents something of a change—in the late 1800s and early 1900s, northern Protestants were distinctly more likely to vote Republican, and northern Catholics were more likely to vote Democratic.

Religious Influence: Religiosity and Evangelicals. Nevertheless, two factors do turn out to be major predictors of political attitudes among members of the various Christian denominations. One is the degree of *religiosity*, or practice of beliefs, and the other is whether the person holds fundamentalist or evangelical views. A high degree of religiosity is usually manifested by very frequent attendance at church services, at least once or twice a week.

Voters who are more devout, regardless of their church affiliation, tend to vote Republican, while voters who are less devout are more often Democrats. In 2000,

---

[7]Thomas B. Edsall, "Voters Thinking Less with Their Wallets," *International Herald Tribune*, March 27, 2001, p. 3.

A Jewish grandmother and granddaughter light the menorah candles during the Hanukkah holiday in December. Despite their modern-day prosperity, a majority of American Jews continue to support liberal politics. Why might Jewish voters continue to be more interested in traditionally liberal values than in "voting their pocketbooks"? (Ariel Skelley/Corbis)

TABLE 6–2 | PERCENTAGE OF UNION HOUSEHOLDS VOTING REPUBLICAN

Although union members are more likely to identify themselves as Democrats than Republicans and labor organizations are far more likely to support Democratic candidates, the data below show that in eight of the last fourteen presidential elections, Republicans have captured at least 40 percent of the votes from union households.

YEAR	UNION HOUSEHOLDS VOTING REPUBLICAN FOR PRESIDENT CANDIDATES	PERCENTAGE
1952	Eisenhower vs. Stevenson	44
1956	Eisenhower vs. Stevenson	57
1960	Kennedy vs. Nixon	36
1964	Johnson vs. Goldwater	17
1968	Nixon vs. Humphrey	44
1972	Nixon vs. McGovern	57
1976	Carter vs. Ford	36
1980	Reagan vs. Carter	45
1984	Reagan vs. Mondale	43
1988	Bush vs. Dukakis	42
1992	Clinton vs. Bush	24
1996	Clinton vs. Dole	30
2000	Bush vs. Gore	37
2004	Bush vs. Kerry	40

Sources: *CQ Researcher*, June 28, 1996, p. 560; *The New York Times*, November 10, 1996, p. 16; and authors' updates.

Teleconferencing has become a relatively inexpensive way to address citizens who may be thousands of miles away. Here, former Senate Majority Leader Bill Frist (R., Tenn.) talks to those attending an evangelical rally in Louisville, Kentucky. Can teleconferencing ever be as effective as speaking in person? (AP Photo/Patti Longmire)

for example, Protestants who regularly attended church gave 84 percent of their votes to Republican candidate George W. Bush, compared with 55 percent of those who attended church less often. Among Catholics, there was a similar pattern: a majority of Catholics who attended church regularly voted Republican, while a majority of Catholics who were not regular churchgoers voted for Democratic candidate Al Gore.[8] There is an exception to this trend: African Americans of all religions have been strongly supportive of Democrats.

Another distinctive group of voters who are also likely to be very religious are those Americans who can be identified as holding fundamentalist or evangelical beliefs. They are usually members of a Protestant denomination, although no one denomination can be labeled as evangelical. In election studies, these individuals are usually identified by a pattern of beliefs: they may describe themselves as "born again" and believe in the literal word of the Bible, among other characteristics. As voters, these Christians tend to be cultural conservatives but not necessarily economic conservatives.

The Influence of Race and Ethnicity.   Although African Americans are, on average, somewhat conservative on certain cultural issues such as same-sex marriage and abortion, they tend to be more liberal than whites on social-welfare matters, civil liberties, and even foreign policy. African Americans voted principally for Republicans until Democrat Franklin Roosevelt's New Deal in the 1930s. Since then, they have largely identified with the Democratic Party. Indeed, Democratic presidential candidates have received, on average, more than 80 percent of the African American vote since 1956. As you learned in Chapter 1, Hispanics also favor the Democrats. Hispanics of Cuban ancestry, however, are predominantly Republican. Most Asian American groups lean toward the Democrats, although often by narrow margins. Muslim American immigrants and their descendants

---

[8]Ronald Brownstein, "Attendance, Not Affiliation, Key to Religious Voters," *The Los Angeles Times*, July 16, 2001, p. A10.

An Asian American family standing outside their new home. The median family income of Asian Americans is about $10,000 more than the median income for all households. As a result, Asian Americans, especially those from Japan, China, and India, are sometimes seen as succeeding through education and hard work. Nonetheless, some Asian Americans continue to live in poverty or experience discrimination. Like many better-off Americans, Asian Americans are more likely to vote Republican than members of most other minority groups. (Ariel Skelley/Corbis)

are an interesting category.[9] In 2000, a majority of Muslim Americans of Middle Eastern ancestry voted for Republican George W. Bush because they shared his cultural conservatism and believed that he would do a better job of defending their civil liberties than Democrat Al Gore. In the 2004 election campaign, however, the civil liberties issue propelled many of these voters toward the Democrats.[10]

The Gender Gap. Until the 1980s, there was little evidence that men's and women's political attitudes were very different. Following the election of Ronald Reagan in 1980, however, scholars began to detect a **gender gap.** A May 1983 Gallup poll revealed that men were more likely than women to approve of Reagan's job performance. The gender gap has reappeared in subsequent presidential elections, with women being more likely than men to support the Democratic candidate (see Figure 6–3 on the following page). In the 2000 elections, 54 percent of women voted for Democrat Al Gore, compared with 42 percent of men. A similar gender gap was evident in the 2002 midterm elections: 55 percent of women favored Democratic candidates, compared with 43 percent of men.

Women also appear to hold different attitudes from their male counterparts on a range of issues other than presidential preferences. They are much more likely than men to oppose capital punishment and the use of force abroad. Studies also have shown that women are more concerned about risks to the environment, more supportive of social welfare, and more in agreement with extending civil rights to gay men and lesbians than are men. In contrast, women are also more concerned than men about the security issues raised by the events of 9/11. This last fact may have pushed women in a more conservative direction, at least for a time. In the 2004 presidential elections, the gender gap narrowed somewhat: 51 percent of women favored Democrat John Kerry, compared with 44 percent of men.

Gender Gap
The difference between the percentage of women who vote for a particular candidate and the percentage of men who vote for the candidate.

---

[9]At least a third of U.S. Muslims actually are African Americans whose ancestors have been in this country for a long time. In terms of political preferences, African American Muslims are more likely to resemble other African Americans than Muslim immigrants from the Middle East.

[10]For up-to-date information on Muslim American issues, see the Web site of the Council on American-Islamic Relations at **www.cair-net.org**.

FIGURE 6-3 | GENDER GAP IN PRESIDENTIAL ELECTIONS, 1980–2004

A gender gap in voting is apparent in the percentage of women and the percentage of men voting in the last seven presidential elections. Even when women and men favor the same candidate, they do so by different margins, resulting in a gender gap.

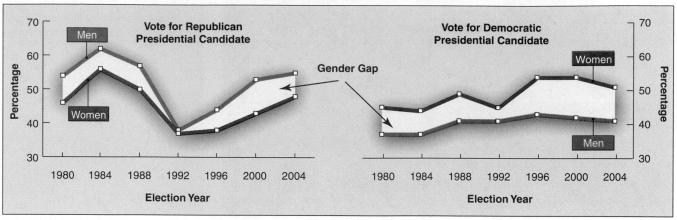

Note: Data in the chart includes votes for Republican and Democratic candidates only. The effect of third party candidates on the gender gap is nominal except in 1992, when H. Ross Perot received 17 percent of the vote among women and 21 percent among men. Perot's impact, if factored into the data, would widen the gap pictured in the chart for 1992, and to a lesser extent in 1996, when his candidacy drew fewer votes.
Sources: Center for American Women and Politics (CAWP); Eagleton Institute of Politics; and Rutgers University.

Reasons for the Gender Gap.   What is the cause of the gender gap? A number of explanations have been offered, including the increase in the number of working women, feminism, and women's concerns over abortion rights and other social issues. Researchers Lena Edlund and Rohini Pande of Columbia University, however, found that the major factor leading to the gender gap has been the disparate economic impact on men and women of not being married. In the last three decades, men and women have tended to marry later in life or stay single even after having children. The divorce rate has also risen dramatically. Edlund and Pande argue that this decline in marriage has tended to make men richer and women relatively poorer. Consequently, support for Democrats is high among single women, particularly single mothers.[11]

Researchers have also found that the gender gap grows wider as men and women become better educated. This result seems to contradict Edlund and Pande's theory, at least in part—it does not seem likely that well-educated women would be suffering economically, and there is some evidence that the gender gap persists even among well-educated married women.[12]

Geographic Region.   Finally, where you live can influence your political attitudes. In one way, regional differences are less important today than just a few decades ago. The former solid (Democratic) South has crumbled in national elections. Only 43 percent of the votes from the southern states went to Democrat Al Gore in 2000, while 55 percent went to Republican George W. Bush.

There is a tendency today, at least in national elections, for the South, the Great Plains, and the Rocky Mountain states to favor the Republicans and for the West Coast and the Northeast to favor the Democrats. Perhaps more important than region is residence—urban, suburban, or rural. People in large cities tend to be liberal and Democratic. Those who live in smaller communities tend to be conservative and Republican.

[11]For an online video presentation of Edlund and Pande's research, go to **www.Columbia.edu/cu/news/media/02/edlund_pande/index.html**.
[12]Susan Page, "'Til Politics Do Us Part: Gender Gap Widens," USA Today, December 18, 2003, pp. 1A–2A.

Election-Specific Factors

Factors such as party identification, perception of the candidates, and issue preferences may have an effect on how people vote in particular elections. Although most people do not change their party identification from year to year, candidates and issues can change greatly, and voting behavior can therefore change as well.

Party Identification.   With the possible exception of race, party identification has been the most important determinant of voting behavior in national elections. Party affiliation is influenced by family and peer groups, by generational effects, by the media, and by the voter's assessment of candidates and issues.

In the middle to late 1960s, party attachment began to weaken. Whereas independent voters were only a little more than 20 percent of the eligible electorate during the 1950s, they constituted more than 30 percent of all voters by the mid-1990s, and their numbers have remained constant since that time. New voters are likely to identify themselves as independent voters although they may be more ready to identify with one of the major parties by their mid thirties. There is considerable debate among political scientists over whether those who call themselves independents are truly so: when asked, most say that they are "leaning" toward one party or the other. (For further discussion of party affiliation, see Chapter 8).

Perception of the Candidates.   The image of the candidate also seems to be important in a voter's choice, especially of a president. To some extent, voter attitudes toward candidates are based on emotions (such as trust) rather than on any judgment about experience or policy. In some years, voters have been attracted to a candidate who appeared to share their concerns and worries. (President Bill Clinton was one example.) In other years, voters have sought a candidate who appeared to have high integrity and honesty. Voters have been especially attracted to these candidates in elections that follow a major scandal, such as Richard Nixon's Watergate scandal (1972–1974) or Clinton's sex scandal (1998–1999).

Issue Preferences.   Issues make a difference in presidential and congressional elections. Although personality or image factors may be very persuasive, most voters have some notion of how the candidates differ on basic issues or at least know which candidates want a change in the direction of government policy.

Historically, economic concerns have been among the most powerful influences on public opinion. When the economy is doing well, it is very difficult for a challenger, especially at the presidential level, to defeat the incumbent. In contrast, inflation, unemployment, or high interest rates are likely to work to the disadvantage of the incumbent. Some studies seem to show that people vote on the basis of their personal economic well-being, while other research suggests that people vote on the basis of the nation's overall economic health.[13]

Measuring Public Opinion

In a democracy, people express their opinions in a variety of ways, as mentioned in this chapter's introduction. One of the most common means of gathering and measuring public opinion on specific issues is, of course, through the use of **opinion polls.**

| DID YOU KNOW . . .
That Britain had a major gender gap for much of the twentieth century—because women were much more likely than men to support the Conservative Party rather than the more left-wing Labor Party?

| Opinion Poll
A method of systematically questioning a small, selected sample of respondents who are deemed representative of the total population.

---

[13]Warren E. Miller and J. Merrill Shanks, *The New American Voter* (Cambridge, Mass.: Harvard University Press, 1996). See page 270 for voting on the basis of personal income and page 196 for voting on the basis of the state of the economy.

The History of Opinion Polls

During the 1800s, certain American newspapers and magazines spiced up their political coverage by doing face-to-face straw polls (unofficial polls indicating the trend of political opinion) or mail surveys of their readers' opinions. In the early twentieth century, the magazine *Literary Digest* further developed the technique of opinion polling by mailing large numbers of questionnaires to individuals, many of whom were its own subscribers, to determine their political opinions. From 1916 to 1936, more than 70 percent of the magazine's election predictions were accurate.

Literary Digest's polling activities suffered a setback in 1936, however, when the magazine predicted, based on more than two million returned questionnaires, that Republican candidate Alfred Landon would win over Democratic candidate Franklin D. Roosevelt. Landon won in only two states. A major problem with the *Digest*'s polling technique was its use of nonrepresentative respondents. In 1936, at possibly the worst point of the Great Depression, the magazine's subscribers were, for one thing, considerably more affluent than the average American. In other words, they did not accurately represent all of the voters in the U.S. population.

Several newcomers to the public opinion poll industry accurately predicted Roosevelt's landslide victory. These newcomers are still active in the poll-taking industry today: the Gallup poll of George Gallup and the Roper poll founded by Elmo Roper. Gallup and Roper, along with Archibald Crossley, developed the modern polling techniques of market research. Using personal interviews with small samples of selected voters (less than two thousand), they showed that they could predict with accuracy the behavior of the total voting population.

By the 1950s, improved methods of sampling and a whole new science of survey research had been developed. Survey research centers sprang up throughout the United States, particularly at universities. Some of these survey groups are the American Institute of Public Opinion at Princeton, in New Jersey; the National Opinion Research Center at the University of Chicago; and the Survey Research Center at the University of Michigan.

A woman in Jenkintown, Pennsylvania, responds to a preelection survey conducted by a personal interviewer. Generally, well-designed polls conducted by interviewers at the home provide the most accurate results, although they are the most expensive to conduct. What possible drawbacks would such a method have? (AP Photo/Joseph Kaczmarek)

Sampling Techniques

How can interviewing fewer than two thousand voters tell us what tens of millions of voters will do? Clearly, it is necessary that the sample of individuals be representative of all voters in the population. Consider an analogy. Let's say we have a large jar containing ten thousand pennies of various dates, and we want to know how many pennies were minted within certain decades (1960–1969, 1970–1979, and so on).

Representative Sampling.   One way to estimate the distribution of the dates on the pennies—without examining all ten thousand—is to take a representative sample. This sample would be obtained by mixing the pennies up well and then removing a handful of them—perhaps one hundred pennies. The distribution of dates might be as follows:

- *1960–1969: 5 percent*
- *1970–1979: 5 percent*
- *1980–1989: 20 percent*
- *1990–1999: 30 percent*
- *2000–present: 40 percent*

If the pennies are very well mixed within the jar, and if you take a large enough sample, the resulting distribution will probably approach the actual distribution of the dates of all ten thousand coins.

The Principle of Randomness.   The most important principle in sampling, or poll taking, is randomness. Every penny or every person should have a known chance, and especially an *equal chance,* of being sampled. If this happens, then a small sample should be representative of the whole group, both in demographic characteristics (age, religion, race, region, and the like) and in opinions. The ideal way to sample the voting population of the United States would be to put all voter names into a jar—or a computer—and randomly sample, say, two thousand of them. Because this is too costly and inefficient, pollsters have developed other ways to obtain good samples. One technique is simply to choose a random selection of telephone numbers and interview the respective households. This technique produces a relatively accurate sample at a low cost.

To ensure that the random samples include respondents from relevant segments of the population—rural, urban, northeastern, southern, and so on—most survey organizations randomly choose, say, urban areas that they will consider as representative of all urban areas. Then they randomly select their respondents within those areas. A generally less accurate technique is known as *quota sampling*. Here, survey researchers decide how many persons of certain types they need in the survey—such as minorities, women, or farmers—and then send out interviewers to find the necessary number of these types. Not only is this method often less accurate, but it also may be biased if, say, the interviewer refuses to go into certain neighborhoods or will not interview after dark.

Generally, the national survey organizations take great care to select their samples randomly, because their reputations rest on the accuracy of their results. The Gallup and Roper polls usually interview about 1,500 individuals, and their results have a very high probability of being correct—within a margin of 3 percentage points. The accuracy with which the Gallup poll has predicted presidential election results is shown in Table 6–3 on the following page.

Problems with Polls

Public opinion polls are snapshots of the opinions and preferences of the people at a specific moment in time and as expressed in response to a specific question. Given

> **DID YOU KNOW . . .**
> That public opinion pollsters typically measure national sentiment among the roughly 200 million adult Americans by interviewing only about 1,500 people?

TABLE 6–3 | GALLUP POLL ACCURACY RECORD

YEAR	GALLUP FINAL SURVEY, PERCENTAGE		ELECTION RESULTS, PERCENTAGE		DEVIATION
2004	49.3	Bush	50.7	Bush	−1.7
2000	50.0	Bush	48.0	Bush	+2.0
1996	52.0	Clinton	49.0	Clinton	+3.0
1992	49.0	Clinton	43.2	Clinton	+5.8
1988	56.0	Bush	53.9	Bush	+2.1
1984	59.0	Reagan	59.1	Reagan	−0.1
1980	47.0	Reagan	50.8	Reagan	−3.8
1976	48.0	Carter	50.0	Carter	−2.0
1972	62.0	Nixon	61.8	Nixon	+0.2
1968	43.0	Nixon	43.5	Nixon	−0.5
1964	64.0	Johnson	61.3	Johnson	+2.7
1960	51.0	Kennedy	50.1	Kennedy	+0.9
1956	59.5	Eisenhower	57.8	Eisenhower	+1.7
1952	51.0	Eisenhower	55.4	Eisenhower	−4.4
1948	44.5	Truman	49.9	Truman	−5.4
1944	51.5	Roosevelt	53.3	Roosevelt	−1.8
1940	52.0	Roosevelt	55.0	Roosevelt	−3.0
1936	55.7	Roosevelt	62.5	Roosevelt	−6.8

Sources: *The Gallup Poll Monthly*, November 1992; *Time*, November 21, 1994; *The Wall Street Journal*, November 6, 1996; and authors' updates.

that definition, it is fairly easy to understand situations in which the polls are wrong. For example, opinion polls leading up to the 1980 presidential election showed President Jimmy Carter defeating challenger Ronald Reagan. Only a few analysts noted the large number of "undecided" respondents a week before the election. Those voters shifted massively to Reagan at the last minute, and Reagan won the election.

The famous photo of Harry Truman showing the front page of the newspaper that declared his defeat in the 1948 presidential elections is another tribute to the weakness of polling. Again, the poll that predicted his defeat was taken more than a week before election day.

Sampling Errors.   Polls may also report erroneous results because the pool of respondents was not chosen in a scientific manner; that is, the form of sampling and the number of people sampled may be too small to overcome **sampling error,** which is the difference between the sample result and the true result if the entire population had been interviewed. The sample would be biased, for example, if the poll interviewed people by telephone and did not correct for the fact that more women than men answer the telephone and that some populations (college students and very poor individuals, for example) cannot be found so easily by telephone. Unscientific mail-in polls, telephone call-in polls, Internet polls, and polls completed by the workers in a campaign office are usually biased and do not give an accurate picture of the public's views. Because of these and other problems with polls, some have suggested that polling be regulated by the government.

As poll takers get close to election day, they become even more concerned about their sample of respondents. Some pollsters continue to interview eligible voters, meaning those over age eighteen and registered to vote. Many others use a series of questions in the poll and other weighting methods to try to identify "likely voters" so that they can be more accurate in their election-eve predictions. When a poll changes its method from reporting the views of eligible voters to reporting those of likely voters, the results tend to change dramatically.

Poll Questions.   It makes sense to expect that the results of a poll will depend on the questions that are asked. Depending on what question is asked, voters could be

| Sampling Error
The difference between a sample's results and the true result if the entire population had been interviewed.

President Harry Truman holds up the front page of the *Chicago Daily Tribune* issue that predicted his defeat on the basis of a Gallup poll. The poll had indicated that Truman would lose the 1948 contest for his reelection by a margin of 55.5 to 44.5 percent. The Gallup poll was completed more than a week before the election, so it missed a shift by undecided voters to Truman. Truman won the election with 49.9 percent of the vote.
(AP Photo/Byron Rollins)

said either to support a particular proposal or to oppose it. One of the problems with many polls is the yes/no answer format. For example, suppose the poll question asks, "Do you favor or oppose the war in Iraq?" Respondents might wish to answer that they favored the war at the beginning but not as it is currently being waged or that they favor fighting terrorism but not a military occupation. They have no way of indicating their true position with a yes or no answer. Respondents also are sometimes swayed by the inclusion of certain words in a question: more respondents will answer in the affirmative if the question asks, "Do you favor or oppose the war in Iraq as a means of fighting terrorism?" Furthermore, respondents' answers are also influenced by the order in which questions are asked, by the possible answers from which they are allowed to choose, and, in some cases, by their interaction with the interviewer. To a certain extent, people try to please the interviewer. They answer questions about which they have no information and avoid some answers to try to measure up to the interviewer's expectations.

Push Polls.   Some campaigns have begun using "push polls," in which the respondents are given misleading information in the questions asked to persuade them to vote against a candidate. Obviously, the answers given are likely to be influenced by such techniques. Are push polls unfair, and if they are, what can be done about them? We take a closer look at push polls in this chapter's *Politics and Polls* feature on the following page.

Because of these problems with polls, you need to be especially careful when evaluating poll results. For some suggestions on how to be a critical consumer of public opinion polls, see the *Making a Difference* feature at the end of this chapter. Some have suggested that during times of crisis, it is particularly important for pollsters to avoid these kinds of problems and try to obtain accurate results.

The Accuracy of the 2006 Polls

The 2006 election forecasts were mostly on the mark. Indeed, pollsters were publicly ecstatic about how closely their preelection forecasts matched the results. Two

"One final question: Do you now own or have you ever owned a fur coat?"

POLITICS AND POLLS | The Issue of Push Polls

The notion that candidates can use polls to "push" the respondents into voting for the candidate sponsoring the poll is relatively new to politics. Nonetheless, this type of polling is increasingly being used in political campaigns.

WHAT IS A PUSH POLL?

The National Council on Public Polls defines a *push poll* as

> a technique in which telephone calls are used to canvass vast numbers of potential voters, feeding them false and damaging "information" about a candidate under the guise of taking a poll to see how this "information" affects voter preferences. In fact, the intent is to "push" the voters away from one candidate and toward the opposing candidate.

Push polls are typically used in an effort to reach a high percentage of voters just before the close of an election campaign. Whereas a normal polling interview lasts from a few minutes to over thirty minutes, a push poll typically lasts no longer than sixty seconds, and sometimes only twenty seconds.

THE INCREASING USE OF PUSH POLLS

Designing polling questions so as to influence the respondents' votes has become common. Indeed, the practice has spread throughout all levels of U.S. politics—local, state, and

federal. In 1996, in a random survey of forty-five candidates, researchers found that thirty-five of them claimed to have been victimized by negative push-polling techniques used by their opponents.* Now even advocacy groups, as well as candidates for political offices, are using push polls.

During the 2000 presidential primaries, Republican presidential hopeful John McCain accused the Bush camp of making more than 200,000 "advocacy" calls, asking voters about their likely choices in the elections. The calls used long questions containing information about McCain's record. The Bush camp said that the information was accurate. In contrast, McCain saw this as negative "push polling."

Push polling continued during the campaigns in 2004 and the congressional campaigns in 2006. Its use was widespread in campaigns for governorships and other state offices.

FOR CRITICAL ANALYSIS

Is it possible to tell whether a survey question is worded "neutrally" or is worded in a biased manner in an effort to elicit a particular response?

*Karl T. Feld, "When Push Comes to Shove: A Polling Industry Call to Arms," *Public Perspective,* September/October 2001, p. 38.

---

pollsters, Mark Blumenthal and John McIntyre, took the average of five polls taken by major organizations (including Harris, Roper, and Gallup) on each of the last five days before the elections. The averaged forecasts were correct for every candidate leading the last-five-day poll. In addition, the average of polls had Democrats picking up six Senate seats, which they did. According to Blumenthal, "The reason polls continue to do reasonably well is that people who actually vote are people who take the trouble to be interviewed."

Technology and Opinion Polls

Public opinion polling is based on scientific principles, particularly with respect to randomness. Today, technological advances allow polls to be taken over the Internet, but serious questions have been raised about the ability of pollsters to obtain truly random samples using this medium. The same was said not long ago when another technological breakthrough changed public opinion polling—the telephone.

The Advent of Telephone Polling

During the 1970s, telephone polling began to predominate over in-person polling. Obviously, telephone polling is less expensive than sending interviewers to poll respondents in their homes. Additionally, telephone interviewers do not have to worry about safety problems, particularly in high-crime areas. Finally, telephone interviews can be conducted relatively quickly. They allow politicians or the media to poll one evening and report the results the next day.

Telephone Polling Problems.   Somewhat ironically, the success of telephone polling has created major problems for the technique. The telemarketing industry in general has become so pervasive that people increasingly refuse to respond to telephone polls. More than 40 percent of households now use either caller ID or some other form of call screening. This has greatly reduced the number of households that polling organizations can reach. Calls may be automatically rejected, or the respondent may not pick up the call. A potentially greater problem for telephone polling is the popularity of cell phones. Cellular telephone numbers are not yet included in random digit dialing programs or listed in telephone directories. Furthermore, individuals with cell phones may be located anywhere in the United States or the world, thus confounding attempts to reach people in a particular area. As more people, and especially younger Americans, choose to use only a cell phone and do not have a landline at all, polling accuracy is further reduced because these individuals cannot be included in any sample for a poll.

Nonresponse Rates Have Skyrocketed.   Nonresponses in telephone polling include unreachable numbers, refusals, answering machines, and call-screening devices. The nonresponse rate has increased to as high as 80 percent for most telephone polls. Such a high nonresponse rate undercuts confidence in the survey results. In most cases, polling only 20 percent of those on the list cannot lead to a random sample. Even more important for politicians is the fact that polling organizations are not required to report their response rates.

Enter Internet Polling

Obviously, Internet polling is not done on a one-on-one basis, since there is no voice communication. In spite of the potential problems, the Harris Poll, a widely respected national polling organization, conducted online polls during the 1998 elections. Its election predictions were accurate in many states. Nonetheless, it made a serious error in one southern gubernatorial election. The Harris group subsequently refined its techniques and continues to conduct online polls. This organization believes that proper weighting of the results will achieve the equivalent of a random-sampled poll.

Public opinion experts argue that the Harris Poll procedure violates the mathematical basis of random sampling. Nonetheless, the Internet population is looking more like the rest of America: almost as many women (71 percent) go online as men (74 percent), 61 percent of African American adults are online, and so are 72 percent of Hispanics (compared with 73 percent of non-Hispanic whites).[14]

"Nonpolls" on the Internet.   Even if organizations such as the Harris Poll succeed in obtaining the equivalent of a random sample when polling on the Internet, another problem will remain: the proliferation of "nonpolls" on the Internet. Every media outlet that maintains a Web site allows anyone to submit her or his opinion. Numerous organizations and for-profit companies send polls to individuals via e-mail. Mister Poll (**www.mrpoll.com**) bills itself as the Internet's largest online polling database. Mister Poll allows you to create your own polls just for fun or to include them on your home page. In general, Mister Poll, like many other polling sites, asks a number of questions on various issues and seeks answers from those who log on to its site. Although the Mister Poll Web site states, "None of these polls is scientific," sites such as this one undercut the efforts of legitimate pollsters to use the Internet scientifically.

---

[14]Pew Internet and American Life Project, *May–June 2006 Tracking Survey.* The Pew Internet surveys are online at **www.pewinternet.org**.

Will Internet Polling Contribute to the Devaluation of Polling Results? Although nonpolls certainly existed before the Internet, the ease with which they can be conducted and disseminated or it is accelerating another trend: the indiscriminate use of polling by all concerned. Though Americans may not want to be bothered by telemarketers or unwanted telephone polls, they seem to continue to want reports of polling results during presidential elections and news stories about the president's approval ratings and similar topics. When asked, a majority of Americans say that polling results are interesting to them. Yet the proliferation of polls, often on the Internet, with little effort to ensure the accuracy of the results presents perhaps the greatest threat to the science of polling.

As we have noted, totally nonscientific polls sometimes get as much "hype" from the media as more scientifically conducted surveys. Poll results are broadcast on the Internet with no authentication at all, and news media regularly encourage viewers to call in to their own unscientific polls. This indiscriminate use of polling may encourage Americans to see all polls as equally truthful or equally fraudulent. The value placed on polling results may diminish to the level placed on advertising. If so, voters' cynicism about all polls may increase.

Public Opinion and the Political Process

Public opinion affects the political process in many ways. Politicians, whether in office or in the midst of a campaign, see public opinion as important to their careers. The president, members of Congress, governors, and other elected officials realize that strong support by the public as expressed in opinion polls is a source of power in dealing with other politicians. It is far more difficult for a senator to say no to the president if the president is immensely popular and if polls show approval of the president's policies. Public opinion also helps political candidates identify the most important concerns among the people and may help them shape their campaigns successfully.

Nevertheless, surveys of public opinion are not equivalent to elections in the United States. Although opinion polls may influence political candidates or government officials, elections are the major vehicle through which Americans can bring about changes in their government.

Political Culture and Public Opinion

Americans are divided into a multitude of ethnic, religious, regional, and political subgroups. Given the diversity of American society and the wide range of opinions contained within it, how is it that the political process continues to function without being stalemated by conflict and dissension? One explanation is rooted in the concept of the American political culture, which can be described as a set of attitudes and ideas about the nation and the government. As discussed in Chapter 1, our political culture is widely shared by Americans of many different backgrounds. To some extent, it consists of symbols, such as the American flag, the Liberty Bell, and the Statue of Liberty. The elements of our political culture also include certain shared beliefs about the most important values in the American political system, including (1) liberty, equality, and property; (2) support for religion; and (3) community service and personal achievement. The structure of the government—particularly federalism, the political parties, the powers of Congress, and popular rule—is also an important value.

Political Culture and Support for Our Political System. The political culture provides a general environment of support for the political system. If the people share certain beliefs about the system and a reservoir of good feeling exists toward the institutions of government, the nation will be better able to weather periods of crisis. Such was the case after the 2000 presidential elections when, for several weeks, it was not certain who the next president would be and how that determination

The Pentagon Honor Guard renders honors during a memorial ceremony commemorating the fifth anniversary of the September 11, 2001, terrorist attacks on the United States. When Americans express high levels of confidence in the military, which events or which people are they likely to be thinking about? (Mass Communication Specialist 1st Class Chad J. McNeeley/ U.S. Navy)

would be made. At the time, some contended that the nation was facing a true constitutional crisis. Certainly, in many nations of today's world this would be the case. In fact, however, the broad majority of Americans did not believe that the uncertain outcome of the elections had created a constitutional crisis. Polls taken during this time found that, on the contrary, most Americans were confident in our political system's ability to decide the issue peaceably and in a lawful manner.[15]

Political Trust.   The political culture also helps Americans evaluate their government's performance. At times in our history, **political trust** in government has reached relatively high levels. As you can see in Table 6–4, a poll taken two weeks after the 9/11 attacks found that trust in government was higher than it had been for more than three decades. At other times, political trust in government has fallen to low levels. For example, in the 1960s and 1970s, during the Vietnam War and the Watergate scandals, surveys showed that the overall level of political trust in government had declined steeply. A considerable proportion of Americans seemed to feel that they could not trust government officials and that they could not count on officials to care about the ordinary person. This index of political trust reached an all-time low in the early 1990s but then climbed steadily until 2001.

At times it can be instructive to look at the level of trust that the rest of the world has in the U.S. government. For many years, the United States was a trusted leader in world affairs with many allies. In recent years, however, world opinion

| Political Trust
The degree to which individuals express trust in the government and political institutions, usually measured through a specific series of survey questions.

[15]As reported in *Public Perspective*, March/April 2002, p. 11, summarizing the results of Gallup/CNN/ *USA Today* polls conducted between November 11 and December 10, 2000.

TABLE 6–4 | TRENDS IN POLITICAL TRUST

QUESTION: How much of the time do you think you can trust the government in Washington to do what is right—just about always, most of the time, or only some of the time?

	1972	1976	1978	1980	1982	1984	1986	1988	1990	1992	1994	1996	1998	2000	2001	2002	2003	2005	2006
Percentage saying: Always/Most of the time	53	33	29	25	32	46	42	44	27	23	20	25	34	40	64	46	33	30	32
Some of the time	45	63	67	73	64	51	55	54	73	75	79	71	66	59	35	52	58	65	64

Sources: *New York Times*/CBS News Surveys; University of Michigan Survey Research Center, National Election Studies; Pew Research Center for the People and the Press; Council for Excellence in Government; *Washington Post* poll, September 25–27, 2001; and Gallup polls, Fall 2002, 2003, 2005, and 2006.

BEYOND OUR BORDERS | World Opinion of the United States

In the immediate aftermath of the September 11, 2001, terrorist attacks, most of the world expressed a great deal of sympathy toward the United States. Few nations objected to the subsequent American invasion of Afghanistan in 2001 to oust the Taliban government or to the Bush administration's vow to hunt down the terrorists responsible for the 9/11 attacks. When the United States announced plans to invade Iraq in 2003, however, world opinion began to sour. By 2006, world opinion had become decidedly anti-American, as the United States' ongoing "war on terrorism"—and the Bush administration in particular—rankled observers around the globe.

NEGATIVE VIEWS OF AMERICAN UNILATERALISM

The invasion of Iraq in 2003 marked a key turning point in world public opinion toward the United States. Most nations opposed the United States' plan to attack Iraq. They favored continued inspections to search for weapons of mass destruction there and called for proof that Iraqi dictator Saddam Hussein had ties to terrorist groups, but the United States decided to lead an invasion of Iraq anyway. Although Saddam Hussein had very few supporters in the world community, most nations still did not believe that attacking Iraq was justified. The willingness of American leaders to ignore world opinion with regard to the Iraq situation incensed people across the globe.

Moreover, at times, many foreigners have accused President George W. Bush of being divisive, arrogant, and irresponsible. Few of those abroad queried in opinion polls were confident that Bush would "do the right thing" regarding world affairs. Only 18 percent of Spaniards and 25 percent of French poll respondents, for example, expressed "a lot" or "some" confidence in Bush. Even in Britain, the United States' leading ally in the war on terrorism, only 38 percent thought positively of Bush. Only India had an overall favorable opinion toward Bush, at 54 percent.

ARAB AND MUSLIM OPINION TOWARD AMERICA AND ITS IDEALS

Among Arabs and Muslims, opinion of the United States is particularly low. The primary reason for anti-Americanism around the globe is opposition to U.S. foreign policy. That opposition is most vehement in the Middle East. In 2005, for example, 85 percent of Jordanians opposed the U.S.-led war on terrorism. In Turkey, a relatively secular nation in the region that has been a U.S. ally in the past, the opposition was a stunning 71 percent. That figure is even more telling considering that only 7 percent of Turks expressed a favorable opinion of al Qaeda leader Osama bin Laden.

Many Arabs and Muslims resent the United States' interventionism and presence in the Middle East. This does not mean that they reject all aspects of the United States or its ideals, however. The majority of Muslims do not support religious extremism or terrorism in their own nations. Nor are Arabs and Muslims dismissive of democracy. Recent polls have shown declining support for terrorist groups among Arabs and Muslims, with only 13 percent of Moroccans and 25 percent of Pakistani Muslims expressing positive views toward terrorism. There has also been broad support for democracy in the Middle East. Many individuals are suspicious of American motives in the region, however, and believe that democracy is a real possibility in their own country. Indeed, 83 percent of Lebanese and 80 percent of Jordanians believe that democracy could work in their respective nations.

FOR CRITICAL ANALYSIS

How might the United States reverse its negative image in the world? Some polls have shown that younger Muslims and Arabs have a more positive opinion toward the United States. Why might that be the case?

toward the United States has soured, as discussed in this chapter's *Beyond Our Borders* feature.

Public Opinion about Government

A vital component of public opinion in the United States is the considerable ambivalence with which the public regards many major national institutions. Table 6–5 shows trends from 1983 to 2006 in opinion polls asking respondents, at regularly spaced intervals, how much confidence they had in the institutions listed. Over the years, military and religious organizations have ranked highest. Note, however, the decline in confidence in churches in 2002 following a substantial number of sex-abuse allegations against Catholic priests. Note also the somewhat heightened regard for the military after the first Gulf War in 1991. Since that time, the public has consistently had more confidence in the military than in any of the

TABLE 6–5 | CONFIDENCE IN INSTITUTIONS TREND

QUESTION: I am going to read a list of institutions in American society. Would you please tell me how much confidence you, yourself, have in each one—a great deal, quite a lot, some, or very little?

	PERCENTAGE SAYING "A GREAT DEAL" OR "QUITE A LOT"														
	1983	1985	1987	1989	1991	1993	1995	1997	1999	2001	2002	2003	2004	2005	2006
Military	53	61	61	63	69	67	64	60	68	66	79	82	75	74	73
Church or organized religion	62	66	61	52	56	53	57	56	58	60	45	50	53	53	52
Banks and banking	51	51	51	42	30	38	43	41	43	44	47	50	53	49	49
U.S. Supreme Court	42	56	52	46	39	43	44	50	49	50	50	47	46	41	40
Public schools	39	48	50	43	35	39	40	40	36	38	38	40	41	37	37
Television	25	29	28	NA	24	21	33	34	34	34	35	35	30	28	31
Newspapers	38	35	31	NA	32	31	30	35	33	36	35	33	30	28	30
Congress	28	39	NA	32	18	19	21	22	26	26	29	29	30	22	19
Organized labor	26	28	26	NA	22	26	26	23	28	26	26	28	31	24	24
Big business	28	31	NA	NA	22	23	21	28	30	28	20	22	24	22	18

NA = Not asked.
Source: Gallup poll, May 21–23, 2004.

other institutions shown in Table 6–5. In 2002 and 2003, confidence in the military soared even higher, most likely because Americans recognized the central role being played by the military in the war on terrorism.

The United States Supreme Court and the banking industry have scored well over time. Less confidence is expressed in newspapers, television, big business, and organized labor. In 1991, following a scandal involving congressional banking practices, confidence in Congress fell to a record low of 18 percent. Confidence in Congress has yet to return to the levels reported in the 1970s and 1980s.

At times, popular confidence in all institutions may rise or fall, reflecting optimism or pessimism about the general state of the nation. For example, between 1979 and 1981 there was a collapse of confidence affecting most institutions. This reflected public dissatisfaction with the handling of the hostage crisis in Iran and with some of the highest levels of inflation in U.S. history. Some of this confidence was restored by 1985, however, when conditions had improved.

Although people may not have much confidence in government institutions, they nonetheless turn to government to solve what they perceive to be the major problems facing the country. Table 6–6, which is based on Gallup polls conducted

TABLE 6–6 | MOST IMPORTANT PROBLEM TREND, 1975 TO PRESENT

1977	High cost of living, unemployment	1992	Unemployment, budget deficit
1978	High cost of living, energy problems	1993	Health care, budget deficit
1979	High cost of living, energy problems	1994	Crime, violence, health care
1980	High cost of living, unemployment	1995	Crime, violence
1981	High cost of living, unemployment	1996	Budget deficit
1982	Unemployment, high cost of living	1997	Crime, violence
1983	Unemployment, high cost of living	1998	Crime, violence
1984	Unemployment, fear of war	1999	Crime, violence
1985	Fear of war, unemployment	2000	Morals, family decline
1986	Unemployment, budget deficit	2001	Economy, education
1987	Unemployment, economy	2002	Terrorism, economy
1988	Economy, budget deficit	2003	Terrorism, economy
1989	War on drugs	2004	War in Iraq, economy
1990	War in Middle East	2005	War in Iraq
1991	Economy	2006	War in Iraq, gas prices

Sources: *New York Times*/CBS News poll, January 1996; and Gallup polls, 2000 through 2006.

from the years 1977 to 2006, shows that the leading problems have changed over time. The public tends to emphasize problems that are immediate and that have been the subject of many stories in the media. When coverage of a particular problem increases suddenly, the public is more likely to see that as the most important problem. Thus, the fluctuations in the "most important problem" cited in Table 6–6 may, in part, be attributed to media agenda setting. In recent years, terrorism, the war in Iraq, and the economy have reached the top of the list.

Public Opinion and Policymaking

If public opinion is important for democracy, are policymakers really responsive to public opinion? A study by political scientists Benjamin I. Page and Robert Y. Shapiro suggests that in fact the national government is very responsive to the public's demands for action.[16] In looking at changes in public opinion poll results over time, Page and Shapiro show that when the public supports a policy change, the following occurs: policy changes in a direction consistent with the change in public opinion 43 percent of the time, policy changes in a direction opposite to the change in opinion 22 percent of the time, and policy does not change at all 33 percent of the time. Page and Shapiro also show, as should be no surprise, that when public opinion changes dramatically— say, by 20 percentage points rather than by just 6 or 7 percentage points—government policy is much more likely to follow changing public attitudes.

Setting Limits on Government Action. Although opinion polls cannot give exact guidance on what the government should do in a specific instance, the opinions measured in polls do set an informal limit on government action. For example, consider the highly controversial issue of abortion. Most Americans are moderates on this issue; they do not approve of abortion as a means of birth control, but they do feel that it should be available under certain circumstances. Yet sizable groups of people express very intense feelings both for and against legalized abortion. Given this distribution of opinion, most elected officials would rather not try to change policy to favor either of the extreme positions. To do so would clearly violate the opinion of the majority of Americans. In this case, as in many others, *public opinion does not make public policy; rather, it restrains officials from taking truly unpopular actions.* If officials do act in the face of public opposition, the consequences will be determined at the ballot box.

To what degree should public opinion influence policymaking? It would appear that members of the public view this issue differently than policy leaders do. The results of a recent poll about polls showed that whereas 68 percent of the public feel that public opinion should have a great deal of influence on policy, only 43 percent of policy leaders hold this opinion.[17] Why would a majority of policy leaders *not* want to be strongly influenced by public opinion? One answer to this question is that public opinion polls can provide only a limited amount of guidance to policymakers.

The Limits of Polling. Policymakers cannot always be guided by opinion polls. In the end, politicians must make their own choices. When they do so, their choices necessarily involve trade-offs. If politicians vote for increased spending to improve education, for example, by necessity there must be fewer resources available for other worthy projects.

Individuals who are polled do not have to make such trade-offs when they respond to questions. Indeed, survey respondents usually are not even given a choice of trade-offs in their policy opinions. Pollsters typically ask respondents whether they want more or less spending in a particular area, such as education. Rarely, though, is a dollar amount assigned. Additionally, broad poll questions often

---

[16]See the extensive work of Page and Shapiro in Benjamin I. Page and Robert Y. Shapiro, *The Rational Public: Fifty Years of Trends in Americans' Policy Preferences* (Chicago: University of Chicago Press, 1992).
[17]Mollyann Brodie *et al.*, "Polling and Democracy: The Will of the People," *Public Perspective*, July/August 2001, pp. 10–14.

provide little guidance for policymakers. What does it mean if a majority of those polled want "free" medical treatment for everyone in need? Obviously, medical care is never free. Certain individuals may receive medical care free of charge, but society as a whole has to pay for it. In short, polling questions usually do not reflect the cost of any particular policy choice. Moreover, to make an informed policy choice requires an understanding not only of the policy area but also of the consequences of any given choice. Virtually no public opinion polls make sure that those polled have such information.

Finally, government decisions cannot be made simply by adding up individual desires. Politicians engage in a type of "horse trading." All politicians know that they cannot satisfy every desire of every constituent. Therefore, each politician attempts to maximize the *net* benefits to his or her constituents, while keeping within whatever the politician believes the government can afford.

MAKING A DIFFERENCE | Being a Critical Consumer of Opinion Polls

Americans are inundated with the results of public opinion polls. The polls purport to tell us a variety of things: whether the president's popularity is up or down, whether gun control is more in favor now than previously, or who is leading the pack for the next presidential nomination. What must be kept in mind with this blizzard of information is that all poll results are not equally good or equally believable.

Why Should You Care?

As a critical consumer, you need to be aware of what makes one set of public opinion poll results valid and other results useless or even dangerously misleading. Knowing what makes a poll accurate is especially important if you plan to participate actively in politics. Successful participation depends on accurate information, and that includes knowing what your fellow citizens are thinking. If large numbers of other people really agree with you that a particular policy needs to be changed, there may be a good chance that the policy can actually be altered. If almost no one agrees with you on a particular issue, there may be no point in trying to change policy immediately; the best you can do is to try to sway the opinions of others, in the hope that someday

enough people will agree with you to make policy changes possible.

What Can You Do?

Pay attention only to opinion polls that are based on scientific, or random, samples. In these so-called *probability samples,* a known probability is used to select each person interviewed. Do not give credence to the results of opinion polls that consist of shopping-mall interviews or the like. The main problem with this kind of opinion taking is that not everyone has an equal chance of being in the mall when the interview takes place. Also, it is almost certain that the people in the mall are not a reasonable cross section of a community's entire population.

Probability samples are useful because you can calculate the range within which the results would have fallen if everybody had been interviewed. Well-designed probability samples will allow the pollster to say, for example, that he or she is 95 percent sure that 61 percent of the public, plus or minus 4 percentage points, supports national health insurance. It turns out that if you want to be twice as precise about a poll result, you need to collect a sample four times as large. This tends to make

accurate polls expensive and difficult to conduct.

Pay attention as well to how people were contacted for the poll—by mail, by telephone, in person in their homes, or in some other way (such as via the Internet). Because of its lower cost, polling firms have turned more and more to telephone interviewing. This method can produce highly accurate results. Its disadvantage is that telephone interviews typically need to be short and to deal with questions that are fairly easy to answer. Interviews in person are better for getting useful information about why a particular response was given. They take much longer to complete, however. Results from mailed questionnaires should be taken with a grain of salt. Usually, only a small percentage of people send them back.

When viewers or listeners of television or radio shows are encouraged to call in their opinions to an 800 telephone number, the polling results are meaningless. Users of the Internet also have an easy way to make their views known. Only people who own computers and are interested in the topic will take the trouble to respond, however, and that group is not representative of the general public.

Key Terms

agenda setting 195	generational effect 196	opinion poll 203	public opinion 192
consensus 192	lifestyle effect 196	peer group 194	sampling error 206
divisive opinion 192	media 195	political socialization 193	socioeconomic status 197
gender gap 201	opinion leader 194	political trust 211	Watergate break-in 197

Chapter Summary

1 Public opinion is the aggregate of individual attitudes or beliefs shared by some portion of the adult population. A consensus exists when a large proportion of the public appears to express the same view on an issue. Divisive opinion exists when the public holds widely different attitudes on an issue. Sometimes, a poll shows a distribution of opinion indicating that most people either have no information about an issue or are not interested enough in the issue to form a position on it.

2 People's opinions are formed through the political socialization process. Important factors in this process are the family, educational experiences, peer groups, opinion leaders, the media, and political events. The influence of the media as a socialization factor may be growing relative to the family. Voting behavior is influenced by demographic factors such as education, economic status, religion, race and ethnicity, gender, and region. It is also influenced by election-specific factors such as party identification, perception of the candidates, and issue preferences.

3 Most descriptions of public opinion are based on the results of opinion polls. The accuracy of polls depends on sampling techniques that include a representative sample of the population being polled and that ensure randomness in the selection of respondents.

4 Problems with polls include sampling errors (which may occur when the pool of respondents is not chosen in a scientific manner), the difficulty of knowing the degree to which responses are influenced by the type and order of questions asked, the use of a yes/no format for answers to the questions, and the interviewer's techniques. Many are concerned about the use of "push polls" (in which the questions "push" the respondent toward a particular candidate).

5 Advances in technology have changed polling techniques over the years. During the 1970s, telephone polling came to be widely used. Today, largely because of extensive telemarketing, people often refuse to answer calls, and nonresponse rates in telephone polling have skyrocketed. Due to the difficulty of obtaining a random sample in the online environment, Internet polls are often "nonpolls." Whether Internet polls can overcome this problem remains to be seen.

6 Public opinion affects the political process in many ways. The political culture provides a general environment of support for the political system, allowing the nation to weather periods of crisis. The political culture also helps Americans to evaluate their government's performance. At times, the level of trust in government has been relatively high; at other times, the level of trust has declined steeply. Similarly, Americans' confidence in government institutions varies over time, depending on a number of circumstances. Generally, though, Americans turn to government to solve what they perceive to be the major problems facing the country. In 2004, Americans ranked the war in Iraq and the economy as the two most significant problems facing the nation.

7 Public opinion also plays an important role in policymaking. Although polling data show that a majority of Americans would like policy leaders to be influenced to a great extent by public opinion, politicians cannot always be guided by opinion polls. This is because the respondents often do not understand the costs and consequences of policy decisions or the trade-offs involved in making such decisions. An important function of public opinion is to set limits on government action through public pressure.

|Selected Print and Media Resources

SUGGESTED READINGS

Asher, Herbert. *Polling and the Public: What Every Citizen Should Know.* Washington, D.C.: CQ Press, 2004. This clearly written and often entertaining book explains what polls are, how they are conducted and interpreted, and how the wording and ordering of survey questions, as well as the interviewer's techniques, can significantly affect the respondents' answers.

Bardes, Barbara A., and Robert W. Oldendick. *Public Opinion: Measuring the American Mind,* 3rd ed. Belmont, Calif.: Wadsworth Publishing Co., 2006. This examination of public opinion polling looks at the uses of public opinion data and recent technological issues in polling in addition to providing excellent coverage of public opinion on important issues over a period of decades.

Berinsky, Adam J. *Silent Voices: Public Opinion and Political Participation in America.* Princeton, N.J.: Princeton University Press, 2004. Berinsky argues that people who do not respond to survey questions may differ significantly from those who do.

Lynch, Marc. *Voices of the New Arab Public: Iraq, al-Jazeera, and Middle East Politics Today.* New York: Columbia University Press, 2006. The author takes an in-depth look at how al-Jazeera and other Arab satellite television stations have transformed Middle Eastern politics over the past decade. Lynch also discusses how this new era of political socialization has affected relations with the United States.

Newport, Frank. *Polling Matters: Why Leaders Must Listen to the Wisdom of the People.* New York: Warner Books, 2004. Newport, the editor-in-chief of the Gallup Poll, offers a spirited defense of the polling process. Newport believes that polls reflect the country's collective wisdom, and he disputes the argument that citizens are too uninformed to offer useful opinions.

MEDIA RESOURCES

Faith and Politics: The Christian Right—This 1995 documentary was hosted by Dan Rather and produced by CBS News. It focuses on the efforts of the Christian conservative movement to affect educational curriculums and public policy. Members of the Christian right who are interviewed include Ralph Reed and Gary Bauer. Critics of the Christian right who are interviewed include Senator Arlen Specter.

Vox Populi: Democracy in Crisis—A PBS special focusing on why public confidence in government, which has plummeted during recent decades, still has not recovered.

Wag the Dog—A 1997 film that provides a very cynical look at the importance of public opinion. The film, which features Dustin Hoffman and Robert De Niro, follows the efforts of a presidential political consultant who stages a foreign policy crisis to divert public opinion from a sex scandal in the White House.

E·MOCRACY | Online Polling and Poll Data

News organizations, interest groups, not-for-profit groups, and online e-zines are now using online polling to gather the opinions of their readers and viewers. All the user has to do is log on to the Web site and click on the box indicating the preferred response. People can respond to online polls more easily than to call-in polls, and in most cases, they are free to the user. Realize, though, that online polls are totally nonscientific because the respondents are all self-selected. Essentially, Internet polls are pseudopolls because only those who choose to do so respond, making the polls much more likely to be biased and based on an unrepresentative sample.

At the same time, the Internet is an excellent source for finding reliable polling reports and data. All of the major polling organizations have Web sites that include news releases about polls they have conducted. Some sites make the polling data available for free to users; others require that a user pay a subscription fee before accessing the polling archives on the site.

Logging On

Yale University Library, one of the world's great research institutions, offers access to social science libraries and information services. If you want to browse through library sources of public opinion data, this is an interesting site to visit. Go to

www.library.yale.edu/socsci/opinion

According to its home page, the mission of National Election Studies (NES) "is to produce high-quality data on voting, public opinion, and political participation that serves the research needs of social scientists, teachers, students, and policymakers concerned with understanding the theoretical and empirical foundations of mass politics in a democratic society." This is a good place to obtain information on public opinion. Find it at

www.umich.edu/~nes

The Polling Report Web site offers polls and their results organized by topic. It is up to date and easy to use:

www.pollingreport.com

The Gallup organization's Web site offers not only polling data (although a user must pay a subscription fee to obtain access to many polling reports) but also information on how polls are constructed, conducted, and interpreted. Go to

www.gallup.com

Another site that features articles and polling data on public opinion is the Web site of the Zogby poll at

www.zogby.com

Online Review

At **www.politicalscience.wadsworth.com/ schmidt12**, you will find a free Study Guide to this book. For each chapter, there are two online quizzes to help you master the material.

• The PoliPrep Self-Study Assessment provides a pretest for each major section of the chapter. PoliPrep then generates a customized study plan. After you complete the study plan, a posttest evaluates your progress.

• The Tutorial Quiz for each chapter provides questions on the chapter contents, including the features. The questions are organized to match the major sections of the chapter.

7 | Interest Groups

What If . . .
Retired Government Employees Could Not Work for Interest Groups?

BACKGROUND

Many interest groups employ lobbyists to influence legislation and the administrative decisions of government. About half of the paid lobbyists in Washington are former government employees or former members of Congress. Interest groups place a high value on lobbyists who "know their way around Washington." Former government employees and elected officials qualify in this regard. Often, retired government employees or congresspersons retain personal friendships with their former colleagues. There are rules in place to prevent former government employees from lobbying their former colleagues for a limited period of time after retirement. Congresspersons and their staff members also face such limits. Still, retirees can immediately engage in activities that do not technically qualify as lobbying, and they can begin full-scale lobbying as soon as the time limits expire.

WHAT IF RETIRED GOVERNMENT EMPLOYEES COULD NOT WORK FOR INTEREST GROUPS?

Some people have argued that interest groups gain improper influence by hiring former government employees. Therefore, these critics say, such hiring should not merely be restricted but should be banned altogether. If this were to happen, interest groups that frequently hire former government employees would be less effective. Which groups are these, and what do they seek to accomplish?

A large number of interest groups represent particular industries. Typically, such groups are concerned with legislation and administrative rules that are specific to their industry and are of little interest to the general public. Therefore, the press pays little attention to these laws and regulations. Industry lobbying can "fly under the radar." A retired government employee with expert knowledge of the specific subject matter and

of the processes and people involved in making administrative rules can be a formidable lobbyist.

Likewise, a former member of Congress can offer invaluable assistance when an interest group seeks to affect lawmaking. If these knowledgeable retirees were not available to interest groups, those groups would have less influence on administrative rulemaking and on legislation. Of course, campaign contributions by interest groups are also part of the process of influencing Congress. (You will learn more about campaign finance later in this chapter and in Chapter 9.)

CORPORATE WELFARE

As an example of an interest group, the pharmaceutical industry spends nearly $100 million per year on lobbying, and more than half of its 600-plus registered lobbyists are former members of Congress or former government employees. The pharmaceutical industry has a history of slipping

favorable elements into pending legislation. In 2004, for example, the Medicare Reform Bill was passed with a prescription drug benefits program that does not allow Medicare bureaucrats to negotiate the prices of approved drugs as private health insurance companies normally do to control costs.

Industry-specific legislation can include tariffs on imports, tax breaks, and direct subsidies. The cost of this legislation adds up. The Cato Institute, a libertarian research group, estimates that what it calls "corporate welfare" costs nearly $100 billion a year. Barring former government employees from working for interest groups might reduce these kinds of corporate subsidies.

Interest groups that address issues of broader concern generally do not need to hire experts with government experience to be effective. There can be little doubt, for example, that the influence of the National Rifle Association

does not depend on its ability to hire retired government employees.

THE IMPACT ON FORMER EMPLOYEES

Some government employees—and many congresspersons—look forward to lobbying as a final stage of their careers. A government career may be more attractive if it ends with a few years of highly paid, comfortable employment. Banning such employment might make government service less appealing to some. The long-term result might be that fewer well-qualified individuals would choose to enter government and politics as a lifelong career.

FOR CRITICAL ANALYSIS

1. Why would interest groups argue that a ban on hiring retired government employees would be an unfair (or even an unconstitutional) restriction on their activities?
2. In what ways might a ban on hiring retired government employees be unfair to the former employees themselves?

The structure of American government invites the participation of **interest groups** at various stages of the policymaking process. For example, interest groups played a role in the legislation passed by Congress after the terrorist attacks of September 11, 2001. In a show of national unity, the House of Representatives and the Senate voted overwhelmingly to give President George W. Bush authority to use military force in response to the attacks and passed a $40 billion emergency spending bill to pay for the response.

Two weeks after the attacks, life on Capitol Hill returned to the more normal process of dissension and debate. The president's requests for further antiterrorism legislation spurred furious action by interest groups, which quickly sent their **lobbyists** to persuade Congress to adopt their positions on these bills. The airlines, which constitute a powerful interest group, expressed their need for congressional help. They were gratified by an airline bailout bill to make up for the sizable losses they suffered as a result of the closure of U.S. airspace after the attacks and the drop in the number of passengers in the weeks that followed. After the bill passed, however, lobbyists for the many other industries—including car rental firms, the hotel industry, and travel and tourism companies—that were hurt by the attacks began asking for their own assistance packages.

| Interest Group
An organized group of individuals sharing common objectives who actively attempt to influence policymakers.

| Lobbyist
An organization or individual who attempts to influence legislation and the administrative decisions of government.

Interest Groups: A Natural Phenomenon

Alexis de Tocqueville observed in 1834 that "in no country of the world has the principle of association been more successfully used or applied to a greater multitude of objectives than in America."[1] The French traveler was amazed at the degree to which Americans formed groups to solve civic problems, establish social

[1] Alexis de Tocqueville, *Democracy in America*, Vol. 1, edited by Phillips Bradley (New York: Knopf, 1980), p. 191.

Lobbying activity becomes most intense the day a vote is being taken on an important issue. Not surprisingly, lobbyists are often found in the lobbies of Congress. What functions do lobbyists fulfill? (Dennis Brack/Stock Photo)

Alexis de Tocqueville (1805–1859), a French social historian and traveler, commented on Americans' predilection for joining groups. (Musees Nationaux/Art Resource NY)

| Social Movement
A movement that represents the demands of a large segment of the public for political, economic, or social change.

relationships, and speak for their economic or political interests. Perhaps James Madison, when he wrote *Federalist Paper* No. 10 (see Appendix C), had already judged the character of his country's citizens similarly. He supported the creation of a large republic with many states to encourage the formation of multiple interests. The multitude of interests, in Madison's view, would work to discourage the formation of an oppressive majority interest.

Surely, neither Madison nor de Tocqueville foresaw the formation of more than a hundred thousand associations in the United States. Poll data show that more than two-thirds of all Americans belong to at least one group or association. Although the majority of these affiliations could not be classified as "interest groups" in the political sense, Americans do understand the principles of working in groups.

Today, interest groups range from the elementary school parent-teacher association and the local "Stop the Sewer Plant Association" to the statewide association of insurance agents. They include small groups such as local environmental organizations and national groups such as the Boy Scouts of America, the American Civil Liberties Union, the National Education Association, and the American League of Lobbyists.

Interest Groups and Social Movements

Interest groups are often spawned by mass **social movements.** Such movements represent demands by a large segment of the population for change in the political, economic, or social system. Social movements are often the first expression of latent discontent with the existing system. They may be the authentic voice of weaker or oppressed groups in society that do not have the means or standing to organize as interest groups. For example, most mainstream political and social leaders disapproved of the women's movement of the 1800s. Because women were unable to vote or take an active part in the political system, it was difficult for women who desired greater freedoms to organize formal groups. After the Civil War, when more women became active in professional life, the first real women's rights group, the National Woman Suffrage Association, came into being.

Social movements, such as the push for women's suffrage, have spawned interest groups. Shown here is the cover of an official program for the National American Women's Suffrage Association. The scene depicts suffragettes marching in a Washington, D.C., procession during 1913. How have women's rights groups expanded their agendas since winning suffrage? (Library of Congress)

African Americans found themselves in an even more disadvantaged situation after the end of the Reconstruction period. They were unable to exercise political rights in many southern and border states, and their participation in any form of organization could lead to economic ruin, physical harassment, or even death. The civil rights movement of the 1950s and 1960s was clearly a social movement. Although the movement received support from several formal organizations—including the Southern Christian Leadership Conference, the National Association for the Advancement of Colored People, and the Urban League—only a social movement could generate the kinds of civil disobedience that took place in hundreds of towns and cities across the country.

Social movements are often precursors of interest groups. They may generate interest groups with specific goals that successfully recruit members through the incentives the group offers. In the case of the women's movement of the 1960s, the National Organization for Women was formed in part out of a demand to end gender-segregated job advertising in newspapers.

Why So Many?

Whether based in a social movement or created to meet an immediate crisis, interest groups continue to form and act in American society. One reason for the multitude of interest groups is that the right to join a group is protected by the First Amendment to the U.S. Constitution (see Chapter 4). Not only are all people guaranteed the right "peaceably to assemble," but they are also guaranteed the right "to petition the Government for a redress of grievances." This constitutional provision encourages Americans to form groups and to express their opinions to the government or to their elected representatives as members of a group. Group membership makes the individual's opinions appear more powerful and strongly conveys the group's ability to vote for or against a representative.

In addition, our federal system of government provides thousands of "pressure points" for interest group activity. Americans can form groups in their neighborhoods or cities and lobby the city council and their state government. They can join statewide groups or national groups and try to influence government policy through Congress or through one of the executive agencies or cabinet departments. Representatives of giant corporations may seek to influence the president personally at social events or fund-raisers. When attempts to influence government through the executive and legislative branches fail, interest groups turn to the courts, filing suit in state or federal court to achieve their political objectives. Pluralist theorists, as discussed in Chapter 1, point to the openness of the American political structure as a major factor in the power of groups in American politics.

| Why Do Americans Join Interest Groups?

One puzzle that has fascinated political scientists is why some people join interest groups, whereas many others do not. Everyone has some interest that could benefit from government action. For many individuals, however, those concerns remain unorganized interests, or **latent interests.**

According to political theorist Mancur Olson,[2] it simply may not be rational for individuals to join most groups. In his classic work on this topic, Olson introduced the idea of the "collective good." This concept refers to any public benefit that, if available to any member of the community, cannot be denied to any other member, whether or not he or she participated in the effort to gain the good.

> **DID YOU KNOW . . .**
> That at least half of all lobbyists in Washington, D.C., are women?

Latent Interests
Public-policy interests that are not recognized or addressed by a group at a particular time.

---

[2]Mancur Olson, *The Logic of Collective Action* (Cambridge, Mass.: Harvard University Press, 1965).

Free Rider Problem
The difficulty interest groups face in recruiting members when the benefits they achieve can be gained without joining the group.

Solidary Incentive
A reason or motive having to do with the desire to associate with others and to share with others a particular interest or hobby.

Material Incentive
A reason or motive having to do with economic benefits or opportunities.

Purposive Incentive
A reason for supporting or participating in the activities of a group that is based on agreement with the goals of the group. For example, someone with a strong interest in human rights might have a purposive incentive to join Amnesty International.

Although collective benefits are usually thought of as coming from such public goods as clean air or national defense, benefits are also bestowed by the government on subsets of the public. Price subsidies to dairy farmers and loans to college students are examples. Olson used economic theory to propose that it is not rational for interested individuals to join groups that work for group benefits. In fact, it is often more rational for the individual to wait for others to procure the benefits and then share them. How many college students, for example, join the American Association of Community Colleges, an organization that lobbies the government for increased financial aid to students? The difficulty interest groups face in recruiting members when the benefits can be obtained without joining is referred to as the **free rider problem.**

If so little incentive exists for individuals to join together, why are there thousands of interest groups lobbying in Washington? According to the logic of collective action, if the contribution of an individual *will* make a difference to the effort, then it is worth it to the individual to join. Thus, smaller groups, which seek benefits for only a small proportion of the population, are more likely to enroll members who will give time and funds to the cause. Larger groups, which represent general public interests (the women's movement or the American Civil Liberties Union, for example), will find it relatively more difficult to get individuals to join. People need an incentive—material or otherwise—to participate.

Solidary Incentives

Interest groups offer **solidary incentives** for their members. Solidary incentives include companionship, a sense of belonging, and the pleasure of associating with others. Although the National Audubon Society was originally founded to save the snowy egret from extinction, today most members join to learn more about birds and to meet and share their pleasure with other individuals who enjoy bird-watching as a hobby. Even though the incentive might be solidary for many members, this organization nonetheless also pursues an active political agenda, working to preserve the environment and to protect endangered species. Most members may not play any part in working toward larger, more national goals unless the organization can convince them to take political action or unless some local environmental issue arises.

Material Incentives

For other individuals, interest groups offer direct **material incentives.** A case in point is AARP (formerly the American Association of Retired Persons), which provides discounts, insurance plans, and organized travel opportunities for its members. Because of its exceptionally low dues ($12.50 annually) and the benefits gained through membership, AARP has become the largest—and a very powerful—interest group in the United States. AARP can claim to represent the interests of millions of senior citizens and can show that they actually have joined the group. For most seniors, the material incentives outweigh the membership costs.

Many other interest groups offer indirect material incentives for their members. Such groups as the American Dairy Association and the National Association of Automobile Dealers do not give discounts or freebies to their members, but they do offer indirect benefits and rewards by, for example, protecting the material interests of their members from government policymaking that is injurious to their industry or business.

Purposive Incentives

Interest groups also offer the opportunity for individuals to pursue political, economic, or social goals through joint action. **Purposive incentives** offer individuals

AARP's Web site lists the many benefits and discounts available to members for an annual fee of $12.50. If many members of an organization join purely for the membership benefits, is it appropriate for the organization to lobby aggressively for specific policies that not all members may endorse?

the satisfaction of taking action when the goals of a group correspond to their beliefs or principles. The individuals who belong to a group focusing on the abortion issue or gun control, for example, do so because they feel strongly enough about the issues to support the group's work with money and time.

Some scholars have argued that many people join interest groups simply for the discounts, magazine subscriptions, and other tangible benefits and are not really interested in the political positions taken by the groups. According to William P. Browne, however, research shows that people really do care about the policy stance of an interest group. Members of a group seek people who share the group's views and then ask them to join. As one group leader put it, "Getting members is about scaring the hell out of people."[3] People join the group and then feel that they are doing something about a cause that is important to them.

Types of Interest Groups

Thousands of groups exist to influence government. Among the major types of interest groups are those that represent the main sectors of the economy. In addition, a number of "public-interest" organizations have been formed to represent the needs of the general citizenry, including some "single-issue" groups. The interests of foreign governments and foreign businesses are also represented in the American political arena. The names and Web addresses of some major interest groups are shown in Tables 7–1 and 7–2 on the following page.

---

[3]William P. Browne, *Groups, Interests, and U.S. Public Policy* (Washington, D.C.: Georgetown University Press, 1998), p. 23.

TABLE 7-1 | *FORTUNE*'S "POWER 25"—THE TWENTY-FIVE MOST EFFECTIVE INTEREST GROUPS

1. National Rifle Association of America (the NRA—opposed to gun control): **www.nra.org**
2. AARP (formerly the American Association of Retired Persons): **www.aarp.org**
3. National Federation of Independent Business: **www.nfibonline.com**
4. American Israel Public Affairs Committee (AIPAC—a pro-Israel group): **www.aipac.org**
5. Association of Trial Lawyers of America: **www.atla.org**
6. American Federation of Labor–Congress of Industrial Organizations (the AFL-CIO—a federation of most U.S. labor unions): **www.aflcio.org**
7. Chamber of Commerce of the United States of America (an association of businesses): **www.uschamber.org**
8. National Beer Wholesalers Association: **www.nbwa.org**
9. National Association of Realtors: **www.realtor.com**
10. National Association of Manufacturers (NAM): **www.nam.org**
11. National Association of Home Builders of the United States: **www.nahb.org**
12. American Medical Association (the AMA—representing physicians): **www.ama-assn.org**
13. American Hospital Association: **www.aha.org**
14. National Education Association of the United States (the NEA—representing teachers): **www.nea.org**
15. American Farm Bureau Federation (representing farmers): **www.fb.org**
16. Motion Picture Association of America (representing movie studios): **www.mpaa.org**
17. National Association of Broadcasters: **www.nab.org**
18. National Right to Life Committee (opposed to legalized abortion): **www.nrlc.org**
19. America's Health Insurance Plans: **www.ahip.org**
20. National Restaurant Association: **www.restaurant.org**
21. National Governors' Association: **www.nga.org**
22. Recording Industry Association of America: **www.riaa.com**
23. American Bankers Association: **www.aba.com**
24. Pharmaceutical Research and Manufacturers of America: **www.phrma.org**
25. International Brotherhood of Teamsters (a labor union): **www.teamster.org**

Source: *Fortune*, May 2005.

TABLE 7-2 | SOME OTHER IMPORTANT INTEREST GROUPS (NOT ON *FORTUNE*'S "POWER 25" LIST)

American Civil Liberties Union (the ACLU): **www.aclu.org**
American Legion (a veterans' group): **www.legion.org**
American Library Association: **www.ala.org**
The American Society for the Prevention of Cruelty to Animals (the ASPCA): **www.aspca.org**
Amnesty International USA (promotes human rights): **www.amnesty.org**
Handgun Control, Inc. (favors gun control): **www.bradycampaign.org**
League of United Latin American Citizens (LULAC): **www.lulac.org**
Mothers Against Drunk Driving (MADD): **www.madd.org**
NARAL Pro-Choice America (formerly the National Abortion and Reproductive Rights Action League—favors legalized abortion): **www.naral.org**
National Association for the Advancement of Colored People (the NAACP—represents African Americans): **www.naacp.org**
National Audubon Society (an environmentalist group): **www.audubon.org**
National Gay and Lesbian Task Force: **www.ngltf.org**
National Organization for Women (NOW—a feminist group): **www.now.org**
National Urban League (a civil rights organization): **www.nul.org**
National Wildlife Federation: **www.nwf.org**
The Nature Conservancy: **www.nature.org**
Sierra Club (an environmentalist group): **www.sierraclub.org**
Veterans of Foreign Wars of the United States: **www.vfw.org**
World Wildlife Fund: **www.wwf.org**

Economic Interest Groups

More interest groups are formed to represent economic interests than any other set of interests. The variety of economic interest groups mirrors the complexity of the American economy. The major sectors that seek influence in Washington, D.C., include business, agriculture, labor unions and their members, government workers, and professionals.

Business Interest Groups. Thousands of business groups and trade associations work to influence government policies that affect their respective industries. "Umbrella groups" represent certain types of businesses or companies that deal in a particular type of product. The U.S. Chamber of Commerce, for example, is an umbrella group that represents businesses, and the National Association of Manufacturers is an umbrella group that represents only manufacturing concerns. The American Pet Products Manufacturers Association works for the good of manufacturers of pet food, pet toys, and other pet products, as well as for pet shops. This group strongly opposes increased regulation of stores that sell animals and restrictions on importing pets. Other major organizations that represent business interests, such as the Better Business Bureaus, take positions on policies but do not actually lobby in Washington, D.C.[4]

Vice President Dick Cheney speaks about the President's Job and Growth Package at the U.S. Chamber of Commerce. Do business interests have undue influence on our government's economic policies? (White House photo/David Bohrer)

Some business groups are decidedly more powerful than others. The U.S. Chamber of Commerce, which has more than 200,000 member companies, can bring constituent influence to bear on every member of Congress. Another powerful lobbying organization is the National Association of Manufacturers. With a staff of more than sixty people in Washington, D.C., the organization can mobilize dozens of well-educated, articulate lobbyists to work the corridors of Congress on issues of concern to its members.

Although business interest groups are likely to agree on anything that reduces government regulation or taxation, they often do not concur on the specifics of policy, and the sector has been troubled by disagreement and fragmentation within its ranks. For example, should states be able to collect sales tax on purchases made using the Internet? Businesses have come down on both sides of this issue, which we discuss in this chapter's *Which Side Are You On?* feature on the following page.

Business groups and trade associations used to lobby at cross-purposes because they had no way to coordinate their messages. Faced with increasing efforts by organized labor to support Democratic candidates for Congress, business interests agreed in 1996 to form "the Coalition," an informal organization that raises funds specifically to help Republican candidates for Congress.[5]

Agricultural Interest Groups. American farmers and their employees represent less than 2 percent of the U.S. population. Nevertheless, farmers' influence on legislation beneficial to their interests has been significant. Farmers have succeeded in their aims because they have very strong interest groups. They are geographically dispersed and therefore have many representatives and senators to speak for them.

---

[4]Charles S. Mack, *Business, Politics, and the Practice of Government Relations* (Westport, Conn.: Quorum Books, 1997), p. 14.

[5]H. R. Mahood, *Interest Groups in American National Politics: An Overview* (New York: Prentice Hall, 2000), p. 34.

WHICH SIDE ARE YOU ON? | Should the Internet Be Taxed?

Sales taxes are one of the most important ways in which state governments can raise revenue. But what happens when consumers in one state buy goods and services in another, using the mail, the telephone, or the Internet? Many states impose a *use tax* on such transactions that is identical to their sales tax. If you buy something through the Internet or a mail-order catalogue, however, the vendor you are dealing with might not collect a tax for your state. The United States Supreme Court ruled in *Quill Corp. v. North Dakota* (1992) that no state can compel a business located outside the state to collect use taxes from the state's residents.* The only way a state can collect these taxes is to go after customers directly, but the states usually have no idea who the customers are or what they bought.

States could tax Internet access instead. In 1998, however, Congress banned such taxes. Congress has not prohibited use taxes, but as noted, they are hard to collect. The United States Supreme Court, however, explicitly stated in the *Quill* decision that Congress could establish a nationwide system for collecting state use taxes under its power to regulate interstate commerce. Should Congress take such a step?

TAXATION IS NOT FAIR UNLESS EVERYONE PAYS

Most state governments favor such a step. State governments constitute an important lobby in Washington, and they are under financial pressure. Businesses that must collect sales taxes because they operate "brick-and-mortar" stores also support this viewpoint. These businesses argue that competitors who are not required to collect taxes have an unfair advantage.

Many state government officials believe they are losing billions of dollars in revenues because they cannot collect

use taxes on e-commerce. If that revenue could be collected, some of the current pressure on state government finances might be relieved.

THE INTERNET IS SPECIAL

Opponents of any plan to make use taxes collectible include almost every interest group involved with the Internet—online and mail-order vendors, the computer and telecommunications industries, and e-commerce shoppers. Opponents argue that taxing the Internet might impede the growth of e-commerce. Also, mail-order and Internet vendors must charge shipping fees, which sometimes exceed the sales taxes collected by brick-and-mortar stores. The large number of different tax rates would complicate any use-tax collection system. Further, stores such as Wal-Mart receive benefits that include police and fire protection, garbage collection, and road construction, all of which are paid for by sales taxes. Online vendors do not enjoy these benefits. Finally, those who want to limit taxes in general argue that e-commerce may force states to keep sales taxes low so that local merchants can compete.

WHAT'S YOUR POSITION?

Should Congress make it possible for states to collect use taxes? Why do the antitax forces have the upper hand at this time?

GOING ONLINE

Annette Nellen of San Jose State University sponsors a Web site that provides a substantial amount of material on e-commerce taxation. To view this site, go to **www.cob.sjsu.edu/facstaff/ nellen_a/e-links.html**.

*504 U.S. 298 (1992). Under the ruling in the *Quill* case, a state can require a business to collect sales or use taxes only if the business has a "substantial physical presence" in the state.

The American Farm Bureau Federation, established in 1919, has several million members (many of whom are not actually farmers) and is usually seen as conservative. It was instrumental in getting government guarantees of "fair" prices during the Great Depression in the 1930s.[6] Another important agricultural interest organization is the National Farmers' Union (NFU), which is considered more liberal. As farms have become larger and "agribusiness" has become a way of life, single-issue farm groups have emerged. The American Dairy Association, the Peanut Growers Group, and the National Soybean Association, for example, work to sup-

---

[6]The Agricultural Adjustment Act of 1933 (declared unconstitutional) was replaced by the 1938 Agricultural Adjustment Act and later changed and amended several times.

port their respective farmers and associated businesses. In recent years, agricultural interest groups have become active on many new issues. Among other things, they have opposed immigration restrictions and are very involved in international trade matters as they seek new markets. One of the newest agricultural groups is the American Farmland Trust, which supports policies to conserve farmland and protect natural resources.

As proof of how powerful the agricultural lobby still is in the United States, in May 2002 President George W. Bush signed the Farm Security and Rural Investment Act, which authorized the largest agricultural subsidy in U.S. history.

Labor Interest Groups. Interest groups representing the **labor movement** date back to at least 1886, when the American Federation of Labor (AFL) was formed. In 1955, the AFL joined forces with the Congress of Industrial Organizations (CIO). Today, the combined AFL-CIO is a large union with a membership of nearly 9 million workers and an active political arm called the Committee on Political Education. In a sense, the AFL-CIO is a union of unions.

The AFL-CIO experienced severe discord within its ranks during 2005, however, when four key unions left the federation and formed the Change to Win Coalition. The new Change to Win Coalition represents about one-third of the 13 million workers who formerly belonged to the AFL-CIO. Many labor advocates fear that the split will further weaken organized labor's waning political influence. Indeed, the role of unions in American society has declined in recent years, as witnessed by the decrease in union membership (see Figure 7–1). In the age of automation and with the rise of the **service sector,** blue-collar workers in basic industries (autos, steel, and the like) represent a smaller and smaller percentage of the total working population.

Because of this decline in the industrial sector of the economy, national unions are looking to nontraditional areas for their membership, including migrant farm workers, service workers, and, most recently, public employees—such as police

| Labor Movement
Generally, the economic and political expression of working-class interests; politically, the organization of working-class interests.

| Service Sector
The sector of the economy that provides services—such as health care, banking, and education—in contrast to the sector that produces goods.

FIGURE 7–1 | DECLINE IN UNION MEMBERSHIP, 1948 TO PRESENT

As shown in this figure, the percentage of the total workforce that is represented by labor unions has declined precipitously over the last two decades. Note, however, that in contrast to the decline in union representation in the private sector, the percentage of government workers who are unionized has increased significantly since about 1960.

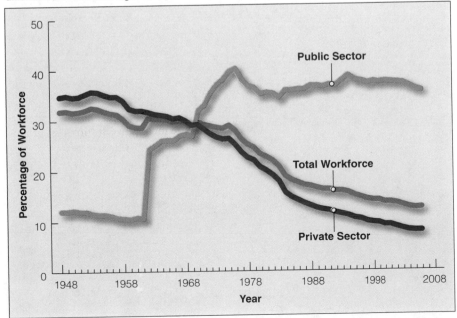

Source: Bureau of Labor Statistics, 2006.

officers, firefighting personnel, and teachers, including college professors and graduate assistants. Indeed, public-sector unions are the fastest-growing labor organizations.

Although the proportion of the workforce that belongs to a union has declined over the years, American labor unions have not given up their efforts to support sympathetic candidates for Congress or for state office. Currently, the AFL-CIO, under the leadership of John J. Sweeney, has a large political budget, which it uses to help Democratic candidates nationwide. Although interest groups that favor Republicans continue to assist their candidates, the efforts of labor are more sustained and more targeted. Labor offers a candidate (such as Democratic presidential candidate John Kerry in 2004) a corps of volunteers in addition to campaign contributions. A massive turnout by labor union members in critical elections can significantly increase the final vote totals for Democratic candidates.

Public Employee Unions.   The degree of unionization in the private sector has declined since 1965, but this has been partially offset by growth in the unionization of public employees. Figure 7–1 on the previous page displays the growth in public-sector unionization. With a total membership of more than 7.1 million, public-sector unions are likely to continue expanding.

Both the American Federation of State, County, and Municipal Employees and the American Federation of Teachers are members of the AFL-CIO's Public Employee Department. Over the years, public employee unions have become quite militant and are often involved in strikes. Most of these strikes are illegal, because almost no public employees have the right to strike.

A powerful interest group lobbying on behalf of public employees is the National Education Association (NEA), a nationwide organization of about 2.8 million teachers and others connected with education. Many NEA locals function as labor unions. The NEA lobbies intensively for increased public funding of education.

Interest Groups of Professionals.   Numerous professional organizations exist, including the American Bar Association, the Association of General Contractors of

Members of the Operating Engineers, Laborers, and Carpenters unions protest the policies of a construction company, claiming that this company's actions are undermining union wages and benefits. Labor unions have wielded considerable political power since the early 1900s. Why has that power declined somewhat in recent years? (AP Photo/*The Capital Times*/David Sandell)

Members of the American Bar Association (ABA) gather at the organization's national convention. The delegates are discussing a proposed overhaul of the code of ethics for lawyers. Many members of Congress are lawyers. Would it benefit the country if more legislators were drawn from other occupations? Why or why not?
(AP Photo/Charles Bennett)

America, the Institute of Electrical and Electronic Engineers, and others. Some professional groups, such as lawyers and doctors, are more influential than others because of their social status. Lawyers have a unique advantage—a large number of members of Congress share their profession. In terms of money spent on lobbying, however, one professional organization stands head and shoulders above the rest—the American Medical Association (AMA). Founded in 1847, it is now affiliated with more than 2,000 local and state medical societies and has a total membership of about 300,000.

The Unorganized Poor. Some have argued that the system of interest group politics leaves out poor Americans or U.S. residents who are not citizens and cannot vote. Americans who are disadvantaged economically cannot afford to join interest groups; if they are members of the working poor, they may hold two or more jobs just to survive, leaving them no time to participate in interest groups. Other groups in the population—including non-English-speaking groups, resident aliens, single

The president of the organization Unidad Honduruena (or Honduran Unity) counsels a young immigrant about taking the proper steps to maintain his temporary protected status. In this case, an interest group formed to protect nonvoters. How can such an interest group leverage its power when it does not represent voters?
(AP Photo/Wilfredo Lee)

Theodore Roosevelt (left) and John Muir stand on Glacier Point in what is today part of Yosemite National Park in California. Muir founded the Sierra Club, which today is one of the most powerful interest groups dedicated to protecting the environment. What are some reasons why the membership rolls of many environmental interest groups have grown in recent years? (Library of Congress)

| Public Interest
The best interests of the overall community; the national good, rather than the narrow interests of a particular group.

Ralph Nader, testifying on automobile safety before a Senate Government Operations subcommittee in 1966. Nader, an attorney, was the author of the book *Unsafe at Any Speed.* Nader campaigned for president in 2000 and 2004 but received only a small share of the votes. How might his political ambitions have affected the public-interest organizations that he helped found? (AP Photo)

parents, disabled Americans, and younger voters—probably do not have the time or expertise even to find out what group might represent them. Consequently, some scholars suggest that interest groups and lobbyists are the privilege of upper-middle-class Americans and those who belong to unions or other special groups.

R. Allen Hays examines the plight of poor Americans in his book *Who Speaks for the Poor?*[7] Hays studied groups and individuals who have lobbied for public housing and other issues related to the poor and concluded that the poor depend largely on indirect representation. Most efforts on behalf of the poor come from a policy network of groups—including public housing officials, welfare workers and officials, religious groups, public-interest groups, and some liberal general interest groups—that speak loudly and persistently for the poor. Poor Americans themselves remain outside the interest group network and have little direct voice of their own.

Environmental Groups

Environmental interest groups are not new. We have already mentioned the National Audubon Society, which was founded in 1905 to protect the snowy egret from the commercial demand for hat decorations. The patron of the Sierra Club, John Muir, worked for the creation of national parks more than a century ago. But the blossoming of national environmental groups with mass memberships did not occur until the 1970s. Since the first Earth Day, organized in 1970, many interest groups have sprung up to protect the environment in general or unique ecological niches. The groups range from the National Wildlife Federation, with a membership of more than 5 million and an emphasis on education, to the more elite Environmental Defense Fund, with a membership of 300,000 and a focus on influencing federal policy. Other groups include the Nature Conservancy, which uses members' contributions to buy up threatened natural areas and either give them to state or local governments or manage them itself, and the more radical Greenpeace Society and Earth First.

Public-Interest Groups

Public interest is a difficult term to define because, as we noted in Chapter 6, there are many publics in our nation of about 300 million. It is almost impossible for one particular public policy to benefit everybody, which makes it practically impossible to define the public interest. Nonetheless, over the past few decades, a variety of lobbying organizations have been formed "in the public interest."

Nader Organizations. The best-known and perhaps the most effective public-interest groups are those organized under the leadership of consumer activist Ralph Nader. Nader's rise to the top began in 1965 with the publication of his book *Unsafe at Any Speed,* a lambasting critique of the purported attempt by General Motors (GM) to keep from the public detrimental information about its rear-engine Corvair. Partly as a result of Nader's book, Congress

---

[7]R. Allen Hays, *Who Speaks for the Poor?* (New York: Routledge, 2001).

began to consider an automobile safety bill. GM made a clumsy attempt to discredit Nader's background. Nader sued, the media exploited the story, and when GM settled out of court for $425,000, Nader became a recognized champion of consumer interests. Since then, Nader has turned over much of his income to the more than sixty public-interest groups that he has formed or sponsored. Nader ran for president in 2000 on the Green Party ticket and again in 2004 as an independent.

Other Public-Interest Groups. Partly in response to the Nader organizations, numerous conservative public-interest law firms have sprung up that are often pitted against the consumer groups in court. Some of these are the Mountain States Legal Defense Foundation, the Pacific Legal Foundation, the National Right-to-Work Legal Defense Foundation, the Washington Legal Foundation, the Institute for Justice, and the Mid-Atlantic Legal Foundation.

One of the largest public-interest groups is Common Cause, founded in 1970. Its goal is to reorder national priorities toward "the public" and to make governmental institutions more responsive to the needs of the public. Anyone willing to pay dues of $20 a year can become a member. Members are polled regularly to obtain information about local and national issues requiring reassessment. Some of the activities of Common Cause have been (1) helping to ensure the passage of the Twenty-sixth Amendment (giving eighteen-year-olds the right to vote), (2) achieving greater voter registration in all states, (3) supporting the complete withdrawal of all U.S. forces from South Vietnam in the 1970s, and (4) promoting legislation that would limit campaign spending.

Other public-interest groups include the League of Women Voters, founded in 1920. Although nominally nonpartisan, it has lobbied for the Equal Rights Amendment and for government reform. The Consumer Federation of America is an alliance of about two hundred local and national organizations interested in consumer protection. The American Civil Liberties Union dates back to World War I (1914–1918), when, under a different name, it defended draft resisters. It generally enters into legal disputes related to Bill of Rights issues.

A crowd of people in New York City gather during the first Earth Day awareness celebration in 1970. How might such mass gatherings, often organized by interest groups, influence political action? (Photo by Hulton Archive/Getty Images)

Other Interest Groups

Single-interest groups, being narrowly focused, may be able to call attention to their causes because they have simple, straightforward goals and because their members tend to care intensely about the issues. Thus, such groups can easily motivate their members to contact legislators or to organize demonstrations in support of their policy goals.

A number of interest groups focus on just one issue. The abortion debate has created various groups opposed to abortion (such as the Right to Life organization) and groups in favor of abortion rights (such as NARAL Pro-Choice America). Other single-issue groups are the National Rifle Association, the Right to Work Committee (an antiunion group), and the American Israel Public Affairs Committee (a pro-Israel group).

Still other groups represent Americans who share a common characteristic, such as age or ethnicity. Such interest groups may lobby for legislation that benefits their members in terms of rights or just represent a viewpoint.

AARP, as mentioned earlier, is one of the most powerful interest groups in Washington, D.C., and, according to some, the strongest lobbying group in the

The job of lobbyists never stops. These Washington lobbyists are scrutinizing news reports to ascertain the positions of members of Congress on policy issues relevant to the interests that the lobbyists represent. Although many critics of lobbyists and interest groups argue that they distort the actions of government, the First Amendment prohibits the government from regulating their speech. (Tom McCarthy/PhotoEdit)

United States. It is certainly the nation's largest interest group, with a membership of about 36 million. AARP has accomplished much for its members over the years. It played a significant role in the creation of Medicare and Medicaid, as well as in obtaining cost-of-living increases in Social Security payments. In 2003, AARP supported the Republican bill to add prescription drug coverage to Medicare. (The plan also made other changes to the system.) Some observers believe that AARP's support tipped the balance and allowed Congress to pass the measure on a closely divided vote.

Foreign Governments

Homegrown interests are not the only players in the game. Washington, D.C., is also the center for lobbying by foreign governments as well as private foreign interests. The governments of the largest U.S. trading partners, such as Canada, the European Union (EU) countries, Japan, and South Korea, maintain substantial research and lobbying staffs. Even smaller nations, such as those in the Caribbean, engage lobbyists when vital legislation affecting their trade interests is considered. Frequently, these foreign interests hire former representatives or former senators to promote their positions on Capitol Hill. To learn more about how foreign interests lobby the U.S. government, see this chapter's *Beyond Our Borders* feature.

What Makes an Interest Group Powerful?

At any time, thousands of interest groups are attempting to influence state legislatures, governors, Congress, and members of the executive branch of the U.S. government. What characteristics make some of those groups more powerful than others and more likely to have influence over government policy? Generally, interest groups attain a reputation for being powerful through their membership size, financial resources, leadership, and cohesiveness.

Size and Resources

No legislator can deny the power of an interest group that includes thousands of his or her own constituents among its members. Labor unions and organizations such as AARP and the American Automobile Association are able to claim voters in every congressional district. Having a large membership—nearly 9 million in the case of the AFL-CIO—carries a great deal of weight with government officials. AARP now has about 36 million members and a budget of $435 million for its operations. In addition, AARP claims to represent all older Americans, who constitute close to 20 percent of the population, whether they join the organization or not. AARP played a significant role in derailing President George W. Bush's proposed Social Security reforms, as you will read in this chapter's *Politics and Interest Groups* feature on page 236.

Having a large number of members, even if the individual membership dues are relatively small, provides an organization with a strong financial base. Those funds pay for lobbyists, television advertisements, mailings to members, a Web site, and many other resources that help an interest group make its point to politicians. The business organization with the largest membership is probably the U.S. Chamber of Commerce, which has more than 200,000 members. The Chamber uses its members' dues to pay for staff and lobbyists, as well as a sophisticated communications network

BEYOND OUR BORDERS | Lobbying and Foreign Interests

Domestic groups are not alone in lobbying the federal government. Many foreign entities hire lobbyists to influence policy and spending decisions in the United States. American lobbying firms are often utilized by foreign groups seeking to advance their agendas. The use of American lobbyists assures greater access and increases the possibility of success. With the United States holding such a dominant position in the global economy and world affairs, it is hardly surprising that foreign entities regularly attempt to influence the U.S. government.

FOREIGN CORPORATIONS AND THE GLOBAL ECONOMY

Economic globalization has had an incalculable impact on public policy worldwide. Given the United States' prominence in the global economy, international and multinational corporations have taken a keen interest in influencing the U.S. government. Foreign corporations spend millions of dollars each year on lobbying in an effort to create favorable business and trade conditions.

As an example of the importance of cultivating good relations with the U.S. government, consider the attempt by a Chinese oil company, CNOOC, to purchase California-based Unocal in 2005. CNOOC made a highly competitive offer, but several lawmakers in Congress threatened to pass legislation that would block such a deal. These members of Congress claimed that foreign ownership of an American oil company would represent a national security risk. Citing an unfavorable political climate, CNOOC withdrew its offer, and Unocal was eventually purchased by another American firm, Chevron.

Foreign corporations frequently hire former members of Congress to lobby on their behalf. Indeed, many overseas companies enlist the most influential lobbyists in Washington. In recent years, however, a few of these companies have found themselves involved in scandals. Some overseas companies had hired lobbyist Jack Abramoff, who pleaded guilty in January 2006 to three felony charges involving fraud in his lobbying activities. Although foreign interests generally are not allowed to donate to political campaigns, recent investigations of the campaign finances of lawmakers such as former House Majority Leader Tom DeLay (R., Tex.) have uncovered various violations.

INFLUENCE FROM OTHER NATIONS

Foreign nations also lobby the U.S. government. After it became clear that several Saudi Arabian citizens participated in the September 11, 2001, terrorist attacks, Saudi Arabia became very concerned about its image in the United States. The Saudi government hired Qorvis Communications, LLC, a public and government affairs consulting firm, to spread the message that Saudi Arabia backed the U.S.-led war on terrorism and was dedicated to peace in the Middle East. In 2002 alone, Saudi Arabia spent $14.6 million on lobbying and public relations services provided by Qorvis.

Foreign governments lobby for more specific agendas as well. Numerous developing nations have lobbied Congress to cut back on domestic farm subsidies. If the subsidies were reduced or eliminated, nations with cheaper labor costs could sell their agricultural products in the United States at a lower cost than those produced on American farms.

In recent years, the Mexican government has increased its lobbying efforts regarding immigration policy. One of the Mexican government's aims is to secure the right to work for millions of illegal immigrants now residing in the United States. Mexican immigrants working in the United States send billions of dollars home annually to help support family members still living in Mexico.

FOR CRITICAL ANALYSIS

Considering recent lobbying scandals, how might foreign efforts to influence the U.S. government present unique problems? Should special efforts be made to monitor foreign lobbying? Why or why not?

so that it can contact members in a timely way. All of the members can receive e-mail and check the Web site to get updates on the latest legislative proposals.

Other organizations may have fewer members but nonetheless can muster significant financial resources. The pharmaceutical lobby, which represents many of the major drug manufacturers, is one of the most powerful interest groups in Washington due to its financial resources. This lobby has over six hundred registered lobbyists and spent close to $200 million in the last presidential election cycle for lobbying and campaign expenditures.

POLITICS AND INTEREST GROUPS | Social Security Reform

After his reelection in 2004, President George W. Bush vowed to tackle the growing problems in the United States' federal pension program, Social Security. Bush proposed a partial privatization of Social Security, which would allow workers to invest a specified portion of their Social Security payroll taxes in the stock market and possibly in other investment options. Bush's plan received some initial support, particularly among younger Americans. A number of interest groups quickly began attacking the president's plan, however, saying that it threatened to leave millions of Americans destitute in their retirement years.

THE POLITICAL CLOUT OF OLDER AMERICANS

As you have read in this chapter, interest groups lobby Congress and the executive branch on behalf of their constituents or members. Older Americans make up a powerful political demographic group because they vote in higher numbers than other age groups and often have the financial means to contribute to political causes. As a result, a wide array of interest groups cater to older Americans. Similarly, elected officials are highly responsive to the needs and wishes of these citizens.

When Bush unveiled his ideas for partial privatization of Social Security, interest groups that advocate on behalf of older Americans raised serious objections to the proposed reforms. These groups worried that the president's plan would only exacerbate shortfalls in tax revenues that support current benefit levels promised to retirees. Many older Americans feared that the monthly pension checks that they rely on as a source of retirement income would gradually diminish. Others were concerned that Social Security in its present form might cease to exist altogether.

AARP LEADS THE WAY

One group in particular, AARP (formerly known as the American Association of Retired Persons), led the effort to

AARP chief executive officer William D. Novelli speaks to seniors about President Bush's plan for allowing younger workers to divert a portion of their Social Security payroll taxes into private investment, in Amherst, New York, during March 2005. (AP Photo/David Duprey)

squelch talk of altering Social Security. With its large membership and millions in its annual operations budget, AARP is the largest, and arguably the most influential, interest group in the United States.

Immediately following the 2004 elections, before AARP and other interest groups launched a blitz of lobbying and advertising, partial privatization had received some support, and many Americans were undecided about the proposal. By the summer of 2005, however, the president's plan had become a political liability, as a clear majority of Americans reported being opposed to partial privatization. AARP took credit for this almost complete turnaround in public opinion.

FOR CRITICAL ANALYSIS

What might younger Americans do to better communicate their views on important issues such as Social Security reform?

Leadership

Money is not the only resource that interest groups need to have. Strong leaders who can develop effective strategies are also important. For example, the American Israel Public Affairs Committee (AIPAC) has long benefited from strong leadership. AIPAC lobbies Congress and the executive branch on issues related to U.S.-Israeli relations, as well as general foreign policy in the Middle East. AIPAC has been successful in facilitating the close relationship that the two nations have enjoyed, which includes between $6 billion and $8 billion in foreign aid that the United States annually bestows on Israel. Despite its modest membership size,

Celebrated actor and NRA president Charlton Heston holds up a musket as he tells an NRA convention that "they [the government] can have my gun when they pry it from my cold dead hands." Heston, who received a standing ovation, was forced to step down in 2003 due to ill health. The NRA is one of the most powerful interest groups in the country. Why is it so effective? (AP Photo/Ric Feld)

AIPAC has won bipartisan support for its agenda and is consistently ranked among the most influential interest groups in America.

Other interest groups, including some with few financial resources, succeed in part because they are led by individuals with charisma and access to power, such as Jesse Jackson of the Rainbow Coalition. Sometimes, choosing a leader with a particular image can be an effective strategy for an organization. The National Rifle Association (NRA) had more than organizational skills in mind when it elected actor Charlton Heston as its president. The strategy of using an actor identified with powerful roles as the spokesperson for the organization worked to improve its national image.

Cohesiveness

Regardless of an interest group's size or the amount of funds in its coffers, the motivation of an interest group's members is a key factor in determining how powerful it is. If the members of a group hold their beliefs strongly enough to send letters to their representatives, join a march on Washington, or work together to defeat a candidate, that group is considered powerful. As described earlier, the American labor movement's success in electing Democratic candidates made the labor movement a more powerful lobby.

In contrast, although groups that oppose abortion rights have had little success in influencing policy, they are considered powerful because their members are vocal and highly motivated. Other measures of cohesion include the ability of a group to get its members to contact Washington quickly or to give extra money when needed. The U.S. Chamber of Commerce excels at both of these strategies. In comparison, AARP cannot claim that it can get its 36 million members to contact their congressional representatives, but it does seem to influence the opinions of older Americans and their views of political candidates.

Interest Group Strategies

Interest groups employ a wide range of techniques and strategies to promote their policy goals. Although few groups are successful at persuading Congress and the president to completely endorse their programs, many are able to block—or at least weaken—legislation injurious to their members. The key to success for interest groups is access to government officials. To gain such access, interest groups and their representatives try to cultivate long-term relationships with legislators and government officials. The best of these relationships are based on mutual respect and cooperation. The interest group provides the official with excellent sources of information and assistance, and the official in turn gives the group opportunities to express its views.

The techniques used by interest groups can be divided into direct and indirect techniques. With **direct techniques,** the interest group and its lobbyists approach the officials personally to present their case. With **indirect techniques,** in contrast, the interest group uses the general public or individual constituents to influence the government on behalf of the interest group.

Direct Techniques

Lobbying, publicizing ratings of legislative behavior, building coalitions, and providing campaign assistance are the four main direct techniques used by interest groups.

Lobbying Techniques.   As might be guessed, the term *lobbying* comes from the activities of private citizens regularly congregating in the lobbies of legislative chambers before a session to petition legislators. In the latter part of the 1800s, railroad and industrial groups openly bribed state legislators to pass legislation beneficial to their interests, giving lobbying a well-deserved bad name. Most lobbyists today are professionals. They are either consultants to a company or interest group or members of one of the Washington, D.C., law firms that specialize in providing such services. As described in this chapter's opening *What If . . .* feature, such firms employ hundreds of former members of Congress and former government officials—for example, former presidential candidates Bob Dole and Walter Mondale. Lobbyists are valued for their network of contacts in Washington. As Ed Rollins, a former White House aide, put it, "I've got many friends who are all through the agencies and equally important, I don't have many enemies. . . . I tell my clients I can get your case moved to the top of the pile."[8] Lobbyists of all types are becoming more numerous. The number of lobbyists in Washington, D.C., has more than doubled since 2000.

Lobbyists engage in an array of activities to influence legislation and government policy. These include the following:

1. Engaging in private meetings with public officials, including the president's advisers, to make known the interests of the lobbyists' clients. Although acting on behalf of their clients, lobbyists often furnish needed information to senators and representatives (and government agency appointees) that these officials could not easily obtain on their own. It is to the lobbyists' advantage to provide accurate information so that policymakers will rely on this source in the future.
2. Testifying before congressional committees for or against proposed legislation.
3. Testifying before executive rulemaking agencies—such as the Federal Trade Commission or the Consumer Product Safety Commission—for or against proposed rules.
4. Assisting legislators or bureaucrats in drafting legislation or prospective regulations. Often, lobbyists furnish advice on the specific details of legislation.
5. Inviting legislators to social occasions, such as cocktail parties, boating expeditions, and other events, including conferences at exotic locations. Most lobbyists believe that meeting legislators in a relaxed social setting is effective.

| **Direct Technique**
An interest group activity that involves interaction with government officials to further the group's goals.

| **Indirect Technique**
A strategy employed by interest groups that uses third parties to influence government officials.

[8]As quoted in Mahood, *Interest Groups in American National Politics*, p. 51.

6. Providing political information to legislators and other government officials. Often, the lobbyists have better information than the party leadership about how other legislators are going to vote. In this case, the political information they furnish may be a key to legislative success.

7. Supplying nominations for federal appointments to the executive branch.

The Ratings Game.   Many interest groups attempt to influence the overall behavior of legislators through their rating systems. Each year, the interest group selects legislation that it believes is most important to the organization's goals and then monitors how legislators vote on it. Each legislator is given a score based on the percentage of times that he or she voted in favor of the group's position. The usual scheme ranges from 0 to 100 percent. In the ratings scheme of the liberal Americans for Democratic Action, for example, a rating of 100 means that a member of Congress voted with the group on every issue and is, by that measure, very liberal.

Ratings are a shorthand way of describing members' voting records for interested citizens. They can also be used to embarrass members. For example, an environmental group identifies the twelve representatives who the group believes have the worst voting records on environmental issues and labels them "the Dirty Dozen," and a watchdog group describes those representatives who took home the most "pork" for their districts or states as the biggest "pigs."

Building Alliances.   Another direct technique used by interest groups is to form a coalition with other groups concerned about the same legislation. Often, these groups will set up a paper organization with an innocuous name to represent their joint concerns. In the early 1990s, for example, environmental, labor, and consumer groups formed an alliance called the Citizens Trade Campaign to oppose the passage of the North American Free Trade Agreement.

Members of such a coalition share expenses and multiply the influence of their individual groups by combining their efforts. Other advantages of forming a coalition are that it blurs the specific interests of the individual groups involved and makes it appear that larger public interests are at stake. These alliances also are efficient devices for keeping like-minded groups from duplicating one another's lobbying efforts.

Another example of an alliance developed when the Republicans launched the K Street Project. The project, named for the street in Washington, D.C., where the

Interest groups from every imaginable ideological point of view issue scorecards of individual legislators' voting records as it relates to the organization's agenda. Shown here are a few such scorecards. How much value can voters place on these kinds of ratings? (Photo illustration assembled from various Web sites.)

largest lobbying firms have their headquarters, was designed to alter the lobbying community's pro-Democratic tilt. Republicans sought to pressure lobbying firms to hire Republicans in top positions, offering loyal lobbyists greater access to lawmakers in return. An indication of the success of the project is the increase in the donations given to Republican lawmakers by lobbyists, which rose from $1.2 million in 1994 to nearly $12 million in 2006. But the K Street Project also had a troubling aspect, as revelations of legislative favors being granted to special interests in return for campaign donations have made clear. This trend, and the numerous examples of corruption attendant on it, will be discussed further in Chapter 11.

Campaign Assistance. Interest groups have additional strategies to use in their attempts to influence government policies. Groups recognize that the greatest concern of legislators is to be reelected, so they focus on the legislators' campaign needs. Associations with large memberships, such as labor unions, are able to provide workers for political campaigns, including precinct workers to get out the vote, volunteers to put up posters and pass out literature, and people to staff telephone banks for campaign headquarters.

In many states where certain interest groups have large memberships, candidates vie for the groups' endorsements in the campaign. Gaining those endorsements may be automatic, or it may require that the candidates participate in debates or interviews with the interest groups. Endorsements are important because an interest group usually publicizes its choices in its membership publication and because the candidate can use the endorsement in her or his campaign literature. Traditionally, labor unions have endorsed Democratic Party candidates. Republican candidates, however, often try to persuade union locals at least to refrain from any endorsement. Making no endorsement can then be perceived as disapproval of the Democratic Party candidate.

Despite attempts at campaign-finance reform, the 2004 election boasted record campaign spending. The usual array of interest groups—labor unions, professional groups, and business associations—gathered contributions to their political action committees and distributed them to the candidates. Most labor contributions went to Democratic candidates, while a majority of business contributions went to Republicans. Some groups, such as real estate agents, gave evenly to both parties. At the same time, the new campaign groups, the so-called 527 organizations—tax-exempt associations focused on influencing political elections—raised more than $400 million in unregulated contributions and used them for campaign activities and advertising. Some national interest groups, such as the Laborers' Union, the National Association of Realtors, and the Sierra Club, created their own 527 organizations to spend funds for advertising and other political activities. The flood of unregulated funds supported massive advertising campaigns in the last months of the campaign.

Indirect Techniques

Interest groups can also try to influence government policy by working through others, who may be constituents or the general public. Indirect techniques mask the interest group's own activities and make the effort appear to be spontaneous. Furthermore, legislators and government officials are often more impressed by contacts from constituents than from an interest group's lobbyist.

Generating Public Pressure. In some instances, interest groups try to produce a "groundswell" of public pressure to influence the government. Such efforts may include advertisements in national magazines and newspapers, mass mailings, television publicity, and demonstrations. The Internet and satellite links make communication efforts even more effective. Interest groups may commission polls to find out what the public's sentiments are and then publicize the results. The intent of this activity is to convince policymakers that public opinion overwhelmingly supports the group's position.

Some corporations and interest groups also engage in a practice that might be called **climate control.** With this strategy, public relations efforts are aimed at improving the public image of the industry or group and are not necessarily related to any specific political issue. Contributions by corporations and groups in support of public television programs, sponsorship of special events, and commercials extolling the virtues of corporate research are some ways of achieving climate control. For example, to improve its image in the wake of litigation against tobacco companies, Philip Morris began advertising its assistance to community agencies, including halfway houses for teen offenders and shelters for battered women. By building a reservoir of favorable public opinion, groups believe that their legislative goals will be less likely to encounter opposition by the public.

Using Constituents as Lobbyists. Interest groups also use constituents to lobby for the group's goals. In the "shotgun" approach, the interest group tries to mobilize large numbers of constituents to write, phone, or send e-mails to their legislators or the president. Often, the group provides postcards or form letters for constituents to fill out and mail. These efforts are effective on Capitol Hill only when there is a very large number of responses, however, because legislators know that the voters did not initiate the communications on their own. Artificially manufactured grassroots activity has been aptly labeled *Astroturf lobbying.*

A more powerful variation of this technique uses only important constituents. With this approach, known as the "rifle" technique or the "Utah plant manager theory," the interest group might, for example, ask the manager of a local plant in Utah to contact the senator from Utah.[9] Because the constituent is seen as responsible for many jobs or other resources, the legislator is more likely to listen carefully to the constituent's concerns about legislation than to a paid lobbyist.

---

[9]Kay Lehman Schlozman and John T. Tierney, *Organized Interests and American Democracy* (New York: Harper & Row, 1986), p. 293.

| Climate Control
The use of public relations techniques to create favorable public opinion toward an interest group, industry, or corporation.

A group of protestors against Bush administration policies on pollution demonstrate along a highway to gain public and media attention for their cause. Members of the Sierra Club, Common Cause, and Public Citizen are pictured. How might pooling resources help interest groups with overlapping agendas? (AP Photo/Adele Starr)

| Boycott
A form of pressure or protest—an organized refusal to purchase a particular product or deal with a particular business.

Unconventional Forms of Pressure.   Sometimes, interest groups may employ forms of pressure that are outside the ordinary political process. These can include marches, rallies, civil disobedience, or demonstrations. Such assemblies, as long as they are peaceful, are protected by the First Amendment. In Chapter 5, we described the civil disobedience techniques of the African American civil rights movement in the 1950s and 1960s. The 1963 March on Washington in support of civil rights was one of the most effective demonstrations ever organized. The women's suffrage movement of the early 1900s also employed marches and demonstrations to great effect.

Demonstrations, however, are not always peaceable. Violent demonstrations have a long history in America, dating back to the antitax Boston Tea Party described in Chapter 2. The Vietnam War (1964–1975) provoked a large number of demonstrations, some of which were violent. In 1999, at a meeting of the World Trade Organization in Seattle, demonstrations against "globalization" turned violent. These demonstrations were repeated throughout the 2000s at various sites around the world. Still, violent demonstrations can be counterproductive—instead of putting pressure on the authorities, they may simply alienate the public. For example, historians continue to debate whether the demonstrations against the Vietnam War were effective or counterproductive.

Another unconventional form of pressure is the **boycott**—a refusal to buy a particular product or deal with a particular business. To be effective, boycotts must command widespread support. One example was the African American boycott of buses in Montgomery, Alabama, during 1955, described in Chapter 5. Another was the boycott of California grapes that were picked by nonunion workers, as part of a campaign to organize Mexican American farmworkers. The first grape boycott lasted from 1965 to 1970; a series of later boycotts was less effective.

Regulating Lobbyists

Congress made its first attempt to control lobbyists and lobbying activities through Title III of the Legislative Reorganization Act of 1946, otherwise known as the Federal Regulation of Lobbying Act. The act actually provided for public disclosure more than for regulation, and it neglected to specify which agency would enforce its provisions. The 1946 legislation defined a *lobbyist* as any person or organization that received money to be used principally to influence legislation before Congress. Such persons and individuals were supposed to "register" their clients and the purposes of their efforts and report quarterly on their activities.

The legislation was tested in a 1954 Supreme Court case, *United States v. Harriss*,[10] and was found to be constitutional. The Court agreed that the lobbying law did not violate due process, freedom of speech or of the press, or the freedom to petition. The Court narrowly construed the act, however, holding that it applied only to lobbyists who were influencing federal legislation *directly*.

The Results of the 1946 Act

The immediate result of the act was that a minimal number of individuals registered as lobbyists. National interest groups, such as the National Rifle Association and the American Petroleum Institute, could employ hundreds of staff members who were, of course, working on legislation but only register one or two lobbyists who were engaged *principally* in influencing Congress. There were no reporting requirements for lobbying the executive branch, federal agencies, the courts, or congressional staff.

Approximately seven thousand individuals and organizations registered annually as lobbyists, although most experts estimated that ten times that number were actually employed in Washington to exert influence on the government.

[10]347 U.S. 612 (1954).

The Reforms of 1995

The reform-minded Congress of 1995–1996 overhauled the lobbying legislation, fundamentally changing the ground rules for those who seek to influence the federal government. Lobbying legislation passed in 1995 included the following provisions:

1. A *lobbyist* is defined as anyone who spends at least 20 percent of his or her time lobbying members of Congress, their staffs, or executive-branch officials.
2. Lobbyists must register with the clerk of the House and the secretary of the Senate within forty-five days of being hired or of making their first contacts. The registration requirement applies to organizations that spend more than $20,000 in one year or to individuals who are paid more than $5,000 annually for lobbying work.
3. Semiannual reports must disclose the general nature of the lobbying effort, specific issues and bill numbers, the estimated cost of the campaign, and a list of the branches of government contacted. The names of the individuals contacted need not be reported.
4. Representatives of U.S.-owned subsidiaries of foreign-owned firms and lawyers who represent foreign entities also are required to register.
5. The requirements exempt "grassroots" lobbying efforts and those of tax-exempt organizations, such as religious groups.

As they debated the 1995 law, both the House and the Senate adopted new rules on gifts and travel expenses: the House adopted a flat ban on gifts, and the Senate limited gifts to $50 in value and to no more than $100 in gifts from a single source in a year. There are exceptions for gifts from family members and for home-state products and souvenirs, such as T-shirts and coffee mugs. Both chambers banned all-expenses-paid trips, golf outings, and other such junkets. An exception applies for "widely attended" events, however, or if the member is a primary speaker at an event. These gift rules stopped the broad practice of taking members of Congress to lunch or dinner, but the various exemptions and exceptions have caused much controversy as the Senate and House Ethics Committees have considered individual cases.

Recent Lobbying Scandals

The regulation of lobbying activity again surfaced in 2005 when a number of scandals came to light. At the center of a number of the publicized incidents was a highly influential and corrupt lobbyist, Jack Abramoff. Using his ties with numerous Republican, and a handful of Democratic, lawmakers, Abramoff brokered numerous deals for the special interest clients that he represented in return for campaign donations, gifts, and various perks.

In January 2006, Abramoff pled guilty to three criminal felony counts related to the defrauding of American Indian tribes and the corruption of public officials. Investigations have not ceased, however, as lawmakers and Bush administration officials connected with Abramoff and his colleagues are under continued scrutiny. Numerous politicians have attempted to distance themselves from the embattled lobbyist by giving Abramoff's campaign donations to charity.

Congress has discussed numerous lobbying reform bills, but significant legislation has yet to be passed. Any proposed reform would amend the 1995 Lobbying Disclosure Act.

Jack Abramoff (far left), the lobbyist convicted of corruption and defrauding clients, poses at St. Andrews golf course in Scotland with several influential public officials. Abramoff frequently arranged trips to desirable destinations in an attempt to influence government officials. Should elected officials be allowed to partake in such travel paid for by lobbyists? (AP Photo/U.S. District Court)

Interest Groups and Representative Democracy

The role played by interest groups in shaping national policy has caused many to question whether we really have a democracy at all. Most interest groups have a middle-class or upper-class bias. Members of interest groups can afford to pay the membership fees, are generally fairly well educated, and normally participate in the political process to a greater extent than the "average" American.

Furthermore, leaders of interest groups tend to constitute an "elite within an elite" in the sense that they usually are from a higher social class than their members. The most powerful interest groups—those with the most resources and political influence—are primarily business, trade, or professional groups. In contrast, public-interest groups or civil rights groups make up only a small percentage of the interest groups lobbying Congress.

Interest Groups: Elitist or Pluralist?

Remember from Chapter 1 that the elite theory of politics presumes that most Americans are uninterested in politics and are willing to let a small, elite group of citizens make decisions for them. Pluralist theory, in contrast, views politics as a struggle among various interest groups to gain benefits for their members. The pluralist approach views compromise among various competing interests as the essence of political decision making. In reality, neither theory fully describes American politics.

If interest groups led by elite, upper-class individuals are the dominant voices in Congress, then what we see is a conflict among elite groups—which would lend as much support to the elitist theory as to the pluralist approach.

Interest Group Influence

The results of lobbying efforts—congressional legislation—do not always favor the interests of the most powerful groups, however. In part, this is because not all interest groups have an equal influence on government. Each group has a different combination of resources to use in the policymaking process. While some groups are composed of members who have high social status and significant economic resources, such as the National Association of Manufacturers, other groups derive influence from their large memberships. AARP, for example, has more members than any other interest group. Its large membership allows it to wield significant power over legislators. Still other groups, such as environmentalists, have causes that can claim strong public support even from people who have no direct stake in the issue. Groups such as the National Rifle Association are well organized and have highly motivated members. This enables them to channel a stream of mail or electronic messages toward Congress with a few days' effort.

Even the most powerful interest groups do not always succeed in their demands. Whereas the U.S. Chamber of Commerce may be accepted as having a justified interest in the question of business taxes, many legislators might feel that the group should not engage in the debate over the future of Social Security. In other words, groups are seen as having a legitimate concern in the issues closest to their interests but not necessarily in broader issues. This may explain why some of the most successful groups are those that focus on very specific issues—such as tobacco farming, funding of abortions, or handgun control—and do not get involved in larger conflicts.

Complicating the question of interest group influence is the fact that many groups' lobbyists are former colleagues, friends, or family members of current members of Congress.

MAKING A DIFFERENCE | The Gun Control Issue

Some interest groups focus on issues that concern only a limited number of people. Others are involved in causes in which almost everyone has a stake. Gun control is one of the issues that concerns a large number of people. The question of whether the possession of handguns should be regulated or even banned is at the heart of a long-running heated battle among organized interest groups. The fight is fueled by the one million gun incidents occurring in the United States each year—murders, suicides, assaults, accidents, and robberies in which guns are involved.

Why Should You Care?

The passionate feelings that are brought to bear on both sides of the gun control issue are evidence of its importance. The problem of crime is central to the gun control issue. Public opinion poll respondents cited crime as one the nation's most important problems throughout the 1990s, and it continues to be a major concern in the 2000s.

Does the easy availability of handguns promote crime? Do people have a right to possess firearms to defend home and hearth? In other words, are guns part of the problem of crime—or part of the solution? Either way, the question is important to you personally. Even if you are fortunate enough not to be victimized by crime, you will probably find yourself limiting your activities from time to time out of a fear of crime.

What Can You Do?

Almost every year, Congress and the various state legislatures debate measures that would alter gun laws for the nation or for the individual states. As a result, there are plenty of opportunities to get involved.

Issues in the debate include child-safety features on guns and the regulation of gun dealers who sell firearms at gun shows. Proponents of gun control seek safety locks and more restrictions on gun purchases—if not to ban handguns entirely. Proponents of firearms claim that possessing firearms is a constitutional right and meets a vital defense need for individuals. They contend that the problem lies not in the sale and ownership of weapons but in their use by criminals.

The National Coalition to Ban Handguns favors a total ban, taking the position that handguns "serve no valid purpose, except to kill people." Such a ban is opposed by the National Rifle Association of America (NRA). The NRA, founded in 1871, is currently one of the most powerful single-issue groups in the United States. The NRA believes that gun laws will not reduce the number of crimes. It is illogical to assume, according to the NRA, that persons who refuse to obey laws prohibiting rape, murder, and other crimes will obey a gun law.

Many proponents of gun control insist that controlling the purchase of weapons would reduce the availability of guns to children. In response, some states have passed laws that hold adults liable for not locking away their firearms. In addition, a number of cities have sued gun manufacturers for not controlling the flow of their products to dealers who sell guns to criminals and gang members.

To find out more about the NRA's position, contact that organization at the following address:

The National Rifle Association
11250 Waples Mill Rd.
Fairfax, VA 22030
703-267-1000
www.nra.org

To learn about the positions of gun control advocates, contact:

The Coalition to Stop Gun Violence
1023 15th St. N.W., Suite 600
Washington, DC 20036
202-408-0061
www.csgv.org

Brady Center to Prevent Gun Violence
1225 Eye St. N.W., Suite 1100
Washington, DC 20005
202-289-7319
www.bradycampaign.org

Key Terms

boycott 242

climate control 241

direct technique 238

free rider problem 224

indirect technique 238

interest group 221

labor movement 229

latent interests 223

lobbyist 221

material incentive 224

public interest 232

purposive incentive 224

service sector 229

social movement 222

solidary incentive 224

Chapter Summary

1 An interest group is an organization whose members share common objectives and actively attempt to influence government policy. Interest groups proliferate in the United States because they can influence government at many points in the political structure and because they offer solidary, material, and purposive incentives to their members. Interest groups are often created out of social movements.

2 Major types of interest groups include business, agricultural, labor, public employee, professional, and environmental groups. Other important groups may be considered public-interest groups. In addition, special interest groups and foreign governments lobby the government.

3 Interest groups use direct and indirect techniques to influence government. Direct techniques include testifying before committees and rulemaking agencies, providing information to legislators, rating legislators' voting records, aiding political campaigns, and building alliances. Indirect techniques to influence government include campaigns to rally public sentiment, letter-writing campaigns, efforts to influence the climate of opinion, and the use of constituents to lobby for the group's interest. Unconventional methods of applying pressure include demonstrations and boycotts.

4 The 1946 Legislative Reorganization Act was the first attempt to control lobbyists and their activities through registration requirements. The United States Supreme Court narrowly construed the act as applying only to lobbyists who directly seek to influence federal legislation.

5 In 1995, Congress approved new legislation requiring anyone who spends 20 percent of his or her time influencing legislation to register. Also, any organization spending $20,000 or more and any individual who is paid more than $5,000 annually for his or her work must register. Semiannual reports must include the names of clients, the bills in which they are interested, and the branches of government contacted. Grassroots lobbying and the lobbying efforts of tax-exempt organizations are exempt from the rules.

Selected Print and Media Resources

SUGGESTED READINGS

Berry, Jeffrey M., and Clyde Wilcox. *Interest Group Society*, 4th ed. New York: Longman, 2006. This work examines the expanding influence of interest groups as well as their relationship to the party system.

Goldstein, Kenneth M. *Interest Groups, Lobbying, and Participation in America*. New York: Cambridge University Press, 2003. What kind of people join interest groups, and how do such people seek to influence legislation? The author looks for answers using survey data and interviews with activists.

Patrick, Brian Anse. *The National Rifle Association and the Media: The Motivating Force of Negative Coverage*. Vol. 1 of *Frontiers in Political Communications*. New York: Peter Lang Publishing, 2004. Patrick argues that the NRA (the National Rifle Association) actually benefits from negative media coverage, which has served to mobilize participants in the "gun culture."

Sifry, Micah, and Nancy Watzman. *Is That a Politician in Your Pocket? Washington on $2 Million a Day*. New York: John Wiley & Sons, 2004. The authors, who are staff members at Public Campaign, provide a clearly written and detailed exposé of how financial contributions by interest groups drive politics. Chapters cover pharmaceuticals, gun control, agribusiness, oil and chemical corporations, and cable TV.

MEDIA RESOURCES

Bowling for Columbine—Michael Moore's documentary won an Academy Award in 2003. Moore seeks to understand why the United States leads the industrialized world in firearms deaths. While the film is hilarious, it takes a strong position in favor of gun control and is critical of the National Rifle Association.

Norma Rae—A 1979 Hollywood movie about an attempt by a northern union organizer to unionize workers in the southern textile industry; stars Sally Field, who won an Academy Award for her performance.

Organizing America: The History of Trade Unions—A 1994 documentary that incorporates interviews, personal accounts, and archival footage to tell the story of the American labor movement. The film is a Cambridge Educational Production.

The West Wing—A popular television series that was widely regarded as being an accurate portrayal of the issues and political pressures faced by a liberal president and his White House staff.

E·MOCRACY Interest Groups and the Internet

The Internet may have a strong equalizing effect in the world of lobbying and government influence. The first organizations to use electronic means to reach their constituents and drum up support for action were the large economic coalitions, including the Chamber of Commerce and the National Association of Manufacturers. Groups such as these, as well as groups representing a single product such as tobacco, quickly realized that they could set up Web sites and mailing lists to provide information more rapidly to their members. Members could check the Web every day to see how legislation was developing in Congress or anywhere in the world. National associations could send e-mail to all of their members with one keystroke, mobilizing them to contact their representatives in Congress.

Logging On

Almost every interest group or association has its own Web site. To find one, use your favorite search engine (Lycos, Google, or another search engine) and search for the association by name. For a sense of the breadth of the kinds of interest groups that have Web sites, take a look at one or two of those listed here.

Those interested in the gun control issue may want to visit the National Rifle Association's site at

www.nra.org

You can learn more about the labor movement by visiting the AFL-CIO's site at

www.aflcio.org

AARP (formerly the American Association of Retired Persons) has a site at

www.aarp.org

Information on environmental issues is available at a number of sites. The Environmental Defense Fund's site is

www.environmentaldefense.org/home.cfm

You can also go to the National Resources Defense Council's site for information on environmental issues. Its URL is

www.nrdc.org

Online Review

At **www.politicalscience.wadsworth.com/schmidt12**, you will find a free Study Guide to this book. For each chapter, there are two online quizzes to help you master the material.

• The PoliPrep Self-Study Assessment provides a pretest for each major section of the chapter. PoliPrep then generates a customized study plan. After you complete the study plan, a posttest evaluates your progress.

• The Tutorial Quiz for each chapter provides questions on the chapter contents, including the features. The questions are organized to match the major sections of the chapter.

What If . . .
Parties Were Supported Solely by Public Funding?

BACKGROUND

Today's major political parties are supported by hundreds of millions of dollars offered by unions, corporations, other groups, and individuals. Not surprisingly, some Americans lament that the winning candidates are merely the "best that money can buy." For years, members of both political parties have been linked to lobbying and campaign-contribution scandals, leading some critics to call for dramatic reforms. One of those reforms would be the public financing of political parties. Such public financing would, of course, come from taxpayers.

WHAT IF PARTIES WERE SUPPORTED SOLELY BY PUBLIC FUNDING?

One question that would immediately arise is: What level of funding would be required? Both major political parties now spend many millions of dollars each year to educate the public, register voters, recruit candidates, and support election campaigns. If that amount were significantly reduced, the effectiveness of the political parties would also be reduced.

Also, if the public were funding the national parties, there would almost certainly be prohibitions on contributions from corporations, individuals, and interest groups. This would be a much different situation than exists now, because corporations and interest groups currently give to candidates who they believe will support their interests. For example, labor unions give to Democratic political action committees and chambers of commerce are more likely to give to Republican political action committees. The number of paid employees at the major political parties would also fall if they were publicly funded, though more people might volunteer.

THE EFFECT ON LOBBYISTS

Currently, candidates for election receive public funds in certain states, such as Arizona, Maine, and Vermont, and a limited amount of public financing is provided for presidential candidates. All such public financing of candidates' campaigns carries with it restrictions on acceptable sources of other funds. If both the major parties and candidates for election were publicly financed, the role of lobbies and lobbyists would be changed. No longer would they be holding fund-raising social events for candidates and parties. Instead, they would have to rely on their ability to inform or persuade legislators.

THE FLOW OF MONEY AND POWER

The public financing of the major national parties would most likely weaken their influence over candidates, voters, and campaigns. Because the financing of political parties would only affect the national party organizations, contributors would channel their campaign contributions to the state and local party organizations. Those organizations would then support campaigns in the same way that national organizations do now. The public financing of political parties would increase spending by individuals and groups, which are largely unregulated. Candidates would also increase their own fund-raising if they could not depend on the national parties to do it for them. Already, most legislators have their own PACs (political action committees), and those would multiply. Having candidates be responsible for their own funding might make them more independent of their parties, weakening party cohesion. In the long run, this might also weaken the attachment of voters to their party identification, making it possible for them to join a third party.

MORE POLITICAL PARTIES WOULD BE POSSIBLE

Who is to say that public funding of political parties would be limited to only the two major parties? If we adopted the French system, for example, public funds would be available for numerous political parties. The only requirement would be a minimum number of party members. As you might imagine, the result in France has been the emergence of dozens of small political parties. After all, if public funds are available, someone will figure out a way to obtain them. That means those with strong political ideas would be able to gather like-minded Americans to create a party, spend some effort to obtain like-minded members, and apply for public funds.

The major political parties would still be the only serious players in this country, however. In our winner-take-all electoral system, few independent party candidates can win public office.

FOR CRITICAL ANALYSIS

1. If political parties were publicly funded, what would be the appropriate level of funding? More than the parties are spending today, the same, or less?
2. Currently, both major political parties have paid employees who function as "upper management." Would the type of person seeking such a job change if the parties were supported solely by public funds? Why or why not?

Every two years, usually starting in early fall, the media concentrate on the state of the political parties. For example, near the end of the 2004 campaigns, the media offered continuous commentaries on how Democratic candidate John F. Kerry and Republican incumbent George W. Bush were faring. As the elections drew near, the polls also concentrated on discovering to which political party each potential voter believed he or she "belonged." Prior to an election, a typical poll usually asks the following question: "Do you consider yourself to be a Republican, a Democrat, or an independent?" Generally, the responses indicate that Americans divide fairly evenly among these three choices, with about one-third describing themselves as **independents.** Of course, independents as such are not represented in Congress. This situation could change if parties were publicly funded, thereby possibly allowing for the creation of more parties, as discussed in the chapter-opening *What If . . .* feature.

After the elections are over, the media publish the election results. Among other things, Americans learn which party controls the presidency and how many Democrats and Republicans will be sitting in the House of Representatives and the Senate when the new Congress convenes.

Notice that in the first paragraph, when discussing party membership, we put the word *belonged* in quotation marks. We did this because hardly anyone actually "belongs" to a political party in the sense of being a card-carrying member. To become a member of a political party, you do not have to pay dues, pass an examination, or swear an oath of allegiance. Therefore, at this point we can ask an obvious question: If it takes nothing to be a member of a political party, what, then, is a political party?

What Is a Political Party?

A **political party** might be formally defined as a group of political activists who organize to win elections, operate the government, and determine public policy. This definition explains the difference between an interest group and a political party. Interest groups do not want to operate the government, and they do not put forth political candidates—even though they support candidates who will promote their interests if elected or reelected. Another important distinction is that interest groups tend to sharpen issues, whereas American political parties tend to blur their issue positions to attract voters.

Political parties differ from **factions,** which are smaller groups that are trying to obtain power or benefits.[1] Factions generally preceded the formation of political parties in American history, and the term is still used to refer to groups within parties that follow a particular leader or share a regional identification or an ideological viewpoint. For example, the Republican Party is sometimes seen as having a northeastern faction that holds more moderate positions than the dominant conservative majority of the party. Factions are subgroups within parties that may try to capture a nomination or get a position adopted by the party. A key difference between factions and parties is that factions do not have a permanent organization, whereas political parties do.

Political parties in the United States engage in a wide variety of activities, many of which are discussed in this chapter. Through these activities, parties perform a number of functions for the political system. These functions include the following:

1. *Recruiting candidates for public office.* Because it is the goal of parties to gain control of government, they must work to recruit candidates for all elective offices. Often, this means recruiting candidates to run against powerful incumbents. If parties did not search out and encourage political hopefuls, far more offices would be uncontested, and voters would have limited choices.

Independent
A voter or candidate who does not identify with a political party.

Political Party
A group of political activists who organize to win elections, operate the government, and determine public policy.

Faction
A group or bloc in a legislature or political party acting in pursuit of some special interest or position.

[1]See James Madison's comments on factions in Chapter 2.

One of the functions of political parties is to act as the organized opposition to the party in power. Here, a group of Democratic lawmakers, before the Democrats took control of Congress after the 2006 elections, address the media to decry ethics scandals involving Republican members of Congress. A few Democrats also made news for ethics scandals, however. Why might the public react skeptically to such an attempt to portray a problem in strictly partisan terms? (Photo Courtesy of the House Democratic Whip's Office.)

2. *Organizing and running elections.* Although elections are a government activity, political parties actually organize the voter-registration drives, recruit the volunteers to work at the polls, provide most of the campaign activity to stimulate interest in the election, and work to increase voter participation.

3. *Presenting alternative policies to the electorate.* In contrast to factions, which are often centered on individual politicians, parties are focused on a set of political positions. The Democrats or Republicans in Congress who vote together do so because they represent constituencies that have similar expectations and demands.

4. *Accepting responsibility for operating the government.* When a party elects the president or governor and members of the legislature, it accepts the responsibility for running the government. This includes staffing the executive branch with loyal party supporters and developing linkages among the elected officials to gain support for policies and their implementation.

5. *Acting as the organized opposition to the party in power.* The "out" party, or the one that does not control the government, is expected to articulate its own policies and oppose the winning party when appropriate. By organizing the opposition to the "in" party, the opposition party forces debate on the policy alternatives.

The major functions of American political parties are carried out by a small, relatively loose-knit nucleus of party activists. This arrangement is quite different from the more highly structured, mass-membership party organization typical of many European parties. American parties concentrate on winning elections rather than on signing up large numbers of deeply committed, dues-paying members who believe passionately in the party's program.

A History of Political Parties in the United States

Although it is difficult to imagine a political system in the United States with four, five, six, or seven major political parties, other democratic systems have three-party, four-party, or even ten-party systems. In some European nations, parties are clearly tied to ideological positions; parties that represent Marxist, socialist, liberal, conservative, and ultraconservative positions appear on the political continuum. Some nations have political parties representing regions of the nation that have separate cultural identities, such as the French-speaking and Flemish-speaking regions of Belgium. Some parties are rooted in religious differences. Parties also exist that represent specific economic interests—agricultural, maritime, or industrial—and some, such as monarchist parties, speak for alternative political systems.

The United States has a **two-party system,** and that system has been around since about 1800. The function and character of the political parties, as well as the emergence of the two-party system itself, have much to do with the unique historical forces operating from this country's beginning as an independent nation. Indeed, James Madison (1751–1836) linked the emergence of political parties to the form of government created by the Constitution.

Generally, we can divide the evolution of the nation's political parties into seven periods:

1. The creation of parties, from 1789 to 1816.
2. The era of one-party rule, or personal politics, from 1816 to 1828.
3. The period from Andrew Jackson's presidency to just before the Civil War, from 1828 to 1860.
4. The Civil War and post–Civil War period, from 1860 to 1896.
5. The Republican ascendancy and the progressive period, from 1896 to 1932.
6. The New Deal period, from 1932 to about 1968.
7. The modern period, from approximately 1968 to the present.

The Formative Years: Federalists and Anti-Federalists

The first partisan political division in the United States occurred before the adoption of the Constitution. As you will recall from Chapter 2, the Federalists were those who pushed for adoption of the Constitution, whereas the Anti-Federalists were against ratification.

In September 1796, George Washington, who had served as president for almost two full terms, decided not to run again. In his farewell address, he made a somber assessment of the nation's future. Washington felt that the country might be destroyed by the "baneful [harmful] effects of the spirit of party." He viewed parties as a threat to both national unity and the concept of popular government. Early in his career, Thomas Jefferson did not like political parties either. In 1789, he stated, "If I could not go to heaven but with a party, I would not go there at all."[2]

Nevertheless, in the years after the ratification of the Constitution, Americans came to realize that something more permanent than a faction would be necessary to identify candidates for office and represent political differences among the people. The result was two political parties.

One party was the Federalists, which included John Adams, the second president (1797–1801). The Federalists represented commercial interests such as merchants and large planters. They supported a strong national government.

[2]Letter to Francis Hopkinson written from Paris while Jefferson was minister to France. In John P. Foley, ed., *The Jeffersonian Cyclopedia* (New York: Russell & Russell, 1967), p. 677.

| DID YOU KNOW . . .
That the political party with the most seats in the House of Representatives chooses the Speaker of the House, makes any new rules it wants, gets a majority of the seats on each important committee and chooses committee chairs, and hires most of the congressional staff?

| **Two-Party System**
A political system in which only two parties have a reasonable chance of winning.

Thomas Jefferson, founder of the first Republican Party. His election to the presidency in 1800 was one of the world's first transfers of power through a free election. (Library of Congress)

Andrew Jackson earned the name "Old Hickory" for exploits during the War of 1812. In 1828, Jackson was elected president as the candidate of the new Democratic Party. (Corbis/Bettmann)

| **Era of Good Feelings**
The years from 1817 to 1825, when James Monroe was president and there was, in effect, no political opposition.

| **Democratic Party**
One of the two major American political parties evolving out of the Republican Party of Thomas Jefferson.

| **Whig Party**
A major party in the United States during the first half of the nineteenth century, formally established in 1836. The Whig Party was anti-Jackson and represented a variety of regional interests.

Thomas Jefferson led the other party, which came to be called the Republicans, or Jeffersonian Republicans. (These Republicans should not be confused with the later Republican Party of Abraham Lincoln. To avoid confusion, some scholars refer to Jefferson's party as the Democratic-Republicans, but this name was never used during the time that the party existed.) Jefferson's Republicans represented artisans and farmers. They strongly supported states' rights. In 1800, when Jefferson defeated Adams in the presidential contest, one of the world's first peaceful transfers of power from one party to another was achieved.

The Era of Good Feelings

From 1800 to 1820, a majority of U.S. voters regularly elected Republicans to the presidency and to Congress. By 1816, the Federalist Party had virtually collapsed, and two-party competition did not really exist. Although during elections the Republicans opposed the Federalists' call for a stronger, more active central government, they undertook such active government policies as acquiring the Louisiana Territory and Florida and establishing a national bank. Because there was no real political opposition to the Republicans and thus little political debate, the administration of James Monroe (1817–1825) came to be known as the **era of good feelings.** Since political competition now took place among individual Republican aspirants, this period can also be called the *era of personal politics*.

National Two-Party Rule: Democrats and Whigs

Organized two-party politics returned in 1824. With the election of John Quincy Adams as president, the Republican Party split in two. The followers of Adams called themselves National Republicans. The followers of Andrew Jackson, who defeated Adams in 1828, formed the **Democratic Party.** Later, the National Republicans took the name **Whig Party,** which had been a traditional name for British liberals. The Whigs stood, among other things, for federal spending on "internal improvements," such as roads. The Democrats opposed this policy. The Democrats, who were the stronger of the two parties, favored personal liberty and opportunity for the "common man." It was understood implicitly that the "common man" was a white man—hostility toward African Americans was an important force holding the disparate Democratic groups together.[3]

The Democrats' success was linked to their superior efforts to involve common citizens in the political process. Mass participation in politics and elections was a new phenomenon in the 1820s, as the political parties began to appeal to popular enthusiasm and themes. The parties adopted the techniques of mass campaigns, including rallies and parades. Lavishing food and drink on voters at polling places also became a common practice. Perhaps of greatest importance, however, was the push to cultivate party identity and loyalty. In large part, the spirit that motivated the new mass politics was democratic pride in participation. By making citizens feel that they were part of the political process, the parties hoped to win lasting party loyalty at the ballot box.

The Civil War Crisis

In the 1850s, hostility between the North and South over the issue of slavery divided both parties. The Whigs were the first to split in two. The Whigs had been

---

[3]Edward Pessen, *Jacksonian America: Society, Personality, and Politics* (Homewood, Ill.: Dorsey Press, 1969). See especially pages 246–247. The small number of free blacks who could vote were overwhelmingly Whig.

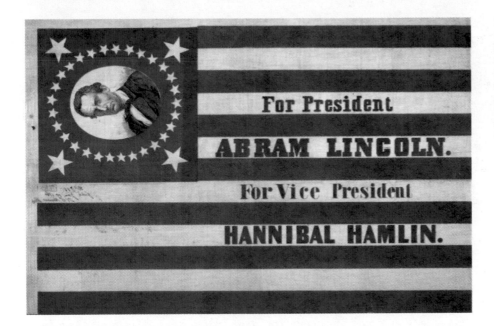

This banner was used in the election campaign of 1860 for Republican candidate Abraham Lincoln. Such banners and handbills served the same purpose as today's lawn signs and direct-mail advertisements, appealing directly to the voters with the candidate's patriotic image. Why do you think the flag is invoked so often in campaign advertisements? (Library of Congress)

the party of an active federal government, but southerners had come to believe that "a government strong enough to build roads is a government strong enough to free your slaves." The southern Whigs therefore ceased to exist as an organized party. The northern Whigs united with antislavery Democrats and members of the radical antislavery Free Soil Party to form the modern **Republican Party.**

Republican Party
One of the two major American political parties. It emerged in the 1850s as an antislavery party and consisted of former northern Whigs and antislavery Democrats.

The Post–Civil War Period

After the Civil War, the Democratic Party was able to heal its divisions. Southern resentment of the Republicans' role in defeating the South and fears that the federal government would intervene on behalf of African Americans ensured that the Democrats would dominate the white South for the next century.

"Rum, Romanism, and Rebellion."   Northern Democrats feared a strong government for other reasons. The Republicans thought that the government should promote business and economic growth, but many Republicans also wanted to use the power of government to impose evangelical Protestant moral values on society. Democrats opposed what they saw as culturally coercive measures. Many Republicans wanted to limit or even prohibit the sale of alcohol. They favored the establishment of public schools—with a Protestant curriculum. As a result, Catholics were strongly Democratic. In 1884, Protestant minister Samuel Burchard described the Democrats as the party of "rum, Romanism, and rebellion." This remark was offensive to Catholics, and Republican presidential candidate James Blaine later claimed that it cost him the White House. Offensive as it may have been, Burchard's characterization of the Democrats contained an element of truth.

The Triumph of the Republicans.   In this period, the parties were very evenly matched in strength. The abolition of the three-fifths rule, described in Chapter 2, meant that African Americans would be counted fully when allocating House seats and electoral votes to the South. The Republicans therefore had to carry almost every northern state to win, and this was not always possible. In the 1890s, however, the Republicans gained a decisive edge. In that decade, the populist movement emerged in the West and South to champion the interests of small farmers, who were often heavily in debt. Populists supported inflation, which benefited debtors by reducing the real value of outstanding debts. In 1896, when William Jennings Bryan became the Democratic candidate for president, the Democrats embraced populism.

As it turned out, the few western farmers who were drawn to the Democrats by this step were greatly outnumbered by urban working-class voters who believed that inflation would reduce the purchasing power of their paychecks and who therefore became Republicans. William McKinley, the Republican candidate, was elected with a solid majority of the votes. Figure 8–1 shows the states taken by Bryan and McKinley. The pattern of regional support shown in Figure 8–1 persisted for many years. From 1896 until 1932, the Republicans were successfully able to present themselves as the party that knew how to manage the economy.

The Progressive Interlude

In the early 1900s, a spirit of political reform arose in both major parties. Called *progressivism*, this spirit was compounded of a fear of the growing power of great corporations and a belief that honest, impartial government could regulate the economy effectively. In 1912, the Republican Party temporarily split as former Republican president Theodore Roosevelt campaigned for the presidency on a third-party Progressive, or Bull Moose, ticket. The Republican split permitted the election of Woodrow Wilson, the Democratic candidate, along with a Democratic Congress.

Like Roosevelt, Wilson considered himself a progressive, although he and Roosevelt did not agree on how progressivism ought to be implemented. Wilson's progressivism marked the beginning of a radical change in Democratic policies. Dating back to its very foundation, the Democratic Party had been the party of limited government. Under Wilson, the Democrats became for the first time at least as receptive as the Republicans to government action in the economy. (Wilson's progressivism did not extend to race relations—for African Americans, the Wilson administration was something of a disaster.)

The New Deal Era

The Republican ascendancy resumed after Wilson left office. It ended with the election of 1932, in the depths of the Great Depression. Republican Herbert Hoover was

Republican presidential candidate William McKinley campaigned in 1896 on a platform draped with the American flag. More than a century later, candidates are still using the same type of decorations. What sort of messages are modern-day candidates attempting to send by frequent displays of the flag? (Ralph E. Becker Collection/ Smithsonian Institution)

FIGURE 8–1 | THE 1896 PRESIDENTIAL ELECTION

In 1896, the agrarian, populist appeal of Democrat William Jennings Bryan (blue states) won western states for the Democrats at the cost of losing more populous eastern states to Republican William McKinley (red states). This pattern held in subsequent presidential elections.

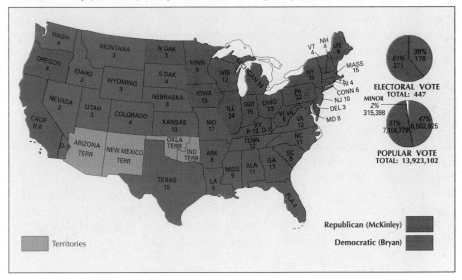

president when the depression began in 1929. Although Hoover took some measures to fight the depression, they fell far short of what the public demanded. Significantly, Hoover opposed federal relief for the unemployed and the destitute. In 1932, Democrat Franklin D. Roosevelt was elected president by an overwhelming margin.

The Great Depression shattered the working-class belief in Republican economic competence. Under Roosevelt, the Democrats began to make major interventions in the economy in an attempt to combat the depression and to relieve the suffering of the unemployed. Roosevelt's New Deal relief programs were open to all citizens, both black and white. As a result, African Americans began to support the

Unemployed workers filing benefit claims in the 1930s. Unemployment insurance was introduced during the "New Deal" of Democratic president Franklin D. Roosevelt. The Great Depression did not end until 1941 (with the economic stimulus of World War II), but Roosevelt's attempts to alleviate suffering caused by the depression made him very popular. (Franklin D. Roosevelt Presidential Library and Museum)

Democratic Party in large numbers—a development that would have stunned any American politician of the 1800s.

Roosevelt's political coalition was broad enough to establish the Democrats as the new majority party, in place of the Republicans. In the 1950s, Republican Dwight D. Eisenhower, the leading U.S. general during World War II, won two terms as president. Otherwise, with minor interruptions, the Democratic ascendancy lasted until 1968.

An Era of Divided Government

The New Deal coalition managed the unlikely feat of including both African Americans and whites who were hostile to African American advancement. This balancing act came to an end in the 1960s, a decade that was marked by the civil rights movement, by several years of "race riots" in major cities, and by increasingly heated protests against the Vietnam War. For many economically liberal, socially conservative voters, especially in the South, social issues had become more important than economic ones, and these voters left the Democrats. These voters outnumbered the new voters who joined the Democrats—newly enfranchised African Americans and former liberal Republicans in New England and the upper Midwest.

The Parties in Balance.   The result, since 1968, has been a nation almost evenly divided in politics. In presidential elections, the Republicans have had more success than the Democrats. Until 1994, Congress remained Democratic, but official party labels can be misleading. Some of the Democrats were southern conservatives who normally voted with the Republicans on issues. As these conservative Democrats retired, they were largely replaced by Republicans.

In the thirty-eight years between the elections of 1968 and 2006, there were only ten years when one of the two major parties controlled the presidency, the House of Representatives, and the Senate. The Democrats controlled all three institutions during the presidency of Jimmy Carter (1977–1981) and during the first two years of the presidency of Bill Clinton (1993–2001). The Republicans controlled all three institutions during the third through sixth years of George W. Bush's presidency.[4] Before the 1992 elections, the electorate seemed to prefer, in most circumstances, to match a Republican president with a Democratic Congress. Under Bill Clinton, that state of affairs was reversed, with a Democratic president facing a Republican Congress. After the 2006 elections, a Republican president again faced a Democratic Congress.

Red State, Blue State.   The pattern of a Republican Congress and a Democratic president would have continued after the election of 2000 if Democratic presidential candidate Al Gore had prevailed. Gore won the popular vote, but lost the electoral college by a narrow margin. Despite the closeness of the result, most states had voted in favor of either Bush or Gore by a fairly wide margin. To many observers, America had become divided between states that were solidly Republican or Democratic in their leanings, with a handful of "swing states." States that had shown strong support for a Republican candidate were deemed "red states" and so-called Democratic states were labeled "blue states."

Despite the presidential victory of Republican George W. Bush and the larger Republican margins of control in the House and Senate, the 2004 elections revealed a nation that continued to be closely divided between the two parties. As you can see in Figure 8–2, the electoral margin of victory for Bush was slim. Cultural politics may have played a more important role than was expected by most observers

---

[4]The Republicans also were in control of all three institutions for the first four months after Bush's inauguration. This initial period of control came to an end when Senator James Jeffords of Vermont left the Republican Party, giving the Democrats control of the Senate.

FIGURE 8–2 | THE PRESIDENTIAL ELECTION OF 2004

The 2004 presidential election proved very close in the electoral college. Although Republican incumbent George W. Bush won the popular vote by over 3 million votes, Democratic challenger John F. Kerry could have carried the election if the state of Ohio, and its 20 electoral votes, had fallen in his column.

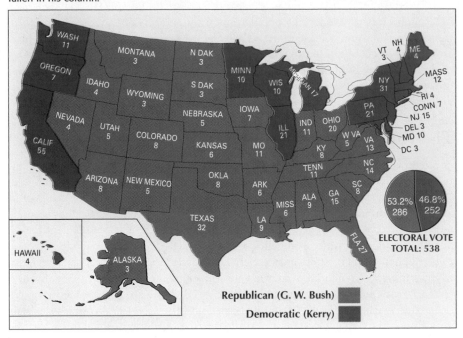

before the elections. In exit polls, more voters chose "moral values" as the most important election issue rather than the war in Iraq or the economy in the exit poll. While this result suggests the importance of cultural issues, the choice of "moral issues" was never offered to voters in prior elections. The fact that same-sex marriage referenda were on the ballot in many states may have increased the number of conservative voters who turned out and voted Republican. Democratic senator John F. Kerry, with his New England reserve, could not easily appeal to these voters, although clearly he tried. In the wake of the elections, some Democrats called for a candidate in 2008 who, like presidents Bill Clinton and Jimmy Carter, could make a stronger appeal to religious voters.

Partisan Trends in the 2006 Elections

While the campaign rhetoric was hot, heavy, and oftentimes nasty, the 2006 midterm elections showed that the American public is not as polarized as recent commentators have suggested. Many victory speeches right after the elections, particularly by Democrats, used the words "new direction." This notion of a new direction for American politics, though, was probably grossly exaggerated. Indeed, the most successful Democratic candidates moved toward moderate positions on many issues, as did those Americans who voted for them. In contrast, the Republican Party saw the perils of being too conservative as several of the most conservative members lost in both houses of Congress. There is some evidence, nonetheless, of a trend away from the Republican Party. In monthly surveys starting in January 2004 and ending with the 2006 elections, the percentage of American adults saying that they were affiliated with the Republican Party dropped from 37.2 percent to just under 32 percent. The number of Democrats grew only slightly during the same period from 36.1 percent to 37.3 percent. The remainder, of course, are independents. There was some evidence that a majority of independents decided in the last few days of the campaign to vote Democratic.

The Two Major U.S. Parties Today

It is sometimes said that the major American political parties are like Tweedledee and Tweedledum, the twins in Lewis Carroll's *Through the Looking Glass*. Labels such as "Repubocrats" are especially popular among supporters of third parties, such as the Green Party and the Libertarian Party. Third-party advocates, of course, have an interest in claiming that there is no difference between the two major parties—their chances of gaining support are much greater if the major parties are seen as indistinguishable. Despite such allegations, the major parties do have substantial differences, both in their policies and in their constituents.

The Parties' Core Constituents

You learned in Chapter 6 how demographic factors affect support for the two parties. Democrats receive disproportionate support not only from the least well educated voters but also from individuals with advanced degrees. Upper-income voters are generally more Republican than lower-income voters; businesspersons are much more likely to vote Republican than labor union members. The Jewish electorate is heavily Democratic; white evangelical Christians who are regular churchgoers tend to be Republicans. Hispanics are strongly Democratic; African Americans are overwhelmingly so. Women are somewhat more Democratic than men. City dwellers tend to be Democrats; rural people tend to be Republicans. In presidential elections, the South, the Rocky Mountain states, and the Great Plains states typically vote Republican; the West Coast and the Northeast are more likely to favor the Democrats. These tendencies represent the influences of economic interests and cultural values, which are often in conflict with each other.

Economic Beliefs

A coalition of the labor movement and various racial and ethnic minorities has been the core of Democratic Party support since the presidency of Franklin D. Roosevelt. The social programs and increased government intervention in the economy that made up Roosevelt's New Deal were intended to ease the pressure of economic hard times on these groups. This goal remains important for many Democrats today. In general, Democratic identifiers are more likely to approve of social-welfare spending, to support government regulation of business, to endorse measures to improve the situation of minorities, and to support assisting the elderly with their medical expenses. Republicans are more supportive of the private marketplace and believe more strongly in an ethic of self-reliance and limited government.

These traditional party beliefs are reflected in the public opinion poll results in Figure 8–3. On economic and health-care issues, respondents considered the Democrats more trustworthy than Republicans. Republicans showed strength on security issues.

Economic Convergence?   In his 1996 State of the Union address, Democratic president Bill Clinton announced that "the era of big government is over." One might conclude from this that both parties now favor limited government. Some political observers, however, argue the reverse. These observers believe that despite the tax cuts that Republicans have implemented, both parties in practice now favor "big government."

Harvard University professor Jeffrey Frankel goes even further. "When it comes to White House economic policy," Frankel writes, "the Republican and Democratic parties have switched places since the 1960s." Frankel points out that budget deficits rose during the administrations of Republicans Ronald Reagan (1981–1989)

FIGURE 8–3 | REPUBLICAN ISSUES AND DEMOCRATIC ISSUES

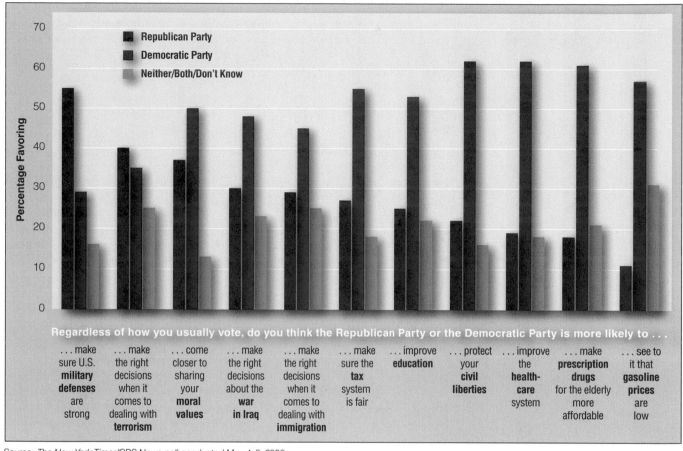

Source: *The New York Times*/CBS News poll conducted May 4–8, 2006.

and George W. Bush but fell under Bill Clinton. Federal employment grew under Reagan and George W. Bush but fell under Clinton. Reagan and Bush both introduced "protectionist" measures to restrict imports, such as Bush's tariffs on imported steel and timber. Clinton, despite the protectionist beliefs of many Democrats in Congress, was in practice more supportive of free trade.[5] Despite these facts, Clinton was not really a supporter of limited government. If his 1993 plan for universal health insurance had been accepted by Congress, the size and cost of the federal government would have increased considerably.

Republican and Democratic Budgets. Other observers have noted a contrast in budgets. Reagan faced a Congress controlled by the Democrats. Clinton in turn faced a Republican Congress for most of his administration. Reagan regularly submitted budgets larger than the ones that the Democratic Congress eventually passed, however, while Clinton's budgets were typically smaller than those approved by the Republican Congress. During the first three years of George W. Bush's presidency, discretionary federal spending rose by 27 percent, compared with 10 percent under Clinton's two full terms in office. Finally, it was a Republican majority in Congress that passed a new Medicare prescription drug benefit in 2003.

---

[5]Jeffrey Frankel, "Republican and Democratic Presidents Have Switched Economic Policies," *Milken Institute Review*, Vol. 5, No. 1 (First Quarter 2003), pp. 18–25.

Despite these paradoxes, the perception is that the Democrats still tend to favor the less well off, while the Republicans tend to favor the prosperous. Democrats have argued, for example, that President Bush's tax cuts were weighted heavily toward the upper end of the economic spectrum. In addition, there is another class of issues on which the differences between the parties have become greater than ever—cultural issues.

Cultural Politics

In recent years, cultural values may have become more important than they previously were in defining the beliefs of the two major parties. For example, in 1987, Democrats were almost as likely to favor stricter abortion laws (40 percent) as Republicans were (48 percent). Today, Republicans are twice as likely to favor stricter abortion laws (50 percent to 25 percent).

Cultural Politics and Socioeconomic Status.   Thomas Frank, writing in *Harper's Magazine*, reported seeing the following bumper sticker at a gun show in Kansas City: "A working person voting for the Democrats is like a chicken voting for Colonel Sanders." (Colonel Sanders is the iconic founder of KFC, the chain of fried chicken restaurants.) In light of the economic traditions of the two parties, this seems to be an odd statement. In fact, the sticker is an exact reversal of an earlier one directed against the Republicans.

You can make sense of such a sentiment by remembering what you learned in Chapter 6—although economic conservatism is associated with higher incomes, social conservatism is relatively more common among lower-income groups. The individual who displayed the bumper sticker, therefore, was in effect claiming that cultural concerns—in this example, presumably the right to own handguns—are far more important than economic ones. Frank argues that despite Republican control of the national government during the George W. Bush administration, cultural conservatives continued to view themselves as embattled "ordinary Americans" under threat from a liberal, cosmopolitan elite.[6]

Also, according to Republican commentator Karl Zinsmeister, many police officers, construction workers, military veterans, and rural residents began moving toward the Republican Party in the 1960s and 1970s. In contrast, many of America's rich and superrich elite, including financiers, media barons, software millionaires, and entertainers, started slowly, but surely, drifting toward the Democratic Party. Arguably, the major financial backing for Democrats is from the rich and superrich. In contrast, for the Republicans, in the last two presidential elections, less than 10 percent of voters in pro-Bush counties earned over $100,000 per year.

All that can be said today is that it is difficult to stereotype what socioeconomic groups support which party.

The Regional Factor in Cultural Politics.   Conventionally, some parts of the country are viewed as culturally liberal, and others as culturally conservative. On a regional basis, cultural liberalism (as opposed to economic liberalism) may be associated with economic dynamism. The San Francisco Bay Area can serve as an example. The greater Bay Area contains Silicon Valley, the heart of the microcomputer industry; it has the highest per capita personal income of any metropolitan area in America. It also is one of the most liberal regions of the country. San Francisco liberalism is largely cultural—one sign of this liberalism is that the city has a claim to be the "capital" of gay America. There is not much evidence, however, that the region's wealthy citizens are in favor of higher taxes.

To further illustrate this point, we can compare the political preferences of relatively wealthy states with relatively poor ones. Of the ten states with the highest per

---

[6]Thomas Frank, "Lie Down for America," *Harper's Magazine*, April 2004, p. 33.

capita personal incomes in 2004, eight voted for Democrat John Kerry in the presidential election of that year. Of the twenty-five states with the lowest per capita incomes in 2004, twenty-three voted for Republican George W. Bush.

Given these data, it seems hard to believe that upper-income voters really are more Republican than lower-income ones. Within any given state or region, however, upscale voters are more likely to be Republican regardless of whether the area as a whole leans Democratic or Republican. States that vote Democratic are often northern states that contain large cities. At least part of this **reverse-income effect** may simply be that urban areas are more prosperous, culturally liberal, and Democratic than the countryside, and that the North is more prosperous, culturally liberal, and Democratic than the South.

The 2004 Elections: Economics and National Security

Despite the importance of cultural beliefs in determining party allegiance, Republican incumbent George W. Bush and Democratic challenger John F. Kerry avoided cultural issues in the 2004 elections whenever possible. Both candidates believed that national security and economic concerns would be the most important issues for undecided voters.

Kerry at first stressed economics. He claimed that the economic recovery of 2003 and 2004 had not created significant numbers of new jobs. Bush campaigned as the national security candidate—a leader who merited reelection on the basis of his actions in the years following the terrorist attacks of September 11, 2001. These contrasting campaigns were based on the traditional beliefs of the two parties. Kerry's appeal to economic fairness was an expression of the value of equality; Bush's emphasis on security was an expression of the value of order, a key value for cultural conservatives. (These values were defined and described in Chapter 1 of this text.)

During the Democratic National Convention, however, Kerry sought to portray himself as a better choice for commander in chief by playing up his Vietnam War record and by using patriotic symbolism. Kerry claimed that Bush had needlessly antagonized our traditional allies. Meanwhile, Bush continued to attack Kerry's credibility as a potential president by branding him as a "flip-flopper."

The Three Faces of a Party

Although American parties are known by a single name and, in the public mind, have a common historical identity, each party really has three major components. The first component is the **party-in-the-electorate.** This phrase refers to all those individuals who claim an attachment to the political party. They need not participate in election campaigns. Rather, the party-in-the-electorate is the large number of Americans who feel some loyalty to the party or who use partisanship as a cue to decide who will earn their vote. Party membership is not really a rational choice; rather, it is an emotional tie somewhat analogous to identifying with a region or a baseball team. Although individuals may hold a deep loyalty to or identification with a political party, there is no need for members of the party-in-the-electorate to speak out publicly, to contribute to campaigns, or to vote all Republican or all Democratic. Needless to say, the party leaders pay close attention to the affiliation of their members in the electorate.

The second component, the **party organization,** provides the structural framework for the political party by recruiting volunteers to become party leaders; identifying potential candidates; and organizing caucuses, conventions, and election campaigns for its candidates, as will be discussed in more detail shortly. It is the party organization and its active workers that keep the party functioning between elections, as well as make sure that the party puts forth electable candidates and

Reverse-Income Effect
A tendency for wealthier states or regions to favor the Democrats and for less wealthy states or regions to favor the Republicans. The effect appears paradoxical because it reverses traditional patterns of support.

Party-in-the-Electorate
Those members of the general public who identify with a political party or who express a preference for one party over another.

Party Organization
The formal structure and leadership of a political party, including election committees; local, state, and national executives; and paid professional staff.

Party-in-Government
All of the elected and appointed officials who identify with a political party.

clear positions in the elections. If the party-in-the-electorate declines in numbers and loyalty, the party organization must try to find a strategy to rebuild the grass-roots following.

The **party-in-government** is the third component of American political parties. The party-in-government consists of those elected and appointed officials who identify with a political party. Generally, elected officials do not also hold official party positions within the formal organization, although they often have the informal power to appoint party executives.

Party Organization

Each of the American political parties is often seen as having a pyramid-shaped organization, with the national chairperson and committee at the top and the local precinct chairperson on the bottom. This structure, however, does not accurately reflect the relative power of the individual components of the party organization. If it did, the national chairperson of the Democratic Party or the Republican Party, along with the national committee, could simply dictate how the organization was to be run, just as if it were the ExxonMobil Corporation or Ford Motor Company. In reality, the political parties have a confederal structure, in which each unit has significant autonomy and is linked only loosely to the other units.

The National Party Organization

National Convention
The meeting held every four years by each major party to select presidential and vice-presidential candidates, to write a platform, to choose a national committee, and to conduct party business.

Party Platform
A document drawn up at each national convention, outlining the policies, positions, and principles of the party.

Each party has a national organization, the most clearly institutional part of which is the **national convention,** held every four years. The convention is used to nominate the presidential and vice-presidential candidates. In addition, the **party platform** is developed at the national convention. The platform sets forth the party's position on the issues and makes promises to initiate certain policies if the party wins the presidency.

After the convention, the platform frequently is neglected or ignored by party candidates who disagree with it. Because candidates are trying to win votes from a wide spectrum of voters, it is counterproductive to emphasize the fairly narrow and sometimes controversial goals set forth in the platform. Political scientist Gerald M. Pomper discovered decades ago, however, that once elected, the parties do try to carry out platform promises and that roughly three-fourths of the promises eventually become law.[7] Of course, some general goals, such as economic prosperity, are included in the platforms of both parties.

Convention Delegates.   The party convention provides the most striking illustration of the difference between the ordinary members of a party, or party identifiers, and party activists. As a series of studies by the *New York Times* shows, delegates to the national party conventions are quite different from ordinary party identifiers. Delegates to the Democratic National Convention, as shown in Table 8–1, are far more liberal than ordinary Democratic voters. Typically, delegates to the Republican National Convention are far more conservative than ordinary Republicans. Why does this happen? In part, it is because a person, to become a delegate, must gather votes in a primary election from party members who care enough to vote in a primary or be appointed by party leaders. Also, the primaries generally pit presidential candidates against each other on intraparty issues. Competition within each party tends to pull candidates away from the center, and delegates even more so. Often, the most important activity for the convention is making peace among the delegates who

---

[7]Gerald M. Pomper and Susan S. Lederman, *Elections in America: Control and Influence in Democratic Politics*, 2d ed. (New York: Longman, 1980).

TABLE 8-1 | CONVENTION DELEGATES AND VOTERS: HOW DID THEY COMPARE ON THE ISSUES IN 2004?

	PERCENTAGE OF . . .				
	DEMOCRATIC DELEGATES	DEMOCRATIC VOTERS	ALL VOTERS	REPUBLICAN VOTERS	REPUBLICAN DELEGATES
SCOPE OF GOVERNMENT					
Government should do more to . . .					
solve the nation's problems	79	48	42	35	7
promote traditional values	15	26	40	61	55
ECONOMIC POLICY					
The budget deficit is a very serious problem for the country	86	68	51	28	13
All or most of the tax cuts Congress has passed since 2000 should be made permanent	7	33	49	68	95
FOREIGN POLICY					
The United States did the right thing in taking military action against Iraq	7	21	46	78	96
It is extremely important for the United States to work through the United Nations to solve international problems	79	66	49	31	7
DOMESTIC POLICY					
New antiterrorism laws excessively restrict the average person's civil liberties	77	53	43	25	15
Gay couples should be allowed to legally marry	44	36	26	11	3
Abortion should be generally available to those who want it	75	49	34	17	13
The penalty for murder should be death, rather than life in prison without chance of parole	19	39	50	65	57
IDEOLOGY					
Your political ideology is . . .					
liberal	41	34	20	8	1
moderate	52	45	42	30	33
conservative	3	19	36	61	63

Source: *The New York Times*, July 25, 2004 and August 29, 2004.

Delegates at the 2004 Republican National Convention in New York (left photos) and at the Democratic National Convention in Boston (right photos). Do national party conventions still have a function in an era in which presidential candidates are actually chosen by primary elections and caucuses open to all party members? (Photos Courtesy of DNC and RNC.)

| National Committee
A standing committee of a national political party established to direct and coordinate party activities between national party conventions.

support different candidates and persuading them to accept a party platform that will appeal to the general electorate.

The National Committee. At the national convention, each of the parties formally chooses a national standing committee, elected by the individual state parties. This **national committee** directs and coordinates party activities during the following four years. The Democrats include at least two members (a man and a woman) from each state, from the District of Columbia, and from the several territories. Governors, members of Congress, mayors, and other officials may be included as at-large members of the national committee. The Republicans, in addition, include state chairpersons from every state carried by the Republican Party in the preceding presidential, guber-natorial, or congressional elections. The selections of national committee members are ratified by the delegations to the national convention.

One of the jobs of the national committee is to ratify the presidential nominee's choice of a national chairperson, who in principle acts as the spokesperson for the party. The national chairperson and the national committee plan the next campaign and the next convention, obtain financial contributions, and publicize the national party.

Picking a National Chairperson. In general, the party's presidential candidate chooses the national chairperson. (If that candidate loses, however, the chairperson is often changed.) The national chairperson performs such jobs as establishing a national party headquarters, raising campaign funds and distributing them to state parties and to candidates, and appearing in the media as a party spokesperson. The national chairperson, along with the national committee, attempts to maintain some sort of liaison among the different levels of the party organization. The fact, though, is that the real strength and power of a national party are at the state level.

Ken Mehlman (left), chairman of the Republican National Committee and Howard Dean (right) Chairman of the Democratic National Committee. Is the function of a national party chairperson similar to the function of a chairperson of a corporate board of directors? (Photos Courtesy of the Republican and Democratic National Committees)

The State Party Organization

There are fifty states in the Union, plus the District of Columbia and the territories, and an equal number of party organizations for each major party. Therefore, there are more than a hundred state parties (and even more, if we include local parties and minor parties). Because every state party is unique, it is impossible to describe what an "average" state political party is like. Nonetheless, state parties have several organizational features in common.

Each state party has a chairperson, a committee, and a number of local organizations. In theory, the role of the **state central committee**—the principal organized structure of each political party within each state—is similar in the various states. The committee, usually composed of members who represent congressional districts, state legislative districts, or counties, has responsibility for carrying out the policy decisions of the party's state convention. In some states the state committee can issue directives to the state chairperson.

Also, like the national committee, the state central committee has control over the use of party campaign funds during political campaigns. Usually, the state central committee has little, if any, influence on party candidates once they are elected. In fact, state parties are fundamentally loose alliances of local interests and coalitions of often bitterly opposed factions.

State parties are also important in national politics because of the **unit rule,** which awards electoral votes in presidential elections as an indivisible bloc (except in Maine and Nebraska). Presidential candidates concentrate their efforts in states in which voter preferences seem to be evenly divided or in which large numbers of electoral votes are at stake.

State Central Committee
The principal organized structure of each political party within each state. This committee is responsible for carrying out policy decisions of the party's state convention.

Unit Rule
A rule by which all of a state's electoral votes are cast for the presidential candidate receiving a plurality of the popular vote in that state.

Local Party Machinery: The Grassroots

The lowest layer of party machinery is the local organization, supported by district leaders, precinct or ward captains, and party workers. Much of the work is coordinated by county committees and their chairpersons.

Patronage and City Machines. In the 1800s, the institution of **patronage**—rewarding the party faithful with government jobs or contracts—held the local

Patronage
Rewarding faithful party workers and followers with government employment and contracts.

Florida Democratic Party chairperson Scott Maddox holds a voter-registration form during a campaign to sign up university students. In past elections, younger citizens have been less likely to vote than older ones. Why do you think that would happen? (AP Photo/Steve Cannon)

organization together. For immigrants and the poor, the political machine often furnished important services and protections. The big-city machine was the archetypal example. Tammany Hall, or the Tammany Society, which dominated New York City government for nearly two centuries, was perhaps the most notorious example of this political form.

The last big-city local political machine to exercise substantial power was run by Chicago's Mayor Richard J. Daley, who was also an important figure in national Democratic politics. Daley, as mayor, ran the Chicago Democratic machine from 1955 until his death in 1976. The current mayor of Chicago, Richard M. Daley, son of the former mayor, does not have the kind of machine that his father had.

City machines are now dead, mostly because their function of providing social services (and reaping the reward of votes) has been taken over by state and national agencies. This trend began in the 1930s, when the social legislation of the New Deal established Social Security and unemployment insurance. The local party machine has little, if anything, to do with deciding who is eligible to receive these benefits.

Local Party Organizations Today.   Local political organizations—whether located in cities, in townships, or at the county level—still can contribute a great deal to local election campaigns. These organizations are able to provide the foot soldiers of politics—individuals who pass out literature and get out the vote on election day, which can be crucial in local elections. In many regions, local Democratic and Republican organizations still exercise some patronage, such as awarding courthouse jobs, contracts for street repair, and other lucrative construction contracts. The constitutionality of awarding—or not awarding—contracts on the basis of political affiliation has been subject to challenge, however. The United States Supreme Court has ruled that firing or failing to hire individuals because of their political affiliation is an infringement of the employees' First Amendment rights to free expression.[8] Local party organizations are also the most important vehicles for recruiting young adults into political work, because political involvement at the local level offers activists many opportunities to gain experience.

---

[8]*Rutan v. Republican Party of Illinois*, 497 U.S. 62 (1990).

The Party-in-Government

After the election is over and the winners are announced, the focus of party activity shifts from getting out the vote to organizing and controlling the government. As you will learn in Chapter 11, party membership plays an important role in the day-to-day operations of Congress, with partisanship determining everything from office space to committee assignments and power on Capitol Hill. For the president, the political party furnishes the pool of qualified applicants for political appointments to run the government. (Although it is uncommon to do so, presidents can and occasionally do appoint executive personnel, such as cabinet members, from the opposition party.) As we will note in Chapter 12, there are not as many of these appointed positions as presidents might like, and presidential power is limited by the permanent bureaucracy. Judicial appointments also offer a great opportunity to the winning party. For the most part, presidents are likely to appoint federal judges from their own party.

Divided Government. All of these party appointments suggest that the winning political party, whether at the national, state, or local level, has a great deal of control in the American system. Because of the checks and balances and the relative lack of cohesion in American parties, however, such control is an illusion. One reason is that for some time many Americans have seemed to prefer a **divided government,** with the executive and legislative branches controlled by different parties. The trend toward **ticket splitting**—splitting votes between the president and members of Congress—has increased sharply since 1952. This practice may indicate a lack of trust in government or the relative weakness of party identification among many voters. Voters have often seemed comfortable with having a president affiliated with one party and a Congress controlled by the other.

The Limits of Party Unity. There are other ways in which the power of the parties is limited. Consider how major laws are passed in Congress. Traditionally, legislation has rarely been passed by a vote strictly along party lines. Although most Democrats may oppose a bill, for example, some Democrats may vote for it. Their votes, combined with the votes of Republicans, may be enough to pass the bill. Similarly, support from some Republicans may enable a bill sponsored by the Democrats to pass. This is not to say that Congress *never* votes along strict party lines. A notable example of such partisan voting occurred in the House of Representatives in 1998. The issue at hand was whether to impeach President Bill Clinton. Almost all votes were strictly along party lines—Democrats against, and Republicans for.

One reason that the political parties find it so hard to rally all of their members in Congress to vote along party lines is that parties in this country do not have a "boss system." In other words, the head of a political party in most instances cannot handpick candidates who share his or her views and who will be beholden to that boss and to that party. In the United States, the candidates who win most elections largely do so on their own, without significant help from a political party. A candidate generally gains a nomination through her or his own hard work and personal political organization. This means, though, that the parties have very little control over the candidates who run under the party labels. In fact, a candidate could run as a Republican, for example, and advocate beliefs repugnant to the national party, such as racism. No one in the Republican Party organization could stop this person from being nominated or even elected.

Party Polarization. Despite the forces that act against party-line voting, there have been times when the two parties in Congress have been polarized, and defections from the party line have been rare. One such period was the mid-1990s, after

Divided Government
A situation in which one major political party controls the presidency and the other controls the chambers of Congress, or in which one party controls a state governorship and the other controls the state legislature.

Ticket Splitting
Voting for candidates of two or more parties for different offices. For example, a voter splits her ticket if she votes for a Republican presidential candidate and for a Democratic congressional candidate.

the Republicans gained control of both the House and the Senate. Under House Speaker Newt Gingrich, the Republicans maintained strict discipline in an attempt to use their new majority to sponsor a specific legislative agenda. In 2003, polarization peaked again. "People genuinely hate each other," lamented Louisiana senator John Breaux, a moderate Democrat.[9]

One cause of polarization is the use of sophisticated computer programs to create House districts that are "safe" for each party. A safe Republican district, for example, would contain such a large share of Republican voters that no Democratic candidate would have a chance of winning. (You will learn more about congressional redistricting in Chapter 11.) With **safe seats,** Republicans and Democrats alike find it advantageous to appeal to their party's most committed supporters, rather than to independents. The close party division in Congress also enhances the spirit of political competition.

Safe Seat
A district that returns the legislator with 55 percent of the vote or more.

Writers and advocates in the media, who find that stridency sells, also tend to encourage an atmosphere of polarization. Some commentators, however, do not believe that this spirit of polarization extends very far into the general electorate. They contend that a majority of Americans are strongly committed to tolerance of opposing political views.[10]

Why Has the Two-Party System Endured?

There are several reasons why two major parties have dominated the political landscape in the United States for almost two centuries. These reasons have to do with (1) the historical foundations of the system, (2) political socialization and practical considerations, (3) the winner-take-all electoral system, and (4) state and federal laws favoring the two-party system.

The Historical Foundations of the Two-Party System

As we have seen, at many times in American history there has been one preeminent issue or dispute that divided the nation politically. In the beginning, Americans were at odds over ratifying the Constitution. After the Constitution went into effect, the power of the federal government became the major national issue. Thereafter, the dispute over slavery divided the nation by section, North versus South. At times—for example, in the North after the Civil War—cultural differences have been important, with advocates of government-sponsored morality (such as banning alcoholic beverages) pitted against advocates of personal liberty.

During much of the 1900s, economic differences were preeminent. In the New Deal period, the Democrats became known as the party of the working class, while the Republicans became known as the party of the middle and upper classes and commercial interests.

When politics is based on an argument between two opposing points of view, advocates of each viewpoint can mobilize most effectively by forming a single, unified party. Also, when a two-party system has been in existence for almost two centuries, it becomes difficult to imagine an alternative.

Political Socialization and Practical Considerations

Given that the majority of Americans identify with one of the two major political parties, it is not surprising that most children learn at a fairly young age to think of themselves as either Democrats or Republicans. This generates a built-in mechanism to perpetuate a two-party system. Also, many politically oriented people who

[9]Jackie Calmes, "Set This House on Fire," *The Wall Street Journal Europe,* December 1, 2003, p. A7.
[10]Robert J. Samuelson, "Polarization Myths," *The Washington Post,* December 3, 2003, p. A29.

Many young people learn at a fairly early age to think of themselves as either Democrats or Republicans. Here, supporters of George W. Bush and John Kerry clash in front of the elections office in Jacksonville, Florida, on Election Day 2004. What influences might play a role in an individual's party affiliation or lack thereof? (AP/*The Florida Times-Union*, Bob Mack)

aspire to work for social change consider that the only realistic way to capture political power in this country is to be either a Republican or a Democrat.

The Winner-Take-All Electoral System

At virtually every level of government in the United States, the outcome of elections is based on the **plurality,** winner-take-all principle. In a plurality system, the winner is the person who obtains the most votes, even if that person does not receive a majority (over 50 percent) of the votes. Whoever gets the most votes gets everything. Most legislators in the United States are elected from single-member districts in which only one person represents the constituency, and the candidate who finishes second in such an election receives nothing for the effort.

Presidential Voting. The winner-take-all system also operates in the election of the U.S president. Recall that the voters in each state do not vote for a president directly but vote for **electoral college** delegates who are committed to the various presidential candidates. These delegates are called *electors*.

In all but two states (Maine and Nebraska), if a presidential candidate wins a plurality in the state, then *all* of the state's votes go to that candidate. For example, let us say that the electors pledged to a particular presidential candidate receive a plurality of 40 percent of the votes in a state. That presidential candidate will receive all of the state's votes in the electoral college. Minor parties have a difficult time competing under such a system. Because voters know that minor parties cannot win any electoral votes, they often will not vote for minor-party candidates, even if the candidates are in tune with them ideologically.

Popular Election of the Governors and the President. In most European countries, the chief executive (usually called the prime minister) is elected by the legislature, or parliament. If the parliament contains three or more parties, as is usually the case, two or more of the parties can join together in a coalition to choose the prime minister and the other leaders of the government. In the United States, however, the people elect the president and the governors of all fifty states. There is no opportunity for two or more parties to negotiate a coalition. Here, too, the winner-take-all principle discriminates powerfully against any third party.

| Plurality
A number of votes cast for a candidate that is greater than the number of votes for any other candidate but not necessarily a majority.

| Electoral College
A group of persons, called electors, who are selected by the voters in each state. This group officially elects the president and the vice president of the United States.

Proportional Representation. Many other nations use a system of proportional representation with multimember districts. If, during the national election, party X obtains 12 percent of the vote, party Y gets 43 percent of the vote, and party Z gets the remaining 45 percent of the vote, then party X gets 12 percent of the seats in the legislature, party Y gets 43 percent of the seats, and party Z gets 45 percent of the seats. Because even a minor party may still obtain at least a few seats in the legislature, the smaller parties have a greater incentive to organize under such electoral systems than they do in the United States. To read more about nations that utilize a proportional representation system, see this chapter's *Beyond Our Borders* feature.

The relative effects of proportional representation versus our system of single-member districts are so strong that many scholars have made them one of the few "laws" of political science. "Duverger's Law," named after French political scientist Maurice Duverger, states that electoral systems based on single-member districts tend to produce two parties, while systems of proportional representation produce multiple parties.[11] Still, many countries with single-member districts have more than two political parties—Britain and Canada are examples.

State and Federal Laws Favoring the Two Parties

Many state and federal election laws offer a clear advantage to the two major parties. In some states, the established major parties need to gather fewer signatures to place their candidates on the ballot than minor parties or independent candidates do. The criterion for determining how many signatures will be required is often based on the total party vote in the last general election, thus penalizing a new political party that did not compete in that election.

At the national level, minor parties face different obstacles. All of the rules and procedures of both houses of Congress divide committee seats, staff members, and other privileges on the basis of party membership. A legislator who is elected on a minor-party ticket, such as the Conservative Party of New York, must choose to be counted with one of the major parties to obtain a committee assignment. The Federal Election Commission (FEC) rules for campaign financing also place restrictions on minor-party candidates. Such candidates are not eligible for federal matching funds in either the primary or the general election. In the 1980 election, John Anderson, running for president as an independent, sued the FEC for campaign funds. The commission finally agreed to repay part of his campaign costs after the election in proportion to the votes he received. Giving funds to a candidate when the campaign is over is, of course, much less helpful than providing funds while the campaign is still under way.

| The Role of Minor Parties in U.S. Politics

For the reasons just discussed, minor parties have a difficult, if not impossible, time competing within the American two-party political system. Nonetheless, minor parties have played an important role in our political life. Parties other than the Republicans or Democrats are usually called third parties. (Technically, of course, there could be fourth, fifth, or sixth parties as well, but we use the term *third party* because it has endured.) Third parties can come into existence in a number of ways. They may be founded from scratch by individuals or groups who are committed to a particular interest, issue, or ideology. They can split off from one of the major parties when a group becomes dissatisfied with the major party's policies. Finally, they can be organized around a particular charismatic leader and serve as that person's vehicle for contesting elections.

| Third Party
A political party other than the two major political parties (Republican and Democratic).

---

[11]As cited in Todd Landman, *Issues and Methods in Comparative Politics* (New York: Routledge, 2003), p. 14.

BEYOND OUR BORDERS | Multiparty Systems—The Rule Rather Than the Exception

The United States has a two-party system. Occasionally, a third-party candidate enters the race, but really has little chance of winning. Throughout the world, though, many democracies have multiparty systems.

SOME EXAMPLES

In its first legislative elections ever, Afghanistan saw the emergence of six major parties and seven minor parties. In the 2005 Iraqi National Assembly Election, there were a total of 15 parliamentary alliances and parties, plus 20 other parties. In any national election in India, there are 6 major parties, and in the states, there are a total of 30 parties. (There are also over 700 registered, but unrecognized, parties in India.)

In the latest elections in Germany, there were major parties and numerous minor ones. In any given presidential election in France, there are even more parties. They include the National Front that represents the extreme right, anti-immigrant part of the electorate. But there was also a party for hunting, fishing, nature, and traditions and one for the Revolutionary Communist League. All in all, there are at least fifteen French parties, most of which obtain some public funding.

PROPORTIONAL REPRESENTATION AND COALITIONS

In the German elections of September 2005, the Christian Democrats received about 30 percent of the vote and obtained about 30 percent of the seats in the German Federal Congress, called the *Bundestag*. The Christian Social Union of Bavaria obtained about 8 percent of the votes and almost 8 percent of the seats. Together these two right-of-center parties obtained 36.8 percent of the seats in Germany's equivalent of our House of Representatives. The opposition on the left, called

the Social Democratic Party of Germany, obtained almost the same—36.2 percent. Not surprisingly, neither the right nor the left in Germany had a high enough percentage of seats in the *Bundestag* to move forward. Consequently, a coalition government was formed, one that had to take account of the more extreme parties represented in the *Bundestag*, including the Free Democratic Party and the so-called Greens (ecologists).

In the latest French elections, the Union for a Presidential Minority, along with assorted other right-of-center parties, obtained a clear majority and therefore did not have to form coalitions with opposition parties on the left.

Coalitions are almost a certainty in a multiparty system. Why? Because usually the leading party does not have a majority of votes in the legislature. The leading party therefore has to make compromises to obtain votes from other parties. These coalitions see changes all the time, depending on the legislation to be voted. Coalitions represent the bargaining among interest groups.

If we had a multiparty system in the United States, we might have a farmers' party, a Hispanic party, a western party, a labor party, and others. To gain support for her or his program, a president would have to build a coalition of several parties by persuading each that its members would benefit from the coalition. The major difficulty in a multiparty system is, of course, that the parties will withdraw from the coalition when they fail to benefit from it. Holding a coalition together for more than one issue is sometimes impossible.

FOR CRITICAL ANALYSIS

Are multiparty systems necessarily more representative than the two-party system in the United States? Why or why not?

Third parties have acted as barometers of changes in the political mood. Such barometric indicators have forced the major parties to recognize new issues or trends in the thinking of Americans. Political scientists believe that third parties have acted as safety valves for dissident groups, preventing major confrontations and political unrest. In some instances, third parties have functioned as way stations for voters en route from one of the major parties to the other. Table 8–2 on the next page lists significant third-party presidential campaigns in American history; Table 8–3 on p. 275 provides a brief description of third-party beliefs.

Ideological Third Parties

The longest-lived third parties have been those with strong ideological foundations that are typically at odds with the majority mind-set. The Socialist Party is an

TABLE 8–2 | THE MOST SUCCESSFUL THIRD-PARTY PRESIDENTIAL CAMPAIGNS SINCE 1864

The following list includes all third-party candidates winning over 5 percent of the popular vote or any electoral votes since 1864. (We ignore isolated "unfaithful electors" in the electoral college who fail to vote for the candidate to which they are pledged.)

Year	Major Third Party	Third-Party Presidential Candidate	Percent of of the Popular Vote	Electoral Votes	Winning Presidential Candidate and Party
1892	Populist	James Weaver	8.5	22	Grover Cleveland (D)
1912	Progressive	Theodore Roosevelt	27.4	88	Woodrow Wilson (D)
	Socialist	Eugene Debs	6.0	—	
1924	Progressive	Robert LaFollette	16.6	13	Calvin Coolidge (R)
1948	States' Rights	Strom Thurmond	2.4	39	Harry Truman (D)
1960	Independent Democrat	Harry Byrd	0.4	15*	John Kennedy (D)
1968	American Independent	George Wallace	13.5	46	Richard Nixon (R)
1980	National Union	John Anderson	6.6	—	Ronald Reagan (R)
1992	Independent	Ross Perot	18.9	—	Bill Clinton (D)
1996	Reform	Ross Perot	8.4	—	Bill Clinton (D)

*Byrd received fifteen electoral votes from unpledged electors in Alabama and Mississippi.

Source: *Dave Leip's Atlas of U.S. Presidential Elections,* at **www.uselectionatlas.org**.

example. The party was founded in 1901 and lasted until 1972, when it was finally dissolved. (A smaller party later took up the name.)

Ideology has at least two functions. First, the members of the minor party regard themselves as outsiders and look to one another for support; ideology provides great psychological cohesiveness. Second, because the rewards of ideological commitment are partly psychological, these minor parties do not think in terms of immediate electoral success. A poor showing at the polls therefore does not dissuade either the leadership or the grassroots participants from continuing their quest for change in American government (and, ultimately, American society).

Currently active ideological parties include the Libertarian Party and the Green Party. As you learned in Chapter 1, the Libertarian Party supports a *laissez-faire* ("let it be") capitalist economic program, together with a hands-off policy on regulating matters of moral conduct. The Green Party began as a grassroots environmentalist organization with affiliated political parties across North America and Western Europe. It was established in the United States as a national party in 1996 and nominated Ralph Nader to run for president in 2000. Nader campaigned

Independent presidential candidate Ralph Nader (shown here) and former candidate Howard Dean debated the legitimacy of third-party campaigns in July 2004. After Dean's own bid for the presidency failed, the former governor of Vermont became the Democratic Party's leading critic of Nader's campaign. What might have happened if Dean himself had mounted a third-party effort, as some of his supporters wished? (Reuters/Molly Riley/Landov)

**TABLE 8–3 | POLICIES OF SELECTED AMERICAN
THIRD PARTIES SINCE 1864**

Populist: This pro-farmer party of the 1890s advocated progressive reforms. It also advocated replacing gold with silver as the basis of the currency in hopes of creating a mild inflation in prices. (It was believed by many that inflation would help debtors and stimulate the economy.)

Socialist: This party advocated a "cooperative commonwealth" based on government ownership of industry. It was pro-labor, often antiwar, and in later years, anti-Communist. It was dissolved in 1972 and replaced by nonparty advocacy groups (Democratic Socialists of America and Social Democrats USA).

Communist: This left-wing breakaway from the Socialists was the U.S. branch of the worldwide Communist movement. The party was pro-labor and advocated full equality for African Americans. It was also closely aligned with the Communist-led Soviet Union, which provoked great hostility among most Americans.

Progressive: This name was given to several successive splinter parties built around individual political leaders. Theodore Roosevelt, who ran in 1912, advocated federal regulation of industry to protect consumers, workers, and small businesses. Robert LaFollette, who ran in 1924, held similar viewpoints.

American Independent: Built around George Wallace, this party opposed any further promotion of civil rights and advocated a militant foreign policy. Wallace's supporters were mostly former Democrats who were soon to be Republicans.

Libertarian: This party opposes most government activity.

Reform: The Reform Party was initially built around businessman Ross Perot but later was taken over by others. Under Perot, the party was a middle-of-the-road group opposed to federal budget deficits. Under Patrick Buchanan, it came to represent right-wing nationalism and opposition to free trade.

Green: The Greens are a left-of-center pro-environmental party; they are also generally hostile to globalization.

against what he called "corporate greed," advocated universal health insurance, and promoted environmental concerns.[12] He ran again for president as an independent in 2004.

Splinter Parties

Some of the most successful minor parties have been those that split from major parties. The impetus for these **splinter parties,** or factions, has usually been a situation in which a particular personality was at odds with the major party. The most successful of these splinter parties was the Bull Moose Progressive Party, formed in 1912 to support Theodore Roosevelt for president. The Republican national convention of that year denied Roosevelt the nomination, despite the fact that he had won most of the primaries. He therefore left the Republicans and ran against Republican "regular" William Howard Taft in the general election. Although Roosevelt did not win the election, he did split the Republican vote, enabling Democrat Woodrow Wilson to become president.

Third parties have also been formed to back individual candidates who were not rebelling against a particular party. Ross Perot, for example, who challenged Republican George H. W. Bush and Democrat Bill Clinton in 1992, had not previously been active in a major party. Perot's supporters, likewise, probably would have

Splinter Party
A new party formed by a dissident faction within a major political party. Often, splinter parties have emerged when a particular personality was at odds with the major party.

---

[12]Ralph Nader offers his own entertaining account of his run for the presidency in 2000 in *Crashing the Party: How to Tell the Truth and Still Run for President* (New York: St. Martin's Press, 2002).

Theodore Roosevelt (left) served as president of the United States from 1901 to 1909 as a Republican. Later, after he was unable to secure the Republican nomination for president in 1912, Roosevelt formed a splinter group known as the Bull Moose Progressive Party. Roosevelt was ultimately unsuccessful in his bid to regain the presidency as a minor-party candidate. Does a minor-party candidate have a realistic chance of winning a presidential election today? (Library of Congress)

split their votes between Bush and Clinton had Perot not been in the race. In theory, Perot ran in 1992 as a nonparty independent; in practice, he had to create a campaign organization. By 1996, Perot's organization was formalized as the Reform Party.

The Impact of Minor Parties

Third parties have rarely been able to affect American politics by actually winning elections. (One exception is that third-party and independent candidates have occasionally won races for state governorships—for example, Jesse Ventura was elected governor of Minnesota on the Reform Party ticket in 1998.) Instead, the impact of third parties has taken two forms. First, third parties can influence one of the major parties to take up one or more issues. Second, third parties can determine the outcome of a particular election by pulling votes from one of the major-party candidates in what is called the "spoiler effect."

Influencing the Major Parties.   One of the most clear-cut examples of a major party adopting the issues of a minor party took place in 1896, when the Democratic Party took over the Populist demand for "free silver"—that is, a policy of coining enough new money to create an inflation. As you learned on pages 255 and 256, however, absorbing the Populists cost the Democrats votes overall.

Affecting the Outcome of an Election.   The presidential election of 2000 was one instance in which a minor party may have altered the outcome. Green candidate Ralph Nader received almost 100,000 votes in Florida, a majority of which would probably have gone to Democrat Al Gore if Nader had not been in the race. The real question, however, is not whether the Nader vote had an effect—clearly, it did—but whether the effect was important.

The problem is that in an election as close as the presidential election of 2000, *any* factor with an impact on the outcome can be said to have determined the results of the election. Discussing his landslide loss to Democrat Lyndon Johnson in 1964, Republican Barry Goldwater wrote, "When you've lost an election by that much, it isn't the case of whether you made the wrong speech or wore the wrong necktie. It was just the wrong time."[13] With the opposite situation, a humorist might speculate that Gore would have won the election had he worn a better tie! Nevertheless, given that Nader garnered almost three million votes nationwide, many people believe that the Nader campaign was an important reason for Gore's loss. Should voters ignore third parties to avoid spoiling the chances of a preferred major-party candidate? We discuss this question in this chapter's *Which Side Are You On?* feature.

| Mechanisms of Political Change

What does the twenty-first century hold for the Democrats and the Republicans? Support for the two major parties is roughly balanced today. In the future, could one of the two parties decisively overtake the other and become the "natural party of government"? The Republicans held this status from 1896 until 1932, and the Democrats enjoyed it for many years after the election of Franklin D. Roosevelt in 1932. Not surprisingly, political advisers in both parties dream of circumstances that could grant them lasting political hegemony, or dominance.

---

[13]Barry Goldwater, *With No Apologies* (New York: William Morrow, 1979).

WHICH SIDE ARE YOU ON? | Should Voters Ignore Third-Party Candidates?

Many people argue that if Green Party presidential candidate Ralph Nader had not run in 2000, a majority of his votes would have gone to Democrat Al Gore. In turn, Gore would have defeated Republican George W. Bush. But did Green voters "shoot themselves in the foot" by not supporting Gore, who was arguably the "greenest" major-party presidential candidate in U.S. history?

VOTERS SHOULD VOTE THEIR CONSCIENCES, REGARDLESS

Third-party advocates claim that a vote for their candidate is the only way to bring new issues into the national debate. The major-party candidates, fearful of offending any large constituency, will always blur the issues and avoid controversy. Furthermore, why should anyone assume that third-party voters would support a particular major-party candidate if the third party were not in the race? It is just as likely that these voters would stay home if no candidate represented their beliefs.

Voters should consider how close either of the two major candidates is to the positions they prefer. Gore may have been a rather green Democrat, but what if the Libertarian Party truly represents your beliefs? Bush, Gore, and 2004 Democratic candidate John Kerry were all a long way from having a libertarian philosophy.

A final point is that not all elections are close. In 2004, third-party voters in Massachusetts knew that Kerry was sure to carry his home state, and everyone knew that nothing could keep Texas from going for Bush. In these states, third-party supporters could vote for their preferred candidate secure in the knowledge that their votes would not affect the election outcome.

ACTIONS SHOULD BE JUDGED BY THEIR CONSEQUENCES

Third-party opponents argue that pure intentions may get you into heaven, but elections are a part of this world. Nader supporters cannot escape the simple truth that they helped elect Bush in 2000. Furthermore, backing the Green Party was not necessary to get environmental concerns onto the table. Gore's 1992 book, *Earth in the Balance: Ecology and the Human Spirit,** was so controversial that it may have done his campaign as much damage as Nader was able to inflict. Instead of

*Albert Gore, Jr., *Earth in the Balance: Ecology and the Human Spirit* (1992; repr., New York: Houghton Mifflin Co., 2000).

In February 2004, a Nader supporter exchanged harsh words with a demonstrator who wanted Nader to stay out of the 2004 presidential race. Later that year, Nader failed to win the nomination of the Green Party but continued to run as an independent. What effect, if any, could Nader's failure to win the nomination have had on those who were considering whether to support him? (Reuters/Jonathan Ernst/Landov)

getting Gore, the Greens got Bush, who wanted to open new federally owned lands for logging and oil drilling, who opposed many steps to address global warming, and who sought to roll back some pollution-control standards for the benefit of industry.

WHAT'S YOUR POSITION?

Should voters support a third-party candidate even if they prefer one of the major-party candidates to the other? What considerations should such a voter take into account?

GOING ONLINE

Anyone who is contemplating a vote for a third party should first learn what that party believes. Visiting the party's Web site is a good place to begin. You can find the Green Party at www.gp.org and the Libertarian Party at www.lp.org. You can find a comprehensive list of parties and partylike organizations at www.politics1.com/parties.htm.

Realignment

Realignment
A process in which a substantial group of voters switches party allegiance, producing a long-term change in the political landscape.

One mechanism by which a party might gain dominance is called realignment. In this process, major constituencies shift their allegiance from one party to another, creating a long-term alteration in the political environment. Realignment has often been associated with particular elections, called *realigning elections*. The election of 1896, which established a Republican ascendancy, was clearly a realigning election. So was the election of 1932, which made the Democrats the leading party.

Realignment: The Myth of Dominance. A number of myths have grown up around the concept of realignment. One is that in realignment, a newly dominant party must replace the previously dominant party. Actually, realignment could easily strengthen an already dominant party. Alternatively, realignment could result in a tie. This has happened—twice. One example was the realignment of the 1850s, which resulted in Abraham Lincoln's election as president in 1860. After the Civil War, the Republicans and the Democrats were almost evenly matched nationally.

The most recent realignment—which also resulted in two closely matched parties—has sometimes been linked to the elections of 1968. Actually, the realignment was a gradual process that took place over many years. In 1968, Democrat Hubert Humphrey, Republican Richard Nixon, and third-party candidate George Wallace of Alabama all vied for the presidency. Following the Republican victory in that election, Nixon adopted a "southern strategy" aimed at drawing dissatisfied southern Democrats into the Republican Party.[14] At the presidential level, the strategy was an immediate success, although years would pass before the Republicans could gain dominance in the South's delegation to Congress or in state legislatures. Nixon's southern strategy helped create the political environment in which we live today. Another milestone in the progress of the Republicans was Ronald Reagan's sweeping victory in the presidential election of 1980.

Realignment: The Myth of Predictability. A second myth concerning realignments is that they take place, like clockwork, every thirty-six years. Supposedly, there were realigning elections in 1860, 1896, 1932, and 1968, and therefore 2004 must have been a year for realignment. No such event appears to have taken place. In fact, there is no force that could cause political realignments at precise thirty-six-year intervals. Further, as we observed earlier in this section, realignments are not always tied to particular elections. The most recent realignment, in which conservative southern Democrats became conservative southern Republicans, was not closely linked to a particular election. The realignment of the 1850s, following the creation of the modern Republican Party, also took place over a number of years.

Is Realignment Still Possible? The nature of American political parties created the pattern of realignment in American history. The sheer size of the country, combined with the inexorable pressure toward a two-party system, resulted in parties made up of voters with conflicting interests or values. The pre–Civil War party system involved two parties—Whigs and Democrats—with support in both the North and the South. This system could survive only by burying, as deeply as possible, the issue of slavery. We should not be surprised that the structure eventually collapsed. The Republican ascendancy of 1896–1932 united capitalists and industrial workers under the Republican banner, despite serious economic conflicts between the two. The New Deal Democratic coalition after 1932 brought African Americans and ardent segregationists into the same party.

For realignment to occur, a substantial body of citizens must come to believe that their party can no longer represent their interests or values. The problem must be

---

[14]The classic work on Nixon's southern strategy is Kirkpatrick Sales, *The Emerging Republican Majority* (New Rochelle, N.Y.: Arlington House, 1969).

fundamental and not attributable to the behavior of an individual politician. It is not easy to identify groups of Republicans or Democrats today who might reach such a conclusion. Despite the confusion that the major parties sometimes display on policy matters, the values that unite each party are relatively coherent, and their constituents are reasonably compatible. Therefore, the current party system should be more stable than in the past, and a major realignment is not likely to take place in the foreseeable future.

Dealignment

Among political scientists, one common argument has been that realignment is no longer likely because voters are not as committed to the two major parties as they were in the 1800s and early 1900s. In this view, called dealignment theory, large numbers of independent voters may result in political volatility, but the absence of strong partisan attachments means that it is no longer easy to "lock in" political preferences for decades.

Dealignment
A decline in party loyalties that reduces long-term party commitment.

Independent Voters. Figure 8–4 shows trends in party identification, as measured by standard polling techniques from 1937 to the present. The chart displays a rise in the number of independent voters throughout the period combined with a fall in support for the Democrats from the mid-1960s on. The decline in Democratic identification may be due to the consolidation of Republican support in the South since 1968, a process that by now may be substantially complete. In any event, the traditional Democratic advantage in party identification has vanished.

Party Identification
Linking oneself to a particular political party.

Not only has the number of independents grown over the last half-century, but voters are also less willing to vote a straight ticket—that is, to vote for all the candidates of one party. In the early 1900s, straight-ticket voting was nearly universal. By midcentury, 12 percent of voters engaged in ticket splitting. In recent presidential elections, between 20 and 40 percent of the voters engaged in split-ticket voting. This trend, along with the increase in the number of voters who call themselves independents, suggests that parties have lost much of their hold on the loyalty of the voters.

Straight-Ticket Voting
Voting exclusively for the candidates of one party.

FIGURE 8–4 | PARTY IDENTIFICATION FROM 1937 TO THE PRESENT

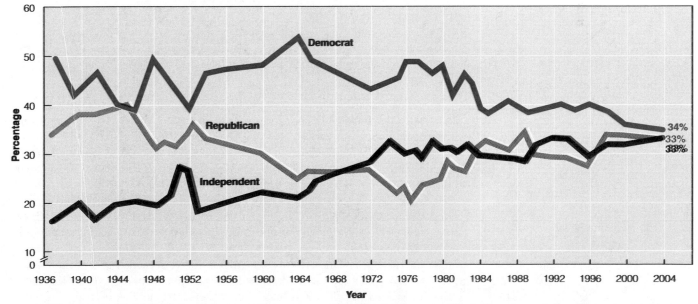

Sources: *Gallup Report*, August 1995; *New York Times*/CBS poll, June 1996; *Gallup Report*, February 1998; The Pew Research Center for the People and the Press, November 2003; and authors' update.

Swing Voters
Voters who frequently swing their support from one party to another.

Not-So-Independent Voters. A problem with dealignment theory is that many "independent" voters are not all that independent. Polling organizations estimate that of the 33 percent of voters who identify themselves as independents, 11 percent vote as if they were Democrats in almost all elections, and 12 percent vote as if they were Republicans. If these "leaners" are deducted from the independent category, only 10 percent of the voters remain. These true independents are swing voters—they can swing back and forth between the parties. These voters are important in deciding elections. Some analysts believe, however, that swing voters are far less numerous today than they were two or three decades ago.

Tipping

Realignment is not the only mechanism that can alter the political landscape. Political transformation can also result from changes in the composition of the electorate. Even when groups of voters never change their party preferences, if one group becomes more numerous over time, it can become dominant for that reason alone. We call this kind of demographically based change tipping. Immigration is one cause of this phenomenon.

Tipping
A phenomenon that occurs when a group that is becoming more numerous over time grows large enough to change the political balance in a district, state, or country.

Tipping in Massachusetts. Consider Massachusetts, where for generations Irish Catholics confronted Protestant Yankees in the political arena. Most of the Yankees were Republican; most of the Irish were Democrats. The Yankees were numerically dominant from the founding of the state until 1928. In that year, for the first time, Democratic Irish voters came to outnumber the Republican Yankees. Massachusetts, which previously had been one of the most solidly Republican states, cast its presidential vote for Democrat Al Smith. Within a few years, Massachusetts became one of the most reliably Democratic states in the nation.

Tipping in California? California may have experienced a tipping effect during the 1990s. From 1952 until 1992, California consistently supported Republican presidential candidates, turning Democratic only in the landslide election of Lyndon Johnson in 1964. In 1992, however, the California electorate gave Democrat Bill Clinton a larger percentage of its votes than he received in the country as a whole. Since then, no Republican presidential candidate has managed to carry California.

The improved performance of the Democrats in California is almost certainly a function of demography. In 1999, California became the third state, after Hawaii and New Mexico, in which non-Hispanic whites do *not* make up a majority of the population. Hispanics and African Americans both give most of their votes to the Democrats. Even before 1999, these groups were numerous enough to tip California into the Democratic column.

On to the Future

Some speculation about the future is reasonable, as long as we remember that unexpected events can make any prediction obsolete. We can anticipate that party advocates will continue to hope that events will propel their party into a dominant position. Either party could lose substantial support if it were identified with a major economic disaster. Noneconomic events could have an impact as well.

Republican strategists will seek to encourage substantial numbers of voters to abandon the Democrats, perhaps on the basis of cultural issues. Some of these strategists believe that the relative conservatism of Hispanic Americans on cultural matters may provide an opening for the Republicans. Others point to the increasing numbers of Americans with investments in the stock market as a possible indicator of growing economic conservatism. Finally, Republicans look at the decline in Democratic Party identification since the 1960s (see Figure 8–4 on page 279) and project that trend into the future.

Democratic strategists hope that the tolerant spirit of many younger voters (in attitudes toward gay rights, for example) may work to their advantage. Hispanic voters are of interest to the Democrats as well. Demographic changes have turned once reliably Republican states such as Florida into swing states that can decide national elections. As noted in Chapter 1, some time after 2015, Texas—now among the most Republican states—will no longer have a non-Hispanic white majority. If the Republicans do not succeed in detaching Hispanics from the Democratic Party, Texas could eventually tip into the Democratic column and possibly tip the country as a whole to the Democrats as well.

MAKING A DIFFERENCE | Electing Convention Delegates

The most exciting political party event, staged every four years, is the national convention. State conventions also take place on a regular basis. Surprising as it might seem, there are opportunities for the individual voter to become involved in nominating delegates to a state or national convention or to become a delegate.

Why Should You Care?

How would you like to exercise a small amount of real political power yourself—power that goes beyond simply voting in an election? You might be able to become a delegate to a county, district, or even state party convention. Many of these conventions nominate candidates for various offices. For example, in Michigan, the state party conventions nominate the candidates for the Board of Regents of the state's three top public universities. The regents set university policies, so these are nominations in which students have an obvious interest. In Michigan, if you are elected as a party precinct delegate, you can attend your party's state convention.

In much of the country, there are more openings for district level delegates than there are people willing to serve. In such circumstances, almost anyone can become a delegate by collecting a handful of signatures on a nominating petition or by mounting a small-scale write-in campaign. You are then eligible to take part in one

of the most educational political experiences available to an ordinary citizen. You will get a firsthand look at how political persuasion takes place, how resolutions are written and passed, and how candidates seek out support among their fellow party members. In some states, party caucuses bring debate even closer to the grassroots level.

What Can You Do?

When the parties choose delegates for the national convention, the process begins at the local level—either the congressional district or the state legislative district. Delegates may be elected in party primary elections or chosen in neighborhood or precinct caucuses.

If the delegates are elected in a primary, persons who want to run for these positions must first file petitions with the board of elections. If you are interested in committing yourself to a particular presidential candidate and running for the delegate position, check with the local county committee or with the party's national committee about the rules you must follow.

It is even easier to get involved in the grassroots politics of presidential caucuses. In some states—Iowa being the earliest and most famous example—delegates are first nominated at the local precinct caucus. According to the rules of the Iowa caucuses, anyone can participate in a caucus if he or she is eighteen years old, a resident of

the precinct, and registered as a party member. These caucuses, in addition to being the focus of national media attention in January or February, select delegates to the county conventions who are pledged to specific presidential candidates. This is the first step toward the national convention.

At both the county caucus and the convention levels, both parties try to find younger members to fill some of the seats. Contact the state or county political party to find out when the caucuses or primaries will be held. Then gather local supporters and friends, and prepare to join in an occasion during which political debate is at its best.

For further information about these opportunities (some states hold caucuses and state conventions in every election year), contact the state party office or your local state legislator for specific dates and regulations. You can also write to the national committee for information on how to become a delegate.

Republican National Committee
Republican National Headquarters
310 First St. S.E.
Washington, DC 20003
202-863-8500
www.rnc.org

Democratic National Committee
Democratic National Headquarters
430 Capital St. S.E.
Washington, DC 20003
202-863-8000
www.democrats.org/index.html

Key Terms

dealignment 279	party identification 279	Republican Party 255	tipping 280
Democratic Party 254	party-in-government 264	reverse-income effect 263	two-party system 253
divided government 269	party-in-the-electorate 263	safe seat 270	unit rule 267
electoral college 271	party organization 263	splinter party 275	Whig Party 254
era of good feelings 254	party platform 264	state central committee 267	
faction 251	patronage 267	straight-ticket voting 279	
independent 251	plurality 271	swing voters 280	
national committee 266	political party 251	third party 272	
national convention 264	realignment 278	ticket splitting 269	

Chapter Summary

1 A political party is a group of political activists who organize to win elections, operate the government, and determine public policy. Political parties recruit candidates for public office, organize and run elections, present alternative policies to the voters, assume responsibility for operating the government, and act as the opposition to the party in power.

2 The evolution of our nation's political parties can be divided into seven periods: (a) the creation and formation of political parties from 1789 to 1816; (b) the era of one-party rule, or personal politics, from 1816 to 1828; (c) the period from Andrew Jackson's presidency to the Civil War, from 1828 to 1860; (d) the Civil War and post–Civil War period, from 1860 to 1896; (e) the Republican ascendancy and progressive period, from 1896 to 1932; (f) the New Deal period, from 1932 to about 1968; and (g) the modern period, from approximately 1968 to the present.

3 Many of the differences between the two parties date from the time of Franklin D. Roosevelt's New Deal. The Democrats have advocated government action to help labor and minorities, and the Republicans have championed self-reliance and limited government. The constituents of the two parties continue to differ. A close look at policies actually enacted in recent years, however, suggests that despite rhetoric to the contrary, both parties are committed to a large and active government. Today, cultural differences are at least as important as economic issues in determining party allegiance.

4 A political party consists of three components: the party-in-the-electorate, the party organization, and the party-in-government. Each party component maintains linkages to the others to keep the party strong. Each level of the party— local, state, and national—has considerable autonomy. The national party organization is responsible for holding the national convention in presidential election years, writing the party platform, choosing the national committee, and conducting party business.

5 The party-in-government comprises all of the elected and appointed officeholders of a party. The linkage of party members is crucial to building support for programs among the branches and levels of government.

6 Two major parties have dominated the political landscape in the United States for almost two centuries. The reasons for this include (a) the historical foundations of the system, (b) political socialization and practical considerations, (c) the winner-take-all electoral system, and (d) state and federal laws favoring the two-party system. For these reasons, minor parties have found it extremely difficult to win elections.

7 Minor, or third, parties have emerged from time to time, sometimes as dissatisfied splinter groups from within major parties, and have acted as barometers of changes in the political mood. Splinter parties have emerged when a particular personality was at odds with the major party, as when Theodore Roosevelt's differences with the Republican Party resulted in the formation of the Bull Moose Progressive Party. Other minor parties, such as the Socialist Party, have formed around specific issues or ideologies. Third parties can affect the political process (even if they do not win) if major parties adopt their issues or if they determine which major party wins an election.

8 One mechanism of political change is realignment, in which major blocs of voters switch allegiance from one party to another. Realignments were manifested in the elections of 1896 and 1932. Realignment need not leave one party dominant—it can result in two parties of roughly equal strength. Some scholars speak of dealignment—that is, the loss of strong party attachments. In fact, the share of the voters who describe themselves as independents has grown since the 1930s, and the share of self-identified Democrats has shrunk since the 1960s. Many independents actually vote as if they were Democrats or Republicans, however. Demographic change can also "tip" a district or state from one party to another.

Selected Print and Media Resources

SUGGESTED READINGS

Black, Earl, and Merle Black. *The Rise of Southern Republicans*. Cambridge, Mass.: Belknap Press, 2003. This book analyzes the shift in politics in the southern states over the last four decades.

Frank, Thomas. *What's the Matter with Kansas?: How Conservatives Won the Heart of America*. New York: Henry Holt & Company, 2005. This book looks at how the Republican Party gained its current dominance in the American heartland. The author examines why so many Americans vote against their own economic interests.

Gould, Lewis. *Grand Old Party: A History of the Republicans*. New York: Random House, 2003. A companion volume to the history of the Democrats by Jules Witcover, listed below. Gould provides a sweeping history of the Republican Party from its origins as an antislavery coalition to the present. A major theme of the work is the evolution of the Republicans from a party of active government to the more conservative party that it is today.

Green, John C., and Paul S. Hernson, eds. *Responsible Partisanship: The Evolution of American Political Parties since 1950*. Lawrence: University Press of Kansas, 2003. This collection of scholarly essays explores the roles and functions of political parties, both as parties-in-the-electorate and as parties-in-government.

McAuliffe, Terry. *What a Party!: My Life among Democrats*. New York: St. Martin's Press, 2007. The former chairman of the Democratic National Committee discusses his years of experience on the inside of a major political party.

Nader, Ralph. *Crashing the Party: How to Tell the Truth and Still Run for President*. New York: St. Martin's Press, 2002. This is Nader's own entertaining and detailed account of his run for the presidency as a Green in 2000.

Sager, Ryan. *The Elephant in the Room: Evangelicals, Libertarians, and the Battle to Control the Republican Party*. New York: Wiley, 2006. The author describes the current coalition of subgroups within the Republican Party and predicts an eventual splintering as the individual groups struggle for greater power within the party.

Witcover, Jules. *Party of the People: A History of the Democrats*. New York: Random House, 2003. A companion volume to the history of the Republicans by Lewis Gould, listed above. Witcover describes the transformation of the Democrats from a party of limited government to a party of national authority, but he also finds a common thread that connects modern Democrats to the past—a belief in social and economic justice.

MEDIA RESOURCES

The American President—A 1995 film starring Michael Douglas as a president who must balance partisanship and friendship (Republicans in Congress promise to approve the president's crime bill only if he modifies an environmental plan sponsored by his liberal girlfriend).

The Best Man—A 1964 drama based on Gore Vidal's play of the same name. The film, which deals with political smear campaigns by presidential party nominees, focuses on political party power and ethics.

The Last Hurrah—A classic 1958 political film starring Spencer Tracy as a corrupt politician who seeks his fifth nomination for mayor of a city in New England.

A Third Choice—A film that examines America's experience with third parties and independent candidates throughout the nation's political history.

E-MOCRACY | Political Parties and the Internet

Today's political parties use the Internet to attract voters, organize campaigns, obtain campaign contributions, and the like. Voters, in turn, can go online to learn more about specific parties and their programs. Those who use the Internet for information on the parties, though, need to exercise some caution. Besides the parties' official sites, there are satirical sites mimicking the parties, sites distributing misleading information about the parties, and sites that are raising money for their own causes rather than for political parties.

Logging On

The political parties all have Web sites. The Democratic Party is online at

www.democrats.org

The Republican National Committee is at

www.rnc.org

The Libertarian Party has a Web site located at

www.lp.org

The Green Party of the United States can be found at

www.gp.org

Politics1.com offers extensive information on U.S. political parties, including the major parties and fifty minor parties. Go to

www.politics1.com/parties.htm

The Pew Research Center for the People and the Press offers survey data online on how the parties fared during the most recent elections, voter typology, and numerous other issues. To access this site, go to

people-press.org

Online Review

At **www.politicalscience.wadsworth.com/ schmidt12**, you will find a free Study Guide to this book. For each chapter, there are two online quizzes to help you master the material.

• The PoliPrep Self-Study Assessment provides a pretest for each major section of the chapter. PoliPrep then generates a customized study plan. After you complete the study plan, a posttest evaluates your progress.

• The Tutorial Quiz for each chapter provides questions on the chapter contents, including the features. The questions are organized to match the major sections of the chapter.

What If . . .
Spending Limits Were Placed on Campaigns?

BACKGROUND

In the 2004 presidential elections, the Republican and Democratic nominees each received almost $75 million in government funding for the general election. In addition, President George W. Bush collected $367 million in contributions prior to the election, and Democrat John Kerry took in $326 million. The 2004 elections were the most expensive presidential elections ever, and two years later the 2006 congressional elections also saw contributions hit all-time highs. By midsummer of that year, more than $42 million had been raised for the New York Senate race alone. By the same date, lawyers and law firms had already made campaign contributions of $70 million, most of which went to support Democratic candidates. Finally, retired Americans and real estate agents had ponied up more than $100 million to support primarily Republican candidates.

WHAT IF SPENDING LIMITS WERE PLACED ON CAMPAIGNS?

Given the federal government's expanding role in our economy and society, more is at stake in every election, particularly at the federal level. It is not surprising, then, that elections are becoming more expensive. After all, in the business world, if there is an opportunity for higher profits, more competitors will invest in that area in an attempt to attain those higher profits. So, too, those affected by the federal government's policies have an incentive to "invest" in politicians by making campaign contributions.

A limit on campaign spending could therefore be counter to the natural tendencies of those concerned with the political process. One thing that would happen with such a restriction would be a decline in the number of candidates with "deep pockets." In other words, fewer of the very rich would attempt to run for office because they would not be able to use their personal wealth in the effort to win.

A limit on campaign spending would also mean a limit on campaign contributions. Consequently, special interest groups and lobbying organizations would necessarily diminish in numbers. The lobbying industry would shrink because one of the best ways to influence legislation is to make sure that the candidate of choice is elected or reelected. Contributions are certainly helpful in winning elections.

THE IMPACT ON TELEVISION

The television industry would also be affected. Just as the bulk of the public's entertainment time is spent on television, so too is the bulk of campaign spending. Consider that in just the last week of the presidential campaigns in 2004, the two candidates spent more than $40 million on TV ads. By Election Day of that year, the two political parties had spent more than $400 million on television (and radio) ads. A limit on total campaign spending would, by necessity, dramatically reduce spending on television advertising. Consequently,

the fortunes of media companies would probably be impaired every election year. That would also mean that commercial advertisers would face less competition during September and October in election years, so the prices for advertising slots for commercial products and services would be lower.

It is possible, though, that overall television spending might not decline that much. Although fewer explicitly political TV ads would be aired due to campaign spending limits, more subtle forms of "advertising" might occur. For example, rich candidates might produce their own television shows aimed at informing the public about specific campaign issues, all the while attempting to appear unbiased. We might therefore see a slew of new types of political television programming. (Whether anyone would watch these shows is another matter.)

WE HAVE ALREADY ATTEMPTED TO REFORM CAMPAIGNS

Complaints about "excessive" campaign

spending are not new. Even sitting politicians have attempted to "clean up" elections. The Bipartisan Campaign Reform Act of 2002 was one such attempt. The law became effective in January 2003. This law prohibited, among other things, so-called soft money contributions and expenditures that were clearly being used to influence federal elections. It also banned supposedly nonpartisan "issue ads" that were funded by corporations and labor unions. Such ads cannot appear thirty days prior to a primary election or sixty days before a general election. As we saw earlier, however, campaign spending overall has increased dramatically since the act became effective.

FOR CRITICAL ANALYSIS

1. Why would it be extremely difficult to effectively limit campaign spending?
2. If campaign spending limits were effective, who would be hurt more—those politicians already in office or those attempting to win an election for the first time? Explain your answer.

Free elections are the cornerstone of the American political system. Voters choose one candidate over another to hold political office by casting ballots in local, state, and federal elections. In 2004, the voters chose George W. Bush and Dick Cheney to be president and vice president of the United States for the next four years. In addition, voters elected all of the members of the House of Representatives and one-third of the members of the Senate. The campaigns were bitter, long, and extremely expensive. The total cost for all federal elections in the 2003–2004 cycle was well into the billions of dollars.

Voters and candidates frequently criticize the American electoral process. It is said to favor wealthier candidates, to further the aims of special interest groups, and to be dominated by older voters and those with better education and higher incomes. Recent reforms of the campaign-finance laws were tested for the first time in 2004. Although the new laws had some effect on campaign strategy, fund-raising outside the system and extensive use of television advertising dominated the election season. During the congressional campaigns in 2006, television advertising continued to dominate. Some have argued in favor of strict limits on campaign spending, a topic we discussed in the *What If . . .* feature that opened this chapter.

Who Wants to Be a Candidate?

For an election to be competitive, there must be more than one strong candidate seeking office. If there is only one candidate for any office, the election may be regarded as undemocratic. Who, then, are the people who seek to run for office?

There are thousands of elective offices in the United States. The political parties strive to provide a slate of candidates for every election. Recruiting candidates is easier for some offices than for others. Political parties may have difficulty finding candidates for the board of the local water control district, but they generally have a sufficient number of candidates for county commissioner or sheriff. The "higher" the office and the more prestige attached to it, the more candidates are likely to want to run. In many areas of the country, however, one political party may be considerably stronger than the other. In those situations, the minority party may have more difficulty finding nominees for elections in which victory is unlikely.

The presidential campaign provides the most colorful and exciting look at candidates and how they prepare to compete for office—in this instance, the highest office in the land. The men and women who wanted to be candidates in the 2004 presidential campaign faced a long and obstacle-filled path. First, they needed to raise sufficient funds to tour the nation, particularly the states with early presidential primaries, to see if they had enough local supporters. They needed funds to create an organization, to devise a plan to win primary votes, and to win the party's nomination at the national convention. Finally, they required funds to finance a successful campaign for president. Always, at every turn, there was the question of whether they would have enough funds to wage a campaign.

Presidential Primary
A statewide primary election of delegates to a political party's national convention, held to determine a party's presidential nominee.

Why They Run

People who choose to run for office can be divided into two groups—the "self-starters" and those who are recruited. The volunteers, or self-starters, get involved in political activities to further their careers, to carry out specific political programs, or in response to certain issues or events. Ralph Nader's campaigns for the presidency in 2000 and 2004 were rooted in his belief that the two major parties were ignoring vital issues, such as environmental protection and the influence of corporate wealth on American politics. Howard Dean's primary campaign in 2004 stemmed from his desire to get Americans, especially young voters, engaged in politics.

Issues are important, but self-interest and personal goals—status, career objectives, prestige, and income—are central in motivating some candidates to enter political life. Political office is often seen as the stepping-stone to achieving certain career goals. A lawyer or an insurance agent may run for office only once or twice and then return to private life with enhanced status. Other politicians may aspire to long-term political office—for example, county offices such as commissioner or sheriff sometimes offer attractive opportunities for power, status, and income and are in themselves career goals. Finally, we think of ambition as the desire for ever more important

The top row shows a sampling of Senate Republican incumbents who lost to Democratic challengers in 2006. The bottom row shows Senate Democratic incumbents who faced Republican challengers in 2006 yet won reelection. Generally, how do you explain the Democrats' success in the 2006 congressional races? (Photos Courtesy of the candidates' campaign organizations)

2006 SENATE REPUBLICAN INCUMBENTS IN RACES WITH DEMOCRATIC CHALLENGERS

2006 SENATE DEMOCRATIC INCUMBENTS IN RACES WITH REPUBLICAN CHALLENGERS

offices and higher status. Politicians who run for lower offices and then set their sights on Congress or a governorship may be said to have "progressive" ambitions.[1]

The Nomination Process

Individuals become official candidates through the process of nomination. Generally, nominating processes for all offices are controlled by state laws and usually favor the two major political parties. For most minor offices, individuals become candidates by submitting petitions to the local election board. Political parties may help individuals obtain the petitions, pay whatever filing fee is required, and gather signatures. In most states, a candidate from one of the two major parties faces far fewer requirements to get on the ballot than a candidate who is an independent or who represents a minor or new party.

The American system of nominations and primary elections is one of the most complex in the world. In a majority of European nations, the political party's choice of candidates is final, and no primary elections are ever held.

Who Is Eligible?

There are few constitutional restrictions on who can become a candidate in the United States. As set out in the Constitution, the formal requirements for national office are as follows:

1. *President.* Must be a natural-born citizen, have attained the age of thirty-five years, and be a resident of the country for fourteen years by the time of inauguration.
2. *Vice president.* Must be a natural-born citizen, have attained the age of thirty-five years, and not be a resident of the same state as the candidate for president.[2]
3. *Senator.* Must be a citizen for at least nine years, have attained the age of thirty by the time of taking office, and be a resident of the state from which elected.
4. *Representative.* Must be a citizen for at least seven years, have attained the age of twenty-five by the time of taking office, and be a resident of the state from which elected.

The qualifications for state legislators are set by the state constitutions and likewise include age, place of residence, and citizenship. (Usually, the requirements for the upper chamber of a legislature are somewhat more stringent than those for the lower chamber.) The legal qualifications for running for governor or other state office are similar.

Who Runs?

In spite of these minimal legal qualifications for office at both the national and state levels, a quick look at the slate of candidates in any election—or at the current members of the U.S. House of Representatives—will reveal that not all segments of the population take advantage of these opportunities. Holders of political office in the United States are overwhelmingly white and male. Until the twentieth century, presidential candidates were of northern European origin and of Protestant heritage.[3] Laws that effectively denied voting rights made it impossible to elect African American public officials in many areas in which African Americans constituted a

---

[1]See the discussion of this topic in Linda Fowler, *Candidates, Congress, and the American Democracy* (Ann Arbor: University of Michigan Press, 1993), pp. 56–59.
[2]Technically, a presidential and vice-presidential candidate can be from the same state, but if they are, one of the two must forfeit the electoral votes of their home state.
[3]A number of early presidents were Unitarian. The Unitarian Church is not Protestant, but it is historically rooted in the Protestant tradition.

Hillary Rodham Clinton succeeded in winning one of New York State's seats in the U.S. Senate in 2000, even though she had been a resident of that state for a relatively short time. When she won reelection in 2006, she appeared to be a possible front-runner for the Democratic nomination for the presidency in 2008. What barriers does a female candidate face in attaining the presidency? (Photo Courtesy of Senator Clinton)

significant portion of the population. As a result of the passage of major civil rights legislation in the 1960s, however, the number of African American public officials has increased throughout the United States.

Women as Candidates.   Until recently, women generally were considered to be appropriate candidates only for lower-level offices, such as state legislator or school board member. The last twenty years have seen a tremendous increase in the number of women who run for office, not only at the state level but for the U.S. Congress as well. Figure 9–1 shows the increase in female candidates. In 2006, 151 women ran for Congress, and 78 were elected. Women were not recruited in the past because they had not worked their way up through the party organization or because they were thought to have no chance of winning. Women also had a more difficult time raising campaign funds. Today, it is clear that women are just as likely as men to participate in many political activities, and a majority of Americans say they would vote for a qualified woman for president of the United States.

Lawyers as Candidates.   Candidates are likely to be professionals, particularly lawyers. Political campaigning and officeholding are simply easier for some occupational groups than for others, and political involvement can make a valuable contribution to certain careers. Lawyers, for example, have more flexible schedules than do many other professionals, can take time off for campaigning, and can leave their jobs to hold public office full-time. Furthermore, holding political office is good publicity for their professional practice, and they usually have partners or associates to keep the firm going while they are in office. Perhaps most important, many jobs that lawyers aspire to—federal or state judgeships, state attorney offices, or work in a federal agency—can be attained by political appointment. Such appointments often go to loyal partisans who have served their party by running for and holding office. For certain groups, then, participation in the political arena may further personal ambitions, whereas it could be a sacrifice for others whose careers demand full-time attention for many years.

The Twenty-First-Century Campaign

After the candidates have been nominated, the most exhausting and expensive part of the election process begins—the general election campaign. The contemporary political campaign is becoming more complex and more sophisticated with every election. Even with the most appealing of candidates, today's campaigns require a strong organization; expertise in political polling and marketing; professional assistance in fund-raising, accounting, and financial management; and technological capabilities in every aspect of the campaign.

The Changing Campaign

The goal is the same for all campaigns—to convince voters to choose a candidate or a slate of candidates for office. Part of the reason for the increased intensity of campaigns in the last decade is that they are now centered on the candidate, not on the party. The candidate-centered campaign emerged in response to several developments: changes in the electoral system, the increased importance of television in campaigns, technological innovations such as computers, and the increased cost of campaigning.

FIGURE 9–1 | WOMEN RUNNING FOR CONGRESS (AND WINNING)

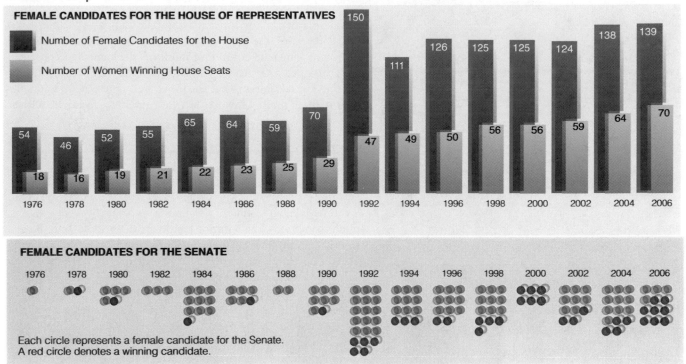

To run a successful and persuasive campaign, the candidate's organization must be able to raise funds for the effort, obtain coverage from the media, produce and pay for political commercials and advertising, schedule the candidate's time effectively, convey the candidate's position on the issues to the voters, conduct research on the opposing candidate, and get the voters to go to the polls. When party identification was stronger among voters and before the advent of television campaigning, a strong party organization at the local, state, or national level could furnish most of the services and expertise that the candidate needed. Political parties provided the funds for campaigning until the 1970s. Parties used their precinct organizations to distribute literature, register voters, and get out the vote on election day. Less effort was spent on advertising each candidate's positions and character, because the party label presumably communicated that information to many voters.

One of the reasons that campaigns no longer depend on parties is that fewer people identify with them (see Chapter 8), as is evident from the increased number of political independents. In 1952, about one-fifth of adults identified themselves as independents, whereas in 2006, about one-third considered themselves independents. Political independents include not only adults who are well educated and issue oriented but also many individuals who are not very interested in politics or well informed about candidates or issues.

The Professional Campaign

Whether the candidate is running for the state legislature, for the governor's office, for the U.S. Congress, or for the presidency, every campaign has some fundamental tasks to accomplish. Today, in national elections, the lion's share of these tasks is handled by paid professionals rather than volunteers or amateur politicians.

The most sought-after and possibly the most criticized campaign expert is the political consultant, who, for a large fee, devises a campaign strategy, thinks up a

Political Consultant
A paid professional hired to devise a campaign strategy and manage a campaign.

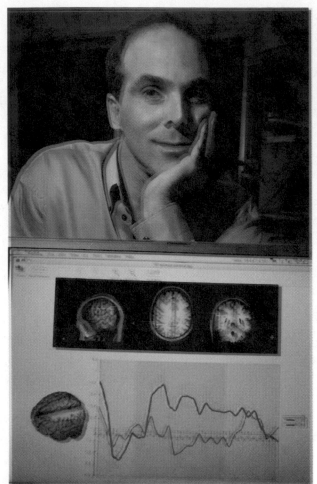

This researcher at UCLA believes that magnetic resonance imaging (MRI) can be used to judge the effectiveness of political ads on television. The graph he shows in this photo is the average of responses of Republicans (red line) and Democrats (blue line) as they watched a pro–George W. Bush video. Clearly, the Republican viewers demonstrated a more positive response than did the Democrats. Why might political consultants be interested in such research? (AP Photo/Reed Saxon)

| **Tracking Poll**
A poll taken for the candidate on a nearly daily basis as election day approaches.

campaign theme, oversees the advertising, and possibly chooses the campaign colors and the candidate's official portrait. Political consultants began to displace volunteer campaign managers in the 1960s, about the same time that television became a force in campaigns. The paid consultant monitors the campaign's progress, plans all media appearances, and coaches the candidate for debates. The consultants and the firms they represent are not politically neutral; most will work only for candidates from one party.

The Strategy of Winning

In the United States, unlike some European countries, there are no rewards for a candidate who comes in second; the winner takes all. A winner-take-all system is also known as a *plurality voting system*. In most situations, the winning candidate does not have to have a majority of the votes. If there are three candidates, the one who gets the most votes wins—that is, "takes it all"—and the other two candidates get nothing. Given this system, the campaign organization must plan a strategy that maximizes the candidate's chances of winning. In American politics, candidates seek to capture all the votes of their party's supporters, to convince a majority of the independent voters to vote for them, and to gain a few votes from supporters of the other party. To accomplish these goals, candidates must consider their visibility, their message, and their campaign strategy.

Candidate Visibility and Appeal

One of the most important concerns is how well known the candidate is. If she or he is a highly visible incumbent, there may be little need for campaigning except to remind the voters of the officeholder's good deeds. If, however, the candidate is an unknown challenger or a largely unfamiliar character attacking a well-known public figure, the campaign must devise a strategy to get the candidate before the public.

In the case of the independent candidate or the candidate representing a minor party, the problem of name recognition is serious. Such candidates must present an overwhelming case for the voter to reject the major-party candidates. Both Democratic and Republican candidates use the strategic ploy of labeling third-party candidates as "not serious" and therefore not worth the voter's time.

The Use of Opinion Polls

Opinion polls are a major source of information for both the media and the candidates. Poll taking is widespread during the primaries. Presidential hopefuls have private polls taken to make sure that there is at least some chance they could be nominated and, if nominated, elected. During the presidential campaign itself, polling is even more frequent. Polls are taken not only by the regular pollsters—Roper, Harris, Gallup, and others—but also privately by each candidate's campaign organization. These private polls are for the exclusive and secret use of the candidate and his or her campaign organization. As the election approaches, many candidates use **tracking polls,** which are polls taken almost every day, to find out how well they are competing for votes. Tracking polls enable consultants to fine-tune the advertising and the candidate's speeches in the last days of the campaign.

Focus Groups

Another tactic is to use a **focus group** to gain insights into public perceptions of the candidate. Professional consultants organize a discussion of the candidate or of certain political issues among ten to fifteen ordinary citizens. The citizens are selected from specific target groups in the population—for example, working women, blue-collar men, senior citizens, or young voters. Recent campaigns have tried to reach groups such as "soccer moms," "Wal-Mart shoppers," or "NASCAR dads."[4] The group discusses personality traits of the candidate, political advertising, and other candidate-related issues. The conversation is digitally video recorded (and often observed from behind a mirrored wall). Focus groups are expected to reveal more emotional responses to candidates or the deeper anxieties of voters—feelings that consultants believe often are not tapped by more impersonal telephone surveys. The campaign then can shape its messages to respond to these feelings and perceptions.

Financing the Campaign

In a book published in 1932 entitled *Money in Elections*, Louise Overacker had the following to say about campaign financing:

> The financing of elections in a democracy is a problem which is arousing increasing concern. Many are beginning to wonder if present-day methods of raising and spending campaign funds do not clog the wheels of our elaborately constructed mechanism of popular control, and if democracies do not inevitably become [governments ruled by small groups].[5]

Although writing more than seventy years ago, Overacker touched on a sensitive issue in American political campaigns—the connection between money and elections. More than $3.5 billion was spent at all levels of campaigning during the 2003–2004 election cycle. Total spending by the presidential candidates in 2004 amounted to about $750 million. For the midterm senatorial election in 2006 in New York State alone, the two candidates together amassed $50 million in contributions for their campaigns. Arizona, Michigan, Minnesota, Missouri, Nebraska, Pennsylvania, and Washington all saw senatorial campaigns costing between $15 million and $30 million. As might be expected, candidates spend much less to retain or obtain a seat in the House of Representatives because representatives must run for election every two years as opposed to six years for senators. (There are other reasons, too.) Except for the presidential campaigns, all of these funds had to be provided by the candidates and their families, borrowed, or raised by contributions from individuals or *political action committees*, described later in this chapter. For the presidential campaigns, some of the funds come from the federal government.

Regulating Campaign Financing

The way campaigns are financed has changed dramatically in the last two and a half decades. Today, candidates and political parties must operate within the constraints imposed by complicated laws regulating campaign financing.

A variety of federal **corrupt practices acts** have been designed to regulate campaign financing. The first, passed in 1925, limited primary and general election expenses for congressional candidates. In addition, it required disclosure of election expenses and, in principle, put controls on contributions by corporations. There were many loopholes in the restrictions, and the acts proved to be ineffective.

DID YOU KNOW . . .
That a candidate can buy lists of all the voters in a precinct, county, or state for only about 2 cents per name from a commercial firm?

Focus Group
A small group of individuals who are led in discussion by a professional consultant in order to gather opinions on and responses to candidates and issues.

Corrupt Practices Acts
A series of acts passed by Congress in an attempt to limit and regulate the size and sources of contributions and expenditures in political campaigns.

---

[4]NASCAR stands for the "National Association of Stock Car Auto Racing."
[5]Louise Overacker, *Money in Elections* (New York: Macmillan, 1932), p. vii.

| Hatch Act
An act passed in 1939 that restricted the political activities of government employees. It also prohibited a political group from spending more than $3 million in any campaign and limited individual contributions to a campaign committee to $5,000.

The **Hatch Act** (Political Activities Act) of 1939 is best known for restricting the political activities of civil servants. The act also, however, made it unlawful for a political group to spend more than $3 million in any campaign and limited individual contributions to a political group to $5,000. Of course, such restrictions were easily circumvented by creating additional political groups.

In the 1970s, Congress passed additional legislation to reshape the nature of campaign financing. In 1971, it passed the Federal Election Campaign Act to reform the process. Then in 1974, in the wake of the Watergate scandal (see Chapter 6), Congress enacted further reforms.

The Federal Election Campaign Act

The Federal Election Campaign Act (FECA) of 1971, which became effective in 1972, essentially replaced all past laws. The act placed no limit on overall spending but restricted the amount that could be spent on mass media advertising, including television. It limited the amount that candidates could contribute to their own campaigns (a limit later ruled unconstitutional) and required disclosure of all contributions and expenditures over $100. In principle, the FECA limited the role of labor unions and corporations in political campaigns. It also provided for a voluntary $1 (now $3) check-off on federal income tax returns for general campaign funds to be used by major-party presidential candidates.

Further Reforms in 1974.   For many, the 1971 act did not go far enough. Amendments to the FECA passed in 1974 did the following:

1. *Created the Federal Election Commission.* This commission consists of six nonpartisan administrators whose duties are to enforce compliance with the requirements of the act.

2. *Provided public financing for presidential primaries and general elections.* Any candidate running for president who is able to obtain sufficient contributions in at least twenty states can obtain a subsidy from the U.S. Treasury to help pay for primary campaigns. In 2004, however, neither George W. Bush nor John Kerry accepted public financing for the primaries. This allowed both of them to spend much more on advertising and other expenses than they could have if they had accepted public funding. Each of the two did accept $74.62 million for the general election campaign.

3. *Limited presidential campaign spending.* Any candidate accepting federal support must agree to limit campaign expenditures to the amount prescribed by federal law.

4. *Limited contributions.* Under the 1974 amendments, citizens could contribute up to $1,000 to each candidate in each federal election or primary; the total limit on all contributions from an individual to all candidates was $25,000 per year. Groups could contribute up to a maximum of $5,000 to a candidate in any election. (As you will read shortly, some of these limits were changed by the 2002 campaign-reform legislation.)

5. *Required disclosure.* Each candidate must file periodic reports with the Federal Election Commission, listing who contributed, how much was spent, and for what the funds were spent.

Buckley v. Valeo.   The 1971 act had limited the amount that each individual could spend on his or her own behalf. The Supreme Court declared the provision unconstitutional in 1976, in *Buckley v. Valeo*,[6] stating that it was unconstitutional to restrict in any way the amount congressional candidates could spend on their own behalf: "The candidate, no less than any other person, has a First Amendment

---

[6]424 U.S. 1 (1976).

right to engage in the discussion of public issues and vigorously and tirelessly to advocate his own election."

The *Buckley v. Valeo* decision, which has often been criticized, was directly countered by a 1997 Vermont law. The law, known as Act 64, imposed spending limits ranging from $2,000 to $300,000 (depending on the office sought) by candidates for state offices in Vermont. A number of groups, including the American Civil Liberties Union and the Republican Party, challenged the act, claiming that it violated the First Amendment's guarantee of free speech. In a landmark decision in August 2002, a federal appellate court disagreed and upheld the law. The court stated that Vermont had shown that, without spending limits, "the fund-raising practices in Vermont will continue to impair the accessibility which is essential to any democratic political system. The race for campaign funds has compelled public officials to give preferred access to contributors, selling their time in order to raise campaign funds."[7]

In 2006, the U.S. Supreme Court declared that Vermont's campaign spending and donation limits were unconstitutional, thereby in a sense reaffirming the *Buckley v. Valeo* decision.

Attorney James Bopp is shown leaving the Supreme Court building in Washington, D.C., where he argued against the Vermont law that put limits on campaign spending and donations. He won the case, for the Supreme Court, in 2006 in *Randell v. Sorrell,* ruled that Vermont's law was unconstitutional. Can another state, nonetheless, pass a similar law? Why or why not?
(AP Photo/J. Scott Applewhite)

Interest Groups and Campaign Money

In the last two decades, interest groups and individual companies have found new, very direct ways to support elected officials through campaign donations. Elected officials, in turn, have become dependent on these donations to run increasingly expensive campaigns. Interest groups and corporations funnel money to political candidates through several devices: **political action committees (PACs)**, **soft money** contributions, and **issue advocacy advertising.** These devices developed as a means of circumventing the campaign-financing reforms of the early 1970s, which limited contributions by individuals and unions to set amounts.

PACs and Political Campaigns

The 1974 and 1976 amendments to the Federal Election Campaign Act of 1971 allow corporations, labor unions, and other interest groups to set up PACs to raise funds for candidates. For a federal PAC to be legitimate, the funds must be raised from at least fifty volunteer donors and must be given to at least five candidates in the federal election. PACs can contribute up to $5,000 to each candidate in each election. Each corporation or each union is limited to one PAC. As you might imagine, corporate PACs obtain funds from executives and managers in their firms, and unions obtain PAC funds from their members.

The number of PACs has grown significantly since 1976, as has the amount they spend on elections. There were about 1,000 PACs in 1976; today, there are more than 4,500. Total spending by PACs grew from $19 million in 1973 to more than

| **Political Action Committee (PAC)**
A committee set up by and representing a corporation, labor union, or special interest group. PACs raise and give campaign donations.

| **Soft Money**
Campaign contributions unregulated by federal or state law, usually given to parties and party committees to help fund general party activities.

| **Issue Advocacy Advertising**
Advertising paid for by interest groups that support or oppose a candidate or a candidate's position on an issue without mentioning voting or elections.

---

[7]*Randell v. Vermont Public Interest Research Group,* 300 F.3d 129 (2d Cir. 2002).

$900 million in 2003–2004. About 44 percent of all campaign funds raised by House candidates in 2004 came from PACs.[8]

Interest groups funnel PAC funds to the candidates they think can do the most good for them. Frequently, they make the maximum contribution of $5,000 per election to candidates who face little or no opposition. The summary of PAC contributions given in Figure 9–2 shows that the great bulk of campaign contributions goes to incumbent candidates rather than to challengers. Table 9–1 shows the amounts contributed by the top twenty PACs during the 2005–2006 election cycle.

As Table 9–1 also shows, many PACs give most of their contributions to candidates of one party. Other PACs, particularly corporate PACs, tend to give funds to Democrats in Congress as well as to Republicans, because, with both chambers of Congress so closely divided, predicting which party will be in control after an election is almost impossible. Why, you might ask, would business leaders give to Democrats who may be more liberal than themselves? Interest groups see PAC contributions as a way to ensure *access* to powerful legislators, even though the groups may disagree with the legislators some of the time. PAC contributions are, in a way, an investment in a relationship.

Campaign-financing regulations clearly limit the amount that a PAC can give to any one candidate, but there is no limit on the amount that a PAC can spend on issue advocacy, either on behalf of a candidate or party or in opposition to one.

Campaign Financing beyond the Limits

Within a few years after the establishment of the tight limits on contributions, new ways to finance campaigns were developed that skirted the reforms and made it possible for huge sums to be raised, especially by the major political parties.

---

[8]Center for Responsive Politics, 2006, at **www.opensecrets.org**.

FIGURE 9–2 | PAC CONTRIBUTIONS TO CONGRESSIONAL CANDIDATES, 1991 TO 2004

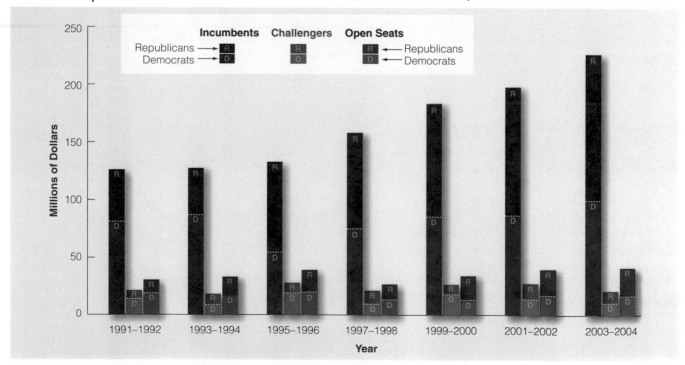

Source: Federal Election Commission, **www.fec.gov/press/press2005/20050609candidate/allhistory2004.xls**.

TABLE 9–1 | THE TOP TWENTY CONTRIBUTORS TO FEDERAL CANDIDATES, 2005–2006 ELECTION CYCLE*

PAC Name	Total Amount	Dem. %	Rep. %
National Association of Realtors	$1,953,005	48%	52%
Association of Trial Lawyers of America	1,806,000	95	4
International Brotherhood of Electrical Workers	1,793,650	96	3
National Beer Wholesalers Association	1,762,500	27	73
Operating Engineers Union	1,697,135	77	22
AT&T, Inc.	1,691,433	33	67
Credit Union National Association	1,631,599	43	57
United Parcel Service	1,565,709	30	70
American Bankers Association	1,555,174	33	67
National Auto Dealers Association	1,541,100	31	69
National Association of Home Builders	1,421,250	25	75
Teamsters Union	1,383,275	90	10
United Auto Workers	1,381,850	98	1
Laborers Union	1,375,150	82	18
Carpenters and Joiners Union	1,349,640	66	33
American Federation of State, County, and Municipal Employees	1,306,671	97	2
International Association of Fire Fighters	1,163,705	71	28
American Federation of Teachers	1,137,000	99	1
Air Line Pilots Association	1,096,500	81	18
Machinists/Aerospace Workers Union	1,069,000	99	0

*Includes subsidiaries and affiliated PACs, if any.
Source: Center for Responsive Politics, 2006.

Contributions to Political Parties. Candidates, PACs, and political parties found ways to generate *soft money*—that is, campaign contributions to political parties that escaped the limits of federal election law. Although the FECA limited contributions that would be spent on elections, there were no limits on contributions to political parties for activities such as voter education and voter-registration drives. This loophole enabled the parties to raise millions of dollars from corporations and individuals. It was not unusual for some corporations to give more than $1 million to the Democratic National Committee or to the Republican Party.[9] As shown in Table 9–2, nearly twice as much soft money was raised in the 1999–2000 presidential election cycle as in the previous (1995–1996) presidential election cycle. The parties spent these funds for their conventions, for registering voters, and for advertising to promote the general party position. The parties also sent a great deal to state and local party organizations, which used the soft money to support their own tickets. Although soft money contributions to the national parties were outlawed after Election Day 2002 (as you will read shortly), political parties saw no contradiction in raising and spending as much soft money as possible during the 2001–2002 election cycle.

[9]Paul Allen Beck, *Party Politics in America*, 8th ed. (New York: Longman, 1997), pp. 293–294.

TABLE 9–2 | SOFT MONEY RAISED BY POLITICAL PARTIES, 1993 TO 2002

	1993–1994	1995–1996	1997–1998	1999–2000	2001–2002
Democratic Party	$ 45.6 million	$122.3 million	$ 92.8 million	$243.0 million	$199.6 million
Republican Party	59.5 million	141.2 million	131.6 million	244.4 million	221.7 million
Total	105.1 million	263.5 million	224.4 million	487.4 million	421.3 million

Source: **www.opensecrets.org**, 2006.

TOLES ©2004 *The Washington Post.* Reprinted with permission of Universal Press Syndicate.

| Independent Expenditures
Nonregulated contributions from PACs, organizations, and individuals. The funds may be spent on advertising or other campaign activities so long as those expenditures are not coordinated with those of a candidate.

Independent Expenditures.   Business corporations, labor unions, and other interest groups discovered that it was legal to make **independent expenditures** in an election campaign so long as the expenditures were not coordinated with those of the candidate or political party. Hundreds of unique committees and organizations blossomed to take advantage of this campaign tactic. Although a 1990 United States Supreme Court decision, *Austin v. Michigan State Chamber of Commerce,*[10] upheld the right of the states and the federal government to limit independent, direct corporate expenditures (such as for advertisements) on behalf of *candidates,* the decision did not stop business and other types of groups from making independent expenditures on *issues.*

Issue Advocacy.   Indeed, issue advocacy—spending unregulated funds on advertising that promotes positions on issues rather than candidates—has become a common tactic in recent years. Interest groups routinely wage their own issue campaigns. For example, the Christian Coalition, which is incorporated, annually raises millions of dollars to produce and distribute voter guidelines and other direct-mail literature to describe candidates' positions on various issues and to promote its agenda. In 2004, the interest group "MoveOn.org" began running issue ads attacking the Bush record shortly after Senator John Kerry had clinched the Democratic nomination. The Bush campaign responded by beginning its own advertising campaign.

Although promoting issue positions is very close to promoting candidates who support those positions, the courts repeatedly have held, in accordance with the *Buckley v. Valeo* decision mentioned earlier, that interest groups have a First Amendment right to advocate their positions. In a 1996 decision,[11] the Supreme Court clarified this point, stating that political parties may also make independent expenditures on behalf of candidates—as long as the parties do so *independently* of the candidates. In other words, the parties must not coordinate such expenditures with the candidates' campaigns.

---

[10]494 U.S. 652 (1990).
[11]*Colorado Republican Federal Campaign Committee v. Federal Election Commission,* 518 U.S. 604 (1996).

The Bipartisan Campaign Reform Act of 2002

Campaign reform had been in the air for so long that it was almost anticlimactic when President George W. Bush signed the Bipartisan Campaign Reform Act on March 27, 2002. This act, which amended the 1971 FECA, took effect on the day after the congressional elections were held on November 5, 2002.

Key Elements of the New Law. The 2002 law bans the large, unlimited contributions to national political parties that are known as soft money. It places curbs on, but does not entirely eliminate, the use of campaign ads by outside special interest groups advocating the election or defeat of specific candidates. Such ads are allowed up to sixty days before a general election and up to thirty days before a primary election.

In 1974, contributions by individuals to federal candidates were limited to $1,000 per individual. The 2002 act increased this limit to $2,000. In addition, the maximum amount that an individual can give to all federal candidates was raised from $25,000 per year to $95,000 over a two-year election cycle.

The act did not ban soft money contributions to state and local parties. These parties can accept such contributions as long as they are limited to $10,000 per year per individual.

Challenges to the 2002 Act. Almost immediately, the 2002 act faced a set of constitutional challenges brought by groups negatively affected. In December 2003, however, the Supreme Court upheld almost all of the clauses of the act.[12]

Soon thereafter, a coalition of conservative and liberal groups called Wisconsin Right to Life brought a lawsuit claiming that the 2002 act infringed on legitimate grassroots lobbying. Wisconsin Right to Life argued that part of the act violated its right to free speech. In 2006, the Supreme Court unanimously ruled that the Wisconsin group could go back to court to challenge a specific part of the 2002 act—the federal ban on issue-oriented ads that mention a particular candidate just before an election.[13]

Once the Supreme Court upheld the bulk of the 2002 law, it was left to the Federal Election Commission (FEC) to interpret the statute. Slowly but surely, the FEC opened loopholes that allowed campaign finance to return to "business as usual." In 2004, a U.S. district court struck down more than a dozen such commission regulations. When the FEC asked for these rulings to be reversed, a federal appeals court in Washington did not agree.

The Rise of the 527s. Interest groups that previously gave soft money to the parties responded to the 2002 Bipartisan Campaign Reform Act by setting up new organizations outside the parties, called "527" organizations after the section of the tax code that provides for them. These tax-exempt organizations, which rely on soft money contributions for their funding and generally must report their contributions and expenditures to the Internal Revenue Service, first made a major impact in the 2003–2004 election cycle. The groups focus on encouraging voter registration and running issue ads aimed at energizing supporters. Often 527 groups run ads that take a strong position for or against a candidate.

Among the most successful 527 groups during the 2004 presidential elections were America Coming Together (ACT), the Media Fund, and MoveOn.org Voter Fund, which together spent $33 million on television ads attacking Bush's record. The three groups spent another $85 million to register new voters and to run ads explaining the liberal position on issues ranging from health care to international trade. Billionaire George Soros contributed more than $15 million to the three

A MoveOn.org television commercial that has an image of former President Nixon morphing into the image of President George W. Bush. This ad was targeted generally against the Republican Party in the run-up to the 2006 elections. How can independent expenditures on political advertisements create problems for a party that is the apparent beneficiary of the ads? (Photos Courtesy of MoveOn.org)

---

[12]*McConnell v. Federal Election Commission,* 540 U.S. 93 (2003).
[13]*Wisconsin Right to Life, Inc. v. Federal Election Commission,* 126 S.Ct. 1016 (2006).

A still frame image from an TV ad produced and paid for by a 527 organization called Swift Vets and POWs for Truth, or SwiftVets.com. This group ran a controversial but very effective series of ads during the 2004 presidential campaign that attacked Senator Kerry's military record in Vietnam and criticized his activist work following his service in the war. (Photo Courtesy of Swift Vets and POWs for Truth)

groups. Overall, 527 groups spent more than $600 million in the 2003–2004 election cycle. They continued to be active during the 2005–2006 election cycle, as you can see in Table 9–3.

In principle, charitable organizations are not allowed to participate directly in any type of political activity. Nonetheless, the Internal Revenue Service has found that some charities are not following the rules, as you will learn in this chapter's *Politics and Campaigns* feature.

Campaign Financing and the 2006 Elections

Some political commentators have maintained that all politics is local. The 2006 congressional elections were at least an exception to that rule. The results of surveys before the election and during exit polls placed the situation in Iraq and terrorism as the two top issues that were extremely important in determining how people voted. The economy, illegal immigration, corruption, and ethics in government were important, too, in deciding campaign issues. In any event, the 2006 campaign set a record for political spending because of so many hotly contested races. Estimated total spending in the last midterm election in 2002 was about $1.6 billion. In 2006, this total was almost twice that, at $3.1 billion. Campaign spending at the state level, particularly for contested governorships such as the one in California, reached record highs also. Both Democrats and Republicans participated in the creation of what some political analysts claimed was the most toxic campaign environment in modern times.

Running for President: The Longest Campaign

The American presidential election is the culmination of two different campaigns linked by the parties' national conventions. The presidential primary campaign lasts from January until June of the election year. Traditionally, the final campaign heats up around Labor Day, although in 2004 it began much earlier.

Primary elections were first mandated in 1903 in Wisconsin. The purpose of the primary was to open the nomination process to ordinary party members and to weaken the influence of party bosses in the nomination procedure. Until 1968, however, there were fewer than twenty primary elections for the presidency. They were often **"beauty contests"** in which the candidates competed for popular votes, but the results had little or no impact on the selection of delegates to the national convention. National conventions were meetings of the party elite—legislators, mayors, county chairpersons, and loyal party workers—who were mostly appointed to their delegations. National conventions saw numerous trades and bargains among competing candidates, and the leaders of large blocs of delegates could direct their delegates to support a favorite candidate.

| "Beauty Contest"
A presidential primary in which contending candidates compete for popular votes but the results do not control the selection of delegates to the national convention.

TABLE 9–3 | 527 COMMITTEE ACTIVITY IN 2005–2006 BY TYPE OF GROUP OR INTEREST

TYPE OF GROUP OR INTEREST	TOTAL RECEIPTS	TOTAL EXPENDITURES
Republican/conservative	$17,179,412	$34,150,184
Democratic/liberal	15,045,233	18,001,892
Miscellaneous unions	14,354,031	17,512,894
Public-sector unions	8,957,147	11,335,565
Building trade unions	7,079,956	4,322,358
Women's issues	5,120,785	4,211,303
Environment	2,549,357	1,019,757
Industrial unions	2,496,305	2,773,894
Human rights	1,710,332	2,143,076

Source: Internal Revenue Service.

POLITICS AND CAMPAIGNS | Charities and Politics Are Not Supposed to Mix

Charities are typically tax-exempt organizations. Under the rules of the Internal Revenue Service (IRS), to maintain tax-exempt status, a charitable organization must not participate in political campaigns. Apparently, though, some tax-exempt groups have been violating the law. So, after the 2004 elections, certain "watchdog" organizations filed complaints with the IRS about purportedly illegal political activities of certain charities, especially churches.

THE IRS INVESTIGATES

In 2005, the IRS reviewed more than eighty churches, charities, and other tax-exempt organizations. The IRS looked for such banned activities as the distribution of printed materials encouraging members to vote for a specific candidate, contributions of cash to candidates' campaigns, and ministers' use of their pulpits to oppose or endorse specific candidates. The result? In 2006, IRS Commissioner Mark Everson announced, "Our examination substantiated a disturbing amount of political intervention in the 2004 election cycle." The IRS then issued guidelines to clear up any confusion about what charities could or could not do before the 2006 elections.

CHURCHES' ROLE IN THE 2004 ELECTIONS

The IRS found that churches played a particularly important role in the 2004 elections. For example, well-known fundamentalist Baptist minister Jerry Falwell used his Web site to endorse President Bush and to urge visitors to the site to donate $5,000 to the Campaign for Working Families. At the All Saints Church in Pasadena, California, a pastor gave a sermon in which he imagined a debate among Senator John Kerry, President George Bush, and Jesus Christ. Although Jesus won, the press reported that the hypothetical debate came out in favor of John Kerry.

Of the eighty-two churches, charities, and other tax-exempt organizations that the IRS examined, more than 75 percent engaged in prohibited political activity during the 2003–2004 election cycle. The IRS proposed to revoke the tax-exempt status of at least three of these organizations.

FOR CRITICAL ANALYSIS

What is the reasoning behind the prohibition on political activities by tax-exempt organizations?

Reforming the Primaries

In recent decades, the character of the primary process and the make-up of the national convention have changed dramatically. The public, rather than party elites, now generally controls the nomination process. After the disruptive riots outside the doors of the 1968 Democratic convention in Chicago, many party leaders pushed for serious reforms of the convention process. They saw the general dissatisfaction with the convention, and the riots in particular, as being caused by the inability of the average party member to influence the nomination system.

The Democratic National Committee appointed a special commission to study the problems of the primary system. Called the McGovern-Fraser Commission, the group over the next several years formulated new rules for delegate selection that had to be followed by state Democratic parties.

The reforms instituted by the Democratic Party, which were imitated in most states by the Republicans, revolutionized the nomination process for the presidency. The most important changes require that a majority of the convention delegates not be nominated by party elites; they must be elected by the voters in primary elections, in caucuses held by local parties (discussed later), or at state conventions. Delegates are normally pledged to a particular candidate, although the pledge is not always formally binding at the convention. The delegation from each state must also include a proportion of women, younger party members, and representatives of the minority groups within the party. At first, virtually no special privileges were given to elected party officials, such as senators and governors. In 1984, however, many of these officials returned to the Democratic convention as **superdelegates.**

| Superdelegate
A party leader or elected official who is given the right to vote at the party's national convention. Superdelegates are not elected at the state level.

Demonstrations outside the 1968 Democratic convention in Chicago were shown on national television. Dissatisfaction with the convention influenced the party to reform its delegate selection rules. Forty years later, do the national conventions generate much controversy? Why or why not? (AP Photo/Michael Boyer)

Types of Primaries

Before discussing the types of primaries, we must first examine how some states use a party **caucus.** A caucus is typically a small local meeting of party regulars who agree on a nominee. Sometimes the results of caucuses are voted on by a broader set of party members in a primary election. (If the party's chosen candidates have no opponents, however, a primary election may not be necessary.)

Alternatively, there may be a local or state party convention at which a slate of nominees of loyal party members is chosen. In any event, the resulting primary elections differ from state to state. The most common types are discussed here.

Caucus
A meeting of party members designed to select candidates and propose policies.

Closed Primary. In a **closed primary,** only avowed or declared members of a party can vote in that party's primary. In other words, voters must declare their party affiliation, either when they register to vote or at the primary election. A closed-primary system tries to make sure that registered voters cannot cross over into the other party's primary in order to nominate the weakest candidate of the opposing party or to affect the ideological direction of that party.

Closed Primary
A type of primary in which the voter is limited to choosing candidates of the party of which he or she is a member.

Open Primary. An **open primary** is a primary in which voters can vote in either party primary without disclosing their party affiliation. Basically, the voter makes the choice in the privacy of the voting booth. The voter must, however, choose one party's list from which to select candidates. Open primaries place no restrictions on independent voters.

Open Primary
A primary in which any registered voter can vote (but must vote for candidates of only one party).

Blanket Primary. A *blanket primary* is one in which the voter can vote for candidates of more than one party. Alaska, Louisiana, and Washington have blanket primaries. Blanket-primary campaigns may be much more costly because each candidate for every office is trying to influence all the voters, not just those in his or her party.

In 2000, the United States Supreme Court issued a decision that altered significantly the use of the blanket primary. The case arose when political parties in California challenged the constitutionality of a 1996 ballot initiative authorizing the use of the blanket primary in that state. The parties contended that the blanket primary violated their First Amendment right of association. Because the nominees represent the party, they argued, party members—not the general electorate—should have the right to choose the party's nominee. The Supreme Court ruled in favor of the parties, holding that the blanket primary violated parties' First Amendment associational rights.[14]

The Court's ruling called into question the constitutional validity of blanket primaries in other states as well. The question before these states is how to devise a primary election system that will comply with the Supreme Court's ruling yet offer independent voters a chance to participate in the primary elections.

RunOff Primary.   Some states have a two-primary system. If no candidate receives a majority of the votes in the first primary, the top two candidates must compete in another primary, called a *runoff primary.*

Front-Loading the Primaries

As soon as politicians and potential presidential candidates realized that winning as many primary elections as possible guaranteed them the party's nomination for president, their tactics changed dramatically. For example, candidates running in the 2004 primaries, such as Howard Dean, concentrated on building organizations in states that held early, important primary elections. Candidates realized that winning early contests, such as the Iowa caucuses or the New Hampshire primary election (both in January), meant that the media instantly would label the winner as the **front-runner,** thus increasing the candidate's media exposure and escalating the pace of contributions to his or her campaign fund.

The Rush to Be First.   The states and state political parties began to see that early primaries had a much greater effect on the outcome of the presidential election and, accordingly, began to hold their primaries earlier in the season to secure that advantage. While New Hampshire held on to its claim to be the first primary, other states moved theirs to the following week. A group of mostly southern states decided to hold their primaries on the same date, known as Super Tuesday, in the hope of nominating a moderate southerner at the Democratic convention. When California, which had held the last primary (in June), moved its primary to March, the primary season was curtailed drastically. Due to this process of **front-loading** the primaries, in 2000 the presidential nominating process was over in March, with both George W. Bush and Al Gore having enough convention delegate votes to win their nominations. This meant that the campaign was essentially without news until the conventions in August, a gap that did not appeal to the politicians or the media. Both parties discussed whether more changes in the primary process were necessary.

In 2006, the Democratic Party announced that the Nevada caucus and the South Carolina primary would be held in the same time frame traditionally dominated by New Hampshire and Iowa. The Democrats reasoned that they wanted to add diversity to an early-primary calendar that has been dominated by the predominantly white, rural voices of New Hampshire and Iowa. Nevada boasts a quickly growing Hispanic population and South Carolina has a long-standing African American community.

Consequences of Early Primaries.   Despite the apparent problems with the front-loaded primary season in 2000, the Democratic Party decided to hold some of its

DID YOU KNOW . . .
That David Leroy Gatchell changed his middle name to None of the Above, but when he ran for the U.S. Senate representing Tennessee, a court ruled that he could not use his middle name on the ballot?

Front-Runner
The presidential candidate who appears to be ahead at a given time in the primary season.

Front-Loading
The practice of moving presidential primary elections to the early part of the campaign to maximize the impact of these primaries on the nomination.

---

[14]*California Democratic Party v. Jones,* 530 U.S. 567 (2000).

The first 2004 Democratic presidential candidate debate was held in Albuquerque, New Mexico, in September 2003. The Democratic presidential candidates (from the left) were Senator Bob Graham, Representative Dick Gephardt, former senator Carol Moseley Braun, Senator John Kerry, Representative Dennis Kucinich, Senator John Edwards, Senator Joe Lieberman, and former governor Howard Dean. To win such debates, do candidates take a moderate stance or a "radical" stance on the issues debated? Why? (EPA/POOL/Landov)

primaries even earlier in the 2003–2004 presidential election cycle. For example, the Democratic Iowa caucus was advanced to January 19, to be followed eight days later by the New Hampshire primary. The Democrats' goal in moving up their primaries was obvious: settle on a candidate early so that she or he would have a long time during which to raise funds to unseat the incumbent president, George W. Bush.

In 2005, a private commission headed by former president Jimmy Carter and former secretary of state James A. Baker III proposed a number of steps to avoid the consequences of early primaries. The Commission on Federal Election Reform was organized by American University. The commission argued in favor of keeping the Iowa caucuses and New Hampshire's early primary because "they test the candidates by genuine retail, door-to-door campaigning." After that, though, the commission had a radical suggestion—eliminate the state primaries and hold four regional presidential primaries. These regional primaries would be held at monthly intervals in March, April, May, and June, with the order rotated every four years.

The 2004 Primary Contest.   The contest for the Democratic nomination drew a large and diverse field of candidates in 2004. Former Vermont governor Howard Dean got off to the strongest start, in part due to his effective use of the Internet to recruit supporters and raise funds. Senators John Kerry of Massachusetts and John Edwards of North Carolina were also strong contenders. A late entry to the race was General Wesley Clark, who claimed expertise in national security and defense. Two African American candidates made a run for the nomination—former Illinois senator Carol Moseley Braun and the Reverend Al Sharpton. Other candidates included Connecticut senator Joe Lieberman, a former vice-presidential candidate; Ohio representative Dennis Kucinich; and representative Dick Gephardt of Missouri.

The Dean campaign had great momentum before the primaries actually began, but by January all of the other Democratic candidates were attacking Dean on his positions and experience. Senator John Kerry, who won the Iowa caucuses, was catapulted into the lead, while Howard Dean destroyed his own campaign by seeming to lose control during a speech to his followers. It was an amazing example of how one moment in a campaign, shown over and over on television, can affect an election. In the primaries that followed, Edwards was Kerry's only real competition. By March 2, Kerry had clinched the nomination.

On to the National Convention

Presidential candidates have been nominated by the convention method in every election since 1832. The delegates are sent from each state and are apportioned on the basis of state representation. Extra delegates are allowed to attend from states that had voting majorities for the party in the preceding elections. Parties also accept delegates from the District of Columbia, the territories, and certain overseas groups.

Seating the Delegates. At the convention, each political party uses a credentials committee to determine which delegates may participate. The credentials committee usually prepares a roll of all delegates entitled to be seated. Controversy may arise when rival groups claim to be the official party organization for a county, district, or state. The Mississippi Democratic Party split along racial lines in 1964 at the height of the civil rights movement in the Deep South. Separate all-white and mixed white and African American sets of delegates were selected, and both factions showed up at the national convention. After much debate on party rules, the committee decided to seat the pro–civil rights delegates and exclude those who represented the traditional "white" party.

| Credentials Committee
A committee used by political parties at their national conventions to determine which delegates may participate. The committee inspects the claim of each prospective delegate to be seated as a legitimate representative of his or her state.

Convention Activities. The typical convention lasts only a few days. The first day consists of speech making, usually against the opposing party. During the second day, there are committee reports, and during the third day, there is presidential balloting. Because delegates generally arrive at the convention committed to presidential candidates, no convention since 1952 has required more than one ballot to choose a nominee, and since 1972, candidates have usually come into the convention with enough committed delegates to win. On the fourth day, a vice-presidential candidate is usually nominated, and the presidential nominee gives the acceptance speech.

In 2004, the outcome of the two conventions was so predictable that the national networks devoted only three hours of prime-time coverage to each convention—barely enough time to include speeches by the candidates. Several cable networks and Internet sites provided gavel-to-gavel coverage, however.

| The Electoral College

Many people who vote for the president and vice president think that they are voting directly for a candidate. In actuality, they are voting for electors who will cast their ballots in the electoral college. Article II, Section 1, of the Constitution outlines in detail the method of choosing electors for president and vice president. The framers of the Constitution wanted to avoid the selection of president and vice president by the "excitable masses." Rather, they wished the choice to be made by a few supposedly dispassionate, reasonable men (but not women).

| Elector
A member of the electoral college, which selects the president and vice president. Each state's electors are chosen in each presidential election year according to state laws.

The Choice of Electors

Each state's electors are selected during each presidential election year. The selection is governed by state laws. After the national party convention, the electors normally are pledged to the candidates chosen. The total number of electors today is 538, equal to 100 senators, 435 members of the House, and 3 electors for the District of Columbia (the Twenty-third Amendment, ratified in 1961, added electors for the District of Columbia). Each state's number of electors equals that state's number of senators (two) plus its number of representatives. A graphic inside the front cover of this book shows how the electoral votes are apportioned by state.

The Electors' Commitment

When a plurality of voters in a state chooses a slate of electors except in Maine and Nebraska, where electoral votes are based on congressional districts, those electors are pledged to cast their ballots on the first Monday after the second Wednesday in December in the state capital for the presidential and vice-presidential candidates of their party. The Constitution does not, however, *require* the electors to cast their ballots for the candidates of their party.

The ballots are counted and certified before a joint session of Congress early in January. The candidates who receive a majority of the electoral votes (270) are certified as president-elect and vice president–elect. According to the Constitution, if no candidate receives a majority of the electoral votes, the election of the president is decided in the House from among the candidates with the three highest numbers of votes, with each state having one vote (decided by a plurality of each state delegation). The selection of the vice president is determined by the Senate in a choice between the two candidates with the most votes, each senator having one vote. Congress was required to choose the president and vice president in 1801 (Thomas Jefferson and Aaron Burr), and the House chose the president in 1825 (John Quincy Adams).[15]

It is possible for a candidate to become president without obtaining a majority of the popular vote. There have been many minority presidents in our history, including Abraham Lincoln, Woodrow Wilson, Harry Truman, John F. Kennedy, Richard Nixon (in 1968), Bill Clinton, and George W. Bush (in 2000). Such an event becomes more likely when there are important third-party candidates.

Perhaps more distressing is the possibility of a candidate's being elected when an opposing candidate receives a plurality of the popular vote. This has occurred on four occasions—in the elections of John Quincy Adams in 1824, Rutherford B. Hayes in 1876, Benjamin Harrison in 1888, and George W. Bush in 2000, all of whom won elections in which an opponent received a plurality of the popular vote.

Criticisms of the Electoral College

Besides the possibility of a candidate's becoming president even though an opponent obtains more popular votes, there are other complaints about the electoral college. The idea of the Constitution's framers was to have electors use their own discretion to decide who would make the best president. But electors no longer perform the selecting function envisioned by the founders, because they are committed to the candidate who has a plurality of popular votes in their state in the general election.[16]

One can also argue that the current system, which in most states gives all of the electoral votes to the candidate who has a statewide plurality, is unfair to other candidates and their supporters. The current system of voting also means that presidential campaigning will be concentrated in those states that have the largest number of electoral votes and in those states in which the outcome is likely to be close. The other states may receive second-class treatment during the presidential campaign. It can also be argued that there is something of a bias favoring states with smaller populations, because including Senate seats in the electoral vote total partly offsets the edge of the more populous states in the House. Wyoming (with two senators and one representative) gets an electoral vote for roughly every 164,594 inhabitants (based

---

[15]For a detailed account of the process, see Michael J. Glennon, *When No Majority Rules: The Electoral College and Presidential Succession* (Washington, D.C.: Congressional Quarterly Press, 1993), p. 20.

[16]Note, however, that there have been revolts by so-called *faithless electors*—in 1796, 1820, 1948, 1956, 1960, 1968, 1972, 1976, 1988, and 2000.

on the 2000 census), for example, whereas Iowa gets one vote for every 418,046 inhabitants, and California has one vote for every 615,848 inhabitants. Note that many of the smallest states have Republican majorities.

Many proposals for reform of the electoral college system have been advanced, particularly after the turmoil resulting from the 2000 elections. The most obvious is to get rid of it completely and simply allow candidates to be elected on a popular-vote basis; in other words, have a direct election, by the people, of the president and vice president. Because abolishing the electoral college would require a constitutional amendment, however, the chances of electing the president by a direct vote are remote.

The major parties are not in favor of eliminating the electoral college, fearing that it would give minor parties a more influential role. Also, less populous states are not in favor of direct election of the president because they believe they would be overwhelmed by the large-state vote.

How Are Elections Conducted?

The United States uses the **Australian ballot**—a secret ballot that is prepared, distributed, and counted by government officials at public expense. Since 1888, all states have used the Australian ballot. Before that, many states used the alternatives of oral voting and differently colored ballots prepared by the parties. Obviously, knowing which way a person was voting made it easy to apply pressure on the person to change his or her vote, and vote buying was common.

Office-Block and Party-Column Ballots

Two types of Australian ballots are used in the United States in general elections. The first, called an **office-block ballot,** or sometimes a **Massachusetts ballot,** groups all the candidates for a particular elective office under the title of that office. Parties

Australian Ballot
A secret ballot prepared, distributed, and tabulated by government officials at public expense. Since 1888, all states have used the Australian ballot rather than an open, public ballot.

Office-Block, or Massachusetts, Ballot
A form of general election ballot in which candidates for elective office are grouped together under the title of each office. It emphasizes voting for the office and the individual candidate, rather than for the party.

| **Party-Column, or Indiana, Ballot**
A form of general-election ballot in which all of a party's candidates for elective office are arranged in one column under the party's label and symbol. It emphasizes voting for the party, rather than for the office or individual.

| **Coattail Effect**
The influence of a popular candidate on the electoral success of other candidates on the same party ticket. The effect is increased by the party-column ballot, which encourages straight-ticket voting.

dislike the office-block ballot because it places more emphasis on the office than on the party; it discourages straight-ticket voting and encourages split-ticket voting.

A **party-column ballot** is a form of general election ballot in which all of a party's candidates are arranged in one column under the party's label and symbol. It is also called the **Indiana ballot.** In some states, it allows voters to vote for all of a party's candidates for local, state, and national offices by simply marking a single "X" or by pulling a single lever. Most states use this type of ballot. As it encourages straight-ticket voting, the two major parties favor this form. When a party has an exceptionally strong presidential or gubernatorial candidate to head the ticket, the use of the party-column ballot increases the **coattail effect** (the influence of a popular candidate on the success of other candidates on the same party ticket).

Voting by Mail

Although voting by mail has been accepted for absentee ballots for many decades (for example, for those who are doing business away from home or for members of the armed forces), only recently have several states offered mail ballots to all of their voters. The rationale for using the mail ballot is to make voting easier for the voters. A startling result came in a special election in Oregon in spring 1996: with the mail-only ballot, turnout was 66 percent, and the state saved more than $1 million. In the 2000 presidential elections, in which Oregon voters were allowed to mail in their ballots, voter participation was over 80 percent. Although voters in a number of states now have the option of voting by mail, Oregon is the only state to have abandoned precinct polling places completely. A nationwide system of voting by mail would have many pros and cons, which we explore in this chapter's *Which Side Are You On?* feature.

Vote Fraud

Vote fraud is something regularly suspected but seldom proved. Voting in the 1800s, when secret ballots were rare and people had a cavalier attitude toward the open buying of votes, was probably much more conducive to fraud than modern elections are. Larry J. Sabato and Glenn R. Simpson, however, claim that the potential for vote fraud is high in many states, particularly through the use of phony voter registrations and absentee ballots.[17]

[17]Larry J. Sabato and Glenn R. Simpson, *Dirty Little Secrets: The Persistence of Corruption in American Politics* (New York: Random House, 1996).

These protesters want to remind all Americans that every vote should be counted. After the 2000 elections, and since, there have been numerous instances of alleged miscounts of votes because of faulty voting equipment, inexperienced voting booth personnel, and outright fraud. (AP Photo/J. Pat Carter)

WHICH SIDE ARE YOU ON? | Should Voting by Mail Be Universal?

As pointed out in the text, so far Oregon is the only state to have eliminated precinct polling places. Washington State has also been a leader in adopting voting by mail. The majority of that state's counties now use a vote-by-mail system.

Typically, with a vote-by-mail system ballots are mailed to the homes of registered voters, who then fill them out and return them via the postal system. Usually, ballots are sent out about three weeks before the election date. Local voting authorities determine the cutoff date for returning the ballots. In some vote-by-mail jurisdictions, volunteers pick up ballots at voters' homes and take them to drop-off booths or to drive-in quick-drop locations.

VOTE BY MAIL: THE REAL WINNER IS DEMOCRACY

Many proponents of voting by mail believe that it is the best way to increase voter participation. (Internet voting would be even easier.) In spite of some initial concerns that voters would not return their ballots, Oregon has seen the highest percentage of voter participation ever, reaching 87 percent in the 2004 elections.

When questions arise about the accuracy of ballot counts, mail-in votes provide an automatic paper trail. Each vote-by-mail ballot is normally read by optical scanners, and the paper version remains available should a hand recount become necessary. Certainly, the elimination of polling places reduces the expense of elections for any jurisdiction. Oregon estimates that it has reduced costs by more than 30 percent since it went to a statewide vote-by-mail system.

Proponents of voting by mail argue that it is preferable to some alternative national standard that would apply new rules to an outdated system of polling places. Voting by mail is low tech, low cost, and convenient.

VOTE BY MAIL: A SUBVERSION OF THE ELECTION PROCESS

Political scientist Norman Ornstein, an early critic of mail-in voting, argues that mail balloting subverts the whole election process. He points out that voters can cast their ballots well before meaningful debates and other exchanges occur between the candidates. As a result, the voter may be casting an uninformed ballot.* The constitution project at Georgetown University as well as a consortium of the Massachusetts Institute of Technology and the California Institute of Technology came to the same conclusion after an examination of the 2004 elections.

Critics additionally argue that mail-in voting deprives voters of the secrecy guaranteed by voting at a polling place. They also believe that mail-in voting provides more opportunities for fraud. Finally, they contend that it represents the abandonment of an important civic duty of going to the polls on Election Day.

WHAT'S YOUR POSITION?

Do you believe that the chances of voting fraud are greater or less with a mail-in voting system than with the current polling-place system? Explain your answer.

GOING ONLINE

To learn more about voting by mail, visit the Oregon secretary of state's Web page dedicated to the topic at **www.sos.state.or.us/elections**. The site includes frequently asked questions and a brief history of voting by mail.

*Norman Ornstein, "Vote-by-Mail: Is It Good for Democracy?" *Campaigns and Elections,* May 1996, p. 47.

The Danger of Fraud. In California, for example, it is very difficult to remove a name from the polling list even if the person has not cast a ballot in the last two years. Thus, many persons are still on the rolls even though they no longer live in California. Enterprising political activists could use these names for absentee ballots. Other states have registration laws that are meant to encourage easy registration and voting. Such laws can be taken advantage of by those who seek to vote more than once.

After the 2000 elections, Larry Sabato again emphasized the problem of voting fraud. "It's a silent scandal," said Sabato, "and the problem is getting worse with increases in absentee voting, which is the easiest way to commit fraud." He noted that in 2000, one-third of Florida's counties found that more than 1,200 votes were cast illegally by felons, and in one county alone nearly 500 votes were cast by

This registrar of voters in New Orleans reviews absentee ballots sent via fax in April 2006. The fax machines worked day and night prior to that city's first municipal elections after Hurricane Katrina. Are there problems when many voters never step inside a voting booth? If so, what are they? (AP Photo/Cheryl Gerber)

unregistered voters. In two precincts, the number of ballots cast was greater than the number of people who voted.[18]

Mistakes by Voting Officials.   Some observers claim, however, that errors leading to fraud are trivial in number and that a few mistakes are inevitable in a system involving millions of voters. These people argue that an excessive concern with vote fraud makes it harder for minorities and poor people to vote.

For example, in 2000, Katherine Harris, Florida's top election official, oversaw a purge of the voter rolls while simultaneously serving as co-chair of the Florida Bush campaign. According to the *New York Times*, when attempting to remove the names of convicted felons from the list of voters:

> Ms. Harris's office overruled the advice of the private firm that compiled the felon list and called for removing not just names that were an exact match, but ones that were highly inexact. Thousands of Florida voters wound up being wrongly purged . . . . In Missouri, elected officials charged for years that large numbers of St. Louis residents were casting votes from vacant lots. A study conducted by *The* [St. Louis] *Post Dispatch* in 2001 found that in the vast majority of cases, the voters lived in homes that had been wrongly classified by the city.[19]

In both the Florida and Missouri examples, a majority of the affected voters were African American.

As a result of the confusion generated by the 2000 elections, many states are now in the process of improving their voting systems and procedures. Some claim that certain reforms, such as requiring voters to show a voter-registration card or photo identification when they go to the polls, will help to curb voting fraud.

---

[18]As cited in "Blind to Voter Fraud," *The Wall Street Journal,* March 2, 2001, p. A10.
[19]"How America Doesn't Vote," *The New York Times: The News of the Week in Review,* February 15, 2004, p. 10.

Turning Out to Vote

In 2004, the voting-age population was about 221.3 million people. Of that number, 123.7 million, or 55.3 percent of the voting-age population, actually went to the polls. When only half of the voting-age population participates in elections, it means, among other things, that the winner of a close presidential election may be voted in by only about one-fourth of the voting-age population (see Table 9–4).

Figure 9–3 on the following page shows **voter turnout** for presidential and congressional elections from 1904 to 2006. According to these statistics, the last good year for voter turnout was 1960, when almost 65 percent of the voting-age population actually voted. Each of the peaks in the figure represents voter turnout in a presidential election. Thus, we can also see that turnout for congressional elections is influenced greatly by whether there is a presidential election in the same year. Whereas voter turnout during the presidential elections of 2004 was over 50 percent, it dropped to 40 percent in the midterm elections of 2006.

The same is true at the state level. When there is a race for governor, more voters participate both in the general election for governor and in the election for state representatives. Voter participation rates in gubernatorial elections are also greater in presidential election years. The average turnout in state elections is about 14 percentage points higher when a presidential election is held.

Now consider local elections. In races for mayor, city council, county auditor, and the like, it is fairly common for only 25 percent or less of the electorate to vote. Is something amiss here? It would seem that people should be more likely to vote in elections that directly affect them. At the local level, each person's vote counts more (because there are fewer voters). Furthermore, the issues—crime control, school

| Voter Turnout

The percentage of citizens taking part in the election process; the number of eligible voters that actually "turn out" on election day to cast their ballots.

TABLE 9–4 | ELECTED BY A MAJORITY?

Most presidents have won a majority of the votes cast in the election. We generally judge the extent of their victory by whether they have won more than 51 percent of the votes. Some presidential elections have been proclaimed *landslides,* meaning that the candidates won by an extraordinary majority of votes cast. As indicated below, however, no modern president has been elected by more than 38 percent of the total voting-age population.

YEAR—WINNER (PARTY)	PERCENTAGE OF TOTAL POPULAR VOTE	PERCENTAGE OF VOTING-AGE POPULATION
1932—Roosevelt (D)	57.4	30.1
1936—Roosevelt (D)	60.8	34.6
1940—Roosevelt (D)	54.7	32.2
1944—Roosevelt (D)	53.4	29.9
1948—Truman (D)	49.6	25.3
1952—Eisenhower (R)	55.1	34.0
1956—Eisenhower (R)	57.4	34.1
1960—Kennedy (D)	49.7	31.2
1964—Johnson (D)	61.1	37.8
1968—Nixon (R)	43.4	26.4
1972—Nixon (R)	60.7	33.5
1976—Carter (D)	50.1	26.8
1980—Reagan (R)	50.7	26.7
1984—Reagan (R)	58.8	31.2
1988—Bush (R)	53.4	26.8
1992—Clinton (D)	43.3	23.1
1996—Clinton (D)	49.2	23.2
2000—Bush (R)	47.8	24.5
2004—Bush (R)	51.0	27.6

Sources: *Congressional Quarterly Weekly Report,* January 31, 1989, p. 137; *The New York Times,* November 5, 1992; *The New York Times,* November 7, 1996; and *The New York Times,* November 12, 2004.

bonds, sewer bonds, and so on—touch the immediate interests of the voters. The facts, however, do not fit the theory. Potential voters are most interested in national elections, when a presidential choice is involved. Otherwise, voter participation in our representative government is very low (and, as we have seen, it is not overwhelmingly great even at the presidential level).

The Effect of Low Voter Turnout

There are two schools of thought concerning low voter turnout. Some view low voter participation as a threat to representative democratic government. Too few individuals are deciding who wields political power in society. In addition, low voter participation presumably signals apathy about the political system in general. It also may signal that potential voters simply do not want to take the time to learn about the issues. When only a handful of people take the time to research the issues, it will be easier, say the alarmists, for an authoritarian figure to take over our government.

Others are less concerned about low voter participation. They believe that low voter participation simply indicates more satisfaction with the status quo. Also, they believe that representative democracy is a reality even if a very small percentage of eligible voters vote. If everyone who does not vote believes that the outcome of the election will accord with his or her own desires, then representative democracy is working. The nonvoters are obtaining the type of government—with the type of people running it—that they want to have anyway.

Is Voter Turnout Declining?

During many recent elections, the media have voiced concern that voter turnout is declining. Indeed, Figure 9–3 appears to show somewhat lower voter turnout in recent years than during the 1960s. Pundits have blamed the low turnout on negative campaigning and broad public cynicism about the political process. But is voter turnout actually as low as it seems?

FIGURE 9–3 | VOTER TURNOUT FOR PRESIDENTIAL AND CONGRESSIONAL ELECTIONS, 1904 TO 2006

The peaks represent turnout in presidential election years; the troughs represent turnout in off-presidential-election years.

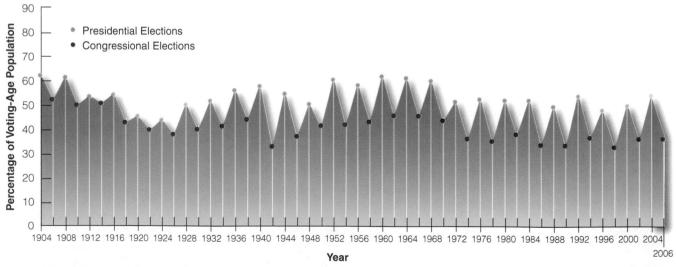

Sources: Historical Data Archive, Inter-university Consortium for Political and Social Research; U.S. Department of Commerce, *Statistical Abstract of the United States: 1980*, 101st ed. (Washington, D.C.: U.S. Government Printing Office, 1980), p. 515; William H. Flanigan and Nancy H. Zingale, *Political Behavior of the American Electorate*, 5th ed. (Boston: Allyn and Bacon, 1983), p. 20; *Congressional Quarterly*, various issues; and authors' updates.

One problem with widely used measurements of voter turnout—as exemplified by Figure 9–3—is that they compare the number of people who actually vote with the voting-age population, not the population of *eligible voters*. These figures are not the same. The figure for the voting-age population includes felons and ex-felons who have lost the right to vote. Above all, it includes new immigrants who are not yet citizens. Finally, it does not include Americans living abroad, who can cast absentee ballots.

In 2004, the measured voting-age population included 3.2 million ineligible felons and ex-felons and an estimated 17.5 million noncitizens. It did not include 3.3 million Americans abroad. As stated earlier in this chapter, the voting-age population in 2004 was 221.3 million people. The number of eligible voters, however, was only 204 million. That means that voter turnout in 2004 was not 55.3 percent, as often reported, but 58.8 percent.

As you learned in Chapter 1, the United States has experienced high rates of immigration in recent decades. Political scientists Michael McDonald and Samuel Popkin argue that the apparent decline in voter turnout since 1972 is entirely a function of the increasing size of the ineligible population, chiefly due to immigration.[20]

Factors Influencing Who Votes

A clear association exists between voter participation and the following characteristics: age, educational attainment, minority status, income level, and the existence of two-party competition.

1. *Age.* Look at Table 9–5, which shows the breakdown of voter participation by age group for the 2004 presidential elections. It would appear from these figures that age is a strong factor in determining voter turnout on election day. The reported turnout increases with older age groups. Greater participation with age is very likely due to the fact that older voters are more settled in their lives, are already registered, and have had more time to experience voting as an expected activity.

2. *Educational attainment.* Education also influences voter turnout. In general, the more education you have, the more likely you are to vote. This pattern is clearly evident in the 2004 election results, as you can see in Table 9–6. Reported turnout was 30 percentage points higher for those who had some college education than it was for people who had never been to high school.

3. *Minority status.* Race and ethnicity are important, too, in determining the level of voter turnout. Non-Hispanic whites in 2004 voted at a 67.2 percent rate, whereas the non-Hispanic African American turnout rate was 60.0 percent. For Hispanics, the turnout rate was 44.2 percent, and for Asian Americans the rate was slightly lower, at 44.1 percent. These low rates are largely due to the fact that many Hispanic and Asian American immigrants are not yet citizens.

4. *Income level.* Differences in income also correlate with differences in voter turnout. Wealthier people tend to be overrepresented among voters who turn out on election day. In the 2004 presidential elections, voter turnout for those with the highest annual family incomes was almost three times the turnout for those with the lowest annual family incomes.

5. *Two-party competition.* Another factor in voter turnout is the extent to which elections are competitive within a state. More competitive states generally have higher turnout rates, and turnout increases considerably in states where there is an extremely competitive race in a particular year. In addition, turnout can be increased through targeted get-out-the-vote drives among minority voters.

[20]Michael P. McDonald and Samuel L. Popkin, "The Myth of the Vanishing Voter," *American Political Science Review*, Vol. 95, No. 4 (December 2001), p. 963.

TABLE 9–5 | VOTING IN THE 2004 PRESIDENTIAL ELECTIONS BY AGE GROUP

Turnout is given as a percentage of the voting-age citizen population.

AGE	REPORTED TURNOUT
18–24	46.7
25–34	55.7
35–44	64.0
45–54	68.7
55–64	72.8
65–74	73.3
75 years and over	68.5

Source: U.S. Bureau of the Census, May 26, 2005.

TABLE 9–6 | VOTING IN THE 2004 PRESIDENTIAL ELECTIONS BY EDUCATION LEVEL

Turnout is given as a percentage of the voting-age citizen population.

YEARS OF SCHOOL COMPLETED	REPORTED TURNOUT
Less than 9th grade	38.8
9th to 12th grade, no diploma	39.8
High school graduate	56.4
Some college or associate degree	68.9
Bachelor's degree	77.5
Advanced degree	84.2

Source: U.S. Bureau of the Census, May 26, 2005.

These statistics reinforce one another. White voters are likely to be wealthier than African American voters, who are also less likely to have obtained a college education.

Why People Do Not Vote

For many years, political scientists believed that one reason voter turnout in the United States was so much lower than in other Western nations was that it was very difficult to register to vote. In most states, registration required a special trip to a public office far in advance of elections. Many experts are now proposing other explanations for low U.S. voter turnout.

Uninformative Media Coverage and Negative Campaigning.   Some scholars contend that one of the reasons why some people do not vote has to do with media coverage of campaigns. Many researchers have shown that the news media tend to provide much more news about "the horse race," or which candidates are ahead in the polls, than about the actual policy positions of the candidates. Thus, voters are not given the kind of information that would provide an incentive to go to the polls on election day. Additionally, negative campaigning is thought to have an adverse effect on voter turnout. By the time citizens are ready to cast their ballots, most of the information they have heard about the candidates has been so negative that no candidate is appealing.

According to a year-long study conducted in 2000 by Harvard University's Center on the Press, Politics, and Public Policy, nonvoters and voters alike shared the same criticisms of the way the media cover campaigns: most thought the media treated campaigns like theater or entertainment. Nonvoters, however, were much more cynical about government and politicians than were voters. As the director of the study put it, "All the polls, the spin, the attack ads, the money and the negative news have soured Americans on the way we choose our president."[21]

The Rational Ignorance Effect.   Another explanation of low voter turnout suggests that citizens are making a logical choice in not voting. If citizens believe that their votes will not affect the outcome of an election, then they have little incentive to seek the information they need to cast intelligent votes. The lack of incentive to obtain costly (in terms of time, attention, and so on) information about politicians and political issues has been called the **rational ignorance effect.** That term may seem contradictory, but it is not. Rational ignorance is a condition in which people purposely and rationally decide not to obtain information—to remain ignorant.

Why, then, do even one-third to one-half of U.S. citizens bother to show up at the polls? One explanation is that most citizens receive personal satisfaction from the act of voting. It makes them feel that they are good citizens and that they are doing something patriotic. Even among voters who are registered and who plan to vote, if the cost of voting goes up (in terms of time and inconvenience), the number of registered voters who actually vote will fall. In particular, bad weather on Election Day means that, on average, a smaller percentage of registered voters will go to the polls.

Plans for Improving Voter Turnout.   Mail-in voting, Internet voting, registering to vote when you apply for a driver's license—these are all ideas that have been either suggested or implemented in the hope of improving voter turnout. Nonetheless, voter turnout remains low.

| **Rational Ignorance Effect**
An effect produced when people purposely and rationally decide not to become informed on an issue because they believe that their vote on the issue is not likely to be a deciding one; a lack of incentive to seek the necessary information to cast an intelligent vote.

---

[21]Thomas E. Patterson, *The Vanishing Voter: Public Involvement in an Age of Uncertainty* (New York: Knopf, 2002). You can continue to track the Vanishing Voter Project at the study's Web site, **www. vanishingvoter.org**.

Two other ideas seemed promising. The first was to allow voters to visit the polls up to three weeks before election day. The second was to allow voters to vote by absentee ballot without having to give any particular reason for doing so. The Committee for the Study of the American Electorate discovered, however, that in areas that had implemented these plans, neither plan increased voter turnout. Indeed, voter turnout actually fell in those jurisdictions. In other words, states that did *not* permit early voting or unrestricted absentee voting had better turnout rates than states that did. Apparently, these two innovations appeal mostly to people who already intended to vote.

What is left? One possibility is to declare Election Day a national holiday. In this way, more eligible voters will find it easier to go to the polls.

Legal Restrictions on Voting

Legal restrictions on voter registration have existed since the founding of our nation. Most groups in the United States have been concerned with the suffrage issue at one time or another.

Historical Restrictions

In colonial times, only white males who owned property with a certain minimum value were eligible to vote, leaving a greater number of Americans ineligible than eligible to take part in the democratic process.

Property Requirements.   Many government functions concern property rights and the distribution of income and wealth, and some of the founders of our nation believed it was appropriate that only people who had an interest in property should vote on these issues. The idea of extending the vote to all citizens was, according to Charles Pinckney, a South Carolina delegate to the Constitutional Convention, merely "theoretical nonsense."

The logic behind the restriction of voting rights to property owners was questioned seriously by Thomas Paine in his pamphlet *Common Sense*:

> Here is a man who today owns a jackass, and the jackass is worth $60. Today the man is a voter and goes to the polls and deposits his vote. Tomorrow the jackass dies. The next day the man comes to vote without his jackass and cannot vote at all. Now tell me, which was the voter, the man or the jackass?[22]

The writers of the Constitution allowed the states to decide who should vote. Thus, women were allowed to vote in Wyoming in 1870 but not in the entire nation until the Nineteenth Amendment was ratified in 1920. By about 1850, most white adult males in virtually all the states could vote without any property qualification. North Carolina was the last state to eliminate its property test for voting—in 1856.

Further Extensions of the Franchise.   Extension of the franchise to black males occurred with the passage of the Fifteenth Amendment in 1870. This enfranchisement was short lived, however, as the "redemption" of the South by white racists had rolled back these gains by the end of the century. As discussed in Chapter 5, it was not until the 1960s that African Americans, both male and female, were able to participate in the electoral process in all states. Women received full national voting rights with the Nineteenth Amendment in 1920. The most recent extension

African American voters in New York circa 1945. Until the 1965 Voting Rights Act, African Americans faced obstacles when trying to exercise their right to vote, especially in the South. If part of the population cannot vote, what impact is that likely to have on the types of legislation passed by Congress or state legislatures? (Library of Congress/NAACP Collection)

---

[22]Thomas Paine, *Common Sense* (London: H. D. Symonds, 1792), p. 28.

of the franchise occurred when the voting age was reduced to eighteen by the Twenty-sixth Amendment in 1971. In the years since the amendment was passed, however, young people have traditionally had a low turnout.

Is the Franchise Still Too Restrictive?   There continue to be certain classes of people who do not have the right to vote. These include noncitizens and, in most states, convicted felons who have been released from prison. They also include current prison inmates, election law violators, and people who are mentally incompetent. Also, no one under the age of eighteen can vote. Some political activists have argued that some of these groups should be allowed to vote. Most other democracies do not prevent persons convicted of a crime from voting after they have completed their sentences. In the 1800s, many states let noncitizen immigrants vote. In Nicaragua, the minimum voting age is sixteen.

One discussion concerns the voting rights of convicted felons who are no longer in prison or on parole. Some contend that voting should be a privilege, not a right, and we should not want the types of people who commit felonies participating in decision making. Others believe that it is wrong to further penalize those who have paid their debt to society. These people argue that barring felons from the polls injures minority groups because minorities make up a disproportionately large share of former prison inmates.

A Republican campaign worker registers a citizen to vote during the 2004 campaign in New York's Times Square. How do voter-registration drives affect election outcomes? (AP Photo/Jennifer Szymaszek)

Current Eligibility and Registration Requirements

Voting generally requires **registration,** and to register, a person must satisfy the following voter qualifications, or legal requirements: (1) citizenship, (2) age (eighteen or older), and (3) residency—the duration varies widely from state to state and with types of elections. Since 1972, states cannot impose residency requirements of more than thirty days.

Each state has different qualifications for voting and registration. In 1993, Congress passed the "motor voter" bill, which requires that states provide voter-registration materials when people receive or renew driver's licenses, that all states allow voters to register by mail, and that voter-registration forms be made available at a wider variety of public places and agencies. In general, a person must register well in advance of an election, although voters in Idaho, Maine, Minnesota, Oregon, Wisconsin, and Wyoming are allowed to register up to, and on, Election Day. North Dakota has no voter registration at all.

Some argue that registration requirements are responsible for much of the nonparticipation in our political process. Certainly, since their introduction in the late 1800s, registration laws have had the effect of reducing the voting participation of African Americans and immigrants. There also is a partisan dimension to the debate over registration and nonvoting. Republicans generally fear that an expanded electorate would help to elect more Democrats.

The question arises as to whether registration is really necessary. If it decreases participation in the political process, perhaps it should be dropped altogether. Still, as those in favor of registration requirements argue, such requirements may prevent fraudulent voting practices, such as multiple voting or voting by noncitizens. Indeed, several states have passed legislation that requires a would-be voter to show a government-issued photo identification before casting a ballot. The courts, though, have often ruled against these states, arguing that such requirements discriminate against those who do not have a driver's license, passport, or other government-issued identification.

Extension of the Voting Rights Act

In the summer of 2006, President Bush signed legislation that extended the Voting Rights Act for twenty-five more years. As we discussed in Chapter 5, the Voting Rights Act was enacted to assure that African Americans had equal access to the polls. Most of the provisions of the 1965 Voting Rights Act became permanent law. The 2006 act extended certain temporary sections and clarified certain amendments. For example, any new voting practices or procedures in jurisdictions with a history of discrimination in voting have to be approved by the U.S. Department of Justice or the federal district court in Washington, D.C., before being implemented. Section 203 of the 2006 act ensures that American citizens with limited proficiency in English can obtain the necessary assistance to enable them to understand and cast a ballot. Further, the act authorizes the U.S. attorney general to appoint federal election observers when there is evidence of attempts to intimidate minority voters at the polls. Those who supported the 2006 act believe that such provisions will ensure continuing voter participation by minority groups in America.

Registration
The entry of a person's name onto the list of registered voters for elections. To register, a person must meet certain legal requirements of age, citizenship, and residency.

MAKING A DIFFERENCE | Registering and Voting

In nearly every state, before you are allowed to cast a vote in an election, you must first register. Registration laws vary considerably from state to state. Depending in part on how difficult a state's laws make it to register, some states have much lower rates of registration and voting participation than do others.

Why Should You Care?

To vote, you must register. But why bother to vote? After all, the electorate is large, many elections are not close, and often your vote will not have an important effect on the election outcome. If you do vote, however, you increase the amount of attention that politicians pay to people like you. When Congress, state legislatures, or city councils consider new laws and regulations, these bodies typically give more weight to the interests of groups that are more likely to vote. So even if your single vote does not determine the outcome of an election, it does add, to a small degree, to the voter turnout for your constituency. Your vote therefore increases the chances of legislation that benefits you or that meets with your approval.

What Can You Do?

What do you have to do to register and cast a vote? In general, you must be a citizen of the United States, at least eighteen years old on or before election day, and a resident of the state in which you intend to register.

Most states require that you meet minimum-residency requirements. In other words, you must have lived in the state in which you plan to be registered for a specified period of time. If you have not lived in the state long enough to register before an upcoming election, you may retain your previous registration in another state and cast an absentee vote, if that state permits it. Minimum-residency requirements vary among the states. By a ruling of the United States Supreme Court, no state can require more than thirty days of residency. Some states require a much shorter period—for example, ten days in New Hampshire and Wisconsin and one day in Alabama. Twenty states do not have a minimum-residency requirement at all.

Nearly every state also specifies a closing date by which you must be registered before an election. In other words, even if you have met a residency requirement, you still may not be able to vote if you register too close to the day of the election. The closing date is different in certain states (Connecticut, Delaware, and Louisiana) for primary elections than for other elections. The closing date for registration varies from Election Day itself (Idaho, Maine, Minnesota, Oregon, Wisconsin, and Wyoming) to thirty days before the election (Arizona). In North Dakota, no registration is necessary.

In most states, your registration can be revoked if you do not vote within a certain number of years. This process of automatically "purging" the voter-

registration lists of nonactive voters happens every two years in about a dozen states, every three years in Georgia, every four years in more than twenty other states, every five years in Maryland and Rhode Island, every eight years in North Carolina, and every ten years in Michigan. Ten states do not require this purging at all.

Let us look at Iowa as an example. Iowa voters normally register through the local county auditor or when they obtain a driver's license (under the "motor voter" law of 1993). A voter who moves to a new address within the state must change his or her registration by contacting the auditor. Postcard registrations must be postmarked or delivered to the county auditor no later than the twenty-fifth day before an election. Voters can declare or change their party affiliation when they register or reregister, or they can change or declare a party when they go to the polls on Election Day. Postcard registration forms in Iowa are available at many public buildings, from labor unions, at political party headquarters, at the county auditors' offices, or from campus groups. Registrars who will accept registrations at other locations may be located by calling a party headquarters or a county auditor.

For more information on voting registration, contact your county or state officials, party headquarters, labor union, or local chapter of the League of Women Voters.

League of Women Voters
www.lwv.org

Key Terms

Australian ballot 307

"beauty contest" 300

caucus 302

closed primary 302

coattail effect 308

corrupt practices acts 293

credentials committee 305

elector 305

focus group 293

front-loading 303

front-runner 303

Hatch Act 294

independent expenditures 298

issue advocacy advertising 295

office-block, or Massachusetts, ballot 307

open primary 302

party-column, or Indiana, ballot 308

political action committee (PAC) 295

political consultant 291

presidential primary 287

rational ignorance effect 314

registration 317

soft money 295

superdelegate 301

tracking poll 292

voter turnout 311

Chapter Summary

1 People may choose to run for political office to further their careers, to carry out specific political programs, or in response to certain issues or events. The legal qualifications for holding political office are minimal at both the state and local levels, but holders of political office still are predominantly white and male and are likely to be from the professional class.

2 American political campaigns are lengthy and extremely expensive. In the last decade, they have become more candidate centered rather than party centered in response to technological innovations and decreasing party identification. Candidates have begun to rely less on the party and more on paid professional consultants to perform the various tasks necessary to wage a political campaign. The crucial task of professional political consultants is image building. The campaign organization devises a campaign strategy to maximize the candidate's chances of winning. Candidates use public opinion polls and focus groups to gauge their popularity and to test the mood of the country.

3 The amount of money spent in financing campaigns is increasing steadily. A variety of corrupt practices acts have been passed to regulate campaign finance. The Federal Election Campaign Act of 1971 and its amendments in 1974 and 1976 instituted major reforms by limiting spending and contributions; the acts allowed corporations, labor unions, and interest groups to set up political action committees (PACs) to raise money for candidates. New techniques, including "soft money" contributions to the parties and independent expenditures, were later developed. The Bipartisan Campaign Reform Act of 2002 banned soft money contributions to the national parties, limited advertising by interest groups, and increased the limits on individual contributions.

4 After the Democratic convention of 1968, the McGovern-Fraser Commission formulated new rules for primaries, which were adopted by all Democrats and by Republicans in many states. These reforms opened up the nomination process for the presidency to all voters.

5 A presidential primary is a statewide election to help a political party determine its presidential nominee at the national convention. Some states use the caucus method of choosing convention delegates. The primary campaign recently has been shortened to the first few months of the election year.

6 The voter technically does not vote directly for president but chooses between slates of presidential electors. In most states, the slate that wins the most popular votes throughout the state gets to cast all the electoral votes for the state. The candidate receiving a majority (270) of the electoral votes wins. Both the mechanics and the politics of the electoral college have been sharply criticized. There have been many proposed reforms, including a proposal that the president be elected on a popular-vote basis in a direct election.

7 The United States uses the Australian ballot, a secret ballot that is prepared, distributed, and counted by government officials. The office-block ballot groups candidates according to office. The party-column ballot groups candidates according to their party labels and symbols.

8 Voter participation in the United States is low compared with that of other countries. Some view low voter turnout as a threat to representative democracy, whereas others believe it simply indicates greater satisfaction with the status quo. There is an association between voting and a person's age, education, minority status, and income level. Another factor affecting voter turnout is the extent to which elections are competitive within a state. It is also true that the number of eligible voters is smaller than the number of people of voting age because of ineligible felons and immigrants who are not yet citizens.

9 In colonial times, only white males with a certain minimum amount of property were eligible to vote. The suffrage issue has concerned, at one time or another, most groups in the United States. Today, to be eligible to vote, a person must satisfy registration, citizenship, and age and residency requirements. Each state has different qualifications. Some claim that these requirements are responsible for much of the nonparticipation in the political process in the United States.

Selected Print and Media Resources

SUGGESTED READINGS

Green, Donald P., and Alan S. Gerber. *Get Out the Vote: How to Increase Voter Turnout*. Washington, D.C.: Brookings Institution Press, 2004. This volume is a practical guide for activists seeking to mount get-out-the-vote (GOTV) campaigns. It differs from other guides in that it is based on research and experiments in actual electoral settings—Green and Gerber are political science professors at Yale University. The authors discover that many widely used GOTV tactics are less effective than is often believed.

Jamieson, Kathleeen Hall, *et al.*, eds. *Capturing Campaign Dynamics, 2000 and 2004: The National Annenberg Election Survey*. Philadelphia: University of Pennsylvania Press, 2006. During the contentious 2000 and 2004 presidential elections, the Annenberg Public Policy Center conducted one of the largest studies ever of the American electorate. The data show the dynamic effects of political events as they unfolded during these two important presidential elections.

Lau, Richard R., *et al.*, eds. *How Voters Decide: Information Processing in Election Campaigns*. Cambridge: Cambridge University Press, 2006. The researchers who wrote this book attempted to get "inside the heads" of citizens who confront huge amounts of information during modern presidential campaigns. The researchers argued that we should care not just about which candidates receive the most votes but also about how many citizens voted "correctly"—that is, in accordance with their own interests.

MoveOn. *MoveOn's 50 Ways to Love Your Country: How to Find Your Political Voice and Become a Catalyst for Change*. Makawao, Maui, Hawaii: Inner Ocean Publishing, 2004. This book contains fifty short chapters in which individuals describe how they sought to make a difference by getting involved in the political process. MoveOn has been called a "shadow party" to the Democrats. Nevertheless, the techniques described here could be used just as easily by Republicans. The volume is also available on audiotape.

Thurber, James A., and Candice J. Nelson, eds. *Campaigns and Elections American Style: Transforming American Politics*. New York: Westview Press, 2004. The articles in this book consider the basics of American campaigns and discuss practical campaign politics. They examine the evolution of campaigns over time, including town meetings, talk radio, infomercials, and focus groups. In this book, you will discover how campaign themes and strategies are determined.

Wayne, Stephen J. *The Road to the White House, 2004: The Politics of Presidential Elections*. Belmont, Calif.: Wadsworth Publishing, 2003. Stephen Wayne examines the changes in the election process since 1996 and provides an excellent analysis of the presidential selection process.

MEDIA RESOURCES

Bulworth—A 1998 satirical film starring Warren Beatty and Halle Berry. Jay Bulworth, a senator who is fed up with politics and life in general, hires a hit man to carry out his own assassination. He then throws political caution to the wind in campaign appearances by telling the truth and behaving the way he really wants to behave.

The Candidate—A 1972 film, starring the young Robert Redford, that effectively investigates and satirizes the decisions that a candidate for the U.S. Senate must make. A political classic.

If You Can't Say Anything Nice—Negative campaigning seems to have become the norm in recent years. This 1999 program looks at the resulting decline in popularity of politics among the electorate and suggests approaches to restoring faith in the process.

Money Talks: The Influence of Money on American Politics—Bill Moyers reports on the influence of money on our political system. Produced in 1994.

Primary Colors—A 1998 film starring John Travolta as a southern governor who is plagued by a sex scandal during his run for the presidency.

E·MOCRACY | Elections and the Web

Today's voters have a significant advantage over those in past decades. It is now possible to obtain extensive information about candidates and issues simply by going online. Some sites present point-counterpoint articles about the candidates or issues in an upcoming election. Other sites support some candidates and positions and oppose others. The candidates themselves all now have Web sites that you can visit if you want to learn more about them and their positions. You can also obtain information online about election results by going to sites such as those listed in the *Logging On* section. While the Internet has proved to be a valuable vehicle for communicating information about elections, it is not clear whether it will be used for actual voting in national elections at some future time. Although Internet voting seems like a great idea, it also raises many concerns, particularly about security.

Logging On

For detailed information about current campaign-financing laws and for the latest filings of finance reports, see the site maintained by the Federal Election Commission at

www.fec.gov

To find excellent reports on where campaign money comes from and how it is spent, be sure to view the site maintained by the Center for Responsive Politics at

www.opensecrets.org

You can learn about the impact of different voting systems on election strategies and outcomes at the Center for Voting and Democracy, which maintains the following Web site:

www.fairvote.org

Another Web site for investigating voting records and campaign-financing information is that of Project Vote Smart. Go to

www.vote-smart.org

Online Review

At **www.politicalscience.wadsworth.com/ schmidt12**, you will find a free Study Guide to this book. For each chapter, there are two online quizzes to help you master the material.

• The PoliPrep Self-Study Assessment provides a pretest for each major section of the chapter. PoliPrep then generates a customized study plan. After you complete the study plan, a posttest evaluates your progress.

• The Tutorial Quiz for each chapter provides questions on the chapter contents, including the features. The questions are organized to match the major sections of the chapter.

10 | The Media and Cyberpolitics

What If . . .
The Media Had to Reveal All of Their Sources?

BACKGROUND

Reporters, whether they work for newspapers, newswire services, television stations, magazines, or Internet blogs, typically attempt to "protect their sources." Many of these sources are willing to talk to reporters only on the condition that they remain anonymous. Consequently, untold news stories include phrases such as "informed sources said . . ." or "an anonymous source revealed . . ." Typically, these sources are confident that their names will not be disclosed because so-called shield laws protect reporters from being forced to disclose their sources in court or in other judicial proceedings. In 1972, the U.S. Supreme Court stated that "news gathering is not without First Amendment protections."* The majority on the Court, though, did not see those protections as absolute and held, among other things, that the First Amendment did not protect reporters from federal grand jury subpoenas seeking their confidential sources. In response, state legislatures and courts created their own shield laws.

WHAT IF THE MEDIA HAD TO REVEAL ALL OF THEIR SOURCES?

Assume that at both the federal and state levels, shield laws were abolished. In other words, imagine a world in which reporters could continue to cite anonymous sources but would be subject to subpoenas that legally would require them to reveal their sources. Clearly, news gatherers who could not guarantee confidentiality for many of their sources would find those sources refusing to provide information.

In these circumstances, investigative reporting in general could "take a hit." Investigative reporters would discover that fewer and fewer individuals would be willing to talk to them, except about minor matters that were not controversial.

Many jurists have predicted the same

outcome. One judge stated that compelling a reporter to disclose confidential sources "unquestionably threatens a journalist's ability to secure information that is made available to him only on a confidential basis." The judge continued by saying that the "negative effect of such disclosure on future undercover investigative reporting would be serious and threatens freedom of the press and the public's need to be informed."†

INCREASED LITIGATION POSSIBLE

If news gatherers' sources were fair game without any shield-law protection, there would probably be a big increase in litigation. Imagine a person who is unhappy about a story written about him or her. If that person were sufficiently motivated, he or she could go to court to demand the names of

the anonymous sources who had provided the information on which the reporter based the detrimental story. The sources might then face a lawsuit.

THE RISE OF THE BLOGGERS

If they were no longer protected by shield laws, reporters might turn to other techniques to disseminate news, including those used by spammers. To avoid fines and other punishments, spammers—those who send out unsolicited ads on the Internet—use a variety of methods to avoid detection. For example, some send their spam from offshore servers that route the spam through other servers that retain the spammers' anonymity.

If the media had to reveal all of their sources, news gatherers might take similar actions. They would create blogs to inform the public but remain anonymous by using nontraceable methods of

Internet dissemination. Not only would it be difficult for the government to ascertain who created the information, but the public would also be in the dark about the source of the information.

Today, most people tend to rely on trusted news sources and dismiss what might be considered gossip. If trusted news sources engaged in less investigative reporting, though, anonymous bloggers might become increasingly important.

FOR CRITICAL ANALYSIS

1. Is it fair that reporters can shield their sources today? If your answer is yes, under what circumstances might shielding sources be considered unfair?
2. Why do anonymous sources wish to keep their identities secret?

*Branzburg v. Hayes, 408 U.S. 665 (1972).

†Baker v. F & F Investment, 470 F.2d 778 (1972).

The study of people and politics—of how people gain the information that they need to be able to choose among political candidates, to organize for their own interests, and to formulate opinions on the policies and decisions of the government—must take into account the role played by the media. Historically, the print media played the most important role in informing public debate. The print media developed, for the most part, our understanding of how news is to be reported. Today, however, more than 90 percent of Americans use television news as their primary source of information. In addition, the Internet has become a source for political communication and fund-raising. As Internet use grows, the system of gathering and sharing news and information is changing from one in which the media have a primary role to one in which the individual citizen may play a greater part. With that in mind, it is important to analyze the current relationship between the media and politics. Requiring the media to reveal all of their sources would have an impact on this relationship, as we pointed out in the chapter-opening *What If . . .* feature.

The Media's Functions

The mass media perform a number of different functions in any country. In the United States, we can list at least six. Almost all of them can have political implications, and some are essential to the democratic process. These functions are as follows: (1) entertainment, (2) reporting the news, (3) identifying public problems, (4) socializing new generations, (5) providing a political forum, and (6) making profits.

Entertainment

By far the greatest number of radio and television hours are dedicated to entertaining the public. The battle for prime-time ratings indicates how important successful entertainment is to the survival of networks and individual stations.

Although there is no direct linkage between entertainment and politics, network dramas often introduce material that may be politically controversial and that may

The media are present during virtually every campaign event. Here, reporters surround Ned Lamont (right) after he defeated longtime Senate incumbent Joseph Lieberman of Connecticut in the Democratic primary in August 2006. Lieberman went on to run as an independent. To what extent do the media create campaign news? (AP Photo/Jessica Hill)

stimulate public discussion. Examples include the TV series *The West Wing* and *Commander in Chief,* which people believe promoted liberal political values. Made-for-TV movies have focused on a number of controversial topics, including AIDS, incest, and wife battering.

Reporting the News

A primary function of the mass media in all their forms—newspapers and magazines, radio, television, cable, and online news services—is the reporting of news. The media provide words and pictures about events, facts, personalities, and ideas. The protections of the First Amendment are intended to keep the flow of news as free as possible, because it is an essential part of the democratic process. If citizens cannot obtain unbiased information about the state of their communities and their leaders' actions, how can they make voting decisions? One of the most incisive comments about the importance of the media was made by James Madison, who said, "A people who mean to be their own governors must arm themselves with the power knowledge gives. A popular government without popular information or the means of acquiring it, is but a prologue to a farce or a tragedy or perhaps both."[1]

Identifying Public Problems

| Public Agenda
Issues that are perceived by the political community as meriting public attention and governmental action.

The power of the media is important not only in revealing what the government is doing but also in determining what the government ought to do—in other words, in setting the **public agenda.** The mass media identify public issues, such as convicted sex offenders living in residential neighborhoods on their release from prison. The media then influence the passage of legislation, such as "Megan's Law," which requires police to notify neighbors about the release and/or resettlement of certain offenders. American journalists also work in a long tradition of uncovering public wrongdoing, corruption, and bribery and of bringing such wrongdoing to the public's attention. Closely related to this investigative function is that of presenting policy alternatives. Public policy is often complex and difficult to make entertaining, but programs devoted to public policy increasingly are being scheduled for prime-time television. Most networks produce shows with a "news magazine" format that sometimes include segments on foreign policy and other issues.

Socializing New Generations

As mentioned in Chapter 6, the media, and particularly television, strongly influence the beliefs and opinions of Americans. Because of this influence, the media play a significant role in the political socialization of the younger generation, as well as immigrants to this country. Through the transmission of historical information (sometimes fictionalized), the presentation of American culture, and the portrayal of the diverse regions and groups in the United States, the media teach young people and immigrants about what it means to be an American. TV talk shows, such as the *Oprah Winfrey Show,* sometimes focus on controversial issues (such as abortion or assisted suicide) that relate to basic American values (such as liberty). Many children's shows are designed not only to entertain young viewers but also to instruct them in the traditional moral values of American society. In recent years, the public has become increasingly concerned about the level of violence depicted on children's programs and on other shows during prime time.

---

[1]James Madison, "Letter to W. T. Barry" (August 4, 1822), in Gaillard P. Hunt, ed., *The Writings of James Madison* 103 (1910).

Republican presidential candidate George W. Bush chats with talk-show host Oprah Winfrey. What types of voters would Bush appeal to by appearing on this show? (AP Photo/Wilfredo Lee)

As more young Americans turn to the Internet for entertainment, they are also finding an increasing amount of social and political information there. America's youth today are the Internet generation. Young people do not use the Internet just for chat and e-mail. They also participate in political forums, obtain information for writing assignments, and increasingly watch movies and even news shows online.

Providing a Political Forum

As part of their news function, the media also provide a political forum for leaders and the public. Candidates for office use news reporting to sustain interest in their campaigns, while officeholders use the media to gain support for their policies or to present an image of leadership. Presidential trips abroad are an outstanding way for the chief executive to get colorful, positive, and exciting news coverage that makes the president look "presidential." The media also offer ways for citizens to participate in public debate, through letters to the editor, televised editorials, or electronic mail. The question of whether more public access should be provided will be discussed later in this chapter.

Making Profits

Most of the news media in the United States are private, for-profit corporate enterprises. One of their goals is to make profits for expansion and for dividends to the stockholders who own the companies. In general, profits are made as a result of charging for advertising. Advertising revenues usually are related directly to circulation or to listener/viewer ratings.

For the most part, the media depend on advertisers to obtain revenues to make profits. Media outlets that do not succeed in generating sufficient revenues from advertising either go bankrupt or are sold. Consequently, reporters may feel pressure from media owners and from advertisers. Media owners may take their cues from what advertisers want. If an important advertiser does not like the political bent of a particular reporter, the reporter could be asked to alter his or her "style" of writing. The

Project for Excellence in Journalism discovered that 53 percent of local news directors said that advertisers try to tell them what to air and what not to air.[2]

Advertisers have been known to pull ads from newspapers and TV stations whenever they read or view negative publicity about their own companies or products. For example, CBS ran a *60 Minutes* show about Dillard's and other department stores that claimed store security guards used excessive force and racial profiling. In response, Dillard's pulled its ads from CBS. This example can be multiplied many times over.

Several well-known media outlets, in contrast, are publicly owned—public television stations in many communities and National Public Radio. These operate without extensive commercials, are locally supported, and are often subsidized by the government and corporations. A complex relationship exists among the for-profit and nonprofit media, the government, and the public. Throughout the rest of this chapter, we examine some of the many facets of this relationship.

A History of the Media in the United States

Many years ago Thomas Jefferson wrote, "Were it left to me to decide whether we should have a government without newspapers, or newspapers without a government, I should not hesitate a moment to prefer the latter."[3] Although the media have played a significant role in politics since the founding of this nation, they were not as overwhelmingly important in the past as they are today. For one thing, politics was controlled by a small elite who communicated personally. For another, during the early 1800s and before, news traveled slowly. If an important political event occurred in New York, it was not known until five days later in Philadelphia; ten days later in the capital cities of Connecticut, Maryland, and Virginia; and fifteen days later in Boston.

Roughly three thousand newspapers were being published by 1860. Some of these, such as the *New York Tribune*, were mainly sensation mongers that concentrated on crimes, scandals, and the like. The *New York Herald* specialized in self-improvement and what today would be called practical news. Although sensational and biased reporting often created political divisiveness (this was true particularly during the Civil War), many historians believe that the growth of the print media also played an important role in unifying the country.

The Rise of the Political Press

Americans may cherish the idea of an unbiased press, but in the early years of the nation's history, the number of politically sponsored newspapers was significant. The sole reason for the existence of such periodicals was to further the interests of the politicians who paid for their publication. As chief executive of our government during this period, George Washington has been called a "firm believer" in **managed news.** Although acknowledging that the public had a right to be informed, he believed that some matters should be kept secret and that news that might damage the image of the United States should be censored (not published). Washington, however, made no attempt to control the press.

The Development of Mass-Readership Newspapers

Two inventions in the nineteenth century led to the development of mass-readership newspapers. The first was the high-speed rotary press; the second was the telegraph. Faster presses meant lower per-unit costs and lower subscription prices. In addition,

Managed News
Information generated and distributed by the government in such a way as to give government interests priority over candor.

---

[2]Project for Excellence in Journalism, "Gambling with the Future," *Columbia Journalism Review*, November/December 2001.
[3]Thomas Jefferson, "Letter to Edward Carrington" (1787), in Andrew A. Lipscomb and Albert E. Bergh, eds., *The Writings of Thomas Jefferson*, Memorial Edition (Washington, D.C., 1903–04), p. 57.

by 1848, the Associated Press had developed the telegraph into a nationwide apparatus for the dissemination of all types of information on a systematic basis.

Along with these technological changes came a growing population and increasing urbanization. A larger, more urban population could support daily newspapers, even if the price per paper was only a penny. Finally, the burgeoning, diversified economy encouraged the growth of advertising, which meant that newspapers could obtain additional revenues from merchants who seized the opportunity to promote their wares to a larger public.

The Popular Press and Yellow Journalism

Students of the history of journalism have ascertained a change in the last half of the 1800s, not in the level of biased news reporting but in its origin. Whereas politically sponsored newspapers had expounded a particular political party's point of view, the post–Civil War mass-based newspapers expounded whatever political philosophy the owner of the newspaper happened to have.

Even if newspaper owners did not have a particular political axe to grind, they often allowed their editors to engage in sensationalism and what is known as **yellow journalism.** The questionable or simply personal activities of a prominent businessperson, politician, or socialite were front-page material. Newspapers, then as now, made their economic way by maximizing readership. As the *National Enquirer* demonstrates with its current circulation of almost two million, sensationalism is still rewarded by high levels of readership.

The Age of the Electromagnetic Signal

The first scheduled radio program in the United States featured politicians. On the night of November 2, 1920, KDKA-Pittsburgh transmitted the returns of the presidential election race between Warren G. Harding and James M. Cox. The listeners were a few thousand people tuning in on very primitive, homemade sets.

By 1924, there were nearly 1,400 radio stations. But it was not until 8 P.M. on November 15, 1926, that the electronic media came into their own in the United States. On that night, the National Broadcasting Company (NBC) made its debut with a four-hour program broadcast by twenty-five stations in twenty-one cities. Network broadcasting had become a reality.

| Yellow Journalism
A term for sensationalistic, irresponsible journalism. Reputedly, the term is an allusion to the cartoon "The Yellow Kid" in the old *New York World*, a newspaper especially noted for its sensationalism.

©1997 Jim Borgman, *Cincinnati Enquirer.* Reprinted with permission of King Feature Syndicate.

" INTERESTING.....IT'S LIKE A PORTABLE 500K FILE and YOU DON'T HAVE TO WAIT FOR IT TO DOWNLOAD.... AND YOU SAY IT'S CALLED A NEWSPAPER ? "

| Electronic Media
Communication channels that involve electronic transmissions, such as radio, television, and, to an increasing extent, the Internet.

Even with the advent of national radio in the 1920s and television in the late 1940s, many politicians were slow to understand the significance of the **electronic media.** The 1952 presidential campaign was the first to involve a real role for television. Television coverage of the Republican convention helped Dwight Eisenhower win over delegates and secure the nomination. His vice-presidential running mate, Richard Nixon, put TV to good use. Accused of hiding a secret slush fund, Nixon replied to his critics with his famous "Checkers" speech. He denied the attacks, cried real tears, and said that the only thing he ever received from a contributor for his personal use was his dog, Checkers, and a "Republican cloth coat" for his wife, Pat. It was a highly effective performance.

Today, television dominates the campaign strategy of every would-be national politician, as well as that of every elected official. Politicians think of ways to continue to be newsworthy, thereby gaining access to the electronic media. Attacking the president's programs is one way of becoming newsworthy; other ways include holding highly visible hearings on controversial subjects, going on "fact-finding" trips, and employing gimmicks (such as taking a walking tour of a state).

The Revolution in the Electronic Media

Just as technological change was responsible for the end of politically sponsored periodicals, technology is increasing the number of alternative news sources today. The advent of pay TV, cable TV, subscription TV, satellite TV, and the Internet has completely changed the electronic media landscape. With hundreds, if not thousands, of potential outlets for specialized programs, the electronic media are becoming more and more like the print media in catering to specialized tastes. This is sometimes referred to as **narrowcasting.** Cable and satellite television and the Internet offer the public unparalleled access to specialized information on everything from gardening and home repair to sports and religion. Most viewers are able to choose among several sources for their favorite type of programming.

| Narrowcasting
Broadcasting that is targeted to one small sector of the population.

The Web site of the Fox News cable network. All of the major TV news providers now have Web sites at which viewers can find up-to-the-minute breaking stories. Fox News has been widely accused of bias in favor of conservative causes and the Republican Party. The network claims, however, that it is impartial. How might you judge the political bias of a network?

In recent years, narrowcasting has become increasingly prevalent. The broadcast networks' audiences are declining. Between 1982 and 2006, their share of the audience fell from 72 percent to 54 percent. At the same time, the percentage of households having access to the Internet grew from zero to more than 68 percent.

Talk-Show Politics and Satellite Radio

Multiple news outlets have given rise to literally thousands of talk shows on television, radio, and the Internet. By 2007, there were more than two dozen national television talk shows; their hosts ranged from Jerry Springer, who is regarded as a sensationalist, to Larry King, whose show has become a political necessity for candidates. In 2003, Arnold Schwarzenegger actually announced his candidacy for governor of California on Jay Leno's *Tonight Show*.

The real blossoming of "talk" has occurred on the radio. The number of radio stations that program only talk shows has increased from about 300 in 1989 to more than 1,200 today. The topics of talk shows range from business and investment, to psychology, to politics. There has been considerable criticism of the political talk shows, especially those hosted by Rush Limbaugh, G. Gordon Liddy, and other conservatives, on the ground that these shows focus on personal attacks rather than policy issues. Critics contend that such shows increase the level of intolerance and irrationality in American politics. The listeners to those shows are self-selected and tend to share the viewpoint of the host.

Responding to conservative dominance of "talk radio," in 2003 and 2004 a number of liberal groups began considering the possibilities of left-of-center talk shows. In 2004, liberal comedian Al Franken went live on Air America Radio with his highly partisan take on the news. Franken has been willing to match rhetoric with conservative talk-show hosts such as Rush Limbaugh.

Satellite radio may also become an important player in talk-show politics. Howard Stern, who was considered an outspoken force on both traditional radio

Radio talk-show host Rush Limbaugh has a very large number of enthusiastic listeners across the country. Limbaugh, who is strongly conservative, is famous for the harsh language he aims at liberals and liberal ideas. What are the political implications of the conservative dominance of talk radio? Does it unbalance the national discourse— or does it balance liberal voices in other branches of the media?
(AP Photo/Lennox McLendon)

and TV, moved to Sirius satellite radio in 2006. Though Stern spends much of his time on nonpolitical topics, he does interview political guests (whom he usually harasses). A competing satellite radio system, XM, has its own political commentators, including Bob Edwards, who conducts interviews on XM Public Radio. XM also carries America Right, a channel that features *The G. Gordon Liddy Show* and another show hosted by Michael Reagan, son of the late president Ronald Reagan.

The Internet, Blogging, and Podcasting

For at least ten years, every politician has felt the necessity of having a Web site. On the national level, political Web sites were created for the two major-party candidates for president for the first time in 1996. Since then, even the lowliest local politician feels obligated to have a Web site that is updated at least on occasion. Political candidates have used the Internet to raise tens of million of dollars. Howard Dean did so in a significant way during the Democratic primaries in the last presidential election cycle.

Within the last few years, politicians have also felt obligated to post regular blogs on their Web sites. The word *blog* comes from Web log, a regular updating of one's ideas at a specific Web site. Of course, many people besides politicians are also posting blogs. Not all of the millions of blogs posted daily are political in nature, but many are and they can have a dramatic influence on events, giving rise to the term *blogosphere politics*. During the 2004 presidential campaign, CBS's Dan Rather reported on television that documents showed that President George W. Bush had failed to fulfill his obligations to the National Guard during the 1970s. Within four hours, a blogger on Freerepublic.com pointed out that the documents shown on CBS appeared to have been created in Microsoft Word, even though personal computers and Microsoft Word did not even exist in the 1970s. Another blogger, Charles Johnson (Littlegreenfootballs.com), showed that by using Word default settings he could create documents that matched those from CBS. Eleven days later, CBS admitted that an error had been made, and Dan Rather ultimately lost his job as a news anchor.

This official home page of the Republican National Committee features blogs from many contributors, including President George W. Bush and his wife, Laura. There are also links to podcasts. Users can sign up for RSS (really simple syndication) feeds on specific topics. Thus, those who use RSS feeds are automatically e-mailed links to blogs and podcasts of interest. Under what circumstances would individuals or organizations wish to use RSS services?

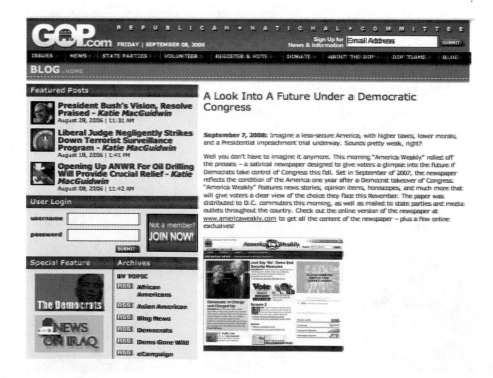

Blogs are clearly threatening the mainstream media. They can be highly specialized, highly political, and highly entertaining. And they are cheap. The *Washington Post* requires thousands of employees, paper, and ink to generate its offline product and incurs delivery costs to get it to readers. A blogging organization such as RealClearPolitics can generate its political commentary with fewer than ten employees.

Once blogs—written words—became well established, it was only a matter of time before they would end up as spoken words. Enter podcasting, so called because the first Internet-communicated spoken blogs were downloaded onto Apple's iPods. Podcasts, though, can be heard on one's computer or downloaded onto any portable listening device. Podcasting can also include videos. Hundreds of thousands of podcasts are now being generated everyday. Basically, anyone who has an idea can easily create a podcast and make it available for downloading. Like blogs, podcasting threatens traditional media sources. Even video podcasting costs virtually nothing with today's inexpensive technology.

Although politicians have been slower to adopt this form of communication, many now are using podcasts to keep in touch with their constituents. By the time you read this, there will be thousands, if not tens of thousands, of political podcasts. Certainly, podcasting will be a major part of campaigning during the 2007–2008 election cycle.

> **DID YOU KNOW . . .**
> That the number of people watching the television networks during prime time has declined by almost 25 percent in the last ten years?

Podcasting
A method of distributing multimedia files, such as audio or video files, for downloading onto mobile devices or personal computers.

The Primacy of Television

Television is the most influential medium. It is also big business. National news TV personalities such as Katie Couric and Brian Williams may earn millions of dollars per year from their TV contracts alone. They are paid so much because they command large audiences, and large audiences command high prices for advertising on national news shows. Indeed, news *per se* has become a major factor in the profitability of TV stations.

The Increase in News-Type Programming

In 1963, the major networks—ABC, CBS, and NBC—devoted only eleven minutes daily to national news. A twenty-four-hour-a-day news cable channel—CNN—started operating in 1980. With the addition of CNN–Headline News, CNBC, MSNBC, Fox News, and other news-format cable channels since the 1980s, the amount of news-type programming has continued to increase. By 2007, the amount of time the networks devoted to news-type programming each day had increased to about three hours. In recent years, all of the major networks have also added Internet sites to try to capture that market, but they face hundreds of competitors on the Web.

Television's Influence on the Political Process

Television's influence on the political process today is recognized by all who engage in the process. Television news is often criticized for being superficial, particularly compared with the detailed coverage available in the print media, such as the *New York Times*. In fact, television news is constrained by its technical characteristics, the most important being the limitations of time—stories must be reported in only a few minutes.

The most interesting aspect of television is, of course, the fact that it relies on pictures rather than words to attract the viewer's attention. Therefore, the digital videos or slides that are chosen for a particular political story have exaggerated importance.

Jon Stewart of *The Daily Show,* an award-winning production of the Comedy Central channel. Stewart was highly critical of the Bush administration during 2004. The program regularly features political guests—Democratic senator John Edwards formally announced his candidacy for president on the show. Many voters report that they get most of their political news from programming that is primarily slanted toward entertainment. How would such information differ from the news that is available on the evening news shows? (Courtesy of *The Daily Show*)

Sound Bite
A brief, memorable comment that can easily be fit into news broadcasts.

Viewers do not know what other photos may have been taken or what other events may have been digitally recorded—they see only those appearing on their screens. Television news can also be exploited for its drama by well-constructed stories. Some critics suggest that there is pressure to produce television news that has a "story line," like a novel or movie. The story should be short, with exciting pictures and a clear plot. In the extreme case, the news media are satisfied with a sound bite, a several-second comment selected or crafted for its immediate impact on the viewer.

It has been suggested that these formatting characteristics—or necessities—of television increase its influence on political events. (Newspapers and news magazines are also limited by their formats, but to a lesser extent.) As you are aware, real life is usually not dramatic, nor do all events have a neat or an easily understood plot. Political campaigns are continuing events, lasting perhaps as long as two years. The significance of their daily turns and twists is only apparent later. The "drama" of Congress, with its 535 players and dozens of important committees and meetings, is also difficult for the media to present. What television requires is dozens of daily three-minute stories.

Some commentators, including M. B. Zuckerman, editor in chief of *U.S. News and World Report,* claim that "policymaking is held hostage to imagery." Zuckerman argues that television networks "distort the meaning of events by failing to provide the context that would help us make sense of these images." The TV newsroom cliché has been and probably always will be "if it bleeds, it leads." It is not news to show one hundred rebuilt schools in Iraq, but it is news to show a car bombing that injures or kills civilians.

The Media and Political Campaigns

All forms of the media—television, newspapers, radio, magazines, blogs, and podcasts—have a significant political impact on American society. Media influence is most obvious during political campaigns. News coverage of a single event, such as the results of the Iowa caucuses or the New Hampshire primary, may be the most

Vice President Dick Cheney unclips his microphone after a live TV interview at the Bush-Cheney 2004 national campaign headquarters in Arlington, Virginia. How much of an impact do vice-presidential candidates have on a presidential race? (AP Photo/Gerald Herbert)

important factor in having a candidate be referred to in the media as the front-runner in a presidential campaign. It is not too much of an exaggeration to say that almost all national political figures, starting with the president, plan every public appearance and statement to attract media coverage.

Because television is still the primary news source for the majority of Americans, candidates and their consultants spend much of their time devising strategies that use television to their benefit. Three types of TV coverage are generally employed in campaigns for the presidency and other offices: advertising, management of news coverage, and campaign debates.

Advertising

Perhaps one of the most effective political ads of all time was a thirty-second spot created by President Lyndon Johnson's media adviser in 1964. In this ad, a little girl stood in a field of daisies. As she held a daisy, she pulled the petals off and quietly counted to herself. Suddenly, when she reached number ten, a deep bass voice cut in and began a countdown: "10, 9, 8, 7, 6 . . . ." When the voice intoned "zero," the unmistakable mushroom cloud of an atomic bomb began to fill the screen. Then President Johnson's voice was heard: "These are the stakes. To make a world in which all of God's children can live, or to go into the dark. We must either love each other or we must die." At the end of the commercial, the message read, "Vote for President Johnson on November 3."

To understand how effective this "daisy girl" commercial was, you must know that Johnson's opponent was Barry Goldwater, a Republican conservative candidate known for his expansive views on the role of the U.S. military. The ad's implication was that Goldwater would lead the United States into nuclear war. Although the ad was withdrawn within a few days, it has a place in political campaign history as the classic negative campaign advertisement. The ad's producer, Tony Schwartz, describes the effect in this way: "It was comparable to a person going to a psychiatrist and seeing dirty pictures in a Rorschach pattern. The daisy commercial evoked Goldwater's pro-bomb statements. They were like dirty pictures in the audience's mind."[4]

Since the daisy girl advertisement, negative advertising has come into its own. Candidates vie with one another to produce "attack" ads and then to counterattack when the opponent responds. The public claims not to like negative advertising, but as one consultant put it, "Negative advertising works." The most important effect of negative advertisements may not be to transfer votes from the candidate who is under attack to the candidate running the ads. Rather, the negative ads can demoralize the supporters of the candidate who is under attack. Some supporters, as a result, may not bother to vote. The widespread use of negative ads, therefore, can lead to reduced political participation and a general cynicism about politics.

Political advertising has become increasingly important for the profitability of television station owners. Hearst-Argyle Television, for example, obtains well over 10 percent of its revenues from political ads during an election year. Political advertising is not restricted to television, however. In addition to typical print ads, online political advertising has been on the rise. The Interactive Advertising Bureau estimates that during the 2008 presidential campaign, as much as $10 billion could be spent on Internet advertising.

[4]As quoted in Kathleen Hall Jamieson, *Packaging the Presidency: A History and Criticism of Presidential Campaign Advertising*, 3d ed. (New York: Oxford University Press, 1996), p. 200.

President Lyndon Johnson's "daisy girl" ad contrasted the innocence of childhood with the horror of an atomic attack.

VOTE FOR PRESIDENT JOHNSON ON NOVEMBER 3.

These images are from still frames of television ads for opposing candidates in the Senate race in Pennsylvania in 2006. The top-row images are for the Democratic challenger, Robert Casey. The bottom row shows those for incumbent Republican Rick Santorum. What is most noticeable are the last frames—each shows the candidates in a family or traditional American environment stressing family and other well-accepted values. Why would opposing candidates use the same "pitch"? (Photos Courtesy of Candidates' Campaign Offices)

Management of News Coverage

Using political advertising to get a message across to the public is a very expensive tactic. Coverage by the news media, however, is free; it simply demands that the campaign ensure that coverage takes place. In recent years, campaign managers have shown increasing sophistication in creating newsworthy events for journalists to cover. As Doris Graber points out, "To keep a favorable image of their candidates in front of the public, campaign managers arrange newsworthy events to familiarize potential voters with their candidates' best aspects."[5]

The campaign staff uses several methods to try to influence the quantity and type of coverage the campaign receives. First, the campaign staff understands the technical aspects of media coverage—camera angles, necessary equipment, timing, and deadlines—and plans political events to accommodate the press. Second, the campaign organization is aware that political reporters and their sponsors—networks or newspapers—are in competition for the best stories and can be manipulated through the granting of favors, such as a personal interview with the candidate. Third, the scheduler in the campaign has the important task of planning events that will be photogenic and interesting enough for the evening news. A related goal, although one that is more difficult to attain, is to convince reporters that a particular interpretation of an event is correct.

Today, the art of putting the appropriate spin on a story or event is highly developed. Each candidate's or elected official's press advisers, often referred to as spin doctors, try to convince the journalists that their interpretations of the political events are correct. For example, throughout 2005 and 2006 George W. Bush's camp tried to persuade the media that criticisms of the administration's handling of the Iraq war were inappropriate. The same type of persuasion was used to justify the administration's Middle East policies in general. More recently, journalists have begun to report on the different spins used by candidates and elected officials to try to manipulate news coverage.

Going for the Knockout Punch—Presidential Debates

In presidential elections, perhaps just as important as political advertisements is the performance of the candidate in televised presidential debates. After the first such debate in 1960, in which John Kennedy, the young senator from Massachusetts,

| Spin
An interpretation of campaign events or election results that is favorable to the candidate's campaign strategy.

| Spin Doctor
A political campaign adviser who tries to convince journalists of the truth of a particular interpretation of events.

[5]Doris Graber, *Mass Media and American Politics,* 7th ed. (Washington, D.C.: Congressional Quarterly Press, 2005), p. 63.

A family watches the 1960 Kennedy-Nixon debates on television. After the debate, TV viewers thought Kennedy had won, whereas radio listeners thought Nixon had won. (Library of Congress)

took on the vice president of the United States, Richard Nixon, candidates became aware of the great potential of television for changing the momentum of a campaign. In general, challengers have much more to gain from debating than do incumbents. Challengers hope that the incumbent will make a mistake in the debate and undermine the "presidential" image. Incumbent presidents are loath to debate their challengers because it puts their opponents on an equal footing with them, but the debates have become so widely anticipated that it is difficult for an incumbent to refuse.

Debates can affect the outcome of a race. Some people believe that Democrat Al Gore hurt himself during the 2000 debates by appearing arrogant. In 2004, John

Senator John Kerry (left) speaks as President George W. Bush (right) listens during the first 2004 presidential candidates' debate. The debate was held at the University of Miami in Florida on September 30, 2004. Coming into the debates, Kerry was trailing in the Gallup Poll and in other polls. After the first debate, however, Gallup reported that Kerry and Bush were tied. The race was again too close to call, as it had been for much of 2004. Who has the most to lose in such debates when an incumbent is running? Why? (Dennis Brack/Bloomberg News/Landov)

Kerry came close to saving his campaign with a strong debate performance, though in the end George W. Bush won the election. During the debates, Kerry appeared calm and forceful—in a word, presidential. Kerry badly needed to project this image to counter repeated Republican accusations that he lacked the character to serve as commander in chief. In contrast, Bush seemed somewhat rattled by Kerry's criticisms, especially during the first debate.

Although debates are justified publicly as an opportunity for the voters to find out how candidates differ on the issues, what the candidates want is to capitalize on the power of television to project an image. They view the debate as a strategic opportunity to improve their own images or to point out the failures of their opponents. Candidates also know that the morning-after interpretation of the debate by the news media may play a crucial role in what the public thinks. Regardless of the risks of debating, the potential for gaining votes is so great that candidates undoubtedly will continue to seek televised debates.

Political Campaigns and the Internet

Without a doubt, the Internet has become an important vehicle for campaign advertising and news coverage, as well as for soliciting campaign contributions. This was made clear during the 2004 presidential elections, when 7 percent of all Internet users participated in online campaign activities. (Internet users included about two-thirds of all American adults.) As pointed out previously, Democratic presidential hopeful Howard Dean (now head of the Democratic Party) used his Internet site and e-mailings to generate millions of dollars in campaign contributions, most of which were very small, such as $50 or $100. Certainly, with the increased use of blogs and podcasts, the Internet will be used even more during the 2007–2008 election cycle. Instead of just receiving an e-mail presenting a candidate's positions, you will receive an e-mail containing a link to her or his latest video podcast, which will not only set out the candidate's positions, but also ask for a contribution.

Today, the campaign staff of every candidate running for a significant political office includes an Internet campaign strategist—a professional hired to create and maintain the campaign Web site, blogs, and podcasts. The work of this strategist includes designing a user-friendly and attractive Web site for the candidate, managing the candidate's e-mail communications, and tracking campaign contributions made through the site. Additionally, virtually all major interest groups in the United States now use the Internet to promote their causes. Prior to elections, various groups engage in issue advocacy from their Web sites. At little or no cost, they can promote positions taken by favored candidates and solicit contributions.

Only a few years ago, some speculated that the Internet would soon dominate political campaign advertising and news coverage. The traditional media— television, radio, and printed newspapers and magazines—would play a far less significant role than in the past. Will this, in fact, happen? We examine this question in this chapter's *Which Side Are You On?* feature on the next page.

The Media's Impact on the Voters

The question of how much influence the media have on voting behavior is difficult to answer. Generally, individuals watch television, read newspapers, or log on to a Web site with certain preconceived ideas about political issues and candidates. These attitudes and opinions act as a kind of perceptual screen that filters out information that makes people feel uncomfortable or that does not fit with their own ideas.

Voters watch campaign commercials and news about political campaigns with "selective attentiveness"—that is, they tend to watch those commercials that support the candidates they favor and tend to pay attention to news stories about their

WHICH SIDE ARE YOU ON? | Are Internet Campaigns the Wave of the Future?

In December 2002, Vermont governor Howard Dean did not look like a candidate who could win the Democratic presidential nomination, although his fiery speeches were popular among the faithful. By December 2003, Dean was propelled to the head of the Democratic pack by a campaign that took unique advantage of the Internet. In January 2004, however, Dean's support collapsed. While Dean was on the rise, many observers claimed that Internet-based campaigns were indeed the wave of the future. But after January, some pundits compared Dean's campaign to the tech boom of the 1990s—"an overinflated bubble that left its naïve believers drenched in soap scum."*

THE INTERNET WILL DEMOCRATIZE POLITICAL CAMPAIGNS

Internet advocates say that new technology can bring more people into the democratic process. Activists can sign up online for face-to-face meetings through Web sites such as Meetup.com. Supporters can create independent blogs that give them a stake in the campaign. Both supporters and candidates can create audio or video podcasts and send out information on them via e-mail lists. Above all, the Web is a very effective way of mobilizing campaign contributions. Finally, the Web can be used to distribute advertisements at almost no cost. Web ads can be more hard hitting than TV ads because the Internet is not yet subject to government regulation.

*Steven Levy, "Dean's Net Effect Is Just the Start," *Newsweek*, March 29, 2004, p. 73.

THE INTERNET IS SERIOUSLY OVERSOLD

Web critics question whether the Web is truly transformative. After all, Dean failed. Through their inexperience, many of the young campaign workers he recruited through the Web may have turned off more voters than they were able to mobilize. A "flash mob" psychology can lead Web users to rally behind candidates who have not been tested by the pressure of a national campaign. The Web also promotes extreme political positions. This can pull campaigns away from the political center, where most of the votes are located. Finally, the Internet cannot be used to persuade marginal voters to get out and vote, and get-out-the-vote drives have been key to the success of most recent campaigns.

WHAT'S YOUR POSITION?

Do you think that Internet campaigns are essential or that they are overhyped? Might the Web be more useful for lobbying than for organizing campaigns?

GOING ONLINE

You can find the Meetup service at **www.meetup.com**. Meetup participants can set the location and agenda of a meeting online. You can obtain information on registering to vote at **www.declareyourself.org**. Web site technologies for candidates are for sale at **www.electionmall.com**, an entertaining site.

own candidates. This selectivity also affects their perceptions of the content of a news story or commercial and whether it is remembered. Apparently, the media have the most influence on those persons who have not formed an opinion about political candidates or issues. Studies have shown that the flurry of television commercials and debates immediately before Election Day has the greatest impact on those voters who are truly undecided. Few voters who have already formed their opinions change their minds under the influence of the media.

In 2004, as in earlier years, the media focused on the "horse race" aspects of the presidential campaigns. While some media outlets did present careful analyses of the issues and critiques of the candidates' advertising spots, most of the television coverage focused on the ever-present polls. Both presidential candidates, John Kerry and George W. Bush, took advantage of every opportunity to be on prime-time television: they visited with Oprah, David Letterman, and Larry King, among others. In fact, a national poll has indicated that some 20 percent of the voters said that they learned about politics from late-night talk shows.

The Role of the Media in the 2006 Elections

As in many past elections, broadcast television dominated media spending during the campaign. In the last midterm elections, $912 million was spent on TV ads. In the 2006 elections, $1.6 billion was spent. Moving away from traditional television, the big news during the 2006 campaign was the ease with which short video clips of candidates' bloopers could be propagated with lightening speed over the Internet. All it takes is an onlooker's digital movie camera and a connection to YouTube.com. A number of candidates discovered, to their peril, that seemingly racial slurs and other offensive statements soon found their way to YouTube. One candidate's embarrassing remarks were downloaded from YouTube by hundreds of thousands of news organizations, campaign opponents, and potential voters within days. In the 2006 election, YouTube became a source of viral word-of-mouth. Indeed, the Internet has become the source of political news for over 43 percent of likely voters.

The Media and the Government

The mass media not only wield considerable power when it comes to political campaigns, but they also, in one way or another, can wield power over the affairs of government and over government officials. For example, in April 2004 President George W. Bush tried to keep Condoleezza Rice, then the national security adviser, from testifying before the bipartisan 9/11 investigation commission by citing the doctrine of executive privilege. After several weeks during which this decision was widely criticized in the print and electronic media, Bush reversed himself and allowed Rice to testify.

Prepackaged News

In recent years, the public learned that the Bush administration had spent millions of dollars on public relations, including "news" programs that were often created specifically to be rebroadcast on television. In 2005, for example, the Bush administration had to acknowledge that it paid a number of conservative commentators to write in support of administration-backed programs. Specifically, conservative commentator Armstrong Williams received $240,000 to write favorably about the No Child Left Behind Act and the Department of Education. Additionally, the Bush administration created a video about the new education law that was designed to look like a legitimate news program. The administration used the same technique to promote the law providing a new prescription drug benefit for Medicare recipients.

Before the telecast of the 2004 Super Bowl, hundreds of local television stations broadcast an interview with White House drug czar John Waters by news anchor Mike Morris. What the stations did not know, however, was that the interview was produced by Waters's Office of National Drug Control Policy and that Morris was actually under contract to the federal government. Is the use of taxpayer dollars to create prepackaged news legal? Some argue that it is because the government is not forcing anyone to broadcast this "covert" propaganda. Others, however, question the ethical underpinnings of government advocacy at the expense of both unbiased journalism and taxpayers' dollars.

This still frame is taken from a Department of Education video that was used to promote the Bush administration's education law, entitled the No Child Left Behind Act. The video made it appear that the reporting was unbiased, but failed to point out that the reporter creating the video was in fact paid by the federal government with taxpayers' funds. Are there any circumstances when it is appropriate to use taxpayers' funds to market pending federal legislation? If so, what are they? If no, why not? (AP Photo/Education Department)

| **White House Press Corps**
The reporters assigned full-time to cover the presidency.

| **Press Secretary**
The presidential staff member responsible for handling White House media relations and communications.

The Media and the Presidency

The relationship between the media and the president usually is reciprocal: each needs the other to thrive. Because of this codependency, both the media and the president work hard to exploit one another. The media need news to report, and the president needs coverage.

In the United States, the prominence of the president is accentuated by a **White House press corps** that is assigned full-time to cover the presidency. These reporters even have a lounge in the White House where they spend their days, waiting for a story to break. Most of the time, they simply wait for the daily or twice-daily briefing by the president's **press secretary.** Because of the press corps' physical proximity to the president, the chief executive cannot even take a brief stroll around the presidential swimming pool without its becoming news. Perhaps no other nation allows the press such access to its highest government official. Consequently, no other democratic nation has its airwaves and print media so filled with absolute trivia regarding the personal lives of the chief executive and his or her family.

One of the first presidents to make truly effective use of the media was President Franklin D. Roosevelt (1933–1945), who brought new spirit to a demoralized country and led it through the Great Depression with his radio broadcasts. His "fireside chats" brought hope to millions. Through his speeches, Roosevelt was able to forge a common emotional bond among his listeners. His decisive announcement in 1933 on the reorganization of the banks, for example, calmed a jittery nation and prevented the collapse of the banking industry. (Nervous depositors were withdrawing their assets, which threatened to create a "run" on the banks.) His famous Pearl Harbor speech, following the Japanese attack on the U.S. Pacific fleet on December 7, 1941 ("a day that will live in infamy"), mobilized the nation for World War II.

Setting the Public Agenda

According to a number of studies, the media play an important part in setting the public agenda. Evidence is strong that whatever public problems receive the greatest media treatment will be cited by the public in contemporary surveys as the most important problems. Although the media do not make policy decisions, they do

President Ronald Reagan (1981–1989) in a speech from the White House. Reagan was called "the great communicator" for his effective use of the media. He was an actor before entering politics, and that experience helped him develop his skills. Reagan accumulated decades of political experience before becoming president. Still, some people held his acting career against him. Why might that be so? (AP Photo/Barry Thumma)

President Franklin D. Roosevelt, the first president to fully exploit the airwaves for his benefit, reported to the nation through radio "fireside chats." How did such capabilities change the nature of the presidency? (Franklin D. Roosevelt Presidential Library and Museum)

influence to a significant extent the policy issues that will be decided—and this is an important part of the political process. Because those who control the media are not elected representatives of the people, the agenda-setting role of the media necessarily is a controversial one. The relationship of the media to agenda setting remains complex, though, because politicians are able to manipulate media coverage to control some of its effects, as well as to exploit the media to further their agendas with the public.

Government Regulation of the Media

The United States has one of the freest presses in the world. Nonetheless, regulation of the media does exist, particularly of the electronic media. Many aspects of this regulation were discussed in Chapter 4, when we examined First Amendment rights and the press.

The First Amendment does not mention electronic media, which did not exist when the Bill of Rights was written. For many reasons, the government has much greater control over the electronic media than it does over printed media. Through the Federal Communications Commission (FCC), which regulates communications by radio, television, wire, and cable, the number of radio stations has been controlled for many years, even though technologically we could have many more radio stations than now exist. Also, the FCC created a situation in which the three major TV networks dominated the airwaves.

Controlling Ownership of the Media

Many FCC rules have dealt with ownership of news media, such as how many stations a network can own. In the past, the FCC auctioned off hundreds of radio frequencies, allowing the expansion of cellular telephone applications.

In 1996, Congress passed legislation that had far-reaching implications for the communications industry—the Telecommunications Act. The act ended the rule that kept telephone companies from entering the cable business and other communications markets. What this means is that a single corporation—whether Time Warner or Disney—can offer long-distance and local telephone services, cable television, satellite television, Internet services, and, of course, libraries of films and entertainment. The act opened the door to competition and led to more options for consumers, who now can choose among multiple competitors for all of these services delivered to the home. At the same time, it launched a race among competing companies to control media ownership.

Media Conglomerates.   Many media outlets are now owned by corporate conglomerates. A single entity may own a television network; the studios that produce shows, news, and movies; and the means to deliver that content to the home via cable, satellite, or the Internet. The question to be faced in the future is how to ensure competition in the delivery of news so that citizens have access to multiple points of view from the media.

All of the prime-time television networks are owned by major American corporations, including such corporate conglomerates as General Electric (owner of NBC) and Disney (owner of ABC). The Turner Broadcasting/CNN network was also purchased by a major corporation, Time Warner. Later, Time Warner was acquired by America Online (AOL), a merger that combined the world's then-largest media company with the world's then-largest online company. Fox Television has always been a part of Rupert Murdoch's publishing and media empire. In addition to taking part in mergers and acquisitions, many of these companies have formed partnerships with computer software makers, such as Microsoft, for joint electronic publishing ventures.

Increased Media Concentration.   The FCC promulgates rules on what media conglomerates can own. One measure of a conglomerate's impact is "audience reach," or the percentage of the national viewing public that has access to the conglomerate's outlets. The FCC places an upper limit on audience reach, known as the "audience-reach cap." A few years ago, the FCC raised the national audience-reach cap from

The Reverend Jesse Jackson leads a protest outside the headquarters of the Federal Communications Commission (FCC) in Washington, D.C. In 2003, the FCC voted to relax its media-ownership rules, opening the door for media conglomerates to buy more local television stations and newspapers. Why might someone believe that the media coverage would be less balanced under conglomerate ownership?
(Chris Kleponis/*Bloomberg News*/Landov)

35 percent to 45 percent and also allowed a corporation to own a newspaper and a television station in the same market. Congress rebelled against this new rule, however, and pushed the national audience-reach cap back below 40 percent. Nevertheless, a corporation can still own up to three TV stations in its largest market. The reality today is that there are only a few independent news operations left in the entire country.

This media concentration has led to the disappearance of localism in the news. Obviously, costly locally produced news cannot be shown anywhere except in that local market. In contrast, the costs of producing a similar show for national broadcast can be amortized over millions and millions of viewers and paid for by higher revenues from national advertisers. Another concern, according to former media mogul Ted Turner, is that the rise of media conglomerates may lead to a decline in democratic debate. The emergence of independent news Web sites, blogs, and podcasts provides an offset to this trend, however. Consequently, the increased concentration of traditional media news organizations may not matter as much as in the past.

Government Control of Content

On the face of it, the First Amendment would seem to apply to all media. In fact, the United States Supreme Court has often been slow to extend free speech and free press guarantees to new media. For example, in 1915, the Court held that "as a matter of common sense," free speech protections did not apply to cinema. Only in 1952 did the Court find that motion pictures were covered by the First Amendment.[6] In contrast, the Court extended full protection to the Internet almost immediately by striking down provisions of the 1996 Telecommunications Act.[7] Cable TV also received broad protection in 2000.[8] (To learn about nations that exercise far more control over media content, see this chapter's *Beyond Our Borders* feature on the following page.)

Control of Broadcasting. While the Court has held that the First Amendment is relevant to radio and television, it has never extended full protection to these media. The Court has used a number of arguments to justify this stand—initially, the scarcity of broadcast frequencies. The Court later held that the government could restrict "indecent" programming based on the "pervasive" presence of broadcasting in the home.[9] On this basis, the FCC has the authority to fine broadcasters for indecency or profanity.

Indecency in broadcasting became a major issue in 2004. In the first three months of that year, the FCC levied fines that exceeded those imposed in the previous nine years combined. Including older fines, radio personality Howard Stern cost his employers almost $2 million. Another triggering episode was singer Janet Jackson's "wardrobe malfunction" during a 2004 Super Bowl halftime performance. Legislation was introduced in Congress to increase the maximum fine that the FCC can impose to $500,000 per incident.

Government Control of the Media during the Second Gulf War. During the First Gulf War in 1991, the U.S. government was strongly criticized for not providing accurate information to the media. Stung by this criticism, the Bush administration tried a two-pronged strategy during the Second Gulf War in 2003. Every day, reporters at the central command post in Qatar were able to hear briefings from top

| DID YOU KNOW . . .
That a thirty-second television advertisement shown during the Super Bowl costs more than $2.3 million?

---

[6]*Joseph Burstyn, Inc. v. Wilson,* 343 U.S. 495 (1952).

[7]*Reno v. American Civil Liberties Union,* 521 U.S. 844 (1997).

[8]*United States v. Playboy Entertainment Group,* 529 U.S. 803 (2000).

[9]*FCC v. Pacifica Foundation,* 438 U.S. 230 (1978). In this case, the Court banned seven swear words (famously used by comedian George Carlin) during hours when children could hear them.

BEYOND OUR BORDERS | Government-Controlled Media Abroad

The First Amendment to the Constitution guarantees freedom of expression in the United States. While there are certainly some restrictions on what Americans say on the radio and television, or even publish, those restrictions are few indeed. Not so in many other countries today, even though their constitutions may also guarantee freedom of expression.

IRAN'S CONTROL OF THE MEDIA

Broadcasting is run by the state in Iran. The state-run media reflect the views of President Mahmoud Ahmadinejad and those of his allies in the conservative clerical establishment.

In Iran, there are no independent newspapers that can present views contrary to the government's conservative clerical views. Every newspaper has to be licensed. Virtually all reformist newspapers have been closed down. In a less-than-totally successful attempt to skirt such censorship, reformist journalists have gone to the Internet.

Because the Internet has become increasingly important as a source of news, Iran has one of the most sophisticated Internet censorship systems in the world, probably as good as or even better than the one used in China (see Chapter 4). Although ostensibly Internet filtering is used to prevent pornographic or immoral materials, the government in reality uses such blocking to censor political content.

THE RUSSIANS HAVE LOST MANY PRESS FREEDOMS, TOO

After the end of communism in Russia, a thriving independent press came about. On television, radio, and in newspapers, Russians could read all sorts of political views. Since Vladimir Putin took over the presidency, though, virtually all opposition journalists have been in one way or another silenced. In particular, Putin has spent most of his tenure eliminating privately owned television stations. Russians are now fed a steady diet of Putin's pronouncements on TV. There is virtually no criticism of Putin's regime that the average Russian can view on TV or hear on the radio. Russians have to seek the foreign press to find out about the corruption that surrounds Putin's administration.

Of course, the Internet and blogs still present a problem to the Russian political hierarchy, but Putin's government attempts to filter the Internet, although less successfully than in Iran or China.

Russian President Vladimir Putin makes one of his many speeches, which are duly broadcast and rebroadcast on nearly all available television channels throughout the country. There is virtually no independent television programming in Russia today. (Photo courtesy of Russian Presidential Press and Information Office/Sergeja Velichkina)

THERE ARE WORSE EXAMPLES, OF COURSE

Currently, if you want to find the worst case of lack of freedom of expression, you have to examine North Korea. The country's dictator, Kim Jong Il, makes sure that North Korea's inhabitants have almost no knowledge of the outside world. To a much lesser degree, there are various restrictions on freedom of the press in Cuba, Egypt, Lebanon, Myanmar (formerly Burma), Saudi Arabia, Syria, Venezuela, and Yemen. In short, the government controls the media in countries in which democracy is either unknown or weak.

FOR CRITICAL ANALYSIS

How has technology helped reduce various government's control of the media?

During the Second Gulf War, the U.S. military allowed journalists to join military units for the duration of their presence in the Middle East. This program was called "embedding." Here, Chris Tomlinson, right, of the Associated Press, eats a "meal ready to eat" or MRE, at a temporary camp in the desert with U.S. Army soldiers from the A Company 3rd Battalion, 7th Infantry Regiment about 100 miles south of Baghdad. How might such close contact between reporters and soldiers affect what the reporters write? (AP Photo/John Moore)

commanders. (Reporters complained, however, that they did not hear enough about the true progress of the war.) The administration also allowed more than five hundred journalists to travel with the combat forces as "embedded" journalists. Reports from the field were very favorable to the military. This was understandable, given that the journalists quickly identified with the troops and their difficulties. The Bush administration, however, was unable to control reports from foreign and Arab media.

The Government's Attempt to Control the Media during the Current War on Terrorism. Certainly, since September 11, 2001, there has been increased government secrecy, sometimes apparently with the public's acceptance. Senator Patrick Leahy (D., Vt.) argues that the First Amendment would have trouble winning ratification today if it were proposed as a constitutional amendment. He based this assertion on a Knight Foundation survey that found that almost 40 percent of 110,000 students believed that newspapers should have to get "government approval" of news articles before they are published.

In any event, the charter for the Department of Homeland Security, created soon after the 9/11 terrorist attacks, includes a provision that allows certain groups to stamp "critical infrastructure information" on the top of documents when they submit information to Homeland Security. The public has no right to see this information. Additionally, more and more government documents have been labeled "secret" so that they do not have to be revealed to the public.

Despite such measures, since the war on terror and the second war in Iraq started, there have been numerous intelligence leaks to the press. The public did find out about the government's monitoring of domestic phones that were used in communications with suspected terrorists abroad. The tension between needed intelligence secrecy and the public's "right to know" continues to create both legal and military problems.

The Public's Right to Media Access

Does the public have a right to **media access**? Both the FCC and the courts gradually have taken the stance that citizens do have a right of access to the media, particularly the electronic media. The argument is that because the airwaves are public,

Media Access
The public's right of access to the media. The Federal Communications Commission and the courts gradually have taken the stance that citizens do have a right to media access.

|Bias
An inclination or a preference that interferes with impartial judgment.

the government has the right to dictate how they are used. The government could, for example, require the broadcast networks to provide free airtime to candidates. Republican senator John McCain of Arizona, a major proponent of campaign-finance reform, has proposed—so far without success—legislation that would provide such free airtime.

Technology is giving more citizens access to the electronic media and, in particular, to television. As more cable operators have more airtime to sell, some of it will remain unused and will be available for public access. At the same time, the Internet makes media access by the public very easy, although not everyone has the resources to take advantage of it.

| Bias in the Media

Many studies have been undertaken to try to identify the sources and direction of **bias** in the media, and these studies have reached different conclusions. Some claim that the press has a liberal bias. Others conclude that the press shows a conservative bias. Still others do not see any notable partisan bias.

Do the Media Have a Partisan Bias?

In a classic study conducted in the 1980s, researchers found that media producers, editors, and reporters (the "media elite") exhibited a notably liberal and "left-leaning" bias in their news coverage.[10] Since then, the contention that the media have a liberal bias have been repeated time and again. Joining the ranks of those who assert that the media has a liberal bias is Bernard Goldberg, a veteran CBS broadcaster. Goldberg argues that liberal bias is responsible for the declining number of viewers who watch network news. He claims that this liberal bias, which "comes naturally to most reporters," has given viewers less reason to trust the big news networks.[11] Conservative journalist William McGowan also claims that the press exhibits a liberal bias. He maintains that most news reporters have liberal views on the issues they cover (he cites a survey of journalists in which over 80 percent of the respondents said that they were in favor of abortion rights) and that this bias prevents them from investigating and reporting on opposing viewpoints.[12]

In 2005, the University of Connecticut's Department of Public Policy surveyed 300 journalists nationwide. These journalists were asked whom they voted for in the 2004 presidential election. The Democratic challenger, John Kerry, received 52 percent of their votes, while Bush received only 19 percent (27 percent of those queried either refused to disclose their vote or did not vote).[13]

In that same year, there was heated debate about the liberal bias of the government-funded Public Broadcasting Service (PBS). President Bush had already named a Republican, Kenneth Y. Tomlinson, to chair the underlying Corporation for Public Broadcasting. Tomlinson contracted with an outside consultant to track PBS's political leanings on the program *Now with Bill Moyers*. Apparently, Tomlinson wanted proof that PBS had a liberal bias. To counter this supposed liberal bias, Tomlinson encouraged PBS officials to broadcast *The Journal Editorial Report*, a program hosted by Paul Gigot, editor of the conservative editorial page of the *Wall Street Journal*. In his defense, Tomlinson stated that "my goal here is to see programming that satisfies a broad con-

[10]S. Robert Lichter, Stanley Rothman, and Linda S. Lichter, *The Media Elite* (New York: Adler and Adler, 1986).
[11]Bernard Goldberg, *Bias: A CBS Insider Exposes How the Media Distort the News* (Washington, D.C.: Regnery Publishing, 2001).
[12]William McGowan, *Coloring the News: How Political Correctness Has Corrupted American Journalism* (San Francisco: Encounter Books, 2003).
[13]University of Connecticut, "National Polls of Journalists and the American Public," May 16, 2005.

POLITICS AND DIVERSITY | Racial Profiling in the Media

Racial profiling is the act of routinely making negative assumptions about individuals based on race. The term was first used to describe the behavior of certain police officers who habitually stopped African American motorists more frequently than white ones, often on minor pretexts. African Americans have described these incidents as stops for "driving while black." Some observers have charged that the media—television in particular—engage in racial profiling in their reporting on minority group members.

IMAGES ON TV

Those who believe that the media engage in racial profiling point to common stereotypes that journalists often use when illustrating news stories. For example, a study found that while African Americans constituted 29 percent of the nation's poor, they made up 65 percent of the images of the poor shown on leading network news programs. In addition to being disproportionately portrayed as black, the poor were also largely represented by the persons least likely to command sympathy—unemployed adults. The elderly and the working poor were underrepresented.* Critics of racial profiling also argue that

*Martin Gilens, "Race and Poverty in America: Public Misperceptions and the American News Media," *Public Opinion Quarterly*, vol. 6 (1996).

African Americans are regularly used to illustrate drug abusers or dealers, even though a majority of users are white, and that images of criminals in general are disproportionately black.

Americans of Middle Eastern ancestry have also complained about profiling. In this instance, the stereotype is of the Arab terrorist. Of course, such people exist, but like African American criminals, they make up a small part of the group's population.

DIVERSITY IN THE NEWSROOM

Today's newsrooms are increasingly diverse. One survey revealed that minority group members made up 18 percent of the employees in television journalism, and African Americans made up 10 percent. Such a substantial minority presence may serve to prevent egregious examples of racial profiling. Some even argue that racial and ethnic diversity in the workforce leads television journalists to "pull their punches" when reporting on minority group members.

FOR CRITICAL ANALYSIS

Although part of the newsroom workforce is made up of minority group members, network executives and news directors are predominantly white and male. In what ways could this reduce minority influence?

stituency."[14] (Tomlinson was forced to quit after it was discovered that he improperly used his office for personal gain.)

A Commercial Bias?

According to Andrew Kohut, director of the Pew Research Center in Washington, D.C., however, the majority of those responding to Pew Research Center polls see no ideological or partisan pattern in media bias. Rather, what people mean when they say the press is biased in its political reporting is that it is biased toward its own self-interest—the need to gain higher ratings and thus more advertising revenues.

Interestingly, even though Bernard Goldberg, as just mentioned, argues that there is a liberal bias in the media, some of the examples he provides in his book would indicate that the bias in the press is more toward commercialism and elitism. For example, he states that during "sweeps" months (when ratings are important), the networks deliberately avoid featuring blacks, Hispanics, and poor or unattractive people on their prime-time news magazine shows. This, asserts Goldberg, is because such coverage might "turn off" the white, middle-class viewers that the networks want to attract so that they can build the ratings that advertisers want. When the media do cover minority groups, are the images they use misleading? We examine this question in this chapter's *Politics and Diversity* feature.

[14]"Republican Chairman Exerts Pressure on PBS, Alleging Biases," *Washington Times*, May 2, 2005, p. 7.

MAKING A DIFFERENCE | Being a Critical Consumer of the News

Television and newspapers provide a wide range of choices for Americans who want to stay informed. Still, critics of the media argue that a substantial amount of programming and print is colored either by the subjectivity of editors and producers or by the demands of profit making. Few Americans take the time to become critical consumers of the news.

Why Should You Care?

Even if you do not plan to engage in political activism, you have a stake in ensuring that your beliefs are truly your own and that they represent your values and interests. To guarantee this result, you need to obtain accurate information from the media and avoid being swayed by subliminal appeals, loaded terms, or outright bias. If you do not take care, you could find yourself voting for a candidate who is opposed to what you believe in or voting against measures that are in your interest.

Even when journalists themselves are relatively successful in an attempt to remain objective, they will of necessity give airtime to politicians and interest group representatives who are far from impartial. You need the ability to determine what motivates the players in the political game and to what extent they are "shading" the news or even propagating outright lies. You also need to determine which news outlets are reliable.

What Can You Do?

To become a critical news consumer, you must practice reading a news-paper with a critical eye toward editorial decisions. For example, ask yourself what stories are given prominence on the front page of the paper and which ones merit a photograph. What is the editorial stance of the newspaper? Which columnists are given space on the "op-ed" page opposite the paper's own editorial page? For a contrast to most daily papers, occasionally pick up an outright political publication such as the *National Review* or the *New Republic* and take note of the editorial positions.

Watching the evening news can be far more rewarding if you look at how much the news depends on video effects. You will note that stories on the evening news tend to be no more than three minutes long, that stories with excellent videotape get more attention, and that considerable time is taken up with "happy talk" or human interest stories.

Another way to critically evaluate news coverage is to compare how the news is covered in different media. For example, you might compare the evening news with the daily paper. You will see that the paper is perhaps half a day behind television in reporting the news but that the printed story contains far more information.

If you wish to obtain more information on the media, you can contact one of the following organizations:

National Association of Broadcasters
1771 N St. N.W.
Washington, DC 20036
202-429-5300
www.nab.org

National Newspaper Association
129 Neff Annex
Columbia, MO 65211
1-800-829-4NNA
www.nna.org

Accuracy in Media
(a conservative group)
4455 Connecticut Ave. N.W.,
Suite 330
Washington, DC 20008
202-364-4401
www.aim.org

People for the American Way
(a liberal group)
2000 M St. N.W., Suite 400
Washington, DC 20036
202-467-4999
www.pfaw.org

Key Terms

Chapter Summary

1 The media are enormously important in American politics today. They perform a number of functions, including (a) entertainment, (b) news reporting, (c) identifying public problems, (d) socializing new generations, (e) providing a political forum, and (f) making profits.

2 The media have always played a significant role in American politics. In the 1800s and earlier, however, news traveled slowly, and politics was controlled by small groups whose members communicated personally. The high-speed rotary press and the telegraph led to self-supported newspapers and mass readership.

3 Broadcast media (television and radio) have been important means of communication since the early twentieth century. New technologies, such as cable television and the Internet, are giving broadcasters the opportunity to air a greater number of specialized programs.

4 The media wield great power during political campaigns and over the affairs of government and government officials by focusing attention on their actions. Today's political campaigns use political advertising and expert management of news coverage. For presidential candidates, how they appear in presidential debates is of major importance.

5 The relationship between the media and the president is close; each uses the other—sometimes positively, sometimes negatively. The media play an important role in investigating the government, in getting government officials to understand better the needs and desires of American society, and in setting the public agenda.

6 The electronic media are subject to government regulation. Many Federal Communications Commission rules have dealt with ownership of TV and radio stations. Legislation has removed many rules about co-ownership of several forms of media, although the most recent steps taken by Congress have been to halt any further deregulation.

7 Studies of bias in the media have reached different conclusions. Some claim that the press has a liberal bias; others contend that the press shows a conservative bias. Still others conclude that the press is biased toward its own self-interest—the need to gain higher ratings and thus more advertising revenues. Other studies have found other types of biases, such as a bias in favor of the status quo or a bias against losers.

Selected Print and Media Resources

SUGGESTED READINGS

Alterman, Eric. *What Liberal Media? The Truth about Bias and the News.* New York: Basic Books, 2003. Based on extensive research, Alterman's book argues that the media have a conservative bias overall, especially on economic issues.

Gillmor, Dan. *We the Media: Grassroots Journalism by the People, for the People.* Sebastopol, Calif.: O'Reilly, 2004. Blogs have become an increasingly important part of the media. In 2004, for the first time, bloggers were awarded press credentials to cover the national political conventions. Newspaper journalist Dan Gillmor, a blogger himself, covers the new movement.

Goldberg, Bernard. *Arrogance: Rescuing America from the Media Elite.* New York: Warner, 2003. This is Goldberg's second book in which he argues that the media have a liberal bias and is a follow-up to *Bias: A CBS Insider Exposes How the Media Distort the News.* Goldberg argues that the media elite constitute an inbred, insular group.

Kuypers, Jim. *Bush's War: Media Bias and Justification for War in a Terrorist Age.* Lanham, Md.: Rowman & Littlefield Publishers, 2006. This researcher examines how the public understood President George W. Bush's justification of military actions since September 11, 2001, as that information was filtered through the new media. The author contends that the public perception of what the president says is shaped by media bias.

Tremayne, Mark, ed. *Blogging, Citizenship, and the Future of Media.* Oxford: Routledge Publishing, 2006. This collection of essays examines the population's growing dependence on blogs for political information. Some of the essays also look at how blog readers differ from the rest of the population. Finally, the book explores the future of traditional media in light of the blogging phenomenon.

MEDIA RESOURCES

All the President's Men—A film, produced by Warner Brothers in 1976, starring Dustin Hoffman and Robert Redford as the two *Washington Post* reporters, Bob Woodward and Carl Bernstein, who broke the story on the Watergate scandal. The film is an excellent portrayal of the *Washington Post* newsroom and the decisions that editors make in such situations.

Citizen Kane—A 1941 film, based on the life of William Randolph Hearst and directed by Orson Welles, that has been acclaimed as one of the best movies ever made. Welles himself stars as the newspaper tycoon. The film also stars Joseph Cotten and Alan Ladd.

Leveraging Technology for Your Legislative Campaigns: Effectively Using E-Newsletters, E-Mail Alerts, Podcasts, and Your Web Site—This is a series of audio compact discs and MP3 files created by Robert McLean and TheCapitol.net for Capitol Learning that gives you the ins and outs of how modern campaign managers use blogging and podcasts.

E·MOCRACY | The Media and the Internet

Today, the Internet offers a great opportunity to those who want to access the news. All of the major news organizations, including radio and television stations and newspapers, are online. Most local newspapers include at least some of their news coverage and features on their Web sites, and all national newspapers are online. Even foreign newspapers can now be accessed online within a few seconds. Also available are purely Web-based news publications, including e-zines (online news magazines) such as *Slate*, *Salon*, and *Hotwired*. Because it is relatively simple for anyone or any organization to put up a home page or Web site, a wide variety of sites have appeared that critique the news media or give alternative interpretations of the news and the way it is presented.

| Logging On

The Web site of the *American Journalism Review* includes features from the magazine and original content created specifically for online reading. Go to

www.ajr.org

The *Drudge Report* home page, posted by Matt Drudge, provides a handy guide to the Web's best spots for news and opinions. Its mission is one-click access to breaking news and recent columns. It provides links to specific columnists and opinion pages for magazines and major daily newspapers. Go to

www.drudgereport.com

The American Review Web page critiques the media, promotes media activism, and calls for media reform. Its URL is

www.americanreview.us

To view *Slate*, the e-zine of politics and culture published by Microsoft, go to

www.slate.msn.com

Blogs have become a major feature of the Internet. A large number of blogs deal with political topics. For a listing of several hundred political blogs, go to the Blog Search Engine at

www.blogsearchengine.com

For an Internet site that provides links to news media around the world, including alternative media, go to

www.mediachannel.org

| Online Review

At **www.politicalscience.wadsworth.com/ schmidt12**, you will find a free Study Guide to this book. For each chapter, there are two online quizzes to help you master the material.

• The PoliPrep Self-Study Assessment provides a pretest for each major section of the chapter. PoliPrep then generates a customized study plan. After you complete the study plan, a posttest evaluates your progress.

• The Tutorial Quiz for each chapter provides questions on the chapter contents, including the features. The questions are organized to match the major sections of the chapter.

11 | The Congress

What If . . .
Nonpartisan Panels Drew Congressional Districts?

BACKGROUND

It used to be that on Election Day, Americans chose their representatives. Today, in contrast, the opposite seems to be occurring—the representatives are choosing the voters through the political redistricting process. Once someone gets elected to the House of Representatives, that person becomes an incumbent. Incumbents who choose to run for reelection have an extraordinarily good chance of winning. Reelection rates for members of the House have been as high as 98 percent.

Don't be fooled, though, into thinking that this dramatic success rate is due just to the incumbents having done a good job for their constituents while in Congress. Rather, reelection is practically guaranteed in most jurisdictions because in most states congressional districts are carved out so as to reduce competition between the two parties. In almost all states, district lines are drawn by a small group of party leaders in the state legislature. In this manner, both Democrats and Republicans have arranged congressional districts every decade so that most districts are "safe seats" where an incumbent has an almost 100 percent chance of being reelected. Consider that in the 2004 elections, only 23 of the 435 congressional districts were decided by 10 percentage points or less. In the 2006 elections, the results were similar.

Such lack of competition is not surprising, given that in most states during 2001, sophisticated computer modeling was used to create new districts that would be "safe seats." In response to such blatant partisan redistricting, California governor Arnold Schwarzenegger and others have proposed that the responsibility for redrawing congressional district lines be taken away from politicians and given to a panel of nonpartisan retired judges.

WHAT IF NONPARTISAN PANELS DREW CONGRESSIONAL DISTRICTS?

If nonpartisan panels or state commissions were used to draw congressional districts every ten years, an immediate question would be, Who should be the members? As mentioned above, some politicians have suggested retired judges. Other possible participants might be current or retired law professors, political scientists teaching at major universities, or some combination of these.

Above all, the members of the panels or commissions would have to be nonpartisan. In other words, panel participants could receive no benefit from the outcome of the redistricting. Perhaps prospective panel members would have to declare that they favored neither Republicans nor Democrats. Alternatively, a panel could

consist of an equal number of declared Democrats and Republicans.

NONPARTISAN PANELS ALREADY EXIST

Nonpartisan boards for redistricting already exist in Britain and Canada, where they apparently have been highly successful. The boundaries are universally respected, and the legislative seats are often more competitive than in the United States. Some states, such as Arizona, Iowa, and Minnesota, already use nonpartisan redistricting, employing a panel of retired judges to draw district lines. Many who live in those states claim that the districts are more competitive than those in other states.

IMPLICATIONS OF MORE COMPETITIVE CONGRESSIONAL ELECTIONS

Assuming that nonpartisan panels were able to redistrict in an unbiased

way, the result would be more competitive congressional races. One consequence would be increased spending by challengers because the probability of a challenger winning would be greater. Today, there are races with almost no campaign spending because the challengers know that they have little chance of winning. Of course, incumbents facing viable challengers would have to step up their spending, too. We would therefore expect to see increased spending on television and Internet ads during every election cycle. We would also expect both candidates to make use of blogs and podcasts to get their messages across. In short, average campaign spending per district would increase.

The make-up of Congress would also change. Fewer members would remain in the House of Representatives for

decades. Hence, there would be more turnover in the powerful committee chairs. In other words, there would be fewer "old-timers" holding the reins of power in Congress and the House of Representatives. On the one hand, having many newcomers in power could bring new ideas, but on the other hand, more turnover could result in the loss of many experienced members.

FOR CRITICAL ANALYSIS

1. What types of people do you think would be the most unbiased participants in a redistricting panel or commission? Why?
2. Some argue that less politically homogeneous districts might result in divisive elections. Do you believe this might be a problem? Why or why not?

Most Americans view Congress in a less than flattering light. In recent years, Congress has appeared to be deeply split, highly partisan in its conduct, and not very responsive to public needs. Polls show that only about 40 percent of the public have favorable opinions about Congress as a whole. Yet individual members of Congress often receive much higher approval ratings from the voters in their districts. This is one of the paradoxes of the relationship between the people and Congress. Members of the public hold the institution in relatively low regard compared with the satisfaction they express with their individual representatives.

Part of the explanation for these seemingly contradictory appraisals is that members of Congress spend considerable time and effort serving their **constituents.** If the federal bureaucracy makes a mistake, the senator's or representative's office tries to resolve the issue. What most Americans see of Congress, therefore, is the work of their own representatives in their home states. Indeed, as you read in the chapter-opening *What If . . .* feature, members of Congress have exceptionally high reelection rates.

Congress, however, was created to work not just for local constituents but also for the nation as a whole. Understanding the nature of the institution and the process of lawmaking is an important part of understanding how the policies that shape our lives are made. In this chapter, we describe the functions of Congress, including constituent service, representation, lawmaking, and oversight of the government. We review how the members of Congress are elected and how Congress organizes itself when it meets. We also examine how bills pass through the legislative process.

Constituent
One of the persons represented by a legislator or other elected or appointed official.

Why Was Congress Created?

The founders of the American republic believed that the bulk of the power that would be exercised by a national government should be in the hands of the legislature. The leading role envisioned for Congress in the new government is apparent from its primacy in the Constitution. Article I deals with the structure, the powers, and the operation of Congress, beginning in Section 1 with an application of the basic principle of separation of powers: "All legislative Powers herein granted shall be vested in a Congress of the United States, which shall consist of a Senate and House of Representatives." These legislative powers are spelled out in detail in Article I and elsewhere.

The **bicameralism** of Congress—its division into two legislative houses—was in part the result of the Connecticut Compromise, which tried to balance the large-state population advantage, reflected in the House, and the small-state demand for equality in policymaking, which was satisfied in the Senate. Beyond that, the two chambers of Congress also reflected the social class biases of the founders. They wished to balance the interests and the numerical superiority of the common citizens with the property interests of the less numerous landowners, bankers, and merchants. They achieved this goal by providing in Sections 2 and 3 of Article I that members of the House of Representatives should be elected directly by "the People," whereas members of the Senate were to be chosen by the elected representatives sitting in state legislatures, who were more likely to be members of the elite. (The latter provision was changed in 1913 by the passage of the Seventeenth Amendment, which provides that senators also are to be elected directly by the people.)

Bicameralism
The division of a legislature into two separate assemblies.

The logic of separate constituencies and separate interests underlying the bicameral Congress was reinforced by differences in length of tenure. Members of the House are required to face the electorate every two years, whereas senators can serve for a much more secure term of six years—even longer than the four-year term provided for the president. Furthermore, the senators' terms are staggered so that only one-third of the senators face the electorate every two years, along with all of the House members.

The Functions of Congress

The bicameral structure of Congress was designed to enable the legislative body and its members to perform certain functions for the political system. These functions include the following: lawmaking, representation, service to constituents, oversight, public education, and conflict resolution. Of these, the two most important and the ones that are most often in conflict are lawmaking and representation.

The Lawmaking Function

Lawmaking
The process of establishing the legal rules that govern society.

The principal and most obvious function of any legislature is **lawmaking.** Congress is the highest elected body in the country charged with making binding rules for all Americans. Lawmaking requires decisions about the size of the federal budget, about health-care reform and gun control, and about the long-term prospects for war or peace. This does not mean, however, that Congress initiates most of the ideas for legislation that it eventually considers. A majority of the bills that Congress acts on originate in the executive branch, and many other bills are traceable to interest groups and political party organizations. Through the processes of compromise and **logrolling** (offering to support a fellow member's bill in exchange for that member's promise to support your bill in the future), as well as debate and discussion, backers of legislation attempt to fashion a winning majority coalition to create policies for the nation.

Logrolling
An arrangement in which two or more members of Congress agree in advance to support each other's bills.

The Representation Function

Representation
The function of members of Congress as elected officials representing the views of their constituents.

Representation includes both representing the desires and demands of the constituents in the member's home district or state and representing larger national interests such as farmers or the environment. Because the interests of constituents in a specific district may be in conflict with the demands of national policy, the representation function is often at variance with the lawmaking function for individual lawmakers and sometimes for Congress as a whole. For example, although it may be in the interest of the nation to reduce defense spending by closing military bases, such closures are not in the interest of the states and districts that will lose jobs and

Democratic Congresswoman Betty McCollum (right) from Minnesota was only the second woman in that state's history to be elected to Congress when she first won her seat in 2000. Here, she is shown in a recent parade celebration in South St. Paul, which also allowed her supporters to push for her reelection. How effective are a representative's personal appearances at such functions? (Photo Courtesy of Betty McCollum)

local spending. Every legislator faces votes that set representational issues against lawmaking realities.

How should the legislators fulfill the representation function? There are several views on how this should be accomplished.

The Trustee View of Representation.   The first approach to the question of how representation should be achieved is that legislators should act as **trustees** of the broad interests of the entire society. They should vote against the narrow interests of their constituents if their conscience and their perception of national needs so dictate. For example, a number of Republican legislators have supported strong laws regulating the tobacco industry in spite of the views of some of their constituents.

The Instructed-Delegate View of Representation.   Directly opposed to the trustee view of representation is the notion that the members of Congress should behave as **instructed delegates;** that is, they should mirror the views of the majority of the constituents who elected them to power in the first place. On the surface, this approach is plausible and rewarding. For it to work, however, we must assume that constituents actually have well-formed views on the issues that are decided in Congress and, further, that they have clear-cut preferences about these issues. Neither condition is likely to be satisfied very often.

Generally, most legislators hold neither a pure trustee view nor a pure instructed-delegate view. Typically, they combine both perspectives in a pragmatic mix that is often called the "politico" style.

Service to Constituents

Individual members of Congress are expected by their constituents to act as brokers between private citizens and the imposing, often faceless federal government. This function of providing service to constituents usually takes the form of **casework.** The legislator and her or his staff spend a considerable portion of their time in casework

Trustee
A legislator who acts according to her or his conscience and the broad interests of the entire society.

Instructed Delegate
A legislator who is an agent of the voters who elected him or her and who votes according to the views of constituents regardless of personal beliefs.

Casework
Personal work for constituents by members of Congress.

Congressman Tim Bishop (D., N.Y., at the podium) meets with constituents to discuss measures to help drivers afford gasoline. Bishop was elected to represent New York's 1st Congressional District in 2002 in one of the closest contests in the nation. In 2004, he was reelected with 56 percent of the vote. Bishop claimed that he had brought more than $65 million in federal funding to his district in his first term. Does "bringing home the bacon," as this activity is often called, constitute part of a representative's function? (Photo Courtesy of Tim Bishop)

| Ombudsperson
A person who hears and investigates complaints by private individuals against public officials or agencies.

activities, such as tracking down a missing Social Security check, explaining the meaning of particular bills to people who may be affected by them, promoting a local business interest, or interceding with a regulatory agency on behalf of constituents who disagree with proposed agency regulations.

Legislators and many analysts of congressional behavior regard this **ombudsperson** role as an activity that strongly benefits the members of Congress. A government characterized by a large, confusing bureaucracy and complex public programs offers innumerable opportunities for legislators to come to the assistance of (usually) grateful constituents. Morris P. Fiorina once suggested, somewhat mischievously, that senators and representatives prefer to maintain bureaucratic confusion to maximize their opportunities for performing good deeds on behalf of their constituents:

> Some poor, aggrieved constituent becomes enmeshed in the tentacles of an evil bureaucracy and calls upon Congressman St. George to do battle with the dragon. . . . In dealing with the bureaucracy, the congressman is not merely one vote of 435. Rather, he is a nonpartisan power, someone whose phone call snaps an office to attention. He is not kept on hold. The constituent who receives aid believes that his congressman and his congressman alone got results.[1]

Some members of Congress will go to great lengths to please their constituents. In 2006, for example, when gasoline prices increased to more than $3 per gallon, Senate Republicans argued in favor of sending $100 rebate checks to millions of taxpayers, while Senate Democrats campaigned for a sixty-day gasoline tax holiday. The latter plan would have cut the price of gasoline by about twenty cents a gallon. Did members of Congress actually believe that a $100 rebate or a sixty-day tax holiday would do anything to reduce high gasoline prices in the long run? Certainly not. In private, members of Congress who supported these schemes admitted that they would have been little more than a gesture. Nevertheless, all members of Congress wanted to show their constituents that they were doing something about the problem.

The Oversight Function

| Oversight
The process by which Congress follows up on laws it has enacted to ensure that they are being enforced and administered in the way Congress intended.

Oversight of the bureaucracy is essential if the decisions made by Congress are to have any force. **Oversight** is the process by which Congress follows up on the laws it has enacted to ensure that they are being enforced and administered in the way Congress intended. This is done by holding committee hearings and investigations, changing the size of an agency's budget, and cross-examining high-level presidential nominees to head major agencies. Sometimes Congress establishes a special commission to investigate a problem. For example, after Hurricane Katrina devastated New Orleans and parts of surrounding states, Congress created a commission to determine how and why the federal government, particularly the Federal Emergency Management Agency (FEMA), had mishandled government aid both during and after that natural disaster. Sometimes a commission may take several years to complete its work. This was the case with the so-called 9/11 Commission, which investigated why the United States was so unprepared for the terrorist attacks in 2001.

Senators and representatives increasingly see their oversight function as a critically important part of their legislative activities. In part, oversight is related to the concept of constituency service, particularly when Congress investigates alleged arbitrariness or wrongdoing by bureaucratic agencies.

The Public-Education Function

Educating the public is a function that is performed whenever Congress holds public hearings, exercises oversight over the bureaucracy, or engages in committee and

---

[1]Morris P. Fiorina, *Congress: Keystone of the Washington Establishment*, 2d ed. (New Haven, Conn.: Yale University Press, 1989), pp. 44, 47.

floor debate on such major issues and topics as political assassinations, aging, illegal drugs, and the concerns of small businesses. In so doing, Congress presents a range of viewpoints on pressing national questions. Congress also decides what issues will come up for discussion and decision; this **agenda setting** is a major facet of its public-education function.

The Conflict-Resolution Function

Congress is commonly seen as an institution for resolving conflicts within American society. Organized interest groups and representatives of different racial, religious, economic, and ideological interests look on Congress as an access point for airing their grievances and seeking help. This puts Congress in the position of trying to resolve the differences among competing points of view by passing laws to accommodate as many interested parties as possible. To the extent that Congress meets pluralist expectations in accommodating competing interests, it tends to build support for the entire political process.

The Powers of Congress

The Constitution is both highly specific and extremely vague about the powers that Congress may exercise. The first seventeen clauses of Article I, Section 8, specify most of the **enumerated powers** of Congress—that is, powers expressly given to that body.

Enumerated Powers

The enumerated, or expressed, powers of Congress include the right to impose taxes and import tariffs; borrow funds; regulate interstate commerce and international trade; establish procedures for naturalizing citizens; make laws regulating bankruptcies; coin (and print) money and regulate its value; establish standards of weights and measures; punish counterfeiters; establish post offices and postal routes; regulate copyrights and patents; establish the federal court system; punish illegal acts on the

| **Agenda Setting**
Determining which public-policy questions will be debated or considered.

| **Enumerated Power**
A power specifically granted to the national government by the Constitution. The first seventeen clauses of Article I, Section 8, specify most of the enumerated powers of Congress.

A U.S. Postal Service employee collects tax returns from last-minute filers outside a Massachusetts post office on the night of April 15. The most important of Congress's domestic powers is the right to impose taxes, including taxes on income. Should Congress be held responsible for not raising taxes high enough to prevent running a budget deficit? (AP Photo/Christopher Evans/ *The Republican*)

high seas; declare war; raise and regulate an army and a navy; call up and regulate the state militias to enforce laws, to suppress insurrections, and to repel invasions; and govern the District of Columbia.

The most important of the domestic powers of Congress, listed in Article I, Section 8, are the rights to collect taxes, to spend, and to regulate commerce. The most important foreign policy power is the power to declare war. Other sections of the Constitution allow Congress to establish rules for its own members, to regulate the electoral college, and to override a presidential veto. Congress may also regulate the extent of the Supreme Court's authority to review cases decided by the lower courts, regulate relations among states, and propose amendments to the Constitution.

Powers of the Senate.   Some functions are restricted to one chamber. The Senate must advise on, and consent to, the ratification of treaties and must accept or reject presidential nominations of ambassadors, Supreme Court justices, and "all other Officers of the United States." But the Senate may delegate to the president or lesser officials the power to make lower-level appointments. In 2005, President George W. Bush faced two vacancies on the Supreme Court. After Justice Sandra Day O'Connor announced her retirement, Bush nominated John Roberts to the Court and the Senate appeared likely to approve the appointment. Then, when the death of Chief Justice William Rehnquist created a second vacancy, Bush immediately changed Roberts's nomination to that of chief justice, and the Senate approved. When Bush nominated a relatively inexperienced lawyer, Harriet Miers, however, it quickly became clear that the Senate would not approve her nomination. Therefore, Bush named an experienced federal appeals court judge, Samuel Alito, who was confirmed.

Constitutional Amendments.   Amendments to the Constitution provide for other congressional powers. Congress must certify the election of a president and a vice president or itself choose these officers if no candidate has a majority of the electoral vote (Twelfth Amendment). It may levy an income tax (Sixteenth Amendment) and determine who will be acting president in case of the death or incapacity of the president or vice president (Twentieth Amendment and Twenty-fifth Amendment). In addition, Congress explicitly is given the power to enforce, by appropriate legislation, the provisions of several other amendments.

The Necessary and Proper Clause

Beyond these numerous specific powers, Congress enjoys the right under Article I, Section 8 (the "elastic," or "necessary and proper," clause), "[t]o make all Laws which shall be necessary and proper for carrying into Execution the foregoing Powers [of Article I], and all other Powers vested by this Constitution in the Government of the United States, or in any Department or Officer thereof." As discussed in Chapter 3, this vague statement of congressional responsibilities provided, over time, the basis for a greatly expanded national government. It also constituted, at least in theory, a check on the expansion of presidential powers.

House-Senate Differences

Congress is composed of two markedly different—but co-equal—chambers. Although the Senate and the House of Representatives exist within the same legislative institution, each has developed certain distinctive features that clearly distinguish one from the other. A summary of these differences is given in Table 11–1.

TABLE 11–1 | DIFFERENCES BETWEEN THE HOUSE AND THE SENATE

House*	Senate*
Members chosen from local districts	Members chosen from an entire state
Two-year term	Six-year term
Originally elected by voters	Originally (until 1913) elected by state legislatures
May impeach (indict) federal officials	May convict federal officials of impeachable offenses
Larger (435 voting members)	Smaller (100 members)
More formal rules	Fewer rules and restrictions
Debate limited	Debate extended
Less prestige and less individual notice	More prestige and more media attention
Originates bills for raising revenues	Has power to advise the president on, and to consent to, presidential appointments and treaties
Local or narrow leadership	National leadership
More partisan	Less party loyalty

*Some of these differences, such as the term of office, are provided for in the Constitution. Others, such as debate rules, are not.

Size and Rules

The central difference between the House and the Senate is simply that the House is much larger than the Senate. The House has 435 representatives, plus delegates from the District of Columbia, Puerto Rico, Guam, American Samoa, and the Virgin Islands, compared with just 100 senators. This size difference means that a greater number of formal rules are needed to govern activity in the House, whereas correspondingly looser procedures can be followed in the less crowded Senate.

The effect of the difference in size is most obvious in the rules governing debate on the floors of the two chambers. The Senate normally permits extended debate on all issues that arise before it. In contrast, the House operates with an elaborate system in which its **Rules Committee** normally proposes time limitations on debate for any bill, and a majority of the entire body accepts or modifies those suggested time limits. As a consequence of its stricter time limits on debate, the House, despite its greater size, often is able to act on legislation more quickly than the Senate.

In 2005, then Speaker Dennis Hastert (R., Ill.) and other Republicans in the House pushed through rule changes that effectively shut down the House ethics committee. This meant that there was no formal mechanism for investigating the allegedly unethical behavior by then House Majority Leader Tom DeLay (R.,Tex.). With the highly partisan atmosphere in the House, suppressing the ethics committee was unsuccessful. Several months later, the House reinstated the ethics committee framework to investigate DeLay.

Debate and Filibustering

The Senate tradition of the **filibuster,** or the use of unlimited debate as a blocking tactic, dates back to 1790. In that year, a proposal to move the U.S. capital from New York to Philadelphia was stalled by such time-wasting maneuvers. This unlimited-debate tradition—which also existed in the House until 1811—is not absolute, however. In 2005, use of the filibuster became the subject of national debate. Senate Democrats had been using the filibuster for some time to block confirmation votes on many of President Bush's most controversial nominees to the federal courts of appeals. Frustrated by this tactic, Republican senators threatened to utilize what

Rules Committee
A standing committee of the House of Representatives that provides special rules under which specific bills can be debated, amended, and considered by the House.

Filibuster
The use of the Senate's tradition of unlimited debate as a delaying tactic to block a bill.

Orrin Hatch (R., Utah), former chair of the Senate Judiciary Committee, speaks in the Senate chamber. Hatch spoke during the thirty-ninth hour of a marathon session organized by Republicans to protest Democratic filibusters. The Democrats were blocking Bush nominees for federal court judgeships. Why might senators seek to block a president's judicial candidates? (AP Photo/APTN)

some called the "nuclear option," under which Senate rules would be revised to disallow filibusters against judicial nominees. In the end, though, a bipartisan group engineered a temporary compromise to preserve the filibuster.

Under Senate Rule 22, debate may be ended by invoking *cloture*. Cloture shuts off discussion on a bill. Amended in 1975 and 1979, Rule 22 states that debate may be closed off on a bill if sixteen senators sign a petition requesting it and if, after two days have elapsed, three-fifths of the entire membership (sixty votes, assuming no vacancies) vote for cloture. After cloture is invoked, each senator may speak on a bill for a maximum of one hour before a vote is taken.

In 1979, the Senate refined Rule 22 to ensure that a final vote must take place within one hundred hours of debate after cloture has been imposed. It further limited the use of multiple amendments to stall postcloture final action on a bill.

Prestige

As a consequence of the greater size of the House, representatives generally cannot achieve as much individual recognition and public prestige as can members of the Senate. Senators are better able to gain media exposure and to establish careers as spokespersons for large national constituencies. To obtain recognition for his or her activities, a member of the House generally must do one of two things. He or she might survive in office long enough to join the ranks of the leadership on committees or within the party. Alternatively, the representative could become an expert on some specialized aspect of legislative policy—such as tax laws, the environment, or education.

Congresspersons and the Citizenry: A Comparison

Members of the U.S. Senate and the U.S. House of Representatives are not typical American citizens. Members of Congress are older than most Americans, partly because of constitutional age requirements and partly because a good deal of political experience normally is an advantage in running for national office. Members of

Congress are also disproportionately white, male, and trained in high-status occupations. Lawyers are by far the largest occupational group among congresspersons, although the proportion of lawyers in the House is lower now than it was in the past. Compared with the average American citizen, members of Congress are well paid. In 2006, annual congressional salaries were $165,200. Increasingly, members of Congress are also much wealthier than the average citizen. Whereas fewer than 1 percent of Americans have assets exceeding $1 million, about one-third of the members of Congress are millionaires. Table 11–2 summarizes selected characteristics of the members of Congress.

Compared with the composition of Congress over the past two hundred years, however, the House and Senate today are significantly more diverse in gender and ethnicity than ever before. There are almost sixty women in the House of Representatives (about 16 percent) and fourteen women in the Senate (14 percent). Minority group members fill over 15 percent of the seats in the House. The 110th Congress has significant numbers of members born in 1946 or later, the so-called Baby Boomers. A majority of House members and an even larger minority of the Senate belong to this postwar generation. This shift in the character of Congress may prompt consideration of the issues that will affect the Boomers, such as Social Security and Medicare.

Congress after the 2006 Elections

During the campaign leading up to the 2006 elections, Republican candidates predicted that giving control of Congress to the Democrats would be disastrous for the nation. Clearly, the voters disagreed, and when the elections were over, the Democrats held the majority of seats in both chambers of Congress. It is unclear, though, whether a Democrat-controlled Congress can be very energetic during the life of the 110th Congress. With all eyes on the 2008 election, Congress is likely to accomplish less than promised during the heat of electioneering. Nonetheless, political analysts believe that

TABLE 11–2 | CHARACTERISTICS OF THE 110TH CONGRESS, 2007–2009

CHARACTERISTIC	U.S. POPULATION (2000)*	HOUSE	SENATE
Age (median)	35.3	56.0	61.9
Percentage minority	24.9	15.9	5
Religion			
Percentage church members	61.0	90.6	99
Percentage Roman Catholic	39.0	29.4	24
Percentage Protestant	56.0	55.6	56
Percentage Jewish	4.0	6.7	13
Percentage female	50.9	16.1	16
Percentage with advanced degrees	5.0	66.7	78
Occupation			
Percentage lawyers	0.4	38.4	58
Percentage blue-collar workers	20.1	1.6	3
Family income			
Percentage of families earning over $50,000 annually	22.0	100.0	100
Personal wealth			
Percentage with assets over $1 million†	0.7	16.0	33

Source: *Congressional Quarterly.*
*Estimates based on 2000 census.
†108th Congress.

the Democratic Congress will pass a minimum wage bill. Moreover, there will probably be no drilling allowed in the Arctic National Wildlife Preserve. As for additional legislation, the new majority will have to work with the president, like it or not. The Democratic majority is not large enough to override the president's veto. Hence, new legislation will require compromise between Congress and the executive branch.

Congressional Elections

The process of electing members of Congress is decentralized. Congressional elections are conducted by the individual state governments. The states, however, must conform to the rules established by the U.S. Constitution and by national statutes. The Constitution states that representatives are to be elected every second year by popular ballot, and the number of seats awarded to each state is to be determined every ten years by the results of the census. Each state has at least one representative, with most congressional districts having about half a million residents. Senators are elected by popular vote (since the passage of the Seventeenth Amendment) every six years; approximately one-third of the seats are chosen every two years. Each state has two senators. Under Article I, Section 4, of the Constitution, state legislatures are given control over "[t]he Times, Places and Manner of holding Elections for Senators and Representatives"; however, "the Congress may at any time by Law make or alter such Regulations."

Only states can elect members of Congress. Therefore, territories such as Puerto Rico and Guam are not represented, though they do elect nonvoting delegates who sit in the House. The District of Columbia is also represented only by a nonvoting delegate. Should D.C. be allowed to elect representatives who can vote? We examine this question in this chapter's *Politics and Diversity* feature.

Candidates for Congressional Elections

Candidates for congressional seats may be self-selected. In districts where one party is very strong, however, there may be a shortage of candidates willing to represent the weaker party. In such circumstances, leaders of the weaker party must often actively recruit candidates. Candidates may resemble the voters of the district in ethnicity or religion, but they are also likely to be very successful individuals who have been active in politics before. House candidates are especially likely to have local ties to their districts. Candidates usually choose to run because they believe they would enjoy the job and its accompanying status. They also may be thinking of a House seat as a stepping-stone to future political office as a senator, governor, or president.

Congressional Campaigns and Elections.   Congressional campaigns have changed considerably in the past two decades. Like all other campaigns, they are much more expensive, with the average cost of a winning Senate campaign now $7.1 million and a winning House campaign averaging more than $1.1 million. Campaign funds include direct contributions by individuals, contributions by political action committees (PACs), and "soft money" funneled through state party committees. As you read in Chapter 9, all of these contributions are regulated by laws, including the Federal Election Campaign Act of 1971, as amended, and most recently the Bipartisan Campaign Reform Act of 2002. Once in office, legislators spend time almost every day raising funds for their next campaign.

Most candidates for Congress must win the nomination through a **direct primary,** in which **party identifiers** vote for the candidate who will be on the party ticket in the general election. To win the primary, candidates may take more liberal or more conservative positions to get the votes of party identifiers. In the general election,

| Direct Primary
An intraparty election in which the voters select the candidates who will run on a party's ticket in the subsequent general election.

| Party Identifier
A person who identifies with a political party.

POLITICS AND DIVERSITY | Representation for the District of Columbia

Washington, D.C., casts three electoral votes in presidential elections, the same number as the state with the smallest population. The citizens of the capital also elect a delegate who sits in the House of Representatives, but that delegate cannot vote. The District is not represented in the Senate at all. There have been a number of proposals to give D.C. voting representation in Congress. In 1978, Congress approved a constitutional amendment to give the District the representation it would have if it were a state, including two senators. The amendment was not ratified, however. More recently, District citizens have campaigned to make D.C. a state. New states can be admitted to the union without amending the Constitution.

POLITICAL CONSEQUENCES

About 60 percent of Washington's population is African American, and District voters are heavily Democratic. If D.C. were a state, its congressional delegation would probably always be Democratic. Clearly, the Republican Party has no interest in such a result. Also, conservatives in both parties do not like the liberal tendencies of D.C.'s voters. The only state with a smaller population than the District is Wyoming. Another consideration was raised by James Madison, who thought that it would be unfair for any given state to be the host of the nation's capital. He argued that such a state and its elected officials would enjoy unwarranted "imputation of awe or influence."

ALTERNATIVE SOLUTIONS

In 2003, Representative Tom Davis, a Republican from Virginia, proposed a plan to give the District a voting representative. His plan would also give an additional representative to the strongly Republican state of Utah.

Historian John Steele Gordon has another proposal. He notes that until 1801, Washington's inhabitants voted as if they were residents of Maryland. (Article 1, Section 8, Clause 17, of the Constitution created the District of Columbia as the seat of government of the United States. Both Virginia and Maryland had given land for the District, but Virginia's grant was returned because it was believed it would not be needed. Today, the District covers 69 square miles.) Gordon suggests that District

Dressed as George Washington, a demonstrator protests the District of Columbia's lack of congressional representation at a rally for the D.C. delegates to the Democratic National Convention. The delegates gathered at Union Station in Washington before a train trip to Boston. Why do you think the two major parties grant the District representation at their national conventions? (AP Photo/Lauren Burke)

citizens again vote as if they lived in Maryland. In 2004, he drafted a constitutional amendment that would allow this. Actually, an amendment might not be necessary, although the legislature of Maryland would probably have to agree to any proposal. Many District residents oppose both of these plans because neither would give D.C. two senators. In any event, some still argue strongly that the city should be returned to Maryland and that the federal enclave should be reduced to the very core of Capitol Hill.

FOR CRITICAL ANALYSIS

Which solution to the D.C. representation issue would be the most just? Why?

---

they may moderate their views to attract the votes of independents and voters from the other party.

Presidential Effects. Congressional candidates are always hopeful that a strong presidential candidate on the ticket will have "coattails" that will sweep in senators and representatives of the same party. In fact, coattail effects have been quite limited and in recent presidential elections have not materialized at all. One way to measure the coattail effect is to look at the subsequent midterm elections, held in the even-numbered years following the presidential contests. In these years, voter

TABLE 11-3 | MIDTERM GAINS AND LOSSES BY THE PARTY OF THE PRESIDENT, 1942 TO 2006

SEATS GAINED OR LOST BY THE PARTY OF THE PRESIDENT IN THE HOUSE OF REPRESENTATIVES	
1942	−45 (D.)
1946	−55 (D.)
1950	−29 (D.)
1954	−18 (R.)
1958	−47 (R.)
1962	−4 (D.)
1966	−47 (D.)
1970	−12 (R.)
1974	−48 (R.)
1978	−15 (D.)
1982	−26 (R.)
1986	−5 (R.)
1990	−8 (R.)
1994	−52 (D.)
1998	+5 (D.)
2002	+5 (R.)
2006	−30 (R.)

turnout falls sharply. In the past, the party controlling the White House normally lost seats in Congress in the midterm elections, in part because the coattail effect ceased to apply. Members of Congress who were from contested districts or who were in their first term were more likely not to be reelected. In recent years, however, this "midterm effect" has often failed to materialize. Table 11–3 shows the pattern for midterm elections since 1942. Even if presidents typically had coattail effects in midterm elections, it's not clear that they would apply to George W. Bush's second term. His job approval ratings have been uncommonly low, sometime falling below 40 percent. In 2005 and 2006, the Gallup poll consistently found that voters would favor congressional candidates who opposed the president's policies.

The Power of Incumbency

The power of incumbency in the outcome of congressional elections cannot be overemphasized, as we pointed out in the chapter-opening *What If . . .* feature. Table 11–4 shows that a sizable majority of representatives and a slightly smaller proportion of senators who decide to run for reelection are successful. This conclusion holds for both presidential-year and midterm elections. A number of scholars contend that the pursuit of reelection is the strongest motivation behind the activities of members of Congress. The reelection goal is pursued in several ways. Incumbents can use the mass media, make personal appearances with constituents, and send newsletters—all to produce a favorable image and to make the incumbent's name a household word. Members of Congress generally try to present themselves as informed, experienced, and responsive to people's needs. Legislators also can point to things that they have done to benefit their constituents—by fulfilling the congressional casework function or bringing money for mass transit to the district, for example. Finally, incumbents can demonstrate the positions that they have taken on key issues by referring to their voting records in Congress.

Party Control of Congress after the 2006 Elections

In 2006, in the most surprising midterm election outcomes since 1994 (when the Republicans took control of Congress for the first time in forty years), the voters returned Democratic majorities to both the Senate and House of Representatives.

TABLE 11-4 | THE POWER OF INCUMBENCY

	ELECTION YEAR													
	1980	1982	1984	1986	1988	1990	1992	1994	1996	1998	2000	2002	2004	2006
House														
Number of incumbent candidates	398	393	411	394	409	406	368	387	384	402	403	393	404	405
Reelected	361	354	392	385	402	390	325	349	361	395	394	383	397	382
Percentage of total	90.7	90.1	95.4	97.7	98.3	96.0	88.3	90.2	94.0	98.3	97.8	97.5	98.3	94.3
Defeated	37	39	19	9	7	16	43	38	23	7	9	10	7	23
In primary	6	10	3	3	1	1	19	4	2	1	3	3	1	2
In general election	31	29	16	6	6	15	24	34	21	6	6	7	6	21
Senate														
Number of incumbent candidates	29	30	29	28	27	32	28	26	21	29	29	28	26	29
Reelected	16	28	26	21	23	31	23	24	19	26	23	24	25	23
Percentage of total	55.2	93.3	89.6	75.0	85.2	96.9	82.1	92.3	90.5	89.7	79.3	85.7	96.2	79.3
Defeated	13	2	3	7	4	1	5	2	2	3	6	4	1	6
In primary	4	0	0	0	0	0	1	0	1	0	0	1	0	1*
In general election	9	2	3	7	4	1	4	2	1	3	6	3	1	6

*Joe Lieberman of Connecticut lost the Democratic primary but won the general election as an independent. He plans to organize with the Senate Democrats.
Sources: Norman Ornstein, Thomas E. Mann, and Michael J. Malbin, *Vital Statistics on Congress, 2001–2002* (Washington, D.C.: The AEI Press, 2002); and authors' update.

Majorities in both chambers mean that the Democrats will now occupy the leadership positions in Congress. Democrats also had little choice but to name loyal and long-serving liberal members to key committee chairs. Clearly, though, the agenda of these more liberal elements in the Democratic Party will have to be tempered somewhat to meet the demands of the more moderate Democrats and independents who helped to bring about the Democrats' victory in the elections. Indeed, the new Speaker of the House, Nancy Pelosi, who considers herself to be a traditional liberal, will face an uphill battle whenever she attempts to push for legislation that greatly deviates from the moderate positions of both parties. Consequently, Democrats will have to reach across the aisle to enlist Republican support if they are to succeed in getting legislation passed. This is particularly true in the Senate, in which the Democrats have only a two-seat majority.

> **DID YOU KNOW . . .**
> That 2004 was the first time since 1866 that Republicans increased their majority in the House of Representatives in two consecutive elections?

Congressional Apportionment

Two of the most complicated aspects of congressional elections are apportionment issues—**reapportionment** (the allocation of seats in the House to each state after each census) and **redistricting** (the redrawing of the boundaries of the districts within each state). In a landmark six-to-two vote in 1962, the United States Supreme Court made the apportionment of state legislative districts a **justiciable** (that is, a reviewable) **question.**[2] The Court did so by invoking the Fourteenth Amendment principle that no state can deny to any person "the equal protection of the laws." In 1964, the Court held that *both* chambers of a state legislature must be apportioned so that all districts are equal in population.[3] Later that year, the Court applied this "one person, one vote" principle to U.S. congressional districts on the basis of Article I, Section 2, of the Constitution, which requires that members of the House be chosen "by the People of the several States."[4]

Severe malapportionment of congressional districts before 1964 resulted in some districts containing two or three times the populations of other districts in the same state, thereby diluting the effect of a vote cast in the more populous districts. This system generally benefited the conservative populations of rural areas and small towns and harmed the interests of the more heavily populated and liberal cities. In fact, suburban areas have benefited the most from the Court's rulings, as suburbs account for an increasingly larger proportion of the nation's population, while cities include a correspondingly smaller segment of the population.

Reapportionment
The allocation of seats in the House of Representatives to each state after each census.

Redistricting
The redrawing of the boundaries of the congressional districts within each state.

Justiciable Question
A question that may be raised and reviewed in court.

Gerrymandering

Although the general issue of apportionment has been dealt with fairly successfully by the one person, one vote principle, the **gerrymandering** issue has not yet been resolved. This term refers to the legislative boundary-drawing tactics that were used under Elbridge Gerry, the governor of Massachusetts, in the 1812 elections (see Figure 11–1 on the next page). A district is said to have been gerrymandered when its shape is altered substantially by the dominant party in a state legislature to maximize its electoral strength at the expense of the minority party.

In 1986, the Supreme Court heard a case that challenged gerrymandered congressional districts in Indiana. The Court ruled for the first time that redistricting for the political benefit of one group could be challenged on constitutional grounds. In this specific case, *Davis v. Bandemer,*[5] however, the Court did not agree that

Gerrymandering
The drawing of legislative district boundary lines for the purpose of obtaining partisan or factional advantage. A district is said to be gerrymandered when its shape is manipulated by the dominant party in the state legislature to maximize electoral strength at the expense of the minority party.

---

[2]*Baker v. Carr*, 369 U.S. 186 (1962). The term *justiciable* is pronounced juhs-tish-a-buhl.
[3]*Reynolds v. Sims*, 377 U.S. 533 (1964).
[4]*Wesberry v. Sanders*, 376 U.S. 1 (1964).
[5]478 U.S. 109 (1986).

FIGURE 11-1 | THE ORIGINAL GERRYMANDER

The practice of "gerrymandering"—the excessive manipulation of the shape of a legislative district to benefit a certain incumbent or party—is probably as old as the republic, but the name originated in 1812. In that year, the Massachusetts legislature carved out of Essex County a district that historian John Fiske said had a "dragonlike contour." When the painter Gilbert Stuart saw the misshapen district, he penciled in a head, wings, and claws and exclaimed, "That will do for a salamander!" Editor Benjamin Russell replied, "Better say a Gerrymander" (after Elbridge Gerry, then governor of Massachusetts).

Source: *Congressional Quarterly's Guide to Congress*, 3d ed. (Washington, D.C.: Congressional Quarterly Press, 1982), p. 695.

the districts were drawn unfairly, because it could not be proved that a group of voters would consistently be deprived of influence at the polls as a result of the new districts.

Redistricting after the 2000 Census

In the meantime, political gerrymandering continues. For example, New York Democratic Representative Maurice Hinchey's district resembles a soup ladle. Why? That shape guarantees that he will always be able to pick up enough votes in Ithaca and Binghamton to win reelection. Right next to that district is Republican Representative Sherwood Boehlert's district, which has been said to resemble a "napping Bugs Bunny."

Redistricting decisions are often made by a small group of political leaders within a state legislature. Typically, their goal is to shape voting districts in such a way as to maximize their party's chances of winning state legislative seats as well as seats in Congress. Two of the techniques they use are called "packing" and "cracking." With the use of powerful computers and software, they *pack* voters supporting the opposing party into as few districts as possible or *crack* the opposing party's supporters into different districts. Consider that in Michigan, the Republicans who dominated redistricting efforts succeeded in packing six Democratic incumbents into only three congressional seats.

Clearly, partisan redistricting aids incumbents. The party that dominates a state's legislature will be making redistricting decisions. Through gerrymandering tactics such as packing and cracking, districts can be redrawn in such a way as to ensure that party's continued strength in the state legislature or Congress. As pointed out before, some have estimated that only between 30 and 50 of the 435 seats in the House of Representatives were open for any real competition in the most recent elections.

In 2004, the United States Supreme Court reviewed an obviously political redistricting scheme in Pennsylvania. The Court concluded, however, that the federal judiciary would not address purely political gerrymandering claims.[6] Two years later, the Supreme Court reached a similar conclusion with respect to most of the new congressional districts created by the Republicans in the Texas legislature in 2003.

---

[6]*Vieth v. Jubelirer*, 541 U.S. 267 (2004).

Again, except for one district in Texas, the Court refused to intervene in what was clearly a political gerrymandering plan.[7]

"Minority-Majority" Districts

In the early 1990s, the federal government encouraged a type of gerrymandering that made possible the election of a minority representative from a "minority-majority" area. Under the mandate of the Voting Rights Act of 1965, the Justice Department issued directives to states after the 1990 census instructing them to create congressional districts that would maximize the voting power of minority groups—that is, create districts in which minority voters were the majority. The result was a number of creatively drawn congressional districts—see, for example, the depiction of Illinois's Fourth Congressional District in Figure 11–2, which is commonly described as "a pair of earmuffs."

Constitutional Challenges

Many of these "minority-majority" districts were challenged in court by citizens who claimed that creating districts based on race or ethnicity alone violates the equal protection clause of the Constitution. In 1995, the Supreme Court agreed with this argument when it declared that Georgia's new Eleventh District was unconstitutional. The district stretched from Atlanta to the Atlantic, splitting eight counties and five municipalities along the way. The Court referred to the district as a "monstrosity" linking "widely spaced urban centers that have absolutely nothing to do with each other." The Court went on to say that when a state assigns voters on the basis of race, "it engages in the offensive and demeaning assumption that voters of a particular race, because of their race, think alike, share the same political interests, and will prefer the same candidates at the polls." The Court also chastised the Justice Department for concluding that race-based districting was mandated under

[7]*League of United Latin American Citizens v. Perry,* 399 F.Supp. 2d 756 (2006).

FIGURE 11–2 | THE FOURTH CONGRESSIONAL DISTRICT OF ILLINOIS

This district, which is mostly within Chicago's city limits, was drawn to connect two Hispanic neighborhoods separated by an African American majority district.

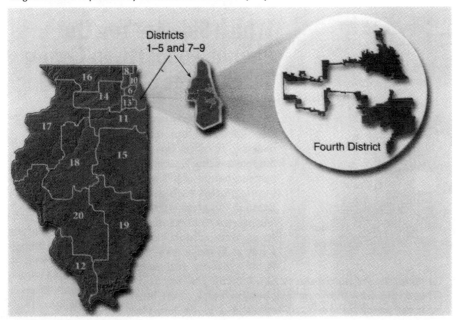

Source: *The New York Times,* July 15, 2001, p. 16.

the Voting Rights Act of 1965: "When the Justice Department's interpretation of the Act compels race-based districting, it by definition raises a serious constitutional question."[8] In subsequent rulings, the Court affirmed its position that when race is the dominant factor in the drawing of congressional district lines, the districts are unconstitutional.

Changing Directions

In the early 2000s, the Supreme Court seemed to take a new direction on racial redistricting challenges. In a 2000 case, the Court limited the federal government's authority to invalidate changes in state and local elections on the basis that the changes were discriminatory. The case involved a proposed school redistricting plan in Louisiana. The Court held that federal approval for the plan could not be withheld simply because the plan was discriminatory. Rather, the test was whether the plan left racial and ethnic minorities worse off than they were before.[9]

In 2001, the Supreme Court reviewed, for a second time, a case involving North Carolina's Twelfth District. The district was 165 miles long, following Interstate 85 for the most part. According to a local joke, the district was so narrow that a car traveling down the interstate highway with both doors open would kill most of the voters in the district. In 1996, the Supreme Court had held that the district was unconstitutional because race had been the dominant factor in drawing the district's boundaries. Shortly thereafter, the boundaries were redrawn, but the district was again challenged as a racial gerrymander. A federal district court agreed and invalidated the new boundaries as unconstitutional. In 2001, however, the Supreme Court held that there was insufficient evidence for the lower court's conclusion that race had been the dominant factor when the boundaries were redrawn.[10] The Twelfth District's boundaries remained as drawn.

| Perks and Privileges

Legislators have many benefits that are not available to most workers. For example, members of Congress are granted generous **franking** privileges that permit them to mail newsletters, surveys, and other correspondence to their constituents. The annual cost of congressional mail has risen from $11 million in 1971 to over $70 million today. Typically, the costs for these mailings rise substantially during election years.

Permanent Professional Staffs

More than 30,000 people are employed in the Capitol Hill bureaucracy. About half of them are personal and committee staff members. The personal staff includes office clerks and secretaries; professionals who deal with media relations, draft legislation, and satisfy constituency requests for service; and staffers who maintain local offices in the member's home district or state.

The average Senate office on Capitol Hill employs about thirty staff members, and twice that number work on the personal staffs of senators from the most populous states. House office staffs typically are about half as large as those of the Senate. The number of staff members has increased dramatically since 1960. With the bulk of those increases coming in assistants to individual members, some scholars question whether staff members are really advising on legislation or are primarily aiding constituents and gaining votes in the next election.

| Franking
A policy that enables members of Congress to send material through the mail by substituting their facsimile signature (frank) for postage.

---

[8]*Miller v. Johnson*, 515 U.S. 900 (1995).
[9]*Reno v. Bossier Parish School Board*, 528 U.S. 320 (2000).
[10]*Easley v. Cromartie*, 532 U.S. 234 (2001).

Congress also benefits from the expertise of the professional staffs of agencies that were created to produce information for members of the House and Senate. For example, the Congressional Research Service, the Government Accountability Office, and the Congressional Budget Office all provide reports, audits, and policy recommendations for review by members of Congress.

Privileges and Immunities under the Law

Members of Congress also benefit from a number of special constitutional protections. Under Article I, Section 6, of the Constitution, they "shall in all Cases, except Treason, Felony and Breach of the Peace, be privileged from Arrest during their Attendance at the Session of their respective Houses, and in going to and returning from the same; and for any Speech or Debate in either House, they shall not be questioned in any other Place." The arrest immunity clause is not really an important provision today. The "speech or debate" clause, however, means that a member may make any allegations or other statements he or she wishes in connection with official duties and normally not be sued for libel or slander or otherwise be subject to legal action.

Congressional Caucuses: Another Source of Support

All members of Congress are members of one or more caucuses. The most important caucuses are those established by the parties in each chamber. These Democratic and Republican meetings provide information to the members and devise legislative strategy for the party. Other caucuses have been founded, such as the Democratic Study Group and the Congressional Black Caucus, to support subgroups of members. In 1995, concerned with the growth of caucuses supported by public funds, the Republican majority in the House passed a rule that prohibited using free space for caucuses or using public funds to finance them.

The number of caucuses has not declined, however. Instead, the number has increased. There are now more than two hundred caucuses, including small ones (the Albanian Issues Caucus, the Potato Caucus) and large ones (the Sportsmen's Caucus). These organizations, which are now funded by businesses and special interests, provide staff assistance and information for members of Congress and help them build support among specific groups of voters.

The congressional Hispanic Caucus gathers in Albuquerque, New Mexico, the site of the first debate among the 2004 Democratic presidential hopefuls. From the left are Hispanic Caucus chair Ciro Rodriguez, (D., Tex.); Democratic National Committee chair Terry McAuliffe; and New Mexico governor Bill Richardson (who is Hispanic despite his Anglo-sounding name). What impact, if any, do congressional caucuses have on election outcomes? (AP Photo/ Pat Vasquez-Cunningham/*The Albuquerque Journal*)

The Committee Structure

Most of the actual work of legislating is performed by the committees and sub-committees within Congress. Thousands of bills are introduced in every session of Congress, and no single member can possibly be adequately informed on all the issues that arise. The committee system is a way to provide for specialization, or a division of the legislative labor. Members of a committee can concentrate on just one area or topic—such as taxation or energy—and develop sufficient expertise to draft appropriate legislation when needed. The flow of legislation through both the House and the Senate is determined largely by the speed with which the members of these committees act on bills and resolutions.

The Power of Committees

Sometimes called "little legislatures," committees usually have the final say on pieces of legislation.[11] Committee actions may be overturned on the floor by the House or Senate, but this rarely happens. Legislators normally defer to the expertise of the chairperson and other members of the committee who speak on the floor in defense of a committee decision. Chairpersons of committees exercise control over the scheduling of hearings and formal action on a bill. They also decide which sub-committee will act on legislation falling within their committee's jurisdiction.

Committees only very rarely are deprived of control over a bill—although this kind of action is provided for in the rules of each chamber. In the House, if a bill has been considered by a standing committee for thirty days, the signatures of a majority (218) of the House membership on a **discharge petition** can pry a bill out of an uncooperative committee's hands. From 1909 to 2007, however, although over nine hundred such petitions were initiated, only slightly more than two dozen resulted in successful discharge efforts. Of those, twenty resulted in bills that passed the House.[12]

---

[11]The term *little legislatures* is from Woodrow Wilson, *Congressional Government* (New York: Meridian Books, 1956 [first published in 1885]).

[12]Congressional Quarterly, Inc., *Guide to Congress*, 5th ed. (Washington, D.C.: CQ Press, 2000); and authors' update.

| Discharge Petition
A procedure by which a bill in the House of Representatives may be forced (discharged) out of a committee that has refused to report it for consideration by the House. The petition must be signed by an absolute majority (218) of representatives and is used only on rare occasions.

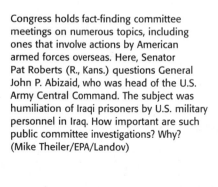

Congress holds fact-finding committee meetings on numerous topics, including ones that involve actions by American armed forces overseas. Here, Senator Pat Roberts (R., Kans.) questions General John P. Abizaid, who was head of the U.S. Army Central Command. The subject was humiliation of Iraqi prisoners by U.S. military personnel in Iraq. How important are such public committee investigations? Why? (Mike Theiler/EPA/Landov)

Types of Congressional Committees

Over the past two centuries, Congress has created several different types of committees, each of which serves particular needs of the institution.

Standing Committees.   By far the most important committees in Congress are the standing committees—permanent bodies that are established by the rules of each chamber of Congress and that continue from session to session. A list of the standing committees of the 110th Congress is presented in Table 11–5. In addition, most of the standing committees have created subcommittees to carry out their work. For example, in the 109th Congress, there were sixty-eight subcommittees in the Senate and eighty-eight in the House.[13] Each standing committee is given a specific area of legislative policy jurisdiction, and almost all legislative measures are considered by the appropriate standing committees.

Because of the importance of their work and the traditional influence of their members in Congress, certain committees are considered to be more prestigious than others. Seats on standing committees that handle spending issues are especially sought after because members can use these positions to benefit their constituents. Committees that control spending include the Appropriations Committee in either chamber and the Ways and Means Committee in the House. Members also normally seek seats on committees that handle matters of special interest to their constituents. A member of the House from an agricultural district, for example, will have an interest in joining the House Agriculture Committee.

Select Committees.   In principle, a select committee is created for a limited time and for a specific legislative purpose. For example, a select committee may be formed to investigate a public problem, such as child nutrition or aging. In practice

---

[13]*Congressional Directory* (Washington, D.C.: U.S. Government Printing Office, various editions).

| Standing Committee
A permanent committee in the House or Senate that considers bills within a certain subject area.

| Select Committee
A temporary legislative committee established for a limited time period and for a special purpose.

TABLE 11–5 | STANDING COMMITTEES OF THE 110TH CONGRESS, 2007–2009

HOUSE COMMITTEES	SENATE COMMITTEES
Agriculture	Agriculture, Nutrition, and Forestry
Appropriations	Appropriations
Armed Services	Armed Services
Budget	Banking, Housing, and Urban Affairs
Education and the Workforce	Budget
Energy and Commerce	Commerce, Science, and Transportation
Financial Services	Energy and Natural Resources
Government Reform	Environment and Public Works
Homeland Security	Finance
House Administration	Foreign Relations
International Relations	Governmental Affairs
Judiciary	Health, Education, Labor, and Pensions
Resources	Judiciary
Rules	Rules and Administration
Science	Small Business and Entrepreneurship
Small Business	Veterans Affairs
Standards of Official Conduct	
Transportation and Infrastructure	
Veterans Affairs	
Ways and Means	

Global terrorism is the topic of many hearings in the House and the Senate. Here, members of the Senate confer with various intelligence community heads before one such hearing. Second from the left is National Intelligence Director John Negroponte; third from the right in the back is then director of the CIA, Porter Goss. How much information of an intelligence nature should be discussed in an open hearing?
(AP Photo/Manuel Balce Ceneta)

a select committee, such as the Select Committee on Intelligence in each chamber, may continue indefinitely. Select committees rarely create original legislation.

Joint Committees.   A joint committee is formed by the concurrent action of both chambers of Congress and consists of members from each chamber. Joint committees, which may be permanent or temporary, have dealt with the economy, taxation, and the Library of Congress.

Conference Committees.   Special joint committees—conference committees—are formed for the purpose of achieving agreement between the House and the Senate on the exact wording of legislative acts when the two chambers pass legislative proposals in different forms. No bill can be sent to the White House to be signed into law unless it first passes both chambers in identical form. Sometimes called the "third house" of Congress, conference committees are in a position to make significant alterations to legislation and frequently become the focal point of policy debates.

The House Rules Committee.   Because of its special "gatekeeping" power over the terms on which legislation will reach the floor of the House of Representatives, the House Rules Committee holds a uniquely powerful position. A special committee rule sets the time limit on debate and determines whether and how a bill may be amended. This practice dates back to 1883. The Rules Committee has the unusual power to meet while the House is in session, to have its resolutions considered immediately on the floor, and to initiate legislation on its own.

The Selection of Committee Members

In both chambers, members are appointed to standing committees by the Steering Committee of their party. The majority-party member with the longest term of continuous service on a standing committee is given preference when the committee selects its chairperson. This is not a law but an informal, traditional process, and it applies to other significant posts in Congress as well. The seniority system, although it deliberately treats members unequally, provides a predictable means of assigning

Joint Committee
A legislative committee composed of members from both chambers of Congress.

Conference Committee
A special joint committee appointed to reconcile differences when bills pass the two chambers of Congress in different forms.

Seniority System
A custom followed in both chambers of Congress specifying that the member of the majority party with the longest term of continuous service will be given preference when a committee chairperson (or a holder of some other significant post) is selected.

positions of power within Congress. The most senior member of the minority party is called the *ranking committee member* for that party.

The general pattern until the 1970s was that members of the House or Senate who represented **safe seats** would be reelected continually and eventually would accumulate enough years of continuous committee service to enable them to become the chairpersons of their committees. In the 1970s, a number of reforms in the chairperson selection process somewhat modified the seniority system. The reforms introduced the use of a secret ballot in electing House committee chairpersons and allowed for the possibility of choosing a chairperson on a basis other than seniority. The Democrats immediately replaced three senior chairpersons who were out of step with the rest of their party. In 1995, under Speaker Newt Gingrich, the Republicans chose relatively junior House members as chairpersons of several key committees, thus ensuring conservative control of the committees. The Republicans also passed a rule limiting the term of a chairperson to six years.

| Safe Seat
A district that returns a legislator with 55 percent of the vote or more.

The Formal Leadership

The limited amount of centralized power that exists in Congress is exercised through party-based mechanisms. Congress is organized by party. When the Democratic Party, for example, wins a majority of seats in either the House or the Senate, Democrats control the official positions of power in that chamber, and every important committee has a Democratic chairperson and a majority of Democratic members. The same process holds when Republicans are in the majority.

We consider the formal leadership positions in the House and Senate separately, but you will note some broad similarities in the way leaders are selected and in the ways they exercise power in the two chambers.

Leadership in the House

The House leadership is made up of the Speaker, the majority and minority leaders, and the party whips.

The Speaker.   The foremost power holder in the House of Representatives is the **Speaker of the House.** The Speaker's position is technically a nonpartisan one, but in fact, for the better part of two centuries, the Speaker has been the official leader of the majority party in the House. When a new Congress convenes in January of odd-numbered years, each party nominates a candidate for Speaker. All Democratic members of the House are expected to vote for their party's nominee, and all Republicans are expected to support their candidate. The vote to organize the House is the one vote in which representatives must vote with their party. In a sense, this vote defines a member's partisan status.

| Speaker of the House
The presiding officer in the House of Representatives. The Speaker is always a member of the majority party and is the most powerful and influential member of the House.

The influence of modern-day Speakers is based primarily on their personal prestige, persuasive ability, and knowledge of the legislative process—plus the acquiescence or active support of other representatives. The major formal powers of the Speaker include the following:

1. Presiding over meetings of the House.
2. Appointing members of joint committees and conference committees.
3. Scheduling legislation for floor action.
4. Deciding points of order and interpreting the rules with the advice of the House parliamentarian.
5. Referring bills and resolutions to the appropriate standing committees of the House.

Nancy Pelosi (D., Calif.), on the left, became Democratic Speaker of the House of Representatives in 2007, after the Democrats won control of the House in the 2006 elections. Dennis Hastert (R., Ill.), on the right, was Speaker of the House from 1999 to 2007. What benefits could a state receive when one of its senators or representatives wins a leadership post? (Photos Courtesy of the U.S. Congress)

A Speaker may take part in floor debate and vote, as can any other member of Congress, but recent Speakers usually have voted only to break a tie. Since 1975, the Speaker, when a Democrat, has also had the power to appoint the Democratic Steering Committee, which determines new committee assignments for House party members.

In general, the powers of the Speaker are related to his or her control over information and communications channels in the House. This is a significant power in a large, decentralized institution in which information is a very important resource. With this control, the Speaker attempts to ensure the smooth operation of the chamber and to integrate presidential and congressional policies.

Majority Leader of the House
A legislative position held by an important party member in the House of Representatives. The majority leader is selected by the majority party in caucus or conference to foster cohesion among party members and to act as spokesperson for the majority party in the House.

The Majority Leader.　　The **majority leader of the House** is elected by a caucus of the majority party to foster cohesion among party members and to act as a spokesperson for the party. The majority leader influences the scheduling of debate and acts as the chief supporter of the Speaker. The majority leader cooperates with the Speaker and other party leaders, both inside and outside Congress, to formulate the party's legislative program and to guide that program through the legislative process in the House. The Democrats often recruit future Speakers from those who hold that position.

Minority Leader of the House
The party leader elected by the minority party in the House.

The Minority Leader.　　The **minority leader of the House** is the candidate nominated for Speaker by a caucus of the minority party. Like the majority leader, the leader of the minority party has as her or his primary responsibility the maintaining of cohesion within the party's ranks. The minority leader works for cohesion among the party's members and speaks on behalf of the president if the minority party controls the White House. In relations with the majority party, the minority leader consults with both the Speaker and the majority leader on recognizing members who wish to speak on the floor, on House rules and procedures, and on the scheduling of legislation. Minority leaders have no actual power in these areas, however.

Whips. The leadership of each party includes assistants to the majority and minority leaders, known as **whips.** The whips are members of Congress who assist the party leaders by passing information down from the leadership to party members and by ensuring that members show up for floor debate and cast their votes on important issues. Whips conduct polls among party members about the members' views on legislation, inform the leaders about whose vote is doubtful and whose is certain, and may exert pressure on members to support the leaders' positions. In the House, serving as a whip is the first step toward positions of higher leadership.

Leadership in the Senate

The Senate is less than one-fourth the size of the House. This fact alone probably explains why a formal, complex, and centralized leadership structure is not as necessary in the Senate as it is in the House.

The two highest-ranking formal leadership positions in the Senate are essentially ceremonial in nature. Under the Constitution, the vice president of the United States is the president (that is, the presiding officer) of the Senate and may vote to break a tie. The vice president, however, is only rarely present for a meeting of the Senate. The Senate elects instead a **president pro tempore** ("pro tem") to preside over the Senate in the vice president's absence. Ordinarily, the president pro tem is the member of the majority party with the longest continuous term of service in the Senate. The president pro tem is mostly a ceremonial position. Junior senators take turns actually presiding over the sessions of the Senate.

The real leadership power in the Senate rests in the hands of the **Senate majority leader,** the **Senate minority leader,** and their respective whips. The Senate majority and minority leaders have the right to be recognized first in debate on the floor and generally exercise the same powers available to the House majority and minority leaders. They control the scheduling of debate on the floor in conjunction with the

> **DID YOU KNOW . . .**
> That the Constitution does not require that the Speaker of the House of Representatives be an elected member of the House?

Whip
A member of Congress who aids the majority or minority leader of the House or the Senate.

President Pro Tempore
The temporary presiding officer of the Senate in the absence of the vice president.

Senate Majority Leader
The chief spokesperson of the majority party in the Senate, who directs the legislative program and party strategy.

Senate Minority Leader
The party officer in the Senate who commands the minority party's opposition to the policies of the majority party and directs the legislative program and strategy of his or her party.

After the Democrats took control of Congress in the 2006 elections, Republican senator Mitch McConnell of Kentucky, left, was elected Senate minority leader for the 110th Congress. Democratic senator Harry Reid, right, who had been elected Senate minority leader at the beginning of the 109th Congress, became the Senate majority leader. It is very rare for a congressional leader to become president. How might a leadership position interfere with presidential aspirations? (Left: Courtesy of Senator McConnell; right: Courtesy of Senator Reid)

DID YOU KNOW . . .
That in 2004, on the urging of representative Don Young (R., Alaska), the House approved a new bridge to connect a town of 7,845 people with an island of 50 residents—a $200 million structure with a longer span than the George Washington Bridge in New York?

majority party's Policy Committee, influence the allocation of committee assignments for new members or for senators attempting to transfer to a new committee, influence the selection of other party officials, and participate in selecting members of conference committees. The leaders are expected to mobilize support for partisan legislative initiatives or for the proposals of a president who belongs to their party. The leaders act as liaisons with the White House when the president is of their party, try to obtain the cooperation of committee chairpersons, and seek to facilitate the smooth functioning of the Senate through the senators' unanimous consent. The majority and minority leaders are elected by their respective party caucuses.

Senate party whips, like their House counterparts, maintain communication within the party on platform positions and try to ensure that party colleagues are present for floor debate and important votes. The Senate whip system is far less elaborate than its counterpart in the House, simply because there are fewer members to track.

A list of the formal party leaders of the 110th Congress is presented in Table 11–6. Party leaders are a major source of influence over the decisions about public issues that senators and representatives must make every day.

How Members of Congress Decide

Each member of Congress casts hundreds of votes in each session. Each member compiles a record of votes during the years that he or she spends in the national legislature. There are usually a number of different reasons why any particular vote is cast. Research shows that the best predictor of a member's vote is party affiliation. Obviously, party members do have common opinions on some, if not all, issues facing the nation. In addition, the party leadership in each house works hard to build cohesion and agreement among the members through the activities of the party caucuses and conferences. In recent years, the increase in partisanship in both the House and the Senate has meant that most Republicans are voting in opposition to most Democrats.

TABLE 11–6 | PARTY LEADERS IN THE 110TH CONGRESS, 2007–2009

Position	Incumbent	Party/State	Leader since
House			
Speaker	Nancy Pelosi	D., Calif.	Jan. 2007
Majority leader	Steny Hoyer	D., Md.	Jan. 2007
Majority whip	James Clyburn	D., S.C.	Jan. 2007
Chair of the Democratic Caucus	Rahm Emanuel	D., Ill.	Jan. 2007
Minority leader	John Boehner	R., Ohio	Jan. 2007
Minority whip	Roy Blunt	R., Mo.	Jan. 2007
Chair of the Republican Conference	Adam Putnam	R., Fla.	Jan. 2007
Senate			
President pro tempore	Robert Byrd	D., W.Va.	Jan. 2007
Majority leader	Harry Reid	D., Nev.	Jan. 2007
Majority whip	Dick Durbin	D., Ill.	Jan. 2007
Vice Chair of the Democratic Conference	Charles E. Schumer	D., N.Y.	Jan. 2007
Minority leader	Mitch McConnell	R., Ky.	Jan. 2007
Minority whip	Trent Lott	R., Miss.	Jan. 2007
Chair of the Republican Conference	Jon Kyl	R., Ariz.	Jan. 2007

The Conservative Coalition

Political parties are not always unified. In the 1950s and 1960s, the Democrats in Congress were often split between northern liberals and southern conservatives. This division gave rise to the **conservative coalition,** a voting bloc made up of conservative Democrats and conservative (which is to say, most) Republicans. This coalition was able to win many votes over the years. Today, however, most southern conservatives are Republicans, so the coalition has almost disappeared.

Conservative Coalition
An alliance of Republicans and southern Democrats that can form in the House or the Senate to oppose liberal legislation and support conservative legislation.

"Crossing Over"

On some votes, individual representatives and senators will vote against their party, "crossing over to the other side," because the interests of their states or districts differ from the interests that prevail within the rest of their party. In some cases, members vote a certain way because of the influence of regional or national interests. Other voting decisions are based on the members' religious or ideological beliefs. Votes on issues such as abortion or gay rights may be motivated by a member's religious views.

There are, however, far too many voting decisions for every member to be fully informed on each issue. Research suggests that many voting decisions are based on cues provide by trusted colleagues or the party leadership. A member who sits on the committee that wrote a law may become a reliable source of information about that law. Alternatively, a member may turn to a colleague who represents a district in the same state or one who represents a similar district for cues on voting. Cues may also come from fellow committee members, from leaders, and from the administration.

How a Bill Becomes Law

Each year, Congress and the president propose and approve many laws. Some are budget and appropriations laws that require extensive bargaining but must be passed for the government to continue to function. Other laws are relatively free of controversy and are passed with little dissension. Still other proposed legislation is extremely controversial and reaches to the roots of differences between Democrats and Republicans and between the executive and legislative branches.

As detailed in Figure 11–3 on the following page, each law begins as a bill, which must be introduced in either the House or the Senate. Often, similar bills are introduced in both chambers. A "money bill," however, must start in the House. In each chamber, the bill follows similar steps. It is referred to a committee and its subcommittees for study, discussion, hearings, and rewriting ("mark up"). When the bill is reported out to the full chamber, it must be scheduled for debate (by the Rules Committee in the House and by the leadership in the Senate). After the bill has been passed in each chamber, if it contains different provisions, a conference committee is formed to write a compromise bill, which must be approved by both chambers before it is sent to the president to sign or veto.

Another form of congressional action, the *joint resolution*, differs little from a bill in how it is proposed or debated. Once it is approved by both chambers and signed by the president, it has the force of law.[14] A joint resolution to amend the Constitution, however, after it is approved by two-thirds of both chambers, is sent not to the president but to the states for ratification.

---

[14]In contrast, *simple resolutions* and *concurrent resolutions* do not carry the force of law but rather are used by one or both chambers of Congress, respectively, to express facts, principles, or opinions. For example, a concurrent resolution is used to set the time when Congress will adjourn.

FIGURE 11–3 | HOW A BILL BECOMES LAW

This illustration shows the most typical way in which proposed legislation is enacted into law. Most legislation begins as similar bills introduced into the House and the Senate. The process is illustrated here with two hypothetical bills, House bill No. 100 (HR 100) and Senate bill No. 200 (S 200). The path of HR 100 is shown on the left, and that of S 200, on the right.

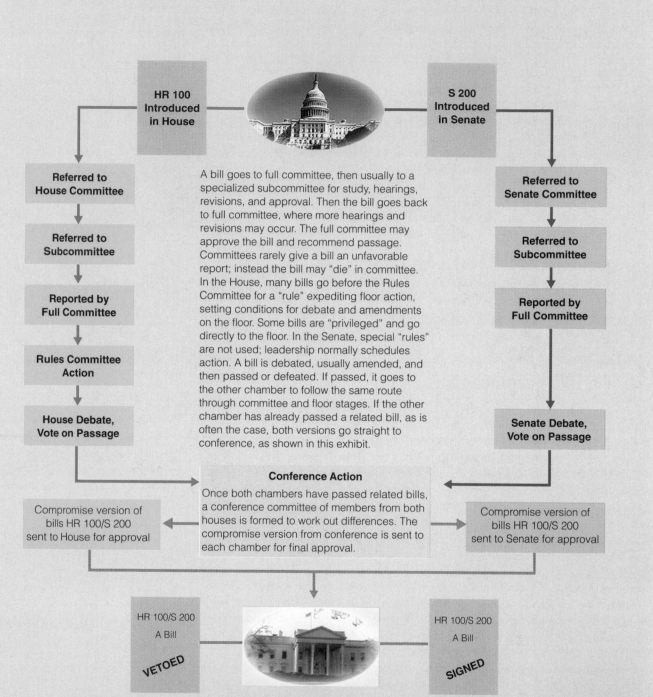

A compromise bill approved by both houses is sent to the president, who can sign it into law or veto it and return it to Congress.

Congress may override a veto by a two-thirds majority vote in both houses; the bill then becomes law without the president's signature.

How Much Will the Government Spend?

The Constitution is very clear about where the power of the purse lies in the national government: all taxing or spending bills must originate in the House of Representatives. Today, much of the business of Congress is concerned with approving government expenditures through the budget process and with raising the revenues to pay for government programs.

From 1922, when Congress required the president to prepare and present to the legislature an **executive budget,** until 1974, the congressional budget process was so disjointed that it was difficult to visualize the total picture of government finances. The president presented the executive budget to Congress in January. It was broken down into thirteen or more appropriations bills. Some time later, after all of the bills had been debated, amended, and passed, it was more or less possible to estimate total government spending for the next year.

Frustrated by the president's ability to impound, or withhold, funds and dissatisfied with the entire budget process, Congress passed the Budget and Impoundment Control Act of 1974 to regain some control over the nation's spending. The act required the president to spend the funds that Congress had appropriated, ending the president's ability to kill programs by withholding funds. The other major accomplishment of the act was to force Congress to examine total national taxing and spending at least twice in each budget cycle.

The budget cycle of the federal government is described in the rest of this section. (See Figure 11–4 for a graphic illustration of the budget cycle.)

Preparing the Budget

The federal government operates on a **fiscal year (FY)** cycle. The fiscal year runs from October through September, so that fiscal 2008, or FY08, runs from October 1, 2007, through September 30, 2008. Eighteen months before a fiscal year starts, the executive branch begins preparing the budget. The Office of Management and Budget (OMB) receives advice from the Council of Economic Advisers and the Treasury Department. The OMB outlines the budget and then sends it to the various departments and agencies. Bargaining follows, in which—to use only two of

Executive Budget
The budget prepared and submitted by the president to Congress.

Fiscal Year (FY)
A twelve-month period that is used for bookkeeping, or accounting, purposes. Usually, the fiscal year does not coincide with the calendar year. For example, the federal government's fiscal year runs from October 1 through September 30.

FIGURE 11–4 | THE BUDGET CYCLE

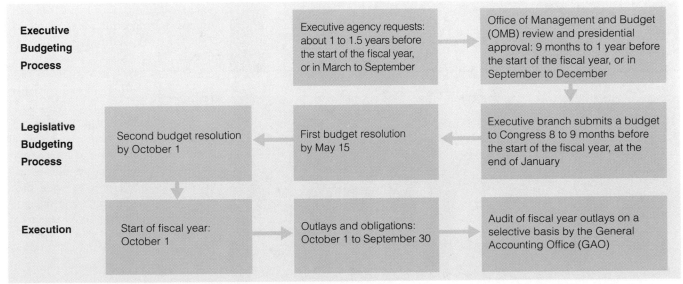

Executive Budgeting Process	Executive agency requests: about 1 to 1.5 years before the start of the fiscal year, or in March to September	Office of Management and Budget (OMB) review and presidential approval: 9 months to 1 year before the start of the fiscal year, or in September to December
Legislative Budgeting Process	Second budget resolution by October 1 ← First budget resolution by May 15	Executive branch submits a budget to Congress 8 to 9 months before the start of the fiscal year, at the end of January
Execution	Start of fiscal year: October 1	Outlays and obligations: October 1 to September 30	Audit of fiscal year outlays on a selective basis by the General Accounting Office (GAO)

many examples—the Department of Health and Human Services argues for more welfare spending, and the armed forces argue for more defense spending.

Even though the OMB has only six hundred employees, it is one of the most powerful agencies in Washington. It assembles the budget documents and monitors federal agencies throughout each year. Every year, it begins the budget process with a **spring review**, in which it requires all of the agencies to review their programs, activities, and goals. At the beginning of each summer, the OMB sends out a letter instructing agencies to submit their requests for funding for the next fiscal year. By the end of the summer, each agency must submit a formal request to the OMB.

In actuality, the "budget season" begins with the **fall review**. At this time, the OMB looks at budget requests and, in almost all cases, routinely cuts them back. Although the OMB works within guidelines established by the president, specific decisions often are left to the OMB director and the director's associates. By the beginning of November, the director's review begins. The director meets with cabinet secretaries and budget officers. Time becomes crucial. The budget must be completed by January so that it can be included in the *Economic Report of the President*.

Congress Faces the Budget

In January, nine months before the fiscal year starts, the president takes the OMB's proposed budget, approves it, and submits it to Congress. Then the congressional budgeting process takes over. The budgeting process involves two steps. First, Congress must authorize funds to be spent. The **authorization** is a formal declaration by the appropriate congressional committee that a certain amount of funding may be available to an agency. Congressional committees and subcommittees look at the proposals from the executive branch and the Congressional Budget Office in making the decision to authorize funds. After the funds are authorized, they must be appropriated by Congress. The appropriations committees of both the House and the Senate forward spending bills to their respective bodies. The **appropriation** of funds occurs when the final bill is passed.

The budget process involves large sums. For example, President George W. Bush's proposed budget for fiscal year 2007 called for expenditures of $2.77 trillion, or $2,770,000,000,000. When forming the budget for a given year, Congress and the president must take into account revenues, primarily in the form of taxes, as well as expenditures to balance the budget. If spending exceeds the amount brought in by taxes, the government runs a budget deficit (and increases the public debt). For example, although President Bush's proposed budget for fiscal year 2007 called for expenditures of approximately $2.77 trillion, projected revenues from taxes amounted to only about $2.416 trillion—leaving a deficit of $354 billion.

With these large sums in play, representatives and senators who chair key committees find it relatively easy to slip spending proposals into a variety of bills. These proposals may have nothing to do with the ostensible purpose of the bill. Are such earmarked appropriations good policy? We look at the issue of pork-barrel spending in this chapter's *Which Side Are You On?* feature.

Spring Review
The annual process in which the Office of Management and Budget requires federal agencies to review their programs, activities, and goals and submit their requests for funding for the next fiscal year.

Fall Review
The annual process in which the Office of Management and Budget, after receiving formal federal agency requests for funding for the next fiscal year, reviews the requests, makes changes, and submits its recommendations to the president.

Authorization
A formal declaration by a legislative committee that a certain amount of funding may be available to an agency. Some authorizations terminate in a year; others are renewable automatically without further congressional action.

Appropriation
The passage, by Congress, of a spending bill specifying the amount of authorized funds that actually will be allocated for an agency's use.

President George W. Bush walks to a press conference with members of his economic team in 2006 at Camp David, Maryland. From left is Vice President Dick Cheney, Secretary of Labor Elaine Chao, Director of the Office of Management and Budget Rob Portman, Bush, and Chairman of the Council of Economic Advisers Edward Lazear. How much can any president control the economy? (AP Photo/Evan Vucci)

WHICH SIDE ARE YOU ON? | Should We Prohibit Pork-Barrel Legislation?

"Bringing home the pork" is just a variation on "bringing home the bacon." The idea is that a congressperson can obtain funding for his or her constituents' favorite projects. This process is also known as *earmarking,* a term that comes from the practice of cutting out a V-shaped piece from a calf's left ear so that the animal can be identified. Through earmarking, members of Congress secure federal dollars for their pork projects by attaching the proposals to huge spending bills. In 1987, President Ronald Reagan vetoed a spending bill because it had too many earmarks—121. Just ten years ago, about 1,200 earmarks were included in legislation each year. Now in any given year there are more than 15,000 earmarks totaling around $30 billion.

DEFINITELY, LET'S PROHIBIT EARMARKS

Contrary to what some members of Congress have said, pork-barrel spending does not have a long history in the United States: it's a relatively recent phenomenon. James Madison said that the general welfare clause of the Constitution was not intended to give Congress unlimited spending power—in other words, it was not to be used as a blank check. More recently, Senator Tom Coburn (R., Okla.) has said that pork-barrel legislation is "the root cause of the unholy relationship between some members of Congress, lobbyists, and donors. Inside Congress, the pork process is effectively a black-market economy." He further believes that "earmarks are a gateway drug in the road to spending addiction."* Given that the federal government runs a large deficit every year, indiscriminate pork-barrel spending must be stopped, say those who want to eliminate it.

*"Just Say No to Earmarks." The Wall Street Journal, Editorial, October 4, 2006.

WITHOUT PORK-BARREL SPENDING, CULTURE WOULD SUFFER

Opponents of any change in the current pork-barrel legislation system point out that many earmarks provide funding to build or expand museums, create or repair dams and bridges, and maintain other important infrastructure. As Speaker of the House Dennis Hastert has said, pork is "what members do," and members are best positioned to know where to put a "red light in their district." Moreover, if Congress debated all pork-barrel projects individually, the legislative process would grind to a screeching halt. Consider also that $30 billion in pork-barrel spending is a minuscule part of the almost $3 trillion federal budget. In other words, even today's historically high level of pork-barrel spending represents only about 1 percent of the federal budget.

WHAT'S YOUR POSITION?

If you had control over congressional spending procedures, would you eliminate all pork-barrel spending? Why or why not?

GOING ONLINE

Each year the taxpayer watchdog group Citizens Against Government Waste compiles its "Pig Book," which lists and describes all congressional earmarks. You can utilize the full-text searchable Pig Books at **www.cagw.org/site/ PageServer?pagename=reports_pigbook2006**.

Budget Resolutions

The **first budget resolution** by Congress is scheduled to be passed in May. It sets overall revenue goals and spending targets. During the summer, bargaining among all the concerned parties takes place. Spending and tax laws that are drawn up during this period are supposed to be guided by the May congressional budget resolution.

By September, Congress is scheduled to pass its **second budget resolution,** one that will set "binding" limits on taxes and spending for the fiscal year beginning October 1. Bills passed before that date that do not fit within the limits of the budget resolution are supposed to be changed.

In actuality, between 1978 and 1996, Congress did not pass a complete budget by October 1. In other words, generally, Congress does not follow its own rules. Budget resolutions are passed late, and when they are passed, they are not treated as binding. In each fiscal year that starts without a budget, every agency operates on the basis of a **continuing resolution,** which enables the agency to keep on doing whatever it was doing the previous year with the same amount of funding. Even continuing resolutions have not always been passed on time.

First Budget Resolution
A resolution passed by Congress in May that sets overall revenue and spending goals for the following fiscal year.

Second Budget Resolution
A resolution passed by Congress in September that sets "binding" limits on taxes and spending for the following fiscal year.

Continuing Resolution
A temporary funding law that Congress passes when an appropriations bill has not been decided by the beginning of the new fiscal year on October 1.

MAKING A DIFFERENCE | Learning about Your Representatives

Do you know the names of your senators and your representative in Congress? A surprising number of Americans do not. Even if you know the names and parties of your elected delegates, there is still much more you could learn about them that would be useful.

Why Should You Care?

The legislation that Congress passes can directly affect your life. Consider, for example, the Medicare prescription drug benefit passed in November 2003. Some might think that such a benefit, which only helps persons over the age of sixty-five, would be of no interest to college students. Actually, legislation such as this could affect you long before you reach retirement age. Funding the new benefit may mean that you will have to pay higher taxes when you join the workforce. Also, some students may be affected even sooner than that. Most students are part of a family, and family finances are often important in determining whether a family will help pay for the student's tuition. There are families in which the cost of medicine for the oldest members is a substantial burden.

    You can make a difference in our democracy simply by going to the polls on Election Day and voting for the candidates you would like to represent you in Congress. It goes with-out saying, though, that to cast an informed vote, you need to know how your congressional representatives stand on the issues and, if they are incumbents, how they have voted on bills that are important to you.

What Can You Do?

To contact a member of Congress, start by going to the Web sites of the U.S. House of Representatives (at **www.house.gov**) and the U.S. Senate (at **www.senate.gov**).

    Although you can communicate easily with your representatives by e-mail, using e-mail has some drawbacks. Representatives and senators are now receiving large volumes of e-mail from constituents, and they rarely read it themselves. They have staff members who read and respond to e-mail instead. Many interest groups argue that U.S. mail, or even express mail or a phone call, is more likely to capture the attention of the representative than e-mail. You can contact your representatives using one of the following addresses or phone numbers:

United States House of Representatives
Washington, DC 20515
202-224-3121

United States Senate
Washington, DC 20510
202-224-3121

Performance Evaluations

Interest groups also track the voting records of members of Congress and rate the members on the issues. Project Vote Smart tracks the performance of over 13,000 political leaders, including their campaign finances, issue positions, and voting records. You can contact Project Vote Smart at:

Project Vote Smart
One Common Ground
Philipsburg, MT 59858
Voter Hotline toll-free: 1-888-VOTE-SMART (1-888-868-3762)
www.vote-smart.org

    Finally, if you want to know how your representatives funded their campaigns, contact the Center for Responsive Politics (CRP), a research group that tracks money in politics, campaign fund-raising, and similar issues. You can contact the CRP at:

The Center for Responsive Politics
1101 14th St. N.W., Suite 1030
Washington, DC 20005
202-857-0044
www.opensecrets.org

| Key Terms

agenda setting 359	conservative coalition 379	executive budget 381	gerrymandering 367
appropriation 382	constituent 355	fall review 382	instructed delegate 357
authorization 382	continuing resolution 383	filibuster 361	joint committee 374
bicameralism 355	direct primary 364	first budget resolution 383	justiciable question 367
casework 357	discharge petition 372	fiscal year (FY) 381	lawmaking 356
conference committee 374	enumerated power 359	franking 370	logrolling 356

|Chapter Summary

1 The authors of the Constitution believed that the bulk of national power should be in the legislature. The Constitution states that Congress will consist of two chambers. A result of the Connecticut Compromise, this bicameral structure established a balanced legislature, with the membership in the House of Representatives based on population and the membership in the Senate based on the equality of states.

2 The functions of Congress include (a) lawmaking, (b) representation, (c) service to constituents, (d) oversight, (e) public education, and (f) conflict resolution.

3 The first seventeen clauses of Article I, Section 8, of the Constitution specify most of the enumerated, or expressed, powers of Congress, including the right to impose taxes, to borrow money, to regulate commerce, and to declare war. Besides its enumerated powers, Congress enjoys the right to "make all Laws which shall be necessary and proper for carrying into Execution the foregoing Powers, and all other Powers vested by this Constitution in the Government of the United States, or in any Department or Officer thereof." This is called the elastic, or necessary and proper, clause.

4 There are 435 members in the House of Representatives and 100 members in the Senate. Owing to its larger size, the House has a greater number of formal rules. The Senate tradition of unlimited debate dates back to 1790 and has been used over the years to frustrate the passage of bills. Under Senate Rule 22, cloture can be used to shut off debate on a bill.

5 Members of Congress are not typical American citizens. They are older and wealthier than most Americans, disproportionately white and male, and more likely to be trained in professional occupations.

6 Congressional elections are operated by the individual state governments, which must abide by rules established by the Constitution and national statutes. Most candidates for Congress must win nomination through a direct primary. The overwhelming majority of incumbent representatives and a smaller proportion of senators who run for reelection are successful. A complicated aspect of congressional elections is apportionment—the allocation of legislative seats to con-stituencies. The Supreme Court's "one person, one vote" rule has been applied to equalize the populations of congressional and state legislative districts.

7 Members of Congress are well paid and enjoy benefits such as franking privileges. Members of Congress have personal and committee staff members available to them and also enjoy a number of legal privileges and immunities.

8 Most of the actual work of legislating is performed by committees and subcommittees within Congress. Legislation introduced into the House or Senate is assigned to the appropriate standing committees for review. Select committees are created for a limited time for a specific purpose. Joint committees are formed by the concurrent action of both chambers and consist of members from each chamber. Conference committees are special joint committees set up to achieve agreement between the House and the Senate on the exact wording of legislative acts passed by both chambers in different forms. The seniority rule, which is usually followed, specifies that the longest-serving member of the majority party will be the chairperson of a committee.

9 The foremost power holder in the House of Representatives is the Speaker of the House. Other leaders are the House majority leader, the House minority leader, and the majority and minority whips. Formally, the vice president is the presiding officer of the Senate, with the most senior member of the majority party serving as the president pro tempore to preside when the vice president is absent. Actual leadership in the Senate rests with the majority leader, the minority leader, and their whips.

10 A bill becomes law by progressing through both chambers of Congress and their appropriate standing and joint committees to the president.

11 The budget process for a fiscal year begins with the preparation of an executive budget by the president. This is reviewed by the Office of Management and Budget and then sent to Congress, which is supposed to pass a final budget by the end of September. Since 1978, Congress generally has not followed its own time rules.

Selected Print and Media Resources

SUGGESTED READINGS

Barone, Michael, and Grant Ujifusa. *The Almanac of American Politics, 2006.* Washington, D.C.: National Journal, 2005. This book, which is published biannually, is a comprehensive summary of current political information on each member of Congress, his or her state or congressional district, recent congressional election results, key votes, ratings by various organizations, sources of campaign contributions, and records of campaign expenditures.

Davidson, Roger H., and Walter J. Oleszek. *Congress and Its Members,* 10th ed. Washington, D.C.: CQ Press, 2005. This classic looks carefully at the "two Congresses," the one in Washington and the role played by congresspersons at home.

Just, Ward S. *The Congressman Who Loved Flaubert.* New York: Carrol and Graf Publishers, 1990. This fictional account of a career politician was first published in 1973 and is still a favorite with students of political science. Ward Just is renowned for his political fiction, and particularly for his examination of character and motivation.

Mann, Thomas B., and Norman J. Ornstein. *The Broken Branch: How Congress Is Failing America and How to Get It Back on Track.* New York: Oxford University Press, 2006. These two political scientists believe that Congress is more dysfunctional now than ever before. They argue that there is too much partisan dickering and internal rancor. These two scholars of government and politics present a blueprint for reform.

Rangel, Charles B., and Leon Wynter. *. . . And I Haven't Had a Bad Day Since: The Memoir of Charles B. Rangel's Journey from the Streets of Harlem to the Halls of Congress.* New York: Scribner, 2007. This biographical account of one of Congress's most flamboyant members tells his story from (obviously) the streets of Harlem to the halls of Congress. Rangel, a high school dropout, became a lawyer and then a member of Congress. He helped create the earned income tax credit for working families.

MEDIA SOURCES

The Congress—In one of his earliest efforts (1988), filmmaker Ken Burns profiles the history of Congress. Narration is by David McCullough, and those interviewed include David Broker, Alistair Cooke, and Cokie Roberts. PBS Home Video rereleased this film on DVD in 2003.

Congress: A Day in the Life of a Representative—From political meetings to social functions to campaigning, this 1995 program examines what politicians really do. Featured representatives are Tim Roemer (a Democrat from Indiana) and Sue Myrick (a Republican from North Carolina).

Mr. Smith Goes to Washington—A 1939 film in which Jimmy Stewart plays the naïve congressman who is quickly educated in Washington. A true American political classic.

The Seduction of Joe Tynan—A 1979 film in which Alan Alda plays a young senator who must face serious decisions about his political role and his private life.

E·MOCRACY | Elections and the Web

Almost all senators and representatives now have Web sites that you can find simply by keying in their names in a search engine. As you read in this chapter's *Making a Difference* feature, you can easily learn the names of your congressional representatives by going to the Web site of the House or Senate (see the following *Logging On* section for the URLs for these sites). Once you know the names of your representatives, you can go to their Web sites to learn more about them and their positions on specific issues. You can also check the Web sites of the groups listed in the *Making a Difference* feature to track your representatives' voting records and discover the names of their campaign contributors.

Note that some members of Congress also provide important services to their constituents via their Web sites. Some sites, for example, allow constituents to apply for internships in Washington, D.C., apply for appointments to military academies, order flags, order tours of the Capitol, and register complaints electronically. Other sites may provide forms from certain government agencies, such as the Social Security Administration, that constituents can use to request assistance from those agencies or register complaints.

Logging On

To find out about the schedule of activities taking place in Congress, use the following Web sites:

www.senate.gov

www.house.gov

The Congressional Budget Office is online at

www.cbo.gov

The URL for the Government Printing Office is

www.gpoaccess.gov

For the real inside facts on what's going on in Washington, D.C., you can look at the following resources:

RollCall, the newspaper of the Capitol:

www.rollcall.com

Congressional Quarterly, a publication that reports on Congress:

www.cq.com

The Hill, which investigates various activities of Congress:

www.hillnews.com

Online Review

At **www.politicalscience.wadsworth.com/ schmidt12**, you will find a free Study Guide to this book. For each chapter, there are two online quizzes to help you master the material.

• The PoliPrep Self-Study Assessment provides a pretest for each major section of the chapter. PoliPrep then generates a customized study plan. After you complete the study plan, a posttest evaluates your progress.

• The Tutorial Quiz for each chapter provides questions on the chapter contents, including the features. The questions are organized to match the major sections of the chapter.

12 | The President

What If . . .
There Were No Executive Privilege?

BACKGROUND

When a U.S. president wishes to keep information secret, he or she can invoke *executive privilege.* Typically, administrations use executive privilege to safeguard national security secrets. Although there is no mention of executive privilege in the Constitution, presidents from George Washington to George W. Bush have invoked this privilege in response to perceived encroachments on the executive branch by Congress and by the judiciary. For example, in 2006 when two congressional committees were investigating the federal government's response to Hurricane Katrina, the Bush administration cited the need for confidentiality of executive-branch communications as justification for refusing to turn over certain documents, including e-mail correspondence involving White House staff members. The administration had previously refused to release the names of oil company executives who had advised Vice President Cheney on energy policy.

Nonetheless, Congress could pass a law prohibiting the executive branch from using executive privilege as a defense to requests for information. Alternatively, the Supreme Court could hold that executive privilege is an unconstitutional exercise of executive power.

WHAT IF THERE WERE NO EXECUTIVE PRIVILEGE?

If there were no executive privilege, a president would have to be aware that all of his or her words, documents, and actions could be made public. We know from twentieth-century history that when a president does not have full executive privilege to protect information, the results can be devastating. President Richard Nixon (1969–1974) had tape-recorded hundreds of hours of conversations in the Oval Office. During a scandal involving a cover-up (the Watergate scandal, as you will read later in this chapter), Congress requested those tapes. Nixon invoked executive privilege and refused to turn them over. Ultimately, the Supreme Court ordered him to do so, however, and the tapes provided damning information about Nixon's role in the purported cover-up of illegal activities. Rather than face impeachment, Nixon resigned the presidency.

Clearly, if executive privilege were eliminated, it is unlikely that conversations between the president and other members of the executive branch would be recorded or otherwise documented. As a result, we would have fewer records of an administration's activities than we do today.

EXECUTIVE PRIVILEGE IN A WORLD FILLED WITH TERRORISM

Following the terrorist attacks on September 11, 2001, Attorney General John Ashcroft advised federal agencies "to lean toward withholding information whenever possible." In some instances, the Bush administration attempted to withhold information from Congress and the courts, not just the public. In one troubling example, a top civil servant was threatened with firing if he told Congress the true projected cost of the administration's Medicare prescription drug bill.

Of course, without executive privilege, the president might experience problems in waging a war on terrorism. While Congress and the courts have procedures that can be used to guard sensitive information, both branches of government are unaccustomed to keeping secrets, and often find it hard to do so.

PAST, PRESENT, AND FUTURE PRESIDENTIAL PAPERS

The White House is allowed to decide what is classified as top secret. Even if Congress requests top secret material, the White House does not have to release it. In general, not all transcripts of private conversations between past presidents and foreign heads of state are made available to congressional committees, for example.

The Bush administration has attempted to control not only its own records but also those of former presidents, even against their wishes. Soon after September 11, 2001, President Bush signed Executive Order 13233, which provided that former presidents' private papers can be released only with the approval of both the former president in question and the current one. Former President Bill Clinton publicly objected, saying that he wanted all of his papers released to the public. Nevertheless, the Bush administration denied access to documents surrounding the 177 pardons that Clinton granted in the last days of his presidency.

If executive privilege were eliminated, the White House would have a difficult time regulating the flow of past presidential records into the public forum. Future presidents, of course, would know that virtually every word and act could be released to the public. The behavior of presidents and their administrations would certainly change. They might simply insist that there be no record of sensitive conversations. If so, future Americans would lose much of the historical background for America's domestic and international actions.

FOR CRITICAL ANALYSIS

1. The history of executive privilege dates back to 1796, when President George Washington refused a request by the House for certain documents. Given the changes that have taken place since that time, should executive privilege be eliminated? Or should it be retained as even more necessary today than it was at that time?
2. What would be the costs to the nation if executive privilege were eliminated?

The writers of the Constitution created the presidency of the United States without any models to follow. Nowhere else in the world was there a democratically selected chief executive. What the founders did not want was a king. In fact, given their previous experience with royal governors in the colonies, many of the delegates to the Constitutional Convention wanted to create a very weak executive who could not veto legislation. Other delegates, especially those who had witnessed the need for a strong leader in the Revolutionary Army, believed a strong executive would be necessary for the new republic. The delegates, after much debate, created a chief executive who had enough powers granted in the Constitution to balance those of Congress.[1]

The power exercised by each president who has held the office has been scrutinized and judged by historians, political scientists, the media, and the public. The executive privilege enjoyed by presidents has also been subject to scrutiny and debate, as you learned in the chapter-opening *What If . . .* feature. Indeed, it would seem that Americans are fascinated by presidential power and by the persons who hold the office. In this chapter, after looking at who can become president and at the process involved, we examine closely the nature and extent of the constitutional powers held by the president.

Who Can Become President?

The requirements for becoming president, as outlined in Article II, Section 1, of the Constitution, are not overwhelmingly stringent:

> No person except a natural born Citizen, or a Citizen of the United States, at the time of the Adoption of this Constitution, shall be eligible to the Office of President; neither shall any Person be eligible to that Office who shall not have attained to the Age of thirty-five Years, and been fourteen Years a Resident within the United States.

---

[1]Forrest McDonald, *The American Presidency: An Intellectual History* (Lawrence, Kans.: University Press of Kansas, 1994), p. 179.

DID YOU KNOW . . .
That George Washington's salary of $25,000 in 1789 was the equivalent of about $600,000 in today's dollars?

Harry Truman, left, when he was the proprietor of a Kansas City, Missouri, men's clothing store, about 1920. Ronald Reagan, right, is shown as a frontier marshal in the movie *Law and Order,* released in 1953. Compared to members of Congress, presidents have had a more varied background. How would varied life experiences benefit a president? (Truman Photo Courtesy of Truman Presidential Library and Museum; Reagan Photo by Corbis)

The only question that arises about these qualifications relates to the term *natural born Citizen*. Does that mean only citizens born in the United States and its territories? What about a child born to a U.S. citizen (or to a couple who are U.S. citizens) visiting or living in another country? Although the Supreme Court has never directly addressed the question, it is reasonable to expect that someone would be eligible if her or his parents were Americans. The first presidents, after all, were not even American citizens at birth, and others were born in areas that did not become part of the United States until later. These questions were debated when George Romney, who was born in Chihuahua, Mexico, made a serious bid for the Republican presidential nomination in the 1960s.[2]

When Arnold Schwarzenegger became governor of California, many of his supporters suggested that he might be a potential presidential candidate. But Schwarzenegger, who was born in Austria, is a naturalized U.S. citizen and therefore is ineligible to become president under the Constitution. So a movement began to amend the Constitution to allow *naturalized* citizens to become president. As Schwarzenegger's popularity has waned, however, so has support for such an amendment.

The American dream is symbolized by the statement that "anybody can become president of this country." It is true that in modern times, presidents have included a haberdasher (Harry Truman—for a short period of time), a peanut farmer (Jimmy Carter), and an actor (Ronald Reagan). But if you examine the list of presidents inside the back cover of this book, you will see that the most common previous occupation of presidents in this country has been the law. Out of forty-three presidents, twenty-six have been lawyers, and many have been wealthy. (There have been fewer lawyers in the last century, however.)

Although the Constitution states that the minimum-age requirement for the presidency is thirty-five years, most presidents have been much older than that when they assumed office. John F. Kennedy, at the age of forty-three, was the youngest elected president, and the oldest was Ronald Reagan, at age sixty-nine. The average age at inauguration has been fifty-four. There has clearly been a demographic bias in the selection of presidents. All have been male, white, and from the Protestant tradition, except for John F. Kennedy, a Roman Catholic. Presidents have been men of great stature—such as George Washington—and men in whom leadership qualities were not so pronounced—such as Warren Harding (1921–1923). A presidential candidate usually has experience as a vice president, senator, or state governor. Former governors have been especially successful at winning the presidency.

The Process of Becoming President

Major and minor political parties nominate candidates for president and vice president at national conventions every four years. As discussed in Chapter 9, the nation's voters do not elect a president and vice president directly but rather cast ballots for presidential electors, who then vote for president and vice president in the electoral college.

Because the election is governed by a majority in the electoral college, it is conceivable that someone could be elected to the office of the presidency without having a plurality of the popular vote cast. Indeed, in four cases, candidates won elections even though their major opponents received more popular votes. One of those cases occurred in 2000, when George W. Bush won the electoral college vote

---

[2]George Romney was governor of Michigan from 1963 to 1969. Romney was not nominated for the presidency, and the issue remains unresolved.

and became president even though his opponent, Al Gore, won the popular vote. In elections when more than two candidates were running for office, many presidential candidates have won with less than 50 percent of the total popular votes cast for all candidates—including Abraham Lincoln, Woodrow Wilson, Harry Truman, John F. Kennedy, Richard Nixon, and, in 1992, Bill Clinton. Independent candidate Ross Perot garnered a surprising 19 percent of the vote in 1992. Remember from Chapter 9 that no president has won a majority of votes from the entire voting-age population.

On occasion, the electoral college has failed to give any candidate a majority. At this point, the election is thrown into the House of Representatives. The president is then chosen from among the three candidates having the most electoral college votes, as noted in Chapter 9. Only two times in our past has the House had to decide on a president. Thomas Jefferson and Aaron Burr tied in the electoral college in 1800. This happened because the Constitution had not been explicit in indicating which of the two electoral votes was for president and which was for vice president. In 1804, the **Twelfth Amendment** clarified the matter by requiring that the president and vice president be chosen separately. In 1824, the House again had to make a choice, this time among William H. Crawford, Andrew Jackson, and John Quincy Adams. It chose Adams, even though Jackson had more electoral and popular votes.

Twelfth Amendment
An amendment to the Constitution, adopted in 1804, that specifies the separate election of the president and vice president by the electoral college.

The Many Roles of the President

The Constitution speaks briefly about the duties and obligations of the president. Based on this brief list of powers and on the precedents of history, the presidency has grown into a very complicated job that requires balancing at least five constitutional roles. These are (1) head of state, (2) chief executive, (3) commander in chief of the armed forces, (4) chief diplomat, and (5) chief legislator of the United States. Here we examine each of these significant presidential functions, or roles. It is worth noting that one person plays all these roles simultaneously and that the needs of these roles may at times come into conflict.

Head of State
The role of the president as ceremonial head of the government.

Head of State

Every nation has at least one person who is the ceremonial head of state. In most democratic governments, the role of **head of state** is given to someone other than the chief executive, who leads the executive branch of government. In Britain, for example, the head of state is the queen. In much of Europe, the prime minister is the chief executive, and the head of state is the president. But in the United States, the president is both chief executive and head of state. According to William Howard Taft, as head of state the president symbolizes the "dignity and majesty" of the American people.

As head of state, the president engages in a number of activities that are largely symbolic or ceremonial, such as the following:

- Decorating war heroes.
- Throwing out the first ball to open the baseball season.
- Dedicating parks and post offices.
- Receiving visiting heads of state at the White House.
- Going on official state visits to other countries.
- Making personal telephone calls to astronauts.
- Representing the nation at times of national mourning, such as after the terrorist attacks of September 11, 2001, after the loss of the space shuttle *Columbia* in 2003, and after the destruction from Hurricane Katrina in 2005.

From left to right, the first U.S. cabinet—Henry Knox, Thomas Jefferson, Edmund Randolph, Alexander Hamilton—and the first U.S. president, George Washington. (National Archives)

Some students of the American political system believe that having the president serve as both the chief executive and the head of state drastically limits the time available to do "real" work. Not all presidents have agreed with this conclusion, however—particularly those presidents who have skillfully blended these two roles with their role as politician. Being head of state gives the president tremendous public exposure, which can be an important asset in a campaign for reelection. When that exposure is positive, it helps the president deal with Congress over proposed legislation and increases the chances of being reelected—or getting the candidates of the president's party elected.

Chief Executive

| **Chief Executive**
The role of the president as head of the executive branch of the government.

| **Signing Statement**
A written declaration that a president may make when signing a bill into law. Usually, such statements point out sections of the law that the president deems unconstitutional.

According to the Constitution, "The executive Power shall be vested in a President of the United States of America . . . . [H]e may require the Opinion, in writing, of the principal Officer in each of the executive Departments, upon any Subject relating to the Duties of their respective Offices . . . and he shall nominate, and by and with the Advice and Consent of the Senate, shall appoint . . . Officers of the United States. . . . [H]e shall take Care that the Laws be faithfully executed."

As **chief executive,** the president is constitutionally bound to enforce the acts of Congress, the judgments of federal courts, and treaties signed by the United States. The duty to "faithfully execute" the laws has been a source of constitutional power for presidents. Is the president allowed to reject certain parts of legislation if he or she believes that they are unconstitutional? This question relates to so-called **signing statements,** which are written declarations made by presidents that accompany legislation. Presidents have been issuing such statements for decades, but President George W. Bush has used them more than previous presidents to raise constitutional objections to parts of a bill. (See this chapter's *Politics and the Presidency* feature.)

President George W. Bush pictured in the Oval Office. This oval-shaped office in the White House is often used to represent the power of the presidency and of the United States. (AP Photo/Doug Mills)

POLITICS AND THE PRESIDENCY | Does the President Have the Power to Execute Only Part of the Laws of the Land?

In the hot summer of 2006, Senator Arlen Specter (R., Pa.), the chair of the Judiciary Committee, announced on the Senate floor that he was preparing legislation that would authorize Congress "to undertake judicial review of [President Bush's] signing statements with the view to having [those] acts declared unconstitutional." Specter was following in the footsteps of an American Bar Association task force that had concluded that, by attaching conditions to legislation, the president was avoiding his constitutional duty to sign a bill, veto it, or take no action.

THE PRACTICE IS NOT NEW

For at least 175 years, presidents have used signing statements to make substantive constitutional pronouncements on the bill being signed. In 1830, President Andrew Jackson created a controversy when he signed a bill and at the same time sent to Congress a message that restricted the reach of the statute. In 1842, President John Tyler expressed misgivings in a signing statement about the constitutionality and policy of an entire act. Presidents Abraham Lincoln, Andrew Johnson, Theodore Roosevelt, Woodrow Wilson, and Franklin Roosevelt all used signing statements.

As for the legality of the practice, the Department of Justice has advised the last four administrations that the Constitution provides the president with the authority to decline to enforce a clearly unconstitutional law. Four justices of the Supreme Court joined in an opinion that the president may resist laws that encroach upon presidential powers by "disregarding them when they're unconstitutional."[*]

PRESIDENT BUSH HAS USED SIGNING STATEMENTS MORE THAN ANY OTHER PRESIDENT

Since George W. Bush took office, he has issued signing statements on more than eight hundred statutes, more than all of

the previous presidents combined. He has also tended to use the statements for a different purpose. When earlier presidents issued signing statements, they were normally used to instruct agencies on how to execute the laws or for similar purposes. In contrast, many, if not most, of Bush's signing statements have served notice that he believes parts of bills that he signs are unconstitutional or might violate national security.

Bush's signing statements typically include language such as the following:

> The Supreme Court of the United States has stated that the President's authority to classify and control information bearing on the national security flows from the Constitution and does not depend on a legislative authority.[†]

> The executive branch shall construe the provisions . . . calling for furnishing information to entities outside the executive branch . . . in a manner consistent with the President's constitutional authority to supervise the unitary executive branch.[§]

NOT ALL MEMBERS OF CONGRESS ARE SO CONCERNED

Some members of Congress are not so concerned about Bush's signing statements. Senator John Cornyn (R., Tex.) says that Bush's signing statements are only "expressions of presidential opinion" and carry no legal weight. According to Cornyn, federal courts would be unlikely to consider the statements when interpreting the laws with which they were issued.

FOR CRITICAL ANALYSIS

How might Bush's extensive use of signing statements be related to the expansion of presidential powers during the war on terrorism?

[†]Statement on Signing the Emergency Supplemental Appropriations Act for Defense, the Global War on Terror, and Hurricane Katrina, June 15, 2006.
[§]Statement on Signing the USA Patriot Improvement and Reauthorization Act of 2005, March 9, 2006.

[*]*Freytag v. C.I.R.,* 501 U.S. 868 (1991).

The Powers of Appointment and Removal. To assist in the various tasks of the chief executive, the president has a federal bureaucracy (see Chapter 13), which consists of over 2.7 million federal civilian employees. You might think that the president, as head of the largest bureaucracy in the United States, wields enormous power. The president, however, only nominally runs the executive bureaucracy. Most government positions are filled by **civil service** employees, who generally gain government employment through a merit system rather than presidential

| Civil Service
A collective term for the body of employees working for the government. Generally, civil service is understood to apply to all those who gain government employment through a merit system.

| Appointment Power

The authority vested in the president to fill a government office or position. Positions filled by presidential appointment include those in the executive branch and the federal judiciary, commissioned officers in the armed forces, and members of the independent regulatory commissions.

appointment.[3] Therefore, even though the president has important **appointment power,** it is limited to cabinet and subcabinet jobs, federal judgeships, agency heads, and about two thousand lesser jobs. This means that most of the 2.7 million federal employees owe no political allegiance to the president. They are more likely to owe loyalty to congressional committees or to interest groups representing the sector of the society that they serve. Table 12–1 shows what percentage of the total employment in each executive department is available for political appointment by the president.

The president's power to remove from office those officials who are not doing a good job or who do not agree with the president is not explicitly granted by the Constitution and has been limited. In 1926, however, a Supreme Court decision prevented Congress from interfering with the president's ability to fire those executive-branch officials whom the president had appointed with Senate approval.[4] There are ten agencies whose directors the president can remove at any time. These agencies include the Arms Control and Disarmament Agency, the Commission on Civil Rights, the Environmental Protection Agency, the General Services Administration, and the Small Business Administration. In addition, the president can remove all heads of cabinet departments, all individuals in the Executive Office of the President, and all of the 6,280 political appointees listed in Table 12–1.

Harry Truman spoke candidly of the difficulties a president faces in trying to control the executive bureaucracy. On leaving office, he referred to the problems that Dwight Eisenhower, as a former general of the army, was going to have: "He'll sit here and he'll say do this! do that! and nothing will happen. Poor Ike—it won't be a bit like the Army. He'll find it very frustrating."[5]

[3]See Chapter 13 for a discussion of the Civil Service Reform Act.
[4]*Meyers v. United States,* 272 U.S. 52 (1926).
[5]Quoted in Richard E. Neustadt, *Presidential Power: The Politics of Leadership* (New York: Wiley, 1960), p. 9. Truman may not have considered the amount of politics involved in decision making in the upper echelon of the army.

TABLE 12–1 | TOTAL CIVILIAN EMPLOYMENT IN CABINET DEPARTMENTS AVAILABLE FOR POLITICAL APPOINTMENT BY THE PRESIDENT

Executive Department	Total Number of Employees	Political Appointments Available	Percentage
Agriculture	100,084	384	0.43
Commerce	39,151	324	1.13
Defense	670,568	655	0.06
Education	4,581	260	4.06
Energy	15,689	469	2.75
Health and Human Services	63,323	418	0.61
Homeland Security	165,085	453	0.27
Housing and Urban Development	10,154	152	1.53
Interior	72,982	283	0.32
Justice	126,711	569	0.39
Labor	16,016	219	1.17
State	28,054	1,287	3.79
Transportation	64,131	271	0.42
Treasury	159,274	175	0.14
Veterans Affairs	223,137	361	0.14
TOTAL	1,593,855	6,280	0.33

Sources: *Policy and Supporting Positions* (Washington, D.C.: Government Printing Office, 2006); U.S. Office of Personnel Management, 2006.

The Power to Grant Reprieves and Pardons. Section 2 of Article II of the Constitution gives the president the power to grant **reprieves** and **pardons** for offenses against the United States except in cases of impeachment. All pardons are administered by the Office of the Pardon Attorney in the Department of Justice. In principle, a pardon is granted to remedy a mistake made in a conviction.

The United States Supreme Court upheld the president's power to grant reprieves and pardons in a 1925 case concerning a pardon granted by the president to an individual convicted of contempt of court. The judiciary had contended that only judges had the authority to convict individuals for contempt of court when court orders were violated and that the courts should be free from interference by the executive branch. The Court simply stated that the president could grant reprieves or pardons for all offenses "either before trial, during trial, or after trial, by individuals, or by classes, conditionally or absolutely, and this without modification or regulation by Congress."[6]

In a controversial decision, President Gerald Ford pardoned former president Richard Nixon for his role in the Watergate affair before any charges were brought in court. Just before George W. Bush's inauguration in 2001, President Bill Clinton announced pardons for almost two hundred persons. Some of these pardons were controversial.

Commander in Chief

The president, according to the Constitution, "shall be Commander in Chief of the Army and Navy of the United States, and of the Militia of the several States, when called into the actual Service of the United States." In other words, the armed forces are under civilian, rather than military, control.

Wartime Powers. Certainly, those who wrote the Constitution had George Washington in mind when they made the president the **commander in chief.** Although we do not expect our president to lead the troops into battle, presidents as commanders in chief have wielded dramatic power. Harry Truman made the awesome decision to drop atomic bombs on Hiroshima and Nagasaki in 1945 to force Japan to surrender and thus bring World War II to an end. Lyndon Johnson ordered bombing missions against North Vietnam in the 1960s, and he personally selected some of the targets. Richard Nixon decided to invade Cambodia in 1970. Ronald Reagan sent troops to Lebanon and Grenada in 1983 and ordered U.S. fighter planes to attack Libya in 1986. George H. W. Bush sent troops to Panama in 1989 and to the Middle East in 1990. Bill Clinton sent troops to Haiti in 1994 and to Bosnia in 1995, ordered missile attacks on alleged terrorist bases in 1998, and sent American planes to bomb Serbia in 1999. Most recently, George W. Bush ordered the invasion of Iraq in 2003.

The president is the ultimate decision maker in military matters. Everywhere the president goes, so too goes the "football"—a briefcase filled with all the codes necessary to order a nuclear attack. Only the president has the power to order the use of nuclear force.

Presidents have probably exercised more authority in their capacity as commander in chief than in any other role. Constitutionally, Congress has the sole power to declare war, but the president can send the armed forces into a country in situations that are certainly the equivalent of war. Harry Truman dispatched troops to Korea in 1950. Kennedy, Johnson, and Nixon waged an undeclared war in Southeast Asia, where more than 58,000 Americans were killed and 300,000 were wounded. In neither of these situations had Congress declared war.

DID YOU KNOW . . .
That President Richard Nixon served 56 days without a vice president, and that President Gerald Ford served 132 days without a vice president?

Reprieve
A formal postponement of the execution of a sentence imposed by a court of law.

Pardon
A release from the punishment for or legal consequences of a crime; a pardon can be granted by the president before or after a conviction.

Commander in Chief
The role of the president as supreme commander of the military forces of the United States and of the state National Guard units when they are called into federal service.

---

[6]*Ex parte Grossman,* 267 U.S. 87 (1925).

President George W. Bush gives a Memorial Day speech in 2006 in the amphitheater of the Arlington National Cemetery. Congress officially proclaimed this day in 1868, when it was called Decoration Day. What is the relationship between the president and the armed services? (Chief Photographer's Mate Johnny Bivera/U.S. Navy)

The War Powers Resolution. In an attempt to gain more control over such military activities, in 1973 Congress passed the **War Powers Resolution**—over President Nixon's veto—requiring that the president consult with Congress when sending American forces into action. Once they are sent, the president must report to Congress within forty-eight hours. Unless Congress approves the use of troops within sixty days or extends the sixty-day time limit, the forces must be withdrawn. The War Powers Resolution was tested in the fall of 1983, when Reagan requested that troops be left in Lebanon. The resulting compromise was a congressional resolution allowing troops to remain there for eighteen months. Shortly after the resolution was passed, however, more than 240 sailors and Marines were killed in a suicide bombing of a U.S. military housing compound in Beirut. That event provoked a furious congressional debate over the role American troops were playing in the Middle East, and all troops were withdrawn shortly thereafter.

In spite of the War Powers Resolution, the powers of the president as commander in chief are more extensive today than they were in the past. (President Bush's use of these powers has led to some controversy, which we examine in this chapter's *Which Side Are You On?* feature.) These powers are linked closely to the president's powers as chief diplomat, or chief crafter of foreign policy.

Chief Diplomat

The Constitution gives the president the power to recognize foreign governments; to make treaties, with the **advice and consent** of the Senate; and to make special agreements with other heads of state that do not require congressional approval. In addition, the president nominates ambassadors. As **chief diplomat,** the president dominates American foreign policy, a role that has been supported many times by the Supreme Court.

| **War Powers Resolution**
A law passed in 1973 spelling out the conditions under which the president can commit troops without congressional approval.

| **Advice and Consent**
Terms in the Constitution describing the U.S. Senate's power to review and approve treaties and presidential appointments.

| **Chief Diplomat**
The role of the president in recognizing foreign governments, making treaties, and effecting executive agreements.

WHICH SIDE ARE YOU ON? | Should the President Have the Power to Authorize Warrantless Domestic Surveillance?

The president is empowered by the Constitution to fight this nation's wars. According to the Bush administration's lawyers, that means that the president can fight wars, including the "war on terror," however he sees fit. These lawyers even argue that the president can violate international treaties when necessary to fight the war on terror. Not everyone has accepted these claims, however. Much of the controversy has centered on the president's use of the National Security Agency (NSA) to engage in domestic wiretapping without warrants.

LET THE PRESIDENT DO WHATEVER IS NECESSARY TO KEEP OUR COUNTRY SAFE

Those who are in favor of allowing presidential powers to include authorizing warrantless domestic wiretapping believe that the president's job requires such actions—and more. They argue that the president should be able to act on his own because he has what can be called inherent powers as commander in chief. In any event, these proponents of the NSA's domestic wiretapping insist that the agency was not listening to conversations between ordinary Americans. Rather, the agency was only listening to calls that came from abroad from suspected terrorists. Consider how ineffective the administration would be if, every time a suspected terrorist called someone in the United States, the government had to obtain a warrant to listen to the conversation. If we are to win the war on terror, the president must have a wide range of "war powers," even though we are not officially at war with any specific nation. Given the nature of terrorism today, the president must be able to act quickly to do whatever is necessary.

PRESIDENTIAL POWER DOES NOT INCLUDE THE RIGHT TO VIOLATE THE FOURTH AMENDMENT

Critics of the NSA's wiretapping program say that when Congress authorized the president to use force in the war on terrorism after the terrorist attacks in 2001, this authorization did not give President Bush a blank check to violate the Constitution and other existing laws. Under the Fourth Amendment to the Constitution, domestic wiretapping requires a warrant. Therefore, the NSA's warrantless domestic surveillance program was unlawful, and the president exceeded his power when he authorized the NSA to undertake this prohibited activity. Presidential power should be used wisely and always in compliance with the Constitution and other laws of the land, say these critics. To be sure, the current debate over the trade-off between national security and civil

This is the National Security Agency headquarters, which is located in Fort Meade, Maryland. Thousands of mathematicians, linguists, engineers, data flow experts, and computer scientists work at the NSA. At least one job that the NSA does is intercept phone calls worldwide in an attempt to, among other things, track terrorist activities. (NSA Photo)

liberties is not new—similar questions have been raised during earlier conflicts. But given that the war on terror could continue indefinitely, we should not allow the president to violate our civil liberties in the name of that war.

WHAT'S YOUR POSITION?

When is the situation so dangerous that we should allow the president the maximum wide-ranging powers in the war on terrorism?

GOING ONLINE

The Electronic Frontier Foundation is dedicated to defending privacy rights and Internet freedom. You can read about its position on the NSA surveillance issue at **www.eff.org/ Privacy/Surveillance/NSA**. To read more about the Bush administration's official position on the surveillance, visit **www. whitehouse.gov/news/releases/2006/01/20060122.html**.

| Diplomatic Recognition
The formal acknowledgment of a foreign government as legitimate.

Diplomatic Recognition.   An important power of the president as chief diplomat is that of **diplomatic recognition,** or the power to recognize—or refuse to recognize—foreign governments. In the role of ceremonial head of state, the president has always received foreign diplomats. In modern times, the simple act of receiving a foreign diplomat has been equivalent to accrediting the diplomat and officially recognizing his or her government. Such recognition of the legitimacy of another country's government is a prerequisite to diplomatic relations or treaties between that country and the United States.

Deciding when to recognize a foreign power is not always simple. The United States, for example, did not recognize the Soviet Union until 1933—sixteen years after the Russian Revolution of 1917. It was only after all attempts to reverse the effects of that revolution—including military invasion of Russia and diplomatic isolation—had proved futile that Franklin Roosevelt extended recognition to the Soviet government. U.S. presidents faced a similar problem with the Chinese Communist revolution. In December 1978, long after the Communist victory in China in 1949, Jimmy Carter granted official recognition to the People's Republic of China.[7]

A diplomatic recognition issue that faced the Clinton administration involved recognizing a former enemy—the Republic of Vietnam. Many Americans, particularly those who believed that Vietnam had not been forthcoming in the efforts to find the remains of missing American soldiers or to find out about former prisoners of war, opposed any formal relationship with that nation. After the U.S. government had negotiated with the Vietnamese government for many years over the missing-in-action issue and engaged in limited diplomatic contacts for several years, President Clinton announced on July 11, 1995, that the United States would recognize the government of Vietnam and move to establish normal diplomatic relations.

Proposal and Ratification of Treaties.   The president has the sole power to negotiate treaties with other nations. These treaties must be presented to the Senate, where they may be modified and must be approved by a two-thirds vote. After ratification, the president can approve the senatorial version of the treaty. Approval

---

[7]The Nixon administration first encouraged new relations with the People's Republic of China by allowing a cultural exchange of Ping-Pong teams.

Allied leaders attend the Versailles Peace Conference in 1919 after World War I. U.S. President Woodrow Wilson is second from the left. Wilson failed to get the resulting peace treaty approved by the U.S. Senate. To what extent should Congress defer to the president in making foreign policy? (National Archives)

poses a problem when the Senate has tacked on substantive amendments or reservations to a treaty, particularly when such changes may require reopening negotiations with the other signatory governments. Sometimes a president may decide to withdraw a treaty if the senatorial changes are too extensive—as Woodrow Wilson did with the Versailles Treaty in 1919. Wilson believed that the senatorial reservations would weaken the treaty so much that it would be ineffective. His refusal to accept the senatorial version of the treaty led to the eventual refusal of the United States to join the League of Nations.

President Carter was successful in lobbying for the treaties that provided for the return of the Panama Canal to Panama by the year 2000 and neutralizing the canal. President Bill Clinton won a major political and legislative victory in 1993 by persuading Congress to ratify the North American Free Trade Agreement (NAFTA). In so doing, he had to overcome opposition from Democrats and most of organized labor. In 1998, he worked closely with Senate Republicans to ensure Senate approval of a treaty governing the use of chemical weapons. In 2000, President Clinton won another major legislative victory when Congress voted to normalize trade relations with China permanently.

Before September 11, 2001, President George W. Bush indicated his intention to steer the United States in a unilateral direction on foreign policy. He rejected the Kyoto Agreement on global warming and proposed ending the 1972 Anti-Ballistic Missile (ABM) Treaty that was part of the first Strategic Arms Limitation Treaty (SALT I). After the terrorist attacks of September 11, 2001, however, President Bush sought cooperation from U.S. allies in the war on terrorism. Bush's return to multilateralism was exemplified in the signing of a nuclear weapons reduction treaty with Russia in 2002. Nonetheless, his attempts to gain international support for a war against Iraq to overthrow that country's government were not as successful as he had hoped. During the continuing occupation of Iraq, the Bush administration has seen even more erosion in other countries' support of his actions.

Executive Agreements. Presidential power in foreign affairs is enhanced greatly by the use of **executive agreements** made between the president and other heads of state. Such agreements do not require Senate approval, although the House and Senate may refuse to appropriate the funds necessary to implement them. Whereas treaties are binding on all succeeding administrations, executive agreements require each new president's consent to remain in effect.

Among the advantages of executive agreements are speed and secrecy. The former is essential during a crisis; the latter is important when the administration fears that open senatorial debate may be detrimental to the best interests of the United States or to the interests of the president.[8] There have been far more executive agreements (about 9,000) than treaties (about 1,300). Many executive agreements contain secret provisions calling for American military assistance or other support. For example, Franklin Roosevelt (1933–1945) used executive agreements to bypass congressional isolationists when he traded American destroyers for British Caribbean naval bases and when he arranged diplomatic and military affairs with Canada and Latin American nations.

Chief Legislator

Constitutionally, presidents must recommend to Congress legislation that they judge necessary and expedient. Not all presidents have wielded their powers as **chief legislator** in the same manner. Some presidents have been almost completely

Executive Agreement
An international agreement made by the president, without senatorial ratification, with the head of a foreign state.

Chief Legislator
The role of the president in influencing the making of laws.

[8]The Case Act of 1972 requires that all executive agreements be transmitted to Congress within sixty days after the agreement takes effect. Secret agreements are transmitted to the foreign relations committees as classified information.

unsuccessful in getting their legislative programs implemented by Congress. Presidents Franklin Roosevelt and Lyndon Johnson, however, saw much of their proposed legislation put into effect. (Some political systems combine the activities and powers of chief executive and chief legislator in a single position, called the head of government. In many democratic countries, the head of government is not directly elected by the voters for that position, as this chapter's *Beyond Our Borders* feature explains.)

In modern times, the president has played a dominant role in creating the congressional agenda. In the president's annual **State of the Union message**, which is required by the Constitution (Article II, Section 3) and is usually given in late January shortly after Congress reconvenes, the president as chief legislator presents a program. The message gives a broad, comprehensive view of what the president wishes the legislature to accomplish during its session. It is as much a message to the American people and to the world as it is to Congress. Its impact on public opinion can determine the way in which Congress responds to the president's agenda.

Getting Legislation Passed.   The president can propose legislation. Congress, however, is not required to pass—or even introduce—any of the administration's bills. How, then, does the president get those proposals made into law? One way is by exercising the power of persuasion. The president writes to, telephones, and meets with various congressional leaders; makes public announcements to influence public opinion; and, as head of the party, exercises legislative leadership through the congresspersons of that party.

A president whose party holds a majority in both chambers of Congress may have an easier time getting legislation passed than does a president who faces a hostile Congress. Note, though, that even with a Republican-dominated Congress, President George W. Bush failed to obtain Social Security reform legislation or to make headway with his proposed Federal Marriage Amendment to the Constitution.

Saying No to Legislation.   The president has the power to say no to legislation through use of the veto, by which the White House returns a bill unsigned to

| **State of the Union Message**
An annual message to Congress in which the president proposes a legislative program. The message is addressed not only to Congress but also to the American people and to the world.

Each year, the president presents the State of the Union message, which is required by Article II, Section 3, of the Constitution and is usually given in late January. Attendees include all members of Congress and usually the justices of the United States Supreme Court and the heads of most of the executive departments. The vice president and the Speaker of the House normally sit behind the president. To what extent do presidents use this occasion to present a purely political message? (Kevin Lamarque/Pool via *Bloomberg News*/Landov)

BEYOND OUR BORDERS | Heads of Government Are Not Always Elected As Such

In the United States, the president is the head of state and the head of government. In many democratic societies, however, voters do not directly elect the head of government. This is true in the British parliamentary system and in parliamentary systems throughout the world that follow the Westminster system, named after the Palace of Westminster (also known as the Houses of Parliament), the building where the British Parliament meets. Canada uses this system, as do Australia, India, Ireland, Jamaica, Malaysia, New Zealand, Singapore, and Malta.

THE PRIME MINISTER IN GREAT BRITAIN

Under the British Westminster system, the head of government is the prime minister, who is typically the leader of the party that has a majority of the seats in the House of Commons (Parliament also includes the House of Lords, but it plays little role in the government.) Although prime ministers do not have to be members of Parliament themselves, they typically are. Thus, most prime ministers are elected by popular vote for a seat in Parliament, but not necessarily as head of government.

In Great Britain, the monarch, as the head of state, asks the leader of the majority in Parliament to form a government. The process of forming a government requires the prime minister to designate members of Parliament as heads of the various cabinet departments, not too dissimilar to the cabinet in the United States. All ministers must support the policy of the government, irrespective of any reservations they might have privately.

Officially, the appointment of the prime minister is a royal prerogative. In reality, however, the naming of the prime minister is merely ceremonial, and the monarch would never designate a prime minister who belonged to the minority party in Parliament. Also note that because Britain does not have a written constitution, the office of prime minister existed long before it was mentioned in official state documents. The first reference to the prime minister in an act of Parliament did not occur until the early twentieth century.

CANADA'S SYSTEM IS SIMILIAR

As in Britain, the office of the prime minister of Canada does not formally exist in the constitution. The office evolved *de facto* into what it is today, starting in the mid-nineteenth century. Also as in Britain, the prime minister is the leader of the political party with the most seats in the Canadian House of Commons. Technically, the prime minister along with his or her cabinet is appointed by the governor general. The prime minister in Canada does not serve for a fixed number of years in office.

FOR CRITICAL ANALYSIS

Would you feel comfortable having a head of government whom you did not actually elect as the person to take that position? Why or why not?

Congress with a **veto message** attached.[9] Because the Constitution requires that every bill passed by the House and the Senate be sent to the president before it becomes law, the president must act on each bill.

1. If the bill is signed, it becomes law.
2. If the bill is not sent back to Congress after ten congressional working days, it becomes law without the president's signature.
3. The president can reject the bill and send it back to Congress with a veto message setting forth objections. Congress then can change the bill, hoping to secure presidential approval and repass it. Or Congress can simply reject the president's objections by overriding the veto with a two-thirds roll-call vote of the members present in both the House and the Senate.
4. If the president refuses to sign the bill and Congress adjourns within ten working days after the bill has been submitted to the president, the bill is killed for that session of Congress. This is called a **pocket veto.** If Congress wishes the bill to be reconsidered, the bill must be reintroduced during the following session.

| **Veto Message**
The president's formal explanation of a veto when legislation is returned to Congress.

| **Pocket Veto**
A special veto exercised by the chief executive after a legislative body has adjourned. Bills not signed by the chief executive die after a specified period of time. If Congress wishes to reconsider such a bill, it must be reintroduced in the following session of Congress.

---

[9]*Veto* in Latin means "I forbid."

Presidents employed the veto power infrequently until after the Civil War, but it has been used with increasing vigor since then (see Table 12–2). The total number of vetoes from George Washington through the middle of George W. Bush's second term in office was 2,552, with about two-thirds of those vetoes being exercised by Grover Cleveland, Franklin Roosevelt, Harry Truman, and Dwight Eisenhower.

Not since Martin Van Buren (1837–1841) has a president served a full term in office without exercising the veto power. George W. Bush, who had the benefit of a Republican Congress that passed legislation he was willing to sign, did not veto any

TABLE 12–2 | PRESIDENTIAL VETOES, 1789 TO PRESENT

Years	President	Regular Vetoes	Vetoes Overridden	Pocket Vetoes	Total Vetoes
1789–1797	Washington	2	0	0	2
1797–1801	J. Adams	0	0	0	0
1801–1809	Jefferson	0	0	0	0
1809–1817	Madison	5	0	2	7
1817–1825	Monroe	1	0	0	1
1825–1829	J. Q. Adams	0	0	0	0
1829–1837	Jackson	5	0	7	12
1837–1841	Van Buren	0	0	1	1
1841–1841	Harrison	0	0	0	0
1841–1845	Tyler	6	1	4	10
1845–1849	Polk	2	0	1	3
1849–1850	Taylor	0	0	0	0
1850–1853	Fillmore	0	0	0	0
1853–1857	Pierce	9	5	0	9
1857–1861	Buchanan	4	0	3	7
1861–1865	Lincoln	2	0	5	7
1865–1869	A. Johnson	21	15	8	29
1869–1877	Grant	45	4	48	93
1877–1881	Hayes	12	1	1	13
1881–1881	Garfield	0	0	0	0
1881–1885	Arthur	4	1	8	12
1885–1889	Cleveland	304	2	110	414
1889–1893	Harrison	19	1	25	44
1893–1897	Cleveland	42	5	128	170
1897–1901	McKinley	6	0	36	42
1901–1909	T. Roosevelt	42	1	40	82
1909–1913	Taft	30	1	9	39
1913–1921	Wilson	33	6	11	44
1921–1923	Harding	5	0	1	6
1923–1929	Coolidge	20	4	30	50
1929–1933	Hoover	21	3	16	37
1933–1945	F. Roosevelt	372	9	263	635
1945–1953	Truman	180	12	70	250
1953–1961	Eisenhower	73	2	108	181
1961–1963	Kennedy	12	0	9	21
1963–1969	L. Johnson	16	0	14	30
1969–1974	Nixon	26*	7	17	43
1974–1977	Ford	48	12	18	66
1977–1981	Carter	13	2	18	31
1981–1989	Reagan	39	9	39	78
1989–1993	G. H. W. Bush	29	1	15	44
1993–2001	Clinton	37†	2	1	38
2001–	G. W. Bush	1	0	0	1
TOTAL		1,486	106	1,066	2,552

*Two pocket vetoes by President Nixon, overruled in the courts, are counted here as regular vetoes.
†President Clinton's line-item vetoes are not included.
Source: Office of the Clerk.

legislation during his first term. Only in the summer of 2006 did Bush finally issue a veto, saying "no" to stem-cell research legislation passed by Congress. He occasionally threatened to use the veto and certainly used it when he was governor of Texas.

The Line-Item Veto.   Ronald Reagan lobbied strenuously for Congress to give another tool to the president—the **line-item veto,** which would allow the president to veto *specific* spending provisions of legislation that was passed by Congress. In 1996, Congress passed the Line Item Veto Act, which provided for the line-item veto. Signed by President Clinton, the law granted the president the power to rescind any item in an appropriations bill unless Congress passed a resolution of disapproval. Of course, the congressional resolution could be, in turn, vetoed by the president. The law did not take effect until after the 1996 election.

The act was soon challenged in court as an unconstitutional delegation of legislative powers to the executive branch. In 1998, by a six-to-three vote, the United States Supreme Court agreed and overturned the act. The Court stated that "there is no provision in the Constitution that authorizes the president to enact, to amend or to repeal statutes."[10]

On the occasion of Bush's first veto, which was against legislation providing federal funding for stem-cell research, he presented remarks in Cypress, Texas. Why might Bush have chosen this particular legislation to exercise his first veto? (White House Photo by Kimberlee Hewitt)

Congress's Power to Override Presidential Vetoes.   A veto is a clear-cut indication of the president's dissatisfaction with congressional legislation. Congress, however, can override a presidential veto, although it rarely exercises this power. Consider that two-thirds of the members of each chamber who are present must vote to override the president's veto in a roll-call vote. This means that if only one-third plus one of the members voting in one of the chambers of Congress do not agree to override the veto, the veto holds. It was not until the administration of John Tyler (1841–1845) that Congress overrode a presidential veto. In the first sixty-five years of American federal government history, out of thirty-three regular vetoes, Congress overrode only one, or about 3 percent. Overall, only about 7 percent of all regular vetoes have been overridden.

| Line-Item Veto
The power of an executive to veto individual lines or items within a piece of legislation without vetoing the entire bill.

Other Presidential Powers

The powers of the president just discussed are called **constitutional powers,** because their basis lies in the Constitution. In addition, Congress has established by law, or statute, numerous other presidential powers—such as the ability to declare national emergencies. These are called **statutory powers.** Both constitutional and statutory powers have been labeled the **expressed powers** of the president, because they are expressly written into the Constitution or into law.

Presidents also have what have come to be known as **inherent powers.** These depend on the statements in the Constitution that "the executive Power shall be vested in a President" and that the president should "take Care that the Laws be faithfully executed." The most common example of inherent powers are those emergency powers invoked by the president during wartime. Franklin Roosevelt, for example, used his inherent powers to move the Japanese and Japanese Americans living in the United States into internment camps for the duration of World War II.

Clearly, modern U.S. presidents have many powers at their disposal. According to some critics, among the powers exercised by modern presidents are certain powers that rightfully belong to Congress but that Congress has yielded to the executive branch.

| Constitutional Power
A power vested in the president by Article II of the Constitution.

| Statutory Power
A power created for the president through laws enacted by Congress.

| Expressed Power
A power of the president that is expressly written into the Constitution or into statutory law.

| Inherent Power
A power of the president derived from the statements in the Constitution that "the executive Power shall be vested in a President" and that the president should "take Care that the Laws be faithfully executed"; defined through practice rather than through law.

[10]*Clinton v. City of New York,* 524 U.S. 417 (1998).

The President as Party Chief and Superpolitician

Presidents are by no means above political partisanship, and one of their many roles is that of chief of party. Although the Constitution says nothing about the function of the president within a political party (the mere concept of political parties was abhorrent to most of the authors of the Constitution), today presidents are the actual leaders of their parties.

The President as Chief of Party

Patronage
The practice of rewarding faithful party workers and followers with government employment and contracts.

As party leader, the president chooses the national committee chairperson and can try to discipline party members who fail to support presidential policies. One way of exerting political power within the party is through **patronage**—appointing political supporters to government or public jobs. This power was more extensive in the past, before the establishment of the civil service in 1883 (see Chapter 13), but the president retains important patronage power. As we noted earlier, the president can appoint several thousand individuals to jobs in the cabinet, the White House, and the federal regulatory agencies.

Perhaps the most important partisan role that the president played in the late 1900s and early 2000s was that of fund-raiser. The president is able to raise large amounts for the party through appearances at dinners, speaking engagements, and other social occasions. President Clinton may have raised more than half a billion dollars for the Democratic Party during his two terms. President George W. Bush was even more successful than Clinton.

Presidents have a number of other ways of exerting influence as party chief. The president may make it known that a particular congressperson's choice for federal judge will not be appointed unless that member of Congress is more supportive of the president's legislative program.[11] The president may agree to campaign for a particular program or for a particular candidate. Presidents also reward loyal members of Congress with support for the funding of local projects, tax breaks for regional industries, and other forms of "pork."

The President's Power to Persuade

According to political scientist Richard E. Neustadt, without the power to persuade, no president can lead very well. After all, even though the president is in the news

---

[11]"Senatorial courtesy" (see Chapter 14) often puts the judicial appointment in the hands of the Senate, however.

President George W. Bush and Representative Paul Ryan (R., Wis.) arrive in Milwaukee for a political fund-raiser. How could the president's role as party leader affect campaign fund-raising for his political party? (AP Photo/Morry Gash)

virtually every day, the Constitution gives Congress most of the authority in the U.S. political system. The Constitution does not give the executive branch enough constitutional power to keep the president constantly in a strong leadership position. Therefore, the president must convince Congress to do what the president wants. As Neustadt argues, "presidential power is the power to persuade."[12]

Neustadt argues that one can find a high correlation between effective presidents and those who are best at persuasion. Presidents have to persuade the public, too. Many have argued that the reason George W. Bush has so little support is that he is not persuasive when he appears on television and in person.

Constituencies and Public Approval

All politicians worry about their constituencies, and presidents are no exception. Presidents are also concerned with public approval ratings.

Presidential Constituencies. Presidents have many constituencies. In principle, they are beholden to the entire electorate—the public of the United States—even those who did not vote. They are certainly beholden to their party because its members helped to put them in office. The president's constituencies also include members of the opposing party whose cooperation the president needs. Finally, the president must take into consideration a constituency that has come to be called the **Washington community.** This community consists of individuals who—whether in or out of political office—are intimately familiar with the workings of government, thrive on gossip, and measure on a daily basis the political power of the president.

Public Approval. All of these constituencies are impressed by presidents who maintain a high level of public approval, partly because this is very difficult to accomplish. Presidential popularity, as measured by national polls, gives the president an extra political resource to use in persuading legislators or bureaucrats to pass legislation. After all, refusing to do so might be going against public sentiment. President Bill Clinton showed significant strength in the public opinion polls for a second-term chief executive, as Figure 12–1 indicates.

[12]Richard E. Neustadt, *Presidential Power and the Modern Presidents: The Politics of Leadership from Roosevelt to Reagan*, rev. ed. (New York: Free Press, 1991).

> | DID YOU KNOW . . .
> That the 2008 presidential elections will be only the second in the last twenty-eight years without a Bush on the ballot?

| **Washington Community**
Individuals regularly involved with politics in Washington, D.C.

FIGURE 12–1 | PUBLIC POPULARITY OF MODERN PRESIDENTS

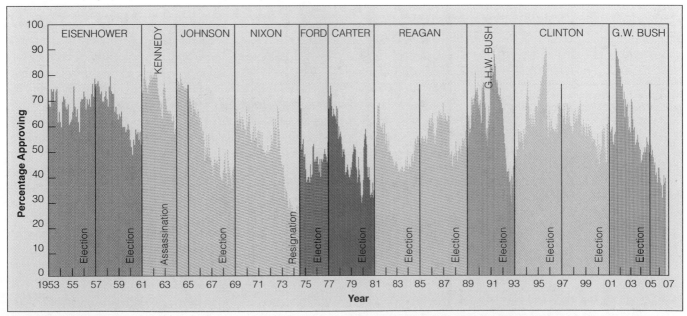

Sources: The Roper Center for Public Opinion Research; Gallup and *USA Today*/CNN polls, March 1992 through November 2006.

"I don't think you can distance yourself from the White House on this one. After all, you are the President."

George W. Bush and the Public Opinion Polls.   The impact of popular approval on a president's prospects was placed in sharp relief by the experiences of President Bush. Immediately after 9/11, Bush had the highest approval ratings ever recorded. His popularity then entered a steep decline that was interrupted only briefly by high ratings during the early phases of the Second Gulf War. Such a decline appeared to threaten his reelection. In the end, however, Bush's popularity stabilized at just over 50 percent, reflecting the continued support of his political "base." Bush's support may have come from a narrow majority of the voters, but their support was firm. During his second term, Bush's approval ratings reached new lows, falling to 31 percent during May 2006. During the summer of that year, more than 56 percent of citizens polled disapproved of the job he was doing as president.

"Going Public."   Since the early 1900s, presidents have spoken more to the public and less to Congress. In the 1800s, only 7 percent of presidential speeches were addressed to the public; since 1900, 50 percent have been addressed to the public. One scholar, Samuel Kernell, has proposed that the style of presidential leadership has changed since World War II, owing partly to the influence of television, with a resulting change in the balance of national politics.[13] Presidents frequently go over the heads of Congress and the political elites, taking their cases directly to the people.

This strategy, which Kernell dubbed "going public," gives the president additional power through the ability to persuade and manipulate public opinion. By identifying their own positions so clearly, presidents make compromises with Congress much more difficult and weaken the legislators' positions. Given the increasing importance of the media as the major source of political information for citizens and elites, presidents will continue to use public opinion as part of their arsenal of weapons to gain support from Congress and to achieve their policy goals.

---

[13]Samuel Kernell, *Going Public: New Strategies of Presidential Leadership,* 3d ed. (Washington, D.C.: Congressional Quarterly Press, 1997).

Special Uses of Presidential Power

Presidents have at their disposal a variety of special powers and privileges not available in the other branches of the U.S. government. These include (1) emergency powers, (2) executive orders, and (3) executive privilege.

Emergency Powers

If you read the Constitution, you will find no mention of the additional powers that the executive office may exercise during national emergencies. Indeed, the Supreme Court has indicated that an "emergency does not create power."[14] But it is clear that presidents have used their inherent powers during times of emergency, particularly in the realm of foreign affairs. The **emergency powers** of the president were first enunciated in the Supreme Court's decision in *United States v. Curtiss-Wright Export Corp.*[15] In that case, President Franklin Roosevelt, without authorization by Congress, ordered an embargo on the shipment of weapons to two warring South American countries. The Court recognized that the president may exercise inherent powers in foreign affairs and that the national government has primacy in these affairs.

Examples of emergency powers are abundant, coinciding with crises in domestic and foreign affairs. Abraham Lincoln suspended civil liberties at the beginning of the Civil War (1861–1865) and called the state militias into national service. These actions and his subsequent governance of conquered areas and even of areas of northern states were justified by claims that they were essential to preserve the Union. Franklin Roosevelt declared an "unlimited national emergency" following the fall of France in World War II (1939–1945) and mobilized the federal budget and the economy for war.

President Harry Truman authorized the federal seizure of steel plants and their operation by the national government in 1952 during the Korean War. Truman claimed that he was using his inherent emergency power as chief executive and commander in chief to safeguard the nation's security, as an ongoing strike by steelworkers threatened the supply of weapons to the armed forces. The Supreme Court did not agree, holding that the president had no authority under the Constitution to seize private property or to legislate such action.[16] According to legal scholars, this was the first time a limit was placed on the exercise of the president's emergency powers.

Executive Orders

Congress allows the president (as well as administrative agencies) to issue **executive orders** that have the force of law. These executive orders can do the following: (1) enforce legislative statutes, (2) enforce the Constitution or treaties with foreign nations, and (3) establish or modify rules and practices of executive administrative agencies.

An executive order, then, represents the president's legislative power. The only apparent requirement is that under the Administrative Procedure Act of 1946, all executive orders must be published in the *Federal Register,* a daily publication of the U.S. government. Executive orders have been used to establish procedures to appoint noncareer administrators, to implement national affirmative action regulations, to restructure the White House bureaucracy, to ration consumer goods and to administer wage and price controls under emergency conditions, to classify government information as secret, to regulate the export of restricted items, and to establish military tribunals for suspected terrorists.

---

[14]*Home Building and Loan Association v. Blaisdell,* 290 U.S. 398 (1934).
[15]299 U.S. 304 (1936).
[16]*Youngstown Sheet and Tube Co. v. Sawyer,* 343 U.S. 579 (1952).

DID YOU KNOW . . .
That the shortest inaugural address was George Washington's second one at 135 words?

Emergency Power
An inherent power exercised by the president during a period of national crisis.

Executive Order
A rule or regulation issued by the president that has the effect of law. Executive orders can implement and give administrative effect to provisions in the Constitution, to treaties, and to statutes.

Federal Register
A publication of the U.S. government that prints executive orders, rules, and regulations.

Executive Privilege

| Executive Privilege
The right of executive officials to withhold information from or to refuse to appear before a legislative committee.

Another inherent executive power that has been claimed by presidents concerns the ability of the president and the president's executive officials to withhold information from or refuse to appear before Congress or the courts. This is called **executive privilege,** and it relies on the constitutional separation of powers for its basis.

As discussed in this chapter's opening *What If . . .* feature, presidents have frequently invoked executive privilege to avoid having to disclose information to Congress on actions of the executive branch. For example, President George W. Bush claimed executive privilege to keep the head of the newly established Office of Homeland Security, Tom Ridge, from testifying before Congress. The Bush administration also resisted attempts by the congressional Government Accountability Office to obtain information about meetings and documents related to Vice President Dick Cheney's actions as chair of the administration's energy policy task force. Bush, like presidents before him, claimed that a certain degree of secrecy is essential to national security. Critics of executive privilege believe that it can be used to shield from public scrutiny actions of the executive branch that should be open to Congress and to the American citizenry.

Limiting Executive Privilege.   Limits to executive privilege went untested until the Watergate affair in the early 1970s. Five men had broken into the headquarters of the Democratic National Committee and were caught searching for documents that would damage the candidacy of the Democratic nominee, George McGovern. Later investigation showed that the break-in was planned by members of Richard Nixon's campaign committee and that Nixon and his closest advisers had devised a strategy for impeding the investigation of the crime. After it became known that all of the conversations held in the Oval Office had been tape-recorded on a secret system, Nixon was ordered to turn over the tapes to the special prosecutor.

As you read in this chapter's opening *What If . . .* feature, Nixon refused to do so, claiming executive privilege. He argued that "no president could function if the private papers of his office, prepared by his personal staff, were open to public scrutiny." In 1974, in one of the Supreme Court's most famous cases, *United States v. Nixon,*[17] the justices unanimously ruled that Nixon had to hand over the tapes. The Court held that executive privilege could not be used to prevent evidence from being heard in criminal proceedings.

Clinton's Attempted Use of Executive Privilege.   The claim of executive privilege was also raised by the Clinton administration as a defense against the aggressive investigation of Clinton's relationship with Monica Lewinsky by Independent Counsel Kenneth Starr. The Clinton administration claimed executive privilege for several presidential aides who might have discussed the situation with the president. In addition, President Clinton asserted that his White House counsel did not have to testify before the Starr grand jury due to attorney-client privilege. Finally, the Department of Justice claimed that members of the Secret Service who guard the president could not testify about his activities due to a "protective function privilege" inherent in their duties. The federal judge overseeing the case denied the claims of privilege, however, and the decision was upheld on appeal.

| Abuses of Executive Power and Impeachment

Presidents normally leave office either because their first term has expired and they have not sought (or won) reelection or because, having served two full terms, they are not allowed to be elected for a third term (owing to the Twenty-second

---

[17]318 U.S. 683 (1974).

President Richard Nixon says goodbye outside the White House after his resignation on August 9, 1974, as he prepares to board a helicopter for a flight to nearby Andrews Air Force Base. Nixon addressed members of his staff in the East Room prior to his departure. Was Nixon impeached? (AP Photo/Bob Daughtery)

Amendment, passed in 1951). Eight presidents have died in office. But there is still another way for a president to leave office—by **impeachment** and conviction. Articles I and II of the Constitution authorize the House and Senate to remove the president, the vice president, or other civil officers of the United States for committing "Treason, Bribery, or other high Crimes and Misdemeanors." According to the Constitution, the impeachment process begins in the House, which impeaches (accuses) the federal officer involved. If the House votes to impeach the officer, it draws up articles of impeachment and submits them to the Senate, which conducts the actual trial.

In the history of the United States, no president has ever actually been impeached and also convicted—and thus removed from office—by means of this process. President Andrew Johnson (1865–1869), who succeeded to the office after the assassination of Abraham Lincoln, was impeached by the House but acquitted by the Senate. More than a century later, the House Judiciary Committee approved articles of impeachment against President Richard Nixon for his involvement in the cover-up of the Watergate break-in of 1972. Informed by members of his own party that he had no hope of surviving the trial in the Senate, Nixon resigned on August 9, 1974, before the full House voted on the articles. Nixon is the only president to have resigned from office.

The second president to be impeached by the House but not convicted by the Senate was President Bill Clinton. In September 1998, Independent Counsel Kenneth Starr sent to Congress the findings of his investigation of the president on the charges of perjury and obstruction of justice. The House approved two charges against Clinton: lying to the grand jury about his affair with Monica Lewinsky and obstruction of justice. The articles of impeachment were then sent to the Senate, which acquitted Clinton.

| **Impeachment**
An action by the House of Representatives to accuse the president, vice president, or other civil officers of the United States of committing "Treason, Bribery, or other high Crimes and Misdemeanors."

On December 19, 1998, the House of Representatives voted to impeach President Bill Clinton for perjury and obstruction of justice. That same day, Clinton addressed lawmakers and staff outside the Oval Office, surrounded by supporters. President Clinton was later acquitted by the Senate, but the events raised important issues about presidential privacy and ethics. To what extent should the president's personal life be the subject of public scrutiny while he or she is in office? (AP Photo/Doug Mills)

The Executive Organization

Gone are the days when presidents answered their own mail, as George Washington did. It was not until 1857 that Congress authorized a private secretary for the president, to be paid by the federal government. Woodrow Wilson typed most of his correspondence, even though he did have several secretaries. At the beginning of Franklin Roosevelt's long tenure in the White House, the entire staff consisted of thirty-seven employees. With the New Deal and World War II, however, the presidential staff became a sizable organization.

Today, the executive organization includes a White House Office staff of about 600, including some workers who are part-time employees and others who are borrowed from their departments by the White House. Not all of these employees have equal access to the president, nor are all of them likely to be equally concerned about the administration's political success. The more than 360 employees who work in the White House Office itself are closest to the president. They often include many individuals who worked on the president's campaign. These assistants are most concerned with preserving the president's reputation. Also included in the president's staff are a number of councils and advisory organizations, such as the National Security Council. Although the individuals who hold staff positions in these offices are appointed by the president, they are really more concerned with their own areas than with the president's overall success. The group of appointees who perhaps are least helpful to the president is the cabinet, each member of which is the principal officer of a government department.

The Cabinet

Although the Constitution does not include the word *cabinet*, it does state that the president "may require the Opinion, in writing, of the principal Officer in each of the executive Departments." Since the time of George Washington, there has been an advisory group, or **cabinet,** to which the president turns for counsel.

Members of the Cabinet.   Originally, the cabinet consisted of only four officials— the secretaries of state, treasury, and war, and the attorney general. Today, the cabinet

| **Cabinet**
An advisory group selected by the president to aid in making decisions. The cabinet includes the heads of fifteen executive departments and others named by the president.

numbers fourteen department secretaries and the attorney general. (See Table 12–1 on page 396 for the names of the cabinet departments and Chapter 13 for a detailed discussion of these units.)

The cabinet may include others as well. The president at his or her discretion can, for example, ascribe cabinet rank to the vice president, the head of the Office of Management and Budget, the national security adviser, the ambassador to the United Nations, or others.

Often, a president will use a **kitchen cabinet** to replace the formal cabinet as a major source of advice. The term *kitchen cabinet* originated during the presidency of Andrew Jackson, who relied on the counsel of close friends who often met with him in the kitchen of the White House. A kitchen cabinet is a very informal group of advisers; usually, they are friends with whom the president worked before being elected.

Presidential Use of Cabinets. Because neither the Constitution nor statutory law requires the president to consult with the cabinet, its use is purely discretionary. Some presidents have relied on the counsel of their cabinets more than others. Dwight Eisenhower was used to the team approach to solving problems from his experience as supreme allied commander during World War II, and therefore he frequently turned to his cabinet for advice on a wide range of issues. More often, presidents have solicited the opinions of their cabinets and then did what they wanted to do anyway. Lincoln supposedly said—after a cabinet meeting in which a vote was seven nays against his one aye—"Seven nays and one aye, the ayes have it." In general, few presidents have relied heavily on the advice of their cabinet members.

It is not surprising that presidents tend not to rely on their cabinet members' advice. Often, the departmental heads are more responsive to the wishes of their own staffs or to their own political ambitions than they are to the president. They may be more concerned with obtaining resources for their departments than with achieving the goals of the president. So there is often a strong conflict of interest between presidents and their cabinet members.

| **Kitchen Cabinet**
The informal advisers to the president.

President George W. Bush makes remarks as he meets with his cabinet in the Cabinet Room of the White House in 2006. To what extent are cabinet members part of Bush's team? (AP Photo/Gerald Herbert)

The Executive Office of the President

When President Franklin Roosevelt appointed a special committee on administrative management, he knew that the committee would conclude that the president needed help. Indeed, the committee proposed a major reorganization of the executive branch. Congress did not approve the entire reorganization, but it did create the **Executive Office of the President (EOP)** to provide staff assistance for the chief executive and to help coordinate the executive bureaucracy. Since that time, a number of agencies have been created within the EOP to supply the president with advice and staff help. These agencies include the following:

- White House Office.
- White House Military Office.
- Office of the Vice President.
- Council of Economic Advisers.
- Council on Environmental Quality.
- National Security Council.
- Office of Management and Budget.
- Office of National AIDS Policy.
- Office of National Drug Control Policy.
- Office of Science and Technology Policy.
- Office of the United States Trade Representative.
- President's Critical Infrastructure Protection Board.
- President's Foreign Intelligence Advisory Board.

Several of the offices within the EOP are especially important, including the White House Office, the Office of Management and Budget, and the National Security Council.

The White House Office.   The White House Office includes most of the key personal and political advisers to the president. Among the jobs held by these aides are those of legal counsel to the president, secretary, press secretary, and appointments secretary. Often, the individuals who hold these positions are recruited from the president's campaign staff. Their duties—mainly protecting the president's political interests—are similar to campaign functions. In all recent administrations, one member of the White House Office has been named **chief of staff**. This person, who is responsible for coordinating the office, is also one of the president's chief advisers.

The president may establish special advisory units within the White House to address topics the president finds especially important. Such units include the long-

| Executive Office of the President (EOP)
An organization established by President Franklin D. Roosevelt to assist the president in carrying out major duties.

| White House Office
The personal office of the president, which tends to presidential political needs and manages the media.

| Chief of Staff
The person who is named to direct the White House Office and advise the president.

Condoleezza Rice has served as both national security advisor and secretary of state. She has been frequently called to testify before Congress. What are some of the challenges facing any administration official who gives public testimony? (Greg E. Mathieson/MAI/Landov)

Dr. Condoleezza Rice

established Domestic Policy Council and the National Economic Council. Under George W. Bush, these units also include the Office of Faith-Based and Community Initiatives and the USA Freedom Corps. The White House Office also includes the staff members who support the first lady.

In addition to civilian advisers, the president is supported by a large number of military personnel, who are organized under the White House Military Office. These members of the military provide communications, transportation, medical care, and food services to the president and the White House staff.

Employees of the White House Office have been both envied and criticized. The White House Office, according to most former staffers, grants its employees access and power. They are able to use the resources of the White House to contact virtually anyone in the world by telephone, cable, fax, or electronic mail as well as to use the influence of the White House to persuade legislators and citizens. Because of this influence, staffers are often criticized for overstepping the bounds of the office. It is the appointments secretary who is able to grant or deny senators, representatives, and cabinet secretaries access to the president. It is the press secretary who grants to the press and television journalists access to any information about the president.

White House staff members are closest to the president and may have considerable influence over the administration's decisions. Often, when presidents are under fire for their decisions, the staff is accused of keeping the chief executive too isolated from criticism or help. Presidents insist that they will not allow the staff to become too powerful, but, given the difficulty of the office, each president eventually turns to staff members for loyal assistance and protection.

The Office of Management and Budget. The **Office of Management and Budget (OMB)** was originally the Bureau of the Budget, which was created in 1921 within the Department of the Treasury. Recognizing the importance of this agency, Franklin Roosevelt moved it into the White House Office in 1939. Richard Nixon reorganized the Bureau of the Budget in 1970 and changed its name to reflect its new managerial function. It is headed by a director, who must make up the annual federal budget that the president presents to Congress each January for approval. In principle, the director of the OMB has broad fiscal powers in planning and estimating various parts of the federal budget because all agencies must submit their proposed budget to the OMB for approval. In reality, it is not so clear that the OMB truly can affect the greater scope of the federal budget. Rather, the OMB may be more important as a clearinghouse for legislative proposals initiated in the executive agencies.

The National Security Council. The **National Security Council (NSC)** is a link between the president's key foreign and military advisers and the president. Its members consist of the president, the vice president, and the secretaries of state and defense, plus other informal members. Included in the NSC is the president's special assistant for national security affairs. In 2001, Condoleezza Rice became the first woman to serve as a president's national security adviser.

The Vice Presidency

The Constitution does not give much power to the vice president. The only formal duty is to preside over the Senate—which is rarely necessary. This obligation is fulfilled when the Senate organizes and adopts its rules and when the vice president is needed to decide a tie vote. In all other cases, the president pro tem manages parliamentary procedures in the Senate. The vice president is expected to participate only informally in senatorial deliberations, if at all.

| DID YOU KNOW . . .

That the 2008 presidential elections will be the first since 1952 without an incumbent president or vice president running?

| Office of Management
and Budget (OMB)

A division of the Executive Office of the President. The OMB assists the president in preparing the annual budget, clearing and coordinating departmental agency budgets, and supervising the administration of the federal budget.

| National Security Council (NSC)

An agency in the Executive Office of the President that advises the president on national security.

The Vice President's Job

Vice presidents have traditionally been chosen by presidential nominees to balance the ticket to attract groups of voters or appease party factions. If a presidential nominee is from the North, it is not a bad idea to have a vice-presidential nominee who is from the South. If the presidential nominee is from a rural state, perhaps someone with an urban background would be most suitable as a running mate. Presidential nominees who are strongly conservative or strongly liberal would do well to have vice presidential nominees who are more in the middle of the political road.

Strengthening the Ticket. In recent presidential elections, vice presidents have often been selected for other reasons. Bill Clinton picked Al Gore to be his running mate in 1992 even though both were southern and moderates. The ticket appealed to southerners and moderates, both of whom were crucial to the election. In 2000, both vice presidential selections were intended to shore up the respective presidential candidates' perceived weaknesses. Republican George W. Bush, who was subject to criticism for his lack of government experience and his "lightweight" personality, chose Dick Cheney, a former member of Congress who had also served as secretary of defense. Democrat Al Gore chose Senator Joe Lieberman of Connecticut, whose reputation for moral integrity (as an Orthodox Jew) could help counteract the effects of Bill Clinton's sex scandals. In 2004, Democratic presidential candidate John Kerry made a more traditional choice in Senator John Edwards of North Carolina. Edwards provided regional balance and also a degree of socioeconomic balance because, unlike Kerry, he had been born into relatively humble circumstances.

In 2006, Vice President Dick Cheney addresses an audience assembled at the Pentagon to commemorate the 186 persons killed during the September 11, 2001, attack on that building. To what extent does a vice president actually represent the president? (R. D. Ward/Department of Defense)

Supporting the President. The job of vice president is not extremely demanding, even when the president gives some specific task to the vice president. Typically, vice presidents spend their time supporting the president's activities. During the Clinton administration (1993–2001), however, Vice President Al Gore did much to strengthen the position of vice president by his aggressive support for environmental protection policies on a global basis. He also took a special interest in areas of emerging technology and was instrumental in providing subsidies to public schools for Internet use. Vice President Dick Cheney, as one of President George W. Bush's key advisers, clearly has been an influential figure in the Bush administration. Of course, the vice presidency takes on more significance if the president becomes disabled or dies in office—and the vice president becomes president.

Vice presidents sometimes have become elected presidents in their own right. John Adams and Thomas Jefferson were the first to do so. Richard Nixon was elected president in 1968 after he had served as Dwight D. Eisenhower's vice president during 1953–1961. In 1988, George H. W. Bush was elected to the presidency after eight years as Ronald Reagan's vice president.

Presidential Succession

Eight vice presidents have become president because of the death of the president. John Tyler, the first to do so, took over William Henry Harrison's position after only one month. No one knew whether Tyler should simply be a caretaker until a new president could be elected three and a half years later or whether he actually should be president. Tyler assumed that he was supposed to be the chief executive and he acted as such—although he was commonly referred to as "His Accidency." Since then, vice presidents taking over the position of the presidency because of the incumbent's death have assumed the presidential powers.

But what should a vice president do if a president becomes incapable of carrying out necessary duties while in office? When James Garfield was shot in 1881, he remained alive for two and a half months. What was Vice President Chester Arthur's role?

This question was not addressed in the original Constitution. Article II, Section 1, says only that "[i]n Case of the Removal of the President from Office, or of his Death, Resignation, or Inability to discharge the Powers and Duties of the said Office, the same shall devolve on [the same powers shall be exercised by] the Vice President." There have been many instances of presidential disability. When Dwight Eisenhower became ill a second time in 1958, he entered into a pact with Richard Nixon specifying that the vice president could determine whether the president was incapable of carrying out his duties if the president could not communicate. John Kennedy and Lyndon Johnson entered into similar agreements with their vice presidents. Finally, in 1967, the **Twenty-fifth Amendment** was passed, establishing procedures in case of presidential incapacity.

The Twenty-fifth Amendment

According to the Twenty-fifth Amendment, when a president believes that he or she is incapable of performing the duties of office, the president must inform Congress in writing. Then the vice president serves as acting president until the president can resume normal duties. When the president is unable to communicate, a majority of the cabinet, including the vice president, can declare that fact to Congress. Then the vice president serves as acting president until the president resumes normal duties. If a dispute arises over the return of the president's ability, a two-thirds vote of Congress is required to decide whether the vice president shall remain acting president or whether the president shall resume normal duties.

| **Twenty-fifth Amendment**
A 1967 amendment to the Constitution that establishes procedures for filling presidential and vice-presidential vacancies and makes provisions for presidential disability.

An attempted assassination of President Ronald Reagan occurred on March 31, 1981. In the foreground, two men bend over Press Secretary James Brady, who lies seriously wounded. In the background, President Reagan is watched over by a U.S. Secret Service agent with an automatic weapon. A Washington, D.C., police officer lies to the left after also being shot. (AP Photo/ Ron Edmonds)

In 2002, President George W. Bush formally invoked the Twenty-fifth Amendment for the first time by officially transferring presidential power to Vice President Dick Cheney while the president underwent a colonoscopy, a twenty-minute procedure. He commented that he undertook this transfer of power "because we're at war," referring to the war on terrorism. The only other time the provisions of the Twenty-fifth Amendment have been used was during President Reagan's colon surgery in 1985, although Reagan did not formally invoke the amendment.

When the Vice Presidency Becomes Vacant

The Twenty-fifth Amendment also addresses the issue of how the president should fill a vacant vice presidency. Section 2 of the amendment simply states, "Whenever there is a vacancy in the office of the Vice President, the President shall nominate a Vice President who shall take office upon confirmation by a majority vote of both Houses of Congress." This is exactly what occurred when Richard Nixon's vice president, Spiro Agnew, resigned in 1973 because of his alleged receipt of construction contract kickbacks during his tenure as governor of Maryland. Nixon turned to Gerald Ford as his choice for vice president. After extensive hearings, both chambers of Congress confirmed the appointment. Then, when Nixon resigned on August 9, 1974, Ford automatically became president and nominated as his vice president Nelson Rockefeller. Congress confirmed Ford's choice. For the first time in the history of the country, neither the president nor the vice president had been elected to their positions.

The question of who shall be president if both the president and vice president die is answered by the Succession Act of 1947. If the president and vice president die, resign, or are disabled, the Speaker of the House will become president, after resigning from Congress. Next in line is the president pro tem of the Senate, followed by the cabinet officers in the order of the creation of their departments (see Table 12–3).

TABLE 12-3 | LINE OF SUCCESSION TO THE PRESIDENCY OF THE UNITED STATES

1. Vice president
2. Speaker of the House of Representatives
3. Senate president pro tempore
4. Secretary of state
5. Secretary of the treasury
6. Secretary of defense
7. Attorney general (head of the Justice Department)
8. Secretary of the interior
9. Secretary of agriculture
10. Secretary of commerce
11. Secretary of labor
12. Secretary of health and human services
13. Secretary of housing and urban development
14. Secretary of transportation
15. Secretary of energy
16. Secretary of education
17. Secretary of veterans affairs
18. Secretary of homeland security

MAKING A DIFFERENCE | Communicating with the White House

Writing the president is a traditional way for citizens to express their opinions. Every day, the White House receives several thousand letters and other communications.

Why Should You Care?

Should you consider sending a message to the president? There are reasons why you might want to engage in this form of political participation. Presidents typically claim that they do not set their policies by looking at the public opinion polls. Yet any president must pay attention to public opinion, and few presidents have been able to avoid changing policy when the public is pressing them to do so. President Bush has been no exception.

In 2003 and 2004, in response to the situation in Iraq, a number of Democratic and Republican legislators began raising the idea of reinstating a military draft of young people. Such a measure would probably need the support of the president to succeed. A military draft might affect you or your friends directly. If you have opinions on a topic such as this, you may well want to "cast your vote" by adding your letter to the many others that the president receives on this issue.

What Can You Do?

The most traditional form of communication with the White House is, of course, by letter. Letters to the president should be addressed to

The President of the United States
The White House
1600 Pennsylvania Avenue N.W.
Washington, DC 20500

Letters may be sent to the first lady at the same address. Will you get an answer? Almost certainly. The White House mail room is staffed by volunteers and paid employees who sort the mail for the president and tally the public's concerns. You may receive a standard response to your comments or a more personal, detailed response.

You can also call the White House on the telephone and leave a message for the president or first lady. To call the switchboard, call 202-456-1414, a number publicized by former Secretary of State James Baker when he told the Israelis through the media, "When you're serious about peace, call us at . . . ." The switchboard received more than eight thousand calls in the next twenty-four hours.

The White House also has a round-the-clock comment line, which you can reach at 202-456-1111. When you call that number, an operator will take down your comments and forward them to the president's office.

The home page for the White House is

www.whitehouse.gov

It is designed to be entertaining and to convey information about the president. You can also send your comments and ideas to the White House using e-mail. Send comments to the president at

President@whitehouse.gov

Address e-mail to the first lady at

First.Lady@whitehouse.gov

In 2003, the White House deployed a new and somewhat complicated system for sending messages to President Bush. It involves navigating successive Web pages and filling out a form. You must choose one of a limited number of topics selected by the White House. Once the message is sent, the writer must wait for an automated e-mail response that asks for a confirmation.

Key Terms

Chapter Summary

1 The office of the presidency in the United States, combining as it does the functions of chief of state and chief executive, was, when created, unique. The framers of the Constitution were divided over whether the president should be a weak or a strong executive.

2 The requirements for the office of the presidency are outlined in Article II, Section 1, of the Constitution. The president's roles include both formal and informal duties. The roles of the president include head of state, chief executive, commander in chief, chief diplomat, chief legislator, and party chief.

3 As head of state, the president is ceremonial leader of the government. As chief executive, the president is bound to enforce the acts of Congress, the judgments of the federal courts, and treaties. The chief executive has the power of appointment and the power to grant reprieves and pardons.

4 As commander in chief, the president is the ultimate decision maker in military matters. As chief diplomat, the president recognizes foreign governments, negotiates treaties, signs agreements, and nominates and receives ambassadors.

5 The role of chief legislator includes recommending legislation to Congress, lobbying for the legislation, approving laws, and exercising the veto power. In addition to constitu-

tional and inherent powers, the president has statutory powers written into law by Congress. Presidents are also leaders of their political parties. Presidents use their power to persuade and their access to the media to fulfill this function.

6 Presidents have a variety of special powers not available to other branches of the government. These include emergency power and the power to issue executive orders and invoke executive privilege.

7 Abuses of executive power are dealt with by Articles I and II of the Constitution, which authorize the House and Senate to impeach and remove the president, vice president, or other officers of the federal government for committing "Treason, Bribery, or other high Crimes and Misdemeanors."

8 The president receives assistance from the cabinet and from the Executive Office of the President (including the White House Office).

9 The vice president is the constitutional officer assigned to preside over the Senate and to assume the presidency in the event of the death, resignation, removal, or disability of the president. The Twenty-fifth Amendment, passed in 1967, established procedures to be followed in case of presidential incapacity and when filling a vacant vice presidency.

Selected Print and Media Resources

SUGGESTED READINGS

Bartlett, Bruce R. *Imposter: How George W. Bush Bankrupted America and Betrayed the Reagan Legacy*. New York: Doubleday Publishing, 2006. A former staff member under both Ronald Reagan and George W. Bush, Bartlett offers a scathing critique of Bush's fiscal policy.

Clinton, Bill. *My Life*. New York: Knopf, 2004. President Clinton's autobiography devotes ample space to illuminating stories from his childhood. In contrast, some may find the account of his presidential years excessively detailed. Still, the book is essential source material on one of the most important and controversial political figures of our time.

Frum, David. *The Right Man: The Surprise Presidency of George Bush*. New York: Random House, 2003. The author, who was a speechwriter for George W. Bush during his first year as president, provides an inside look at this period of the Bush presidency.

Genovese, Michael A., and Lori Cox Han, eds. *The Presidency and the Challenge of Democracy*. Boston: Palgrave Macmillan, 2006. This collection of essays by leading scholars probes the current trend of expanding presidential powers.

Mann, James. *Rise of the Vulcans: The History of Bush's War Cabinet*. New York: Viking Books, 2004. This is a collective biography of the foreign policy team (not all of whom were actually in the cabinet) during George W. Bush's first term. The self-described Vulcans included Donald Rumsfeld, secretary of defense; Vice President Dick Cheney; Colin Powell, secretary of state; Paul

Wolfowitz, deputy secretary of defense; Richard Armitage, deputy secretary of state; and Condoleezza Rice, national security adviser. While these individuals were never in perfect agreement, they shared basic values.

MEDIA RESOURCES

CNN—Election 2000—A politically balanced look at the extraordinarily close presidential election of 2000, which pitted Republican George W. Bush against Democrat Al Gore. The race was eventually settled by the United States Supreme Court. CNN's Bill Hemmer narrates this 2001 production.

Fahrenheit 9/11—Michael Moore's scathing 2004 critique of the Bush administration has been called "one long political attack ad." It is also the highest-grossing documentary ever made. While the film may be biased, it is—like all of Moore's productions—entertaining.

LBJ: A Biography—An acclaimed biography of Lyndon Johnson that covers his rise to power, his presidency, and the events of the Vietnam War, which ended his presidency; produced in 1991 as part of PBS's *The American Experience* series.

Nixon—An excellent 1995 film exposing the events of Richard Nixon's troubled presidency. Anthony Hopkins plays the embattled but brilliant chief executive.

Sunrise at Campobello—An excellent portrait of one of the greatest presidents, Franklin Delano Roosevelt; produced in 1960 and starring Ralph Bellamy.

E·MOCRACY | The Presidency and the Internet

Today, the Internet has become such a normal part of most Americans' lives that it is almost hard to imagine what life was like without it. Certainly, accessing the latest press releases from the White House was much more difficult ten years ago than it is today. It was not until the Clinton administration (1993–2001) that access to the White House via the Internet became possible. President Bill Clinton supported making many White House documents available on the White House Web site.

Correspondence with the president and the first lady quickly moved from ordinary handwritten letters to e-mail. During the Clinton presidency, most agencies of the government, as well as congressional offices, also began to provide access and information on the Internet. Today, you can access the White House Web site (see the following *Logging On* section) to find White House press

releases, presidential State of the Union messages and other speeches, historical data on the presidency, and much more.

| Logging On

This site offers extensive information on the White House and the presidency:

www.whitehouse.gov

Inaugural addresses of American presidents from George Washington to George W. Bush can be found at

www.bartleby.com/124

You can find an excellent collection of data and maps describing all U.S. presidential elections at Dave Leip's Atlas of U.S. Presidential Elections. Go to

uselectionatlas.org

| Online Review

At **www.politicalscience.wadsworth.com/ schmidt12**, you will find a free Study Guide to this book. For each chapter, there are two online quizzes to help you master the material.

• The PoliPrep Self-Study Assessment provides a pretest for each major section of the chapter. PoliPrep then generates a customized study plan. After you complete the study plan, a posttest evaluates your progress.

• The Tutorial Quiz for each chapter provides questions on the chapter contents, including the features. The questions are organized to match the major sections of the chapter.

13 | The Bureaucracy

What If . . .
The Public Graded Federal Bureaucracies?

BACKGROUND

Congress has repeatedly reformed the civil service since 1883. In addition, each modern administration has claimed that it would make bureaucrats more accountable. In spite of all efforts, however, bureaucrats are far from accountable to their bosses in the executive branch, to Congress, and, least of all, to the public—the taxpayers who fund their salaries. Would bureaucrats be more accountable if report cards graded their efforts?

WHAT IF THE PUBLIC GRADED FEDERAL BUREAUCRACIES?

On taking office, President George W. Bush created a plan known as performance-based budgeting to increase bureaucratic accountability. As part of this plan, the Office of Management and Budget (OMB) was to examine how well each agency met specific performance criteria and create a report card for each agency.

The government could also prepare report cards that summarize public input. Many commercial businesses actively solicit feedback from their customers on whether staff members were polite, whether problems were resolved quickly, and whether the customer was satisfied with the transaction overall. Similarly, the government could print evaluation forms to be distributed to citizens every time they interacted with the government. Taxpayers could even insert their evaluations of the Internal Revenue Service into the same envelope as their tax returns.

MAKING SENSE OF THE EVALUATIONS

The number of federal agencies is very large, and the average citizen usually deals with only a few of them. Therefore, if report cards were based on responses from a federal agency's "customers," they might not represent the opinions of the general public. For some agencies, this probably would not matter. If customers rated the performance of the Department of Veterans Affairs, their responses would probably not be much different from what the public would have thought.

THE PUBLIC'S IMPLICIT GRADING AFTER HURRICANE KATRINA

In one recent example, public opinion polls provided an actual evaluation of a federal agency's performance. In the immediate aftermath of Hurricane Katrina, residents of New Orleans were extremely critical of the assistance provided by the Federal Emergency Management Agency (FEMA). Criticism of FEMA's management led to a change in leadership at the agency. Interestingly, though, a Gallup poll taken in October 2005, a month after the hurricane, found that half of the city's residents believed that FEMA had been very helpful to them.

Residents were also very critical of President George W. Bush and Louisiana governor Kathleen Blanco for failing to provide more assistance. They were not unhappy with all levels of government, however. In a 2006 Gallup poll, a majority of the residents of New Orleans said that they approved of the performance of Mayor Ray Nagin during the hurricane. In other words, to residents of New Orleans local government seemed to have responded better to their problems than the federal and state governments.

MAKING USE OF THE EVALUATIONS

Under the Bush administration's plan for performance-based budgeting, budgetary payouts were to be linked to specific performance criteria for each program. Unfortunately, it is not always possible to cut the funding of a program that is performing poorly. The program may be so essential that it cannot be cut. It may be performing badly because it is underfunded—and cutting back will only make matters worse.

Bad publicity might be a better tool for making bureaucrats more responsive. Already, numerous private groups are ridiculing the federal government by publicizing laughable programs and actions by federal bureaucrats that virtually no one could justify. If agencies were compared with other agencies and had to fear criticism if their performance fell below average, they might have an incentive to improve the quality of their work.

A BASIS FOR DISCIPLINE

Many observers believe that the greatest obstacle to making the federal bureaucracy responsive is that it is very hard to fire federal bureaucrats. If bureaucrats in private businesses do not perform, their bosses simply fire them. The federal bureaucracy, in contrast, is so extensively governed by rules and regulations about firing that virtually no one is ever dismissed.

Congress could make it easier for bureaucrats to be fired. If it did so, perhaps poor performance on a public report card could lead to discipline and, in due course, discharge. Threats against individual bureaucrats might be more effective than a threat to cut a program's budget—a threat that the government might not be able to carry out.

FOR CRITICAL ANALYSIS

1. What specific items ought to be listed on a report card that is used to evaluate a federal bureaucracy?
2. If Congress tried to make civil servants easier to fire, what political forces might stand in the way?

Faceless bureaucrats—this image provokes a negative reaction from many, if not most, Americans. Polls consistently report that the majority of Americans support "less government." The same polls, however, report that the majority of Americans support almost every specific program that the government undertakes. The conflict between the desire for small government and the benefits that only a large government can provide has been a constant feature of American politics. For example, the goal of preserving endangered species has widespread support. At the same time, many people believe that restrictions imposed under the Endangered Species Act violate the rights of landowners. Helping the elderly pay their medical bills is a popular objective, but hardly anyone enjoys paying the Medicare tax that supports this effort.

In this chapter, we describe the size, organization, and staffing of the federal bureaucracy. We review modern attempts at bureaucratic reform and the process by which Congress exerts ultimate control over the bureaucracy. We also discuss the bureaucracy's role in making rules and setting policy.

The Nature of Bureaucracy

Every modern president, at one time or another, has proclaimed that his administration was going to "fix government." All modern presidents also have put forth plans to end government waste and inefficiency (see Table 13–1). Their success has been, in a word, underwhelming. Presidents generally have been powerless to affect the structure and operation of the federal bureaucracy significantly.

A **bureaucracy** is the name given to a large organization that is structured hierarchically to carry out specific functions. Generally, most bureaucracies are characterized by an organization chart. The units of the organization are divided according to the specialization and expertise of the employees.

| Bureaucracy
A large organization that is structured hierarchically to carry out specific functions.

Public and Private Bureaucracies

We should not think of bureaucracy as unique to government. Any large corporation or university can be considered a bureaucratic organization. The fact is that the handling of complex problems requires a division of labor. Individuals must concentrate their skills on specific, well-defined aspects of a problem and depend on others to solve the rest of it.

Public or government bureaucracies differ from private organizations in some important ways, however. A private corporation, such as Microsoft, has a single set of leaders—its board of directors. Public bureaucracies, in contrast, do not have a single set of leaders. Although the president is the chief administrator of the federal system, all bureaucratic agencies are subject to Congress for their funding, staffing,

TABLE 13–1 | SELECTED PRESIDENTIAL PLANS TO END GOVERNMENT INEFFICIENCY

PRESIDENT	NAME OF PLAN
Lyndon Johnson (1963–1969)	Programming, Planning, and Budgeting Systems
Richard Nixon (1969–1974)	Management by Objectives
Jimmy Carter (1977–1981)	Zero-Based Budgeting
Ronald Reagan (1981–1989)	President's Private Sector Survey on Cost Control (the Grace Commission)
George H. W. Bush (1989–1993)	Right-Sizing Government
Bill Clinton (1993–2001)	Reinventing Government
George W. Bush (2001–2009)	Performance-Based Budgeting

German sociologist Max Weber (1864–1920). (Photo Courtesy of Bavarian Academy of Sciences and Humanities)

| Weberian Model
A model of bureaucracy developed by the German sociologist Max Weber, who viewed bureaucracies as rational, hierarchical organizations in which decisions are based on logical reasoning.

| Acquisitive Model
A model of bureaucracy that views top level bureaucrats as seeking to expand the size of their budgets and staffs to gain greater power.

| Monopolistic Model
A model of bureaucracy that compares bureaucracies to monopolistic business firms. Lack of competition in either circumstance leads to inefficient and costly operations.

and, indeed, their continued existence. Furthermore, public bureaucracies supposedly serve the citizenry.

One other important difference between private corporations and government bureaucracies is that government bureaucracies are not organized to make a profit. Rather, they are supposed to perform their functions as efficiently as possible to conserve the taxpayers' dollars. Perhaps it is this ideal that makes citizens hostile toward government bureaucracy when they experience inefficiency and red tape.

Models of Bureaucracy

Several theories have been offered to help us better understand the ways in which bureaucracies function. Each of these theories focuses on specific features of bureaucracies.

Weberian Model.   The classic model, or **Weberian model,** of the modern bureaucracy was proposed by the German sociologist Max Weber.[1] He argued that the increasingly complex nature of modern life, coupled with the steadily growing demands placed on governments by their citizens, made the formation of bureaucracies inevitable. According to Weber, most bureaucracies—whether in the public or private sector—are organized hierarchically and governed by formal procedures. The power in a bureaucracy flows from the top downward. Decision-making processes in bureaucracies are shaped by detailed technical rules that promote similar decisions in similar situations. Bureaucrats are specialists who attempt to resolve problems through logical reasoning and data analysis instead of "gut feelings" and guesswork. Individual advancement in bureaucracies is supposed to be based on merit rather than political connections. Indeed, the modern bureaucracy, according to Weber, should be an apolitical organization.

Acquisitive Model.   Other theorists do not view bureaucracies in terms as benign as Weber's. Some believe that bureaucracies are acquisitive in nature. Proponents of the **acquisitive model** argue that top level bureaucrats will always try to expand, or at least to avoid any reductions in, the size of their budgets. Although government bureaucracies are not-for-profit enterprises, bureaucrats want to maximize the size of their budgets and staffs because these things are the most visible trappings of power in the public sector. These efforts are also prompted by the desire of bureaucrats to "sell" their products—national defense, public housing, agricultural subsidies, and so on—to both Congress and the public.

Monopolistic Model.   Because government bureaucracies seldom have competitors, some theorists have suggested that these bureaucratic organizations may be explained best by a **monopolistic model.** The analysis is similar to that used by economists to examine the behavior of monopolistic firms. Monopolistic bureaucracies—like monopolistic firms—essentially have no competitors and act accordingly. Because monopolistic bureaucracies usually are not penalized for chronic inefficiency, they have little reason to adopt cost-saving measures or to make more productive use of their resources. Some economists have argued that such problems can be cured only by privatizing certain bureaucratic functions.

Bureaucracies Compared

The federal bureaucracy in the United States enjoys a greater degree of autonomy than do federal or national bureaucracies in many other nations. Much of the insu-

---

[1]Max Weber, *Theory of Social and Economic Organization*, edited by Talcott Parsons (New York: Oxford University Press, 1974).

Ear tags were used to trace the path of a cow that died of mad cow disease in Washington State in 2003. Canadian officials conducted DNA tests on the dead cow to see if it came from Canada. Protection against communicable diseases in animals (and in humans) often requires cooperation among agencies from many countries. (EPA/Barry Sweet/Landov)

larity that is commonly supposed to characterize the bureaucracy in this country may stem from the sheer size of the government organizations needed to implement a budget that is about $3 trillion. Because the lines of authority often are not well defined, some bureaucracies may be able to operate with a significant degree of autonomy.

The federal nature of the American government also means that national bureaucracies regularly provide financial assistance to their state counterparts. Both the Department of Education and the Department of Housing and Urban Development, for example, distribute funds to their counterparts at the state level. In contrast, most bureaucracies in European countries have a top-down command structure so that national programs may be implemented directly at the lower level. This is due not only to the smaller size of most European countries but also to the fact that public ownership of such businesses as telephone companies, airlines, railroads, and utilities is far more common in Europe than in the United States.

The fact that the U.S. government owns relatively few enterprises does not mean, however, that its bureaucracies are comparatively powerless. Indeed, there are many **administrative agencies** in the federal bureaucracy—such as the Environmental Protection Agency, the Nuclear Regulatory Commission, and the Securities and Exchange Commission—that regulate private companies.

| Administrative Agency
A federal, state, or local government unit established to perform a specific function. Administrative agencies are created and authorized by legislative bodies to administer and enforce specific laws.

| The Size of the Bureaucracy

In 1789, the new government's bureaucracy was minuscule. There were three departments—State (with nine employees), War (with two employees), and Treasury (with thirty-nine employees)—and the Office of the Attorney General (which later became the Department of Justice). The bureaucracy was still small in 1798. At that time, the secretary of state had seven clerks and spent a total of $500 (about $8,194 in 2007 dollars) on stationery and printing. In that same year, the Appropriations Act allocated $1.4 million to the War Department (or $22.9 million in 2007 dollars).[2]

---

[2]Leonard D. White, *The Federalists: A Study in Administrative History, 1789–1801* (New York: Free Press, 1948).

FIGURE 13–1 | FEDERAL AGENCIES AND THEIR RESPECTIVE NUMBERS OF CIVILIAN EMPLOYEES

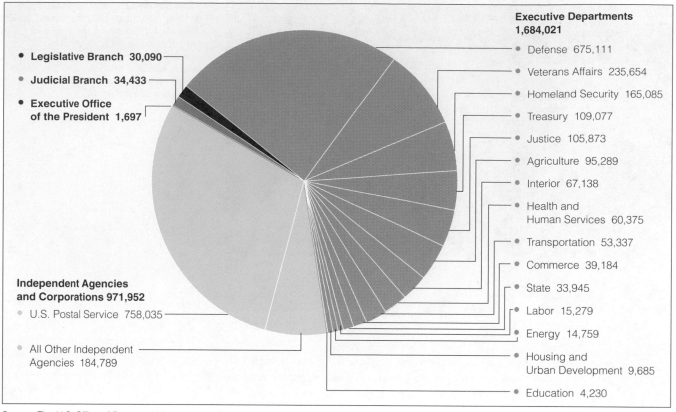

- **Legislative Branch 30,090**
- **Judicial Branch 34,433**
- **Executive Office of the President 1,697**

Independent Agencies and Corporations 971,952

- U.S. Postal Service 758,035
- All Other Independent Agencies 184,789

Executive Departments 1,684,021

- Defense 675,111
- Veterans Affairs 235,654
- Homeland Security 165,085
- Treasury 109,077
- Justice 105,873
- Agriculture 95,289
- Interior 67,138
- Health and Human Services 60,375
- Transportation 53,337
- Commerce 39,184
- State 33,945
- Labor 15,279
- Energy 14,759
- Housing and Urban Development 9,685
- Education 4,230

Source: The U.S. Office of Personnel Management, September 2006.

FIGURE 13–2 | GOVERNMENT EMPLOYMENT AT THE FEDERAL, STATE, AND LOCAL LEVELS

There are more local government employees than federal or state employees combined.

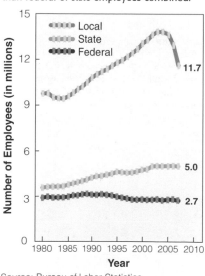

Source: Bureau of Labor Statistics.

Times have changed, as we can see in Figure 13–1, which lists the various federal agencies and the number of civilian employees in each. Excluding the military, the federal bureaucracy includes approximately 2.7 million government employees. That number has remained relatively stable for the last several decades. It is somewhat deceiving, however, because many other individuals work directly or indirectly for the federal government as subcontractors or consultants and in other capacities. In fact, according to some studies, the federal workforce vastly exceeds the number of official federal workers.[3]

The figures for federal government employment are only part of the story. Figure 13–2 shows the growth in government employment at the federal, state, and local levels. Since 1970, this growth has been mainly at the state and local levels. If all government employees are included, more than 16 percent of all civilian employment is accounted for by government.

The costs of the bureaucracy are commensurately high. The share of the gross domestic product accounted for by all government spending was only 8.5 percent in 1929. Today, it exceeds 30 percent. Could we reduce the cost of government by eliminating unnecessary spending? We look at one example of questionable spending in this chapter's *Politics and Subsidies* feature.

---

[3]See, for example, Paul C. Light, *The True Size of Government* (Washington, D.C.: Brookings Institution Press, 1999).

POLITICS AND SUBSIDIES | Trains for the Rich or Poor?

Thirty-five years ago, after several private rail companies went bankrupt, Congress created a public railway system called AMTRAK. Today, AMTRAK links 500 American towns and cities in 46 states with over 22,000 miles of rail. AMTRAK runs 41 long-distance routes such as the "Sunset Limited" between Orlando and Los Angeles, but its most popular routes are along the Northeast corridor. While AMTRAK appears impressive, it has many critics both in and outside Congress.

THE RED INK KEEPS FLOWING

During AMTRAK's existence, American taxpayers have subsidized it to the tune of over $25 billion. Current subsidies typically exceed $1 billion a year—$1.8 billion was requested in 2006 and $2 billion will have been requested for 2007. As Republican representative Harold Rogers of Kentucky has pointed out, "Every time a passenger boards a train, Uncle Sam writes a check for $138.71, on average." For example, the aforementioned Sunset Limited route costs the taxpayers $347 for each passenger served. The subsidy on a round-trip AMTRAK ride between Los Angeles and New York is $1,270. You can buy a cross-country airline ticket from a discounter for around $400 to $500.

In 2005, the Bush administration sent up a trial balloon hinting that the administration would end federal subsidies for AMTRAK's operating expenses. Nothing ever came of this proposal, however.

THE RATIONALE FOR KEEPING SUBSIDIES

Those in favor of the AMTRAK subsidies argue that AMTRAK provides essential transportation for the poor. Actually, the percentage of users with incomes above $40,000 is higher for AMTRAK than for any other intercity transportation option. Upper-middle-income suburbanites in the Northeast are its main users.

AMTRAK supporters believe that it relieves congestion on the highways and at airports. Because so few people use AMTRAK, though, if the system disappeared, the airlines could easily accommodate its customers in seats that are now

An AMTRAK train rolls through a station near Wilmington, Delaware. Publicly owned passenger railroad systems run at a loss in most countries, but few are as unprofitable per mile traveled as AMTRAK. Why might a passenger rail system in the United States be especially unprofitable? (Photo Courtesy of Maine Department of Transportation)

unsold on existing flights. On the majority of AMTRAK routes, if customers used their automobiles instead, only one or two vehicles per lane per hour would be added.

PRIVATIZATION EFFORTS

Some members of Congress have suggested that AMTRAK be sold off to the highest bidder. The U.S. Department of Transportation has also considered allowing states or groups of states to bid on portions of AMTRAK. Under either proposal, AMTRAK's responsibilities as a federal corporation would be phased out. Not surprisingly, AMTRAK's managers have voiced skepticism over privatization efforts.

FOR CRITICAL ANALYSIS

Who might gain and who might lose if AMTRAK were privatized?

The Organization of the Federal Bureaucracy

Within the federal bureaucracy are a number of different types of government agencies and organizations. Figure 13–3 on the next page outlines the several bodies within the executive branch, as well as the separate organizations that provide services to Congress, to the courts, and directly to the president. In Chapter 12, we discussed those agencies that are considered to be part of the Executive Office of the President.

The executive branch, which employs most of the government's staff, has four major types of structures. They are (1) cabinet departments, (2) independent executive agencies, (3) independent regulatory agencies, and (4) government corporations. Each has a distinctive relationship to the president, and some have unusual internal structures, overall goals, and grants of power.

FIGURE 13-3 | ORGANIZATION CHART OF THE FEDERAL GOVERNMENT

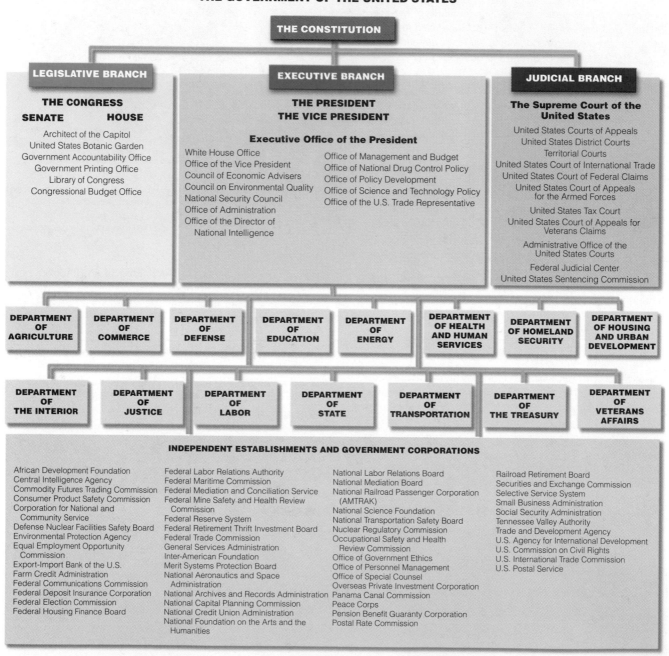

THE GOVERNMENT OF THE UNITED STATES

THE CONSTITUTION

LEGISLATIVE BRANCH

THE CONGRESS
SENATE   HOUSE

Architect of the Capitol
United States Botanic Garden
Government Accountability Office
Government Printing Office
Library of Congress
Congressional Budget Office

EXECUTIVE BRANCH

THE PRESIDENT
THE VICE PRESIDENT

Executive Office of the President

White House Office
Office of the Vice President
Council of Economic Advisers
Council on Environmental Quality
National Security Council
Office of Administration
Office of the Director of
  National Intelligence

Office of Management and Budget
Office of National Drug Control Policy
Office of Policy Development
Office of Science and Technology Policy
Office of the U.S. Trade Representative

JUDICIAL BRANCH

The Supreme Court of the United States

United States Courts of Appeals
United States District Courts
Territorial Courts
United States Court of International Trade
United States Court of Federal Claims
United States Court of Appeals
  for the Armed Forces
United States Tax Court
United States Court of Appeals for
  Veterans Claims
Administrative Office of the
  United States Courts
Federal Judicial Center
United States Sentencing Commission

DEPARTMENT OF AGRICULTURE
DEPARTMENT OF COMMERCE
DEPARTMENT OF DEFENSE
DEPARTMENT OF EDUCATION
DEPARTMENT OF ENERGY
DEPARTMENT OF HEALTH AND HUMAN SERVICES
DEPARTMENT OF HOMELAND SECURITY
DEPARTMENT OF HOUSING AND URBAN DEVELOPMENT

DEPARTMENT OF THE INTERIOR
DEPARTMENT OF JUSTICE
DEPARTMENT OF LABOR
DEPARTMENT OF STATE
DEPARTMENT OF TRANSPORTATION
DEPARTMENT OF THE TREASURY
DEPARTMENT OF VETERANS AFFAIRS

INDEPENDENT ESTABLISHMENTS AND GOVERNMENT CORPORATIONS

African Development Foundation
Central Intelligence Agency
Commodity Futures Trading Commission
Consumer Product Safety Commission
Corporation for National and
  Community Service
Defense Nuclear Facilities Safety Board
Environmental Protection Agency
Equal Employment Opportunity
  Commission
Export-Import Bank of the U.S.
Farm Credit Administration
Federal Communications Commission
Federal Deposit Insurance Corporation
Federal Election Commission
Federal Housing Finance Board

Federal Labor Relations Authority
Federal Maritime Commission
Federal Mediation and Conciliation Service
Federal Mine Safety and Health Review
  Commission
Federal Reserve System
Federal Retirement Thrift Investment Board
Federal Trade Commission
General Services Administration
Inter-American Foundation
Merit Systems Protection Board
National Aeronautics and Space
  Administration
National Archives and Records Administration
National Capital Planning Commission
National Credit Union Administration
National Foundation on the Arts and the
  Humanities

National Labor Relations Board
National Mediation Board
National Railroad Passenger Corporation
  (AMTRAK)
National Science Foundation
National Transportation Safety Board
Nuclear Regulatory Commission
Occupational Safety and Health
  Review Commission
Office of Government Ethics
Office of Personnel Management
Office of Special Counsel
Overseas Private Investment Corporation
Panama Canal Commission
Peace Corps
Pension Benefit Guaranty Corporation
Postal Rate Commission

Railroad Retirement Board
Securities and Exchange Commission
Selective Service System
Small Business Administration
Social Security Administration
Tennessee Valley Authority
Trade and Development Agency
U.S. Agency for International Development
U.S. Commission on Civil Rights
U.S. International Trade Commission
U.S. Postal Service

Source: *United States Government Manual*, 2006–2007 (Washington, D.C.: U.S. Government Printing Office, 2006).

Cabinet Departments

The fifteen **cabinet departments** are the major service organizations of the federal government. They can also be described in management terms as **line organizations.** This means that they are directly accountable to the president and are responsible for performing government functions, such as printing money and training troops. These departments were created by Congress when the need for each department arose. The first department to be created was State, and the most recent one was Homeland Security, established in 2003. (Not everyone agrees that creating the Department of Homeland Security was the right thing to do. We examine this controversy in this chapter's *Which Side Are You On?* feature on the following page.) A president might ask that a new department be created or an old one abolished, but the president has no power to do so without legislative approval from Congress.

Each department is headed by a secretary (except for the Justice Department, which is headed by the attorney general). Each also has several levels of undersecretaries, assistant secretaries, and so on.

Presidents theoretically have considerable control over the cabinet departments, because presidents are able to appoint or fire all of the top officials. Even cabinet departments do not always respond to the president's wishes, though. One reason that presidents are frequently unhappy with their departments is that the entire bureaucratic structure below the top political levels is staffed by permanent employees, many of whom are committed to established programs or procedures and who resist change. Table 13–2 on page 433 shows that each cabinet department employs thousands of individuals, only a handful of whom are under the control of the president. The table also describes some of the functions of each of the departments.

Independent Executive Agencies

Independent executive agencies are bureaucratic organizations that are not located within a department but report directly to the president, who appoints their chief officials. When a new federal agency is created—the Environmental Protection

| **Cabinet Department**
One of the fifteen departments of the executive branch (State, Treasury, Defense, Justice, Interior, Agriculture, Commerce, Labor, Health and Human Services, Homeland Security, Housing and Urban Development, Education, Energy, Transportation, and Veterans Affairs).

| **Line Organization**
In the federal government, an administrative unit that is directly accountable to the president.

| **Independent Executive Agency**
A federal agency that is not part of a cabinet department but reports directly to the president.

In 2006, Homeland Security secretary Michael Chertoff consults with federal authorities responsible for New Orleans's readiness in case of new emergencies. Together, many federal agencies have staffed the New Orleans Emergency Operations Center. To what extent should the federal government be responsible for local natural disasters? Why? (Marvin Nauman/FEMA photo)

WHICH SIDE ARE YOU ON? | Unifying Our Antiterrorism Efforts Was the Right Thing to Do

The creation of the Department of Homeland Security (DHS) in 2003 was the largest reorganization of the U.S. government since 1947. Twenty-two agencies with responsibilities for preventing terrorism were merged into a single department. President George W. Bush argued that combining the Federal Emergency Management Agency (FEMA), Customs and Border Protection, the Coast Guard, the Secret Service, and many other organizations into a single agency would promote efficiency and improve coordination. This sprawling agency now has more than 165,000 employees and an estimated budget of $43 billion in 2007.

THE TIME WAS RIPE TO UNIFY OUR ANTITERRORISM EFFORTS

After September 11, 2001, the nation saw that there was no single agency that was responsible for coordinating antiterrorism efforts. Nor was there one person who could muster a nationwide response to a terrorist attack. Fighting terrorism involves so many different aspects—screening baggage at airports, inspecting freight shipments, and protecting the border, to name just a few—that coordinating them would be impossible unless all these functions were combined in one agency.

Of course, some growing pains were inevitable. You cannot meld twenty-two agencies into one and expect things to go perfectly from the beginning. But in the long run, we will slowly but surely develop the ability to maintain a coordinated fight against terrorism and, if need be, a response to terrorist acts.

It's important to have one person in charge of our antiterrorism efforts. Perhaps the present secretary of DHS is not up to the job, but that problem will be solved over time. Managing more than 165,000 employees is no small task. Management systems will eventually be put in place that will make the DHS more efficient than the uncoordinated actions of the twenty-two agencies that were formerly scattered among various departments.

THE RECORD SO FAR FOR THE DHS IS DISMAL

Those who were against the consolidation of antiterrorism and terrorist response agencies into one department point out

that so far the DHS has not had a shining record. When FEMA became part of the DHS, not only was its funding reduced, but more important, it received less attention because the focus of the DHS has been on fighting terrorism, not on responding to natural disasters. Michael Brown, political supporter of President Bush, was named to head FEMA, but he had no experience in disaster relief. The end result was FEMA's poor performance in the aftermath of Hurricane Katrina.

Perhaps even more important, the DHS did not actually unify all U.S. antiterrorism efforts. The most important antiterrorist agencies are the Federal Bureau of Investigation (FBI) and the Central Intelligence Agency (CIA), but neither is part of the DHS. Many believe that the number-one problem in addressing terrorism is the failure of the FBI and CIA to exchange information with each other. Creating the DHS did nothing to solve that problem. To show that the administration understood this, President Bush created a Terrorist Threat Integration Center in *addition* to the DHS, the FBI, and the CIA.

Today, the danger is a multiplication of additional agencies. Not surprisingly, in 2004 the bipartisan 9/11 Commission recommended a new national intelligence director to centralize efforts spread over six cabinet departments, plus the CIA. Later in 2004, Congress established the new Office of the Director of National Intelligence to coordinate the nation's intelligence efforts, and in 2005 President Bush appointed John Negroponte to be the director of national intelligence.

WHAT'S YOUR POSITION?

Does the centralization of antiterrorism efforts make sense in principle? In practice? Defend your position.

GOING ONLINE

To learn more about the structure and organization of the Department of Homeland Security, visit the department's Web site at **www.dhs.gov/dhspublic/theme_home1.jsp**.

Agency, for example—Congress decides where it will be located in the bureaucracy. In recent decades, presidents often have asked that a new organization be kept separate or independent rather than added to an existing department, particularly if a department may be hostile to the agency's creation. Table 13–3 on page 434 describes the functions of several selected independent executive agencies.

TABLE 13–2 | EXECUTIVE DEPARTMENTS

DEPARTMENT AND YEAR ESTABLISHED	PRINCIPAL FUNCTIONS	SELECTED SUBAGENCIES
State (1789) (33,945 employees)	Negotiates treaties; develops foreign policy; protects citizens abroad.	Passport Agency; Bureau of Diplomatic Security; Foreign Service; Bureau of Human Rights and Humanitarian Affairs; Bureau of Consular Affairs.
Treasury (1789) (109,077 employees)	Pays all federal bills; borrows money; collects federal taxes; mints coins and prints paper currency; supervises national banks.	Internal Revenue Service; U.S. Mint.
Interior (1849) (67,138 employees)	Supervises federally owned lands and parks; supervises Native American affairs.	U.S. Fish and Wildlife Service; National Park Service; Bureau of Indian Affairs; Bureau of Land Management.
Justice (1870)* (105,873 employees)	Furnishes legal advice to the president; enforces federal criminal laws; supervises federal prisons.	Federal Bureau of Investigation; Drug Enforcement Administration; Bureau of Prisons.
Agriculture (1889) (95,289 employees)	Provides assistance to farmers and ranchers; conducts agricultural research; works to protect forests.	Soil Conservation Service; Agricultural Research Service; Food Safety and Inspection Service; Federal Crop Insurance Corporation; Commodity Credit Corporation; Forest Service.
Commerce (1913)† (39,184 employees)	Grants patents and trademarks; conducts a national census; monitors the weather; protects the interests of businesses.	Bureau of the Census; Bureau of Economic Analysis; Patent and Trademark Office; National Oceanic and Atmospheric Administration.
Labor (1913)† (15,279 employees)	Administers federal labor laws; promotes the interests of workers.	Occupational Safety and Health Administration; Bureau of Labor Statistics; Employment Standards Administration; Employment and Training Administration.
Defense (1947)‡ (675,111 employees)	Manages the armed forces (army, navy, air force, and marines); operates military bases; is responsible for civil defense.	National Security Agency; Joint Chiefs of Staff; Departments of the Air Force, Navy, Army; Defense Advanced Research Projects Agency; Defense Intelligence Agency; the service academies.
Housing and Urban Development (1965) (9,685 employees)	Deals with the nation's housing needs; develops and rehabilitates urban communities; oversees resale of mortgages.	Government National Mortgage Association; Office of Community Planning and Development; Office of Fair Housing and Equal Opportunity.
Transportation (1967) (53,337 employees)	Finances improvements in mass transit; develops and administers programs for highways, railroads, and aviation.	Federal Aviation Administration; Federal Highway Administration; National Highway Traffic Safety Administration; Federal Transit Administration.
Energy (1977) (14,759 employees)	Promotes the conservation of energy and resources; analyzes energy data; conducts research and development.	Federal Energy Regulatory Commission; National Nuclear Security Administration.
Health and Human Services (1979)§ (60,375 employees)	Promotes public health; enforces pure food and drug laws; conducts and sponsors health-related research.	Food and Drug Administration; Public Health Service; Centers for Disease Control and Prevention; National Institutes of Health; Centers for Medicare and Medicaid Services.
Education (1979)§ (4,230 employees)	Coordinates federal programs and policies for education; administers aid to education; promotes educational research.	Office of Special Education and Rehabilitation Service; Office of Elementary and Secondary Education; Office of Postsecondary Education; Office of Vocational and Adult Education; Office of Federal Student Aid.
Veterans Affairs (1988) (235,654 employees)	Promotes the welfare of veterans of the U.S. armed forces.	Veterans Health Administration; Veterans Benefits Administration; National Cemetery Systems.
Homeland Security (2003) (165,085 employees)	Attempts to prevent terrorist attacks within the United States, control America's borders, and minimize the damage from natural disasters.	U.S. Customs Service; U.S. Coast Guard; Secret Service; Federal Emergency Management Agency; Bureau of Citizenship and Immigration Services.

*Formed from the Office of the Attorney General (created in 1789).
†Formed from the Department of Commerce and Labor (created in 1903).
‡Formed from the Department of War (created in 1789) and the Department of the Navy (created in 1798).
§Formed from the Department of Health, Education, and Welfare (created in 1953).

TABLE 13–3 | SELECTED INDEPENDENT EXECUTIVE AGENCIES

NAME	DATE FORMED	PRINCIPAL FUNCTIONS
The Smithsonian Institution (5,245 employees)	1846	Runs the government's museums and the National Zoo.
Central Intelligence Agency (CIA) (number of employees not released)	1947	Gathers and analyzes political and military information about foreign countries; conducts covert operations outside the United States.
General Services Administration (GSA) (12,757 employees)	1949	Purchases and manages property of the federal government; acts as the business arm of the federal government in overseeing federal government spending projects; discovers overcharges in government programs.
National Science Foundation (NSF) (1,315 employees)	1950	Promotes scientific research; provides grants to all levels of schools for instructional programs in the sciences.
Small Business Administration (SBA) (3,630 employees)	1953	Protects the interests of small businesses; provides low-cost loans and management information to small businesses.
National Aeronautics and Space Administration (NASA) (18,954 employees)	1958	Is responsible for the U.S. space program, including the building, testing, and operating of space vehicles.
Environmental Protection Agency (EPA) (18,217 employees)	1970	Undertakes programs aimed at reducing air and water pollution; works with state and local agencies to help fight environmental hazards.

Independent Regulatory Agencies

Independent Regulatory Agency
An agency outside the major executive departments charged with making and implementing rules and regulations.

The **independent regulatory agencies** are typically responsible for a specific type of public policy. Their function is to make and implement rules and regulations in a particular sphere of action to protect the public interest. The earliest such agency was the Interstate Commerce Commission (ICC), which was established in 1887 when Americans began to seek some form of government control over the rapidly growing business and industrial sector. This new form of organization, the independent regulatory agency, was supposed to make technical, nonpolitical decisions about rates, profits, and rules that would be for the benefit of all and that did not require congressional legislation. In the years that followed the creation of the ICC, other agencies were formed to regulate communication (the Federal Communications Commission), nuclear power (the Nuclear Regulatory Commission), and so on. (The ICC was abolished on December 30, 1995.)

The Purpose and Nature of Regulatory Agencies. In practice, the regulatory agencies are administered independently of all three branches of government. They were set up because Congress felt it was unable to handle the complexities and technicalities required to carry out specific laws in the public interest. The regulatory commissions in fact combine some functions of all three branches of government—executive, legislative, and judicial. They are legislative in that they make rules that have the force of law. They are executive in that they provide for the enforcement of those rules. They are judicial in that they decide disputes involving the rules they have made.

Members of regulatory agency boards or commissions are appointed by the president with the consent of the Senate, although they do not report to the president. By law, the members of regulatory agencies cannot all be from the same political party. Members may be removed by the president only for causes specified in the law creating the agency. Presidents can influence regulatory agency behavior by appointing people of their own parties or individuals who share their political views when vacancies occur, in particular when the chair is vacant. For example, President George W. Bush placed people on the Federal Communications Commission (FCC) who share his belief in the need to curb obscene language in the media. Not surprisingly, the FCC soon thereafter started to "crack down" on obscenities on the air. One victim of this regulatory effort was Howard Stern, a nationally syndicated radio and television personality. His response was to switch from commercial radio and TV to unregulated satellite radio, where he can be heard every day on Sirius. Table 13–4 describes the functions of selected independent regulatory agencies.

Agency Capture. Over the last several decades, some observers have concluded that these agencies, although nominally independent, may in fact not always be so. They contend that many independent regulatory agencies have been **captured** by the very industries and firms that they were supposed to regulate. The results have been less competition rather than more competition, higher prices rather than lower prices, and less choice rather than more choice for consumers.

Deregulation and Reregulation. During the presidency of Ronald Reagan (1981–1989), some significant deregulation (the removal of regulatory restraints—the opposite of regulation) occurred, much of which had started under President Jimmy Carter (1977–1981). For example, President Carter appointed a chairperson of the Civil Aeronautics Board (CAB) who gradually eliminated regulation of airline fares and routes. Then, under Reagan, the CAB was eliminated on January 1, 1985.

During the administration of George H. W. Bush (1989–1993), calls for reregulation of many businesses increased. Indeed, during that administration, the Americans with Disabilities Act of 1990, the Civil Rights Act of 1991, and the Clean Air Act Amendments of 1991, all of which increased or changed the regulation of many businesses, were passed. Additionally, the Cable Reregulation Act of 1992 was passed.

Under President Bill Clinton (1993–2001), the Interstate Commerce Commission was eliminated, and the banking and telecommunications industries, along with many other sectors of the economy, were deregulated. At the same time, there was extensive regulation to protect the environment.

> **DID YOU KNOW . . .**
> That the Commerce Department's U.S. Travel and Tourism Administration gave away $440,000 in disaster relief to western ski resort operators because there hadn't been enough snow?

Capture
The act by which an industry being regulated by a government agency gains direct or indirect control over agency personnel and decision makers.

TABLE 13–4 | SELECTED INDEPENDENT REGULATORY AGENCIES

NAME	DATE FORMED	PRINCIPAL FUNCTIONS
Federal Reserve System Board of Governors (Fed) (1,068 employees)	1913	Determines policy with respect to interest rates, credit availability, and the money supply.
Federal Trade Commission (FTC) (1,045 employees)	1914	Prevents businesses from engaging in unfair trade practices; stops the formation of monopolies in the business sector; protects consumer rights.
Securities and Exchange Commission (SEC) (3,261 employees)	1934	Regulates the nation's stock exchanges, in which shares of stocks are bought and sold; requires full disclosure of the financial profiles of companies that wish to sell stocks and bonds to the public.
Federal Communications Commission (FCC) (2,051 employees)	1934	Regulates all communications by telegraph, cable, telephone, radio, and television.
National Labor Relations Board (NLRB) (1,931 employees)	1935	Protects employees' rights to join unions and bargain collectively with employers; attempts to prevent unfair labor practices by both employers and unions.
Equal Employment Opportunity Commission (EEOC) (2,589 employees)	1964	Works to eliminate discrimination based on religion, gender, race, color, national origin, age, or disability; examines claims of discrimination.
Nuclear Regulatory Commission (NRC) (3,083 employees)	1974	Ensures that electricity-generating nuclear reactors in the United States are built and operated safely; regularly inspects the operations of such reactors.

| Government Corporation
An agency of government that administers a quasi-business enterprise. These corporations are used when activities are primarily commercial.

Government Corporations

Another form of bureaucratic organization in the United States is the **government corporation.** Although the concept is borrowed from the world of business, distinct differences exist between public and private corporations.

A private corporation has shareholders (stockholders) who elect a board of directors, who in turn choose the corporate officers, such as president and vice president. When a private corporation makes a profit, it must pay taxes (unless it avoids them through various legal loopholes). It either distributes part or all of the after-tax profits to shareholders as dividends or plows the profits back into the corporation to make new investments.

A government corporation has a board of directors and managers, but it does not have any stockholders. We cannot buy shares of stock in a government corporation. If the government corporation makes a profit, it does not distribute the profit as dividends. Also, if it makes a profit, it does not have to pay taxes; the profits remain in the corporation. Table 13–5 describes the functions of selected government corporations.

| Staffing the Bureaucracy

There are two categories of bureaucrats: political appointees and civil servants. As noted earlier, the president is able to make political appointments to most of the top jobs in the federal bureaucracy. The president can also appoint ambassadors to foreign posts. All of the jobs that are considered "political plums" and that usually go to the politically well connected are listed in *Policy and Supporting Positions*, a book published by the Government Printing Office after each presidential election. Informally (and appropriately), this has been called "The Plum Book." The rest of the national government's employees belong to the civil service and obtain their jobs through a much more formal process.

Political Appointees

To fill the positions listed in "The Plum Book," the president and the president's advisers solicit suggestions from politicians, businesspersons, and other prominent

TABLE 13–5 | SELECTED GOVERNMENT CORPORATIONS

Name	Date Formed	Principal Functions
Tennessee Valley Authority (TVA) (13,379 employees)	1933	Operates a Tennessee River control system and generates power for a seven-state region and for the U.S. aeronautics and space programs; promotes the economic development of the Tennessee Valley region; controls floods and promotes the navigability of the Tennessee River.
Federal Deposit Insurance Corporation (FDIC) (5,473 employees)	1933	Insures individuals' bank deposits up to $100,000; oversees the business activities of banks.
Export-Import Bank of the United States (Ex-Im Bank) (394 employees)	1933	Promotes the sale of American-made goods abroad; grants loans to foreign purchasers of American products.
National Railroad Passenger Corporation (AMTRAK) (22,000 employees)	1970	Provides a national and intercity rail passenger service; controls 22,000 miles of track and serves 500 communities.
U.S. Postal Service* (787,818 employees)	1970	Delivers mail throughout the United States and its territories; is the largest government corporation.

*Formed from the Post Office Department (an executive department) in 1970.

A mail clerk unloads mail from a "sweeper" at the main post office in St. Louis during the Christmas rush. The U.S. Postal Service is a government corporation. The United States enjoys one of the lowest rates for domestic letter postage in the industrialized world—$0.39. In U.S. dollars, the rate is $0.51 in Britain, $0.62 in France, and $0.73 in Japan. (UPI Photo/Bill Greenblatt/Landov)

individuals. Appointments to these positions offer the president a way to pay off outstanding political debts. But the president must also take into consideration such things as the candidate's work experience, intelligence, political affiliations, and personal characteristics. Presidents have differed in the importance they attach to appointing women and minorities to plum positions. Presidents often use ambassadorships, however, to reward individuals for their campaign contributions.

We should note here that just because the president has the power to appoint a government official does not mean that such an appointment will pass muster. Before making any nominations, the administration requires potential appointees to undergo a detailed screening process and answer questions such as the following: What are your accomplishments? Did you ever *not* pay taxes for your nannies or housekeepers? What kinds of investments have you made? What have your past partisan affiliations been?

Such a process takes months, and after completing it, the appointees must be confirmed by the Senate. Even with such a screening process, the Bush administration has made some serious errors. For example, as mentioned previously, the president's appointment of Michael Brown to head the Federal Emergency Management Agency turned out to be a big mistake because Brown had no experience in emergency planning and relief efforts. As another example, the president's appointee to the National Aeronautics and Space Administration (NASA) had to resign when officials at Texas A&M University confirmed that he had *not* graduated from that university, contrary to what he indicated on his résumé.

The Aristocracy of the Federal Government. Political appointees are in some sense the aristocracy of the federal government. But their powers, although appearing formidable on paper, are often exaggerated. Like the president, a political appointee will occupy her or his position for a comparatively brief time. Political appointees often leave office before the president's term actually ends. In fact, the average term of service for political appointees is less than two years. As a result, most appointees have little background for their positions and may be mere figureheads. Often, they only respond to the paperwork that flows up from below. Additionally, the professional civil servants who make up the permanent civil service may not feel compelled to carry out their current boss's directives quickly, because they know that he or she will not be around for very long.

The Difficulty in Firing Civil Servants. This inertia is compounded by the fact that it is very difficult to discharge civil servants. In recent years, fewer than one-tenth of 1 percent of federal employees have been fired for incompetence. Because discharged employees may appeal their dismissals, many months or even years can pass before the issue is resolved conclusively. This occupational rigidity helps to ensure that most political appointees, no matter how competent or driven, will not be able to exert much meaningful influence over their subordinates, let alone implement dramatic changes in the bureaucracy itself.

History of the Federal Civil Service

When the federal government was formed in 1789, it had no career public servants but rather consisted of amateurs who were almost all Federalists. When Thomas Jefferson took over as president, few in his party were holding federal administrative jobs, so he fired more than one hundred officials and replaced them with his own supporters. Then, for the next twenty-five years, a growing body of federal administrators gained experience and expertise, becoming in the process professional public servants. These administrators stayed in office regardless of who was elected president. The bureaucracy had become a self-maintaining, long-term element within government.

To the Victor Belong the Spoils. When Andrew Jackson took over the White House in 1828, he could not believe how many appointed officials (appointed before he became president, that is) were overtly hostile toward him and his Democratic Party. As the bureaucracy was reluctant to carry out his programs, Jackson did the obvious: he fired federal officials—more than had all his predecessors combined. The **spoils system**—an application of the principle that to the victor belong the spoils—became the standard method of filling federal positions. Whenever a new president was elected from a party different from the party of the previous president, there would be an almost complete turnover in the staffing of the federal government.

| **Spoils System**
The awarding of government jobs to political supporters and friends.

On September 19, 1881, President James A. Garfield was assassinated by a disappointed office seeker, Charles J. Guiteau. The long-term effect of this event was to replace the spoils system with a permanent career civil service. This process began with the passage of the Pendleton Act in 1883, which established the Civil Service Commission. (Library of Congress)

The Civil Service Reform Act of 1883. Jackson's spoils system survived for a number of years, but it became increasingly corrupt. Also, as the size of the bureaucracy increased by 300 percent between 1851 and 1881, the cry for civil service reform became louder. Reformers began to look to the example of several European countries, in particular, Germany, which had established a professional civil service that operated under a **merit system** in which job appointments were based on competitive examinations.

In 1883, the **Pendleton Act**—or **Civil Service Reform Act**—was passed, placing the first limits on the spoils system. The act established the principle of employment on the basis of open, competitive examinations and created the **Civil Service Commission** to administer the personnel service. Only 10 percent of federal employees were covered by the merit system initially. Later laws, amendments, and executive orders, however, increased the coverage to more than 90 percent of federal employees. The effects of these reforms were felt at all levels of government.

The Supreme Court strengthened the civil service system in *Elrod v. Burns*[4] in 1976 and *Branti v. Finkel*[5] in 1980. In those two cases, the Court used the First Amendment to forbid government officials from discharging or threatening to discharge public employees solely for *not* being supporters of the political party in power unless party affiliation is an appropriate requirement for the position. Additional enhancements to the civil service system were added in *Rutan v. Republican Party of Illinois*[6] in 1990. The Court's ruling effectively prevented the use of partisan political considerations as the basis for hiring, promoting, or transferring most public employees. An exception was permitted, however, for senior policymaking positions, which usually go to officials who will support the programs of the elected leaders.

The Civil Service Reform Act of 1978. In 1978, the Civil Service Reform Act abolished the Civil Service Commission and created two new federal agencies to perform its duties. To administer the civil service laws, rules, and regulations, the act created the Office of Personnel Management (OPM). The OPM is empowered to recruit, interview, and test potential government workers and determine who should be hired. The OPM makes recommendations to the individual agencies as to which persons meet the standards (typically, the top three applicants for a position), and the agencies then decide whom to hire. To oversee promotions, employees' rights, and other employment matters, the act created the Merit Systems Protection Board (MSPB). The MSPB evaluates charges of wrongdoing, hears employee appeals from agency decisions, and can order corrective action against agencies and employees.

Federal Employees and Political Campaigns. In 1933, when President Franklin D. Roosevelt set up his New Deal, a virtual army of civil servants was hired to staff the numerous new agencies that were created. Because the individuals who worked in these agencies owed their jobs to the Democratic Party, it seemed natural for them to campaign for Democratic candidates. The Democrats controlling Congress in the mid-1930s did not object. But in 1938, a coalition of conservative Democrats and Republicans took control of Congress and forced through the Hatch Act—or Political Activities Act—of 1939. The act prohibited federal employees from actively participating in the political management of campaigns. It also forbade the use of federal authority to influence nominations and elections and outlawed the use of bureaucratic rank to pressure federal employees to make political contributions.

Merit System
The selection, retention, and promotion of government employees on the basis of competitive examinations.

Pendleton Act (Civil Service Reform Act)
An act that established the principle of employment on the basis of merit and created the Civil Service Commission to administer the personnel service.

Civil Service Commission
The initial central personnel agency of the national government; created in 1883.

---

[4]427 U.S. 347 (1976).
[5]445 U.S. 507 (1980).
[6]497 U.S. 62 (1990).

The Hatch Act created a controversy that lasted for decades. Many contended that the act deprived federal employees of their First Amendment freedoms of speech and association. In 1972, a federal district court declared the act unconstitutional. The United States Supreme Court, however, reaffirmed the challenged portion of the act in 1973, stating that the government's interest in preserving a nonpartisan civil service was so great that the prohibitions should remain.[7] Twenty years later, Congress addressed the criticisms of the Hatch Act by passing the Federal Employees Political Activities Act of 1993. This act, which amended the Hatch Act, lessened the harshness of the 1939 act in several ways. Among other things, the 1993 act allowed federal employees to run for office in nonpartisan elections, participate in voter-registration drives, make campaign contributions to political organizations, and campaign for candidates in partisan elections.

Modern Attempts at Bureaucratic Reform

As long as the federal bureaucracy exists, there will continue to be attempts to make it more open, efficient, and responsive to the needs of U.S. citizens. The most important actual and proposed reforms in the last several decades include sunshine and sunset laws, privatization, incentives for efficiency, and more protection for so-called whistleblowers.

Sunshine Laws before and after 9/11

In 1976, Congress enacted the **Government in the Sunshine Act.** It required for the first time that all multiheaded federal agencies—agencies headed by a committee instead of an individual—hold their meetings regularly in public session. The bill defined *meetings* as almost any gathering, formal or informal, of agency members, including a conference telephone call. The only exceptions to this rule of openness are discussions of matters such as court proceedings or personnel problems, and these exceptions are specifically listed in the bill. Sunshine laws now exist at all levels of government.

| **Government in the Sunshine Act**
A law that requires all committee-directed federal agencies to conduct their business regularly in public session.

[7]*United States Civil Service Commission v. National Association of Letter Carriers*, 413 U.S. 548 (1973).

"Who do I see to get big government off my back?"

Information Disclosure. Sunshine laws are consistent with the policy of information disclosure that has been supported by the government for decades. For example, beginning in the 1960s, a number of consumer protection laws have required that certain information be disclosed to consumers—when purchasing homes, borrowing funds, and so on. In 1966, the federal government passed the Freedom of Information Act, which required federal government agencies, with certain exceptions, to disclose to individuals, on their request, any information about them contained in government files. (You will learn more about this act in the *Making a Difference* feature at the end of this chapter.)

Curbs on Information Disclosure. Since September 11, 2001, the trend toward government in the sunshine and information disclosure has been reversed at both the federal and state levels. Within weeks after September 11, 2001, numerous federal agencies removed hundreds, if not thousands, of documents from Internet sites, public libraries, and reading rooms found in various federal government departments. Information contained in some of the documents included diagrams of power plants and pipelines, structural details on dams, and safety plans for chemical plants. The military also immediately started restricting information about its current and planned activities, as did the Federal Bureau of Investigation. These agencies were concerned that terrorists could make use of this information to plan attacks. The federal government has also gone back into the archives to remove an increasing quantity of not only sensitive information but also sometimes seemingly unimportant information.

In making public documents inaccessible to the public, the federal government was ahead of state and local governments, but they quickly followed suit. State and local governments control and supervise police forces, dams, electricity sources, and water supplies. Consequently, it is not surprising that many state and local governments followed in the footsteps of the federal government in curbing access to certain public records and information.

Such actions constitute a broad attempt by state and local governments to keep terrorists from learning about local emergency preparedness plans. It is possible, however, that as soon as the public starts to believe that the threat has lessened, some groups will take state and local governments to court in an effort to increase public access to state and local records by reimposing the sunshine laws that were in effect before 9/11.

Sunset Laws

Potentially, the size and scope of the federal bureaucracy can be controlled through **sunset legislation,** which places government programs on a definite schedule for congressional consideration. Unless Congress specifically reauthorizes a particular federally operated program at the end of a designated period, it would be terminated automatically; that is, its sun would set.

The idea of sunset legislation was initially suggested by Franklin D. Roosevelt when he created the plethora of New Deal agencies in the 1930s. His assistant, William O. Douglas, recommended that each agency's charter should include a provision allowing for its termination in ten years. Only an act of Congress could revitalize it. The proposal was never adopted. It was not until 1976 that a state legislature—Colorado's—adopted sunset legislation for state regulatory commissions, giving them a life of six years before their suns set. Today, most states have some type of sunset law.

Pedestrians and traffic clog the 59th Street Bridge in New York City during the power outage of August 14, 2003. Parts of the Northeast, the Midwest, and Canada struggled to resume normal operations after the biggest electrical blackout in North American history. What steps can the federal government take to address the causes of this type of disaster? (James Patrick Cooper/ *Bloomberg News*/Landov)

Sunset Legislation
Laws requiring that existing programs be reviewed regularly for their effectiveness and be terminated unless specifically extended as a result of these reviews.

| Privatization
The replacement of government services
with services provided by private firms.

Privatization

Another approach to bureaucratic reform is **privatization,** which occurs when government services are replaced by services from the private sector. For example, the government might contract with private firms to operate prisons. Supporters of privatization argue that some services could be provided more efficiently by the private sector. Another scheme is to furnish vouchers to "clients" in lieu of services. For example, instead of supplying housing, the government could offer vouchers that recipients could use to "pay" for housing in privately owned buildings.

The privatization, or contracting out, strategy has been most successful on the local level. Municipalities, for example, can form contracts with private companies for such things as trash collection. This approach is not a cure-all, however, as many functions, particularly on the national level, cannot be contracted out in any meaningful way. For example, the federal government could not contract out most of the Defense Department's functions to private firms. Nonetheless, the U.S. military has contracted out many services in Iraq and elsewhere, as you'll learn in this chapter's *Beyond Our Borders* feature.

Incentives for Efficiency and Productivity

An increasing number of state governments are beginning to experiment with a variety of schemes to run their operations more efficiently and capably. They focus on maximizing the efficiency and productivity of government workers by providing incentives for improved performance.[8] For example, many governors, mayors, and city administrators are considering ways in which government can be made more entrepreneurial. Some of the most promising measures have included such tactics as permitting agencies that do not spend their entire budgets to keep some of the difference and rewarding employees with performance-based bonuses.

Government Performance and Results Act.   At the federal level, the Government Performance and Results Act of 1997 was designed to improve efficiency in the federal workforce. The act required that all government agencies (except the Central Intelligence Agency) describe their new goals and establish methods for determining whether those goals are met. Goals may be broadly crafted (for example, reducing the time it takes to test a new drug before allowing it to be marketed) or narrowly crafted (for example, reducing the number of times a telephone rings before it is answered).

The "performance-based budgeting" implemented by President George W. Bush took this results-oriented approach a step further. Performance-based budgeting links agency funding to actual agency performance. Agencies are given specific performance criteria to meet, and the Office of Management and Budget rates each agency to determine how well it has performed. In theory, the amount of funds that each agency will receive in the next annual budget should be determined by the extent to which it has met the performance criteria.

Bureaucracy Changed Little, Though.   Efforts to improve bureaucratic efficiency are supported by the assertion that although society and industry have changed enormously in the past century, the form of government used in Washington, D.C., and in most states has remained the same. Some observers believe that the nation's diverse economic base cannot be administered competently by traditional bureaucratic organizations. Consequently, government must become more responsive to cope with the

---

[8]See, for example, David Osborne and Ted Gaebler, *Reinventing Government: How the Entrepreneurial Spirit Is Transforming the Public Sector* (Reading, Mass.: Addison-Wesley, 1992); and David Osborne and Peter Plastrik, *Banishing Bureaucracy: The Five Strategies for Reinventing Government* (Reading, Mass.: Addison-Wesley, 1997).

BEYOND OUR BORDERS | Privatizing the U.S. Military Abroad

Privatization has been a "hot" topic for several decades now, at least domestically. All levels of government—federal, state, and local—have privatized at least some activities. Less well known, however, is that for more than a decade the U.S. military has been employing private companies abroad to perform a number of functions that were previously done by military personnel. After the American military was downsized following the fall of the Berlin Wall in 1989, the military responded by outsourcing many functions to the private sector. Before the First Gulf War, the Pentagon was already spending about 8 percent of its overall budget on private companies.

PRIVATE CONTRACTORS GALORE

Today, private contractors are everywhere in Iraq. By 2005, there were over 10,000 private contractors/workers on the ground in Iraq. At that time, the British had only 9,000 troops in Iraq.

In addition, the Pentagon says that it is spending at least $4 billion a year to create war-fighting exercises. Through the publicly traded firm of Cubic, Bosnian refugees have come to the United States to re-create their gruesome experiences so that American military personnel can participate in authentic war games.

THE NUMBERS TELL IT ALL

One of the reasons that the U.S. military has felt obligated to hire private contractors in Iraq and elsewhere is that the army in particular has been downsized. During the First Gulf War, active duty troops in the army numbered 711,000. Today, that number has been reduced by almost one-third, to only about 485,000. As a result, the Pentagon says that it has to fill ancillary jobs and programs by contracting with private companies that either send their workers abroad or hire workers there.

FOR CRITICAL ANALYSIS

Is there any national security argument against using private contractors to do U.S. military work?

increasing number of demands placed on it. Political scientists Joel Aberbach and Bert Rockman take issue with this contention. They argue that the bureaucracy has changed significantly over time in response to changes desired by various presidential administrations. In their opinion, many of the problems attributed to the bureaucracy are, in fact, a result of the political decision-making process. Therefore, attempts to "reinvent" government by reforming the bureaucracy are misguided.[9]

Other analysts have suggested that the problem lies not so much with traditional bureaucratic organizations as with the people who run them. According to policy specialist Taegan Goddard and journalist Christopher Riback, what needs to be "reinvented" is not the machinery of government but public officials. After each election, new appointees to bureaucratic positions may find themselves managing complex, multimillion-dollar enterprises, yet they often are untrained for their jobs. According to these authors, if we want to reform the bureaucracy, we should focus on preparing newcomers for the task of "doing" government.[10]

Saving Costs through E-Government.   Many contend that the communications revolution brought about by the Internet has not only improved the efficiency with which government agencies deliver services to the public but also helped to reduce the cost of government. Agencies can now communicate with members of the public, as well as other agencies, via e-mail. Additionally, every federal agency now has a Web site to which citizens can go to find information about agency services instead of calling or appearing in person at a regional agency office. Since 2003, federal agencies have also

---

[9]Joel D. Aberbach and Bert A. Rockman, *In the Web of Politics: Three Decades of the U.S. Federal Executive* (Washington, D.C.: Brookings Institution Press, 2000).

[10]Taegan D. Goddard and Christopher Riback, *You Won—Now What? How Americans Can Make Democracy Work from City Hall to the White House* (New York: Scribner, 1998).

| **Whistleblower**
Someone who brings to public attention gross governmental inefficiency or an illegal action.

been required by the Government Paperwork Elimination Act of 1998 to use electronic commerce whenever it is practical to do so and will save on costs.

Helping Out the Whistleblowers

The term **whistleblower** as applied to the federal bureaucracy has a special meaning: it is someone who blows the whistle on a gross governmental inefficiency or illegal action. Whistleblowers may be clerical workers, managers, or even specialists, such as scientists. The 1978 Civil Service Reform Act prohibits reprisals against whistleblowers by their superiors, and it set up the Merit Systems Protection Board as part of this protection. Many federal agencies also have toll-free hot lines that employees can use anonymously to report bureaucratic waste and inappropriate behavior. About 35 percent of all calls result in agency action or follow-up.

Further protection for whistleblowers was provided in 1989, when Congress passed the Whistle-Blower Protection Act. That act established an independent agency, the Office of Special Counsel (OSC), to investigate complaints brought by government employees who have been demoted, fired, or otherwise sanctioned for reporting government fraud or waste. There is little evidence, though, that potential whistleblowers truly have received more protection as a result of these endeavors. More than 40 percent of the employees who turned to the OSC for assistance in a recent three-year period stated that they were no longer employees of the government agencies on which they blew the whistle.

Some state and federal laws encourage employees to blow the whistle on their employers' wrongful actions by providing monetary incentives to the whistleblowers. At the federal level, the False Claims Act of 1986 allows a whistleblower who has disclosed information about a fraud against the U.S. government to receive a monetary award. If the government chooses to prosecute the case and wins, the whistleblower receives between 15 and 25 percent of the proceeds. If the government declines to intervene, the whistleblower can bring suit on behalf of the government, and if the suit is successful, will receive between 25 and 30 percent of the proceeds.

| **Enabling Legislation**
A statute enacted by Congress that authorizes the creation of an administrative agency and specifies the name, purpose, composition, functions, and powers of the agency being created.

| Bureaucrats as Politicians and Policymakers

Because Congress is unable to oversee the day-to-day administration of its programs, it must delegate certain powers to administrative agencies. Congress delegates the power to implement legislation to agencies through what is called **enabling legislation.** For example, the Federal Trade Commission was created by the Federal Trade Commission Act of 1914, the Equal Employment Opportunity Commission was created by the Civil Rights Act of 1964, and the Occupational Safety and Health Administration was created by the Occupational Safety and Health Act of 1970. The enabling legislation generally specifies the name, purpose, composition, functions, and powers of the agency.

In theory, the agencies should put into effect laws passed by Congress. Laws are often drafted in such vague and general terms, however, that they provide relatively little guidance to agency administrators as to how the laws should be implemented. This means that the agencies themselves must decide how best to carry out the wishes of Congress.

The discretion given to administrative agencies is not accidental. Congress has long realized that it lacks the technical expertise and the resources to monitor the implementation of its laws. Hence, the administrative agency is created to fill the gaps. This gap-filling role requires the agency to formulate administrative rules (regulations) to put flesh on the bones of the law. But it also forces the agency itself to become an unelected policymaker.

The Rulemaking Environment

Rulemaking does not occur in a vacuum. Suppose that Congress passes a new air-pollution law. The Environmental Protection Agency (EPA) might decide to implement the new law through a technical regulation on factory emissions. This proposed regulation would be published in the *Federal Register*, a daily government publication, so that interested parties would have an opportunity to comment on it. Individuals and companies that opposed parts or all of the rule might then try to convince the EPA to revise or redraft the regulation. Some parties might try to persuade the agency to withdraw the proposed regulation altogether. In any event, the EPA would consider these comments in drafting the final version of the regulation following the expiration of the comment period.

Waiting Periods and Court Challenges. Once the final regulation has been published in the *Federal Register*, there is a sixty-day waiting period before the rule can be enforced. During that period, businesses, individuals, and state and local governments can ask Congress to overturn the regulation. After that sixty-day period has lapsed, the regulation can still be challenged in court by a party having a direct interest in the rule, such as a company that expects to incur significant costs in complying with it. The company could argue that the rule misinterprets the applicable law or goes beyond the agency's statutory purview. An allegation by the company that the EPA made a mistake in judgment probably would not be enough to convince the court to throw out the rule. The company instead would have to demonstrate that the rule itself was "arbitrary and capricious." To meet this standard, the company would have to show that the rule reflected a serious flaw in the EPA's judgment.

Controversies. How agencies implement, administer, and enforce legislation has resulted in controversy. Decisions made by agencies charged with administering the Endangered Species Act have led to protests from farmers, ranchers, and others whose economic interests have been harmed. For example, the government decided to cut off the flow of irrigation water from Klamath Lake in Oregon in the summer of 2001. That action, which affected irrigation water for more than one thousand farmers in southern Oregon and northern California, was undertaken to save endangered suckerfish and salmon. It was believed that the lake's water level was so low that further use of the water for irrigation would harm these fish. The results of this decision were devastating for many farmers.

Negotiated Rulemaking

Since the end of World War II (1939–1945), companies, environmentalists, and other special interest groups have challenged government regulations in court. In the 1980s, however, the sheer wastefulness of attempting to regulate through litigation became more and more apparent. Today, a growing number of federal agencies encourage businesses and public-interest groups to become directly involved in drafting regulations. Agencies hope that such participation may help to prevent later courtroom battles over the meaning, applicability, and legal effect of the regulations.

Congress formally approved such a process, which is called *negotiated rulemaking*, in the Negotiated Rulemaking Act of 1990. The act authorizes agencies to allow those who will be affected by a new rule to participate in the rule-drafting process. If an agency chooses to engage in negotiated rulemaking, it must publish in the *Federal Register* the subject and scope of the rule to be developed, the parties affected significantly by the rule, and other information. Representatives of the affected groups and other interested parties then may apply to be members of the negotiating committee. The agency is represented on the committee, but a neutral third party (not the agency) presides over the proceedings. Once the committee members

A northern spotted owl sits in a tree in a national forest in Oregon. Environmentalists filed a lawsuit in 2003 seeking to stop logging on federal lands in southwestern Oregon. They claimed the U.S. Fish and Wildlife Service had ignored the need to protect critical habitat for the owl, a threatened species. How should we balance the desire to protect rare species with our need for natural resources? (Photo Courtesy of Northwest Habitat Institute)

have reached agreement on the terms of the proposed rule, a notice is published in the *Federal Register,* followed by a period for comments by any person or organization interested in the proposed rule. Negotiated rulemaking often is conducted under the condition that the participants promise not to challenge in court the outcome of any agreement to which they were a party.

Bureaucrats Are Policymakers

Theories of public administration once assumed that bureaucrats do not make policy decisions but only implement the laws and policies promulgated by the president and legislative bodies. Many people continue to make this assumption. A more realistic view, which is now held by most bureaucrats and elected officials, is that the agencies and departments of government play important roles in policymaking. As we have seen, many government rules, regulations, and programs are in fact initiated by bureaucrats, based on their expertise and scientific studies. How a law passed by Congress eventually is translated into concrete action—from the forms to be filled out to decisions about who gets the benefits—usually is determined within each agency or department. Even the evaluation of whether a policy has achieved its purpose usually is based on studies that are commissioned and interpreted by the agency administering the program.

The bureaucracy's policymaking role has often been depicted by what traditionally has been called the "iron triangle." Recently, the concept of an "issue network" has been viewed as a more accurate description of the policymaking process.

Iron Triangles.   In the past, scholars often described the bureaucracy's role in the policymaking process by using the concept of an **iron triangle**—a three-way alliance among legislators in Congress, bureaucrats, and interest groups. Consider as an example the development of agricultural policy. Congress, as one component of the triangle, includes two major committees concerned with agricultural policy, the House Committee on Agriculture and the Senate Committee on Agriculture, Nutrition, and Forestry. The Department of Agriculture, the second component of the triangle, has more than 95,000 employees, plus thousands of contractors and consultants. Agricultural interest groups, the third component of the iron triangle in agricultural policymaking, include many large and powerful associations, such as the American Farm Bureau Federation, the National Cattleman's Association, and the Corn Growers Association. These three components of the iron triangle work together, formally or informally, to create policy.

For example, the various agricultural interest groups lobby Congress to develop policies that benefit their groups' interests. Members of Congress cannot afford to ignore the wishes of interest groups because those groups are potential sources of voter support and campaign contributions. The legislators in Congress also work closely with the Department of Agriculture, which, in implementing a policy, can develop rules that benefit—or at least do not hurt—certain industries or groups. The Department of Agriculture, in turn, supports policies that enhance the department's budget and powers. In this way, according to theory, agricultural policy is created that benefits all three components of the iron triangle.

Issue Networks.   To be sure, the preceding discussion presents a much simplified picture of how the iron triangle works. With the growth in the complexity of government, policymaking also has become more complicated. The bureaucracy is larger, Congress has more committees and subcommittees, and interest groups are more powerful than ever. Although iron triangles still exist, often they are inadequate as descriptions of how policy is actually made. Frequently, different interest groups concerned about a certain area of policy have conflicting demands, making agency decisions difficult. Additionally, divided government in some years has

| Iron Triangle
The three-way alliance among legislators, bureaucrats, and interest groups to make or preserve policies that benefit their respective interests.

meant that departments are sometimes pressured by the president to take one approach and by Congress to take another.

Many scholars now use the term *issue network* to describe the policymaking process. An **issue network** consists of individuals or organizations that support a particular policy position on the environment, taxation, consumer safety, or some other issue. Typically, an issue network includes legislators and/or their staff members, interest groups, bureaucrats, scholars and other experts, and representatives from the media. Members of a particular issue network work together to influence the president, members of Congress, administrative agencies, and the courts to affect public policy on a specific issue. Each policy issue may involve conflicting positions taken by two or more issue networks.

Issue Network
A group of individuals or organizations—which may consist of legislators and legislative staff members, interest group leaders, bureaucrats, the media, scholars, and other experts—that supports a particular policy position on a given issue.

Congressional Control of the Bureaucracy

Many political pundits doubt whether Congress can meaningfully control the federal bureaucracy. Nevertheless, Congress does have some means of exerting control.

Ways Congress Does Control the Bureaucracy

These commentators forget that Congress specifies in an agency's "enabling legislation" the powers of the agency and the parameters within which it can operate. Additionally, Congress has the power of the purse and theoretically could refuse to authorize or appropriate funds for a particular agency (see the discussion of the budgeting process in Chapter 11). Whether Congress would actually take such a drastic measure would depend on the circumstances. It is clear, however, that Congress does have the legal authority to decide whether to fund or not to fund administrative agencies. Congress can also exercise oversight over agencies through investigations and hearings.

Congressional committees conduct investigations and hold hearings to oversee an agency's actions, reviewing them to ensure compliance with congressional intentions. The agency's officers and employees can be ordered to testify before a committee about the details of an action. Through these oversight activities, especially in the questions and comments of members of the House or Senate during the hearings, Congress indicates its positions on specific programs and issues.

Congress can ask the Government Accountability Office (GAO) to investigate particular agency actions as well. The Congressional Budget Office (CBO) also conducts oversight studies. The results of a GAO or CBO study may encourage Congress to hold further hearings or make changes in the law. Even if a law is not changed explicitly by Congress, however, the views expressed in any investigations and hearings are taken seriously by agency officials, who often act on those views.

In 1996, Congress passed the Congressional Review Act. The act created special procedures that can be employed to express congressional disapproval of particular agency actions. These procedures have rarely been used, however. Since the act's passage, the executive branch has issued over 15,000 regulations. Yet only eight resolutions of disapproval have been introduced, and none of these was passed by either chamber.

Reasons Why Congress Cannot Easily Oversee the Bureaucracy

Despite the powers just described, one theory of congressional control over the bureaucracy suggests that Congress cannot possibly oversee all of the bureaucracy. Consider two possible approaches to congressional control—(1) the "police patrol" and (2) the "fire alarm" approach. Certain congressional activities, such as annual budget hearings, fall under the police patrol approach. This regular review occasionally catches *some* deficiencies in a bureaucracy's job performance, but it usually fails to detect most problems.

In contrast, the fire alarm approach is more likely to discover gross inadequacies in a bureaucracy's job performance. In this approach, Congress and its committees react to scandal, citizen disappointment, and massive negative publicity by launching a full-scale investigation into whatever agency is suspected of wrongdoing. Clearly, this is what happened when Congress investigated the inadequacies of the Central Intelligence Agency after the 9/11 terrorist attacks. Congress was also responding to an alarm when it investigated the failures of the Federal Emergency Management Agency after Hurricane Katrina.

Fire alarm investigations will not catch all problems, but they will alert bureaucracies that they need to clean up their procedures before a problem arises in their own agencies.[11]

---

[11]Matthew D. McCubbins and Thomas Schwartz, "Congressional Oversight Overlooked: Police Patrols versus Fire Alarms," *American Journal of Political Science*, February 28, 1984, pp. 165–179.

MAKING A DIFFERENCE — What the Government Knows about You

The federal government collects billions of pieces of information on tens of millions of Americans each year. These data are stored in files and sometimes are exchanged among agencies. You are probably the subject of several federal records (for example, in the Social Security Administration; the Internal Revenue Service; and, if you are a male, the Selective Service).

Why Should You Care?

Verifying the information that the government has on you can be important. On several occasions, the records of two people with similar names have become confused. Sometimes innocent persons have had the criminal records of other persons erroneously inserted in their files. Such disasters are not always caused by bureaucratic error. One of the most common crimes in today's world is "identity theft," in which one person makes use of another person's personal identifiers (such as a Social Security number) to commit fraud. In some instances, identity thieves have been arrested or even jailed under someone else's name.

What Can You Do?

The 1966 Freedom of Information Act (FOIA) requires that the federal government release, at your request, any identifiable information it has about you or about any other subject. Ten categories of material are exempted, however (classified material, confidential material on trade secrets, internal personnel rules, personal medical files, and the like). To request material, write directly to the Freedom of Information Act officer at the agency in question (say, the Department of Education). You must have a relatively specific idea about the document or information you want to obtain.

A second law, the Privacy Act of 1974, gives you access specifically to information the government may have collected about you. This law allows you to review records on file with federal agencies and to check those records for possible inaccuracies.

If you want to look at any records or find out if an agency has a record on you, write to the agency head or Privacy Act officer, and address your letter to the specific agency. State that "under the provisions of the Privacy Act of 1974, 5 U.S.C. 522a, I hereby request a copy of (or access to) _____." Then describe the record that you wish to investigate.

The American Civil Liberties Union (ACLU) has published a manual, called *Your Right to Government Information*, that guides you through the steps of obtaining information from the federal government. You can order it online at the following Web site:

www.aclu.org

Alternatively, you can order the manual from the ACLU at the following address:

ACLU Publications
P.O. Box 4713
Trenton, NJ 08650-4713
1-800-775-ACLU

Key Terms

acquisitive model 426

administrative agency 427

bureaucracy 425

cabinet department 431

capture 435

Civil Service Commission 439

enabling legislation 444

government corporation 436

Government in the Sunshine Act 440

independent executive agency 431

independent regulatory agency 434

iron triangle 446

issue network 447

line organization 431

merit system 439

monopolistic model 426

Pendleton Act (Civil Service Reform Act) 439

privatization 442

spoils system 438

sunset legislation 441

Weberian model 426

whistleblower 444

Chapter Summary

1 Bureaucracies are hierarchical organizations characterized by a division of labor and extensive procedural rules. Bureaucracy is the primary form of organization of most major corporations and universities as well as governments.

2 Several theories have been offered to explain bureaucracies. The Weberian model posits that bureaucracies are rational, hierarchical organizations in which decisions are based on logical reasoning. The acquisitive model views top level bureaucrats as pressing for ever-larger budgets and staffs to augment their own sense of power and security. The monopolistic model focuses on the environment in which most government bureaucracies operate, stating that bureaucracies are inefficient and excessively costly to operate because they have no competitors.

3 Since the founding of the United States, the federal bureaucracy has grown from 50 to about 2.7 million employees (excluding the military). Federal, state, and local employees together make up over 16 percent of the nation's civilian labor force. The federal bureaucracy consists of fifteen cabinet departments, as well as a large number of independent executive agencies, independent regulatory agencies, and government corporations. These entities enjoy varying degrees of autonomy, visibility, and political support.

4 A federal bureaucracy of career civil servants was formed during Thomas Jefferson's presidency. Andrew Jackson implemented a spoils system through which he appointed his own political supporters. A civil service based on professionalism and merit was the goal of the Civil Service Reform Act of

1883. Concerns that the civil service be freed from the pressures of politics prompted the passage of the Hatch Act in 1939. Significant changes in the administration of the civil service were made by the Civil Service Reform Act of 1978.

5 There have been many attempts to make the federal bureaucracy more open, efficient, and responsive to the needs of U.S. citizens. The most important reforms have included sunshine and sunset laws, privatization, strategies to provide incentives for increased productivity and efficiency, and protection for whistleblowers.

6 Congress delegates much of its authority to federal agencies when it creates new laws. The bureaucrats who run these agencies may become important policymakers because Congress has neither the time nor the technical expertise to oversee the administration of its laws. In the agency rulemaking process, a proposed regulation is published. A comment period follows, during which interested parties may offer suggestions for changes. Because companies and other organizations have challenged many regulations in court, federal agencies now are authorized to allow parties that will be affected by new regulations to participate in the rule-drafting process.

7 Congress exerts ultimate control over all federal agencies because it controls the federal government's purse strings. It also establishes the general guidelines by which regulatory agencies must abide. The appropriations process may provide a way to send messages of approval or disapproval to particular agencies, as do congressional hearings and investigations of agency actions.

Selected Print and Media Resources

SUGGESTED READINGS

Burrough, Bryan. *Public Enemies: America's Greatest Crime Wave and the Birth of the F.B.I., 1933–1934.* New York: Penguin Press, 2004. Burroughs strips the myths from such romanticized criminals as John Dillinger while simultaneously showing how incompetent the FBI often was in its initial years.

Gronlund, Ake, ed. *Electronic Government: Design, Applications, and Management.* Hershey, Pa.: Idea Group Publishing, 2002. This

collection of essays focuses on how electronic government might improve government services as well as increase citizen participation in democratic processes.

Hilts, Philip J. *Protecting America's Health: The FDA, Business, and One Hundred Years of Regulation.* New York: Knopf, 2003. This history of the Food and Drug Administration (FDA) explains the origin and nature of the drug-approval process and the importance of clinical trials. The book provides a thorough examination of an important regulatory agency. Hilts is sympathetic to the agency and relatively critical of the pharmaceutical industry.

Meier, Kenneth J., and Lawrence J. O'Toole, Jr. *Bureaucracy in a Democratic State: A Governance Perspective.* Baltimore: Johns Hopkins University Press, 2006. This study employs a governance approach to the bureaucracy. The authors examine the details of bureaucracy and demonstrate that bureaucracy can actually promote democracy.

Osborne, David, and Peter Plastrik. *Banishing Bureaucracy: The Five Strategies for Reinventing Government.* San Francisco: David Osborne Publishing, 2006. In 1992, David Osborne (with Ted Gaebler) wrote a best seller entitled *Reinventing Government.*

Vanishing Bureaucracy is his sequel, which goes one step further—it outlines specific strategies that can help transform public systems and organizations into engines of efficiency. The book focuses on clarifying a bureaucracy's purpose, creating incentives, improving accountability, redistributing power, and nurturing the correct culture.

MEDIA RESOURCES

The Bureaucracy of Government: John Lukacs—A 1988 Bill Moyers special. Historian John Lukacs discusses the common political lament over the giant but invisible mechanism called bureaucracy.

Yes, Minister—A new member of the British cabinet bumps up against the machinations of a top civil servant in a comedy of manners. This popular 1980 BBC comedy is now available on DVD.

E·MOCRACY | E-government

All federal government agencies (and virtually all state agencies) now have Web pages. Citizens can access these Web sites to find information and forms that, in the past, could normally be obtained only by going to a regional or local branch of the agency. For example, if you or a member of your family wants to learn about Social Security benefits available on retirement, you can simply access the Social Security Administration's Web site to find that information. A number of federal government agencies have also been active in discovering and prosecuting fraud perpetrated on citizens via the Internet.

| Logging On

Numerous links to federal agencies and information on the federal government can be found at the U.S. government's official Web site. Go to

www.firstgov.gov

You may want to examine two publications available from the federal government to learn more about the federal bureaucracy. The first is the *Federal Register*, which is the official publication for executive-branch documents. You can find it at

www.gpoaccess.gov/fr/browse.html

The second is the *United States Government Manual*, which describes the origins, purposes, and administrators of every federal department and agency. It is available at

www.gpoaccess.gov/gmanual/index.html

"The Plum Book," which lists the bureaucratic positions that can be filled by presidential appointment, is online at

www.gpoaccess.gov/plumbook/index.html

To find telephone numbers for government agencies and personnel, you can go to

www.firstgov.gov/Agencies.shtml

| Online Review

At **www.politicalscience.wadsworth.com/schmidt12**, you will find a free Study Guide to this book. For each chapter, there are two online quizzes to help you master the material.

• The PoliPrep Self-Study Assessment provides a pretest for each major section of the chapter. PoliPrep then generates a customized study plan. After you complete the study plan, a posttest evaluates your progress.

• The Tutorial Quiz for each chapter provides questions on the chapter contents, including the features. The questions are organized to match the major sections of the chapter.

14 | The Courts

EQUAL JUSTICE UNDER LAW

What If . . .
Supreme Court Justices Had Term Limits?

BACKGROUND

The nine justices who sit on the Supreme Court are not elected officials. Rather, they are appointed by the president (and confirmed by the Senate). Barring gross misconduct, they also hold their offices for life. Nevertheless, these justices are among the most important policymakers in this nation because they have the final say on how the U.S. Constitution—the "supreme law of the land"—should be interpreted.

The life tenure of Supreme Court justices came under scrutiny during the latest confirmation hearings for Supreme Court nominees. When Chief Justice William H. Rehnquist died—after thirty-three years on the bench—some people suggested that, with today's longer life spans, lifetime tenure is no longer appropriate for federal judges, and certainly not for Supreme Court justices. Consider that from 1789 to 1970, the average Supreme Court justice served only fifteen years and retired (or died) at age sixty-eight. Since 1970, the average tenure is more than twenty-five years, and the average age at retirement or death is about eighty.

WHAT IF SUPREME COURT JUSTICES HAD TERM LIMITS?

If Supreme Court justices had term limits, what should be the length of the term? Perhaps an appropriate one would be the average time on the bench from the founding of our nation until 1970—fifteen years. In other words, after confirmation by the Senate, a person could serve only fifteen years on the bench and then would have to retire.

Perhaps the most important result of term limits would be a reduction in the rancor surrounding confirmation hearings. Today, the confirmation of a Supreme Court nominee—one chosen by the president to fit his or her views—is a major political event because that person may be on the Court for the next three decades.

Consider the current chief justice, John Roberts. When he took the Supreme Court bench at age fifty, Americans could potentially anticipate that his conservative ideology would influence Supreme Court decisions for as long as thirty years. Knowing this, those who did not share his views or philosophy fought bitterly to prevent him from being confirmed. If term limits were in existence, in contrast, less would have been at stake—probably about half as many years of his influence.

TERM LIMITS WOULD PUT THE UNITED STATES IN LINE WITH OTHER DEMOCRACIES

In having no term limits for federal judges, the United States is somewhat out of step. Not only does just one state—Rhode Island—appoint state supreme court justices for life, but virtually every other major democratic nation has age or term limits for judges. Thus, term limits in the United States for federal judges would not be an anomaly. Even with term limits, Supreme Court justices would still be independent, which is what the framers of the Constitution desired.

MORE INFUSION OF NEW BLOOD

With term limits of, say, fifteen years, vacancies would be created on a more or less regular basis. Consequently, Supreme Court justices would have less temptation to time their retirements for political purposes. Thus, liberal-leaning justices would not necessarily delay their retirements until a Democratic president was in office, and conservative-leaning justices would not necessarily wait for a Republican.

In other words, fewer justices would follow the example of Justice Thurgood Marshall, who often said that he was determined to hang on to his judicial power until a Democratic president was in office to appoint his successor. After many years on the bench, he joked, "I have instructed my clerks that if I should die, they should have me stuffed—and continue to cast my votes."

In short, virtually every president, whether he or she was Republican or Democrat, would get a chance to fill a Supreme Court vacancy every few years. As a result, "new blood" would be infused into the Supreme Court more often. We would no longer face the risk of having Supreme Court justices who become less than enthusiastic about their work and less willing to examine new intellectual arguments. Term limits would also avoid the decrepitude that has occurred with several very old Supreme Court justices. In the last thirty years, some truly have stayed until the last possible minute. The public might prefer at least to have a mandatory retirement age.

FOR CRITICAL ANALYSIS

1. What are the benefits of having lifetime appointments to the Supreme Court?
2. Just because a president can appoint whomever he or she wishes to the Supreme Court, does that necessarily mean that the successful nominee will always reflect the president's political philosophy? Explain your answer.

The justices of the Supreme Court are not elected but rather are appointed by the president and confirmed by the Senate. The same is true for all other federal court judges. This fact does not mean that the federal judiciary is apolitical, however. Indeed, our courts play a larger role in making public policy than courts in most other countries in the world today. Because Supreme Court justices are so important in our governmental system, term limits have been suggested for them, as this chapter's opening *What If . . .* feature indicated.

As Alexis de Tocqueville, a French commentator on American society in the 1800s, noted, "scarcely any political question arises in the United States that is not resolved, sooner or later, into a judicial question."[1] Our judiciary forms part of our political process. The instant that judges interpret the law, they become actors in the political arena—policymakers working within a political institution. The most important political force within our judiciary is the United States Supreme Court.

How do courts make policy? Why do the federal courts play such an important role in American government? The answers to these questions lie, in part, in our colonial heritage. Most of American law is based on the English system, particularly the English *common law tradition*. In that tradition, the decisions made by judges constitute an important source of law. We open this chapter with an examination of this tradition and of the various sources of American law. We then look at the federal court system—its organization, how its judges are selected, how these judges affect policy, and how they are restrained by our system of checks and balances.

The Common Law Tradition

In 1066, the Normans conquered England, and William the Conqueror and his successors began the process of unifying the country under their rule. One of the ways they did this was to establish king's courts. Before the conquest, disputes had been settled according to local custom. The king's courts sought to establish a common or uniform set of rules for the whole country. As the number of courts and cases increased, portions of the most important decisions of each year were gathered together and recorded in *Year Books*. Judges settling disputes similar to ones that had been decided before used the *Year Books* as the basis for their decisions. If a case was unique, judges had to create new laws, but they based their decisions on the general principles suggested by earlier cases. The body of judge-made law that developed under this system is still used today and is known as the **common law.**

The practice of deciding new cases with reference to former decisions—that is, according to **precedent**—became a cornerstone of the English and American judicial systems and is embodied in the doctrine of ***stare decisis*** (pronounced *ster-*ay dih-*si-*ses), a Latin phrase that means "to stand on decided cases." The doctrine of *stare decisis* obligates judges to follow the precedents set previously by their own courts or by higher courts that have authority over them.

For example, a lower state court in California would be obligated to follow a precedent set by the California Supreme Court. That lower court, however, would not be obligated to follow a precedent set by the supreme court of another state, because each state court system is independent. Of course, when the United States Supreme Court decides an issue, all of the nation's other courts are obligated to abide by the Court's decision—because the Supreme Court is the highest court in the land.

The doctrine of *stare decisis* provides a basis for judicial decision making in all countries that have common law systems. Today, the United States, Britain, and several dozen other countries have common law systems. Generally, those countries that were once British colonies, such as Australia, Canada, and India, have retained their English common law heritage. An alternative legal system based on Muslim *sharia* is discussed in this chapter's *Beyond Our Borders* feature on the next page.

Common Law
Judge-made law that originated in England from decisions shaped according to prevailing custom. Decisions were applied to similar situations and gradually became common to the nation.

Precedent
A court rule bearing on subsequent legal decisions in similar cases. Judges rely on precedents in deciding cases.

Stare Decisis
To stand on decided cases; the judicial policy of following precedents established by past decisions.

[1]Alexis de Tocqueville, *Democracy in America* (New York: Harper & Row, 1966), p. 248.

BEYOND OUR BORDERS | The Legal System Based on *Sharia*

Hundreds of millions of Muslims throughout the world are governed by a system of law called *sharia*. In this system, religious laws and precepts are combined with practical laws relating to common actions such as entering into contracts and borrowing funds.

THE AUTHORITY OF *SHARIA*

It is said that *sharia*, or Islamic law, is drawn from two major sources and one lesser source. The first major source is, of course, the Qur'an (Koran) and the specific guidelines laid down in it. The second major source, called *sunnah*, is based on the way the Prophet Muhammad lived his life. The lesser source is called *ijma*; it represents the consensus of opinion in the community of Muslims. *Sharia* law is comprehensive in nature. All possible actions of Muslims are divided into five categories.

1. Obligatory.
2. Meritorious.
3. Permissible.
4. Reprehensible.
5. Forbidden.

WHERE *SHARIA* LAW IS APPLIED

The degree to which *sharia* is used varies throughout Muslim societies today. Several of the countries with the largest Muslim populations do not have Islamic law. These include

Bangladesh, India, and Indonesia. Other Muslim countries have dual systems of *sharia* courts and secular courts. Canada, which has a *sharia* arbitration court in Ontario, is the first North American country to establish a *sharia* court.

Some countries maintain religious courts for all aspects of jurisprudence. They include Iran and Saudi Arabia. Recently, Nigeria has reintroduced *sharia* courts.

THE SCOPE OF *SHARIA* LAW

Sharia law covers many aspects of daily life, including the following:

- Dietary rules.
- Relations between married men and women.
- The role of women.
- Holidays.
- Dress codes, particularly for women.
- Speech with respect to the Prophet Muhammad.
- Crimes, including adultery, murder, and theft.
- Business dealings, including borrowing and lending of funds.

FOR CRITICAL ANALYSIS

Based on this brief and incomplete summary of sharia law, what are the major differences between secular law and Islamic law?

Sources of American Law

The body of American law includes the federal and state constitutions, statutes passed by legislative bodies, administrative law, and case law—the legal principles expressed in court decisions.

Constitutions

The constitutions of the federal government and the states set forth the general organization, powers, and limits of government. The U.S. Constitution is the supreme law of the land. A law in violation of the Constitution, no matter what its source, may be declared unconstitutional and thereafter cannot be enforced. Similarly, the state constitutions are supreme within their respective borders (unless they conflict with the U.S. Constitution or federal laws and treaties made in accordance with it). The Constitution thus defines the political playing field on which state and federal powers are reconciled. The idea that the Constitution should be supreme in certain matters stemmed from widespread dissatisfaction with the weak federal government that had existed previously under the Articles of Confederation adopted in 1781.

The courts are sometimes asked to make decisions that have an impact on our federal system. Here, then New York attorney general Eliot Spitzer (now the governor of New York) points to images of the polar ice caps at a press conference. Eight states and New York City have sued the federal government to compel the Environmental Protection Agency (EPA) to revise national regulations governing power plant emissions. Carbon dioxide emissions from these plants are blamed in part for global warming that is melting the polar ice. If states employ the federal courts in an attempt to change national regulations, the courts may find themselves in controversial territory. (EPA/Jason Szenes/Landov)

Statutes and Administrative Regulations

Although the English common law provides the basis for both our civil and criminal legal systems, statutes (laws enacted by legislatures) increasingly have become important in defining the rights and obligations of individuals. Federal statutes may relate to any subject that is a concern of the federal government and may apply to areas ranging from hazardous waste to federal taxation. State statutes include criminal codes, commercial laws, and laws covering a variety of other matters. Cities, counties, and other local political bodies also pass statutes, which are called ordinances. These ordinances may deal with such issues as zoning proposals and public safety. Rules and regulations issued by administrative agencies are another source of law. Today, much of the work of the courts consists of interpreting these laws and regulations and applying them to circumstances in cases before the courts.

Case Law

Because we have a common law tradition, in which the doctrine of *stare decisis* (described under "The Common Law Tradition" above) plays an important role, the decisions rendered by the courts also form an important body of law, collectively referred to as **case law**. Case law includes judicial interpretations of common law principles and doctrines as well as interpretations of the types of law just mentioned—constitutional provisions, statutes, and administrative agency regulations. As you learned in previous chapters, it is up to the courts, and particularly the Supreme Court, to decide what a constitutional provision or a statutory phrase means. In doing so, the courts, in effect, establish law. (We will discuss this policy-making function of the courts in more detail later in the chapter.)

| Case Law
Judicial interpretations of common law principles and doctrines, as well as interpretations of constitutional law, statutory law, and administrative law.

| The Federal Court System

The United States has a dual court system. There are state courts and federal courts. Each of the fifty states, as well as the District of Columbia, has its own independent system of courts. This means that there are fifty-two court systems in total. Here we focus on the federal courts.

Basic Judicial Requirements

In any court system, state or federal, before a case can be brought before a court, certain requirements must be met. Two important requirements are jurisdiction and standing to sue.

|Jurisdiction
The authority of a court to decide certain cases. Not all courts have the authority to decide all cases. Where a case arises and what its subject matter is are two jurisdictional issues.

Jurisdiction. A state court can exercise jurisdiction (the authority of the court to hear and decide a case) over the residents of a particular geographic area, such as a county or district. A state's highest court, or supreme court, has jurisdictional authority over all residents within the state. Because the Constitution established a federal government with limited powers, federal jurisdiction is also limited.

Article III, Section 1, of the U.S. Constitution limits the jurisdiction of the federal courts to cases that involve either a federal question or diversity of citizenship. A federal question arises when a case is based, at least in part, on the U.S. Constitution, a treaty, or a federal law. A person who claims that her or his rights under the Constitution, such as the right to free speech, have been violated could bring a case in a federal court. Diversity of citizenship exists when the parties to a lawsuit are from different states or (more rarely) when the suit involves a U.S. citizen and a government or citizen of a foreign country. The amount in controversy must be at least $75,000 before a federal court can take jurisdiction in a diversity case, however.

|Federal Question
A question that has to do with the U.S. Constitution, acts of Congress, or treaties. A federal question provides a basis for federal jurisdiction.

|Diversity of Citizenship
The condition that exists when the parties to a lawsuit are citizens of different states, or when the parties are citizens of a U.S. state and citizens or the government of a foreign country. Diversity of citizenship can provide a basis for federal jurisdiction.

Standing to Sue. Another basic judicial requirement is standing to sue, or a sufficient "stake" in a matter to justify bringing suit. The party bringing a lawsuit must have suffered a harm, or have been threatened by a harm, as a result of the action that led to the dispute in question. Standing to sue also requires that the controversy at issue be a justiciable controversy. A *justiciable controversy* is a controversy that is real and substantial, as opposed to hypothetical or academic. In other words, a court will not give advisory opinions on hypothetical questions.

Types of Federal Courts

As you can see in Figure 14–1, the federal court system is basically a three-tiered model consisting of (1) U.S. district courts and various specialized courts of limited

FIGURE 14-1 | THE FEDERAL COURT SYSTEM

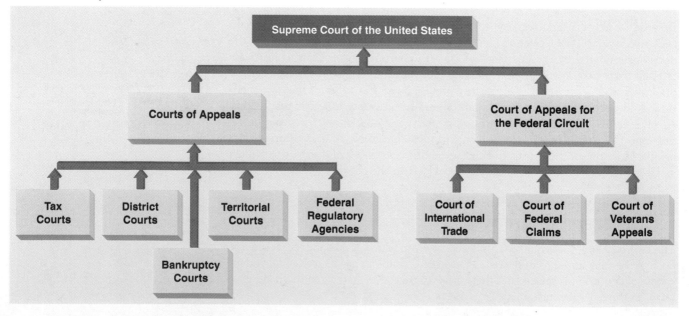

jurisdiction (not all of the latter are shown in the figure), (2) intermediate U.S. courts of appeals, and (3) the United States Supreme Court.

U.S. District Courts. The U.S. district courts are trial courts. A trial court is what the name implies—a court in which trials are held and testimony is taken. The U.S. district courts are courts of general jurisdiction, meaning that they can hear cases involving a broad array of issues. Federal cases involving most matters typically are heard in district courts. The other courts on the lower tier of the model shown in Figure 14–1 are courts of limited jurisdiction, meaning that they can try cases involving only certain types of claims, such as tax claims or bankruptcy petitions.

There is at least one federal district court in every state. The number of judicial districts can vary over time owing to population changes and corresponding case-loads. Currently, there are ninety-four federal judicial districts. A party who is dis-satisfied with the decision of a district court can appeal the case to the appropriate U.S. court of appeals, or federal appellate court. Figure 14–2 shows the jurisdic-tional boundaries of the district courts (which are state boundaries, unless otherwise indicated by dotted lines within a state) and of the U.S. courts of appeals.

U.S. Courts of Appeals. There are thirteen U.S. courts of appeals—also referred to as U.S. circuit courts of appeals. Twelve of these courts, including the U.S. Court of Appeals for the District of Columbia, hear appeals from the federal district courts located within their respective judicial circuits (geographic areas over which they exercise jurisdiction). The Court of Appeals for the Thirteenth Circuit, called the Federal Circuit, has national appellate jurisdiction over certain types of cases, such as cases involving patent law and those in which the U.S. government is a defendant.

| **Trial Court** |
| The court in which most cases begin. |

| **General Jurisdiction** |
| Exists when a court's authority to hear cases is not significantly restricted. A court of general jurisdiction normally can hear a broad range of cases. |

| **Limited Jurisdiction** |
| Exists when a court's authority to hear cases is restricted to certain types of claims, such as tax claims or bankruptcy petitions. |

| **Appellate Court** |
| A court having jurisdiction to review cases and issues that were originally tried in lower courts. |

FIGURE 14–2 | GEOGRAPHIC BOUNDARIES OF FEDERAL DISTRICT COURTS AND CIRCUIT COURTS OF APPEALS

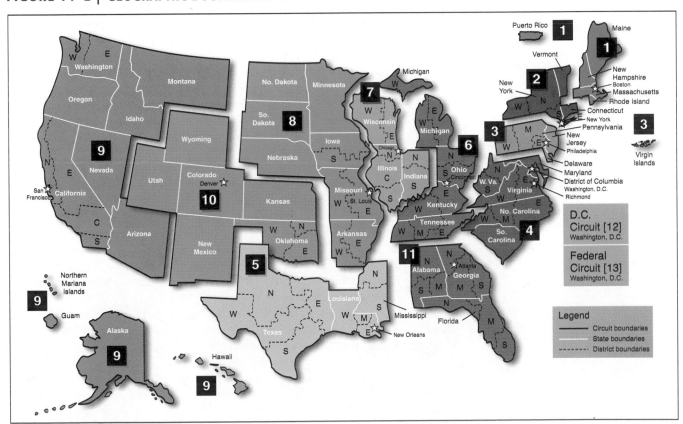

Source: Administrative Office of the United States Courts.

*"Do you ever have one of those days when everything
seems un-Constitutional?"*

Note that when an appellate court reviews a case decided in a district court, the appellate court does not conduct another trial. Rather, a panel of three or more judges reviews the record of the case on appeal, which includes a transcript of the trial proceedings, and determines whether the trial court committed an error. Usually, appellate courts do not look at questions of *fact* (such as whether a party did, in fact, commit a certain action, such as burning a flag) but at questions of *law* (such as whether the act of burning a flag is a form of speech protected by the First Amendment to the Constitution). An appellate court will challenge a trial court's finding of fact only when the finding is clearly contrary to the evidence presented at trial or when there is no evidence to support the finding.

A party can petition the United States Supreme Court to review an appellate court's decision. The likelihood that the Supreme Court will grant the petition is slim, however, because the Court reviews very few of the cases decided by the appellate courts. This means that decisions made by appellate judges usually are final.

The United States Supreme Court.   The highest level of the three-tiered model of the federal court system is the United States Supreme Court. When the Supreme Court came into existence in 1789, it had five justices. In the following years, more justices were added. Since 1869 there have been nine justices on the Court.

According to the language of Article III of the U.S. Constitution, there is only one national Supreme Court. All other courts in the federal system are considered "inferior." Congress is empowered to create other inferior courts as it deems necessary. The inferior courts that Congress has created include the district courts, the federal courts of appeals, and the federal courts of limited jurisdiction.

Although the Supreme Court can exercise original jurisdiction (that is, act as a trial court) in certain cases, such as those affecting foreign diplomats and those in which a state is a party, most of its work is as an appellate court. The Court hears appeals not only from the federal appellate courts but also from the highest state courts. Note, though, that the United States Supreme Court can review a state supreme court decision only if a federal question is involved. Because of its importance in the federal court system, we will look more closely at the Supreme Court starting on page 461.

Specialized Federal Courts and the War on Terrorism

As noted, the federal court system includes a variety of trial courts of limited jurisdiction, dealing with matters such as tax claims or international trade. The government's attempts to combat terrorism have drawn attention to certain specialized courts that meet in secret.

The FISA Court. The federal government created the first secret court in 1978. In that year, Congress passed the Foreign Intelligence Surveillance Act (FISA), which established a court to hear requests for warrants for the surveillance of suspected spies. Officials can request warrants without having to reveal to the suspect or to the public the information used to justify the warrant. The FISA court has approved almost all of the thousands of requests for warrants that the U.S. attorney general's office and other officials have submitted. The seven judges on the FISA court meet in secret, with no published opinions or orders. There is also no public access to the court's proceedings or records. Hence, when the court authorizes surveillance, the majority of the suspects do not even know that they are under scrutiny. Additionally, during the Clinton administration, the court was given the authority to approve physical as well as electronic searches, which means that officials may search a suspect's property without obtaining a warrant in open court and without notifying the subject.

In the aftermath of the terrorist attacks on September 11, 2001, the Bush administration expanded the powers of the FISA court. Previously, the FISA allowed secret domestic surveillance only if the "purpose" was foreign intelligence. Recent amendments to the FISA changed this wording to "a significant purpose"—meaning that warrants may now be requested to obtain evidence that can be used in criminal trials.

Alien "Removal Courts." The FISA court is not the only court in which suspects' rights have been reduced. In response to the Oklahoma City bombing in 1995, Congress passed the Anti-Terrorism and Effective Death Penalty Act of 1996. The act included a provision creating an alien "removal court" to hear evidence against suspected "alien terrorists." The judges rule on whether there is probable cause for deportation. If so, a public deportation proceeding is held in a U.S. district court. The prosecution does not need to follow procedures that normally apply in criminal cases. In addition, the defendant cannot see the evidence that the prosecution used to secure the hearing.

In some cases, the United States Supreme Court has ruled against the Bush administration's efforts to use secret legal proceedings in dealing with suspected terrorists. In 2004, the Supreme Court ruled that enemy combatants who are U.S. citizens and who have been taken prisoner by the United States cannot be denied due process rights. Justice Sandra Day O'Connor wrote that "due process demands that a citizen held in the United States as an enemy combatant be given a meaningful opportunity to contest the factual basis of that detention before a neutral decision maker . . . . A state of war is not a blank check for the president when it comes to the rights of the nation's citizens."[2] The Court also found that noncitizen detainees held at Guantánamo Bay in Cuba were entitled to challenge the grounds for their confinement.[3]

Parties to Lawsuits

In most lawsuits, the parties are the plaintiff (the person or organization that initiates the lawsuit) and the defendant (the person or organization against whom the

---

[2]*Hamdi v. Rumsfeld*, 542 U.S. 507 (2004).
[3]Hamdi was eventually released following a settlement with the government under which he agreed to renounce his U.S. citizenship and return to Saudi Arabia.

| **Litigate**
To engage in a legal proceeding or seek relief in a court of law; to carry on a lawsuit.

| ***Amicus Curiae* Brief**
A brief (a document containing a legal argument supporting a desired outcome in a particular case) filed by a third party, or *amicus curiae* (Latin for "friend of the court"), who is not directly involved in the litigation but who has an interest in the outcome of the case.

| **Class-Action Suit**
A lawsuit filed by an individual seeking damages for "all persons similarly situated."

lawsuit is brought). There may be a number of plaintiffs and defendants in a single lawsuit. In the last several decades, many lawsuits have been brought by interest groups (see Chapter 7). Interest groups play an important role in our judicial system, because they **litigate**—bring to trial—or assist in litigating most cases of racial or gender-based discrimination, virtually all civil liberties cases, and more than one-third of the cases involving business matters. Interest groups also file *amicus curiae* (pronounced ah-*mee*-kous *kur*-ee-eye) **briefs,** or "friend of the court" briefs, in more than 50 percent of these kinds of cases.

Sometimes interest groups or other plaintiffs will bring a **class-action suit,** in which whatever the court decides will affect all members of a class similarly situated (such as users of a particular product manufactured by the defendant in the lawsuit). The strategy of class-action lawsuits was pioneered by such groups as the National Association for the Advancement of Colored People (NAACP), the Legal Defense Fund, and the Sierra Club, whose leaders believed that the courts would offer a more sympathetic forum for their views than would Congress.

Procedural Rules

Both the federal and the state courts have established procedural rules that shape the litigation process. These rules are designed to protect the rights and interests of the parties, to ensure that the litigation proceeds in a fair and orderly manner, and to identify the issues that must be decided by the court—thus saving court time and costs. Court decisions may also apply to trial procedures. For example, the Supreme Court has held that the parties' attorneys cannot discriminate against prospective jurors on the basis of race or gender. Some lower courts have also held that people cannot be excluded from juries because of their sexual orientation or religion.

The parties must comply with procedural rules and with any orders given by the judge during the course of the litigation. When a party does not follow a court's order, the court can cite him or her for contempt. A party who commits *civil* contempt (failing to comply with a court's order for the benefit of another party to the proceeding) can be taken into custody, fined, or both, until the party complies with the court's order. A party who commits *criminal* contempt (obstructing the administration of justice or bringing the court into disrespect) also can be taken into custody and fined but cannot avoid punishment by complying with a previous order.

This criminal trial has a prosecutor, who represents the people. The prosecutor is asking for testimony from an expert witness. Criminal trials require different procedural rules than do other trials. (AP Photo/Charles V. Tines/Pool)

Throughout this text, you have read about how technology is affecting all areas of government. The judiciary is no exception. Today's courts continue to place opinions and other information online. Increasingly, lawyers are expected to file court documents electronically. There is little doubt that in the future we will see more court proceedings being conducted through use of the Internet.

The Supreme Court at Work

The Supreme Court begins its regular annual term on the first Monday in October and usually adjourns in late June or early July of the next year. Special sessions may be held after the regular term ends, but only a few cases are decided in this way. More commonly, cases are carried over until the next regular session.

Of the total number of cases that are decided each year, those reviewed by the Supreme Court represent less than one-half of 1 percent. Included in these, however, are decisions that profoundly affect our lives. In recent years, the United States Supreme Court has decided issues involving capital punishment, affirmative

In her chambers, Justice Ruth Bader Ginsburg works on her caseload with one of her law clerks. Each justice has four law clerks, who typically are culled from the "best and the brightest" graduates from U.S. law schools. Some critics of the Supreme Court's practices argue that the clerks have too much power and influence over the Court's decision making. Would Supreme Court justices be able to decide as many cases as they do now without the help of their clerks? Why or why not? (Paul Conklin/PhotoEdit)

action programs, religious freedom, assisted suicide, abortion, property rights, busing, term limits for congresspersons, sexual harassment, pornography, states' rights, limits on federal jurisdiction, and many other matters with significant consequences for the nation. Because the Supreme Court exercises a great deal of discretion over the types of cases it hears, it can influence the nation's policies by issuing decisions in some types of cases and refusing to hear appeals in others, thereby allowing lower court decisions to stand.

Which Cases Reach the Supreme Court?

Many people are surprised to learn that in a typical case, there is no absolute right of appeal to the United States Supreme Court. The Court's appellate jurisdiction is almost entirely discretionary—the Court can choose which cases it will decide. The justices never explain their reasons for hearing certain cases and not others, so it is difficult to predict which case or type of case the Court might select. Former chief justice William Rehnquist, in his description of the selection process in *The Supreme Court: How It Was, How It Is*,[4] said that the decision of whether to accept a case "strikes me as a rather subjective decision, made up in part of intuition and in part of legal judgment."

Factors That Bear on the Decision.   Factors that bear on the decision include whether a legal question has been decided differently by various lower courts and needs resolution by the highest court, whether a lower court's decision conflicts with an existing Supreme Court ruling, and whether the issue could have significance beyond the parties to the dispute. In its 2006–2007 term, the Court agreed to review a variety of cases of great importance. Questions before the Court included the following: When is a ban on partial birth abortion constitutional? Under what circumstances can a legal immigrant be deported? When can hearsay testimony be used at trial? Is a person owed damages for false arrest? What are the appropriate procedures for presenting a grievance about prison conditions?

Another factor is whether the solicitor general is pressuring the Court to take a case. The solicitor general, a high-ranking presidential appointee within the Justice Department, represents the national government before the Supreme Court and promotes presidential policies in the federal courts. He or she decides what cases the government should ask the Supreme Court to review and what position the government should take in cases before the Court.

Granting Petitions for Review.   If the Court decides to grant a petition for review, it will issue a **writ of *certiorari*** (pronounced sur-shee-uh-*rah*-ree). The writ orders a lower court to send the Supreme Court a record of the case for review. More than 90 percent of the petitions for review are denied. A denial is not a decision on the merits of a case, nor does it indicate agreement with the lower court's opinion. (The judgment of the lower court remains in force, however.) Therefore, denial of the writ has no value as a precedent. The Court will not issue a writ unless at least four justices approve of it. This is called the **rule of four.**[5]

Deciding Cases

Once the Supreme Court grants *certiorari* in a particular case, the justices do extensive research on the legal issues and facts involved in the case. (Of course, some preliminary research is necessary before deciding to grant the petition for review.) Each

| Writ of *Certiorari*
An order issued by a higher court to a lower court to send up the record of a case for review.

| Rule of Four
A United States Supreme Court procedure by which four justices must vote to grant a petition for review if a case is to come before the full court.

---

[4]William H. Rehnquist, *The Supreme Court: How It Was, How It Is* (New York: Morrow, 1987).
[5]The "rule of four" is modified when seven or fewer justices participate, which occurs from time to time. When that happens, as few as three justices can grant *certiorari*.

justice is entitled to four law clerks, who undertake much of the research and preliminary drafting necessary for the justice to form an opinion.[6]

The Court normally does not hear any evidence, as is true with all appeals courts. The Court's consideration of a case is based on the abstracts, the record, and the briefs. The attorneys are permitted to present **oral arguments.** All statements and the justices' questions are tape-recorded during these sessions. Unlike the practice in most courts, lawyers addressing the Supreme Court can be (and often are) questioned by the justices at any time during oral argument.

The justices meet to discuss and vote on cases in conferences held throughout the term. In these conferences, in addition to deciding cases currently before the Court, the justices determine which new petitions for *certiorari* to grant. These conferences take place in the oak-paneled chamber and are strictly private—no stenographers, tape recorders, or video cameras are allowed. Two pages used to be in attendance to wait on the justices while they were in conference, but fear of information leaks caused the Court to stop this practice.[7]

Decisions and Opinions

When the Court has reached a decision, its opinion is written. The **opinion** contains the Court's ruling on the issue or issues presented, the reasons for its decision, the rules of law that apply, and other information. In many cases, the decision of the lower court is **affirmed,** resulting in the enforcement of that court's judgment or decree. If the Supreme Court believes that a reversible error was committed during the trial or that the jury was instructed improperly, however, the decision will be **reversed.** Sometimes the case will be **remanded** (sent back to the court that originally heard the case) for a new trial or other proceeding. For example, a lower court might have held that a party was not entitled to bring a lawsuit under a particular law. If the Supreme Court holds to the contrary, it will remand (send back) the case to the trial court with instructions that the trial go forward.

The Court's written opinion sometimes is unsigned; this is called an opinion *per curiam* ("by the court"). Typically, the Court's opinion is signed by all the justices who agree with it. When in the majority, the chief justice assigns the opinion and often writes it personally. When the chief justice is in the minority, the senior justice on the majority side decides who writes the opinion.

When all justices unanimously agree on an opinion, the opinion is written for the entire Court (all the justices) and can be deemed a **unanimous opinion.** When there is not a unanimous opinion, a **majority opinion** is written, outlining the views of the majority of the justices involved in the case. Often, one or more justices who feel strongly about making or emphasizing a particular point that is not made or emphasized in the unanimous or majority written opinion will write a **concurring opinion.** That means the justice writing the concurring opinion agrees (concurs) with the conclusion given in the majority written opinion, but for different reasons. Finally, in other than unanimous opinions, one or more dissenting opinions are usually written by those justices who do not agree with the majority. The **dissenting opinion** is important because it often forms the basis of the arguments used years later if the Court reverses the previous decision and establishes a new precedent.

Shortly after the opinion is written, the Supreme Court announces its decision from the bench. At that time, the opinion is made available to the public at the office of the clerk of the Court. The clerk also releases the opinion for online publication. Ultimately, the opinion is published in the *United States Reports*, which is the official printed record of the Court's decisions.

Oral Arguments
The verbal arguments presented in person by attorneys to an appellate court. Each attorney presents reasons to the court why the court should rule in her or his client's favor.

Opinion
The statement by a judge or a court of the decision reached in a case. The opinion sets forth the applicable law and details the reasoning on which the ruling was based.

Affirm
To declare that a court ruling is valid and must stand.

Reverse
To annul or make void a court ruling on account of some error or irregularity.

Remand
To send a case back to the court that originally heard it.

Unanimous Opinion
A court opinion or determination on which all judges agree.

Majority Opinion
A court opinion reflecting the views of the majority of the judges.

Concurring Opinion
A separate opinion prepared by a judge who supports the decision of the majority of the court but who wants to make or clarify a particular point or to voice disapproval of the grounds on which the decision was made.

Dissenting Opinion
A separate opinion in which a judge dissents from (disagrees with) the conclusion reached by the majority on the court and expounds his or her own views about the case.

---

[6]For a former Supreme Court law clerk's account of the role these clerks play in the high court's decision-making process, see Edward Lazarus, *Closed Chambers: The First Eyewitness Account of the Epic Struggles inside the Supreme Court* (New York: Times Books, 1998).

[7]It turned out that one supposed information leak came from lawyers making educated guesses.

The Selection of Federal Judges

All federal judges are appointed. The Constitution, in Article II, Section 2, states that the president appoints the justices of the Supreme Court with the advice and consent of the Senate. Congress has provided the same procedure for staffing other federal courts. This means that the Senate and the president jointly decide who shall fill every vacant judicial position, no matter what the level.

There are over 850 federal judgeships in the United States. Once appointed to such a judgeship, a person holds that job for life. Judges serve until they resign, retire voluntarily, or die. Federal judges who engage in blatantly illegal conduct may be removed through impeachment, although such action is rare.

Judicial Appointments

Judicial candidates for federal judgeships are suggested to the president by the Department of Justice, senators, other judges, the candidates themselves, and lawyers' associations and other interest groups. In selecting a candidate to nominate for a judgeship, the president considers not only the person's competence but also other factors, including the person's political philosophy (as will be discussed shortly), ethnicity, and gender.

The nomination process—no matter how the nominees are obtained—always works the same way. The president makes the actual nomination, transmitting the name to the Senate. The Senate then either confirms or rejects the nomination. To reach a conclusion, the Senate Judiciary Committee (operating through subcommittees) invites testimony, both written and oral, at its various hearings. A practice used in the Senate, called senatorial courtesy, is a constraint on the president's freedom to appoint federal district judges. Senatorial courtesy allows a senator of the president's political party to veto a judicial appointment in her or his state. During much of American history, senators from the "opposition" party (the party to which the president did not belong) also enjoyed the right of senatorial courtesy, although their veto power varied over time.

| Senatorial Courtesy
In federal district court judgeship nominations, a tradition allowing a senator to veto a judicial appointment in his or her state.

Republican senators call for an end to a Democratic filibuster. From left to right are senators Kay Bailey Hutchison of Texas, Rick Santorum of Pennsylvania, and Orrin Hatch of Utah. The filibuster blocked a vote on federal appeals court nominee Miguel Estrada, a conservative Hispanic attorney. Should minority-group members support a nominee from their own group even when the nominee's political philosophy might not be shared by most group members? Why or why not? (Brendan McDermid/Reuters/Landov)

Federal District Court Judgeship Nominations. Although the president officially nominates federal judges, in the past the nomination of federal district court judges actually originated with a senator or senators of the president's party from the state in which there was a vacancy. In effect, judicial appointments were a form of political patronage. President Jimmy Carter (1977–1981) ended this tradition by establishing independent commissions to oversee the initial nomination process. President Ronald Reagan (1981–1989) abolished Carter's nominating commissions and established complete presidential control of nominations.

In 2000, Orrin Hatch, Republican chair of the Senate Judiciary Committee, announced that the opposition party (at that point, the Democrats) would no longer be allowed to invoke senatorial courtesy. The implementation of the new policy was delayed when Republican senator James Jeffords of Vermont left the Republican Party. Jeffords's departure turned control of the Senate over to the Democrats. After the 2002 elections, however, when the Republicans regained control of the Senate, they put the new policy into effect.[8]

Federal Courts of Appeals Appointments. Appointments to the federal courts of appeals are far less numerous than federal district court appointments, but they are more important. This is because federal appellate judges handle more important matters, at least from the point of view of the president, and therefore presidents take a keener interest in the nomination process for such judgeships. Also, the U.S. courts of appeals have become "stepping-stones" to the Supreme Court.

Supreme Court Appointments. As we have described, the president nominates Supreme Court justices.[9] As you can see in Table 14–1, which summarizes the background of all Supreme Court justices to 2007, the most common occupational background of the justices at the time of their appointment has been private legal practice or state or federal judgeship. Those nine justices who were in federal executive posts at the time of their appointment held the high offices of secretary of state, comptroller of the treasury, secretary of the navy, postmaster general, secretary of the interior, chairman of the Securities and Exchange Commission, and secretary of labor. In the "Other" category under "Occupational Position before Appointment" in Table 14–1 are two justices who were professors of law (including William H. Taft, a former president) and one justice who was a North Carolina state employee with responsibility for organizing and revising the state's statutes.

The Special Role of the Chief Justice. Although ideology is always important in judicial appointments, as described next, when a chief justice is selected for the Supreme Court, other considerations must also be taken into account. The chief justice is not only the head of a group of nine justices who interpret the law. He or she is also in essence the chief executive officer (CEO) of a large bureaucracy that includes all of the following:

- 1,200 judges with lifetime tenure.
- More than 850 magistrates and bankruptcy judges.
- A staff of 30,000.

The chief justice is also the chair of the Judicial Conference of the United States, a policymaking body that sets priorities for the federal judiciary. That means that the chief justice also indirectly oversees the $5.5 billion budget of this group.

---

[8]John Anthony Maltese, "Anatomy of a Confirmation Mess: Recent Trends in the Federal Judicial Selection Process," April 15, 2004. This article is available as part of a *Jurist* online symposium. Go to **jurist.law.pitt.edu/forum/symposium-jc/index.php**.

[9]For a discussion of the factors that may come into play during the process of nominating Supreme Court justices, see David A. Yalof, *Pursuit of Justices: Presidential Politics and the Selection of Supreme Court Nominees* (Chicago: University of Chicago Press, 1999).

TABLE 14–1 | BACKGROUND OF U.S. SUPREME COURT JUSTICES TO 2007

	NUMBER OF JUSTICES (110 = TOTAL)
Occupational Position before Appointment	
Private legal practice	25
State judgeship	21
Federal judgeship	30
U.S. attorney general	7
Deputy or assistant U.S. attorney general	2
U.S. solicitor general	2
U.S. senator	6
U.S. representative	2
State governor	3
Federal executive post	9
Other	3
Religious Background	
Protestant	83
Roman Catholic	13
Jewish	6
Unitarian	7
No religious affiliation	1
Age on Appointment	
Under 40	5
41–50	32
51–60	59
61–70	14
Political Party Affiliation	
Federalist (to 1835)	13
Jeffersonian Republican (to 1828)	7
Whig (to 1861)	1
Democrat	44
Republican	44
Independent	1
Educational Background	
College graduate	94
Not a college graduate	16
Gender	
Male	108
Female	2
Race	
White	108
African American	2

Sources: Congressional Quarterly, *Congressional Quarterly's Guide to the U.S. Supreme Court* (Washington, D.C.: Congressional Quarterly Press, 1996); and authors' update.

Finally, the chief justice appoints the director of the Administrative Office of the United States Courts. The chief justice and this director select judges who sit on judicial committees that examine international judicial relations, technology, and a variety of other topics

Partisanship and Judicial Appointments

Ideology plays an important role in the president's choices for judicial appointments. In most circumstances, the president appoints judges or justices who belong to the president's own political party. Presidents see their federal judiciary appointments as the one sure way to institutionalize their political views long after they have left office. By 1993, for example, Presidents Ronald Reagan and George H. W. Bush together had appointed nearly three-quarters of all federal court judges. This preponderance of Republican-appointed federal judges strengthened the legal moorings of the conservative social agenda on a variety of issues, ranging from abortion to civil rights. Nevertheless, President Bill Clinton had the opportunity to appoint about two hundred federal judges, thereby shifting the ideological make-up of the federal judiciary.

During the first two years of his second term, President George W. Bush was able to nominate two relatively conservative justices to the Supreme Court—John Roberts, who became chief justice, and Samuel Alito. Both are Catholics and have relatively, but not consistently, conservative views. In fact, during his first term as chief justice, Roberts voted most of the time with the Court's most conservative justices, Antonin Scalia and Clarence Thomas. Nonetheless, Roberts and Alito may not cause the Supreme Court to "tilt to the right" as much as some people anticipated. The reason is that the two newest Supreme Court members replaced justices who were moderate to conservative. Thus, the make-up of the Court did not necessarily change.

Interestingly, some previous conservative justices have shown a tendency to "migrate" to a more liberal view of the law. Sandra Day O'Connor, the first female justice and a conservative, gradually shifted to the left on a number of issues, including abortion. In 1981, during her confirmation hearing before the Senate Judiciary Committee, she said, "I am opposed to it [abortion], as a matter of birth control or otherwise." By 1992, she was part of a five-to-four majority that agreed that the Constitution protects a woman's right to an abortion.

Chief Justice John G. Roberts, Jr. is sworn in as the seventeenth head of the United States Supreme Court on September 29, 2005. This ceremony took place in the East Room of the White House. Why have there been so few chief justices?
(White House Photo by Paul Morse)

Supreme Court nominees must "make the rounds" throughout the Senate to discuss their legal philosophies, among other things, with, at a minimum, the important members of that chamber. In 2005, nominee Samuel Alito met with Senator Mary Landrieu of Louisiana. Why don't nominees spend much, if any, time in the House of Representatives? (Photo Courtesy of Senator Landrieu)

The Senate's Role

Ideology also plays a large role in the Senate's confirmation hearings, and presidential nominees to the Supreme Court have not always been confirmed. In fact, almost 20 percent of presidential nominations to the Supreme Court have been either rejected or not acted on by the Senate. There have been many acrimonious battles over Supreme Court appointments when the Senate and the president have not seen eye to eye about political matters.

The U.S. Senate had a long record of refusing to confirm the president's judicial nominations from the beginning of Andrew Jackson's presidency in 1829 to the end of Ulysses Grant's presidency in 1877. From 1894 until 1968, however, only three nominees were not confirmed. Then, from 1968 through 1987, four presidential nominees to the highest court were rejected. One of the most controversial Supreme Court nominations was that of Clarence Thomas, who underwent an extremely volatile confirmation hearing in 1991, replete with charges against him of sexual harassment. He was ultimately confirmed by the Senate, however.

President Bill Clinton had little trouble gaining approval for both of his nominees to the Supreme Court: Ruth Bader Ginsburg and Stephen Breyer. President George W. Bush's nominees faced hostile grilling in their confirmation hearings, and various interest groups mounted intense media ad blitzes against them. Indeed, Bush had to forgo one of his nominees, Harriet Miers, when he realized that he could not win the confirmation battle. Both Clinton and Bush had trouble securing Senate approval for their judicial nominations to the lower courts. In fact, during the late 1990s and early 2000s, the duel between the Senate and the president aroused considerable concern about the consequences of the increasingly partisan and ideological tension over federal judicial appointments. As a result of Senate delays in confirming nominations, the number of judicial vacancies mounted, as did the backlog of cases pending in the federal courts. Especially given the backlog of judicial appointments, is it appropriate for senators to consider purely political questions when voting on a judicial nominee? We look at this question in this chapter's *Which Side Are You On?* feature on the following page.

WHICH SIDE ARE YOU ON? | Is the Process of Confirming Judicial Nominees Too Political?

On a number of occasions, presidents have appointed federal judges using a temporary "recess appointment." This procedure is always used for the same reason—to avoid the continuation of an acrimonious and perhaps futile Senate confirmation process. Although the confirmation hearings on Supreme Court nominees get all of the media attention, the hearings on nominees for the lower federal courts are equally bitter, leading some to ask whether the politicization of the confirmation process has gone too far.

According to Fifth Circuit Court Judge Edith Jones, judicial nominations have turned into battlegrounds because so many federal judges now view the courts as agents of social change. Jones argues that when judge-made law (as opposed to legislature-made law) enters into sensitive topics, it provokes a political reaction.

JUDICIAL CONFIRMATIONS HAVE BECOME TOO POLITICAL

Since 1987, when the Senate refused to confirm the appointment of Robert Bork to the Supreme Court, serious battles over judicial nominees have become commonplace. Those who believe that the confirmation process has become too political claim that these attempts to block nominees are based on a doctrine of "payback"—making trouble for one party's nominees because that party made trouble for your nominees in the past. Instead, nominees should be assessed on the basis of their qualifications alone. The ideology of a judge should not matter, because judges should base their rulings on the law, not their personal preferences.

POLITICS CANNOT BE AVOIDED

Others say that the system is working as it should. Politics have played a role in selecting judges since the administration of George Washington. Most nominees are confirmed without dispute. As of 2006, the vacancy rate on the federal bench was at its lowest point in fifteen years. Those nominees who run into trouble are usually the most conservative Republican nominees or the most liberal Democratic ones. It is legitimate

Senator Barbara Boxer (D., Calif.) speaks during a thirty-hour filibuster on President George W. Bush's judicial nominees. Next to Boxer is a chart claiming that the Democrats were blocking fewer Bush nominees than the Republicans had blocked when Bill Clinton was president. (AP Photo/APTN)

to evaluate a candidate's judicial ideology when that ideology is strongly held and likely to influence the judge's rulings.

WHAT'S YOUR POSITION?

If it is impossible to eliminate politics completely from the confirmation process, in what ways can the effects of politics be minimized?

GOING ONLINE

You can find an online symposium on the judicial confirmation process at the *Jurist* Web site. Go to **jurist.law.pitt.edu/forum/symposium-jc/index.php**. *Jurist* is a gateway to legal instruction, information, and scholarship. It is edited by a team of professors from law schools across the United States and around the world. *Jurist* is hosted by the University of Pittsburgh.

Policymaking and the Courts

The partisan battles over judicial appointments reflect an important reality in today's American government: the importance of the judiciary in national politics. Because appointments to the federal bench are for life, the ideology of judicial appointees can affect national policy for years to come. Although the primary function of judges in our system of government is to interpret and apply the laws, inevitably judges make policy when carrying out this task. One of the major policymaking tools of the federal courts is their power of judicial review.

Judicial Review

Remember from Chapter 2 that the power of the courts to determine whether a law or action by the other branches of government is constitutional is known as the power of *judicial review*. This power enables the judicial branch to act as a check on the other two branches of government, in line with the system of checks and balances established by the U.S. Constitution.

The power of judicial review is not mentioned in the Constitution, however. Rather, it was established by the United States Supreme Court's decision in *Marbury v. Madison*.[10] In that case, in which the Court declared that a law passed by Congress violated the Constitution, the Court claimed such a power for the judiciary:

> It is emphatically the province and duty of the Judicial Department to say what the law is. Those who apply the rule to a particular case must of necessity expound and interpret that rule. If two laws conflict with each other, the courts must decide on the operation of each.

If a federal court declares that a federal or state law or policy is unconstitutional, the court's decision affects the application of the law or policy only within that court's jurisdiction. For this reason, the higher the level of the court, the greater the impact of the decision on society. Because of the Supreme Court's national jurisdiction, its decisions have the greatest impact. For example, when the Supreme Court held that an Arkansas state constitutional amendment limiting the terms of congresspersons was unconstitutional, laws establishing term limits in twenty-three other states were also invalidated.[11]

Some claim that the power of judicial review gives unelected judges and justices on federal court benches too much influence over national policy. Others argue that the powers exercised by the federal courts, particularly the power of judicial review, are necessary to protect our constitutional rights and liberties. Built into our federal form of government is a system of checks and balances. If the federal courts did not have the power of judicial review, there would be no governmental body to check Congress's lawmaking authority.

Judicial Activism and Judicial Restraint

Judicial scholars like to characterize different judges and justices as being either "activist" or "restraintist." The doctrine of **judicial activism** rests on the conviction that the federal judiciary should take an active role by using its powers to check the activities of Congress, state legislatures, and administrative agencies when those governmental bodies exceed their authority. One of the Supreme Court's most activist eras was the period from 1953 to 1969, when the Court was headed by Chief Justice Earl Warren. The Warren Court propelled the civil rights movement forward by holding, among other things, that laws permitting racial segregation violated the equal protection clause.

In contrast, the doctrine of **judicial restraint** rests on the assumption that the courts should defer to the decisions made by the legislative and executive branches, because members of Congress and the president are elected by the people whereas members of the federal judiciary are not. Because administrative agency personnel normally have more expertise than the courts do in the areas regulated by the agencies, the courts likewise should defer to agency rules and decisions. In other words, under the doctrine of judicial restraint, the courts should not thwart the implementation of legislative acts and agency rules unless they are clearly unconstitutional.

Judicial activism sometimes is linked with liberalism, and judicial restraint with conservatism. In fact, though, a conservative judge can be activist, just as a liberal

Judicial Activism
A doctrine holding that the Supreme Court should take an active role by using its powers to check the activities of governmental bodies when those bodies exceed their authority.

Judicial Restraint
A doctrine holding that the Supreme Court should defer to the decisions made by the elected representatives of the people in the legislative and executive branches.

---

[10]5 U.S. 137 (1803).
[11]*U.S. Term Limits v. Thornton*, 514 U.S. 779 (1995).

judge can be restraintist. In the 1950s and 1960s, the Supreme Court was activist and liberal. Some observers believe that the Rehnquist Court, with its conservative majority, became increasingly activist during the early 2000s. Some go even further and claim that the federal courts, including the Supreme Court, wield too much power in our democracy.

Strict versus Broad Construction

| Strict Construction
A judicial philosophy that looks to the "letter of the law" when interpreting the Constitution or a particular statute.

| Broad Construction
A judicial philosophy that looks to the context and purpose of a law when making an interpretation.

Other terms that are often used to describe a justice's philosophy are *strict construction* and *broad construction*. Justices who believe in **strict construction** look to the "letter of the law" when they attempt to interpret the Constitution or a particular statute. Those who favor **broad construction** try to determine the context and purpose of the law.

As with the doctrines of judicial restraint and judicial activism, strict construction is often associated with conservative political views, whereas broad construction is often linked with liberalism. These traditional political associations sometimes appear to be reversed, however. Consider the Eleventh Amendment to the Constitution, which rules out lawsuits in federal courts "against one of the United States by Citizens of another State, or by Citizens or Subjects of any Foreign State." Nothing is said about citizens suing their *own* states, and strict construction would therefore find such suits to be constitutional. Conservative justices, however, have construed this amendment broadly to deny citizens the constitutional right to sue their own states in most circumstances. John T. Noonan, Jr., a federal appellate court judge who was appointed by a Republican president, has described these rulings as "adventurous."[12]

Broad construction is often associated with the concept of a "living constitution." Supreme Court Justice Antonin Scalia has said that "the Constitution is not a living organism, it is a legal document. It says something and doesn't say other things." Scalia believes that jurists should stick to the plain text of the Constitution "as it was originally written and intended."

Ideology and the Rehnquist Court

William H. Rehnquist became the sixteenth chief justice of the Supreme Court in 1986, after fifteen years as an associate justice. He was known as a strong anchor of the Court's conservative wing until his death in 2005. With Rehnquist's appointment as chief justice, it seemed to observers that the Court would necessarily become more conservative.

Indeed, that is what happened. The Court began to take a rightward shift shortly after Rehnquist became chief justice, and the Court's rightward movement continued as other conservative appointments to the bench were made during the Reagan and George H. W. Bush administrations. During the late 1990s and early 2000s, three of the justices (William Rehnquist, Antonin Scalia, and Clarence Thomas) were notably conservative in their views. Four of the justices (John Paul Stevens, David Souter, Ruth Bader Ginsburg, and Stephen Breyer) held liberal-to-moderate views. The middle of the Court was occupied by two moderate-to-conservative justices, Sandra Day O'Connor and Anthony Kennedy. O'Connor and Kennedy usually provided the "swing votes" on the Court in controversial cases. The ideological alignments on the Court varied, however, depending on the issues involved in particular cases.

Certainly, today's Supreme Court has moved far from the liberal positions taken by the Court under Earl Warren (1953–1969) and under Warren Burger

---

[12]John T. Noonan, Jr., *Narrowing the Nation's Power: The Supreme Court Sides with the States* (Berkeley: University of California Press, 2002).

FIGURE 14-3 | THE ROBERTS COURT

The members of the United States Supreme Court as of 2007.

(1969–1986). Since the mid-1990s, the Court has issued many conservative rulings, some of which you have already read about in this text. It is premature to know whether the Roberts Court (see Figure 14–3) will remain conservative, although there are some early indications that it might.

Federalism. Several of these rulings reflect a conservative approach to constitutional law that emphasizes states' rights. For example, in 1995 the Court curbed—for the first time in sixty years—the national government's constitutional power under the commerce clause to regulate intrastate activities. The Court held that a federal law regulating the possession of guns in school zones had nothing to do with interstate commerce, and therefore Congress had overreached its powers by attempting to regulate this activity.[13] In 2000, the Court held that Congress had overreached its authority under the commerce clause when it included a federal remedy for gender-motivated violence, such as rape or stalking, in the Federal Violence against Women Act of 1994. The Court concluded that the effect of such violence on interstate commerce was not sufficient to justify national regulation of noneconomic, violent criminal conduct.[14]

Although some observers have feared that the Court's decisions on states' rights would threaten the federal structure of the nation, recent decisions tell a different

---

[13]*United States v. Lopez*, 514 U.S. 549 (1995).
[14]*United States v. Morrison*, 529 U.S. 598 (2000).

story. For example, some states have passed medical marijuana laws that allow certain sick persons to obtain this drug legally. These laws go squarely against federal legislation. In a 2005 case, the Court ruled that Congress's power to regulate interstate commerce allowed it to ban marijuana use even when state law permits such use and the growing and use of the drug are strictly local in nature.[15]

Similarly, in view of the Court's support for states' rights, many scholars were surprised when the Court involved itself in the dispute over the manual recounting of the Florida votes after the 2000 elections. Nonetheless, in a historic decision, the Court reversed the Florida Supreme Court's order to manually recount the votes in selected Florida counties—a decision that effectively handed the presidency to George W. Bush.[16]

Civil Rights. In civil rights cases, the Rehnquist Court's generally conservative (strict) interpretation of the Constitution had mixed results. In one decision, the Court refused to extend the constitutional right to privacy to include the right of terminally ill persons to end their lives through physician-assisted suicide. Therefore, a state law banning this practice did not violate the Constitution.[17] (Essentially, the Court left it up to the states to decide whether to ban—or to permit—assisted suicide; to date, only one state, Oregon, has passed a law permitting the practice.) In another decision, the Court held that a federal statute expanding religious liberties was an unconstitutional attempt by Congress to rewrite the Constitution.[18]

A series of cases decided by the Court in 2003 had a major impact on civil rights issues. In two cases involving the University of Michigan, the Court held that limited affirmative action plans in pursuit of diversity were constitutional.[19] In a Texas case, the Court ruled that laws against homosexual conduct violate the due process clause of the Fourteenth Amendment.[20]

---

[15]*Gonzales v. Raich*, 545 U.S. 1 (2005).
[16]*Bush v. Gore*, 531 U.S. 98 (2000).
[17]*Washington v. Glucksberg*, 521 U.S. 702 (1997).
[18]*City of Boerne v. Flores*, 521 U.S. 507 (1997).
[19]*Gratz v. Bollinger*, 539 U.S. 244 (2003); and *Grutter v. Bollinger*, 539 U.S. 306 (2003).
[20]*Lawrence v. Texas*, 539 U.S. 558 (2003).

University of Michigan law students attend a rally outside the United States Supreme Court building to defend the university's affirmative action programs. In 2003, the Court ruled that the affirmative action plan used to select law students was constitutional, but the plan used to choose undergraduates was not. What might happen if all affirmative action programs were ruled unconstitutional? (Alex Wong/Getty Images)

The Roberts Court. As noted before, it is probably too early to talk in terms of a "Roberts Court." During John Roberts's first term (2005–2006) as chief justice, the Court ruled on several important issues, but no clear pattern was discernible in the decisions. Under Roberts, the Court ruled in 2006 that the due process clause of the Constitution does not prohibit Arizona's use of an insanity test stated solely in terms of the accused's capacity to tell whether an act charged as a crime was right or wrong. In the same year, the Court held that federal courts can assess the procedures used in military tribunals when the accused is not a member of the military. With respect to capital punishment, the Roberts Court ruled that the capital sentencing statute in Kansas was constitutional.

What Checks Our Courts?

Our judicial system is one of the most independent in the world. But the courts do not have absolute independence, for they are part of the political process. Political checks limit the extent to which courts can exercise judicial review and engage in an activist policy. These checks are exercised by the executive branch, the legislature, the public, and, finally, the judiciary itself.

Executive Checks

President Andrew Jackson was once supposed to have said, after Chief Justice John Marshall made an unpopular decision, "John Marshall has made his decision; now let him enforce it."[21] This purported remark goes to the heart of **judicial implementation**—the enforcement of judicial decisions in such a way that those decisions are translated into policy. The Supreme Court simply does not have any enforcement powers, and whether a decision will be implemented depends on the cooperation of the other two branches of government. Rarely, though, will a president refuse to enforce a Supreme Court decision, as President Jackson did. To take such an action could mean a significant loss of public support because of the Supreme Court's stature in the eyes of the nation.

| **Judicial Implementation**
The way in which court decisions are translated into action.

More commonly, presidents exercise influence over the judiciary by appointing new judges and justices as federal judicial seats become vacant. Additionally, as mentioned earlier, the U.S. solicitor general plays a significant role in the federal court system, and the person holding this office is a presidential appointee.

Executives at the state level may also refuse to implement court decisions with which they disagree. A notable example of such a refusal occurred in Arkansas after the Supreme Court ordered schools to desegregate "with all deliberate speed" in 1955.[22] Arkansas governor Orval Faubus refused to cooperate with the decision and used the state's National Guard to block the integration of Central High School in Little Rock. Ultimately, President Dwight Eisenhower had to federalize the Arkansas National Guard and send federal troops to Little Rock to quell the violence that had erupted.

Legislative Checks

Courts may make rulings, but often the legislatures at local, state, and federal levels are required to appropriate funds to carry out the courts' rulings. A court, for example, may decide that prison conditions must be improved, but it is up to the legislature to

---

[21]The decision referred to was *Cherokee Nation v. Georgia*, 30 U.S. 1 (1831).
[22]*Brown v. Board of Education*, 349 U.S. 294 (1955)—the second *Brown* decision.

authorize the funds necessary to carry out the ruling. When such funds are not appropriated, the court that made the ruling, in effect, has been checked.

Constitutional Amendments. Courts' rulings can be overturned by constitutional amendments at both the federal and state levels. Many of the amendments to the U.S. Constitution (such as the Fourteenth, Fifteenth, and Twenty-sixth Amendments) check the state courts' ability to allow discrimination, for example. Proposed constitutional amendments that were created in an effort to reverse courts' decisions on school prayer and abortion have failed.

Rewriting Laws. Finally, Congress or a state legislature can rewrite (amend) old laws or enact new ones to overturn a court's rulings if the legislature concludes that the court is interpreting laws or legislative intentions erroneously. For example, Congress passed the Civil Rights Act of 1991 in part to overturn a series of conservative rulings in employment-discrimination cases. In 1993, Congress enacted the Religious Freedom Restoration Act (RFRA), which broadened religious liberties, after Congress concluded that a 1990 Supreme Court ruling restricted religious freedom to an unacceptable extent.[23]

According to political scientist Walter Murphy, "A permanent feature of our constitutional landscape is the ongoing tug and pull between elected government and the courts."[24] Certainly, over the last few decades the Supreme Court has been in conflict with the other two branches of government. Congress at various times has passed laws that, among other things, made it illegal to burn the American flag and attempted to curb pornography on the Internet. In each instance, the Supreme Court ruled that those laws were unconstitutional. The Court also invalidated the RFRA, described above.

Whenever Congress does not like what the judiciary does, it threatens to censure the judiciary for its "activism." One member of the Senate Judiciary Committee, John Cornyn (R., Tex.), claimed that judges are making "political decisions yet are unaccountable to the public." He went on to say that violence against judges in the courtroom can be explained by the public's distress at such activism.

The states can also negate or alter the effects of Supreme Court rulings, when such decisions allow it. A good case in point is *Kelo v. City of New London*.[25] In that case, the Supreme Court allowed a city to take private property for redevelopment by private businesses. Since that case was decided, a majority of states have passed legislation limiting or prohibiting such takings.

Public Opinion

Public opinion plays a significant role in shaping government policy, and certainly the judiciary is not excepted from this rule. For one thing, persons affected by a Supreme Court decision that is noticeably at odds with their views may simply ignore it. Officially sponsored prayers were banned in public schools in 1962, yet it was widely known that the ban was (and still is) ignored in many southern districts. What can the courts do in this situation? Unless someone complains about the prayers and initiates a lawsuit, the courts can do nothing.

The public can also pressure state and local government officials to refuse to enforce a certain decision. As already mentioned, judicial implementation requires

---

[23]*Employment Division, Department of Human Resources of Oregon v. Smith*, 494 U.S. 872 (1990).
[24]As quoted in Neal Devins, "The Last Word Debate: How Social and Political Forces Shape Constitutional Values," *American Bar Association Journal*, October 1997, p. 48.
[25]545 U.S. 469 (2005).

the cooperation of government officials at all levels, and public opinion in various regions of the country will influence whether such cooperation is forthcoming.

Additionally, the courts themselves necessarily are influenced by public opinion to some extent. After all, judges are not "islands" in our society; their attitudes are influenced by social trends, just as the attitudes and beliefs of all persons are. Courts generally tend to avoid issuing decisions that they know will be noticeably at odds with public opinion.[26] In part, this is because the judiciary, as a branch of the government, prefers to avoid creating divisiveness among the public. Also, a court—particularly the Supreme Court—may lose stature if it decides a case in a way that markedly diverges from public opinion. For example, in 2002 the Supreme Court ruled that the execution of mentally retarded criminals violates the Eighth Amendment's ban on cruel and unusual punishment. In its ruling, the Court indicated that the standards of what constitutes cruel and unusual punishment are influenced by public opinion and that there is "powerful evidence that today our society views mentally retarded offenders as categorically less culpable than the average criminal."[27]

In any event, public opinion in most recent years appears to support a judiciary that makes decisions based more on Christian values.[28] When Justice Sandra Day O'Connor announced her retirement from the Supreme Court, almost 50 percent of Americans surveyed in a Gallup poll said that the choice of a new Supreme Court justice mattered a great deal to them.[29] Those most concerned about the philosophy of a new Supreme Court justice attended church weekly.

Judicial Traditions and Doctrines

Supreme Court justices (and other federal judges) typically exercise self-restraint in fashioning their decisions. In part, this restraint stems from their knowledge that the other two branches of government and the public can exercise checks on the judiciary, as previously discussed. To a large extent, however, this restraint is mandated by various judicially established traditions and doctrines. For example, in exercising its discretion to hear appeals, the Supreme Court will not hear a meritless appeal just so it can rule on the issue. Also, when reviewing a case, the Supreme Court typically narrows its focus to just one issue or one aspect of an issue involved in the case. The Court rarely makes broad, sweeping decisions on issues. Furthermore, the doctrine of *stare decisis* acts as a restraint because it obligates the courts, including the Supreme Court, to follow established precedents when deciding cases. Only rarely will courts overrule a precedent.

Hypothetical and Political Questions. Other judicial doctrines and practices also act as restraints. As already mentioned, the courts will hear only what are called justiciable disputes—disputes that arise out of actual cases. In other words, a court will not hear a case that involves a merely hypothetical issue. Additionally, if a political question is involved, the Supreme Court often will exercise judicial restraint and refuse to rule on the matter. A **political question** is one that the Supreme Court declares should be decided by the elected branches of government—the executive branch, the legislative branch, or those two branches acting together. For example, the Supreme Court has refused to rule on the controversy regarding the rights of gay

| Political Question
An issue that a court believes should be decided by the executive or legislative branch.

---

[26]One striking counterexample is the *Kelo v. City of New London* decision mentioned earlier.

[27]*Atkins v. Virginia*, 536 U.S. 304 (2002).

[28]"Americans Judge Their Judiciary: Plurality Thinks Christian Values Aren't Considered Enough," Gallup poll, July 12, 2005.

[29]"Choosing a New Supreme Court Justice," Gallup poll, January 6, 2005.

men and lesbians in the military, preferring instead to defer to the executive branch's decisions on the matter. Generally, fewer questions are deemed political questions by the Supreme Court today than in the past.

The Impact of the Lower Courts. Higher courts can reverse the decisions of lower courts. Lower courts can act as a check on higher courts, too. Lower courts can ignore—and have ignored—Supreme Court decisions. Usually, this is done indirectly. A lower court might conclude, for example, that the precedent set by the Supreme Court does not apply to the exact circumstances in the case before the court; or the lower court may decide that the Supreme Court's decision was ambiguous with respect to the issue before the lower court. The fact that the Supreme Court rarely makes broad and clear-cut statements on any issue makes it easier for the lower courts to interpret the Supreme Court's decisions in a different way.

MAKING A DIFFERENCE | Changing the Legal System

The U.S. legal system may seem too complex to be influenced by one individual, but its power nonetheless depends on the support of individuals. The public has many ways of resisting, modifying, or overturning statutes and rulings of the courts.

Why Should You Care?

Legislative bodies may make laws and ordinances, but legislation is given its practical form by court rulings. Therefore, if you care about the effects of a particular law, you may have to pay attention to how the courts are interpreting it. For example, do you believe that sentences handed down for certain crimes are too lenient—or too strict? Legislative bodies can attempt to establish sentences for various offenses, but the courts inevitably retain considerable flexibility in determining what happens in any particular case.

What Can You Do?

Public opinion can have an effect on judicial policies. One example of the

kind of pressure that can be exerted on the legal system began with a tragedy. In 1980, thirteen-year-old Cari Lightner was hit from behind and killed by a drunk driver while she was walking in a bicycle lane. The driver was a forty-seven-year-old man with two prior drunk-driving convictions. He was at that time out on bail after a third arrest. Cari's mother, Candy, quit her job as a real estate agent to form Mothers Against Drunk Driving (MADD) and launched a campaign to stiffen penalties for drunk-driving convictions.

The organization now has three million members and supporters. Outraged by the thousands of lives lost every year because of drunk driving, the group seeks stiff penalties against drunk drivers. MADD, by becoming involved, has gotten results. Owing to its efforts and the efforts of other citizen-activist groups, many states have responded with stiffer penalties and deterrents. If you feel strongly about this issue and want to get involved, contact:

MADD
P.O. Box 541688
Dallas, TX 75354-1688
1-800-GET-MADD
www.madd.org

If you want information about the Supreme Court, contact the following by telephone or letter:

Clerk of the Court
The Supreme Court of the United States
1 First St., N.E.
Washington, DC 20543
202-479-3000

You can access online information about the Supreme Court at the following site:

www.oyez.org/oyez/frontpage

Key Terms

Chapter Summary

1 American law is rooted in the common law tradition, which is part of our heritage from England. The common law doctrine of *stare decisis* (which means "to stand on decided cases") obligates judges to follow precedents established previously by their own courts or by higher courts that have authority over them. Precedents established by the United States Supreme Court, the highest court in the land, are binding on all lower courts. Fundamental sources of American law include the U.S. Constitution and state constitutions, statutes enacted by legislative bodies, regulations issued by administrative agencies, and case law.

2 Article III, Section 1, of the U.S. Constitution limits the jurisdiction of the federal courts to cases involving (a) a federal question, which is a question based, at least in part, on the U.S. Constitution, a treaty, or a federal law; or (b) diversity of citizenship—which arises when parties to a lawsuit are from different states or when the lawsuit involves a foreign citizen or government. The federal court system is a three-tiered model consisting of (a) U.S. district (trial) courts and various lower courts of limited jurisdiction; (b) U.S. courts of appeals; and (c) the United States Supreme Court. Cases may be appealed from the district courts to the appellate courts. In most cases, the decisions of the federal appellate courts are final because the Supreme Court hears relatively few cases.

3 The Supreme Court's decision to review a case is influenced by many factors, including the significance of the issues involved and whether the solicitor general is pressing the Court to take the case. After a case is accepted, the justices undertake research (with the help of their law clerks) on the issues involved in the case, hear oral arguments from the parties, meet in conference to discuss and vote on the issue, and announce the opinion, which is then released for publication.

4 Federal judges are nominated by the president and confirmed by the Senate. Once appointed, they hold office for life, barring gross misconduct. The nomination and confirmation process, particularly for Supreme Court justices, is often extremely politicized. Democrats and Republicans alike realize that justices may occupy seats on the Court for decades and naturally want to have persons appointed who share their basic views. Nearly 20 percent of all Supreme Court appointments have been either rejected or not acted on by the Senate.

5 In interpreting and applying the law, judges inevitably become policymakers. The most important policymaking tool of the federal courts is the power of judicial review. This power was not mentioned specifically in the Constitution, but John Marshall claimed the power for the Court in his 1803 decision in *Marbury v. Madison*.

6 Judges who take an active role in checking the activities of the other branches of government sometimes are characterized as "activist" judges, and judges who defer to the other branches' decisions sometimes are regarded as "restraintist" judges. The Warren Court of the 1950s and 1960s was activist in a liberal direction, whereas the Rehnquist Court became increasingly activist in a conservative direction. Several politicians and scholars argue that judicial activism has gotten out of hand. It is too early to know what direction the Roberts Court will take.

7 Checks on the powers of the federal courts include executive checks, legislative checks, public opinion, and judicial traditions and doctrines.

Selected Print and Media Resources

SUGGESTED READINGS

Baird, Vanessa. *Answering the Call of the Court: How Justices and Litigants Set the Supreme Court Agenda*. Charlottesville, Va.: University of Virginia Press, 2006. The author attempts to relate the justices' political and philosophical priorities to the way the Court's agenda has expanded in recent years. This is one of the first studies of the Court's agenda-setting process.

Foskett, Ken. *Judging Thomas: The Life and Times of Clarence Thomas*. New York: William Morrow, 2004. Foskett, an Atlanta journalist, delves into the intellectual development of Justice Thomas, one of the nation's most prominent African American conservatives.

Klarman, Michael J. *From Jim Crow to Civil Rights: The Supreme Court and the Struggle for Racial Equality*. New York: Oxford University Press, 2004. Klarman, a professor of constitutional law, provides a detailed history of the Supreme Court's changing attitudes toward equality. Klarman argues that the civil rights movement would have revolutionized the status of African Americans even if the Court had not outlawed segregation.

O'Connor, Sandra Day. *The Majesty of the Law: Reflections of a Supreme Court Justice*. New York: Random House, 2003. As the Supreme Court's most prominent swing vote during her years on the bench, Justice O'Connor may have been the most powerful member of that body. O'Connor gives a basic introduction to the Court, reflects on past discrimination against women in the law, tells amusing stories about fellow justices, and calls for improving the treatment of jury members.

Raskin, Jamin B. *We the Students: Supreme Court Cases for and about Students*, 2d ed. Washington, D.C.: CQ Press, 2003. This book explores, in an interactive format, a number of cases reviewed by the Supreme Court on issues of high interest to students.

Zimmerman, Joseph F. *Interstate Disputes: The Supreme Court's Original Jurisdiction*. Buffalo, N.Y.: State University of New York, 2006. This well-researched study examines the role of the Court in settling disputes between the states. The author concludes that states should enter into more interstate compacts rather than taking their disputes to the Supreme Court.

MEDIA RESOURCES

Amistad—A 1997 movie, starring Anthony Hopkins, about a slave ship mutiny in 1839. Much of the story revolves around the prosecution, ending at the Supreme Court, of the slave who led the revolt.

Court TV—This TV channel covers high-profile trials, including those of O. J. Simpson, the Unabomber, British nanny Louise Woodward, and Timothy McVeigh. (You can learn how to access Court TV from your area at its Web site—see the *Logging On* section in this chapter's *E-mocracy* feature for its URL.)

Gideon's Trumpet—A 1980 film, starring Henry Fonda as the small-time criminal James Earl Gideon, which makes clear the path a case takes to the Supreme Court and the importance of cases decided there.

Justice Sandra Day O'Connor—In a 1994 program, Bill Moyers conducts Justice O'Connor's first television interview. Topics include women's rights, O'Connor's role as the Supreme Court's first female justice, and her difficulties breaking into the male-dominated legal profession. O'Connor defends her positions on affirmative action and abortion.

The Magnificent Yankee—A 1950 movie, starring Louis Calhern and Ann Harding, that traces the life and philosophy of Oliver Wendell Holmes, Jr., one of the Supreme Court's most brilliant justices.

Marbury v. Madison—A 1987 video on the famous 1803 case that established the principle of judicial review.

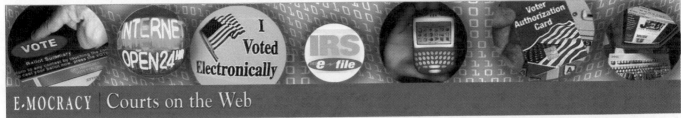

E·MOCRACY | Courts on the Web

Most courts in the United States now have sites on the Web. These sites vary in what they include. Some courts simply display contact information for court personnel. Others include recent judicial decisions along with court rules and forms. Many federal courts permit attorneys to file documents electronically. The information available on these sites continues to grow as courts try to avoid being left behind in the information age. One day, courts may decide to implement *virtual courtrooms,* in which judicial proceedings take place totally via the Internet. The Internet may ultimately provide at least a partial solution to the twin problems of overloaded dockets and the high time and money costs of litigation.

| Logging On

The home page of the federal courts is a good starting point for learning about the federal court system in general. At this site, you can even follow the "path" of a case as it moves through the federal court system. Go to

www.uscourts.gov

To access the Supreme Court's official Web site, on which Supreme Court decisions are made available within hours of their release, go to

supremecourtus.gov

Several Web sites offer searchable databases of Supreme Court decisions. You can access Supreme Court cases since 1970 at FindLaw's site:

www.findlaw.com

The following Web site also offers an easily searchable index to Supreme Court opinions, including some important historic decisions:

www.law.cornell.edu/supct/index.html

You can find information on the justices of the Supreme Court, as well as their decisions, at

www.oyez.org/oyez/frontpage

Court TV's Web site offers information ranging from its program schedule and how you can find Court TV in your area to famous cases and the wills of celebrities. For each case included on the site, you can read a complete history

as well as selected documents filed with the court and court transcripts. You can access this site at

www.courttv.com

| Online Review

At **www.politicalscience.wadsworth.com/ schmidt12**, you will find a free Study Guide to this book. For each chapter, there are two online quizzes to help you master the material.

• The PoliPrep Self-Study Assessment provides a pretest for each major section of the chapter. PoliPrep then generates a customized study plan. After you complete the study plan, a posttest evaluates your progress.

• The Tutorial Quiz for each chapter provides questions on the chapter contents, including the features. The questions are organized to match the major sections of the chapter.

15 | Domestic Policy

What If . . .
We Had Universal Health Care?

BACKGROUND

Currently, roughly 45 million Americans do not have health insurance. Some of those uninsured are between jobs; others are young people who are single and healthy and have chosen *not* to purchase health insurance. Others are unable to purchase health insurance because they are homeless; have preexisting conditions, such as diabetes, AIDS, or cancer; or simply cannot afford it. In the United States, those without such insurance often seek primary care in hospital emergency rooms. According to two Pulitzer Prize–winning journalists, "U.S. health care is second rate at the start of the twenty-first century and destined to get a lot worse and more expensive."[*]

According to Cardinal Joseph Bernardin of the Chicago Archdiocese, "Health care is an essential safeguard of human life and dignity. There is an obligation for society to ensure that every person be able to realize this right."

WHAT IF WE HAD UNIVERSAL HEALTH CARE?

We must first distinguish between universal health insurance and universal health care. Here we are discussing the latter— providing access to health care for those who are uninsured. We are not talking about setting up a universal, government-administered health-insurance system. With universal health care, those in need of basic medical care who lack insurance would have access to physicians, clinics, hospitals, and the like.

THE SAN FRANCISCO EXPERIMENT

To understand how universal health care might work, we can go to San Francisco, California, where a universal health-care plan was approved in the summer of 2006. The San Francisco Health Access Plan, as it is called, is financed by local government, mandatory contributions from employers, and income-adjusted premiums from users.

Enrollment fees range from $3 to $201, and most participants will pay $35 a month. Uninsured San Franciscans can then seek comprehensive primary care in the city's public and private clinics and hospitals. San Francisco Mayor Gavin Newsom described the city's historic undertaking as a "moral obligation."

Not everybody in the city is happy about the new plan, however. To offset the estimated annual price tag of more than $200 million, firms with twenty or more workers have to contribute about a dollar per hour worked by any employee. Those with more than a hundred workers have to pay $1.60 per hour, up to a monthly maximum of $180 per worker.

Many small-business owners in San Francisco predict that new businesses will no longer locate there. They also argue that goods and services within the city will become more expensive as employers pass on the added health-care costs to customers.

THE RELATIONSHIP BETWEEN UNIVERSAL HEALTH-CARE ACCESS AND THE NUMBER OF UNINSURED

Economic analysis yields a simple relationship between price and quantity demanded—the lower the price, the higher the quantity demanded. Medical care is a service like any other. If medical care is provided at a lower price to those who desire it, more medical care will be demanded.

We can predict that if a universal health-care plan is implemented, the number of people without health insurance will increase. To understand this, consider how people will behave if universal health-care access becomes a reality. Over time, some individuals and families will choose not to renew their health insurance because they will know that they can rely on universal health-care access. Consequently, the existence of universal health care will actually increase the number of those who do not have health insurance in the United States.

THE RELATIONSHIP BETWEEN UNIVERSAL HEALTH CARE AND THE BURDEN ON CLINICS AND HOSPITALS

We can predict that, as more individuals and families take advantage of universal health-care access, the burden on existing clinics and hospitals will increase. Health-insurance companies have the data. Those individuals who have health-insurance policies with zero or small deductibles utilize the services of the health-care sector much more than those who have a high deductible. In essence, universal health-care coverage is the equivalent of having a zero deductible for primary care. Note that this does not mean that people will become sicker if they have access to universal health care. It does mean that they will make greater use of health-care facilities.

FOR CRITICAL ANALYSIS

1. Administratively, what is the difference between setting up universal health care and providing universal health insurance?
2. If universal health-care access becomes a reality, what will happen to hospital emergency rooms?

[*]Donald Barlett and James Steele, *Critical Condition* (New York: Broadway Books, 2006).

Typically, whenever a policy decision is made, some groups will be better off and some groups will be hurt. All policymaking generally involves such a dilemma.

Part of the public-policy debate in our nation involves domestic problems. **Domestic policy** can be defined as all of the laws, government planning, and government actions that affect each individual's daily life in the United States. Consequently, the span of such policies is enormous. Domestic policies range from relatively simple issues, such as what the speed limit should be on interstate highways, to more complex ones, such as how best to protect our environment or whether we should have universal health-care access, as discussed in this chapter's opening *What If . . .* feature. Many of our domestic policies are formulated and implemented by the federal government, but a number of others are the result of the combined efforts of federal, state, and local governments.

In this chapter, we look at domestic policy issues involving health care, poverty and welfare, immigration, crime, and the environment. Before we start our analysis, though, we must look at how public policies are made.

> **Domestic Policy**
> Public plans or courses of action that concern internal issues of national importance, such as poverty, crime, and the environment.

The Policymaking Process

How does any issue get resolved? First, of course, the issue must be identified as a problem. Often, policymakers simply have to open their local newspapers—or letters from their constituents—to discover that a problem is brewing. On rare occasions, a crisis, such as that brought about by the terrorist attacks of September 11, 2001, creates the need to formulate policy. Like most Americans, however, policymakers receive much of their information from the national media. Finally, various lobbying groups provide information to members of Congress.

As an example of policymaking, consider the Medicare reform bill. Medicare is a program that pays health-care expenses for Americans over the age of sixty-five. As initially created in the 1960s, Medicare did not cover the cost of prescription drugs. The new bill provided a direct drug benefit beginning in 2006. (Certain discounts were available immediately.)

No matter how simple or how complex the problem, those who make policy follow a number of steps. We can divide the process of policymaking into at least five steps: agenda building, policy formulation, policy adoption, policy implementation, and policy evaluation. (See Figure 15–1 on page 485.)

Agenda Building

First of all, the issue must get on the agenda. In other words, Congress must become aware that an issue requires congressional action. Agenda building may occur as the result of a crisis, technological change, or mass media campaigns, as well as through the efforts of strong political personalities and effective lobbying groups.

Advocates for the elderly, including AARP (formerly the American Association of Retired Persons), had demanded a Medicare drug benefit for years. Traditionally, liberals have advocated such benefits. Yet the benefit was created under President George W. Bush—a conservative Republican. Bush's advocacy of Medicare reform was essential to its success.

Bush had already backed measures, such as outlawing "partial birth" abortions, to solidify his conservative support. He now needed to show moderates that they did not have to vote for a Democrat to get action on domestic issues. A Medicare drug benefit would "steal the clothes of the other party," a time-honored political maneuver. For example, Democratic president Bill Clinton (1993–2001) championed a welfare reform bill that limited the number of years in which any one person could receive benefits. Conservatives were much more pleased with this reform than liberals.

Policy Formulation

During the next step in the policymaking process, various policy proposals are discussed among government officials and the public. Such discussions may take place in the printed media, on television, and in the halls of Congress. Congress holds hearings, the president voices the administration's views, and the topic may even become a campaign issue.

Many Republicans in Congress were opposed to any major new social-spending program. Many also disliked Medicare because they saw it as a government insurance program. These members of Congress believed that insurance programs should be run by private businesses. To win their support, the Republican leadership advocated a degree of "privatization." Under this plan, private companies would administer the drug benefit. In a six-city demonstration project, plans administered by private companies would compete with traditional Medicare. The Democratic leadership opposed privatization, claiming that it threatened the very existence of Medicare.

The Republicans also proposed measures that would benefit the insurance and pharmaceutical industries. For example, the government would not use its immense bargaining power to obtain lower prices for Medicare drugs and would discourage the importation of lower-cost drugs from Canada. Finally, the Republicans proposed that to keep the cost of the bill down, not all drug expenses would be covered. To reduce costs, the Republican plan had a "doughnut hole" in which out-of-pocket drug expenses greater than $2,250 but under $3,600 were not covered. The Democrats wanted more coverage—they wanted the "hole" filled.

Policy Adoption

The third step in the policymaking process involves choosing a specific policy from among the proposals that have been discussed. In the end, the Republican proposals were adopted, and the bill passed by the narrowest of margins. The progress of the bill through Congress revealed some of the intense partisanship that has become common in recent years. For example, the Republicans refused to allow any Democrats from the House to participate in the conference committee that reconciled the House and Senate versions of the bill—a startling departure from tradition.

Almost at the last minute, AARP endorsed the bill, which may have guaranteed its success. A significant minority of the Democratic members of Congress broke with their party to support the bill, and that was enough to balance out the Republicans who refused to vote for it.

Policy Implementation

The fourth step in the policymaking process involves the implementation of the policy alternative chosen by Congress. Government action must be implemented by bureaucrats, the courts, police, and individual citizens. In the example of the Medicare reform bill, the main portion of the legislation was not to come into effect until 2006. For the most part, therefore, implementation did not begin immediately. Some sections of the bill did become effective in 2004, however. These included a series of drug discount cards, sponsored by the government in cooperation with various insurance companies, which would provide some savings on prescription drugs right away. Because the Bush administration hoped to elicit a positive political response to the Medicare reform, it organized a major advertising campaign for the new cards, paid for by taxpayers through the Department of Health and Human Services. In May 2004, however, the federal Government Accountability Office ruled that the advertisements were illegal.

AGENDA BUILDING

June 3, 1997
AARP members rally to show their strong support for Medicare benefits.

July 3, 1997
John Rother, chief lobbyist of AARP, with mail from retirees. "We got Congress to pay attention," he said.

July 12, 2001
President Bush with a copy of a proposed discount card for lower prices on prescription drugs for seniors.

POLICY FORMULATION

June 12, 2003
President Bush speaks to seniors during a round-table discussion about Medicare at a Connecticut hospital.

June 17, 2003
House Minority Leader Nancy Pelosi criticizes a Republican version of the Medicare drug bill in committee hearings.

June 18, 2003
Bush in a bipartisan meeting with senators on Medicare reform in the White House.

POLICY ADOPTION

July 15, 2003
Members of the House-Senate Conference Committee on Medicare legislation begin their meeting at the Capitol.

November 24, 2003
Senate Majority Leader Bill Frist with Republican leaders after the Senate voted to end debate on the Medicare drug bill.

November 25, 2003
AARP executives speak about AARP's support of the Medicare bill during a news conference.

POLICY IMPLEMENTATION

December 8, 2003
President Bush signs the Medicare Prescription Drug, Improvement, and Modernization Act of 2003 at Constitution Hall in Washington, D.C.

May 3, 2004
On the first day senior citizens can sign up for the Medicare prescription drug discount cards, seniors meet with House Speaker Dennis Hastert to raise questions and express confusion about the new program.

June 14, 2004
President Bush meets the employees at a Hy-Vee Pharmacy in Liberty, Missouri and participates in a discussion about health care, including Medicare and the new prescription drug card.

FIGURE 15–1 | THE POLICYMAKING PROCESS: THE MEDICARE REFORM BILL

Four of the five steps of the policymaking process, as exemplified by the Medicare reform bill of 2003. The fifth step—evaluation—could not begin until 2006, when all provisions of the new act went into effect.

AARP protest (Gray Panther Photo)
Lobbyist (AP Photo/Susan Walsh)
Bush with card (White House Photo)

Roundtable (White House Photo by Eric Draper)
Pelosi (AP Photo/Dennis Cook)
Bipartisan (White House Photo by Paul Morse)

Members (Courtesy of the House Committee on Ways and Means)
Frist *et al.* (AP Photo/Terry Ashe)
AARP executives (AP Photo/Susan Walsh)

Bush signs bill (White House Photo by Paul Morse)
Q&As on cards (AP Photo/Stephen J. Carrera)
Bush at pharmacy (AP Photo/Susan Walsh)

Policy Evaluation

After a policy has been implemented, it is evaluated. Groups inside and outside the government conduct studies to determine what actually happens after a policy has been in place for a given period of time. Based on this feedback and the perceived success or failure of the policy, a new round of policymaking initiatives will be undertaken to improve on the effort. Given that the new prescription drug benefit was the most significant expansion of Medicare since its creation forty years ago, there was certain to be mixed feedback. In this instance, much of the feedback was negative. Most of the popular press featured headlines about the confusion plaguing the new drug program. At the beginning of 2006, those who could benefit from the new program had to choose among dozens of competing private insurance plans. More than two-thirds of those who signed up said that they were confused by the multitude of options. Even college graduates had trouble selecting the best plan for their needs.

Almost immediately the secretary of health and human services, Michael Leavitt, had to "face the music." His department hired additional telephone operators to assist pharmacies working with program beneficiaries. Despite all of the confusion, the federal government indicated that it would *not* reimburse states that were covering the costs of prescription drugs for Medicare beneficiaries who had not yet figured out how to obtain the new drug benefit. Undoubtedly, Congress will revise the Medicare program in years to come.

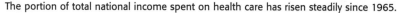

| Health Care

Spending for health care is estimated to account for about 15 percent of the total U.S. economy. In 1965, about 6 percent of our income was spent on health care (as shown in Figure 15–2), but that percentage has been increasing ever since. Per capita spending on health care is greater in the United States than almost anywhere else in the world. Measured by the percentage of the *gross domestic product* devoted to health care, America spends almost twice as much as Australia or Canada—see Figure 15–3. (The gross domestic product, or GDP, is the dollar value of all final goods and services produced in a one-year period.)

FIGURE 15–2 | PERCENTAGE OF TOTAL NATIONAL INCOME SPENT ON HEALTH CARE IN THE UNITED STATES

The portion of total national income spent on health care has risen steadily since 1965.

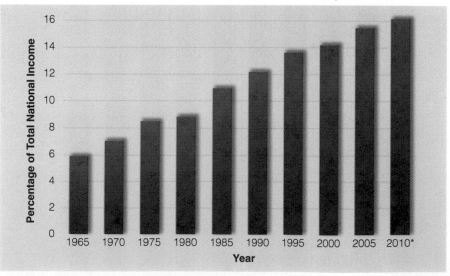

*Estimate

Sources: U.S. Department of Commerce; U.S. Department of Health and Human Services; Deloitte and Touche LLP; and VHA, Inc.

FIGURE 15–3 | COST OF HEALTH CARE
IN ECONOMICALLY ADVANCED NATIONS

Cost is given as a percentage of total gross domestic product (GDP).

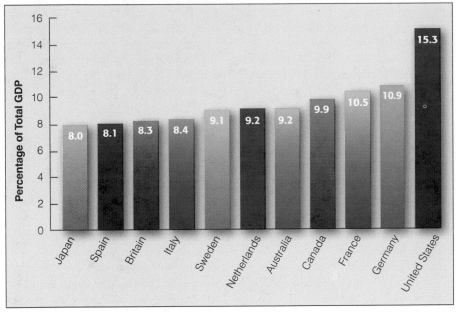

Source: Organization for Economic Cooperation and Development, *OECD Health Data*, 2006.

The Rising Cost of Health Care

There are numerous explanations for why health-care costs have risen so much. At least one has to do with changing demographics—as you learned in Chapter 1, the U.S. population is getting older. Life expectancy has gone up, as shown in Figure 15–4. The top 5 percent of those using health care incur over 50 percent of all health-care costs. The bottom 70 percent of health-care users account for only 10 percent of health-care expenditures. Not surprisingly, the elderly make up most of the top users of health-care services. Nursing home expenditures are generally made by people older than age seventy. The use of hospitals is also dominated by the aged.

FIGURE 15–4 | LIFE EXPECTANCY IN THE UNITED STATES

Along with health-care spending, life expectancy has gone up. Therefore, we are presumably getting some return for our spending.

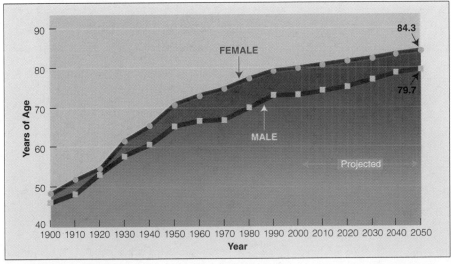

Source: Social Security Administration, Office of the Chief Actuary.

Advanced Technology.   Another reason that health-care costs have risen so dramatically is advancing technology. A CT (computerized tomography) scanner costs around $1 million. An MRI (magnetic resonance imaging) scanner can cost over $2 million. A PET (positron emission tomography) scanner costs around $4 million. All of these machines have become increasingly available in recent decades and are in demand around the country. Typical fees for procedures using them range from $300 to $500 for a CT scan to as high as $2,000 for a PET scan. The development of new technologies that help physicians and hospitals prolong human life is an ongoing process in an ever-advancing industry. New procedures that involve even greater costs can be expected in the future.

The Government's Role in Financing Health Care.   Currently, government spending on health care constitutes about 45 percent of total health-care spending. Private insurance accounts for about 35 percent of payments for health care. The remainder—less than 20 percent—is paid directly by individuals or by philanthropy. Medicare and Medicaid are the main sources of hospital and other medical benefits for 35 million U.S. residents, most of whom are over the age of sixty-five.

Medicare is specifically designed to support the elderly, regardless of income. **Medicaid,** a joint state-federal program, is in principle a program to subsidize health care for the poor. In practice, it often provides long-term health care to persons living in nursing homes. (To become eligible for Medicaid, these individuals must first exhaust their financial assets.) Medicare, Medicaid, and private insurance companies are called *third parties*. Caregivers and patients are the two primary parties. When third parties pay for medical care, the demand for such services increases; health-care recipients have no incentive to restrain their use of health care. One result is some degree of wasted resources.

Medicare

The Medicare program, which was created in 1965 under President Lyndon Johnson (1963–1969), pays hospital and physicians' bills for U.S. residents over the age of

| **Medicare**
A federal health-insurance program that covers U.S. residents over the age of sixty-five. The costs are met by a tax on wages and salaries.

| **Medicaid**
A joint state-federal program that provides medical care to the poor (including indigent elderly persons in nursing homes). The program is funded out of general government revenues.

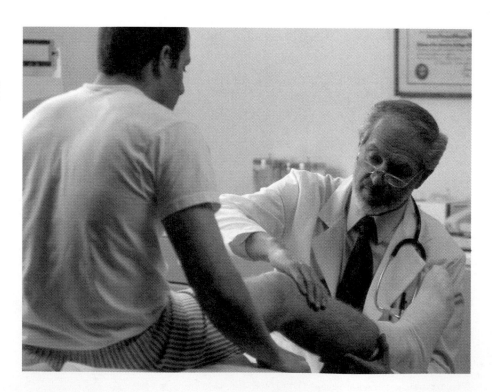

A physician examines a patient. Managed-care programs, which have become popular with employers in recent years, often reimburse only a limited number of health-care providers. How might we allow patients to visit physicians of their own choosing and simultaneously control health-care costs? (Corbis. All rights reserved.)

sixty-five. As already mentioned, beginning in 2006, Medicare also pays for at least part of the prescription drug expenses of the elderly. In return for paying a tax on their earnings (currently set at 2.9 percent of wages and salaries) while in the workforce, retirees are ensured that the majority of their hospital and physicians' bills will be paid for with public funds.

Over the past forty years, Medicare has become the second-largest domestic spending program, after Social Security. Government expenditures on Medicare have routinely turned out to be far in excess of the expenditures forecast at the time the program was put into place or expanded. In Chapter 16, you will learn about Medicare's impact on the current federal budget and the impact it is likely to have in the future. For now, consider only that the total outlays on Medicare are high enough to create substantial demands to curtail its costs.

One response by the federal government to soaring Medicare costs has been to impose arbitrary reimbursement caps on specific procedures. To avoid going over Medicare's reimbursement caps, however, hospitals have sometimes discharged patients too soon or in an unstable condition. The government has also cut rates of reimbursement to individual physicians and physician groups, such as health maintenance organizations (HMOs). One consequence has been a nearly 15 percent reduction in the amount the government pays for Medicare services provided by physicians. As a result, physicians and HMOs have become reluctant to accept Medicare patients. Several of the nation's largest HMOs have withdrawn from certain Medicare programs. A growing number of physicians now refuse to treat Medicare patients.

Medicaid

In a few short years, the joint federal-state taxpayer-funded Medicaid program for the "working poor" has generated one of the biggest expansions of government entitlements in the last fifty years. In 1997, Medicaid spending was around $150 billion. Ten years later it exceeded $300 billion. At the end of the last decade, 34 million people were enrolled in the program. Today, there are more than 50 million. When you add Medicaid coverage to Medicare and the military and federal employee health plans, the government has clearly become the nation's primary health insurer. More than 100 million people—one in three—in the United States have government coverage.

Why Has Medicaid Spending Exploded?   One of the reasons Medicaid has become such an important health-insurance program is that the income ceiling for eligibility has increased to more than $40,000 per year in most states. In other words, a family of four can earn around $40,000 and still obtain health insurance through Medicaid for its children. Indeed, many low-income workers choose Medicaid over health insurance offered by employers. Why? The reason is that Medicaid is less costly and sometimes covers more medical expenses. Indeed, to most recipients, Medicaid is either free or almost free.

Medicaid and the States.   On average, the federal government pays almost 60 percent of Medicaid's cost—the states pay the rest. Certain states, particularly in the South, receive even higher reimbursements. In general, such states are not complaining about the expansion of Medicaid. Other states, however, such as New York, have been overwhelmed by the rate of increase in Medicaid spending. Even with the federal government's partial reimbursement, the portion paid by the states has increased so rapidly that the states are finding themselves financially strapped. Florida, for example, had to drastically revise its Medicaid eligibility rules to reduce the number of families using Medicaid. Otherwise, the state projected a budget deficit that it would not be able to handle.

These concerned citizens argue in favor of better funding for Medicaid-supported health expenses during a rally in Jackson, Mississippi. Why are so many Americans concerned about the level of Medicaid funding? (AP Photo/Rogelio Solis)

The Uninsured

More than 45 million Americans—15 percent of the population—do not have health insurance. The proportion of the population that is uninsured varies from one part of the country to another. In Hawaii and Minnesota, only 7 percent of working adults lack coverage. In Texas, however, the figure is 27 percent. According to the Congressional Black Caucus Foundation, African Americans, Hispanics, and Asian/Pacific Islanders make up more than half of the year-round uninsured, even though they constitute only 29 percent of the total U.S. population. Hispanic Americans are the most likely to be uninsured, with only 35 percent of working Hispanic adults having coverage.

According to surveys, being uninsured has negative health consequences. People without coverage are less likely to get basic preventive care, such as mammograms; less likely to have a personal physician; and more likely to rate their own health as only poor or fair.

The Uninsured Employed.   The uninsured population is relatively young, in part due to Medicare, which covers almost everyone over the age of sixty-five. Also, younger workers are more likely to be employed in entry-level jobs that do not come with health-insurance benefits. The current system of health care in the United States assumes that employers will provide health insurance. Many small businesses, however, simply cannot afford to offer their workers health insurance. Insurance costs are now approaching an average of $9,000 a year for each employee.

Shifting Costs to the Uninsured.   A further problem faced by the uninsured is that when they do seek medical care, they must usually pay much higher fees than would be paid on their behalf if they had insurance coverage. Large third-party insurers, private or public, normally strike hard bargains with hospitals and physicians over how much they will pay for procedures and services. The uninsured have less bargaining power. As a result, hospitals attempt to recover from the uninsured the revenues they lost in paying third-party insurers. A further result is that individual health-insurance policies (those not obtained through an employer) are extremely costly.

In any given year, most people do not require expensive health care. Young, healthy people in particular can be tempted to do without insurance. One benefit of insurance coverage, however, is that it protects the insured against catastrophic costs resulting from unusual events. Medical care for life-threatening accidents or diseases can run into thousands or even hundreds of thousands of dollars. An uninsured person who requires this kind of medical care may be forced into bankruptcy.

One Alternative: National Health Insurance

The United States is the only advanced industrial country with a large pool of citizens who lack health insurance. Western Europe, Japan, Canada, and Australia all provide systems of universal coverage. Such coverage is provided through **national health insurance.** In effect, the government takes over the economic function of providing basic health-care coverage. Private insurers are excluded from this market. The government collects premiums from employers and employees on the basis of their ability to pay and then provides basic services to the entire population.

Because the government provides all basic insurance coverage, national health-insurance systems are often called **single-payer plans.** Such plans can significantly reduce administrative overhead because physicians need only deal with a single set of forms and requirements. The number of employees required to process claims is also lowered. In France, for example, which has national health insurance, administrative overhead is 5 percent of total costs, compared to 14 percent in the United States.[1] The French experience suggests that containing unnecessary procedures may be more difficult with a single-payer plan, however. National health-insurance systems are also sometimes called *socialized medicine*. It should be noted, though, that only health insurance is socialized. The government does not employ most physicians, and in many countries the hospitals are largely private as well.[2] Americans seeking an example of national health insurance often look to the Canadian system, which we examine in this chapter's *Beyond Our Borders* feature on the following page.

Another Alternative: A Health Savings Account

Republicans in Congress have enacted a health savings account (HSA) program as an alternative to completely changing the U.S. health-care industry. Most taxpayers can set up a tax-free HSA, which must be combined with a high-deductible health-insurance policy. Eligible individuals or families can make an annual tax-deductible contribution to an HSA up to a maximum of $2,700 for an individual and $5,450 for a family. Funds in the HSA accumulate tax free, and distributions of HSA funds for medical expenses are also exempt. Any funds remaining in an HSA after an individual reaches age sixty-five can be withdrawn tax free. The benefits can be impressive—a single person depositing around $1,500 each year with no withdrawals will have hundreds of thousands of dollars in the account after forty years.

For those using an HSA, the physician-patient relationship remains intact because third-party payers do not intervene in paying or monitoring medical expenses. The patients, rather than third parties, have an incentive to discourage their physicians from ordering expensive tests for every minor ache and pain because they are allowed to keep any funds saved in the HSA. Some critics argue that HSA participants may also forgo necessary medical attention and develop more

National Health Insurance
A plan to provide universal health insurance under which the government provides basic health-care coverage to all citizens. In most such plans, the program is funded by taxes on wages or salaries.

Single-Payer Plan
A plan under which one entity has a monopoly on issuing a particular type of insurance. Typically, the entity is the government, and the insurance is basic health coverage.

---

[1]Paul V. Dutton, "Health Care in France and the United States: Learning from Each Other," Washington, D.C.: The Brookings Institution, 2002. This article is online at **www.brookings.edu/fp/cusf/ analysis/dutton.htm**.
[2]Britain is an exception. Under the British "National Health," most (but not all) physicians are employed by the government.

BEYOND OUR BORDERS | The Canadian Health-Care System

Canada's national health-insurance system is often viewed as a potential model for solving some the health-care woes affecting many Americans. Canada's program, however, is atypical in many respects. Until very recently, Canada was the only country that in effect outlawed private parallel health-care services.

THE HIDDEN COSTS OF THE CANADIAN HEALTH-CARE SYSTEM

Canadians have found that their "free" health care entails some unexpected costs. Because physicians are unwilling to provide as many services as people wish to purchase at the below-market fees dictated by the Canadian government, long waiting lists are a fixture of the Canadian system. The average waiting time to see a specialist after referral by a general practitioner is more than four months. Individuals experiencing debilitating back pain often must wait at least a year for neurosurgery. Even people diagnosed with life-threatening cancers typically have to wait six weeks before they have an initial examination by a cancer specialist. It is not surprising that a Gallup poll in 2005 found that only 9 percent of Canadians rated their health-care system as "excellent."

CANADIANS GO ELSEWHERE FOR HEALTH CARE

The long waits for officially approved health care in Canada have led to the establishment of private health-care clinics on Native American reservations, where physicians can legally accept private payments. (Until recently, it was strictly illegal for Canadians to purchase private health insurance to pay for care received on these reservations, however.) In addition, rather than wait for years to obtain elective surgeries, about 20,000 Canadians fly to India each year at their own expense and pay physicians in that country to perform surgeries such as hip replacements. In actuality, the "free" Canadian health-care system is very costly to that nation's residents.

FOR CRITICAL ANALYSIS

Why do you suppose that many Canadians who wish to have MRI scans travel to the United States and pay for scans out of their own pockets instead of waiting three months for a "free" MRI scan in Canada?

serious medical problems as a consequence. Also, HSAs do not address the issue of universal access to health care. After all, even if HSAs become common, not everyone will be willing or able to participate.

Poverty and Welfare

Throughout the world, poverty has historically been accepted as inevitable. The United States and other industrialized nations, however, have sustained enough economic growth in the past several hundred years to eliminate mass poverty. In fact, considering the wealth and high standard of living in the United States, the persistence of poverty here appears bizarre and anomalous. How can there still be so much poverty in a nation of so much abundance? And what can be done about it?

A traditional solution has been **income transfers.** These are methods of transferring income from relatively well-to-do to relatively poor groups in society, and as a nation, we have been using such transfers for a long time. Before we examine these efforts, let us look at the concept of poverty in more detail and at the characteristics of the poor.

| **Income Transfer**
A transfer of income from some individuals in the economy to other individuals. This is generally done by government action.

The Low-Income Population

We can see in Figure 15–5 that the number of people classified as poor fell steadily from 1961 to 1968—that is, during the presidencies of John Kennedy and Lyndon

Johnson. The number remained level until the recession of 1981–1982, under Ronald Reagan, when it increased substantially. The number fell during the "Internet boom" of 1994–2000, but then it started to rise again.

The threshold income level that is used to determine who falls into the poverty category was originally based on the cost of a nutritionally adequate food plan designed by the U.S. Department of Agriculture in 1963. The threshold was determined by multiplying the food-plan cost times three, on the assumption that food expenses constitute approximately one-third of a poor family's expenditures. Until 1969, annual revisions of the threshold level were based only on changes in food prices. After 1969, the adjustments were made on the basis of changes in the consumer price index (CPI). The CPI is based on the average prices of a specified set of goods and services bought by wage earners in urban areas.

The low-income poverty threshold thus represents the income needed to maintain a specified standard of living as of 1963, with the purchasing-power value increased year by year to reflect the general increase in prices. For 2006, for example, the official poverty level for a family of four was about $20,000.

The official poverty level is based on pretax income, including cash but not **in-kind subsidies**—food stamps, housing vouchers, and the like. If we correct poverty levels for such benefits, the percentage of the population that is below the poverty line drops dramatically. To put the official U.S. poverty level in perspective, consider that this income level for the United States is twice as high as the world's average per capita income level. Indeed, according to the World Bank, only twenty-six countries have per capita incomes higher than the poverty income threshold defined by the U.S. government.

| In-Kind Subsidy
A good or service—such as food stamps, housing, or medical care—provided by the government to low-income groups.

The Antipoverty Budget

It is not always easy to determine how much the government spends to combat poverty. In part, this is because it can be difficult to decide whether a particular program is an antipoverty program. Are grants to foster parents an antipoverty measure? What about job-training programs? Are college scholarships for low-income students an antipoverty measure? President George W. Bush's federal budget for 2007 allocated $18 billion for such scholarships.

FIGURE 15–5 | THE OFFICIAL NUMBER OF POOR IN THE UNITED STATES

The number of individuals classified as poor fell steadily from 1961 through 1968. It then increased during the 1981–1982 recession. After 1994, the number fell steadily until 2000, when it started to rise again.

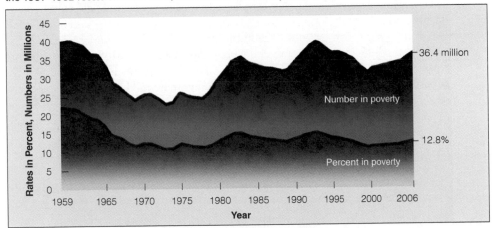

Note: The data points represent the midpoints of the respective years.
Source: U.S. Census Bureau, Current Population Reports, *Income, Poverty, and Health Insurance Coverage in the United States: 2005*, Washington, D.C.: Government Printing Office (2006).

Bush's 2007 budget allocated about $720 billion, or about one-fourth of all federal expenditures, to federal programs that support persons of limited income (scholarships included).[3] Of this amount, $350 billion was for Medicaid, which funds medical services for the poor, as discussed earlier. The states were expected to contribute an additional $243 billion to Medicaid. Medical care is by far the largest portion of the antipoverty budget. One reason medical spending is high is the widespread belief that everyone should receive medical care that at least approximates the care received by an average person. No such belief supports spending for other purposes, such as shelter or transportation. Elderly people receive 70 percent of Medicaid spending.

Basic Welfare

| **Temporary Assistance to Needy Families (TANF)**
A state-administered program in which grants from the national government are used to provide welfare benefits. The TANF program replaced the Aid to Families with Dependent Children (AFDC) program.

The program that most people think of when they hear the word *welfare* is called **Temporary Assistance to Needy Families (TANF).** With the passage in 1996 of the Personal Responsibility and Work Opportunity Reconciliation Act, popularly known as the Welfare Reform Act, the government created TANF to replace an earlier program known as Aid to Families with Dependent Children (AFDC). The AFDC program provided "cash support for low-income families with dependent children who have been deprived of parental support due to death, disability, continued absence of a parent, or unemployment."

Under the TANF program, the U.S. government turned over to the states, in the form of block grants, funds targeted for welfare assistance. The states, not the national government, now bear the burden of any increased welfare spending. For example, if a state wishes to increase the amount of TANF payments over what the national government supports, the state has to pay the additional costs.

One of the aims of the Welfare Reform Act was to reduce welfare spending. To do this, the act made two significant changes in the basic welfare program. One change was to limit most welfare recipients to only two years of assistance at a time. The second change was to impose a lifetime limit on welfare assistance of five years. The Welfare Reform Act has largely met its objectives. During the first five years after the act was passed, the number of families receiving welfare payments was cut in half. The 2007 federal budget allocated $16 billion to the TANF block grants.

Welfare Controversies

Whether known as AFDC or TANF, the basic welfare program has always been controversial. Conservative and libertarian voters often object to welfare spending as a matter of principle, believing that it reduces the incentive to find paid employment. Because AFDC and TANF have largely supported single-parent households, some also believe that such programs are antimarriage. Finally, certain people object to welfare spending out of a belief that welfare recipients are "not like us." In fact, non-Hispanic whites made up only 30 percent of TANF recipients in the mid-2000s. As a result of all these factors, basic welfare payments in the United States are relatively low when compared with similar payments in other industrialized nations. In 2006, the average monthly TANF payment nationwide was about $400 per family.

Other Forms of Government Assistance

| **Supplemental Security Income (SSI)**
A federal program established to provide assistance to elderly persons and persons with disabilities.

The **Supplemental Security Income (SSI)** program was established in 1974 to provide a nationwide minimum income for elderly persons and persons with disabilities who

---

[3]This sum does not include the earned-income tax credit, which is not part of the federal budget.

do not qualify for Social Security benefits. The 2007 budget allocated $41 billion to this program.

The government also issues **food stamps,** benefits that can be used to purchase food; they are usually provided electronically through a card similar to a debit card. Food stamps are available to low-income individuals and families. Recipients must prove that they qualify by showing that they have a low income (or no income at all). Food stamps go to a much larger group of people than TANF payments. President Bush's 2007 budget allocated $40 billion to the food stamp program. The food stamp program has become a major part of the welfare system in the United States, although it was started in 1964 mainly to benefit farmers by distributing surplus food through retail channels.

The **earned-income tax credit (EITC) program** was created in 1975 to help low-income workers by giving back part or all of their Social Security taxes. Currently, about 15 percent of all taxpayers claim an EITC, and an estimated $33 billion a year is rebated to taxpayers through the program.

Homelessness—Still a Problem

The plight of the homeless remains a problem. Indeed, some observers argue that the Welfare Reform Act of 1996 has increased the number of homeless persons. There are no hard statistics on the homeless, but estimates of the number of people without a home on any given night in the United States range from a low of 230,000 to as many as 750,000 people.

It is difficult to estimate how many people are homeless because the number depends on how the homeless are defined. There are *street people*—those who sleep in bus stations, parks, and other areas. Many of these people are youthful runaways. There are the so-called *sheltered homeless*—those who sleep in government-supported or privately funded shelters. Many of these individuals used to live with their families or friends. Whereas street people are almost always single, the sheltered homeless include many families with children. Homeless families are the fastest-growing subgroup of the homeless population. What is the best way to help the *hard-core homeless*, those who have been on the streets for a year or more? (Examine the advantages and disadvantages of one type of program in this chapter's *Which Side Are You On?* feature on the next page.)

The homeless problem pits liberals against conservatives. Conservatives argue that there are not really that many homeless people and that most of them are alcoholics, drug users, or the mentally ill. Conservatives contend that these individuals should be dealt with by either the mental-health system or the criminal justice system. In contrast, many liberals argue that homelessness is caused by a reduction in welfare benefits and by excessively priced housing. They want more shelters to be built for the homeless.

Some cities have "criminalized" homelessness. Many municipalities have outlawed sleeping on park benches and sidewalks, as well as panhandling and leaving personal property on public property. In some cities, police sweeps remove the homeless, who then become part of the criminal justice system.

Since 1993, the U.S. Department of Housing and Urban Development has spent billions of dollars on programs designed to combat homelessness. Yet because there is so much disagreement about the number of homeless persons, the reasons for homelessness, and the possible cures for the problem, there has been no consistent government policy. Whatever policies have been adopted usually have been attacked by one group or another.

Food Stamps
Benefits issued by the federal government to low-income individuals to be used for the purchase of food; originally provided as coupons but now typically provided electronically through a card similar to a debit card.

Earned-Income Tax Credit (EITC) Program
A government program that helps low-income workers by giving back part or all of their Social Security taxes.

An instructor (standing) with a welfare recipient during a workshop at the Philadelphia Workforce Development Corporation (PWDC). The PWDC is a nonprofit organization that helps people on welfare to find employment. (Mike Mergen/*Bloomberg News*/Landov)

WHICH SIDE ARE YOU ON? | Can a "Housing-First" Policy Alleviate Our Homeless Problem?

On any given night, several hundred thousand Americans will "sleep rough." About 10 percent of them will have been doing the same thing for years. These are the so-called hard-core homeless. They are not typical of the homeless population. They are overwhelmingly male, and they usually suffer from some problem such as drug or alcohol abuse, mental illness, disease, or disability. The hard-core homeless cost our major cities large sums every year. In New York alone, it is estimated that one hard-core homeless person costs the city $40,000 annually in shelter costs, hospital stays, emergency room visits, and jail time. This figure goes as high as $150,000 in San Diego. To counter chronic homelessness, more than two hundred cities have adopted a "housing-first" policy. Such policies are based on a cost-benefit analysis: it is cheaper to put the chronically homeless in rooms of their own than to leave them on the street. Additionally, research conducted among the chronically homeless themselves has discovered that they do not want a bed in a shelter or a twelve-step program to rid them of alcoholism. So, under a housing-first program, the government rents rooms or apartments from the private sector or builds permanent housing and then brings social services to the tenants, who are the hard-core homeless.

HOUSING-FIRST PROGRAMS ARE THE ONLY WAY TO RID THE STREETS OF HARD-CORE HOMELESS

Proponents of housing-first programs say that the evidence of their benefits is overwhelming. When a housing-first concept is used, the hard-core homeless stay off the streets. For example, the nonprofit Pathways to Housing placed four hundred chronically homeless mentally ill New Yorkers in rental units. It has had a success rate of almost 90 percent—defined as the percentage of those in the rentals who do not return to the streets for five years or more. Although the cost is high at $22,000 per person per year, that is less expensive than the estimated $40,000 that New York would spend otherwise. Using a similar strategy, San Francisco has seen a 40 percent drop in street homelessness. In the last five years, Philadelphia claims that its street population has declined by 60 percent.

HOUSING-FIRST PROGRAMS IGNORE FAMILIES AND OTHERS

Critics argue that housing-first programs focus too much on single male alcohol and drug abusers and seem almost to reward the hard-core homeless. When housing-first programs are established, fewer funds are available for homeless families and others who do not qualify as hard-core homeless. Moreover, critics say that persons who are not among the hard-core homeless will eventually figure out the system. Then, to obtain housing first, they will do whatever is necessary to qualify as hard-core homeless—faking addiction (or even becoming addicts) or committing petty crimes to end up in jail more often. Finally, there is a moral issue: Are the hard-core homeless more worthy than other homeless people?

WHAT'S YOUR POSITION?

If you were in charge of spending on the homeless, would you create a housing-first program? Why or why not?

GOING ONLINE

To learn more about the "housing-first" movement, visit the Web site of the National Alliance to End Homelessness at **www.naeh.org**.

| Immigration

Time and again, this nation has been challenged and changed—and culturally enriched—by immigrant groups. All of these immigrants have faced the problems involved in living in a new and different political and cultural environment. Most of them have had to overcome language barriers, and many have had to deal with discrimination in one form or another because of their color, their inability to speak English fluently, or their customs. The civil rights legislation passed during and since the 1960s has done much to counter the effects of prejudice against immigrant groups by ensuring that they obtain equal rights under the law.

A vintage print showing immigrant children at Ellis Island, New York. Immigrants usually are younger than the population as a whole. What consequences follow from this fact? (National Archives)

One of the questions facing Americans and their political leaders today is the effect of immigration on American politics and government. Another issue is whether immigration is having a positive or negative impact on the United States and the form immigration reform should take.

The Continued Influx of Immigrants

Today, immigration rates are among the highest they have been since their peak in the early twentieth century. Every year, more than one million people immigrate to this country, and people who were born on foreign soil now constitute more than 10 percent of the U.S. population—twice the percentage of thirty years ago.

Minority Groups' Importance on the Rise. Since 1977, four out of five immigrants have come from Latin America or Asia. Hispanics have overtaken African Americans as the nation's largest minority. If current immigration rates continue, by the year 2060 minority groups collectively will constitute the "majority" of Americans. If Hispanics, African Americans, and perhaps Asians were to form coalitions, they could increase their political power dramatically and would have the numerical strength to make significant changes. According to Ben Wattenberg of the American Enterprise Institute, in the future the "old guard" white majority will no longer dominate American politics.

The Advantages of High Rates of Immigration. Some regard the high rate of immigration as a plus for America because it offsets the low birthrate and aging population. Immigrants expand the workforce and help to support, through their taxes, government programs that benefit older Americans, such as Medicare and Social Security. If it were not for immigration, contend these observers, the United States would be facing even more serious problems than it already does with funding these programs (see Chapter 16). In contrast, nations that do not have high immigration rates, such as Japan, are experiencing serious fiscal challenges due to their aging populations.

Attempts at Immigration Reform

A significant number of U.S. citizens, however, believe that immigration—both legal and illegal—negatively affects America. They argue, among other things, that the large number of immigrants seeking work results in lower wages for Americans, especially those with few skills. They also worry about the cost of providing immigrants with services such as schools and medical care. Not surprisingly, prior to the 2006 elections, members of Congress were in favor of enacting a sweeping immigration reform bill, but the two houses could not agree on what it should do. Some versions of the bill in the House would have made every illegal immigrant in the United States a felon. The Senate, in contrast, came up with a much softer immigration reform system, one that, at least initially, was backed by President Bush. The Senate bill in its various forms in 2006 would have allowed illegal immigrants gradually to become citizens. None of these immigration reform bills came to fruition, however, before Congress recessed for the summer. During the debate on the House bill, illegal immigrants and their supporters held marches and protests, particularly during May 2006. The estimated number of demonstrators exceeded one million with a half million alone in Los Angeles. Most were Hispanics.

Not wanting to commit one way or the other on the issue prior to an election, Congress held numerous hearings during its recess. The political strategy was obvious. Many hearings were held in states with few illegal immigrants. Consequently, members of Congress could show that they were strongly against illegal immigration in such states, because there would be no backlash. In the meantime, a number of cities passed laws or used existing laws to fight what they perceived as "too many" illegal immigrants.

In the late spring of 2006, many immigrants and their supporters rallied around the nation to voice their displeasure with proposed federal restrictions on undocumented aliens. What groups are in favor of relatively loose immigration laws and their enforcement? (AP Photo/Damian Dovarganes)

Crime in the Twenty-First Century

In 2006, overall crime rates in the United States dropped below those in many other countries, such as Britain. Nonetheless, virtually all polls taken in the United States in the last ten years have shown that crime remains one of the major concerns of the public. A related issue that has been on the domestic policy agenda for decades is controlling the use and sale of illegal drugs—activities that are often associated with crimes of violence. More recently, finding ways to deal with terrorism has become a priority for the nation's policymakers.

Crime in American History

In every period in the history of this nation, people have voiced apprehension about crime. Some criminologists argue that crime was probably as frequent around the time of the American Revolution as it is today. During the Civil War, mob violence and riots erupted in several cities. After the Civil War, people in San Francisco were told that "no decent man is in safety to walk the streets after dark; while at all hours, both night and day, his property is jeopardized by incendiarism [arson] and burglary."[4] In 1886, *Leslie's Weekly* reported, "Each day we see ghastly records of crime . . . murder seems to have run riot and each citizen asks . . . 'who is safe?'" From 1860 to 1890, the crime rate rose twice as fast as the population.[5] In 1910, one author stated that "crime, especially in its more violent forms and among the young, is increasing steadily and is threatening to bankrupt the Nation."[6]

From 1900 to the 1930s, social violence and crime increased dramatically. Labor union battles and race riots were common. Only during the three-decade period

---

[4]President's Commission on Law Enforcement and Administration of Justice, *Challenge of Crime in a Free Society* (Washington, D.C.: Government Printing Office, 1967), p. 19.

[5]Richard Shenkman, *Legends, Lies, and Cherished Myths of American History* (New York: HarperCollins, 1988), p. 158.

[6]President's Commission, *Challenge of Crime*, p. 19.

A police officer writes down a woman's report of a crime in her neighborhood. Research indicates that cooperation between the police and ordinary citizens is a highly effective method of combating crime. In what ways can police-community relations be improved? (Michael Newman/PhotoEdit)

from the mid-1930s to the early 1960s did the United States experience, for the first time in its history, stable or slightly declining overall crime rates.

What most Americans are worried about is violent crime. From the mid-1980s to 1994, its rate rose relentlessly. The murder rate per 100,000 people in 1964 was 4.9, whereas in 1994 it was estimated at 9.3, an increase of almost 100 percent. Between 1995 and 2004, violent crime rates declined. Some argue that this decline was due to the growing economy the United States has generally enjoyed since about 1993. Others claim that the $3 billion of additional funds the federal government has spent to curb crime in the last few years has led to less crime. Still others claim that an increase in the number of persons who are jailed or imprisoned is responsible for the reduction in crime. Some have even argued that legalized abortion has reduced the population that is likely to commit crimes. You can see changes in the rates of violent crimes, homicides, and thefts in Figures 15–6, 15–7, and 15–8, respectively.

Many people have heard that the United States has the highest crime rates in the world. This is not actually true. Total crime rates are higher in some other countries, including Britain, Denmark, and Sweden, than in the United States. You are much more likely to be robbed in London than in New York City. What the United States has is not a high total crime rate, but a *murder* rate that is unusually high for an advanced industrialized nation. Explanations for this fact vary from easy access to firearms to a cultural predisposition for settling disputes with violence. It is worth noting, however, that many countries in Asia, Africa, and Latin America have much higher homicide rates than the United States.

Crimes Committed by Juveniles

A disturbing aspect of crime is the number of serious crimes committed by juveniles, although the number of such crimes is also dropping, as shown in Figure 15–9 on page 502. The political response to this rise in serious juvenile crimes has been varied. Some cities have established juvenile curfews. Several states have begun to try more juveniles as adults, particularly juveniles who have been charged with homicides. Still other states are operating "boot camps" to try to "shape up" less violent juvenile criminals. Additionally, victims of juvenile crime and victims' relatives are attempting to pry open the traditionally secret juvenile court system.[7]

---

[7]See Chapter 5 for details on the rights of juveniles in our legal system.

A group of young inmates begin "boot camp" by marching in line at the Sumter County Correctional Institution in Bushnell, Florida. What can be done to reach troubled youths before they commit crimes that lead to imprisonment? (Bettmann/Corbis)

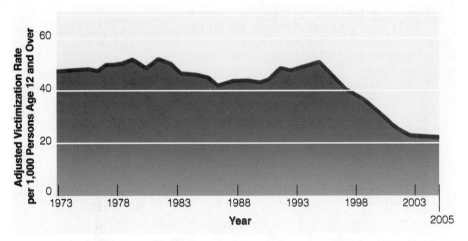

FIGURE 15–6 | VIOLENT CRIME RATES

Violent crime rates have declined since 1994, reaching the lowest level ever recorded in 2002. The crimes included in this chart are rape, robbery, aggravated and simple assault, and homicide.

Sources: U.S. Department of Justice; rape, robbery, and assault data are from the *National Crime Victimization Survey;* the homicide data are from the Federal Bureau of Investigation's *Uniform Crime Reports.*

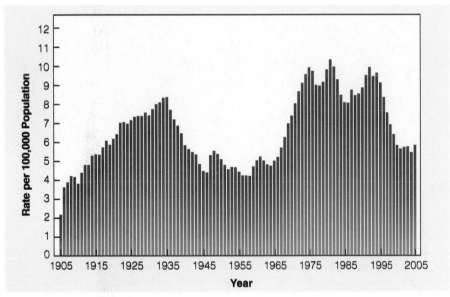

FIGURE 15–7 | HOMICIDE RATE

Homicide rates have recently declined to levels last seen in the late 1960s. The 2001 rate does *not* include deaths attributed to the 9/11 terrorism attacks.

Sources: U.S. Department of Justice; National Center for Health Statistics, *Vital Statistics.*

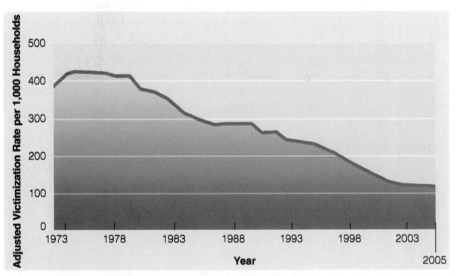

FIGURE 15–8 | THEFT RATES

Theft rates have declined significantly since the 1970s. *Theft* is defined as completed or attempted theft of property or cash without personal contact.

Source: U.S. Department of Justice, *National Crime Victimization Survey.*

FIGURE 15–9 | SERIOUS VIOLENT CRIME BY PERCEIVED AGE OF OFFENDER

The number of serious violent crimes committed by juveniles has generally declined since 1993. The crimes included are rape, robbery, aggravated assault, and homicide.

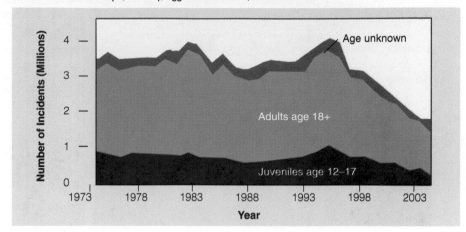

Sources: U.S. Department of Justice; rape, robbery, and assault data are from the *National Crime Victimization Survey*. The homicide data are from the FBI's *Uniform Crime Reports*.

Some worry that the decline in serious juvenile crimes is only temporary. The number of youths between the ages of fifteen and seventeen will rise from about nine million today to almost thirteen million in the year 2010. It is thus understandable that there is grave concern about preventing an even worse juvenile crime problem in the years to come.

The Cost of Crime to American Society

For the perpetrator, crime may pay in certain circumstances—a successful robbery or embezzlement, for example—but crime certainly costs the American public. One study suggests that when everything is added up, including the expenses of the legal system, the costs of private deterrence, losses by victims, and the value of time wasted by criminals and victims, the annual burden of crime in the United States exceeds a trillion dollars each year.[8]

The Office for Victims of Crime, a unit of the U.S. Department of Justice, has estimated that the direct tangible costs to crime victims, including the costs of medical expenses, lost earnings, and victim assistance, are $105 billion annually. Pain, suffering, and reduced quality of life increase the cost to $450 billion annually. Check fraud costs an estimated $10 billion each year. Fraud involving stocks, bonds, and commodities costs about $40 billion a year. Telemarketing fraud costs another $40 billion (though the recently established "do not call" list may have curbed this expense somewhat). Insurance fraud costs about $80 billion a year.[9]

The Prison Population Bomb

Many Americans believe that the best solution to the nation's crime problem is to impose stiff prison sentences on offenders. Such sentences, in fact, have become national policy. By 2007, U.S. prisons and jails held 2.2 million people. About

---

[8]David A. Anderson, "The Aggregate Burden of Crime," *Journal of Law and Economics*, Vol. 42, No. 2 (October 1999).

[9]These estimates are online at **www.ojp.usdoj.gov/ovc/ncvrw/2006/welcome.html**.

two-thirds of the incarcerated population was in state or federal prisons, with the remainder held in local jails. About 60 percent of the persons held in local jails were awaiting court action. The other 40 percent were serving sentences.

The number of incarcerated persons has grown rapidly in recent years. In 1990, for example, the total number of persons held in U.S. jails or prisons was still only 1.1 million. From 1995 to 2002, the incarcerated population grew at an average of 3.8 percent annually. The rate of growth has slowed since 2002, however.

The Incarceration Rate. Some groups of people are much more likely to find themselves behind bars than others. Men are more than ten times more likely to be incarcerated than women. Prisoners are also disproportionately African American. To measure how frequently members of particular groups are imprisoned, the standard statistic is the incarceration rate. This rate is the number of people incarcerated for every 100,000 persons in a particular population group. To put it another way, an incarceration rate of 1,000 means that 1 percent of a particular group is in custody. Using this statistic, we can say that U.S. men have an incarceration rate of 1,309, compared to a rate of 113 for U.S. women. Table 15–1 shows selected incarceration rates by gender, race, and age. Note the very high incarceration rate for African Americans between the ages of twenty-five and twenty-nine—at any given time, almost 12 percent of this group are in jail or prison.

International Comparisons. The United States has more people in jail or prison than any other country in the world. That fact is not necessarily surprising, because the United States also has one of the world's largest total populations. More to the point, the United States has the highest reported incarceration rate of any country on earth.[10] Figure 15–10 compares U.S. incarceration rates, measured by the number of prisoners per 100,000 residents, with incarceration rates in other major countries.

Prison Construction. To house a growing number of inmates, prison construction and management have become sizable industries in the United States. Ten years ago, prison overcrowding was a major issue. In 1994, for example, state prisons had a rated capacity of about 500,000 inmates but actually held 900,000 people. The prisons were therefore operating at 80 percent above capacity. Today, after a major prison construction program, state prisons are operating between at 1 and 16 percent above capacity, although the federal prison system is still 31 percent above capacity. Since 1980, Texas

| Incarceration Rate
The number of persons held in jail or prison for every 100,000 persons in a particular population group.

[10]North Korea probably has a higher incarceration rate than the United States, but that nation does not report its incarceration statistics. The incarceration rate for political prisoners alone is estimated to be between 650 and 900 per 100,000 inhabitants. North Korea also holds an unknown number of prisoners as common criminals. See Pierre Rigoulot, "Comparative Analysis of Concentration Camps in Nazi Germany, the Former Soviet Union, and North Korea," 2002. This article is online at the Web site of Human Rights without Frontiers. Go to **www.hrwf.net/north_korea/cf_north_korea_ _ _political_pri.html**.

TABLE 15–1 | INCARCERATION RATES PER 100,000 PERSONS FOR SELECTED U.S. POPULATION GROUPS

	Men	Women
Non-Hispanic white, total	709	129
Non-Hispanic white, aged 25–29	1,682	220
Non-Hispanic black, total	4,682	347
Non-Hispanic black, aged 25–29	11,955	720
Hispanic, total	1,856	144
Hispanic, aged 25–29	3,884	287
All groups	1,371	129

Source: "Prison and Jail Inmates at Midyear 2005," *Bureau of Justice Statistics Bulletin*, U.S. Department of Justice (2006).

FIGURE 15–10 | INCARCERATION RATES AROUND THE WORLD FROM 2002 TO 2004
Incarceration rates of major nations measured by the number of prisoners per 100,000 residents. Some authorities believe that the estimate for China is too low.

United States 701
Russia 584
Brazil 160
Mexico 156
Britain 140
China 119
Canada 118
Germany 98
France 93
Pakistan 59
Japan 54
Indonesia 38
India 29

Prisoners per 100,000 Residents

Source: International Centre for Prison Studies. The most recent data are online at **www.kcl.ac.uk/depsta/rel/icps/worldbrief/highest_to_lowest_rates.php**.

has built 120 new prisons, Florida has built 84, and California has built 83. In 1923, there were only 61 prisons in the entire United States.

Nationwide, local jails are operating at 93 percent of capacity. That figure conceals major differences among jurisdictions, however. Seventeen of the fifty largest jail jurisdictions are operating at over 100 percent of their rated capacity. Clark County, Nevada (Las Vegas), is 66 percent above capacity and Maricopa County, Arizona (Phoenix), is 52 percent above capacity.

Effects of Incarceration.   When imprisonment keeps truly violent felons behind bars longer, it prevents them from committing additional crimes. The average predatory street criminal commits fifteen or more crimes each year when not behind bars. But most prisoners are in for a relatively short time and are released on parole early, often because of prison overcrowding. Then many find themselves back in prison because they have violated parole, typically by using illegal drugs. Indeed, of the more than 1.5 million people who are arrested each year, the majority are arrested for drug offenses. Given that from twenty to forty million Americans violate one or more drug laws each year, the potential "supply" of prisoners seems virtually limitless. Consequently, it may not matter how many prisons are built; there will still be overcrowding as along as we maintain the same legislation on illegal drugs.

Federal Drug Policy

Illegal drugs are a major cause of crime in America. A rising percentage of arrests are for illegal drug trafficking. The latest major illegal drug has contributed to an increase in the number of drug arrests. That drug is methamphetamine, sometimes known as meth or speed. Methamphetamine is often made in small home laboratories using toxic household chemicals. Raids on meth labs around the country have become common news stories. The violence that often accompanies the illegal drug trade occurs for several reasons. One is that drug dealers engage in "turf wars" over the territories in which drugs can be sold. Another is that when drug deals go bad, drug dealers cannot turn to the legal system for help, so they resort to violence. Finally, drug addicts who do not have the income to finance their habits often engage in crime—assault, robbery, and sometimes murder.

The war on drugs and the increased spending on drug interdiction over the years have had virtually no effect on overall illegal drug consumption in the United States. Mandatory sentences, which have been imposed by the federal government since the late 1980s for all federal offenses, including the sale or possession of illegal drugs, are also not an ideal solution. Mandatory sentences lead to a further problem—overcrowded prisons. Furthermore, almost half of the 1.5 million people arrested each year in the United States on drug charges are arrested for marijuana offenses—and of these, almost 90 percent are charged with possession only.

While the federal government has done little to modify its drug policy, state and local governments have been experimenting with new approaches to the problem. Many states now have special "drug courts" for those arrested for illegal drug use. In these courts, offenders typically are "sentenced" to a rehabilitation program.

Confronting Terrorism

Of all of the different types of crimes, terrorism can be the most devastating. The victims of terrorist attacks can number in the hundreds—or even in the thousands, as was the case when hijacked airplanes crashed into the Pentagon and the World Trade Center on September 11, 2001. Additionally, locating the perpetrators is often extremely difficult. In a suicide bombing, the perpetrators have themselves been killed, so the search is not for the perpetrators but for others who might have conspired with them in planning the attack.

After a plot to mix liquid chemicals to form explosives aboard as many as ten planes going to the United States from London was thwarted, passengers were no longer allowed to carry virtually any liquids and gels on planes. This new rule caused increased delays at all airports, including Dulles International Airport near Washington, D.C. Can any government completely control all possible ways that terrorists can kill or injure civilians? (AP Photo/Kevin Wolf)

Terrorism is certainly not a new phenomenon in the world, but it is a relatively new occurrence on U.S. soil. And certainly, the 9/11 attacks made many Americans aware for the first time of the hatred of America harbored by some foreigners—in this case, a network of religious fundamentalists in foreign countries. As you have read elsewhere in this text, immediately after 9/11 the U.S. government took many actions, including launching a war in Afghanistan, as part of a "war on terrorism." Congress quickly passed new legislation to fund these efforts, as well as a number of other acts, such as the Aviation Security Act.

Some of the actions taken in the wake of 9/11, such as the war in Afghanistan, were widely supported by the public. Others, such as the enactment of the USA Patriot Act and President Bush's executive order establishing military tribunals have been criticized for infringing too much on Americans' civil liberties. Worldwide, of course, terrorists' acts have continued since 9/11. Among others, they include bomb attacks on the subway system and a bus in London, which killed more than fifty people, and bomb attacks on the public transportation system in Madrid, which killed more than two hundred people. In the summer of 2006, the British government foiled what could have been one of the worst terrorist attacks yet. Ten or more individuals had prepared to take clear liquids into planes departing for the United States. These liquids were in fact bomb materials, and they were going to be detonated with electronic devices, such as MP3 players (or, what appeared to be these devices, of course). Certainly, at this point there is no end in sight to the war on terrorism. As with all policies, the nation's policy with respect to terrorism will be evaluated—and perhaps modified—over time.

Environmental Policy

Americans have paid increasing attention to environmental issues in the last three decades. A major source of concern for the general public has been the emission of pollutants into the air and water. Each year, the world atmosphere receives 20 million metric tons of sulfur dioxide, 18 million metric tons of ozone pollutants, and 60 million metric tons of carbon monoxide.

Environmentalism

Environmental issues are not limited to concerns about pollution. A second major concern is the protection of the natural environment. The protection of endangered species is an example of this type of issue. The movement to protect the environment has been based on two major strands of thought since its beginnings in the early 1900s. One point of view calls for *conservation*—that is, a policy under which natural resources should be used, but not abused. A second view advocates *preservation*. Under this policy, natural preserves are established that are isolated from the effects of human activity.

The Environmentalist Movement.   In the 1960s, an environmentalist movement arose that was much more focused on pollution issues than the previous conservation movement. A series of high-profile events served to awaken environmental interest. In 1962, Rachel Carson, of the U.S. Fish and Wildlife Service, published *Silent Spring*,[11] in which she detailed the injurious effects of pesticides on a variety of wild species. In 1969, an oil spill off the coast of Santa Barbara, California, drew national attention. That same year, the Cuyahoga River in Cleveland actually caught fire due to flammable chemicals floating on top of the water.

[11]Boston: Houghton Mifflin, 1962; repr., Boston: Mariner Books, 2002.

These three photos illustrate some of the environmental problems that persuaded Congress to pass the National Environmental Policy Act of 1969.

Top: The Cuyahoga River in 1969—firefighters extinguish a fire that started on the river and spread to a wooden trestle bridge. (Photo Courtesy of the Environmental Protection Agency)

Lower left: Workers clean a beach after a 1969 oil spill in Santa Barbara, California. (Photo Courtesy of the California Environmental Protection Agency)

Lower right: In 1945, municipal workers spray the pesticide DDT at Jones Beach, New York, while children frolic. (Library of Congress)

In 1970, the environmental movement organized the first Earth Day, which proved to be very successful in drawing attention to environmentalism and its concerns. Pollution control was a popular goal, and during the 1960s and 1970s, Congress passed numerous bills aimed at cleaning up the nation's air and water. We will describe some of these efforts in greater detail shortly.

Ecology. In the 1970s, a number of environmental activists began to advocate policies that were more controversial than pollution control. These policies represented a radical elaboration of the older preservationist philosophy and a rejection of the conservationist principle of wise use. Not only did the new line of thought reject the conservation of natural resources for use by people, but some activists also argued that the human race itself was the problem. Along with the new thinking came a new label—the ecology movement. *Ecology* refers to the total pattern of relationships between organisms and their environment.

Cleaning Up the Air and Water

The government has been responding to pollution problems since before the American Revolution, when the Massachusetts Bay Colony issued regulations to try to stop the pollution of Boston Harbor. In the 1800s, states passed laws controlling water pollution after scientists and medical researchers convinced most policymakers that dumping sewage into drinking and bathing water caused disease. At the national level, the Federal Water Pollution Control Act of 1948 provided research and assistance to the states for pollution-control efforts, but little was done.

The National Environmental Policy Act. The year 1969 marked the start of the most concerted national government involvement in solving pollution problems. As mentioned, in that year, the conflict between oil-exploration interests and environmental interests literally erupted when an oil well six miles off the coast of Santa Barbara, California, exploded, releasing 235,000 gallons of crude oil. The result was an oil slick, covering an area of eight hundred square miles, that washed up on the city's beaches and killed plant life, birds, and fish. Hearings in Congress revealed that the Interior Department had no guidance in the energy-environment trade-off. Congress soon passed the National Environmental Policy Act of 1969. This landmark legislation established, among other things, the Council on Environmental Quality. It also mandated that an **environmental impact statement (EIS)** be prepared for all major federal actions that could significantly affect the quality of the environment. The act gave citizens and public-interest groups concerned with the environment a weapon against the unnecessary and inappropriate use of natural resources by the government.

Curbing Air Pollution. Beginning in 1975, the government began regulating tailpipe emissions from cars and light trucks in an attempt to curb air pollution. In 1990, after years of lobbying by environmentalists, Congress passed the Clean Air Act of 1990. The act established tighter standards for emissions of nitrogen dioxide (NO_2) and other pollutants by newly built cars and light trucks. California was allowed to establish its own, stricter standards. By 1994, the maximum allowable NO_2 emissions (averaged over each manufacturer's "fleet" of vehicles) were about a fifth of the 1975 standard. The "Tier 2" system, phased in between 2004 and 2007, reduced maximum fleet emissions by cars and light trucks to just over 2 percent of the 1975 standard. In 2008–2009, the standards will be extended to trucks weighing between 6,000 and 8,500 pounds.

Stationary sources of air pollution were also made subject to more regulation

the United States to cut their emissions 40 percent by 2001. Controls were placed

| Environmental Impact
Statement (EIS)
A report that must show the costs and benefits of major federal actions that could significantly affect the quality of the environment.

A curtain of smog shrouds the Los Angeles skyline. Strict air-pollution standards for automobiles have been phased in over the past several years to curb such air pollution. How do policymakers measure the economic impact of clean-air policies? (AP Photo/Nick Ut)

on other factories and businesses in an attempt to reduce ground-level ozone pollution in ninety-six cities to healthful levels by 2005 (except in Los Angeles, which has until 2010 to meet the standards). The act also required that the production of chlorofluorocarbons (CFCs) be stopped completely by 2002. CFCs are thought to deplete the ozone layer in the upper atmosphere and increase the levels of harmful radiation reaching the earth's surface. CFCs were formerly used in air-conditioning and other refrigeration units.

In 1997, in light of evidence that very small particles (2.5 microns, or millionths of a meter) of soot might be dangerous to our health, the Environmental Protection Agency (EPA) issued new particulate standards for motor vehicle exhaust systems and other sources of pollution. The EPA also established a more rigorous standard for ground-level ozone, which is formed when sunlight combines with pollutants from cars and other sources. Ozone is a major component of smog.

Water Pollution.   One of the most important acts regulating water pollution is the Clean Water Act of 1972, which amended the Federal Water Pollution Control Act of 1948. The Clean Water Act established the following goals: (1) make waters safe for swimming, (2) protect fish and wildlife, and (3) eliminate the discharge of pollutants into the water. The act set specific time schedules, which were subsequently extended by further legislation. Under these schedules, the EPA establishes limits on discharges of types of pollutants based on the technology available for controlling them. The 1972 act also required municipal and industrial polluters to apply for permits before discharging wastes into navigable waters.

The Clean Water Act also prohibits the filling or dredging of wetlands unless a permit is obtained from the Army Corps of Engineers. The EPA defines *wetlands* as "those areas that are inundated or saturated by surface or ground water at a frequency and duration sufficient to support, and that under normal circumstances do support, a prevalence of vegetation typically adapted for life in saturated soil conditions." In recent years, the broad interpretation of what constitutes a wetland subject to the regulatory authority of the federal government has generated substantial controversy.

Perhaps one of the most controversial regulations concerning wetlands was the "migratory-bird rule" issued by the Army Corps of Engineers. Under this rule, any bodies of water that could affect interstate commerce, including seasonal ponds or waters "used or suitable for use by migratory birds" that fly over state borders, were "navigable waters" subject to federal regulation under the Clean Water Act as wetlands. In 2001, after years of controversy, the United States Supreme Court struck down the rule. The Court stated that it was not prepared to hold that isolated and seasonal ponds, puddles, and "prairie potholes" become "navigable waters of the United States" simply because they serve as a habitat for migratory birds.[12]

Cost-Effective Solutions

Before the mid-1980s, environmental politics seemed to be couched in terms of "them against us." "Them" was everyone involved in businesses that cut down rain forests, poisoned rivers, and created oil spills. "Us" was the government, and it was the government's job to stop "them." Today, particularly in the United States, more people are aware that the battle lines are blurred.

According to the EPA, we are spending about $210 billion annually to comply with federal environmental rules. There is a bright side, however. A report issued by

---

[12]*Solid Waste Agency of Northern Cook County v. U.S. Army Corps of Engineers*, 531 U.S. 159 (2001).

the Office of Management and Budget in 2003 concluded that the health and social benefits of enforcing tough new clean-air regulations are five to seven times greater than the costs of compliance. The government has become interested in how to solve the nation's environmental problems at the lowest cost. Moreover, U.S. corporations are becoming increasingly engaged in producing recyclable and biodegradable products, as well as helping to solve some environmental problems.

The Costs of Clean Air.   Cost concerns clearly were on the minds of the drafters of the Clean Air Act of 1990 when they tackled the problem of sulfur emissions from electric power plants. Rather than tightening the existing standards, the law simply limited total sulfur emissions. Companies had a choice of either rebuilding old plants or buying rights to pollute. The result was that polluters had an incentive to not even attempt to deal with exceptionally dirty plants. When closing down such plants, they could sell their pollution rights to those who valued them more. The law is straightforward: An electric utility power plant is allowed to emit up to one ton of sulfur dioxide into the air in a given year. If the plant emits one ton of sulfur dioxide, the allowance disappears. If a plant switches to a fuel low in sulfur dioxide, for example, or installs "scrubbing equipment" that reduces sulfur dioxide, it may end up emitting less than one ton. In this circumstance, it can sell or otherwise trade its unused pollution allowance, or it can bank it for later use.

These rights to pollution allowances are being traded in the marketplace. Indeed, there is a well-established market in "smog futures" offered on the Chicago Board of Trade and the New York Mercantile Exchange.

There Have Been Improvements.   The United States is making fairly substantial strides in the war on toxic emissions. According to the Environmental Protection Agency, in the last thirty years U.S. air pollution has been cut in half. Airborne lead is 3 percent of what it was in 1975, and the lead content of the average American's blood is one-fifth of what it was in that year. Airborne sulfur dioxide concentrations are one-fifth of the levels found in the 1960s. Carbon monoxide concentrations are a quarter of what they were in 1970. Water pollution is also down. Levels of six persistent pollutants in U.S. freshwater fish are about one-fifth of their 1970 levels. One reason for these successes is the increased awareness of the American public of the need for environmental protection. To a large extent, this increased awareness has been brought about through the efforts of various environmental interest groups, which have also exerted pressure on Congress to take action.

The Endangered Species Act

Inspired by the plight of disappearing species, Congress passed the Endangered Species Preservation Act in 1966. In 1973, Congress passed a completely new Endangered Species Act (ESA). The ESA made it illegal to kill, harm, or otherwise "take" a species listed as endangered or threatened. The government could purchase habitat critical to the survival of a species or prevent landowners from engaging in development that would harm a listed species.

The ESA proved to be a powerful legal tool for the ecology movement. In a famous example, environmental groups sued to stop the Tennessee Valley Authority from completing the Tellico Dam on the ground that it threatened habitat critical to the survival of the snail darter, a tiny fish. In 1978, the United States Supreme Court ruled in favor of the endangered fish.[13] Further controversy erupted in 1990, when the Fish and Wildlife Service listed the spotted owl as a threatened species.

---

[13]*Tennessee Valley Authority v. Hill*, 437 U.S. 153 (1978). In 1979, Congress exempted the snail darter from the ESA. In 1980, snail darters were discovered elsewhere, and the species turned out not to be in danger.

Not too many years ago, construction on the multimillion dollar Tellico Dam in Tennessee was stopped dead in its tracks when a group of environmentalists argued that it endangered the snail darter fish, shown on the right. Several years later, the snail darter was found to be thriving in a number of other locations, and shortly thereafter, it was removed from the government's endangered species list. How does a society balance environmental issues with economic ones?
(Courtesy of the Tennessee Valley Authority and the U.S. Fish and Wildlife Service)

The logging industry blamed the ESA for a precipitous decline in national forest timber sales in subsequent years.

The ESA continues to be a major subject of debate. There are signs, however, that the government and environmentalists may be seeking common ground. Both sides are shifting toward incentives for landowners who participate in protection programs. "Regulatory incentives really do result in landowners doing good things for their land," said William Irvin of the World Wildlife Fund.[14] Still, environmental groups accused the Bush administration of underfunding the act and undermining the species-listing process by shifting control from the Fish and Wildlife Service to the secretary of the interior.

Global Warming

In the 1990s, scientists working on climate change began to conclude that average world temperatures will rise significantly in the twenty-first century. Gases released by human activity, principally carbon dioxide, may produce a "greenhouse effect," trapping the sun's heat and slowing its release into outer space. In fact, many studies have shown that global warming has already begun, although the effects of the change are still modest. Christine Todd Whitman, who headed the Environmental Protection Agency from 2001 to 2003, called global warming "one of the greatest environmental challenges we face, if not the greatest."

The Kyoto Protocol.   In 1997, delegates from around the world gathered in Kyoto, Japan, for a global climate conference sponsored by the United Nations. The conference issued a proposed treaty aimed at reducing emissions of greenhouse gases to 5.2 percent below 1990 levels by 2012. Only thirty-eight developed nations were mandated to reduce their emissions, however—developing nations faced only voluntary limits. The U.S. Senate voted unanimously in 1997 that it would not accept a treaty that exempted developing countries, and in 2001 President Bush announced that he would not submit the Kyoto protocol to the Senate for ratification. By 2007, 124 nations had ratified the protocol. Its rejection by the United States, however, raised the question of whether it could ever be effective.

---

[14]"Endangered Species Act Turns 30 as Environmental Strategy Shifts," *The Charleston Post and Courier,* Charleston, S.C., January 2, 2004.

Even in those European countries that most enthusiastically supported the Kyoto protocol and signed it, the results have not been overly positive. Thirteen of the fifteen original European Union signatories will miss their 2010 emission targets. For example, Spain will miss its target by 33 percentage points. Denmark had agreed to reduce its levels of greenhouse gas emissions by 21 percent, but so far its emissions have *increased* by more than 6 percent since 1990. Greece has seen its greenhouse gas emissions increase by 23 percent since 1990. Closer to home, Prime Minister Paul Martin of Canada lambasted the United States for its lack of a "global conscience." But since 1990, Canada's emissions have risen by 24 percent, much faster than the U.S. rate.

The Global Warming Debate. While the majority of scientists who perform research on the world's climate believe that global warming will be significant, there is considerable disagreement as to how much warming will actually occur. It is generally accepted that world temperatures have already increased by at least 0.6 degrees Celsius over the last century. Scenarios by the United Nations Intergovernmental Panel on Climate Change predict increases ranging from 2.0 to 4.5 degrees Celsius by the year 2100. More conservative estimates, such as those by climate experts James Hansen and Patrick Michaels, average around 0.75 degrees Celsius.[15]

Global warming has become a major political football to be kicked back and forth by conservatives and liberals. Some conservatives have seized on the work of scientists who believe that global warming does not exist at all. (Some of these researchers work for oil companies.) If this were true, there would be no reason to limit emissions of carbon dioxide and other greenhouse gases. A more sophisticated argument by conservatives is that major steps to limit emissions in the near future would not be cost effective. Bjorn Lomborg, a critic of the environmental movement, believes that it would be more practical to take action against global warming later in the century, when the world is (presumably) richer and when renewable energy sources have become more competitive in price.[16]

Bjorn Lomborg, director of Denmark's Environment Assessment Institute, speaks at the Copenhagen Consensus conference in 2004. Eight world-renowned professors of economics, among them several Nobel laureates, made up an expert panel that discussed and prioritized solutions to serious global challenges. (EPA/Bjarke Orsted/Landov)

[15]J. E. Hansen, "Defusing the Global Warming Time Bomb," *Scientific American*, March 2004, pp. 69–77. This article is also online at **www.sciam.com/media/pdf/hansen.pdf**.

[16]Bjorn Lomborg, *The Skeptical Environmentalist* (Cambridge, England: Cambridge University Press, 2001), pp. 258–324.

According to a study by the National Aeronautics and Space Administration, Arctic sea ice has been decreasing at a rate of 9 percent per decade since the 1970s. Researchers suspect the loss of Arctic sea ice may be caused by the buildup of greenhouse gases in the atmosphere. The first image shows the minimum sea ice concentration in 1979, and the second shows minimum sea ice in 2003. The red line highlights the change. The changes in Arctic ice may be a harbinger of global climate change. (NASA Images)

MAKING A DIFFERENCE | Environmental Trade-Offs

Environmental problems will undoubtedly be some of the most important domestic issues in the coming decades. For example, every energy policy involves environmental questions. To make things more complicated, the parallel struggles of coping with energy problems and preserving our environment tend to work at cross-purposes.

Land use is another topic that can require difficult political trade-offs. Landowners naturally want the freedom to do whatever they wish with their property. But what if a farm family at some distance from town wants to sell its property so that developers can put up tract housing? Should the state or local government be able to block such a development on the ground that it would foster "urban sprawl"?

Why Should You Care?

The trade-off between energy development and preserving the environment has a direct impact on your pocketbook and your quality of life. In recent years, gasoline prices have risen dramatically. High gas prices affect your mobility. Yet increased oil drilling might despoil nature reserves, and no one wants to live next door to a refinery.

Land-use issues can have an even more direct effect on your life. On the one hand, a housing development might destroy a local scenic view. On the other hand, failure to build new housing will increase the value of existing housing. As a result, you might have to pay more to rent an apartment or, eventually, to buy a house.

What Can You Do?

Energy policy is a national issue, and you can have an impact on policy by getting involved with national organizations through their Web sites. The following environmental groups have taken a special interest in energy issues:

Friends of the Earth
www.foe.org

Wilderness Society
www.wilderness.org

For a contrasting point of view, go to

Heritage Foundation
www.heritage.org.

Look for its list of research issues, and click on "Energy & Environment."

Land-use policies are usually set at the state or local level. There are some national groups that organize around these issues, however. For a slow-growth perspective, visit

Smart Growth Network
www.smartgrowth.org.

For counterarguments, go to

Thoreau Institute
www.ti.org

Key Terms

domestic policy 483

earned-income tax credit (EITC) program 495

environmental impact statement (EIS) 507

food stamps 495

incarceration rate 503

income transfer 492

in-kind subsidy 493

Medicaid 488

Medicare 488

national health insurance 491

single-payer plan 491

Supplemental Security Income (SSI) 494

Temporary Assistance to Needy Families (TANF) 494

Chapter Summary

1 Domestic policy consists of all of the laws, government planning, and government actions that affect the lives of American citizens. Policies are created in response to public problems or public demand for government action. Major policy problems discussed in this chapter include health care, poverty and welfare, immigration, crime, and the environment.

2 The policymaking process is initiated when policymakers become aware—through the media or from their constituents—of a problem that needs to be addressed by the legislature and the president. The process of policymaking includes five steps: agenda building, policy formulation, policy adoption,

policy implementation, and policy evaluation. All policy actions necessarily result in both costs and benefits for society.

3 Health-care spending is about 15 percent of the U.S. economy and is growing. Reasons for this growth include the increasing number of elderly persons, advancing technology, and higher demand because costs are picked up by third-party insurers. A major third party is Medicare, the federal program that pays health-care expenses of U.S. residents over the age of sixty-five. The federal government has tried to restrain the growth in Medicare spending, but it has also expanded the program to cover prescription drugs.

4 About 15 percent of the population does not have health insurance—a major political issue. Most uninsured adults work for employers that cannot afford to offer health benefits. Hospitals tend to charge the uninsured higher rates than they charge insurance companies or the government. One proposal for addressing this problem is a national health-insurance system under which the government provides basic coverage to all citizens. Another alternative is the use of health savings accounts (HSAs) that allow people to save for their medical expenses tax free.

5 In spite of the wealth of the United States, a significant number of Americans live in poverty or are homeless. The low-income poverty threshold represents the income needed to maintain a specified standard of living as of 1963, with the purchasing-power value increased year by year based on the general increase in prices. The official poverty level is based on pretax income, including cash, and does not take into consideration in-kind subsidies (food stamps, housing vouchers, and so on).

6 The 1996 Welfare Reform Act transferred more control over welfare programs to the states, limited the number of years people can receive welfare assistance, and imposed work requirements on welfare recipients. The reform act succeeded in reducing the number of welfare recipients in the United States by at least 50 percent.

7 America has always been a land of immigrants and continues to be so. Today, more than one million immigrants from other nations enter the United States each year, and more than 10 percent of the U.S. population consists of foreign-born persons. The civil rights legislation of the 1960s and later has helped immigrants to overcome some of the effects of prejudice and discrimination against them.

8 There is widespread concern in this country about violent crime, particularly the large number of crimes that are committed by juveniles. The overall rate of violent crime, including crimes committed by juveniles, declined between 1995 and 2004, however. In response to crime concerns, the United States has incarcerated an unusually large number of persons. Crimes associated with illegal drug sales and use have also challenged policymakers. A pressing issue facing Americans and their government today, of course, is terrorism—one of the most devastating forms of crime. Government attempts to curb terrorism will no doubt continue for some time to come.

9 Pollution problems continue to plague the United States and the world. Since the 1800s, a number of significant federal acts have been passed in an attempt to curb the pollution of our environment. The National Environmental Policy Act of 1969 established the Council on Environmental Quality. That act also mandated that environmental impact statements be prepared for all legislation or major federal actions that might significantly affect the quality of the environment. The Clean Water Act of 1972 and the Clean Air Act amendments of 1990 constituted the most significant government attempts at cleaning up our environment. Recent environmental controversies have centered on the Endangered Species Act and global warming.

Selected Print and Media Resources

SUGGESTED READINGS

Davis, Devra Lee. *When Smoke Ran Like Water: Tales of Environmental Deception and the Battle against Pollution*. New York: Basic Books, 2004. Davis, an epidemiologist, describes the health consequences of polluted air. She provides historical examples, such as the Donora Fog of 1948 that sickened a small town in Pennsylvania.

Easterbrook, Gregg. *The Progress Paradox: How Life Gets Better While People Feel Worse*. New York: Random House, 2003. Easterbrook points to real improvements in recent years in fighting crime, cleaning up the environment, and enhancing the material prosperity of most Americans. Nevertheless, pessimism remains widespread.

Ehrenreich, Barbara. *Nickel and Dimed: On (Not) Getting By in America*. New York: Owl Books, 2002. Released on audio CD in 2004. What is life like for the working poor? Commentator and humorist Barbara Ehrenreich sought to live for a few months working at minimum-wage jobs. Here, she describes her experiences.

Hage, Dave. *Reforming Welfare by Rewarding Work: One State's Successful Experiment*. Minneapolis, Minn.: University of Minnesota Press, 2004. Hage describes the Minnesota Family Investment Program, a pilot program in welfare reform. He illustrates the story with firsthand accounts of three families.

Miller, Roger LeRoy, et al. *The Economics of Public Issues*, 15th ed. Reading, Mass.: Addison-Wesley, 2005. Chapters 4, 8, 11, 13, 19, 20, 22, 24, and 27 are especially useful. The authors use short essays of three to seven pages to explain the purely economic aspects of numerous social problems, including health care, the environment, and poverty.

Sered, Susan Starr, and Rushika Fernandopulle. *Uninsured in America: Life and Death in the Land of Opportunity*. Berkeley, Calif.: University of California Press, 2006. Based on interviews with 120 uninsured individuals and numerous policymakers and medical providers, this book looks at the growing ranks of Americans lacking health insurance and the problems with the nation's current health-care policies.

Zuberi, Dan. *Differences that Matter: Social Policy and the Working Poor in the United States and Canada*. Ithaca, NY: Cornell University Press, 2006. The author takes a comparative approach to the lives of the working poor in the United States and Canada, looking at vital issues ranging from health care to labor policies.

MEDIA RESOURCES

... released in 2002, that contains unprecedented interviews with bombers, gunmen, hijackers, and kidnappers. The interviews are combined with photos from police and news archives. The four tapes are *In the Name of Liberation, In the Name of Revolution, In the Name of God,* and *In the Name of the State.*

America's Promise: Who's Entitled to What?—A four-part series that examines the current state of welfare reform and its impact on immigrant and other populations.

A Day's Work, A Day's Pay—This 2002 documentary by Jonathan Skurnik and Kathy Leichter follows three welfare recipients in New York City from 1997 to 2000. When forced to work at city jobs for well below the prevailing wage and not allowed to go to school, the three fight for programs that will help them get better jobs.

Drugs and Punishment: Are America's Drug Policies Fair?—In this 1996 BBC production, British journalist Charles Wheeler examines America's drug use and the hail of new drug laws instituted under the Reagan administration. Former drug czar William Bennett defends the government's position.

Traffic—A 2001 film, starring Michael Douglas and Benicio Del Toro, that offers compelling insights into the consequences of failed drug policies. (Authors' note: Be aware that this film contains material of a violent and sexual nature that may be offensive.)

Young Criminals, Adult Punishment—An ABC program that examines the issue of whether the harsh sentences given out to adult criminals, including capital punishment, should also be applied to young violent offenders.

E·MOCRACY | The Internet and Domestic Policy

Today, the World Wide Web offers opportunities for you to easily access information about any domestic policy issue. The *Logging On* section that follows lists a variety of Web sites where you can learn more about domestic policy issues and how they affect you. Many other sites are available as well. For example, would you like to learn more about prisons and imprisonment rates in different countries? The Web site of the International Center for Prison Studies (ICPS) can help. A URL for the ICPS is **www.kcl.ac.uk/depsta/rel/icps/worldbrief/world_brief.html**. Would you like to take a turn at proposing a federal budget and allocating spending among different programs, domestic or otherwise? You can find a budget simulation game at **www.kowaldesign.com/budget**. Of course, most news media outlets have their own Web sites, which are useful for keeping up to date on the latest domestic policy developments.

| Logging On

To find more information on poverty in the United States and the latest research on this topic, go to the Web site of the Institute for Research on Poverty at

www.ssc.wisc.edu/irp

For current statistics on poverty in the United States, go to

www.census.gov/hhes/www/poverty.html

The National Governors Association offers information on the current status of welfare reform and other topics at

www.nga.org

The Federal Bureau of Investigation offers information about crime rates at its Web site:

www.fbi.gov/ucr/ucr.htm

You can also find statistics and other information on crime in the United States at the Web site of the Bureau of Justice Statistics. Go to

www.ojp.usdoj.gov/bjs

| Online Review

At **www.politicalscience.wadsworth.com/schmidt12**, you will find a free Study Guide to this book. For each chapter, there are two online quizzes to help you master the material.

• The PoliPrep Self-Study Assessment provides a pretest for each major section of the chapter. PoliPrep then generates a customized study plan. After you complete the study plan, a posttest evaluates your progress.

• The Tutorial Quiz for each chapter provides questions on the chapter contents, including the features. The questions are organized to match the major sections of the chapter.

What If . . .
The Federal Government Were Required to Balance Its Budget?

BACKGROUND

Except for a few years in the late 1990s, the federal government has spent more than it received every single year for decades. In other words, the federal government has run a budget deficit. Since the recession of 2001 and the terrorist attacks in that same year, the federal budget deficit has ballooned, averaging more than $380 billion per year from 2001 to 2007. To comprehend the size of the federal budget deficit, consider that it is the equivalent of spending about $44 million per hour, or $1.1 billion per day, for one year. In January 2004, when President George W. Bush started his second term, he promised to cut the deficit in half by the time he leaves office in January 2009.

WHAT IF THE FEDERAL GOVERNMENT WERE REQUIRED TO BALANCE ITS BUDGET?

To understand the ramifications of a balanced federal budget, you first have to consider how it would be balanced. Let's assume that an amendment requiring a balanced budget is added to the U.S. Constitution. Initially, there would be only two possible ways to balance the federal budget. One way would be to raise taxes and increase user fees. The other possibility would be to reduce the amount of federal government spending. Alternatively, a combination of these two actions could be undertaken.

INCREASED TAXES

On the revenue side of the equation, one way to balance the budget is to increase taxes on individuals and corporations. If the government did this by increasing taxes on individuals, then the tax rates paid by the middle class would have to rise significantly. Why? The reason is simply that the middle class is the source of most tax revenues for the federal government. The rich and the superrich pay a more-than-proportionate share in taxes, but they do not pay the bulk of all personal federal income taxes—the middle class does. So middle-class Americans would see their taxes go up rather dramatically.

Taxes on corporations might increase significantly, too. Corporations, though, exist only as legal entities. Therefore, increased corporate taxes would mean reduced income for owners of corporate stock, lower salaries for employees of corporations, and higher prices for consumers.

It would also be possible to increase user fees for all federal government services, perhaps to keep them more in line with the actual costs of the federal government. The fees to visit national parks would likely be raised, as one example.

REDUCED FEDERAL GOVERNMENT SPENDING

On the spending side of the equation, a reduction in federal government spending could mean dramatic changes for many Americans. There might be fewer pork-barrel spending projects, such as the National Cowgirl Museum and Hall of Fame in Fort Worth, Texas; the indoor rain forest in Coralville, Iowa; and the whaling museum in New Bedford, Massachusetts. But such obvious boondoggles, or earmarked spending projects, account for less than 1 percent of the federal budget.

Much more spending would have to be reduced to balance the budget (unless taxes were raised at the same time). So there might be across-the-board cuts of, say, 6 percent in every department. Each department would then have to decide how much to cut from its own programs. Obviously, the public would be outraged as popular programs were either cut back substantially or eliminated altogether.

FOREIGN OWNERSHIP OF U.S. TREASURY BONDS

Another effect of a balanced federal budget would be a reduction in the amount of U.S. Treasury bonds held by foreign residents and governments. When the federal government runs a deficit, it creates debt obligations, usually in the form of U.S. Treasury bonds. Currently, foreigners buy a significant portion of those bonds, up to 50 percent. If the government had to balance its budget, foreigners would no longer be able to buy U.S. debt. Many Americans are uncomfortable knowing that foreigners own so much of our accumulated federal deficits and would therefore view this change as beneficial.

FOR CRITICAL ANALYSIS

1. Of the two methods of reducing the deficit to zero—raising taxes or decreasing government spending—which method do you believe would be less "painful"? Why?
2. How can the federal government spend more than it receives every year, whereas a family would have a hard time doing the same thing year in and year out?

Nowhere are the principles of public policymaking more obvious than in the economic decisions made by the federal government. The president and Congress (and to a growing extent, the judiciary) are constantly faced with questions of economic policy. A major economic policy issue is how to maintain stable economic growth without falling into either excessive unemployment or *inflation* (rising prices). **Inflation** is defined as a sustained upward movement in the average level of prices.

Another policy issue that is always under discussion is the state of the federal budget, because it is rarely balanced. You read about the effects of forcing the federal government to balance its budget in this chapter's opening *What If . . .* feature. Other issues discussed in this chapter include world trade, taxes, and the impact that Social Security will have on the federal budget in future years.

Inflation
A sustained rise in the general price level of goods and services.

Good Times, Bad Times

Other than the fundamental tasks of maintaining law, order, and national security, no governmental objective is more important than the maintenance of economic stability. Like any economy that is fundamentally capitalist, the U.S. economy experiences ups and downs. Good times—booms—are followed by lean years. If a slowdown is so severe that the economy actually shrinks for six or more months, it is called a **recession.** Recessions, in part because they bring increased unemployment, are political poison for a sitting president, even though a president's power to control the economy is actually not that great. The government tries to moderate the effects of such downturns. In contrast, booms are historically associated with another economic problem that the government must address—rising prices, or inflation. We will turn to the topic of inflation shortly. First, we consider the problem of excessive unemployment.

Recession
Two or more successive quarters in which the economy shrinks instead of grows.

Unemployment

One political goal of any administration is to keep the rate of unemployment down. **Unemployment** is the inability of those who are in the workforce to find a job. Individuals may become unemployed for several reasons. Some people enter the labor force for the first time and have to look for a job. Some people are fired or laid off and have to look for a job. Others just want to change occupations. **Full employment** is defined as a level of unemployment that makes allowances for normal movement between jobs. Full employment is widely considered to be a desirable state of affairs, but the nation does not always have it. During recessions, unemployment rises well above the full-employment level. For example, during the last serious business slowdown in 2001–2002, the rate of unemployment increased from 4.0 to 6.5 percent. Since 2005, the unemployment rate has fallen below 5 percent.

Unemployment
The inability of those who are in the labor force to find a job; defined as the total number of those in the labor force actively looking for a job but unable to find one.

Full Employment
An arbitrary level of unemployment that corresponds to "normal" friction in the labor market. In 1986, a 6.5 percent rate of unemployment was considered full employment. Today, it is assumed to be around 5 percent.

Unemployment Becomes an Issue. For much of American history, unemployment was not a problem that the federal government was expected to address. In the early years of the republic, most people would have thought that the national government could not do much about unemployment. Indeed, by the late 1800s, many people had come to believe that as a matter of principle, the government should not fight unemployment. This belief followed from an economic philosophy that was dominant in those years—*laissez-faire economics.* (You learned about the concept of *laissez-faire*— French for "let it be"—in Chapter 1.) Advocates of this philosophy believed then (and believe now) that government intervention in the economy is almost always misguided and likely to lead to negative results. A second barrier to any federal government action against unemployment was the doctrine of *dual federalism*, which was described in Chapter 3. Under this theory, only state governments had the right to address a problem such as unemployment.

The Great Depression of the 1930s ended popular support for dual federalism and *laissez-faire* economics. As the depression took hold, unemployment initially exceeded 25 percent. Relatively high rates of unemployment—over 15 percent—persisted for more than ten years. One of the methods that the Roosevelt administration adopted to combat the effects of the depression was direct government employment of those without jobs.

Since the passage of the Social Security Act of 1935, the federal government has also offered a program of unemployment insurance. The program is the government's single most important source of assistance to the jobless. Not all unemployed workers are eligible, however. In fact, only about one-third of the unemployed receive benefits. Benefits are not available to employees who quit their jobs voluntarily or are fired for cause (for example, constantly showing up late for work). They are also not paid to workers who are entering the labor force for the first time but cannot find a job. Unemployment insurance is a joint state-federal program and is paid for by a tax on employers.

Measuring Unemployment.   Estimates of the number of unemployed are prepared by the U.S. Department of Labor. The Bureau of the Census also generates estimates using survey research data. Figure 16–1 shows how unemployment has gone up and down over the course of American history.

Critics of the published unemployment rate calculated by the federal government believe that it fails to reflect the true numbers of discouraged workers and "hidden unemployed." Though there is no exact definition of discouraged workers or way to measure them, the Department of Labor defines them as people who have dropped out of the labor force and are no longer looking for a job because they believe that the job market has little to offer them.

Inflation

Rising prices, or inflation, can also be a serious political problem for any sitting administration, especially if prices are rising fast. As previously stated, inflation is a sustained upward movement in the average level of prices. Inflation can also be defined as a decline in the purchasing power of money over time. The government

In 1935, young members of the Civilian Conservation Corps (CCC) clear rocks from a trail in Prince George's County, Maryland. Today, government employees' unions, fearing competition, often oppose programs under which the government hires former welfare recipients or other low-paid individuals. How should such concerns be addressed? (Library of Congress/ Photo by Carl Mydans)

FIGURE 16–1 | MORE THAN A CENTURY OF UNEMPLOYMENT

Unemployment reached lows during World Wars I and II of less than 2 percent and a high during the Great Depression of more than 25 percent.

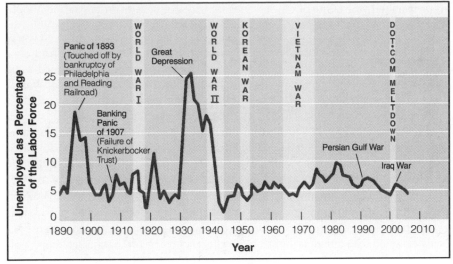

Source: U.S. Department of Labor, Bureau of Labor Statistics.

measures inflation using the **consumer price index,** or **CPI.** The Bureau of Labor Statistics (BLS) identifies a market basket of goods and services purchased by the typical consumer and regularly checks the price of that basket. Over a period of many years, inflation can add up. For example, today's dollar is worth (very roughly) one-twentieth of what a dollar was worth a century ago. Figure 16–2 shows the changing rates of inflation in the United States since 1860. Since the mid-2000s, inflation has again become a more or less constant news item. Predicted inflation rates are still in

Consumer Price Index (CPI)
A measure of the change in price over time of a specific group of goods and services used by the average household.

FIGURE 16–2 | CHANGING RATES OF INFLATION, 1860 TO THE PRESENT

From the Civil War until World War II, the United States experienced alternating inflation and deflation. (*Deflation* is a sustained decrease in the average price level.) Since World War II, deflation has not been a problem. The vertical yellow bars represent wartime.

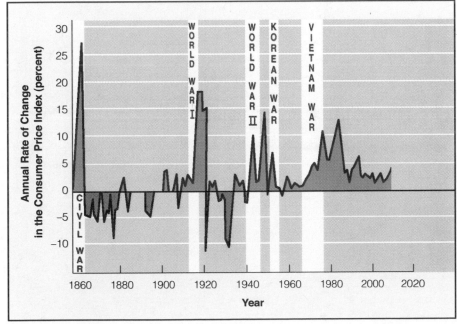

Source: U.S. Department of Labor, Bureau of Labor Statistics.

excess of 3 to 4 percent per year. That might not seem very high, but an inflation rate of 4 percent per year leads to a *doubling* of the price index in 18 years.

The Business Cycle

As noted earlier in the chapter, the economy passes through boom times and recessions. Economists refer to the regular succession of economic expansions and contractions as the *business cycle*. This term may be less appropriate than it used to be because *cycle* implies regular recurrence, and in the years since World War II (1939–1945), contractions and expansions have varied greatly in length. Figure 16–3 shows business cycles since 1880. Note that the long-term upward trend line is shown as horizontal, so all changes in business activity focus around that trend line.

An extremely severe recession is called a *depression*, as in the example of the Great Depression. By 1933, actual output was 35 percent below the nation's productive capacity. By 1932, the net income of farm operators was barely 20 percent of its 1929 level, even though total farm output had risen by 3 percent in the interim. Between 1929 and 1932, more than five thousand banks, one out of every five, failed, and their customers' deposits vanished. Compared with this catastrophe, recessions since 1945 have been mild. Nevertheless, limiting the effects of recessions has been a major policy goal of every administration that has had to confront such a slowdown.

| Fiscal Policy

To smooth out the ups and downs of the national economy, the government has several policy options. One is to change the level of taxes or government spending.

FIGURE 16–3 | NATIONAL BUSINESS ACTIVITY, 1880 TO THE PRESENT

Variations around the trend of U.S. business activity have been frequent since 1880.

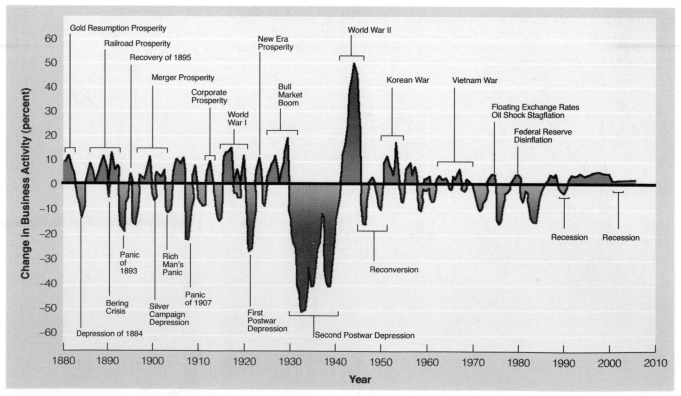

Sources: *American Business Activity from 1790 to Today,* 67th ed. (AmeriTrust Co., January 1996); and authors' updates.

The other possibility involves influencing interest rates and the money side of the economy. We will examine taxing and spending, or fiscal policy, first. Fiscal policy is the domain of Congress. A fiscal policy approach to stabilizing the economy is often associated with a twentieth-century economist named John Maynard Keynes.

Keynesian Economics

The British economist John Maynard Keynes (1883–1946) originated the school of thought called **Keynesian economics,** which supports the use of government spending and taxing to help stabilize the economy. (*Keynesian* is pronounced *kayn*-zee-un.) Keynes believed that there was a need for government intervention in the economy, in part because after falling into a recession or depression, a modern economy may become trapped in an ongoing state of less than full employment.

Government Spending. Keynes developed his fiscal policy theories during the Great Depression. He believed that the forces of supply and demand operated too slowly on their own in such a serious recession. Unemployment meant people had less to spend, and because they could not buy things, more businesses failed, creating additional unemployment. It was a vicious cycle. Keynes's idea was simple: in such circumstances, the *government* should step in and undertake the spending that is needed to return the economy to a more normal state.[1]

Government Borrowing. Government spending can be financed in a number of ways, including increasing taxes and borrowing. For government spending to have the effect Keynes wanted, however, it was essential that the spending be financed by borrowing, and not by taxes. In other words, the government should run a **budget deficit** (which we discussed in the chapter-opening *What If . . .* feature)—it should spend more than it receives. If the government financed its spending during a recession by taxation, the government would be spending funds that would, for the most part, otherwise have been spent by taxpayers.

Normally, businesses constantly borrow funds to expand future production. Consumers also borrow to finance items that cannot be paid for out of current income, such as a house or a car. In a recession, however, borrowing slows down. Businesses may not believe that they can sell the new goods or services that would allow them to repay the funds they might borrow. Consumers may be fearful of incurring long-term obligations at a time when their jobs might be threatened.

When the government borrows during a recession, this borrowing replaces the borrowing that businesses and consumers would normally undertake. By running a budget deficit, therefore, the government makes up not only for reduced spending by businesses and consumers, but for reduced private borrowing as well.

Discretionary Fiscal Policy. Keynes originally developed his fiscal theories as a way of lifting an economy out of a major disaster such as the Great Depression. Beginning with the presidency of John F. Kennedy (1961–1963), however, policymakers have attempted to use Keynesian methods to "fine-tune" the economy. This is discretionary fiscal policy—*discretionary* meaning left to the judgment or discretion of a policymaker. For example, President George W. Bush advertised his tax cuts of 2001 and 2003 as a method of stimulating the economy to halt the economic slowdown of those years. During 2006, Bush repeatedly pointed out that since his tax cuts were put into effect, the economy grew so much that federal tax revenues increased more than anticipated, thereby reducing the federal budget deficit below the level that had been predicted.

---

[1]Robert Skidelsky, *John Maynard Keynes: The Economist as Savior, 1920–1937: A Biography* (New York: Penguin USA, 1994).

| **Fiscal Policy**
The federal government's use of taxation and spending policies to affect overall business activity.

| **Keynesian Economics**
A school of economic thought that tends to favor active federal government policymaking to stabilize economy-wide fluctuations, usually by implementing discretionary fiscal policy.

| **Budget Deficit**
Government expenditures that exceed receipts.

John Maynard Keynes, the famous British economist, at his home in London in 1929. (Corbis. All rights reserved.)

| Wage and Price Controls
Government-imposed controls on the maximum prices that may be charged for specific goods and services, plus controls on permissible wage increases.

| Automatic, or Built-In, Stabilizers
Certain federal programs that cause changes in national income during economic fluctuations without the action of Congress and the president. Examples are the federal income tax system and unemployment compensation.

Kennedy was the first American president to explicitly adopt Keynesian economics. In 1963, during a mild business slowdown, Kennedy proposed a tax cut. Congress did not actually pass the necessary legislation until early 1964, after Kennedy had been assassinated. The economy picked up—the tax cut was a success.

Discretionary Fiscal Policy Failures.   Subsequent presidents did not have the same success as Kennedy with their fiscal policies. Lyndon Johnson, Kennedy's successor, presided over a boom that was partially fueled by spending on the Vietnam War (1964–1975). In principle, Johnson should have asked for a tax increase to pay for the war. He was afraid of the political consequences, however; the Vietnam War was unpopular enough already. Instead of raising taxes, Congress borrowed and ran a budget deficit. This, of course, is the exact opposite of what Keynes would have recommended. One of the results seemed to be inflation.

Ending an inflationary spiral can be politically dangerous. It may result in a recession. Johnson's successors, presidents Richard Nixon, Gerald Ford, and Jimmy Carter, were reluctant to take that risk and, in any event, may have lacked the political support needed for serious anti-inflationary measures. Nixon, in particular, chose to fight inflation not with fiscal or monetary policies but by instituting a comprehensive system of **wage and price controls.** Eventually, Nixon had to lift the controls, and when he did, measured inflation came roaring back stronger than ever. In the end, inflation was halted through the use of monetary policy, which you will read about shortly.

The Thorny Problem of Timing

Attempts to fine-tune the economy face a timing problem. Have you ever taken a shower, turned on the hot water, and had the water come out cold? Then, in frustration, you gave the hot water faucet another turn and were scalded? What happened was that there was a lag between the time you turned on the faucet and the time the hot water actually reached the showerhead. Policymakers concerned with short-run stabilization face similar difficulties.

It takes a while to collect and assimilate economic data. Time may go by before an economic problem can be identified. After an economic problem is recognized, a solution must be formulated. There will be an action time lag between the recognition of a problem and the implementation of policy to solve it. Getting Congress to act can easily take a year or two. Finally, after fiscal policy is enacted, it takes time for the policy to act on the economy. Because fiscal policy time lags are long and variable, a policy designed to combat a recession may not produce results until the economy is already out of the recession.

Automatic Stabilizers

Not all changes in taxes or in government spending require new legislation by Congress. Certain automatic fiscal policies—called **automatic,** or **built-in, stabilizers**—include the tax system itself and government transfer payments such as unemployment insurance.

You know that if you work less, you are paid less, and therefore you pay lower taxes. The amount of taxes that our government collects falls automatically during a recession. Some economists consider this an automatic tax cut. Like other tax cuts, it may help reduce the extent of a recession.

Similar to the tax system, unemployment compensation payments may boost total economy-wide demand. When business activity drops, many laid-off workers automatically become eligible for unemployment compensation from their state governments. They continue to receive income, although certainly it is less than they earned when they were employed.

Deficit Spending and the Public Debt

The federal government typically borrows by selling **U.S. Treasury bonds.** The sale of these federal government bonds to corporations, private individuals, pension plans, foreign governments, foreign businesses, and foreign individuals adds to this nation's *public debt*. In the last few years, foreigners have come to own about 50 percent of the U.S. public debt. Thirty years ago, the share of the U.S. public debt held by foreigners was only 15 percent.

The Public Debt in Perspective.   Did you know that the federal government has accumulated trillions of dollars in debt? Does that scare you? It certainly would if you thought that we had to pay it back tomorrow. But we do not.

There are two types of public debt—gross and net. The **gross public debt** includes all federal government interagency borrowings, which really do not matter. This is similar to your taking an IOU ("I owe you") out of your left pocket and putting it into your right pocket. Currently, federal interagency borrowings account for close to $3 trillion of the gross public debt. What is important is the **net public debt**—the public debt that does not include interagency borrowing. Table 16–1 shows the net public debt of the federal government since 1940.

This table does not take into account two very important variables: inflation and increases in population. A better way to examine the relative importance of the public debt is to compare it to the **gross domestic product (GDP),** as is done in Figure 16–4. (The *gross domestic product* is the dollar value of all final goods and services produced in a one-year period.) There you see that the public debt reached its peak during World War II and fell thereafter. Since about 1960, the net public debt as a percentage of GDP has ranged between 30 and 50 percent.

Are We Always in Debt?   From 1960 until the last few years of the twentieth century, the federal government spent more than it received in all but two years. Some observers consider these ongoing budget deficits to be the negative result of Keynesian policies. Others argue that the deficits actually result from the abuse of Keynesianism. Politicians have been more than happy to run budget deficits in

U.S. Treasury Bond
Debt issued by the federal government.

Gross Public Debt
The net public debt plus interagency borrowings within the government.

Net Public Debt
The accumulation of all past federal government deficits; the total amount owed by the federal government to individuals, businesses, and foreigners.

Gross Domestic Product (GDP)
The dollar value of all final goods and services produced in a one-year period.

FIGURE 16–4 | NET PUBLIC DEBT AS A PERCENTAGE OF THE GROSS DOMESTIC PRODUCT

During World War II, the net public debt as a percentage of GDP grew dramatically. It fell thereafter but rose again from 1975 to 1995. The percentage fell after 1995, began to rise again after the events of 9/11, and then fell again, starting in 2004.

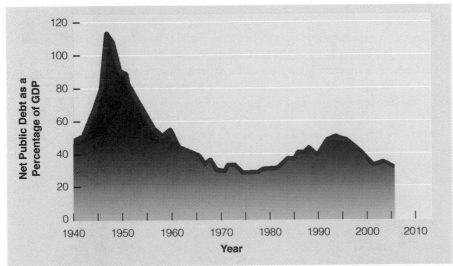

TABLE 16–1 | NET PUBLIC DEBT OF THE FEDERAL GOVERNMENT

YEAR	TOTAL (BILLIONS OF CURRENT DOLLARS)
1940	$ 42.7
1945	235.2
1950	219.0
1960	237.2
1970	284.9
1980	709.3
1990	2,410.1
1992	2,998.6
1993	3,247.5
1994	3,432.1
1995	3,603.4
1996	3,747.1
1997	3,900.0
1998	3,870.0
1999	3,632.9
2000	3,448.6
2001	3,200.3
2002	3,528.7
2003	3,878.4
2004	4,295.0
2005	4,592.0
2006	4,895.0*
2007	5,197.0*
2008	5,501.0*

*Estimate.
Source: U.S. Office of Management and Budget.

Federal Reserve System (the Fed)
The agency created by Congress in 1913 to serve as the nation's central banking organization.

Federal Open Market Committee
The most important body within the Federal Reserve System. The Federal Open Market Committee decides how monetary policy should be carried out.

Benjamin S. Bernanke is chair of the Board of Governors of the Federal Reserve System, which means he is head of the central bank in the United States. Some commentators contend that the chair of "the Fed" is the most powerful person on earth, at least in terms of economics. The Fed controls the rate of growth of the amount of money in circulation and, by implication, the "tightness" or "looseness" of credit markets. (Federal Reserve Board Photo)

recessions, but they have often refused to implement the other side of Keynes's recommendations—to run a *budget surplus* during boom times.

In 1993, however, President Bill Clinton (1993–2001) obtained a tax increase as the nation emerged from a mild recession. For the first time, the federal government implemented the more painful side of Keynesianism. In any event, between the tax increase and the "dot-com boom," the United States had a budget surplus each year from 1998 to 2002. Some commentators predicted that we would be running federal government surpluses for years to come. All of those projections went by the wayside because of several events.

One event was the "dot-com bust" followed by the 2001–2002 recession, which lowered the rate of growth of not only the economy but also the federal government's tax receipts. Another event was a series of large tax cuts passed by Congress in 2001 and 2003 at the urging of President George W. Bush.

The third event took place on September 11, 2001. Basically, as a result of the terrorist attacks, the federal government spent much more than it had planned to spend on security against terrorism. Finally, the government had to pay for the war in Iraq in 2003 and the occupation of that country thereafter. The federal budget deficit for 2006 was close to $300 billion. Few people now think there will be government budget surpluses in the near future.

Monetary Policy

Controlling the rate of growth of the money supply is called *monetary policy*. This policy is the domain of the **Federal Reserve System,** also known simply as the **Fed.** The Fed is the most important regulatory agency in the U.S. monetary system.

The Fed performs a number of important functions. Perhaps the Fed's most important ability is that it is able to regulate the amount of money in circulation, which can be defined loosely as checkable account balances and currency. The Fed also provides a system for transferring checks from one bank to another. In addition, it holds reserves deposited by most of the nation's banks, savings and loan associations, savings banks, and credit unions.

Organization of the Federal Reserve System

A board of governors manages the Fed. This board consists of seven full-time members appointed by the president with the approval of the Senate. The twelve Federal Reserve district banks have twenty-five branches. The most important unit within the Fed is the **Federal Open Market Committee.** This is the body that actually determines the future growth of the money supply and other important economywide financial variables. This committee is composed of the members of the Board of Governors, the president of the New York Federal Reserve Bank, and presidents of four other Federal Reserve banks, rotated periodically.

The Board of Governors of the Federal Reserve System is independent. The president can attempt to influence the board, and Congress can threaten to merge the Fed into the Treasury Department, but as long as the Fed retains its independence, its chairperson and governors can do what they please. Hence, any talk about "the president's monetary policy" or "Congress's monetary policy" is inaccurate. To be sure, the Fed has, on occasion, yielded to presidential pressure, and for a while the Fed's chairperson had to observe a congressional resolution requiring him to report monetary targets over each six-month period. But now, more than ever before, the Fed remains one of the truly independent sources of economic power in the government.[2]

---

[2]Axel Krause, "The American Federal Reserve System: Functioning and Accountability" (Paris, France: Groupement d'études et de recherches, Notre Europe, Research and Policy Paper No. 7, 1999). This paper is available online at **www.notre-europe.asso.fr/IMG/pdf/Etud7-en.pdf**.

Loose and Tight Monetary Policies

The Federal Reserve System seeks to stabilize nationwide economic activity by controlling the amount of money in circulation. Changing the amount of money in circulation is a major aspect of **monetary policy.** You may have read a news report in which a business executive complained that money is "too tight." You may have run across a story about an economist who has warned that money is "too loose." In these instances, the terms *tight* and *loose* refer to the monetary policy of the Fed.

Credit, like any good or service, has a cost. The cost of borrowing—the interest rate—is similar to the cost of any other aspect of doing business. When the cost of borrowing falls, businesspersons can undertake more investment projects. When it rises, businesspersons will undertake fewer projects. Consumers also react to interest rates when deciding whether to borrow funds to buy houses, cars, or other "big-ticket" items.

If the Fed implements a **loose monetary policy** (often called an "expansionary" policy), the supply of credit increases and its cost falls. If the Fed implements a **tight monetary policy** (often called a "contractionary" policy), the supply of credit falls and its cost increases. A loose money policy is often implemented as an attempt to encourage economic growth. You may be wondering why any nation would want a tight money policy. The answer is to control inflation. If money becomes too plentiful too quickly, prices (and ultimately the price level) increase and the purchasing power of the dollar decreases.

Time Lags for Monetary Policy

You learned earlier that policymakers who implement fiscal policy—the manipulation of budget deficits and the tax system—experience problems with time lags. The Fed faces similar problems when it implements monetary policy.

Sometimes accurate information about the economy is not available for months. Once the state of the economy is known, time may elapse before any policy can be put into effect. Still, the time lag when implementing monetary policy is usually much shorter than the lag involved in fiscal policy. The Federal Open Market Committee meets eight times a year and can put a policy into effect relatively quickly. Nevertheless, a change in the money supply may not have an effect for several months.

Time lags were a major reason why the Fed's implementation of monetary policy had dismal results for much of the twentieth century. Researchers point out that until the last two or so decades, the Fed's policies turned out to be procyclical rather than anticyclical—that is, by the time the Fed started pumping money into the economy, it was usually time to do the opposite. By the time the Fed started reducing the rate of growth of the money supply, it was usually time to start increasing it.

The Fed's greatest blunder occurred during the Great Depression. The Fed's policy actions at that time resulted in an almost one-third decrease in the amount of money in circulation. Some economists believe that the Fed was responsible for turning a severe recession into a full-blown depression.

Panicked crowds stand on the top of the Sub Treasury Building across the street from the New York Stock Exchange when collapse of the market was reported due to heavy trading on October 24, 1929. (The National Archives)

The Way Federal Reserve Policy Is Announced

Whatever the Fed's intentions, it signifies its current monetary policy by making announcements about an interest rate target. Nevertheless, when the chair of the Fed states that the Fed is lowering "the" interest rate from, say, 4.75 percent to 4.50 percent, something else is really meant. The interest rate referred to is the *federal funds rate*, or the rate at which banks can borrow excess reserves from other banks. The

direct impact of this interest rate on the economy is modest. To have a significant effect on interest rates throughout the economy, the Fed must increase or restrain the growth in the money supply.

Monetary Policy versus Fiscal Policy

A tight monetary policy is effective as a way of taming inflation. (Some would argue that ultimately, a tight monetary policy is the only way that inflation can be fought.) If interest rates go high enough, people *will* stop borrowing. How effective, though, is a loose monetary policy at ending a recession?

Under normal conditions, a loose monetary policy will spur an expansion in economic activity. At any given time, there are businesses that are considering whether to borrow. If interest rates are low, the businesses are more likely to do so. Low interest rates also reduce the cost of new houses or cars and encourage consumers to spend.

Recall from earlier in the chapter, however, that in a serious recession businesses may not want to borrow no matter how low the interest rate falls. Likewise, consumers may be reluctant to make major purchases even if the interest rate is zero. In these circumstances, monetary policy is ineffective. Indeed, using monetary policy in this situation has been described as "pushing on a string," because the government has no power to *make* people borrow. Here is where fiscal policy becomes important. The borrowing *can* take place—if the government does it itself.

World Trade

Most of the consumer electronic goods you purchase—flat-screen television sets, boom boxes, and digital cameras—are made in other countries. Many of the raw materials used in manufacturing in this country are also purchased abroad. For example, more than 90 percent of bauxite, from which aluminum is made, is brought in from other nations.

World trade, however, is a controversial topic. Since 1999, meetings of major trade bodies such as the World Trade Organization have been marked by large and sometimes violent demonstrations against "globalization." Opponents of globalization often refer to "slave" wages in developing countries as a reason to restrict imports from those nations. Others argue that we should restrict imports from countries that do not follow the same environmental standards as the United States.

Although economists of all political persuasions are strong believers in the value of international trade, this is not true of the general public. In 2006, when a Gallup poll asked a sampling of Americans whether they believe increased trade between the United States and other countries helped or hurt U.S. workers, 65 percent said they thought international trade hurt the workers. In the same poll, 50 percent said that increased international trade hurt U.S. companies.[3]

Imports and Exports

Imports
Goods and services produced outside a country but sold within its borders.

Imports are those goods (and services) that we purchase from outside the United States. Today, imports make up about 15 percent of the goods and services that we buy. This is a significant share of the U.S. economy, but actually it is quite small in comparison with many other countries.

Exports
Goods and services produced domestically for sale abroad.

We not only import goods and services from abroad; we also sell goods and services abroad, called **exports.** Each year we export over $900 billion of goods. In addition, we export about $300 billion of services. The United States exports about

[3]Gallup poll, April 21, 2006.

Police in Hong Kong fire tear gas at protestors in December 2005. These demonstrators were showing their displeasure about globalization and a variety of other issues during a meeting of the World Trade Organization (WTO). Why might some view the growth in world trade—increased globalization—as something against which to fight? (AP Photo/Ming Pao)

13 percent of GDP. Like our imports, our exports are a relatively small part of our economy compared with those of many other countries.

Back in the 1950s, imports and exports comprised only about 4 percent of the U.S. GDP. In other words, international trade has become more important for the United States. This is also true for the world as a whole. Consider Figure 16–5. There you see that since the 1950s, world trade has increased by more than twenty-two times.

FIGURE 16–5 | WORLD TRADE KEEPS GROWING

In this chart, the volume of world trade and world GDP are both represented by indexes. The base year is 1950, which means that the index is set to equal 100 for that year. While world output has increased by about eight times since 1950, world trade has increased by more than twenty-two times.

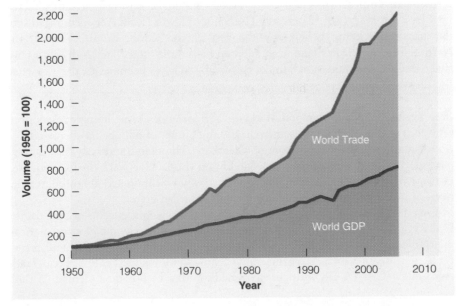

The Impact of Import Restrictions on Exports

What we gain as a country from international trade is the ability to import the things we want. We must export other things to pay for those imports. A fundamental proposition for understanding international trade is the following:

IN THE LONG RUN, IMPORTS ARE PAID FOR BY EXPORTS.

Of course, in the short run, imports can also be paid for by the sale (or export) of U.S. assets, such as title to land, stocks, and bonds, or through an extension of credit from other countries. Other nations, however, will not continue to give us credit forever for the goods and services that we import from them.

Economists point out that if we restrict the ability of the rest of the world to sell goods and services to us, then the rest of the world will not be able to purchase all of the goods and services that we want to sell to them. This argument runs contrary to the beliefs of people who want to restrict foreign competition to protect domestic jobs. Although it is certainly possible to preserve jobs in certain sectors of the economy by restricting foreign competition, there is evidence that import restrictions actually reduce the total number of jobs in the economy. Why? The reason is that ultimately such restrictions lead to a reduction in employment in export industries.

Protecting American Jobs.   When imports are restricted to save jobs, one effect is to reduce the supply of a particular good or service and thus to raise its price to consumers. Economists calculate that restrictions on imports of clothing have cost U.S. consumers $45,000 *per year* for each job saved. In the steel industry, the cost of preserving a job has been estimated at approximately $750,000 per year. How much did it cost to save jobs in the automobile industry? We examine this question in this chapter's *Politics and Trade* feature.

Quotas and Tariffs.   The U.S. government uses two key tools to restrict foreign trade. They are import quotas and tariffs. An **import quota** is a restriction imposed on the value or the number of units of a particular good that can be brought into the United States. **Tariffs** are taxes specifically on imports. Tariffs can be set as a particular dollar amount per unit—say, 10 cents per pound—or as a percentage of the value of the imported commodity.

Tariffs have been a part of the import landscape for two centuries. One of the most famous examples of the use of tariffs was the Smoot-Hawley Tariff Act of 1930. It included tariff schedules for over 20,000 products, raising taxes on affected imports by an average of 52 percent. The Smoot-Hawley Tariff Act encouraged similar import-restricting policies by the rest of the world. Britain, France, the Netherlands, and Switzerland soon adopted high tariffs, too. The result was a massive reduction in international trade. According to many economists, this worsened the ongoing Great Depression.

Free Trade Areas and Common Markets.   To lower or even eliminate restrictions on free trade among nations, some nations and groups of nations have created free trade areas, sometimes called common markets. The oldest and best-known common market is today called the European Union (EU). As of 2007, the EU consisted of twenty-five member nations. These countries have eliminated almost all restrictions on trade in both goods and services among themselves.

On our side of the Atlantic, the best-known free trade zone consists of Canada, the United States, and Mexico. This free trade zone was created by the North American Free Trade Agreement (NAFTA), approved by Congress in 1993. A more recent trade agreement is the Central American–Dominican Republic Free Trade Agreement (CAFTA-DR), which was signed into law by President George W. Bush

| Import Quota
A restriction imposed on the value or number of units of a particular good that can be brought into a country. Foreign suppliers are unable to sell more than the amount specified in the import quota.

| Tariffs
Taxes on imports.

POLITICS AND TRADE | The High Cost of Saving U.S. Jobs

One of the best examples of how import restrictions raise prices to consumers has been in the automobile industry, where "voluntary" restrictions on Japanese car imports were in place for more than a decade. Due in part to the enhanced quality of imported cars, sales of domestically produced automobiles fell from 9 million units per year in the late 1970s to an average of 6 million units annually between 1980 and 1982. As you can imagine, profits of U.S. automobile manufacturers fell as well. The U.S. automakers and the United Automobile Workers demanded protection from import competition.

POLITICIANS RESPONDED WITH TRADE RESTRICTIONS

Politicians from automobile-producing states were sympathetic to the "cause." The result was a "voluntary" agreement entered into by Japanese car companies. This agreement, which restricted U.S. sales of Japanese cars to 1.68 million units per year, began in April 1981 and continued into the 1990s in various forms.

THE COST PER JOB SAVED

Economist Robert W. Crandall estimated how much this "voluntary" trade restriction cost U.S. consumers. According to his estimates, the reduced supply of Japanese cars pushed their prices up by more than $1,500 apiece. The higher price of Japanese imports, in turn, enabled domestic producers to hike their prices an average of more than $600 per car. The total cost in the first full year of the program was more than $6.5 billion (expressed in today's dollars). Crandall also estimated that about 26,000 jobs were saved in automobile-related industries. Dividing $6.5 billion by 26,000 jobs yields a cost to consumers of more than $250,000 every year for each job saved in the automobile industry. U.S. consumers could have saved nearly $2 billion on their car purchases each year if, instead of implicitly agreeing to import restrictions, they had simply given $75,000 annually to every autoworker whose job was preserved by the "voluntary" import restraints.

FOR CRITICAL ANALYSIS

If it is so costly to save U.S. jobs through import restrictions, why do you think that politicians continue to pass import-restricting legislation?

---

in 2005. This agreement was formed by Costa Rica, the Dominican Republic, El Salvador, Guatemala, Honduras, Nicaragua, and the United States. Once the parties agree on an effective date, CAFTA-DR will reduce trade tariffs and improve market access among all of the signatory nations, including the United States.

The World Trade Organization

Since 1997, the principal institution overseeing tariffs throughout the world has been the World Trade Organization (WTO). The goal of the nations that created the WTO was to lessen trade barriers throughout the world so that all nations can benefit from freer international trade.

What the WTO Does. The WTO's many tasks include administering trade agreements, acting as a forum for trade negotiations, settling trade disputes, and reviewing national trade policies. Today, the WTO has more than 140 members, accounting for over 97 percent of world trade. Another 30 countries are negotiating to obtain membership. Since the WTO came into being, it has settled many trade disputes between countries, sometimes involving the United States.

For example, a few years ago, the United States, backed by five Latin American banana-exporting nations, argued before the WTO that the banana import rules of the European Union (EU) favored former European colonies in Africa and the Caribbean at the expense of Latin American growers and U.S. marketing companies.

Specifically, Chiquita Banana claimed that its earnings had fallen because its competitors' bananas received preferential treatment from the EU. Because the EU would not back down, the United States imposed a 100 percent tariff on almost $200 million worth of EU items in nine categories. The right of the United States to impose the tariffs was backed by the WTO. Finally, the WTO brokered a deal between the United States and the EU. The EU agreed to dismantle its banana import policy that favored European multinationals and former European colonies. The United States agreed to drop the 100 percent tariff.

The WTO and Globalization.   Opponents of globalization have settled on the WTO as the embodiment of their fears. As noted earlier, WTO meetings in recent years have been the occasion for widespread and sometimes violent demonstrations. Indeed, the WTO raises serious political questions for many Americans. Although the WTO has arbitration boards to settle trade disputes, no country has veto power. Some people claim that a "vetoless" America will be repeatedly outvoted by the countries of Western Europe and East Asia. Some citizens' groups have warned that the unelected WTO bureaucrats based in Geneva, Switzerland, might be able to weaken environmental, health, and consumer safety laws if such laws affect international trade flows.

The United States is not the only country to have problems with the WTO. Beginning in 2001, the WTO sponsored a new round of trade talks called the Doha round, after the city in Qatar where the first talks were held. In 2003, however, the talks broke down completely at a meeting in Cancún, Mexico. At that meeting, economically advanced countries such as the United States and the nations of Western Europe pressed for new rules on cross-border investments, competition, government procurement, and trade facilitation. Developing countries opposed these priorities. A group of African nations demanded instead that wealthy nations open their markets to exports by poor farmers. When they were rebuffed, the Africans walked out.

In 2006, WTO negotiations suffered their greatest setback. The United States and the European Union would not agree to reduce agricultural subsidies enough to entice other nations to sign a freer trade agreement. The Doha round was effectively declared dead as this book went to press.

Bananas were the subject of a major trade dispute between the United States and Europe. Here, a worker in Honduras carries boxes in a banana-packing plant. If you buy apples, you have many choices, including Golden Delicious, Granny Smith, and McIntosh. Oranges may be mandarins, navels, or others. But in a world of more than five hundred banana varieties, U.S. and European consumers are loyal to just one, the Cavendish. The crop is huge and unvaried—a ready target for disease. Some scientists say it might be time to rethink our banana habits. (AP Photo/Esteban Felix)

The Balance of Trade and the Current Account Balance

You may have heard on the news that the U.S. **balance of trade** is "negative" by some large figure. What does this announcement mean? To begin with, a negative balance of trade exists when the value of goods imported into a country is greater than the value of its exports. This situation is called a *trade deficit*. The United States has consistently had a large trade deficit since the late 1970s.

The Current Account Balance. The balance of trade is limited to trade in goods. A broader concept is the **current account balance,** which includes trade in services and a number of other items. The United States has enjoyed a positive balance of trade in *services* for a long time. (Does the recent practice of "outsourcing" service jobs abroad change this fact? We examine this question in this chapter's *Beyond Our Borders* feature on the following page.) Like the balance of trade, however, the current account balance is negative and has been growing more negative for years. Figure 16–6 shows the growth in the current account deficit.

Are We Borrowing Too Much from Other Countries? If we run a current account deficit, as we have in recent years, we can finance it only by increasing our obligations to other countries. The increasing current account deficit shown in Figure 16–6 can also be viewed as an increase in the claims that foreigners have on our economy.

> **Balance of Trade**
> The difference between the value of a nation's exports of goods and the value of its imports of goods.

> **Current Account Balance**
> A wider concept than the balance of trade. The current account balance includes the balance of trade in services, unilateral transfers, and other items.

FIGURE 16–6 | THE CURRENT ACCOUNT DEFICIT

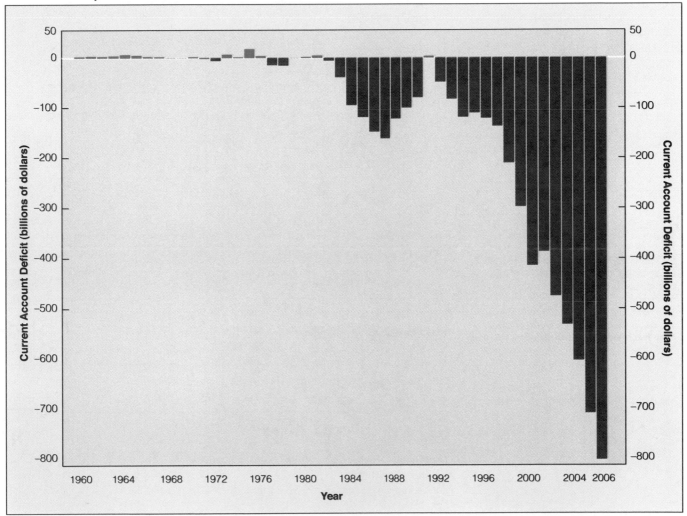

Source: U.S. Department of Commerce, Bureau of Economic Analysis, U.S. International Transactions Accounts Data, Table 1, June 2006.

BEYOND OUR BORDERS | Sending Work Overseas

For hundreds of years, nations have bought goods and services from abroad. Nonetheless, Americans have always perceived the purchase of *services* from other countries as a way of allowing those countries to "steal" American jobs. Today, such activity is called either "offshoring" or "outsourcing." During the 2004 presidential election campaigns, outsourcing was a hot topic.

In that year, Congress even tried to pass a bill to prevent any type of outsourcing by the Department of State and the Department of Defense. Presidential candidate John Kerry called the heads of companies that outsourced telemarketing and customer services "Benedict Arnold CEOs." One CNN business analyst kept a growing list of "unpatriotic" U.S.-based companies that were "sending this country's jobs overseas."

OUTSOURCING PROBABLY EXAGGERATED

The latest data about outsourcing from the McKinsey Global Institute show that about 300,000 jobs per year are lost to overseas outsourcing firms. This may sound like a lot, but we must put that number in perspective: the U.S. labor market is close to 140 million! In any one month, more than 4 million U.S. residents start new jobs with new employers. Also, consider that from 1999 to 2003, according to the Institute for International Economics, the United States lost 125,000 programming jobs to foreign outsourcing, but it added 425,000 jobs for higher-skilled software analysts and engineers.

TODAY'S FAVORITE "VILLAIN" COUNTRIES MAY CHANGE SOON

Outsourcing is here to stay, but the countries to which jobs are outsourced may change. India and China were the leading "villains" in the outsourcing debate a few years ago, but other countries may soon take their place. Why? Wages for outsourcing services are rising rapidly in both of those countries.

Outsourcing service providers in India and China have seen the handwriting on the wall. In response, they are attempting to move into higher-tech activities. In India, for example, calls for customer service are increasingly being handled by automated systems, thereby reducing the demand for low-cost Indian workers in this low-tech field.

FOR CRITICAL ANALYSIS

The head of a major retail organization that boasts low prices argued against outsourcing his company's customer calls to India. At the same time, his company kept its prices low by importing relatively cheaper clothing and electronic consumer items. Is there a difference between outsourcing services and importing low-cost consumer products? Explain your answer.

These obligations to other countries can take a variety of forms. Foreigners can buy stocks on Wall Street. They can buy American businesses or real estate. Above all, they can buy U.S. Treasury bonds issued by the government to fund the federal budget deficit.

Have our obligations abroad, which by 2007 were increasing by over $700 billion per year, become too large? It is true that during the last twenty years, the United States has enjoyed a larger share of the world's economic growth than any country other than China. Many people in other nations therefore consider the United States an attractive place to invest. While foreign appetites for investment in America are not unlimited, the rise in the current account deficit suggests that foreigners are still willing to invest in the United States.

The Politics of Taxes

Taxes are enacted by members of Congress. Today, the Internal Revenue Code encompasses thousands of pages, thousands of sections, and thousands of subsections—our tax system is very complex.

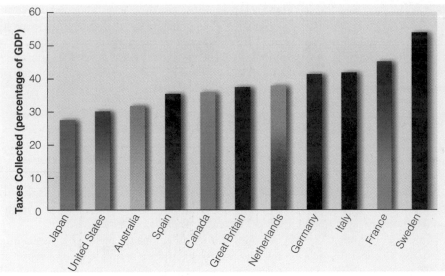

FIGURE 16–7 | TOTAL AMOUNT OF TAXES COLLECTED AS A PERCENTAGE OF GROSS DOMESTIC PRODUCT (GDP) IN MAJOR INDUSTRIALIZED NATIONS

Source: The OECD Observer, *OECD in Figures—Volume 2006*, Supplement 1 (Organization for Economic Cooperation and Development, 2005).

Americans pay a variety of different taxes. At the federal level, the income tax is levied on most sources of income. Social Security and Medicare taxes are assessed on wages and salaries. There is an income tax for corporations, which has an indirect effect on many individuals. The estate tax is collected from property left behind by those who have died. State and local governments also assess taxes on income, sales, and land. Altogether, the value of all taxes collected by the federal government and by state and local governments is about 30 percent of GDP. This is a substantial sum, but it is less than what many other countries collect, as you can see in Figure 16–7.

Federal Income Tax Rates

Individuals and businesses pay taxes based on tax rates. Not all of your income is taxed at the same rate. The first few dollars you make are not taxed at all. The highest rate is imposed on the "last" dollar you make. This highest rate is the *marginal* tax rate. Table 16–2 shows the 2006 marginal tax rates for individuals and married couples. The higher the tax rate—the action on the part of the government—the greater the public's reaction to that tax rate. If the highest tax rate you pay on the income you make is 15 percent, then any method you can use to reduce your taxable income by

TABLE 16–2 | MARGINAL TAX RATES FOR SINGLE PERSONS AND MARRIED COUPLES (2006)

SINGLE PERSONS		MARRIED FILING JOINTLY	
MARGINAL TAX BRACKET	MARGINAL TAX RATE	MARGINAL TAX BRACKET	MARGINAL TAX RATE
$ 0–$ 7,150	10%	$ 0–$ 14,300	10%
$ 7,151–$ 29,050	15%	$ 14,301–$ 58,100	15%
$ 29,051–$ 70,350	25%	$ 58,101–$117,250	25%
$ 70,351–$146,750	28%	$117,251–$178,650	28%
$146,751–$319,100	33%	$178,651–$319,100	33%
$319,101 and higher	35%	$319,101 and higher	35%

one dollar saves you fifteen cents in tax liabilities that you owe the federal government. Individuals paying a 15 percent rate have a relatively small incentive to avoid paying taxes, but consider the individuals who faced a marginal tax rate of 94 percent in the 1940s. They had a tremendous incentive to find legal ways to reduce their taxable incomes. For every dollar of income that was somehow deemed nontaxable, these taxpayers would reduce tax liabilities by ninety-four cents.

Loopholes and Lowered Taxes

Loophole
A legal method by which individuals and businesses are allowed to reduce the tax liabilities owed to the government.

Individuals and corporations facing high tax rates will adjust their earning and spending behavior to reduce their taxes. They will also make concerted attempts to get Congress to add loopholes to the tax law that allow them to reduce their taxable incomes. When Congress imposed very high tax rates on high incomes, it also provided for more loopholes than it does today. For example, special provisions enabled investors in oil and gas wells to reduce their taxable incomes.

In 2001, President George W. Bush fulfilled a campaign pledge by persuading Congress to enact new legislation lowering tax rates for a period of several years. In 2003, rates were lowered again, retroactive to January 2003; these rates are reflected in Table 16–2. As a result of other changes contained in the new tax laws, the U.S. tax code became even more complicated than it was before. In 2006, Bush attempted to renew his tax-rate cuts on a permanent basis.

Progressive Tax
A tax that rises in percentage terms as incomes rise.

Progressive and Regressive Taxation.   As Table 16–2 shows, the greater your income, the higher the marginal tax rate. Persons with large incomes pay a larger share of their income in income tax. A tax system in which rates go up with income is called a **progressive tax** system. The federal income tax is clearly progressive.

The income tax is not the only tax you must pay. For example, the federal Social Security tax is levied on wage and salary income at a flat rate of 6.2 percent. (Employers pay another 6.2 percent, making the total effective rate 12.4 percent.) In 2006, however, there was no Social Security tax on wages and salaries in excess of $94,200. (This threshold changes from year to year.) Persons with very high salaries therefore pay no Social Security tax on much of their wages. In addition, the tax is not levied on investment income (including capital gains, rents, royalties, interest, dividends, or profits from a business). The wealthy receive a much greater share of their income from these sources than do the poor. As a result, the wealthy pay a much smaller portion of their income in Social Security taxes than do the working poor. The Social Security tax is therefore a **regressive tax.**

Regressive Tax
A tax that falls in percentage terms as incomes rise.

Who Pays?   The question of whether the tax system should be progressive—and if so, to what degree—is subject to vigorous political debate. Democrats in general and liberals in particular favor a tax system that is significantly progressive. Republicans and conservatives are more likely to prefer a tax system that is proportional or even regressive. For example, President Bush's tax cuts made the federal system somewhat less progressive, largely because they significantly reduced taxes on nonsalary income.

Overall, what kind of tax system do we have? The various taxes Americans pay pull in different directions. The Medicare tax, as applied to wages and salaries, is entirely flat—that is, neither progressive nor regressive. Because it is not levied on investment income, however, it is regressive overall. Sales taxes are regressive because the wealthy spend a relatively smaller portion of their income on items subject to the sales tax. Table 16–3 lists the characteristics of major taxes. Add everything up, and the tax system as a whole is probably slightly progressive.[4]

TABLE 16–3 | PROGRESSIVE VERSUS REGRESSIVE TAXES

PROGRESSIVE TAXES
Federal Income Tax
State Income Taxes
Federal Corporate Income Tax
Estate Tax

REGRESSIVE TAXES
Social Security Tax
Medicare Tax
State Sales Taxes
Local Real Estate Taxes

[4]Brian Roach, "GDAE Working Paper No. 03–10: Progressive and Regressive Taxation in the United States: Who's Really Paying (and Not Paying) Their Fair Share?" (Medford, Mass.: Global Development and Environment Institute, Tufts University, 2003). This paper is online at www.ase.tufts.edu/gdae/Pubs/wp/03-10-Tax_Incidence.pdf.

The Social Security Problem

Closely related to the question of taxes in the United States is the viability of the Social Security system. Social Security taxes came into existence when the Federal Insurance Contribution Act (FICA) was passed in 1935. Social Security was established as a means of guaranteeing a minimum level of pension benefits to all persons. Today, many people regard Social Security as a kind of "social compact"—a national promise to successive generations that they will receive support in their old age.

To pay for Social Security, as of 2006, a 6.2 percent rate is imposed on each employee's wages up to a maximum of $94,200. Employers must pay in ("contribute") an equal percentage. In addition, a combined employer/employee 2.9 percent tax rate is assessed for Medicare on all wage income, with no upper limit. Medicare is a federal program, begun in 1965, that pays hospital and physicians' bills for persons over the age of sixty-five.

Social Security Is Not a Pension Fund

One of the problems with the Social Security system is that people who pay into Social Security think that they are actually paying into a fund, perhaps with their name on it. This is what you do when you pay into a private pension plan. It is not the case, however, with the federal Social Security system, which is basically a pay-as-you-go transfer system in which those who are working are paying benefits to those who are retired.

Currently, the number of people who are working relative to the number of people who are retiring is declining. Therefore, those who continue to work will have to pay more in Social Security taxes to fund the benefits of those who retire. In 2025, when the retirement of the Baby Boomer generation is complete, benefits are projected to cost almost 25 percent of taxable payroll income in the economy, compared with the current rate of 16 percent. In today's dollars, that amounts to more than $1 trillion of additional taxes annually.

Workers per Retiree

One way to think about the future bill that today's college students (and their successors) could face in the absence of fundamental changes in Social Security is to consider the number of workers available to support each retiree. As you can see in Figure 16–8, roughly three workers now provide for each retiree's Social Security, plus his or her Medicare benefits. Unless the current system is changed, by 2030 only two workers will be available to pay the Social Security and Medicare benefits due each recipient.

The growing number of people claiming the Social Security retirement benefit may pose less of a problem than the ballooning cost of Medicare. In the first place, an older population will require greater expenditures on medical care. In addition, however, medical expenditures *per person* are also increasing rapidly. Given continuing advances in medical science, Americans may logically wish to devote an ever-greater share of the national income to medical care. This choice puts serious pressure on federal and state budgets, however, because a large part of the nation's medical bill is funded by the government.

What Will It Take to Salvage Social Security?

The facts just discussed illustrate why efforts to reform Social Security and Medicare have begun to dominate the nation's public agenda. What remains to be seen is how the government ultimately will resolve the problem. What, if anything, might be done?

Raise Taxes. One option is to raise the combined Social Security and Medicare payroll tax rate. A 2.2 percentage point hike in the payroll tax rate, to an overall

FIGURE 16–8 | WORKERS PER SOCIAL SECURITY RETIREE

The average number of workers per Social Security retiree has declined dramatically since the program began.

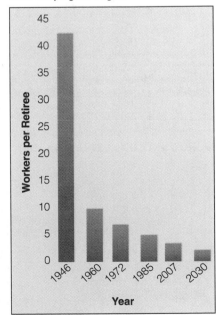

Sources: Social Security Administration; and authors' estimates.

WHICH SIDE ARE YOU ON? | Should Social Security Be Partially Privatized?

A major policy issue that has divided liberals and conservatives is whether Social Security should be privatized, at least partially. Privatization would allow workers to invest a specified portion of their Social Security payroll taxes in the stock market and possibly in other investment options, such as bonds or real estate. Although such a solution would have been unthinkable in past decades, today there is some support for the idea. Indeed, President George W. Bush's proposal that Social Security be partially privatized in this way drew significant support.

PARTIAL PRIVATIZATION COULD INCREASE THE RATE OF RETURN

Those who argue in favor of privatization point to the falling implied rate of return for Social Security contributions if

FIGURE 16–9 | PRIVATE RATES OF RETURN ON SOCIAL SECURITY CONTRIBUTIONS

Although those who paid in to Social Security in earlier years got a good deal, those who are paying in now and those who will contribute in the future are facing low or negative implicit returns.

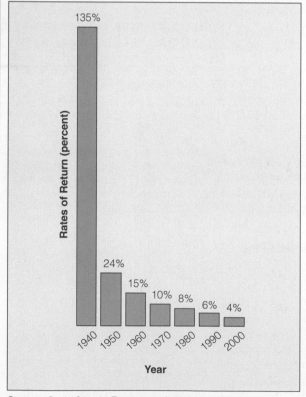

Sources: Social Security Trustees; and authors' estimates.

the program is compared with a private investment plan. Figure 16–9 shows that Social Security was a very good deal for those who paid into it in earlier generations. Today, the implicit rate of return is not so good. Looking into the future, the situation is worse. By 2020, the implicit rate of return may be negative, and it is likely to become increasingly negative in subsequent years. Advocates of privatization believe that investing Social Security contributions would yield greater returns for the average retired worker. In addition, the added investment in the nation's private sector could fuel economic growth, to everyone's benefit.

ANY PRIVATIZATION IS A THREAT TO SOCIAL SECURITY

A number of groups oppose the concept of partial privatization. These groups fear that the diversion of Social Security funds into individual investment portfolios could jeopardize the welfare of future retirees, who could be at the mercy of the volatile stock market. Opponents of partial privatization point out that such a plan might mean that workers would have to pay for two systems for many years—the benefits for today's retirees cannot simply be abolished.

For these people, the rate of return on Social Security contributions is also less of an issue than it might appear. Social Security was never meant to be an investment fund, and the program has always contained a certain "welfare" component that subsidizes the retirement of low-income individuals. This drives down the rate of return for the program as a whole. Finally, opponents worry that such a change could be the first step down a slippery slope toward the end of government-guaranteed retirement income.

WHAT'S YOUR POSITION?

Given the past performance of the stock market, just how risky would it be to invest a part of your Social Security contributions in the private sector?

GOING ONLINE

You can find arguments in favor of Social Security privatization at the Web site of the Cato Institute, a libertarian research organization. You can find Cato's home page at **www.cato.org** and the institute's arguments on Social Security at **socialsecurity.org**. The Social Security Network, a project of the Century Foundation, opposes privatization. Its Web site is at **www.socsec.org**.

rate of 17.5 percent, would yield an $80 billion annual increase in contributions. Such a tax increase would keep current taxes above current benefits until 2020, after which the system would again technically be in "deficit." Another option is to eliminate the current cap on the level of wages to which the Social Security payroll tax is applied; this measure would also generate about $80 billion per year in additional tax revenues. Nevertheless, even a combined policy of eliminating the wage cap and implementing a 2.2 percentage point tax increase would not keep tax collections above benefit payments over the long run.

Other Options.   Proposals are also on the table to increase the age of full benefit eligibility, perhaps to as high as seventy. In addition, many experts believe that increases in immigration offer the best hope of dealing with the tax burdens and workforce shrinkage of the future. Unless Congress changes the existing immigration system to permit the admission of a much larger number of working-age immigrants with useful skills, however, immigration is unlikely to relieve fully the pressure building due to our aging population. Still another proposal calls for partially privatizing the Social Security system in the hope of increasing the rate of return on individuals' retirement contributions. Would this be a workable solution? We examined this issue in this chapter's *Which Side Are You On?* feature.

MAKING A DIFFERENCE | Learning about Social Security

The growing number of elderly people and increases in the cost of medical care will force changes in the Social Security and Medicare programs in years to come. The nature of these changes is still an open question.

| Why Should You Care?

Unless you die before your time, you will grow old. Paying for your retirement will become an important issue. Even while you are still young, you may consider the cost of Social Security taxes on your wages or salary. What should the trade-off be between the interests of the elderly and the interests of younger persons who are members of the workforce? Few questions will have a greater impact on your pocketbook, today and in the future.

| What Can You Do?

Should Social Security and Medicare be changed as little as possible, to keep the system at least close to what

now exists? Or should we make more radical changes, such as replacing the existing programs with a system of private pensions? You can develop your own opinions by learning more about the Social Security issue.

There are a variety of proposals for privatizing Social Security. Some call for a complete replacement of the existing system. Others call for combining a market-based plan with parts of the existing program. In general, advocates of privatization believe that the government should not be in the business of providing pensions and that pensions and health insurance are best left to the private sector. The following organizations advocate privatization:

National Center for Policy Analysis
12655 N. Central Expy.,
   Suite 720
Dallas, TX 75243–1739
972-386-6272
www.ncpa.org
www.teamncpa.org

Institute for Policy Innovation
250 S. Stemmons Freeway,
   Suite 215
Lewisville, TX 75067
972-874-5139
www.ipi.org

A variety of organizations oppose privatization in the belief that it will lead to reduced benefits for some or all older people. Opponents of privatization believe that privatization plans are motivated more by ideology than by practical considerations. Organizations opposing privatization include:

AARP
601 E. Street N.W.
Washington, DC 20049
1-800-424-3410
www.aarp.org/socialsecurity

National Committee to Preserve
   Social Security and Medicare
10 G Street N.E., Suite 600
Washington, DC 20002
202-216-0420
www.ncpssm.org

Key Terms

automatic, or built-in, stabilizers 522

balance of trade 531

budget deficit 521

consumer price index (CPI) 519

current account balance 531

exports 526

Federal Open Market Committee 524

Federal Reserve System (the Fed) 524

fiscal policy 521

full employment 517

gross domestic product (GDP) 523

gross public debt 523

import quota 528

imports 526

inflation 517

Keynesian economics 521

loophole 534

loose monetary policy 525

monetary policy 525

net public debt 523

progressive tax 534

recession 517

regressive tax 534

tariffs 528

tight monetary policy 525

unemployment 517

U.S. Treasury bond 523

wage and price controls 522

Chapter Summary

1 One of the most important policy goals of the federal government is to maintain economic growth without falling into either excessive unemployment or inflation (rising prices). Inflation is commonly measured using the Consumer Price Index (CPI) published by the U.S. Bureau of Labor Statistics. The regular fluctuations in the economy are called business cycles. If the economy fails to grow for six months or more, the nation is experiencing a recession.

2 Fiscal policy is the use of taxes and spending to affect the overall economy. Economist John Maynard Keynes is credited with developing a theory under which the government should run budget deficits during recessions to stimulate the economy. Keynes also advocated budget surpluses in boom times, but political leaders have been reluctant to implement this side of the policy. Time lags in implementing fiscal policy can create serious difficulties.

3 The federal government has run a deficit in most years since the 1930s. The deficit is met by U.S. Treasury borrowing. This adds to the public debt of the U.S. government. Although the budget was temporarily in surplus from 1998 to 2002, deficits now seem likely for many years to come.

4 Monetary policy is controlled by the Federal Reserve System, or the Fed. Monetary policy involves changing the rate of growth of the money supply in an attempt to either stimulate or cool the economy. A loose monetary policy, in which more money is created, encourages economic growth. A tight monetary policy, in which less money is created, may be the only effective way of ending an inflationary spiral. Monetary policy may, however, be ineffectual in pulling the economy out of a severe recession—fiscal policy may be required.

5 World trade has grown rapidly since 1950. The United States imports and exports not only goods but services as well. While economists of all persuasions strongly support world trade, the public is less enthusiastic. Restrictions on imports to protect jobs are often popular. Ultimately, however, imports are paid for by exports. Restricting imports restricts exports as well, with resulting loss of employment in export industries. Trade restrictions also increase the cost of the affected goods to consumers.

6 Groups of nations have established free trade blocs to encourage trade among themselves. Examples include the European Union and the North American Free Trade Association (NAFTA). The World Trade Organization (WTO) is an international organization set up to oversee trade disputes and provide a forum for negotiations to reduce trade restrictions. The WTO has been a source of controversy in American politics.

7 The current account balance includes the balance of trade, which is limited to goods, and also the balance in the trade of services and other items. A possible problem for the future is the growing size of the U.S. current account deficit. This deficit is funded by foreign investments in the United States.

8 U.S. taxes amount to about 30 percent of the gross domestic product, which is not particularly high by international standards. Individuals and corporations that pay taxes at the highest rates will try to pressure Congress into creating exemptions and tax loopholes. Loopholes allow high-income earners to reduce their taxable incomes. The federal income tax is progressive; that is, tax rates increase as income increases. Some other taxes, such as the Social Security tax and state sales taxes, are regressive—they take a larger share of the income of poorer people. As a whole, the tax system is slightly progressive.

9 Closely related to the question of taxes is the viability of the Social Security and Medicare systems. As the number of people who are retired increases relative to the number of people who are working, those who are working may have to pay more for the benefits of those who retire. Proposed solutions to the problem include raising taxes, reducing benefits, allowing more immigration, and partially privatizing the Social Security system in hopes of obtaining higher rates of return on contributions.

Selected Print and Media Resources

SUGGESTED READINGS

Friedman, Milton, and Walter Heller. *Monetary versus Fiscal Policy*. New York: Norton, 1969. This is a classic presentation of the pros and cons of monetary and fiscal policy given by a noninterventionist (Friedman) and an advocate of federal government intervention in the economy (Heller).

Hundt, Reed. *In China's Shadow: The Crisis of American Entrepreneurship*. New Haven, Conn.: Yale University Press, 2006. The author explores the foreseeable challenges that the American economy faces from China.

Kotlikoff, Laurence J., and Scott Burns. *The Coming Generational Storm: What You Need to Know about America's Economic Future*.

Cambridge, Mass.: MIT Press, 2004. The authors explain how an aging population will create a crisis in Social Security and Medicare funding. One possible flaw in the authors' argument is their unquestioning use of very long-term demographic projections, which are inherently uncertain.

MEDIA RESOURCES

Alan Greenspan—This rather laudatory biography of the former chair of the Federal Reserve was released in 1999. Using Greenspan, the film looks at factors that influence the world and national economies.

E-MOCRACY | E-Commerce and Economic Policy

The age of e-commerce has brought with it several challenges for economic policymakers. One economic policy issue has to do with electronic money, or *e-money*. In one type of e-money, a balance of funds is recorded on a magnetic stripe on a card; each time the card is used, a computer terminal debits funds from the balance. Another type uses a microprocessor chip embedded in a so-called *smart card*. E-money is sometimes referred to as *e-cash* because it can be used like cash, meaning that no personally identifiable records are created. The problem for policymakers is that e-cash moves about outside the network of banks, checks, and paper currency. With the growth of e-cash, the traditional definition of money will no longer hold, giving the Federal Reserve less ability to control the money supply.

Logging On

You can keep up with actions taken by the Federal Reserve by checking the home page of the Federal Reserve Bank of San Francisco at

www.frbsf.org

For further information on Social Security, access the Social Security Administration's home page at

www.ssa.gov

For information on the 2007 budget of the U.S. government, go to

www.whitehouse.gov/omb/budget/fy2007

Online Review

At **www.politicalscience.wadsworth.com/schmidt12**, you will find a free Study Guide to this book. For each chapter, there are two online quizzes to help you master the material.

• The PoliPrep Self-Study Assessment provides a pretest for each major section of the chapter. PoliPrep then generates a customized study plan. After you complete the study plan, a posttest evaluates your progress.

• The Tutorial Quiz for each chapter provides questions on the chapter contents, including the features. The questions are organized to match the major sections of the chapter.

17 | Foreign Policy

What If . . .
All American Troops Were Restricted to U.S. Soil?

BACKGROUND

President George Washington warned Americans against getting involved in "foreign entanglements." Nonetheless, American troops have gone to Europe for World Wars I and II, to Asia for World War II and the Korean and Vietnam conflicts, to Afghanistan, and, of course, to Iraq. Particularly since World War II, American troops have been stationed on foreign soil, including parts of Europe, Asia, and the South Pacific. Isolationist sentiments, though, have always existed throughout the United States. Isolationism was prominent after World War I, and it is starting to emerge again as many Americans ask why we are still in Iraq and, to a lesser extent, still involved in Afghanistan. A Gallup poll in the summer of 2006 found that a majority of those surveyed favored withdrawing from Iraq immediately or within one year.

WHAT IF ALL AMERICAN TROOPS WERE RESTRICTED TO U.S. SOIL?

Of course, "bringing the troops home" could not happen overnight. The U.S. government would have to physically extract itself from the nation's overseas commitments in Europe, Asia, and the Middle East. The logistics of bringing all U.S. military personnel back to U.S. soil cannot be underestimated. In addition to transporting the hundreds of thousands of troops serving abroad, the infrastructure created for them would have to be dismantled and shipped back to the United States or its trusts, possessions, and territories.

Once the troops returned to U.S. soil, infrastructure would be needed to house them. Many "mothballed" military bases might have to be reopened. Others would have to be created, at considerable expense.

A DIFFERENT TYPE OF PREPAREDNESS WOULD BE NECESSARY

If the United States wished to continue to maintain its fighting capability in the event of terrorism or war elsewhere, then the current infrastructure would have to change. With all of its troops based on U.S. soil, the military would have less access to the world's "hot spots" if the government wished to send U.S. troops there. Thus, more and better long-range troop transportation systems would have to be developed, and more unmanned aircraft with bombing capabilities (drones) might also be needed.

To ensure that U.S. allies would still be protected, the United States might agree to subsidize the increase in its allies' own troops that would be needed to make up for the withdrawal of U.S. troops from their countries. In parallel, the number of U.S. military personnel could likely be reduced because they would no longer have to be scattered around the world.

IMPLICATIONS FOR SPECIFIC COUNTRIES

The withdrawal of U.S. troops would have important implications for several regions and countries in the world, in particular for East Asia and for Iraq. In East Asia, if U.S. troops left the Korean peninsula, then South Korea would have to deal directly with North Korea. South Korea—and probably Japan as well—would likely need to increase the size of its own military to compensate for the loss of the U.S. presence. The absence of U.S. troops in that area might also encourage China to show its military might more overtly and aggressively. Taiwan might feel more vulnerable and therefore might increase its spending on defense.

As for Iraq, predictions about what might happen if all U.S. troops were withdrawn run the gamut from civil war and chaos to an orderly transition through improvements in the Iraqi domestic policing system. Some argue that if U.S. troops left Iraq, the two major factions, the Sunnis and the Shiites, would have to negotiate and participate in a peaceful coalition government. Those who believe this also think that as a consequence, there would be fewer violent clashes between these two groups of Iraqis if the U.S. troops left.

The third group of Iraqis, the Kurds, would probably secede and become an independent nation. But that may happen even if U.S. troops stay in Iraq. The Kurds already have their own troops, and they control the oil-rich city of Kirkuk.

Some believe that Iran would take over Iraq if the United States did not have a presence there. The Iraqis, however, maintain that they have such a deep sense of nationalism that they would not accept an Iranian occupation.

FOR CRITICAL ANALYSIS

1. How might the U.S. military respond to the idea of "bringing the troops home"?
2. Some believe that if no U.S. military personnel were stationed abroad, terrorists would have less desire to harm Americans and the United States. Do you agree? Why or why not?

On September 11, 2001, Americans were forced to change their view of national security and of our relations with the rest of the world—literally overnight. No longer could citizens of the United States believe that national security issues involved only threats overseas or that the American homeland could not be attacked. No longer could Americans believe that regional conflicts in other parts of the world had no direct impact on the United States.

Within a few days, it became known that the attacks on the World Trade Center and on the Pentagon had been planned and carried out by a terrorist network named al Qaeda that was funded and directed by the radical Islamist leader Osama bin Laden. The network was closely linked to the Taliban government of Afghanistan, which had ruled that nation since 1996.

Americans were shocked by the complexity and the success of the attacks. They wondered how our airport security systems could have failed so drastically. How could the Pentagon, the heart of the nation's defense, have been successfully attacked? Shouldn't our intelligence community have known about and defended against this network? And, finally, how could our foreign policy have been so blind to the anger voiced by Islamist groups throughout the world?

In this chapter, we examine the tools of foreign policy and national security policy in light of the many challenges facing the United States today. Another issue for policymakers is how many U.S. troops should be stationed abroad, a question that we examined in the chapter-opening *What If . . .* feature. One of the major challenges for U.S. foreign policymakers is how best to respond to the threat of terrorism. The chapter concludes with a look at major themes in the history of American foreign policy.

Facing the World: Foreign and Defense Policy

The United States is only one nation in a world with almost two hundred independent countries, many located in regions where armed conflict is ongoing. What tools does our nation have to deal with the many challenges to its peace and prosperity? One tool is **foreign policy.** By this term, we mean both the goals the government wants to achieve in the world and the techniques and strategies to achieve them. For example, if one national goal is to achieve stability in the Middle East and to encourage the formation of pro-American governments there, U.S. foreign policy in that area may be carried out through **diplomacy, economic aid, technical assistance,** or military intervention. Sometimes foreign policies are restricted to statements of goals or ideas, such as helping to end world poverty, whereas at other times foreign policies are comprehensive efforts to achieve particular objectives, such as changing the regime in Iraq.

As you will read later in this chapter, in the United States, the **foreign policy process** usually originates with the president and those agencies that provide advice on foreign policy matters. Congressional action and national public debate often affect foreign policy formulation.

National Security Policy

As one aspect of overall foreign policy, **national security policy** is designed primarily to protect the independence and the political integrity of the United States. It concerns itself with the defense of the United States against actual or potential (real or imagined) enemies, domestic or foreign.

U.S. national security policy is based on determinations made by the Department of Defense, the Department of State, and a number of other federal agencies, including the National Security Council (NSC). The NSC acts as an

---

Foreign Policy
A nation's external goals and the techniques and strategies used to achieve them.

Diplomacy
The process by which states carry on political relations with each other; settling conflicts among nations by peaceful means.

Economic Aid
Assistance to other nations in the form of grants, loans, or credits to buy the assisting nation's products.

Technical Assistance
The practice of sending experts in such areas as agriculture, engineering, or business to aid other nations.

Foreign Policy Process
The steps by which foreign policy goals are decided and acted on.

National Security Policy
Foreign and domestic policy designed to protect the nation's independence and political and economic integrity; policy that is concerned with the safety and defense of the nation.

| Defense Policy
A subset of national security policies having
to do with the U.S. armed forces.

advisory body to the president, but it has increasingly become a rival to the State Department in influencing the foreign policy process.

Defense policy is a subset of national security policy. Generally, defense policy refers to the set of policies that direct the scale and size of the U.S. armed forces. Among the questions defense policymakers must consider is the number of major wars the United States should be prepared to fight simultaneously. Defense policy also considers the types of armed forces units we need to have, such as Rapid Defense Forces or Marine Expeditionary Forces, and the types of weaponry that should be developed and maintained for the nation's security. Defense policies are proposed by the leaders of the nation's military forces and the secretary of defense and are greatly influenced by congressional decision makers.

Diplomacy

Diplomacy is another aspect of foreign policy. Diplomacy includes all of a nation's external relationships, from routine diplomatic communications to summit meetings among heads of state. More specifically, diplomacy refers to the settling of disputes and conflicts among nations by peaceful methods. Diplomacy is the set of negotiating techniques by which a nation attempts to carry out its foreign policy.

Diplomacy can be successful only if the parties are willing to negotiate. Diplomacy clearly failed before the First Gulf War and perhaps before the second (some observers believe that the United States did not give diplomacy long enough time to work to avoid the Second Gulf War). So far, diplomacy has been relatively ineffective in keeping Iran from pursuing its goal of becoming a nuclear power. Nor has diplomacy stopped North Korea from continuing its efforts to develop its own nuclear bomb.

In the summer of 2006, several incidents set off an ever-escalating war between Israel and Hezbollah, a militant Shiite Islamist group based in Lebanon. While Israeli aircraft bombed Hezbollah's positions inside Lebanon and Hezbollah shelled Israeli cities with rockets, diplomatic efforts persisted at the United Nations. The diplomatic goal of establishing a cease-fire was eventually realized, but not until after many Israelis and Lebanese had died.

Morality versus Reality in Foreign Policy

From the earliest years of the republic, Americans have felt that their nation had a special destiny. The American experiment in democratic government and capitalism, it was thought, would provide the best possible life for men and women and be a model for other nations. As the United States assumed greater status as a power in world politics, Americans came to believe that the nation's actions on the world stage should be guided by American political and moral principles. As Harry Truman stated, "The United States should take the lead in running the world in the way that it ought to be run."

| Moral Idealism
A philosophy that sees nations as normally willing to cooperate and to agree on moral standards for conduct.

Moral Idealism

This view of America's mission has led to the adoption of many foreign policy initiatives that are rooted in moral idealism. This philosophy sees the world as fundamentally benign and assumes that most nations can be persuaded to take moral considerations into account when setting their policies.[1] In this perspective, nations should come together and agree to keep the peace, as President Woodrow Wilson (1913–1921) proposed for the League of Nations. Many of the foreign policy initiatives taken by the

This Peace Corps volunteer is helping Ghanaian farmers develop a tourist business. One important component of American foreign policy is moral idealism. (Peace Corps Photo)

---

[1]Eugene R. Wittkopf, Charles W. Kegley, and James M. Scott, *American Foreign Policy*, 6th ed. (Belmont, Calif.: Wadsworth Publishing, 2002).

United States have been based on this idealistic view of the world. The Peace Corps, which was created by President John Kennedy in 1961, is one example of an effort to spread American goodwill and technology that has achieved some of its goals.

Political Realism

In opposition to the moral perspective is **political realism,** often called *realpolitik* (a German word meaning "realistic politics"). Realists see the world as a dangerous place in which each nation strives for its own survival and interests regardless of moral considerations. The United States must also base its foreign policy decisions on cold calculations without regard for morality. Realists believe that the United States must be prepared militarily to defend itself, because all other nations are, by definition, out to improve their own situations. A strong defense will show the world that the United States is willing to protect its interests. The practice of political realism in foreign policy allows the United States to sell weapons to military dictators who will support its policies, to support American business around the globe, and to repel terrorism through the use of force.

American Foreign Policy—A Mixture of Both

It is important to note that the United States has never been guided by only one of these principles. Instead, both moral idealism and political realism affect foreign policymaking. President George W. Bush drew on the tradition of morality in foreign policy when he declared that the al Qaeda network of Osama bin Laden was "evil" and that fighting terrorism was fighting evil. To actually wage war on the Taliban in Afghanistan, however, U.S. forces needed the right to use the airspace of India and Pakistan, neighbors of Afghanistan. The United States had previously criticized both of these South Asian nations because they had developed and tested nuclear weapons. In addition, the United States had taken the moral stand that it would not deliver certain fighter aircraft to Pakistan as long as it continued its weapons program. When it became absolutely necessary to work with India and Pakistan, the United States switched to a realist policy, promising aid and support to both regimes in return for their assistance in the war on terrorism.

The Second Gulf War that began in 2003 also revealed a mixture of idealism and realism. While the primary motive for invading Iraq was realistic (the interests of

In 1983, President Ronald Reagan's special envoy for the Middle East, Donald Rumsfeld, shakes hands with Saddam Hussein in Iraq. Over the next few years, normal diplomatic relations between the United States and Iraq were established, in spite of a report that Hussein had ordered the chemical gassing of Iranian troops during a protracted war between Iran and Iraq. What type of foreign policy did the United States demonstrate by developing diplomatic relations with Iraq during this period? (National Archives)

Political Realism
A philosophy that sees each nation acting principally in its own interest.

Iraqi citizens wait to vote in elections in October 2005. They voted on a newly drafted constitution. What problems faced voters in Iraq that are unheard of in the United States? (Photo by Lance Cpl. Christopher J. Zahn/2nd Marine Division)

U.S. security), another goal of the war reflected idealism—the liberation of the Iraqi people from an oppressive regime and the establishment of a democratic model in the Middle East. Are idealist and realist values associated with the two major political parties? We examine this question in this chapter's *Politics and Foreign Policy* feature.

Challenges in World Politics

The foreign policy of the United States, whether moralistic, realistic, or both, must be formulated to deal with world conditions. Early in its history, the United States was a weak, new nation facing older nations well equipped for world domination. In the twenty-first century, the United States faces different challenges. Now it must devise foreign and defense policies that will enhance its security in a world in which it is the global superpower and has no equal.

The Emergence of Terrorism

Dissident groups, rebels, and other revolutionaries have long engaged in terrorism to gain attention and to force their enemies to the bargaining table. Over the last two decades, however, terrorism has increasingly threatened world peace and the lives of ordinary citizens.

Terrorism and Regional Strife. Terrorism can be a weapon of choice in regional or domestic strife. The conflict in the Middle East between Israel and the Arab states is an example. Until recently, the conflict had been lessened by a series of painfully negotiated agreements between Israel and some of the Arab states. Those opposed to the peace process, however, have continued to disrupt the negotiations through assassinations, mass murders, and bomb blasts in the streets of major cities within Israel. Other regions have also experienced terrorism. In September 2004, terrorists acting on behalf of Chechnya, a breakaway republic of Russia, seized a school at Besian in the nearby Russian republic of North Ossetia. In the end, at least 330 people—most of them children—were dead.

Terrorist Attacks against Foreign Civilians. In other cases, terrorist acts are planned against civilians of foreign nations traveling abroad to make an international statement. One of the most striking attacks was that launched by Palestinian terrorists against Israeli athletes at the Munich Olympics in 1972, during which eleven athletes were murdered. Other attacks have included ship and airplane hijackings, as well as bombings of embassies. For example, in 1998, terrorist bombings of two American embassies in Africa killed 257 people, including 12 Americans, and injured more than 5,500 others.

September 11. In 2001, terrorism came home to the United States in ways that few Americans could have imagined. In a well-coordinated attack, nineteen terrorists hijacked four airplanes and crashed three of them into buildings—two into the World Trade Center towers in New York City and one into the Pentagon in Washington, D.C. The fourth airplane crashed in a field in Pennsylvania, after the passengers fought the hijackers. Why did the al Qaeda network plan and launch attacks on the United States? Apparently, the leaders of the network, including Osama bin Laden, were angered by the presence of U.S. troops on the soil of Saudi Arabia, which they regard as sacred. They also saw the United States as the primary defender of Israel against the Palestinians and as the defender of the royal family that governs Saudi Arabia. The attacks were intended to so frighten and demoralize the

POLITICS AND FOREIGN POLICY | How Much Realism Should There Be?

Realism has led to U.S. support of, for example, the royal family in Saudi Arabia and the less-than-democratic president of Egypt Hosni Mubarak. For decades, realists have supported the status quo in the Middle East, including strong nondemocratic leaders, because they have maintained stability in the region. Are such positions more likely to be found in one political party than the other?

IDEALISM IN CONTRAST TO REALISM

Those who are called idealists have advocated the spread of democracy, among other things. In the past, Democratic presidents Woodrow Wilson (1913–1921), Harry Truman (1945–1953), and John F. Kennedy (1961–1963) promoted idealistic foreign policy. Kennedy once stated that the United States would "pay any price" and "bear any burden" to further liberty in the world.

POLITICAL ROLE REVERSALS

Even though idealism has been associated with Democratic presidents in the past, a role reversal seems to have occurred in recent years. President George W. Bush's administration appears to have adopted an idealistic foreign policy, particularly after 9/11. Bush argues that U.S. security requires the transformation of the Middle East into a zone of democracy to reduce terrorism in that area. His 2004 Democratic opponent,

John Kerry, was not so sure. Kerry spoke more of a *stable* Iraq than of a democratic Iraq. Kerry's argument that the United States should make greater efforts to coordinate its actions with the world's other democratic nations also suggested realism instead of idealism.

Some Democratic candidates who have maintained their idealistic foreign policy views seem to have suffered in recent years. A good example is Senator Joseph I. Lieberman of Connecticut, who has staunchly maintained that the United States should stay in Iraq as long as necessary. He lost in the Democratic primary for the Senate in the summer of 2006. The main argument raised by his opponent (Ned Lamont, a Connecticut millionaire) was simply to be antiwar and to oppose continued occupation in Iraq because it was a failed policy.

Notably, though, Senator Hillary Rodham Clinton (D., N.Y.) has not joined the Democratic Party's antiwar bandwagon. Some believe that given her aspirations for the presidency of the United States, she is trying to find a middle ground, criticizing the Bush administration's conduct of the Iraq war without adopting a completely antiwar platform.

FOR CRITICAL ANALYSIS

Which approach to foreign policy—idealism or realism—is more likely to benefit our national interests?

American people that they would convince their leaders to withdraw American troops from the Middle East.

London Bombings. On July 7, 2005, terrorists carried out synchronized bombings of the London Underground (subway) and bus network. Four suicide bombers, believed to have been of Middle Eastern descent, claimed the lives of fifty-two other people and wounded hundreds more in the attacks. On July 21, a second group of bombers attempted to carry out a similar plot, but no one was killed. Following the attacks, security was heightened in Britain and abroad (including New York City).

In August 2006, British authorities foiled a plot to bring down ten planes scheduled to leave London's Heathrow Airport for the United States (see Chapter 15). If successful, it would have been the biggest terrorist attack since September 11. The alleged bombers planned to blow up the airplanes with liquid chemicals that could be combined to make a bomb. The chemicals were to be carried on in containers for bottled water and other ordinary liquids, mixed together on the plane, and then ignited using triggers installed in what appeared to be MP3 players and other small electronic devices. After the suspects were arrested, the London airport was shut down, flights to the United States were canceled, and travel by air was extremely difficult in England for a few days. Travel in the United States was severely disrupted, too, as carry-on luggage was given extra screening.

Terrorist bombings have become increasingly destructive. Left: The wreckage of a bus with its seats open to the elements and its roof blown off after an explosion in London in 2005. Nearby simultaneous explosions rocked the London subway and a double-decker bus during the morning rush hour, causing 52 deaths and sending bloodied victims fleeing from debris-strewn blast sites. (AP Photo/Sergio Dionisio)
Center: Rescue workers cover bodies following train explosions in Madrid, Spain, just three days before Spain's general elections in 2004. The bombs killed more than 170 and wounded more than 500. (AP Photo/Paul White)
Upper right: The bombing of a nightclub on the island of Bali in Indonesia in 2002 killed more than 180 tourists, most of them Australian. Al Qaeda was blamed for the bombing. (AP Photo/David Guttenfelder)
Bottom right: Palestinians carry sacks of food through the remains of a market in Bethlehem, destroyed after a standoff between Israeli troops and Palestinians in 2002. (AP Photo/Achmad Ibrahim)

The War on Terrorism

After 9/11, President George W. Bush implemented stronger security measures to protect homeland security and U.S. facilities and personnel abroad. The president sought and received congressional support for heightened airport security, new laws allowing greater domestic surveillance of potential terrorists, and new funding for the military. The Bush administration has also conducted two military efforts as part of the war on terrorism.

Military Responses. The first military effort was directed against al Qaeda camps in Afghanistan and the Taliban regime, which had ruled that country since 1996. In late 2001, after building a coalition of international allies and anti-Taliban rebels

A satellite image of lower Manhattan shows the devastation after the collapse of the World Trade Center towers on September 11, 2001. Terrorists crashed two commercial airplanes into the twin towers. About three thousand people were killed in the terrorist attacks at the World Trade Center and the Pentagon. What might be the long-term effects of this horrible event on American foreign policy? (Photo Courtesy of U.S. Department of Defense)

Marine Corps officers address the Marines and Afghan security forces operating out of Camp Blessing in the Kunar province of Afghanistan in 2006. Camp Blessing, a former HIV/AIDS clinic that the Taliban closed, was later used by coalition special forces and is now home to American forces. How much political and security responsibility should the United States assume in Afghanistan following the defeat of the Taliban? (Photo by Cpl. Rich Mattingly/Combined Joint Task Force)

within Afghanistan, the United States defeated the Taliban and fostered the creation of an interim government that did not support terrorism.

Then, during 2002 and early 2003, the U.S. government turned its attention to the threat posed by Saddam Hussein's government in Iraq. (The war in Iraq and the subsequent occupation of that country will be discussed in detail later in this chapter under "Wars in Iraq.")

A New Kind of War. Terrorism has posed a unique challenge for U.S. foreign policymakers. The Bush administration's response has also been unique. In September 2002, President Bush enunciated what has since become known as the "Bush doctrine" or the doctrine of preemption:

> We will . . . [defend] the United States, the American people, and our interests at home and abroad by identifying and destroying the threat before it reaches our borders. While the United States will constantly strive to enlist the support of the international community, we will not hesitate to act alone, if necessary to exercise our right of self-defense by acting preemptively against such terrorists, to prevent them from doing harm against our people and our country.[2]

The concept of "preemptive war" as a defense strategy is a new element in U.S. foreign policy. The concept is based on the assumption that in the war on terrorism, self-defense must be *anticipatory*. As President Bush stated on March 17, 2003, just before launching the invasion of Iraq, "Responding to such enemies only after they have struck first is not self-defense, it is suicide."

The Bush doctrine has not been without its critics. Some point out that preemptive wars against other nations have traditionally been waged by dictators and rogue states—not democratic nations. By employing such tactics, the United States would seem to be contradicting its basic values. Others claim that launching preemptive wars will make it difficult for the United States to further world peace in the future. By endorsing such a policy itself, the United States could hardly argue against the decisions of other nations to do likewise when they feel threatened.

---

[2]George W. Bush, September 17, 2002. The full text of the document from which this statement is taken can be accessed at **www.whitehouse.gov/nsc/nssall.html**.

Wars in Iraq

On August 2, 1990, the Persian Gulf became the setting for a major challenge to the international system set up after World War II (1939–1945). President Saddam Hussein of Iraq sent troops into the neighboring oil sheikdom of Kuwait, occupying that country. This was the most clear-cut case of aggression against an independent nation in half a century.

The Persian Gulf—The First Gulf War.   At the formal request of the king of Saudi Arabia, American troops were dispatched to set up a defensive line at the Kuwaiti border. After the United Nations (UN) approved a resolution authorizing the use of force if Saddam Hussein did not respond to sanctions, the U.S. Congress reluctantly also approved such an authorization. On January 17, 1991, two days after a deadline for Hussein to withdraw, U.S.-led coalition forces launched a massive air attack on Iraq. After several weeks, the ground offensive began. Iraqi troops retreated from Kuwait a few days later, and the First Gulf War ended, although many Americans criticized President George H. W. Bush for not sending troops to Baghdad to depose Saddam Hussein.

As part of the cease-fire that ended the Gulf War, Iraq agreed to abide by all UN resolutions and to allow UN weapons inspectors to search for and oversee the destruction of its medium-range missiles and all weapons of mass destruction, including any chemical and nuclear weapons, and related research facilities. Economic sanctions were to be imposed on Iraq until the weapons inspectors finished their work. In 1999, however, Iraq placed so many obstacles in the path of the UN inspectors that they withdrew from the country.

The Persian Gulf—The Second Gulf War.   After the terrorist attacks on the United States on September 11, 2001, President George W. Bush called Iraq and Saddam Hussein part of an "axis of evil" that threatened world peace. In 2002 and

A collage of images from the Second Gulf War in Iraq. Clockwise from the lower left, the photographs show the initial battles that began in March 2003, the fall of Baghdad, the capture of Saddam Hussein, and the protracted struggle with various insurgents that followed. What has been the greatest challenge facing the United States during this occupation? (Photos Courtesy of the U.S. Armed Forces)

early 2003, Bush called for "regime change" in Iraq and began assembling an international coalition that might support further military action in Iraq.

Having tried and failed to convince the UN Security Council that the UN should take action to enforce its resolutions, Bush decided to take unilateral action against Iraq. In March 2003, supported by a coalition of thirty-five other nations, including Britain, the United States invaded Iraq. Within three weeks, the coalition forces had toppled Hussein's decades-old dictatorship and were in control of Baghdad and most of the other major Iraqi cities.

The process of establishing order and creating a new government in Iraq turned out to be extraordinarily difficult, however. In the course of the fighting, the Iraqi army, rather than surrendering, disbanded itself. Soldiers simply took off their uniforms and made their way home. As a result, the task of maintaining law and order fell on the shoulders of a remarkably small coalition expeditionary force. Coalition troops were unable to put an immediate halt to the wave of looting and disorder that spread across Iraq in the wake of the invasion. Although Hussein himself was found and arrested in December 2003, his capture did nothing to end the insurgent resistance movement that had begun against the coalition forces.

Crew members of the USS *Abraham Lincoln* salute President George W. Bush after he was given a ride on a fighter jet based on the aircraft carrier. A large sign on the carrier declared "Mission Accomplished," referring to major military operations in Iraq. How can identification with the military be politically helpful to a president or a presidential candidate? (Photographer's Mate 3rd Class Tyler J. Clements/U.S. Navy)

Occupied Iraq. The people of Iraq are divided into three principal groups by ethnicity and religion. The Kurdish-speaking people of the north, who had in practice been functioning as an American-sponsored independent state since the First Gulf War, were overjoyed by the invasion. The Arabs adhering to the Shiite branch of Islam live principally in the south and constitute a majority of the population. The Shiites were glad that Saddam Hussein, who had murdered many thousands of Shiites, was gone. They were deeply skeptical of U.S. intentions, however. The Arabs belonging to the Sunni branch of Islam live in the center of the country, west of Baghdad. Although the Sunnis constituted only a minority of the population, they had controlled the government under Hussein. Many of them considered the occupation to be a disaster. Figure 17–1 on the following page shows the distribution of major ethnic and religious groups in Iraq.

Uprisings in Spring 2004. In April 2004, four non-Iraqi civilian security personnel were murdered in the Sunni city of Fallujah, and their bodies were publicly defiled. U.S. Marines entered the city to locate and arrest the perpetrators. Almost at the same time, authorities in Baghdad closed a newspaper run by followers of the Shiite cleric Muqtada al-Sadr. Al-Sadr, a radical, was the son of a famous Shiite martyr. The paper was closed on the ground that it had been fomenting violence. The result was simultaneous uprisings in the "Sunni triangle" west of Baghdad and in neighborhoods dominated by al-Sadr's militia in Baghdad and southern cities.

After several weeks, fighting was confined to Fallujah and the Shiite city of Najaf, where al-Sadr had established his headquarters. Public opinion polls in Iraq revealed that hostility toward the occupation forces had grown dramatically. To make matters worse, in May 2004 graphic photographs were published showing that U.S. guards at Abu Ghraib prison in Baghdad had subjected prisoners to physical and sexual abuse.

While coalition forces were able to maintain control of the country, they were now suffering monthly casualties comparable to those experienced during the initial invasion. Iraq had begun to be a serious political problem for President Bush. By May 2004, a majority of Americans no longer believed that going to war had been

FIGURE 17–1 | ETHNIC/RELIGIOUS GROUPS IN IRAQ

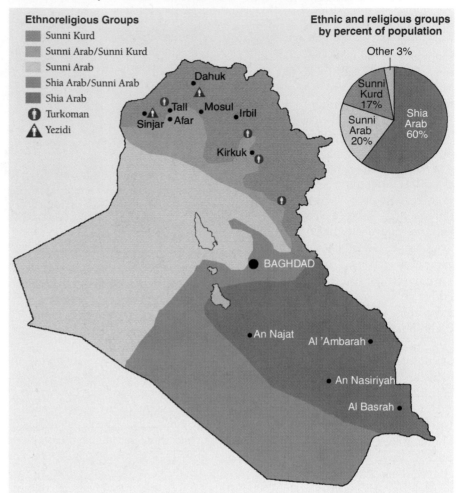

Source: The Central Intelligence Agency, as adapted by **www.globalsecurity.org**.

the right thing to do, and Bush's overall job-approval rating had fallen significantly. The events discussed here formed the backdrop for the first Iraqi elections (see the *Beyond Our Borders* feature on page 273 in Chapter 8).

The Continuing Insurgency.   Certainly, establishing a stable Iraqi government has proved difficult, particularly because of the problems with Sunni participation. As mentioned earlier, the Sunnis dominated the political landscape when Saddam Hussein was in power, even though they were a minority. Now, with Hussein gone, the Shiites, who are a majority of the population, are the dominant political force. The Sunnis clearly are participating in the insurgency to prevent the Shiites from controlling the political scene.

Additionally, the insurgency may be fed by Iran, which is a Shiite country. Indeed, much information shows that Iran is pressing Shiite militia to step up attacks against American-led forces. In August 2006, while the war between Hezbollah and Israel was being waged in Lebanon, tens of thousands of followers of a major Shiite cleric held a rally in Baghdad in support of Hezbollah. Now there is concern that the rise of the majority Shiites in Iraq will lead to the creation of a "Shiite crescent" across the Middle East with groups in Iran, Iraq, and Lebanon working together against such common enemies as Sunni Arabs, Israel, and the United States.

Nuclear Weapons

In 1945, the United States was the only nation to possess nuclear weapons. Several nations quickly joined the "nuclear club," however, including the Soviet Union in 1949, Great Britain in 1952, France in 1960, and China in 1964. Few nations have made public their nuclear weapons programs since China's successful test of nuclear weapons in 1964. India and Pakistan, however, detonated nuclear devices within a few weeks of each other in 1998, and North Korea conducted an underground nuclear explosive test in October 2006. Several other nations are suspected of possessing nuclear weapons or the capability to produce them in a short time.

The United States and the Soviet Union.   More than 32,000 nuclear warheads are known to be stocked worldwide, although the exact number is uncertain because some countries do not reveal the extent of their nuclear stockpiles. Although the United States and Russia have dismantled some of their nuclear weapons systems since the end of the **Cold War** and the dissolution of the Soviet Union in 1991 (discussed later in this chapter), both still retain sizable nuclear arsenals. Even more troublesome is *nuclear proliferation*—that is, the development of nuclear weapons by additional nations.

Cold War
The ideological, political, and economic confrontation between the United States and the Soviet Union following World War II.

Nuclear Proliferation.   The United States has attempted to influence late arrivals to the "nuclear club" through a combination of rewards and punishments. In some cases, the United States has promised aid to a nation to gain cooperation. In other cases, such as those of India and Pakistan, it has imposed economic sanctions as a punishment for carrying out nuclear tests. In the end, Pakistan demonstrated its ability to explode nuclear bombs in 1998. In spite of the United States' disagreement with these countries, President Bush signed a new nuclear pact with India in March 2006.

In 1999, President Bill Clinton presented the Comprehensive Nuclear Test Ban Treaty to the Senate for ratification. The treaty, formed in 1996, prohibits all nuclear test explosions worldwide and provides for the establishment of a global network of monitoring stations. Ninety-three nations have ratified the treaty. Among those that have not are China, Israel, India, and Pakistan. In a defeat for the Clinton administration, the U.S. Senate rejected the treaty in 1999.

President George W. Bush described both North Korea and Iran as members of an "axis of evil," and the fear exists that one of them could supply nuclear materials to terrorists. In addition, Israel is known to possess more than one hundred nuclear warheads. South Africa developed six nuclear warheads in the 1980s but dismantled them in 1990. In 2003, Libya announced that it was abandoning a secret nuclear weapons program. Also, since the dissolution of the Soviet Union in 1991, the security of its nuclear arsenal has declined. There have been reported thefts, smugglings, and illicit sales of nuclear material from the former Soviet Union in the past fifteen years.

For years, the United States, the European Union, and the UN have tried to prevent Iran from becoming a nuclear power. Today, though, many observers believe that Iran has already developed nuclear capability or is close to doing so. Continued diplomatic attempts to at least slow down Iran's quest for a nuclear bomb have proved ineffectual at best.

With nuclear weapons, materials, and technology available worldwide, it is conceivable that terrorists could develop a nuclear device and use it in a terrorist act. In fact, a U.S. federal indictment filed in 1998, after the attack on the American embassies in Kenya and Tanzania, charged Osama bin Laden and his associates with trying to buy components for a nuclear bomb "at various times" since 1992.

This CIA photograph shows Yongbyon in North Korea. The area marked in red contains a nuclear research center and associated reprocessing facilities. What, if anything, can the United States legitimately offer to North Korea if that country abandons its nuclear weapons program? (Globalsecurity.org)

| Normal Trade Relations (NTR) Status

A status granted through an international treaty by which each member nation must treat other members at least as well as it treats the country that receives its most favorable treatment. This status was formerly known as *most-favored-nation status*.

The New Power: China

Since Richard Nixon's visit to China in 1972, American policy has been to gradually engage the Chinese in diplomatic and economic relationships in the hope of turning the nation in a more pro-Western direction. In 1989, however, when Chinese students engaged in extraordinary demonstrations against the government, the Chinese government crushed the demonstrations, killing a number of students and protesters and imprisoning others. The result was a distinct chill in Chinese-American relations.

Chinese-American Trade Ties. After initially criticizing the administration of George H. W. Bush (1989–1993) for not being hard enough on China, President Bill Clinton came around to a policy of diplomatic outreach to the Chinese. An important reason for this change was the large and growing trade ties between the two countries. China was granted *most-favored-nation status* for tariffs and trade policy on a year-to-year basis. To prevent confusion, in 1998 the status was renamed **normal trade relations (NTR) status.** In 2000, over objections from organized labor and human rights groups, Congress approved a permanent grant of NTR status to China.

In 2001, Congress endorsed China's application to join the World Trade Organization (WTO), thereby effectively guaranteeing China's admission to that body. For a country that is officially Communist, China already permits a striking degree of free enterprise, and the rules China must follow as a WTO member will further increase the role of the private sector in China's economy.

Chinese-American Tensions. China has one of the fastest-growing economies in the world. Given China's large population, projections suggest that the gross domestic product of China may match or exceed that of the United States during this century. This prospect has led to alarm in some quarters. Some U.S. observers and officials have argued that China is destined to become a great rival—or even an enemy—of the United States. What problems would be posed if China should become a superpower? We examine this question in this chapter's *Beyond Our Borders* feature.

Relations between the United States and China have not been particularly warm in recent years. In 2001, tensions were heightened by a dispute that followed a collision between a U.S. spy plane and a Chinese fighter jet. Still, after the September 11 attacks, China offered its full support to the United States in the war on terrorism and, for the first time ever, supplied intelligence to the United States about terrorist activities. The Chinese did not support the American military action to overthrow Saddam Hussein, however, and have continued to be unsupportive of the U.S. occupation of Iraq. Moreover, China (along with Russia) has refused to back any efforts to censor or impose sanctions on Iran for its obvious attempt at becoming a nuclear power. Following North Korea's nuclear test in October 2006, however, China did agree with other world leaders to impose sanctions on North Korea.

Regional Conflicts

The United States has played a role—sometimes alone, sometimes with other powers—in many regional conflicts during the 1990s and 2000s.

Cuba. Tensions between the United States and Cuba have been frequent since Fidel Castro took power in Cuba in 1959. Relations with Cuba continue to be politically important in the United States because the Cuban American population can influence election outcomes in Florida, a state that all presidential candidates try to win. When Fidel Castro became seriously ill and was operated on in the summer of 2006,

BEYOND OUR BORDERS | China: The Next Superpower

China has experienced rapid economic growth for the last thirty years and today is one of the world's great economic powers. Adjusted for purchasing power, China's gross domestic product (GDP) is now second only to that of the United States and is almost double that of Japan. This fact does not mean that all Chinese are rich. Indeed, per capita income in China is well below that of the United States and Europe.

Between 2001 and 2007, China's industrial output increased by almost 50 percent. China now produces more steel than America and Japan combined. Such rapid growth, of course, requires massive amounts of raw materials. China today consumes 40 percent of the world's output of cement, for example. China's growing demand for raw materials has contributed to dramatic increases in the world prices of many commodities, including oil. Although economists around the world have been predicting that China's growth will slow down, it had yet to do so by the beginning of 2007.

CHINA'S ECONOMIC PROSPECTS

Goldman Sachs, a U.S. investment firm, has projected that China's GDP will surpass that of the United States by 2039, making China's economy the largest in the world. In fact, this projection may underestimate China's prospects—it uses growth rates that are substantially lower than the actual rates China has posted over the last thirty years.

WHAT ABOUT TAIWAN?

Inevitably, economic power translates into military potential. Is China's economic growth a potential problem for the United States? It could be if China had territorial ambitions. Currently, China does not have an appetite for non-Chinese territory, although it recently purchased oil and mineral rights in a number of South American nations. China, however, has always considered the island of Taiwan to be Chinese territory.

In principle, Taiwan agrees. Taiwan calls itself the "Republic of China" and officially considers its government to be the legitimate ruler of the entire country. This diplomatic friction has been in effect since 1949, when the Chinese Communist Party won a civil war and drove the anti-Communist forces off the mainland. China's position is that, sooner or later, Taiwan must rejoin the rest of China. The position of the United States is that such an action must not come about by force.

Is peaceful reunification possible? China points to Hong Kong as an example. Hong Kong came under Chinese sovereignty peacefully in 1997. The people of Taiwan, however, are far from considering Hong Kong to be an acceptable precedent.

FOR CRITICAL ANALYSIS

If China invades Taiwan, should the United States go to war to protect Taiwan? Why or why not?

---

his brother, Raul, temporarily assumed power. No one believes that if Castro dies, his brother will be any more amenable to normal relations with the United States.

Israel and the Palestinians. As a longtime supporter of Israel, the United States has undertaken to persuade the Israelis to negotiate with the Palestinian Arabs who live in the territories occupied by the state of Israel. The conflict, which began in 1948, has been extremely hard to resolve. The internationally recognized solution is for Israel to yield the West Bank and the Gaza Strip to the Palestinians in return for effective security commitments and abandonment by the Palestinians of any right of return to Israel proper. Unfortunately, the Palestinians have been unwilling to stop terrorist attacks on Israel, and Israel has been unwilling to dismantle all of its settlements in the occupied territories. Further, the two parties have been unable to come to an agreement on how much of the West Bank should go to the Palestinians and on what compensation (if any) the Palestinians should receive for abandoning all claims to settlement in Israel proper.

In December 1988, the United States began talking directly to the Palestine Liberation Organization (PLO), and in 1991, under great pressure from the United States, the Israelis opened talks with representatives of the Palestinians and other Arab states. In 1993, both parties agreed to set up Palestinian self-government in the

West Bank and the Gaza Strip. The historic agreement, signed in Cairo on May 4, 1994, put in place a process by which the Palestinians would assume self-rule in the Gaza Strip and in the town of Jericho. In the months that followed, Israeli troops withdrew from much of the occupied territory, the new Palestinian Authority assumed police duties, and many Palestinian prisoners were freed by the Israelis.

The Collapse of the Israeli-Palestinian Peace Process.   Although negotiations between the Israelis and the Palestinians resulted in more agreements in Oslo, Norway, in 2000, the agreements were rejected by Palestinian radicals, who began a campaign of suicide bombings in Israeli cities. In 2002, the Israeli government responded by moving tanks and troops into Palestinian towns to kill or capture the terrorists. One result of the Israeli reoccupation was an almost complete collapse of the Palestinian Authority. Groups such as Hamas (the Islamic Resistance Movement), which did not accept the concept of peace with Israel even in principle, moved into the power vacuum.

In 2003, President Bush attempted to renew Israeli-Palestinian negotiations by sponsoring a "road map" for peace. First, the road map called for an end to terrorism by the Palestinians. Later, it held out hopes for a Palestinian state alongside Israel. In its weakened condition, however, the Palestinian Authority was unable to make any commitments, and the "road map" process ground to a halt. In February 2004, Israeli Prime Minister Ariel Sharon announced a plan under which Israel would withdraw from the Gaza Strip regardless of whether a deal could be reached with the Palestinians. Sharon's plan met with strong opposition within his own political party, but ultimately the withdrawal took place.

After the death of Palestinian leader Yasir Arafat in 2004, a moderate prime minister was elected. In January 2006, however, the militant group Hamas won a majority of the seats in the Palestinian legislature. American and European politicians hoped that after it became part of the legitimate government, Hamas would agree to rescind its avowed desire to destroy Israel, but so far, it has not done so.

The Israeli-Hezbollah (Lebanon) War.   As mentioned before, in the summer of 2006, Israel went to war with the militant group Hezbollah in Lebanon. The conflict started after Hezbollah captured several Israeli soldiers and commenced firing rockets into Israel. The United States at first did nothing, agreeing with Israel that Hezbollah had to be disarmed and weakened for there to be viable peace in the region. Eventually, though, as more lives were lost on both sides, the United States helped broker a cease-fire.

The photo on the left shows destruction in Haifa, Israel, caused by rockets fired by Hezbollah fighters in nearby Lebanon during the late summer of 2006. The photo on the right shows destruction in a suburb of Beirut, Lebanon, caused by Israel's response to Hezbollah's attacks. Civilians were killed on both sides. The "war" ended through negotiation, but skeptics believe that fighting will renew itself as long as Hezbollah fighters are not completely disarmed. Many of their arms purportedly have been furnished by Iran. (AP Photo/Mahmoud Tawil)

AIDS in Southern Africa. During the early 2000s, the disease AIDS (acquired immune deficiency syndrome) spread throughout southern Africa. This disease infects one-fourth of the populations of Botswana and Zimbabwe and is endemic in most other nations in the southernmost part of the continent. Millions of adults are dying from AIDS, leaving orphaned children. The epidemic is taking a huge economic toll on the affected countries because of the cost of caring for patients and the loss of skilled workers. The disease may be the greatest single threat to world stability emanating from Africa. The Bush administration put in place a special aid package directed at this problem amounting to $15 billion over five years.

African Civil Wars. The year 1994 brought disaster to the African nation of Rwanda. Following the death of that country's president, members of the Hutu tribe launched a campaign of genocide against the Tutsi tribe. More than half a million people were killed in a matter of weeks. The genocide campaign came to an abrupt end as a Tutsi guerrilla force, sponsored by neighboring Uganda, overthrew the Rwandan government. A large number of Hutus then fled from Rwanda. The United States played almost no part in this crisis until small military and civilian contingents were sent to assist the Hutu refugees.

In Angola, wars dating back as far as 1961 came to an end in 2002 with the death of rebel leader Jonas Savimbi, who had received U.S. support for several years in the 1970s. In 1996, civil war broke out in Zaire (now named Democratic Republic of the Congo; also known as Congo-Kinshasa). Rebels were aided by Rwandan and Ugandan forces, while Angolan and Zimbabwean forces entered the country to support the government. The civil war officially came to an end in 2002, and a coalition government was established in 2003. Several million deaths, primarily due to disease and malnutrition, were attributed to the war.

In 2004, the world woke up to a growing disaster in Darfur, a western province of Sudan. In the spring of 2004, Sudan had reached a tenuous agreement with rebels in the southern part of the country, but the agreement did not cover a separate rebellion in Darfur. Government-sponsored militias drove over a million inhabitants of Darfur from their homes and into refugee camps, where they faced starvation. In spite of a cease-fire, fighting renewed during the summer of 2006 and continued to plague the region.

DID YOU KNOW . . .
That the United States invaded and occupied part of Russia in 1919?

Displaced children in the Kalma camp near Nyala in South Darfur wait in the shade while their mother works in nearby fields for income. This work is very dangerous; relief workers report that women who venture from the camps are often targets of Jingaweit attacks, including rape and murder. Why have the continued killings in Darfur not created much outrage throughout the world?
(Photo Courtesy of USAID)

Who Makes Foreign Policy?

Given the vast array of challenges in the world, developing a comprehensive U.S. foreign policy is a demanding task. Does this responsibility fall to the president, to Congress, or to both acting jointly? There is no easy answer to this question, because, as constitutional authority Edwin S. Corwin once observed, the U.S. Constitution created an "invitation to struggle" between the president and Congress for control over the foreign policy process. Let us look first at the powers given to the president by the Constitution.

Constitutional Powers of the President

The Constitution confers on the president broad powers that are either explicit or implied in key constitutional provisions. Article II vests the executive power of the government in the president. The presidential oath of office given in Article II, Section 1, requires that the president "solemnly swear" to "preserve, protect and defend the Constitution of the United States."

War Powers.   In addition, and perhaps more important, Article II, Section 2, designates the president as "Commander in Chief of the Army and Navy of the United States." Starting with Abraham Lincoln, all presidents have interpreted this authority dynamically and broadly. Indeed, since George Washington's administration, the United States has been involved in at least 125 undeclared wars that were conducted under presidential authority. For example, in 1950 Harry Truman ordered U.S. armed forces in the Pacific to counter North Korea's invasion of South Korea. Dwight Eisenhower threatened China and North Korea with nuclear weapons if the Korean peace talks were not successfully concluded. Bill Clinton sent troops to Haiti and Bosnia. In 2001, George W. Bush authorized an attack against the al Qaeda terrorist network and the Taliban government in Afghanistan. As described earlier, in 2003 Bush sent military forces to Iraq to destroy Saddam Hussein's government.

Treaties and Executive Agreements.   Article II, Section 2, of the Constitution also gives the president the power to make treaties, provided that two-thirds of the senators present concur. Presidents usually have been successful in getting treaties through the Senate. In addition to this formal treaty-making power, the president makes use of executive agreements (discussed in Chapter 12). Since World War II (1939–1945), executive agreements have accounted for almost 95 percent of the understandings reached between the United States and other nations.

Executive agreements have a long and important history. During World War II, Franklin Roosevelt reached several agreements with the Soviet Union and other countries. One agreement with long-term results was concluded at Yalta in the Soviet Crimea. In other important agreements, presidents Eisenhower, Kennedy, and Johnson all promised support to the government of South Vietnam. In all, since 1946 more than eight thousand executive agreements with foreign countries have been made. There is no way to obtain an accurate count, because perhaps as many as several hundred of these agreements have been secret.

On August 8, 1964, in the East Room of the White House, President Lyndon B. Johnson signs the "Gulf of Tonkin" resolution (Joint Resolution for the Maintenance of Peace and Security in Southeast Asia). The Resolution is significant because it gave President Johnson approval, without a formal declaration of war by the Congress, "to take all necessary steps, including the use of armed force, to assist any member or protocol state of the Southeast Asia Collective Defense Treaty requesting assistance in defense of its freedom." To what extent can a president "run a war" without the consent of Congress? (LBJ Library Photo by Cecil Stoughton)

Other Constitutional Powers. An additional power conferred on the president in Article II, Section 2, is the right to appoint ambassadors, other public ministers, and consuls. In Section 3 of that article, the president is given the power to recognize foreign governments by receiving their ambassadors.

Informal Techniques of Presidential Leadership

Other broad sources of presidential power in the U.S. foreign policy process are tradition, precedent, and the president's personality. The president can employ a host of informal techniques that give the White House overwhelming superiority within the government in foreign policy leadership.

First, the president has access to information. The Central Intelligence Agency (CIA), the State Department, and the Defense Department make more information available to the president than to any other governmental official. This information carries with it the ability to make quick decisions—and the president uses that ability often. Second, the president is a legislative leader who can influence the funds that are allocated for different programs. Third, the president can influence public opinion. President Theodore Roosevelt once made the following statement:

> People used to say to me that I was an astonishingly good politician and divined what the people are going to think. . . . I did not "divine" how the people were going to think; I simply made up my mind what they ought to think and then did my best to get them to think it.[3]

Presidents are without equal with respect to influencing public opinion, partly because of their ability to command the media. Depending on their skill in appealing to patriotic sentiment (and sometimes fear), they can make people believe that their course in foreign affairs is right and necessary. Public opinion often seems to be impressed by the president's decision to make a national commitment abroad. President George W. Bush's speech to Congress shortly after the September 11 attacks rallied the nation and brought new respect for his leadership. It is worth noting that presidents normally, although certainly not always, receive the immediate support of the American people in a foreign policy crisis.

Finally, the president can commit the nation morally to a course of action in foreign affairs. Because the president is the head of state and the leader of one of the most powerful nations on earth, once the president has made a commitment for the United States, it is difficult for Congress or anyone else to back down on that commitment.

Other Sources of Foreign Policymaking

In addition to the president, there are at least four foreign policymaking sources within the executive branch. These are (1) the Department of State, (2) the National Security Council, (3) the intelligence community, and (4) the Department of Defense.

The Department of State. In principle, the State Department is the executive agency that has primary authority over foreign affairs. It supervises U.S. relations with the nearly two hundred independent nations around the world and with the United Nations and other multinational groups, such as the Organization of American States. It staffs embassies and consulates throughout the world. It has about 32,000 employees. This number may sound impressive, but it is small compared with, say, the 67,000 employees of the Department of Health and Human Services. Also, the State Department had an annual budget of only $9.5 billion in fiscal year 2007, one of the smallest budgets of the cabinet departments.

Henry Kissinger may have been the most influential national security adviser in U.S. history. Here, he is shown walking with President Nixon on the south lawn of the White House in 1971. Kissinger later became Nixon's secretary of state. He has purportedly been a regular and frequent outside adviser to President George W. Bush on foreign policy. (National Archives)

---

[3]Sidney Warren, *The President as World Leader* (New York: McGraw-Hill, 1964), p. 23.

|Negative Constituents
Citizens who openly oppose the government's policies.

President Ford meets with the National Security Council on August 10, 1974. Gerald Ford, on President Nixon's resignation, succeeded to the presidency on August 9, 1974. Seated at the table in the Cabinet Room are (left to right) William E. Colby, CIA Director Robert S. Ingersoll, deputy secretary of state; Henry Kissinger, secretary of state; President Ford; James R. Schlesinger, secretary of defense; William P. Clements, Jr., deputy secretary of defense; George S. Brown, chairman of the joint chiefs of staff. Do the department heads all support the president as if they formed part of a "team"? Why or why not? (Library of Congress)

Newly elected presidents usually tell the American public that the new secretary of state is the nation's chief foreign policy adviser. Nonetheless, the State Department's preeminence in foreign policy has declined since World War II. The State Department's image within the White House Executive Office and Congress (and even with foreign governments) is quite poor—a slow, plodding, bureaucratic maze of inefficient, indecisive individuals. Reportedly, Premier Nikita Khrushchev of the Soviet Union urged President John Kennedy to formulate his own views rather than rely on State Department officials who, according to Khrushchev, "specialized in why something had not worked forty years ago."[4] In any event, since the days of Franklin Roosevelt, the State Department has often been bypassed or ignored when crucial decisions are made.

It is not surprising that the State Department has been overshadowed in foreign policy. It has no natural domestic constituency as does, for example, the Department of Defense, which can call on defense contractors for support. Instead, the State Department has what might be called **negative constituents**—U.S. citizens who openly oppose the government's policies. One of the State Department's major functions, administering foreign aid, often elicits criticisms. There is a widespread belief that the United States spends much more on foreign aid than it actually does. For 2007, President Bush's budget request allocated $25 billion to foreign economic aid, or about eighty-eight cents for every one hundred dollars of federal spending.

The National Security Council. The job of the National Security Council (NSC), created by the National Security Act of 1947, is to advise the president on the integration of "domestic, foreign, and military policies relating to the national security." Its larger purpose is to provide policy continuity from one administration to the next. As it has turned out, the NSC—consisting of the president, the vice president, the secretaries of state and defense, the director of emergency planning, and often the chairperson of the joint chiefs of staff and the director of the CIA—is used in just about any way the president wants to use it.

The role of national security adviser to the president seems to adjust to fit the player. Some advisers have come into conflict with heads of the State Department. Henry A. Kissinger, Nixon's flamboyant and aggressive national security adviser,

---

[4]Theodore C. Sorensen, *Kennedy* (New York: Harper & Row, 1965), pp. 554–555.

rapidly gained ascendancy over William Rogers, the secretary of state. More recently, Condoleezza Rice played an important role as national security adviser during George W. Bush's first term. Rice eventually became secretary of state.

The Intelligence Community. No discussion of foreign policy would be complete without some mention of the **intelligence community.** This consists of the forty or more government agencies or bureaus that are involved in intelligence activities. They are as follows:

1. Central Intelligence Agency (CIA).
2. National Security Agency (NSA).
3. Defense Intelligence Agency (DIA).
4. Offices within the Department of Defense.
5. Bureau of Intelligence and Research in the Department of State.
6. Federal Bureau of Investigation (FBI).
7. Army intelligence.
8. Air Force intelligence.
9. Drug Enforcement Administration (DEA).
10. Department of Energy.
11. Directorate of Information Analysis and Infrastructure Protection in the Department of Homeland Security.
12. Office of the Director of National Intelligence

The CIA, created as part of the National Security Act of 1947, is the key official member of the intelligence community.

Covert Actions. Intelligence activities consist mostly of overt information gathering, but covert actions also are undertaken. Covert actions, as the name implies, are carried out in secret, and the American public rarely finds out about them. The CIA covertly aided in the overthrow of the Mossadegh regime in Iran in 1953 and the Arbenz government of Guatemala in 1954. The agency was instrumental in destabilizing the Allende government in Chile from 1970 to 1973.

During the mid-1970s, the "dark side" of the CIA was partly uncovered when the Senate undertook an investigation of its activities. One of the major findings of the Senate Select Committee on Intelligence was that the CIA had routinely spied on American citizens domestically—supposedly a prohibited activity. Consequently, the CIA came under the scrutiny of oversight committees within Congress, which restricted the scope of its operations. By 1980, however, the CIA had regained much of its lost power to engage in covert activities.

Criticisms of the Intelligence Community. By 2001, the CIA had come under fire for a number of lapses, including the discovery that one of its agents was spying on behalf of a foreign power, the failure to detect the nuclear arsenals of India and Pakistan, and, above all, the failure to obtain advance knowledge about the 9/11 terrorist attacks. With the rise of terrorism as a threat, the intelligence agencies have received more funding and enhanced surveillance powers, but these moves have also provoked fears of civil liberties violations. In 2004, the bipartisan 9/11 commission called for a new intelligence czar to oversee the entire intelligence community, with full control of all agency budgets. After initially balking at this recommendation, President Bush eventually called for a partial implementation of the commission's report. Legislation enacted in 2004 established the Office of the Director of National Intelligence to oversee the intelligence community. In 2005, Bush appointed John Negroponte to be the first director.

President George W. Bush meets with Secretary of State Condoleezza Rice and National Security Adviser Stephen Hadley at the Bush ranch to discuss the Middle East in 2006. How much does a president rely on his aides before he makes foreign policy decisions?
(White House Photo by Eric Draper)

Intelligence Community
The government agencies that gather information about the capabilities and intentions of foreign governments or that engage in covert actions.

An aerial view of the Pentagon, the headquarters of the U.S. Department of Defense (DoD) located between the Potomac River and Arlington National Cemetery. The Pentagon employs approximately 23,000 military and civilian personnel and is one the world's largest office buildings with three times the floor space of the Empire State Building in New York City. In the background, the obelisk of the Washington Monument is visible. When the media refer to "The Pentagon," what do they mean? (Johnny Bivera/U.S. Navy)

The Department of Defense.   The Department of Defense (DoD) was created in 1947 to bring all of the various activities of the American military establishment under the jurisdiction of a single department headed by a civilian secretary of defense. At the same time, the joint chiefs of staff, consisting of the commanders of the various military branches and a chairperson, was created to formulate a unified military strategy.

Although the Department of Defense is larger than any other federal department, it declined in size after the fall of the Soviet Union in 1991. In the subsequent ten years, the total number of civilian employees was reduced by about 400,000, to about 665,000. Military personnel were also reduced in number. The defense budget remained relatively flat for several years, but with the advent of the war on terrorism and the use of military forces in Afghanistan and Iraq, funding has again been increased.

Congress Balances the Presidency

A new interest in the balance of power between Congress and the president on foreign policy questions developed during the Vietnam War (1964–1975). Sensitive to public frustration over the long and costly war and angry at Richard Nixon for some of his other actions as president, Congress attempted to establish limits on the power of the president in setting foreign and defense policy. In 1973, Congress passed the War Powers Resolution over President Nixon's veto. The act limited the president's use of troops in military action without congressional approval (see Chapter 12). Most presidents, however, have not interpreted the "consultation" provisions of the act as meaning that Congress should be consulted before military action is taken. Instead, presidents Ford, Carter, Reagan, George H. W. Bush, and Clinton ordered troop movements and then informed congressional leaders. Critics note that it is quite possible for a president to commit troops to a situation from which the nation could not withdraw without incurring heavy losses, whether or not Congress is consulted.

Congress has also exerted its authority by limiting or denying presidential requests for military assistance to various groups (such as Angolan rebels and the government of El Salvador) and requests for new weapons (such as the B-1 bomber). In general, Congress has been far more cautious in supporting the president in situations in which military involvement of American troops is possible. Recently, however, Congress has shown a willingness to support the administration of George W. Bush in the use of military force to fight the war on terrorism.

Congress has its limits, of course, and often these are based on political considerations about election campaigns. Prior to the 2006 elections, Democrats found that antiwar platforms could be very effective during their campaigns. As we pointed out earlier, one incumbent Democratic senator, Joseph I. Lieberman, lost a primary battle to an antiwar candidate. We can expect to see more congressional Democrats calling for the United States to pull out of Iraq.

Domestic Sources of Foreign Policy

The making of foreign policy is often viewed as a presidential prerogative because of the president's constitutional power in that area and the resources of the executive branch that the president controls. Foreign policymaking is also influenced by a number of other sources, however, including elite and mass opinion and the *military-industrial complex,* described below.

Elite and Mass Opinion

Public opinion influences the making of U.S. foreign policy through a number of channels. Elites in American business, education, communications, labor, and religion try to influence presidential decision making through several strategies. A number of elite organizations, such as the Council on Foreign Relations and the Trilateral Commission, work to increase international cooperation and to influence foreign policy through conferences, publications, and research. The members of the American elite establishment also exert influence on foreign policy through the general public by encouraging debate over foreign policy positions, publicizing the issues, and using the media.

Generally, the efforts of the president and the elites are most successful with the segment of the population called the **attentive public.** This sector of the mass public, which probably constitutes 10 to 20 percent of all citizens, is more interested in foreign affairs than are most other Americans, and members of the attentive public are likely to transmit their opinions to the less interested members of the public through conversation and local leadership.

| Attentive Public
That portion of the general public that pays attention to policy issues.

| Military-Industrial Complex
The mutually beneficial relationship between the armed forces and defense contractors.

The Military-Industrial Complex

Civilian fear of the relationship between the defense establishment and arms manufacturers (the **military-industrial complex**) dates back many years. During President Eisenhower's eight years in office, the former five-star general of the army experienced firsthand the kind of pressure that could be brought against him and other policymakers by arms manufacturers. Eisenhower decided to give the country a solemn and—as he saw it—necessary warning of the consequences of this influence. On January 17, 1961, in his last official speech, he said:

> In the councils of government, we must guard against the acquisition of unwarranted influence, whether sought or unsought, by the military-industrial complex. The potential for the disastrous rise of misplaced power exists and will persist. . . . Only an alert and knowledgeable citizenry can compel the proper meshing of the huge industrial and military machinery of defense with our peaceful methods and goals, so that security and liberty may prosper together.[5]

Here, President Dwight D. Eisenhower is shown making his famous speech in which he stated, "We must guard against the acquisition of unwarranted influence, whether sought or unsought, by the military-industrial complex. The potential for the disastrous rise of misplaced power exists and will persist." (National Archives)

---

[5]*Congressional Almanac* (Washington, D.C.: Congressional Quarterly Press, 1961), pp. 938–939.

The Pentagon has supported a large sector of our economy through defense contracts. It has also supplied retired army officers as key executives to large defense-contracting firms. Perhaps the Pentagon's strongest allies have been members of Congress whose districts or states benefit economically from military bases or contracts. After the Cold War ended in the late 1980s, the defense industry looked abroad for new customers. Sales of some military equipment to China raised serious issues for the Clinton administration. The war on terrorism provoked a new debate about what types of weaponry would be needed to safeguard the nation in the future. When President George W. Bush proposed legislation in 2002 to increase the Defense Department's budget substantially, weapons manufacturers looked forward to increased sales and profits.

The Major Foreign Policy Themes

Although some observers might suggest that U.S. foreign policy is inconsistent and changes with the current occupant of the White House, the long view of American diplomatic ventures reveals some major themes underlying foreign policy. In the early years of the nation, presidents and the people generally agreed that the United States should avoid foreign entanglements and concentrate instead on its own development. From the beginning of the twentieth century until today, however, a major theme has been increasing global involvement. The theme of the post–World War II years was the containment of communism. The theme for at least the first part of the twenty-first century may be the containment of terrorism.

The Formative Years: Avoiding Entanglements

Foreign policy was largely nonexistent during the formative years of the United States. Remember that the new nation was operating under the Articles of Confederation. The national government had no right to levy or collect taxes, no control over commerce, no right to make commercial treaties, and no power to raise an army (the Revolutionary army was disbanded in 1783). The government's lack of international power was made clear when Barbary pirates seized American hostages in the Mediterranean. The United States was unable to rescue the hostages and ignominiously had to purchase them in a treaty with Morocco.

A portrait of President James Monroe by Gilbert Stuart. The Monroe Doctrine essentially made the Western Hemisphere the concern of the United States. (Library of Congress)

The founders of this nation had a basic mistrust of European governments. George Washington said it was the U.S. policy "to steer clear of permanent alliances," and Thomas Jefferson echoed this sentiment when he said America wanted peace with all nations but "entangling alliances with none." This was also a logical position at a time when the United States was so weak militarily that it could not influence European development directly. Moreover, being protected by oceans that took weeks to traverse certainly allowed the nation to avoid entangling alliances. During the 1800s, therefore, the United States generally stayed out of European conflicts and politics. In this hemisphere, however, the United States pursued an actively expansionist policy. The nation purchased Louisiana in 1803, annexed Texas in 1845, gained substantial territory from Mexico in 1848, purchased Alaska in 1867, and annexed Hawaii in 1898.

The Monroe Doctrine. President James Monroe, in his message to Congress on December 2, 1823, stated that the United States would not accept foreign intervention in the Western Hemisphere. In return, the United States would not meddle in European affairs. The

Monroe Doctrine was the underpinning of the U.S. **isolationist foreign policy** toward Europe, which continued throughout the 1800s.

The Spanish-American War and World War I. The end of the isolationist policy started with the Spanish-American War in 1898. Winning the war gave the United States possession of Guam, Puerto Rico, and the Philippines (which gained independence in 1946). On the heels of that war came World War I (1914–1918). In his reelection campaign of 1916, President Woodrow Wilson ran on the slogan "He kept us out of war." Nonetheless, the United States declared war on Germany on April 6, 1917, because that country refused to give up its campaign of sinking all ships headed for Britain, including passenger ships. (Large passenger ships of that time commonly held over a thousand people, so the sinking of such a ship was a disaster comparable to the attack on the World Trade Center.)

In the 1920s, the United States went "back to normalcy," as President Warren G. Harding urged it to do. U.S. military forces were largely disbanded, defense spending dropped to about 1 percent of total annual national income, and the nation returned to a period of isolationism.

The Era of Internationalism

Isolationism was permanently shattered by the bombing of the U.S. naval base at Pearl Harbor, Hawaii, on December 7, 1941. The surprise attack by the Japanese caused the deaths of 2,403 American servicemen and wounded 1,143 others. Eighteen warships were sunk or seriously damaged, and 188 planes were destroyed at the airfields. The American public was outraged. President Franklin Roosevelt asked Congress to declare war on Japan immediately, and the United States entered World War II. This unequivocal response was certainly due to the nature of the provocation. American soil had not been attacked by a foreign power since the occupation of Washington, D.C., by the British in 1814.

The United States was the only major participating country to emerge from World War II with its economy intact, and even strengthened. Britain, France, Germany, Italy, Japan, the Soviet Union, and a number of minor participants in the

Monroe Doctrine
A policy statement made by President James Monroe in 1823, which set out three principles: (1) European nations should not establish new colonies in the Western Hemisphere, (2) European nations should not intervene in the affairs of independent nations of the Western Hemisphere, and (3) the United States would not interfere in the affairs of European nations.

Isolationist Foreign Policy
A policy of abstaining from an active role in international affairs or alliances, which characterized U.S. foreign policy toward Europe during most of the 1800s.

British Prime Minister Winston Churchill, U.S. President Franklin Roosevelt, and Soviet leader Joseph Stalin met at Yalta in February 1945 to resolve their differences over the shape that the international community would take after World War II. (Library of Congress)

The atomic bomb explodes over Nagasaki, Japan, on August 9, 1945. (U.S. Air Force Photo)

war were economically devastated. The United States was also the only country to have control over operational nuclear weapons. President Harry Truman had made the decision to use two atomic bombs, on August 6 and August 9, 1945, to end the war with Japan. (Historians still argue over the necessity of this action, which ultimately killed more than 100,000 Japanese and left an equal number permanently injured.) The United States truly had become the world's superpower.

The Cold War. The United States had become an uncomfortable ally of the Soviet Union after Adolf Hitler's invasion of that country. Soon after World War II ended, relations between the Soviet Union and the West deteriorated. The Soviet Union wanted a weakened Germany, and to achieve this, it insisted that Germany be divided in two, with East Germany becoming a buffer against the West. Little by little, the Soviet Union helped to install Communist governments in Eastern European countries, which began to be referred to collectively as the **Soviet bloc.** In response, the United States encouraged the rearming of Western Europe. The Cold War had begun.[6]

In Fulton, Missouri, on March 5, 1946, Winston Churchill, in a striking metaphor, declared that from the Baltic to the Adriatic Sea "an iron curtain has descended across the [European] continent." The term **iron curtain** became even more appropriate when Soviet-dominated East Germany built a wall separating East Berlin from West Berlin in August 1961.

Containment Policy. In 1947, a remarkable article was published in *Foreign Affairs*. The article was signed by "X." The actual author was George F. Kennan, chief of the policy-planning staff for the State Department. The doctrine of **containment** set forth in the article became—according to many—the Bible of Western foreign policy. "X" argued that whenever and wherever the Soviet Union could successfully challenge the West, it would do so. He recommended that our policy toward the Soviet Union be "firm and vigilant containment of Russian expansive tendencies."[7]

Soviet Bloc
The Soviet Union and the Eastern European countries that installed Communist regimes after World War II and were dominated by the Soviet Union.

Iron Curtain
The term used to describe the division of Europe between the Soviet bloc and the West; coined by Winston Churchill.

Containment
A U.S. diplomatic policy adopted by the Truman administration to contain Communist power within its existing boundaries.

---

[6]See John Lewis Gaddis, *The United Nations and the Origins of the Cold War* (New York: Columbia University Press, 1972).
[7]X, "The Sources of Soviet Conduct," *Foreign Affairs*, July 1947, p. 575.

The containment theory was expressed clearly in the Truman Doctrine, which was enunciated by President Harry Truman in his historic address to Congress on March 12, 1947. In that address, he announced that the United States must help countries in which a Communist takeover seemed likely. Later that year, he backed the Marshall Plan, an economic assistance plan for Europe that was intended to prevent the expansion of Communist influence there. By 1950, the United States had entered into a military alliance with the European nations commonly called the North Atlantic Treaty Organization, or NATO. The combined military power of the United States and the European nations worked to contain Soviet influence to Eastern Europe and to maintain a credible response to any Soviet military attack on Western Europe. Figure 17–2 shows the face-off between the U.S.-led NATO alliance and the Soviet-led Warsaw Pact.

| Truman Doctrine
The policy adopted by President Harry Truman in 1947 to halt Communist expansion in southeastern Europe.

Superpower Relations

During the Cold War, there was never any direct military conflict between the United States and the Soviet Union. Rather, confrontations among "client" nations were used to carry out the policies of the superpowers. Only on occasion did the United States directly enter a conflict in a significant way. Two such occasions were in Korea and in Vietnam.

After the end of World War II, northern Korea was occupied by the Soviet Union, and southern Korea was occupied by the United States. The result was two rival Korean governments. In 1950, North Korea invaded South Korea. Under UN authority, the United States entered the war, which prevented an almost certain South Korean defeat. When U.S. forces were on the brink of conquering North Korea, however, China joined the war on the side of the North, resulting in a stalemate. An armistice signed in 1953 led to the two Koreas that exist today. U.S. forces have remained in South Korea ever since.

The Vietnam War (1964–1975) also involved the United States in a civil war between a Communist North and pro-Western South. When the French army in

FIGURE 17–2 | EUROPE DURING THE COLD WAR

This map shows the face-off between NATO (led by the United States) and the Soviet bloc (the Warsaw Pact). Note that France was out of NATO from 1966 to 1996, and Spain did not join until 1982.

Indochina was defeated by the Communist forces of Ho Chi Minh and the two Vietnams were created in 1954, the United States assumed the role of supporting the South Vietnamese government against North Vietnam. President John Kennedy sent 16,000 "advisers" to help South Vietnam, and after Kennedy's death in 1963, President Lyndon Johnson greatly increased the scope of that support. More than 500,000 American troops were in Vietnam at the height of the U.S. involvement. More than 58,000 Americans were killed and 300,000 were wounded in the conflict. A peace agreement in 1973 allowed U.S. troops to leave the country, and in 1975 North Vietnam easily occupied Saigon (the South Vietnamese capital) and unified the nation. The debate over U.S. involvement in Vietnam became extremely heated and, as mentioned previously, spurred congressional efforts to limit the ability of the president to commit forces to armed combat. The military draft was also a major source of contention during the Vietnam War. Do events in Iraq justify bringing back the draft? We examine this question in this chapter's *Which Side Are You On?* feature.

The Cuban Missile Crisis.   Perhaps the closest the two superpowers came to a nuclear confrontation was the Cuban missile crisis in 1962. The Soviets installed missiles in Cuba, ninety miles off the U.S. coast, in response to Cuban fears of an American invasion and to try to balance an American nuclear advantage. President Kennedy and his advisers rejected the option of invading Cuba and set up a naval blockade around the island instead. When Soviet vessels appeared near Cuban waters, the tension reached its height. After intense negotiations between Washington and Moscow, the Soviet ships turned around on October 25, and on October 28 the Soviet Union announced the withdrawal of its missile operations from Cuba. In exchange, the United States agreed not to invade Cuba in the future and to remove some of its own missiles that were located near the Soviet border in Turkey.

Détente
A French word meaning a relaxation of tensions. The term characterized U.S.-Soviet relations as they developed under President Richard Nixon and Secretary of State Henry Kissinger.

A Period of Détente.   The French word **détente** means a relaxation of tensions. By the end of the 1960s, it was clear that some efforts had to be made to reduce the threat of nuclear war between the United States and the Soviet Union. The Soviet Union gradually had begun to catch up in the building of strategic nuclear delivery vehicles in the form of bombers and missiles, thus balancing the nuclear scales between the two countries. Each nation acquired the military capacity to destroy the other with nuclear weapons.

As the result of lengthy negotiations under Secretary of State Henry Kissinger and President Nixon, the United States and the Soviet Union signed the **Strategic Arms Limitation Treaty (SALT I)** in May 1972. That treaty "permanently" limited the development and deployment of antiballistic missiles (ABMs) and limited the number of offensive missiles each country could deploy. To further reduce tensions, new scientific and cultural exchanges were arranged with the Soviets, as well as new opportunities for Jewish emigration out of the Soviet Union.

Strategic Arms Limitation Treaty (SALT I)
A treaty between the United States and the Soviet Union to stabilize the nuclear arms competition between the two countries. SALT I talks began in 1969, and agreements were signed on May 26, 1972.

The policy of détente was not limited to the U.S. relationship with the Soviet Union. Seeing an opportunity to capitalize on increasing friction between the Soviet Union and the People's Republic of China, Kissinger secretly began negotiations to establish a new relationship with that nation. President Nixon eventually visited China in 1972. The visit set the stage for the formal diplomatic recognition of that country, which occurred during the Carter administration (1977–1981).

The Reagan-Bush Years.   President Ronald Reagan took a hard line against the Soviet Union during his first term, proposing the strategic defense initiative (SDI), or "Star Wars," in 1983. The SDI was designed to serve as a space-based defense against enemy missiles. Reagan and others in his administration argued that the program would deter nuclear war by shifting the emphasis of defense strategy from offensive to defensive weapons systems.

WHICH SIDE ARE YOU ON? | Should We Bring Back the Draft?

By law, male residents of the United States are required to register for the military draft after their eighteenth birthdays. From 1948 through 1973, all American men were subject to the draft, and draftees filled the ranks of the armed forces during war and peace. Since 1973, however, the armed forces have been composed entirely of volunteers.

Beginning in 2004, coalition troops in Iraq faced major uprisings. U.S. forces were stretched thin. The Department of Defense was compelled to extend the tours of duty for units that were about to be brought home. In particular, this meant extending the service of National Guard units. Most members of the National Guard had never anticipated that they would serve in a war zone.

In response, some members of Congress proposed enlarging the army. A few spoke up for bringing back the draft.

BRINGING BACK THE DRAFT WOULD PROMOTE FAIRNESS

Those who advocate bringing back the draft believe that universal service would be fairer than the current system. Now, almost no children of wealthy families enter the military. Only four members of the 107th Congress had children in one of the services. Draft advocates say that the military should not be limited to the lower classes—everyone should give something back to society. Alternative civilian service could be provided for those who do not wish to join the armed forces, but complete exemption should be unavailable.

A draft would prevent the kinds of troop shortages that the military is currently experiencing. In particular, it could eliminate the unfairness involved in stationing National Guard troops abroad for long periods of time. Finally, if there were a universal draft, Congress might be more cautious about endorsing wars.

THE DRAFT IS UNFAIR AND UNNECESSARY

Others fundamentally oppose forcing young people to give up one or more years of their lives to the government. The draft, they say, is a "tax" that falls most strongly on those who value their independence. If the government wants more soldiers, let it offer higher pay and better benefits. A draft would worsen already existing divisions in the country, as it did during the Vietnam War. Furthermore, the military really needs highly trained members who will reenlist, not large numbers of "warm bodies" who will leave as soon as they can.

WHAT'S YOUR POSITION?

If the draft were reinstated, should it include women? Why or why not?

GOING ONLINE

Draft registration is administered by the Selective Service System, which maintains a Web site at **www.sss.gov**. At this site, you can actually register online. An antidraft site that advocates civil disobedience is at **www.draftresistance.com**.

In November 1985, however, President Reagan and Mikhail Gorbachev, the Soviet leader, began to work on an arms reduction compact. The negotiations resulted in a historic agreement signed by Reagan and Gorbachev in Washington, D.C., on December 8, 1987. The terms of the Intermediate-Range Nuclear Force (INF) Treaty, which was ratified by the Senate, required the superpowers to dismantle a total of four thousand intermediate-range missiles within the first three years of the agreement.

Beginning in 1989, President George H. W. Bush continued the negotiations with the Soviet Union to reduce the number of nuclear weapons and the number of armed troops in Europe. Subsequent events, including developments in Eastern Europe, the unification of Germany, and the dissolution of the Soviet Union (in December 1991), made the process much more complex. American strategists worried as much about who now controlled the Soviet nuclear arsenal as about completing the treaty process. In 1992, the United States signed the Strategic Arms Reduction Treaty (START) with four former Soviet republics—Russia, Ukraine, Belarus, and Kazakhstan—to reduce the number of long-range nuclear weapons. President George W. Bush changed directions in 2001, announcing that the United States was withdrawing from the 1972 ABM treaty. Six months later, however, Bush and Russian President Vladimir Putin signed an agreement greatly reducing the number of nuclear weapons on each side over the next few years.

The Dissolution of the Soviet Union. After the fall of the Berlin Wall in 1989, it was clear that the Soviet Union had relinquished much of its political and military control over the states of Eastern Europe that formerly had been part of the Soviet bloc. No one expected the Soviet Union to dissolve into separate states as quickly as it did, however. Though Gorbachev tried to adjust the Soviet constitution and political system to allow greater autonomy for the republics within the union, demands for political, ethnic, and religious autonomy grew. In August 1991, anti-reformist conspirators launched an attempt to overthrow the Soviet government and to depose Gorbachev. These efforts were thwarted by the Russian people and parliament under the leadership of Boris Yeltsin, then president of Russia.

Instead of restoring the Soviet state, the attempted *coup d'état* hastened the process of creating an independent Russian state led by Yeltsin. On the day after Christmas in 1991, the Soviet Union was officially dissolved. Another uprising in Russia, this time led by anti-Yeltsin members of the new parliament who wanted to restore the Soviet Union immediately, failed in 1993. Figure 17–3 shows the new situation in Europe following the collapse of the Soviet Union.

In 2000, Yeltsin resigned due to poor health. He named Vladimir Putin, architect of the Russian military effort against the independence movement in the province of Chechnya, as acting president. A few months later, Putin won the presidency in a national election. As the United States launched its war on terrorism, Putin stood by President George W. Bush's side as an ally. Nonetheless, Russia opposed the use of military forces in Iraq in early 2003, believing that a war against Iraq was unjustified.

Although Putin has claimed that Russia's most important task is to "develop as a free and democratic state," his actions belie his words. Throughout his time in office, he has slowly but surely limited freedom of the press and freedom of speech. In addition, he has reduced the number of political offices that are filled by free elections. Some argue that without the huge revenues that the Russian government is obtaining as a result of the high price of oil, Putin would face popular discontent and would be unable to carry out his antidemocratic actions.

FIGURE 17–3 | EUROPE AFTER THE FALL OF THE SOVIET UNION
This map shows the growth in European unity as marked by the participation in transnational organizations. The United States continues to lead NATO (and would be orange if it were on the map). Note the reunification of Germany and the creation of new states from former Yugoslavia and the former Soviet Union.

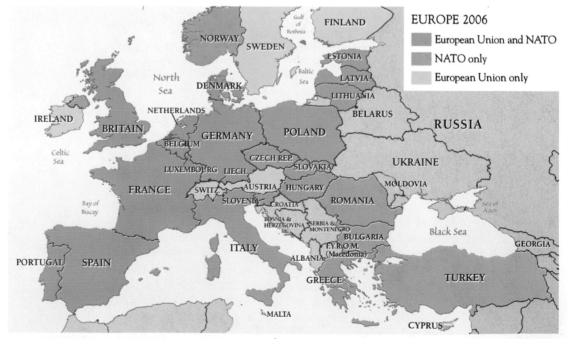

MAKING A DIFFERENCE | Working for Human Rights

In many countries throughout the world, human rights are not protected. In some nations, people are imprisoned, tortured, or killed because they oppose the current regime. In other nations, certain ethnic or racial groups are oppressed by the majority population.

Why Should You Care?

The strongest reason for involving yourself with human rights issues in other countries is simple moral altruism—unselfish regard for the welfare of others. The defense of human rights is unlikely to put a single dollar in your pocket.

A broader consideration, however, is that human rights abuses are often associated with the kind of dictatorial regimes that are likely to provoke wars. To the extent that the people of the world can create a climate in which human rights abuses are unacceptable, they may also create an atmosphere in which national leaders believe that they must display peaceful conduct generally. This, in turn, might reduce the frequency of wars, some of

which could involve the United States. Less war would mean preserving peace and human life, not to mention, reducing the financial burden.

What Can You Do?

What can you do to work for the improvement of human rights in other nations? One way is to join an organization that attempts to keep watch over human rights violations. (Two such organizations are listed at the end of this feature.) By publicizing human rights violations, such organizations try to pressure nations into changing their practices. Sometimes, these organizations are able to apply enough pressure and cause enough embarrassment that victims may be freed from prison or allowed to emigrate.

Another way to work for human rights is to keep informed about the state of affairs in other nations and to write personally to governments that violate human rights or to their embassies, asking them to cease these violations.

If you want to receive general information about the position of the United States on human rights violations, you can contact the State Department:

U.S. Department of State
  Bureau of Democracy,
  Human Rights, and Labor
2201 C St. N.W.
Washington, DC 20520
202-647-4000
www.state.gov/g/drl/hr

The following organizations are well known for their watchdog efforts in countries that violate human rights for political reasons:

Amnesty International U.S.A.
322 Eighth Ave., Floor 10
New York, NY 10001
212-807-8400
www.amnestyusa.org

American Friends Service Committee
1501 Cherry St.
Philadelphia, PA 19102
215-241-7000
www.afsc.org

Key Terms

attentive public 563

Cold War 553

containment 566

defense policy 544

détente 568

diplomacy 543

economic aid 543

foreign policy 543

foreign policy process 543

intelligence community 561

iron curtain 566

isolationist foreign policy 565

**military-industrial
  complex** 563

Monroe Doctrine 565

moral idealism 544

national security policy 543

negative constituents 560

**normal trade relations (NTR)
  status** 554

political realism 545

Soviet bloc 566

**Strategic Arms Limitation
  Treaty (SALT I)** 568

technical assistance 543

Truman Doctrine 567

Chapter Summary

1 Foreign policy includes national goals and the techniques used to achieve them. National security policy, which is one aspect of foreign policy, is designed to protect the independence and the political and economic integrity of the United States. Diplomacy involves the nation's external relationships and is an attempt to resolve conflict without resort to arms. U.S. foreign policy is sometimes based on moral idealism and sometimes on political realism.

2 Terrorism has become a major challenge facing the United States and other nations. The United States waged war on terrorism after the September 11 attacks. U.S. armed forces occupied Afghanistan in 2001 and Iraq in 2003.

3 Nuclear proliferation continues to be an issue due to the breakup of the Soviet Union and loss of control over its nuclear arsenal, along with the continued efforts of other nations to gain nuclear warheads. More than 32,000 nuclear warheads are known to exist worldwide.

4 Ethnic tensions and political instability in many regions of the world provide challenges to the United States. In the Caribbean, Cuba requires American attention because of its proximity. Civil wars have torn apart Rwanda and other countries. The Middle East continues to be a hotbed of conflict despite efforts to continue the peace process. In 1991 and again in 2003, the United States sent combat troops to Iraq. The Second Gulf War, in 2003, succeeded in toppling the decades-long dictatorship in Iraq.

5 The formal power of the president to make foreign policy derives from the U.S. Constitution, which designates the president as commander in chief of the army and navy. Presidents have interpreted this authority broadly. They also have the power to make treaties and executive agreements. In principle, the State Department is the executive agency with primary authority over foreign affairs. The National Security Council also plays a major role. The intelligence community consists of government agencies engaged in activities varying from information gathering to covert operations. In response to presidential actions in the Vietnam War, Congress attempted to establish some limits on the power of the president to intervene abroad by passing the War Powers Resolution in 1973.

6 Three major themes have guided U.S. foreign policy. In the early years of the nation, isolationism was the primary strategy. With the start of the twentieth century, isolationism gave way to global involvement. From the end of World War II through the 1980s, the major goal was to contain communism and the influence of the Soviet Union.

7 During the 1800s, the United States had little international power and generally stayed out of European conflicts and politics, and so these years have been called the period of isolationism. The Monroe Doctrine of 1823 stated that the United States would not accept foreign intervention in the Western Hemisphere and would not meddle in European affairs. The United States pursued an actively expansionist policy in the Americas and the Pacific area, however.

8 The end of the policy of isolationism toward Europe started with the Spanish-American War of 1898. U.S. involvement in European politics became more extensive when the United States entered World War I on April 6, 1917. World War II marked a lasting change in American foreign policy. The United States was the only major country to emerge from the war with its economy intact and the only country with operating nuclear weapons.

9 Soon after the close of World War II, the uncomfortable alliance between the United States and the Soviet Union ended, and the Cold War began. A policy of containment, which assumed an expansionist Soviet Union, was enunciated in the Truman Doctrine. Following the frustrations of the Vietnam War and the apparent arms equality of the United States and the Soviet Union, the United States adopted a policy of détente. Although President Reagan took a tough stance toward the Soviet Union during his first term, his second term saw serious negotiations toward arms reduction, culminating in the signing of the Intermediate-Range Nuclear Force Treaty in 1987. After the fall of the Soviet Union, Russia emerged as a less threatening state and signed the Strategic Arms Reduction Treaty with the United States in 1992. The United States and Russia have agreed on some issues in recent years, such as the fight against terrorism, but have disagreed on other matters, such as the war against Iraq in 2003.

Selected Print and Media Resources

SUGGESTED READINGS

Chomsky, Noam, and Gilbert Achcar. *Perilous Power: The Middle East and U.S. Foreign Policy Dialogues on Terror, Democracy, War, and Justice.* Boulder, Colo.: Paradigm Publishers, 2006. Chomsky is one of the most vocal critics of U.S. foreign policy, and he shows it in the essays in this book. Achcar is a specialist in Middle Eastern affairs who has lived in the region. These authors examine key questions relating to terrorism, conspiracies, democracy, anti-Semitism, and anti-Arab racism. This book can serve as an introduction to understanding the Middle East today.

Hoffmann, Stanley. *Chaos and Violence: What Globalization, Failed States, and Terrorism Mean for U.S. Foreign Policy.* Lanham, Md.: Rowman & Littlefield Publishers, 2006. What is the proper place of the United States in a world that has been defined by the terrorist acts of September 11, 2001? What are the ethics of intervention, and what is the morality of human rights? These are questions the author answers. He also attempts to show how our broken relationship with Europe can be repaired. He believes that America has engaged in too much unilateralism.

Nye, Joseph S., Jr. *The Paradox of American Power: Why the World's Only Superpower Can't Go It Alone.* New York: Oxford University Press, 2002. Former assistant secretary of defense and now dean of Harvard's Kennedy School of Government, Joseph Nye stresses the importance of U.S. cooperation with the international community and indicates why the United States cannot "go it alone" in today's world arena.

O'Hanlon, Michael, and Mike M. Mochizuki. *Crisis in the Korean Peninsula: How to Deal with a Nuclear North Korea.* New York: McGraw-Hill, 2003. The authors provide a comprehensive introduction to the dangers posed by North Korea, which could become a greater threat to world peace than the current terrorist movements. They also offer a possible "grand bargain" to defuse the crisis.

Woodward, Bob. *State of Denial.* New York: Simon and Schuster, 2006. This is the third of Woodward's masterful inside accounts of policymaking in George W. Bush's administration. *Bush at War* (2002) dealt with 9/11 and the war in Afghanistan. *Plan of Attack* (2004) covered the Second Gulf War in Iraq and its aftermath. *State of Denial* provides the fullest, and most critical, account of the development and implementation of the Bush administration's Iraq policy.

MEDIA RESOURCES

The Aftermath: A Visit to Postwar Iraq—A 2003 program that features interviews with Iraqi clerics, businesspersons, scholars, and street protesters, and also with U.S. soldiers and their commanders.

Black Hawk Down—This 2002 film recounts the events in Mogadishu, Somalia, in October 1993, during which two U.S. Black Hawk helicopters were shot down. The film, which is based on reporter Mark Bowden's best-selling book by the same name, contains graphic scenes of terrifying urban warfare.

The Fall of Milošević—A highly acclaimed 2003 documentary by Norma Percy and Brian Lapping. This film covers the final years of the crisis in former Yugoslavia, including the war in Kosovo and the fall of Slobodan Milošević, Serb nationalist leader and alleged war criminal. Except for Milošević himself, almost all top Serb and Albanian leaders are interviewed, as are President Bill Clinton and British Prime Minister Tony Blair.

The 50 Years War—Israel and the Arabs—A two-volume PBS Home Video released in 2000. More balanced than some accounts, this film includes interviews with many leaders involved in the struggle, including: from Israel, Yitzhak Rabin, Shimon Peres, Benjamin Netanyahu, and Ariel Sharon; from the Arab world, Egypt's Anwar al-Sadat, Jordan's King Hussein, and Yasir Arafat; and from the United States, presidents Jimmy Carter, George H. W. Bush, and Bill Clinton.

Osama bin Laden: In the Name of Allah—A 2001 biography of the leader responsible for the terrorist attacks of September 11, 2001.

E·MOCRACY | Attacking Government Computer Systems

Attacks on the government's computer systems occur often and are sometimes successful. In 1996, hackers caused mischief at the computers of the Central Intelligence Agency and the Justice Department and destroyed the Air Force's home page. In early 1998, computer hackers accessed a series of non-classified sites, caused major university and National Aeronautics and Space Administration computers to crash, and defaced military base home pages. It is clear from these episodes that the electronic network used by U.S. military and intelligence organizations is susceptible to access by amateurs, criminals, and spies.

Perhaps even more damage could be caused by interruptions to the global economic and banking systems. During 1997, a survey of banks, universities, and companies showed that more than 60 percent had been accessed "illegitimately" during that year alone. In 2000, a series of computer viruses crippled businesses around the world. One of the most destructive viruses was eventually traced to a graduate student in the Philippines whose thesis had been rejected.

The potential consequences of successful attacks on government or business computer systems are great. Among the networks that, if impaired or destroyed, could interfere with the nation's activities are those that connect the military services; guide satellites for communications and defense; guide submarines; and control all air traffic,

credit-card transactions, interbank transactions, and utility grids throughout the nation. The collapse of the World Trade Center towers in 2001 damaged telecommunications and Internet communications for all of lower Manhattan.

| Logging On

Our government and the governments of other nations maintain hundreds of Web sites on foreign and defense policy. If you are interested in information about visas, passports, and individual countries, you can access the site maintained by the Department of State at

www.state.gov

For information about human rights, national security, and other issues from a European point of view, check a Web site maintained by the Swiss government, the International Relations and Security Network, at

www.css.ethz.ch

The Brookings Institution, a Washington, D.C., think tank, provides access to its research reports at the following Web site:

www.brook.edu

The Global Affairs Agenda, an interest group that promotes a progressive or liberal foreign policy, provides information about many topics at

www.fpif.org

For information about the intelligence community and about foreign countries, go to the Web site of the Central Intelligence Agency at

www.cia.gov

Freedom House, an organization that promotes its vision of democracy around the world, rates all nations on their democratic practices at

www.freedomhouse.org

| Online Review

At **www.politicalscience.wadsworth.com/schmidt12**, you will find a free Study Guide to this book. For each chapter, there are two online quizzes to help you master the material.

• The PoliPrep Self-Study Assessment provides a pretest for each major section of the chapter. PoliPrep then generates a customized study plan. After you complete the study plan, a posttest evaluates your progress.

• The Tutorial Quiz for each chapter provides questions on the chapter contents, including the features. The questions are organized to match the major sections of the chapter.

18 | Texas History and Culture

What If . . .
Texas Had an Official Language?

BACKGROUND

It may surprise many people that, despite the obviously privileged position of English in the United States, this nation does not have an "official" language. Several states, however, have passed legislation making English an official language for the state, with varying policy implications. Official language advocates argue that the majority has the right to create an official language to foster a unified culture and identity. As might be expected, minority language speakers resist these proposals.

As we discuss in the "Cultural Diversity" section at the end of this chapter, Hispanic Americans are expected to become a majority of the Texas population by about the year 2035. Any discussion of an official language for Texas must take that fact into account.

WHAT IF TEXAS HAD AN OFFICIAL LANGUAGE?

For an official language declaration to mean anything, it must require the state government to take specific actions on behalf of the official language. Based on steps taken in other states, it is possible that firefighters, police officers, and other emergency workers would be required or encouraged to use only the official language. Ballots and other public documents might be printed only in the official language.

Bilingual programs might be banned in elementary schools, although the schools would presumably attempt to assist children who were not fluent in the official tongue. No law could prevent speakers of an unofficial language from using it in their own homes. Still, considerable pressure might be exerted to discourage speakers of unofficial languages from using those languages in public.

Proponents of English as an official language in other states have argued that such laws encourage minority language speakers to become fluent in English and become better able to communicate with the majority. This would reduce friction and allow all groups to share a common identity as well as a common language.

THE POLITICAL CONSEQUENCES

The reality would almost certainly be different. An attempt to establish English as the official language of Texas would be widely perceived as an attack on the state's Hispanic American population. Rather than promoting unity, official English would probably be one of the most divisive measures the state government could possibly implement.

In the 2004 presidential elections, Republican George W. Bush split the Hispanic vote in Texas almost evenly with Democrat John F. Kerry.

This is encouraging news for the now-dominant Texas Republican Party. If the Republican Party can win half of the Hispanic vote, it can probably maintain its dominance no matter how many Hispanics there are in Texas. But what if official English became a current political issue?

Almost certainly, Texas Democrats would be more united and fierce in their opposition to an official English measure than the Republicans could possibly hope to be. If such a measure were actually passed, the probable result would be to deliver a large majority of the Hispanic vote to the Democrats for generations to come. This possibility is not lost on the Republican leadership.

OFFICIAL SPANISH?

To better understand the probable Hispanic reaction to official English, consider how the Texas Anglo population (and English-speaking African Americans and Asian Americans) would react if the official language of Texas were to become Spanish. Presumably, by the middle of the twenty-first century, Spanish-speaking Texans would have the votes to implement such a proposal if they so desired. All of the arguments in favor of cultural unity could then be advanced on behalf of official Spanish. Proponents of Spanish could further argue that Texans would then be better able to communicate with the Spanish-speaking peoples of Latin America. This linguistic compatibility would give Texas marketing and production a distinct advantage in the rapidly expanding economies of our southern neighbors.

FOR CRITICAL ANALYSIS

1. Would Hispanic opposition to official English be legitimate? Would such opposition be unpatriotic or un-American?
2. What arguments could opponents of an official language use if such a proposal were seriously made?

Almost a hundred years before the *Mayflower* dropped anchor off Plymouth Rock, Núñez Cabeza de Vaca set foot on what was to become Texas. During the next three centuries, land-hungry settlers pushed the Cherokees and the Caddos from the eastern pine forests; the Karankawas from the sands of the coast; and the Comanches, Apaches, and Kiowas from the western plains. Texas culture and history were made under thirty-seven Spanish governors, fifteen Mexican governors, five presidents of the Republic of Texas, and forty-eight state governors.

The successful end of the Texas Revolution in 1836 saw the English/Scotch-Irish culture, as it had evolved in its passage through the southern United States, become the dominant culture of the state. Anglo Americans were the most numerous population group and controlled most of the political and economic systems in Texas. Anglo American Protestant sects also became the dominant religious groups in Texas. As evidence of the dominance of this culture, all the presidents of the Republic and the governors of the state have been Protestant and had surnames linked to the British Isles.

Politics and Government: The Early Years

Politics in the Republic of Texas was simpler than politics in Texas today. There were no political parties, and conflict revolved around pro-Houston and anti-Houston policies. Sam Houston, the hero of the battle of San Jacinto (1836), advocated peaceful relations with the eastern Native Americans and U.S. statehood for Texas. The anti-Houston forces were led by Mirabeau B. Lamar, who believed that Native American and Anglo American cultures could not coexist. He also envisioned Texas as a great nation extending from the Sabine River to the Pacific.[1]

Joining the Union

Texas voters approved **annexation** to the United States in 1836, almost immediately after Texas achieved independence from Mexico. The slavery controversy in the United States, however, delayed final annexation until pro-annexation Democrat James K. Polk was elected president. On December 29, 1845, Texas officially became the twenty-eighth state in the Union.

Several articles of annexation were more or less peculiar to Texas. Most important was that Texas retained ownership of its public lands because the U.S. Congress refused to accept them in exchange for payment of the republic's $10 million public debt. Although many millions of acres were eventually given away or sold, the remaining public lands continue to produce hundreds of millions of dollars in state revenue, mostly in royalties from the production of oil and natural gas. Today, this revenue primarily benefits the Permanent University Fund and the Permanent School Fund.

The annexation articles also granted Texas the privilege of "creating . . . new states, of convenient size, not exceeding four in number, in addition to said State of Texas."[2] This provision was an attempt by Congress to keep a balanced ratio of slave and free states in the United States (and thus equal representation of slave and free states in the U.S. Senate). The provision suggests fascinating, though unlikely, possibilities. If the land that is now the state of Texas contained five states, the region

| Annexation

The incorporation of a territory into a larger political unit, such as a country, state, county, or city.

This painting of Sam Houston shows him in the prime of life. Houston was commander in chief of the armies of Texas during the war for independence from Mexico and subsequently was elected the first president of the Republic of Texas. His lifelong friendship with the Native Americans and his opposition to secession set him apart from other Texans of his generation. He died in 1863 during the American Civil War. (Courtesy Huntsville Arts Commission)

[1]The information in this and subsequent sections depends heavily on Seymour V. Connor, *Texas: A History* (New York: Thomas Y. Crowell, 1971); Rupert N. Richardson, *Texas: The Lone Star State*, 3d ed. (Englewood Cliffs, N.J.: Prentice Hall, 1970); and T. R. Fehrenbach, *Lone Star: A History of Texas and the Texans* (New York: Collier Books, 1980).

[2]The Annexation of Texas, Joint Resolution of Congress, March 1, 1845, *U.S. Statutes at Large*, Vol. V, pp. 797–798. This document can be found online at **www.pbs.org/weta/thewest/resources/archives/two/texannex.htm**.

would have ten senators and eight more votes in the electoral college. It would thereby gain influence in the U.S. Senate, as well as in presidential politics. Modern Texans, however, seem uninterested in the prospect of carving four additional states out of Texas.

Early Statehood and Secession: 1846–1864

The politics of early statehood immediately began to revolve around pro-Union and secessionist forces. Sam Houston, a strong Unionist alarmed at the support for **secession** in Texas, resigned his seat in the U.S. Senate and in 1857 ran for the office of governor of Texas. He was defeated, primarily because secession forces controlled the dominant Democratic Party. He was elected governor two years later, however.

After Abraham Lincoln was elected president of the United States in 1860, a Texas secessionist convention voted to secede from the Union. Branded as illegal by Sam Houston, the convention was nevertheless upheld as legitimate by the Texas legislature. Although Houston strongly opposed secession, he refused an offer from President Lincoln of five thousand federal troops to force Texas to remain in the Union. Texas then seceded from the United States and was admitted into the Confederate States of America.

Texas politics during the Civil War primarily concerned the military. Besides supplying large numbers of troops to the conflict (primarily Confederate but also Union), Texas was responsible for the defense of the frontier and the Mexican border. Thus, the state—not the central Confederate government—filled the military vacuum created by the withdrawal of federal troops.

Post–Civil War Texas: 1865–1885

Following the collapse of the Confederacy, relative anarchy existed in Texas until it was occupied by federal troops on June 19, 1865. Only then were government functions and stability restored to the state.

Even before the end of the hostilities, a disagreement had arisen between radical and moderate Republicans in the U.S. Congress over Reconstruction policies for the defeated southern states. Some of these states, including Texas, provided ammunition to congressional radicals (called *Radical Republicans*) in this intraparty conflict by electing to office former Confederate officials and by passing **Black Codes** (state laws that severely restricted the rights of freed slaves). Radical Republicans in Congress reacted by enacting legislation that strictly limited both voter registration and eligibility to hold public office for former Confederate soldiers and officials. This restriction even included former mayors and school board members.

The Reconstruction of Texas under E. J. Davis.   From 1865 through 1869, Texas government was under the military rule of the U.S. Army. Following the adoption of the constitution of 1869, E. J. Davis, a Texan and Radical Republican who had fought for the Union in the Civil War, was elected governor of Texas in an election in which the former slaves could vote—but the former leaders of the state could not. Texas was then readmitted to the Union and governed by civilian authority under Davis, who served for one four-year term from 1870 through 1873. Under the 1869 Texas Constitution, political power was centralized in the office of the governor, and the state police and the militia were placed under his direct control.

Charges of corruption were common during the Davis administration, and state indebtedness drastically increased. Republican domination of Texas politics was "a world turned upside down" for most white Texas citizens.

The Fall of Governor Davis.   The perception of the Davis administration as a government imposed on a defeated people in itself made it unpopular and prompted a strong anti-Republican reaction as soon as the Republicans lost power. In 1873, former Confederates were allowed to vote, and in 1874, Democrat Richard Coke was overwhelmingly elected governor in a vicious and hotly contested campaign. The Texas Supreme Court, handpicked by Davis, invalidated the election based on a technicality.

Davis locked himself in the capitol, surrounded it with the state police, requested the support of federal troops from President Ulysses S. Grant, and refused to leave office. In the predawn hours of January 13, 1874, however, Democratic legislators managed to gain access to the unoccupied legislative chambers, declared a quorum present, and officially validated the election of Coke as governor of Texas. Despite Grant's refusal to send in troops and with tension mounting, Davis still refused to leave the capitol. Only when serious violence seemed imminent between the state police and the numerically superior Coke forces did Davis withdraw.

The End of Republicanism.   The new Texas officials immediately began to remove the last vestiges of radical Republicanism. One of the first steps was to rewrite the state constitution. A constitutional convention of ninety members was elected (seventy-five Democrats and fifteen Republicans) that included many former officials of both the Union and Confederate governments. Forty members of the 1875 convention also belonged to the Grange, at that time a nonpartisan organization of farmers. Ratified in 1876, the new constitution cut expenditures, decentralized state government, and strictly limited the flexibility of elected officials. Although often amended, it is still in use today.

Davis established a law practice in Austin and continued to head the Republican Party and control patronage from Washington until his death in 1883. He remained unpopular with most Texans, and his death created a racial division between black and white Republicans. The African American forces, under Norris Wright Cuney of Galveston, gained control of both the state party machinery and party patronage from Washington. The political consequence of Reconstruction and the policies of E. J. Davis was one-party dominance by an all-white Democratic Party with the numerically smaller, predominantly black Republican Party in opposition.

Politics and Government: 1886–1945

After 1886, increasing demands for change forced the Democratic Party to make political adjustments. Many reform measures were enacted and enforced in Texas in the 1880s, especially **antitrust legislation**. The election of James Stephen Hogg as attorney general in 1886 ensured the vigorous enforcement of the new laws against abuses by insurance companies, railroads, and other corporate interests.

Governor Hogg

Hogg, who had strong support among small East Texas farmers, played an important reformist role in Texas politics and rapidly developed a reputation as a champion of the common people. Feeling that he needed more power to regulate the railroad interests that dominated many state governments, Hogg ran for governor. The 1890 Democratic state convention nominated him as candidate for governor in spite of opposition from powerful political and corporate business enemies. A major issue in the campaign that followed was a proposed amendment giving the Texas legislature the power to establish a commission to regulate railroads. The voters gave both Hogg and the amendment a clear victory.

| DID YOU KNOW . . .
That *Juneteenth,* or Emancipation Day, long celebrated by Texas African Americans, became an official state holiday in 1979?

| Antitrust Legislation
Legislation directed against economic monopolies.

The Railroad Commission.   As governor, Hogg was able to persuade the legislature to establish a three-member Railroad Commission, in spite of intense opposition from special interest legislators. His appointment of respected political figures to the commission, notably John H. Reagan as chairman, enabled it to become one of the most important railroad regulatory bodies in the United States.

The constitutionality of a railroad commission still had to be tested in the federal courts, but it was upheld after two years of litigation. The commission was later given the power to regulate the production and transportation of oil and natural gas and to regulate rubber-tired vehicles used in intrastate commerce. In 1994, however, the U.S. Congress determined that the commission's *intrastate* trucking regulations were an obstacle to *interstate* commerce and mandated gradual deregulation of the trucking industry in Texas.

Edward M. House.   In 1894, an early Hogg supporter, Edward M. House, was able to take control of the Democratic Party from Hogg on a "promote unity" platform. House established himself as a behind-the-scenes political power in Texas for the next forty years. House also wielded significant influence in national politics, first as a supporter and later as chief confidant of President Woodrow Wilson (1913–1921). Although he never sought elective office, he was one of the most astute politicians ever to operate in Texas.

Throughout the early 1900s, programs enacted by the legislature continued to identify Texas as one of the most progressive states in the nation. Texas pioneered the regulation of trusts (monopolies), railroads, child labor, and other employer abuses, as well as reform of prisons, taxes, and insurance companies. In 1905, state conventions were replaced with direct primaries to nominate major-party candidates.

Farmer Jim: 1914–1918

James E. Ferguson entered the Texas political scene in 1914 and was a controversial and powerful force in Texas politics for the next twenty years. He had worked as a migrant laborer in California, Nevada, Colorado, and Texas. Although Ferguson had little formal education and only a few months' study of law, he was admitted to the Texas bar in 1897.

By 1914, when he announced his candidacy for governor, Ferguson owned varied business interests and was the president of the Temple State Bank. Ferguson was an antiprohibitionist ("wet") at a time when **Prohibition** was a major political issue, and although his strongest opponent in the Democratic primary was a prohibitionist ("dry"), Ferguson tried to ignore the liquor issue. Although sensitive to the problems and interests of the business community, Ferguson called himself "Farmer Jim" to emphasize his rural background and focused his campaign on the difficulties of the numerous **tenant farmers** in Texas.

Farmer Jim as Governor.   The legislature was unusually receptive to Ferguson's programs, which were in the best tradition of the **progressive movement**, and enacted legislation designed to help alleviate problems of tenant farmers, rural schools, and state courts. Governor Ferguson was reelected in 1916, and although rumors of financial irregularities in the office had begun to gain credibility, his progressive legislative programs were again successful. This was especially true in the areas of public school and college education and the proposal to create a state highway commission. The latter agency was formed to take the construction and maintenance of state roads away from the counties, where there was great variation in quality and consistency.

The Fall of Farmer Jim.   Rumors of financial irregularities such as bribery and embezzlement continued during Ferguson's second term. His fatal step, however,

Prohibition
Outlawing of the production, sale, and consumption of alcoholic beverages.

Tenant Farmer
A farmer who does not own the land that he or she farms but rents it from a landowner.

Progressive Movement
A political movement within both major parties in the early twentieth century. Progressives believed that the power of the government should be used to restrain the growing power of large corporations.

may have been "declaring war" on the University of Texas. After the legislature had adjourned, Ferguson issued an **item veto** of the entire appropriation for the university, apparently because the board of regents had refused to remove certain faculty members whom the governor found objectionable. This step alienated many politically powerful graduates. They immediately demanded action, and Ferguson was indicted by the Travis County grand jury for illegal use of public funds. Ultimately, he was impeached on twenty-one charges. In August 1917, following three weeks of hearings by the state senate, Ferguson was convicted on ten of the charges, removed from office, and barred from holding public office in Texas.

Ferguson was found guilty of accepting funds from secret sources, tampering with state officials, depositing state funds in the Temple State Bank (which he partly owned), and using public funds for personal gain. His successor was Lieutenant Governor W. P. Hobby, Sr. The same legislature, in another called session, ratified the Eighteenth Amendment to the U.S. Constitution, establishing national Prohibition. The prohibitionists had won.

World War I, the Twenties, and the Return of Farmer Jim: 1919–1928

As did the rest of the nation, Texas saw boom years during World War I. Its favorable climate and the Zimmerman Note (in which Germany allegedly urged Mexico to invade Texas) prompted the national government to station additional troops in the state. Texas became an important training area for the military, and many of the training camps later became permanent bases.

Progressive political programs, however, suffered during the war. Several of Governor Hobby's proposals—including women's suffrage, using the state's credit to help individuals purchase homes, and a new constitution—were defeated either by the legislature or by the voters.

In 1921, Pat M. Neff became governor of Texas. His proposals to reorganize the executive branch to eliminate duplication and waste and to rewrite the Texas Constitution both failed, while Prohibition, women's suffrage, crime, education, and the **Ku Klux Klan (KKK)** emerged as issues that demanded attention from the politicians and voters.

Cultural Issues: Prohibition and Women's Suffrage. Bootleggers—traffickers in illegal alcohol—often circumvented Prohibition. Governor Neff, an avid prohibitionist, used the Texas Rangers to find and destroy private stills used to produce illegal spirits. The Rangers were too few in number to be effective, though, and the legislature refused to give Neff the police powers necessary to enforce Prohibition effectively.

The women's suffrage movement gained momentum in Texas during the early years of the twentieth century, and by 1918 many suffrage organizations existed in the state. Groups opposing suffrage were also formed out of concern that the responsibilities of citizenship would be too hard on the "weaker sex." Nevertheless, Texas was one of the first states to ratify the Nineteenth Amendment to the U.S. Constitution, which gave women the right to vote. Other progressive measures during this period included free textbooks for public schools, the establishment of several colleges, and the beginning of the state park system.

Cultural Issues: The Klan. First organized in the late 1860s to intimidate freed African American slaves, the Ku Klux Klan was reborn in the 1920s with a somewhat modified mission. The new Klan saw itself as a patriotic, Christian, fraternal organization for native-born white Protestants. Its members perceived both a general moral decline in society, perpetrated by "modern" young people, and a basic

James "Farmer Jim" Ferguson, former governor of Texas and husband of then governor Miriam "Ma" Ferguson, leaves the White House in Washington, D.C., after visiting president Franklin D. Roosevelt in 1933. (Corbis. All rights reserved.)

Item Veto
The power to veto particular sections or items of an appropriations bill while signing the remainder of the bill into law. The governors of most states have this power.

Ku Klux Klan (KKK)
Any of several white supremacist organizations. The first klans were founded during the Reconstruction era following the Civil War.

threat to the Protestant white Christian "race" and its values by African Americans, Jews, Catholics, Mexican Americans, German Americans, and other "foreigners."

Acting on its paranoia, the 1920s Klan set out to force society to comply with its version of fundamentalist Christian morality. It used intimidation, violence, and torture—tarring and feathering, branding, beating, threats of castration—as means of coercion. As many as eighty thousand Texans may have joined the "invisible empire" in an effort to make the world more to their liking. Many elected officials—U.S. and state legislators as well as county and city officials—were either avowed Klansmen or friendly neutrals. In fact, the Klan influenced Texas society to such an extent that its power was a major political issue from 1921 through 1925.

The Return of the Fergusons. The strongest anti-Klan candidate in the gubernatorial election of 1924 was Miriam A. "Ma" Ferguson, wife of the impeached (and convicted) Farmer Jim. Running successfully on a platform of "Two Governors for the Price of One," she became the first female governor of Texas. Ma's election indicated that Texas voters had forgiven Farmer Jim. Her success in getting legislation passed that prohibited wearing a mask in public led to the end of the Klan as an effective political force in Texas. Ma was criticized, however, for her lenient pardoning policy (occasionally a convicted felon was pardoned before reaching prison) and a highway scandal. In the 1926 election, she was defeated by Attorney General Dan Moody, also a reformer and an anti-Klan candidate.

In 1928, national politics exerted more influence than usual on Texas politics when Al Smith became the Democratic nominee for president. Smith was a Roman Catholic, a "wet," and a big-city politician; Herbert Hoover, the Republican nominee, was a Protestant, a "dry," and an international humanitarian. Hoover won the electoral votes from Texas—the first Republican ever to do so.

The Great Depression: 1929–1939

When the stock market crashed in 1929, Texas, along with the entire nation, was crushed under the blow. Almost overnight, prices dropped, farm products could not be sold, mortgages and taxes could not be paid, and many jobs ceased to exist. Numerous businesses and bank accounts were wiped out.

The Independent Oil Crisis. The discovery of the East Texas oil field near Kilgore in 1930 helped to alleviate the situation until overproduction of oil forced the price to drop to as low as ten cents a barrel (about a dollar in today's currency). Unlike earlier discoveries, the East Texas field was developed and controlled largely by "independents"—oil producers not associated with the major oil companies. The "majors" owned the oil refineries, however, and because of the oil surplus, they often refused to purchase oil from independents for refining. Independents requested assistance from Governor Ross Sterling, but instead he ordered the East Texas field closed because of its threat to the entire oil industry. Outraged independents claimed that he had overreacted and refused to stop production.

Sterling declared martial law and sent in the National Guard. Eventually, the Railroad Commission (RRC) was given the power to control production of oil in Texas (first by executive order, later by law). To give the RRC some authority, the Texas Rangers were pressed into service in 1933 in an attempt to enforce the RRC guidelines. Despite the work of the Rangers, some East Texas independents still circumvented RRC orders by building their own refineries for processing illegal ("hot") oil and selling gasoline through independent retail outlets. A legislative act in 1934 that required refineries to divulge their sources of crude oil eventually ended the expansion of independent operators and refiners. The whole enforcement question soon became unimportant, however, because by 1938 the major oil companies had gained control of 80 percent of the production in the East Texas fields.

After her second term in office ended, Ma Ferguson temporarily retired from politics. She and Farmer Jim jumped back into the fray in 1940, when she joined a field of Democrats in an unsuccessful challenge to the popular incumbent W. Lee "Pappy" O'Daniel. After Farmer Jim's death in 1944, Ma retired for good. Why might Texans have been willing to elect a governor who, to all appearances, would act as her husband's puppet? (Texas State Library and Archives)

"Ma" Ferguson Again.   In 1932, Ma Ferguson, using economy in government as her campaign issue, was reelected governor. In an effort to promote efficiency, she hired a private consulting firm to recommend management changes in Texas government. This firm suggested reforms that included the following:

1. Reorganization of the numerous bureaus and commissions into twenty departments for an estimated savings of $1.5 million per year (about $18 million in today's dollars).
2. Reorganization of the college and university systems for a savings of $2 million per year (about $25 million in today's dollars).

These reforms were never implemented, and similar changes continue to be suggested by reformers in the twenty-first century.

In 1933, the ratification of the Twenty-first Amendment to the U.S. Constitution brought an end to nationwide Prohibition. Prohibition ended in Texas two years later with the adoption of local option elections, although selling liquor by the drink was still forbidden statewide. A board was established to administer taxing and licensing of liquor dealers.

"Pass the Biscuits, Pappy": 1938–1945

W. Lee O'Daniel, certainly one of the most colorful and unusual characters in Texas politics, entered the Democratic gubernatorial primary in 1938. "Pappy" O'Daniel was a highly successful flour salesman and the host of a radio hillbilly music show that was liberally sprinkled with homespun poetry and moral advice. O'Daniel's show had more daily listeners than any show in the history of Texas radio. The leader of O'Daniel's band, the Light Crust Doughboys, was Bob Wills.

In his gubernatorial campaign, O'Daniel used the slogan, "Pass the biscuits, Pappy!" Touring Texas in a bus with the Light Crust Doughboys, O'Daniel ran on a platform of the Ten Commandments, the Golden Rule, and increased old-age pensions.

He had never run for public office, had never voted in Texas, had never paid a poll tax (saying that no politician was worth $1.75), and admitted that he knew nothing about politics. With no campaign manager and no campaign headquarters,

Pappy O'Daniel is shown with the Hillbilly Boys—Pappy is on the right. For all his political and personal failings, O'Daniel was undeniably an important figure in the development of Western Swing. Why might actors have had more success in politics than musicians? (Texas State Library and Archives)

and without a runoff, he defeated thirteen candidates in the Democratic primary—some of whom were well-known, prominent political figures.

"Pappy" as Governor. Governor O'Daniel was not successful as a legislative leader, but he was reelected easily in 1940 against strong opposition in the Democratic primary. Again, he was notably unsuccessful in getting his proposals passed by the legislature. When the senior U.S. senator from Texas died, O'Daniel was urged to appoint himself to the post until a special election could be held. Instead, he appointed Andrew Jackson Houston, the last surviving son of Sam Houston. Houston, at age eighty-seven, became the oldest man ever to enter the U.S. Senate. Indeed, there was some question as to whether he could survive the trip to Washington! He did, but he died eighteen days later.

"Pappy" as Senator.   Pappy then entered the special election for the Senate seat and won, defeating twenty-nine other candidates. (His closest competitor was a young congressman from Central Texas, Lyndon B. Johnson.) Lieutenant Governor Coke R. Stevenson succeeded Pappy as governor. O'Daniel served with a notable lack of distinction in the Senate but was reelected to a full six-year term in 1942. His ineffectiveness in Washington was possibly related to his habit of making derogatory remarks about other politicians, such as "Washington is the only lunatic asylum in the world run by its own inmates."

Politics and Government since World War II

Beauford Jester easily won the gubernatorial election of 1946 after an especially bitter primary victory over Homer P. Rainey, the former president of the University of Texas. A major campaign issue was university autonomy and academic freedom.

The 1948 senatorial campaign (for the seat of the retiring Pappy O'Daniel) is worth special note. Several qualified people announced their candidacies for the position. The runoff in the Democratic primary pitted former governor Coke R. Stevenson against thirty-nine-year-old U.S. Congressman Lyndon B. Johnson.

The campaign was especially controversial, and the election was the closest in the state's history, with both candidates charging election fraud. At first, the election bureau gave the unofficial count as 494,330 votes for Stevenson and 493,968 for Johnson; then the revised returns for counties began to be reported, most of which favored Johnson. The final official election results were 494,191 for Johnson and 494,104 for Stevenson—a difference of 87 votes.

"Box 13" in Jim Wells County, one of several "machine" counties dominated by political boss George Parr (the "Duke of Duval"), was particularly important in these new figures. This box revised Johnson's vote upward by 202 votes and Stevenson's upward by only one. Box 13 was also late in reporting. In the end, after various bitter political and judicial battles, Johnson was certified the victor.

The 1950s

Lieutenant Governor Allan Shivers became governor in 1949 following the death of Governor Jester. He was easily elected governor in 1950, setting the stage for the 1952 Texas political extravaganza in which a president, the governor, and a U.S. senator would be elected.

Both state and national political issues captured the interest of the 1952 Texas voters. Harry Truman, a Democrat, had succeeded to the presidency in 1945 following the death of Franklin Roosevelt. Several scandals marred the Truman administration, and many conservative Texas Democrats were disillusioned with the New Deal and Fair Deal policies of the Roosevelt-Truman era.

The Tidelands Controversy. Another major issue was the **tidelands** question. Following the discovery of oil in the Gulf of Mexico, a jurisdictional conflict arose between the government of the United States and the governments of the coastal states.

Texas claimed three leagues (a Spanish unit of measure equal to about ten miles) as its jurisdictional boundary; the U.S. government said that Texas had rights to only three miles. At stake were hundreds of millions of dollars in royalty revenue.

Governor Shivers and Attorney General Price Daniel, who was campaigning for the U.S. Senate, both attacked the national Democratic administration as being corrupt and soft on communism, eroding the rights of states, and being outright thieves in attempting to steal the tidelands oil from the schoolchildren of Texas. State control would direct much of the oil income to the Permanent School Fund used for public education. State control would also mean a lower school tax burden for Texans. The Democratic presidential nomination of Adlai Stevenson of Illinois, who disagreed with the Texas position on the tidelands, only intensified this opposition.

Loyalists and Shivercrats. The Republicans nominated Dwight Eisenhower, a World War II hero who was sympathetic to the Texas position on the tidelands issue. Eisenhower was born in Texas (but reared in Kansas), and his supporters used the campaign slogan "Texans for a Texan." The presidential campaign crystallized a split in the Texas Democratic Party that lasted for the next forty years. The conservative "Texas Democrats" faction of the party, led by Shivers and Daniel, advocated "splitting the ticket"—voting for Eisenhower for president and for Texas Democrats for state offices. The liberal faction, or "Loyalist Democrats of Texas," led by Judge Ralph "Raff" Yarborough, campaigned for a straight Democratic ticket.

Texas voted for Eisenhower, and the tidelands dispute was eventually settled in favor of Texas. Shivers was reelected governor, and Daniel succeeded in entering the U.S. Senate. Shivers, Daniel, and the Democratic candidates for several other statewide offices (including lieutenant governor and attorney general) were actually endorsed by the Republican Party. These candidates won in the general election as Democrats, however. For some time afterward, those who voted for conservative Democrats at the state level and for Republicans at the national level were known as **Shivercrats.**

Governor Shivers also sought and won an unprecedented third term in 1954; however, veterans' land and insurance scandals soon surfaced that marred his administration. Scandals and corruption continued well into the administration of Shivers's successor, Price Daniel, Sr. Lobbyists' use of the "three Bs" of lobbying ("booze, beefsteak, and broads"), campaign contributions, and all-expense-paid vacations for influential administrators and legislators continued to buy weak laws and lax regulation. In 1959, public outrage forced the legislature to adopt (minimal) controls on lobbyists. During the Daniel administration, Texas's first broadly based tax, the general sales tax, was enacted.

The 1960s

When Lyndon B. Johnson, majority leader of the U.S. Senate and one of the most powerful men in Washington, lost his bid for the Democratic presidential nomination to John F. Kennedy in 1960, he accepted the nomination for vice president. By the grace of the Texas legislature, Johnson was on the ballot of the general election as both vice-presidential and senatorial nominee. When the

| **Tidelands**
An area that extends three leagues (about ten miles) off the Texas coast. The tidelands controversy developed when offshore oil was discovered and the federal government contended that Texas's jurisdiction extended only three miles out from the coast.

| **Shivercrat**
A follower of Governor Allan Shivers of Texas (1949–1957). Shivercrats split their votes between conservative Democrats for state office and Republicans for the U.S. presidency.

Governor Shivers was known for being all business. This photo shows him making a rare exception. To what extent might Shivers's hostility to the national Democratic Party have been the result of its refusal to give Texas the royalties from oil in the tidelands? (Texas State Library and Archives)

| DID YOU KNOW . . .

That historian T. R. Fehrenbach, writing about Lyndon Johnson's 87-vote victory over Coke Stevenson for the U.S. Senate in 1948, said, "There was probably no injustice involved. Johnson men had not 'defrauded' Stevenson, but successfully 'outfrauded' him"?

Democratic ticket was successful, he was elected to both positions, and a special election was necessary to fill the Senate seat he chose to vacate. (The same law allowed Senator Lloyd Bentsen to run for both vice president and senator in 1988. He lost the vice-presidential election but was reelected senator.) In the special election, Republican John Tower was elected to fill Johnson's vacated seat in the Senate—the first Republican since Reconstruction to serve as a U.S. senator from Texas.

Following the assassination of President Kennedy in 1963, Lyndon B. Johnson became president and was then easily elected for a full term in 1964. He chose not to run again in 1968, however, largely because of urban race riots, anti–Vietnam War sentiment, and poor health.

In 1962, John B. Connally, the secretary of the navy in the John F. Kennedy administration, returned to Texas and was elected governor. Connally became a dominant force in Texas politics and was easily reelected to second and third terms. He did not seek reelection for a fourth term and, in 1969, was succeeded by Lieutenant Governor Preston Smith.

The 1970s

The Sharpstown scandal erupted in 1971. It began when attorneys for the U.S. Securities and Exchange Commission (SEC) filed a suit alleging stock fraud against a series of elected Texas officials. The SEC also filed suit against Frank Sharp, owner of the Sharpstown State Bank. Buried in the SEC's supporting material was the allegation that several prominent politicians, including Governor Smith and house speaker Gus Mutscher, had accepted bribes to support legislation favorable to Sharp. Although Governor Smith was not found guilty of any wrongdoing, Mutscher, along with others, was convicted of conspiracy to accept a bribe.[3]

In the wake of the scandal, a large number of "reform" advocates were elected in 1972. Dolph Briscoe, a wealthy Uvalde rancher and banker, won the governorship by a plurality of less than 100,000 votes over his Republican and Raza Unida[4] opponents—the first general election since the institution of the party primary in 1906 in which the Democratic gubernatorial candidate did not receive a majority of the votes. Briscoe was easily reelected in 1974.

In 1974, state legislators served as delegates to a constitutional convention but failed to propose a new constitution to the voters, primarily due to conflict over a proposed *right-to-work* provision. (Under right-to-work laws passed in many states, union membership cannot be a requirement for employment.) The legislature in the next regular session proposed an extensive revision of the Texas Constitution in the form of amendments, but voters rejected them by a margin of almost three to one.

In 1979 William P. Clements became the first Republican governor of Texas since E. J. Davis vacated the office in 1874. The election of a Republican governor did not affect legislative-executive relations, however, since Clements received strong political support from conservative Democrats.

[3]For further discussion of the Sharpstown scandal, see Charles Deaton, *The Year They Threw the Rascals Out* (Austin: Shoal Creek Publishers, 1973); and Sam Kinch, Jr., and Ben Procter, *Texas under a Cloud: Story of the Texas Stock Fraud Scandal* (Austin and New York: Jenkins Publishing Co., 1972).

[4]*La Raza Unida* literally means "A United People." Officially named El Partido Nacional La Raza Unida, this party was organized in the late 1960s as a means of getting Mexican Americans to unite politically and to identify ethnically as one people. Its name is derived from *La Raza Cosmica* ("The Cosmic Race"), written by Mexican intellectual Jose Vasconcelos after the 1910 Mexican Revolution. Vasconcelos argued that the racially mixed Mestizos (whose racial heritage is both European and Native American) constituted a new race, and he urged them to unite regardless of national boundaries. For more information, see <u>larazaunida.tripod.com</u>.

Former Texas governor Price Daniel (left) greets former Texas governor John Connally (right) while George H. W. Bush and his wife, Barbara, look on (center). The occasion is the inauguration of Republican Bill Clements as Texas governor in 1979. Bush, a Republican, was elected president of the United States in 1988. (Texas State Library and Archives)

The 1980s

In 1982, a Democrat, Attorney General Mark White, displaced incumbent governor Bill Clements despite Clements's unprecedented campaign spending. Teachers overwhelmingly supported White, who promised them salary increases and expressed support for education. Clements opposed the salary increases and was perceived as unsympathetic to education.

In 1984, House Bill 72, the first comprehensive educational reform since 1949, became law. The reform increased teachers' salaries, equalized school district income, and—controversially—raised standards for students and teachers. Public school teachers were required to pass a competency test to continue to teach ("no pass, no teach"), and students who failed a course were barred from extracurricular activities for six weeks ("no pass, no play").

In 1986, voter unhappiness with education reform, a sour economy, and decreased state revenue was enough to return Republican Bill Clements to the governor's office in a sweeping victory over Democrat Mark White. In 1988, three Republicans were elected to the Texas Supreme Court and one to the Railroad Commission—the first Republicans elected to statewide office (other than governor or U.S. senator) since Reconstruction.

In 1989, the Texas Supreme Court unanimously upheld an Austin district court's ruling in *Edgewood v. Kirby*[5] that the state's educational funding system violated the Texas constitutional requirement of "an efficient system" for the "general diffusion of knowledge." After several reform laws were also declared unconstitutional, the legislature in 1993 enacted a complex law that left the property tax as the basic vehicle for school funding but required wealthier school districts to share their wealth with poorer districts.

---

[5]777 S.W.2d 391 (Tex. 1989).

| **Down-Ticket**
An elective position located "down-ticket" on the ballot.

The 1990s

In 1990, the State Board of Education adopted the first elementary and high school biology texts since the 1960s that contained a thorough explanation of Darwin's theory of evolution. In 1994, however, the board removed pictures of male and female reproductive systems and discussions of changes that occur at puberty from high school health books.

With the 1990 election of Dan Morales (attorney general), Kay Bailey Hutchison (treasurer), and Rick Perry (agriculture commissioner), Texas elected the first Hispanic ever, and the first Republicans since Reconstruction, to **down-ticket** executive offices. (You will learn more about such offices in Chapter 24.) Austin voters elected the first avowed homosexual to the Texas legislature in 1991.

Texans also elected Ann Richards as their first female governor since Miriam "Ma" Ferguson. Through her appointive powers, she opened the doors of state government to unprecedented numbers of women, Hispanics, and African Americans. In 1992, Texas elected Kay Bailey Hutchison as its first female U.S. senator. She joined fellow Republican Phil Gramm, and they became the first two Republicans to hold U.S. Senate seats concurrently since 1874.

Two-Party Politics.   When the smoke, mud, and sound bites of the 1994 general election settled, a new political age had dawned—Texas had truly become a two-party state. Republican candidates won victories from the top to the bottom of the ballot. For the first time since Reconstruction, with the election of George W. Bush, Republicans held the governor's office and both U.S. Senate seats.

Although both Democratic and Republican incumbents were reelected to down-ticket administrative positions, Republicans held all the Railroad Commission seats and a majority on the State Board of Education and the Texas Supreme Court.

In 1996, Republicans won a majority in the Texas Senate for the first time since Reconstruction. The 1997 legislature failed to enact campaign finance reform, non-

The late Ann Richards was inaugurated governor in 1991. The first woman to be elected Texas governor on her own merits, Richards appointed more women, blacks, and Hispanics to office than any previous governor. Why are Texans (and other Americans) more willing to elect women to high office today than in years past? (Texas State Library and Archives)

partisan election of judges, and Governor Bush's tax initiative to reduce public schools' reliance on local property taxes. The state's first comprehensive water management plan was enacted, however, along with voluntary surgical castration for child molesters, prohibition of tobacco possession by minors, and authorization for patients to sue health-maintenance organizations (HMOs) for malpractice. Voters also ratified an amendment to the Texas Constitution that allows them to use their *home equity* (the current market value of a home minus the outstanding mortgage debt) as collateral for a loan.

Republican Dominance. The 1998 general election was a sweep year for Republicans, who won every statewide (nonlegislative) elective office. This overwhelming achievement also positioned Governor George W. Bush as the frontrunner for the Republican nomination for president in 2000. In the Seventy-sixth Texas Legislature (1999), however, Democrats narrowly retained control of the state house of representatives, and Republican control of the state senate was diminished to a one-vote margin. Legislators deregulated electric companies in Texas and required parents' permission for underage girls to obtain an abortion or have their bodies pierced (except for ears). Physicians were also given the right to collectively bargain with HMOs. The legal blood-alcohol level for driving drunk was reduced to 0.08 percent, cities and counties were prohibited from suing gun manufacturers, and the state's city annexation law was made more restrictive.

Public school teachers received a pay raise, but not enough to bring them up to the national average. A modest property tax reduction was enacted (which would come back to haunt the legislature in subsequent years as the demand for state services grew). A plan for taxpayer-funded vouchers to be used by families to pay for their children's private school education failed. A state program was initiated to provide basic health insurance to approximately 30 percent of the state's children who lacked health-insurance coverage.

The 2000s

The 2001 legislature, after considerable conflict, enacted a "hate crimes" bill that strengthened penalties for crimes motivated by a victim's race, religion, color, gender, disability, sexual preference, age, or national origin. The legislature also criminalized carrying open alcohol containers in most motor vehicles, established partial funding for health insurance for public school employees, and made it easier for poor children to apply for health-care coverage under Medicaid. With little conflict, the legislature agreed to reimburse school districts that grant **tax abatements** to corporations. A Republican proposal to redraw U.S. congressional districts and the effects of the 1999 tax cuts, though, hung menacingly over the 2001 legislature. As a result, work on solutions for many significant state problems was postponed until the 2003 legislature. Without higher taxes, increased funding of public schools, higher education, and transportation infrastructure remained in limbo.

Tax Abatement
A reduction of or exemption from taxes (usually real estate taxes); typically granted by a local government in exchange for broader economic benefits such as employment for local residents.

The Republicans Consolidate Their Power. The Republicans swept Texas statewide offices and both chambers of the legislature in the 2002 elections. A Republican governor, lieutenant governor, and speaker of the house ensured Republican proposals a sympathetic hearing in the 2003 legislative session. A nonpartisan policy, however, remained in effect in the legislature—the lieutenant governor and speaker appointed some Democrats to committee chair and vice-chair positions. Can the new Republican dominance be viewed in terms of the political culture of Texans? We look at the issue of political culture in this chapter's *Politics and Culture* feature on the following page.

POLITICS AND CULTURE | Tradition and Individualism in Texas

Political culture describes the set of political values and beliefs that are dominant in a society. This concept has been useful in the study of American politics, in which federalism has emphasized the diversity among regions, states, and communities—a diversity that cries out for some approach that can effectively explain it. One way to analyze the political culture of Texans and other Americans is to view our political culture as a mix of three subcultures, each prevalent in at least one area of the United States.

• The *moralistic* culture is a product of the Puritan era and, as might be expected, is strongest in New England. As the label suggests, adherents of this tradition are greatly concerned with "right and wrong" in politics; however, the tradition now is associated with secular (nonreligious) attitudes to a striking degree. This is true despite the origin of the tradition in Puritan religious values.
• *Traditional* culture is widespread but comes to us most strongly through the plantation society of the Deep South. This culture is most frequently associated with religious practice today.
• The *individualistic* culture was popular in the commercial centers of the Middle Atlantic states, moving west and south along the Ohio River and its tributaries.*

The mix, as well as the isolation, of these cultures gives American politics its flavor.

POLITICAL CULTURE AND POLITICAL PARTICIPATION

A key point is that the degree of political participation may be determined by political culture.† The moralistic culture sees the discussion of public issues and voting as not only a right but also an opportunity beneficial to the individual and society

*Daniel J. Elazar, *American Federalism: A View from the States,* 3d ed. (New York: Harper & Row, 1984).
†David C. Saffel, *State Politics* (Reading, Mass.: Addison-Wesley Publishing Co., 1984), p. 8.

alike. In contrast, the traditionalistic culture views politics as the special preserve of the social and economic elite—as a process of maintaining the existing order. Believing in personal rather than public solutions to problems, it views political participation as a privilege and accepts social pressure as well as restrictive election laws that limit participation. The individualistic culture blurs the distinction between economic and political life. Here, business and politics are both viewed as appropriate avenues by which an individual can advance her or his interests, and conflicts of interest are fairly commonplace. In this culture, business interests can play a very strong role, and running for office is difficult without their support.

POLITICAL CULTURE IN TEXAS

Voter turnout in Texas is well below the national average (though the figures are not quite so bad if we correct for the large number of noncitizens, prisoners, and ex-felons in the Texas population). Low levels of political participation in Texas may be partly due to the state's political culture, which is a mix of traditionalism and individualism. The traditionalistic aspect is especially characteristic of East Texas, settled primarily by immigrants from the Deep South in the years before the Civil War. The individualistic aspect predominates throughout the rest of the state. As a result, participation in politics is not as highly regarded as it is in some other states, particularly those with a moralistic culture, and politics in Texas is largely the domain of business interests. People *may* be less likely to vote in Texas because they do not value political participation for its own sake and because they tend to think that they have little role to play in politics.

FOR CRITICAL ANALYSIS

To what degree might some Americans who hold traditional values participate in religious activities because religion is traditional, instead of endorsing traditional values because their religion supports these values?

A projected $10 billion budget deficit created an uncomfortable environment for the Republicans. Politically and ideologically opposed to both new taxes and state-provided social services, the legislature and the governor chose to reduce funding for most state programs but especially for education, health care, and social services for the needy.

Attempts to close some tax loopholes failed. For example, businesses and professions of all sizes may continue to organize as "partnerships" to avoid the state corporate franchise tax. The legislature did place limits on pain-and-suffering jury awards for injuries caused by physician malpractice and hospital incompetence and made it more difficult to sue the makers of unsafe, defective products.

The legislature's social agenda was ambitious. It outlawed civil unions for same-sex couples and barred recognition of such unions even when they are registered by other states (Vermont, for example, registers same-sex unions). In addition, a twenty-four-hour wait to be "educated" about the fetus is now required before a woman can have an abortion.

The Redistricting Controversy.   Although the districts for electing U.S. representatives in Texas had been redrawn by a panel of one Democrat and two Republican federal judges following the 2000 census, then U.S. House Majority Leader Tom DeLay was unhappy that more Texas Republicans were not elected to Congress. Governor Rick Perry agreed to call a special session in order to re-redraw the redrawn districts to favor Republican congressional candidates. Minority party Democrats argued that the districts had already been drawn to accommodate the decade's population shifts and that the Republicans were only trying to gerrymander Texas voters. (See Chapter 11 for a further discussion of the gerrymander.)

During Special Session One (June 30, 2003), most house Democrats left the state for Oklahoma to deny the state house of representatives the required two-thirds quorum necessary to conduct its business.

Special Session Two (July 28, 2003), saw Republican Lieutenant Governor David Dewhurst change the senate rule that had required a two-thirds majority vote for bills to be heard on the senate floor, thereby denying the minority senate Democrats a procedural tool to block congressional redistricting. In response, most senate Democrats left the state for New Mexico so that the Texas Senate would not have the required quorum. For Special Session Three (September 15, 2003), senate Democrats were unable to muster enough members to block the quorum, and the new district lines were drawn. The redistricting generated numerous lawsuits challenging its legality. The United States Supreme Court combined four of the cases and in March 2006 considered four legal questions.

1. Can the legislature, on its own initiative, undertake mid-decade redistricting?
2. Did the redistricting of the 23rd and 24th Districts diminish the rights of minority voters under the Voting Rights Act?
3. Is the state obligated to create additional Hispanic districts in South and West Texas?
4. Is the Republican redistricting plan a legitimate use of the political process to correct past redistricting injustices or is it an unconstitutional "partisan gerrymander"?[6]

The School Funding Issue.   The 78th Legislature (2003) voted to revamp sources of funding for public education by ending the revenue-sharing policy whereby property-rich school districts were required to share their tax revenues with poorer school districts, a policy reviled by residents in the wealthier districts. Exactly how public schools were to be funded was left to another day.

Special Session Four was called on April 20, 2004, to attempt to reform school funding. Legislative proposals usually included increasing the "sin" tax on cigarettes and legalizing and taxing gambling. The session ended without resolution.

The issues concerning Texas education funding were then thrown into the lap of the Texas Supreme Court. In November 2005, the court ruled that Texas's decrease in the state's portion of education funding while also placing a statutory limit on school property tax rates had in effect created a statewide property tax and therefore violated the Texas Constitution. This ruling required the legislature to either remove the tax limit or to seek sources of revenue other than the property tax as a means of raising funds for public schools.

---

[6] Allen Pusey, *Dallas Morning News*, March 1, 2006.

Although Texas ranks thirty-second among the states in public school funding, the court declared the current funding level adequate and not in violation of the constitutional mandate of an "efficient" school system. The court further ruled that the disparity in funding between rich and poor school districts did not violate the constitution, but that it may soon become large enough to do so.[7]

Under this judicial ultimatum, the legislature in special session may have changed the school tax code enough to pass judicial muster without alienating the state's more powerful economic interests. School property taxes are to be decreased from a maximum of $1.50 to $1.00 per $100 valuation over a period of two years. To fund this decrease, the corporate franchise tax was increased, and thousands of previously untaxed businesses were included. Separate bills increased the tax on cigarettes by one dollar per pack and designated part of the state "rainy day" surplus to pay for tax reform.

The legislature also gave Texas teachers a $2,000 per-year pay raise, maintained the principle of school equity, required four years of high school math and science, and prohibited the start of the school year before the fourth Monday in August.

Texas Cultural Regions

No single culture has emerged from the various ethnic and cultural groups that settled Texas. The "typical Texan," like the "average American," is an oversimplification used to broadly generalize the distinctive social, religious, economic, and political characteristics of Texans.[8] Actually, the cultural diversity of Texas is more apparent than its homogeneity. One approach to studying this diversity is to examine the cultural regions that developed from various geographic characteristics and migration patterns. Modern Texas has evolved into nine fairly distinct cultural regions, as shown in Figure 18–1. While political boundaries are clear-cut, the effect of the mass media and the mobility of modern Texans often blur cultural boundaries. These regions, however, continue to serve as a useful guide to contemporary Texas culture, attitudes, and beliefs.

East Texas

East Texas is a social and cultural extension of the old South. It is basically rural and biracial. In spite of the changes brought about by civil rights legislation, black "towns" still exist alongside white "towns," and there are many segregated social and economic institutions, such as churches, fraternal lodges, and chambers of commerce.

East Texas counties and towns are often dominated by old families, whose wealth is usually based on real estate, banking, construction, and retail merchandising. Cotton—once "king" of agriculture in the region—has been replaced by beef cattle, poultry, and timber. Owing to a general lack of economic opportunity, young East Texans migrate to metropolitan areas, primarily Dallas–Fort Worth and Houston. The region is dominated spiritually by fundamentalist Protestantism, which permeates its political, social, and cultural activities.

The Gulf Coast

Before 1900, Texas was an economic colony; it sold raw materials to the industrialized North and bought northern manufactured products. In 1901, however, an oil well named **Spindletop** was drilled near Beaumont, and the Texas economy began

| Spindletop
A major oil discovery in 1901 near Beaumont that began the industrialization of Texas.

---

[7]*Neely v. West Orange-Cove Consolidated Independent School District,* 176 S.W.3d 746 (2005).

[8]Information for this section is adapted from D. W. Meinig, *Imperial Texas: An Interpretive Essay in Cultural Geography* (Austin and London: University of Texas Press, 1969).

to change. Since Spindletop, the Gulf Coast has experienced almost continuous growth, especially during World War II, the Cold War defense buildup, and the energy crises of the 1970s and 1980s.

In addition to being an industrial and petrochemical center, the Gulf Coast is one of the most important shipping centers in the nation. Spindletop was backed by out-of-state investors, largely from the northeastern states, and its success stimulated increased out-of-state investment. Local wealth was also generated and largely reinvested in Texas to promote long-range development. Nevertheless, much of the economy is still supported by the sale of raw materials.

A Boom Based in Houston.   With the energy crisis of the 1970s, the petrochemical industry, which is concentrated on the Gulf Coast, experienced unprecedented growth, and a boomtown psychology developed. Rapid growth fed real estate development and speculation for the entire region. The Houston area especially flourished, and despite a downturn in the oil industry, Harris County (Houston) remained the third most populous county in the United States.

In the 1970s and 1980s, there was extensive migration to Texas from the Frost Belt (Great Lake and Mid-Atlantic states), which at the time was undergoing an economic depression due to the metamorphosis of the U.S. economy from an industrial to a service base. This migration included large numbers of well-educated young executives and professionals, as well as skilled and unskilled laborers. The Gulf Coast economy continues to attract heavy immigration from the Americas and Asia.

The continuing influx of job seekers from East Texas and other rural areas of the state has tended to give the Gulf Coast the flavor of rural Texas in an urban setting.

> **DID YOU KNOW . . .**
> That Texas has the second largest population of any state in the country—an estimated 21,487,000 people in 2005?

FIGURE 18–1 | CULTURAL AREAS OF MODERN TEXAS

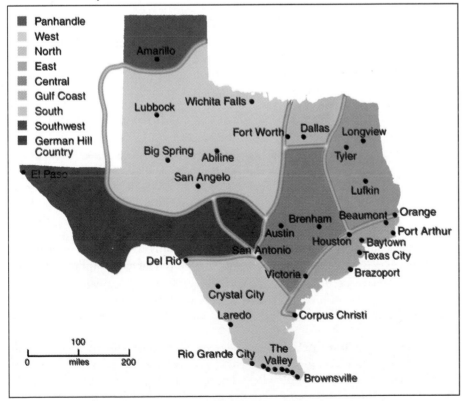

Source: Adapted from D. W. Meinig, *Imperial Texas: An Interpretive Essay in Cultural Geography* (Austin and London: University of Texas Press, 1969). Reproduced by permission of the publisher.
© 1969 D. W. Meinig. All rights reserved.

This rural flavor is diminishing, however, because much of the Coast's population is now second- or third-generation urban and somewhat removed from its rural roots.

The social and economic elite is generally made up of second- and third generation rich whose wealth comes from oil, insurance, construction, land development, or banking. The executives and professional support personnel of international corporations now headquartered in Houston contribute fresh blood to the elite pool.

There are still many large ranches and plantations in the Gulf Coast region. They are owned either by wealthy business executives who live in the large cities or by "old families."

Economic Trouble.   The collapse of the oil boom and drastic declines in the price of oil and other petroleum products in the 1980s and 1990s struck especially hard at the Gulf Coast economy, which relies heavily on the petrochemical industry. Conversely, rising prices in the 2000s may result in another oil-based boom for the region.

The implosion of Houston-based Enron Corporation in the early 2000s affected financial markets and political attitudes nationwide, but it was especially damaging to Houston's economy, labor force, and national image. Enron was intertwined into the fabric of Houston's political, social, cultural, and financial existence to an extent rarely seen in corporate America. A dynamic corporate citizen, Enron made significant contributions to almost every aspect of Houston life. Its collapse left many Houstonians with dramatically decreased retirement incomes and investments. Some top executives, however, sought to ensure a comfortable retirement for themselves as they drew tens of millions of dollars of personal wealth from the Enron corpse.

Enron founder, Kenneth Lay, suffered a heart attack and died in 2006 while awaiting sentencing for his convictions on several conspiracy and fraud charges. All indictments and convictions, as well as criminal proceedings to seize his assets, were dismissed because of his death. Former Enron CEO Jeffrey Skilling was sentenced to twenty-four years in prison for his role in the fraud and was ordered to pay $50 million in restitution to Enron's victims.

The Gulf Coast continues to be a remarkably vibrant and energetic region. Houston, the worldwide oil and gas capital, attracts many corporate relocations from other areas. In addition, as suggested earlier, the dramatic increase in petroleum prices in the late 1990s and early 2000s is a welcome boost to its economy.

South Texas

The earliest area settled by Europeans, South Texas developed a **ranchero culture** based on livestock production that was similar to the feudal institutions in faraway Spain. **Creoles,** who descended from Spanish immigrants, were the economic, social, and political elite, while the first Texas cowboys, the **Mestizos** and the Native Americans, did the ranch work. Anglo Americans first became culturally important in South Texas when they gained title to much of the real estate in the region following the Texas Revolution of 1836.

Modern South Texas still retains elements of the ranchero culture, including some of its feudal aspects. Large ranches, often owned by one family for several generations, are prevalent; however, wealthy and corporate ranchers from outside the area are becoming common.

South Texas Agriculture Today.   Because of the semitropical South Texas climate, **The Valley (of the Rio Grande)** and the **Winter Garden** around Crystal City became major producers of vegetable and citrus products. They were developed by migrants from the northern United States in the 1920s and continue to be important agricultural assets.

| **Ranchero Culture**
The traditions, beliefs, and practices of Creole ranch owners, who defined themselves in contrast to the part-Indian Mestizos.

| **Creole**
A descendant of European Spanish (or in some regions, French) immigrants to the Americas.

| **Mestizo**
A person of both Spanish and American Indian lineage.

| **The Valley (of the Rio Grande)**
An area along the Texas side of the Rio Grande known for its production of citrus fruits.

| **Winter Garden**
An area of South Texas known for its vegetable production.

The development of citrus and vegetable enterprises required intensive manual labor, which brought about increased immigration from Mexico. Modern South Texas Mexican Americans can usually trace their U.S. roots to the 1920s or later, because much of the Hispanic population was driven south of the Rio Grande after the Texas Revolution.

The Mexican Connection. The worldwide drop in oil prices, a high external debt, and the devaluation of the peso depressed the Mexican economy in the 1980s. Because the border cities of South Texas are closely tied to the Mexican economy, they also suffered economic hardship, high unemployment, and economic stagnation. Although Mexico and South Texas are both improving economically, the region remains one of the poorest in the United States.

South Texas also gains economically from *maquiladoras,* factories through which U.S. corporations pump needed revenues into Mexico's border regions by employing inexpensive Mexican labor for assembly and piecework. Unfortunately, lax environmental and safety standards result in high levels of air, ground, and water pollution in the general area. In fact, the Rio Grande is now one of America's most ecologically endangered rivers.

The **North American Free Trade Agreement (NAFTA),** which is still being implemented, has helped remove trade barriers among Canada, Mexico, and the United States, and may be an economic benefit to South Texas because the region is a conduit for much of the commerce from Mexico.

Immigration and National Security. Economic and political disorder and suppression of civil liberties in Mexico, together with poverty, military conflicts, and suppression of civil liberties in Central America, have driven hundreds of thousands of immigrants into the border states of the United States. This flow continues in spite of tightened security measures following September 11, 2001; South Texas remains a major staging ground for the migration of both legal and illegal immigrants into the interior of Texas and the rest of the United States. Some reduction in immigration from Mexico may have resulted from NAFTA, however, because more trade has created better economic opportunities at home for Mexican workers.

South Texas is a "mingling pot" for Mexican American and Anglo American cultures. Roman Catholic Mexican Americans often retain strong links with Mexico through extended family and friends in Mexico and through Spanish-language newspapers. Many Mexican Americans continue to speak Spanish; in fact, Spanish is also the commercial and social language of choice for many of the region's Anglos.

Military expenditures by the U.S. government are also important to the economy of the region. A decision by the U.S. Navy to station a contingent of naval vessels in Ingleside has been an economic boost to the upper South Texas coast.

Southwest Texas

Southwest Texas exhibits many of the same bicultural characteristics as South Texas. Its large Mexican American population often maintains strong ties with relatives and friends in Mexico. The Roman Catholic Church strongly influences social and cultural attitudes.

Southwest Texas is a major commercial and social passageway between Mexico and the United States. El Paso, the "capital city" of Southwest Texas and the fifth largest city in Texas, is a military, manufacturing, and commercial center. El Paso's primary commercial partners are Mexico and New Mexico. The economy of the border cities of Southwest Texas, like that of South Texas, has been affected by the downturn in the Mexican economy but has also benefited from the economic opportunities brought

---

| DID YOU KNOW . . .
That in 2006, among the states only Tennessee and Arkansas had a lower cost of living than Texas?

| *Maquiladora*
A factory in the Mexican border region that assembles goods imported duty-free into Mexico for export. In Spanish, it literally means "twin plant."

| North American Free Trade Agreement (NAFTA)
A treaty among Canada, Mexico, and the United States that calls for the gradual removal of tariffs and other trade restrictions. NAFTA came into effect in 1994.

| Bicultural
Encompassing two cultures.

about by NAFTA. The agricultural economy of much of the region depends on sheep, goat, and cattle production, although there is some irrigated row-crop agriculture. Most of the labor on ranches, as well as in manufacturing and commerce, is Mexican American.

South and Southwest Texas together make up the area known as the "Texas Border." A corresponding "Mexico Border" includes parts of the Mexican states of Chihuahua, Coahuila, Nuevo León, and Tamaulipas. It can be argued that the Texas Border and the Mexico Border are two parts of an economic, social, and cultural region with a substantial degree of communality that sets it off from the rest of the United States and Mexico. The region, which is expanding in size both to the north and to the south, has a **binational,** bicultural, and bilingual subculture in which **internationality** is commonplace and the people, economies, and societies on both sides constantly interact.[9] What will be the impact of Mexican American political participation on Texas? We look at differing attitudes among Latinos in this chapter's *Politics and Diversity* feature.

Binational
Belonging to two nations.

Internationality
Having family and/or business interests in two or more nations.

German Hill Country

The Hill Country was settled primarily by immigrants from Germany but also by immigrants who were Czech, Polish, and Norwegian. Although they mixed with Anglo Americans, they retained much of their culture, language, and architecture. Skilled artisans were common in the towns; farms were usually moderate in size, self-sufficient, and family owned and operated. Most settlers were Lutheran or Roman Catholic, and these remain the most common religions for modern residents.

The German Hill Country is still a distinct and homogeneous cultural region. Its inhabitants have become "Americanized" but cling to many of their cultural traditions. Primarily a farming and ranching area, the Hill Country is socially and politically conservative and has long been a stronghold of the Texas Republican Party.

Migration into the region, primarily by Anglo Americans and Mexican Americans, is increasing. The most significant encroachment into the Hill Country is residential growth from rapidly expanding urban areas, especially San Antonio and Austin. Resorts, country homes, and retirement villages for well-to do urbanites from the Gulf Coast and Dallas–Fort Worth area are also contributing to the cultural transformation of the German Hill Country.

West Texas

The defeat of the Comanches in the 1870s opened West Texas to Anglo American settlement. Migrating primarily from the southern United States, these settlers passed their social and political attitudes and southern Protestant fundamentalism on to their descendants.

There are few African Americans in modern West Texas, but Mexican Americans have begun to migrate into the region in significant numbers, primarily to the cities and the intensively farmed areas. West Texas is socially and politically conservative, and its religion is Bible Belt fundamentalism. West Texas voters traditionally supported conservative Democrats but today favor the Republican Party. Indeed, this is true of many conservative Texans throughout the state.

The southern portion of the area emphasizes sheep, goat, and cattle production. In fact, San Angelo advertises itself as the "Sheep and Wool Capital of the World."

---

[9]John Sharp, Texas Comptroller of Public Accounts, "Bordering the Future: Challenge and Opportunity in the Texas Border Region," July 1998, p. 3; Jorge Bustamante, "A Conceptual and Operative Vision of the Population Problems on the Border," in *Demographic Dynamics on the U.S.-Mexico Border,* ed. John R. Weeks and Roberto Ham Chande (El Paso: Texas Western Press, 1992), cited in Sharp, "Bordering the Future."

POLITICS AND DIVERSITY | Hispanics versus Mexican Americans in Texas

In 2002, Democrat Tony Sanchez unsuccessfully challenged Republican Rick Perry for the Texas governor's seat. Sanchez sought to "make history" by becoming the first Hispanic governor of Texas. To that end, Sanchez, a wealthy businessman, put up almost $60 million of his own money.

Nevertheless, Sanchez received only 39 percent of the votes. This was lower than the 44 percent received in 1996 by Victor Morales, a Mexican American schoolteacher who ran for the U.S. Senate against incumbent Republican Phil Gramm. Unlike Sanchez, Morales campaigned on a shoestring budget. Why, then, did Morales turn in a noticeably better performance than Sanchez?

THE PROBLEM WITH THE "HISPANIC" LABEL

One possible answer is that Rick Perry may have been a more popular, less polarizing figure than Phil Gramm. Another answer, however, is that Morales was more effective than Sanchez in mobilizing Mexican American voters. One problem with Sanchez's approach was the very fact that he billed himself as the "Hispanic" candidate and as a direct descendant of the original Spanish settlers of Laredo, Texas. A majority of Latinos are not particularly fond of the Hispanic label and prefer to identify with their actual country of origin. Cuban Americans, for example, usually prefer to be called exactly that.

THE MEANINGS BEHIND THE LABELS

Fernando Pinon, a professor at San Antonio College, argues that the two appellations—Hispanic and Mexican American— represent alternative frameworks by which Latinos in Texas view themselves in relation to the dominant Anglo population.

The term *Mexican American* brings to mind resistance to the majority that "stole their land and ha[s] since then denied them their culture, suppressed their rights, and turned them into second-class citizens." The word *Hispanic,* in contrast, brings to mind accommodation rather than confrontation. Hispanics have "made it" within the system. "Hispanic Texans represent a Latinized version of Anglo Texan suburbanites," writes Pinon, "and, as such, do not connect with the mostly blue-collar Mestizo Mexican American of the barrio."*

Given these considerations, it is easy to understand the greater success that Morales enjoyed in mobilizing the Latino vote. Morales presented himself as a cultural maverick fighting the establishment. He was able to tap into the historical grievances of the Mexican American population. Tony Sanchez, wealthy and successful, was unable to do the same.

FOR CRITICAL ANALYSIS

In years to come, we can expect that the existing Mexican American population of Texas will become better educated, earn more, and be more completely integrated into the majority culture. What effect will these developments have on Mexican American political attitudes? Could continued high rates of immigration from Mexico have an effect on the political attitudes of Mexican Americans who are already here? If so, how?

*Fernando Pinon, "The Political Culture of 'Hispanics' and 'Mexican Americans' in Texas," *Texas Politics Today,* 11th ed. (Belmont, Calif.: Thomson Wadsworth, 2004), p. 27.

Southern West Texas, which is below the Cap Rock Escarpment, is the major oil-producing area of Texas. The cities of Snyder, Midland, and Odessa owe their existence almost entirely to oil and related industries.

Northern West Texas is part of the Great Plains and High Plains and is primarily agricultural, with cotton, grain, and feedlot cattle production predominating. In this part of semiarid West Texas, the outstanding agricultural production is due to extensive irrigation from the **Ogallala Aquifer.** The large amount of water used for irrigation is resulting in a gradual depletion of the Ogallala. This not only means higher costs to farmers but also serves as a warning signal for the economic future of the region.

The Panhandle

Railroads advancing from Kansas City through the Panhandle brought midwestern farmers into this region. Wheat production was developed largely by these migrants from Kansas. Because the commercial and cultural focus of the region was, and still

| Ogallala Aquifer
A major underground source of water for irrigation and human consumption in northern West Texas and the Texas Panhandle, as well as other states.

| DID YOU KNOW . . .

That the median age of Texans is 32.7 years and that only one state (Utah) has a younger population?

| La Réunion
A failed French socialist colony of the 1800s located within the city limits of modern Dallas. Its skilled and educated inhabitants benefited early Dallas.

| Metroplex
The greater Dallas–Fort Worth metropolitan area.

is, Kansas City rather than the developed areas of Texas, the Panhandle is basically midwestern in both character and institutions. The social and political conservatism of the area is more midwestern Republican than southern Democrat, and its Protestant churches are midwestern in philosophy and practice.

Economically, the Panhandle is similar to northern West Texas, with extensive irrigation of cotton and grains from the Ogallala Aquifer. Feedlots for livestock and livestock production are major economic enterprises. Effective conservation of the Ogallala Aquifer is critical to the economic future of both northern West Texas and the Panhandle.

North Texas

Located between East and West Texas, North Texas exhibits many characteristics of both regions. Early North Texas benefited from the failure of the French socialist colony of **La Réunion,** which included many highly trained professionals in medicine, education, music, and science. (La Réunion was located on the south bank of the Trinity River, across from modern downtown Dallas.) The colonists and their descendants helped give North Texas a cultural and commercial distinctiveness. North Texas today is dominated by the Dallas–Fort Worth **Metroplex.** Dallas is a banking and commercial center of national importance, and Fort Worth is the financial and commercial center of West Texas.

When railroads came into Texas from the North in the 1880s, Dallas became a rail center, and people and capital from the North stimulated its growth. Fort Worth became a regional capital that looked primarily to West Texas. The Swift and Armour meatpacking companies, which moved plants to Fort Worth in 1901, became the first national firms to establish facilities close to Texas's natural resources. More businesses followed, and North Texas began its evolution from an economic colony to an industrially developed area.

North Texas experienced extraordinary population growth after World War II, with extensive migration from the rural areas of East, West, and Central Texas. The descendants of these migrants are now second- and third-generation urbanites and tend to display this in their attitudes and behavior. Recently, migration from other states, especially from the North, has been significant. Many international corporations have established headquarters in North Texas. Their executive and support staffs contribute to the region's diversity and cosmopolitan environment.

Although North Texas is more economically diverse than most other Texas regions, it relies heavily on the defense and aerospace industries. It also produces electronic equipment, computer products, plastics, and food products.

Central Texas

Central Texas is often called the "core area" of Texas. It is roughly triangular in shape, with its three corners being Houston, Dallas–Fort Worth, and San Antonio. The centerpiece of the region is Austin, one of the fastest-growing metropolitan areas in the nation. Already a center of government and education, the Austin metropolitan area has become the "Silicon Valley" of high-tech industries in Texas. Although the worldwide downturn in the high-tech sector after 2000 dealt a serious blow to the area's economy, high-tech industries still make a major economic contribution.

Austin's rapid growth is a result of significant migration from the northeastern United States and the West Coast, as well as from other regions in Texas. The influx of well-educated persons from outside Texas has added to the already substantial pool of accomplished Austinites, making the state's capital the intellectual as well as the economic center of Central Texas. The cultural and economic traits of all the other regions of Texas mingle here, with no single trait being dominant; Central Texas is a microcosm of Texas culture.

Cultural Diversity

Texas is one of the fastest-growing states in the nation. No longer predominantly rural and agrarian, Texas is becoming more culturally diverse than ever as immigrants continue to find it a desirable place to call home.

The 2000 census showed a significant trend toward greater ethnic diversity. Over the ten-year period, the Anglo majority declined from 60.7 to 53.1 percent, while Hispanics increased from 25.5 to 32.0 percent and the rapidly growing "Other" classification (primarily Asians, Pacific Islanders, Middle Easterners, and Native Americans) grew from 2.1 to 3.3 percent. The African American percentage of the total population also fell marginally, from 11.7 to 11.6 percent.

The Texas State Population Estimates and Projections Program is designed to aid government and corporate planners by developing estimates of Texas's future population growth. This group of researchers has proposed three possible population scenarios. One scenario assumes that net migration into Texas will be zero. We find this assumption to be unrealistic and therefore do not include that scenario here. Another scenario, in contrast, assumes that the relatively high immigration levels of the 1980s will continue. We have chosen, however, to use a third, middle-of-the-road scenario, which is the one that the researchers recommend. This mid-range scenario assumes a moderate degree of immigration. All scenarios show Anglo Texans losing their numerical majority by 2010.

The pie charts in Figure 18–2 illustrate the mid-range scenario. The scenario predicts a Texas population of slightly more than 35 million by 2040, with a Hispanic plurality by 2025 and a Hispanic majority by 2035.

A high-immigration scenario, in contrast, projects a Texas population of more than 50 million by 2040. Hispanics achieve plurality status by 2015 and majority

FIGURE 18–2 | TEXAS POPULATION, MID-RANGE SCENARIO

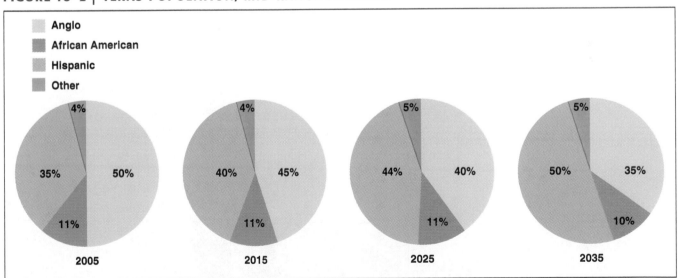

Source: Data from Population Estimates and Projections Program, "Projections of Texas and Counties in Texas by Age, Sex, and Race/Ethnicity for 1990–2040" (San Antonio: Texas State Data Center, Office of the State Demographer, 2004). Methodology and data are online at http://txsdc.utsa.edu/tpepp/2006projections/. Click on "Population Projections for the State of Texas."

FIGURE 18–3 | NET FAMILY INCOME IN TEXAS

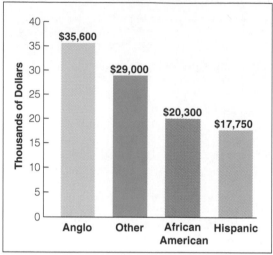

Source: The Henry J. Kaiser Family Foundation, "State Health Facts Online," www.statehealthfacts.kff.org.

FIGURE 18–4 | PERCENTAGE OF PERSONS IN POVERTY IN TEXAS

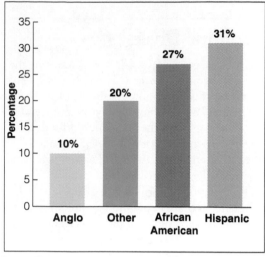

Source: The Henry J. Kaiser Family Foundation, "State Health Facts Online," www.statehealthfacts.kff.org.

status by 2030. Furthermore, the "Other" classification surpasses African Americans and becomes the third largest group by 2040.

Clearly, Texans are becoming more diverse and now have the opportunity to continue to build on their already rich cultural pluralism. Increasing diversity could also have a significant impact on the political culture of Texas, because the interests of more groups would have to be seriously considered as public policy is formulated and implemented.

A downside of Texas diversity is an unequal distribution of wealth and access to medical care. As shown in Figures 18–3, 18–4, and 18–5, Hispanic Americans, African Americans, and "Others" are more likely to live in poverty, have significantly lower family income, and have lower levels of health insurance than the more favored Anglo Americans.

FIGURE 18–5 | HEALTH-INSURANCE STATUS OF PERSONS UNDER THE AGE OF 65 IN TEXAS

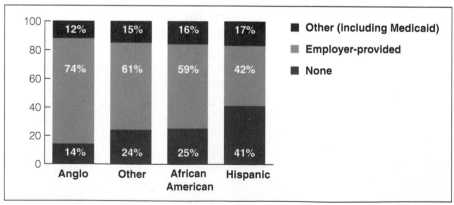

Source: The Henry J. Kaiser Family Foundation, "State Health Facts Online," www.statehealthfacts.kff.org.

MAKING A DIFFERENCE | Learn More about Your Own Culture

The United States is one of the most diverse nations in the world, and Texas is one of the most diverse states. It is made up of a rich variety of nationalities, ethnic groups, and religions that, when joined together, become the American mosaic. This does not mean that we are melted into one and have lost our individual distinctiveness. America is a mixing pot of all the races and nationalities of the world—different but united politically as one. It is our individual uniqueness that makes us different as a people; it is our unity in diversity that makes us different as a nation.

uniqueness. What you learn about your cultural and ethnic history will become a part of your understanding of yourself and can be a priceless gift to pass on to your own children and to their children.

Learning to understand and appreciate the cultural and ethnic histories of others as well can only contribute to our understanding and appreciation of who we all are, both as individuals and as Americans. It is in our individual differences that we can find both our national strength and the danger of conflicts among us. Collectively, our choice will determine which of these possibilities will predominate.

history. Record as much oral history as you can about their personal lives, experiences, and political recollections, as well as family myths and traditions. You may find this information priceless as you someday talk to your own children and grandchildren about their culture.

Broaden your cultural and political experiences. Participate in activities and organizations of ethnic, religious, and ideological groups that are different from your own. This will help you better understand and appreciate the rich diversity of modern American life.

Why Should You Care?

Our individual cultural and ethnic histories are, in a sense, who we are. Gaining knowledge of this history adds to your understanding of your own

What Can You Do?

Talk to grandparents, parents, and uncles and aunts to learn what they know about your culture and family

Key Terms

annexation 577

antitrust legislation 579

bicultural 595

binational 596

Black Codes 578

Creole 594

down-ticket 588

internationality 596

item veto 581

Ku Klux Klan (KKK) 581

La Réunion 598

maquiladora 595

Mestizo 594

Metroplex 598

North American Free Trade Agreement (NAFTA) 595

Ogallala Aquifer 597

progressive movement 580

Prohibition 580

ranchero culture 594

secession 578

Shivercrat 585

Spindletop 592

tax abatement 589

tenant farmer 580

tidelands 585

The Valley (of the Rio Grande) 594

Winter Garden 594

Chapter Summary

1 Originally part of Mexico, Texas was largely settled from the American South. Texas declared its independence from Mexico in 1836 and joined the United States in 1845. Early politics revolved around the slavery issue and the possibility of secession from the Union, which was strongly opposed by Sam Houston, one of the founders of the Texas Republic and the hero of the battle of San Jacinto (1836). After the election of Abraham Lincoln as U.S. president, Texas left the Union and joined the

Confederacy. The collapse of the Confederacy meant anarchy until Union troops occupied Texas in June 1865.

2 After a period of military occupation, radical Republican E. J. Davis (1870–1873) became governor in an election in which African Americans could vote but many former Confederates could not. The Davis administration was enormously unpopular with the white majority in Texas, and after the former Confederates regained the franchise, Davis was swept from office. The Democratic Party was to control Texas politics for more than a hundred years.

3　While conservatives normally dominated the Democratic Party, Texas experienced a degree of progressive reform with the election of several progressive governors between 1890 and 1939, including James Hogg (1891–1895) and both "Farmer Jim" and "Ma" Ferguson (1915–1917, 1925–1927, and 1933–1935). Another colorful governor was radio announcer W. "Pappy" Lee O'Daniel, a popular figure who nonetheless had little legislative success.

4　A key figure in the era following World War II (1939–1945) was governor Allan Shivers (1949–1957). A conservative Democrat, Shivers advocated voting for Republican presidents and conservative Democrats for all other offices. In 1960, Lyndon B. Johnson, U.S. senator from Texas and the Senate majority leader, became vice president under John F. Kennedy. In a special election in 1961, Republican John Tower filled Johnson's seat. Tower was the first Republican since Reconstruction to be elected to an important position in Texas, but he would not be the last. In 1963, following Kennedy's assassination, Johnson became U.S. president.

5　The election of Republican William Clements as governor in 1979 was a sign of the growing importance of the Republican Party. By 1994, Texas was clearly a two-party state. By 2002, the Republicans were in complete control of all levels of state government, including both chambers of the legislature. Texas seemed headed toward a one-party system again, but under a different party. In 2003, the Republicans consolidated their power by redistricting the U.S. House seats. As a result, in 2004 they gained control of the Texas delegation to the U.S. House.

6　Texas can be divided into a series of cultural regions with differing characteristics and traditions. We identify the following regions: (1) East Texas, (2) the Gulf Coast, (3) South Texas, (4) Southwest Texas, (5) the German Hill Country, (6) West Texas, (7) the Panhandle, (8) North Texas, and (9) Central Texas.

7　Projections of population growth and immigration predict a gradual shift in Texas's population away from an Anglo American majority toward a Hispanic American majority. Increased political clout can come with increased population, and Hispanic Americans could begin to challenge the political and economic dominance of Anglo Americans. Regardless of the political outcome of population shifts, Texas is becoming more culturally diverse and now has an opportunity to build on its already rich cultural pluralism.

Selected Print and Media Resources

SUGGESTED READINGS

Brammer, Billy Lee. *The Gay Place.* Austin: University of Texas Press, 1995. This work is really three interlocking novels that use Texas politics as the setting and Texas politicians as the primary characters.

Campbell, Randolph B. *Gone to Texas: A History of the Lone Star State.* New York: Oxford University Press, 2003. A leading Texas historian, Campbell sets early Texas history firmly within the history of Mexico and also keeps African Americans, both slave and free, at the center of his story. Much of the book concerns the state's lively political history. Campbell exhibits considerable skepticism about claims that Texas is unique among the states.

Davidson, Chandler. *Race and Class in Texas Politics.* Princeton, N.J.: Princeton University Press, 1992. The author examines the forces that shape Texas politics. The book is recommended by *The American Political Science Review.*

Lind, Michael. *Made in Texas: George W. Bush and the Southern Takeover of American Politics.* New York: Basic Books, 2003. This book takes a look at how the political tradition of Texas is shaping U.S. and world politics.

Rogers, Mary Beth (with an introduction by Bill Moyers). *Cold Anger: A Story of Faith and Power Politics.* Denton, Texas: University of North Texas Press, 1990. Rogers writes the story of Ernesto Cortes, who employs religion and other tools to develop grassroots Mexican American movements in South Texas.

MEDIA RESOURCES

Lone Star—Producer/director John Sayles explores the cultural and social interaction among Mexicans, Mexican Americans, African Americans, and Anglo Americans along the Texas-Mexico border.

Traffic—Director Steven Soderbergh examines the impact of the "war against drugs" on the people, institutions, and social structures along the border.

The American Experience: Remember the Alamo—This PBS program is available in both Spanish and English versions. A documentary, it explores the life of prominent Mexican Texan José Antonio Navarro and the Tejanos (Mexican Texans) who fought alongside Anglo Texans for Texas independence.

Two Towns of Jasper—Another PBS production from 2002, this program explores the separate reactions and viewpoints of the white and black communities of Jasper, Texas, following the murder of James Byrd, who was dragged to his death while chained to a pickup truck by three white men.

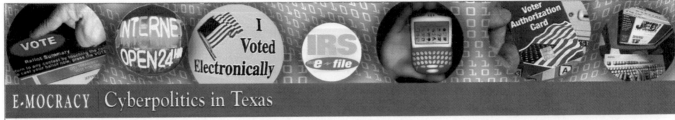

E·MOCRACY | Cyberpolitics in Texas

Welcome to cyberpolitics in Texas. The rapid development of the World Wide Web on the Internet has created unprecedented opportunities for research, communication, and participation in Texas politics. Today, students can easily communicate with the authors of their textbooks, government leaders, and fellow students all across Texas.

To research the Texas cultural regions, we suggest you begin with the home page of the monthly magazine that presents Texas to Texans and to the rest of the country, *Texas Monthly*. Two recommended features are "Links across Texas," which includes a section on government and politics, and the "Texpertise" section, which answers a variety of questions about Texas. The site also lists more than 1,600 links, including a government and politics section and a "Texas Talks" section, which provides the opportunity to ask questions of famous Texans and of editors and writers at the magazine.

Logging On

To facilitate this new educational technology, Wadsworth/Thomson Learning has developed a series of political science Web sites available at

www.wadsworth.com/politicalscience_d

Click on "Student Book Companion Sites" under the "Resources" column on the left, and then scroll down to the entry for *American Government and Politics Today: Texas Edition*. Click on the thumbnail picture of the cover of this text.

Texas Monthly can be found online at

www.texasmonthly.com

Historical maps of interest can be found at the University of Texas Library Online. They include "State of Origin of the Old Stock Anglo-American Population; Black Slaves as a Percentage of Total Population, 1840 and 1860"; "German Element, 1850"; "Spanish and French Surnames, 1850"; and the "Vote on Secession, 1861." Go to

**www.lib.utexas.edu/maps/historical/
history_texas.html**

Look at the state of Texas home page for information on Texas history, early native populations, historical events and dates, historic sites, and population information, projections, and demographics:

www.state.tx.us

The *New Handbook of Texas* is a great source for information on Texas history, culture, and geography. A joint project of the Texas State Historical Association and the University of Texas at Austin, it is an encyclopedia of all things Texan. It can be found online at

www.tsha.utexas.edu/handbook/online

Factual information and statistics can be found in the *Texas Fact Book 2006*, written by Bob Bullock of the Texas State History Museum for the Legislative Budget Board. Go to

**www.lbb.state.tx.us/The_LBB/
Access/Other_Documents.htm**

Lone Star Junction is a nonprofit organization chartered by the state of Texas. It provides an online resource about Texas and its early history at

www.lsjunction.com

Online Review

At **www.politicalscience.wadsworth.com/
schmidt12**, you will find a free Study Guide to this book. For each chapter, there are two online quizzes to help you master the material.

• The PoliPrep Self-Study Assessment provides a pretest for each major section of the chapter. PoliPrep then generates a customized study plan. After you complete the study plan, a posttest evaluates your progress.

• The Tutorial Quiz for each chapter provides questions on the chapter contents, including the features. The questions are organized to match the major sections of the chapter.

19 | The Texas Constitution

What If . . .
Texas Used a More Typical State Constitution?

BACKGROUND

The Texas constitution places more restrictions on state government than do the constitutions of most other states. It is one of the most detailed state constitutions and, with 439 amendments by 2006, the fourth most frequently amended. At approximately 90,000 words, the Texas constitution is longer than that of any other state except Alabama.

WHAT IF TEXAS USED A MORE TYPICAL STATE CONSTITUTION?

While there is no "typical" state constitution, the Texas constitution is extraordinary. If the constitution of Texas were shorter and less detailed, the legislature, governor, and courts would have greater flexibility. The elected state supreme court would have more opportunity to interpret general language in the Texas constitution. Voters would be called on less frequently to vote on technical amendments to change details that they may care little about and may not even understand.

THE LEGISLATURE

The Texas legislature probably would be allowed to meet annually instead of biennially—that is, once every two years—and would be able to sit for longer than 140 days. With longer sessions, the members of the legislature would be less likely to pass legislation they had not read or understood.

(The Texas House of Representatives once unanimously passed a resolution to honor the "Boston strangler" without knowing what it was voting for!) The legislature could pass an annual budget instead of a two-year budget. As a result, it would not need to predict fully two years in advance how many students will enroll in all public schools, colleges, and universities; how many inmates will be sentenced to state prisons; how many patients will be admitted to state mental and tuberculosis hospitals; and even how many potholes will appear on state highways. With the current biennial sessions, in contrast, some state services are underfunded, and others are overfunded. (One can only imagine what happens to funds in overfunded agencies.)

Legislators might be better paid (with salaries more typical of the private sector) and could spend more time on legislative tasks. In larger states, legislators often serve on a full-time basis, and that might happen in Texas as well. Longer and more frequent meetings might also allow legislators to form independent judgments and depend less on the advice of special interest lobbyists.

THE GOVERNOR

The governor of Texas would most likely be able to directly appoint the heads of state agencies instead of appointing members of boards, which in turn appoint agency heads. The governor would not need to compete with so many other elected officers who have their own ambitions. The governor would be able to appoint and direct a cabinet and, like the president, would be able to issue orders to coordinate, supervise, and eliminate duplication among state agencies.

OTHER CHANGES

The Court of Criminal Appeals would probably be eliminated and consolidated with the state supreme court. The new Texas Supreme Court would then have greater power to interpret the Texas constitution.

Voters might be given more power to change the structures of county and special district governments. They could eliminate unneeded offices and establish local structures and functions adapted to their special needs.

In general, there would be a greater concentration of power—something Texans greatly fear. Voters would have more opportunities to influence local government, but they would elect fewer state officers and have less opportunity to vote on constitutional amendments.

FOR CRITICAL ANALYSIS

1. What benefits might result if Texas government —especially the executive branch—were more efficient?
2. What might be some negative consequences of a more active state government in Texas?

The real character of a government is determined less by the provisions of its constitution than by the minds and hearts of its citizens. Government is a process of decision making conditioned by a state's history, its people, and the pressures exerted by individuals, interest groups, and political parties.

Still, our national, state, and local governments would be vastly different were it not for their constitutions. Although the exact meaning of constitutional provisions may be disputed, there is general agreement that a constitution should be respected as the legal basis controlling the fundamentals of government decision making. A constitution serves as a rationalization for actions by courts, legislatures, executives, and the people themselves. Indeed, the very idea of having a written constitution has become part of the basic system of political beliefs in the United States—our political culture.

Constitutions establish major governing institutions, assign them power, and place both implicit and explicit limits on the power that has been assigned. And, because Americans respect constitutions, they promote *legitimacy*, a concept we discussed in Chapter 1 of this text.

Texans' reactions to Reconstruction (1864–1877) led to the adoption of a constitution designed to curb government power. The legislature is hampered by numerous limitations on salary, sessions, and activities; power in the executive branch is fragmented; appeals courts are divided, and judges are elected rather than appointed. A rigid structure and ceilings on debt and tax restrictions limit local government, especially county government.

Therefore, it is difficult for Texas state government to develop new programs without first amending the constitution. Amendments have been adopted for such seemingly minor purposes as abolishing the office of county surveyor in Jackson County and clearing some land titles in Fort Bend County. The division of executive power, which makes it difficult for the governor or any other official to become an effective leader, also obstructs problem solving. Although Texas has had some powerful governors, such as Allan Shivers, John Connally, and George W. Bush, they have become effective despite the constitution, not because of it.

The Texas Constitution in History

Why has Texas adopted one of the longest, most frequently amended, and most restrictive state constitutions? Like all other state constitutions, the Texas constitution reflects the interests and concerns of those who wrote and amended it. Some of its history parallels the histories of other state constitutions, but much of it is unique to Texas.

The First Texas Constitutions

The first constitution of Texas was written in 1836 after Texas had gained its independence from Mexico and become an independent republic. The constitutional convention established a *unitary*, as opposed to a *federal*, government (see Chapter 3). Several other provisions were direct reactions to policies experienced under the government of Mexico.

President George W. Bush and First Lady Laura Bush attend the dedication ceremony for the Bob Bullock Texas History Museum. The museum in downtown Austin tells the story of Texas with three floors of interactive exhibits and Austin's only IMAX theater, featuring *Texas: The Big Picture.* How has Texas history influenced the state's constitution? (AP Photo/Pablo Martinez Monsivais)

The convention provided a constitution with strict separation of church and state, forbidding clergymen of any faith from holding office. It reversed the antislavery policies of the old Mexican government by forbidding masters from freeing their slaves without consent of the republic's congress. Remembering the abuses of Mexican president Santa Anna, Texans limited the terms of their presidents to three years and prohibited them from serving consecutive terms.

Aside from these provisions, the Texas constitution was an almost word-for-word copy of the U.S. Constitution and those of several southern states. It was clearly the product of the political culture from which the early Texans came—the Anglo American traditions of southern planters.

The Constitution of 1845.   The constitution of 1845 was written in preparation for Texas's admission into the United States. Although similar to other southern state constitutions, it also incorporated certain elements of Spanish political culture (some of which would later be adopted by other states). The constitution of 1845 exempted homesteads from **foreclosure**, protected a wife's property rights, and provided for **community property**, meaning that husband and wife would equally own property acquired during their marriage. It also required a two-thirds vote in the Texas House to establish any corporation and made bank corporations illegal altogether. The governor served a two-year term, and legislative sessions were biennial.

The Constitution of 1861.   The constitution of 1861 was basically the same as that of 1845 except for changes required by the fact that Texas had become one of the Confederate states at war with the Union. It increased the debt ceiling and prohibited the emancipation of slaves.

Constitutions after the Civil War

Following the Civil War, the U.S. army occupied Texas, as well as other Confederate states. Texans wrote the constitution of 1866, which they believed would permit the restoration of civilian government under President Andrew Johnson's mild Reconstruction program. The new constitution nullified secession, abolished slavery, and renounced Confederate war debts. Still, it did not fully satisfy the few requirements set down by President Johnson, for the following reasons:

- It did not declare that secession was unconstitutional.
- It failed to ratify the Thirteenth Amendment (abolishing slavery).
- It did not adequately establish the civil status and rights of African Americans.

Texans, however, were correct in assuming that Johnson would accept it. Under its terms, a civilian government was elected and operated for several months despite some interference from the **Freedmen's Bureau** of the national government, which had responsibility for the former slaves.

Johnson's lenient policies were unacceptable to the Republican-controlled U.S. Congress, which took control of Reconstruction in 1867. Under the authority of the Reconstruction Act, the U.S. military purged the civilian-elected authorities and imposed military rule. Texas would be under military occupation until the Reconstruction era ended.

The Constitution of 1869.   Under congressional Reconstruction, top former Confederates and persons who refused to swear an "ironclad oath" of loyalty to the Union were temporarily barred from participation in politics. While

| **Foreclosure**
The legal process by which a lender takes possession of a mortgaged property when the borrower defaults on the loan.

| **Community Property**
Any property that a married couple has acquired during their marriage. In certain states, it is divided equally between them in the event of a divorce.

| **Freedmen's Bureau**
The Bureau of Refugees, Freedmen and Abandoned Lands, a federal bureau established in 1865 to aid refugees of the Civil War (including former slaves) and to administer confiscated property. Among other tasks, it sought to provide education to the former slaves. It was disbanded in 1872.

In this 1868 drawing, a man representing the Freedmen's Bureau stands between armed whites and African Americans. (Library of Congress)

those barred made up only about 10 percent of the population, they included almost the entire former leadership of Texas politics and society. The remaining voters, including newly enfranchised African Americans, elected eighty-one whites and nine blacks to the constitutional convention in 1868. The convention produced a document that centralized state power in the hands of the governor, lengthened the chief executive's term to four years, and allowed the governor to appoint all major state officers, including judges. It provided for annual legislative sessions; weakened local government, which was controlled by traditional elites; and centralized the public school system. The convention in 1868 reflected little of the fear of centralized government power that was later to become the hallmark of Texas government. The constitution it proposed was ratified in 1869.

Reconstruction under the Constitution of 1869.   The constitution of 1869 was to serve as the instrument of government for an era that white Texans would regard as the most abusive in the state's history. An **enabling act** allowed Republican governor E. J. Davis to fill about 8,500 jobs in state government that had been left vacant by enforcement of the ironclad oath. The legislature authorized a state police force that had the authority to operate anywhere in the state, overruling local law enforcement officials. The state police were hated by the white majority because blacks made up a sizable portion of the force and because the force was used to put down violent opposition to Reconstruction. In four counties where law and order broke down, Governor Davis declared martial law and sent in the state police to regain state control. Davis also took control of voter registration, intimidated unsupportive newspapers, and arrested several political opponents.

The economic policies of the Davis administration were also unlike anything that had ever been seen in Texas. Both taxes and spending increased dramatically, in part to fund railroads and public schools. High taxes led to widespread tax evasion, and lavish government spending led to a large state debt. Subsidies to railroad companies, along with other legislation that financially benefited Republican-oriented interests, helped inspire the widespread view that the Davis administration was the most corrupt in Texas history. In 1874, Democrat Richard Coke was elected governor in a landslide. The Republican-dominated state supreme court, however, invalidated the election. Davis wired President Ulysses Grant to send federal troops to thwart the Democratic victory. Grant refused, and Democrats gathered in the legislative chambers to form the new government.

The Fall of Davis.   According to legend, Davis was determined not to give up his office and surrounded himself with armed state police in the capitol. Only when a well-armed group of Coke supporters marched toward the capitol singing "The Yellow Rose of Texas" did Davis finally vacate his offices.

For most white Texans, Reconstruction left a bitter memory of a humiliating, corrupt, extravagant, and even tyrannical government. Some recent historians, however, writing in the wake of the modern civil rights movement, have argued that Davis was not personally corrupt and that during Reconstruction an activist government attempted to play a positive role in people's lives while protecting the civil and political rights of former slaves. (We take an additional look at this argument in this chapter's *Which Side Are You On?* feature on the following page.) Whichever historical view is more accurate, it is clear that the period that followed was a conservative white reaction to the policies of the Davis administration.

The Constitution of 1876

Most Texans were determined to strip power away from state government by writing a new constitution. The Texas Grange (whose members were called Grangers)

| Enabling Act
Legislation that confers on appropriate officials the power to implement or enforce the law.

Democrat Richard Coke was elected governor in 1874 to replace the highly controversial Republican governor E. J. Davis. (Library of Congress)

WHICH SIDE ARE YOU ON? | Was Reconstruction Truly a Disaster for Texas?

Texas and southern legend has it that Reconstruction was a time when the victorious North took savage vengeance on the defeated Confederacy. The North and its henchmen raised taxes, ruined the economy, granted the freed slaves dominion over their former masters, and used armed force to perpetuate regimes that were radical, unjust, and corrupt. In Texas, the administration of Governor E. J. Davis was the last chapter in Reconstruction and was followed by the return of those who, in southern tradition, were called "Redeemers." The victory of the Redeemers was symbolized in Texas by the adoption of the constitution of 1876.

There can be little doubt that the victory of the Redeemers was inevitable. By the 1870s, northern voters of both parties had little appetite for resisting the demands of those who clearly represented the majority in most parts of the South. Yet does it follow that the accusations leveled against Reconstruction governments by the Redeemers were true, at least in part?

This photograph shows E. J. Davis, the Reconstruction-era Republican governor of Texas, during the Civil War. Davis fought as a general in the Union Army. To what degree might white Texans have held Davis's military service against him? (Texas State Library and Archives)

THE DAVIS REGIME WAS INDEED A DISASTER

Traditional Texan writers regard the Davis regime as the most corrupt and abusive in the state's history. Large gifts of public funds were made to interests such as railroads. Tax rates sky-rocketed to pay for ambitious and wasteful public programs. Landowners refused to pay exorbitant property taxes (amounting to as much as one-fifth of personal income). And government accumulated what was for that time an incredible public debt. Law and order collapsed, and much of the state fell prey to desperadoes. Using the state police and militia to maintain his powerful political machine, Davis was a true tyrant.

Even some modern commentators who oppose the frankly reactionary policies of the Redeemers blame Davis for provoking a backlash. Without the centralizing policies of the Davis administration, Texas might not be saddled today with a constitution that cripples any attempt at progressive government action.

DAVIS WAS SIMPLY AHEAD OF HIS TIME

Some modern scholars are much more sympathetic to Reconstruction and to leaders such as Davis. One issue that complicates any modern criticism of Davis is that almost all the measures he sponsored are now generally accepted public policy. Today, Texas lays out large sums for education and road building. Taxes are higher than they ever were under Davis. Racial discrimination is illegal. Nothing Davis did upset white Texans more than the recruitment of African Americans into the state police. Yet African American law enforcement officers are so commonplace today as to attract no notice at all.

Similarly, subsidies to business are hardly absent from the Texas scene today. (And ironically, Davis opposed most railroad subsidies—they were voted through by an alliance of Democrats and conservative Republicans.) Additionally, to blame Davis for the breakdown in law and order that accompanied Reconstruction is more than a little disingenuous. Precisely through the hated state police, Davis took robust and unprecedented action to reestablish the rule of law.

One point rarely stressed by those who call Davis a tyrant is the extent to which violence was employed by the Redeemers. The suppression of African American political participation by organizations such as the Ku Klux Klan would be characterized as terrorism if it happened today.

WHAT'S YOUR POSITION?

Did the Davis administration really harm Texas? If so, how? Is there any chance that Texans might have reacted less negatively to Davis if his government had spent less and imposed fewer taxes?

GOING ONLINE

The *Handbook of Texas Online* is always a good place to start when researching Texas historical topics. Go to **www.tsha.utexas.edu/handbook/online**, enter "reconstruction" in the search field, and click on the "Search" button. The *Handbook* will retrieve dozens of Reconstruction-related articles, including a general overview of the period.

organized in 1873. Campaigning on a platform of "retrenchment and reform," it managed to elect at least forty of its members to the constitutional convention of 1875. Like most of the ninety delegates, they were Democrats who were determined to strike at the heart of big government.

Retrenchment. To reduce expenses, the convention did not publish a journal—reflecting the frugal tone of the final constitution. When the convention ended, some of the funds appropriated for its expenses remained unspent. The constitution created by the convention cut salaries for governing officials, placed strict limits on property taxes, and restricted state borrowing. The new regime was also miserly with the power it granted government officials. Most of the governor's powers were stripped, the term of office was reduced from four to two years, and the salary was cut. In addition, the new constitution required that the attorney general and state judges be elected rather than appointed by the governor.

Restrictions on the Legislature. The legislature did not escape the convention's pruning. Regular legislative sessions were to be held only once every two years, and legislators were encouraged to limit the length of the sessions. Legislative procedure was detailed in the constitution of 1876, with severe restrictions placed on the kinds of policies the legislature might enact. In fact, a number of public policies were written into the Texas constitution itself. Local government was strengthened, and counties were given many of the administrative and judicial functions of the state.

Ratification. The convention had largely reacted to the abuse of state power by attempting to abolish it. Despite opposition from blacks, Republicans, most cities, and railroad interests, voters ratified the constitution in 1876, and it remains in effect today.

The poster shows delegates to the Texas constitutional convention of 1875. The convention severely limited the powers of the state government. Why might Texans traditionally have been so resistant to strong government—an attitude that dates back to well before the Civil War? (Center for American History, University of Texas at Austin)

The Texas Constitution Today

Many students begin their examination of state constitutions with an ideal or model constitution in mind. Comparisons with this ideal then leave them with the feeling that if only this or that provision were changed, state government would somehow find its way to increased honesty, efficiency, and effectiveness. But in truth there is no ideal constitution that would serve well in each of the diverse fifty states. Nor is it possible to write a state constitution that could permanently meet the dynamically changing needs and concerns of the state's citizens. Further, because government is much more than its constitution, honest and effective government must be commanded by the political environment—by leaders, citizens, parties, and interest groups. Constitutions alone cannot guarantee good government. Scoundrels will be corrupt and unconcerned citizens will be apathetic under even the best constitution.

This pragmatic view of the role of state constitutions, however, should not lead to the conclusion that they are only incidental to good government. A workable constitution is necessary for effective government even if it is not sufficient to guarantee it. Low salaries may discourage independent, high-caliber leaders from seeking office. Constitutional restrictions may make it virtually impossible for government to meet the changing needs of its citizens. Institutions may be set up in such a way that they will operate inefficiently and irresponsibly.

The events preceding the adoption of the current Texas constitution in 1876 did not provide the background for developing a constitution capable of serving well under the pressures and changes that would take place in the century to follow. The decade of the 1870s was an era of paranoia and reaction, and the constitution it produced was directed more toward solving the problems arising from Reconstruction than toward meeting the challenges of generations to follow. It was literally a reactionary document.

Separation of Powers

Like the Bill of Rights, Article 2 of the Texas constitution limits government. To prevent the concentration of power in the hands of any single institution, the national government and all states have provided for a *separation of powers* among three branches: legislative, executive, and judicial branches (see Chapter 2).

Because there is still the potential for any of these three branches to abuse whatever powers they have been given, the Texas constitution also follows American tradition in subsequent constitutional articles—it sets up a system of *checks and balances*. So that each branch of government can check the others, functions normally assigned to one branch of government are given to another.

For example, the veto power that deals with lawmaking (a legislative function) is given to the governor (an executive). Impeachment and conviction, which deal with determining guilt (a judicial function), are given to the legislature. The state senate (a chamber of the legislature) confirms appointments made by the governor in the executive branch.

Despite the separation of powers, the checks-and-balances system requires that each branch have the opportunity to influence the others. The three branches specialize in separate functions, but there is some sharing of powers as well.

Legislative Branch

The legislative article (Article 3) is by far the longest in the Texas constitution. It assigns legislative power to a **bicameral** (two-chamber) **legislature** consisting of the 31-member senate and the 150-member house of representatives. Elected for a four-year term from a single-member district, each senator must be:

- At least twenty-six years old.
- A U.S. citizen.
- A resident of the state for five years and of the district for one year.

A representative serves only two years and must be:

- At least twenty-one years old.
- A U.S. citizen.
- A resident of the state for two years and of the district for one year.

The Texas constitutional provisions concerning bicameralism, number of members of the legislature, and length of terms are typical of state constitutions (see Table 19–1). Minimum qualifications for Texas senators, however, are somewhat more restrictive than average.

Salaries of Legislators.   The Texas constitution sets annual salaries at $7,200 unless the Texas Ethics Commission recommends an increase and voters approve it. The commission has made no such recommendation but has exercised its power to increase the *per diem* allowance (for daily expenses) to $125 while the legislature is in session. No other large state sets legislative salaries so low. Table 19–2 (on page 614) lists legislative salaries in the fifty states, along with the frequency of legislative sessions.

Limited Sessions.   Texas is one of very few states that have a constitution restricting their legislatures to biennial **regular sessions.** Because sessions are also limited

| **Bicameral Legislature**
A legislature made up of two chambers. The U.S. Congress, composed of the House of Representatives and the Senate, is a bicameral legislature.

| **Regular Session**
A legislative session scheduled by the constitution. Texas regular sessions are biennial (once every two years) rather than annual as in most states and in Congress.

to 140 days, important legislation may receive inadequate consideration, and many bills are ignored altogether. The 2005 legislature introduced 9,338 bills, concurrent resolutions, and joint resolutions (67 per calendar day). Of these, it passed 4,961 (53 percent).

Unlike legislatures in most states, the Texas legislature may not call itself into **special sessions** or determine the issues to be decided in such sessions. Special sessions are convened by the governor to consider only the legislative matters he or she presents, and the length of a special session is limited to thirty days. Special sessions are more restricted than in any other state.

Ironically, in 1917 Governor James E. Ferguson called the special session that would impeach and convict him. Despite the governor's ordinary power to call special sessions and limit their purpose, the courts later held that impeachment powers were so broad they could be exercised beyond the limits imposed by the governor. The legislature has also adopted laws to permit it to call itself into special session for the sole purpose of impeachment.

Setting Legislative Procedures. The Texas constitution establishes more specific procedural requirements than most other state constitutions. Although the provision is often suspended, the Texas constitution requires that a bill must be read on three separate days unless four-fifths of the legislature set aside the requirement. It stipulates when bills may be introduced and how they will be reported out of committee, signed, and entered in the **house and senate journals** once enacted. It even specifies how the enacting clause will read. (The enacting clause is formal language in any bill that gives the bill the force of law if it is approved.)

| Special Session
Any legislative session that is not specifically scheduled by the constitution or by statute. In some states, the legislature may call itself into special session, but in Texas only the governor may call the legislature into special session.

| House and Senate Journals
The official public records of the actions of the two chambers of the Texas legislature. The two journals are issued daily during sessions.

TABLE 19–1 | REQUIREMENTS FOR ELECTION TO VARIOUS LEGISLATURES

CONSTITUTIONAL AND STATUTORY PROVISIONS FOR LEGISLATIVE BODIES	TEXAS LEGISLATURE	U.S. CONGRESS	THE FIFTY STATE LEGISLATURES
Bicameral	Yes	Yes	Only Nebraska's legislature is unicameral.
Number of members			
Senate	31	2 per state	39.4 is average.
House	150	435 by statute	108.2 is average.
Term			
Senate	4 years	6 years	4 years in 38 states; 2 in the remainder.
House	2 years	2 years	2 years in all but 5 states, which have extended it to 4 years.
Qualifications			
Senate			
Age	26 years	30 years	Only 6 states set higher age requirements than Texas.
Residence in state	5 years	Citizen 9 years and current resident of state	3 years or less in 41 states; 2 states require more than 5 years.
Residence in district	1 year	–	3 states require more than 1 year.
House			
Age	21 years	25 years	Only 6 states set higher age requirements than Texas, while 17 states allow 18-year-olds to serve.
Residence in state	2 years	Citizen 7 years and current resident of state	Only 11 states require more than 2 years.
Residence in district	1 year	None	Only 2 states require more than 1 year.

Source: Council of State Governments, *Book of the States 2005.*

TABLE 19-2 | STATE LEGISLATIVE SESSIONS AND ANNUAL SALARIES

	YEARS SESSIONS ARE HELD	SALARY*
Alabama	Annual	$ 10(d)[†]
Alaska	Annual	24,012[†]
Arizona	Annual	24,000[†]
Arkansas	Odd	14,067[†]
California	Even**	110,880[†]
Colorado	Annual	30,000[†]
Connecticut	Annual	28,000
Delaware	Annual	39,785
Florida	Annual	29,916[†]
Georgia	Annual	16,524[†]
Hawaii	Annual	34,200[†]
Idaho	Annual	15,646[†]
Illinois	Annual	57,619[†]
Indiana	Annual	11,600[†]
Iowa	Annual	21,381[†]
Kansas	Annual	83.14(d)[†]
Kentucky	Annual	170.17(d)[†]
Louisiana	Annual	16,800[†]
Maine	Even	11,384[§†]
Maryland	Annual	40,500[†]
Massachusetts	Biennial**	55,569[†]
Michigan	Annual	79,650[†]
Minnesota	Odd[††]	31,141[†]
Mississippi	Annual	10,000[†]
Missouri	Annual	31,351[†]
Montana	Odd	76.80(d)[†]
Nebraska"	Annual	12,000[†]
Nevada	Odd	130(d)[†]
New Hampshire	Annual	200(b)
New Jersey	Annual	49,000
New Mexico	Annual	0[†]
New York	Annual	79,500[†]
North Carolina	Odd[††]	13,951[†]
North Dakota	Odd	125(d)[†]
Ohio	Odd**	56,261
Oklahoma	Annual	38,400[†]
Oregon	Odd	16,284[†]
Pennsylvania	Odd**	69,647[†]
Rhode Island	Annual	12,646
South Carolina	Biennial	10,400[†]
South Dakota	Annual	12,000[†]
Tennessee	Annual	16,500[†]
Texas	Odd	7,200[†]
Utah	Annual	120(d)[†]
Vermont	Annual	589(w)[†]
Virginia	Annual	18,000[‡‡]
Washington	Annual	34,227[†]
West Virginia	Annual	15,000[†]
Wisconsin	Odd**	45,569[†]
Wyoming	Annual	125(d)[†]

*Salaries annual unless otherwise noted as (d)—per day, (b)—biennium, or (w)—per week.
[†]Plus *per diem* living expenses.
[§]For odd year; $8,655 for even year.
"Unicameral (single-house) legislature.
**Two-year session (that is, it meets every year).
[††]Annual at option of legislature.
[‡‡]Senate; House is $17,640.
Source: Council of State Governments, *Book of the States 2006*.

Mandating a Balanced Budget.   Most states legally require a balanced budget, but the restrictions imposed by the Texas constitution seem more effective than most. Article 3 (Section 49) prohibits the legislature from authorizing state debt except under rare conditions. The comptroller of public accounts is required to certify that funds are available for each appropriations measure adopted. Although specific constitutional amendments have authorized the sale of bonds for such purposes as veterans' real estate programs, student loans, and parks and water development, the largest share of general-obligation debt is for criminal justice. Per capita state debt remains among the lowest in the nation.

Statute-Like Details.   The Texas constitution further confines the legislature by establishing detailed policies on subjects that normally would be handled by legislative statute. Much of the length of Article 3 results from its in-depth description of the veterans' land program, Texas park and water development funds, student loans, welfare programs, a grain warehouse self-insurance fund, and the municipal donation of outdated firefighting equipment. The Texas constitution establishes the design of the great seal of Texas, authorizes the legislature to pass laws concerning fences, and even explains how stationery must be purchased! Article 16 authorizes the legislature to regulate cattle brands; Article 11 permits the building of seawalls.

By including such **statute-like details** in the Texas constitution, its framers guaranteed that even relatively unimportant decisions that might easily be handled by the legislature could instead be changed only by constitutional amendment. Events may outstrip detailed constitutional provisions, leaving behind **deadwood**—provisions that are no longer functional. For example, Article 9, Section 14, provides for establishment of county poorhouses. Only by amending the constitution can Texans remove such provisions. In brief, basic distrust of the legislature, however much it may have been deserved in 1876, put a straitjacket on the state's ability to cope with the challenges of the twenty-first century.

| Statute-Like Details
Detailed state constitutional provisions characterized by the narrow scope usually found in statutory law.

| Deadwood
In the context of state government, constitutional provisions made inoperative by changing circumstances or by conflicting federal constitutional or statutory law.

Executive Branch

Article 4 establishes the executive branch, with the governor as its head. The governor must be:

- A citizen.
- At least thirty years of age.
- A resident of the state for five years preceding his or her election.

Since the passage of a constitutional amendment in 1974, the governor is elected to a four-year term. The governor's salary is no longer constitutionally limited; according to statute, it is $115,345. Table 19–3 compares the governor of Texas with other governors and the U.S. president.

TABLE 19–3 | CONSTITUTIONAL PROVISIONS FOR CHIEF EXECUTIVES' QUALIFICATIONS

CONSTITUTIONAL PROVISIONS	TEXAS GOVERNOR	U.S. PRESIDENT	THE FIFTY STATES' GOVERNORS
Age	30 years	35 years	34 states set the minimum age at 30.
Residence	5 years	14 years	5 years or less in 39 states.
Term	4 years with no limit on the number of terms	4 years (limited to two terms or 10 years)	48 states allow a 4-year term, but unlike Texas, 36 states impose term limits.

Source: Council of State Governments, *Book of the States 2006*.

| **Plural Executive**
An executive branch with power divided among several independent officers and a weak chief executive.

| **Removal Power**
The power to dismiss government officials. In Texas, the governor can remove an official that he or she appointed only with the consent of two-thirds of the state senate.

| **Indirect Appointive Power**
In Texas, the power of the governor to appoint supervisory boards (but not operational directors) for most state agencies. The supervisory boards and commissions usually appoint the actual heads of most state agencies in Texas.

| **Directive Authority**
The power to issue binding orders to state agencies. This power is severely limited for the governor of Texas.

| **Budgetary Power**
The power to propose a spending plan to the legislature. The governor of Texas has limited budgetary power because of the competing authority of the Legislative Budget Committee.

| **Item Veto**
The power to veto particular sections or items of an appropriations bill while signing the remainder of the bill into law. The governors of most states have this power.

A Plural Executive.   Provisions for terms, qualifications, and salary may be somewhat less restrictive than in most states, but there are much more severe constitutional restrictions on the power of the office. Indeed, the governor of Texas remains among the weakest in the nation. Although the Texas constitution provides that the governor is the chief executive, it actually establishes a **plural executive** by dividing executive powers among a number of independently elected officers—the governor, the lieutenant governor, the attorney general, the comptroller of public accounts, the commissioner of the general land office, and three railroad commissioners. There are also provisions for a state board of education to be either elected or appointed.

Few states elect as many officials as Texas. Seven states have abolished the office of lieutenant governor as an independently elected executive, and a few have made offices as important as the attorney general appointive rather than elective. Comptrollers—and land, educational, and agricultural officers—are rarely elected in states other than Texas.

In the tradition of the constitutional plural executive, the legislature by statute has established an elected commissioner of agriculture and has exercised its option to have the state board of education elected independently of the governor. Most of the remaining agencies the legislature establishes to administer state programs are headed by appointed multimember boards with substantial independence from the governor. Generally, the governor appoints only supervisory boards for the agencies, with the approval of two-thirds of the state senate. Each board in turn appoints the agency's director. The governor does not appoint the agency administrator directly. Texas is one of eight states lacking a formal cabinet.

The Governor's Powers over the Executive Branch.   The governor has narrow **removal powers** to supplement the **indirect appointive powers** described in the preceding paragraph. Officers appointed by the current governor (but not her or his predecessors) may be fired, but only if two-thirds of the senators agree that there is just cause for removal—making firing almost as difficult as impeachment and conviction. **Directive authority** (to issue binding orders) is quite restricted, and **budgetary power** (to recommend to the legislature how much it should appropriate for various executive agencies) is limited by the competing influence of the Legislative Budget Board. (We will describe the Legislative Budget Board in depth in Chapter 23. This board, which is controlled by the presiding officers of the two chambers of the legislature, prepares a draft of the state budget that is often more important than the draft prepared by the governor.) Weak control by the chief executive can lead to duplication of functions and to lack of planning, coordination, and accountability.

The Governor's Veto Powers.   The statutes and the constitution combine to make the governor a relatively weak executive; however, the veto gives the governor effective influence over legislation. Only once in the past half-century has the legislature mustered the two-thirds vote necessary to override a governor's veto. (That override took place in 1979, the year when William P. Clements became the first Republican governor of Texas in a century.) The Texas legislature often lacks the opportunity to override a veto, however, because major legislation may be adopted during the last days of the session. Once the legislature delivers a bill to the governor, the governor must either sign it or veto it within ten days. If the bill is passed during the last ten days of the session, the governor can simply wait until the legislature adjourns before vetoing it. The governor has twenty days to act after the legislature adjourns.

Texas is among forty-three states that give the governor **item veto** power to strike out particular sections of an appropriations bill without vetoing the entire bill.

(Several states—but not Texas—also allow the item veto to be used on matters other than appropriations.) The governor of Texas lacks both the **reduction veto** (to reduce appropriations without striking them out altogether) and the **pocket veto** (to kill bills simply by ignoring them after the end of the session).

The Courts

Just as the Texas constitution limits the power of the chief executive, it also fragments the court system, which is governed by Article 5. Texas is the only state other than Oklahoma that has two courts of final appeal. The highest court for civil matters is the nine-member Texas Supreme Court; the other, for criminal matters, is the nine-member Court of Criminal Appeals. Leaving some flexibility as to number and jurisdiction, the constitution also creates intermediate courts of appeals and district, county, and justice of the peace courts. (The structure of the Texas court system is displayed in Figure 19–1.) The same article describes the selection of grand and trial juries and such administrative officers as sheriff, county clerk, and county and district attorney.

Judicial Problems. The number and variety of courts confuse the average citizen, and coordination among courts is minimal, as is supervision of lower-level judges. Some have also claimed that the state courts lack qualified judges. The Texas constitution specifies only general qualifications for county judges and justices of the peace, who need not be lawyers. There may have been good reason for nonlawyers to serve as judges in a simple, rural setting, but today such judges may be an anachronism.

Partisan Election of Judges. The manner of selecting judges is another factor that affects their qualifications—Texas judges are chosen in **partisan elections** in which they run as Democrats or Republicans. Trial judges are elected to four-year terms and appeals court judges to six-year terms, but the governor has frequent opportunities to fill temporary vacancies when judges leave office before the end of their terms.

Although a majority of states elect their judges, critics regard this effort at popular control as undesirable. A judge may become too much the politician and too little the independent magistrate to apply the law uniformly. Several states have

| Reduction Veto
The power of governors in some states (but not Texas) to reduce amounts in an appropriations bill without striking them out altogether.

| Pocket Veto
A special veto power exercised by the chief executive after a legislative body has adjourned. Bills not signed by the chief executive die after a specified period of time. If the legislature wishes to reconsider such a bill, it must reintroduce the bill in the following session. The governor of Texas does not have a pocket veto.

| Partisan Election
An election between candidates who are nominated by their parties and whose party affiliation is designated on the ballot. In Texas, all state and county officials (including judges) are selected in this manner. Only municipal and some special district elections are nonpartisan in Texas.

FIGURE 19–1 | THE TEXAS COURT SYSTEM

Texas is the only state in the country, other than Oklahoma, with two "supreme courts."

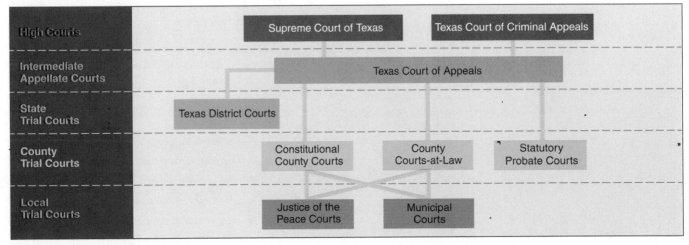

Source: University of North Texas libraries.

attempted to solve these problems by providing for nonpartisan election of judges. Others use an appointive-elective (merit) system in which the governor makes an initial appointment from a list nominated by a judicial qualifying commission. The electorate then decides whether to retain the appointed judge based on his or her record. The appointive-elective merit system is commonly known as the **Missouri Plan**. Still other states allow the governor or the legislature to appoint judges without a nominating commission, and a few do not require an election to retain the judge in office. Figure 19–2 illustrates the methods used initially to select supreme court judges in various states.

Local Government

The Texas constitution decentralizes governmental power by assigning many functions to units of local government, especially counties. Much of the counties' rigid organizational structure is set down in Articles 9 and 16. As a result of these provisions, voters of the entire state were once required to approve constitutional amendments to allow individual counties to abolish unneeded offices such as treasurer, weigher, surveyor, and inspector of hides and animals. The Texas constitution now authorizes county voters to abolish a number of offices, but there is no provision for county **home rule**. As in state government, the constitution divides and diffuses county powers through a plural executive system.

The legislature, which has the power to set up structures for city governments, has offered municipalities several standard alternative **general-law charters**. Cities with populations of more than five thousand may adopt home-rule charters and

| **Missouri Plan**
A method of selecting judges that combines appointment and election. Under the plan, the state governor or another official selects judges from nominees chosen by a nonpartisan committee. After a year on the bench, the judges face a popular election to determine whether the public wishes them to remain in office.

| **Home Rule**
The right of a local government to write a charter establishing any organizational structure or program that does not conflict with state law. In Texas, home rule is reserved for municipalities with populations over five thousand.

| **General-Law Charter**
A city structure established by statute. Most smaller Texas cities choose among several available options allowed by the state legislature.

FIGURE 19–2 | STATE-BY-STATE SELECTION METHODS OF SUPREME COURT JUDGES

Most states use a variety of methods to select their judges, with different procedures in different jurisdictions. The information presented here identifies the predominant method in each state.

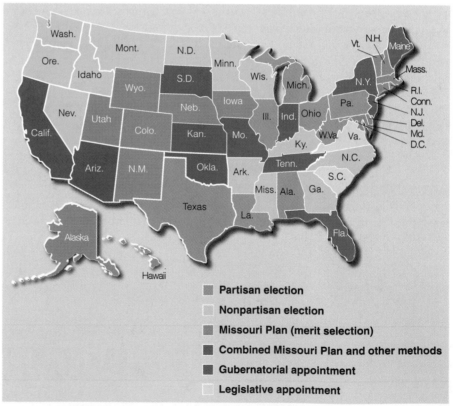

- Partisan election
- Nonpartisan election
- Missouri Plan (merit selection)
- Combined Missouri Plan and other methods
- Gubernatorial appointment
- Legislative appointment

Source: American Judicature Society.

establish any organizational structure or program that does not conflict with state law or the Texas constitution.

Generally, the legislature has the power to provide for the establishment of limited-purpose local governments known as **special districts.** Numerous special districts are also established by the Texas constitution itself, and to eliminate one of them requires a constitutional amendment. Many of the districts have been created to perform functions that general-purpose local governments, such as counties and cities, cannot afford because of constitutional tax and debt limits. Special districts have multiplied taxing and spending authorities and, except for school districts, operate largely outside the public's view.

| **Special District**
A local government that provides services to a jurisdiction that are not provided by general-purpose governments. Examples are municipal utility districts, hospital authorities, and transit authorities.

| The Constitution and the People

The Texas constitution defines the relationship between the state's government and its people, and in doing so it reflects basic American political culture. For example, its bill of rights contains provisions similar to those found in other state constitutions and the U.S. Constitution. Important areas in which the constitution affects the people of Texas include civil rights and liberties and voting rights.

Civil Rights and Liberties

As you learned in Chapter 4, the United States Supreme Court has interpreted the Fourteenth Amendment to extend many national constitutional guarantees to the states. The U.S. Constitution establishes only minimum standards for the states, however. The Texas bill of rights (Article 1) guarantees additional rights not specifically mentioned by the U.S. Constitution.

Texans' Rights under the State Constitution. Notably, Texas has adopted an amendment to prohibit discrimination based on gender. Similar guarantees were proposed as an Equal Rights Amendment to the U.S. Constitution, but it was never ratified by the states (see Chapter 5). The Texas constitution also guarantees victims' rights and forbids imprisonment for debt. A person who is mentally ill may not be committed for an extended period without a jury trial. The constitution also prohibits the suspension of the writ of *habeas corpus* under any circumstances. Article 16 protects homesteads and prohibits garnishment of wages except for court-ordered child support. (We describe the effect of these protections on bankruptcy proceedings in this chapter's *Politics and Civil Liberties* feature on the following page.) There is general agreement that the Texas bill of rights and other provisions guarantee the average citizen a greater variety of protections than most other state constitutions.

Rights Established by the Courts and the Legislature. Texas courts have interpreted some state constitutional provisions in a way that broadens basic rights beyond the minimum standards set by the U.S. Constitution. While the United States Supreme Court has refused to interpret the Fourteenth Amendment as guaranteeing equal public school funding,[1] the Texas Supreme Court interpreted the efficiency clause of the Texas Constitution (Article 7, Section 1) to require greater equality in public school funding between rich and poor school districts.[2]

Using Texas constitutional and **statutory law** (law passed by the legislature), Texas courts have struck down polygraph (lie-detector) tests for public employees, required workers' compensation for farm workers, expanded free speech rights of private employees, and affirmed free speech rights at privately owned shopping malls.

| **Statutory Law**
Law passed by legislatures and eventually compiled in law codes.

[1] *San Antonio Independent School District v. Rodriguez,* 411 U.S. 1 (1973).
[2] *Edgewood v. Kirby,* 777 S.W.2d 391 (Texas 1989).

POLITICS AND CIVIL LIBERTIES | Protecting the Homesteads of Bankrupt Texans

The Bankruptcy Reform Act of 2005 limited the Texas homestead exemption. Now, any homestead acquired within three and a half years preceding the date of bankruptcy filing has a maximum exemption of $125,000. Nevertheless, the federal government has allowed the states some flexibility in setting the rules under which bankruptcies occur. In particular, the federal government has let the states determine what kinds of property will be exempt from seizure by creditors as part of a bankruptcy proceeding.

The Texas constitution gives Texans perhaps the most generous exemptions in the nation. Current wages, no matter how high, are exempt from seizure to pay creditors. Income from pensions, annuities, and life insurance trusts is likewise exempt. A married couple may shelter up to $60,000 of personal possessions, including cars, clothes, jewelry, household effects, professional equipment, and animals. Most crucially, there is no limit on how much home equity can be exempt from seizure. (In most states, the limit is $60,000.) Furthermore, in rural areas, up to 200 acres of land are exempt—and 10 acres in a city.

BEATING THE SYSTEM

With such a system, Texas can be very generous to wealthy bankrupts. Doug Mall, a University of Houston law professor, observes, "Good lawyers are advising these people to sell all they can and sink it into equity in a big house."* Individuals who appear to have taken such advice include executives of Enron, the Houston energy firm that went bankrupt under scandalous circumstances, destroying the retirement savings of thousands of Enron employees. Kenneth Lay, former chairman of the Enron board of directors, who died in July 2006, lived in a condo appraised at $7.1 million. (Because of Lay's death, his fraud convictions were vacated and the government may not be able to collect from his estate regardless.) Former chief executive officer Jeff Skilling lived in a $4.2 million house before he was sentenced to twenty-four years in prison. Enron executives are the targets of dozens of multimillion-dollar lawsuits, but their home equity is exempt from seizure.

THE FEDS HAVE ANOTHER IDEA

The U.S. Congress has considered legislation that would cap home equity exclusions set by the states. Still, such legislation

This photo shows the Houston home of former Enron chief executive officer Jeffrey Skilling. Although Skilling's residence is protected against seizure under the Texas constitution, a federal forfeiture proceeding could override the state constitution. (AP Photo/David J. Phillip)

could not be applied retroactively to any bankruptcies filed before the law went into effect. Federal prosecutors working on the Enron cases, however, have come up with a possible way to seize the homes of Skilling and other Enron figures. This method is based on civil forfeiture, which we discussed in Chapter 1.

The provision of the Texas constitution that protects the homes of bankrupts can be overridden by federal forfeiture laws if the federal government can show that the houses were bought with tainted funds. "The federal forfeiture laws trump all manner of man-made and natural laws," says lawyer David Berg. "It is the black hole of Draconian law."†

FOR CRITICAL ANALYSIS

Why do you think the authors of the Texas constitution provided bankrupts such generous protection from creditors, especially given that many of the authors were wealthy men who were creditors themselves? What circumstances might these people, living in 1875, have envisioned as typical in a bankruptcy proceeding?

---

*Mary Flood, "Executives May Lose Suits, but All Is Not Lost for Them," *Houston Chronicle,* April 8, 2002.

†Kristen Hays, "Officials Seeking Former Enron Executives' Homes," *Laredo Morning Times,* February 28, 2004.

Suffrage

A major way in which state and local governments determine the character of our democracy is by setting suffrage requirements and administering elections. Article 6 of the Texas constitution deals with suffrage requirements. It denies the right to vote to persons under age eighteen, to certain convicted felons, and to those found mentally incompetent by a court of law.

Although constitutional restrictions on the qualifications of voters are now as minimal in Texas as in any other state, Texas voters still lack certain opportunities to participate in state government. The **initiative** (a vote on statutory or constitutional changes brought about by petition), the **referendum** (a vote on laws submitted to the people by the legislature or by initiative), and the **recall** (a special election to remove an official before his or her term expires) are available in many other states and even in some Texas cities, but not for statewide issues in Texas. Texas limits voters to ratifying constitutional amendments, approving a state income tax, and increasing legislative salaries. Political parties in Texas sometimes place referenda on their primary ballots, but they are not legally binding.

Initiative
A procedure by which voters can propose a law or a constitutional amendment.

Referendum
An electoral device whereby voters decide on proposals submitted by the legislature or by initiative.

Recall
A procedure allowing the people to vote to dismiss an elected official from state office before his or her term has expired.

Amending and Revising the Constitution

Given the level of detail in the Texas constitution, the ability to amend that document is of great importance. It is much easier to amend the Texas constitution than the U.S. Constitution.

Rules for Amending the Constitution

The Texas constitution provides that constitutional amendments must be proposed by two-thirds of the total membership of each chamber of the legislature (at least twenty-one senators and one hundred representatives). **Ratification** requires approval by a majority of those persons voting on the amendment in either a general or a special election. Since 1876, Texans have amended their constitution 439 times, more than twice as frequently as the average state. Only three states have amended their constitutions more than Texas: Alabama (766), California (513), and South Carolina (485). Table 19–4 compares the process of amending the Texas constitution with the methods used to amend the constitutions of the federal government and the other states.

Ratification
Formal approval.

TABLE 19–4 | PROCEDURES FOR AMENDING CONSTITUTIONS

AMENDING PROCEDURES	TEXAS CONSTITUTION	U.S. CONSTITUTION	THE FIFTY STATES' CONSTITUTIONS
Proposal	Two-thirds of the entire membership of both chambers of the legislature	(1) Two-thirds of those voting in both chambers of Congress or (2) a national convention called by petition of two-thirds of the states	20 states require a two-thirds vote, but 11 permit a three-fifths vote, and 18 permit a simple majority vote; 18 permit proposal by initiative.
Ratification	A majority of those voting on the amendment	(1) Three-fourths of state legislatures or (2) three-fourths of state ratifying conventions	44 other states have the same requirement as Texas; 4 require a majority of those voting in the entire election; New Hampshire requires a two-thirds vote; Delaware requires no ratification by voters; and some states allow alternative methods.

Source: Council of State Governments, *Book of the States 2006.*

Difficulties in Revising the Constitution

Although the Texas constitution has been frequently amended, successive attempts to revise it have met with failure. Ironically, in 1972 Texas voters had to amend the constitution in order to provide for its revision. Under the provisions of that amendment, the legislature established a constitutional revision commission of thirty-seven members appointed by the governor, lieutenant governor, speaker of the house, attorney general, chief justice of the supreme court, and presiding judge of the Court of Criminal Appeals.

The Proposed Constitution of 1975.   The commission made several proposals for revising the constitution. Meeting in 1974, the legislature acted as a constitutional convention and agreed to many of these recommendations. Ultimately, though, the convention divided over the issue of a "right-to-work" provision (under which workers have the right not to join labor unions), and supporters could not muster the two-thirds vote needed to submit the final document to the electorate.

The New Constitution Goes to the People.   The proposed revision remained alive, however, in another form. In the 1975 regular session, the legislature proposed eight constitutional amendments to the voters. Together, these amendments were substantially the same as the proposal defeated in the convention. If the amendments had been adopted, they would have shortened the constitution by 75 percent through reorganization and through elimination of statute-like detail and deadwood. The legislature would have been strengthened by annual sessions, and a salary commission would have set the legislators' salary. Although limited to two terms, the governor would have been designated as the chief planning officer and given removal powers and certain powers of fiscal control. The court system would have been unified and its administrative procedure simplified. Local governments would have operated under broader home-rule provisions, and counties would have been authorized to pass ordinances and abolish offices.

The People Turn It Down.   Opponents' chief arguments against the amendments focused on fear that they would result in more power for the legislature, greater government costs, and the possibility of an income tax—all of which are serious issues for many Texans. Because the legislature had written the proposals, it was easy for Texas voters to see such things as annual sessions and changes in legislative salaries as a "grab for power" that would substantially increase government expenditures. Despite an emotional campaign, only 23 percent of registered voters cast ballots in the election, and they overwhelmingly rejected the proposed amendments.

| The Texas Constitution Compared

The U.S. Constitution is widely regarded as a model and is revered by most scholars. State constitutions, including the Texas constitution, have attracted more criticism. Here, we compare the various constitutions and examine the reasons that many state constitutions have been so frequently criticized.

The National Constitution

As of 2007, the U.S. Constitution had been in effect for 218 years but had been formally amended only twenty-seven times. It has endured mammoth and fundamental changes in government and society largely because it does not lock government into a rigid framework. Because the U.S. Constitution deals only with the most basic elements of government and leaves much to Congress, the president, and the courts, few formal amendments have been necessary.

Although the U.S. Constitution provides for a representative government, the nation's government was hardly democratic in the earliest years. During the Jeffersonian and Jacksonian eras, it became more democratic as political parties developed, states lowered suffrage requirements, and voters were allowed to choose electors in the electoral college.

The 1800s saw the growth of the new nation from thirteen fledgling agricultural states on the Atlantic coast to a vast industrial nation stretching across a continent. In the modern era, America moved from the position of a third-rate international power to a dominant role in the world. Since the New Deal of the 1930s, government has increasingly provided a safety net for disadvantaged Americans. Much of the nature of the national government is determined by statute, executive order, and court interpretation, so these changes did not require changing the language of the U.S. Constitution.

Criticisms of State Constitutions

Although state constitutions vary considerably (see Table 19–5), most are much longer than the national Constitution, and they frequently deal with details of both structure and policy. Consequently, as changing political and social conditions require changes in government structure and policy, formal constitutional amendments are necessary. Critics of existing state constitutions have advanced several reasons for both the amount of detail in these constitutions and the frequency with which they are amended:

1. Public officials, interest groups, and voters seem to view their state constitutions as more than the basic law of the state. They fail to make a clear distinction between what ought to be and what ought not to be in the constitution. Thus, critics claim, all sorts of inappropriate details are included in the documents. A constitution is fundamental law; it deals with the basic principles of government. It is organic law—the superior law that establishes governing institutions and organizes their formal power relationships. Accordingly, constitutions ideally should describe how decisions will be made but should not actually establish policies that must change with political and social conditions.

2. States have added detailed amendments to overturn the effects of controversial court interpretations of general constitutional provisions. For example, supreme courts in Hawaii, Massachusetts, and Vermont found that denying the benefits of marriage to same-sex couples was a violation of their state constitutions.[3] As a

| Organic Law
The superior law that establishes governing institutions and organizes their formal power relationships.

---

[3]*Baehr v. Lewin*, 852 P.2d 44 (Hawaii 1993); *Baker v. Vermont*, 744 A.2d 864 (Vt. 1999); and *Goodridge v. Department of Public Health*, 798 N.E.2d 941 (Mass. 2003).

TABLE 19–5 | STATE CONSTITUTIONS' LENGTH AND NUMBER OF AMENDMENTS

CONSTITUTIONAL CHARACTERISTICS	TEXAS CONSTITUTION	U.S. CONSTITUTION	AVERAGE FOR STATE CONSTITUTIONS
Length (words)	90,000	7,575	36,332
Amendments	439	27	139
Age (years)	131	218	105
Frequency of amendment	3.4 per year	Once every 8 years	1.3 per year

Source: Council of State Governments, *Book of the States 2006*.

result, Hawaii and a majority of other states (including Texas) added amendments to define marriage as an exclusively heterosexual right.

3. Institutions and interest groups frequently feel safer when their interests are protected in a constitution, which is usually more difficult to change than ordinary law. As a result, many state constitutions include long lists of protections for vested interests.

4. State governments have a peculiar position in the federal system. They are presumed to have all the powers that have not been explicitly denied them. Thus, citizens fearing strong governments have felt the need to impose detailed constitutional restrictions.

5. When state governments misuse their powers, the response is usually to place constitutional limitations and restrictions on such powers. The result is a longer constitution but—it is argued—not a more responsible government. A government bound by a rigid constitution may be unable to respond effectively to changing needs. Excessive restrictions might actually guarantee unresponsive, and thus irresponsible, government.

6. Critics maintain that state constitutions are poorly written and arranged. Some provisions are so ambiguously drafted that they are interpreted to be even more restrictive than the constitution's framers intended.

Criticisms of the Texas Constitution

The Texas constitution has been characterized as an example of poor writing. Only two state constitutions are as concise as the U.S. Constitution (fewer than 10,000 words). Nevertheless, at almost 90,000 words, the Texas Constitution is one of the least concise in the nation. One sentence rambles on for 765 words, and several approach 300 words in length. The document is ambiguous, overlapping, and poorly organized. For example, the provisions dealing with local government are scattered throughout Articles 3, 5, 8, 9, 11, and 16. This poor draftsmanship has led to a restrictive interpretation of the constitution's provisions and, on the part of Texas citizens, ignorance of its contents and confusion as to its intentions.

The continuing need to amend a detailed and restrictive state constitution means that citizens are frequently called on to pass judgment on proposed amendments. Although some maintain that giving Texas voters the opportunity to express themselves on constitutional amendments reaffirms popular control of government, there is little voter interest in amendment elections. Faced with trivial, confusing, or technical amendments, often as few as 10 to 15 percent of the voting-age population vote on constitutional amendments, and turnout has occasionally dropped even lower.

MAKING A DIFFERENCE | Amending the Texas Constitution

The Texas constitution is often criticized because it is so frequently amended. On the one hand, as you know, frequent amendment of the constitution has a number of drawbacks. On the other hand, it gives you an extraordinary opportunity to participate in the continual rewriting of the state's fundamental law.

Why Should You Care?

Because so many detailed provisions of Texas law are spelled out in the state constitution, much legislative business is of necessity placed before the voters at large. This gives you and other Texas citizens a degree of control over legislation that may affect your life. Such control is not possible at the national level and indeed is available in few other states to the same extent as in Texas.

What Can You Do?

You can express your approval or disapproval of proposed constitutional amendments by voting in general and special elections, by writing letters to the local newspaper or other publications, or by participating in campaigns for or against an amendment. Although many amendments deal with technicalities and details, they will be explained in local newspapers, and summaries are available through the Texas Legislative Council, a research body set up by the legislature. Constitutional amendment analyses can be found in Texas Legislative Council publications and at the council's Web site at **www.tlc. state.tx.us**. The League of Women Voters often provides good analyses as well. Local chapters of the League of Women Voters can be found in large-city telephone directories. Be aware that special interest groups often pay for television and newspaper ads on amendments, and their ads often reflect their biases.

Key Terms

bicameral legislature 612	general-law charter 618	partisan election 617	removal power 616
budgetary power 616	home rule 618	plural executive 616	special district 619
community property 608	house and senate journals 613	pocket veto 617	special session 613
deadwood 615	indirect appointive power 616	ratification 621	statute-like details 615
directive authority 616	initiative 621	recall 621	statutory law 619
enabling act 609	item veto 616	reduction veto 617	
foreclosure 608	Missouri Plan 618	referendum 621	
Freedmen's Bureau 608	organic law 623	regular session 612	

Chapter Summary

1 A constitution sets forth fundamental law that establishes basic governing principles and structures. Some constitutions, like that of Texas, also go on to establish many details of routine government and require frequent amendment to reflect new realities. In such circumstances, it is difficult for the state government to develop effective programs without first amending the constitution. Numerous amendments dealing with minor issues are added, like patches, to the constitution.

2 Constitutions are always the result of a political process in which framers reflect their values, hopes, and fears. The current Texas constitution was written in the period following Reconstruction after the U.S. Civil War. Most white Texans viewed the Reconstruction state government as extravagant, tyrannical, and abusive. In 1875, an elected state constitutional convention reacted to the Reconstruction regime by limiting state government in almost every imaginable way. Voters overwhelmingly approved the convention's work in 1876.

3 The Texas constitution strictly limits the sessions and salaries of state legislators and includes many statute-like details that the legislature cannot change without a constitutional amendment. Special sessions are especially restricted, and procedures in both regular and special sessions are circumscribed.

4 The governor of Texas is limited in his or her role as chief executive because Texas has a plural executive system that includes many independently elected executives over which the governor has no control. The governor lacks most of the powers of typical executives to hire, fire, direct, and budget. Although Texas has had some powerful governors, such as Allan Shivers and John Connally (discussed in Chapter 18), they became effective despite the constitution—not because of it.

5 The power of the courts to interpret the Texas constitution is limited by its detail. Texas divides its final court of appeal into two bodies—the Court of Criminal Appeals and the Texas Supreme Court—and also establishes intermediate courts of appeals and district, county, and justice of the peace courts. Judges are chosen in partisan elections. Critics say that judges elected in this way may become too concerned with political matters.

6 County and special district governments are particularly limited by constitutional and statutory requirements. Only large cities have the considerable flexibility of home rule. All local governments face debt and tax restrictions.

7 The Texas constitution includes a bill of rights that is more expansive than that in most constitutions. At the state level, the constitution does not provide for the initiative, referendum, or recall, though such mechanisms may be available at the municipal level.

8 Critics find the Texas constitution confusing. It contains not only the fundamentals of government but also detailed provisions concerning matters that might better be left to the ongoing institutions of government. It is long, it contains much deadwood, and many say that it is poorly drafted and disorganized. Reformers argue that a constitution should include only organic law; that is, it should organize responsible institutions of government. If it goes beyond fundamentals, it becomes a rigid legislative code, difficult to change and baffling to voters.

9 Texas has one of the longest, most detailed, and most frequently amended state constitutions in the United States, but it does reflect Texans' general political culture and their skeptical view of government. It is clear why Texans wrote such a constitution and have held to its principles for so long.

Selected Print and Media Resources

SUGGESTED READINGS

Angell, Robert H. *A Compilation and Analysis of the 1998 Texas Constitution and the Original 1876 Text.* Lewiston, N.Y.: Edwin Mellon Press, 1998. This work contains a version of the Texas constitution with amendments placed in appropriate spots and obsolete text deleted, thus yielding a more coherent document. In his thoroughgoing analysis of the text, Angell argues against assertions that the original 1876 constitution was excessively limited.

Campbell, Randolph B. *Grass-Roots Reconstruction in Texas, 1865–1880.* Baton Rouge: Louisiana State University Press, 1998. Campbell, who later authored *Gone to Texas: A History of the Lone Star State,* uses statistics and case studies to determine the actual impact of Reconstruction at the county level. Campbell notes that the counties with the largest number of freed slaves experienced the greatest degree of political controversy and armed violence.

May, Janice C. *The Texas State Constitution: A Reference Guide.* Reference Guides to the State Constitutions of the United States, no. 26. Westport, Conn.: Greenwood Press, 1996. May, of the University of Texas, is an expert on the Texas constitution. Her work analyzes Texas constitutional and political history from Spanish and Mexican rule to the present. An analytical commentary on the current constitution, with amendments, makes up the heart of the book.

Moneyhon, Carl H. *Texas after the Civil War: The Struggle of Reconstruction.* College Station: Texas A&M University Press, 2004. This new account of Reconstruction in Texas may become a standard. Moneyhon argues that the Civil War shook, but did not destroy, antebellum society. He pays due attention to the violence that accompanied the end of Reconstruction.

E·MOCRACY | Constitutions Online

You can easily research constitutions and constitutional documents using the Internet. A wide variety of sites provide annotated copies of the U.S. Constitution. Other sites provide collections of URLs that lead you to constitutions of nations around the world. Finally, several sites can direct you to the constitutions of the various American states. Cornell University and FindLaw sponsor two sites that provide access to state constitutions. The FindLaw site is of particular interest because it is probably the most comprehensive source of free legal information on the Internet. The addresses of the Cornell and FindLaw sites are in the following *Logging On* section. For additional Web resources on constitutional topics, see the *Logging On* section in Chapter 2 of this text.

| Logging On

The U.S. Constitution sets the context for the powers of the state of Texas in relation to the national government and the other forty-nine state governments. Search for key cases such as *Marbury v. Madison, Fletcher v. Peck,* and *McCulloch v. Maryland* at

www.findlaw.com

Search for the U.S. Constitution—Articles 4 and 6 and the Tenth and Eleventh Amendments. Click on annotations to read United States Supreme Court interpretations of these important constitutional provisions.

The complete text of the Texas constitution, with all seventeen articles, is at

tlo2.tlc.state.tx.us/txconst/toc.html

Click on "3—Legislative Department." Then click on "Sec. 29" and notice that even the enacting clause for legislation is included in the constitution. Click on "16—General Provisions" and then "Sec. 6" and notice the detail. Read deadwood provisions in Article 9, Section 14. Contrast the legislative and executive articles (3 and 4) of the Texas constitution with those of Illinois (Articles 4 and 5) at

ilga.gov/commission/lrb/conmain.htm

Read constitutional amendments that have been proposed by the Texas legislature at

www.lrl.state.tx.us

Several sites on the Web provide collections of links to state constitutions.

The Cornell University Law School maintains one such collection. Go to

www.law.cornell. edu/states/listing.html

Another collection is part of the highly useful FindLaw site at

www.findlaw.com/ 11stategov/indexconst.html

| Online Review

At **www.politicalscience.wadsworth.com/ schmidt12**, you will find a free Study Guide to this book. For each chapter, there are two online quizzes to help you master the material.

• The PoliPrep Self-Study Assessment provides a pretest for each major section of the chapter. PoliPrep then generates a customized study plan. After you complete the study plan, a posttest evaluates your progress.

• The Tutorial Quiz for each chapter provides questions on the chapter contents, including the features. The questions are organized to match the major sections of the chapter.

20 | Texas Interest Groups

What If . . .
Campaign Contributions Had
to Be Reported within Twenty-Four Hours?

BACKGROUND

Voters need information to make intelligent decisions. Representative democracy requires that information be provided to citizens continuously. Yet one piece of information that does not appear in advertisements, party platforms, or candidate speeches is the source of a candidate's funds. The citizen who knows the source of campaign funds knows what kinds of interests support a candidate and may seek his or her favor in the policy arena. This knowledge is incomplete—after all, other factors influence an officeholder's behavior—but may be worth having. Laws that require reporting may also influence who gives and how much. Thus, laws on this subject need to be well thought out.

Texas requires candidates to report the source of campaign contributions of more than fifty dollars to the Texas Ethics Commission. Officeholders not running for reelection must also report contributions. Texas law requires campaign contributions to be reported thirty days and again eight days before a primary or general election. The second reporting period is very close to the election. Contributors may time their giving to avoid public awareness of the contribution before the vote. As a result, information about the contribution may not be available until after the voters have made their choices.

State and local officials who receive reports from candidates are not required by law to post or publish the information. Whether the public learns the contents of candidates' campaign-finance reports depends on whether the media examine them and report their findings in a timely fashion. The media vary in their diligence in reporting this information. Furthermore, the press often focuses more on who has failed to file a report than on which interests are supporting particular candidates.

WHAT IF CAMPAIGN CONTRIBUTIONS HAD TO BE REPORTED WITHIN TWENTY-FOUR HOURS?

As an alternative to the current system, candidates might be required to do the following within twenty-four hours of receiving a campaign contribution:

- Report the name, address, and affiliation of the donor.
- Post the information on the candidate's Web site.
- Transmit the information in electronic format to the Texas Ethics Commission for posting at its site.

If candidates had to report contribution data in this way, citizens could obtain the information quickly. This is especially valuable now that the election law allows early voting weeks before Election Day. Up to 40 percent of ballots cast are now submitted early.

If information were available via this method, candidates might be more careful to avoid actions that appear to value special interests over the general interest. Contributors also might seek to avoid making donations that might be viewed as corrupt.

YEAR-ROUND REPORTING

Reporting between elections is also important. The present law acknowledges this but requires only annual disclosure. Members of the legislature are forbidden to receive contributions thirty days before the regular session and during the session. As a result, the period running from the election to thirty days before the session begins is prime time for contributions from interests with issues before the legislature. This is also the last opportunity for an interest that has backed a losing candidate to make amends through a "late-train" contribution to the winner.

With twenty-four-hour reporting, the problems of undue influence that result from contributions during the presession period could be reduced. Further benefits could follow from disallowing contributions to the governor before and during a legislative session, because the governor's support of or opposition to a measure may be critical to its fate. Other executive officials could be required to report continuously in the same manner as legislators. After all, elected executive officials below the gubernatorial level are lobbied heavily, because each has the power to promulgate administrative rules that have the force of law. Judges, too, could be included in such a plan.

FOR CRITICAL ANALYSIS

1. Why might making information readily available not result in increased public knowledge about candidates' interests?
2. What arguments could be made on the basis of privacy rights to restrict public knowledge about contributions?

People in the United States unhesitantly endorse participation in the political process. Constitutions and laws guarantee the right to do so. Public education encourages it, yet many citizens fail to participate. Whether people choose to be involved depends on a host of factors, including their personality types, the time they have available, their degree of understanding of government's impact on their lives, their confidence in themselves, their trust in government, and their concern for others. People also differ in their concepts of **civic duty.**

Participation is most effective when it is undertaken collectively—that is, by interest groups—rather than by isolated individuals. This chapter identifies what interest groups are and do, explores the constitutional protections for interest groups, classifies groups by type, and discusses the craft of lobbying and the interaction that occurs between the public and government in policymaking. As an example of interest group activities, the chapter concludes with a discussion of the struggle over funding for public schools in Texas.

| Civic Duty
A citizen's understood obligation to register, to vote, to be knowledgeable, and to take action to make the community a better place.

What Are Interest Groups?

Individuals may act alone to influence government, and millions do. As discussed in Chapter 7, when individuals join with others in an organizational structure designed to express their preferences to government, however, they act as an *interest group*. The media frequently speak of the interests of women, minorities, or employers, but individuals who share an interest must unite in a cooperative effort to promote some policy objective before they can be thought of as an interest group.

In summary, interest groups are collections of individuals having shared interests who are organized to influence government decision makers. Usually, they hire *lobbyists* to represent them to public officials. Many interest groups are private institutions pursuing public-policy goals on behalf of their members. Government agencies also may function as interest groups. The concerns of interest groups are narrower than those of political parties. Unlike parties, they do not nominate candidates for office, but because the individuals who hold office affect what government does, interest groups often endorse and support candidates favorable to their cause. At the same time, they often work with members of both parties to secure their goals.

Interest groups are also sometimes called *pressure groups*. The two terms basically mean the same thing. The term *pressure group* comes from the fact that interest groups try to apply pressure on decision makers as they seek favorable policy outputs. Pressure on the officeholder can come from the voting power of the group and the value of its endorsement, campaign contributions, and volunteer help in elections.

Constitutional Guarantees

The constitutions of the United States and of Texas guarantee to citizens the right to political participation through voting, speaking, and writing and petitioning government "for redress of grievances." To peaceably assemble *for political expression* is likewise clearly encouraged. The Texas constitution says it very well:

> The citizens shall have the right . . . to . . . apply to those invested with the powers of government for redress of grievances or other purposes, by petition, address or remonstrance [formal protest]. (Article I, Section 27)

The First Amendment to the U.S. Constitution makes our liberties even more clear:

> Congress shall make no law . . . abridging the freedom of speech, or of the press; or the right of the people peaceably to assemble, and to petition government for redress of grievances.

In these constitutional expressions, free speech, a free press, and the right to join together in political parties and interest groups are guaranteed. These guarantees and the right to vote are essential to democracy. Representative democracy, however, creates dangers. The liberty that comes with it requires citizens to inform themselves about political issues and involve themselves in the choices to be made. Both extreme zealousness and apathy can present dangers to democracy. Highly organized and active groups can threaten the well-being of the unorganized majority. The organized and zealous can be expected to triumph over the apathetic or unorganized. Hence, small factions of the population, rather than the majority, may control selected policy areas.

What Interest Groups Do

The primary goal of interest groups is to influence the branches of government to produce policies favorable to their members. It follows that groups also seek to block policies harmful to their members. Very few, if any, government policies affect all classes of citizens equally. Some benefit, some suffer inconvenience, and others experience economic loss from any policy adopted.

There are direct and indirect ways to influence policymaking. Lobbying, filing suit in a court of law, serving on state boards and commissions, and mounting demonstrations are direct means of influencing government decisions. Indirect methods include electioneering, making campaign contributions, educating the public, and socializing with public officials.

Interest groups are instrumental in drawing citizens into political participation to influence public policies, but most often they draw in *selected* citizens in a way that promotes interests that may be narrow and selfish. Indeed, there are two views of interest groups, one positive and one negative.

Positive Views of Interest Groups.   The favorable characterization of interest groups focuses on their ability to draw citizens into the political processes of communicating with public officials and voting. Certainly, democracy calls for politically attentive and active citizens. Interest groups, in this view, educate their members about issues and mobilize them to participate in constitutionally approved ways. Simultaneously, interest groups inform and educate public officials.

Negative Views of Interest Groups.   Critics, in contrast, focus on the harm that can result when powerful groups demand that public policy reflect their values. Private meetings with public officials present no opportunity for rebuttal of the views that are advanced. Critics worry about corruption and intimidation of public officials by what they call "special interests." The need for campaign contributions, they believe, makes elected officials especially vulnerable to pressure. We give an example of a possible **conflict of interest** in this chapter's *Politics and Conflicts of Interest* feature.

The bottom line for critics is their concern that special interests will prevail over the desires of the general public. As Bob Stein, a professor and dean at Rice University, has said, "Long before the legislature sits down and writes a bill, the lobbyists are there."[1] Table 20–1 summarizes the positive and negative aspects of interest groups.

Types of Interest Groups

Interest groups can be classified in a multitude of ways. The most simple is to categorize them as economic, noneconomic, or mixed. Table 20–2 on page 634 provides classification and examples of Texas interest groups.

| Conflict of Interest
A situation that arises when a legislator, bureaucrat, executive official, or judge can make an official decision that results in a personal economic advantage. The result is a potential or real conflict between the personal interests of the officeholder and the general interests of the public.

---

[1]Clay Robison, "Weak State Government Paved Way for Lobbyists," *Houston Chronicle*, December 29, 2002, p. A1.

POLITICS AND CONFLICTS OF INTEREST | Lobbying by Government Officials

A *conflict of interest* is a situation that arises when a legislator, bureaucrat, executive official, or judge can make an official decision that results in a personal economic advantage. The result is a potential or real conflict between the personal interests of the officeholder and the general interests of the public.

An illustration of the type of activity that many people might consider a conflict of interest came to light just before the legislative session that began in January 2003. State senator Jeff Wentworth, representing the four-hundred-member law firm of Locke, Liddell and Sapp, met with top officials of the Houston Community College System (HCCS) at a private luncheon to discuss a lobbying contract between the law firm and the college. No members of the public or the media attended.

The discovery of this event raised questions about whether a public body—in this example, HCCS—should spend taxpayers' money to lobby, as well as about the apparent conflict of interest that may result when a state senator attempts to secure a lobbying contract for the law firm for which he works.*

FOR CRITICAL ANALYSIS

Texas law does not prohibit lawmakers from representing interest groups, even when the groups are lobbying on issues scheduled for legislative attention. Given the part-time nature of the Texas legislature, some would claim that prohibiting legislators from working for such clients would impose an undue economic burden on the lawmakers. How much weight should be given to this argument, and how might the possible conflicts of interest resulting from such practices be addressed?

*Ron Nissimov, "HCCS Hires Firm after Closed Lunch," *Houston Chronicle*, January 3, 2003, p. A29.

Economic.   Economic interests operating at the state level include business and the professions, education, local government, agriculture, and labor. Each interest seeks financial advantages for its members. Business and agriculture are always interested in keeping their taxes low, securing benefits called **subsidies,** avoiding regulation, and obtaining government contracts. Labor unions seek legislation to obtain workers' compensation and workplace safety benefits and to make it easier to organize (unionize) labor.

Noneconomic.   Noneconomic groups seek the betterment of society as a whole or reform of the political, social, or economic system in ways that do not directly affect their members' pockets. Environmental and political reformers maintain that society in general benefits from their programs. Clean air, clean water, and fair elections are said to promote the well-being of all. Patriotic, civic, and religious groups also fall within this classification.

Government.   Levels and branches of government also lobby. They are not generally recognized as interest groups, but they are affected by what other political institutions and jurisdictions decide. Governors have staff that promotes their political agenda in the legislature. Cities, school districts, and other local governments are seriously affected by legislative decisions on finances and local government authority.

| Subsidies
Grants or special tax exemptions provided by the government to individuals or businesses in the private sector.

TABLE 20–1 | POSITIVE AND NEGATIVE ASPECTS OF INTEREST GROUPS

POSITIVE	NEGATIVE
Increased political representation	Narrow interests
Political participation/mobilization	Secret communications with officials
Education of membership	Corruption/intimidation of public officials

TABLE 20–2 | EXAMPLES OF TEXAS INTEREST GROUPS

ECONOMIC		NONECONOMIC		MIXED	
TYPE OF GROUP	**EXAMPLES**	**TYPE OF GROUP**	**EXAMPLES**	**TYPE OF GROUP**	**EXAMPLES**
Agriculture	Texas Farm Bureau	**Patriotic**	American Legion	**Education**	Texas State Teachers Association Texas Association of School Administrators
Business	Texas Association of Business and Chambers of Commerce	**Public interest**	Texas Common Cause Texans for Public Justice	**Race and ethnicity**	League of United Latin American Citizens NAACP (African Americans)
Labor	American Federation of Labor–Congress of Industrial Organizations (AFL-CIO)	**Religious**	Texas Christian Life Commission	**Local government**	Texas Municipal League Texas County Judges and Commissioners Association
Occupations and professions	Texas Association of Realtors Texas Trial Lawyers Association	**Environment and recreation**	Texas Nature Conservatory Texas Committee on Natural Resources		

They are also affected by rules set by state executive-branch agencies. Therefore, they must protect and/or promote their interests by employing lobbyists or reassigning employees to be lobbyists as needed.

At times local governments may even have to sue their creator, the state, to satisfy their needs. The case of *Neeley v. West Orange-Cove Consolidated Independent School District*[2] is a well-known example from 2005. The strategy here was to force the state to adequately fund public education. A state district court, later upheld by the Texas Supreme Court, agreed that reliance on local property taxes to fund education created such disparities among districts that any semblance of equal funding for children was lost. The decision led to two regular and three special sessions of a legislature consumed in conflict over who should pay how much to constitutionalize funding.

Mixed. Many groups do not fit neatly into economic or noneconomic classifications because they pursue social goals that have clear economic effects. For example, discrimination on the basis of age, disability, ethnicity, gender, or native language is a social problem that also has negative consequences on wages and promotion within the workplace. Groups pursuing equality in society and the workplace can thus be classified as mixed or hybrid organizations.

Similarly, education and local government groups want economic benefits such as greater state support and increased salaries and benefits for their employees. In addition, blocking **unfunded mandates** imposed by the state and obtaining more local control over their affairs are often objectives. Many of the goals of such groups can also be characterized as noneconomic. Improvements to the educational system, for example, can be seen as contributing to the betterment of persons other than the educators themselves.

| Unfunded Mandate
A requirement imposed on a lower level of government by a higher level of government. The requirement is not accompanied by the funds to pay for the resulting expenses.

---

[2]176 S.W.3d 746 (2005).

Why People Join Interest Groups

As explained in Chapter 7, people join interest groups for many reasons. To influence government, you need to be a joiner. Most individuals lack the status, knowledge, political skills, and funds to operate alone and be successful. Joining together creates a network of like-minded people who can pool their talents and other resources to obtain their political ends. Furthermore, work and family obligations leave little time for most people to become experts on the complexities of policy issues. The solution is to create or "hire" an organization to advocate or protect their economic, recreational, social, or political interests. The organization can monitor activities in the capital and alert its members to the need to call or write public officials and influence decisions relevant to the members. A group with many members contacting officials at the same time has a better chance of obtaining favorable results.

The Benefits of Socializing. Joining a group can advance career and social goals as well. Certainly, belonging to a collectivity that meets periodically will increase your circle of friends and business contacts. Getting to know people in your trade or profession can lead to job offers, knowledge exchange, and enjoyment of others who share your interests. Hence, active membership leads to networking that has economic, social, and political benefits.

Other Benefits. Sometimes people in a particular profession join a group because the culture of the profession requires membership—that is, it may be seen as unprofessional not to be a member. People are expected to stay current in their fields, and participation in a professional group may help meet this goal. All organizations exist to disseminate information or knowledge, but an organization may also offer other tangible benefits. For example, malpractice insurance is available to teachers, attorneys, and medical personnel through organizational memberships. A monthly or quarterly magazine or newsletter may attract membership. Publications of nature and conservation groups are often so beautiful that one might join simply to enjoy such groups' magazines.

The Ultimate Goal. Whatever people's reasons for joining, we should not be surprised to learn that their ultimate goal is to influence government. After all, the government regulates our occupations and professions. It decides who pays how

Shown in front is Texas state representative Paul C. Moreno giving a news conference where he accused the Texas attorney general of placing economic interests ahead of the rights of persons with disabilities. Are there economic issues that might be addressed by a group representing such persons? Are there noneconomic issues? Would you classify such a group as economic, noneconomic, or mixed? (AP Photo/Harry Cabluck)

much in taxes and who receives the benefits of those tax dollars through public spending programs. Few aspects of life are untouched by the political system. Those who do not pay attention to what is going on in Washington, Austin, and city hall will nonetheless feel the effects of what occurs there.

Influencing Government

As you learned earlier in this chapter and in Chapter 7, the techniques used by interest groups can be divided into direct and indirect techniques. With *direct techniques,* groups attempt to influence government officials by dealing with them personally. With *indirect techniques,* groups attempt to influence officials by influencing other parties, such as the electorate at large.

Direct Techniques of Exercising Influence

Using lobbyists to contact government officials is the most obvious direct technique. Lawsuits and demonstrations can also fall under this heading.

Lobbying the Legislative and Executive Branches. Lobbying is direct contact between an interest group representative and a legislative- or executive-branch official or employee for the purpose of influencing a specific public policy outcome.[3] Most people understand that the legislature creates, finances, and changes government programs. Therefore, it comes as no surprise that individuals and groups affected by these decisions attempt to participate in the lawmaking process by lobbying legislators. Awareness that privilege, prestige, and funds are at stake in the executive decision-making process that follows the lawmaking is not so common.

The executive branch, or the administration, is charged with the **implementation** of legislative policy. The legislature delegates a great deal of **discretion** to executive agencies, both directly and indirectly. This freedom allows the administrative agencies to complete the policymaking process by issuing rules or regulations that specify how the law will be applied to actual situations. Interest groups seek to shape the regulations that will apply to them.

In short, because what government does is not simply a function of legislative decisions, lobbyists must actively monitor and seek to influence executive branch rulemaking and enforcement as well. The importance of this is revealed in the Texas Ethics Commission Report of 2002—a year when the legislature was not in session—which showed that nearly two thousand registered lobbyists were at work in Texas.

Filing Suit in Court. There are several reasons why organized interests use the courts to further their causes. One is lack of funds or public support. It can be less expensive to file a suit than to successfully influence the legislature. Furthermore, public opinion is supposed to be irrelevant to judicial outcomes.

A second reason for using the courts is to seek a more favorable interpretation of the law than the one employed by the enforcing agency. "More favorable" can mean less costly to the profession, business, or individuals who must obey the rules set by the overseeing agency. Additionally, an interest group that has lost the political struggle may be able to challenge the constitutionality of the law or the means of enforcement selected by the administering agency.

A third reason is to delay the implementation of a new law or rule. Courts often postpone implementation of the law or rule while the case is pending. The members of the group bringing the litigation can then continue to operate as before, in (presumably) a more profitable and unrestrained manner. Filing suit, even when one expects to lose, may delay application of costly rules. If the interest group does

Implementation
The carrying out of laws by executive officials and the bureaucrats who work for them.

Discretion
An official's power to make decisions based on personal judgment rather than on the specific requirements of the law; the freedom to decide or make choices.

---

[3]Texas Government Code Section 305.003a.

prevail in court, two positive outcomes for the interest are possible: (1) the previous way of doing things may be restored, or (2) the state may have to wait until the next session of the legislature to take action.

A fourth reason to file suit is to gain public attention. Media coverage of the suit brings the issue to the attention of the branch or level of government that has the power to produce the change the group seeks. The publicity that results from being sued may provide an incentive for the government to enter into negotiation with the lawsuit's filer to change the policy without the necessity of judicial action.

Suits, then, can be utilized to delay, stop, or start action. The goal depends on the needs of the interest group.

Advising and Serving on State Boards.   State law in Texas generally requires that a majority of the members of appointed boards come from the profession, occupation, business, or activity the board is regulating. The mere existence of such a requirement is testimony to the power of special interest groups to shape government decisions in Texas. The board members and commissioners appointed as a result of this requirement are part-time officials but full-time practitioners of the activity that they have the power to regulate. They simultaneously exercise power as state officials and function as members of a special interest group that may testify and present information to the agency.

We can call this blurring of the line between the state and the special interest co-optation. Critics of interest groups believe that the public interest is endangered when state officials can act as representatives of the group the agency regulates. As mentioned earlier, a conflict of interest exists when the decision maker is personally affected by the decision she or he makes.

The newly created Texas Residential Construction Commission (2003) is testimony to the power of Texas home builders to create an agency to protect themselves, for the law requires home buyers to take complaints to mediation rather than to the courts. The law requires that four members come from the home-building industry and the remainder represent "citizens." Governor Rick Perry has filled four citizen seats with supporters having ties to the construction industry. Thus, the nine-member commission has eight members with ties to either home building or construction, even though the job of the commission is to be an "impartial" judge of complaints against the home builder.

Public Demonstrations.   Marches and demonstrations are used periodically to obtain publicity for a cause. Press coverage is all but guaranteed. This sort of "theater" is especially suited to television news. Texas correctional officers used demonstrations at the state capitol to attract attention to their low pay in the summer of 2000, for example.[4] The challenge for interest groups using this method of pressuring the state is to simultaneously enlist enough members to be impressive and still keep control of the activity. Violating the law, blocking traffic, damaging property, and using obscenities are usually counterproductive. Such conduct may antagonize fellow citizens or the public officials with the power to change the conditions at which the protest is aimed.

Indirect Techniques of Influencing Government

Attempts to influence the voting public are the most obvious indirect technique used by interest groups. We can also characterize as indirect those interactions with government officials that are not specific attempts to address a particular piece of

Faculty, staff, and students of the University of Texas at Austin and UT Hearts of Texas volunteers form the "Heart of Texas" on the main mall of the campus in Austin. The UT Hearts of Texas promotes charitable giving and volunteerism and participates in the Texas State Employee Charitable Campaign. Organizations affiliated with UT and other large universities are important interest groups. (AP Photo/UT Austin)

| Co-optation
The "capturing" of an agency by members of an interest group. In effect, governmental power comes to be exercised by a private interest.

---

[4]Michael Kurtz, "Prison Guards March for Pay Increase," *Austin American-Statesman,* July 5, 2000, p. B1.

legislation or a particular administrative rule. Socializing at parties and other recreational events may allow lobbyists to create a positive impression on officials they may later seek to influence.

Electioneering.   Although interest groups do not nominate candidates for office, one candidate may be more favorable to their cause than another. The organization may endorse that candidate and recommend that its members vote for that person. The organization's newsletter or magazine will be used to carry this message.

A second means of helping candidates favorable to the group's interests is to create a **political action committee (PAC)**. This structure, separated from the interest group legally, has as its sole purpose the funneling of funds to candidates for office.

Educating the Public.   An interest group clearly benefits from providing the general public with messages that build a positive image of the interest the group supports. Everyone knows that reputation is important. Industry interest groups may employ the services of public relations people to enhance the industry's reputation for honesty, satisfactory products and services, concern for the well-being of customers, and good citizenship. Organizational magazines, annual reports to stockholders, and press releases to newspapers are some of the ways to build a reputation and educate the public about the wisdom of policy proposals supported by the organization. Occasionally, a group purchases advertisements on radio and television and in magazines and newspapers to shape and mobilize public opinion on behalf of the interest or to neutralize opposition to what the interest wants to do.

It is important to those who seek government action that they articulate the need or problem in exactly the right language. Their goal must be to evoke a favorable response and to stay in control of the definition of the problem. It is advantageous to educate public officials before an issue becomes public. Once an issue is public, opponents may try to reverse the interest group's definition—that is, to redefine the issue and put the interest group's position in a negative light. For example, those who favor vouchers that can be used to pay for tuition at private schools, including church-sponsored schools, may emphasize their belief that vouchers will improve the education of children who are ill served by the existing system. Opponents may attempt to convince the voters that such aid violates the principle of separation of church and state. Most political struggles are group-against-group battles, and words are the weapons of political combat.

Socializing.   Interest group representatives know that friendships can be formed at social functions. Informal occasions allow people to interact in comfortable settings. A lobbyist may invite a public official to lunch or to a social gathering to establish a positive relationship. Formal occasions designed to honor a person can also serve to build positive relationships. Invitations to speak before a group are another way to cultivate public officials.

The purpose of social invitations is to establish a positive impression that pays off in favorable votes or other friendly decisions by government officials. Interest groups view socializing with public officials as a good "investment," whether or not there is an immediate need for the official's support.

Access to public officials is the prerequisite for influencing public decisions. Lobbyists seek to "get in the door" to discuss a matter of concern in time to shape the public-policy outcome. Indirect techniques of influencing government often pave the road for direct techniques. Groups that have established good relations with public officials are more likely to enjoy access, but even the most successful groups can expect to lose sometimes.

| **Political Action Committee (PAC)**
A committee set up by and representing a corporation, labor union, or special interest group. PACs raise and give campaign donations on behalf of the organizations or groups they represent. In Texas, they must report their income and expenditures to the Texas Ethics Commission.

| **Access**
The ability to contact an official either in person or by telephone. Campaign contributions are often given in hopes of gaining access to elected officials.

Which Interests Are Powerful?

Twenty years ago, businesses and the professions tended to be the most powerful interests in Texas. They still are, in spite of an explosion in the number of interest groups in recent years. Generally speaking, the newer interest groups, such as the environmentalists, have not supplanted the old. In conservative, pro-business Texas, that is not surprising. Politicians typically identify the most powerful interests in Texas as the following:

- The Texas Trial Lawyers Association.
- The Texas Medical Association.
- The Texas Association of Realtors.
- The Texas State Teachers Association.
- The Texas Oil and Gas Association.

Other groups have more than average influence:

- The Texas Motor Transport Association.
- The Texas American Federation of Labor–Congress of Industrial Organizations (AFL-CIO).
- The Texas Independent Producers and Royalty Owners Association (oil and gas).
- The Texas Association of Business and Chambers of Commerce.
- The Texas Municipal League.
- Savings and loan associations (S&Ls).
- SBC Communications (now renamed AT&T).[5]

These groups have the funds to maintain permanent headquarters in Austin and to employ clerical and research staff, as well as lobbyists, to make their presence felt. These resources, when competently managed, enable some interest groups to create a need for themselves within the halls of government. Research shows that the

[5]Ronald Hrebenar and Clive Thomas, "Who's Got Clout? Interest Group Power in the States," *State Legislatures,* April 1999; and Keith Hamm and Charles Wiggins, "The Transformation from Personal to Informational Lobbying," in Ronald Hrebenar and Clive Thomas, eds., *Interest Group Politics in the Southern States* (Tuscaloosa: University of Alabama Press, 1992), pp. 158–162.

A physician representing Physicians for Social Responsibility refers to a map that locates mercury pollution sites in Texas during a news conference. She joined a group of environmentalists who laid out a legislative agenda to reduce pollution and protect public health. How might other interest groups argue against additional environmental legislation? (AP Photo/Harry Cabluck)

number-one element determining the political power of a group is how much public officials need the group. Officials may need the group's expertise to help the state solve problems. They may depend on the group for campaign contributions. Perhaps the state's economy depends on the economic sector the group represents. There are many explanations of public officials' need for a particular interest group.[6]

The Strength of the Business Lobby

Records of registered lobbyists kept by the Texas Ethics Commission show that two-thirds of the registered groups represent some form of business. Business is a comprehensive category. Therefore, we should not think of all business interests as being alike. There are both powerful and weak interests within this classification. Furthermore, independent and small businesses frequently seek policy outcomes opposed by larger enterprises.

The number of lobbyists by subject-matter category, shown in Table 20–3, reflects the importance of business interests. Unraveling the lobbyist registration reports to determine the number of lobbyists representing specific trade groups, business associations, or other interests is challenging. A number of organizations listed may be supported by the same benefactors and represent the same industry, business, or activity. It is easier to identify the lobbyists representing a particular company, profession, union, or employee association. Among business interests, 57 percent are associated with an identifiable company. Many companies, however, are also represented through **umbrella organizations,** in which industries, wholesalers, producers, retailers, and others join together to promote their collective interests. In other words, a firm may employ lobbyists directly and also through these umbrella organizations. (Refer back to Table 20–2 on page 634.)

The Effects of Poverty

Not all interests are well represented in the political system. Low levels of political participation in Texas are associated with the below-average educational attainment of many Texas citizens. Education and income are also related. Compared with the rest of the country, Texas has a relatively high proportion of poor people

| Umbrella Organization
An organization created by interest groups to promote common goals. A number of interest groups may choose this mechanism to coordinate their efforts to influence government when they share the same policy goals. The umbrella organization may be temporary or permanent.

---

[6]Hrebenar and Thomas, "Who's Got Clout?"

TABLE 20–3 | NUMBER OF LOBBYISTS REPORTING BY SUBJECT-MATTER CATEGORY, 2005

SUBJECT-MATTER CATEGORY	NUMBER OF LOBBYISTS
Business and commerce	1,058
Corporations and associations	792
City government	604
Taxation	965
Civil remedies	542
State agencies, boards, and commissions	943
Consumer protection	586
County government	562
Insurance	811
Health and health care	812
Environment	711
Economic and industrial development	757
Tort reform	731
State finance	779
Utilities	778

Source: Texans for Public Justice, *Austin's Oldest Profession: Texas's Top Lobby Clients and Those Who Support Them, 2005 Edition.* Available at **www.tpj.org/reports/austinsoldest06/clients.html**.

in its population. The poor and marginalized do not participate actively in politics. These factors bias the political system toward the upper-middle and upper classes. For the most part, people in these classes have the income to obtain education that pays off economically and socially.

How Groups Use Their Power

A well-organized interest group will attempt to inform its membership, through newsletters or other means, about important matters likely to come before the legislature and executive agencies. Groups also seek to organize their membership into telephone chains or mail chains, or both. When a "hot" issue is about to come to a vote, an "action alert" can be dispatched. Members are asked to contact public officials and express the group's position on the issue. The intent is to apply outside (grassroots) pressure while lobbyists work inside with public officials in Austin.

Special interests with full-time staffs and multiple lobbyists that also disperse sizable sums of money in campaign contributions achieve more than interests that cannot support such activities. There are, however, additional factors involved in interest group success. The media can sway the opinions of the public and of government officials on many issues. The governor may intervene in affairs before executive agencies or in legislative issues and change the outcome. Access and goodwill "bought" by campaign contributions can be nullified by media exposure, public opinion, and the countervailing power of rival interest groups. Thus, as we observed earlier, powerful groups may win more often than they lose, but they are not guaranteed success.

Iron Triangles and Issue Networks

Political scientist Ernest Griffin observed nearly seventy years ago that the relationships and interactions among members of the legislature are generally weaker than the relationships between the legislators and the lobbyists, academics, and high-ranking bureaucrats who interact to address specific needs and solve specific problems.[7] When these participants are active, they become a subsystem of the legislative or administrative decision-making process.

Iron Triangles. In the literature of political science, a stable interaction pattern among legislative committee members, high-ranking bureaucrats, and representatives of special interests is called an *iron triangle*, which we first discussed in Chapter 13. The members of such a triangle can be very powerful when they operate out of public view. Indeed, they may control policy outcomes. This is especially likely if the policy issue is very narrow and affects only a small segment of society.

Issue Networks. The iron triangle arrangement does not describe the environment of all or even most decision making. Another kind of arrangement, called an *issue network*, was also discussed in Chapter 13. Participants in a network are interested in a general policy area, such as health, transportation, or rural economic development, but as the specific topics change, the participants may change. For example, some participants concerned about health care focus on cost and access to services, while others are concerned more with professionalism and the supply of health-care providers. Thus, people representing interests move into and out of the subsystem as the issue focus changes.[8]

---

[7]Ernest Stacey Griffin, *The Impasse of Democracy* (New York: Harrison-Hilton Books, 1939), p. 182.
[8]Hugh Heclo, "Issue Networks and the Executive Establishment," in Anthony King, ed., *The New American Political System*, 2d ed. (Washington: American Enterprise Institute Press, 1990).

Another key difference between issue networks and iron triangles is that typically, networks exist that are opposed to each other on policy issues. As a result, more players are drawn into issue networks than are likely to participate in an iron triangle. While issue networks have more participants than iron triangles, the numbers involved are still small. The general public is absent from most public policy-making and policy-implementing events.

Broad and Narrow Concerns.   Iron triangles are most likely to control rather routine decisions. Economic concerns dominate their agenda. Often, what motivates the actors is subsidies in the form of grants or tax deductions that favor specific economic interests.

Issue networks are broader in their interests and, hence, have more participants. Their focus may be either economic or social, or both. The participants may be members of professional and social organizations that are national in scope and that distribute information through newsletters and other publications. They may strive to bring legislative and bureaucratic actors together in agreement on an approach to a problem.

Factors That Affect Interest Group Power

The Texas political environment has its peculiarities, and it differs from the national political environment and the environments in many other states. The special characteristics of Texas politics affect organized interest groups in a number of ways. Here, we look at a variety of factors that determine the strength of interest groups in general relative to other players in the political game.

A Culture of Nonparticipation

One hundred and fifty years of one-party politics has probably given many Texans less incentive to participate in political affairs than citizens living in states with competitive parties. The absence of two competitive parties has also helped to empower elites and strengthen special interests. Historically, conservative Texas political elites used their control of state government to enact laws that discouraged mass political participation. The poll tax, annual voter registration, and the white primary were examples. (We discussed historical barriers to voting in Chapters 5 and 9.) These barriers to participation promoted a culture of nonparticipation by the masses that has yet to be undone.

Party Competition

Studies by political scientists consistently show that where political parties are weak, interest groups are strong. States with a long history of two-party competition have weaker interest groups than states with weak party development.[9] Parties in competitive states must appeal to the majority of the population to have a chance of winning elections. They cannot limit themselves to one issue or a limited number of issues, as interest groups do, and expect to win a majority of the votes.

In Texas, one-party politics has left the parties weak. In the 1990s, the growth of the Republican Party raised the possibility that Texas would, for the first time, enjoy competition between two strong parties. The elections since 2002, however, suggest that Texas has simply been in transition from one dominant party (Democratic) to another (Republican). The two-party system in Texas may simply have been a passing fancy. Republican Party control now extends to the two highest courts in the state, both houses of the legislature, and all elected officers in the executive branch.

[9]Hrebenar and Thomas, "Who's Got Clout?"

We can expect that a one-party Republican system will be as vulnerable to interest group domination as a one-party Democratic system.

The Part-Time Legislature

With more than 23 million people, Texas is the second most populous state in the Union. It is the only large state with legislative sessions that are limited in length and frequency. In addition, legislative pay is very low, and member turnover is fairly high. The result is a legislative body that is easily influenced by special interest groups. Professor Cal Jillson of Southern Methodist University has put it this way: "If you meet only occasionally, get paid little and have weak staffs, you are at the disposal of the lobby because you have to go to them to get information."[10]

There is no question that the quality of staff in the legislative and executive branches has significantly improved since the 1950s. Better sources of information and research are now available within the government itself. Therefore, public officials may depend somewhat less on special interests for information. Still, this change may be nullified by the dependence of elected officials on campaign funds. The Center for Public Integrity claims that the percentage of Texas legislators with financial ties to special interests is the highest in the United States.[11] The author of this report suggests that the low pay of Texas legislators makes them highly vulnerable to interest group pressure. While that may be true, it is also clear that in the political culture of Texas, politicians accept large campaign contributions as "the way it is done," and the public is resigned to this system.

The Decentralization of Executive-Branch Power

Texas has a plural executive. Power is divided among numerous independently elected executives—the governor, the lieutenant governor, the attorney general, the comptroller, an agricultural commissioner, a land commissioner, and the multiple members of the Railroad Commission and the State Board of Education.

---

[10]Clay Robison, "Weak State Government Paved Way for Lobbyists," *Houston Chronicle*, December 29, 2002, p. A1.

[11]John Dunbar, "Low-Paid Texas Lawmakers Tops in Connections to Lobbyists: Is Their Pay a Factor?" *The Public-I*, October 28, 2000.

Texas lieutenant governor David Dewhurst, left, applauds with Texas Railroad Commission chairperson Victor Carrillo during the commission's oil and gas industry annual meeting. In other states, administrators appointed by the governor wield the powers that in Texas are exercised by the elected Railroad Commission. What kinds of issues might be raised during an election campaign for a seat on the commission? (AP Photo/Jack Plunkett)

| Fragmentation
In state government, a division of power among separately elected executive officials. A plural executive is a fragmented executive.

Government by Commission. The fragmentation, or division of power, within the executive branch is enhanced by the practice of establishing independent boards and commissions as structures for implementing the law. The governor appoints the membership of most unelected boards and commissions—usually a third of the membership every two years—but has little power to remove those appointed. Reformists have argued that if each agency were headed by a single executive who was appointed and removable by the governor, agencies would be more responsive to the broader values represented by the governor rather than those of the specific clientele the agencies serve.

Fragmentation and Interest Group Power. The plural executive and fragmentation of authority mean that there is no strong central executive authority with the legal power to control the executive branch of government. This situation increases the vulnerability of each executive agency to special interest influence. The result may be policies established with less regard for the general public interest than for special interests. Increasing this likelihood is the requirement (previously discussed) that a majority of members on many boards and commissions be engaged in the profession, business, or activity that the board or commission regulates.

Laws

Reformers have long advocated laws to regulate the relationship between public officials and private parties who seek special favors from government. Texas, as we see later in this chapter, does have laws that define lobbying and require reporting of information about the lobbyist, his or her employer, and the expenses associated with trying to influence government decisions. The Texas Ethics Commission makes this information generally available. The press has a special obligation to examine this information and report it to the public in a usable form. If the voters receive this information, they may be able to act on it.

The Media

The media are essential to the democratic system. Radio, television, Internet, and print journalists serve as watchdogs of government. Public officials and bureaucrats know that every decision they make, as well as their general conduct, is fair game for the news media. In a democracy, the public has a right to know what public officials are doing, and the public relies on the media to tell it.

The media not only relay the activities of government to the people but also transmit the people's moods and messages to the leaders of the state. In addition, members of the media communicate their own opinions to both the public and the government. The media are a link between the people and the government, but they are not necessarily a neutral one.

The Media and Open Government. The media's interests are allied with the interests of the people when the media demand that the government's business be conducted in public view. The media work to promote open meetings, open records, and recorded votes on policy decisions in the legislature and in administrative boards and commissions. Openness is the enemy of conflicts of interest and other questionable conduct, and the press delights in exposing such behavior to the public. Thus, the interaction of lobbyists and public officials is a matter of interest to the media.

Coverage of News from the Capital. The media, however, labor under self-imposed restraints on reporting. These restraints may be based on the fact that newspapers,

Governor Rick Perry talks with the media. Any governor of Texas has a high profile and can therefore use the media to communicate his or her agenda to the public effectively. How do the media create problems for a governor? (AP Photo/Harry Cabluck)

news magazines, and radio and television stations are businesses concerned with making a profit. Austin, the state capital, is not the home of the largest newspapers or broadcasting channels in Texas It is costly for media outlets not located in the capital to employ journalists stationed in Austin, and declining newspaper readership has led to the closing of several Austin news bureaus. In 2004, the last of the TV news bureaus, A. H. Belo Corporation (owner of the *Dallas Morning News* and WFFA), "destaffed" its Austin operation. KHOU Houston and KENS San Antonio had previously closed their operations except for the presence of the local Austin news manager.

This has affected TV coverage of state government as well, because media chains generally own newspapers as well as radio and TV stations in their market areas. Increasingly, local station managers de-emphasize coverage of the legislature, governor, and high courts, saying that members of the public are disinterested.

Duplication of Effort.   Some observers argue that if the media combined their staffs and worked cooperatively, there would be sufficient press personnel to cover many more aspects of state government. Breadth and depth of reporting could be improved by pooling staffs, and there would be no increase in cost to the individual media companies.

The Media versus the Government.   The media thrive on scandals, corruption, inefficiencies, mistakes, and conspiracies in the public sector. Money in politics and cozy relationships between public officials and interest groups make good news stories. This seems true even though most of the Texas mass-distribution dailies appear to share the conservative politics that are dominant in Texas. It is true even though competition between newspapers and broadcast media is limited because major newspapers own radio stations and can own at least one key television station in their market area.

Evidence that Texas media, slimmed down as they are, remain important in informing the public and pointing out potential wrongdoing in Texas can be appreciated from the following headlines and programming:

- "Craddick Denies Pushing Insurance Law to Help Daughter," *Austin American-Statesman*, December 4, 2002.
- "Questioning the Ethics of Perry's Bahamas Trip" (editorial), *Houston Chronicle*, April 25, 2004.
- "Special Session's Winners: Lobbyists," *Dallas Morning News*, May 9, 2004.
- "Special Session," KLRU and selected PBS stations in Texas, 2006.

New Technologies

Perhaps the biggest change affecting existing power relationships in the state in recent years is the increasing use of the computer as a political tool. Databases allow groups to keep track of members and finances more easily than in the past. Also, interest groups that are starved for economic resources now have a medium—the Internet—that connects them to their members and to state decision makers. Contacting public officials has never been easier. The Internet cannot completely overcome the disadvantages of scarce funds and other resources, but it does make possible the raising of new and underrepresented voices.

It is too early to know whether the Internet will compensate for the increasing concentration of ownership in print and electronic media. The Internet's political uses are rapidly increasing, nonetheless. The giant media empires will continue to play the major role as news suppliers—but countless individuals and independent opinion and news sources may use the emerging technologies to engage in the political arena.

Constituent Influence

Interest group strength on any issue is affected by the values, attitudes, and beliefs of the voters. No elected official can consistently ignore the "folks back home." Most state representatives and senators have lived in their districts for a long time and may have been born and raised there. They know the culture of their home regions. On many issues before the legislature, they know what the voters would want them to do. In other words, even in the absence of public input, legislators may understand the preferences of their constituents.

Constituent Influence and the Part-Time Legislature.   Texas has a part-time legislature that is only in regular session for 140 days every odd-numbered year. Hence, members are home in their districts 590 days out of 730 in every two-year period. Furthermore, they are home almost every weekend during the four and a half months of the session. Members do not have to exert much effort to find out what their constituents want (presuming that the constituents *know* what they want).

When District Opinion Is Clear.   To please a special interest, would an elected representative vote against the desires of his or her constituents when these desires are clear and known? The answer is "probably not." Further, if an experienced interest group knows that the voters in a legislator's district disagree with the interest group's positions, it probably will not seek to punish the legislator for representing her or his district. In contrast, when the voters back home have no consensus on an issue, then interest groups, fellow legislators, the governor, and the legislator's party may struggle for the legislator's vote.

Interest Groups as Checks on Other Interest Groups

On issues of major public importance, an interest group is likely to be confronted by one or more other interests that do not want the same outcome. In such circumstances, the groups may offset each other's influence. On more obscure issues, a group may be fortunate enough to find itself without opposition. Whether one or many special interests are involved in the policymaking process, however, the status, resources, size, reputation, and lobbying skills of a group affect its ability to influence legislators and agency heads. These factors, plus the substance of what the group is seeking and the financial condition of the state, combine to shape policy outcomes.

Obscure Issues. When the outcome a special interest seeks is very narrow or specific, the general public and other interest groups may not be aware of the issue. Even if they are, they may see no reason to intervene; the matter may simply be of no concern to them. Under such circumstances, the special interest that is concerned may need to persuade only a few key people, such as legislative committee chairs and presiding officers, to win its objective. If the committee approves, the vote on the floor will most likely be favorable.

Broad or Controversial Issues. When a special interest seeks a policy change that affects the political, social, or economic balance of power, however, there will be much greater participation and conflict. Group will be pitted against group, and the general public may be drawn in because the media will transmit stories of conflict to their readers, listeners, and viewers.

As the number of participants in any political debate increases, the possibilities for conflict increase, and the influence of each participating interest group diminishes. Many groups and ordinary citizens are interested in broad or controversial issues, such as tax policy, education, campaign-finance reform, gun control, and abortion. Such issues may generate substantial political conflict. The challenge for the public officials involved is to lead the warring groups to a compromise. Without that, no policy output will be produced.

How to defend homeland security without damaging the border economy is one example of an issue that pits interest groups against each other at the national level. For most Texas interests, however, the health of the border economy is the greater value.

Campaign Contributions

Money in politics is a "hot" topic, in part because of a startling increase in the amount of funds raised and spent by candidates for elective office at all levels. A candidate for state representative in a metropolitan area of Texas may spend over $200,000 to win an office that pays $7,200 a year.

Campaign contributions for legislative and statewide offices often come from large donors. These donors may represent banks, insurance companies, the petrochemical industry, physicians, trial lawyers, real estate agents, teachers, individual corporations, and others who use political action committees (PACs) to funnel money to candidates. These donors participate because the state legislature, the governor, the Railroad Commission, and other agencies and officers make decisions that affect their economic well-being. Donors contribute to gain access to public officials. A substantial contribution may create a sense of obligation on the part of an elected official to listen when the contributor calls. Ordinary citizens may find access more difficult.

According to Texans for Public Justice, statewide and legislative candidates raised $195 million in the 2002 election cycle, supplying $68 million of it from their

A member of Texans for Public Justice, a group that monitors money in Texas politics, shows a report entitled, "Ain't Nobody's Business." The report concluded that few politicians and officials in Texas fully report lobbyists' payments. How might Texas do a better job of tracking lobbying activities? (AP Photo/Harry Cabluck)

own pockets and obtaining the other $127 million from donors. According to FollowtheMoney.org, preliminary data from the 2006 election cycle for all statewide and legislative races indicated expenditures may have ran as much as $258 million.

Just 382 donors accounted for almost one-half ($60 million) of the $127 million supplied by donors. PACs and businesses contributed $50 million. Individuals contributed $77 million. With the exception of two attorneys and two lobbyists, the top fifty individual contributors in the state were all business executives. Yet 60 percent of the races for district-level offices went uncontested, and just 20 percent of those races were truly competitive, with the winner receiving less than 60 percent of the vote.[12]

"Late-Train" Contributions

One of the biennial rituals in Austin occurs after each election when special interest groups hold fund-raising events to honor selected legislators. State law forbids giving and accepting campaign contributions thirty days before the start of a legislative session and throughout the session, causing a rush of fund-raising activity during the five weeks following Election Day. Note that the fund-raising occurs after the election, not before. The reason, as one lobbyist has said, is to "pay the price of admission," or to obtain good access to legislators. Postelection contributions, or **"late-train" contributions,** are commonly given to the winning candidates in the executive branch as well. Losers are rarely the beneficiaries of such largess. During this five-week period in 2002, $30 million was distributed among the (winning) candidates.[13]

| Late-Train Contribution
A contribution given to a candidate in the period that begins after an election and ends thirty days before a regular legislative session.

The Effect of Contributions on the System

Do campaign contributions buy sponsorship of bills and special favors? The press—and much of the public—thinks that they do.[14] Lobbyists and legislators claim they do not.

---

[12]*Money in PoliTex: A Guide to Money in the 2002 Texas Elections* (Austin: Texans for Public Justice, 2003). Available at **www.tpj.org/publications/reports/index.html**.

[13]*Ibid.*

[14]James Gibbons, "Officials Come and Go; the Lobby Rules," *Austin American-Statesman*, January 27, 2003.

The increasing volume of campaign contributions noted earlier and the 98 percent increase in the number of lobbyists from 1988 to 2005 are evidence that would tend to support the perceptions of the press and the public.[15] In 1999, lobbyists outnumbered legislators approximately nine to one.[16] Records of the 2003 legislative session show that lobbyists earned between $132 million and $276 million trying to influence decisions of the Texas legislature. These figures do not include expenditures to influence the members of the executive branch.

The Regulation of Lobbying

Lobbyists and organizations that spend more than a specified amount attempting to shape public decisions are required to register and file reports with the Texas Ethics Commission. Appropriate behavior of both lobbyists and public officials is spelled out in Chapter 305 of the Government Code of Texas.

Who Must Register and Report Lobbying Costs?

Not all lobbyists are required by state law to register and report their activities. Classes of lobbyists not required to register and report include state officials and state employees who lobby, even if lobbying is their principal function. Also exempt are individuals from the private sector who are not paid for their services and do not directly spend any money to influence legislative or administrative action.

Those who do have to register and report are private-sector lobbyists who pass the "compensation threshold" of $1,000 in salary per quarter year or the "expenditure threshold" of $500 per quarter year. These rules seem simple and straightforward, but an examination of the law reveals that not all compensation and expenditures are counted as lobbying. Exempted from reporting are the following:

- Compensation received to prepare for lobbying.
- Office expenses, including telephone, fax, copying, office supplies, postage, dues and subscriptions, transportation, and the costs of clerical help.
- Costs associated with events to which all members of the legislature are invited.[17]

These and other exemptions in the law mean that a very incomplete picture of the "investment" in lobbying by interest groups is made available to the people.

What Must a Lobbyist Report?

The lobbyist registration form requires the lobbyist to reveal the following:

- For whom he or she lobbies—information about these clients and employers.
- The policy areas of concern.
- The compensation category into which the salary or reimbursement received falls.
- The name of, and information about, anyone who assists the principal lobbyist through direct contact with public officials.

Activity reports must be filed by the tenth day of each month for any lobbyist who foresees expending more than $1,000 per year. Those who spend less need only file annually.[18]

---

[15]*Austin American-Statesman*, May 5, 1999, p. B2.
[16]Texans for Public Justice, *Austin's Oldest Profession: Texas's Top Lobby Clients and Those Who Support Them*, 2005 Edition. Available at **www.tpj.org/reports/austinsoldest06/facts.html**.
[17]Texas Ethics Commission, *Lobbying in Texas*, Part IIIA.
[18]*Ibid.*

Reporting on Clients. Very often, a firm or entity represents multiple clients before the state legislature and administrative agencies. The reporting law requires a lobbyist working for a lobbying firm to report who pays the firm to represent its interests to the government. Without such a requirement, those who wanted to influence legislative and executive officials anonymously could simply hire someone else to lobby on their behalf. For many years, in fact, this guarantee of anonymity existed in Texas.

Financial Reporting. As noted, the lobbyist's compensation and expenditures are reported in broad categories rather than in actual amounts. Some believe that this practice understates the influence of money on policymaking. We consider two examples of financial reports to illustrate the problem.

One report was filed with the Texas Ethics Commission by Electronic Data Systems Corporation (EDS) of Dallas in 1995. Forty-two lobbyists were identified in four pay categories: thirty-one were paid from $0.00 to $9,999.99; two received from $50,000.00 to $99,999.99; seven obtained from $150,000.00 to $199,999.99; and one was paid from $200,000.00 to $999,999.99. EDS, in other words, spent somewhere between $1,400,000 and $3,008,990, but the exact amount is unknown.[19] (In 1999, EDS reported using twenty-eight lobbyists and paying between $1.8 million and $2.5 million. Why the difference? Issues before the legislature were of less concern to EDS four years later.[20])

As another example, in 2003 Southwestern Bell Telephone reported having twelve paid and fourteen unpaid lobbyists at the time of filing and sixty-five "prospective" lobbyists with salaries set but not paid. The payroll for the session was between $3,935,000 and $7,600,000. Again in 2005, Southwestern Bell, renamed AT&T, led all others in lobby contracts and expenditures.[21]

Criticisms of the Reporting Standards. Some critics of the law maintain that its provisions continue to leave the public ill-informed about the extent of lobbying. One area of concern, as already indicated, is financial reporting. Critics have suggested that the actual compensation and expenditures of a lobbyist should be disclosed, rather than broad categories. This additional detail would require little effort, because the lobbyist must have the actual figures to know which category to mark on the form.

Reporting on which policy area a lobbyist seeks to influence can also be rather vague. The lobbyist, again, need only check a box on the form. Such a requirement may hide as much as it reveals. Requiring lobbyists to reveal more specifically what they are lobbying about would enable the public to see where corporations, trade associations, labor unions, and individuals were concentrating their efforts.

To provide a clear picture of lobbying activity, Texas could require lobbyists to list the numbers of the bills they have lobbied for and the rulemaking hearings before executive agencies at which they have testified. This, of course, would require more time and expense in filling out the activity forms. Many believe that Texas does not require this additional information because special interests have successfully lobbied the legislature to keep the lobbying law relatively weak.

What We Know about Lobbying. Thanks to the research of Texans for Public Justice and the Texas Ethics Commission, several interesting facts about the lobbying industry in Texas are clear:

---

[19]Texas Ethics Commission, *List of Employers and Clients*, 1995, pp. 63–65.
[20]Texas Ethics Commission, *List of Employers/Clients with Lobbyists Sorted by Employer/Client Name*, 1999, pp. 59–60.
[21]Texans for Public Justice, *Austin's Oldest Profession: Texas's Top Lobby Clients and Those Who Service Them: 2004 Edition*, Part II, "Lobby Clients," p. 1; Texans for Public Justice, *Austin's Oldest Profession: Texas's Top Lobby Clients and Those Who Support Them*, 2005 Edition. Available at **www.tpj.org/reports/ austinsoldest06/facts.html**.

- Special interests entered into 7,455 lobby contracts with 1,525 lobbyists in 2005.[22]
- Sixteen identifiable industry groupings spent more than $1 million each to have their interests protected or advanced.[23]
- Most lobbyists are affiliated with law firms in Texas.

Table 20–4 shows details on the industries spending the most money to influence Texas state government and the number of lobby contracts entered into by each.

We also have information about expenditures in a few categories that do require detailed reporting. Expenditures of over fifty dollars a day on members of the state legislature for food, drink, transportation, or lodging or in the form of a gift must be reported by name, date, place, and purpose.[24] Expenditures for broadcast or print advertisements, mass mailings, and other communications designed to support or oppose legislation or administrative actions also must be identified.

What Is Not Reported as Lobbying. Campaign and late-train contributions to public officials are not lobbying expenses as defined by law, even though the state recognizes their potential to influence policymaking. As noted earlier, such contributions cannot be made less than thirty days before a legislative session or during the session. This restriction is intended to prevent corruption or the appearance of corruption. Campaign contributions are thus reported to the Texas Ethics Commission separately from lobbying expenses.

Registration and the Legislature

Members of the Texas legislature are provided with a list of registered lobbyists and their clients by February 1 of each legislative (odd-numbered) year.[25] The public may obtain copies of registration and activity reports from the Texas Ethics Commission. Much of the information is available from the Ethics Commission on the Internet or on paper.

---

[22]Ibid.

[23]Ibid.

[24]Texas Ethics Commission, *Lobbying in Texas*, Part IVB.

[25]Texas Government Code Section 305.011.

TABLE 20–4 | NUMBER AND MAXIMUM VALUE OF LOBBY CONTRACTS ISSUED BY INDUSTRY GROUPINGS

INDUSTRY GROUPNG	NUMBER OF CONTRACTS	VALUE OF CONTRACTS
Finance	538	$10,275,279
Insurance	536	8,565,309
Real estate	336	8,770,123
Energy and natural resources	910	20,790,311
Communications	400	9,400,143
Health	911	17,970,371
Miscellaneous business	870	16,398,372
Agriculture	179	3,230,072
Transportation	348	5,039,182
Lawyers and lobbyists	334	9,380,153
Ideological and single issue	1,224	20,035,596
Construction	242	4,630,134
Electronics and computers	313	6,310,091
Labor	137	2,690,042
Unknown	66	810,033
Other	91	1,440,033
Total	**7,455**	**$304,122,043**

Source: Texans for Public Justice, *Austin's Oldest Profession: Texas's Top Lobby Clients and Those Who Service Them*, 2005 Edition. Available at **www.tpj.org/reports/austinsoldest06/clients.html**.

There is much evidence that lawmakers' regulation of lobbying remains, in the public's mind, "unfinished business" and controversial. The legislature "tweaks" the laws frequently in response to suspected or verifiable scandal. In 2001, for example, a new conflict of interest statute directed the Ethics Commission to write rules requiring lobbyists to provide written notice to the commission and to their clients when they represent multiple clients who may have incompatible legislative goals. It is a common practice for a lobbyist in Texas to represent multiple clients. Because many firms represent many clients, the possibility of a conflict exists when different people in the firm represent clients with opposing legislative objectives. It can be argued, of course, that this change to the law benefits the interests that hire lobbyists more than it does the general public.

The Craft of Lobbying

Those who directly contact public officials to influence their behavior will find their work easier if they are extroverted and enjoy socializing. The lobbyist's first job is to become known and recognized by members of the legislature and by any executive officials relevant to the interest he or she represents.

Lobbying Before the Legislative Session Begins

Before a legislative session begins, a lobbyist must have successfully completed several tasks:

- Learn who is predisposed to support the lobbyist's cause, who is on the other side, and which members can be swayed.
- Memorize the faces of the members, their nonlegislative occupations, the counties they represent, and a little about their families.
- Establish rapport through personal contact with the members of the legislature.
- Get to know the staffs of legislators, because the members can be influenced through them.
- Know the legislative issues, including the arguments of opponents.

Honesty Is the Best Policy.   To maintain relationships with legislators, the lobbyist must provide sound, accurate information about the legislation the lobbyist's group supports or opposes. This includes "off-the-record" admission of the pluses and minuses of the legislation. Honesty is, in fact, often the best policy for a lobbyist when dealing with a public official.

Wining and Dining Also Helps.   A lobbyist can befriend a legislator in several ways that may eventually pay off in support. Lobbyists have information that may be valuable to a legislator, and they may be able to help draft an important piece of legislation for her or him. Providing an occasional free meal or acknowledging a helpful legislator at a banquet in his or her honor also has merit from the lobbyist's perspective. All these actions are necessary to create and maintain goodwill, without which nothing is possible. (It should also be noted that a group sponsoring "liberal" legislation in Texas or promoting sweeping change is not going to be successful, no matter how competent the lobbyist.)

Approaching the Legislators.   How does a lobbyist approach a member of the legislature or a member of the leadership? How do you get in the door, and what do you say when you get in? How important is the staff of a legislator to a lobbyist? Is it necessary to see all 181 members of the legislature, the lieutenant governor, and the governor?

Given that there are only 140 days in a session, lobbying must precede the convening of the legislature. The eighteen-month period between regular sessions leaves ample time to do the following:

- Work on relationships.
- Learn what proposals have a chance of receiving favorable responses.
- Draft legislation.
- Line up sponsors to introduce bills in the house and senate at the beginning of the next session.

Key Endorsements. Not all members of the legislature are equal. Establishing rapport with, and obtaining feedback from, the powerful presiding officers—the speaker of the house and the lieutenant governor, who presides over the senate—are especially useful. There are no endorsements more important to an interest group than those of the presiding officers. If an endorsement for the group's legislative proposal is not forthcoming, the lobbyist must at least persuade the presiding officers to remain neutral in the legislative struggle.

Securing the endorsement of the chairs of committees through which the legislation must pass before it can go to the floor for a vote is an advantage second only to that of securing the support of the presiding officers. In addition, legislation sought by a local government must have the endorsement of the members representing the relevant legislative districts, or it is doomed to fail.

Lobbying Administrative Agencies

Administrators and interest group representatives seek each other out to provide and obtain information. For example, the Texas Educational Diagnosticians Association (TEDA) and the state colleges of education may wish to know whether the examination for the certification of diagnosticians is scheduled for revision. They will therefore contact the State Board for Educator Certification to obtain an answer. The issue is important to the TEDA because the content and difficulty of the exam affect the number of recruits to the profession. Colleges of education know that changes in the state exam mean changes in the curriculum. Inquiries about the exam also allow the interest groups to communicate their professional opinion about the current exam and make suggestions about any changes.

Administrators seek to discover the impact of their programs and rules on the clientele they serve. They may well seek input from those they serve about present and planned programs. In so doing, they surrender some of their power to the clientele to maintain the political support that is in turn necessary to retain the support of the legislature and governor. An agency's clientele is especially interested in influencing the rules and guidelines that control how they do business, because these rules directly affect profits.

The Rulemaking Process. Agencies issue formal rules that prescribe the standards of conduct to be followed by citizens who are subject to the law. Agencies also issue guidelines to govern the actions of their staffs in applying the law. The rulemaking process in Texas gives all interested parties an opportunity to influence an agency's decision. Notice of intent to make a rule must be published in the *Texas Register.* A time for written public comment on the proposed rule is established. At the close of the comment period, the agency analyzes the public's views. It then publishes a "final rule" having the force of law.

While all citizens have the right to participate in the rulemaking process, it is obvious that only those aware of, and interested in, the proposed rule will participate. Ordinary citizens do not subscribe to the *Texas Register.* Corporations, labor

| *Texas Register*
A publication that contains all official notices of the Texas state government and some notices of regional bodies. It is found in all university libraries and large municipal libraries in Texas.

unions, law firms, and interest groups do. Hence, they know when to mobilize their members to influence decision making.

The Co-optation of Agencies. There is a natural linkage from agency to clientele and clientele to agency. As you learned earlier in this chapter, most state agencies are headed by boards and commissions drawn from the industry, trade, profession, or activity the agency regulates. It is normal for individuals who engage in an economic activity to join the state board or commission regulating that activity and then return to the private sector and resume the regulated activity.

The purpose of this staffing system is to fill the need for expertise in board membership. The question is how the interests of the larger society can be protected when roles become so blurred. Can those regulating an economic activity be objective public servants when they have been, and will be, participants in that activity? Many observers argue that such arrangements endanger the public interest and benefit only special interests. The *Economist* has noted that in Texas, "the state's business and political elites are hopelessly intertwined."[26]

Lobbying the Courts

Filing suit to affect government activities is not lobbying or pressure politics. Rather, it involves using a long-established set of legal procedures to challenge the substance of laws, administrative rules, or other government actions. Only persons licensed to practice law can handle cases in the state's major trial courts.

Grounds for Lawsuits. Anyone negatively affected by a law, an administrative rule, or a government action may seek relief from the courts. The challenge may be made on the ground that the agency failed to follow proper procedures in making the rule or that it misinterpreted the law in writing guidelines or rules. The allegation that the laws or rules are applied unfairly is another basis for suit.

Using the courts is typically a last resort. Nevertheless, major corporations, labor unions, interest groups, and local governments employ staff attorneys to protect their interests. Smaller and less wealthy organizations may keep attorneys on retainer or use attorneys on their boards of directors to represent their interests as needed.

The Impact of Judicial Elections. In a state that elects judges, the question arises as to whether wealthy corporations and other interest groups can influence judicial decisions through campaign contributions. Between 1994 and 2006, CBS has run programs about "justice for sale" on *60 Minutes* alleging that the Texas Supreme Court overwhelmingly identifies with specific interests. These reports have led to demands for campaign-finance regulations to reduce any possible conflicts of interest caused by justices accepting campaign contributions. Thus far, however, the legislature has resisted enactment of anything but voluntary compliance standards for judicial campaigns.[27]

Large campaign contributions to judicial candidates are newsworthy because judges are held to a higher standard than elected legislators and executives. Legislators and elected executives are expected to be highly partisan. Judges are expected to be as impartial as humanly possible. Reformers will therefore continue to seek changes in the method of selecting judges, even when they do not advocate changes in the other branches of government.

---

[26]"The Future Is Texas," *The Economist*, December 19, 2002.

[27]Clay Robison, "Campaign 96: 'Justice for Sale' Charges Leveled Anew," *Houston Chronicle*, September 22, 1996, p. 1A.

Dan Lambe, executive director of Texas Watch, displays what he calls the ten most harmful Texas Supreme Court decisions for consumers. He says that the Texas Supreme Court routinely favors business over consumer and family rights in deciding cases. Does this type of campaign have any chance of influencing the Texas court? (AP Photo/Harry Cabluck)

The Dilemma of School Finance

The issue of how to fund the public schools can serve as an example of the way in which interest groups attempt to influence the political process. Large sums have been introduced into the system as part of this political argument.

As most Texans know, the public schools are largely financed by the local property tax. Texas has many "poor" school districts in which the value of taxable property is limited. Many years ago, the courts ruled that it was contrary to the Texas constitution for the quality of the education available to children to be determined by the district in which they live. The state then had to formulate a system to equalize funding across Texas.

The resulting plan called for "rich" districts to share their wealth with less fortunate districts. Needless to say, this "Robin Hood" system had its detractors. The rich districts resented sharing the wealth, and over time the property tax, even with subsidies from wealthy districts, could not sustain fairness in per-pupil expenditures. More and more districts had to raise the tax rate to the maximum allowable, $1.50 per $100 of property value. Homeowners and businesses began to scream more and more loudly about the burden. The problem was that any change involved finding new sources of revenue to avoid creating, once again, unconstitutional differences in per-pupil spending based on whether the pupil lived in a rich or a poor district. Something had to be done, but the governor had promised no new taxes!

Gambling as a "Solution" to the School Finance Issue

In early February 2004, Governor Rick Perry stated that he would call a special April session of the Texas legislature for the express purpose of restructuring school finance. Perry suggested that slot-machine gambling at racetracks and Indian reservations be legalized and the taxes from this source be used to finance the public schools.

Records at the Texas Ethics Commission show that in Perry's four-year tenure between 2000 and 2004, he and members of the state legislature were the beneficiaries of $7.2 million from racetrack owners and slot-machine manufacturers.[28] After Perry's call for a special session, campaign contributions valued at $307,745 arrived at the governor's office. Sixty-seven of the contributions came from interests identified with horse racing, horse breeding, or gambling.[29]

The Financial Background of the Gambling Plan

The key recipients of campaign contributions from pro-gambling forces in Texas during the 2000–2004 period included the governor, comptroller, lieutenant governor, attorney general, and speaker of the Texas House. Before records from the April special session were complete, forty-seven lobbyists, paid somewhere between $1.2 million and $2.3 million, had been retained by pro–slot machine forces to work in the legislature. Antigambling forces had employed fifteen lobbyists at a cost of $380,000 to $825,000.[30]

The Failure to Solve the School Finance Dilemma

In the end, the Texas legislature was unable to come to an agreement on school finance in the 2004 special session, and the proposal to fund the schools with gambling revenues died. The problem did not go away, however. It became more acute as the constitutionality of the funding system was challenged in *Neeley v. West Orange-Cove Consolidated Independent School District*,[31] mentioned earlier in this chapter. Nearly 700 of the state's roughly 1,000 school districts were at or near the tax-rate cap of $1.50 per $100 property valuation when the decision in this case was rendered in December 2004. These districts were literally in danger of not being able to raise enough revenue through local real estate taxes to properly fund the schools.

State district judge John Dietz ruled that the existing school finance system was unconstitutional and did not provide districts enough funding for the schools. While the state appealed this ruling to the Texas Supreme Court, Dietz's ruling effectively imposed a deadline on the legislature, forcing it to address the school financing issue in the 2005 regular session. Proposals advanced by various state leaders included a revival of the gambling plan, a state property tax (combined with a reduction in local property taxes), and a reform of the state franchise tax on businesses. (Due to loopholes, only one business in six currently pays the franchise tax.) Again, the session ended in failure, and again, the governor called a special session—but the end result was exactly the same.

In November 2005, the Texas Supreme Court confirmed that the state's reliance on local property tax to fund the operating costs of the public schools, coupled with an increasing number of districts having to tax at the maximum rate, constituted a *de facto* unconstitutional state property tax. The legislature was given until June 1, 2006, to find an appropriate way to fund the public schools. The governor would be forced to call a special session in an election year. He could ill afford to fail again. The Republican Party might refuse to renominate him in the March primary, or the voters might refuse to reelect him in November.

This time the governor appointed former Democratic state comptroller John Sharp to head a Texas Tax Reform Commission made up largely of state business elites to formulate recommendations to solve the dilemma. The end result was the formulation of a plan to overcome the court's objections. A special session was called after the primary. Success! With little apparent conflict, the house and senate promptly processed five bills encompassing the key recommendations of the Sharp Commission. Two and a half years of conflict and ineptitude came to an end.

---

[28]Texans for Public Justice, 2004.
[29]Texans for Public Justice, "Did Bundled Bucks Rush Perry to Play the Ponies?" 2004, p. 1.
[30]Texans for Public Justice, "The Pro-Slots Lobby," 2004, p. 3.
[31]176 S.W.3d 746 (2005).

Five conditions made the difference in 2006: (1) the court deadline imposed on the legislature for action, (2) the exhaustion of the state's ability to appeal the decision, (3) the ability of the state elites to come to agreement, (4) disparagement of the state political leadership (the governor, lieutenant governor, and speaker of the house) engendered by repeated failure to solve the issue, and (5) the forthcoming election for governor.

The governor, calling a thirty-day special legislative session for April 17, 2006, left no time for issue avoidance, and failure to produce a solution would be worse than changing the tax code. State elites were directly brought into the process and were anxious to resolve the dilemma, as the issue was negatively affecting the Texas business climate. The political leadership was tarnished by previous failure to resolve the issue, and the governor was particularly vulnerable to defeat in the November election. A review of press coverage before and during the special session reveals very few references to special interests and conflict among them. Business will return to normal at the next regular session.

MAKING A DIFFERENCE | Getting Involved by Joining an Interest Group

The Texas legislature decided in 2003 to allow each university to set tuition, rather than having it set by the legislature. This decision has led to rapidly rising tuition costs in Texas. Were you represented during the policy formulation and policy adoption stages of that policymaking event? Probably not. Indeed, many students may not know why tuition has risen.

Why Should You Care?

The new tuition policy in Texas affects how many people can go to the state universities and which institutions they can afford to attend. We can see similar effects in other policy areas.

State policies, in other words, affect the quality of life of each and every citizen. That is why groups organize to control the political agenda and policy outcomes. Those who do not participate do not have a say about what rules apply to them or how state programs may benefit or harm them.

What Can You Do?

Time is precious. Working, studying, sleeping, and socializing consume the lion's share of any student's time. Citizens, however, still have the opportunity to become informed and use their knowledge to influence the decisions of their state and local governments. How? Become a joiner. Allow an organization that shares your values to monitor government activities and represent you at the state capitol and city hall.

Organizations can analyze the political environment and summarize the information that you need to know to understand the political situation. The organization you join can notify you whenever a phone call, e-mail, or letter from you could help affect the outcome of votes and rulemaking activities. Such participation will not take much of your time.

Almost every organized interest has a Web site that you can locate using popular search engines. Size and wealth are assets that help groups to become powerful, but good leadership and good issues are also important. One group that you might consider is Common Cause of Texas. Founded over thirty years ago, it has never had a membership in excess of six thousand or a budget in excess of $100,000, yet it is constantly called on for advice by the Texas Ethics Commission and the state legislature. Why? Because of the consistency of its opinions, the length of time it has spent in the political arena, the stability of its leadership, and its focus on "good government" issues. You can contact Common Cause at

Common Cause of Texas,
603 W. 13th, Suite 2-D,
Austin, TX 78701,
512-474-2374
e-mail: **commoncause@ccsi.com**
www.commoncause.org

Click on "State Organizations" and then on Texas on the U.S. map.

Key Terms

access 638

civic duty 631

conflict of interest 632

co-optation 637

discretion 636

fragmentation 644

implementation 636

late-train contribution 648

political action
   committee (PAC) 638

subsidies 633

Texas Register 653

umbrella organization 640

unfunded mandate 634

Chapter Summary

1 Interest groups are organizations of people who agree on policy issues that affect their members. Interest groups do not nominate candidates for office but do care about the ideologies of those who stand for election. They therefore may form political action committees (PACs) to support candidates favorable to their causes.

2 The constitutions of the United States and Texas promote political expression. The right to organize to petition officials is explicit. This right recognizes that representatives of the people can represent their constituents only when they are informed of their wishes. Interest groups are therefore constitutionally protected.

3 Groups with sufficient resources employ staff to monitor the government. They proactively bring issues before decision makers and reactively move into the political process to stop or alter proposals that negatively affect their membership.

4 Business groups are among the strongest interests. Large corporations lobby decision makers both through umbrella organizations and directly. It is not uncommon for large interests to have more than twenty paid lobbyists working for them during a legislative session. Between sessions, groups conduct research, draft proposed legislation for the next session, and monitor and influence the executive branch, which writes the rules to carry out laws.

5 Interest groups have been powerful in Texas due to the historical absence of competitive two-party politics, restrictive election laws, low voter turnout, and the below-average educational attainment of many citizens.

6 As happens at the national level, "iron triangles" often form in Texas. These triangles unite interest groups that represent a particular industry or activity with the bureaucracy that regulates the activity and with the members of the legislative committee that oversees the bureaucracy. Iron triangles are especially potent in Texas because regulatory boards and commissions are required to have members who actively participate in the regulated activity. This requirement almost guarantees conflicts of interest. Looser alliances called issue networks also form. These may consist of legislators, legislative staff members, interest group leaders, bureaucrats, journalists, scholars, and others who support a particular policy position on a given issue.

7 The media, a few nonprofit and officially nonpartisan special interests, and the Texas Ethics Commission are the sources of most of the information we have about the relationship between interest groups and public officials in Texas. Most lobbyists are required to file reports with the Ethics Commission, which in turn publishes the names, addresses, employers, expenditures, and salaries (in broad categorical ranges) of lobbyists. The media and the nonpartisan interests "blow the whistle" about conflicts of interest and official behavior that is suspect.

Selected Print and Media Resources

SUGGESTED READINGS

Hrebenar, Ronald, and Clive Thomas. *Interest Group Politics in the Southern States.* Tuscaloosa: University of Alabama Press, 1992 (reprinted in 2002). This is one of four regional analyses of special interest power in the United States by these authors. It gives a comprehensive look at power structures, types of interests, lobbying tactics, and state regulations. Very good, although somewhat dated, information.

———. "Who's Got Clout? Interest Group Power in the States." *State Legislatures,* April 1999. This article serves to update the authors' previous works. The title pinpoints the focus.

Prindle, David. *Petroleum Politics in Texas and the Texas Railroad Commission.* Austin: University of Texas Press, 1981. This work looks inside one of the most powerful regulatory agencies in the United States, the Texas Railroad Commission. Internal politics, conflicts of interest, external pressure groups and their agents,

methods of operation, and consequences of the commission's policy choices are all examined.

Texans for Public Justice. *Austin's Oldest Profession: Texas's Top Lobby Clients and Those Who Service Them.* Austin: Texans for Public Justice, published annually. Through this publication, Texans for Public Justice compiles information from the Texas Ethics Commission and disseminates it widely throughout the state in press releases, in publications, and electronically. Registered lobbyists in Texas are identified, along with their employers. Lobbyists are grouped by interests, such as energy and natural resources, ideological and single issues, health, and miscellaneous business.

Texas Ethics Commission. *Lobbying in Texas.* Austin: Texas Ethics Commission, published annually. This document defines lobbying and summarizes the law governing lobbying. Information on who should register, how to fill out reports, and dates of submission are included. Available in paper and online.

E·MOCRACY | Texas Interest Groups on the Web

The Internet has given interest groups a very useful tool to mobilize and inform their members. Indeed, an organization cannot really claim to be "in the game" if it does not have a Web site. Mailing lists are another tool for disseminating information and soliciting donations. At the national level, some of the larger interest groups have organized their home pages so as to tempt their more ardent supporters to use the home pages as gateways to the entire Internet. Texas interest groups and the Texas branches of national interest groups also strive to maintain a Web presence, as you can see from the examples in *Logging On* section that follows.

Logging On

You can view the Web sites of leading economic interest groups in Texas at the addresses given below. The Texas Association of Business is at

www.txbiz.org/index.html

The Texas Association of Mexican-American Chambers of Commerce (TAMACC) is at

www.tamacc.org

For the American Federation of Labor–Congress of Industrial Organizations (AFL-CIO) in Texas, go to

www.texasaflcio.org

For the Texas Trial Lawyers Association, go to

www.ttla.com/tx

For the Texas Farm Bureau, go to

www.txfb.org

Education-oriented groups are well represented on the Web. For the Texas State Teachers Association (TSTA), go to

www.tsta.org

For interesting information available on the TSTA Web site, click on "Legislative" and then "Guide to Lobbying." For the Texas Association of School Boards (TASB), go to

tasb.org

Hispanics in Texas are represented by a variety of groups. The Texas branch of the League of United Latin American Citizens (LULAC), for example, has a site at

www.txlulac.org

You can find out who made major campaign contributions on a state-by-state or even ZIP-code-by-ZIP-code basis at the Web site of the Center for Responsive Politics at

www.opensecrets.org

For Web sites of selected think tanks in Texas, go to the following addresses:

The Center for Public Policy Priorities is at

www.cppp.org

Texas Citizens for a Sound Economy have a Web site at

www.freedomworks.org/texas

The Texas Public Policy Foundation can be found at

www.texaspolicy.com

Online Review

At **www.politicalscience.wadsworth.com/schmidt12**, you will find a free Study Guide to this book. For each chapter, there are two online quizzes to help you master the material.

• The PoliPrep Self-Study Assessment provides a pretest for each major section of the chapter. PoliPrep then generates a customized study plan. After you complete the study plan, a posttest evaluates your progress.

• The Tutorial Quiz for each chapter provides questions on the chapter contents, including the features. The questions are organized to match the major sections of the chapter.

21 | Political Parties in Texas

What If . . .
the Redistricting Process in Texas Were Nonpartisan?

BACKGROUND

Every ten years following the census, Texas, like all other states, is required to redraw the lines for state and federal legislative districts to ensure that these districts are equal in population. The process of redistricting in Texas is highly political. The dominant party and its incumbents engage in gerrymandering—that is, they attempt to redraw district boundaries to increase and protect their seats in the legislative body. The ability of parties and incumbents to control redistricting has been made easier by the development of sophisticated software that makes it possible to configure districts according to very specific criteria.

After the 2002 election, in which Republicans gained control of both chambers of the Texas state legislature, Republican leaders initiated a plan to redraw congressional district boundaries. What ensued was a partisan legislative battle that lasted six months, involved three special sessions, and had Democratic legislators fleeing the state twice to try to block the Republican redistricting plan.

Such partisan battles have prompted some to call for reform of the redistricting process. These reformers claim that independent or nonpartisan commissions not only would decrease the partisan bickering that occurs with redistricting but also would increase the competitiveness of elections in general.

WHAT IF THE REDISTRICTING PROCESS IN TEXAS WERE NONPARTISAN?

Examples of nonpartisan redistricting processes exist in other states and countries. In Britain, impartial boundary commissions recommend new redistricting plans every eight to twelve years. The commissioners, who are not part of any government department, work independently of national and regional parliaments.

In the United States, five states—Arizona, Hawaii, Iowa, New Jersey, and Washington—give independent commissions first and final say over redistricting. In general, these commissions are bipartisan. In Hawaii, no commissioner can run for office in the two elections following redistricting. In Washington, no commissioner can be a public official.

In Iowa, lines are drawn by legislative staff and approved in the traditional way by the legislature and governor. Iowa law, however, requires strict adherence to principles such as compactness, contiguity, and local government boundaries, and it prohibits partisan considerations. In fact, Iowa state house and senate districts, as well as U.S. House districts, are developed without any political data or information, including the addresses of incumbents.

THE IMPACT OF A NONPARTISAN REDISTRICTING PROCESS ON DEMOCRACY

Proponents of nonpartisan redistricting point to the redistricting process as the primary culprit in reducing the competitiveness of state and national legislative races. This decline in competitive elections has increased the polarization of state and national political parties and made it harder to defeat those who hold office. As evidence to support their position, those who favor nonpartisan redistricting cite Iowa, where four out of the five congressional districts are now competitive largely as a result of the nonpartisan redistricting process.

Opponents of nonpartisan redistricting believe that it is undemocratic. They argue that government should be responsive to the voters' wishes—that is, partisan redistricting reflects the wishes of those who have elected officials to positions of power. For example, Republicans in Texas maintain that the state's congressional districts should reflect the shift to Republican dominance.

Traditionally, the United States Supreme Court took the position that partisan (as opposed to racial) gerrymandering was essentially political and therefore outside the Court's jurisdiction. More recently, the Court has claimed jurisdiction over partisan gerrymandering, but it has set the bar so high for finding a gerrymander unacceptable that no state plan has ever been rejected. This may be about to change, though, as the Court begins to hear new redistricting cases.

In previous decades, redistricting in Texas was less controversial because the Democratic Party overwhelmingly controlled the legislature. As party control of the legislature becomes more evenly divided and partisanship in the redistricting process intensifies, it may be that reforms advocating a more nonpartisan approach to redistricting will receive more attention.

FOR CRITICAL ANALYSIS

1. Are state legislative redistricting plans that gerrymander on a partisan basis unfair?
2. What would you consider an effective nonpartisan or bipartisan process for redistricting? How would your plan accomplish the goal of more competitive elections?

The American founders created our complicated federal system and provided for the election of a president and Congress. But the U.S. Constitution makes no mention of political parties. Indeed, early American leaders held negative attitudes about parties. George Washington warned of the "baneful effects of the spirit of party" in his farewell address. James Madison, in *Federalist Paper* No. 10 (see Appendix C), criticized parties or "factions" as divisive, although he admitted they were inevitable. Madison and others thought that parties would encourage conflict and undermine consensus on public policy. Yet despite their condemnation of parties, these early American politicians engaged in partisan politics and initiated a competitive two-party system, as described in Chapter 8.

Parties, then, are apparently something we cannot live without. They have been with us from the start of this country and will be with us for the foreseeable future, influencing our government and public policy. It is important, therefore, to gain an understanding of what they are all about.

Functions of Political Parties

What is a political party? This question conjures up various stereotypes: smoke-filled rooms where party leaders or bosses make important behind-the-scenes decisions; activists or regulars who give time, funding, and enthusiastic support to their candidates; and voters who proudly identify themselves as Democrats or Republicans. Essentially, though, a political party is simply a broad-based coalition with the primary purpose of winning elections. Gaining control of government through popular elections is the most important goal for political parties, and most of the activities parties pursue are directed toward this purpose. Parties recruit and nominate their members for public office. They form coalitions of different groups and interests to build majorities so that they can elect their candidates.

Political parties are vital to democracy in that they provide a link between the people and government. Parties make it possible for the ordinary citizen and voter to participate in the political system. They provide the means for organizing support for particular candidates. In organizing this support, parties unify various groups and interests and mobilize them on behalf of candidates who support the parties' positions.

Political parties developed and survived because they perform important functions. We described these functions in Chapter 8 and review them here:

- The first function of parties, as already mentioned, is to nominate and elect their members to public office. Except for many local elections in which parties are forbidden by law to participate, political parties nominate candidates, and parties run the election process.
- The second function of political parties is to simplify the issues for voters so that there are fewer positions on a question of public policy. In other words, parties educate the public. They help to make sense of the issues and provide voters with cues on how to vote.
- The third function of parties is to mobilize voters by encouraging participation in the electoral process. Individuals are persuaded to become active in support of party candidates. Contributing funds to campaigns, telephoning, and door-to-door canvassing are all examples of how parties mobilize supporters. The more organized the party, the more effective it becomes in getting out the vote for its candidates.
- The fourth function of parties is to run the government. The president, members of Congress, governors, state representatives, and in Texas, state judges are all elected to public office under the party label. Once elected, these officials try to push forward the positions of their party. In our political system, however, it is often difficult for parties to manage the government because the same party may not capture all the separate branches of government.

Characteristics of American Political Parties

In examining American political parties, we must look at three distinct characteristics not always found in parties elsewhere in the world: (1) pragmatism, (2) decentralization, and (3) the effects of the two-party system.

Pragmatism

| Pragmatism
The philosophy that ideas should be judged by their practical results rather than on an ideological basis. American political parties are usually pragmatic because they are typically more interested in winning elections than in taking clear stands on issues.

| Decentralization
In American party politics, distribution of power to state and local party organizations rather than concentration of power in the national organization. In government, distribution of authority to local and regional governments rather than concentration of authority in a central government.

| Grassroots
The lowest organizational level of a political party.

Pragmatism in politics means that ideas should be judged on the basis of their practical results rather than on an ideological basis. In other words, a pragmatist is interested in what works. American parties are willing to compromise principles to appeal successfully to a majority of voters and gain public office. They willingly bargain with most organized groups and take stands that appeal to a large number of interests to build a winning coalition.

Pragmatism often means taking clear-cut positions only on issues on which there is broad agreement. The natural outcome of a campaign strategy designed to attract all groups (and to repel none) is that the party's ideology is not easily brought into sharp focus. Taking clear-cut stands on controversial issues may alienate potential members of the party's electoral coalition. Political parties and their candidates, including those in Texas, thus prefer to de-emphasize issues and instead attempt to project a positive but vague image. Broad, fuzzy campaign themes that stress leadership potential, statesmanship, family life, and personality often take precedence over issues.

It would be a mistake, nonetheless, to assume that parties do not differ from one another. To succeed, they must satisfy their traditional supporters—voters, public opinion leaders, interest groups, and campaign contributors. The candidates are not blank slates but have their own beliefs, prejudices, biases, and opinions. In most elections, broad ideological differences are apparent. Voters in Texas who participated in the presidential elections of 2004 could easily identify the conservative and liberal orientations of Republican George W. Bush and Democrat John F. Kerry.

Decentralization

At first glance, American party organizations may appear to be neatly ordered and hierarchical, with power flowing from national to state to local parties. In reality, American parties are not nearly so hierarchical. Instead, they reflect the American federal system, with its **decentralization** of power to national, state, and local levels. Political party organizations operate at the precinct, or **grassroots,** level; the local government level (city, county, or district); the state level; and the national level.

Figure 21–1 illustrates the nature of power in American political parties. State and local party organizations are semi-independent actors that exercise considerable discretion on most party matters. The practices that state and local parties follow, the candidates they recruit, the campaign funds they raise, the innovations they introduce, the organized interests to which they respond, the campaign strategies they create, and most important, the policy orientations of the candidates who run under their labels are all influenced by local and state political cultures, leaders, traditions, and interests.

The Service Role of the National Parties. We have seen that the American party system is decentralized. Some observers have argued, though, that in recent years power has shifted to the national party organizations. Both the Democratic and Republican national parties have become stronger and more involved in state and local party activities. By using new campaign technologies—computer-based mailing lists, direct-mail solicitations, and the Internet—the national parties have

FIGURE 21–1 | THE DECENTRALIZED NATURE OF AMERICAN POLITICAL PARTIES AND THE STRENGTHENING OF THE NATIONAL PARTY'S SERVICE FUNCTION
This chart represents intraparty relationships during the era of soft money. Since the passage of the McCain-Feingold Act of 2002 (see Chapter 9), the influence of the national parties has been diminished.

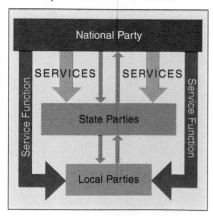

raised millions of dollars. Thus, the national party organizations have assumed a greater "service" role by providing unprecedented levels of assistance to state parties and candidates. This assistance includes a variety of services—candidate recruitment, research, public opinion polling, computer networking, production of radio and television commercials, and direct mailing. As national parties provide more funds and services to state and local parties, they consequently call more and more of the shots.

The End of Soft Money and the Rise of the 527s. If the national parties have gained influence in recent years, the underlying cause has been the large amounts of "soft money" raised by the parties. Soft money was given to political parties by companies, unions, and individuals and not directly to candidates. Because it was used for "party-building activities," it was largely unregulated. Now that the McCain-Feingold Act of 2002 has abolished soft money contributions to the parties, as we explained in Chapter 9, we might expect the influence of national parties to dwindle.

Soft money contributions are still an important part of political campaigns, however. This is because of the development of 527s, organizations that are created by interest groups and get their name from Section 527 of the Internal Revenue Code. (We also described these organizations in Chapter 9.) Many 527s run by special interest groups raise unlimited soft money, which they use for voter mobilization and certain types of issue advocacy, but not for efforts that expressly promote the election or defeat of a federal candidate or that amount to "electioneering communications." Thus, some observers have complained that, rather than eliminating the use of unregulated soft money, we have simply redirected it from parties to interest groups.

The Two-Party System

In a majority of states, political competition usually comes down to competition between the two major parties, the Democrats and the Republicans. As mentioned earlier in Chapter 8, we call this the *two-party system*. Third parties have often tried to gain office but have had little success, because the major parties make a pragmatic, conscientious effort to absorb them by adopting their platforms. (Consider, for example, how the original Populist Party was absorbed by the Democratic Party, as described in Chapter 8.) Voters, potential campaign contributors, and political activists also behave pragmatically; they tend to avoid supporting losing causes. Our electoral system—the **single-member district system**—encourages this pragmatic behavior. If only one representative can be elected in a district, voters normally will cast their ballots for the candidates who have the best chance of winning. Third parties face the problem of historical inertia, too. Voters usually vote for the major parties because they have always done so.

> **Single-Member District System**
> A system that allows only one candidate to be elected from each electoral district. This system discourages the formation of third parties.

The national campaign for the presidency in 1992 by Texas billionaire Ross Perot illustrates the difficulty faced by third-party or independent candidates in American politics. Perot was able to appear on the ballots of all fifty states only because his supporters organized mass petition drives in every state. In the 1992 presidential election, Perot received 19 percent of the national vote and 22 percent of the vote in his home state of Texas. Nonetheless, both nationally and in Texas, Perot's support was diffuse. His support was not concentrated enough in any one state to win that state's electoral votes, the votes needed to actually win the presidency.

In Texas, third parties, such as the Libertarian and Green parties, must have received at least 5 percent of the vote in the previous election to be automatically included on the ballot in the current election. A party that fails to gain this 5 percent can appear on the ballot only by launching petition drives to collect the signatures of a specified number of registered voters who did not vote in the primary of either major party. (We discussed primaries in Chapters 8 and 9 and describe them again in the following section.) Independent candidates must also meet this standard. For example, in order to compete against incumbent governor Rick Perry in the November 2006 gubernatorial election, independent candidates Carole Keeton Strayhorn and Kinky Friedman were forced to collect 45,000 signatures from eligible voters who had not voted in the March 7 primary.

Development of the Texas Party System

Although the two-party system characterizes American politics, many states and localities—Texas, for one—have been dominated by just one party at various times in history. Texas was formerly a one-party Democratic state, but that is no longer the case. To understand political parties in Texas, it is necessary to examine the history of one-party dominance by the Democratic Party, the emergence of two-party competition in the state, and the emerging Republican Party domination of Texas, which can be expected to last years into the future.

The One-Party Tradition in Texas

Under the Republic of Texas, there was little party activity. Political divisions were usually oriented around support of, or opposition to, Sam Houston (a leading founder of the Republic). After Texas became a state, however, the Democratic Party dominated Texas politics until the 1990s. This legacy of dominance was firmly established by the Civil War and the era of Reconstruction, as described in Chapters 18 and 19. During this period, northern troops occupied the South under the direction of a Republican U.S. Congress. From the time Republican and former Union soldier Edmund J. Davis's single term as governor ended in 1874 until Republican Bill Clements's surprising victory in the 1978 gubernatorial election, the Democrats exercised almost complete control over Texas politics.

The Populist Challenge.   The Democratic Party was, at times, challenged by the emergence of more liberal third parties. The most serious of these challenges came in the late 1800s with the Populist revolt. The Populist Party grew out of the dissatisfaction of small farmers, who demanded government regulation of rates charged by banks and railroads, as well as an inflationary monetary policy.

Official photograph of the 1928 Democratic National Convention, held in Houston. Holding the convention in Texas did little to help the Democratic nominee, Governor Al Smith of New York. Smith was the first Catholic ever nominated as a presidential candidate by a major party, and he lost many southern states, including Texas. Why might many Protestants have been unwilling to accept a Catholic presidential candidate in those days? (Calvin Wheat Studio/Library of Congress)

OFFI
NATIONAL D
HC
©

These farmers—joined by sharecroppers, laborers, and African Americans—mounted a serious election bid in 1896 by taking 44 percent of the vote for governor. Eventually, however, the Democratic Party diffused the threat of the Populists by co-opting many of the issues of the new party. The Democrats also effectively disenfranchised African Americans and poor whites in 1902 with the establishment of a poll tax.

The Democratic Primary.   Two events in the early twentieth century solidified the position of the Democrats in Texas politics. The first was the institution of party primary reforms in 1906. For the first time, voters could choose the party's nominees by a vote in a **direct primary**. Thereafter, the Democratic primary became the substitute for the two-party contest—the general election. In the absence of Republican competition, the Democratic primary was the only game in town, and it provided a competitive arena for political differences within the state.

The Great Depression.   The second event that helped the Democrats was the Great Depression. Although Republican presidential candidate Herbert Hoover carried Texas in 1928, the Republicans were blamed for failing to do enough to combat the Great Depression of the 1930s. The effect of this crisis, added to the effects of the Civil War and Reconstruction, ensured Democratic dominance in state government until the early 1990s.

Ideological Basis of Factionalism: Conservatives and Liberals

Although members of a political party may be similar in their views, *factions*, or divisions, within the party inevitably develop. These conflicts may involve a variety of different personalities and issues, but the most important basis for division is ideology.

To understand the ideological basis for factionalism in political parties in Texas, it is necessary to define the terms *conservative* and *liberal*—a difficult task, because the meanings change with time and may mean different things to different people. You learned about conservative and liberal ideologies in Chapter 1; we review these concepts here.

Conservatives.   Modern conservatives typically combine support for the free market with support for traditional values. Conservatives believe that individuals should be

| Direct Primary
An intraparty election in which the voters select the candidates who will run on a party's ticket in the subsequent general election. In Texas, nominees must win a majority of the votes, which often means that there are primary runoff elections between the top two candidates.

left alone to compete in a free market unfettered by government control; they prefer that government regulation of the economy be kept to a minimum. Conservatives, though, often support government subsidies and promotion of business. They may favor construction of highways, tax incentives for investment, and other government aids to business. The theory is that these aids will encourage economic development and hence prosperity for the entire society. In contrast, conservatives are likely to oppose government programs that involve redistribution of wealth, such as welfare, health-care assistance, and unemployment compensation.

As the label suggests, conservatives may view change suspiciously. They may tend to favor the status quo—things as they are now and as they have been in the recent past. They emphasize traditional values associated with the family and close communities, and they often favor government action to preserve what they see as the proper moral values of society. Because conservatives hold a more skeptical view of human nature than do liberals, they are more likely to be tougher on perceived threats to personal safety and the public order. For example, conservatives are more likely to favor stiffer penalties for criminals, including capital punishment.

Liberals.   Modern liberals believe that it is often necessary for government to regulate the economy. They point to concentrations of wealth and power that have threatened to control government, destroy economic competition, and weaken individual freedom. Government power, they believe, should be used to protect the disadvantaged and to promote equality. Liberals generally support the social-welfare programs that conservatives oppose. They are also more likely to favor *progressive* taxes, which increase in percentage terms as incomes increase (see Chapter 16). The best example of a progressive tax is the federal tax on individual incomes.

Liberals possess a more optimistic view of human nature than conservatives. They tend to believe that individuals are essentially rational and, therefore, that consciously planned change will ultimately bring improvements in the human condition. Liberals want government to protect the civil rights and liberties of individuals and are critical of interference with the exercise of constitutional rights of free speech, press, religion, assembly, association, and privacy. They are often suspicious of conservatives' attempts to "legislate morality" because of the potential for interference with individual rights.

Conservative and Liberal Factions in the Democratic Party

For many years, factions within the Texas Democratic Party resembled a two-party system, and the election to select the Democratic Party's nominees—the primary—was the most important election in Texas. Until the 1990s, conservative Democrats were much more successful than their liberal counterparts in these primaries, in part because Republican voters, facing no significant primary race of their own, regularly "crossed over" and supported conservative Democratic candidates. Voters in the general elections, faced with a choice between a conservative Democrat and a conservative Republican, usually went with the traditional party—the Democrats. These Republican crossover votes enabled conservative Democrats, with few exceptions, to control the party and state government for many years—until 1978, when Bill Clements was elected as the first Republican governor of Texas in 105 years.

Conservative Democrats.   Conservative Democrats in Texas provided a good example of the semi-independent relationship of national, state, and local party organizations (as illustrated in Figure 21–1 on page 664). Texas conservatives traditionally voted Democratic in state and local races but often refused to support the national Democratic candidates for president. Indeed, the development of the conservative Democratic faction in Texas was an outgrowth of conservative dissatisfaction with many New Deal proposals of Franklin D. Roosevelt in the 1930s and Fair Deal proposals of Harry Truman in the late 1940s. Conservative Democrats in Texas continued their cool relationship with the national party when many of them supported Republican presidential candidates Dwight D. Eisenhower in 1952 and 1956, Richard Nixon in 1968 and 1972, and Ronald Reagan in 1980 and 1984.

The Success of the Conservative Democrats. In the past, the conservative wing of the Democratic Party enjoyed almost continuous success in Texas politics. This faction supplied almost every governor elected from the mid-1930s to the 1970s. These governors included Allan Shivers (1949–1957), John Connally (1963–1969), and Preston Smith (1969–1973), all of whom later switched to the Republican Party. It also included governors Dolph Briscoe (1973–1979) and Mark White (1983–1987). Until recently, conservative Democrats held almost all of the state's congressional seats; they also dominated both chambers of the Texas legislature.

Several factors accounted for this success, but the most important were the power and resources of the conservative constituency. Conservatives have traditionally made up the state's "power elite" and represent such interests as the oil, gas, and sulfur industries; other large corporations; bigger farms and ranches, or "agribusiness"; owners and publishers of most of the state's major daily newspapers; and veterans. In other words, the most affluent persons in the state have been able and willing to contribute their considerable resources to the campaigns of like-minded politicians. These segments of the population are also the most likely to turn out to vote in elections. This was a significant advantage to conservative Democrats competing in the party primaries, where turnout has generally been low.

The Impact of Governor Shivers. As described in Chapter 18, Governor Allan Shivers, elected in 1948, did more than any individual to establish the dominance of the conservative faction of the Democratic Party. The Shivers faction (labeled *Shivercrats* by liberals) announced its support for the 1952 Republican presidential nominee, Dwight D. Eisenhower, and urged Texas Democrats to vote Republican for president and Democratic for state offices. That same year, Shivers, along with all other Democratic state officeholders at the time (with the exception of state agriculture commissioner John White), received the nomination of both the Democratic and Republican parties. This dual nomination was a unique situation in Texas politics.

Liberal Democrats. Liberals in the Texas Democratic Party consist of those groups that have supported the national Democratic Party ticket and its presidents (Roosevelt, Truman, Kennedy, Johnson, Carter, and Clinton). These groups include the following:

- Organized labor, in particular the AFL-CIO.
- African American groups, such as the National Association for the Advancement of Colored People (NAACP).
- Mexican American groups, such as the American G.I. Forum, the League of Latin American Citizens (LULAC), Mexican American Democrats (MAD), and the Mexican American Legal Defense and Educational Fund (MALDEF).
- Various professionals, lawyers, teachers, and intellectuals.
- Small farmers and ranchers, sometimes belonging to the Texas Farmers Union.
- Environmental groups, such as the Sierra Club.
- Abortion rights groups, such as the Texas Abortion Rights Action League.
- Trial lawyers—that is, lawyers who represent plaintiffs in civil suits and defendants in criminal cases.

Governor Allan Shivers (right) was nationally known for his break with the Democratic Party over the tidelands issue. Shivers endorsed Dwight Eisenhower's presidential candidacy in 1952 and was instrumental in delivering the electoral votes of Texas to the Republicans. A few months after taking office, Eisenhower signed a law that endorsed the state's claim to the tidelands. (Texas State Library and Archives)

Success for liberal Democratic politicians in Texas has been infrequent and has rarely persisted for more than a few years. The heyday of Texas liberalism came in a period from the 1890s through the 1930s with the election of several progressive governors. The latter included governors James Hogg (1891–1895), "Pa" and "Ma" Ferguson (1915–1917, 1925–1927, and 1933–1935), Dan Moody (1927–1931), and James V. Allred (1935–1939). Since the Great Depression of the 1930s, liberals have been able to capture a U.S. Senate seat only once, in 1957, with the election of Ralph Yarborough. In 1970, Yarborough was defeated for reelection by the moderate-to-conservative Democrat Lloyd Bentsen, who held the seat until he became President Clinton's treasury secretary in 1992.

Today, liberal Texas Democrats enjoy more success in capturing their party's nomination, largely because conservatives are voting in the Republican primary. In recent years, liberal or moderate Democrats have been routinely nominated for all the statewide offices. This presents an irony for liberal Democrats—although they have gained strength within the party from the defection of conservatives, this very defection has permitted the Republicans to dominate Texas politics.

The Rise of the Republican Party

Before the presidential election of 1988, only three modern-day Republicans had won statewide races in Texas: U.S. senator John Tower (1961–1985), Governor Bill Clements (1979–1983 and 1987–1991), and U.S. senator Phil Gramm (1985–2003). Why had the Republican Party failed to compete in Texas in the past? As we have seen, the most important reason was the bitter memory that was left by the state's experience in the Civil War and during Reconstruction. The Republican administration of Governor E. J. Davis (1870–1874) was widely considered by the white majority to be the most corrupt and abusive in Texas history. Only in the last few years has the Republican Party been able to shake its image as "the party of Reconstruction."

The Republicans Become Competitive. The revival of the Republican Party was foreshadowed in the 1950s by the development of the so-called presidential Republicans (those who vote Republican for national office but Democratic for state and local office). Conservative Democrats objected to the liberal policies of the national Democratic Party and often voted for Republican presidential candidates.

The first major step in the rejuvenation of the Republican Party in Texas came in 1961, when John Tower, a Republican, was elected to the U.S. Senate. Tower won a special nonpartisan election held when Lyndon Johnson gave up his Senate seat to assume the vice presidency. Tower initially won with the help of many liberal Democrats and was reelected until he retired in 1984. The Republicans retained his seat with the election of former congressman Phil Gramm over his liberal Democratic opponent Lloyd Doggett in 1984. In November 2002, John Cornyn, a Republican and the state's former attorney general, was elected to replace Gramm.

In November 1978, the Republicans achieved their most stunning breakthrough when Republican Bill Clements defeated Democrat John Hill in the race for governor. After losing the governor's seat to moderate-to-conservative Democrat Mark White in 1982, the Republicans regained their momentum in 1986, when Clements turned the tables on White and recaptured the governor's chair.

The Republicans Become Dominant. Developments in the 1990s and early 2000s have many observers believing that Texas is now "Republican country." With the election in 1992 of U.S. senator Kay Bailey Hutchison, Republicans held both U.S. Senate seats for the first time since Reconstruction. In 1994, Republican George W. Bush (son of former president George H. W. Bush) defeated incumbent Democratic governor Ann Richards.

By far the most impressive gains for the Republicans came in the November 1998 elections, when incumbent governor George W. Bush led the Republicans to victory in every statewide election. For the first time in living memory, no Democrats occupied any statewide executive or judicial office. In addition, Republicans won races for the U.S. Senate, the Railroad Commission, the Texas Supreme Court, and the Court of Criminal Appeals. Republicans have continued to maintain their monopoly on statewide offices.

The Republican Party is also extremely competitive in lower-level offices in the state, where Democrats have been most firmly entrenched. In 1974 the GOP held only 53 offices at the county level; in 2004 they held 1,608 offices at the county level. In 1996, the Republicans gained a majority of seats in the state senate, the first time in 126 years that Republicans had held a majority in either chamber of the legislature; and in 2002, they captured the state house of representatives.

Table 21-1 shows the dramatic increases by Republicans in the Texas legislature and the Texas delegation to the U.S. House of Representatives. The extent to which these gains signal a Republican-dominated party system in Texas is discussed later in this chapter.

Sources of Republican Strengths and Weaknesses.   Republican voting strength in recent years has been concentrated in several clusters of counties (see Figure 21-2 on the following page):

- The Houston area.
- The Dallas–Fort Worth area.
- The Midland-Odessa area.
- The northern Panhandle.
- The East Texas oil field counties of Smith, Rusk, and Gregg.
- The Hill Country–Edwards Plateau area.

Results from the 2006 Agricultural Commissioner's race reveal that the Republican Party is weaker in the following areas:

- South and South Central Texas.
- Pockets of Northwest Texas.
- Far West Texas.
- Far pockets of East Texas.

The Republican Party seems to appeal primarily to the following groups:

- Middle- and upper-class individuals in urban and suburban communities.
- Rural, high-income ranchers.
- White Anglo-Saxon Protestants (WASPs).
- German Americans whose ancestors were strong supporters of the Union during the Civil War.
- Active and retired military officers.
- Traditional conservatives who find themselves in a new urban setting.

TABLE 21-1 | CHANGES IN THE NUMBER OF REPUBLICAN AND DEMOCRATIC OFFICEHOLDERS IN TEXAS

	1973		2006	
	DEMOCRATS	REPUBLICANS	DEMOCRATS	REPUBLICANS
Texas House of Representatives	132	17	69	81
Texas Senate	28	3	11	20
U.S. House of Representatives	20	4	13	19
U.S. Senate	1	1	0	2

FIGURE 21-2 | 2006 TEXAS AGRICULTURE COMMISSIONER ELECTION: DEMOCRAT HANK GILBERT VERSUS REPUBLICAN TODD STAPLES

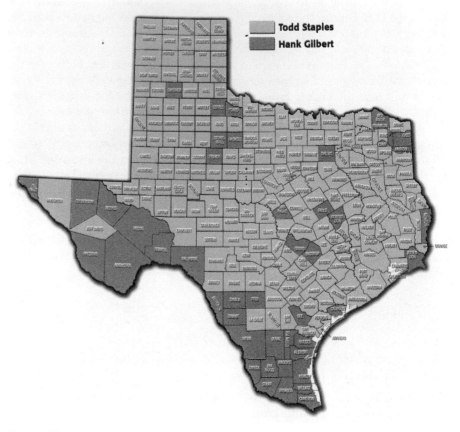

Todd Staples

Hank Gilbert

Source: Office of the Texas Secretary of State.

The party has benefited from the economic growth and prosperity that occurred in Texas from the end of World War II to the early 1980s. During this period, newcomers from more Republican parts of the country were lured to the state by a sympathetic business climate or by the promise of jobs. These transplanted Texans joined more prosperous native Texans to provide a political climate more conducive to Republican Party politics.

Conservative and Moderate Factions within the Republican Party

As the Republican Party becomes more prominent in Texas politics, it is beginning to experience some of the factional differences that characterized the Democratic Party in Texas for years. For example, a bloc of conservative Christians, sometimes loosely referred to as **evangelical** or fundamentalist Christians, has increasingly dominated the Texas Republican Party.[1] This group is concerned with such issues as

| Evangelical
Having to do with a broad spectrum of Protestant Christianity that emphasizes salvation and traditional values. Evangelical voters are likely to support culturally conservative politics.

---

[1]Actually, a majority of American Protestants can be characterized as evangelical. Not all are politically conservative. Some are politically liberal, such as former Democratic presidents Jimmy Carter and Bill Clinton. Conservative Protestants are also sometimes referred to as *fundamentalists*. Fundamentalists are a subset of evangelicals who believe in a number of doctrines not held by all evangelicals. In particular, fundamentalists believe in *biblical inerrancy*—that is, that every word of the Bible is literally true. In politics, fundamentalists are notably more conservative than other evangelicals; liberal fundamentalists are rare. See George M. Marsden, *Understanding Fundamentalism and Evangelicalism* (Grand Rapids, Mich.: Eerdmans Publishing, 1991); and Karen Armstrong, *The Battle for God* (New York: Ballantine Books, 2001).

family, religion, and community morals, and it has been effective in influencing the *party platform*.

The Success of the Conservative Christian Bloc. In 1992, conservative Christians in the Texas Republican Party easily gained control of the Republican state convention and strengthened the antiabortion and antihomosexuality planks in the party's platform. They also captured more than half the seats on the Republican State Executive Committee. Since 1994, the state party chair and a majority of the members of the state executive committee have been conservative Christians. This dominance of leadership positions has given the conservative Christians a degree of control of the party machinery that continues today.

Republican Moderates. The control of the state's Republican Party by the conservative, or right, wing is opposed by the more moderate, or centrist, wing. Many of these moderates fear that the radicalism of the right will interfere with the party's ability to win elections. Many moderates represent business interests, and they are more concerned with keeping taxes low and limiting the government's interference in business decision making than with moral issues.

Republicans and Minorities

In general, the Republican Party has failed to generate much support among the state's minority voters. African American identification with the Republicans consistently hovers around 5 percent. Party strategists have made no great effort to attract African Americans, since they are unlikely to switch parties.

Although George W. Bush did well among Texas Hispanic voters in the 2004 presidential elections, Mexican Americans in Texas have traditionally identified with the Democratic Party. Democrats typically capture elections in heavily Hispanic counties such as those found in the southern and southwestern areas of the state. Nevertheless, observers note that a substantial number of Hispanic voters are *swing voters* (see Chapter 8) not bound by party identification. The Democratic Party cannot afford to take this portion of the electorate for granted, and the Republican Party cannot assume that Hispanic party identification will trend its way. Do the Republicans have a chance of winning enough of the Hispanic vote to maintain their dominance in the state? We examine this question in this chapter's *Politics and Diversity* feature on the following page.

An Example of a Third Party: The Libertarian Party

Chances are if you have voted in a Texas election, you have seen many Libertarian candidates on the ballot. In recent years, the Libertarian Party has become an active, if not always influential, force in Texas politics. The Libertarian Party has a "hands-off" philosophy of government that combines the conservative emphasis on free markets with the liberal skepticism toward legislating morality. The party's general philosophy is one of individual liberty and personal responsibility. Applying their doctrine to the issues, Libertarians oppose Social Security, campaign-finance reform, and military intervention abroad. The Libertarian Party faces the same hurdles as other third parties: poor financing, a lack of media coverage, and in some states, getting access to the ballot. A key problem for the Libertarians is that some of their ideas may be taken over by one of the major parties, in particular the Republicans. They have managed, however, to elect more than three hundred Libertarians to public office at the local and state levels throughout the country.

A lawn sign supporting Bob Smither, the Libertarian Party's candidate for District 22 in the 2006 elections. This district was vacated by the scandal-plagued Tom DeLay. Smither received 6 percent of the vote, breaking the Texas Libertarian Party's record for a congressional candidate. (Nick Lampson won.) In total, the Libertarian Party of Texas had 168 candidates on the ballot, its highest count ever. (Photo Courtesy of Advocates for Self-Government and Bob Smither's campaign)

POLITICS AND DIVERSITY | The Republican Appeal to Hispanics

In the 1992 presidential elections, even as formerly Democratic Texas swung to the Republicans, formerly Republican California swung to the Democrats. Many observers believe that California was transformed politically by the growing number of Democratically inclined Mexican American voters in the state.

Could the same transformation eventually take place in Texas? It will not happen if the Texas Republican Party can prevent it. The Texas Republican leadership knows that if the party is to maintain its dominance in the future, it must find a way of appealing to Mexican American voters.

HOW CONSERVATIVE ARE TEXAS HISPANICS?

If the Republicans are to succeed, Texas Hispanics will have to be more receptive to conservative politics than California Hispanics have been. In fact, public opinion polls suggest that Texas Hispanics are more conservative than California Hispanics on both cultural and economic issues. Still, Texas Hispanics are much more liberal on economic issues than Texas Anglos.

Hispanics around the country appear to be pulled politically in the same direction as their Anglo neighbors. As a result, Hispanics in conservative states such as Texas tend toward greater conservatism. A fact that may reinforce this tendency is that a large number of Mexican Americans in Texas come from the northeastern part of Mexico, where PAN (*Partido de Acción Nacional*—the National Action Party) is strong. PAN, the party of former Mexican president Vicente Fox, supports free enterprise and the Catholic Church and strongly resembles the Republican Party. California's Mexican immigrants, in contrast, are more likely to come from the central and southern parts of the country, where PAN is weak.

THE 2004 ELECTIONS

Initial exit-poll results from the 2004 elections suggested that Republican presidential candidate George W. Bush won 44 percent of the Hispanic vote nationwide and handily carried the Hispanic vote in Texas. Many Republicans concluded that their campaign to win the Hispanic vote was on the brink of success.

Yet Bush's showing may have been purely personal, or perhaps familial. Members of the Bush dynasty—President George H. W. Bush (1989–1993), President George W. Bush, and Florida governor Jeb Bush—have regularly attracted more Hispanic votes than other Republican candidates. The Bushes speak Spanish and have many ties to Mexico and to leading Mexican politicians.

Furthermore, the initial reports of Hispanic support for Bush were in error. Pollsters now believe that in 2004, between 33 and 40 percent of Hispanic voters nationwide supported Bush, a showing only marginally better than Bush posted in the 2000 elections. In late November 2004, the Associated Press (AP), one of the sources of the early erroneous reports, revised its estimate of the Hispanic vote in Texas. The AP now has Democratic candidate John Kerry defeating Bush by one percentage point within the Hispanic community. It appears that if the Republicans wish to actually carry the Hispanic vote in Texas, they have some distance yet to travel.

FOR CRITICAL ANALYSIS

What steps could the Republicans take to increase their appeal among Mexican Americans in Texas? What could the Democrats do to counteract this appeal?

How the Party Machinery Is Organized in Texas

To better understand how political parties are organized in Texas, we can divide the party machinery into two parts: the temporary, consisting of a series of short-lived conventions at various levels; and the permanent, consisting of people elected to continuing leadership positions in the party (see Figure 21–3).

Temporary Party Organization

Conventions are held at all levels of party organization in Texas. Conventions draw in a much larger number of party members than the ongoing permanent bodies can mobilize.

FIGURE 21-3 | TEXAS POLITICAL PARTY ORGANIZATION

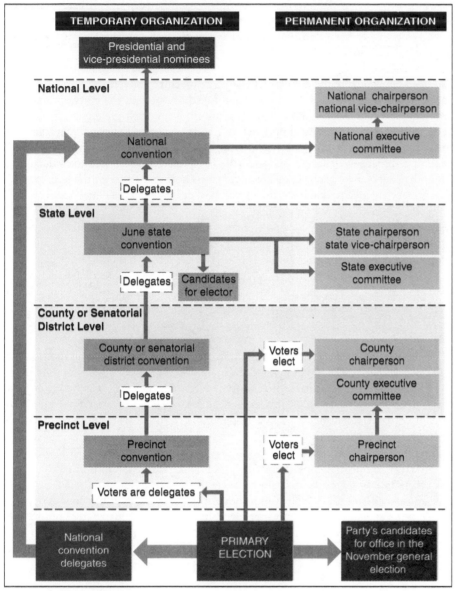

The Precinct Convention. The voting precinct is the starting point of party activity, for it is the scene of the precinct convention, a gathering of the faithful that is open to all who voted earlier in the day in that party's primary. It is also the key to getting involved in politics. (See the *Making a Difference: Grassroots Politics at the Precinct Level* feature at the end of this chapter.)

On a Tuesday early in March in even-numbered years, both the Democratic and the Republican parties hold conventions in almost all the voting precincts in the state. The ticket of admission is usually a voter-registration card stamped to indicate that the holder voted in the party's primary earlier in the day. The agenda of the precinct convention includes the following:

- Adoption of resolutions to be passed on to the county or state senatorial district convention.
- Selection of delegates to the county or senatorial district convention.

Although eligibility for participation in this grassroots level of democracy is open to all who vote in the first primary election, the attendance is low—usually only 2 or 3 percent of those who vote. This low attendance makes it possible for a small, determined minority of the electorate to assume control of the precinct convention and dominate its affairs.

Political Divisions at the Precinct Level.   A precinct convention normally starts with signing in those present and certifying that they voted in the party's primary. In presidential election years, those signing in also indicate their preference for a presidential candidate, while in nonpresidential election years, delegates may organize themselves in different ways, such as by indicating support for a "conservative caucus," "moderate-progressive caucus," and so forth. The preferences are used to evaluate the strength of support for each candidate or caucus. Those factions with the largest numbers present are able to dominate the selection of delegates to the county convention.

If contending factions in a precinct are closely divided, one side or the other may walk out if it loses a key vote and claim a grave injustice was done. Such a group may conduct its own convention, called a **rump convention,** going through the same procedures; then both precinct groups will appeal to a credentials committee appointed by the county executive committee. The credentials committee will decide which set of rival delegates is to be officially seated at the county convention. Although fairness and justice sometimes determine the results, the decision on which group to seat usually depends on which faction is in the majority on the credentials committee.

County and Senatorial District Conventions.   In the weeks following the primary and precinct conventions, county and state senatorial district conventions are held. In the most populous counties, the county convention has given way to state senatorial district conventions within those counties, yielding several state senatorial district conventions instead of one county convention. Delegates vote on adoption of resolutions to be considered at the state convention and select delegates and alternates to attend that convention.

As with the precinct convention, liberal or conservative factions or factions representing different presidential candidates will seek to dominate the selection of delegates. Walkouts followed by rump conventions may occur at the county or even the state level, as well as the precinct level. In Texas, bitter intraparty conflict has historically characterized the Democratic Party to a greater extent than the Republican Party, but that is changing as Republican primaries and conventions grow in importance.

State Convention.   Both the Democratic and Republican parties in Texas hold state conventions in June of even-numbered years. The major functions of these biennial state conventions are as follows:

- To elect state party officers.
- To elect the sixty-two members of the state executive committee (one member for each senatorial district).
- To adopt a party platform. (See excerpts from both major parties' platforms in Table 21–2.)
- To certify the candidates nominated by the party in its March primary to the secretary of state.

In addition, in presidential election years, the state convention performs the following tasks:

- Elects the party's nominees from Texas to the national committee of the party.
- Selects the thirty-four candidates to the electoral college who, if chosen, will vote for the party's candidate for U.S. president.

| Rump Convention
A meeting of members from a larger convention who secede and organize their own convention elsewhere.

TABLE 21–2 | EXCERPTS FROM THE TEXAS DEMOCRATIC AND REPUBLICAN PARTY PLATFORMS

TEXAS DEMOCRATS	TEXAS REPUBLICANS
• Oppose "any form of private school vouchers because vouchers would drain resources essential to guarantee a quality public education for all our children." • Support "sufficient state funding for all education costs to equalize the ability of all communities to offer an exemplary program, without passing the burden to local property taxpayers." • Support abortion rights because "no government, no politician, and no bureaucrat should interfere in an individual's private and personal decisions." • Support "a meaningful increase in the federal minimum wage, to at least $7 per hour, aimed at giving all workers the ability to live dignified lives."	• Support school voucher programs because "parents have the right, as well as the duty, to direct their children's education." • Support the repeal of the "Robin Hood" school funding reallocation system by requiring that local school taxes be used only within that school district. • Oppose legalized abortion because "all human life must be respected and safeguarded from fertilization until natural death." • Oppose increases in the minimum wage and believe "that wages should be determined by the free market conditions prevalent in each market."

Sources: Texas Democratic Party at **www.txdemocrats.org**; and Republican Party of Texas at **www.texasgop.org**.

• Elects some of the delegates to the party's national nominating convention, held in July or August. The number of delegates selected is determined by national party rules.

The role of state convention delegates in selecting delegates to the national convention has diminished in recent years. Most of the delegates for both parties are now selected on the basis of the party's **presidential primary.** A presidential primary allows voters in the party primary to vote directly on the party's presidential nominee.

In 2004, Texas held its presidential primary on March 9. Both Democrats and Republicans, voting in their separate primaries, indicated their selections for presidential candidates, as well as candidates for state and local offices. Texas Democrats selected 55 percent of their 232 delegates to the national convention on the basis of the March 9 primary. Another 68 delegates were selected by the state Democratic convention. The remaining 37 *superdelegates* were chosen from high-ranking elected and national party officials. Thus, Democrats combined a primary and convention system to select most of their delegates. Texas Republicans, in contrast, selected 135 of 138 of their delegates on the basis of the March 9 primary vote.

Permanent Party Organization

The permanent structure of the party consists of people selected to lead the party organization and provide continuity between election campaigns.

Precinct-Level Organization. At the bottom, or grassroots, level of the party structure is the precinct chair. Voters in the precinct's primary election choose the precinct chair for a two-year term. Often the position is uncontested, and in some precincts the chair is elected by write-in votes. The chair's role is to serve as party organizer in the precinct, regularly contacting known and potential party members. He or she may help to organize party activities in the neighborhood, such as voter-registration drives.

| **Presidential Primary**
A statewide primary election of delegates to a political party's national convention to help a party determine its presidential nominee. Such delegates are either pledged to a particular candidate or unpledged.

The precinct chair is responsible for arranging and presiding over the precinct convention and serving as a member of the county executive committee.

County-Level Organization. The county chair has a much more active and important role than the precinct chair. The voters choose the county chair for a two-year term in the party primary. The chair presides over the county executive committee, which is composed of all precinct chairs.

The county chair determines where the voting places will be for the primaries and appoints all primary **election judges.** (These choices must later be approved by the county commissioners court.) Accepting candidates for places on the primary ballot and printing paper ballots or renting voting machines are also the chair's responsibilities. Finally, the chair, along with the county executive committee, must certify the names of official nominees of the party to the secretary of state's office.

The county executive committee has three major functions:

- To assemble the temporary roll of delegates to the county convention.
- To canvass (that is, examine and certify) the returns from the primary for local offices.
- To help the county chair prepare the primary ballot, accept filing fees, and determine the order of candidates' names on the ballot. The order of names is an important consideration if there is a great deal of "blind voting" in which ill-informed voters opt for the first name they come to on the ballot.

State-Level Organization. Delegates to the state convention choose the state chair—the titular head of the party—for a two-year term. The duties of the chair are to preside over meetings of the state executive committee, to call the state convention to order, to handle the requests of statewide candidates on the ballot, and to certify any runoff primary election winners to the state convention.

Each party's state executive committee has sixty-four members and is led by a chair and a vice chair (who must be of opposite genders). In addition, the Democratic and Republican state convention delegates choose one man and one woman from each of the thirty-one state senate districts. The main legal duties of the state executive committee are as follows:

- To determine the site of the next state convention—sometimes a crucial factor in determining whose loyal supporters can attend, since the party does not pay delegates' expenses.
- To canvass statewide primary returns and certify the nomination of party candidates.

The state executive committee also has some political duties, including issuing press releases and other publicity, encouraging organizational work in precincts and counties, raising money, and coordinating special projects. The state committee may work closely with the national party. These political chores are so numerous that the executive committees of both parties now employ full-time executive directors and staff assistants.

| Election Judge
A public official who is responsible for enforcing election rules at a polling place on Election Day.

| A New Era of Republican Dominance

In the elections of 2006, the Democrats fielded a full slate of candidates for state offices. Yet even with a national political climate that led to Democratic control of Congress, incumbent governor Rick Perry led the Republicans to victory in every statewide office. The results of the election demonstrate that although two-party competition now exists in Texas, in practice the Republican Party dominates Texas politics.

Republicans hold 81 of the 150 seats in the Texas House and 20 of the 31 seats in the Texas Senate. In 1978, the Republicans held just 92 elected offices across all of Texas. Following the November 2004 elections, the total was well over 2,100. Clearly, the old pattern of Texans' voting Republican at the top of the ticket and Democratic at the bottom of the ticket is much less true today than in the past.

TABLE 21-3 | PRIMARY VOTING PATTERNS IN TEXAS FROM 1972 TO 2004

YEAR	RACE	REPUBLICAN PRIMARY VOTE	DEMOCRATIC PRIMARY VOTE	REPUBLICANS AS % OF DEMOCRATS
1972	President	114,007	2,192,903	5.2
1974	Governor	69,101	1,521,306	4.5
1976	President	356,307	1,529,168	23.3
1978	Governor	158,403	1,812,896	8.7
1980	President	526,769	1,377,767	38.2
1982	Governor	265,794	1,318,663	20.2
1984	President	336,814	1,463,449	23.0
1986	Governor	544,719	1,096,552	49.7
1988	President	1,014,956	1,767,045	57.4
1990	Governor	855,231	1,487,260	57.5
1992	President	797,146	1,482,075	53.8
1994	Governor	557,340	1,036,944	53.7
1996	President	1,019,803	921,256	110.7
1998	Governor	596,839	664,532	90.0
2000	President	1,159,645	793,825	146.1
2002	Governor	620,463	1,003,388	61.8
2004	President	687,615	839,231	81.9

Source: The Republican Party of Texas.

While Democrats still have considerable resources in many local governments, especially in some central cities and South and Southwest Texas, the Republican Party has made considerable progress at the grassroots level.

Strong evidence for Republican gains has come in the party primaries. In 1974, only 168 of Texas's 254 counties held Republican primaries. In 1996, for the first time ever, all 254 counties held Republican primaries. Table 21–3 shows that Republican turnout in the primaries, as a percentage of total Democratic turnout, increased from 5 percent in 1972, to 50 percent in 1986, to a striking 146 percent in the 2000 primary. (The drop in the 2002 and 2004 figures is attributable to competitive races for the Democratic gubernatorial and Democratic presidential candidates, respectively.)

Most observers now agree that Texas has experienced a political *realignment*— that is, a transition from one stable party system to another. After a hundred years of Democratic Party domination following the Civil War, the pendulum has swung to the Republican Party. (We discussed realignment in Chapter 8.)

Emergence of Republican Party Dominance

Realignment involves more than just casting a vote for a Republican Party candidate. It refers to a shift in *party identification*. Evidence that Texas is becoming a two-party or even a Republican-dominated state comes from public opinion polls that show more Texans are identifying with the Republican Party than in the past. Table 21–4 indicates that in 1952, an overwhelming percentage of those who identified with a political party

TABLE 21-4 | DEMOCRATIC AND REPUBLICAN PARTY IDENTIFIERS

	DEMOCRATS (%)	REPUBLICANS (%)	TOTAL (%)
1952	66	6	72
1972	57	14	71
1990	34	30	64
2002	25	37	62

Sources: Statewide polls in 1952 and 1972 conducted by Belden Associates of Dallas and archived at the Roper Center. Data for 1990 from the Texas poll, Texas A&M University Policy Resources Laboratory, Harte-Hanks Communications. Data for 2002 from American National Election Studies; Center for Public Policy, University of Houston, Texas polls.

in Texas were Democrats. In 2002, polls showed that the number of voters who identified with the Republican Party exceeded the number who identified with the Democratic Party. For more on the political challenges facing the Texas Republican-dominated party system, read this chapter's *Politics and Political Parties* feature.

The Slow Progress of Realignment in Texas. As we have already suggested, there are several reasons for the rise of Republican Party dominance in Texas. The first was the shift among existing voters as conservative middle- and upper-class white Democrats gradually switched their allegiance to the Republican Party during the decades following 1968. After years of voting Republican in presidential elections but identifying themselves as Democrats, these conservatives began thinking of themselves as Republicans. Many white voters defected to the Republican Party because they were alienated by the national Democratic Party's emphasis on civil rights in the 1960s and 1970s. The existence of popular and powerful Democratic leaders from Texas, such as President Lyndon B. Johnson (1963–1969), may have slowed the transition briefly but could not stop it.

This shift in partisan identification was also spurred, in part, by the election of an extremely popular Republican president. Ronald Reagan, elected in 1980 and reelected in 1984, combined clearly conservative positions with a charismatic personality that attracted conservative Democrats into the Republican camp. The impact of Reagan's leadership was reinforced by the election of George W. Bush to the presidency in 2000 and 2004. Bush had been a very popular governor, and his election to the presidency helped solidify the Republican realignment in Texas.

Interstate Immigration, Industrialization, and Urbanization. Party switching by native Texans has not been the only cause of realignment. Another factor involves newcomers to the state. A majority of recent migrants to Texas from other states have been Republicans or independents. These newcomers, who came to Texas in large numbers in the 1970s and 1980s, have helped break down traditional partisan patterns.

Finally, long-term economic trends have provided opportunities for political change. Texas has slowly become an industrialized and urbanized state, a pattern that accelerated after the 1940s. Industrialization, urbanization, and the rise of an affluent middle class have created a new environment for many Texans, and many Texans have been willing to adopt a new party as part and parcel of their new lives. In some parts of the country, urbanization and affluence have been associated with support for the Democratic Party, but in Texas these phenomena may have benefited the Republicans.

The Elections of 2002 and 2004

The elections of 2002 and 2004 support the claim that Texas has experienced a realignment, with the majority of voters now supporting the Republican Party. In 2002 (with the strong support of President George W. Bush), John Cornyn, the Republican nominee for the U.S. Senate, beat his opponent, Ron Kirk, and led a Republican sweep of statewide offices. For the first time since Reconstruction, the Republicans controlled the governor's office and both chambers of the state legislature. In 2004, the Republicans completed the sweep after a Republican-led redistricting plan allowed them to capture a majority of the state's delegation to the U.S. House of Representatives.

Can the Democrats Still Be Competitive?

Some observers still believe that Texas will continue as a competitive two-party state. Supporters of this view cite the unique influence of George W. Bush, a popular governor and later president. Without Bush's coattails in 2008, it will be harder for Republicans to win in close races. These observers also predict that a Texas

POLITICS AND POLITICAL PARTIES | The Political Parties Face New Political Challenges

Today, Texas shows all the signs of a Republican-dominated party system. Texas Republicans are busy promoting issues that may attract culturally conservative voters—private education vouchers for parents with children attending public schools (which we will discuss in Chapter 26), prohibitions against gay foster parents, a constitutional ban on gay marriage, and a requirement that minors obtain parental consent before receiving an abortion.

FACTIONALISM IN THE REPUBLICAN MAJORITY

The Republicans, however, also face challenges that typically follow from being the controlling majority party. Factions within the party are emerging and competing against one another. The most obvious sign of this is the political maneuvering that took place among the three most viable candidates for governor in 2006—incumbent governor Rick Perry, Republican U.S. senator Kay Bailey Hutchison, and state comptroller Carole Keeton Strayhorn.

Perry supporters, considered the most conservative of the three factions, actively discouraged Senator Hutchison from running, saying it would cause serious conflict within the party. In addition, the disputes between Governor Perry and Comptroller Strayhorn were legendary. In 2004, the comptroller criticized the governor for supporting cuts to the state's Children's Health Insurance Program. The governor retaliated with a successful move to strip the comptroller's office of some its traditional powers. Strayhorn made no secret that she was a candidate for the governor's job. The sniping continued during the 2006 gubernatorial campaign.

THE CHALLENGES OF GOVERNING

Republican lawmakers, who control the house 81–69 and the senate 20–11, are finding fissures among their members as well. Once fairly unified in their opposition to Democratic programs, the Republican representatives are being asked to support legislation of their own party's creation. There have been divisions on legislation concerning such diverse issues as limits on increases in property appraisals, gambling, campaign finance, and a state property tax. The Republicans are still relatively united on traditional social issues, but the party is discovering that "leading the herd" has become considerably more challenging as it assumes its position as the governing party.

HARD TIMES FOR THE DEMOCRATS

The Democratic minority has its own set of challenges. Political and demographic changes within the state have been the most

apparent reasons for the Democratic Party's decline, but the quality and effectiveness of the party organization are also a matter of concern for the Democrats. The Democratic Party's financial condition is one indicator of its organizational woes. In the last few years, the party has had problems raising campaign funds. In 2002, after being in the red for fifteen years, it was finally able to retire its debt. In 2006, the Republicans continued to raise large sums of campaign funds. For example, for his reelection, Rick Perry had more than $25 million.

Even more serious than its financial problems is the Democratic Party's absence from statewide executive and judicial office. Elected state officials are able to communicate a party's policy goals to the media and to a statewide constituency. Without leadership positions, the Democrats face a serious disadvantage in serving as the opposition. They are unable to effectively communicate their platform as a viable alternative to Republican policy positions. These two trends—financial hardship and lack of visible leadership—reinforce each other and may help perpetuate the Democrats as the minority party for some time in the future.

PROCEDURAL RULES GIVE DEMOCRATS SOME INFLUENCE

Democrats still exercise some influence in the state legislative process because of the two-thirds rule in the senate. This rule stipulates that legislation must have at least twenty-one of the thirty-one votes in the senate before it can be considered in debate. In the 2005 legislative session, Democrats used the rule to block a bill that would have required Texans to show a photo ID and two other forms of identification before voting.

PARTY COHESIVENESS BREAKS DOWN OVER THE CHEERLEADERS' BILL

Some proposals, of course, generate bipartisan agreement (or opposition). In the 2005 session, the House voted 85–55 to ban sexually suggestive dance routines by school cheerleaders and dance teams. The bill's sponsor, a Democrat, faced some of his most vociferous opposition from his own party members, one of whom stated, "This is a ridiculous bill. It's stupid and it's insulting." The measure received a flood of media attention and became the source of many jokes. Unfortunately for its supporters, the Texas Senate refused to consider the bill.

FOR CRITICAL ANALYSIS

Can we now say that there is serious competition between the two major parties in Texas? Why or why not?

economy that continues to be sluggish will place pressures on the state budget that Republicans will be hard pressed to address. They note that Democrats still have considerable resources in many local governments, especially in some central cities and South and Southwest Texas. Finally, they point to a growing population of Hispanic voters who tend to support Democratic candidates.

Dealignment

There is also some speculation that what is occurring in Texas is not realignment but *dealignment*, meaning that the voters are refusing to identify with either political party and are more inclined to call themselves independents. Evidence for dealignment comes from evaluating the percentage of voters engaging in *ticket splitting*—that is, voting for candidates of both parties in the general election rather than voting for all the candidates of one party or the other (a straight ticket). Increased numbers of ticket splitters suggest that dealignment is occurring. Recent surveys show that in both parties, straight-ticket and split-ticket voting occur in equal proportions—about 50 percent each. This pattern probably means that in Texas, both realignment and dealignment are occurring at the same time. In other words, voters are less willing to identify with either political party (dealignment) and also are more willing to change their professed party (realignment).

MAKING A DIFFERENCE | Grassroots Politics at the Precinct Level

Have you ever wondered how politicians get their start? Chances are they become involved with a political party at the grassroots level. In Texas, as in many other states, the most basic level of partisan participation is the party precinct. Precincts are this country's smallest political unit and are generally composed of about two thousand to three thousand voters. Political activity at the precinct level involves personal face-to-face activity such as registering voters in your precinct, attending the precinct conventions, and getting voters to the polls on Election Day.

Why Should You Care?

Political participation is one of the most important principles of democracy. The American federal system provides many access points for participation; some would say the most important point of access is the

local level. Through your involvement, you influence the leadership and activities of your party and, ultimately, the issues that directly affect your life. In a practical sense, a strong and vital precinct organization is a key component in building the success of your county or district and state party organizations.

What Can You Do?

Participating at the precinct level can include a number of activities, but one of the most important is participating in the precinct convention. In early March, during even-numbered years, both the Democratic and Republican parties in Texas hold their primary elections. Voters in the party primary may attend their party's precinct convention, which begins around 7:15 P.M. after the polls close at 7:00 P.M. Resolutions are passed, and delegates to the next level of party

conventions (the county or senate district level) are selected. Since attendance is often sparse, an individual has a good chance of being heard and even being elected as a delegate. Delegates at the county or district level will pass more resolutions and will elect delegates to the state level. If you are persistent and lucky, you may be selected as a delegate to the state party convention. At this point, you will have become a significant player in politics.

For further information on Texas party conventions and events, leaders, rules, and issue positions, you can check the Web sites of both state political parties at

Texas Democratic Party
www.txdemocrats.org

Texas Republican Party
www.texasgop.org

Key Terms

decentralization 664

direct primary 667

election judges 678

evangelical 672

grassroots 664

pragmatism 664

presidential primary 677

rump convention 676

single-member district system 665

Chapter Summary

1 Despite the hostility of the founders, political parties have become an important part of American political life. This is because parties perform critically important functions in a democracy. They nominate and elect their members to public office, educate and mobilize voters and provide them with cues on how to vote, and run the government at whatever level (local, state, or national) they are active.

2 In discussing political parties in the United States, we must look at three fundamental characteristics: (1) pragmatism, (2) decentralization, and (3) the effects of the two-party system. Pragmatism follows from the major goal of American parties, which is to build majority coalitions and win elections. This means that both Republican and Democratic Party candidates are often fuzzy on issues. The candidates try to accommodate many different interests and viewpoints and alienate as few voters as possible. Because there are few voters on the extremes, left or right, serious third parties have great difficulty developing and surviving, and they are often co-opted by one of the two major parties.

3 Parties are relatively decentralized, with much of the control of the nominating process (the primary) and party machinery in the hands of state and local voters and their leaders. In the recent past, however, both the Democratic and Republican national party organizations have increased their control over state and local parties because of their capacity to raise large amounts of money and provide various services. The McCain-Feingold Act of 2002 may end this trend by cutting off the flow of "soft money" to the major parties.

4 For much of its history, Texas was a one-party Democratic state. Until recently, one-party dominance meant that the election to select the Democratic Party's nominees—the Democratic primary—was the most important election in Texas. Moderate and conservative factions within the Democratic Party became the key political players.

5 After years of domination by the Democratic Party, Texas began to experience strong two-party competition. As a result, both parties strengthened their party machinery and made aggressive appeals to their traditional constituencies. By the late 1990s, the Republicans had became the dominant party in Texas. The transition from a party system in which the Democrats were overwhelmingly dominant to a new system in which the Republicans have a clear edge can be described as a political realignment. The realignment process was foreshadowed in the 1950s by the Shivercrats, Democrats who advocated voting for Republican presidential candidates and conservative Democrats at the state level. After the 1960s, the Republicans slowly but surely gained strength at the state level. In 1978, they gained the governorship. By 2002, they controlled both chambers of the state legislature. The Republicans will no doubt remain dominant in the foreseeable future.

6 Republicans have attracted voters in the expanding suburban areas of the state and have increased their appeal to white voters in rural areas. Democrats have attracted votes in inner cities and among ethnic minorities. The state's increasing ethnic diversity could thus augur well for the Democratic Party.

7 A second political mechanism that may be at work, in addition to realignment, is political dealignment. In this process, voters become detached from both political parties and begin to see themselves as independents.

Selected Print and Media Resources

SUGGESTED READINGS

Black, Earl, and Merle Black. *The Rise of Southern Republicans.* Cambridge, Mass.: Harvard University Press, 2002. This book discusses the slow but sure rise of Republican strength in the previously solid Democratic South over the past five decades.

Burnham, Walter Dean. *Critical Elections and the Mainsprings of American Politics.* New York: W. W. Norton, 1970. This classic work develops the concept of critical elections and electoral realignments. According to Burnham, critical elections establish new dominant parties. Burnham's theories have been criticized on the ground that political realignments are not always tied to specific elections.

Davidson, Chandler. *Race and Class in Texas Politics.* Princeton, N.J.: Princeton University Press, 1992. This work on Texas politics explores the complicated relations between the politically disorganized Texas blue-collar class and the wealthy elite and illustrates the tactics used by the latter to largely control policymaking in the state.

Keefe, William J., and Marc J. Hetherington. *Parties, Politics, and Public Policy in America*. Washington, D.C.: Congressional Quarterly Press, 2003. This fine, up-to-date textbook examines the two-party system in America. The authors discuss how parties have changed and what role partisanship plays among the elites and among ordinary voters.

Key, V. O. *Southern Politics*. New York: Knopf, 1949. This classic work describes the one-party Democratic system that existed in the South until recent years.

Richards, David. *Once Upon a Time in Texas: A Liberal in the Lone Star State*. Austin: University of Texas Press, 2002. This is a lively account of the experiences of Texas liberals from the 1950s to the 1990s. It includes a description of policy battles and profiles of prominent politicians and journalists.

MEDIA RESOURCES

Giant—A 1956 film that tells the story of rival ranchers in Texas in the middle years of the twentieth century. It stars Elizabeth Taylor, Rock Hudson, James Dean, and Carroll Baker.

Last Man Standing: Politics Texas Style—A 2004 PBS video that documents the successful challenge to a Republican incumbent legislator by a twenty-four-year-old Democratic "upstart." It features comments by such important figures as Bush strategist Karl Rove, former Democratic governor Ann Richards, and Clinton appointees Henry Cisneros and Paul Begala.

Lone Star—A 1996 film that offers a realistic portrait of the political machine in a South Texas border town. The story involves characters from the middle and younger generations of three ethnic communities who uncover and confront the surprising truth about their elders' past.

E·MOCRACY | Texas Political Parties and the Internet

The Internet offers a variety of information about Texas political parties. Citizens of the state can locate official party platforms, research party rules for participating in grassroots and state conventions, learn about the party history of Texas, and even view video clips of party officials. The Internet also makes it easy for political parties to mobilize supporters and seek donations.

For those who like a more informal or opinionated discussion of party views and activities, there are several unofficial Web logs, or "blogs," that offer individuals and columnists a chance to express their own views. These vary from the columns of media professionals to individual sites that may be fleeting. Be very careful when using information gleaned from a blog. Often individuals who publish Web logs are highly opinionated, although most are straightforward about their ideological leanings.

By accessing the Web sites of the parties listed below in the *Logging On* section, you can see how the parties promote themselves. Voter registration is a major concern for both parties. Try accessing the home pages of the Texas Democratic and Republican parties. List at least three major differences in the official platforms of the two parties. Then go to the sites of the blogs mentioned or find others by using the search engines described. Read through columns and comments from these blogs, and compare the information with that on the official sites. Can you identify points that may legitimately support either platform? Can you identify columns or statements that should be viewed skeptically?

Logging On

The two major political parties have Web sites both nationally and in Texas. See the Republicans in Texas at

www.texasgop.org

See the Republicans nationally at

www.gop.com

See the Democrats in Texas at

www.txdemocrats.org

See the Democrats nationally at

www.democrats.org

The University of Texas offers an excellent Web site describing Texas politics in general. The site has a unit on Texas political parties that includes the history and functions of political parties in the state, as well as features such as graphs and video clips. To access this site, go to

texaspolitics.laits.utexas.edu

Blog search engines allow you to find blogs of all types. One site that lists such engines is

www.faganfinder.com/blogs

A popular blog search engine is

www.blogsearchengine.com

Instead of using this search engine, you can simply click on "political and government blogs" and immediately see a list of such blogs. Another site with a list of political blogs is

www.blogsuniverse.com

Online Review

At **www.politicalscience.wadsworth.com/schmidt12**, you will find a free Study Guide to this book. For each chapter, there are two online quizzes to help you master the material.

• The PoliPrep Self-Study Assessment provides a pretest for each major section of the chapter. PoliPrep then generates a customized study plan. After you complete the study plan, a posttest evaluates your progress.

• The Tutorial Quiz for each chapter provides questions on the chapter contents, including the features. The questions are organized to match the major sections of the chapter.

What If . . .
Voting Were Required by Law?

BACKGROUND

The 2004 presidential elections were fairly close. Nationally, Republican George W. Bush received a 2.4 percent larger share of the votes than Democrat John Kerry (or about 3 million more votes). Only about 60 percent of those who were eligible to vote actually did so, however. In Texas, about 54 percent of the eligible population turned out to vote.

In the United States and most other countries, voting is voluntary, and people can decide whether or not to go to the polls. In some countries, however, voting is mandatory. In Australia, for example, all citizens are required to vote. Those who do not vote risk a fine and even imprisonment. The same is true in a handful of other countries, including Belgium. Turnout in these countries (not surprisingly) is high.

WHAT IF VOTING WERE REQUIRED BY LAW?

Suppose voting had been required by law in the 2004 presidential elections. Would it have made a difference at the national level? In other words, would Kerry have emerged victorious? What about in Texas? Bush took 60 percent of the Texas vote in 2004, but what would have happened if the 46 percent of the eligible population that did not vote had turned out?

Voters and nonvoters are different. Voters are on average better educated. They also tend to have better jobs and higher incomes. Not surprisingly, voters tend to be more Republican than nonvoters. It would seem to follow that if everyone voted, Democratic candidates would do better on Election Day. But is this true? Do Democrats stand to gain and Republicans to lose? We cannot be sure what would happen if everyone voted. Based on what we know about how people with certain characteristics vote, however, we can

simulate how nonvoters would behave. Such an analysis suggests that most of the time, Democrats would gain more than Republicans, but by only a small margin.

There are two main reasons for this prediction. First, the differences in the preferences of voters and nonvoters are actually not very great.[*] Second, nonvoters are more likely to be influenced by short-term forces such as the state of the economy.[†] Therefore, their support might go disproportionately to the victor. Expanding the voting population might merely widen the winner's margin. Some evidence for this argument comes from the 2004 presidential elections, where voter turnout was up significantly from 2000. Kerry received about

[*]See the report by Benjamin Highton and Raymond Wolfinger at **www.igs.berkeley.edu/publications/par/July1999/HightonWolfinger.html**.

[†]Glenn Mitchell II and Christopher Wlezien, "The Impact of Legal Constraints on Voter Registration, Turnout, and the Composition of the American Electorate," *Political Behavior*, June 1995, pp. 179–202.

8 million more votes nationally than Democrat Al Gore did in 2000, but Bush received about 11.5 million more votes than he did four years previously.

WHAT IF EVERYONE VOTED IN TEXAS?

Even if the partisan balance at the national level remained largely unchanged, it might conceal some measure of variance among individuals, states, and localities. This may be especially true in states such as Texas. It would take a very large change to overcome the current state-level Republican dominance. In state legislative races, however, the parties are often more closely balanced, and turnout is much lower. In local races, turnout tends to be lower still. In such races, expanding participation could have significant effects.

OTHER EFFECTS

Mandatory voting might have effects in addition to altering the balance between the parties. Some

believe that it could cause a "dumbing down" of election campaigns as parties and candidates targeted the votes of people participating only to avoid paying a fine or going to jail. Alternatively, the new voters might seek to learn more about politics. Either result might change the political preferences of those who currently do not vote.

FOR CRITICAL ANALYSIS

1. Consider whether mandatory voting would work in the United States and specifically in Texas. Would the public support mandatory voting? How could we enforce it?
2. Would mandatory voting change the types of candidates who run for office and the positions they take? Might it ultimately change public policies?

Democracy makes demands on its citizens in terms of both time and finances. It takes time for voters to inform themselves about the large number of candidates who compete in the spring for nomination in the party primaries. Then in the November general election, roughly 4,200 of these nominees ask the Texas voters to elect them to local, state, and national offices.

Voting in elections is the most basic and common form of political participation, but other forms of participation exist. Many people discuss political issues with friends and co-workers, write letters to local representatives or to newspaper editors, distribute campaign literature, make contributions to campaigns, or place bumper stickers on their cars. Some people are members of interest groups, such as neighborhood or trade associations, or serve on political party committees or as delegates to conventions. Voting is fundamental, yet not everyone votes, as we pointed out in the *What If . . .* feature at the beginning of this chapter.

Political Participation

Elections are a defining characteristic of representative democracies. It is through our votes that we hold elected officials accountable. Votes are what matter to politicians, at least those interested in winning and holding office. If we vote—and thereby reward or punish elected officials for what they do while in office—politicians have an incentive to do what we want. If we do not vote, elected officials are largely free to do what they want. Clearly, voting is important in a representative democracy.

The Participation Paradox

A problem with voting is that a single individual's vote usually does not make a difference in an election. Imagine that you voted in the 2006 Texas gubernatorial election. Did your vote matter? In other words, did your vote swing the election, ensuring Rick Perry's victory or dooming him to defeat? It did not. Governor Perry won reelection despite your vote.

Our individual votes rarely have any effect on the outcome, yet people still vote. Among political scientists, this is known as the **participation paradox.** The purpose for mentioning this paradox is not to say that people should not vote. Rather, it is to point out that people vote for other reasons (and chiding people to vote because their votes "make a difference" probably is not very effective).

| **Participation Paradox**
The fact that people vote even though their individual votes rarely influence the outcome of an election.

Who Votes?

Over the years, political scientists have learned much about why people go to the polls. It now is clear that a relatively small number of demographic and political variables are especially important.[1]

Education, Income, and Age.   The most important demographic variables are education, income, and age. The more education a person has, the more likely the person is to vote. The same is true for income, regardless of how much education a person has. Age also matters. As people grow older, they are more likely to vote, at least until they become very old. Why do these factors matter? The answer is straightforward: People who are educated, have high incomes, and are older are more likely to care about, and pay attention to, politics. Thus, they are more likely to vote.

---

[1]Raymond E. Wolfinger and Steven Rosenstone, *Who Votes?* (New Haven, Conn.: Yale University Press, 1980). Also see Sydney Verba and Norman H. Nie, *Participation in America* (New York: Harper & Row, 1972).

Interest in Politics and Partisan Identification.   In addition to demographic factors, certain political factors influence the likelihood of voting, especially a person's expressed interest in politics and intensity of identification with a political party. The greater the interest in politics, the more likely a person is to vote. The effect is obvious but nevertheless quite important. A person who does not have much education or income still is very likely to vote if she or he has an intense interest in politics.

Identification with either of the political parties also makes a person more likely to vote. People who are strong partisan identifiers, on average, care much more about politics than those who do not identify with the parties. Parties also attempt to mobilize their identifiers—that is, the more you identify with a party, the more likely it is that you will be contacted by the party and its candidates during election campaigns.

Deciding to Vote.   In one sense, deciding to vote is much like deciding to attend a sporting event such as a professional baseball game. We do not go to a game to affect the outcome. We go for other reasons—because we like baseball and care about it. The same is true for voting: education, income, age, interest, and party identification are important indicators of our desire to participate.

While other factors may contribute to electoral participation, the small group of demographic and political variables just discussed tells us quite a bit. With this information, we can make a good prediction as to whether a person will or will not vote in a particular election. We also can account for most of the differences in turnout among different groups, such as African Americans, Asian Americans, Mexican Americans, and Anglo Americans.

The Practice of Voting

The legal qualifications for voting in Texas are surprisingly few and simple. Anyone who meets the following requirements is eligible to register and vote in Texas:

1. Be a citizen of the United States.
2. Be at least eighteen years of age.
3. Be a resident of the state.

The only individuals prohibited from voting in Texas are those who have been declared "mentally incompetent" in formal court proceedings and those convicted

Voters exercised their rights by casting votes in the 2006 elections. In the 1800s, ballots were not secret. They were often provided by the parties and printed on colored paper, thus allowing everyone to see which party's ballot a voter was using from the color of the paper. What results may have followed from such practices? (Flickr! Public Photo by "Haverchuk")

of a felony whose civil rights have not been restored by a pardon or by the passage of two calendar years from the completion of the sentence.

Registration. Meeting these qualifications does not mean that a person can simply walk into the voting booth on Election Day. To vote, a person must be registered. As a result of the Voting Rights Acts of 1965 and 1970, a number of United States Supreme Court rulings, and recent congressional action, the registration procedure is almost as simple as voting itself. A person may register in person or by mail at any time of the year up to thirty days before the election. Since the passage of federal "motor voter" legislation, a person can also register when renewing a driver's license—indeed, every person renewing a driver's license is asked whether he or she wants to register. Spouses, parents, or offspring also can register the applicant, provided they are qualified voters.

The present Texas registration system is as open and modern as that of any other state that requires advance registration. (Note that a number of states, including Maine, Minnesota, and Wisconsin, permit Election Day registration, while North Dakota requires no registration at all. There, you simply walk in, show your identification, and vote.) The Texas system, established by law in 1975, provides for the mailing of a new two-year voter-registration certificate to every registered voter by January 1 in even-numbered years. The system is permanent; once a voter is on the rolls, he or she will not be removed unless the nonforwardable certificate is returned. Since 1977, Texas law requires the secretary of state to make postage-free registration applications available at any county clerk's office. They are also available at various other public offices.

The "Strike List." Names on returned certificates are stricken from the list of eligible voters and placed on a "strike list." The strike list is attached to the list of voters for each precinct. What if you move? For three months, registered voters who have moved and whose names are therefore on the strike list can vote in their old precincts—provided they have filled out a new voter-registration card for the new residence. They can vote, however, only for those offices that both residences have in common. Coroner's death reports, lists of felony convictions, and adjudications of mental incompetence are also used to purge the list of eligible voters.

Residency Requirements. Establishing residence for voting is no longer a matter of living at a place for a specified time. Residence is defined primarily in terms of intent (that is, people's homes are where they intend them to be). No delay in qualifying to vote is permitted under United States Supreme Court rulings except for a short period of time during which the application is processed and the registrant's name is entered on the rolls. Under a federal court ruling, that delay in Texas is fixed at thirty days.[2]

Voting. Once a person is registered, voting is easy. This is especially true in Texas, which has passed a number of laws to make voting easier. In 1975, for example, the legislature required that all ballots and election materials be printed in Spanish as well as English in counties with a Hispanic population of 5 percent or more. In 1991, the legislature established early voting, which allows people to vote at a number of different sites before Election Day.[3]

Anyone can purchase the computer-generated voter list for any county in the state. Political parties and candidates make extensive use of voter lists when trying to identify likely voters during election campaigns.

---

[2]*Beare v. Smith*, 321 F.Supp. 1100 (1971). In later cases—*Burns v. Fortson*, 410 U.S. 686 (1973) and *Martson v. Lewis*, 410 U.S. 679 (1973)—the United States Supreme Court upheld delays of up to fifty days in Georgia and Arizona.

[3]Texas was one of the first states to institute early voting for all voters.

Voter Turnout in the United States and Texas

Easier registration and voting was expected to result in increased *voter turnout*—that is, the proportion of Americans who vote. Many people believe that instead, voter turnout has fallen during recent decades. Political scientists and pundits alike have made this claim. Some commentators have blamed the falling turnout on negative campaigning and broad public cynicism about the political process. Of course, the striking upturn in voter turnout during the 2004 presidential elections has tended to put this issue to rest, at least for now.

Is Voter Turnout Declining?

Is it true that voter turnout had been declining in the years before 2004? If you look at the percentage of the **voting-age population (VAP)** that actually cast a ballot, there seems to be some evidence of this decline. The national voter turnout as measured by the voting-age population is shown by the green bars in Figure 22–1.

One problem with using the VAP figure to gauge voter turnout is that it is not a very accurate measure of the number of *eligible voters*. The VAP figure includes felons who have lost the right to vote. Above all, it includes new immigrants who are not yet citizens. Finally, it does not include Americans living abroad, who can cast absentee ballots. As we stated in Chapter 9, the national voting-age population in 2004 was 221 million people. The number of eligible voters, however, was only 204 million. We call this second, more accurate figure the **vote-eligible population (VEP)**. Using the VEP measure, voter turnout in 2004 was not 55.3 percent, as it is sometimes reported, but 60.0 percent.

As you read in Chapter 1, the United States has experienced high rates of immigration in recent decades. Political scientists Michael McDonald and Samuel Popkin argue that the apparent decline in voter turnout since 1972 is entirely a function of the increasing size of the ineligible population, chiefly due to immigration. Voter turnout as measured by McDonald and Popkin using VEP figures that they have calculated is shown by the upper (orange) bars in Figure 22–1. (Even if voter turnout has not declined in the United States, however, it is low by international standards, as we explain in this chapter's *Beyond Our Borders* feature.)

Voting-Age Population (VAP)
The total number of persons in the United States or a state who are eighteen years of age or older, regardless of citizenship, military status, felony conviction, or mental state.

Vote-Eligible Population (VEP)
The total number of persons actually eligible to cast a ballot, excluding noncitizens, felons, and other ineligible persons but including citizens who are temporarily abroad (and who may vote absentee).

FIGURE 22–1 | U.S. VOTER TURNOUT IN PRESIDENTIAL ELECTIONS SINCE 1948

This figure shows voter turnout in presidential elections based both on the vote-eligible population (VEP) and on the voting-age population (VAP). Note that a drop-off in voter turnout took place in 1972, in part because the minimum voting age was lowered to eighteen and young people are less likely to vote. As measured by the more accurate VEP figure, turnout since then has gone up and down but has shown no consistent tendency to drop.

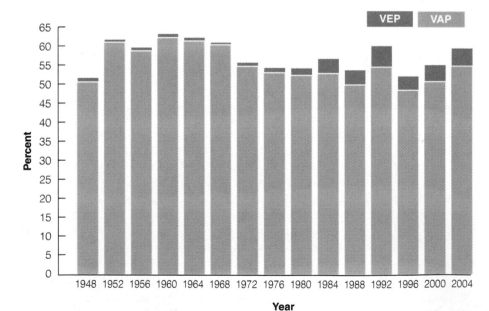

Sources: Data through 2000 are from Michael P. McDonald and Samuel Popkin. "The Myth of the Vanishing Voter," *American Political Science Review*, vol. 95, no. 4 (2001), pp. 963–974. The 2004 figures are from the United States Elections Project and are available at **elections.gmu.edu/voter_turnout.htm.**

BEYOND OUR BORDERS | American Voter Turnout Compared with Turnout in Other Countries

Turnout in American general elections is significantly lower than voter turnout in other industrialized democracies of the world. A study found that among the thirteen most comparable nations—those without compulsory voting—the turnout between 1972 and 1980 averaged 80 percent, substantially higher than the rate in the United States.[*] The more comprehensive numbers in Figure 22–2 show much the same pattern.

[*]G. Bingham Powell, Jr., "American Voter Turnout in Comparative Perspective," *American Political Science Review,* vol. 80 (March 1986), pp. 17 and 23.

They also show that U.S. turnout figures are well below those attained by many economically underdeveloped nations.

Some have argued that Americans are less likely to vote than Europeans because welfare spending is much lower (on a per capita basis) in the United States than in most European countries. Because low-income persons in the United States are less likely to depend on government spending than low-income persons in Europe, they have less of an incentive to follow politics and may find it easier to believe that election results are irrelevant to their lives. As we have seen, low-income persons are much less likely to vote than high-income individuals.

FIGURE 22–2 | VOTER TURNOUT IN SELECTED COUNTRIES AROUND THE WORLD

The turnout figures given here are based on the voting-age population (VAP) and not the vote-eligible population (VEP). The extent to which this makes a difference varies by country (we know that it depresses the U.S. figure). The turnout figures are not for any particular election but represent an average of national elections held since 1945. The U.S. figure is an average of presidential and midterm elections.

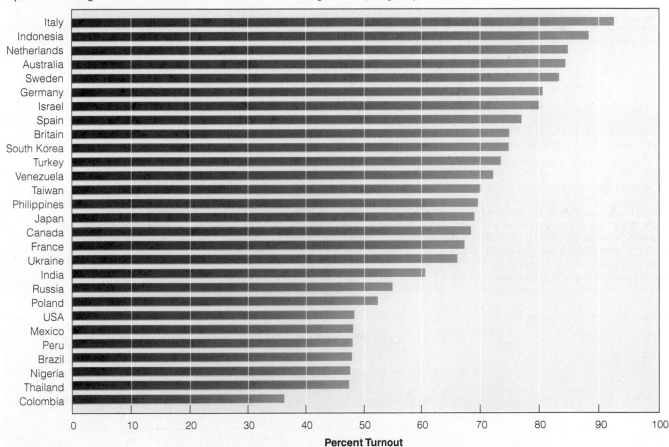

Source: International Institute for Democracy and Electoral Assistance, *Voter Turnout since 1945: A Global Report* (Stockholm, Sweden: 2002). The specific data shown above are available at **www.idea.int/vt/survey/voter_turnout2.cfm**.

Midterm Elections. The national elections that take place halfway between presidential elections are called *midterm elections*. Voter turnout for midterm elections is substantially lower than for presidential elections, even though many states—including Texas—choose their governors in these elections. As measured by VEP, presidential election turnout has fluctuated around an average of 55 percent since 1972. Turnout for the midterm elections has been more constant, rarely moving very far from an average of 40 percent.[4]

Young Voters. As we have observed, young people are much less likely to vote than the average American. Since 1972, citizens in the eighteen- to twenty-year-old age group have rarely posted turnout rates as high as 40 percent, even in a presidential year. In fact, there is some evidence that turnout rates among the youngest voters have fallen since 1972, reaching a low point of 30 percent in 2000.

Young citizens increased their turnout markedly in 2004, however (as did all other groups). In 2004, turnout among the eighteen- to twenty-four-year-old age group rose by almost 6 percentage points over 2000.[5]

Voter Turnout in Texas

In past years, voter turnout in Texas (and in most of the South) has been consistently lower than the turnout nationwide. Figure 22–3 shows that turnout in Texas (as measured by VEP) has tracked national turnout but has regularly been 6 to 7 percentage points lower than the national number. In 2004, only four states posted lower turnout rates than Texas.

---

[4]Michael P. McDonald and Samuel Popkin, "The Myth of the Vanishing Voter," *American Political Science Review*, vol. 95, no. 4 (2001), p. 966.

[5]*Ibid.* For 2004 figures, see reports issued by the Center for Information and Research on Civic Learning and Engagement (CIRCLE) at **www.civicyouth.org**.

FIGURE 22–3 | TEXAS VERSUS NATIONAL VOTER TURNOUT

The chart shows turnout in presidential election years since 1980. The figures do not appear to show any long-term trend upward or downward, though some elections have clearly been more interesting to the voters than others. The difference between the Texas voting-age population (VAP) and vote-eligible population (VEP) figures has grown, primarily because of a growing number of noncitizen residents.

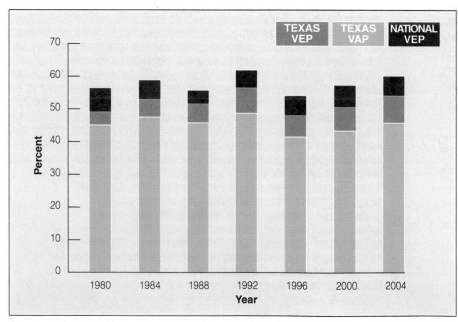

Sources: National VEP figures through 2000 are from Michael P. McDonald and Samuel Popkin, "The Myth of the Vanishing Voter," *American Political Science Review*, vol. 95, no. 4 (2001), pp. 963–974. Texas VEP and VAP figures are from Michael P. McDonald, "State Turnout Rates among Those Eligible to Vote," *State Politics and Policy Quarterly*, vol. 2, no. 2 (2002). All 2004 figures are from the United States Elections Project and are available at **elections.gmu.edu/voter_turnout.htm**.

Turnout for midterm elections in Texas shows a greater amount of variation. Since 1982, it has fluctuated between 30 and 40 percent. The turnout rate was especially good in 1990 and 1994, at 36.2 percent and 38.9 percent, respectively. These relatively high figures may have resulted from fierce competition between Republicans and Democrats at the state level in those years.[6] In 2006, turnout surged to over 40 percent, seemingly due to the open field of four candidates, which included not only Republican governor Perry and Democrat challenger Chris Bell but two independent candidates as well—Republican state comptroller Carole Keeton Strayhorn (who ran as an independent) and Kinky Friedman.

Reasons for Low Voter Turnout in Texas

Most Texans probably think that Texas is in the mainstream of American society. Why, then, is there such a difference between Texas and other urbanized and industrialized states in political behavior? Why is Texas closer to the states of the Deep South in voter turnout? The answer may lie in its laws, socio-economic characteristics, political structure, and political culture.

Legal Constraints.   Traditionally, scholars interested in the variation in turnout across the American states have focused on laws regulating registration and voting. Clearly, the most important of these laws were restrictions on who was allowed to vote, such as the poll tax, property ownership requirements, and the outright exclusion of African Americans and women.

Although these restrictions disappeared some time ago, other barriers to registration and voting persisted, and some remain in effect today.[7] We can ask: Does a state promote political participation by setting the minimum necessary limitations and making it as convenient as possible for the individual to vote? Or does a state repeatedly place barriers on the way to the polls, making the act of voting physically, financially, and psychologically as difficult as the local sense of propriety will allow? There is no doubt into which category Texas once fell—the application has been uneven, but historically Texas was among the most restrictive states of the Union in its voting laws.

Today, nearly all of these restrictions have been abolished by amendments to the U.S. Constitution, changes to state and national laws, rulings by the U.S. Department of Justice, and judicial decisions. Even a cursory examination of the restrictions and the conditions under which they were removed makes us appreciate the extent to which Texas elections were at one time closed. Consider these changes in Texas voting policies:

1. *Poll tax.* The payment of a **poll tax** was made a prerequisite for voting in 1902. The cost was $1.75 ($1.50 plus $0.25 optional for the county) and represented more than a typical day's wages at that time. Many poor Texans were therefore kept from voting. When the Twenty-fourth Amendment was ratified in 1964, it voided the poll tax in national elections. Texas was one of only two states to keep it for state elections until it was held unconstitutional in 1966.[8]
2. *Women's suffrage.* Texas made an attempt to grant the ballot to women in 1917, but the effort failed by four votes in the Texas legislature. Women were allowed to vote in the primaries of 1918, but not until ratification of the Nineteenth Amendment in 1920 did women gain full suffrage in Texas.

In 2006, voter turnout actually dipped to 26 percent despite an open field of four gubernatorial candidates, including Republican Governor Rick Perry and Democrat challenger, Chris Bell, and two independent candidates—Republican State Comptroller Carole Keeton Strayhorn and singer-writer Richard "Kinky" Friedman (above). Do you think that Friedman's campaign increased or decreased voter turnout? Why or why not?

| Poll Tax
A special tax that must be paid as a qualification for voting. The Twenty-fourth Amendment to the Constitution outlawed the poll tax in national elections, and in 1966 the United States Supreme Court declared it unconstitutional in all elections.

---

[6]Michael P. McDonald, "State Turnout Rates among Those Eligible to Vote," *State Politics and Policy Quarterly*, vol. 2, no. 2 (2002). The 2002 and 2004 figures are from the United States Elections Project and are available at **elections.gmu.edu/voter_turnout.htm**.
[7]See Glenn Mitchell II and Christopher Wlezien, "The Impact of Legal Constraints on Voter Registration, Turnout, and the Composition of the American Electorate," *Political Behavior*, June 1995, pp. 179–202.
[8]*U.S. v. Texas*, 384 U.S. 155 (1966).

3. *The white primary.* African Americans were barred from participating when the first Democratic Party primary was held in 1906. This measure was based on the theory that the Democratic Party was a private institution, as we explained in Chapter 5. When movement toward increased participation seemed likely, Texas took several steps to avoid a United States Supreme Court ruling allowing African Americans to vote. Not until 1944 were the legislature's efforts to deny African Americans access to the primaries finally overturned.[9]

4. *The military vote.* Until 1931, members of the National Guard were not permitted to vote. Members of the regular military began to enjoy the full rights of suffrage in Texas in 1965, when the United States Supreme Court voided the Texas constitutional exclusion.[10]

5. *Long residence requirement.* The Texas residency requirement of one year in the state and six months in the county was modified slightly by the legislature to allow new residents to vote in the presidential part of the ballot, but not until a United States Supreme Court ruling in 1972 were such requirements abolished altogether.[11]

6. *Property ownership.* Texas required property ownership for voting in bond elections until the United States Supreme Court ruled out property ownership as a requirement for revenue bond elections in 1969[12] and for tax elections in 1969 and in 1975.[13]

7. *Annual registration.* Even after the poll tax was voided, Texas continued to require voters to register every year until annual registration was prohibited by the federal courts in 1971.[14]

8. *Early registration.* Texas voters were required to meet registration requirements by January 31, earlier than the cutoff date for candidates' filings and more than nine months before the general election. This restriction was also voided in 1971.[15]

9. *Jury duty.* Texas law provided that the names of prospective jurors must be drawn from the voting rolls. Some Texans did not want to serve on juries, and not registering to vote ensured against a jury summons. (Texas counties now use driver's licenses for jury lists.)

| **Grandfather Clause**

A device used by southern states to exempt whites from state taxes and literacy laws originally intended to disenfranchise African Americans. It restricted voting to those who could prove their grandfathers had voted before 1867.

Texas used almost every technique available except the literacy test and the **grandfather clause**[16] to deny the vote to some citizens or to make voting time consuming, expensive, and psychologically difficult. This is not the case today. Most barriers to voting in Texas have been removed. In fact, as mentioned previously, the legislature has instituted a number of provisions that make voting easier than in most states. Thus, the laws in Texas may help us understand why turnout was low in the past and, with the relaxing of restrictions, why turnout has increased somewhat since 1960. The current laws do not help us understand why turnout in Texas remains low today. For this, we need to look elsewhere.

Socioeconomic Factors.   Texas, with its cattle barons and oil tycoons, is known as the land of the "big rich." What is not so well known is that Texas is also the land of the "big poor" and that more persons live in poverty in Texas than in any other state of the Union. While nationally the proportion of people living below the poverty level in 2002–2003 was 12.3 percent, in Texas the proportion was 16.3 percent. More than 25 percent of African American and Mexican American Texans have incomes

[9]*Smith v. Allwright*, 321 U.S. 649 (1944).

[10]*Carrington v. Rash*, 380 U.S. 89 (1965).

[11]*Dunn v. Blumstein*, 405 U.S. 330 (1972).

[12]*Kramer v. Union Free District No. 15*, 395 U.S. 621 (1969).

[13]*Cipriano v. City of Houma*, 395 U.S. 701 (1969); and *Hill v. Stone*, 421 U.S. 289 (1975).

[14]*Beare v. Smith*, 321 F.Supp. 1100 (1971).

[15]*Ibid.*

[16]Grandfather clauses were found unconstitutional by the United States Supreme Court in *Guinn v. United States*, 238 U.S. 347 (1915).

below the poverty level. More than 3 million individuals in Texas live in poverty, and more than 1 million of these are children. Understandably, formal educational achievement also is low. Of all Texans who are older than age twenty-five, one out of four has not graduated from high school. Among African Americans, the ratio is slightly less than one out of three, and among Mexican Americans it is almost one out of two.[17]

Given that income and education are such important determinants of electoral participation, low voter turnout is exactly what we should expect in Texas. Because income and education levels are particularly low among African Americans and especially Mexican Americans, turnout is particularly low for these groups. Voting by Texas minorities is on the rise, however, and this has led to much greater representation of both groups in elected offices, as we will see. These trends should continue as income and education levels among minorities increase.

Political Structure.   Another deterrent to voting in Texas is the length of the ballot and the number of different elections. Texas uses a long ballot that provides for the popular election of a large number of public officers. (Critics believe that some of these officers should be appointed rather than elected.) In an urban county, the ballot may call for the voter to choose among 150 and 200 candidates vying for fifty or more offices. The frequency of referendums on constitutional amendments also contributes to the length of the ballot in Texas. In addition, voters are asked to go to the polls for various municipal, school board, bond, and special district elections. Government simply is far more fragmented in Texas than in other states, and this makes particular elections less meaningful and perhaps more frustrating to voters.

Political Culture.   We discussed the impact of political culture on voter turnout in the *Politics and Culture* feature in Chapter 18 on page 590. Low voter turnout in Texas may be partly due to the state's political culture. As we observed, Texas citizens may be less likely to vote than citizens of other states because many Texans do not value political participation in itself and tend to think that they have little role to play in politics.

Primary, General, and Special Elections in Texas

Winning an office typically is a two-stage process. First, the candidate must win the Democratic or Republican nomination in the primary election. Second, the candidate must win the general election against the nominee of the other party. It is possible for a candidate to get on the general-election ballot without winning a primary election (as we explain shortly), but this is rare. As in most other states, elections in Texas are dominated by the Democratic and Republican parties.

Primary Elections

Three devices for selecting political party nominees have been used in U.S. history, each perceived as a cure for the ills of a previous system that was considered corrupt, inefficient, or inadequate. The first was the *caucus,* consisting of the elected party members serving in the legislature. The "insider" politics of the caucus room motivated the reformers of the Jacksonian era to institute the party convention system in 1828. In this system, ordinary party members select delegates to a party convention, and these delegates then nominate the party's candidates for office and write a party platform. The convention system was hailed as a "sure-fire" method of ending party nominations by the legislative bosses.

---

[17]U.S. Census Bureau. The definition of *poverty* depends on the size and composition of the family. For a family of four, two of whom are children, the poverty-level threshold in 2005 was $19,806.

Direct Primary
An intraparty election in which the voters select the candidates who will run on the party's ticket in the next general election.

The Direct Primary.   By 1890, however, the backroom politics of the convention halls again moved reformers to action, and the result was the **direct primary,** which most states adopted between 1890 and 1920. The first direct primary in Texas was held in 1906, under the Terrell Election Law (passed in 1903). This law enables party members to participate directly in their party's selection of candidates to represent them in the general election.

The White Primary.   Traditionally regarded as private activities, primaries were at one time largely beyond the concern of legislatures and courts. Costs of party activities, including primaries, were paid through donations and through assessments of candidates who sought a party's nomination. Judges attempted to avoid suits among warring factions of the parties in the same way that they avoided those suits involving church squabbles over the division of church property. On the basis of the theory that primaries were private activities, the United States Supreme Court in 1935 upheld the decision of the Texas Democratic Party convention to continue barring African Americans from participating in the Democratic Party primary.[18]

Recognizing that political party activities were increasingly circumscribed by law, the Court reversed itself in 1944 and threw out the white primary system.[19] The Court argued that in a one-party state, which Texas was at the time, the party primary may be the only election in which any meaningful choice is possible. Because the Democratic Party seldom had any real opposition in the general election, winning the nomination was, for all practical purposes, winning the office. Therefore, African Americans could not constitutionally be prevented from participating in the primary.

Who Must Hold a Primary?   Texas, like most other states, has for decades required that "major" political parties—those whose candidates for governor received a fixed minimum number of votes in the last general election—select their nominees through the primary. Other parties, however, were at one time allowed to nominate candidates by primary or convention, whichever they chose. In 1973, the Texas legislature amended the Texas election code to provide that any party receiving 20 percent or more of the gubernatorial vote must hold a primary and that all other parties must use the convention system.[20]

Limits on New Parties.   New parties must meet additional requirements if their nominees are to be on the general-election ballot. In addition to holding a convention, these parties must file with the secretary of state a list of supporters equal to 1 percent of the total vote for governor in the last general election. The list may consist of the names of those who participated in the party's convention, those who signed a nominating petition, or a combination of the two groups. Persons named as supporters must be registered voters who have not participated in the activities (primaries or conventions) of either of the two major parties. Each page (though not each name) on the nominating petition must be notarized. This requirement is, as intended, difficult to meet and therefore inhibits the creation of new political parties.

User-Benefit Theory
The principle that the people who benefit from certain types of governmental services should also be the ones to pay the costs for those services.

Financing the Primaries.   From their beginning in 1906 through 1970, the Texas political party primaries were financed under the **user-benefit theory,** in which users paid the cost through fees or assessments. The "users" were those who sought to become their party's nominees for public office. For all statewide and some local

---

[18]*Grovey v. Townsend,* 295 U.S. 45 (1935).
[19]*Smith v. Allwright,* 321 U.S. 649 (1944).
[20]La Raza Unida Party challenged this limitation. The U.S. Justice Department and federal courts sustained the challenge, but only as applied to La Raza Unida, which was permitted to conduct a primary in 1978. Otherwise, the law stands as written.

offices, nominal fixed-dollar fees were assessed. The major costs of the primaries were borne by candidates for district, county, and precinct offices. The county executive committees assessed candidates on the basis of the estimated costs of the primaries in their respective counties.

Since 1971, however, primary elections have been funded mostly from the state treasury. State and county executive committees initially make the expenditures, but the secretary of state reimburses each committee for the difference between the filing fees collected and the actual cost of the primary. To get on the primary ballot, a candidate need only file an application with the state or county party chair and pay the prescribed fee. The categories of fees, applicable also for special elections, are summarized in Table 22–1.

Getting on the Ballot through a Petition. So that no person is forced to bear an unreasonable expense when running for political office, the legislature (prodded by the federal courts) provided the petition as an alternative to the filing fee. For those seeking nomination to statewide office, the petition must bear the names of five thousand voters. For district and lesser offices, the number of signatures must equal 2 percent of the votes cast for the party's candidate for governor in the last election, up to a maximum of five hundred required signatures. A sample county primary ballot is reproduced in Figure 22–4 on the following page.

Administering Primaries. In a county primary, the chair and the county executive committee of each party receive applications and filing fees and hold drawings to determine the order of names on the ballot for both party and government offices. They then certify the ballot, select an election judge for each voting precinct (usually the precinct chair), select the voting devices (paper ballots, voting machines, or punch cards), and arrange for polling places and for printing. After the primary, the county chair and the executive committee canvass (count) the votes and certify the results to their respective state executive committees.

In the state primaries, the state party chair and the state executive committee of each political party receive applications of candidates for state offices, conduct drawings to determine the order of names, certify the ballot to the county-level officials, and canvass the election returns after the primary.

The Dual Primary. In Texas, as in other southern states that once had a Democratic one-party system (except Tennessee and Virginia), nominations are decided by a majority (50 percent plus one) of the popular vote. If no candidate receives a majority of votes cast for a particular office in the first primary, a second, runoff primary is required, in which the two candidates receiving the highest number of votes are pitted against each other.

| Runoff Primary
A second primary election that pits the two top vote-getters from the first primary against each other. Such an election is held in states such as Texas when the winner of the first primary did not receive a majority of the votes.

TABLE 22–1 | FEES FOR APPEARING ON A PARTY PRIMARY BALLOT IN TEXAS

Office	Fee Schedule
U.S. senator	$5,000
All other statewide officers	$3,700
U.S. representative	$3,125
State senator	$1,200
State representative	$750
County commissioner	$750–$1,250
District judge	$1,500–$2,500
Justice of the peace, constable	$375–$1,000
Public weigher, surveyor, and hide inspector	$75

FIGURE 22-4 | SAMPLE BALLOT FOR 2006 REPUBLICAN PARTY PRIMARY ELECTION

Vote Both Sides   *Vote en Ambos Lados de la Página*

March 7, 2006 Joint Primary Election
Elección Primaria Junta 7 de marzo de 2006
Travis County
Condado de Travis
March 07, 2006 - *07 Marzo 2006*   Precinct *Precinto*   **REP SAMPLE**

Instruction Note:
Use a BLUE or BLACK pen to mark your ballot. To vote, completely fill in the square to the left of your candidate or proposition choice. To vote for a write-in candidate, completely fill in the square to the left of "Write-in" and enter the name of the certified write-in candidate on the line provided.

Nota de Instruccion:
Marque su boleta con una pluma negra o azul. Para votar, llene completamenta el espacio cuadrado a la izquierda del nombre del candidato o selección de proposición de su preferencia. Para votar por un candidato por voto escrito, llene completamente el espacio cuadrado a la izquierda de Voto Escrito y escriba el nombre del candidato certificado en la linea provista.

UNITED STATES SENATOR - REP
SENADOR DE LOS ESTADOS UNIDOS - REP
☐ Kay Bailey Hutchison

DISTRICT 10, UNITED STATES REPRESENTATIVE - REP
DISTRITO NÚM. 10, REPRESENTANTE DE LOS ESTADOS UNIDOS - REP
☐ Michael T. McCaul

DISTRICT 21, UNITED STATES REPRESENTATIVE - REP
DISTRITO NÚM. 21, REPRESENTANTE DE LOS ESTADOS UNIDOS - REP
☐ Lamar Smith

GOVERNOR - REP
GOBERNADOR - REP
☐ Rhett R. Smith
☐ Larry Kilgore
☐ Rick Perry
☐ Star Locke

LIEUTENANT GOVERNOR - REP
GOBERNADOR TENIENTE -REP
☐ David Dewhurst
☐ Tom Kelly

ATTORNEY GENERAL - REP
PROCURADOR GENERAL - REP
☐ Greg Abbott

COMPTROLLER OF PUBLIC ACCOUNTS - REP
CONTRALOR DE CUENTAS PÚBLICAS - REP
☐ Susan Combs

COMMISSIONER OF THE GENERAL LAND OFFICE - REP
COMISIONADO DE LA OFICINA GENERAL DE TIERRAS - REP
☐ Jerry Patterson

COMMISSIONER OF AGRICULTURE - REP
COMISIONADO DE AGRICULTURA - REP
☐ Todd Staples

RAILROAD COMMISSIONER - REP
COMISIONADO DE FERROCARRILES - REP
☐ Major Buck Werner
☐ Elizabeth Ames Jones

CHIEF JUSTICE, SUPREME COURT, UNEXPIRED TERM - REP
JUEZ PRESIDENTE, CORTE SUPREMA, DURACIÓN RESTANTE DEL CARGO - REP
☐ Wallace Jefferson

PLACE 2, JUSTICE, SUPREME COURT - REP
LUGAR NÚM. 2, JUEZ, CORTE SUPREMA - REP
☐ Steve Smith
☐ Don Willett

PLACE 4, JUSTICE, SUPREME COURT - REP
LUGAR NÚM. 4, JUEZ, CORTE SUPREMA - REP
☐ David M. Medina

PLACE 6, JUSTICE, SUPREME COURT - REP
LUGAR NÚM. 6, JUEZ, CORTE SUPREMA - REP
☐ Nathan Hecht

PLACE 8, JUSTICE, SUPREME COURT, UNEXPIRED TERM - REP
LUGAR NÚM. 8, JUEZ, CORTE SUPREMA, DURACIÓN RESTANTE DEL CARGO - REP
☐ Phil Johnson

PRESIDING JUDGE, COURT OF CRIMINAL APPEALS - REP
JUEZ PRESIDENTE, CORTE DE APELACIONES CRIMINALES - REP
☐ Sharon Keller
☐ Tom Price

PLACE 7, JUDGE, COURT OF CRIMINAL APPEALS - REP
LUGAR NÚM. 7, JUEZ, CORTE DE APELACIONES CRIMINALES - REP
☐ Barbara Parker Hervey

PLACE 8, JUDGE, COURT OF CRIMINAL APPEALS - REP
JUEZ, CORTE DE APELACIONES CRIMINALES, LUGAR NÚM. 8 - REP
☐ Robert W. Francis
☐ Charles Holcomb
☐ Terry Keel

DISTRICT 5, MEMBER, STATE BOARD OF EDUCATION - REP
DISTRITO NÚM. 5, MIEMBRO DE LA JUNTA ESTATAL DE EDUCACIÓN PÚBLICA - REP
☐ Ken Mercer
☐ Mark Loewe
☐ Dan Montgomery

DISTRICT 10, MEMBER, STATE BOARD OF EDUCATION - REP
DISTRITO NÚM. 10, MIEMBRO DE LA JUNTA ESTATAL DE EDUCACIÓN PÚBLICA - REP
☐ Tony Dale
☐ Cythnia Dunbar

STATE SENATOR, DISTRICT 25 - REP
SENADOR ESTATAL, DISTRITO NÚM. 25 - REP
☐ Jeff Wentworth

DISTRICT 47, STATE REPRESENTATIVE - REP
DISTRITO NÚM. 47, REPRESENTANTE ESTATAL - REP
☐ Dick Reynolds
☐ Bill Welch
☐ Rich Phillips
☐ Terry Dill
☐ Alex Castano

DISTRICT 48, STATE REPRESENTATIVE - REP
DISTRITO NÚM. 48, REPRESENTANTE ESTATAL - REP
☐ Ben Bentzin

Sample Ballot   Sample Ballot

210004331100   1000000021   18520300

Vote Both Sides   *Vote en Ambos Lados de la Página*

Primary elections in Texas are held on the second Tuesday in March of even-numbered years. The runoff primary is scheduled for the second Tuesday in April, or a month after the initial primary election. Although there are earlier presidential primaries, no other state schedules primaries to nominate candidates for state offices so far in advance of the general election in November.

Presidential Aspirations and Early Primaries.   Until 1960, the primaries were held much later in the year, on the fourth Saturday in July and the fourth Saturday in August. The dates were moved up so that presidential aspirant Lyndon B. Johnson could "lock up" his renomination to the U.S. Senate before the Democratic National Convention began in Los Angeles.

The presidential ambitions of another Texan, vice president George H. W. Bush, contributed to the adoption of an even earlier primary. Believing an early primary victory in Texas would benefit their candidate, Bush's Republican supporters joined conservative Democrats in urging Texas to join most other southern states holding a regional primary on "Super Tuesday." In a special session in 1986, the Texas legislature rescheduled the primary to nominate all state officials on the second Tuesday in March in both presidential and midterm election years. In 1996, Super Tuesday included primary elections in Florida, Louisiana, Mississippi, Oklahoma, Oregon, Tennessee, and Texas. (In later years, several states made further changes to their primary schedules, and these changes broke up the Super Tuesday primary.)

Turnout in Primaries. Turnout in Texas primaries is much lower than in general elections. Take 2002, for example: although 4.5 million Texans voted in the general election, only 1.6 million participated in either the Democratic or the Republican primary—that is, approximately 12 percent of the population eligible to vote. Matters were even worse in 2006, when 1.2 million people, less than 10 percent of the eligible population, voted in either primary. Turnout in presidential election years is higher but still averages below 30 percent. The people who vote in primary elections are not representative of the overall population—they tend to be better educated, more affluent, and more extreme ideologically.

Open versus Closed Primaries. Party primaries are defined as either open or closed. These terms specify whether or not participation is limited to party members. Because the purpose of a primary is to choose the party's nominee, it would seem logical to exclude anyone who is not a party member. Not every state accepts this argument, however. Alaska and Washington use the blanket primary, in which voters can "mix and match" among the various parties' candidates. Seven states have an *open primary,* in which voters decide at the polls in which primary they will participate. Texas and the remaining forty states use what is called a *closed primary.*

The Closed Primary in Texas. Although Texas is classified technically as a closed-primary state, it operates as an open-primary state in practice. As in other closed-primary states, the primary voter is morally—but not legally—bound to vote only in his or her own party's elections. This means that people can participate in either the Democratic or the Republican primary whether they are party members or not. Only two minor legal restrictions make Texas technically a closed-primary state:

1. A person is forbidden to vote in more than one primary on the day of the primary elections.
2. Once a person has voted in the first primary, he or she cannot switch parties and participate in the runoff election or convention of any other party.

Closed Primaries in Other States. In contrast, the closed primary used in many other states requires that when registering to vote, a person must specify a party preference. The party's name is then stamped on the registration card at the time it is issued. A voter may change his or her party registration between elections, up to a set time (often thirty days) before the primary or convention. Voters are limited to participating in the activities of the party for which they have registered. Furthermore, an individual who registers as an independent (no party preference) is excluded from the primaries and conventions of all parties. Note that how a person votes (or fails to vote) in any type of primary does not limit in any way that person's choice in the general election in November.

Crossover Voting. The opportunity always exists in Texas for members of one political party to invade the other party's primary. This is called **crossover voting.** It is often done to increase the chances that the nominee from the other party will be someone whose philosophy is similar to that of the invader's own party. For example, if Republicans can ensure the nomination of a strong conservative in the

| **Crossover Voting**
A circumstance in which members of one political party vote in the other party's primary to influence which nominee is selected by the other party.

Democratic primary, either of the two major party's candidates may be quite acceptable in November.

In the past, the Republican Party "institutionalized" crossover voting to a degree by not holding a Republican primary in some counties. In those counties, Republicans had no place to go except to the Democratic primary. The decision to forgo the primary was not necessarily based on a lack of support for Republican candidates. Although that was true in some counties, it was certainly not true of all. Of the twenty-two counties that did not hold a Republican primary in 1980, President Ronald Reagan carried ten; in 1984 he carried eighteen of twenty-six. This is because a large number of Democrats voted for Reagan in the general election.

The Effects of Crossover Voting.   Crossover voting has long been the liberal Democrat's nemesis in Texas, because many persons who will vote for Republicans in the general election cross over to support conservatives in the Democratic primary. The candidacy of Lloyd Bentsen for the U.S. Senate in 1970 illustrates the point. In the Democratic primary, Bentsen outpolled Senator Ralph Yarborough, the liberal incumbent, in eighty-seven voting precincts in Dallas County, the great majority of which were located in the affluent areas of northern Dallas. In the general election, though, Bentsen received a far smaller share of the votes in these precincts and lost most of them to the Republican candidate, George H. W. Bush. In another twist, there is some evidence that Republicans in other parts of the state voted for Yarborough because they believed he would be easier to defeat.

Crossover voting is a two-edged sword, as the Republicans learned in 1976 when Texas Democrats apparently crossed over in many areas to vote for Ronald Reagan in the presidential primary. The result was that Republican president Gerald Ford was shut out. With the help of conservative Democrats, the Reaganites captured all one hundred delegates to the Republican National Convention. Many were startled that this could happen to an incumbent president (Ford). Mindful thereafter of the hazards of crossover voting, many Republicans have supported a "party-purity" law that would require voters to register their party affiliation and be limited to participating in the primaries of that party.

General Elections

The purpose of party primaries is to choose each party's candidates from among the competing intraparty factions. General elections, in contrast, allow the voters to choose the people who will actually serve in national, state, and county offices from among the competing political party nominees and write-in candidates. General elections differ from primaries in at least two other important ways. First, general elections are administered completely by public (as opposed to party) officials of state and county governments. Second, unlike Texas primaries, in which a majority vote is required, the general election is decided by plurality vote, in which the winning candidate only need receive at least one more vote than any opponent.

Scheduling General Elections.   General elections in Texas are held biennially on the same day as national elections—the first Tuesday after the first Monday in November of even-numbered years. In years divisible by four, Americans elect the president, the vice president, all U.S. representatives, and one-third of the U.S. senators. In Texas, the voters elect all 150 members of the state house in these elections and roughly half (15 or 16) of the 31 senators. Texas voters also elect the winners of a number of board and court positions at the state level, as well as about half of the county positions.

Most major state executive positions (governor, lieutenant governor, attorney general, and others) are not filled until the midterm election, when all U.S. representatives and one-third of U.S. senators (but not the president) again face the vot-

| **Plurality**
The number of votes cast for a candidate who receives more votes than any other candidate but not necessarily a majority. Most national, state, and local election laws provide for winning elections by a plurality vote.

ers. All state house representatives and half of the state senators are elected in these years. Some board members, judges, and county officers are chosen as well.

The Effects of Simultaneous State and National Elections.   Holding simultaneous national and state elections has important political ramifications. During the administration of Andrew Jackson, parties first began to tie the state and the national governments together politically. A strong presidential candidate and an effective candidate for state office can benefit significantly by cooperating and campaigning under the party label. This usually works best, of course, if the candidates are in fundamental agreement on political philosophy and the issues.

In Texas, which is more politically conservative than the average American state, such fundamental agreement has often been lacking. This has been especially true for the Democrats. Popular Democrats in the state have often disassociated themselves from the more liberal presidential nominee of the party. As you learned in Chapter 18, Democratic governor Allan Shivers openly endorsed and worked for the election of the Republican candidate for president in 1952 and again in 1956. In 1980, four former governors (all Democrats) joined Republican governor Bill Clements in endorsing Ronald Reagan for president. State leaders are often hesitant to be identified with a presidential nominee who may "drag them down" because the candidate is less popular with the Texas voters than they are.

President Ronald Reagan and First Lady Nancy Reagan are joined on the podium by his vice-presidential running mate, George H. W. Bush and his wife Barbara at the Republican National Convention in Dallas, Texas, in 1984. How much benefit do you think the Republicans gained from holding the convention for Reagan's nomination to his second term in Texas? How much might Reagan have benefited from having a Texan—George H. W. Bush—as his vice-presidential running mate? (Courtesy of Reagan Presidential Library)

The Effects of Separating State and National Elections.   When the Texas Constitution was amended in 1972 to extend the terms of the governor and other major administrative officials from two years to four years, the elections for these offices were scheduled for the midterm election years. This change had two major effects. First, the separation of presidential and state campaigns insulates public officials from the ebb and flow of presidential politics and allows them to disassociate themselves from the national political parties. Elections for statewide office now largely reflect Texas issues and interests.

Second, the separation reduces voter turnout in statewide elections and makes the outcomes much more predictable. As was shown earlier, turnout is much lower in midterm elections than in presidential elections, when many people are lured to the polls by the importance and the visibility of the presidential campaign. Independent and marginal voters are more likely to turn out, and election results for congressional and state-level offices are less predictable. In midterm election years, however, the less informed and the less predictable voters are more likely to stay home, and the contest is largely confined to party regulars. Most incumbent state politicians prefer to cast their lot with this more limited and predictable midterm electorate.

Special Elections

As the name implies, special elections are held to meet special or emergency needs, such as to ratify a constitutional amendment or to fill a vacant office. Special elections are held to fill vacancies only in those legislative bodies having general (rather than limited) lawmaking power. Legislative bodies with general power are the U.S. Senate and House of Representatives, state legislatures, and city councils in home-rule cities. All other vacancies, including judgeships and county commissioner seats, are filled by appointment. The special election fills a vacancy only until the end of the regular term or until the next general election, whichever comes first.

Republican Senator Kay Bailey Hutchison of Texas. In today's political environment, why might Republican women be strong candidates for legislative posts? (Photo Courtesy of Senator Hutchison)

Special elections are nonpartisan, and so the process of getting on the ballot is relatively easy and does not involve a primary.[21] All that is required is the filing of the application form in a timely and appropriate manner and the payment of the designated filing fee. Unlike the winner of a general election, the winner of a special election must receive a majority of the votes. Thus, a runoff special election may be necessary when no candidate wins an absolute majority the first time around.

Senator Yarborough.   The runoff requirements for special elections in Texas have been enacted in piecemeal fashion—an illustration of how public policy is often established for the political advantage of a particular candidate or political ideology. Before 1957, all special elections could be won with a plurality vote. During a special election in 1957, however, liberal Democratic candidate Ralph Yarborough appeared likely to win. Therefore, the Texas House of Representatives (controlled by conservative Democrats) quickly passed a bill requiring a runoff in any election to fill a vacant U.S. Senate seat whenever the top candidate fails to win a majority.

A few liberal legislators, however, were able to delay the bill in the state senate until after the special election, in which Yarborough led the field of twenty-three candidates. Given that Yarborough received only 38 percent of the popular vote, it is possible that he would have lost in a runoff. Sixteen days after the election, the state senate passed the runoff bill, and it was signed into law by the governor—too late to prevent Yarborough's victory. Once in office, Yarborough was able to capitalize on his incumbency and served for thirteen years.

Senator Hutchison.   In 1993, after U.S. senator Lloyd Bentsen was nominated to serve as secretary of the treasury by President Bill Clinton, a special election was necessary to fill the vacancy. Democratic governor Ann Richards appointed Robert Krueger, a former member of Congress and ambassador-at-large, to fill in until the special election, in which he was the Democratic candidate. Republican Kay Bailey Hutchison ultimately won the special election, however, becoming the first woman elected to represent Texas in the U.S. Senate.

The Conduct and Administration of Elections

Texas has entered a new era in the administration of elections. Gone are the days of almost complete decentralization of responsibility for elections. In the past, some Texas counties did not include certain contests on their ballots or refused to hold elections at all. Because of the problem of local officials' ignoring state law, in 1967 the Texas legislature designated the secretary of state as the chief election officer of Texas. In this capacity, the secretary of state interprets legislation and issues guidelines. Under the Voting Rights Act, the U.S. Department of Justice must approve these decisions, so they appear to carry the weight of federal authority as well.

Since 1973, the secretary of state has had the responsibility for disbursing funds to the state and county party executive committees to pay for the primary elections. The secretary of state is the keeper of election records, both party and governmental. The secretary also receives certificates of nomination from parties that have conducted primaries and conventions and uses these certificates to prepare the ballot for statewide offices. The governor, the secretary of state, and a gubernatorial appointee are the members of a three-person board that canvasses election returns for state and district offices.

---

[21]Here, *nonpartisan* means only that the party label does not appear on the ballot and certification by the party is not necessary. Special elections are, in fact, often partisan because regular party supporters work for "their" candidates.

County-Level Administration

Except for the preparation of the statewide portion of the ballot, county-level officials actually conduct general elections. In 1977, the legislature created three options from which the counties may choose when administering general elections.

The Traditional System. The first option is to maintain the decentralized system that the counties have used for decades. Under this system, the major responsibility rests with the county clerk. By the time the clerk receives the state portion of the ballot from the secretary of state, she or he will have certified the candidates' names for the county-level and precinct-level portions of the ballot. The board of elections—consisting of the county judge, sheriff, and clerk and the chairs of the county executive committees of the two major parties—arranges for polling places and for the printing of ballots. The county tax assessor-collector processes all voter applications and updates the voting rolls. The county commissioners' court draws precinct voting lines, appoints election judges, selects voting devices, canvasses votes, and authorizes payment of all election expenses from the county treasury.

Alternative County Options. The two other options are designed to promote efficiency. One is for the county commissioners' court to transfer the voter-registration function from the office of the tax assessor-collector to that of the county clerk, thus removing the assessor-collector from the electoral process.

The third option, available for the first time in 1979, involves more extensive changes and may represent the direction that election administration will take in the future. It calls for all election-related duties of both the assessor-collector and the county clerk to be transferred to a county election administrator. This officer is appointed for a term of two years by the county elections commission, which, in counties that choose this option, replaces the board of elections. (The membership of the commission is the same as that of the board, except that the sheriff is not included.)

Ballot Construction

Like so many other features of an election system, ballot construction reflects both practical and political considerations. Two basic types of general-election ballots are available—the party-column ballot and the office-block ballot.

The Party-Column Ballot. In the *party-column ballot* (which we first described in Chapter 9), the names of all the candidates of each party are listed in parallel columns. This is the type of ballot that has traditionally been used in Texas. For an example, see Figure 22–5 on the following page. This ballot itemizes the offices as prescribed by law in descending order of importance, and the candidates are listed in each row. Beside each name is a box (on paper ballots) or lever (on voting machines) that the voter must mark or pull if she or he wishes to vote a split ticket. At the top of each column is the party's name and a box or lever. To vote a straight ticket, the voter need only mark the box or pull the lever for the party of his or her choice.

The Office-Block Ballot. In the *office-block ballot,* which we also described in Chapter 9, the names of the candidates for each office are listed underneath the title of the office. (See Figure 22–6 on the next page for an example.) To vote a straight party ticket, a voter must pick his or her party's candidate for each office. Several states use the office-block ballot, which also is called the Massachusetts ballot because it originated there. Minor parties in Texas (which once included the Republican Party) and independent voters advocate the use of this ballot type because it makes straight-ticket voting for the major parties more difficult.

FIGURE 22-5 | PARTY-COLUMN BALLOT USED IN TEXAS FOR THE 2004 GENERAL ELECTION

GENERAL ELECTION (ELECCION GENERAL)
(Condado de) SAMPLE COUNTY, TEXAS
NOVEMBER 2, 2004 (2 de noviembre de 2004)
SAMPLE BALLOT (BOLETA DE MUESTRA)

No. 0000

INSTRUCTION NOTE: Vote for the candidate of your choice in each race by placing an "X" in the square beside the candidate's name. You may cast a straight-party vote (that is, cast a vote for all the nominees of one party) by placing an "X" in the square beside the name of the party of your choice. If you cast a straight-party vote for all the nominees of one party and also cast a vote for an opponent of one of that party's nominees, your vote for the opponent will be counted as well as your vote for all the other nominees of the party for which the straight-party vote was cast.

(NOTA DE INSTRUCCION: Vote por el candidato de su preferencia para cada candidatura marcando una "X" en el espacio cuadrado a la izquierda del nombre del candidato. Usted podrá votar por todos los candidatos de un solo partido político ("straight ticket") marcando una "X" en el espacio cuadrado a la izquierda del nombre de ese partido político. Si usted vota por uno de los partidos políticos y también vota por el contrincante de uno de los candidatos de dicho partido político, se contará su voto por el contrincante, tanto como su voto por todos los demás candidatos del partido político de su preferencia.)

Candidates for: (Candidates para:)	☐ REPUBLICAN PARTY (Partido Republicano)	☐ DEMOCRATIC PARTY (Partido Democrático)	☐ LIBERTARIAN PARTY (Partido Libertariano)	☐ INDEPENDENT (Independiente)	☐ WRITE-IN: (Voto Escrito)
President and Vice President (Presidente y Vice Presidente)	☐ George W. Bush/ Dick Cheney	☐ John F. Kerry/ John Edwards	☐ Michael Badnarik/ Richard V. Campagna		☐
United States Representative, District ___ (Representante de los Estados Unidos, Distrito Núm. ___)					☐
Railroad Commissioner (Comisionado de Ferrocarriles)	☐ Victor G. Carrillo	☐ Bob Scarborough	☐ Anthony Garcia		
Justice, Supreme Court, Place 3 (Juez, Corte Suprema, Núm. 3)	☐ Harriet O'Neill				
Justice, Supreme Court, Place 5 (Juez, Corte Suprema, Núm. 5)	☐ Paul Green				
Justice, Supreme Court, Place 9 (Juez, Corte Suprema, Núm. 9)	☐ Scott Brister	☐ David Van Os			
Judge, Court of Criminal Appeals, Place 2 (Juez, Corte de Apelaciones Criminales, Lugar Núm. 2)	☐ Lawrence "Larry" Meyers		☐ Quanah Parker		
Judge, Court of Criminal Appeals, Place 5 (Juez, Corte de Apelaciones Criminales, Lugar Núm. 5)	☐ Cheryl Johnson		☐ Tom Oxford		
Judge, Court of Criminal Appeals, Place 6 (Juez, Corte de Apelaciones Criminales, Lugar Núm. 6)	☐ Michael E. Keasler	☐ J.R. Molina			

FIGURE 22-6 | OFFICE-BLOCK BALLOT USED IN MASSACHUSETTS

The Politics of Ballot Construction.   Understandably, supporters of the major Texas political parties strongly support the use of the party-column ballot. It enables lesser-known candidates to ride on the coattails of the party label or of a popular candidate running for major office. There also may be an extra advantage in the use of this type of ballot for the party that is listed in the first column.

In the past, candidates of the once-dominant Democratic Party were always listed first, and the practice was accepted without challenge. In 1963, however, the legislature enacted a requirement that the parties be slated from left to right on the ballot according to the proportion of votes that each party's candidate for governor received in the most recent gubernatorial election. Next come candidates of parties that were not on the ballot in the last election, and last come independents. After the election of Governor Bill Clements in 1979, the Republicans achieved the favored ballot position.

Beginning with the 2002 elections, many Texas counties moved away from a strict party-column ballot. Partly due to the adoption of electronic voting systems (discussed later), ballots in these counties combine features of the office-block and party-column designs. As with the office-block ballot, candidates are listed underneath each office. As with the party-column ballot, however, one can vote a straight party ticket with a single mark; that is, before turning to specific offices, voters are first given the option to vote a straight ticket.

Getting on the Ballot

For a candidate to get his or her name on the general-election ballot, the candidate must be either a party nominee or an independent. If a party received at least 5 percent of the vote for any statewide office in the previous general election, its full slate of candidates is placed on the ballot automatically. Thus, the Democratic and Republican parties have no problems, and certification by the appropriate party officials of the winner of a primary or convention is routine.

Making Life Hard for Third Parties and Independents.   Minor parties have a more difficult time. For instance, neither the Libertarian Party nor the Green Party received the necessary votes in 2002, and both had to petition to get their candidates on the ballot in 2004. Independent candidates for president have the most difficult challenge, for they must present a petition with signatures equaling 1 percent of the total state vote for president in the last election. For John Anderson, an independent candidate who ran in 1980, that meant a minimum of 40,719 names on the petition. In 1992, Ross Perot's supporters presented 54,275 signatures to get his name on the ballot.

For all offices except president, the total vote for governor is the basis for determining the required number of signatures for both independents and third-party candidates. A candidate for statewide office needs signatures equaling 1 percent of the total gubernatorial vote in the entire state. For multicounty district offices, the requirement is 3 percent of the gubernatorial vote in the district. For all other district and local offices, it is 5 percent of the gubernatorial vote in the district (a maximum of five hundred signatures at the local level).

Further requirements add to the difficulty of gaining access to the ballot by petition. Signers must be registered voters and must not have participated in the selection of a nominee for that office in another party's primary. In addition, each page of the petition must be notarized.[22]

---

[22]In 1976, the secretary of state interpreted the law as requiring that each *signature* be notarized. The next year, the legislature specified that a notary need only sign each page of the petition. Difficulties involving technical aspects of the law and adverse interpretations of the law represent only part of the harassment that minor parties and independents have traditionally encountered in their quest for a place on the ballot. See Ernest Crain, *et al.*, *Understanding Texas Politics*, 12th edition, (Belmont, Calif.: Wadsworth Publishing Company, 2006).

As a general rule, candidates using the petition route seek twice the required number of signatures to ensure the petition's certifiability. For example, in 1980 the Libertarian Party submitted 55,000 signatures and the Socialist Workers Party (SWP) turned in 30,000 to ensure that each had 23,698 persons who were legally qualified to sign. Only the Libertarians succeeded in placing their candidates' names on the ballot, however. The SWP fell below the minimum when almost half of the petitioners' signatures were found to be those of persons not qualified to sign.[23]

Write-in Candidates.   Write-in candidates are seldom successful. Often, they are individuals who have entered a party primary and lost. A different kind of write-in candidacy developed in 1976, however, following a Democratic primary election for the nomination for associate justice of the Texas Supreme Court. Charles W. Barrow, chief justice of the Fourth Court of Civil Appeals in San Antonio, was thought to be virtually unopposed. The legal establishment was stunned when Don Yarbrough, a young Houston attorney involved in a number of legal entanglements, upset Barrow in the quest for the Democratic nomination. Apparently, the voters had confused the young attorney's name with that of former gubernatorial candidate Don Yarborough. No one had filed in the Republican primary, so there was no Republican candidate to challenge Yarbrough in the general election. Yarbrough appeared to be a shoo-in.

Embarrassed, the legal establishment sought to have the primary winner disqualified from the ballot. Failing that, they mounted a write-in campaign supported strongly by the leaders of both political parties. Playing the name game themselves, they chose as their candidate district judge Sam Houston Jones. The write-in campaign failed miserably.

Don Yarbrough's victory was short lived, however. Under threat of removal by the legislature, he resigned after serving approximately six months. He was replaced through gubernatorial appointment by Charles W. Barrow—his opponent in the Democratic primary. (Some reformers have advocated a system under which all judges would be appointed by the governor, at least initially. We discuss this plan in this chapter's *Which Side Are You On?* feature.)

Write-in candidates may have an easier task in the future as a result of a law subsequently passed by the legislature. It requires a candidate to register with the secretary of state before the start of absentee voting in general elections and forty-five days before a primary election. The names of write-in candidates must be posted at the election site, possibly in the election booth. A candidate not properly registered cannot win, regardless of the number of votes he or she receives. Write-ins in primary elections are permitted only for party offices.

The Secret Ballot and the Integrity of Elections

Most people believe that the right to vote includes the rights to cast a ballot in secret, have the election conducted fairly, and have the ballots counted correctly. These rights have not always been available, however. The *Australian ballot*, adopted by Texas in 1892, includes names of the candidates of all political parties on a single ballot printed at public expense and available only at the voting place.[24] Given a reasonably private area in which to mark the ballot, the voter was offered a secret ballot for the first time.

Election Judges and Poll Watchers.   Protection of the integrity of the electoral process in Texas is primarily addressed through "political" remedies. As a result,

---

[23]The SWP was founded in 1938 by followers of the Russian Communist leader Leon Trotsky, who was Joseph Stalin's chief opponent in the struggle for control of the Soviet Union. (Trotsky lost.) In recent decades, the SWP has looked less to Trotsky for inspiration and more to Cuban leader Fidel Castro.

[24]Optional at first, the Australian ballot was made mandatory in 1903.

WHICH SIDE ARE YOU ON? | Should Texas Change the Way It Elects Judges?

In Texas, candidates for judgeships run under a party label. Law firms, businesses, and ideological groups channel millions of dollars in campaign contributions to candidates for the Texas Supreme Court and other positions. These contributions raise serious questions of judicial independence. Polls and surveys have revealed that 48 percent of judges, 79 percent of lawyers, and 83 percent of the general public believe that campaign contributions have a very significant or somewhat significant impact on judicial decisions. Texas is the only state in which a judge can legally solicit campaign contributions from lawyers and litigants who are actually involved in cases the judge is deciding.

Texas Supreme Court chief justice Tom Phillips, who retired in 2004 after sixteen years on the bench, has said, "I know very few lawyers that don't think solicitations from judges who are not opposed and are not likely to be opposed is not something that borders on a shakedown." In large part because of the problem of campaign contributions, Phillips advocates replacing the current system of partisan elections with a process sometimes known as the "Missouri plan," in which the governor appoints judges who then face nonpartisan retention elections. Phillips lobbied vigorously for this plan during the 2003 legislative session, but it was rejected by both parties. Should a plan such as the one Phillips advocated be adopted by Texas?

THE MISSOURI PLAN WOULD GIVE US BETTER JUDGES

Reformers argue that under the current partisan election system, judges must devote a major portion of their time to fund-raising. Major contributors attempt to influence candidates for the judiciary in the same way they attempt to influence legislative candidates. Under a merit plan for selecting judges, such as the Missouri plan, the governor fills court vacancies from a list of nominees submitted by a judicial commission, which may consist of judges, lawyers, and laypersons. Judges chosen by the governor then face a retention election in which the voters decide whether they should be retained. Most are. Under such a system, fund-raising and campaigning would be almost completely eliminated, and judges could concentrate on handing down impartial justice.

DEMOCRACY IS THE BEST SOLUTION

Those who defend the existing system argue that the people deserve the right to select their judges. So-called merit plans are as thoroughly political as choosing judges through contested elections—but the politics is hidden and confined to an elite. Even requiring judges to run with party labels is a benefit to the public. Voters often have limited knowledge of a candidate's judicial philosophy, and the party label offers this information. Finally, campaign contributions are not as dangerous to judicial independence as many people believe. Even Chief Justice Phillips admits that the problem is mostly one of appearance and that true abuses are rare.

WHAT'S YOUR POSITION?

Do campaign contributors have too much influence with judges in Texas? Would a merit plan for judicial selection result in judges who are more impartial?

GOING ONLINE

For one perspective on the problems surrounding judicial campaign contributions in Texas and where the solution may lie, read the article, "Different Chief Justice, but Same Story," on the Texans for Justice's Web site at **www.tpj.org/page_view.jsp?pageid=611&pubid=362**.

---

minor parties have reason to be concerned that irregularities in elections administered by members of the majority parties may not be observed and, if observed, may not be reported.

Traditional practice has been that, in general and special elections, the county board of elections appoints as election judges the precinct chairs of the political party that has a majority on the elections board. Since 1967, each election judge has been required to select at least one election clerk from each of the lists submitted by the county chairs of the two major political parties. Moreover, law now recognizes the status of "poll watchers," and both primary candidates and county chairs are authorized to appoint them. These oversight options mark a significant improvement over the days when the only possible (and usually ineffective) remedy was to go to court.

Rechecks and Recounts.   If there is a question about the election results, candidates can ask for either a recheck or a recount of the ballots. A recheck applies primarily to voting machines. It checks for counting errors and costs three dollars per precinct. The loser of an election also can ask for a recount (this is discussed in greater detail on page 710). The candidate who requests a recount must put up a deposit and is liable for the entire cost unless she or he wins or ties in the recount. Moreover, a recount (but not a recheck) must include all precincts. In a large county, the cost of a recount can be prohibitive.

Multilingualism

Ballots in most Texas counties are printed in English. In over a hundred counties, the ballot is printed in both English and Spanish. In some parts of the United States, other languages are required, including Chinese, Eskimo, Filipino, Japanese, and Korean. In Los Angeles County alone, ballots are printed in seven different languages.

Vietnamese Ballots in Houston.   In 2002, the U.S. Department of Justice ordered a number of counties around the country, including Harris County (which contains Houston), to provide ballots and voting materials in Vietnamese as well as Spanish. Harris County was the only county in Texas required to provide Vietnamese ballots and the only county outside California to face this requirement. The requirement was due to the Voting Rights Act of 1965 and its 1992 amendments. According to Section 203 of the act, a political subdivision (typically a county) must provide such help if significant numbers of voting-age citizens are members of a single-language minority who do not speak or understand English "well enough to participate in the electoral process."

When Are Multilingual Ballots Required?   Specifically, the legal requirement is triggered when more than 5 percent of the voting-age citizens or 10,000 of these citizens meet the criteria. The 2000 census showed that more than 55,000 people living in Harris County identified themselves as Vietnamese. The Department of Justice determined that at least 10,000 of them were old enough to vote and not proficient in English. Thus, the requirement was triggered. Given the current record levels of immigration into the United States, the number of ballot languages is almost certain to increase. We show a sample multilingual ballot in Figure 22–7.

Voting Absentee and Voting Early

All states allow members of the U.S. armed forces to vote absentee, and Texas, along with forty other states, also permits absentee voting for reasons such as illness or anticipated absence from the county. Traditionally, absentee voting in Texas (and other states) was mostly a convenience for the middle class and served as a boost for conservative candidates.

Current Rules for Absentee Voting.   In 1987, the legislature made changes that appear to have far-ranging effects:

- To vote absentee in person (rather than by mail), you need not swear that you intend to be out of the city or county on Election Day.
- Absentee ballots can be cast in substations in the urban counties.

Since 1989, the absentee-voting period has begun twenty-two days before the election and ended on the sixth day before the election. Moreover, substation voting places now remain open twelve hours a day Monday through Friday, with shorter hours on Saturdays and Sundays. As a result, absentee voting has increased tremendously. Whether cast by mail or in person, on paper ballots or by punch card or electronic machines, absentee votes are not counted until Election Day.

FIGURE 22–7 | ENGLISH-VIETNAMESE LANGUAGE BALLOT USED IN HARRIS COUNTY FOR THE 2006 GENERAL ELECTION

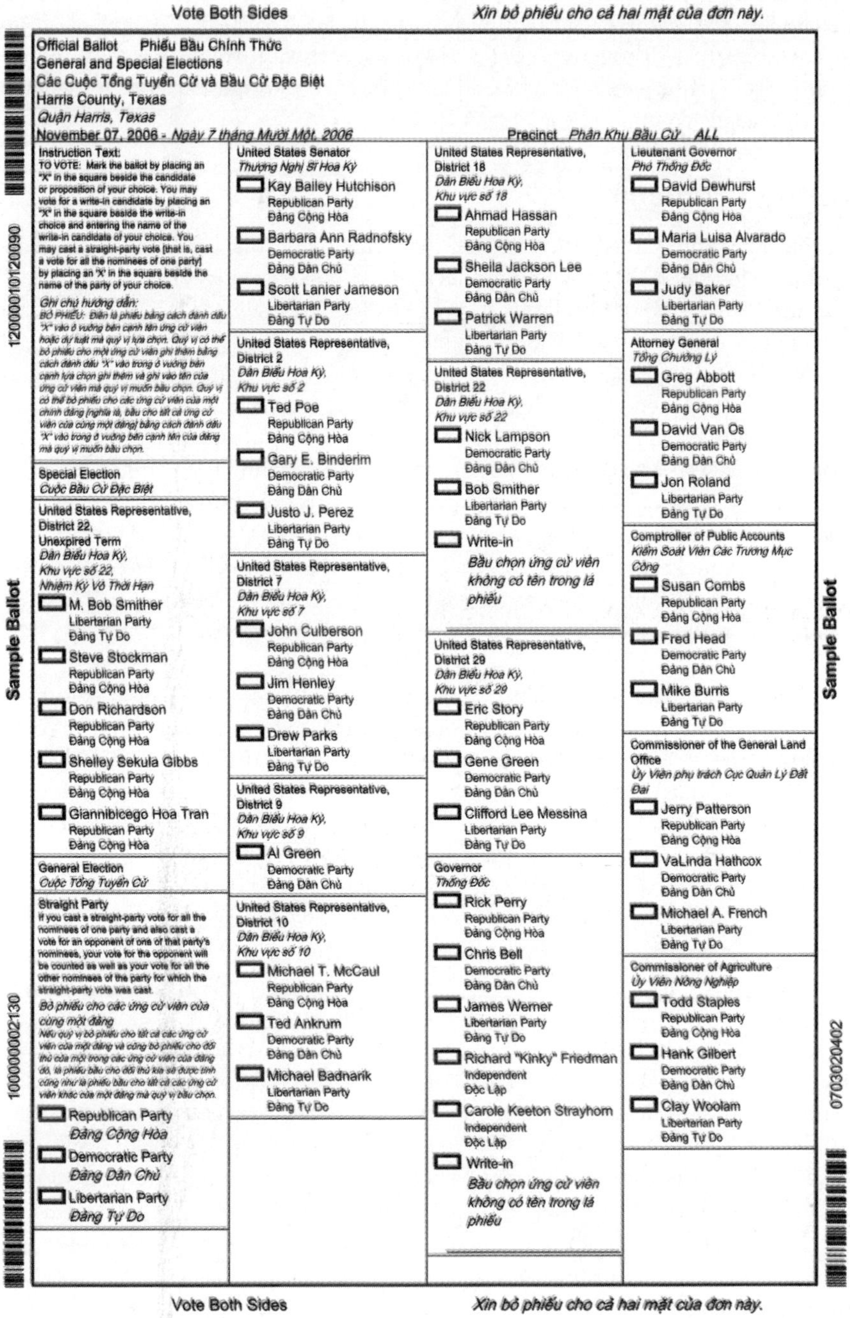

Vote Both Sides   Xin bỏ phiếu cho cả hai mặt của đơn này.

Official Ballot   Phiếu Bầu Chính Thức
General and Special Elections
Các Cuộc Tổng Tuyển Cử và Bầu Cử Đặc Biệt
Harris County, Texas
Quận Harris, Texas
November 07, 2006 - Ngày 7 tháng Mười Một, 2006   Precinct Phận Khu Bầu Cử ALL

Instruction Text:
TO VOTE: Mark the ballot by placing an "X" in the square beside the candidate or proposition of your choice. You may vote for a write-in candidate by placing an "X" in the square beside the write-in choice and entering the name of the write-in candidate of your choice. You may cast a straight-party vote [that is, cast a vote for all the nominees of one party] by placing an "X" in the square beside the name of the party of your choice.

Ghi chú hướng dẫn:
BỎ PHIẾU: Điền lá phiếu bằng cách đánh dấu "X" vào ô vuông bên cạnh tên ứng cử viên hoặc dự luật mà quý vị lựa chọn. Quý vị có thể bỏ phiếu cho một ứng cử viên ghi thêm bằng cách đánh dấu "X" vào trong ô vuông bên cạnh lựa chọn ghi thêm và ghi vào tên của ứng cử viên mà quý vị muốn bầu chọn. Quý vị có thể bỏ phiếu cho các ứng cử viên của một chính đảng (nghĩa là, bầu cho tất cả các ứng cử viên của cùng một đảng) bằng cách đánh dấu "X" vào trong ô vuông bên cạnh tên của đảng mà quý vị muốn bầu chọn.

Special Election
Cuộc Bầu Cử Đặc Biệt

United States Representative, District 22, Unexpired Term
Dân Biểu Hoa Kỳ, Khu vực số 22, Nhiệm Kỳ Vô Thời Hạn
- [ ] M. Bob Smither — Libertarian Party — Đảng Tự Do
- [ ] Steve Stockman — Republican Party — Đảng Cộng Hòa
- [ ] Don Richardson — Republican Party — Đảng Cộng Hòa
- [ ] Shelley Sekula Gibbs — Republican Party — Đảng Cộng Hòa
- [ ] Giannibicego Hoa Tran — Republican Party — Đảng Cộng Hòa

General Election
Cuộc Tổng Tuyển Cử

Straight Party
If you cast a straight-party vote for all the nominees of one party and also cast a vote for an opponent of one of that party's nominees, your vote for the opponent will be counted as well as your vote for all the other nominees of the party for which the straight-party vote was cast.
Bỏ phiếu cho các ứng cử viên của cùng một đảng
Nếu quý vị bỏ phiếu cho tất cả các ứng cử viên của một đảng nào và cũng bỏ phiếu cho đối thủ của một trong các ứng cử viên của đảng đó, lá phiếu bầu cho đối thủ kia sẽ được tính cũng như là lá phiếu bầu cho tất cả các ứng cử viên khác của một đảng mà quý vị bầu chọn.
- [ ] Republican Party — Đảng Cộng Hòa
- [ ] Democratic Party — Đảng Dân Chủ
- [ ] Libertarian Party — Đảng Tự Do

United States Senator
Thượng Nghị Sĩ Hoa Kỳ
- [ ] Kay Bailey Hutchison — Republican Party — Đảng Cộng Hòa
- [ ] Barbara Ann Radnofsky — Democratic Party — Đảng Dân Chủ
- [ ] Scott Lanier Jameson — Libertarian Party — Đảng Tự Do

United States Representative, District 2
Dân Biểu Hoa Kỳ, Khu vực số 2
- [ ] Ted Poe — Republican Party — Đảng Cộng Hòa
- [ ] Gary E. Binderim — Democratic Party — Đảng Dân Chủ
- [ ] Justo J. Perez — Libertarian Party — Đảng Tự Do

United States Representative, District 7
Dân Biểu Hoa Kỳ, Khu vực số 7
- [ ] John Culberson — Republican Party — Đảng Cộng Hòa
- [ ] Jim Henley — Democratic Party — Đảng Dân Chủ
- [ ] Drew Parks — Libertarian Party — Đảng Tự Do

United States Representative, District 9
Dân Biểu Hoa Kỳ, Khu vực số 9
- [ ] Al Green — Democratic Party — Đảng Dân Chủ

United States Representative, District 10
Dân Biểu Hoa Kỳ, Khu vực số 10
- [ ] Michael T. McCaul — Republican Party — Đảng Cộng Hòa
- [ ] Ted Ankrum — Democratic Party — Đảng Dân Chủ
- [ ] Michael Badnarik — Libertarian Party — Đảng Tự Do

United States Representative, District 18
Dân Biểu Hoa Kỳ, Khu vực số 18
- [ ] Ahmad Hassan — Republican Party — Đảng Cộng Hòa
- [ ] Sheila Jackson Lee — Democratic Party — Đảng Dân Chủ
- [ ] Patrick Warren — Libertarian Party — Đảng Tự Do

United States Representative, District 22
Dân Biểu Hoa Kỳ, Khu vực số 22
- [ ] Nick Lampson — Democratic Party — Đảng Dân Chủ
- [ ] Bob Smither — Libertarian Party — Đảng Tự Do
- [ ] Write-in — Bầu chọn ứng cử viên không có tên trong lá phiếu

United States Representative, District 29
Dân Biểu Hoa Kỳ, Khu vực số 29
- [ ] Eric Story — Republican Party — Đảng Cộng Hòa
- [ ] Gene Green — Democratic Party — Đảng Dân Chủ
- [ ] Clifford Lee Messina — Libertarian Party — Đảng Tự Do

Governor
Thống Đốc
- [ ] Rick Perry — Republican Party — Đảng Cộng Hòa
- [ ] Chris Bell — Democratic Party — Đảng Dân Chủ
- [ ] James Werner — Libertarian Party — Đảng Tự Do
- [ ] Richard "Kinky" Friedman — Independent — Độc Lập
- [ ] Carole Keeton Strayhorn — Independent — Độc Lập
- [ ] Write-in — Bầu chọn ứng cử viên không có tên trong lá phiếu

Lieutenant Governor
Phó Thống Đốc
- [ ] David Dewhurst — Republican Party — Đảng Cộng Hòa
- [ ] Maria Luisa Alvarado — Democratic Party — Đảng Dân Chủ
- [ ] Judy Baker — Libertarian Party — Đảng Tự Do

Attorney General
Tổng Chưởng Lý
- [ ] Greg Abbott — Republican Party — Đảng Cộng Hòa
- [ ] David Van Os — Democratic Party — Đảng Dân Chủ
- [ ] Jon Roland — Libertarian Party — Đảng Tự Do

Comptroller of Public Accounts
Kiểm Soát Viên Các Trương Mục Công
- [ ] Susan Combs — Republican Party — Đảng Cộng Hòa
- [ ] Fred Head — Democratic Party — Đảng Dân Chủ
- [ ] Mike Burris — Libertarian Party — Đảng Tự Do

Commissioner of the General Land Office
Ủy Viên phụ trách Cục Quản Lý Đất Đai
- [ ] Jerry Patterson — Republican Party — Đảng Cộng Hòa
- [ ] VaLinda Hathcox — Democratic Party — Đảng Dân Chủ
- [ ] Michael A. French — Libertarian Party — Đảng Tự Do

Commissioner of Agriculture
Ủy Viên Nông Nghiệp
- [ ] Todd Staples — Republican Party — Đảng Cộng Hòa
- [ ] Hank Gilbert — Democratic Party — Đảng Dân Chủ
- [ ] Clay Woolam — Libertarian Party — Đảng Tự Do

Sample Ballot   Sample Ballot

Vote Both Sides   Xin bỏ phiếu cho cả hai mặt của đơn này.

Early Voting. In 1991, the Texas legislature instituted early voting.[25] All Texas voters now are able to cast their ballots before Election Day. Unlike absentee voting, early voting is available to any registered voter. In addition to traditional Election Day voting sites, such as schools and fire stations, there are a number of other places to vote early, including grocery and convenience stores.

---

[25]For a description of early voting and a preliminary assessment of its effects, see Robert M. Stein and Patricia A. Garcia-Monet, "Voting Early but Not Often," *Social Science Quarterly*, vol. 78 (December 1997), pp. 657–671.

This innovation clearly has made voting easier in Texas, and people are taking advantage of it. In 1992, for example, about 25 percent of all votes were cast before Election Day. In 1996, approximately 33 percent of votes were cast early. In 2000, the number was slightly less than 39 percent. In 2004, over 50 percent of all votes were cast early. Although people are voting earlier, turnout has not increased greatly. Still, the tendency to vote early may have serious implications for when and how politicians campaign.

Voting Problems

We take for granted that when we vote, the system will work correctly. As we learned in Florida in the 2000 presidential elections, this is not always ensured. The first machine count of ballots in Florida showed George W. Bush with a 1,725-vote lead. In a mandatory machine recount of the same ballots, the same machines cut his lead to 327. We also learned that some ballots were not counted because they were defective, and other ballots were so poorly designed that they may have led voters to pick the wrong candidate. Claims were also raised that some ineligible persons (typically former felons) cast votes. What does this mean? The answer is simple. Even machines make mistakes. Some ballots are not counted. Some votes may be counted for the wrong candidate. Some people vote who are not supposed to do so.

Experts have known for a long time that voting involves a degree of error. By most accounts, the error rate averages 1 to 2 percent, although it can be higher, depending on the system used.

The Punch-Card Ballot Problem.   The error rate is largest for punch-card ballots, which have commonly been used in big cities in Texas and other states. To vote, you insert the ballot into a slot in the voting booth and then punch holes corresponding to candidates' names, which are printed on lists, usually in the form of a booklet.

There are two sources of error with these ballots. First, some voters do not fully punch out the pieces of paper from the perforated holes—that is, these pieces of paper, which are called **chads,** remain attached to the ballot.

Second, even where the chads are completely detached, machines do not read each and every ballot. This is of importance to voters. It typically is of little consequence for election outcomes, however. Counting errors tend to cancel out, so that no candidate gains a great number of votes. Thus, the errors are important only when elections are very close—within half of a percentage point or less, which is not very common. When it does happen, the losing candidate can request a recount.

Recounts.   Texas has specific laws about recounts. A candidate can request a recount if he or she loses by less than 10 percent. This is a fairly generous rule compared with other states. The candidate who requests the recount does have to pay for it, however, which means that most candidates do not request a recount unless the margin is much closer, say, 1 percentage point.

The Texas election code states that "only one method may be used in the recount [and] a manual recount shall be conducted in preference to an electronic recount." The procedures are fairly detailed. What may be most interesting is the set of rules for how chads should be interpreted. Indeed, canvassing authorities are allowed to determine whether "an indentation on the chad from the stylus or other object is present" and whether "the chad reflects by other means a clearly ascertainable intent of the voter to vote."[26] This leaves ample room for discretion on the part of canvassing authorities in the various Texas counties.

| Chad
A small fragment of paper produced by the punching of a data card, such as a punch-card ballot.

---

[26] Texas Code 127.130. Also see Carlos Guerra, "Texas Is Far Friendlier to All Our Chad," *San Antonio Express-News,* November 25, 2000, p. B-1.

Under Texas election law, hand recounts include "hanging chads." Here, an election worker holds a ballot filled with undetached chads (squares of paper that are pushed out of punch-card ballots) that will have to be manually removed before the ballot can be counted. Why might some states refuse to count ballots unless they are perfectly formed? (AP Photo/Ted S. Warren)

Electronic Voting. Partly in response to the events in Florida in the 2000 presidential elections—and the potential for similar problems in Texas—a number of counties introduced electronic voting in the 2002 midterm election. Instead of punching holes in ballots or filling in empty circles on sheets that can be read by machine, voters in Dallas, Houston, and San Antonio voted by touching screens.

The technology is similar to what is used for e-ticket check-in at many airports and promises an exact count of votes. Electronic voting is being used in various jurisdictions throughout the United States. As with any new technology, however, problems have occurred with the new systems in Texas and elsewhere.[27]

Election Campaigns in Texas

The aim of party activity is to nominate candidates in the party primary or convention and then get them elected in the general election. The pattern in Texas before 1978 was for Republicans and other minor parties to run only token, poorly financed candidates for most contested offices, so the real choices were made in the Democratic primary. Today, the battle has moved from the Democratic primary to the general election itself.

Who Gets Elected

It is useful to think of the elective offices in Texas as a pyramid. At the bottom of the pyramid are the most local of offices; at the top is the governor. Moving from bottom to top, the importance of the office increases, and the number of office-holders decreases. It thus becomes more and more difficult for a politician to ascend higher up the pyramid, and only the best politicians rise to the top. This tells us much about candidates and elections in Texas and elsewhere.

Candidates for Statewide Office. In the most local elections, the pool of candidates is diverse. Contenders may vary in educational background, income, and profession. As we move up the pyramid, however, candidates become more

---

[27]Rachel Konrad, "Reports of Electronic Voting Trouble Top 1,000," *USA Today*, November 4, 2004, available at **www.usatoday.com/tech/news/techpolicy/evoting/2004-11-04-1000-reports_x.htm**.

homogeneous. For statewide office, the typical candidate is middle or upper class, is from an urban area, and has strong ties to business and professional interests in the state. Most officers who are elected statewide, including the governor, lieutenant governor, and attorney general, must be acceptable to the state's major financial and corporate interests and to its top law firms. These interests help a statewide candidate to raise the large volume of funds that is critical to a successful race.

Successful candidates for statewide office in Texas traditionally have been white Protestant males. Before 1984, when Raul Gonzalez was elected to the state supreme court, no Mexican American or African American had been elected to statewide office, although these two ethnic groups combined represent half of the state's population. The only female governor had been Miriam A. "Ma" Ferguson, who in the 1920s served as surrogate for her husband, Jim. In 1982, Ann Richards was elected state treasurer, becoming the second woman ever to be elected to statewide office in Texas.

Gains by Women and Minorities.   Since then, women and minority group members have made substantial gains in statewide offices. In 1990, Democrat Ann Richards (1933–2006) became the first woman elected governor in her own right. That same year, Republican Kay Bailey Hutchison captured the state treasurer's office. In 1993, Hutchison won a special election to become the first woman from Texas elected to the U.S. Senate. Dan Morales became the first Mexican American to win a state executive office when he was elected attorney general in 1990.[28] More history was made in 1992 when Morris Overstreet of Amarillo won a seat on the Texas Court of Criminal Appeals and became the first African American elected to a statewide office.

Women and ethnic groups are starting to make inroads in other elected offices in Texas as well. In the seventy-ninth legislature (2005–2006), 31 women were elected to the 150-member house and 4 to the 31-member senate. Women have also held the post of mayor in five of the state's largest cities—Austin, Dallas, El Paso, Houston, and San Antonio. Mexican Americans hold 35 seats in the state legislature, and African Americans occupy 16 seats. Among the state's 32 U.S. congressional representatives are 3 women, 6 Mexican Americans, and 3 African Americans. Clearly, Texas politics has changed considerably.

The General-Election Campaign

To a large extent, election outcomes are predictable. Despite all the media attention paid to conventions, debates, advertising, and other elements of political campaigns, there are certain things that powerfully structure the vote in national and state elections.[29] In state elections, two factors predominate: party identification and incumbency.

Party Identification.   First, if the voters in a state tend to identify more with one political party than the other, the candidates of the favored party have an advantage in general elections. When most Texans identified with the Democratic Party, Democratic candidates dominated elected offices throughout the state. As Texans have become more Republican in their identification, Republican candidates have done very well. Indeed, as we pointed out in Chapter 21, Republicans now hold every statewide elective office.

Party identification varies considerably within Texas, however, and this has implications for state legislative elections. In some parts of the state, particularly in

---

[28]Morales was convicted of mail and tax fraud in 2003 and was sentenced to four years in prison.

[29]Most of the research has focused on presidential elections. See Christopher Wlezien, "On Forecasting the Presidential Vote," *PS: Political Science and Politics,* vol. 34 (March 2001), pp. 25–31, available at **www.apsanet.org/imgtest/CJ312-ElectionIntro%5B23-24%%5D.pdf**. There is some research on state gubernatorial and legislative elections. See, for example, Mark E. Tompkins, "The Electoral Fortunes of Gubernatorial Incumbents," *Journal of Politics,* vol. 46 (May 1984), pp. 520–543; and Ronald E. Weber, Harvey J. Tucker, and Paul Brace, "Vanishing Marginals in State Legislative Elections," *Legislative Studies Quarterly,* vol. 16 (February 1991), pp. 29–47.

POLITICS AND REDISTRICTING | The Republican Redistricting Coup of 2003

In August 2003, eleven Democratic Texas state senators fled from Austin and encamped at a hotel in Albuquerque, New Mexico. This was by no means the first such incident in Texas history. The previous year, Democratic members of the Texas house had holed up in Ardmore, Oklahoma. You might ask why Texas legislators occasionally flee the state—a practice unique to Texas.

WHY THE DEMOCRATS FLED

A short answer is that both chambers of the Texas legislature have quorums of two-thirds of the total membership. (A **quorum** is the number of members who must be present if a body is to transact business.) This is an unusually high figure. In Texas, 11 members of the 31-member senate or 51 members of the 150-member house can stall business by not showing up.

But why leave the state—why not just stay at home? Because officers of the house or senate can order the Texas Department of Public Safety (DPS) to arrest absent legislators and forcibly return them to the capitol. The DPS has no jurisdiction outside Texas, however, and the U.S. Department of Justice has refused to help Texas arrest recalcitrant lawmakers.

WHAT THE DEMOCRATS HOPED TO ACCOMPLISH

What kind of business were the legislative exiles attempting to stop? In both instances, the target was a Republican plan to redraw the boundaries of the districts that elect members of the U.S. House. Redistricting normally takes place every ten years immediately after the census. Redistricting after the 2000 census became mired in controversy, and a three-judge federal panel eventually defined the districts. In doing so, the judges made only the minimum necessary changes to the old districts—which had been drawn in 1991 by a Democratic legislature to benefit the Democrats.

These districts resulted in a Texas delegation to the U.S. House of seventeen Democrats and fifteen Republicans, even though 55 percent of the votes cast statewide in House contests in 2002 went to Republican candidates. Texas Republicans were not happy with these districts and hit on the plan of designing new ones. Redistricting *between* censuses was unprecedented in American history—but apparently legal.

THE REPUBLICANS WIN

On September 2, John Whitmire, one of the Democrats in Albuquerque, gave up the fight. The Republicans had preserved Whitmire's senate seat in the 2001 remap of Texas senate districts, and apparently "his marker was called." Three weeks later, in a special session, the Texas senate approved the Republican redistricting plan.

By the time of the 2004 elections, one Democrat in the U.S. House had switched to the Republicans, resulting in a delegation of 16 Democrats and 16 Republicans. After the 2004 elections, the Texas delegation consisted of 21 Republicans and 11 Democrats. Clearly, the Republican plan was classic political **gerrymandering**—the artful drawing of district lines to benefit one political party. (We first described gerrymandering in Chapter 11.)

In Texas, as in other states, redistricting remains a highly volatile issue. The federal courts in general have approved even obvious gerrymandering, usually stating that politically based gerrymandering is not under the purview of the judiciary.

FOR CRITICAL ANALYSIS

Why might Texas have established such a high quorum for its legislative bodies? What interests might be served by such a provision?

---

urban districts, a majority of the voters identify with the Democratic Party. Democratic candidates typically represent those areas in the state house and senate. Thus, party identification in the state and in the various districts has much to do with which candidates win general elections. How the boundaries of the various districts are drawn also has an important effect on the outcome, as we show in this chapter's *Politics and Redistricting* feature.

Incumbency. Second, incumbent candidates—those who hold office and are up for reelection—are more likely to win in general elections. This is particularly true in state legislative elections, where the districts are fairly homogeneous and the campaigns are not very visible, but incumbency also is important in elections for statewide office. Incumbents have a number of advantages over challengers, the

Quorum
The number of members of a legislative chamber or other body that must be present for the body to conduct business.

Gerrymandering
The drawing of legislative district boundary lines for the purpose of gaining a partisan or factional advantage. A district is said to be gerrymandered when its shape is manipulated by the dominant party in the state legislature to maximize that party's electoral strength at the expense of the minority party.

most important of which is that they have won before. To become an incumbent, a candidate has to beat an incumbent or else win in an open-seat election, which usually includes a number of strong candidates. By definition, therefore, incumbents are good candidates. In addition, incumbents have the advantages of office. They are in a position to do things for their constituents and thus increase their support among voters.

While party identification and incumbency are important in Texas elections, they are not the whole story. What they really tell us is the degree to which candidates are advantaged or disadvantaged as they embark on their campaigns. Other factors also matter on Election Day, and we consider some of those factors next.[30]

Mobilizing Groups. Groups play an important role in elections for any office. A fundamental part of campaigns is getting out the vote among those groups that strongly support the candidate. To a large extent, candidates focus on groups aligned with the political parties.[31] At the state level, business interests and teachers are particularly important; Republican candidates tend to focus their efforts on the former and Democratic candidates on the latter.

Candidates also attempt to mobilize other groups, including African Americans and Mexican Americans. Traditionally, Democratic candidates emphasized these minority groups, though Governor George W. Bush broke somewhat with this tradition and focused substantial attention on the Hispanic community in Texas. Mobilizing groups does not necessarily involve taking strong public stands on their behalf. Indeed, the mobilization of such groups may be conducted quietly, often through targeted mailings and phone calls.

Choosing Issues. Issues play a role in any campaign. In campaigns for state office, taxes, education, and crime are relevant, and the abortion issue is important in many states. As with the mobilization of groups, the issues candidates select tend to reflect their party affiliations, but issue stands are often not so clear-cut. Very few candidates, after all, are in favor of higher taxes and less spending on education and crime prevention.

Where candidates do differ is in their emphasis on particular issues and their policy proposals. Their choices depend heavily on carefully crafted opinion polls. Using polls, candidates attempt to identify the issues that the public considers important and then develop policy positions to address those issues. The process is ongoing, and candidates pay close attention to changes in public opinion and, perhaps most important, to the public's response to the candidates' own positions. Polling is thus fundamental in modern political campaigns in America.

The Campaign Trail. Deciding where and how to campaign is a critical part of campaign strategy. Candidates spend countless hours "taking the stump," or traveling about the state or district to speak before diverse groups. In a state as large as Texas, candidates for statewide office must pick and choose areas so as to maximize their exposure. This means that candidates spend most of their time in urban areas.

Today, no candidate is elected by stumping alone. The most direct route to the voters is through the media. There are some 17 media markets in Texas. These include approximately 200 television and cable stations and more than 500 radio

---

[30]For a detailed analysis of election campaigns in Texas in a single election year, see Richard Murray, "The 1996 Elections in Texas," in Kent L. Tedin, Donald S. Lutz, and Edward P. Fuchs, eds., *Perspectives on American and Texas Politics*, 5th ed. (Dubuque, Iowa: Kendall/Hunt, 1998), pp. 247–286.

[31]For an analysis of how membership in various demographic groups influences voting behavior, see Robert S. Erikson, Thomas B. Lancaster, and David W. Romero, "Group Components of the Presidential Vote, 1952–1984," *Journal of Politics*, vol. 50 (May 1988), pp. 337–346. For an analysis of how identification with various social groups influences voting behavior, see Christopher Wlezien and Arthur H. Miller, "Social Groups and Political Judgments," *Social Science Quarterly*, vol. 78 (December 1997), pp. 625–640.

stations. In addition, there are 79 daily and 403 weekly papers dispersed throughout the state's 254 counties.[32] Candidates hire public relations firms in their effort to take advantage of all these media outlets, and media consultants and advertising play a large role.

These days, a successful campaign often relies on **negative campaigning,** in which candidates attack opponents' issue positions or character. As one campaign consultant said, "Campaigns are about definition. Either you define yourself and your opponent or they do . . . . Victory goes to the aggressor."[33] While many consider negative campaigning an unfortunate part of American politics, such campaigning can provide voters with information about the candidates and their issue positions.

Timing.   The timing of the campaign effort can be very important. Unlike presidential campaigns, campaigns for state offices, including the governorship, begin fairly late in the election cycle. Indeed, it is common to hear little from gubernatorial candidates until after Labor Day and not much from candidates for the legislature until a month before the election.

Candidates often reserve a large proportion of their campaign advertising budget for a last-minute media "blitz." Early voting may affect this strategy, however. In 2004, half of the votes in Texas were cast early, which means that any final campaign blitz came far too late to have any effect on those voters. Because of this, in the future candidates may be less likely to concentrate their efforts on the final days of the campaign.

Financing Political Campaigns

Political campaigns are expensive, which means that candidates need to raise substantial funds to be competitive. The amount a candidate raises can be the deciding factor in the campaign. How much a candidate needs depends on the level of the campaign and the competitiveness of the race. High-level campaigns for statewide office are usually multimillion-dollar affairs.

In recent years, the race for governor has become especially expensive. In 1990, Republican Clayton Williams spent a reported $20 million but lost to Democrat Ann Richards, who spent almost $12 million. George W. Bush spent almost $15 million to defeat Ann Richards in 1994. In 2002, Tony Sanchez spent almost $70 million, mostly his own funds, but lost to incumbent governor Rick Perry, who spent slightly less than $30 million.

Although lower-level races in Texas are usually not million-dollar affairs, they too can be expensive. This is certainly true if a contested office is an open seat (where the incumbent is not running for reelection) or if the district is a marginal one (where the incumbent won office with less than 55 percent of the vote). It is not unusual for a candidate in a competitive race for the state house to spend between $100,000 and $200,000.

Where Does the Funding Come From?   Where do contributions of this size come from? Candidates often try to solicit small individual contributions through direct-mail campaigns. But to raise the millions required for a high-level state race, they must solicit "big money" from wealthy friends or from business and professional interests that have a stake in the outcome of the campaign. Banks, corporations, law firms, and professional associations—such as those representing physicians, real estate agents, or teachers—organize and register their political action committees (PACs) with the secretary of state's office. PACs serve as the vehicle through which

| Negative Campaigning
A strategy in political campaigns of attacking the opposing candidate's issue positions or—especially—his or her character.

---

[32]*Gale Directory of Publications and Broadcast Media,* vol. 2, 129th ed. (Detroit, Mich.: Gale Research, 1997).

[33]Quoted in Dave McNeely, "Campaign Strategists Preparing Spin Systems," *Austin American-Statesman,* October 21, 1993, p. A11.

interest groups collect donations and then contribute them to political candidates. (You learned about PACs at the national level in Chapter 9.)

Another source of "big money" is loans. Candidates often borrow heavily from banks or wealthy friends or even from themselves.[34]

Where Do the Contributions Go?   Today's political campaign involves a multitude of different expenses. Newspaper ads, billboards, radio messages, bumper stickers, yard signs, and phone banks are all staples in the traditional campaign. Candidates for statewide and urban races must rely on media advertising, particularly television, to get the exposure they need in the three- or four-month campaign period. These candidates are likely to hire consulting firms to manage their campaigns. Consultants contract with public opinion pollsters, arrange advertising, and set up direct-mail campaigns that can target certain areas of the state.

We can get some idea about spending in campaigns from what candidates pay for advertising and political consultants in Houston (and Harris County):[35]

- A thirty-second TV spot costs about $1,500 for a daytime ad, $2,000 to $5,000 for an ad during the evening news, and $5,000 to $20,000 for an ad during a prime-time show, depending on the show's popularity rating. For some very popular programs, such as *CSI*, the cost can be even higher, as much as $25,000.
- Prime time for most radio broadcasting corresponds with "drive time" (5:00 A.M. to 10:00 A.M. and 3:00 P.M. to 8:00 P.M.), when the largest number of people are driving to or from work. Drive-time rates range from $250 to $2,000 per sixty-second spot.
- Billboards can run anywhere from $600 to $15,000 a month, depending on the location. Understandably, billboards on busy freeways are the most expensive.
- Newspaper ads cost from $300 to $500 per column inch in the Sunday paper and $250 per column inch in the daily paper. In November 2004, a half-page ad in the *Houston Chronicle* run on the day before election cost about $15,000. Advertising rates for political campaigns actually are higher than the rates charged commercial customers because campaigns are not given the discounts that regular advertisers receive.
- Hiring a professional polling organization to conduct a poll in Harris County costs $15,000 to $30,000.
- Hiring a political consulting firm to manage a campaign in Harris County costs up to $50,000, plus a percentage of the media buys. (Technically, the latter cost is paid by the television and radio stations.) Most firms also get a bonus ranging from $5,000 to $25,000 if the candidate wins.

Clearly, finance is important in political campaigns. While the candidate who spends the most does not always win, a certain amount of spending is necessary for a candidate to be competitive. Speaking with his tongue halfway in his cheek, one prominent politician noted, in regard to high-level statewide races in Texas, that even if "you don't have to raise $10 million, you have to raise $8 million."[36]

Controlling Campaign Finance.   Prompted by the increasing use of television in campaigns and the increasing amount of funds needed to buy television advertisements, the federal government and most state governments passed laws regulating campaign finance in the early 1970s. (We first discussed campaign finance in

[34]For a comprehensive treatment of campaign finance, see Frank J. Sorauf, *Inside Campaign Finance: Myths and Realities* (New Haven: Yale University Press, 1992).

[35]Nancy Sims of Pierpont Communications, with offices in both Austin and Houston, graciously provided this information.

[36]"The Senate Can Wait," interview with Jim Hightower in *The Texas Observer*, January 27, 1989, p. 6.

Chapter 9.) The Federal Elections Campaign Act of 1971, substantially amended in 1974, established regulations that apply only to federal elections (president, vice president, and members of Congress). It provided for public financing of presidential campaigns through tax dollars, limited the size of the contributions that individuals and PACs could make to campaigns, and required disclosure of campaign donations. In 1976, the United States Supreme Court declared that it was unconstitutional to set spending limits for campaigns that are not publicly funded. This means there are no spending limits for congressional races.[37]

Growing Campaign Expenditures.   Not surprisingly, expenditures in election campaigns continue to increase. The Federal Election Commission reported that $211.8 million was spent in the 1976 election of the president and members of Congress, with $122.8 million spent in the presidential race alone. Of the $60.9 million spent in the elections of the 435 House members, more was spent on behalf of candidates in Texas ($4.5 million) than on those of any other state except California. Such expenditure levels appear modest by today's standards. In 1998, outlays for all congressional races (House and Senate combined) totaled $740 million.[38] In the same year, candidates for the thirty U.S. House seats allocated to Texas spent $27 million in their election efforts, an average of almost $1 million per seat. In 2002, spending totaled over $40 million, more than $1.25 million each for the thirty-two seats Texas has after redistricting. Costs of campaigns for state offices in Texas are at least proportionately high, and Texas has joined other states in enacting legislation designed to control the flow of funds.

Current Texas Campaign Law.   The most important provisions of current Texas law on campaign finance are as follows:

1. Candidates may not raise or spend funds until an official campaign treasurer is appointed.
2. Candidates and PACs may not accept contributions in currency for more than an aggregate of $100.
3. Direct contributions from corporations and labor unions are prohibited.
4. Candidates and treasurers of campaign committees are required to file sworn statements listing all contributions and expenditures for a designated reporting period to the Texas secretary of state's office.
5. Both criminal and civil penalties are imposed on those who violate the law's provisions. Primary enforcement of campaign regulations is the responsibility of the Texas Ethics Commission.

Although these provisions may sound imposing, in fact raising and spending funds in Texas campaigns still is fairly wide open. For example, while corporations and labor unions may not give directly to a candidate, they may give through their PACs. Note that there are no limits on the amount a candidate may spend of his or her own funds. Probably the most important effect of the campaign-finance law in Texas comes from the disclosure requirements. How much a candidate raises, who makes contributions, and how campaign funds are spent are matters of open record. This information may be newsworthy to reporters or other individuals motivated to inform the public.

Soft Money and Independent Expenditures.   In 1979, amendments to the Federal Elections Campaign Act made it legal for political parties to raise and spend unlimited

> **DID YOU KNOW . . .**
> That PACs active in Texas include AQUAPAC (the Water Quality Association), NUTPAC (the Nut Processors Association), SIX-PAC (the National Beer Wholesalers Association), WAFFLEPAC (Waffle House, Inc.), and WHATAPAC (Whataburger Corporation of Texas)?

---

[37]*Buckley v. Valeo*, 424 U.S. 1 (1976).
[38]Federal Election Commission data, reported in *Congressional Quarterly Almanac 1977* (Washington, D.C.: Congressional Quarterly, 1977), p. 35A; and *Congressional Quarterly Weekly Report*, March 5, 1989, p. 478. Since 1976, the federal government actually has expanded the role of contributions in elections.

amounts of *soft money*. Party funds could be used to help candidates in a variety of ways, especially through voter-registration and get-out-the-vote drives. The United States Supreme Court further opened up spending in 1985 by deciding that *independent expenditures* could not be limited.[39] As a result, individuals and organizations can spend as much as they want to promote a candidate so long as they are not working or communicating directly with the candidate's campaign organization. (Soft money and independent expenditures were discussed in Chapter 9.)

In 2002, the Campaign Reform Act deprived the parties of their soft money resources, but activists simply set up nonparty organizations to collect and disperse such funds. Understandably, it has been very difficult to effectively control spending in political campaigns.

---

[39]Federal Election Commission data are available at **www.fec.gov**.

MAKING A DIFFERENCE | "Think Globally, Act Locally"

"Think globally, act locally" is a common slogan in American politics. The phrase reflects a simple and well-known logic. While it may be a good thing to care about the really big issues, such as global warming and the war in Iraq, it makes more sense to act locally, where the effects of our actions are much greater. The math is quite convincing. If I am 1 of 100,000,000, my contribution is likely to be a small share of the total. If I am 1 of 50, however, I can make a noticeable difference.

Ironically, we are much more likely to vote in national-level elections, where we have an almost imperceptible effect, than in local-level elections, where we can make a big impact. To have really tangible effects, we should play a bigger role in local politics.

Why Should You Care?

Elections for local office seem much less important than national elections, and there is truth in this perception.

Whether we go to war in Iraq is a question decided by our national politicians. The largest taxes are collected nationally. Social Security is a federal program. The states are the next biggest players. Much of the funding for higher education and welfare comes from the states.

Counties and cities still have a big role to play, however, as do other local governing bodies. They are largely responsible for streets and garbage collection. These services may seem basic, but they are important, as you probably know all too well.

Take roads, for instance. Poorly designed roads can create unnecessary gridlock. Badly managed traffic lights can have the same effect. Potholes have an obvious impact on our cars and our patience. Local governments also largely fund and oversee our schools. Do we tax a lot or a little for education? Do we fund classrooms or teachers or athletic facilities?

These are big decisions, obviously, and they are largely in the hands of local governments. In addition to

basic services and schools, local governments are responsible for policing the streets where we live, work, and shop. Whether the police are well trained, well equipped, and properly managed clearly matters. Indeed, it can be a matter of life or death.

What Can You Do?

The obvious thing to do is to get involved in local elections. First, find out more about local politics. Newspapers are a good source, and the Internet is, too; but do not forget about your family and your fellow students. They also can be sources of information. You might be surprised by how much of what happens locally is not only interesting but also important. You may find yourself getting involved in an election campaign or an interest group. There, you could really make a difference.

Key Terms

chad 710

crossover voting 699

direct primary 696

gerrymandering 713

grandfather clause 694

negative campaigning 715

participation paradox 687

plurality 700

poll tax 693

quorum 713

runoff primary 697

user-benefit theory 696

vote-eligible population
(VEP) 690

voting-age population
(VAP) 690

Chapter Summary

1 Elections are the defining characteristic of representative democracy. It is through our votes that we hold elected officials accountable.

2 A small number of demographic and political variables are important in predicting who will vote. The most important demographic variables are education, income, and age. Certain political factors also influence the likelihood of voting, especially a person's level of interest in politics and intensity of identification with a political party. Other factors are important as well, but with this small set of demographic and political variables, we can make a good prediction as to whether a person will vote in a particular election.

3 Voting in Texas (and most other states) is a two-stage process. Before you can vote, you must first register. Traditionally a barrier for women and minorities, the registration procedure today is as simple as voting itself—perhaps even simpler. Since the passage of federal "motor voter" legislation, a person can register when renewing a driver's license.

4 Traditionally, voter turnout was measured as a percentage of the voting-age population (VAP). That figure has become increasingly inaccurate, mainly because it includes a growing number of noncitizens, who cannot vote. We can use estimates of the vote-eligible population (VEP) instead. By that measure, national turnout in presidential elections has fluctuated around 55 percent in recent years. In midterm elections, turnout is around 40 percent. These numbers are significantly lower than what we find in other advanced democracies. Voter turnout in Texas is even below the U.S. national average.

5 Low voter turnout in Texas may be due in part to the state's socioeconomic characteristics. A comparatively large percentage of the population live below the poverty level. An even larger percentage have not graduated from high school, and these people are not very likely to vote. Income and education levels are low for African Americans and Mexican Americans, so turnout is particularly low for these groups. Political factors, such as political structure and political culture, may also play a role in low turnout.

6 In Texas, as in other southern states that once were predominantly Democratic, a majority rule is used in primary elections. If no candidate receives a majority of the votes cast for a particular office in the first primary, a second, runoff primary is used to determine the winner. Outside the South, only a plurality of the votes is typically required.

7 Ballot design is an important factor in elections. Texas traditionally has used the party-column ballot, in which the names of all the candidates of each party are listed in parallel columns. The main alternative is the office-block ballot, in which the names of candidates are listed underneath each office. Beginning with the 2002 election, many Texas counties adopted electronic voting systems, which combine features of the office-block and party-column designs.

8 Texas is a diverse state, and the pool of candidates for local offices reflects this diversity. As we move up the pyramid of elected offices, however, the candidates become much more homogeneous. Successful candidates for statewide office traditionally have been white males. While this remains true today, women and minorities have made substantial gains, and these gains are likely to continue as more women and minorities enter politics.

9 In a state as large as Texas, media advertising, political consultants, and polling are required for any candidate seeking to win statewide office or the most competitive state legislative and local elections. These services are expensive.

10 Without a certain amount of funding, it is impossible to be competitive in Texas elections. The high and rising cost of campaigns means that serious candidates must collect contributions from a variety of sources. Most candidates must rely on PACs and wealthy individuals. Although the Texas legislature has passed laws regulating campaign finance in state races, raising and spending funds is still fairly wide open.

Selected Print and Media Resources

SUGGESTED READINGS

Brischetto, Robert, David Richards, Chandler Davidson, and Bernard Grofman. "Texas," in Chandler Davidson and Bernard Grofman, eds., *Quiet Revolution in the South: The Impact of the Voting Rights Act, 1965–1990*. Princeton, N.J.: Princeton University Press, 1994. This chapter chronicles how the Voting Rights Act influenced Texas elections and politics in the twenty-five years after its enactment.

Davidson, Chandler. *Race and Class in Texas Politics*. Princeton, N.J.: Princeton University Press, 1992. This wide-ranging book by a Texas sociologist highlights the power of business interests in Texas politics.

Murray, Richard. "The 1996 Elections in Texas," in Kent L. Tedin, Donald S. Lutz, and Edward P. Fuchs, eds., *Perspectives on American and Texas Politics*, 5th ed. Dubuque, Iowa: Kendall/Hunt, 1998. In this article, a leading analyst of Texas elections and politics offers a view of Texas campaigns through the prism of the 1996 elections.

Murray, Richard, and Sam Attlesey. "Texas: Republicans Gallop Ahead," in Alexander Lamis, ed., *Southern Politics in the 1990s*. Baton Rouge: Louisiana State University Press, 1999. This very accessible chapter traces the rise of Republicans in Texas state politics during the 1990s.

Stein, Robert M. "Early Voting," *Public Opinion Quarterly*, vol. 62, no. 1 (1998), pp. 57–69. This article by a well-known Texas political scientist analyzes the effects of early voting in Texas on both the level of turnout and the composition of the electorate.

Tolleson-Rinehart, Sue, and Jeanie Ricketts Stanley. *Claytie and the Lady: Ann Richards, Gender, and Politics in Texas*. Austin: University of Texas Press, 1994. The authors of this book examine the influence of gender in Texas politics, focusing especially on the 1990 gubernatorial election, in which Ann Richards defeated Clayton Williams after a truly fascinating campaign.

E·MOCRACY | All Those Elections

One of the distinguishing features of Texas politics is the number and variety of elections held in the state. Texas elects a very large number of officials to do different things at different levels of government. See for yourself: go to your county Web site and locate a sample ballot. To find your county's URL, go to

www.state.tx.us

From this home page, click on "Texas Counties."

Once you have located your county Web site, find a sample ballot. Ballots usually are stored on the county clerk's section of the site. You may be able to click on a link marked "Elections" or "County Clerk," though a site's structure is sometimes not so straightforward. In some instances, you may find that your county simply does not post a sample ballot. You might mention this in an e-mail to the county clerk. Perhaps the clerk's office will send you one.

If your county has no sample ballot, you can go to another county site, such as that of Bexar, Dallas, Denton, Harris, Jefferson, or Travis, all of which include a full sample ballot. Examine the ballot

from top to bottom, keeping in mind that it may take a while. Indeed, in some areas, people may be asked to vote for more than one hundred different offices, from governor to railroad commissioner, from state representative to city council member, from state judges to county judges, justices of the peace, and constables. There are other offices as well, and often a constitutional amendment or two.

Logging On

A very large number of Web sites relate to voting, elections, and campaigns. The political parties have Web sites, as do most political candidates, and there are many independent sites. For a wide-ranging list of political resources on the Web, go to

www.polsci.wvu.edu/polycy

For specific information about voting and elections in Texas, go to the secretary of state's election page at

www.sos.state.tx.us

The Southwest Voter Registration Education Project, which is specifically

interested in enrolling Hispanic Americans, is at

www.svrep.org

Online Review

At **www.politicalscience.wadsworth.com/schmidt12**, you will find a free Study Guide to this book. For each chapter, there are two online quizzes to help you master the material.

• The PoliPrep Self-Study Assessment provides a pretest for each major section of the chapter. PoliPrep then generates a customized study plan. After you complete the study plan, a posttest evaluates your progress.

• The Tutorial Quiz for each chapter provides questions on the chapter contents, including the features. The questions are organized to match the major sections of the chapter.

23 | The Texas Legislature

What If . . .
the Texas House of Representatives Were Organized by Political Party?

BACKGROUND

The U.S. House of Representatives and most other legislative bodies in the world are organized by political party. Each chamber has a majority party or coalition and one or more organized opposition parties. For example, the majority party in the U.S. House picks the congressional leaders and committee chairpersons, and it determines which members of the majority party serve on each committee. The minority party chooses its leaders and the **ranking minority members** of committees, and it determines which minority party members fill the minority's allotted committee positions.

Although members of the Texas House of Representatives are elected as either Republicans or Democrats, the house is organized under a "no-party" system—a holdover from the days of one-party Democratic rule. There are no majority leaders or minority leaders in the Texas system, and the speaker of the house may appoint both Republicans and Democrats as committee chairs. The speaker, although normally a member of the majority party, receives many votes from members of the minority party who seek to join the speaker's "team." As team members, these minority party members can obtain favorable committee assignments or even become committee chairpersons. By becoming team players, however, the minority members blur their role as members of the opposition party.

WHAT IF THE TEXAS HOUSE OF REPRESENTATIVES WERE ORGANIZED BY POLITICAL PARTY?

If the Texas House had an official minority party, there would be a clear opposition to the majority. The minority could develop and articulate a rival political philosophy and propose specific policy alternatives. The philosophy and policies could be presented by the minority leader of the house, rather than by individual house members who do not officially represent their party.

Such alternatives could invigorate the media and lead to better-informed citizens. This system would inform both the press and the citizens of policy options other than those advocated by the majority party. Journalists and other Texans could then better evaluate the legitimacy and desirability of both the majority and minority proposals.

Distinct party positions would also make it easier for everyone to follow the actions of the legislative parties and the general stream of legislation—as in a football game, where the two teams wear uniforms of different colors. Citizens could evaluate the actions of the legislature more easily.

INDEPENDENCE FROM THE SPEAKER

The minority party could control which of its members filled its allotted committee seats. As a result, members of the minority would not need to make political compromises to join the speaker's team and receive desirable committee seats. An official minority with control over committee assignments could lessen the speaker's influence over the minority members of the house, giving these representatives more independence to represent their constituents.

IS ORGANIZATION BY PARTY LIKELY IN THE NEAR FUTURE?

The viability of the no-party system may be nearing its end as state politics becomes more partisan. The Republicans have attracted conservative Democrats to the Republican Party both as voters and as legislators, leaving the Democratic Party more liberal. With ideological differences along party lines more pronounced, the house Democratic caucus has begun to function as an embryonic opposition party countering the leadership of Speaker Tom Craddick. If the Democrats were to revive as a political force in the future, organization by party would become a real possibility. Republicans might accept partisan organization as a way of fending off the Democrats, or the Democrats might choose such a system if they ever reestablished control.

FOR CRITICAL ANALYSIS

1. Why is political opposition important in a democratic republic?
2. What interests might be against the creation of an organized opposition? Why might these interests be against it?

The legislature is one of the basic components of the three-branch concept of government and is often considered to be the branch closest to the people. In this chapter, we examine the organization, structure, and processes of the Texas legislature.

The Texas legislature, like the U.S. Congress and all other state legislatures except that of Nebraska, is a **bicameral** (two-chamber) **legislature** composed of a senate and a house of representatives. Although the two chambers have approximately equal power, the smaller, 31-member Texas Senate is more prestigious, and its individual members generally exercise greater power and influence than the 150 members of the Texas House. The Texas legislature has a number of unusual features. One such feature is the great power of the **presiding officers** in each body. A second is the "no-party" system of organizing the two chambers, which allows each presiding officer to recruit members of the other party to his or her "team." We described this system in this chapter's *What If . . .* feature.

> **Ranking Minority Members**
> The senior members of the minority party on a legislative committee.

> **Bicameral Legislature**
> A legislature made up of two chambers.

> **Presiding Officers**
> In Texas, the chief officers of the state senate and house. They are the lieutenant governor, who presides over the senate, and the speaker of the house.

The Limited Session

The Texas legislature meets on the second Tuesday in January in odd-numbered years for a 140-day session. It is the only legislature among those of the ten most populous states that meets biennially. Although forty-three states have instituted annual sessions to conduct state business, Texas has refused to do so. Many Texans believe that the legislature does more harm than good when it is in session and that a longer session would simply give legislators more time to make mischief.

In these short, infrequent sessions, the volume of legislation can overwhelm legislators. Most bills are passed or killed with little consideration. As a result, many important bills are never granted a legislative hearing. In 2005, for example, the Texas legislature debated two very important issues, school financing and college admission rules. As you will learn in this chapter's *Politics and Education* feature on the following page, neither issue saw a passed bill.

Special Sessions

The short biennial sessions and the increasingly complex problems of a modern society make thirty-day special sessions, which can be called only by the governor, more frequent. They are, however, usually unpopular with both the general public and the legislators. The public tends to see the added expense as wasteful, and legislators may

Lawmakers and family members crowded the chamber of the Texas House of Representatives as the 79th Texas Legislature began its regular session in January 2005. What is special about Texas legislative sessions? (AP Photo/Harry Cabluck)

POLITICS AND EDUCATION | The Texas Legislature Grapples with Education

Without question, the most important issue before the 2005 legislative session in Texas was how to pay for the public schools. The legislature also confronted the issue of college admissions in Texas.

PUBLIC SCHOOL FINANCE: "ROBIN HOOD" SURVIVES— FOR THE MOMENT

In 1989, the Texas Supreme Court ruled in *Edgewood v. Kirby* that the grossly unequal funding of public schools from one district to another violated the Texas constitutional requirements for a suitable and "efficient" public school system.* In response, the legislature constructed a new funding plan, popularly known as the "Robin Hood" plan because it requires wealthier districts to share their wealth with property-poor districts.

Ultimately, the issues concerning Texas education funding were put before the Texas Supreme Court which ruled that the Robin Hood plan amounted to a constitutionally forbidden statewide property tax.[†] This ruling effectively required the legislature to seek sources of revenue other than property tax as a means of raising public school funds.

Appealing to constituents in upscale suburbs, the governor and legislative leaders campaigned on the promise of abolishing Robin Hood. In 2005, the legislature attempted to pass two education bills prepared by the house. The attempts failed at the very last minute.

HB2 would have overhauled the state finance formulas to provide aid to school districts for bilingual education, as well as to districts in disadvantaged or rural areas. HB3 would have reduced school districts' heavy reliance on the local prop-

erty tax and placed a cap on property tax rates for homes and businesses. The state would then have picked up a larger share of education costs by increasing the general sales tax by 1 percent. Business taxes would also have gone up—but by much less than business would have gained from the property tax cuts. The Center for Public Policy Priorities calculated that HB3 heavily favored families with the highest incomes.

Democrats and moderate Republicans were in a much stronger position in the senate than in the conservative-dominated house, and senators were concerned about the impact of a 1 percent rise in the sales tax on poorer Texans. The senate demanded a one-half percent sales tax increase instead and more taxes on business. "You can't shift business taxes to consumers. It's not fair," said Lieutenant Governor David Dewhurst, a Republican. The house, led by Speaker Tom Craddick, refused to budge. Senate negotiator Kenneth Brimer, Republican of Fort Worth, observed, "When I give a plan to house members and an hour later a lobbyist comes up to me with a faxed copy of all seven pages, I know who's doing their negotiating over there. That's frustrating."[‡]

THE 10 PERCENT RULE

Under the 10 percent rule, Texas high school graduates ranking in the top 10 percent of their class are automatically admitted to any Texas state university. This law is an effort to increase diversity in Texas universities following

federal court's rejection of affirmative action programs in *Hopwood v. Texas*.[§] The rule has had a greater impact on the student bodies at Texas A&M and the University of Texas (UT) than at other schools. Over a seven-year period, the percentage of Top Ten freshmen at UT-Austin and Texas A&M has increased from 37 percent to 72 percent. University officials argue that the law makes class rank the only factor in determining admission and limits their ability to recruit other credible applicants using different criteria.

Several bills were proposed in 2005 to alter the rule or to restrict the number of students admitted to UT and A&M under the rule. The Texas Senate's proposals required that the incoming freshmen take a more demanding "recommended curriculum" to gain automatic admission and called for giving extra weight to advanced placement, honors, and college-level courses. The senate also stipulated a standardized grade point average produced by the Texas Education Agency as another admission consideration. The senate bill died in a house committee, however.

The house bill was more direct and limited Top Ten applicants at UT and A&M to 50 percent of the freshman class. These universities would accept applicants by percentile, taking the top 1 percent of graduates first, the top 2 percent next, and so on until the 50 percent cap was reached. The house bill died in committee. Ten Percent opponents promise to revisit the issue in 2007.

FOR CRITICAL ANALYSIS

Should a district's property value affect the quality of a child's education? What should determine admission to the University of Texas and Texas A&M?

---

*777 S.W.2d 391 (Texas 1989).
[†]*Neeley v. West Orange-Cove Consolidated Independent School District,* 176 S.W.3d 746 (2005).

[‡]Clay Robison and R. G. Ratcliffe, "As Clock Ticks, Tax Bill Seems Doomed," *Houston Chronicle,* May 29, 2005; and Peggy Fikac and Gary Scharrer, "Hopes Dim for School Finance," *Houston Chronicle,* May 28, 2005.
[§]84 F.3d 720 (5th Cir. 1996).

be distressed by calls away from homes, families, and primary occupations. Furthermore, any interest that was able to get the legislature to kill an item of legislation during the regular session will strongly oppose a special session to reconsider the item that was already killed.

Time Pressures

Because most of the legislative work is done during the regular session, time is valuable. The harassed legislator, lacking adequate staff support, finds it difficult to obtain even rudimentary knowledge of the content of much of the legislation that must be considered, whether in committee or on the *floor*, which will be discussed later in this chapter. The time constraints dictated by the limited session tend to isolate individual legislators and deepen their reliance on the information provided by lobbyists, administrators, and the legislative leadership. Thus, bills that lack interest group, administrative agency, or legislative leadership support have no chance of passage or even serious consideration.

Historically, much questionable legislation was passed in the last days of the session. In 1993, the house adopted new rules to address the end-of-session legislative crunch. During the last seventeen days of the session, the house may consider only bills that originated in the senate or that received previous house approval. The new rules also give house members twenty-four hours to study major legislation before taking floor action. These reforms diminish the volume of last-minute legislation and give legislators time to become better acquainted with bills.

Qualifications, Terms, and Compensation of Members

Texas has "citizen legislators" who meet for only 140 days every other year and receive most of their income from outside sources. It is reasonable to expect the lawmakers to be more focused on their full time careers and outside sources of income than on the Texas public's business.

Formal Qualifications

Although an individual must meet legal, or formal, qualifications before he or she can serve in the Texas legislature, the criteria are broad enough to allow millions of Texas residents the opportunity to run. To be a state senator, a person must be a U.S. citizen, a registered voter, and at least twenty-six years of age and must have lived for five years in the state and one year in the district in which he or she seeks election. Qualifications for house membership are even more easily met. To be a representative, an individual must be a U.S. citizen, be at least twenty-one years of age, and have lived in Texas for two years and in the district for one year.

Terms

Texas senators are elected for four-year staggered terms; representatives are elected for two-year terms. This means that the entire house and half the senate are elected every two years.

Redistricting, which is based on the census, takes place every ten years and triggers a special senate procedure in the first election following redistricting. The last such election took place in 2002. Because of redistricting, the entire senate was up for election. At the start of the first session after the redistricting, senators drew lots to determine who would serve a four-year term and who would serve for two years. Unlucky senators faced reelection in 2004, while the lucky ones did not have to run for reelection until 2006. Thereafter, all senators will serve four-year terms until the

DID YOU KNOW . . .
That on April Fools' Day in 1971, the Texas House unanimously passed a resolution recognizing Albert De Salvo for his "noted activities and unconventional techniques involving population control and applied psychology" and that the house withdrew this recognition when it discovered that De Salvo was the Boston Strangler, an infamous serial killer?

| Texas Ethics Commission
A constitutionally authorized body that has the power to investigate ethics violations and to penalize violators of Texas ethics laws.

election that follows the next census (in 2012). The relative competitiveness of a senator's district determines whether the result of the lottery is only an inconvenience or an incident of major significance.

Texas legislators experience a more rapid turnover than their counterparts in the U.S. Congress, where seniority brings political power. Frustrated by low salaries and the inability to achieve legislative goals not supported by powerful interests or the presiding officers, many house members leave office to pursue full time careers or to seek higher political office. Senators and the members of the house power structure tend to serve longer. Redistricting also brings significant legislative turnover when district lines are redrawn and power bases shift. The median length of service for senators is about twelve years and for house members, about seven.

Compensation

Legislators receive an annual salary of $7,200 plus $128 *per diem* (per day) for expenses during both regular and special sessions. They also have a travel allowance on a reimbursement basis when the legislature is in session. The **Texas Ethics Commission** is constitutionally empowered to propose salary increases, subject to voter approval, for legislators and the lieutenant governor.

The Texas Ethics Commission. The eight-member Texas Ethics Commission enforces state ethics and campaign-finance law. The governor, lieutenant governor, and speaker appoint the commission from a list provided by the Democratic and Republican legislative caucuses. Legislators are excluded from serving on the commission. For more background on the Texas Ethics Commission and a recent ethical issue it faced, read this chapter's *Politics and Ethics* feature on page 729.

Conflicts of Interest. There is little motivation for a Texas legislator to keep his or her position solely for the salary. Present legislative salaries are so low that legislators must receive their primary income from other sources. While Texans require that their legislators seek additional income to subsist, they rarely question the nature of this income. People tend to be responsible to those who pay them, and it is not the public that furnishes most of the legislators' income.[1]

The potential for conflict between the public interest and the interests of a lawmaker's business or employer is obvious. Some legislators recognize the dilemma. For example, Bob Bullock faced it in 1991 when he left the comptroller's office, which paid $74,698 per year, and became the lieutenant governor for a salary of $7,200. Although many employers were eager to hire the lieutenant governor, the appearance of a conflict of interest concerned Bullock enough that he rejected several lucrative offers and accepted employment as a counselor and consultant with View Point Recovery Centers, a network of alcohol rehabilitation hospitals. His salary from View Point, his state employees' retirement income, and his salary as lieutenant governor gave Bullock approximately the same income he had received as comptroller. Unfortunately, many Texas officials have not shared Bullock's desire to avoid even the appearance of impropriety. (Bullock retired in 1998 and died in 1999. The Texas State History Museum is named in his honor.)

| Legislative Districts

The members of the Texas House of Representatives, like the members of the Texas Senate, are elected from single-member districts—one member per house district (see Figure 23–1) and one senator per senate district (see Figure 23–2 on page 728).

---

[1]See Chapter 24 for a further discussion of the interaction among administrators, lobbyists, and legislators.

FIGURE 23–1 | STATE HOUSE DISTRICTS, 80TH LEGISLATURE, 2007–2008

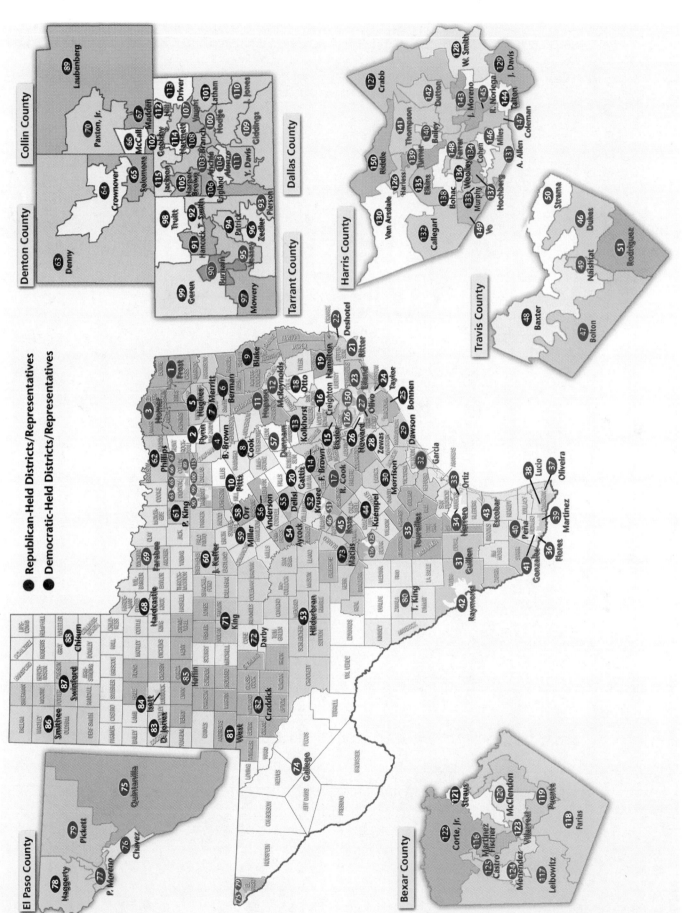

- ● Republican-Held Districts/Representatives
- ● Democratic-Held Districts/Representatives

FIGURE 23-2 | STATE SENATE DISTRICTS, 80TH LEGISLATURE, 2007-2008

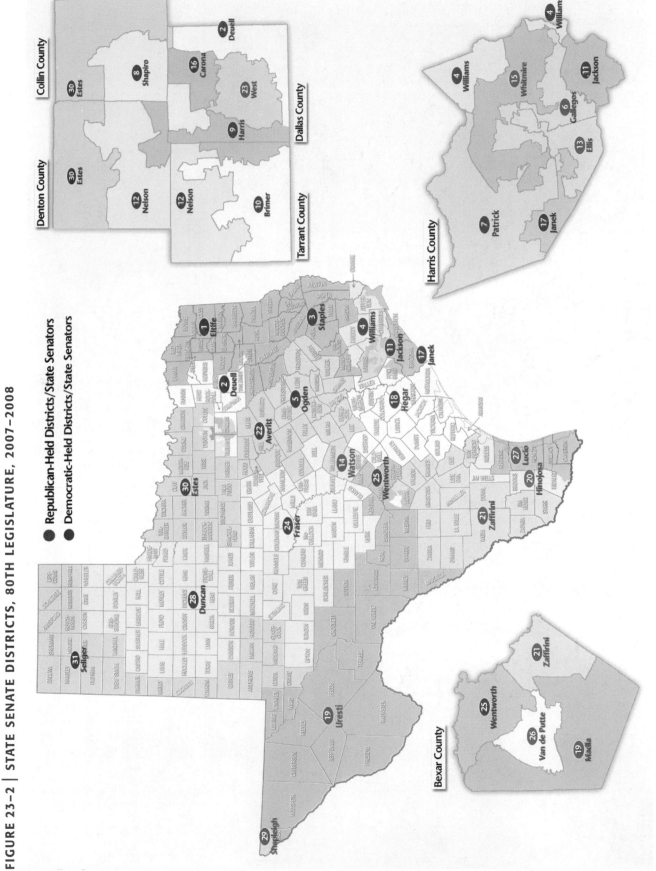

● Republican-Held Districts/State Senators
● Democratic-Held Districts/State Senators

Source: Texas Legislative Council.

POLITICS AND ETHICS | The Texas Ethics Commission

The Texas Ethics Commission was created to regulate elections and to protect the public's right "to apply to their government for the redress of grievances." It is responsible for collecting and maintaining campaign records, leveling fines for late filings, monitoring lobbying practices, taking questions from the public, and investigating complaints of code violations.

The Texas Ethics Commission has only about thirty-five employees, and in the years since a state constitutional amendment established the commission in 1992, it has never completed a thorough audit, subpoenaed a single document, or even met in person with a witness.

BACKGROUND ON A RECENT ISSUE

Bill Ceverha, a lobbyist and former Texas legislator, was treasurer of The Republican Majority Political Action Committee (TRMPAC), a major contributor to the Republican candidates who successfully gained control of the Texas House of Representatives in 2002. The new Republican house majority then elected Tom Craddick as speaker.

The committee, however, received hundreds of thousands of dollars in corporate contributions that are illegal under Texas law. In May 2005, a district court ordered Ceverha to personally pay $197,000 to house Democrats defeated in the 2002 election. Ceverha declared bankruptcy to avoid paying the judgment.

THE MEANING OF THE WORD *DESCRIBE*

Speaker Craddick then appointed Ceverha to the board of the Employees' Retirement System of Texas, which oversees the state employees' $20 billion pension fund. While in this capacity, Ceverha was given a gift of money by Bob Perry, a Houston homebuilder and a major contributor to Republican causes.

Ceverha was now a state official and was required by law to report any gift over $250 to the Texas Ethics Commission, *describe* the gift, and identify the giver. Using the precedent established by a 1999 Ethics Commission ruling that the value of the gift need not be reported, Ceverha described the gift only as a "check."

A public watchdog organization, Texans for Public Justice (TPJ), asked that the Ethics Commission overturn the prior ruling and require Ceverha to divulge the size of the gift. TPJ argued that the description was not adequate because in this instance the gift was not an item like a shotgun or an automobile but money—and the public had the right to know how much.

Attorneys for Ceverha argued that the size of the gift need not be public because Perry had no business with the Employees' Retirement System.

The Texas Ethics Commission, which is chaired by Craddick appointee Cullen Looney, refused to grant a hearing for the TPJ petition. The donor and donee later voluntarily revealed that the amount of the check was $50,000.

FOR CRITICAL ANALYSIS

Do you believe that the value of gifts to public officials should be public knowledge? Why has the Ethics Commission used such a lenient interpretation of the word describe? *Who do you think benefits from this policy? Why do you think the commission refused to hear the TPJ petition?*

Sources: Rick Casey, "Ethics in Wonderland," *Houston Chronicle,* March 28, 2006; and Lisa Sandberg and Kelly Guckian, "Lobbyists' Money Talks—Softly but It's Heard," *San Antonio Express-News,* April 12, 2006.

These districts are required by the U.S. Constitution to be approximately equal in population.[2] Following every ten-year census, each state must undertake a redistricting process to correct for changes in the populations of the districts. Today, the average population of an electoral district for the Texas House is approximately 150,000. State senators represent an average of about 728,000 people. Because the state senate has thirty-one members and the Texas delegation to the U.S. Congress includes thirty-two representatives, U.S. congressional districts are about the same size as senate districts and contain an average of 705,000 people (see Figure 23–3 on the next page).

In Texas, as in most other states, the state legislature redraws its own districts as well as those of the state's delegation to the U.S. Congress. In the event the Texas legislature fails to redistrict, the state constitution provides for the function to be performed by the Legislative Redistricting Board. The board is *ex officio,* which

| Ex Officio
Having a position by virtue of holding a particular office. For example, the lieutenant governor of Texas serves *ex officio* as the presiding officer of the Texas Senate.

[2]*Reynolds v. Sims,* 377 U.S. 533 (1964).

FIGURE 23-3 | U.S. CONGRESSIONAL DISTRICTS, 110TH CONGRESS, 2007–2009

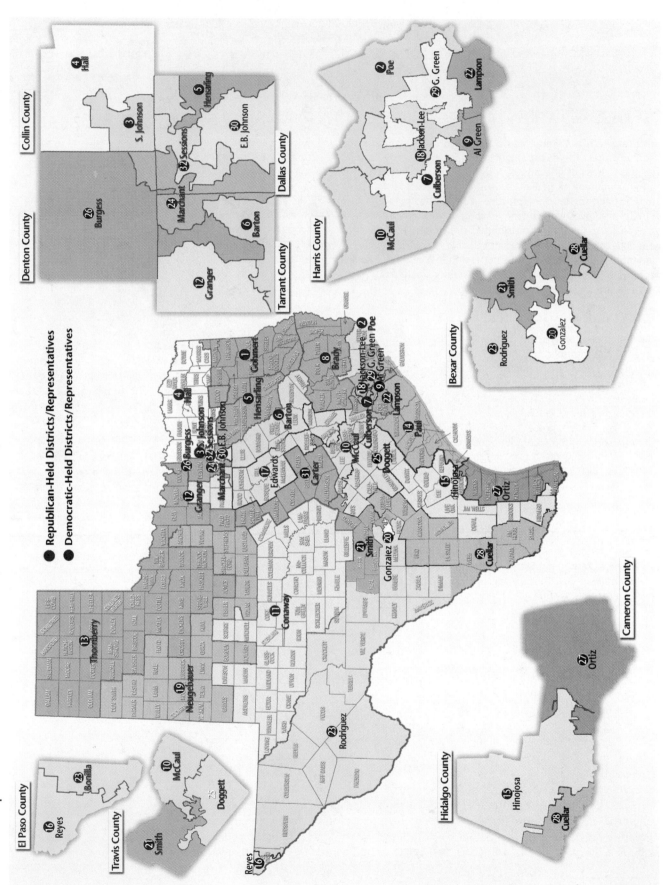

● Republican-Held Districts/Representatives
● Democratic-Held Districts/Representatives

Note: District 23 decided in special runoff election in 2006. Districts 15, 21, 23, 25, and 28 redrawn by U.S. District Court order in *LULAC v. Perry* (2006).
Source: Texas Legislative Council.

means that members hold other offices. It is made up of the lieutenant governor, the speaker of the house, the attorney general, the comptroller, and the commissioner of the General Land Office.

Gerrymandering

The once-per-decade ritual of redistricting may take place with little notice by the casual observer of politics. For the political practitioner and the political activist, however, it may resemble a life-or-death struggle. The way districts are drawn at any level of government to a large extent determines the political, ideological, and ethnic make-up of the legislative body. When districts are subject to *gerrymandering*, political careers may be made or broken, public policy determined for at least a decade, and the power of ethnic or political minorities enhanced or diminished. (Gerrymandering was discussed in Chapters 11 and 22.) Three gerrymandering techniques are common: cracking, packing, and pairing.

Cracking and Packing.   One technique is to diffuse a concentrated political or ethnic minority among several districts so that its votes within any one district are negligible (*cracking*). A second tactic is used if the minority's numbers are great enough when diffused to affect the outcome of elections in several districts. In this circumstance, the minority is concentrated within the smallest possible number of districts (*packing*), thereby ensuring that it will influence the fewest possible elections and that its influence within the legislature as a whole will be minimal. (See Figure 23–4.)

Pairing Incumbents.   A third tactic is the **pairing** technique, which redistricts in such a way that two or more **incumbent** legislators must run in the same district— thereby ensuring that one will be defeated. Pairing can be used to punish legislators who have fallen from grace with the legislative leadership.

Redistricting after the 1990 and 2000 Censuses

Redistricting after the last two censuses substantially changed the make-up of both the Texas legislature and the Texas delegation to the U.S. House of Representatives.

Redistricting after 1990.   Following the 1990 census, it took a special session of the Texas legislature, eleven lawsuits, and various other legal actions in both state and federal courts from 1990 through 1994 to settle the placement of district boundaries. Republican membership in the Texas Senate immediately increased from nine in 1991 to thirteen in 1993. By 1996, Republicans controlled the Texas Senate, although Democrats continued to be the majority in the house.

State House and Senate Redistricting after 2000.   Controversy flared again after the 2000 census. Republican lawmakers refused to accept the legislative redistricting that followed the census and forced the redistricting effort into the Legislative Redistricting Board, where Republicans enjoyed a four-to-one majority. Subsequent to the board's redistricting, the 2002 election increased the senate Republican majority to nineteen and gave Republicans a majority in the Texas House for the first time since Reconstruction.

Redistricting for the U.S. Congress after 2000.   Following a series of lawsuits, the Texas districts that elect members of the U.S. House were redesigned in 2000 by a panel of one Democratic and two Republican U.S. district judges. Despite the political tendencies of the judges, the Democrats still maintained a 17–15 majority in the Texas congressional delegation after the 2002 elections. Given the narrow majority that the Republicans possessed in the U.S. House, its former majority

FIGURE 23–4 | CRACKING AND PACKING

The diagram at the top is balanced, having eight red "voters" and eight blue "voters" represented by the dots in each of the four "districts." Redrawing the electoral districts in the lower example results in a guaranteed three-to-one advantage in representation for the blue voters. Here, fourteen red dots are "packed" into the green-tinted district and the remaining eighteen are "cracked" across the three gray-tinted districts.

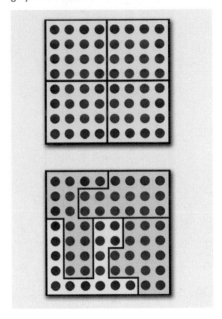

| Pairing
In political redistricting, placing two incumbent officeholders from the same party in the same district. (Only one of these officeholders can be reelected.)

| Incumbent
The current holder of an office.

Nicholas V. "Nick" Lampson, shown here campaigning in September 2006, was a Democratic member of Congress representing Texas's 9th district from 1997 to 2005. After the redistricting orchestrated by former Republican majority leader Tom DeLay, the 9th district was renumbered the 2nd and radically redrawn to favor the Republican Ted Poe, who won the district from Lampson in the 2004 election. In 2006, following the scandal-tainted resignation of DeLay, Lampson delivered DeLay's seat in the 22nd district to the Democrats. Does this mean that Texas is truly becoming a two-party state? (Flickr! Photo by Bryan Bankston)

leader Tom DeLay (a Texan) encouraged Republican-controlled legislatures in Texas, Colorado, and other states to redraw congressional districts before the 2010 census to favor Republican candidates.

In Texas, Governor Rick Perry called a special session to revise the 2000 judicial plan. The first two special sessions were unsuccessful because first the house and then the senate Democrats fled the state, as described in the *Politics and Redistricting* feature in Chapter 22 on page 713. The congressional district boundaries were finally redrawn in a third special session in 2003.

As is shown by the irregular district shapes in Figure 23–3 on page 730, the Republican majority in the third legislative special session used classic gerrymandering techniques to redraw the boundaries for the Texas congressional districts. Although the federal courts prohibit racial gerrymandering, they are reluctant to become involved in political gerrymandering.[3]

Following the 2006 elections, the Texas congressional delegation still had a Republican majority. Anglo American Democratic members of Congress and rural constituents appear to have been the principal losers.

Who Can Become a Member of the Legislature?

We have already described the legal requirements for holding legislative office in Texas. The most important requirements, though, are not the legal ones but the informal ones. Political, social, and economic criteria largely determine who is elected not only to the state legislature but also to offices at all levels of government—national, state, county, city, and special district.

[3]The United States Supreme Court, by a 6–3 vote, refused to hear an appeal from Colorado Republicans following a Colorado Supreme Court ruling that nullified political gerrymandering similar to that in Texas. The gerrymandering was found by the state court to be in conflict with the Colorado Constitution.

Race and Gender

The majority of Texans are white and Protestant, and they elect legislators who share these characteristics. Likewise, a predominantly Mexican American district usually elects a Catholic Mexican American legislator, and an African American district usually elects an African American representative.

Hispanics make up 32 percent of the Texas population but hold just over 20 percent of the legislative seats. African Americans, with just over 11 percent of the population, are represented by about 9 percent of the legislature. The numerical representation of these two ethnic groups should increase dramatically over the next decade, because the combined population of African Americans and Mexican Americans is predicted to equal the Anglo American population by 2010. Because the Anglo ethnic group tends to be overrepresented, however, the redrawing of the legislative lines will determine the extent of minority representation.[4]

Although women are becoming more active and successful as candidates, they remain the most underrepresented group in the Texas legislature. Women make up over 50 percent of the population but only about 20 percent of the legislature.

Campaign Funding

Another qualification for winning legislative office is access to campaign funds. Many competent, motivated individuals who want to serve are excluded because they are unable to raise the funds necessary to finance an adequate campaign. Thus, the voters' pool of potential candidates may be limited to persons who can appeal to the economic interests that provide most campaign contributions. Securing office space, printing campaign literature, buying postage stamps, building a campaign organization, and purchasing advertisements are all among the necessary ingredients for a successful campaign—and all are expensive. The minimum amount necessary to run a modest campaign in a competitive district is about $160,000 for the house and $600,000 for the senate. The key ingredient in Texas politics is money![5]

Business and the Law as Sources of Legislators.   Few wage earners or small-business owners can afford to leave their jobs and businesses for four and a half months every other year to take a temporary job that pays $600 per month. In contrast, persons who serve as executives in large businesses, practice law, or engage in certain other professions may more easily find the time required for service in the state legislature. Legislators from these groups may actually increase their incomes through political service if the prestige and contacts they develop as members of the legislature benefit their law firms or companies. Economic interests may retain the services of an attorney from a particular firm or steer business toward a specific company to ingratiate themselves with a legislator. Paying a public official in exchange for legislative influence is illegal, but paying for goods and services is not.[6]

Even when there is no overt intent to bribe a legislator, an individual who works closely with a particular industry or organization and is handsomely compensated for that work may find that superhuman effort is required to distinguish between the public interest and the client's interest. Because some legislators do not appear to strive very hard to separate the two, an interest can, in effect, "buy a legislator."

When Legislators Appear before Boards and in Court.   Legislators who are lawyers may also be employed to represent clients in adversary proceedings before

---

[4]See Chapter 18 for projections of the future Texas ethnic population.

[5]See www.followthemoney.org for comprehensive information on Texas campaign contributions.

[6]See John Dunbar, "Public Service, Personal Gain in Texas," Center for Public Integrity, available at www.publicintegrity.org/oi/iys.aspx?st=TX&sub=pub.

the various state administrative boards and commissions. The legislature is responsible for the appropriations to state boards and commissions, and the fact that the concerned agency may be generous in evaluating the legal arguments of a lawyer-legislator is not lost on the litigants. In this instance, both the lawyer and her or his client may benefit from the lawyer's legislative position.

A state judge may also grant a trial delay in civil or criminal litigation to a lawyer serving in the legislature. This right of delay lasts from thirty days before a legislative session begins until thirty days after it ends. Either the plaintiff or the defendant may benefit from such a delay. Thus, when either party to a suit seeks a delay, and the legislature is in session, that party may find a lawyer-legislator desirable as a counsel.

Organization of the Texas Legislature

The Texas legislative system places an unusual degree of power in the hands of the presiding officers of each chamber. As in most legislative bodies, the house and senate committees do much of the actual work of the legislature. The presiding officers appoint the chairpersons of committees and most of the committee members. In the Texas legislature, committees are often seen as extensions of the presiding officers' power.

The Presiding Officers

The presiding officers in the Texas legislature are the lieutenant governor in the senate and the speaker of the house of representatives. Although these are primarily legislative offices, their holders exercise significant influence throughout Texas government.

Lieutenant Governor.   The presiding officer in the Texas Senate is the lieutenant governor, who serves as its president. The lieutenant governor is not a senator and is elected in a statewide, partisan election. In the event the office becomes vacant through death, disability, or resignation, the senate elects one of its members to serve as acting lieutenant governor until the next regular election. The senators have adopted rules that grant the lieutenant governor extensive legislative, organizational, procedural, administrative, and planning authority.

The election of the lieutenant governor, who serves a four-year term, attracts far less public attention than the power of the office merits; the lieutenant governor is one of the most influential officials in Texas government. Organized interests are well aware of the importance of the office and contribute sizable sums to influence the election.

Although lieutenant governors in many states exercise a hybrid executive-legislative function, their influence rarely approaches that of the lieutenant governor of Texas. The political power of the lieutenant governor of Texas is largely based on senate rules and could be weakened by a majority of the senate. Therefore, the lieutenant governor must maintain a working relationship with the majority of the senators. The Republican-dominated Seventy-ninth Senate (2005), however, enacted rules that maintained the power of the Republican lieutenant governor.

Speaker of the House.   The Texas House of Representatives, by a majority vote of its membership, chooses its presiding officer from among its members by a recorded vote. The actual campaign can be very competitive and may attract candidates from all parts of the ideological spectrum. Yet because the vote for speaker is not secret, the successful candidate may take punitive action against opponents and their supporters. As a result, incumbent speakers have rarely faced serious opposition. When

Republicans gained a majority in the Texas House in 2002, however, they ousted the Democratic incumbent and elected the first Republican speaker since Reconstruction.

House members who support the winning candidate can become part of the speaker's "team," even if they are members of the opposition party. As mentioned earlier, this Texas legislative idiosyncrasy is known as the no-party system. The speaker appoints team members to serve on prestigious committees and selects her or his most reliable supporters as committee chairs. Lobbyists attempt to form alliances with powerful team members by making campaign contributions and supporting their legislative agendas.

Running for Speaker.　Funds raised and spent during a campaign for the speakership are part of the public record. Candidates for speaker are required to file a complete statement of loans, campaign contributions, and expenditures with the secretary of state. No corporation, labor union, or organization may contribute, and individual contributions are limited to $100. All expenditures over $10 must be reported. These requirements represent an attempt to reduce the influence of lobbyists and interest groups on the speaker's race by limiting and making public their campaign contributions. Still, the support of **"The Lobby"** (the major Texas economic interests) remains necessary to become speaker. In an attempt to curtail abuses of power, a law against "legislative bribery" prohibits the use of threats or promises of important appointments during the campaign to become speaker. The law is difficult to enforce, and it is simply understood that the speaker's supporters will be appointed to important committees.

Legislative Committees

Because several thousand bills are introduced into the Texas legislature each session, a division of labor is necessary for an orderly operation. The committee system exists to carry out this distribution of tasks. Each committee has a chair and a vice chair. The chair controls the committee's agenda, its schedule of hearings, the witnesses to be called, and the voting schedule.

Types of Committees.　Committees are classified based on function and longevity. *Standing committees* are permanent committees that are created for the entire legislative term. **Ad hoc committees** are temporary committees that are created for a specific purpose and then are disbanded. Committees may also be classified either as *substantive committees*, which actually legislate, or *procedural committees*, which deal with the rules, organization, and processes of the legislative body.

Standing Committees.　Most committees are standing substantive committees. Each committee of this type is given authority over a subject of political interest, such as education, taxes, appropriations, or agriculture. Each committee also may have subcommittees with authority over specific topics within the general subject area of the committee. Substantive committees have been called "little legislatures" because they normally conduct the real legislative business of conflict, compromise, and accommodation.

Each bill brought before the Texas legislature is assigned to a substantive standing committee in each chamber, where witnesses—both for and against the proposal—may be heard, debates are held, and bills are **marked up** (changed) or killed. Successful bills are seldom reported out of a committee in their original form. Because standing committees do the basic legislative work, the general membership relies heavily on them for guidance on how to vote on a bill being considered on the floor. In fact, attempting to amend some bills, or even questioning the work of the committee, violates the norms of the Texas Senate.

| DID YOU KNOW . . .
That in Texas, less than 0.3 percent of total state expenditures goes toward legislative staff salaries, services, and accommodations？

| "The Lobby"
Collectively, the most politically and economically powerful special interest groups in Texas.

| Ad Hoc Committee
A temporary committee.

| Mark Up
In legislation, to amend, change, or rewrite bills while they are in committee.

The most important standing procedural committee is the Calendars Committee in the house of representatives. It controls the flow of legislation from the substantive committees to the floor of the house. No bill can reach the floor of the house without authorization from the Calendars Committee (or the much less important Local and Consent Calendars Committee).

Pigeonholing Bills.   An important function of committees in the Texas legislature is to serve as a burying ground for bills. A legislator may introduce a bill as a favor to some group or constituent who feels very strongly about the matter, even though the legislator knows full well that the bill will be killed, or pigeonholed, in committee (and that the committee will take the blame). Other bills may be assigned to hostile committees with the expectation that they will be totally rewritten, if not pigeonholed.

Killing legislation by denying it a hearing is a convenient method of affecting public policy. Legislators do not have to go on record as being in opposition to a bill and thereby provide campaign fodder for political opponents. They can claim that they simply never had a chance to vote on the measure—even though they may have been instrumental in presiding over the bill's death in a substantive committee or subcommittee or in one of the calendars committees.

Expertise.   Where a seniority system is used, committee members and committee chairs are usually returned to the same committee posts each session, and legislators can thus become reasonably well informed, if not expert, on a given subject. This expertise is important because members must hear interest group lobbyists and administrative officials and evaluate their arguments on the merits of proposed legislation.

Compared with the U.S. Congress and most other state legislatures, the Texas legislature operates under a very limited seniority system. Therefore, the expertise of committee members may come from their occupational backgrounds rather than from legislative experience. Texas legislators, as we have seen, are seldom politicians to the exclusion of other occupations, and their interest in their primary occupations may create conflicts with the public interest. For example, if the primary occupation of a legislator is banking, then that lawmaker may be more sensitive to the interests of the banking industry than to the interests of the public. The same problem arises with any occupation.

Bureaucratic Oversight.   In the United States, legislatures function as watchdogs over the executive branch—that is, the legislature oversees the administrative bureaucracy as it executes the law and implements public programs. The vehicle for oversight is usually the legislative committee. Legislators wish to determine whether the bureaucrats are administering the laws in the way the legislature intended. They also must determine if new or revised legislation is needed. Accordingly, committees hold hearings and ask bureaucrats under their jurisdiction about the laws and programs that they are implementing.

Ostensibly, the committees are watching out for the public good by checking on whether the bureaucrats perform their duties in ways consistent with the public interest. More often than not, however, the committees serve as legislative advocates for the bureaucrats and the interests and viewpoints of their clientele. Therefore, a committee may not undertake a truly critical scrutiny of the agencies under its jurisdiction.[7]

Legislative Staff

The Texas legislature has seen fit to provide only minimal funds for hiring competent staff. Monthly staff allotments are about $8,500 per month for house members

---

[7]See Chapter 24 for a more complete discussion of alliances of legislative, executive, and group interests.

and about $25,000 per month for senators, who also receive reimbursement for other "reasonable and necessary" office expenses. These funds are not for personal use, but for staff salaries, office expenses, and official travel.

The Consequences of Limited Staff Support.   As a result of limited funds, neither individual legislators nor legislative committees have professional staff comparable to that of special interest groups. With minimal staff support, individual legislators and committees have no way of challenging the expert testimony and arguments of interest group lobbyists and agency liaisons. Powerful interests and administrative agencies have a distinct advantage when they alone possess information and expertise, and legislators become dependent on them for research data, advice, and other services.

Some house and senate members with shared political views have pooled their expense allocations to hire staff personnel. This tactic provides the participants with a rudimentary level of independent information.

Barriers to Greater Staff Funding.   Whenever the legislature considers larger appropriations to hire competent staff members, both the general public and special interests voice strong opposition. Members of the public are usually swayed by arguments against increased government spending and do not recognize the potential benefits of an informed legislature. Special interests, of course, understand very well how limited staff resources work to their benefit.

> **DID YOU KNOW . . .**
> That the most powerful Texas House committees are Appropriations, Ways and Means, and State Affairs and that the most powerful Texas Senate committees are Finance, Jurisprudence, and State Affairs?

The Presiding Officers and the Legislative Committees

To understand how the Texas legislature works, one must understand the powers exercised by the lieutenant governor in the Texas Senate and the speaker in the Texas House of Representatives. These powers can be roughly divided into two general categories: procedural powers, which are directly related to the legislative process, and institutional powers, which cover administrative policies such as budgeting, planning, and management.

A Summary of the Powers of the Presiding Officers

Both state law and the rules of each chamber, formal and informal, give the presiding officers the procedural power to do the following:

1. Appoint most committee members.
2. Appoint committee chairs.
3. Assign bills to committees.
4. Schedule legislation for floor action.
5. Recognize members on the floor for amendments and points of order.
6. Interpret the procedural rules when conflict arises.
7. Appoint the chairs and members of conference committees.

In addition, laws or legislative rules grant the presiding officers nonprocedural, institutional power to do the following:

1. Serve as joint chairs and appoint the other members of the Legislative Budget Board.
2. Serve as joint chairs and appoint the other members of the Legislative Council.
3. Serve on and appoint the members of the Legislative Audit Committee.
4. Serve on and appoint the members of the Sunset Advisory Commission.

Power in the Texas legislature is thus concentrated in the offices of the lieutenant governor and the speaker of the house. In the rest of this chapter, we describe the powers just summarized in greater detail.

Control of Committees

Committees are central to the legislative process. Those who have the authority to name a committee's members are able to influence the policy decisions of the legislative body. In Texas, this authority belongs to the lieutenant governor and the speaker. Control of committees also provides a degree of control over scheduling, though the presiding officers have additional tools to control scheduling.

Committee Membership in the House. In the house, the speaker appoints the total membership as well as the chairs and vice chairs of the procedural committees. The speaker also appoints all members of the powerful Appropriations Committee, whose members serve as *ex officio* chairs of the subcommittees for budget and oversight of the substantive committees. Thus, the speaker's appointees to the Appropriations Committee also control the budget requests of the other committees. The Appropriations Committee strongly influences funding for all divisions of state government.

The house Calendars Committee controls the flow of legislation from the committees to the house floor. The speaker uses his or her influence with this procedural committee to determine if and when bills are heard on the house floor.

For all substantive committees other than Appropriations, a limited seniority system in the house determines up to one-half of the membership; the speaker appoints the other half. The speaker also appoints the committee's chair and vice chair, which ensures that the committee leadership, as well as a numerical majority of each substantive committee, will be speaker appointees. The standing committee chairs appoint the membership and the chairs and vice chairs of the subcommittees.

Committee Membership in the Senate. The lieutenant governor officially appoints the total membership, as well as the chairs and vice chairs, of all senate committees and permanent subcommittees. In practice, an informal seniority system allows the most senior senators to choose the committee on which they wish to serve until one-third of the committee's positions are filled. This ensures that senior senators will serve on the more powerful committees. The chairs of the standing committees, at their discretion, may appoint subcommittees from the committee membership.

Results of Control by the Presiding Officers. The appointive power of the presiding officers means that the action of a committee on specific legislation is usually predictable. The presiding officers can also use the power of appointment to reward friends and supporters as well as to punish opponents. Interest groups often attempt to influence the presiding officer's decision to their advantage. It is of vital importance to interest groups to have sympathetic members on a committee that reviews legislation important to their interests.

The relative power of the committee and the legislator's position on it (as committee or subcommittee chair) can largely determine that person's influence with administrators, lobbyists, and other legislators. Members actively seek appointments to committees that consider taxes, spending, or legislation for powerful economic interests or that control the house calendar.

There is no way to determine precisely all the coalitions, compromises, and bargains that can relate to a desirable committee appointment. Negotiations for committee positions are intense, and conflicts over committee appointments arise in all legislative bodies. Concentrating the power over committee selection in the presiding officers is one way to resolve such conflicts.

Selection of Committee Chairs. Because the chairs of legislative committees play an important role in determining the ultimate success or failure of legislation, conflict over their selection must be resolved. In some states, the majority of the committee selects the committee chair. In others, a seniority system is used. In Texas, as already explained, the presiding officers make these decisions. Owing to the power of each chair over the committee's organization, procedure, and subcommittees, the fate of much public policy can be determined when the chair is selected.

The presiding officers, by virtue of their power to appoint the chairs of all committees, have a tool that works like a magnet to attract legislators to their teams. If legislators want to "get along" in the legislature, they "go along" (with the presiding officers). This power also increases the bargaining position of the presiding officers relative to interest groups. The lobbyist who can help get a sympathetic legislator appointed as chair of an important committee has earned the salary paid by the interest group that employs her or him. At the same time, the lobbyist owes the presiding officer a real favor for appointing the "right" committee chair.

The appointive power of the presiding officers, although significant, does not provide absolute power over the legislature. The presiding officers may also appoint to important positions legislators who have political power in their own right, such as legislators with close ties to powerful special interest groups. The presiding officers may then have the support of some of the most powerful members of the legislature in a reciprocally beneficial relationship. The presiding officers can usually count on the loyalty of the chairs, who in turn can usually depend on support from the presiding officers.

The No-Party System. The Texas legislature has historically been organized on the basis of ideology, rather than political party, with a coalition of Republicans and conservative-to-moderate Democrats usually in control. Under this no-party system, party affiliation has less significance than ideology and interest group ties.

Historically, the conservative Democratic speakers appointed mostly Democrats—but some Republicans—to committee chair positions. Today, the no-party system has been modified and continued under conservative Republican leadership, with the ratio of Republican to Democrat chairs reversed. The chairs of the most powerful committees are usually, but not always, appointed from the presiding officers' party.

It is important to understand that although the Texas legislature is organizationally a no-party system, party differences are important on matters of policy. Political party caucuses do not fill the positions of power as they do in the U.S. Congress, and members of the minority party may join the presiding officers' team, serve on important committees, and become committee chairs. Differences on public-policy issues are sometimes intense, however, and are becoming increasingly partisan.

Committee Action

Committee members can deliver to the leadership such things as substantial changes in bills, support for legislation favored by the leadership team, and opposition to legislation the leadership wants to defeat. A politically knowledgeable leadership that astutely uses its power over committee members can thus consolidate support for its policies.

Committee Jurisdiction. The presiding officers in the Texas legislature are responsible for assigning bills to particular committees. Because committee jurisdiction in the Texas legislature is often poorly defined, the officers have considerable discretion when making these assignments. The speaker may even reconsider a bill's assignment and change its committees during the legislative session.

The presiding officers do not hesitate to assign a bill they oppose to a committee they know will act unfavorably on the bill—and likewise, assign a bill they support to a committee that will report on it positively. Because the presiding officers can stack the committees to their liking, this is a simple process.

> **DID YOU KNOW . . .**
> That the house legislative calendars are Emergency, Major State, Constitutional Amendments, General State, Local, Consent, Resolutions, and Congratulatory and Memorial Resolutions?

Killing Bills. There are several reasons why a presiding officer may oppose a specific bill (other than that the bill is simply bad public policy):

1. The backers and financial supporters of the presiding officer may view the bill as a threat to their economic or political well-being.
2. The presiding officer and his or her team may feel that supporters of the bill have been uncooperative in the past and should be punished.
3. The supporters of the bill may be outbargained by the bill's opponents.
4. The presiding officer and his or her supporters may believe that the bill, if it became law, would take funds away from programs that they favor.

When a legislator who does not serve on the committee opposes a bill, the legislator may bargain with the members of the committee to pigeonhole it. There are several reasons for this. The most obvious is that the legislator—or an interest that she or he represents—is ideologically opposed to the substance of the bill. In addition, a legislator may want to kill a bill on which his or her political supporters are evenly divided, for no matter how the legislator voted, he or she would lose political support and face political or economic repercussions from angered interest groups or constituents. We give one example of a bill that died in committee in this chapter's *Which Side Are You On?* feature.

| Tagging
In the Texas Senate, a rule that allows a senator to halt a standing committee's consideration of a bill for forty-eight hours.

Tagging in the Senate. The Texas Senate also practices **tagging.** Once each session, any senator may require the chair of a senate committee to give that senator forty-eight hours' advance notice as to when the committee will hold hearings on a bill. This means that, in effect, the senator can delay the hearings for forty-eight hours. The tagging procedure is not debatable; any committee action on the bill within the forty-eight-hour period is void. If the bill's sponsors can get the senator to remove the tag, however, the bill can be immediately cleared for committee hearings. The effect of tagging would be minimal if it were not for the limited legislative session. Under the existing system, tagging late in the session enables a single senator to kill or force the modification of a bill.

The Discharge Petition. All legislative bodies have some procedure whereby bills can be extracted from reluctant committees, but it is usually difficult to accomplish. Legislators, even though they may support a bill that is buried in a committee, are reluctant to vote to discharge it. They see the **discharge petition** as a threat to the privileges of the entire committee system—privileges that they too enjoy.

| Discharge Petition
A seldom-used legislative procedure whereby a bill can be forced out of a committee (discharged) for consideration by the chamber as a whole.

The Relative Weakness of Committees in Texas. The importance of legislative committees within the political system varies from state to state. In Texas, the power of legislative committees is proportionately less, and the power of the bureaucracy and special interests is proportionately more, than in some other political jurisdictions. The reasons include the following:

1. Because legislative sessions are infrequent and short, committees seldom meet and cannot provide ongoing oversight.
2. Members often move from one committee to another, hampering the development of expertise and long-term working relationships.
3. Texas legislators serve for relatively short periods compared with top administrators and lobbyists.

Restraints on the Powers of the Presiding Officers

Although taken together, the organizational, procedural, and institutional powers of the speaker and the lieutenant governor seem to be—and at times are—overwhelming, there are certain restraints that curtail arbitrary and absolute use of these powers.

WHICH SIDE ARE YOU ON? | Should the Production of Horsemeat Be Legal in Texas?

State legislatures sometimes find themselves addressing unusual topics. One example is the horsemeat controversy in Texas. Generally, Americans do not eat horsemeat. Horsemeat is not illegal *per se,* but if horses were slaughtered in the United States for domestic consumption, the processing would have to take place under U.S. Department of Agriculture (USDA) supervision. No slaughterhouses in the country currently choose to ship USDA-approved horsemeat.

THEY EAT HORSES, DON'T THEY?

Horsemeat is eaten in some countries, however, and it is produced for export in the United States. Two small foreign-owned slaughterhouses in North Texas process all U.S. horsemeat for export to Europe and Japan (and to certain U.S. zoos, where it is fed to lions and tigers). Apparently, French and Belgian horsemeat connoisseurs find Texas horsemeat to be unusually flavorful. Horsemeat consumption in Europe has actually risen in the last few years due to concerns that beef might be infected with "mad cow" disease.

As you might expect, there are a number of people who want to ban the slaughter of horses for food. In 2002, animal rights activists discovered that in 1949, the Texas legislature made it illegal to slaughter, possess, sell, and transport horsemeat for human consumption. The law was passed to prevent unscrupulous butchers from passing horsemeat off as beef at a time when horsemeat was much cheaper than beef.

Activists demanded that the two Texas slaughterhouses be shut down. At the request of a member of the house, the Texas attorney general issued an official opinion that the 1949 law was still valid. The slaughterhouses sued in federal court to block enforcement of the law. In 2003, a bill to legalize horse slaughter passed the Texas House, 83–53, but eventually died in committee in the senate. Several senators reported receiving more letters and phone calls about the bill than about all other issues combined.

This slaughterhouse, owned by the Beltex Corporation, processes horsemeat in Fort Worth. Many Americans may oppose eating horsemeat, but a national effort to ban the slaughter of horses for export has had trouble getting through the U.S. Congress. (AP Photo/Donna McWilliam)

ECONOMIC LIBERTY SHOULD OUTWEIGH CULTURAL PREJUDICES

Normally, an animal rights proposal that called for shutting down existing enterprises would get nowhere in famously pro-business Texas, and defenders of the slaughterhouses believe that is as it should be. Under the U.S. Constitution, Texas has no right to interfere with interstate and international commerce—and none of the horsemeat is for consumption in Texas. Those who are opposed to eating horses should simply avoid horsemeat and should not attempt to impose their values on Europeans. Finally, the slaughterhouses offer a humane alternative for horse owners who need to put down unwanted animals.

EATING HORSES IS UNACCEPTABLE AND SHOULD BE STOPPED

Opponents of the slaughterhouses have only one principal argument—but it is a powerful one. Opponents believe that slaughtering horses for human consumption is simply wrong and should not be allowed by law. "Horses are not like cows and pigs and goats," says Jerry Finch, founder of Habitat for Horses, a group organized to rescue abused horses. "They're like pets, and the idea of eating them is repulsive."[*] Horses are special in Texas tradition. In an opinion poll, 72 percent of Texans opposed horse slaughter for human consumption. Further, the very existence of groups such as Habitat for Horses is proof that there are more humane alternatives for unwanted animals than the slaughterhouse.

WHAT'S YOUR POSITION?

Should the slaughterhouses be closed? Why or why not?

GOING ONLINE

While a number of bloggers have championed the right to eat horsemeat, opponents of horse slaughter are much better organized on the Web. For an example, see "Mary Nash's Horsemeat Website" at **www.kaufmanzoning.net/horsemeat**. Nash, incidentally, owns a farm that is immediately adjacent to one of the slaughterhouses.

*Kris Axtman, *Christian Science Monitor,* April 28, 2003.

Personality.   The personalities of the individual presiding officers and the way they view their offices determine their approach to legislative leadership. They may use their powers to develop strong, aggressive leadership, ruthlessly overpowering opposition, or they may be accommodating and compromising, accomplishing the desired results with only the implied possibility of reprisal.

The Team.   The presiding officers require a strong coalition of legislative support to accomplish their aims despite the concentration of powers they enjoy. Support from other legislators may come because of friendship or ideological agreement. Legislators may believe that it is in the best interest of their constituents and supporters for them to be "team players" and back the presiding officers. The speaker and the lieutenant governor are usually able to build on, and add cohesiveness to, this support through use of their powers to reward or punish.

The Lobby and the Bureaucracy.   The relationship between the presiding officers, "The Lobby," and their bureaucratic allies is of great importance in determining the chance of success for specific legislation. When the lieutenant governor, the speaker, bureaucrats, and powerful lobbyists all agree and work together toward a common goal, legislative victory is almost ensured.

In the event of conflict between the lobby-bureaucracy coalition and the speaker or the lieutenant governor, the program of the presiding officer may be either diluted or defeated, depending on such complex factors as the amount of support that can be mustered from the governor, other interest groups, and other legislators. Against a strong coalition of an interest group and the bureaucracy, all of the formal and informal powers of the presiding officers may not be enough to control the legislation. A conflict of this nature is unusual, however, and the presiding officers are usually in basic agreement with the more powerful interests, which often have given political and financial support to their campaigns.

The Governor.   Veto power and influence with lobbyists are the most useful instruments the governor has to achieve changes in the substance of bills while they are still in the legislature. The veto powers given the governor by the Texas Constitution are among her or his most important powers. They include the veto over legislative acts and the item veto over appropriations. These formal powers place the governor in a strong bargaining position, and the governor's support for or opposition to specific programs is an important determinant of their success.

The governor also has the support of friendly interest groups, which can often be enlisted to exert pressure on the presiding officers and other legislators. Interest group support complements the governor's formal legislative power and enhances his or her influence.

A governor who tends toward activism can exercise substantial influence over legislation and thereby moderate the powers of the presiding officers. In fact, successful legislation usually requires a coalition among the governor, the lieutenant governor, and the speaker, with each affecting the content of legislation. Of course, the governor has lost a battle with the legislative leadership if forced to veto a bill after attempting to influence it. If the governor chooses a passive legislative role, her or his influence is significantly decreased—inaction or restraint affects public policy as profoundly as does activist leadership.

The Political Climate.   The general public is seldom aware of events in Austin. Rare exceptions arise when news of a scandal spreads across the state, as in the examples of the veterans' land scandals of the 1950s, the Sharpstown bank scandal of the 1970s, and the delinquent property tax scandal of the 1990s. Although public interest is stimulated by a scandal, most citizens seem content to find and punish a few "bad apples" instead of demanding serious institutional inquiry and the systemic reform of government procedures and regulations.

Scandal does have the benefit of making the presiding officers aware of public scrutiny and temporarily more aware of public criticism. In fact, the political climate following both the Sharpstown and the delinquent property tax scandals resulted in ethics reform legislation. Without scandal, the legislative leadership is all but free from public attention, with only interest groups, administrators, a few concerned citizens, some members of the press, and the governor monitoring legislative activity.

If two-party competition ever returns to Texas, the competition might weaken the authority of the presiding officers, especially the lieutenant governor. It is true that if partisan politics dominated the house, the house majority might simply choose a member of the majority party as speaker and retain the somewhat authoritarian house rules. In contrast, if a lieutenant governor were elected who belonged to a different party than the senate majority, that majority might change the senate rules to seriously reduce the lieutenant governor's powers. In this event, the senate majority would have to institute other mechanisms to broker power and resolve conflict.

Political or Economic Ambition. Through effective management of the press, accumulation of political credits to be cashed in at some future date, and consolidation of interest group support, the offices of speaker and lieutenant governor can serve as stepping-stones for advancement in politics. The presiding officers must not, however, antagonize powerful economic and political forces in the process. Consequently, ambition can serve as a very real restraint on their independence.

Interest group support, campaign finances, and the backing of established politicians are all necessary for political advancement. Presiding officers must play their political cards right if they want to build an economic and political base solid enough to attain higher office.

Other Legislators. Many committee chairs and other legislators exercise a political influence in their own right through their mastery of the intricacies of legislative rules and procedures, strong support of powerful interest groups, and the respect or fear they can generate in other legislators. Because of the ties these individuals have built through the years with administrators, interest groups, and other legislators, the presiding officers may need to solicit their backing on key legislation. Generally, however, these individuals are the exception in an environment heavily influenced by the lieutenant governor or speaker.

The Calendar and the Floor

The instrument for controlling the flow of legislation from the committees to the floor is the **calendar.** Control of the calendar of bills is important in any legislative body. In Texas, it is of paramount importance because of the short biennial sessions.

With the calendar schedules, as with other important aspects of the legislative process, power in the Texas legislature is centralized in the offices of the presiding officers. Unlike many of their other organizational and procedural powers, however, the ability of the speaker and the lieutenant governor to control scheduling is based as much on their influence with other legislators as on the formal powers of the offices.

Because timing a bill for consideration on the floor is critical to its eventual passage or defeat, control of the schedule is a powerful weapon that can be used to aid or to hinder legislation, to reward allies, or to punish enemies. For example, any of the following situations may occur:

1. Supporters may want floor consideration of a bill delayed until they can muster the necessary votes to get it passed. (Opponents, in contrast, may favor quick action because they have the necessary votes to defeat the bill but believe those votes could erode if the supporters are given time to consolidate their forces.)

| DID YOU KNOW . . .

That in 1965, twenty-two members of the Texas House voted against the U.S. Bill of Rights when it was introduced as "an act to protect our fundamental liberties" by Representative Jake Johnson, a liberal from San Antonio?

| Calendar

In the Texas legislature, the schedule that serves as a conduit for legislation between the committees and the primary legislative body.

Democratic representative Terri Hodge of Dallas sits at a desk in the Texas House after learning that several members had bills hung up in the Local and Consent Calendars Committee. Why might the leadership use this committee to pigeonhole a bill of purely local interest? (AP Photo/Harry Cabluck)

| **Suspension of the Rule**
Setting aside of the rules of a legislative body so that another set of rules can be used.

| **Blocking Bill**
In Texas, a bill placed early on the senate calendar that will never actually be considered. A rule—which can be suspended by a two-thirds vote—requires that the senate address bills in chronological order. The blocking bill ensures that a measure must win the vote of two-thirds of the senate even to be considered.

2. Conversely, supporters may want early consideration of a bill because the opposition appears to be gaining strength. (Opponents would want delay under these circumstances.)

3. If a bill has been placed far down on the calendar, opponents can kill it through the filibuster, tagging, or parliamentary maneuvers even if they are in the minority.

House Calendars

The speaker of the house exercises no formal control over the house calendars. The Calendars Committee (and the much less important Local and Consent Calendars Committee) performs this function. This apparent decentralization of power, however, is more illusion than reality. The members and the chairs of the two committees are appointed by the speaker, are allies of the speaker, and can usually be persuaded to be amenable to the speaker's wishes.

There are several calendars for different kinds of bills. Unimportant or trivial bills are placed on special schedules and are usually disposed of promptly with little debate by the body of the house. The process is not so automatic for major or controversial legislation, however. In fact, the speaker and the committee chair often use the Calendars Committee as a "black hole" into which bills simply disappear. The process was once even more opaque than it is today. In a much-applauded action, the 1993 house under Speaker Pete Laney adopted rules making the process more open to the general house membership.

The Senate Calendar

Unlike the house, the senate has only one calendar. Officially, the senate has a rule that requires bills to be placed on the calendar and then considered on the senate floor in the same chronological order in which they were reported from the committees. In practice, bills are taken off the calendar for senate consideration only by a suspension of this rule. The **suspension of the rule** requires a two-thirds majority vote of the entire membership of the senate.

The Blocking Bill. The procedure for consideration goes something like this: The first bill placed on the senate calendar each session is called a **blocking bill.** It is usually a bill dealing with a proposed horticultural change somewhere around the state capitol. It will never be taken off the calendar. It does, however, block all other bills' access to the floor except by the two-thirds vote to suspend the rule.

A Two-Thirds Majority for Action. This senate practice affects the senate's entire legislative process. The irony is that while only a simple majority is necessary for final passage in the senate, a two-thirds majority is necessary to get the bill to the floor for consideration. It can be said that this process protects the minority from the majority. It is also a means whereby the senate can kill a bill without having a floor vote for or against—the bill simply fails to reach the floor and so dies on the calendar. Although lobbyists are keenly interested in which bills die for lack of two-thirds support in a consideration vote, the general public and some members of the press are often unaware that an important vote has even occurred.

The two-thirds rule is a tool that can be used to enhance the powers of the presiding officer. By using this requirement, the lieutenant governor can keep a bill from reaching the floor of the senate by simply persuading eleven members to vote against it. The bill then lacks the necessary two-thirds majority and cannot advance to the floor of the senate. Any coalition of eleven senators can, of course, achieve the same result—occasionally against the wishes of the lieutenant governor.

A practical example of the application of the rule occurred during the 2003 legislative session. Although Republicans possessed a 19–12 senate majority, the twelve Democratic senators had the numerical strength to prevent the suspension of the rule and thereby deny some partisan bills access to the senate floor.

The Quorum Requirement

At least two-thirds of the members of each chamber must be present to conduct business. Absence of eleven or more senators brings any senate action to a halt, as does the absence of fifty-one or more house members. The quorum rule is written into the state constitution, and lack of a quorum is an absolute bar to legislative action. This fact has led to a series of incidents in which members have absented themselves to halt business. We describe the most recent of these attempts—the "Killer D's" episode—in this chapter's *Politics and the Quorum* feature on the next page.

Texas has an unusually high figure for a legislative quorum. Half the membership is a more common rule, and the U.S. Constitution establishes that quorum for the U.S. House and Senate.

The Floor

The Texas Constitution requires that bills must be "read on three consecutive days in each house." The purpose of this action on the **floor** is to ensure that laws are not passed without adequate opportunity for debate. Bills are read once on being introduced before the presiding officer assigns them to a committee. In practice, the entire bill is seldom read at this time. Instead, a caption, or brief summary, is read to acquaint the members of the legislature with the subject of the bill. The bill is read the second time before floor debate in each chamber, and if an entire bill is to be read, it is usually on this second reading. The third reading usually occurs at least one day after floor passage.

Bills containing a statement that they are "cases of imperative public necessity" may be read for the third time on the same day as floor passage, as long as four-fifths of the membership agree. All bills now routinely contain this provision and usually receive the third reading immediately following floor passage. A simple majority is required for passage on the third reading, while a two-thirds majority is necessary for the addition of an amendment.

The House Floor.   As bills reach the floor of the house, a loudspeaker system allows the members and visitors to follow the debate. **Floor leaders** usually stand at the front of the chamber, answer questions, and speak in favor of or against the bill. Microphones located elsewhere in the house chamber serve opponents of the bill and other concerned lawmakers as they speak against the bill, speak for the bill, or simply ask questions.

The consideration of bills on the floor of the house would seem to be a study in confusion and inattention. Throughout the process, members of the house may be laughing, talking, reading papers, or sleeping at their desks. Because many members often know very little about a bill under consideration, however, this is an excellent opportunity for both proponents and opponents of the legislation to seek support for their positions. Eloquent speeches seldom change votes. In fact, many members vote for or against legislation based on who is supporting it or who is against it and only then ask what the bill was all about. This practice is especially true of specialized bills that have generated little statewide interest. Voting time usually brings both supporters and opponents of the bill up and down the aisles pleading with either one finger (vote yes) or two fingers (vote no).

Floor
The place where a legislative body debates, amends, votes on, enacts, and defeats proposed legislation; the entire house or senate acting as a whole.

Floor Leaders
Legislators who are responsible for getting party members to vote for or against particular legislation.

POLITICS AND THE QUORUM | The Killer Bees and the Killer Wasps

The Texas Constitution requires that a quorum of at least two-thirds of the total membership of either of the two chambers be present before that chamber can conduct business. In several incidents, members have been absent on purpose in an attempt to thwart the wishes of the majority.*

THE BEES

In 1979, supporters of former Texas governor John Connally in his bid for the Republican nomination for president proposed to split the Texas presidential primary away from the other primaries. Presumably, holding the presidential primary early would have benefited Connally. This step was opposed by at least twelve of the thirty-one state senators, who were dubbed the "Killer Bees." The senators had taken a "blood oath" to deny the split primary bill access to the senate floor. When it became clear that the Bees could stop floor action, Lieutenant Governor William Hobby removed the two-thirds calendar requirement rule for the presidential primary bill. Conservative Democrats who supported Connally were thereby ensured both a floor hearing and, as they had a majority in the senate, passage of the bill. Because twenty-one of the thirty-one senators must be present to constitute a quorum, however, the twelve Bees simply refused to be present.

Hobby ordered the senate sergeant at arms and the Texas Rangers to find the absent senators and force them to attend the session. The Killer Bees went into hiding. The Rangers proved to be inept in implementing the order and, in fact, arrested the brother of one of the Bees in Houston and forcibly transported him to Austin, where a legislative assistant correctly identified him.

The Bees were never found but returned to the senate chamber to complete the important business of the session,

*This feature is adapted and updated from Ernest Crain, Charles Deaton, and William Earl Maxwell, *The Challenge of Texas Politics* (St. Paul: West Publishing Co., 1980), pp. 94–95.

following the assurances of Lieutenant Governor Hobby that the usual senate rules would be followed. In the end, the conservatives got the last laugh—the Killer Bee stunt proved to be highly unpopular with the voters, and several of the Bees were not reelected.

THE WASPS

In the 1993 regular session, the "Killer Wasps" (the senate's thirteen Republican members) briefly denied the senate a quorum. They instituted a one-day walkout to protest a resolution calling for the settlement of a lawsuit on judicial elections. The suit called for electing state district judges in urban areas by single-member districts rather than by the county at-large system. Mexican Americans and African Americans originated the suit to foster the election of more minorities to the state judiciary. If large urban counties were split up into districts, minorities would be in the majority in at least some of the districts, even if they could not hope to prevail in the county as a whole. The U.S. Fifth Circuit Court of Appeals eventually rejected the settlement, however, leaving the at-large system in place.

The Killer Wasp episode proved to be an embarrassment to the Republicans in 2003, when Republicans denounced the Democratic "Killer D's" who were boycotting the special session called by Governor Perry to gerrymander congressional districts favorable to Republicans. Democrats were able to claim that Republicans had used the same tactic—and for a less worthy cause. The Republican response was that the Killer Wasp incident had lasted only one day.

FOR CRITICAL ANALYSIS

Were the Bees', Wasps', and Ds' actions a legitimate use of the quorum requirement?

Electronic Voting in the House.   House members insert cards into a voting panel on their desks that allows them to push buttons to record a vote of yes, no, or present, but not voting. The tallies are displayed on a large electronic scoreboard with green, red, and white bulbs next to each legislator's name. (Green means yes, red means no, and white means present, but not voting.)

Although the use of the electronic voting machine in the Texas House is a major innovation, one result is that house rules now prohibit "ghost voting," whereby legislators cast votes for absent colleagues. Suspecting that the defeat of a 1993 bill to increase the penalties for having drugs or weapons near schools was due to ghost voting, the bill's supporters requested a roll-call vote. Ten members, eight of whom had voted against the bill, had been present only in spirit. The bill was then passed 65–58 by the roll-call vote.

Points of Order in the House.   Throughout the voting, the speaker recognizes members from the floor, rules on **points of order,** and so forth. If a point of order is sustained late in the session, there may not be time to correct the error, and in that case the bill dies.

Although raising a point of order is not uncommon, it seldom has the impact that it did during the 1997 legislature. Representative Debra Danburg, a Democrat from Houston, raised a point of order that killed a bill requiring parental notification before a minor could have an abortion. In reaction, Arlene Wohlgemuth, a Republican representative from Burleson and a proponent of the antiabortion bill, raised points of order that killed some eighty pending bills, many of which were supported by Governor George W. Bush and other Republican legislators.[8]

The Senate Floor. The senate scene may be similar to that in the house in one sense—usually, few members are paying attention to the debate. Senate debates on even important bills are usually much shorter than debates in the house, primarily due to the all-important rule that requires a two-thirds vote before a bill can be brought to the floor out of its calendar sequence. Bringing a bill to the floor requires the cooperation of the lieutenant governor (who can recognize senators from the floor) and at least twenty-one senators. Such support suggests that compromises have been made and deals have been brokered well before the legislation ever reaches the floor.

The senate may also form itself into a **committee of the whole,** at which time the lieutenant governor appoints a senator to preside. Only a simple majority rather than the usual two-thirds is necessary to consider legislation, and the lieutenant governor may debate and vote on all questions. Otherwise, the senate rules are observed. No journal is kept of the proceedings.

Filibustering in the Senate.   The *filibuster*, which was discussed in Chapter 11, is a threat to bills in the Texas Senate, just as it is in the U.S. Senate. The difference in the Texas Senate is that a member may not give the floor to other senators who also want to filibuster. In Texas, the lieutenant governor controls the floor, so in effect only one senator may filibuster for as long as he or she can physically last. Then the vote is taken. **Cloture** to force a vote is not an option in the Texas Senate.

The purpose of a filibuster is either to attract public attention to a bill that is sure to pass without the filibuster or to delay legislation in the closing days of the session. In fact, the mere threat of a filibuster may be enough to compel a bill's supporters to change the content of the bill to reach a compromise with the disgruntled senator. If a filibuster does occur, it means that no compromise was possible—usually because the senators who favor the bill, by virtue of their numbers, refuse to be intimidated by the threat of a filibuster.

Senator Bill Meier set the world record for a filibuster in the 1977 legislative session by talking for forty-three hours. This feat broke the old record of forty-two hours and thirty-three minutes set in 1972 by Senator Mike McKool. There have been a number of other notable filibusters in the Texas Senate. In 1993, Senator Gonzalo Barrientos filibustered for seventeen hours and fifty minutes in an attempt to kill legislation that overturned an Austin ordinance designed to protect the Barton Springs watershed from development. During the filibuster, Barrientos was required to stand and was restricted to a three-square-foot area. The bill eventually passed 22–7.[9]

Finally, the Senate Votes.   Following the debate, the senators usually vote by hand signals directed toward a recording clerk—one finger for a yes vote and two fingers

---

Point of Order
A formal question to the chairperson about the legitimacy of a parliamentary process. A successful point of order can result in the postponement or defeat of legislation.

Committee of the Whole
An entire legislative body (such as the Texas Senate) acting as a committee. The committee's purpose is to allow the body to relax its rules and thereby expedite legislation.

Cloture
An action by which legislative debate is ended so that a floor vote must be taken.

---

[8]*Austin American-Statesman*, May 30, 1997, p. B7.
[9]Diana R. Fuentes, *San Antonio Express-News*, May 1, 1993, p. 17A.

for a no. During the voting process, senators plead for their colleagues' votes using the same hand signals directed toward the senators. Only a simple majority is necessary for passage.

Conference Committees

A unique by-product of bicameralism is the need to resolve differences in similar bills passed by the two chambers. A temporary, or ad hoc, committee known as a *conference committee* is appointed for each bill to resolve these differences. To determine the acceptability of proposed compromises, the membership of this committee remains in contact with interested legislators, lobbyists, administrators, and the presiding officers.

Conference Committee Membership.   In Texas, conference committees are composed of five members from each chamber, appointed by each chamber's presiding officer. The compromise proposal must win the support of a majority of the committee members from each chamber to be reported out of the conference committee. Because the members of the committee may alter or even kill a bill, the attitudes of the legislators appointed to the committee are of crucial concern to the various interests involved. Bargaining before the selection of the committee is common, and bargaining continues among the committee members during deliberations. Both the presiding officers and the conference committee members are well placed to affect the outcome.

Conference Committee Reports.   After a bill has been reported from the conference committee, it cannot be amended by either chamber but must be accepted or rejected as written or sent back to the conference committee for further compromise. In practice, due to the volume of legislation that must be considered and the limited time available, the Texas legislature tends to accept conference committee reports on most legislation.

How a Bill Becomes a Law

Bills may be introduced in either chamber or, to speed the process, in both chambers at the same time. Consider as an example a bill that is introduced in the senate before it is sent to the house. The numbers in Figure 23–5 correspond to the numbers in the following discussion.

1. *Introduction in the Senate.* A senator must introduce a bill in the senate. It is not difficult to find a legislator who is willing to perform this somewhat clerical function. More difficult is finding a sponsor who will use her or his political skills and bargaining prowess to help get the bill through the intricacies of the legislative process. On introduction, the bill is assigned a number—for example, Senate Bill 13 (SB 13).

2. *Assignment to a Senate Committee.* The lieutenant governor assigns bills to committees in the senate and can, for many bills, choose between two or more committees. It is very important to proponents of the bill that the chosen committee not oppose the spirit of the bill. If possible, proponents of the bill and their allies will gain the lieutenant governor's support and receive a friendly committee assignment. This may be granted in exchange for their support of or opposition to some other bill of particular interest to the lieutenant governor.

3. *Senate Committee Action.* In the relevant subcommittee, supporters and opponents of the bill are allowed to testify. Witnesses are often lobbyists or concerned bureaucrats affected by the bill. The subcommittee then marks up (makes changes to) the bill and sends it to the whole committee. The committee may hear addi-

tional testimony and further mark up the bill. Some senate committees do not have subcommittees. In that circumstance, the entire committee initially hears testimony and marks up the bill. The committee may then report on the bill favorably or unfavorably or may refuse to report on it at all.

4. The Senate Calendar. The senate has only one calendar of bills, and it is rarely followed. In the usual procedure, as described earlier, a senator makes a motion to suspend the regular calendar order and consider a proposed bill out of its sequence. For this parliamentary maneuver to succeed, prior arrangements must be made for the lieutenant governor to recognize the senator who will make the motion. If two-thirds of the senators agree to the motion, the bill, with the blessings of the lieutenant governor, is ready for action on the senate floor.

5. The Senate Floor. The president of the senate (the lieutenant governor) has the power to recognize senators who wish to speak and to interpret rules and points of order. Rarely does the senate overrule these interpretations. Unlimited debate is the rule in the Texas Senate. This does not mean that the Texas Senate is a deliberative body, for it is not; such luxury is not possible in the short legislative session. Unlimited debate could, however, lead to a filibuster—an attempt to either "talk

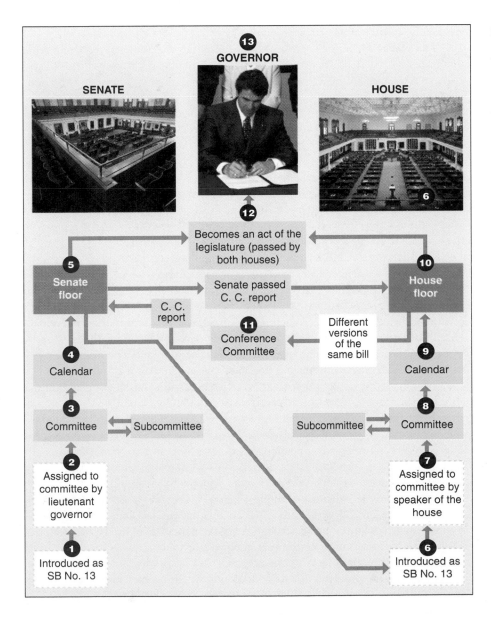

FIGURE 23–5 | HOW A BILL BECOMES A LAW IN TEXAS

The procedure shown in this figure follows a bill that is first introduced in the Texas Senate and eventually reaches the governor's desk. If a bill is first introduced in the Texas House of Representatives, the procedure is much the same, but the diagram would be a mirror image of what you see here, and the bill would be introduced as HB 13.

the bill to death", or force a compromise. If a bill is successful in reaching the senate floor, it has already cleared its major obstacle (the two-thirds majority necessary for senate consideration) and will usually pass in some form. A simple majority is necessary for a bill to pass. The lieutenant governor may vote only to break ties.

6. Introduction to the House. Following senate passage, the bill is sent to the house. A procedure similar to that in the senate is followed there.

7. Assignment to a House Committee. The speaker of the house assigns each bill to a committee. The speaker, like the lieutenant governor, has some freedom of choice in selecting a committee, because the jurisdiction of house committees is vague.

8. House Committee Action. Committee action in the house is similar to that in the senate. Each bill is assigned to a committee and then to a subcommittee, which may hold public hearings. The subcommittee as well as the committee may amend, totally rewrite, pigeonhole, or report favorably or unfavorably on a bill.

9. House Calendars. A bill that is reported favorably by a standing committee, or receives a favorable minority report by the required number of committee members, is placed on one of the eight house calendars by one of the two calendars committees. This establishes the approximate order in which the whole house will consider the legislation. If a calendars committee fails to assign the bill to a calendar, it can be forced to do so by the action of a simple majority of the house. If a bill has the blessings of the speaker, however, it is sure to be promptly placed on the appropriate calendar.

10. The House Floor. The speaker of the house has the power to recognize representatives on the house floor and also to interpret the rules and points of order. Although the speaker may be overruled, he or she seldom is. The size of the house necessitates that debate be more limited than in the senate—usually each member is allowed ten minutes. A bill may be amended, **tabled** (which usually kills the measure), defeated, or sent back to committee. The "yes" votes of only a simple majority of members present and voting are necessary for a bill to pass.

11. Conference Committee. If the house makes a change in the senate-passed version of a bill, a conference committee is necessary to reconcile the differences between the two versions of the bill. The lieutenant governor appoints five senators and the speaker appoints five representatives to sit on the committee. The compromise bill must be approved by a majority of both the senators and the representatives before it can be reported out of the conference committee.

12. Final Passage. A bill reported out of a conference committee is sent first to the chamber where it originated and then to the other chamber for final approval. Neither one may amend the reported bill but must accept it, reject it, or send it back to the conference committee. If both the senate and the house pass the conference committee version of the bill, it becomes an act of the legislature and is sent to the governor.

13. The Governor. The governor has several options for dealing with an act of the legislature. First, she or he may sign it into law. Second, he or she may choose not to sign it, in which circumstance it becomes law in ten days if the legislature is in session or in twenty days if the legislature is not in session. Third, the governor may choose to veto the act, but the veto can be overridden by a two-thirds vote in each chamber. (The Texas legislature almost never overrides a governor's vetoes, in large part because the legislature typically is no longer in session when the veto is issued.) The governor cannot veto a portion of an act unless it is a clause that actually appropriates funds. The governor may strike out an item of appropriation, but he or she does not have a reduction veto (to reduce spending for an item).

If the governor signs an act of the legislature, it becomes a law in ninety days— or sooner if it is an appropriations act or an act that the legislature has designated as emergency legislation. If the act requires the expenditure of funds, the comptroller of public accounts must certify that adequate revenue is available for its implementation. If revenue is lacking, the act goes back to the legislature, where either adequate funds are provided or a four-fifths majority in each chamber approves the act. If neither option is successful, the act cannot be implemented.

| **Table**
In a legislature or similar body, to cease action on a particular measure. A motion to table is not debatable.

Institutional Tools of Leadership

The Texas legislature has established a series of bodies that are active even when the legislature is not in session. To a limited degree, the work of these bodies may counteract the negative effects of the very short legislative sessions.[10]

Legislative Budget Board

Most states, the U.S. government, and most countries have only one budget. Texas has two. Each agency in the state government presents its budget requests both to the governor's office and to the **Legislative Budget Board.** The board then provides to the governor and the legislature a draft of the appropriations bill. The Legislative Budget Board has also been given broad authority over strategic planning for the state, bill analyses, and policy and impact analyses affecting education, criminal justice, and other policy areas.

The Legislative Budget Board operates continuously, even when the legislature is not in session. It is made up of the lieutenant governor and the speaker (who serve as joint chairs), as well as four members from each chamber who are appointed by their presiding officers. These ten members include the chairs of the senate Finance Committee and the house Ways and Means and Appropriations Committees. The board appoints an administrative director.

Clearly, the control of the board is in the hands of the two presiding officers, who are in a position to strongly influence state government from the budgeting stage through the final appropriations stage. The board staff assists the appropriating committees and their chairs, and it also has the watchdog function of overseeing to some extent the expenditures of the executive agencies and departments. Thus, in this critical area of finance, the concentration of power in the hands of the presiding officers is even greater than in other legislative areas.

| **Legislative Budget Board**
The primary budgeting entity for Texas state government.

Legislative Council

Another instrument of influence is the fourteen-member **Legislative Council,** which includes six senators, the chair of the house Administration Committee, five other representatives, and the lieutenant governor and the speaker of the house, who serve as joint chairs. The lieutenant governor appoints the senate members, and the speaker appoints the house members. A director and staff who serve at the pleasure of the council perform the administrative work.

The Legislative Council functions as a source of information and support to the legislature, state agencies, and other governmental institutions. It provides research support to legislators and helps draft legislative proposals.

| **Legislative Council**
In Texas, a body that provides research support, information, and bill-drafting assistance to legislators.

Legislative Audit Committee

The primary function of the **Legislative Audit Committee** is to audit (formally check) the expenditures of the state agencies and departments. The committee is composed of the presiding officers and the chairs of the taxing committees, the house Appropriations Committee, and the senate State Affairs Committee. The state auditor, who serves at the pleasure of the committee, heads the State Auditor's Office. Here, too, management of the fiscal affairs of the Texas government is firmly under the influence of the presiding officers.

| **Legislative Audit Committee**
In Texas, a committee that performs audits of state agencies and departments for the legislature.

[10]Sources for this material are *Guide to Texas State Agencies,* 9th ed. (Austin: Lyndon B. Johnson School of Public Affairs, University of Texas at Austin, 1996); the Legislative Budget Board Web site at **www.lbb.state.tx.us**; the Texas Legislative Council Web site at **www.tlc.state.tx.us**; the State Auditor's Office Web site at **www.sao.state.tx.us**; and the Sunset Advisory Commission Web site at **www.sunset.state.tx.us**.

Sunset Advisory Commission

The Texas Sunset Act requires that most state agencies undergo reevaluation, usually on a twelve-year cycle, to determine the need for their continuance. Agencies are automatically terminated if they are not renewed—that is, the "sun sets" on those agencies not specifically renewed by the legislature. Reauthorization may result in altered scope and authority for the agency.

The twelve-member Sunset Advisory Commission enforces the act. The lieutenant governor appoints four senators and one public member, and the speaker appoints four representatives and one public member. The presiding officers also serve on the commission. Public members are appointed for two-year terms and legislators for four-year staggered terms, with two positions from each chamber filled every two years. The commission appoints the agency's chief executive officer.

Sunset Advisory Commission
In Texas, a body that periodically evaluates most government agencies and departments. The commission may recommend the restructuring, abolition, or alteration of the jurisdiction of an agency.

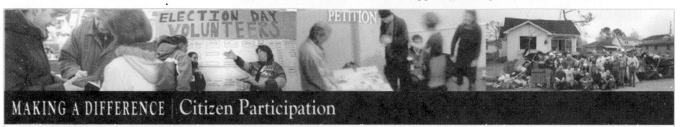

MAKING A DIFFERENCE | Citizen Participation

A democratic republic such as ours is a unique form of government. Under most other forms of government, citizen participation is neither important nor encouraged, but a democratic republic does not function well without the participation of its citizens. All of us have interests and issues that concern us directly, and it is important for us to become informed and to support the legislators and interest groups that are our allies.

Why Should You Care?

What is your opinion of your legislators' positions on the issues? Do your elected representatives work in your best interest? In our political system, it is our business to find out where our legislators stand on the issues. If you raise your voice—and if those who share your views raise their voices as well—you may be able to sway your legislator on an issue of concern to you.

Learn who finances the campaigns of your elected representatives. Go to "Follow the Money: The Institute on Money in State Politics" at **www.followthemoney.org**. Under "State-at-a-Glance," scroll to Texas, and use the date of the last election. In the "Election Summary" section, click on "House" or "Senate," and then click on your representative or senator. You will find a list of his or her top contributors, along with contributions by industry, by economic interest, and by geographic location. This information can help you understand who has access to your representative and, to a large extent, where she or he stands on various issues.

What Can You Do?

You can follow legislation. The best time to learn how the legislature works is when the legislature is in session. By going to **www.capitol.state.tx.us**, you can find a bill that affects you

personally. Click on "Legislation," then scroll to and click on "Bills by Subject." Now click on the legislative session desired and then on your subject of interest. There will be a list of bills from which to choose.

1. Adopt a bill as your project, and follow the bill through the legislative process. Did your bill pass, or was it killed? If it was killed, where did it die?
2. Try to determine what interest groups favored or opposed your bill. Why did they take these positions? Most interest groups have Web pages, and you can go to a group's Web page to learn about the group and its view on the issues before the legislature.
3. What action did the governor take on the bill? If your bill became law, which agency is responsible for its administration?

Key Terms

Chapter Summary

1 The Texas legislature meets on odd-numbered years for 140 days. Texas alone, among the large states, has such a restricted period of time in which to conduct legislative business. The Texas legislator tends to be a white male Protestant businessperson or lawyer with enough personal wealth or interest group support to adequately finance a campaign.

2 There are 31 senators and 150 representatives. The Texas two-chamber legislature is presided over by the lieutenant governor in the senate and the speaker in the house of representatives. Actual power in the legislative process rests with these presiding officers. Through appointive, jurisdictional, and other procedural powers, they are able to strongly influence state policy.

3 Historically, Texas government has been dominated by a coalition of conservative Democrats and Republicans. This coalition dominated the legislature through ideology rather than using party membership as the basis for control. Under Republican control of the legislature, the no-party system of legislative organization remains superficially intact, and Democrats continue to be appointed to chair committees under Republican leadership. The viability of the no-party system may be nearing its end as state politics becomes more partisan.

4 Legislative action is based on the committee system. The presiding officers appoint the committee chairs and many of the committee members. The officers assign bills to committees and have discretion over which committee to use. If a committee does not report on a bill (but instead pigeonholes or tables it), the measure is most likely dead for the session.

5 To reach the floor of the house, a bill must also be placed on a calendar by one of the two calendar committees. These committees are firmly under the control of the speaker. A bill that does not receive a calendar assignment is probably out of the running.

6 The senate calendar is an artificial device. The first item on the calendar is a "blocking bill," which is never brought to the floor. Actually bringing a bill to the floor requires a vote by two-thirds of the senators to "suspend the rule" and vote on the bill out of its calendar order. Given that two-thirds of the senate must vote in the affirmative even to bring a measure to the floor, most bills that reach the floor are approved.

7 To become an act of the legislature, a bill must pass both chambers with identical language. To iron out any differences, bills are sent to a conference committee, a special joint committee with members from both chambers. The presiding officers appoint these committees. Once a conference committee report is accepted by both chambers, the bill is sent to the governor.

8 The governor can sign or refuse to sign a bill (in which circumstance it eventually becomes law without the governor's signature). The governor can also veto a bill. If the bill contains an appropriations clause, the governor can strike it out with an item veto. In theory, the legislature could override a veto, but by the time the veto is issued, the legislature is usually no longer in session.

9 The institutional powers of the presiding officers include control over legislative boards and commissions that manage the budgeting function of state government (the Legislative Budget Board), the auditing function (the Legislative Audit Committee), and policy research (the Legislative Council).

Selected Print and Media Resources

SUGGESTED READINGS

Crawford, Ann Fears, and Frances "Sissy" Farenthold. *Frankie: Mrs. R. D. Randolph and Texas Liberal Politics.* Austin, Tex.: Eakin Press, 1999. Mrs. Randolph was the founder of the *Texas Observer*, a patron of liberal Democratic candidates, and an unelected leader of liberal Democrats in their conflicts with Shivercrats and Republicans.

Hanna, Betty Elliott. *Ladies of the House: How to Survive as the Wife of a Texas Legislator.* Austin, Tex.: Eakin Press, 1993. Texas politics from the spousal viewpoint.

Jones, Nancy Baker. *Capitol Women: Texas Female Legislators, 1923–1999.* Austin: University of Texas Press, 2000. The lives, memories, and political strategies of eighty-seven female Texas legislators.

Kinch, Sam, and Anne Marie Kilday. *Too Much Money Is Not Enough: Political Power and Big Money in Texas Politics.* Austin, Tex.: Campaigns for People, 2001. Interviews with Texas legislators and commentary about Texas's campaign-finance system and the resulting concentration of political power in the hands of wealthy contributors.

Spaw, Patsy McDonald, ed. *Texas Senate, Volume 1: Republic to Civil War, 1836–1861;* and *Texas Senate, Volume 2: Civil War to the Eve of Reform, 1861–1889.* College Station: Texas A&M University Press, 1991 and 1999. Written by the Senate Engrossing and Enrolling Department, this two-volume set is a narrative account of issues, personalities, and events that shaped the economy, politics, and personality of the state.

MEDIA RESOURCES

Last Man Standing: Politics—Texas Style—In a documentary shown on the PBS program *POV* in 2004, Paul Stekler highlights two 2002 election campaigns. One pits the Democratic "dream team" of Tony Sanchez, Ron Kirk, and John Sharp against Rick Perry and the Republican political operatives of President George W. Bush and Karl Rove for, as Stekler says, "the future of Texas politics." The second campaign pits an Anglo American Republican against an Anglo American Democrat in a race for the Texas House of Representatives. The documentary is available in DVD format through Netflix.com.

NOW with Bill Moyers—Moyers interviews columnist Molly Ivins about the redistricting conflict in the Texas legislature.

Tussle in Texas—In a 2003 interview available on PBS's *Online NewsHour*, Tom Bearden reports on Texas congressional redistricting designed to increase the number of Republicans in the U.S. Congress.

E·MOCRACY | Find Your Legislators

Texas Legislature Online—the Web site of the Texas legislature—serves as the front door to a wide variety of information. Be sure to check out the links to the presiding officers' sites, "Speaker of the House" and "Lieutenant Governor." Another interesting feature of the site is "Who Represents Me?" Click on this link, and it will take you to a form that lets you find your state representative, state senator, U.S. representative, and State Board of Education member. Additional links then let you visit the home pages of these individuals. Use the "Who Represents Me?" feature to identify your legislators, and send them e-mail about an issue that concerns you.

Logging On

The Texas Legislature Online site is at

www.capitol.state.tx.us

The lieutenant governor has a site at

www.senate.state.tx.us/75r/LtGov/ Ltgov.htm

The Web site of the speaker of the house is at

www.house.state.tx.us/speaker/ welcome.htm

The Legislative Budget Board, which helps the legislature to prepare the budget, has a site at

www.lbb.state.tx.us

The Texas State Library is a source for legislative, administrative, and judicial research, as well as general information about many political, economic, and social aspects of Texas. The library's Web site is at

www.tsl.state.tx.us

The Legislative Research Library is another good source of information about the Texas legislature. Go to

www.lrl.state.tx.us

For information on the Texas Legislative Council, go to

www.tlc.state.tx.us

The State Auditor's Office is at

www.sao.state.tx.us

The Sunset Advisory Commission is at

www.sunset.state.tx.us

You can find the Web site for any state newspaper at the following site:

www.refdesk.com/tx.html

Online Review

At **www.politicalscience.wadsworth.com/ schmidt12**, you will find a free Study Guide to this book. For each chapter, there are two online quizzes to help you master the material.

• The PoliPrep Self-Study Assessment provides a pretest for each major section of the chapter. PoliPrep then generates a customized study plan. After you complete the study plan, a posttest evaluates your progress.

• The Tutorial Quiz for each chapter provides questions on the chapter contents, including the features. The questions are organized to match the major sections of the chapter.

24 | The Texas Executive Branch

What If . . .
Texas Used the National Executive Branch as a Model?

BACKGROUND

In Texas, the executive branch is splintered. The governor shares power with other officers who are elected separately from the governor. Texas elects numerous state officials independently from the governor because, like many southern states, it follows the tradition of Jacksonian democracy originating in the 1820s and 1830s. Consistent with that tradition, the Texas executive branch still hires major political supporters as higher-level employees (a spoils or patronage system). It lacks a civil service system with hiring based on merit.

Texans have long feared a strong chief executive who might assume the powers exercised during Reconstruction by Governor E. J. Davis (1870–1873). In that era, many Texans who had been active in the Confederacy were denied the right to vote, and national policies were imposed to grant rights to the former slaves and to punish disloyalty to the United States. The state's military was active in suppressing dissent and promoting the political interests of the governor. Texas reacted by adopting a state constitution strictly limiting the governor's power. As a result, the governor is not a true chief executive, because many executive offices and agencies are beyond the governor's effective control.

Powerful special interest groups, bureaucrats, the legislature, and the general public continue to prefer decentralization. As a result, Texas government has evolved into a hodgepodge of independent administrative entities, with no single official being responsible for initiating or implementing policy. Duplication and a lack of coordination and accountability are the result.

WHAT IF TEXAS USED THE NATIONAL EXECUTIVE BRANCH AS A MODEL?

Texans continue to fear a strong chief executive. Nevertheless, if Texans today adopted a strong executive patterned after the national government, it is unlikely that Texas would develop a dictatorship. No U.S. president has ever become a dictator.

If Texas used the national executive branch as a model, Texans would cast only one vote for chief executive. The governor and lieutenant governor would be elected as a team. Citizens would not be called on to vote for relatively minor officials, such as agriculture and land commissioners, whose duties voters frequently do not care about or understand.

Instead, the governor would appoint executive officers, and if scandal, corruption, or inefficiency were exposed, voters would be able to hold accountable a highly visible officer—the governor. The governor would appoint perhaps fifteen cabinet members to head state administrative departments. These appointees would serve as advisers to the governor. Conflicts would arise, but the governor would be allowed to issue executive orders to command coordination and to eliminate duplication and inefficiency. About two hundred state boards and commissions might be eliminated, and their agencies would be made accountable to officers who answered to the governor.

AGENCIES AND STAFF MEMBERS

The governor would have the power to propose a single budget to the state legislature as his or her suggestion for spending by each state agency. Every state agency would have to come to the governor's office to make its budget request for funds from the legislature.

Ordinary lower-level employees would not be hired randomly or haphazardly. Rather, systematic standards based on qualifications eventually would be established for hiring, promoting, and firing employees. Employees would be more difficult to fire solely for political reasons.

THE NEED FOR AN EXECUTIVE OFFICE

It would be difficult for the governor to control the dozens of agencies and the thousands of government employees who work in those agencies. One means by which the governor can hold the bureaucracy accountable is through the staff members of an executive office. This executive staff, although relatively invisible to the public, would be accountable to the governor and could be used to control the bureaucracy.

FOR CRITICAL ANALYSIS

1. Would the governor be overwhelmed by such an increase in power? Is Texas's executive branch controllable by any single person? Would the governor abuse his or her political power to appeal to special interests and ensure reelection?
2. Does a civil service system make government employees too hard to fire? Explain.

Whereas it is the legislative function to create the law, it is the executive function to carry it out. For example, it is the legislative function to determine who will pay how much in taxes, but it is the executive function to actually collect those taxes. It is the legislative function to determine how much will be appropriated for each agency and to set financial priorities, but it is the executive function to actually spend the appropriations—write the checks and make the contracts. It is the legislative function to define crime and prescribe punishment, but it is the executive function to arrest, prosecute, and punish criminals. It is the legislative function to determine which services will be provided, but it is the executive function to actually provide those services—to hire personnel and manage their day-to-day conduct. The executive function is basically to do what the government does, regardless of how centralized or decentralized the executive may be, as discussed in the *What If . . .* feature at the beginning of this chapter.

Structure and Politics of the Governor's Office

More than two hundred state agencies (the bureaucracy) carry out Texas public policy. The state constitution designates the governor as the chief executive (chief bureaucrat) but then proceeds to systematically deny him or her the power to control state agencies. The executive branch of the Texas government is divided into many elective and appointive offices, primarily because Texans traditionally have feared concentration of power anywhere in government, particularly in the executive branch. The effect of this fear is compounded by legislators' reluctance to pass laws that would increase the powers of the chief executive relative to their own powers. As a result, the Texas executive branch has evolved into a mixture of elective offices, boards, and commissions, all separate from, and largely independent of, the governor.

In spite of these constitutional and statutory restrictions, however, the governor can influence state policy by persuading and bargaining with others. The governor's legislative powers, media access, party influence, and appointive powers can enable an astute, politically savvy officeholder to exert meaningful influence on both legislative and administrative decisions.

Texas governor Rick Perry delivers his State of the State address at the state capitol in Austin. As the most prominent leader in the state, the governor has the opportunity to supplement his or her rather limited formal powers by appealing to the people. How might the governor turn popular support to his or her advantage when seeking new legislation? (Photo Courtesy of the Governor's Office)

Who Can Become Governor?

As is usual with elective offices, the legal requirements for becoming governor are minimal: a candidate must be thirty years of age, an American citizen, and a citizen of Texas for five years before election. While the formal qualifications for governor are easily met, the informal criteria are more restrictive.

White Protestant.   Since the Texas Revolution, governors have all been white Protestants, usually Methodists or Baptists. They have also been Anglo, with family names originating in the British Isles.

Male.   The governor is historically male. The only female governor of Texas before Ann Richards (1991–1995) was Miriam A. Ferguson, who served for two nonconsecutive terms (1925–1927 and 1933–1935). Ferguson ran on the slogan "Two Governors for the Price of One" and did not really represent a deviation from male domination of Texas politics, because it was clear that her husband, former governor James E. Ferguson, actually exercised the power of the office.[1] Only Ann Richards was a female governor in her own right.

Middle-Aged Businessperson or Attorney.   The governor will probably be successful in business or law—more than half of the governors who have served in the last one hundred years have been lawyers. The governor will most likely be between forty and sixty years old; have a record of elective public service in state government or some other source of name recognition; and be a participant in service, social, and occupational organizations.

Today, a Republican.   Democrats historically dominated Texas politics. Between 1952 and 1988, the Republicans became competitive in top-of-the-ticket elections—president, U.S. senator, and governor—but the state was basically Democratic for most other offices. Texas became an authentic two-party state with the 1990 election of two Republicans to the down-ticket offices of state treasurer and commissioner of agriculture.

Fourteen years later, Texas had completed its evolution into a strongly Republican state. Republicans first swept statewide offices in 1998, electing the governor, lieutenant governor, and all elected down-ticket administrators, including members of the Texas Railroad Commission. The down-ticket Republican victories have additional political significance. Statewide elective offices can provide political experience and name recognition. They also can serve as a springboard to higher office, as Kay Bailey Hutchison demonstrated by moving from state treasurer to the U.S. Senate. In 1998, Rick Perry rose from commissioner of agriculture to lieutenant governor, and in 2002 he was elected governor. That same year, Texas attorney general John Cornyn was elected to the U.S. Senate. The state's electorate now strongly favors Republican candidates for public office.

The Democrats' Problem.   The Democratic gubernatorial primary is usually a match among moderate-to-liberal candidates. The Democratic nominee must forge an unlikely coalition of business leaders, central cities, ethnic minorities, unions, intellectuals, teachers, and consumer advocates. To win the general election, Democrats would have to win a substantial number of rural votes. Traditionally Democratic rural voters, however, are largely deserting the Democrats, giving the Republicans a distinct advantage in all statewide elections. It is unlikely that a Democrat will win any major statewide elective office in the near future. The Republican primary will nominate the near-certain winner. This primary is a joust

[1]Rupert N. Richardson, *Texas: The Lone Star State*, 2d ed. (Englewood Cliffs, N.J.: Prentice Hall, 1958), p. 317.

between conservative-to-moderate candidates, with the more conservative candidate usually winning.

Support by Interest Groups. Most successful candidates for governor have substantial interest group support. For example, the expenses of the 2003 inauguration of Governor Perry and Lieutenant Governor David Dewhurst were mostly paid by large corporations, including AT&T, Philip Morris, SBC Communications, Sprint, insurance companies, and the state's primary Medicaid contractor. Consumer lobbyists voiced concern about the likely impact on the pending agenda for insurance, health-care, and other legislation facing the 2003 legislature. The festivities cost about $1.5 million, of which $500,000 was raised by ticket sales to the event.[2]

Well-Funded Campaigns. In the general election, Republican gubernatorial candidates usually have the campaign funds to outspend their Democratic opponents. This allows them to develop the necessary political image and name recognition and also to identify and define the issues of the campaign. Candidates who spend the most usually win in competitive races. Paul Taylor, executive director of the Alliance for Better Campaigns, has said that "the legacy is a political culture in which we auction off the right to free speech thirty seconds at a time to the highest political bidder."[3]

A hefty bankroll is necessary even for serious consideration. Challengers usually must spend more than incumbents to buy name recognition. Spending does not buy all elections, however. In the 2002 Texas gubernatorial election, Democrat Tony Sanchez and Republican Rick Perry together spent $95 million to win a $115,345-a-year job. The incumbent, Perry, spent $29.9 million, and the challenger, Sanchez, spent $67.2 million, including $60 million of his own personal wealth. Sanchez spent $36 per vote and lost; Perry spent "only" $9 per vote and won. Regardless of campaign spending, Texans seem to strongly favor Republican issues and values.

Tenure, Removal, and Succession

Texas governors serve a four-year term, as do governors in forty-seven other states. Unlike most states, however, Texas imposes no limit on the number of terms a governor may serve.

The governor may be removed from office before the end of his or her term only by impeachment by the Texas House of Representatives and conviction by the Texas Senate. Impeachment is the legislative equivalent of **indictment** and requires only a simple majority of members present. Conviction requires a two-thirds majority.

If the governor is removed or vacates the office, the lieutenant governor becomes governor for the remainder of the elected term. The Texas Senate then elects a senator as acting lieutenant governor, who also serves as president pro tem until the next general election.

| Indictment
A formal accusation issued by a grand jury against a party charged with a crime when the jury determines that there is sufficient evidence to bring the accused to trial.

Compensation

The governor's annual salary is set by the legislature. Now at $115,345, it stands in marked contrast to the low salaries paid to legislators. Nine other Texas state officials earn more than the governor.

The governor receives free use of the governor's mansion, and there is an expense account to keep it maintained and staffed. The governor has a professional staff with offices in the capitol. This is important, because a modern chief executive depends heavily on staff personnel to carry out the duties of office.

---

[2]Associated Press, *Dallas Morning News*, January 2, 2003, available at **www.dallasnews.com**; and J. Taylor Rushing, *Fort Worth Star-Telegram*, January 21, 2003, available at **www.dfw.com**.
[3]Colleen McCain Nelson, *Dallas Morning News*, November 7, 2002.

Staff

The growing role of the executive in legislative affairs, the need to make appointments, and increased demands on government by the general public have placed greater claims on the time and resources of the executive branch. The Texas governor, like all executives in modern government, depends on others for advice, information, and assistance when making decisions and recommendations. A good staff is a key resource for a successful chief executive.

Assisting the Governor. Some administrative assistants head executive offices that compile and write budget recommendations and manage and coordinate activities within the governor's office. Staff personnel also exercise administrative control over the governor's schedule of ceremonial and official duties. The governor's staff, although primarily designed to assist in the everyday duties of the office, also attempts to persuade legislators, administrators, and the representatives of various local governments to follow the governor's leadership in solving common problems.

Governor Perry's Chief of Staff. Consumer groups expressed fear of excessive corporate influence on the office of the governor when, in 2002, Governor Perry appointed Mike Toomey, a prominent lobbyist for corporate interests, as his chief of staff. Perry said that Texans should not worry, because "Texas leaders have a long tradition of turning to lobbyists to fill high-level state jobs." In disagreement, Tom "Smitty" Smith, director of Texas Public Citizen (one of the public-interest groups founded by Ralph Nader), said that Toomey's "clients sort of form a who's who of those who cost consumers significantly in Texas." Toomey's selection came only days after Republican Tom Craddick of Midland, soon to be elected speaker of the house, announced that his transition team included many corporate lobbyists.[4]

Evaluating Appointees. Among the most important concerns of the governor's staff are political appointments. Each year, the governor makes several hundred appointments to various boards, commissions, and executive agencies. He or she also fills newly created judicial offices and those vacated because of death or resignation. Staff evaluation of potential appointees is necessary because the governor may not personally know many of the individuals under consideration.

Legislative Liaison. Legislative assistants act as liaisons between the office of the governor and the legislature. Their job is to stay in contact with key legislators, committee chairs, and the legislative leadership. These assistants are, in fact, the governor's lobbyists. They keep legislators informed and attempt to persuade them to support the governor's position on legislation. Often, the success of the governor's legislative program rests on the ability and political expertise of the staff.

The Governor's Powers of Persuasion

A governor's ability to influence the creation and execution of government policy depends in part on his or her bargaining skills, persuasiveness, and ability to broker effectively among competing interests—the tools of persuasion. Thus, the **informal powers** of office are as important as the **formal powers** (those granted by the constitution or by law). The ability to use informal powers is largely determined by the extent of the formal powers.

Compared with the governors of other states (especially other populous, industrialized states), the governor of Texas has very weak formal administrative powers.

Informal Powers
Powers not directly granted by law. The governor's informal powers may follow from powers granted by law but may also come from the governor's persuasive abilities, which are affected by the governor's personality, popularity, and political support.

Formal Powers
Legal powers granted to the governor by constitution or statute. Powers of this type, when exercised by the U.S. president, are called expressed powers.

---

[4]Associated Press, *Dallas Morning News*, December 4, 2002.

Yet some Texas governors have been able to exert significant influence on policy formulation and execution. Generally, this occurs when the governor's formal and informal powers are enhanced by a blending of other conditions, such as the following:

- A strong personality.
- Political expertise.
- Prestige.
- A knack for public relations and political drama.
- Good relations with the press.
- Supporters with political and economic strength.
- A favorable political climate.

The Governor as Chief of State

The governor, as the first citizen of Texas, serves as a symbol of Texas as surely as the bluebonnet or the pecan tree. A significant part of the governor's job is related to the pomp and ceremony of the office. These ceremonial duties include throwing out the first baseball of the season; greeting Boy Scout troops at the state capitol; visiting disaster areas; and riding in parades for peanut festivals, county fairs, and cow chip–throwing contests.

The ceremonial role of **chief of state** is important because it can contribute indirectly to the governor's leadership effectiveness through increased popularity and prestige. The governor also broadens the image of first citizen to that of first family of Texas whenever possible. Voters identify with the governor's family, and the governor's spouse often is included in photo opportunities—particularly if the spouse is photogenic and articulate.

Chief of State
Nationally, the head of state—the president of the United States, for example. In Texas and other states, the governor—who serves as the symbol of the state and performs ceremonial duties—is the chief of state.

The Governor as Party Chief

The governor usually maintains the leadership of his or her party by controlling the membership of its executive committee (though there may be varying degrees of competition from other elected officials and from political activists). The chair and a majority of the executive committee of the party are formally elected at the party's state convention but are typically selected by the governor.

Control of the party is a useful channel of influence for a governor. It permits what many consider to be one of the most effective tools of gubernatorial persuasion—rewarding supporters with political patronage. Influential party members who support the governor's party choices and proposals and who contribute to his or her election may be permitted to influence the several hundred appointments the governor makes each year.

The Governor as National Party Leader. The Texas governor can also be a major player in national politics if she or he is so inclined. Unless the governor suffers from serious public relations problems, any candidate for president would want the support of the governor of the nation's second most populous state. The large number of electoral votes that Texas casts also makes the governor an attractive candidate for president or vice president. A governor's support for a winning presidential candidate provides influence over the political patronage that flows from Washington to the state. Of course, patronage can be dramatically increased if a Texas governor actually becomes president.

Taking Positions on National Issues. National politics also affords the governor an opportunity to build a clear public image within Texas. The governor can take positions on political issues that do not involve the Texas government and that the governor cannot control (such as foreign aid and national defense) but that nevertheless are of great concern to the voters. State government issues are often hard for voters to understand (due to the complexities of the issues or because of inadequate reporting by the media). As a result, the electorate can more easily make political identifications through national issues.

Legislative Tools of Persuasion

Ironically, the governor's most important bargaining tools are often legislative. How these tools are used frequently determines the governor's effectiveness.

The Veto. One of the most powerful formal legislative tools of the governor is the veto. After a bill has passed both chambers of the legislature as described in Chapter 23, it is sent to the governor. If the governor signs the bill, it becomes law. If the governor vetoes the bill, it is sent back to the legislature with a message stating the reasons for the governor's opposition. The legislature has the constitutional power to override a veto by a two-thirds vote, but in practice vetoes are usually final.

Because legislative sessions in Texas are short, the vast majority of important bills are passed and sent to the governor in the final days of the session. The governor need take no action on the legislation for ten days when the legislature is in session (twenty days when it is not in session), so he or she can often wait until the legislature has adjourned and thereby ensure that a veto will not be overridden. In fact, it is so difficult to override a veto that this has happened only once since World War II (1939–1945). Thus, the veto gives the Texas governor a strong bargaining position with legislators.

In 2001, Governor Perry frustrated and surprised many lawmakers by vetoing seventy-eight bills on one day. The governor had not previously indicated any dissatisfaction with these measures. Dubbing the event the "Father's Day Veto Massacre," disgruntled legislators claimed Perry had played unfairly by not allowing them to address his concerns during the session. In all, Perry vetoed eighty-two bills in 2001, which is only nine fewer than Governor George W. Bush had vetoed in three sessions and twenty-two more than Governor Ann Richards had vetoed in two sessions.[5]

No Pocket Veto. The Texas governor lacks the pocket veto that is available to many other chief executives, including the president of the United States. A pocket veto permits an executive to kill legislation passed at the end of a session by ignoring it. If the Texas governor neither signs nor vetoes a bill, it becomes law without her or his signature. By not signing a bill and allowing it to become law, the governor may register protest against the bill or some of its sections.

The Item Veto. The single most important bill that the legislature passes is the appropriations bill. If it should be vetoed in its entirety, funds for the operation of the government would be cut off, and a special session would be necessary. Thus, Texas, like most other states, allows the governor an *item veto*, which can be used to veto funds for specific items or projects without killing an entire bill.

The item veto is potentially a very effective legislative tool. Funding is necessary to administer laws, so by vetoing an item or a category of items, the governor can in effect kill either programs or classes of programs. Because the appropriations bill is normally passed at the end of the session, the governor usually employs the item veto after the legislature has adjourned. As a result, there is no opportunity for an override.

---

[5]"Limits of the Veto," a subsection of "The Executive Branch." Developed by *Texas Politics*, a project of Liberal Arts Instructional Technology Services at the University of Texas at Austin. Available at **texaspolitics.laits.utexas.edu/html/exec/0502.html**.

Governor Rick Perry often gives news conferences. In this photo, he is announcing that he vetoed the state's $35.3 billion public education budget. He then called a special session of the legislature in an attempt to find a solution to the school-financing problem in 2005. Does the governor of Texas have the power to call for special sessions at any time? (AP Photo/Harry Cabluck)

The Threat of a Veto.   An informal legislative power of the governor nowhere mentioned in the constitution or the law is the **threat to veto.** This nevertheless is a very real and effective tool, which depends on the formal power of the veto.

Both the veto and the item veto are negative tools that simply kill bills or programs—they do not help the governor shape legislation. Threatening a veto is effective in this regard, however, because the legislature knows how difficult it is to override a veto, and usually lawmakers will at least partially meet the governor's wishes in response to such a threat.

The governor can also use the threat of an item veto to influence bureaucrats who seek funding for programs and projects. The governor may influence the administration of existing agency programs by threatening to veto funds or other bills actively supported by the agency. In addition, the governor can use the threat of an item veto to pressure the agency's legislative liaison personnel (its lobbyists) to support the governor's legislative program.

Finally, the threat of a veto can be used to consolidate support for the governor's legislative proposals among lobbyists in general. Lobbyists may offer to support the governor's position on legislation if the governor will agree not to veto a particular bill that is considered vital to the interests of the lobbyists' employers. The governor can thus bargain with both supporters and opponents of legislation to gain political allies. We give an example of how Governor Perry has affected policy through the threat of a veto in this chapter's *Beyond Our Borders* feature on the following page.

Bargaining.   The governor's bargaining with legislators, lobbyists, and administrators is often intense. These other political forces may attempt to convince the governor to support, oppose, or maintain neutrality toward certain legislation. If the governor or the governor's political and financial supporters have not made this legislation an explicit part of their legislative program, avenues are left open for political bartering. Whoever seeks the governor's support must be willing to give something of real political value in return. All sides of the negotiation want to gain as much as possible and give as little as they can. There is, of course, a vast difference in political resources among politicians, just as there is among interest groups.

Presession Bargaining.   If, before the legislative session begins, the governor, the legislative leadership, concerned administrators, and special interest groups can

| **Threat to Veto**
An informal power by which a state governor (or the U.S. president) threatens to veto legislation so as to affect the content of the legislation while it is still in the legislature.

BEYOND OUR BORDERS | Should Texas Recognize Identity Cards Issued by Mexico?

Mexico issues an identity card called the *matrícula consular* (consular registration) to its citizens in the United States. Applicants for the card must appear in person at a Mexican consular office and present a Mexican birth certificate or an official Mexican identification document that contains a photograph. The *matrícula* card resembles a U.S. state driver's license and has many security features to prevent forgery.

The state of Texas currently does not accept the *matrícula* card as a valid form of identification, but thirteen other states accept it, as do several dozen Texas cities, counties, and police departments, including those of Dallas and Houston. At least eighty-five bank systems accept the card as identification for opening an account.*

This image from the consulate general of Mexico shows a sample of the *matrícula consular* identity card. The cards do not indicate the immigration status of the cardholder. (Photo by the Consulate General of Mexico/Getty Images)

PROPOSALS IN TEXAS

In 2003, lawmakers unsuccessfully introduced several bills that would have required the Texas Department of Public Safety to accept the *matrícula* card as proof of identity for obtaining a Texas driver's license. Then Mexican president Vincente Fox lobbied Governor Rick Perry on behalf of the card in 2003, but Perry continued to object to it based on questions about its security and reliability. In 2001, Perry vetoed a bill that would have recognized Mexican birth certificates, and he appeared poised to veto recognition of the *matrícula* card should such a measure ever pass the legislature.

HOW SECURE IS THE *MATRÍCULA* CARD?

Opponents of the card have claimed that it is insufficiently secure, that it can be forged, that Mexican officials do not adequately check the documents used to obtain it, and that there is no unified database of cardholders that can be checked by Texas officials. Supporters of the card claim that it meets the same standards as U.S. driver's licenses, which can also be forged, and point out that Mexico instituted a centralized database to track the cards in 2004. Supporters also argue that it is better if as many Texans as possible have acceptable, official identification. If cardholders can obtain driver's licenses, there will be fewer unlicensed, uninsured drivers on the road. Use of the card would make it easier for police agencies and other government bodies to carry out their functions.

THE ISSUE OF ILLEGAL IMMIGRATION

Technically, recognition of the *matrícula* card has no effect on a cardholder's immigration status. There is little question, how-

ever, that recognition of the card would make life much easier for undocumented—illegal—immigrants. Legal immigrants do not need the card because they have other acceptable forms of identification.

Card advocates argue that enforcement of the immigration laws is a federal responsibility in which the state government should not involve itself. In contrast, opponents believe that Texas has both the right and the responsibility to uphold national law and that allowing illegal immigrants to readily integrate themselves into mainstream society is poor policy. The belief that the *matrícula* card may facilitate illegal immigration could, in fact, be the most powerful argument against recognizing the card, although it is one that many politicians may be reluctant to make for fear of appearing anti-Hispanic.

FOR CRITICAL ANALYSIS

The matrícula consular *and the methods used for issuing it appear to match the standards of an American driver's license. Those who argue to the contrary seem to be grasping at straws. Yet there is ample evidence that, historically, Mexican officials have been much more susceptible to bribery and corruption than American ones. Even if the technical standards of the card are high, therefore, it is possible to raise questions about the staff administering the program. Why might elected officials be reluctant to make this point explicitly?*

*See Texas House of Representatives, House Research Organization, *"Matrícula Consular:* Should Texas Recognize Mexican-Issued Identity Cards Held by Immigrants?" by Kellie Dworaczyk, *Interim News*, No. 78–2, January 20, 2004.

arrive at successful bargains and compromises, the prospect for passage of the agreed-on proposals is greatly enhanced. **Presession bargaining** is a way of seeking compromises, but harmonious relationships seldom develop immediately.

Representatives of powerful competing political forces may continue bargaining throughout the legislative session. Failure to reach an amicable settlement usually means either defeat of a bill in the legislature or a veto by the governor.

Advance agreement on a given bill can result in several advantages:

1. The advocates of the bill are assured that both the legislative leadership and the governor are friendly to the legislation.

2. The governor need not threaten a veto to influence the content of the bill. This keeps the chief executive on better terms with the legislature.

3. The legislative leaders can guide the bill through their respective chambers, secure in the knowledge that the legislation will not be opposed or vetoed by the governor.

The magnitude and intensity of presession bargaining depend on several factors, including the degree of support for a particular proposal shown by the governor, the members of the legislature, and interest groups. We summarize the elements that go into determining the intensity of the bargaining in Figure 24–1.

Limits of Presession Bargaining. Presession bargaining does not always help the governor. Legislative sources revealed that in late 2002, Governor Rick Perry, Lieutenant Governor David Dewhurst, and Tom Craddick, who was expected to

| Presession Bargaining
In Texas and other states, negotiation that lets the governor and legislative leaders reach compromises on particular bills before the beginning of the legislative session. This usually ensures the passage of the bills.

FIGURE 24–1 | FACTORS THAT DETERMINE THE GOVERNOR'S FLEXIBILITY AND INTENSITY IN BARGAINING

1 The depth of the governor's commitment to a bill.	If the governor is committed to a position, because of either a political debt or ideological belief, his or her position may not be open to negotiation.
2 Timing.	Politicians often try to be the ones to tip the scales for the winning side.
3 Political and financial support given the governor during a campaign.	This does not mean that all campaign contributions buy political decisions, but they do increase the chances that contributors will get a favorable hearing.
4 Future campaign support.	Bargaining may involve financial or political support for the reelection or advancement of an ambitious politician.
5 The identity of a bill's supporters and opponents.	The governor may not want to align with a group that is unpopular either with the governor's financial supporters or with the general electorate. Examples of unpopular groups include advocates for the legalization of marijuana or a graduated state income tax.
6 The amount of firm legislative support for or opposition to a proposal.	Even if the chief executive is inclined toward a particular position, backing a losing cause could mean a loss of prestige.
7 The political benefits to be gained.	Some groups may be more willing or able than others to pay a high price for the governor's support. Thus, an important consideration is the relative strength of the supporters and the opponents of a bill and their ability to pay their political and financial debts. For example, because medical patients in Texas have no organization and few political allies, their interests are not as well represented as those of the Texas Medical Association, health-maintenance organizations, or insurance companies. These interests have strong organizations and political and financial resources.
8 The attitude of interests that could provide postgubernatorial economic opportunities or political assistance.	Some governors have extensive investments and are unlikely to make political decisions that could mean personal financial loss.

become speaker of the Texas House, were negotiating the extent of influence that the governor's office would have on the 2003–2004 state budget. Past budgets had been written largely by the Legislative Budget Board, which is controlled by the lieutenant governor and the speaker. Perry's argument was that because all officers were Republicans, the governor should have more input into the process. The specific decision made in these negotiations is not known, but Governor Perry either declined or was denied the opportunity to contribute to the budget process. He therefore submitted a "budget" in 2003 with no monetary recommendations.[6]

Special Sessions. As mentioned in Chapter 23, the constitution gives the governor exclusive power to call the legislature into *special session* and to determine the legislative subjects to be considered by the session. The legislature may, however, consider nonlegislative subjects, such as confirmation of appointments, resolutions, impeachment, and constitutional amendments, even if the governor does not include them in the call. Special sessions are limited to thirty days' duration, but the governor may call them as often as he or she wants.

Often, when coalitions of legislators and lobbyists request a special session so that a "critical issue" can be brought before the legislature, other coalitions of legislators and interests oppose consideration of the issue and therefore oppose calling the special session. Because there is seldom any legislation that does not hurt some interests and help others, the governor has an opportunity to use the choice of whether to call a special session as a bargaining tool. He or she may or may not call a special session based on some concession or support to be delivered in the future. The supporters and opponents of specific legislation may also have to bargain with the governor over the inclusion or exclusion of specific policy proposals in the special session.

Of course, if the governor has strong feelings about the proposal and is determined to call (or not to call) a special session, this position may not be open to negotiation. If the governor does think that an issue is critical, the attention of the entire state can be focused on the proposal during the special session much more effectively than during the regular session.

Message Power. As a constitutional requirement, the governor must deliver a State of the State message at the beginning of each legislative session. This message includes the outline for the governor's legislative program. Throughout the session, the governor may also submit messages calling for action on individual items of legislation. The receptiveness of the legislature to the various messages is influenced by the governor's popularity, the amount of favorable public opinion generated for the proposals, and the governor's political expertise.

The message power of the governor is a formal power that is enhanced by the visibility of the office. Through the judicious use of the mass media (an informal power), the governor can focus public attention on a bill when it might otherwise be buried in the legislative maze. He or she must not overuse the mass media, however, for too many attempts to urge legislative action can result in public apathy toward all gubernatorial appeals. An effective governor "goes to the people" only for legislation considered vital to the interest of the state or to her or his political and financial supporters.

| Message Power
The ability of a governor (or a U.S. president) to focus the attention of the press, legislators, and citizens on legislative proposals that he or she considers important. The visibility of the office gives the chief executive instant public attention.

| Blue-Ribbon Commission
A commission composed of public personalities or authorities on the subject that is being considered. In Texas, such a commission may have both fact-finding and recommending authority.

Fact-Finding Commissions. Governors sometimes appoint blue-ribbon commissions consisting of influential citizens, politicians, and members of concerned special interest groups. Such commissions can serve either as trial balloons to measure public acceptance of a proposal or as a means to provide information and increase public and interest group support for a proposal. Blue-ribbon commissions are also

[6]W. Gardner Selby, *San Antonio Express-News*, December 18, 2002, p. 5B; and John Moritz, *Fort Worth Star-Telegram*, January 18, 2003.

commonly used to delay the actual consideration of a political "hot potato" until it has cooled. Politicians know that the attention span of the public is short and that other personally important issues, such as the Dallas Cowboys, jobs, and families, draw people's attention away from politics.

The Governor as Chief Executive

The Texas Constitution charges the governor, as the chief executive, with broad responsibilities. Yet it systematically denies the governor the power to meet these responsibilities through direct executive action. In fact, four other important elective executive offices are established in the same section of the constitution and are legally independent of the governor, thus undermining his or her executive authority:

1. The lieutenant governor.
2. The comptroller of public accounts.
3. The attorney general.
4. The commissioner of the General Land Office.

Other provisions in the constitution further fragment executive power. For example, the constitution establishes the Railroad Commission and states that its members are to be elected. It provides that the State Board of Education can be either elected or appointed. (It is elected independently of the governor.) Moreover, the Texas legislature, by statute, has systematically continued to assume executive functions such as budgeting and auditing. The legislature has also created the Department of Agriculture and a multitude of boards and commissions that are independent of direct gubernatorial control to administer state laws. Elected officials in Texas are shown in Figure 24–2. Given the present fragmented executive branch in Texas, few executive bargaining tools are available to the governor, making that officer one of the weakest state chief executives in the nation.

FIGURE 24–2 | ELECTED ADMINISTRATIVE OFFICIALS IN TEXAS

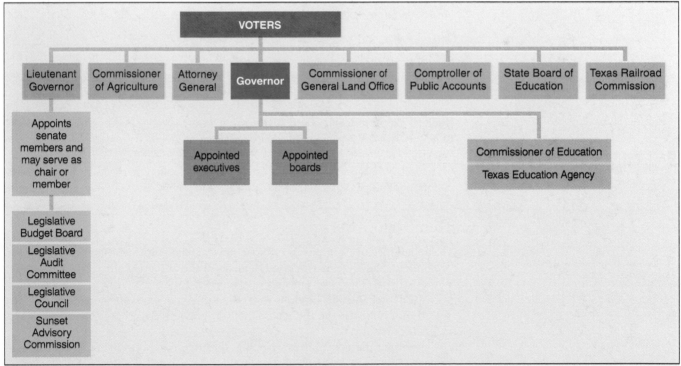

| Boards and Commissions
In Texas, bodies consisting of three to eighteen members that supervise most state agencies.

Appointive Powers

An effective governor will use the power of appointment to the maximum. Probably the most important appointments the governor makes are to certain independent boards and commissions. The members of these boards establish general administrative and regulatory policy for state agencies or institutions and choose the top administrators to carry out these policies.

The governor's ability to affect board policy through appointments is not immediate, however, as the boards are usually appointed for fixed, six-year staggered terms. Because only one-third of these positions become vacant every two years, the governor will have appointed a majority of the members of most boards only in the second half of his or her term.

Interest Group Concerns. Interest groups in Texas are vitally concerned with seeing that the "right kind" of appointees are selected to serve on boards and commissions. In the present age of consumerism, industry interest groups are particularly anxious to have industry advocates (often former lobbyists or industry executives) appointed to the boards that oversee and set policy for "their" agencies. Appointment of a consumer advocate could disturb the close relationship that usually exists between an industry and its agency. Furthermore, competing interest groups within one industry may bargain individually with the governor, each promoting an appointee who is favorable to its particular viewpoint. Thus, appointments to important boards often result in intense lobbying by special interest groups, which gives the governor opportunities to develop support for policies and to help secure funds for future political campaigns. We examine how interest groups influenced a new corporate relocation policy in this chapter's *Politics and Interest Groups* feature.

The Influence of the Senate. The Texas Senate must confirm appointments, and individual senators have some influence over appointments from their districts due to the practice of *senatorial courtesy*. The senate will usually refuse to vote for confirmation if a senator announces that an appointee from his or her district is "personally obnoxious." The senators thereby show courtesy to the disgruntled senator by refusing to confirm his or her political enemy.

Bureaucratic Concerns. Administrators also want commissioners appointed to their agency who are sympathetic to their problems and who share their goals. Appointments friendly to the administrators' interests can strengthen a governor's influence with these administrators.

Judicial Appointments. The governor can exert a great deal of influence on the state's judiciary. It is common for judges to retire or resign before their terms end. The governor is empowered to fill these vacancies until the next general election. The result is that the governor is able to repay political supporters with judicial appointments, and the appointees enjoy the advantage of incumbency in the general election.

Removal Powers

Although the governor possesses broad powers of appointment, powers of removal are limited. She or he may remove members of the executive office and a few minor administrators. The governor may also remove, for cause and with the consent of two-thirds of the senate, his or her own appointees to boards and commissions. (The governor cannot remove those appointed by previous governors even through this difficult procedure.)

In general, the governor cannot issue directives or orders to state agencies, nor remove executive officials who do not abide by her or his wishes. If the governor

POLITICS AND INTEREST GROUPS | Governor Perry and the Enterprise Fund: Boon to Texas or Corporate Welfare?

In the early 2000s, Texas trailed many other states in attracting corporate relocations. Although there were state programs available to encourage relocations, they were widely viewed as bureaucratic and restrictive. Local government enticements were helpful but confusing. They often attracted opposition from citizen groups.

THE TEXAS ENTERPRISE AND EMERGING TECHNOLOGY FUNDS

After Governor Rick Perry took office, the Governor's Task Force on Economic Development issued a report stating that Texas needed a large pool of ready cash that could be given to corporations without strings attached to entice them to move to the state. As a result, in 2003 Governor Perry asked the legislature to create an Enterprise Fund. Although the political environment was difficult—deep and controversial cuts were being made to many parts of the budget—funds were freed up by moving $295 million from the state's "rainy-day" fund.

The Enterprise Fund is managed by the Economic Development and Tourism Division of the governor's office, which is where corporate applications for funds are received and evaluated. Governor Perry, Lieutenant Governor David Dewhurst, and House Speaker Tom Craddick make the final decision on who gets the funding and how much they receive. The process is selective, secretive, streamlined, and not burdened with either legislative oversight or public input. Indeed, the Enterprise Fund decision makers are the three most important elected officials in the state, so the fund represents a substantial centralization of power.

Fewer than twenty corporations have been funded out of more than two hundred applicants. Nevertheless, some argue that the Enterprise Fund has been a major factor in making Texas the number-one site for corporate relocation.[*] Responding to this success, in 2005 the governor asked the legislature for another $300 million to replenish the capital base of the Enterprise Fund, plus another $300 million to establish a sister fund for emerging technology. The Emerging Technology Fund is designed to attract researchers, technology companies, and support industries to Texas. About one-quarter of the funds are to be given to Texas research universities to establish more research units and to recruit highly skilled staff members. The University of Texas at Austin is already a major player in research commercialization—the university develops technology, licenses it to private corporations, and collects royalties on its commercial application.

ARE THE FUNDS CORPORATE WELFARE?

Critics claim that the Texas legislature raided the "rainy-day" fund to give subsidies to some of the wealthiest corporations in the world, while in the same session it was making major cuts in spending for human services and education. According to Greg LeRoy, the executive director of Good Jobs First, state and local tax abatement, job training, and subsidy programs influence only 2 to 3 percent of corporate relocations, are a waste of funds, and mostly benefit corporations that have already made their decisions based on other inputs.[†]

Don Baylor of the Center for Public Policy Priorities says that it is difficult, if not impossible, to track the benefits received from subsidies to large corporations. Baylor believes that the emphasis should be on creating small businesses in rural and high-unemployment areas instead of the metropolitan areas, where 73 percent of the enterprise funding has gone.

Public-interest group representatives point out that the Texas corporate subsidy program lacks transparency and accountability. Funding is not accompanied by requirements—for example, that corporations provide health insurance and a living wage to their employees. Baylor argues that Texas "throws money at corporations up front," while other states, such as Oklahoma, dispense benefits "only when certain employment milestones have been met."[‡] Furthermore, it is difficult for the state treasury to recoup subsidies from inefficient sources of revenue such as lottery tickets.

FOR CRITICAL ANALYSIS

Why would large corporations require taxpayers' funds for relocation to Texas?

---

[*]Mike Ward, "How Texas Plays 'Let's Make a Deal' for Jobs," *Austin-American Statesman,* February 21, 2005.

[†]Paul Sweeney, "Texas: The Corporate Welfare State," *Texas Observer,* April 15, 2005.
[‡]*Ibid.*

believes that an official is administering the law so as to violate its spirit, there is no official way to force that official to administer the law differently. Only by focusing public attention on the agency and garnering public support can the governor force an administrator to change positions or resign. We give an example of how a governor can exert such power in the *Politics and Gubernatorial Influence* feature on page 770.

POLITICS AND GUBERNATORIAL INFLUENCE | Regulating the Insurance Industry

One campaign pledge by Governor Ann Richards (1991–1995) was that she would change the direction of the State Board of Insurance, which she believed established regulatory policies that favored the interests of the insurance industry to the detriment of the insurance consumer. The governor, however, is limited to indirect influence over most state agencies, and in this instance Governor Richards could only appoint members to the state board, who then established policy. Because the three board members were appointed for six-year staggered terms, Richards would have been able to achieve a board majority only in the second two years of her term.

THE GOVERNOR GOES TO WAR

Wanting more immediate action, Richards focused high-visibility attention on the board by testifying at a board hearing, issuing press releases, and calling for the resignation of Governor William Clements's appointees Richard Reynolds and James Saxon. She also threatened to bring the board under state receivership. Saxon resigned, thereby allowing the governor to appoint a board majority early in her first year in office. She had accomplished informally that which she could not do with her formal powers.

THE TEXAS DEPARTMENT OF INSURANCE

The governor's influence on insurance regulation became direct and immediate in 1993, when the legislature created the Texas Department of Insurance to replace the State Board of Insurance. The director of the department is appointed directly by the governor for a two-year fixed term, subject to senate confirmation.

FOR CRITICAL ANALYSIS

Why do you think that members of the State Board of Insurance caved in to Richards's pressure?

Planning Powers

Mostly because of national government requirements concerning federal grants, the governor has gained some powers to engage in planning for state and local governments. With federal encouragement, the state government developed rudimentary coordination and cooperation activities to link the various government units and subunits in the state. The natural center for such statewide planning is the governor's office, which is in a position to determine whether grant requests are in accord with statewide plans. The result is some centralization of planning in the governor's office. The governor also serves as a member of (or appoints representatives to) many multistate organizations and conferences that work to coordinate relations between Texas and other states.

Texas created the Office of State-Federal Relations in Washington, D.C., to facilitate the governor's job of coordinating the activities of state agencies and local governments with the federal government. The governor appoints (and may remove) the director. The office provides information to state officials about federal initiatives and also advocates for the interests of the Texas government with Congress, the administration, and federal agencies. The governor may request federal aid when the state has suffered disaster, drought, or economic calamity. As chief of state, he or she often flies over or visits a disaster area to make a personal assessment of the damage—and also to show the unfortunate victims that the governor is concerned for their welfare.

Budget Powers

Many state executives find their power to propose a budget to the legislature important in dealing with state agencies. The Texas governor also is legally designated as the state's chief budget officer, and each biennium the various agencies and institutions submit their appropriation requests to the governor's staff and to the staff of the Legislative Budget Board (LBB). Working from these estimates, the governor and staff may prepare a budget based on both the state's estimated income and the estimated cost of program proposals. When completed, the budget is submitted to the legislature.

The independent Legislative Budget Board also submits a plan for state spending, however. Because the LBB includes the legislature's most powerful officers, the governor's budget may be largely ignored in favor of the LBB proposals.

Law Enforcement Powers

The governor has little law enforcement power. In the basic tradition of Texas government, law enforcement is decentralized. The governor does have the power to extradite fugitives from Texas law and to grant or refuse such requests from other states.

At the state level, the Texas Rangers and the Highway Patrol conduct law enforcement. Both agencies are under the administrative direction of a director of public safety, who is appointed by an independent board, the Public Safety Commission. At the local level, police functions are under the jurisdiction of county sheriffs and constables (who are elected) and city chiefs of police (who are appointed by city officials).

Criminal acts are prosecuted either by elected district or county attorneys or by appointed city attorneys. The judiciary, which tries and sentences criminals, is elective (except for municipal judges, who are appointed by city officials).

Military Powers

The governor is commander in chief of the state militia, which has two basic parts: the Texas National Guard and the Texas State Guard. The governor appoints (and can remove) an **adjutant general,** who exercises administrative control over both units.

The governor may send units of the militia to keep the peace and protect public property (usually following a natural disaster). She or he may also employ the militia to "suppress insurrection, repel invasions, and protect the frontier from hostile incursions by Indians or other predatory bands"—a power that has not been necessary for many decades. The governor does not have the power to order evacuations in the event of terrorist attacks, hurricanes, or other natural disasters; only county judges have that power.

The Texas National Guard is made up of both army and air force components and is financed by the U.S. government. It must meet federal standards and may be called to active duty by the president. In the event the Guard is "nationalized," command passes from the governor to the president.

The Texas State Guard was established during World War II and serves as a back-up organization in the event the National Guard is called to active duty by the president. It cannot be called into active duty by the federal government, and its members receive no pay unless mobilized by the governor.

Clemency Powers

The 1876 constitution granted the governor virtually unlimited power to pardon, parole, and grant reprieves. Several governors were very generous with these powers, resulting in a 1936 constitutional amendment that established the Board of Pardons and Paroles. Many of the powers that had been held by the governor were transferred to the

| Adjutant General
The principal staff officer of an army, who passes communications to the commanding general and distributes the general's orders to subordinates. In the example of the Texas National Guard and Texas State Guard, the "commanding general" is the governor. *Adjutant* comes from a Latin word meaning "helper."

Governor Perry visits Texas troops in Baghdad. (Photo Courtesy of the Governor's Office)

Clemency
Relief from criminal punishment granted by an executive. In Texas, the power of the governor to grant clemency is strictly limited.

board, which grants, revokes, and determines the conditions for parole and makes **clemency** recommendations to the governor. The governor appoints the board's membership and can grant less clemency than recommended by the board, but not more. He or she can no longer exercise a check on the parole process by blocking early releases from prison. The governor can postpone executions for thirty days.

The Texas Bureaucracy

The most distinctive characteristic of the Texas administration is that no one is really in charge of the administrative apparatus. As in many other states, the administration of laws in Texas is fragmented into several elective and many appointive positions. There is no single official in the Texas government who bears the ultimate responsibility for the actions of the Texas bureaucracy. And there is no single official who can coordinate either planning or program implementation among the many agencies, commissions, and departments. The Texas bureaucracy can be visualized as more than two hundred separate entities, each following its own path, often oblivious to the goals and ambitions of other agencies. Texas, in other words, has a *plural executive* system.

We can categorize the various divisions of the executive branch according to whether they have as their top policymaker or policymakers:

1. A single elected administrator.
2. A single appointed executive.
3. A multimember board or commission, which may be elected, appointed, or serve *ex officio* (serve automatically—discussed further in a later subsection).

Elected Executives

The constitutional and statutory requirement that several administrators (in addition to the governor) be elected was a deliberate effort to decentralize administrative power and prevent any one official from gaining control of the government. Under the Texas plural executive system, the governor shares executive power with several other independently elected executives and boards.

These elected officials are directly responsible to the people rather than to the governor. The fact that few Texans can name the individuals who hold these offices, much less judge their competence or honesty, tends to weigh against the theory that the popular election of multiple administrators enhances democracy.

Lieutenant Governor.   Although the lieutenant governor technically is part of the executive branch, the source of his or her power comes from the legislative branch. The lieutenant governor, as president of the senate, is the *ex officio* co-chair of the Legislative Budget Board, the Legislative Council, and the Legislative Audit Board and, if he or she desires, exercises considerable personal influence in the Sunset Advisory Commission and the Legislative Criminal Justice Board. (You learned about most of these bodies in Chapter 23.) These legislative boards and commissions are not part of the bureaucracy, but they conduct continuing studies of administrative policies and make recommendations to the legislature.

Attorney General.   The attorney general is elected for a four-year term and holds one of the four most powerful offices in Texas government. The attorney general is the lawyer for all officials, boards, and agencies in state government. The legal functions of the office range from antitrust actions and consumer protection to activities concerning insurance, banking, and securities. A broad spectrum of the state's business—oil and gas, law enforcement, environmental protection, highways, trans-

Lieutenant Governor David Dewhurst is shown here during a campaign stop in 2006. He won the election with almost 60 percent of the vote. Does the lieutenant governor in Texas necessarily work with the governor to form a "team"? Why or why not? (Photo Courtesy of the Lieutenant Governor's Office)

Texas Attorney General Greg Abbott with a playground behind him discusses with the media his crackdown on child sex predators. (Photo Courtesy of the Attorney General's Office)

portation, and charitable trusts, to name only a few—is included under the overall jurisdiction of the attorney general.

The attorney general performs two major functions—to give advisory opinions to state officers and to represent the state in major civil actions. As the state's lawyer, the attorney general advises his or her client on the meaning of state law and the constitution. Theoretically, these **attorney general's opinions** are no more than the advice a lawyer might give a client. In practice, if an official ignores the opinions, the attorney general will not defend the action in court. Public officials usually respect the attorney general's opinion, however; in effect, the opinions of the attorney general supplement the rulings of the Texas Supreme Court. Like other American courts, the Texas Supreme Court will not issue advisory opinions or rule on hypothetical cases. The attorney general's opinions fill this gap.

The attorney general also represents the state and the state government in civil litigation, including conflicts with the national government. The attorney general has defended Texas positions on such past issues as the poll tax and segregation and on current issues such as:

- Abortion.
- Obscenity laws.
- Challenges to state legislative districts.
- Affirmative action programs.

The attorney general also initiates suits in cooperation with the governments of other states on antitrust violations or consumer protection. For example, the Texas attorney general, along with the attorneys general from most other states, sued the tobacco industry to recover the state's Medicaid expenses for tobacco-related injuries. The attorney general's power to prosecute crimes is relatively narrow, however, because the primary responsibility for criminal prosecution in Texas lies with the locally elected district and county attorneys.

Comptroller of Public Accounts. The comptroller, who has become one of the state's most powerful officials, is elected for a term of four years to manage most

| Attorney General's Opinion
In Texas and other states, an interpretation of the state's constitution or laws by the state attorney general. Officials may request such opinions, and although the opinions are not legally binding, they are usually followed.

Carole Keeton Strayhorn is the Texas state comptroller. As manager of the state's financial activities, she holds a powerful position. In 2006, Strayhorn ran an unsuccessful campaign for governor, placing third in a five-way race, with 18 percent of the vote. (Photo Courtesy of Texas Comptroller of Public Accounts)

| Permanent School Fund
In Texas, a fund that provides support to the public school system. Leases, rents, and royalties from designated public school lands are deposited into the fund.

financial activities of state government. She or he is the state's chief tax collector and accountant. The constitution requires that the comptroller certify the estimated two-year state revenue, and the state legislature may not constitutionally appropriate more than the comptroller certifies.

The comptroller also certifies the financial condition of the state at the close of each fiscal year. The governor and legislature are anxious to learn if they must reduce spending or increase taxes. (Unlike the federal government, Texas cannot simply balance the books by borrowing.) In recent years, the economy has forced them to do both. In better times, the legislature has had the luxury of increasing spending.

Commissioner of the General Land Office. The commissioner of the General Land Office is elected for a four-year term. Principal duties of the commissioner are managing public lands and leasing mineral rights beneath them and overseeing riverbeds, tidelands, bays, and inlets.

The land commissioner also serves *ex officio* on several boards and chairs the important Veterans' Land Board and the School Land Board, whose programs are administered by the General Land Office. The Veterans' Land Board lends sums to veterans for land purchases and home purchases and improvements. The School Land Board oversees approximately 20 million acres of public land and mineral rights properties, a large portion of which are dedicated to the **Permanent School Fund** (for public schools) and the Permanent University Fund, which benefits the University of Texas and Texas A&M University.

Commissioner of Agriculture. The commissioner of agriculture is elected for a four-year term to oversee the Texas Department of Agriculture. The department has more than five hundred employees and is responsible for the administration of all laws relating to agriculture, as well as research, educational, and regulatory activities. The duties of the department range from checking the accuracy of scales in meat markets and gas pumps at service stations to determining labeling procedures for pesticides and promoting Texas agricultural products in national and world markets. The commissioner also administers the Texas Agricultural Finance Authority, which provides grants and low-interest loans to businesses that produce, process, market, and export Texas agricultural products. The possibility of conflict between the interests of producers and the interests of consumers is ever present in the department's activities, as we discuss in this chapter's *Politics and Administrative Law* feature.

Appointed Executives

The governor of Texas does have the power to appoint a limited number of officials. In general, these officials are less powerful than the ones who are directly elected by the public.

Secretary of State. The governor appoints the secretary of state with confirmation by the state senate. The secretary of state is keeper of the seal of the state. She or he serves as the chief election officer for Texas, administers Texas election laws, maintains voter-registration records, and receives election results. The office of the secretary of state provides a repository for official, business, and commercial records required to be filed with the office. The secretary publishes government rules and regulations and commissions notaries public. By executive order, Governor Rick Perry has also directed the secretary of state to serve as his liaison for Texas border and Mexican affairs and to represent him and the state at international and diplomatic occasions.

POLITICS AND ADMINISTRATIVE LAW | The Department of Agriculture and the Pesticide Issue

The Texas Department of Agriculture is charged with administering laws that protect consumers and workers, as well as other laws related to the agribusiness industry. Conflicts between the interests of consumers and labor on the one hand and business on the other are almost inevitable. Controversy is especially likely if the department begins to protect consumers to the perceived disadvantage of more concentrated economic interests.

COMMISSIONER HIGHTOWER TAKES A STAND

Just such a conflict emerged over the issue of pesticide regulation. Agriculture commissioner Jim Hightower (who served from 1983 to 1991) sought to impose new regulations on pesticide use to protect agricultural workers and consumers from the possible physical dangers of contamination. In response, agribusiness interests tried to limit the department's budget, reduce its authority to regulate pesticides, and make the office appointive.

This conflict resulted in the creation of a new commission, the Agriculture Resources Protection Authority. The new body coordinates pesticide management policies and programs for the Department of Agriculture and several other state agencies. The authority is currently made up of six appointed and nine *ex officio* members, including the commissioner of agriculture.

COMMISSIONER HIGHTOWER SUFFERS DEFEAT

This is a classic example of a situation in which an agency has two constituencies with conflicting interests and is given the function of protecting each interest from the other. The threat perceived by agribusiness interests was resolved in 1990 when Rick Perry (now the governor) was elected commissioner with agribusiness support. Perry became the first Republican ever to hold the office. Former commissioner Hightower's political error was that his attempt to protect the largely unorganized consumers and farmworkers was perceived as a threat to the interests of agribusiness, which sees itself as the principal constituency of the department.

FOR CRITICAL ANALYSIS

Should state governments undertake activities such as regulating pesticides—or should such regulation be a purely national responsibility to be carried out by the federal government?

Adjutant General. The adjutant general (see page 771) is appointed by the governor with the consent of the senate for a two-year term. The adjutant general serves as the state's top-ranking military officer and exercises administrative jurisdiction over the Texas National Guard and Texas State Guard. These are among the few state agencies under the direct administrative control of the governor.

Commissioner of Health and Human Services. The office of commissioner of health and human services was created in the first special session in 1991 and is filled by the governor with the consent of the senate for a two-year term. The commissioner heads an umbrella agency that oversees and manages eleven health and welfare agencies.

Insurance Commissioner. The commissioner of insurance is appointed directly by the governor for a two-year term, subject to senate confirmation. The commissioner oversees the Department of Insurance, which monitors and regulates the Texas insurance industry. The department provides consumer information; monitors corporate solvency; prosecutes violators of insurance law; licenses agents and investigates complaints against them; develops statistics for rate determination; and regulates specific lines of insurance such as property, liability, and life insurance.

Boards and Commissions

Texas government includes at least two hundred boards and commissions. These administrative bodies may be elective, appointive, *ex officio* or some combination of the three. Members may be salaried or may serve only for reimbursement of expenses. Boards differ considerably in their political power. Generally speaking, the most important boards are those that affect the largest number of people and have the largest budgets. Other important boards charter or regulate the state's business, industrial, and financial powers. Their rules and regulations, which often have the force of law, are called **administrative law.**

| Administrative Law
Rules and regulations written by administrators to implement laws. The effectiveness of a law is often determined by how the corresponding administrative law is written.

Elective Boards—The Railroad Commission.   One of the most important state regulatory boards in the United States has been the Texas Railroad Commission, a constitutionally authorized elective board whose three members serve for overlapping six-year terms. The governor fills any midterm vacancies on the board, and these appointees serve until the first election, at which time they may win election to the board in their own right.

The board is politically partisan, and its members must first win their party's nomination before running in the general election. The chair position is rotated so that each member becomes the chair during the last two years of his or her term. This forces any candidate who is challenging an incumbent commissioner to run against the chair of the commission.

The commission regulates gas utilities, oil and gas pipelines, oil and gas drilling and pumping activities, and intrastate railroad transportation. It is also responsible for regulation of waste disposal by the oil and gas industry and the protection of both surface and subsurface water supplies from oil- or gas-related residue. Formerly, the Railroad Commission regulated truck freight in Texas, but the national government has preempted the commission's powers in this area.

Elective Boards—The State Board of Education.   The elected State Board of Education (SBOE) sets policy for the Texas Education Agency (TEA), which oversees and regulates the Texas public school system below the college level and administers national and state education law and SBOE rules and regulations. The TEA writes regulations for and compels local compliance with legislative and judicial mandates and reforms, dispenses state funds, serves as a conduit for some funds from the national government to the local schools, and approves the textbooks to be purchased at state expense for use by local districts.

Members of the SBOE are elected on a partisan basis from fifteen single-member districts and serve four-year staggered terms. The governor appoints the chair for a two-year term from the SBOE membership. The SBOE establishes policy, implements policy established by law, and, as mentioned, oversees the TEA. The board also recommends three nominees for commissioner of education (the TEA's chief executive officer), who is appointed by the governor with the senate's consent to a four-year term.

Ex Officio **Boards.**   A number of boards have memberships that are completely or partially *ex officio*—that is, some or all of their members belong automatically because of other offices they hold. There are two basic reasons for creating such boards. One is that when travel to Austin was expensive and time consuming, it seemed logical to establish a board consisting of persons already in Austin. Another reason is that *ex officio* members may have relevant subject-matter expertise.

These photos show the three Republican members of the Texas Railroad Commission. From the left are Elizabeth A. Jones with Governor Perry, Michael L. Williams, and Victor Carrillo (chair) being sworn into office by the governor. To what extent may declining production of oil and natural gas reduce the importance of the commission in the future? (Photos Courtesy of the Texas Railroad Commission and the Governor's Office)

The Texas Bond Review Board is an example of an *ex officio* board. It has four *ex officio* members—the governor, the lieutenant governor, the speaker of the house, and the comptroller of public accounts—and has twelve full time employees. It reviews and approves all bonds and other long-term debt issued by state agencies and universities. It also engages in various other functions pertaining to state and local long-term debt.

A number of agencies' boards have some *ex officio* members. The Agriculture Resources Protection Authority (fifteen members, nine *ex officio*), the Texas Cosmetology Commission (seven members, one *ex officio*), and the Texas Turnpike Authority (twelve members, three *ex officio*) are examples of such boards.

Appointive Boards. Appointive boards vary extensively in importance, administrative power, and salary. The members of these boards, who are usually nonsalaried, set the policies for their agencies and appoint their own chief administrators. The governor, with the consent of the senate, usually appoints board members, but there are many mixed boards whose members are appointed by the governor or by some other official or whose membership is partially *ex officio*. Due to the usual practice of appointing members to staggered terms, six years may lapse before a governor can appoint a complete board.

Board appointees are often representatives of groups that have an economic interest in the rules and policies of the board. Appointments may be either a reward for political support or an attempt to balance competing interest groups whose economic well-being is affected by board rules and policies.

The governor can remove board members before the expiration of their terms only if he or she appointed those board members, and then only with the concurrence of two-thirds of the senate. The governor may "encourage" board members to resign, however, by publicly criticizing the members or policies of a board.

The Bureaucracy and Public Policy

Texans have not only decentralized public functions, but they have also attempted to depoliticize the bureaucracy by establishing the independent board and commission system. This is an attempt to insulate the bureaucracy from the politics of the legislature and the governor.

Attempts to depoliticize the bureaucracy, however, have simply replaced one kind of politics with another. Most political observers today agree that the Texas bureaucracy is deeply engaged in politics, that politics strongly affects public policy, and that policy formulation cannot be separated from policy administration. Public administration is "in politics" because it operates in a political environment and must seek political support from somewhere if it is to accomplish goals, gain appropriations, or even survive.

The result of strong political support for an agency is increased size, jurisdiction, influence, and prestige. The less successful agency may suffer reduced appropriations, static employment, narrowed administrative jurisdiction, and possibly extinction. Where, then, does a unit of the bureaucracy look for the political support so necessary for its well-being? It may look to clientele interest groups, the legislature, the chief executive, and the public. Political power also comes from factors within the bureaucracy, such as expertise, control of information, and discretion in the interpretation and administration of laws.

Public Support

Good public relations benefits any agency, both in appropriations and jurisdictional battles with other agencies. Favorable propaganda, myth, and literature create broadly based public support for such agencies as the Texas Department of Criminal Justice, the Texas Rangers, and to some extent, the Texas Highway Patrol.

Clientele
Persons represented by a government agency or a politician.

Clientele Groups. The most natural allies for an agency are its **clientele** (or constituent) interest groups—the private groups that benefit directly from agency programs. At the national level, examples of close-knit alliances of interest groups and agencies are defense contractors and the Department of Defense, agribusiness and the Department of Agriculture, and the airlines and the Federal Aviation Administration. In Texas, close bedfellows include the Texas Good Roads and Transportation Association and the Texas Department of Transportation; oil, gas, and transportation industries and the Texas Railroad Commission; the banking industry and the Department of Banking; and the Texas Medical Association and the Department of Health.

The Agency-Clientele Alliance. Agitation by interest groups often leads to the establishment of a state agency, and the agency's power and importance may be directly related to the power and influence of its clientele groups and the intensity of their support. The agency and its clientele groups are therefore usually allied from the very beginning, and this alliance continues to grow and mature as mutual convenience, power, and prosperity increase. Economic and political ties are cemented by mutual self-interest. Agencies and clients share information, have common attitudes and goals, exchange employees, and lobby together with the legislature for both agency appropriations and government policies that favor the interest groups.

Reciprocity. Mutual accommodation has become so accepted that clientele groups often speak of "our agency" and devote considerable time and funds to lobbying for it. The agency reciprocates by protecting its clients within the administration. Of course, both the bureaucracy and the various clientele groups are made up of many entities, and there is often competition for appropriations, so both agencies and special interests seek allies in the legislative branch.

The Legislature, the Lieutenant Governor, and the Speaker

Bureaucratic power is enhanced by the support of powerful legislators, often including the chairperson of the committee that exercises legislative oversight over the agency. The agency depends on legislative allies for laws that expand its powers, increase the scope of its duties, protect it from unfriendly interests, and appropriate the funds for its operation. Therefore, administrators seek the favor of influential lawmakers.

Although the committee chairs are important in the Texas legislature, the short session and the power of the presiding officers limit their influence. For this reason, an agency seeks the support of the lieutenant governor and the speaker of the house, as well as members of the finance and appropriations committees, the Legislative Budget Board, and the Legislative Council.

Campaigns for the Leadership. The importance of legislative support explains the intense lobbying activity that surrounds the appointment of legislators to powerful committees and the campaign activity that precedes election to positions of legislative leadership. If an interest group and its agency are unable to get allies appointed or elected to positions of influence in the legislature, they are forced to try to win support after the influential legislators are chosen—a more difficult endeavor.

The "Revolving Door." Relationships among interest groups, agencies, and lawmakers can be enhanced by the exchange of personnel. The practice by which corporations employ former administrators and legislators as executives, lobbyists, or consultants is known as the **revolving door.** A government employee may resign and accept lucrative employment with an individual, a corporation, or some other organization that has profited financially by that employee's actions. In this envi-

Revolving Door
The interchange of employees among the legislature, government agencies, and related private special interest groups.

ronment, legislators, administrators, and regulators often become promoters of the regulated industry. The revolving door negatively affects public perception of public servants and prompts cynicism toward government.

The Governor

Although the governor has few direct administrative powers, agencies still need support from the governor. The governor's cooperation is especially important because of his or her power to appoint policymaking boards and commissions. Moreover, the governor's support gives the agency greater bargaining power with legislators and interest groups. The Texas governor can influence and shape agency programs and success through veto power as well as through appointments.

Agency employees develop shared attitudes, an esprit de corps, and a sense of communality with the employees of the agency's clientele interest groups. Because an agency's interests are usually similar to those of its clientele, both want the governor to appoint board members who will advance their mutual political goals.

The Iron Texas Star

The iron triangle model, as discussed earlier in Chapter 13, is commonly used to provide a conceptual understanding of the alliance among legislative committees, administrative agencies, and economic special interest groups (clientele groups). The iron triangle, however, is better as a description of the common interests that develop at the federal level than as a description of what happens in Texas. The Texas system can better be described using the **iron Texas star** model. The iron star has five points, not three. Figure 24–3 shows a model of the national iron triangle, while Figure 24–4 displays the iron Texas star.

The Five Points of the Star. The coalitions that make policy in Texas can be thought of as consisting of the following five players:

1 and 2. Due to the hands-on authority exercised by the lieutenant governor and the speaker of the house of representatives, each of the *presiding officers and the legislative*

FIGURE 24–3 | THE NATIONAL IRON TRIANGLE

| **Iron Texas Star**
The Texas version of the iron triangle. A policymaking coalition that includes interest groups; the lieutenant governor and the speaker of the house; standing committees of the legislature; the governor; and administrators, boards, and commissions.

FIGURE 24–4 | THE IRON TEXAS STAR

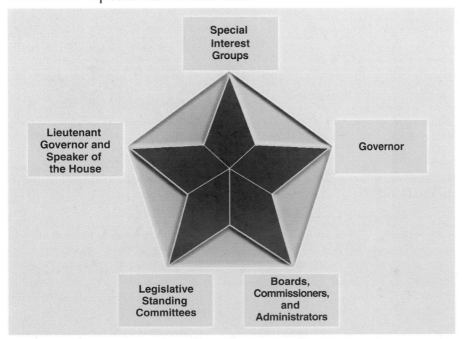

institutions and committees that they control warrant a point on the Texas star. The lieutenant governor and the speaker select most of the membership and all of the chairs of the standing committees, the conference committees, and the legislative boards and commissions.

3. The *governor* is also included due to the veto power and the power to appoint members of various policymaking boards and commissions.

4. The virtual absence of a civil service system for Texas government employees makes them vulnerable to influence by the appointed boards and ultimately the governor. Still, the *boards and the bureaucrats* together can be considered to be a point on the star.

5. *Economic interest groups* provide campaign funds for elected officials, political and financial support for friendly legislators and administrators, and employment opportunities for former state officials. They provide the mortar that builds and holds together the five-cornered coalition that we call the Texas government.

Acquiring "Friends." The basic goal for special interests is to accumulate "friends" in the policymaking and regulatory areas of government. It is equally critical for political operatives to acquire "friends" among economically powerful individuals and special interest groups. The members of the coalition also support the friends of their friends at the other points of the iron star and thereby develop a system of mutual support from which all can benefit.

Legislators, administrators, the presiding officers, and the governor rely to varying degrees on the support of their interest group friends for campaign contributions, supplemental income, political advancement, financial advice and opportunity, and after-office employment and income. As time passes and members of the coalition become more interdependent, each looks to the others for support. Legislators bargain for the interest of the coalition in the legislature. Administrators issue favorable regulations and support their friends' viewpoints in administrative decisions. The presiding officers may shepherd the proposals of their friends through the legislative process and also place the friends of economic special interests on powerful legislative committees and legislative boards and commissions. Finally, the governor appoints friends and friends of friends to various boards and commissions that make policy affecting these same friends. Other government officials may also broker with political operatives for decisions favorable to their friends in the iron star coalition.

Again, the Revolving Door. Appointees to boards and administrative positions are usually chosen from the industry concerned, and the policy decisions they make tend to benefit the most influential operatives in the industry. In turn, when government employees leave government service, many find jobs in the industry where their expertise lies. This interchange of employees between the public and private sectors is the "revolving door" we mentioned earlier in this chapter, and it undermines the independence of government employees. Literally hundreds of former administrators and legislators work for special interests as lobbyists, consultants, and executives.

Bureaucratic Accountability

Throughout the history of the United States, people have tried to hold government responsible for its policies. The rise of the bureaucratic state is the most recent challenge to responsible government. The growing size and political power of modern bureaucracy make the problem of administrative accountability ever more acute. Various organizational arrangements and legal restrictions have been used in attempts to make the bureaucracy accountable to the citizenry, or at least to someone whom the citizens can hold responsible.

Elective Accountability

The simplest approach has been to make the bureaucracy directly accountable to the people through the democratic process—a system of **elective accountability.** In Texas, this plan was established through election of the governor, lieutenant governor, attorney general, treasurer, comptroller of public accounts, commissioner of the General Land Office, commissioner of agriculture, Railroad Commission, and State Board of Education. The reasoning was that the public, if given an opportunity, would keep a close watch on elected administrators and refuse to reelect those who were incompetent or dishonest. Administrators, therefore, would be sensitive to the wishes of the voters and would administer the laws only in the interest of the general public.

Difficulties of Applying the Concept. Several problems exist with the application of elective accountability. Perhaps the most obvious is the difficulty an elected official faces in determining the will of the people or even in determining the public interest. Texas is made up of many divergent groups, each with its own interests, and often these interests are incompatible. Frequently, pleasing one group means displeasing another.

The Invisibility of Many Elected Officials. Another major problem is the relative invisibility of elected executives. As shown in Figure 24–2 on page 767, the list of elected executives is long enough that few voters are even aware of the names of many officeholders, much less their administrative competence. Ineptitude, inefficiency, corruption, and incompetence go unnoticed by the public and the press. Administrators, once elected, are usually returned to office until they die, retire, anger powerful special interests, or commit an act so flagrantly unethical that the voters finally "throw the rascals out."

Elective accountability may be practical for local offices, especially in rural areas, where voters are more likely to be acquainted with their elected officials. In an increasingly urban society, however, elective accountability seems an ineffective method of either influencing administrative behavior or making administrators more responsive to the public.

Legislative Accountability

Some advocates of administrative reform argue that the bureaucracy should be accountable to the legislature, because the legislature is the branch of government closest to the people. According to this argument, because the legislature is elected to protect constituent interests, and because legislators establish policies, elected representatives should determine whether those policies are being administered according to legislative intent. This principle has been implemented in Texas by establishing various auditing, budgeting, and oversight boards as well as legislative committees to try to hold administrators accountable.

The Sunset Advisory Commission. As an important oversight step, the Texas legislature established the Sunset Advisory Commission in 1977 to make recommendations on whether to alter, terminate, or continue some 177 state boards, commissions, and agencies. Agencies and their operations are reviewed periodically, usually in twelve-year cycles. At the end of its cycle, an agency ceases to exist unless the legislature takes specific action to renew it. If an agency is renewed, the Sunset Commission evaluates its compliance with legislative directives. In addition, agency functions may be expanded, diminished, or reassigned to other agencies by legislative action. The state auditor also evaluates any management changes recommended by

Elective Accountability
A condition in which officials are directly accountable to the voters for their actions.

the commission. Some argue that periodic legislative evaluation together with agency self-evaluation should result in better, more efficient administration.

Problems with Legislative Accountability.   In practice, accountability to the legislature also has limited effectiveness. The assumption that the legislative branch best represents the people is debatable. Legislators' independent judgment may be compromised by financial conflicts of interest, campaign contributions from special interest groups, and political ambition. Although legislative oversight may serve the purposes of individual legislators and special interests, the general public does not necessarily benefit. Another problem is the invisibility of committee hearings and decision-making processes in the legislature. The public is not aware of many policy decisions made in its name by the legislature.

Finally, because the Texas legislature is seldom in session, permanent legislative institutions, such as the Legislative Budget Board and the Legislative Council, are given the task of overseeing the administration. These institutions, by themselves, cannot enforce accountability on autonomous agencies in Texas government, and they also lack the visibility necessary for effective operation in the public interest. A major problem of responsible government is knowing who is "watching the watchers."

Accountability to the Chief Executive

Some reformers advocate a Texas administration patterned after the cabinet system of the federal government. As shown in Figure 24–5, establishing a **cabinet system** would entail reorganizing the executive branch. Existing departments would be consolidated into larger departments, and the governor would have the power to appoint and remove top administrators and to control the budget. Administrative authority would be concentrated at the top. Advocates argue that this is only proper, because the governor usually receives the blame for administrative blunders anyway and would have a powerful incentive to hold the appointed bureaucrats accountable for their actions.

Theoretically, several benefits could result from accountability to the governor. The office is visible to the general public, so the problem of who watches the watchers would be solved. There would be no question of who has the ultimate responsibility for any corruption or incompetence in the administration. Administrative control could be simplified, resulting in coordinated planning and policy implementation. Waste and duplication could be reduced.

The Need for an Executive Office.   Clearly, no single person can control dozens of agencies, their chiefs, and their thousands of employees. Analysis of the national government, however, demonstrates that one means by which the president can hold the bureaucracy accountable is through the Executive Office of the President—in particular, the Office of Management and Budget. If public administration in Texas were reorganized on the federal model, the governor would need similar staff organizations. The governor's executive staff, although relatively invisible to the public, would nevertheless be accountable to the governor.

Continued Problems under a Cabinet System.   This chain of accountability—administrative agency, to appointed executive, to staff, to governor, to the people—is weakened by the close ties usually found among administrators, constituent interest groups, and legislators. Interest groups would continue to influence administrative appointments and removals in "their agencies" just as they influence appointments to boards and commissions under the present system. Even under a cabinet system, the governor would have problems enforcing the accountability of agencies that have allies among powerful interest groups and legislators.

| **Cabinet System**
At the state government level, a form of executive organization that allows the governor to appoint and remove top-level administrators, giving the governor more control over the administration.

FIGURE 24–5 | **THE USUAL CABINET SYSTEM**

Bureaucratic Responsibility

To whom is a Texas administrator really responsible? The answer may well be to the interest groups that benefit from the programs that the officer administers. Politics works on the basic principles of mutual accommodation among allies, conflict among opponents, coalition building, and compromise. Agency officials are often obligated to administer the laws and make policy decisions in ways that support the goals and aspirations of their political allies among private economic interests.

Open Meetings and Open Records.   How, then, can the Texas administration be made more accountable to the public? There is no single answer. More openness in government offers one possibility. A basic concept of democratic government is that policy made in the name of the public should be made in full view of the public. Texas has made great strides in this area.

Open-meetings laws require that meetings of government bodies at all levels be open to the general public except when personnel, land acquisition, and litigation are discussed. The laws further prohibit holding unannounced sessions and splitting up to avoid a quorum, and they require that public notice be posted for both open and closed sessions. These laws are continuously being tested by policymakers, however, who feel more comfortable operating in secret.

Openness is further encouraged by the state's **open-records law,** which requires that records of all government proceedings and decisions be available to the public. The only cost in obtaining such records is the expense involved in assembling and reproducing them—which is low using the Internet.

Whistleblowers and Ombudspersons.   Another source of openness is whistleblowers—government employees who expose bureaucratic excesses, blunders, corruption, or favoritism. These employees could be commended and protected from retribution, but too often they are instead exiled to the minor agencies or fired for their effort. To its credit, the Texas whistleblowers' law prohibits governments from acting against employees who report law violations. Enforcement is difficult and time consuming, however. Whistleblowers must often hire attorneys at great expense and lose years of their careers.

Still another option is for government to provide an **ombudsperson,** an official who hears and investigates complaints by private individuals against public officials or agencies. The appointment of ombudspersons at every level of government would give individuals increased access to the bureaucracy and a single impartial office with which to lodge complaints against administrative decisions.

| **Open-Meetings Law**
A law that requires meetings of government decision-making bodies to be open to public scrutiny (with some exceptions).

| **Open-Records Law**
A law requiring that records of all government proceedings and decisions be available to the public.

| **Ombudsperson**
An official who hears and investigates complaints by private individuals against public officials or agencies. The original word—*ombudsman*—is Swedish and means "commissioner."

MAKING A DIFFERENCE | Become a Smart Consumer of State Services

The state's executive branch follows many antiquated traditions, but state agencies are beginning to join the information age and provide a wealth of information and conveniences to residents. Some agency Web sites are not user friendly, but many provide information that can serve as an excellent original source for academic research. Quite a few of these sites also offer online services that can make life easier for Texans.

Why Should You Care?

Democracy depends on an informed electorate. In addition, Texas state agencies provide vital services, and students may benefit directly from many of those services. Some of the best information about crime is available online at the Texas

Department of Public Safety site, for example. The most comprehensive analyses of tax and spending issues are available through the Texas Office of the Comptroller of Public Accounts and the Legislative Budget Board.

What Can You Do?

You can browse through the Legislative Budget Board's latest *Fiscal Size-Up, 2006–2007* at **www.lbb.state.tx.us** to see what services the state offers. From which of these can you benefit? Guaranteed student loans and grants are one possibility.

You can contact the Consumer Protection Division of the Office of the Attorney General to learn about your rights and how to exercise them. Also available are copies of the Deceptive Practices Act and consumer brochures.

The office provides instructions on how to file a complaint, along with a copy of a consumer complaint form. You can contact the office at

Consumer Protection Division
Office of the Attorney General,
P.O. Box 12548
Austin, TX 78711-2548
www.oag.state.tx.us/consumer/consumer.shtml

Complaints against health-care professionals can be lodged with the

Health Professions Council
800-821-3205

Privately owned electric utility rates will no longer be set by the Texas Public Utility Commission. In the new competitive environment, shop for lower utility bills at **www.powertochoose.org**.

Key Terms

Chapter Summary

1 The government of Texas was conceived in the post-Reconstruction era, following an unfortunate and unhappy experience with a centralized, unpopular, minority government. Texas government has been systematically weakened and decentralized by both constitution and statute, reflecting voters' basic distrust of government in general and the executive branch in particular.

2 Distrust of the chief executive's power led the constitution's authors to establish a weak governorship as part of a plural executive system in which executive power is shared among many independently elected officers, as well as appointed boards and commissions.

3 As the executive branch evolved, the legislature established as many as two hundred state agencies headed by appointed boards and commissions. These boards and commissions make general rules and appoint chief administrative directors. Although a governor has extensive powers to appoint members of boards and commissions, this appointive power does not give the governor effective control of state agencies. The governor usually does not appoint the actual administrators of state agencies.

4 The governor lacks meaningful removal, budgetary, or directive powers (to issue executive orders to state agencies). The result is an executive branch that is fragmented, uncoordinated, and insufficiently supervised. The governor is not a true chief executive.

5 To be effective, the governor, as the state's most highly visible officer, must develop the personal power to persuade. In addition to appealing to the public, the governor has strong legislative powers to veto bills (or, with the item veto, parts of bills) and to call special sessions. The patronage power to appoint board and commission members can be used to reward political allies and punish enemies.

6 In the absence of effective gubernatorial power, interest groups and legislative leaders usually fill the power vacuum. Bureaucrats and agency heads have greater latitude to follow their own agendas.

7 Important elected officials other than the governor include the following: (1) the lieutenant governor, who has a powerful role as the presiding officer in the senate; (2) the attorney general, who serves as the lawyer for the state and can issue opinions on the legality of various measures and practices in response to official requests; (3) the comptroller of public accounts, who handles tax collection and state accounting tasks; (4) the commissioner of the General Land Office, who manages state-owned land and mineral rights; and (5) the commissioner of agriculture, who both serves the agricultural industry and oversees consumer protection laws.

8 Important officials who are appointed by the governor include (1) the secretary of state, who oversees elections and records; (2) the adjutant general, who is in charge of the Texas National Guard and Texas State Guard; (3) the commissioner of health and human services; and (4) the insurance commissioner. Major elective boards and commissions include the Railroad Commission, which regulates the oil and gas industries as well as intrastate rail services, and the State Board of Education, which oversees the Texas Education Agency.

9 Texas has adopted some administrative reforms. Although the state continues to use a patronage system of hiring with no systematic requirements to hire the most qualified, Texas has passed sunset legislation, open-meetings and open-records laws, and laws to protect whistleblowers. As with all modern governments around the world, the goal of holding bureaucrats accountable remains elusive.

| Selected Print and Media Resources

SUGGESTED READINGS

Gantt, Fred, Jr. *The Chief Executive in Texas*. Austin: University of Texas Press, 1964. This is the classic study of the governor's office in Texas.

Gantt, Fred, Jr. *The Impact of the Texas Constitution on the Executive*. Houston: Institute for Urban Studies, University of Houston, 1973. This book presents an analysis of the state constitution as it affects the executive branch and provides some insights by comparing the Texas governor with governors of other states. Some provisions in the Texas Constitution have been changed since the book was written.

Gray, Virginia, and Russell L. Hanson. *Politics of the American States: A Comparative Analysis*. Washington, D.C.: Congressional Quarterly, 2003. This publication offers an interesting comparison of politics in the various states.

Prindle, David F. *Petroleum Politics and the Texas Railroad Commission*. Austin: University of Texas Press, 1981. This book offers perhaps the best description available of relations between a Texas agency and its clientele group.

MEDIA RESOURCES

The Best Little Whorehouse in Texas—A lighthearted play and later a movie starring Dolly Parton and Burt Reynolds. It shows the governor's frustration with Texas values and the tradition of local control. Although based partly on fact, neither the play nor the movie reveals that the Texas attorney general finally closed the house with a public-nuisance civil suit.

E·MOCRACY   Contacting the Governor

You can send e-mail to the governor of Texas about an issue of concern to you. First, go to the governor's Web site, listed below. Click on "Major Initiatives." Select one of the priority issues for the governor in the upcoming term. Do some research on the issue by using a search engine or by visiting a few of the sites listed in other chapters of this textbook.

Once you have completed your research, go back to the governor's Web site to send a message. At the bottom of the home page is a button labeled "Contact." Click on that button, and scroll to the bottom of the next page. Click on "Electronic Mail," and an e-mail form will appear that will allow you to send your message to the governor's office.

| Logging On

The governor's Web site is located at

www.governor.state.tx.us

From the governor's home page, you can investigate the governor's legislative initiatives. To check out the governor's appointive power, go to

www.governor.state.tx.us/ divisions/appointments

The governor's mansion, which is open to the public, is displayed at

www.governor.state.tx.us/about/mansion

For the governor's commander-in-chief powers, visit the site of the Texas adjutant general at

www.agd.state.tx.us

Each of the statewide elected executives has a Web site. Notice how these officials try to outdo one another on their Web sites. The attorney general is at

www.oag.state.tx.us

The comptroller of public accounts is at

www.cpa.state.tx.us

The commissioner of the General Land Office is at

www.glo.state.tx.us

The commissioner of agriculture is at

www.agr.state.tx.us

The lieutenant governor is at

www.senate.state.tx.us/ 75r/LtGov/Ltgov.htm

The key appointed executives also have Web sites. The site of the adjutant general is given above. The secretary of state is at

www.sos.state.tx.us

The key elected boards have sites as well. The Texas Railroad Commission is at

www.rrc.state.tx.us

The Texas Education Agency is at

www.tea.state.tx.us

The Texas State Board of Education is at

www.tea.state.tx.us/sboe

For a list of all state agencies, go to

info.texas.gov

Scroll to "Government" and click on "State Agencies" to research the Texas bureaucracy. Select one agency, and go to its site to find out all you can. Does the agency have an e-mail address that you can use to contact it for more information?

| Online Review

At **www.politicalscience.wadsworth.com/ schmidt12**, you will find a free Study Guide to this book. For each chapter, there are two online quizzes to help you master the material.

• The PoliPrep Self-Study Assessment provides a pretest for each major section of the chapter. PoliPrep then generates a customized study plan. After you complete the study plan, a posttest evaluates your progress.

• The Tutorial Quiz for each chapter provides questions on the chapter contents, including the features. The questions are organized to match the major sections of the chapter.

25 | The Texas Judiciary, Law, and Due Process

What If . . .
Texas Abolished the Death Penalty?

BACKGROUND

Between 1976 and 2005, southern states carried out 82 percent of all executions in the United States. Texas led the nation (355), and Virginia ranked second (94). By 2005, 410 offenders remained on Texas's death row--30.5 percent of them were white, 41.2 percent were black, 27.3 percent were Hispanic, and 1 percent were members of other ethnic groups. When the United States Supreme Court outlawed the death penalty for juveniles in 2005, Texas had more juveniles on death row than any other state.

WHAT IF TEXAS ABOLISHED THE DEATH PENALTY?

One way of evaluating what might happen if capital punishment were abolished in Texas is to run down the list of reasons why the state punishes criminals.

One goal of any punishment is to remove the guilty from society to prevent further crimes. Obviously, the death penalty accomplishes this, and Texas now allows an alternative—a life sentence without parole.

A second goal is to deter future crimes through the fear of punishment. Some believe that the death penalty is not a strong deterrent to murder, however. They argue that murderers either commit their crimes in the passion of the moment or do not consider the possibility of punishment. Therefore, many believe that the murder rate would not go up if the death penalty were abolished.

A third goal is rehabilitation to allow the convict to return to society as a productive citizen. This goal is irrelevant to the death penalty because the condemned are never meant to return to society. Even a person serving a life sentence may experience redemption, however, and some point to Nobel Prize nominee and Crips gang founder Stanley Tookie Williams as an example. He was executed in California despite his years attempting to steer youngsters away from gangs.

A fourth goal is justice—settling accounts with those who have violated society's norms. Supporters of the death sentence find it the only appropriate punishment for outrageous crimes such as mass murder and serial killings. Supporters argue that without the sentence, there would be no chance for appropriate social vengeance, and victims' families would be denied closure.

In contrast, some argue that killing is rarely just. Certain religious groups, including the Roman Catholic Church, support a "culture of life" and, therefore, oppose the death penalty.

MISCARRIAGES OF JUSTICE

Critics of the Texas death penalty argue that its abolition would reduce the danger of miscarriages of justice. Some death row inmates have later been proved innocent through the use of such methods as DNA testing. The death penalty can be an irreversible error. Elimination of the penalty would also prevent it from being carried out in a discriminatory fashion. The poor often receive inadequate legal representation, and Texas has no public defender system. Instead, the indigent are represented by appointed attorneys, who rarely have any experience in capital cases. Racial bias is also an issue—especially when the accused is black and the victim is white. Finally, opponents argue that killing in the name of the state can never be appropriate. They believe that abolishing the penalty would move the Texas justice system from one centered on retribution to one that seeks to reduce the damage inflicted by crime.

FOR CRITICAL ANALYSIS

1. Texas juries are no more likely to impose the death penalty in a murder case than juries in other states. Texas executes a large number of prisoners because it has a large population and a high murder rate and because an execution is more likely to actually be carried out in Texas. What implications do these facts have for the death penalty debate?
2. Which of these issues is most important to your sense of justice? Why?

American society has increasingly turned to the judiciary to find answers to personal, economic, social, and political problems. Courts are often asked to determine our rights. Important legal questions touch almost every aspect of our lives. For example, what level of privacy should we expect in our cars, offices, and homes? What treatment should people of different races, genders, or ages expect? In a divorce proceeding, with which parent should the children live? Should a convicted person go to jail, and if so, for how long? What about the death penalty, which we discussed in the *What If . . .* feature at the beginning of this chapter? Additionally, should a woman be allowed to terminate her pregnancy? Should a patient be allowed to refuse potential life-saving treatment? These are among the thousands of questions asked and answered daily by courts in the United States.

In this chapter, our focus will be the Texas judicial system and general attributes of American legal procedure and *due process*. What will quickly become clear is the sheer size and complexity of the Texas court system. We also describe various political influences on the courts and the controversies surrounding the selection of Texas judges.

> **DID YOU KNOW . . .**
> That in 2004, Texas had the nation's sixth-highest crime rate—5,035 crimes per each 100,000 in population?

Civil Law and Criminal Law

America is often considered the most litigious (anxious to go to court to settle differences) society in the world. We have approximately one-quarter of the world's lawyers.[1] There are almost one million attorneys in the United States today.[2] Whereas in 1951, 1 out of every 700 people was a lawyer, that figure is now about 1 out of 300.[3] Cases in American courts have included, for example, a legal action by parents blaming McDonald's food for obesity in teens, a lawsuit by parents against school officials for disciplining their children for cheating, a case in which a wife sued her husband for not shoveling the snow in front of their home, and a lawsuit in which a woman asked for $12 million because she was "pawed" and "humiliated" when a fur-costumed actor interacted with her during a Broadway performance of the musical *Cats*.[4] You should understand, though, that even if people file outrageous-sounding suits, it does not follow that they will win in court. There are few restrictions on what kinds of suits Americans can bring, even if they have little or no chance of success.

Litigation in Texas

Texas clearly fits into this general pattern of using the courts often. In recent years, Texas has ranked eighteenth among the states in terms of litigation.[5] In 2000, it had an attorney for every 309 people.[6] Texas also has more than 2,600 courts and approximately 3,200 justices or judges.[7] These courts dealt with more than 12 million cases

---

[1]G. Alan Tarr, *Judicial Process and Judicial Policymaking*, 3d ed. (Belmont, Calif.: Wadsworth Publishing, 2003), p. 107.

[2]Lawrence Baum, *American Courts*, 5th ed. (Boston: Houghton Mifflin, 2001), p. 60.

[3]U.S. Department of State. "Outline of the United States Legal System: Lawyers, Litigants, and Interest Groups in the Judicial Process," December 2004, at **usinfo.state.gov/products/pubs/legalotln/lawyers.htm** (accessed April 2, 2006).

[4]*Newsweek*, December 15, 2003, p. 45; *Dallas Morning News*, January 23, 2003, p. 4A, and February 8, 1997, p. C6.

[5]*Forbes*, January 17, 1994, p. 70.

[6]The Fred Parks Law Library, *Footnotes Newsletter Online*, vol. 13, no. 5, and figures from the census of 2000. Available at **www.stcl.edu/library/FN13-5Jones.html**.

[7]*Texas Judicial System Annual Report, 2003* (Austin: Texas Judicial Council and Office of Court Administration, 2004), p. 32; Texas Judiciary Online, "Court Structure of Texas," Texas Judicial Council, March 1, 2006 (accessed April 2, 2006), at **www.courts.state.tx.us/oca/PublicInfo/2006_Judicial_ Directory/zCourt_Structure_Chart_March_2006.pdf**. We also wish to acknowledge Michele Budz and Joy Crabaugh for their efforts in this project.

In practice, judges determine our legal rights. Indeed, a large part of our system of laws is judge-made and dates back before the Texas Revolution—or even the American Revolution. This system is the "common law," and it can be traced back to medieval England, when judges began codifying standard answers to legal questions. When a state legislature or the U.S. Congress passes a law, the new statute takes precedence over the common law. Judges must also interpret the meaning of every new statute whenever there is a question that bears on a case. (AP Photo/Irwin Thompson)

in 2003—on average, more than one case for every two residents of the state.[8] In addition, in recent years Texas courts have heard important or controversial cases involving topics such as flag-burning, the death penalty, school desegregation, school finance, sexual orientation, and the freedom-of-association rights of the Ku Klux Klan, as well as a case involving two large oil companies in which one was found liable for more than $10 billion.

Civil Law versus Criminal Law

In the American legal system, court actions are generally classified as cases under either the civil law or the criminal law. **Civil law** concerns private rights and remedies and usually involves private parties or organizations (for example, *Smith v. Jones*), although the government may be involved. A personal-injury suit, a divorce case, a child-custody dispute, a breach of contract case, a challenge to utility rates, and a dispute over water rights are all examples of civil suits.

Criminal law involves violations of laws established by the government. If convicted, the lawbreaker may be punished by a fine or imprisonment, or both. The action is taken by the state against the accused (for example, *State of Texas v. Smith*). Typical examples of grounds for prosecution are arson, rape, murder, armed robbery, speeding, jaywalking, and embezzlement. With exceptions, the characteristics laid out in Figure 25–1 generally distinguish civil and criminal cases.

One of the most important distinctions between civil and criminal cases involves the issue of **burden of proof.** In civil cases, the standard used is a "preponderance of the evidence." This means that whichever party has more evidence or proof on its side should win the case. In a criminal case, however, the burden of proof falls heavily on the government, or prosecution. The prosecution must prove that the defendant is guilty "beyond a reasonable doubt." The evidence must overwhelmingly (without serious question or doubt) point to the defendant's guilt, or the defendant should be found not guilty.

| Civil Law

The law regulating conduct between private persons, as opposed to criminal law. Under civil law, the government provides a forum for the settlement of disputes between private parties in such matters as contracts, domestic relations, and business relations.

| Criminal Law

The law that defines crimes and provides punishments for violations. In criminal cases, the government is the prosecutor.

| Burden of Proof

In a court case, a party's duty to convince a judge or jury that the party's version of the facts is true. The standard of proof is higher in a criminal case than in a civil one.

| Docket

The schedule of court activity.

| Issues in Civil Law

Some argue that society has become too litigious. These people claim that frivolous lawsuits overcrowd court **dockets,** and excessive damages awards unnecessarily drive

[8]*Texas Judicial System Annual Report, 2003*, p. 32.

up insurance premiums and other business costs. When then Texas governor George W. Bush urged **tort reform** to limit awards for injury, he was supported by groups representing conservatives and defendants in civil actions, by the Texas Civil Justice League, by insurance companies, and by a wide range of business and medical interest groups.

As a result, the Texas legislature passed bills to restrict lawsuits by prison inmates, reduce frivolous lawsuits, limit liability in civil cases involving multiple defendants and government employees, enforce residency requirements for plaintiffs, and cap **punitive damages awards.** Texans narrowly approved a constitutional amendment to allow the legislature to limit all medical malpractice and other damages, such as those for pain and suffering, except actual economic damages. Are allegedly frivolous lawsuits sometimes more serious than one might gather from media reports? We look at one example in this chapter's *Politics and Consumerism* feature on the following page.

Tort Reform

In civil law, a tort is a wrong or injury (other than a breach of contract). Tort reform is an effort to limit liability in tort cases.

Punitive Damages Award

A financial payment that may be awarded to a plaintiff in a civil case to punish the defendant and deter similar conduct in the future.

Issues and Elements in Criminal Law

Crime is a national issue, but despite the popularity of "law and order" as a campaign slogan in national elections, only 5 percent of crimes are prosecuted under federal law. The activities of the criminal justice system are primarily state, not federal, functions.

Congress has made the following crimes, among many others, federal offenses:

1. Those committed on the high seas.
2. Those committed on federal property, territories, and reservations.
3. Those that involve the crossing of state or national boundaries.
4. Those that interfere with interstate commerce.
5. Those committed against the national government or its employees while they are engaged in official duties.

Otherwise, most crimes are violations of state rather than federal law.

The Crime

As commonly used, the word *crime* refers to an act that violates whatever an authorized body (usually a state legislature) defines as the law. Many people obey the law simply because it is the law; others may obey out of fear of punishment. Attitudes and values usually determine whether a person will respect or disobey a law. If a law

FIGURE 25–1 | **CIVIL LAW VERSUS CRIMINAL LAW**

Civil Law	Criminal Law
1 Deals primarily with individual or property rights. Civil law involves a concept of responsibility but not guilt.	1 Deals with public concepts of proper behavior and morality as defined in law. The case is initiated by a government prosecutor on behalf of the public.
2 The plaintiff, or petitioner, is often a private party, as is the defendant, or respondent.	2 Specific charges of wrongdoing are spelled out in a grand jury indictment or a writ of information.
3 A dispute is usually set out in a petition.	3 On arraignment, the defendant enters a plea of guilty or not guilty.
4 A somewhat more relaxed procedure is used to weigh the evidence than in criminal law; the side with the preponderance of the evidence wins the suit.	4 Strict rules of procedure are used to evaluate evidence. The standard of proof is guilt beyond a reasonable doubt.
5 The final court remedy is relief from or compensation for the violation of legal rights.	5 Determination of guilt results in punishment.

POLITICS AND CONSUMERISM | The Issue of Frivolous Lawsuits

In an attempt to market his book, a retired air force major from Fort Worth sued Elvis Presley Enterprises for violating his civil rights by monopolizing the Elvis memorabilia market and perpetuating the myth of Elvis's death. The major says he knows Elvis is alive because of his frequent telephone conversations with the rock-and-roll star.

Although courts often dismiss such suits because they have no merit, insurance and business groups have an interest in highlighting the cases in a campaign to limit civil lawsuits. Most sensational media reports on these cases provide few facts and little follow-up.

THE MCDONALD'S COFFEE CASE

As an example, the famous McDonald's coffee case was often used in arguments against "frivolous" lawsuits because a woman initially won $2,700,000 for being scalded by a cup of McDonald's coffee in a car. In fact, the eighty-one-year-old plaintiff had suffered third degree burns on her groin, thighs, and buttocks requiring skin grafts and a seven-day stay in the hospital. She was not driving when the injuries occurred.

At the time of this incident, McDonald's kept its coffee twenty degrees hotter than competing restaurants and was quite aware that doing so could cause severe injuries (it had settled seven hundred cases involving similar injuries to customers). Consumer groups had been asking McDonald's to reduce the temperature of its coffee for several years, to no avail. In this case, McDonald's testified that it would not change its policy or post warning signs and had refused even to pay the victim's medical bills.

Lawyers for the scalded woman made sure that the jury knew of the past cases, the consumer complaints, and the refusal by McDonald's to address the issue. Clearly, the jury intended to send McDonald's a message. In fact, the large award and the consequent publicity succeeded where all previous steps had failed—it induced McDonald's to cool off its coffee (though the current temperature is still above the industry average). The original award (equivalent to about two days' coffee sales) was reduced on appeal to $480,000.

ARGUMENTS IN FAVOR OF LAWSUITS

Punitive damages are uncommon, and when they are awarded, the amount is usually small. Consumer and environmentalist groups, Public Citizen, Texas Citizen Action, and the Texas Trial Lawyers Association generally oppose sweeping changes in the current system. They argue that isolated anecdotal instances of lawsuit abuse should not be used as a justification to restrict the fundamental right to trial by jury. They argue that only a jury hearing all evidence presented by both sides can make appropriate judgments in cases of extreme negligence and abuse of an individual's rights. They see tort reform as a big-business attack on the laws protecting consumers against defective products and deceptive trade practices.

FOR CRITICAL ANALYSIS

Are lawsuits the only means by which manufacturers and professionals can be held responsible for their actions or companies be forced to improve safety procedures?

---

reflects the values of most of society, as the law against murder does, then it is usually obeyed. If, however, a large part of society does not accept the values protected by law, as happened with the national prohibition of alcoholic beverages in the 1920s, then violations become widespread.

Felonies are serious crimes. *Murder* is the illegal, willful killing of another human being. *Robbery* is attempting to take something from a person by force or threat of force. It is inaccurate to say that "a house was robbed"—only people can be robbed. Buildings are *burglarized*—unlawfully entered for the purpose of committing a felony or theft.

Theft (larceny) is simply taking property from the rightful possession of another. Grand larceny—taking something valued at over $1,500—is a felony. In Texas, regardless of value, livestock rustling is a felony.

In Texas, it is a crime for a commercial fisher to possess a flounder less than twelve inches in length. Minors may not possess alcohol. Most traffic violations are crimes, and the resulting fine is a form of punishment. Such minor crimes are called **misdemeanors,** punishable by a sentence in a county jail, a fine, or both. We list the various types of felonies and misdemeanors in Texas in Table 25–1.

| **Felony**
A crime—such as arson, murder, rape, or robbery—that carries the most severe sanctions, usually ranging from one year in prison to death.

| **Misdemeanor**
A lesser crime than a felony, punishable by a fine or imprisonment for up to one year.

TABLE 25–1 | CRIME AND PUNISHMENT UNDER THE TEXAS PENAL CODE

OFFENSE	TERMS*	MAXIMUM FINE
CAPITAL MURDER Including murder of a police officer, firefighter, prison guard, or child under age six; murder for hire; murder committed during another felony, such as rape, robbery, burglary, or arson; and mass murder.	Life sentence or execution	
FIRST DEGREE FELONY Including aggravated sexual assault, theft of more than $200,000, robbery, noncapital murder, and sale of more than four grams of "hard" drugs such as heroin.	5 to 99 years	$10,000
SECOND DEGREE FELONY Including theft of more than $100,000 and burglary of a habitation.	2 to 20 years	$10,000
THIRD DEGREE FELONY Including theft of more than $20,000, drive-by shootings (that do not result in murder), and involuntary manslaughter.	2 to 10 years	$10,000
STATE JAIL FELONY Including theft of more than $1,500, burglary of a building other than a habitation, sale of less than one gram of narcotics, auto theft, and forgery.	180 days to 2 years probation†	$10,000
CLASS A MISDEMEANOR Including theft of more than $500, driving while intoxicated, resisting arrest, and stalking.	1 year maximum	$4,000
CLASS B MISDEMEANOR Including theft of more than $50, possession of small amounts of marijuana, and reckless conduct (such as pointing a gun at someone).	180 days maximum	$2,000
CLASS C MISDEMEANOR Including theft of less than $50, smoking on a public elevator, and disorderly conduct (such as indecent exposure).	None	$500

*Punishments may be reduced for murder committed in "sudden passion" or may be enhanced to the next level if gang activity (involving three or more persons) or the use of deadly weapons is involved, if the person who committed the crime has had previous convictions, or if the murder is a hate crime (motivated by bias based on ethnicity, religion, or sexual orientation).
†Although probation must be granted, a judge may order a sixty-day jail sentence as a condition for probation. If the conviction is for narcotics, the term may be one year. Repeat offenders are not given automatic probation.

The Criminal

What causes people to commit crimes? What leads them to adopt values different from those reflected in the criminal laws of society? Persons who become criminals vary across the broad spectrum of human personality and may come from any socioeconomic class. Yet the persons who commit most serious crimes are similar. For one reason or another, they are unwilling to accept the *mores* (beliefs about "right" and "wrong") of those who write the laws. Lawbreakers are disproportionately young and poor; many have acute emotional and social problems. They have little stake in the values that lawmakers hold dear.

With the decline of traditional family life and the rise of single-parent households, many young people are inadequately socialized by adults and do not have useful and rewarding roles in society. They lack the sense of responsibility that usually accompanies a job or a family. A young person who has dropped out of school or who is unemployed has difficulty functioning in legitimate society.

Street Gangs. In some neighborhoods, street gangs offer the only center for social life and capitalistic endeavor. Gangs may be the only source of approval, protection, and a sense of belonging for their members, and they become traditional neighborhood training grounds in crime for successive generations. Lessons not learned on the streets may be picked up from the thousands of demonstrations of crime seen in movies and on television.

Juvenile Crime. Whether as gangs or individuals, persons under age seventeen commit a disproportionate share of crime. In Texas, juveniles (under age seventeen) accounted for 21 percent of all arrests for theft in 2004, 25 percent of all arrests for

FBI Index Crimes
A set of crimes reported by the FBI and commonly used as a way of measuring the overall crime rate. The index crimes are murder and nonnegligent manslaughter, forcible rape, robbery, aggravated assault, burglary, theft, and motor vehicle theft.

Ellis Unit in Huntsville, Texas, holds the state's death row inmates. Since 1976, the state of Texas has led the nation in state-sanctioned executions. What is at least one reason why this is so? (Greg Smith/Corbis)

burglary, and 40 percent of all arrests for arson.[9] Americans under the age of eighteen accounted for 18 percent of all arrests nationwide for **FBI index crimes**.[10] Used as the barometer for the crime rate, the FBI index crimes are murder and nonnegligent manslaughter, forcible rape, robbery, aggravated assault, burglary, theft, and motor vehicle theft.

Some people may refuse to recognize that the young are major contributors to crime, and others are convinced that young offenders "will grow out of it." In fact, disproportionate numbers of young people commit crimes, and rather than growing out of it, many graduate to more serious crime. Nevertheless, little is done to rehabilitate juveniles early in their criminal careers. Juvenile courts in Texas provide only limited social services for delinquents, and many of these young offenders have no access to vocational training, employment placement, emergency shelter, foster homes, or halfway houses. Because they are limited in resources, Texas juvenile facilities not only fail to correct, but also serve as breeding grounds for adult crime.

Men and Crime. Far more men than women are arrested for crimes. In 2004, males accounted for 87 percent of Texans arrested for burglary, 87 percent of those arrested for robbery, and 79 percent of those arrested for aggravated assault.[11] Perhaps the traditional male social roles and the accompanying psychological attitudes make it difficult for men to accept certain of society's mores. Aggressive and assertive attitudes, violent sports, protectiveness, and working for pay are often regarded as essentials of a boy's training for manhood. Apparently, many young men fail to learn the distinction between the kind of assertiveness that society approves of and the kind it condemns.

Crime and Minority Groups. Minority group members are arrested disproportionately for crimes. In 2004, 42 percent of Texans arrested for robbery, 31 percent of those arrested for murder, and 24 percent of those arrested for rape were African American. Hispanics accounted for 37 percent of the arrests for murder, 35 percent for rape, and 34 percent for robbery.[12] Prejudice among members of law enforcement agencies may account for some minority arrests, but it is also clear that the actual crime rate is higher among minority group members.

Poverty. Ethnic minorities are disproportionately poor, but poverty is by no means unique to them. Perhaps more important, poverty is often accompanied by low educational attainment and psychological problems. The poor, regardless of racial or ethnic background, are more likely to commit violent crimes than are the middle and upper classes.

Urbanization. Crime is more likely in large metropolitan areas. More than three-fourths of all Texans live in metropolitan areas of more than fifty thousand people. The character of urban life may contribute to crime. Cities are more anonymous than rural areas and small towns, and social sanctions seem less effective in this setting. Not only is there greater freedom in the city to act criminally, but there are also gangs and other organizations that may openly encourage criminal activity. A majority of inmates in Texas prisons are from the San Antonio, Dallas, and Houston areas.

Illegal Drugs. Drug addiction contributes to crime in a variety of ways. In 2004, 112,677 Texans were arrested for narcotics violations,[13] and it is impossible to estimate what percentage of robberies, burglaries, and thefts are committed to finance

---

[9]*Crime in Texas: Calendar Year 2004* (Austin: Texas Department of Public Safety, 2005), pp. 30–36.
[10]Federal Bureau of Investigation, *Uniform Crime Reports: Crime in the United States 2004* (Washington, D.C.: U.S. Government Printing Office, 2005), p. 265.
[11]*Crime in Texas: Calendar Year 2004*, pp. 25–30.
[12]*Ibid.*, pp. 21–26.
[13]*Ibid.*, p. 41.

illegal habits. Narcotics and alcohol also reduce inhibitions, and at least one-third of crimes are committed under their influence.

White-Collar Crime. Most violent crimes are committed by those who in one way or other are on the fringes of society. In many instances, these perpetrators simply live in an environment that promotes despair, low self-esteem, and weak emotional ties to the "legitimate" society. Some criminals consciously identify themselves as victims and rationalize their conduct based on their supposed victim status.

In contrast, few think of successful businesspersons or professionals as being criminals, yet these people may violate federal income tax laws, keep fraudulent business accounts, or pollute the environment. Because they seldom rob, rape, murder, or commit other violent acts, however, these white-collar criminals are often punished less severely. Crimes such as bribery, tax fraud, business fraud, price fixing, and embezzlement are committed largely by the white-collar criminal, who has often benefited from the very best that society has to offer.

The Victim

The American people have paid the costs of white-collar crime for many years. For example, fraudulent financial reporting by Enron and MCI likely resulted in a greater loss of confidence in the economy and stock values than all robberies, burglaries, and thefts during the past decade combined. Yet the outrage against crime is still directed largely toward violent crimes such as murder, rape, and robbery, as well as certain property crimes such as burglary, larceny, and auto theft. In general, the public is more concerned about physical security than financial loss. Figure 25–2 and Figure 25–3 (on the next page) give some facts about crime rates in Texas.

Such crimes as prostitution, gambling, and illegal drug possession are sometimes called **victimless crimes** because they do not have an obvious victim; the primary

> **DID YOU KNOW . . .**
> That Tennessee makes it illegal for anyone except a zoo to import skunks; West Virginia makes it illegal to taunt someone fighting a duel; Rhode Island requires that a driver must make a loud noise when passing on the left; North Carolina limits bingo games to five hours; New Jersey makes it illegal to wear a bulletproof vest while committing murder; and in Wisconsin, it is a crime for restaurants to serve margarine unless requested by the customer?

> **Victimless Crime**
> A crime in which there does not appear to be a victim; a consensual crime. (Alternatively, the person breaking the law may be considered the primary victim.) Examples often cited include prostitution, gambling, and illegal drug possession.

FIGURE 25–2 | TEXAS CRIME RATES SINCE 1991

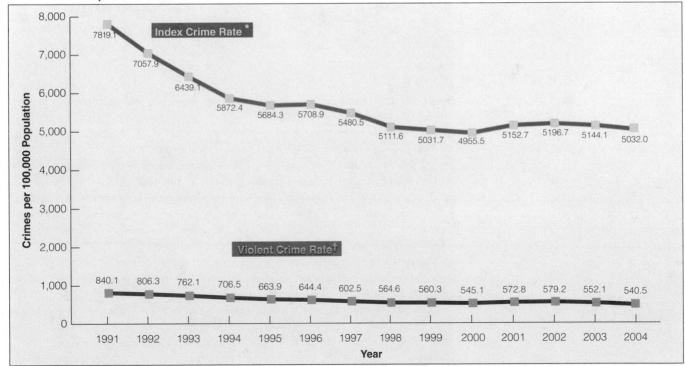

*Total of violent and property crimes (burglary, theft, and motor vehicle theft) per 100,000 population.
†Murder, rape, robbery, and aggravated assault.
Source: *Crime in Texas: Calendar Year 2004* (Austin: Texas Department of Public Safety, 2005), pp. 10–11.

FIGURE 25-3 | THE TEXAS TIME CLOCK: CRIME OBSERVATIONS, 2004

Despite these alarming statistics and violence-centered news coverage, the actual crime rate generally has declined since 1991.

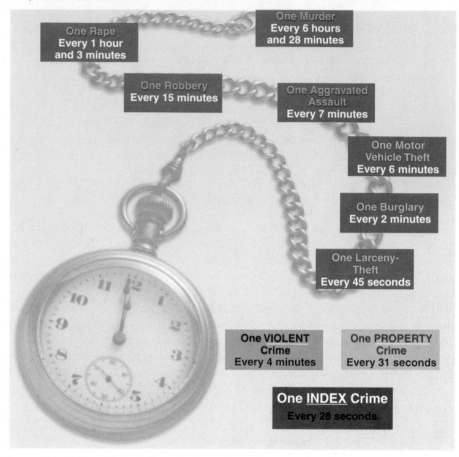

One Rape
Every 1 hour
and 3 minutes

One Murder
Every 6 hours
and 28 minutes

One Robbery
Every 15 minutes

One Aggravated
Assault
Every 7 minutes

One Motor
Vehicle Theft
Every 6 minutes

One Burglary
Every 2 minutes

One Larceny-
Theft
Every 45 seconds

One VIOLENT
Crime
Every 4 minutes

One PROPERTY
Crime
Every 31 seconds

One INDEX Crime
Every 28 seconds

Source: *Crime in Texas: Calendar Year 2004* (Austin: Texas Department of Public Safety, 2005), p. 13.

victims may be the criminals themselves. The families of these criminals and society at large also pay a price for these activities, however, and victimless crimes are often linked to more serious crimes.

Even though more affluent areas of the state and nation sometimes are victimized by crime, police reports continue to demonstrate that the highest rates of victimization are in the poor areas of our cities. Crime is largely a neighborhood affair and is often committed against friends and families of the criminal. Acquaintance rape, or date rape, has been well publicized. Moreover, at least 46 percent of Texas killers are acquainted with their victims, and 17 percent of all murders occur within the family. Minorities and young people suffer most from crime—in a typical recent year, 41 percent of Texas murder victims were Hispanic.[14]

Victims now have the right to be informed of investigations and court proceedings against the accused and to have their victim-impact statements taken into account during sentencing and **parole** actions. The Crime Victims' Compensation Fund is administered by the attorney general and financed by small fees collected from criminals when they are convicted. These meager funds are available to victims who have suffered extreme personal hardship resulting from physical injury during a crime. Most victims are not eligible, however, nor is there compensation for the billion dollars' worth of property stolen each year.

| Parole
Early release from prison under official supervision.

[14]*Ibid.*, p. 21.

Due Process of Law

It is the courts that enforce the most general concepts of justice and the broadest norms of society against specific individuals. The courts must blend two conflicting goals of society:

1. To protect society according to the state's legal concepts of right and wrong.
2. To protect the rights of the individual charged with wrongdoing.

As a result of these conflicting goals, elaborate traditions of court process and procedure have developed over the centuries, dating back to when the American states were still colonies of Britain. Many of these traditional procedures derive from the English experience, while others were developed more recently in the American states. Some court procedures have been written into state and national constitutions and statutes; others are included in written and unwritten traditional codes of court process. Such procedures are designed to promote justice and protect the individual from the government, and together they constitute what is called **due process.**

Unfortunately, the guaranteed rights of the accused are very nearly meaningless unless courts, prosecutors, and law enforcement agents protect them. Sometimes, due process becomes more a philosophy of how justice should be carried out than a description of what really happens.

Pretrial Court Activities

Following arrest, the suspect is jailed while reports are completed and the district attorney's office decides whether to file charges and what bail to recommend. As soon as is practical, the accused is presented before a justice of the peace or other magistrate for **arraignment,** at which time the court performs the following actions:

1. It explains the charges against the accused.
2. It reminds the suspect of the rights to remain silent, to be represented by counsel, and to request a written acknowledgment that the *Miranda* warning (see Chapter 4) was given and understood.
3. It sets bail.
4. It informs the accused of the right to an **examining trial.**

The Right to Know the Nature of the Accusation.   The suspect is usually told the charges (1) on arrest, (2) in the arraignment, and (3) again in subsequent proceedings. Being told the nature of the charges against you is one of the most fundamental aspects of due process. Because the states have governments of "laws and not men," no one should be held in custody on a whim, but only for legal cause. Although a person need not necessarily be guilty of a crime to be held, there must be "probable cause" for the confinement. If it is determined that a person is being held unlawfully, counsel may secure release by a **writ of *habeas corpus*** (a court order requiring that the prisoner be presented in person and legal cause shown for imprisonment).

The Right to Legal Counsel.   The right to counsel is vital to the accused. Aside from clearly understanding the constitutional rights of an accused person, an attorney will be familiar with the baffling intricacies of the law. So important is the assistance of counsel that many suspects will contact an attorney before they appear in front of a magistrate. Yet this right to counsel has never been absolute.

Guaranteed in both the U.S. and Texas constitutions, the right to counsel was traditionally interpreted to mean that a person had a right to counsel if he or she could afford it. In 1932, the United States Supreme Court ruled that the Sixth Amendment requires state courts to appoint counsel for the poor, but only in capital

DID YOU KNOW . . .

That in 1999, the federal Fifth Circuit Court of Appeals reversed the death penalty conviction of Calvin Burdine because his attorney had slept during much of the trial?

Due Process
Established rules and principles for the administration of justice designed to safeguard the rights of the individual. The right to due process of law is provided by the U.S. Constitution and most state constitutions.

Arraignment
The first act in a criminal proceeding, in which the defendant is brought before a court to hear the charges against him or her and to enter a plea of guilty or not guilty.

Examining Trial
A relatively uncommon procedure that may be requested by felony defendants in Texas. In an examining trial, a justice of the peace reviews the facts and decides whether a defendant should have to face trial in criminal court.

Writ of *Habeas Corpus*
An order that requires a jailer to bring a person before a court or judge and explain why the person is being held. *Habeas corpus* is Latin and literally means "you have the body."

cases.[15] Later, the Court extended the indigent's right to counsel to other felony cases and serious misdemeanor cases in which imprisonment might be involved, but the right does not extend to petty offenses such as traffic violations.[16]

The right to court-appointed counsel does not necessarily guarantee equal justice for the poor. An indigent defendant usually is not assigned an attorney until a district judge can respond to the defendant's written request. The attorney's fee, paid by the county, is considerably less than most attorneys receive from paying clients. Although some lawyers may be diligent in indigent cases, other lawyers will act on the assumption that time spent defending poor people does not significantly advance either their practices or their incomes. In addition, lawyers who specialize in civil matters may be appointed at random to defend indigents in criminal cases. Indigents therefore may not receive the kind of expert defense they would have if they could choose among attorneys who specialize in criminal cases.

The Right to Bail. Bail is the security required for the release of a suspect awaiting trial. When the suspect appears at trial, the bail is refunded. Some persons released on bail fail to appear in court, and their security is forfeited. Others commit still more crimes while on bail. The legal system presumes, however, that an individual is innocent unless convicted, and bail supports this assumption by permitting the accused to resume his or her professional and social life while preparing a defense.

The Texas Constitution guarantees the right to bail immediately after arrest, except when proof is "evident" in capital cases or when the defendant is being charged with a third felony after two prior felony convictions. The state constitution allows bail to be denied if the defendant is charged with committing a felony while released on bail or under indictment for another felony.

In practice, the right to bail exists only for those who can afford it. Private licensed bonding companies may be willing to post bond for a fee (usually 10 to 50 percent of the bail as set by the court), which, unlike bail, is not refunded. Many cannot afford even this fee, and unless these prisoners are released on **personal recognizance** (their personal promise to appear), they will await trial in jail. In our criminal justice system, bail procedures may create more problems for the poor than any other single practice.

The Right to an Examining Trial. Although few defendants request one, in Texas the accused has the right to an examining trial in felony cases, as mentioned earlier. In an examining trial, a justice of the peace reviews the facts and decides whether the case should be recommended for criminal proceedings. If the facts warrant, the charges may be dismissed or bail adjusted.

Formal Charges

Although an *indictment*, or formal charge, sometimes precedes arrest, a felony case is usually bound over to a **grand jury** for indictment following arraignment. A grand jury should not be confused with a petit, or trial, jury. Grand juries do not determine a person's guilt or innocence, as trial juries do. Often, the accused does not even appear before the grand jury. The grand jury primarily weighs the evidence in the hands of the prosecutor to determine whether the case will be taken to trial. If the grand jury determines that the evidence could be sufficient to convict, it issues an indictment, which constitutes a formal charge that enables the case to go to trial.

| **Personal Recognizance**
A defendant's personal promise to appear in court.

| **Grand Jury**
A jury that sits in pretrial proceedings to determine if sufficient evidence exists to try an individual and, therefore, approve an indictment.

---

[15]*Powell v. Alabama*, 287 U.S. 45 (1932).
[16]*Gideon v. Wainwright*, 372 U.S. 335 (1963); and *Argersinger v. Hamlin*, 407 U.S. 25 (1972).

A determination that the evidence is sufficient to convict is necessary because if the prosecutor does not have enough evidence to convict, there is no point in bringing the case to trial. Trying a case on flimsy evidence not only costs the taxpayers financially, it also costs the accused in terms of needless expense, lost time, and damaged reputation. The right to a grand jury indictment is guaranteed in both the Texas and the federal courts to protect innocent citizens against harassment on unjustified charges.

In practice, the grand jury is often made up of untrained citizens, who frequently cannot critically evaluate a case. A grand jury usually acts as a rubber stamp for the prosecutor. Some states have abolished the grand jury in favor of **writs of information,** in which a judge evaluates the evidence to determine if it is sufficient to go to trial. Texas guarantees the right to a grand jury indictment in all felony cases but uses the writ of information to charge people with misdemeanors.

Pretrial Hearings

After the indictment, the defendant has the right to another hearing, sometimes called the second arraignment. A district judge (rather than a justice of the peace) presides as the formal indictment is read and the defendant enters a plea. If the plea is guilty, a later hearing is scheduled to set punishment. Most often, the defendant pleads not guilty at this point, and the case is placed on the docket (schedule of court activity) for subsequent trial. A variety of motions may be presented, including a motion for delay or for the suppression of certain evidence.

The Insanity Defense.   Another subject of pretrial hearings concerns possible insanity. A person cannot be held morally and criminally responsible for a crime if, at the time of the offense, mental disorder made it impossible for him or her to recognize that it was wrong. There is considerable controversy as to the effects of mental disorder, so professional testimony may be necessary to establish legal insanity, and psychiatric opinion is frequently divided. The courts rarely find a defendant not guilty by reason of insanity.

Change of Venue.   A change in the site of a trial (a **change of venue**) may be necessary when the news media have so publicized a case that an unbiased jury cannot be selected or when inflamed public opinion may prevent a fair trial. A real tension exists between the rights of the free press and the rights of the accused.

Plea Bargaining

Ideally, the trial is the final step in society's elaborate guarantees of due process. Yet for most of those who are accused of a crime, the final day in court never comes. In fact, the system is designed to discourage and even punish those who choose to exercise the right to a trial. Most cases end in a secret bargaining session with the prosecutor **(plea bargaining).**

Faced with overcrowded dockets and limited staffs, prosecuting attorneys usually meet with the accused and offer a "deal" in exchange for a plea of guilty, which eliminates the necessity of a trial. The usual deal is to offer to drop some of the charges, to recommend probation or a lighter sentence, or to charge the accused with a lesser crime. The prosecutor may agree to delay prosecution **(deferred adjudication)** and later drop charges if the defendant agrees to meet certain probation-like conditions. Such agreements save tax expenditures and court time and may be useful to law enforcement when defendants are given a lighter sentence in exchange for acting as witnesses and testifying against fellow criminals.

The guilty obviously benefit from plea bargaining because they are not punished for the full measure of their crimes. Defense attorneys frequently encourage their

Writ of Information
In criminal law, a formal accusation filed by a prosecutor against a party charged with a crime. It is an alternative to an indictment and does not involve a grand jury.

Change of Venue
A change in the site of a trial.

Plea Bargaining
Negotiations that take place between the prosecution and the defense in a criminal case in which the defendant normally is offered a lighter sentence or other benefits in return for a guilty plea.

Deferred Adjudication
A procedure that allows a judge to postpone final sentencing in a criminal case; charges are dismissed if the defendant completes a satisfactory probationary period.

clients to accept the bargain to save them the effort of a courtroom trial, and some become as much implicit agents for the prosecution as advocates for the defense. The innocent and those who are unwilling to trade their rights for a secret backroom bargain take the chance of being punished more severely for demanding trial.

The Trial

Unless the defense waives the right to a trial by jury, the first major step in the trial is the selection of a jury. The right to a jury trial is often regarded as one of the most valuable rights available in the criminal justice system. In fact, every state provides for trial by jury in all but the most minor cases, and Texas goes even further, providing for the right to trial by jury in every criminal case.[17]

Nevertheless, the right to trial by jury in a criminal case is one of the most frequently waived rights, especially in cases in which the defendant is an object of community prejudice (a member of an unpopular political group or ethnic minority) or in which the alleged crime is particularly outrageous. If the right to a jury trial is waived, the presiding judge determines the verdict. Regardless of whether or not a person chooses to exercise the right to trial by jury, that right remains a valuable alternative to decisions by possibly arbitrary judges.

Selecting the Jurors.   During an initial questioning, prospective jurors may be asked about possible biases, their prior knowledge of the case, or any opinions they may have formed about the case. Either the prosecution or the defense may challenge a prospective juror for reason of prejudice, and the presiding judge will evaluate that challenge.

In addition to asking the judge to dismiss a prospective juror on the ground that he or she is prejudiced, both the prosecution and the defense may dismiss a number of jurors by *peremptory challenges* (challenges without cause). Experienced attorneys and prosecutors use peremptory challenges to eliminate jurors who may be hostile to their side of the case. The defense and the prosecution may consider the occupations, social status, and attitudes of possible jurors. In principle, race and gender are not legitimate grounds for peremptory challenges, but bias is hard to prove. Some lawyers have been known to employ psychologists to assist in the selection process, and lucrative consulting businesses have developed to assist attorneys in jury selection.

| Adversary System
A legal system in which parties to a legal action are opponents and are responsible for bringing the facts and law related to their case before the court.

The Adversary System.   The United States has an **adversary system,** in which two parties to the case (the prosecution and the defense in criminal cases) arm themselves with whatever evidence they can muster and battle in court, under the rules of law, to final judgment. An adversary system cannot operate fairly unless both the defense and the prosecution have an equal opportunity to influence the decision of the court. Hence, procedural guarantees are designed to ensure that both sides have equal access to (1) knowledge of the law and (2) the evidence. So that equal knowledge of the law is guaranteed, the legal knowledge of the prosecution is balanced by the right of the defendant to have legal counsel. Because the government (in the person of the prosecutor) has the power to seize evidence and to force witnesses to testify under oath, the defense must be given that same power (called *compulsory process*).

Presenting Evidence.   In the adversary system, each side can challenge the material evidence and cross-examine the witnesses presented by the opposition. Only

---

[17]The United States Supreme Court held, in the case of *Duncan v. Louisiana,* 391 U.S. 145, 149 (1968), that trial by jury is an essential part of due process when state criminal proceedings involve more than petty offenses.

evidence that is presented can be evaluated in court. The fact that both parties to a case have opposite biases means that each has an interest in concealing evidence that could benefit the opposition.

As it is the legal responsibility of the prosecutor to prove guilt beyond reasonable doubt (the burden of proof lies with the state), the counsel for the defense has no responsibility to present evidence of the defendant's guilt, nor can the defendant be forced to take the stand to testify. Because the prosecutor has the responsibility to convict the guilty rather than the innocent, however, it is a violation of due process for the government to withhold evidence that could benefit the accused—but it happens. There is no way of knowing how many unjust verdicts have been handed down because not all the evidence was presented.

In jury trials, once the evidence has been presented, the presiding judge reads the charge to the jury; this charge constitutes the judge's instructions and the law that applies in the case. He or she will instruct the jurors to ignore such things as hearsay testimony and other illegal evidence to which they may have been exposed during the course of the trial. (Still, it is difficult for jurors to erase from their minds the impact of illegal testimony.) The judge is supposedly neutral and cannot comment on the weight of the evidence that has been presented.

Concluding the Trial.   Following the judge's charge to the jury, the prosecution and defense are allowed to summarize the case. During their summary remarks, the prosecutor will argue that the evidence points toward guilt, and the defense will conclude that the evidence is insufficient to prove guilt beyond a reasonable doubt.

The jury then retires to decide between verdicts of guilty and not guilty. Texas law requires that all the jurors agree on the verdict in criminal cases. If the jury cannot agree, it is said to be a hung jury, and the judge will declare a mistrial, but the defendant may be tried again.

Sentencing.   Regardless of whether the judge or the jury determines guilt, the judge usually prescribes a sentence, unless the defendant demands that the jury do so. After considering the character of the defendant, any past criminal record, and the circumstances surrounding the crime, the judge may assess a penalty between the minimum and maximum provided by law.

A first offender may be given probation, which allows her or him to serve the sentence in free society according to specific terms and restrictions and under the supervision of a probation officer. Similarly, deferred adjudication allows judges to postpone final sentencing in criminal cases; and after a satisfactory probationary period, the charges are dismissed. Judges have a great deal of latitude in assessing penalties, so the fate of a defendant will depend in large part on the attitudes of the presiding judge. Different judges sometimes assess vastly different penalties for similar crimes committed under similar circumstances.

After sentencing, the prisoner may be sent to one of the state's penal institutions. Time served in jail before and during trial is usually deducted from the sentence of the guilty. (For the innocent, however, the time served awaiting trial is a casualty of an imperfect system of justice—underlining the necessity for care in accusing and trying our citizens.)

Posttrial Proceedings

To protect the accused from double jeopardy, a person who is acquitted (found not guilty) cannot be tried again for the same offense. Protection from double jeopardy is much more limited than many citizens realize. In the event of a mistrial or an error in procedure, the trial may end in neither a conviction nor an acquittal. The defendant may then be tried for the same offense on the theory that he or she was never put in jeopardy by the first trial.

| Mistrial
A trial judged to be invalid because of fundamental error. When a mistrial is declared, the trial may start again, beginning with the selection of the jury.

| Probation
A sentencing alternative to imprisonment in which the court releases convicted defendants under supervision as long as certain conditions are observed.

| Acquitted
Found not guilty.

Multiple Charges.   A person found not guilty of one crime may be tried for a related offense. For example, a person accused of driving seventy-five miles per hour through a school zone, going the wrong way on a one-way street, striking down a child in the crosswalk, and then leaving the scene of the accident may have committed several crimes. Being acquitted for speeding does not free the defendant of possible charges for each of the other offenses—they were separate crimes.

Likewise, such acts as bank robbery and kidnapping may violate both federal and state law, and the accused may be tried by both jurisdictions. Finally, even if a person is found not guilty of a crime, a victim of that crime can sue the defendant under civil law. Because the standards of proof under civil law are lower than under criminal law, an acquitted individual may still be forced to pay monetary damages to the alleged victim or the alleged victim's heirs.

Appeals.   A defendant may, of course, appeal a guilty verdict. Although the state cannot appeal a not-guilty verdict, because doing so would constitute double jeopardy, prosecutors may appeal the reversal of a guilty verdict by a higher court. Appellate procedure is designed to review the law as applied by lower courts. In most cases, the appellate court will not assess the evidence. Its major concern is procedure. If serious procedural errors are found, the appellate court may return the case to a lower court for retrial. Such a retrial does not constitute double jeopardy.

Having exhausted the rights of appeal in the Texas courts, a very few defendants appeal their cases to the federal courts, which have jurisdiction in federal law. A ground for appeal to federal courts is the assertion that the state courts have violated the U.S. Constitution or other federal laws.

Texas Court Organization

Figure 25–4 outlines the organizational structure of the Texas court system. This figure shows the various types and levels of courts in the system. It should be noted that some courts within this rather large and complicated system have overlapping jurisdiction.

Municipal Courts

Municipal courts in Texas were once known as *corporation courts*, but the name was changed to *municipal courts* in 1969. Although authorized by state statute, they are set up by incorporated cities and towns. Their status and organization are normally recognized in the city charter or municipal ordinances.

Legally, the municipal courts have exclusive jurisdiction to try violations of city ordinances. They also handle minor violations of state law—class C misdemeanors for which the punishment is a fine of $500 or less and does not include a jail sentence. (Justice of the peace courts have overlapping jurisdiction to handle such minor violations.) Approximately 85 percent of the cases filed in municipal courts involve traffic violations.[18]

Courts of Record?   The legislature has authorized city governments to determine whether their municipal courts are courts of record. Normally, they are not. When a municipal court is designated as a court of record, however, its records are the basis of appeal to the appropriate county court. (Barely more than 1 percent of total cases are appealed from municipal courts.)[19] Otherwise, records are not kept, and defendants may demand a completely new trial in overworked county courts, in which most such

---

[18]Texas Judiciary Online, "Activity Report for Municipal Courts: January 1, 2005 to December 31, 2005," Texas Judicial Council, April 2, 2006, at **www.courts.state.tx.us/trial/municour.asp**.
[19]*Ibid.*

FIGURE 25–4 | COURT STRUCTURE IN TEXAS

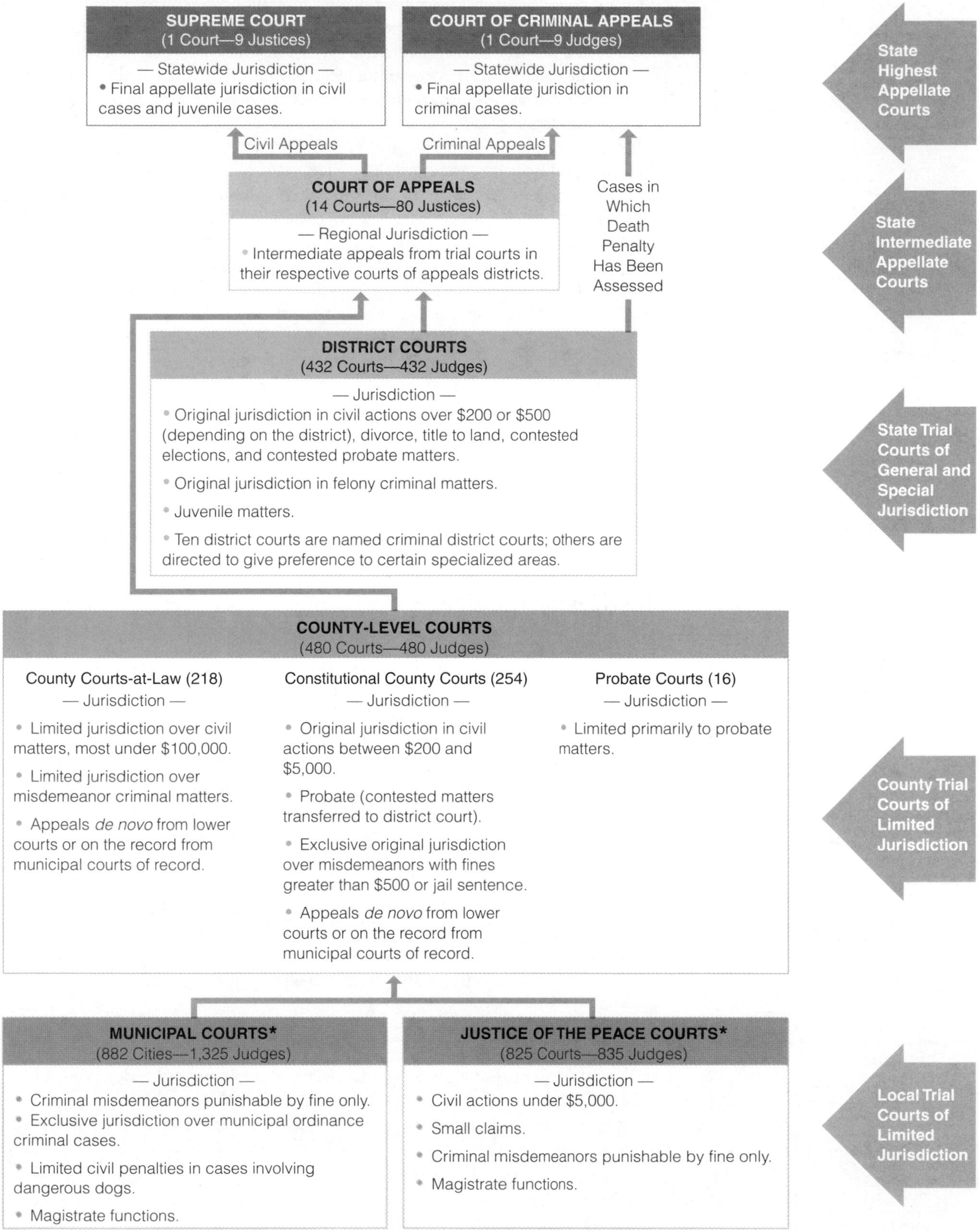

SUPREME COURT
(1 Court—9 Justices)

— Statewide Jurisdiction —
• Final appellate jurisdiction in civil cases and juvenile cases.

COURT OF CRIMINAL APPEALS
(1 Court—9 Judges)

— Statewide Jurisdiction —
• Final appellate jurisdiction in criminal cases.

State Highest Appellate Courts

Civil Appeals   Criminal Appeals

COURT OF APPEALS
(14 Courts—80 Justices)

— Regional Jurisdiction —
• Intermediate appeals from trial courts in their respective courts of appeals districts.

Cases in Which Death Penalty Has Been Assessed

State Intermediate Appellate Courts

DISTRICT COURTS
(432 Courts—432 Judges)

— Jurisdiction —

• Original jurisdiction in civil actions over $200 or $500 (depending on the district), divorce, title to land, contested elections, and contested probate matters.

• Original jurisdiction in felony criminal matters.

• Juvenile matters.

• Ten district courts are named criminal district courts; others are directed to give preference to certain specialized areas.

State Trial Courts of General and Special Jurisdiction

COUNTY-LEVEL COURTS
(480 Courts—480 Judges)

County Courts-at-Law (218)
— Jurisdiction —

• Limited jurisdiction over civil matters, most under $100,000.

• Limited jurisdiction over misdemeanor criminal matters.

• Appeals *de novo* from lower courts or on the record from municipal courts of record.

Constitutional County Courts (254)
— Jurisdiction —

• Original jurisdiction in civil actions between $200 and $5,000.

• Probate (contested matters transferred to district court).

• Exclusive original jurisdiction over misdemeanors with fines greater than $500 or jail sentence.

• Appeals *de novo* from lower courts or on the record from municipal courts of record.

Probate Courts (16)
— Jurisdiction —

• Limited primarily to probate matters.

County Trial Courts of Limited Jurisdiction

MUNICIPAL COURTS*
(882 Cities—1,325 Judges)

— Jurisdiction —
• Criminal misdemeanors punishable by fine only.
• Exclusive jurisdiction over municipal ordinance criminal cases.
• Limited civil penalties in cases involving dangerous dogs.
• Magistrate functions.

JUSTICE OF THE PEACE COURTS*
(825 Courts—835 Judges)

— Jurisdiction —
• Civil actions under $5,000.
• Small claims.
• Criminal misdemeanors punishable by fine only.
• Magistrate functions.

Local Trial Courts of Limited Jurisdiction

*All justice of the peace courts and most municipal courts are not courts of record. Appeals from these courts result in completely new trials in the county-level courts or, in some instances, the district courts. Some municipal courts are courts of record. Appeals from those courts are taken on the record to the county-level court.

Source: Office of Court Administration, Texas Judicial Council, *Seventy-fifth Annual Report, Fiscal Year 2003*, p. 32.

cases are simply dismissed. Where it is available, drivers frequently use this procedure to avoid traffic convictions and higher auto insurance rates.

Those favoring the court-of-record concept point to the large amount of revenue lost because new trials usually result in dismissal. Those opposing the concept argue that municipal courts are too often a means of raising revenue rather than achieving justice. Municipal courts collect over $500 million per year, giving some support to the latter argument.

Judicial Qualifications and Selection.   Judges of the municipal courts meet whatever qualifications are set by the city charter or ordinances. Some cities require specific legal training or experience. Other charters say very little about qualifications. In 2004, less than one-third of municipal court judges were licensed attorneys. Judges may serve one year or indefinitely. Most are appointed for two-year terms but serve at the pleasure of the governing bodies that have selected them. Furthermore, these judges' salaries are paid entirely by their respective cities and vary widely. Where statutes permit, some cities have established more than one municipal court or more than one judge for each court. In view of the volume of cases pending before these courts, the need for a number of judges is obvious.

As will be discussed below in relation to justice of the peace courts, public confidence in municipal courts is low. Out-of-town, out-of-county, or out-of-state residents often expect to be found guilty regardless of the evidence presented. In 2005, 44 percent of all cases filed in municipal courts were settled before trial.[20] Such large percentages of settlement could indicate either guilt or fear that the legal process will not be fair. It could also indicate people's desire to avoid the inconvenience or expense of going through a trial.

Justices of the Peace

The justice of the peace courts in Texas are authorized by the Texas Constitution, which requires that the county commissioners in each county establish at least one, and not more than eight, justice precincts (the areas from which justices of the peace are elected for four-year terms). County commissioners determine how many justices of the peace will be elected (based on the population) and where their courts will sit. Changes are made continuously, making it difficult to determine how many justices of the peace there are at any given time. The Texas Judicial Council determined that there were 825 justices of the peace during 2005.[21]

The functions of the justice of the peace courts are varied. The courts have jurisdiction over criminal cases for which the fine is under $500. They also have **original jurisdiction** in civil cases in which the dispute involves less than $5,000. Justices of the peace may issue warrants for search and arrest, serve *ex officio* as notaries public, conduct preliminary hearings, perform marriages, serve as coroners in counties having no medical examiner, and hear cases involving small claims. Approximately 91 percent of cases filed in justice courts are criminal, and most involve traffic violations.[22]

Qualifications.   All the functions just mentioned are performed by an official whose only qualification is to be a registered voter. No statutory or constitutional provisions require that a justice of the peace be a lawyer, and indeed only about 6 percent of Texas's justices of the peace are lawyers.

When a justice of the peace is not a licensed attorney, he or she is required by statute to take a forty-hour course in the performance of the duties of the office, plus

Original Jurisdiction
The authority of a court to consider a case in the first instance; the power to try a case, as opposed to appellate jurisdiction, which involves the power to review cases decided by other courts.

[20]*Ibid.*
[21]Texas Judiciary Online, "Court Structure of Texas."
[22]Texas Judiciary Online, "Activity Report for Justice of the Peace Courts: January 1, 2005 to December 31, 2005," Texas Judicial Council, April 2, 2006, at **www.courts.state.tx.us/trial/jpcourts.asp**.

a twenty-hour course each year thereafter, at an accredited state-supported institution of higher education. Some people have questioned the constitutionality of this provision because it adds a qualification for the office not specified in the constitution.

Compensation.   For many years, counties in Texas varied widely as to whether they paid their justices of the peace a specific salary or paid them fees based on services performed. Some counties had a mixed system wherein some justices were salaried while others were paid according to a fee system. Since January 1973, all justices of the peace have been paid a salary,[23] but the salary may vary a great deal from county to county and from justice to justice within the same county.

The Negative Image of Justices of the Peace.   The public's perception of justices of the peace is often not flattering. Many justices are regarded as biased, untrained in the law, and incompetent. The average citizen is skeptical about getting a fair trial, which may be a major factor in the settlement of a high percentage of cases before trial (67 percent of criminal cases in 2005).[24] What about a person who goes before a justice of the peace in a county in which he or she does not live? The general assumption is that fairness and decency in this situation are the exception rather than the rule.

There are justices of the peace who are conscientious, objective, and fair, but they find it difficult to overcome the stereotype just described. This negative image is reinforced by the activities of justices of the peace who act as coroners. The function of the coroner is to determine the cause of death in specified cases. For decades, stories have been told about coroners' verdicts that left more questions than answers.

Thus, despite changes in the qualifications, salaries, and responsibilities of justices of the peace, they still do not inspire confidence in many people. Defenders of the system traditionally refer to the justice of the peace courts as the "people's courts" and maintain that elimination of the "justice courts" would remove the close contact between officials and the public that many treasure. Eliminating these courts, defenders say, would limit judicial power to professionals and would ignore the value of amateur status and "commonsense" law. This position is in line with the view, widely held in Texas, that government is best when it is closest to the people. Critics counter that incompetence and bias are not justified simply because these courts are close to the people.

County Courts

Each of the 254 counties in Texas has a county court presided over by the county judge. (The county judge is sometimes referred to as the constitutional county judge, and his or her court may be called the constitutional county court). The Texas Constitution requires that county judges be elected by voters for four-year terms and be "well informed in the law of the state," which can mean almost anything.

Their salaries are paid by the county and vary greatly. About 12 percent of county judges are licensed to practice law. County courts handle probate and other civil matters in which the amount in dispute is between $200 and $5,000. Their criminal jurisdiction is confined to serious misdemeanors for which punishment is a fine of over $500, a jail sentence, or both.

County Courts-at-Law.   Because the constitutional county judge also has administrative responsibilities as presiding officer of the commissioners court (the governing body for Texas counties and not a judicial entity at all), the judge may have

---

[23]Article 16.61 of the Texas Constitution, as amended in November 1972.
[24]Texas Judiciary Online, "Activity Report for Justice of the Peace Courts."

These photos show 4 of the 254 county courthouses in Texas. Clockwise from the upper left are the courthouses that serve Tarrant County, Somervell County, Hood County, and Anderson County. In 1999, the Texas legislature and then governor George W. Bush established the Texas Historic Courthouse Preservation Program. The program provides partial matching grants to Texas counties for the restoration of their historic county courthouses. The legislature has approved $145 million for the program since it began. (Photos Courtesy of Texas Historical Commission)

County Courts-at-Law
In Texas, county courts in addition to the constitutional county court. They are established by the legislature in all but the smallest Texas counties and may have criminal or civil jurisdiction. They form a level of courts superior to justice of the peace and municipal courts but inferior to district courts.

little time to handle judicial matters. The legislature has responded by establishing **county courts-at-law** in certain counties to act as auxiliary, or supplemental, courts. Their judges are elected for four-year terms. There are 218 of these statutory courts-at-law in seventy-four Texas counties.[25] For example, Dallas County has 15 and Harris County, 19. They have either civil or criminal jurisdiction or a combination of both, as determined by the legislative act that established them. Their civil jurisdiction includes cases involving claims of under $100,000. Their criminal jurisdiction includes misdemeanors that are more serious than those tried by the justice of the peace and municipal courts, or misdemeanors that include a jail sentence or a fine in excess of $500.

The qualifications of the judges of the statutory county courts-at-law vary according to the statute that established the particular court. In addition to residence in the county, a court-at-law judge usually must have four years' experience as a practicing attorney or judge.

Over two-thirds of cases filed in county-level courts are criminal. Cases involving theft and driving while intoxicated or under the influence of drugs are the most common. Civil cases include probate matters and suits to collect debt.

Popular Perceptions of County Judges.   Administration of justice in Texas county courts is widely considered to be uneven. Many of the judges are competent and run their courts in an orderly manner, but others regard their courts and official jurisdictions as personal fiefdoms, paying little attention to finer points of law or accepted procedures. If the county judge is performing as a judicial officer as well as the chief administrative officer of the county, the opportunities for arbitrary action are compounded.

---

[25]Texas Judiciary Online, "Court Structure of Texas."

District Courts

The district courts are often described as the chief trial courts of the state, and as a group these courts are called the general trial courts. The names of the courts and their jurisdictions vary. There are constitutional district courts, civil district courts, criminal district courts, and so on, through more than forty other jurisdictions.

Texas has 432 district courts, all of which are single-judge courts.[26] Each judge must be at least twenty-five years of age, a resident of the district for two years, and a citizen of the United States and a judge or a licensed practicing attorney for four years. Judges are elected for four-year terms by voters in their districts.

The state of Texas pays $101,700 of the salary of each district judge. Each county may supplement the salary, but the total salary must be at least $1,000 below that received by justices of the courts of appeals.

Jurisdiction of the District Courts. District courts have jurisdiction in felony cases, which make up about one-third of their caseloads. Civil cases in which the claim exceeds $200 may also be tried in district courts, and such cases constitute the greatest share of their workload (approximately 66 percent). Juvenile cases are usually tried in district courts. While most district courts exercise both criminal and civil jurisdiction, there is a tendency for courts in metropolitan areas to specialize in criminal, civil, or family law matters.

Plea Bargaining. The caseload for district courts is heavy, and it is at this level that plea bargaining is often used to dispose of criminal cases. Plea bargaining saves the state a great amount of time and expense. It is estimated that about 90 percent of criminal cases in district courts are disposed of in this way.[27] If plea bargaining were not used in many urban areas, court delays would be increased by months, if not years. While efficient, plea bargaining raises many issues concerning equity and justice. It often encourages innocent people to plead guilty and allows guilty people to escape with less punishment than the law provides.

Civil Settlements. Similarly, many civil lawsuits are resolved through negotiated settlements between the parties. At times, settlements may be appropriate and just.

In many urban areas, however, there is such a backlog of civil cases before the courts that it can take years for a matter to be heard and settled. Therefore, litigants often choose to settle their cases out of court for reasons other than justice.

Courts of Appeals

Fourteen courts of appeals hear immediate appeals in both civil and criminal cases from district- and county-level courts in their areas. These courts are said to have **appellate jurisdiction.** Only a small percentage of trial court cases are appealed. For example, during 2005, the courts of appeals disposed of 12,058 cases.[28] In these cases, the appeals courts reversed, at least in part, the decision of the trial court 7.4 percent of the time.[29]

The state pays each chief appeals justice $107,850 and each associate justice $107,350. Counties may pay a supplement to appeals judges, but the total salary must be at least $1,000 less than that of Texas Supreme Court judges, and the total supplement cannot exceed $15,000 per year. Appeals judges are elected from their

| Appellate Jurisdiction
The authority vested in an appellate court to review and revise the judicial actions of inferior courts.

---

[26]*Ibid.*

[27]*Texas Crime, Texas Justice* (Austin: Comptroller's Office, 1994), p. 51.

[28]Texas Judiciary Online, "District Courts: Activity for the Fiscal Year Ended August 31, 2005," Texas Judicial Council, April 4, 2006, at **www.courts.state.tx.us/oca/PublicInfo/AR2005/coas/4_Activity_Detail_2005.xls**.

[29]*Ibid.*

districts for six-year terms. They must be at least thirty-five years of age, with at least ten years' experience as a lawyer or judge.

Court of Criminal Appeals

An 1891 constitutional amendment established the present system of dual courts of last resort. The Texas Supreme Court is the highest state appellate court in civil matters, and the Court of Criminal Appeals is the highest state appellate court in criminal matters. Only Oklahoma has a similar system.

Although most criminal cases decided by the fourteen courts of appeals go no further, some are heard by the Court of Criminal Appeals, which consists of a presiding judge and eight other judges. In 2005, Criminal Appeals Court judges wrote 474 opinions, of which 365 (77 percent) were "determinative opinions" that disposed of cases, and the remainder were dissents, concurrences, or opinions on rehearings.[30]

Criminal Appeals Court judges are elected statewide in partisan elections for six-year overlapping terms. They must be at least thirty-five years old and be lawyers or judges with ten years' experience. The presiding judge of the Court of Criminal Appeals receives a salary of $115,000; the other judges receive $113,000.

Reversing Criminal Verdicts.   Historically, the Texas Court of Criminal Appeals has generated a large measure of public controversy due to its alleged "coddling" of criminals. Between 1900 and 1927, the court reversed 42 percent of all the cases it reviewed. As early as 1910, the court was cited by the American Institute of Criminal Law as being "one of the foremost worshippers, among the American appellate courts, of the technicality." In the 1940s, largely in response to both professional and public criticism, the reversal rate began to drop, and by 1966 it was only 3 percent.[31]

The nature of its work makes the Court of Criminal Appeals a highly visible court, even if its individual members are not so visible. When the court reverses

---

[30]Texas Judiciary Online, "Court of Criminal Appeals Activity: FY 2005," Texas Judicial Council, April 4, 2006, at **www.courts.state.tx.us/oca/PublicInfo/AR2005/cca/2_CCA_Activity_2005.pdf**.

[31]Paul Burka, "Trial by Technicality," *Texas Monthly*, April 1982, p. 131.

A man hugs his daughters in 2003 after his release at the Swisher County courthouse in Tulia, Texas. He was one of forty-six Tulia residents—15 percent of the town's African American population—who were arrested in 1999 during a drug "sting." That operation was conducted by a lone police officer, Tom Coleman. No drugs, money, or weapons were seized in any of the cases. Still, all defendants were convicted and sentenced to prison terms running from 20 to 434 years. Coleman's uncorroborated testimony was later discredited, Governor Rick Perry pardoned the wrongly convicted, and Swisher County paid $5 million in damages to forty-five of the defendants. In 2005, Coleman was convicted of perjury and sentenced to ten years' probation and a $7,500 fine. (AP Photo/LM Otero)

convictions based on inadmissible arguments by prosecutors or the introduction of unacceptable or tainted evidence, protests are sure to follow from prosecutors, newspaper editorial writers, and civic club luncheon speakers. Remarks concerning legal technicalities are frequent when a conviction is overturned, even though the real reason for the reversal might be the "overkill" of a zealous prosecutor or other inappropriate behavior by the state. Ordinarily, a reversal means only that the case will be retried.

The Court of Criminal Appeals and the Texas Bill of Rights. The Court of Criminal Appeals has been involved in another controversy. Previously criticized for its "nit-picking" opinions, the court has recently been accused of unfounded interpretations of the Texas Bill of Rights. For example, in a 1991 decision, *William Randolph Heitman v. State*, the court ruled that the Texas Constitution provides criminal defendants more protection against illegal searches and seizures than the U.S. Constitution does.[32] Critics argue that the court should guarantee the accused no broader rights than those protected by the U.S. Constitution. Those supporting the court's decisions point out that the bill of rights in the Texas Constitution is not identical to the Bill of Rights in the U.S. Constitution and therefore lends itself to different interpretations.

The Death Penalty. The Court of Criminal Appeals has exclusive jurisdiction over automatic appeals in death penalty cases. In 2005, the court received twenty-four death penalty appeals.[33] Since the United States Supreme Court restored the use of capital punishment in 1976, Texas has executed far more individuals than any other state. By 2005, the state had executed more than three hundred convicted murderers (more than three times as many as the state with the second-highest total). For a number of years, the rate of executions averaged approximately twenty-five to thirty per year (including a record of forty in 2000).[34] This rate has recently been dropping, however (nineteen individuals were executed in 2005).[35] Death penalty cases have led to a number of headline stories, including controversies over executing a woman (Karla Faye Tucker), a sixty-six-year-old man, persons who were juveniles when they committed the crimes for which they were sentenced to death, individuals who were mentally retarded or mentally ill, those who had received poor legal counsel (including a sleeping attorney), and persons who might actually have been innocent of the crimes.[36]

The State Supreme Court

The Texas Supreme Court is the final court of appeals in civil and juvenile cases. The court has original jurisdiction over issuing writs and conducting proceedings for involuntary retirement or removal of judges. In its other cases, the court has appellate jurisdiction. The court also has the power to make rules for the administration of justice—rules of civil practice and procedure for courts having civil jurisdiction. In addition, it makes rules governing licensing of members of the state bar.

---

[32] 815 S.W.2d 681 (1991).

[33] Texas Judiciary Online, "Court of Criminal Appeals Activity."

[34] "Retarded Man's Impending Execution Prompts Scrutiny of Death-Penalty Laws," *Dallas Morning News*, February 15, 2000; "Who Really Deserves to Die," *Fort Worth Star-Telegram*, January 14, 2001.

[35] "Man Executed for 4 Slayings," *Dallas Morning News*, January 26, 2006.

[36] "Karla Faye Tucker Executed," *Dallas Morning News*, February 4, 1998; "Questions of Competence Arise in Death Row Appeal," *Dallas Morning News*, September 11, 2000; "Man Denied New Trial Despite Sleeping Lawyer," *Fort Worth Star-Telegram*, October 28, 2000; "Death-Penalty Trials Rife with Errors, Study Finds," *Dallas Morning News*, June 12, 2000; "Man Executed for 1988 Revenge Killing," *Fort Worth Star-Telegram*, November 21, 2002; "Death Penalty Debate Reopens," *Fort Worth Star-Telegram*, November 8, 2002; "At Last Name Is Cleared," *Dallas Morning News*, October 6, 2004; "Supreme Court, 5–4, Forbids Execution in Juvenile Crime," *The New York Times*, March 2, 2005, p. A1.

The Texas Supreme Court consists of one chief justice and eight associate justices. All are elected statewide after being nominated in party primaries. Three of the nine justices are elected every two years for six-year terms. The Texas Constitution specifies that a justice must be at least thirty-five years of age and a citizen of the United States and of Texas and must have been a lawyer or judge of a court of record for at least ten years. The salary of the chief justice is $115,000, and the salary of associate justices is $113,000.

The Supreme Court's Workload. During 2005, the court acted on 3,676 matters.[37] The justices wrote 136 opinions, of which 108 (79.4 percent) were deciding opinions that disposed of cases.[38] The court also reversed (at least in part) approximately 72.4 percent of the 105 cases that came to it from the fourteen courts of appeals on petitions for review (formerly "applications for writs of error").[39]

The Role of the Texas Supreme Court. The Texas Supreme Court spends much of its time deciding which petitions for review will be granted, because not all appeals are heard. Generally, it only takes the cases it views as presenting the most significant legal issues. It should also be noted that the Texas Supreme Court plays a policymaking role in the state. As discussed in Chapter 20, for example, in 1989 the court unanimously decided the *Edgewood v. Kirby* case.[40] In this decision, the court ordered major changes in how public schools were financed in Texas. It found unacceptable the huge disparities between rich and poor school districts in the state.

Selection of Judges

Officially, Texas elects its judges (except municipal court judges) in partisan elections. This statement oversimplifies the process, however, and can be somewhat misleading.

Former chief justice Robert W. Calvert referred many times to the system as an "appointive-elective" one. Approximately 45 percent of the trial judges (those who serve in district courts, criminal district courts, county courts-at-law, and probate courts) first assume office through appointment to fill vacancies created when judges leave office before their terms expire.[41] Likewise, about 40 percent of the judges of the appellate courts first assume office through appointment. These appointments between elections are made by the governor with the advice and consent of the senate. In the elections for judicial offices, approximately 80 percent of all Texas judges are reelected unopposed. Furthermore, open competition for judicial posts between nonincumbents is uncommon.

The system of judicial selection in Texas, and practices related to it, have been under attack. Some critics have alleged that Texas has the "best justice that money can buy." In fact, the court system has received negative national exposure on the TV program *60 Minutes*. In the following sections, we explain the reasons for the criticisms and outline the essentially political nature of the system.

An Uninformed Electorate

Because Texas elects judges, a natural question arises: How knowledgeable are voters in these judicial elections? In other words, do voters know who the candidates

[37]Texas Judiciary Online, "Supreme Court Activity," Texas Judicial Council, April 4, 2006, at **www.courts.state.tx.us/oca/PublicInfo/AR2005/sc/2_SC_Activity_2005.pdf**.

[38]*Ibid.*

[39]*Ibid.*

[40]777 S.W.2d 391 (Tex. 1989).

[41]"Profile of Appellate and Trial Judges." *Texas Judicial System Annual Report, 2002* (Austin: Office of Court Administration), p. 54.

are and what their records in office look like? Research on the United States Supreme Court has repeatedly shown that the vast majority of the public knows little about its rulings and actions.[42] If most Americans know very little about the United States Supreme Court, the court that receives the most media attention in this country, how much can we expect voters to know about state and local courts?

A voter in Texas could be asked to vote for candidates running for the Texas Supreme Court, the Court of Criminal Appeals, a court of appeals, a district court, and a county court, as well as justice of the peace. Not surprisingly, polls and research indicate that most voters enter the voting booth with scant knowledge of the candidates running for various judicial posts.[43] For example, a poll taken in Texas after a presidential general election found that only 14.5 percent of voters could recall the name of one of the candidates for either the Texas Supreme Court or the Court of Criminal Appeals.

In addition to systematic research, anecdotal evidence also indicates that most voters in Texas are unaware of candidates' qualifications or experience. Thus, name recognition of any sort can lead people to cast their votes for a candidate. Consequently, candidates with names the same as or similar to those of movie stars, historical figures, or public personages are often candidates for judicial positions.

In 1976, for example (as discussed earlier in this text), Don Yarbrough, an unknown attorney, was elected to the Texas Supreme Court. It is believed that many voters confused him with former senator Ralph Yarborough or with Don Yarborough, who had run for governor. Soon after winning a seat on the court,

---

[42]For example, see John Kessel, "Public Perceptions of the Supreme Court," *Midwest Journal of Political Science* 10 (1966): 167–191; Kenneth Dolbeare, "The Public Views the Supreme Court," in Herbert Jacob, ed., *Law, Politics, and the Federal Courts* (Boston: Little, Brown, 1967); Gregory Casey, "Popular Perceptions of Supreme Court Rulings," *American Politics Quarterly* 4 (1976): 3–45; *Gallup Report* 264 (1987): 29–30; Thomas Marshall, *Public Opinion and the Supreme Court* (New York: Longman, 1989); and Lee Epstein *et al., The Supreme Court Compendium* (Washington, D.C.: CQ Press, 2003).

[43]For example, see Philip Dubois, *From Ballot to Bench: Judicial Elections and the Quest for Accountability* (Austin: University of Texas Press, 1980); and Anthony Champagne and Gregory Thielemann, "Awareness of Trial Court Judges," *Judicature* 74 (1991): 271–276.

Yarbrough resigned because criminal charges had been filed against him. He was later convicted of perjury and, after fleeing the country, was eventually apprehended and imprisoned in Texas.

Party Identification

Because voters know so little about individual candidates, they may use party identification as a cue to determine how to vote. In other words, if a voter has no knowledge of the views or backgrounds of the candidates on the ballot, he or she may make a choice based on the candidates' political party affiliation. In Texas, this appears to be a common way for voters to make selections in judicial elections.

The Rise of the Republicans.   Historically, Texas was part of the "Solid South," and as in other southern states, the Democratic Party monopolized politics. This monopoly was reflected in the judicial posts throughout the state. When Texas became a competitive two-party state in the 1980s, many Republicans were elected judges. One researcher noted, "In one decade the Republican party moved from a position of being locked out of power in the court house to controlling 36 of 37 district seats" in the city of Dallas.[44] This dramatic change included both the Texas Supreme Court and the Court of Criminal Appeals. Indeed, at the end of 2004, both high courts were entirely Republican (in fact, only two Democrats ran for the six seats voted on in 2004). This trend has led to a considerable degree of party switching to the Republican Party by incumbent judges.[45]

The Effects of Partisan Voting.   It has been argued that because judges, especially at the appellate level, make significant policy decisions, it is reasonable for voters to select judges on the basis of political party affiliation.[46] Party affiliation may provide accurate information concerning the general ideology and, thus, the decision-making patterns of judges. Even if this is true, voting based solely on a candidate's political party can lead to controversial results. Some critics point to the 1994 election of Steve Mansfield to the Texas Court of Criminal Appeals as evidence of what can happen when voters do not educate themselves about a candidate's qualifications or background. During the campaign, it was revealed that Mansfield had very limited legal experience and that he had lied in his campaign literature about his experience and his personal and political background. He won nonetheless, apparently because many voters supported every Republican on the ballot (that is, they voted a *straight ticket*).

Judicial Campaign Spending

Because voters often look for simple voting cues (such as name familiarity or party identification), candidates often want to spend as much as possible to make their names or candidacy well known. In recent years, spending in judicial races has risen dramatically. Candidates need to win two elections: their party's nomination and the general election. This can be an expensive endeavor. In the 1988 races for six open seats on the Texas Supreme Court, the candidates spent over $10 million.[47] In the 1996 races for the same seats, three of four incumbent Republican candidates raised about $1 million each (the fourth incumbent received about $700,000, although he was running unopposed).[48]

---

[44]Champagne and Thielemann, "Awareness of Trial Court Judges."

[45]Anthony Champagne, "The Selection and Retention of Judges in Texas," *Southwestern Law Journal* 40 (May 1986): 79–80.

[46]Dubois, *Judicial Elections.*

[47]Anthony Champagne, "Campaign Contributions in Texas Supreme Court Races," *Crime, Law, and Social Change* 17 (1992): 91–106; Kyle Cheek and Anthony Champagne, "Money in Texas Supreme Court Elections: 1980–1998," *Judicature* 84 (2000): 20–25.

[48]"Republican Judges Lead Money Race," *Dallas Morning News*, October 27, 1996, p. A45.

None of the three Democrats in the race raised even $100,000. For example, Chief Justice Tom Phillips received over $1.1 million, while his challenger raised a little over $15,000.[49] Not surprisingly, all four Republicans were reelected. In the three races in 1998 in which the Republicans most outspent their rivals, the funding ratio was fifteen to one (nearly $2.9 million collected compared with $190,000 for the Democrats).[50] In 2002, the results were similar. The Republicans won or held on to all five seats that were up for election and outspent Democrats approximately three to one (even with Chief Justice Phillips accepting no new campaign contributions).[51]

An Appearance of Impropriety. Campaign finances have raised questions concerning fairness and the advantages of incumbency. In addition, many (including 60 *Minutes*) have asked whether justice is for sale in Texas. More precisely, individuals and organizations often appear before judges after having contributed to their election campaigns. Do such contributions affect a judge's impartiality in deciding a case? If nothing else, such a system gives the appearance of possible impropriety or bias.

A notable example was the *Pennzoil v. Texaco*[52] case. This lawsuit involved billions of dollars, and it was decided by justices on the Texas Supreme Court, who had received hundreds of thousands of dollars in campaign contributions from the opposing attorneys and their respective law firms. Research has indicated that 40 percent of campaign contributions to Texas Supreme Court justices came from those with cases before the court.[53] Recently, a public advocacy group sued Texas over this system, claiming it violates due process and the right to a fair trial.[54] The group cited surveys indicating that 83 percent of the Texas public, 79 percent of Texas lawyers, and 48 percent of Texas judges believe that campaign contributions significantly affect judicial decisions.[55]

Consumer Lawsuits. Another example of possible impropriety involves the battle between plaintiffs' attorneys and defense attorneys in civil cases. Texas has traditionally been a conservative, pro-business state. This perspective has usually been reflected in the decisions of the judiciary, which have often favored big business and professional groups (such as the medical profession).

Plaintiffs' lawyers and their related interest group, the Texas Trial Lawyers Association, have made a concerted effort in the past few decades to make the judiciary more open to consumer suits. Such suits are often filed against businesses, physicians, and their insurance companies. The plaintiffs' lawyers have poured millions of dollars into the political funds of candidates they believed would be more favorable to their perspective. Defense and business attorneys have responded with millions of dollars of their own contributions. Plaintiff and defense lawyers alike then often appear before the very judges to whom they have given these large sums.

Minority Representation

A final major criticism of the current partisan elective system involves questions about diversity and minority representation. In 1988, African American and Hispanic groups challenged in federal court the way judges were elected in urban areas of Texas, citing the Voting Rights Act of 1965, as amended. They argued that the at-large (countywide) election of district and county court judges in Bexar, Dallas, Ector, Harris, Jefferson, Lubbock, Midland, Tarrant, and Travis counties

---

[49]*Ibid.*

[50]"Justice Spector Hopes to Win Tough Race against Well-Financed Republican O'Neill," *Dallas Morning News*, October 18, 1998, p. A47.

[51]"Report: Justice Candidates Raise about $3 Million," *Fort Worth Star-Telegram*, August 28, 2002.

[52]748 S.W.2d 631 (Tex. App. 1988).

[53]"Lawyers Give Most to High Court Hopefuls," *Dallas Morning News*, February 28, 1998, p. A26.

[54]"State Sued over Judicial Elections," *Fort Worth Star-Telegram*, April 4, 2000.

[55]*Ibid.*

made the election of minority candidates difficult because it diluted minority voting strength. Attorney General Dan Morales pointed out that African Americans and Hispanics made up 40 percent of Texas's population but held only 5 percent of state district judgeships. In August 1993, the full federal Court of Appeals for the Fifth Circuit upheld the current system. In January 1994, the United States Supreme Court rejected an appeal of the decision without comment.

In recent decades, however, minority judicial candidates have won several high-profile victories. For example, in 1984 Raul A. Gonzalez became the first Hispanic to serve on the Texas Supreme Court. In 1990, Morris Overstreet became the first African American to serve on the Texas Court of Criminal Appeals. In 2001, Governor Perry filled two vacancies on the Texas Supreme Court with minorities—and one of these individuals, Wallace Jefferson, was appointed chief justice in 2004.[56] Still, the changes have been modest. In 2002, only 10.6 percent of 396 district court judges were Hispanic, and only 3.1 percent were African American.[57]

---

[56]"First Black Named to Texas High Court," *Fort Worth Star-Telegram*, March 15, 2001.
[57]League of Women Voters, "The Texas Judicial System," December 2003, at **www.lwvtexas.org/PDF Files/ IS_ JudSysE.pdf**.

MAKING A DIFFERENCE | Dealing Intelligently with Law Enforcement Officers in Texas

Many students may become involved in the criminal justice process as victims, witnesses, or perpetrators. (Legally, traffic offenses are crimes.) As a victim or witness of crime, you must decide whether to report it.

A large number of criminals get away with their crimes because many citizens (especially in minority communities) fear dealing with law enforcement. Others fear that crime reports will increase their insurance rates. Some fail to report crimes because the perpetrator is a friend or relative. Still others fear the perpetrator's vengeance. Some (especially rape victims) are embarrassed by the fact they have become victims. Failure to report crime, however, creates an environment that supports it. The individual must personally evaluate the costs and benefits of filing a report.

Why Should You Care?

Sooner or later, many of us will be arrested—if only through a traffic stop. Do not take such an arrest lightly. In some instances, your life, liberty,

property, and reputation may be at stake. Even a traffic ticket can affect your insurability, and accumulating several tickets may now result in a $1,000 annual state fee to keep your driver's license.

What Can You Do?

Let's consider how you might deal with traffic violations. The best advice is to avoid them. Law enforcement officers do not often ticket drivers traveling less than ten miles per hour above the posted speed limit except in school zones—there, twenty miles per hour means exactly that, and absolutely no more! Regardless of posted speed limits, Texas law provides that you must travel at safe and reasonable speeds, and this provision is usually taken to mean that about one-sixth of the traffic will pass you.

Since 1998, it has been illegal to possess open alcoholic beverages in a car in Texas. Therefore, keep any opened alcoholic beverage containers in the trunk of the car or, if the vehicle has no trunk, behind the last seat.

If you are arrested for a traffic or

any other violation, be respectful and obey the officer or officers. Sometimes a polite, reasoned explanation can prevent the ordeal of a traffic ticket. Do not confess guilt or argue your innocence—these matters will be settled in court later.

If you believe a police order is unlawful, you should comply nonetheless. You may, however, politely state that you believe the order is unlawful and that you are complying against your will. Without probable cause, it is not legal for an officer to demand that you open any locked compartment.

If you ultimately are given a ticket, take advantage of the opportunity to take a safe-driving course to absolve your responsibility. Other alternatives include hiring a lawyer to have the ticket dismissed or obtaining a plea bargain with the prosecutor or judge to plead guilty to the crime of "failure to appear" in exchange for having the ticket dismissed. Deferred adjudications are also a real possibility.

Good drivers may get help finding lower insurance rates through the Texas Department of Insurance.

Key Terms

acquitted 801

adversary system 800

appellate jurisdiction 807

arraignment 797

burden of proof 790

change of venue 799

civil law 790

county courts-at-law 806

criminal law 790

deferred adjudication 799

docket 790

due process 797

examining trial 797

FBI index crimes 794

felony 792

grand jury 798

misdemeanor 792

mistrial 801

original jurisdiction 804

parole 796

personal recognizance 798

plea bargaining 799

probation 801

punitive damages award 791

tort reform 791

victimless crime 796

writ of *habeas corpus* 797

writ of information 799

Chapter Summary

1 Within the American legal system, cases are classified as either civil or criminal. Civil cases primarily involve the rights of private parties or organizations (for example, *Smith v. Jones*). Resolution is based on the concept of responsibility rather than guilt. Tort actions are common in civil law—a tort is a wrong suffered by a party. Disputes are usually set out in a petition, and the side with the preponderance of the evidence wins the suit. The Texas legislature, in an effort to lighten overcrowded court dockets and limit allegedly unnecessary suits, has undertaken tort reform. It has, for example, passed bills that restrict lawsuits by prison inmates, reduce frivolous lawsuits, and cap punitive damages awards.

2 Criminal cases deal with public concepts of proper behavior and morality as defined by law. Punishment for a conviction ranges from a fine to imprisonment to a combination of both. Initiated by a government prosecutor on behalf of the public, a criminal case is brought by the state against the accused (for example, *State of Texas v. Smith*). Specific charges of wrongdoing are spelled out in a grand jury indictment or a writ of information. In addition, in criminal cases the prosecutor must prove that the defendant is guilty beyond a reasonable doubt, a much higher standard than in civil cases.

3 The court procedures that constitute due process aim to promote justice and protect individuals from the govern-

ment. These procedures are generally either written into state and national constitutions and statutes or included in written and unwritten traditional codes of court process. Court procedures have been greatly influenced by tradition. Unfortunately, the goal of due process is often an ideal rather than a reality. It is largely through due process, though, that the courts aim to blend two conflicting goals of society: (1) to protect society according to the state's legal concepts of right and wrong and (2) to protect the rights of the individual charged with wrongdoing.

4 The Texas court system is a large and complicated structure. There are many municipal courts, fewer county-level courts, still fewer district courts and courts of appeals, and only one Texas Supreme Court and one Court of Criminal Appeals. With jurisdictions frequently overlapping, the organization of courts in Texas is often confusing.

5 The system of judicial selection in Texas has been described as appointive-elective. The system has come under attack due to its political nature. For example, voters are often ignorant of the candidates and their records in office, qualifications, and experience. Many vote along party lines. Finally, individuals or organizations often appear before judges after contributing large amounts to their election campaigns, thereby fueling perceptions of apparent or real conflicts of interest.

Selected Print and Media Resources

SUGGESTED READINGS

Abraham, Henry. *The Judicial Process*, 7th ed. New York: Oxford University Press, 1998. This work is a comparative review of courts and court systems throughout the world.

Abramson, Jeffrey. *We, the Jury.* New York: Basic Books, 1994. Abramson reviews various issues surrounding the jury system and its connection to democracy.

Baum, Lawrence. *American Courts: Process and Policy*, 5th ed. Boston: Houghton Mifflin, 2001. This volume is a broad review of lawyers, judges, and U.S. courts.

Cannon, Mark, and David O'Brien, eds. *Views from the Bench.* Chatham, N.J.: Chatham House Publishers, 1985. This edited collection of jurisprudential policy statements covers many aspects of constitutional law and the judicial process.

Dubois, Philip. *From Ballot to Bench: Judicial Elections and the Quest for Accountability*. Austin: University of Texas Press, 1980. Dubois discusses the concepts of competition and accountability in judicial elections.

Epstein, Lee, ed. *Contemplating Courts*. Washington, D.C.: CQ Press, 1995. This edited collection of essays in political science deals with the law, the courts, and the judicial process.

Marquart, James W., Sheldon Ekland-Olson, and Jonathan R. Sorensen. *The Rope, the Chair, and the Needle: Capital Punishment in Texas, 1923–1990*. Austin: University of Texas Press, 1994. James W. Marquart, now director of the Crime Victims Institute at Sam Houston State University, and his co-authors explore the history of the death penalty in Texas and discuss some of the most interesting issues surrounding it.

Marshall, Thomas. *Public Opinion and the Supreme Court*. New York: Longman, 1989. This book focuses on the relationship between public opinion and the United States Supreme Court by comparing polling results with decisions by the Court.

Segal, Jeffrey, and Harold Spaeth. *The Supreme Court and the Attitudinal Model*. New York: Cambridge University Press, 1993. This research attempts to show how the behavior and decision making of justices are affected by their personal policy preferences and attitudes.

MEDIA RESOURCES

Dead Man Walking—A movie starring Susan Sarandon and Sean Penn that examines both sides of the death penalty issue.

The Executed—A PBS *Frontline* case study of an execution in Texas.

The Exonerated—A play by Jessica Blank and Erik Jenson that brings together characters whose lives were affected by wrongful death sentences, including some that occurred in Texas. It is based on real-life interviews.

Justice for Sale—A provocative film that critically examines the election of judges in three states, including Texas. It is available from the Center for Investigative Reporting and the WGBH Education Foundation.

Not Guilty by Reason of Insanity—An A&E production that questions why the mentally ill find their way into the criminal justice system and whether it is difficult to get out of it.

The Plea—A video produced by PBS *Frontline* that focuses on the judicial process and trial by jury.

To Kill a Mockingbird—A 1962 film, based on Harper Lee's Pulitzer Prize–winning novel, that combines a coming-of-age story with a racially charged rape trial in 1930s Alabama.

Twelve Angry Men—A classic 1957 movie starring Henry Fonda. Almost the entire film takes place in a jury room. In the film, we witness how twelve strangers come together to make a decision concerning the life of a young man, and we see the interplay of the law and personal biases during the jury's high-pressure decision making.

E·MOCRACY   Filing Court Documents Online

The Internet has brought about changes in court procedures and practices, including new methods for filing pleadings and other documents and for issuing decisions and opinions. Older methods that involved filing paper pleadings impose significant burdens on the courts' personnel and facilities. Legal firms and their clients also incur costs for the delivery and processing of these documents. The filing, tracking, and processing of paper pleadings create inefficiency and higher costs throughout the system.

Texas Online, a project of the Texas state government, has developed "eFiling" to address these issues. The Texas Online Authority approved electronic filing in July 2002, and the service was developed with the Judicial Committee on Information Technology, the Office of Court Administration, and the Office of the Attorney General. Texas is the first state to implement a statewide system based on a common "electronic post office" for all courts.

Logging On

Texas Online is located at

www.texasonline.state.tx.us

You can access the courts of the state of Texas online at the Texas Judicial Server, located at

www.courts.state.tx.us

The fourteen courts of appeal can be accessed from this site. Click on the number of the appellate court you want to visit.

The Court of Criminal Appeals is at

www.cca.courts.state.tx.us

The Texas Supreme Court is at

www.supreme.courts.state.tx.us

Find out who the municipal court judges are in your community. These are

the judges who hear cases concerning traffic tickets and violations of municipal ordinances. Go to

www.courts.state.tx.us

Choose "Judicial Directory" from the Resource Materials link. From there, select "Municipal Courts" and choose your county. A list of names of all the municipal judges in your county will appear.

The Texas Civil Justice League supports tort reform to limit civil court awards. Go to

www.tcjl.com

Note the types of interests represented on this organization's board. On the other side of the issue are plaintiffs' attorneys, represented by the Texas Trial Lawyers Association at

www.ttla.com

You can renew your driver's license or identify registered sex offenders in your neighborhood through online services provided by the Texas Department of Public Safety (DPS) at

www.txdps.state.tx.us

The DPS site also provides the latest state crime statistics at

www.txdps.state.tx.us

You can compare these figures with the national index crime figures in the Uniform Crime Reports provided by the FBI at

www.fbi.gov/ucr/ucr.htm

The state attorney general's office has a Criminal Victims Services Division. Go to

www.oag.state.tx.us

and click on "Crime Victims Compensation Program."

Younger teens can participate in teen courts and be judged by their peers. For local organizations, go to

www.texasteencourt.com/ memberlist.aspx

One of the recent controversies affecting the Texas criminal justice system has been its large number of executions. Contrast the arguments against the death penalty offered by the Texas Coalition to Abolish the Death Penalty at

www.tcadp.org

with the arguments of death penalty supporters at

www.prodeathpenalty.com

Review case profiles and the role DNA testing plays in the exoneration of persons sentenced to death at

http://www.innocenceproject.org

Extensive data on executed inmates are available at

www.deathpenaltyinfo.org

Online Review

At **www.politicalscience.wadsworth.com/ schmidt12**, you will find a free Study Guide to this book. For each chapter, there are two online quizzes to help you master the material.

• The PoliPrep Self-Study Assessment provides a pretest for each major section of the chapter. PoliPrep then generates a customized study plan. After you complete the study plan, a posttest evaluates your progress.

• The Tutorial Quiz for each chapter provides questions on the chapter contents, including the features. The questions are organized to match the major sections of the chapter.

26 Texas Public Policy

CHAPTER CONTENTS

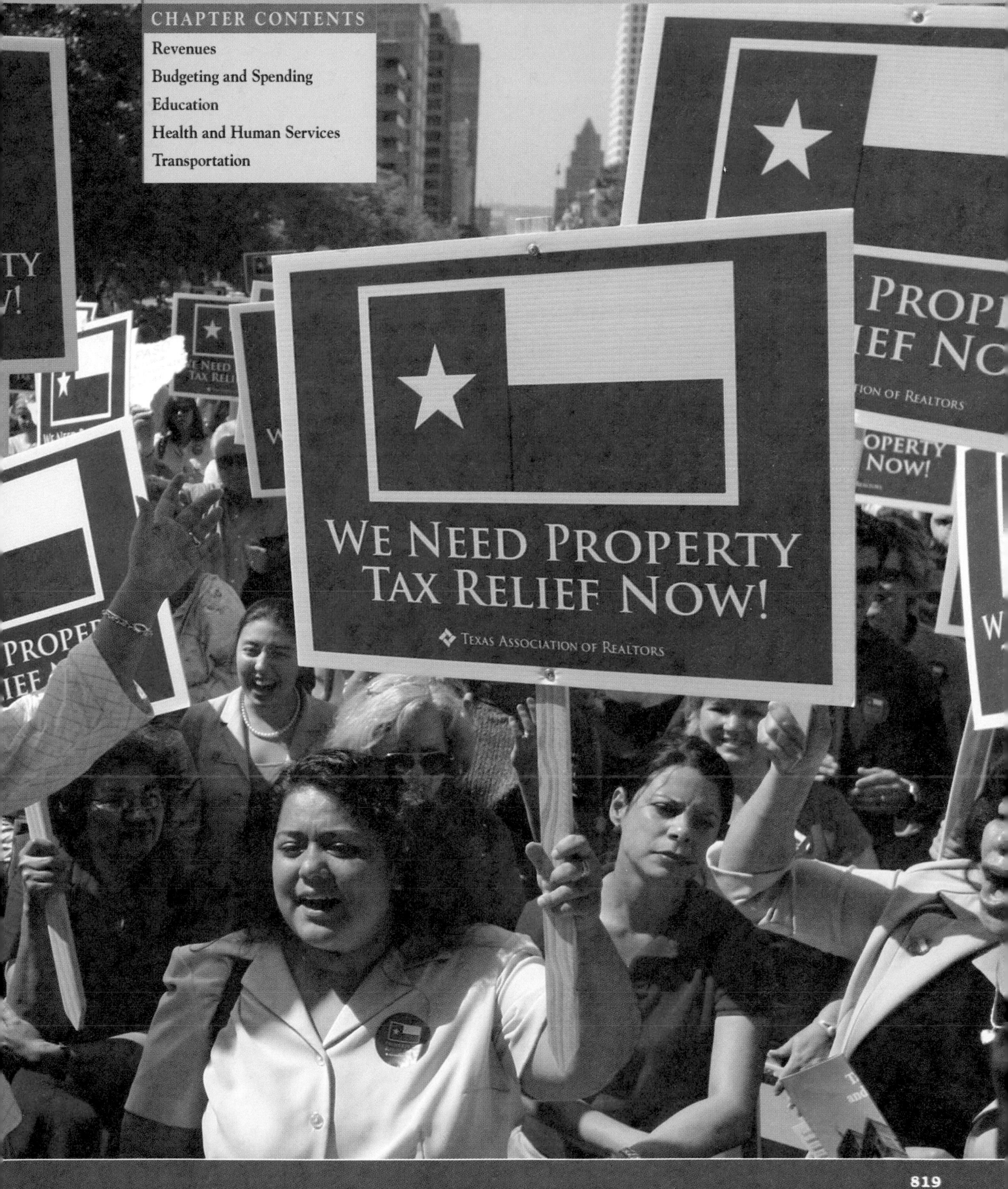

What If . . .
Texas Adopted a School Voucher Plan?

BACKGROUND

Free market economist Milton Friedman proposed that public funds be used to finance vouchers (grants to families) to help pay for private school tuition. Florida, Cleveland, Milwaukee, and Washington D.C., have adopted versions of such plans. Maine and Vermont have voucher plans for rural students, and Utah allows vouchers for special education students. The Texas legislature defeated voucher proposals in several sessions, however.

VOUCHER POLITICS

In 2005, the Texas legislature considered a Republican-sponsored school voucher plan to allow some children to leave underperforming public schools and to transfer to private schools (mostly schools sponsored by religious groups, such as Catholic parochial schools). State funding would have followed the children to whatever schools they attended.

Support was especially strong among religious and economic conservatives, and polls showed considerable public support for vouchers in poorer, central-city minority neighborhoods. Lobbyists for the Texas Catholic bishops launched a campaign to encourage Catholic legislators (many of whom were Democrats) to support vouchers.

Opponents, including many parents of children in better-performing public schools and groups such as the Texas Federation of Teachers and the state's Parent-Teacher Association, fought the voucher proposal. In the end, more than a dozen rural and suburban Republicans voted with Democrats to kill the voucher plan in the Texas House of Representatives.

THE OUTCOMES

If Texas adopts a voucher plan in the future, supporters argue that poorer parents will have the choice to transfer their children out of underperforming public schools, an alternative now available only to wealthier families. They believe that increasing competition between public and private schools would stimulate improvements in both types of schools. "School choice" would allow parents to select schools based on their children's educational needs rather than the neighborhoods in which they live.

Opponents charge that vouchers would damage public schools by draining their financial resources and some of their best students, leaving public schools to educate students with special problems. They argue that public funds should not subsidize special private privileges; therefore, any fair voucher plan must include requirements that private schools adopt open-admissions, open-meetings, and open-records policies.

State funding might invite state controls and threaten the separation of church and state (85 percent of private schools are religious). In addition, the state does not need a voucher system to offer school choice and foster competitiveness within the public school system; a number of programs can provide the same benefits. Local school districts have established magnet schools, for example; charter schools and district home rule are other available options.

Finally, it is not clear whether a school voucher program would have the desired effect. Parents of children using vouchers in other areas generally have been satisfied with the programs, however.

LEGAL ISSUES

Whatever the educational outcome, legal issues would be settled in state court. In 2002, the United States Supreme Court ruled that a Cleveland voucher program does not violate the establishment clause of the U.S. Constitution because the program provides funding to individuals rather than religious organizations. Since those individuals can choose to use the benefits at any private or parochial school, it does not favor religious over nonreligious education.[*]

In Texas, though, the state constitution would remain an issue. In 2006, Florida's state supreme court ruled that the state's voucher program undermined public schools and violated a state constitutional provision requiring a uniform, free public school system. If Texas adopted such a program, it might violate Texas's Constitution, because Article 1, Section 7, prohibits appropriations for the benefit of any sect or religious society.

FOR CRITICAL ANALYSIS

1. What factors should be used to measure success in schools?
2. How would a voucher program affect social development and cultural diversity?

[*]*Zelman v. Simmons-Harris*, 536 U.S. 639 (2002).

At the end of its 2005 session, the Texas legislature passed and sent to the governor the largest budget in the state's history—a total of almost $138.2 billion for fiscal years 2006 and 2007. Texas has the third largest state budget, exceeded only by those of California and New York.

In a sense, though, the size of the most recent Texas budget is not surprising. Each successive budget over the past several years has been larger than the preceding one, resulting in a long succession of record expenditures, as shown in Figure 26–1.

Inflation alone explains some of the rise in government spending, as you can see in the figure. Just as there has been an increase in the cost of what individuals and families buy, there has also been an increase in the cost of what government buys. Nevertheless, inflation has also driven up the salaries and profits with which residents pay their taxes.

Population growth also has played a role in the growth in state spending. Texas's population has grown more rapidly than that of most other states. Each new person must be served, protected, and educated. Of course, the demands of a larger population for increased state services are offset by the fact that more people are also paying taxes to support them. Adjusted for population and inflation, state spending has grown at an average annual rate of 1.5 percent during the past sixteen years.

Revenues

What are the sources of the funds that the state spends? In 2006–2007, the state comptroller's office estimated that almost half of the state's revenues (45.7 percent) would come from various taxes. Federal funding, mostly grants-in-aid, accounted for 35.5 percent, interest and investment income for 3.7 percent, and other sources for the remaining 15.1 percent, as shown in Figure 26–2 on the following page. In addition, the Texas legislature has some limited ability to borrow funds.

FIGURE 26–1 | TRENDS IN TEXAS STATE EXPENDITURES, ALL FUNDS, FISCAL YEARS 1991–2007

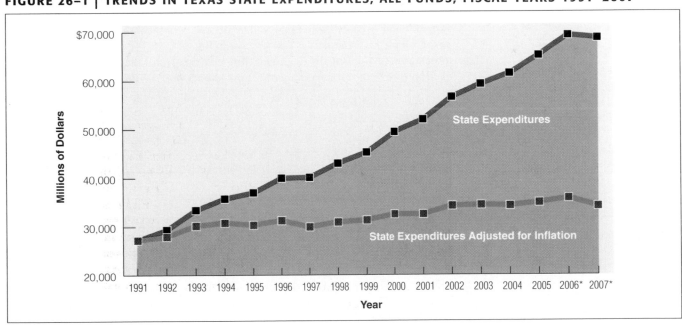

*Estimated.
Source: Legislative Budget Board, *Fiscal Size-Up, 2006–2007* (Austin: Legislative Budget Board, 2005), p. 8.

FIGURE 26-2 | SOURCES OF ESTIMATED STATE REVENUES, 2006-2007 BUDGET PERIOD

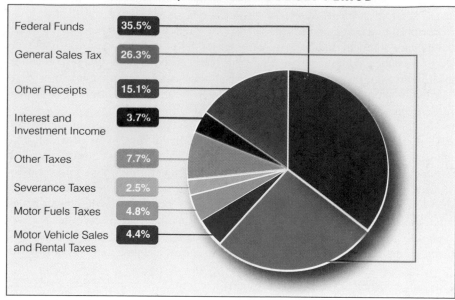

Federal Funds	35.5%
General Sales Tax	26.3%
Other Receipts	15.1%
Interest and Investment Income	3.7%
Other Taxes	7.7%
Severance Taxes	2.5%
Motor Fuels Taxes	4.8%
Motor Vehicle Sales and Rental Taxes	4.4%

Source: Legislative Budget Board, *Fiscal Size-Up, 2006–2007* (Austin: Legislative Budget Board, 2005), p. 21.

Taxation

Property taxes (which are *ad valorem taxes*) were once the major source of state revenue, but property values collapsed during the Great Depression of the 1930s, and with them went the property tax base. At the same time, demands for economic assistance and other public services skyrocketed. Forced to seek other revenue sources, states came to rely on various sales taxes. Texas adopted a tax on cigarettes in 1931, on beer in 1933, and on distilled spirits in 1935. Additional selective sales taxes were adopted in the 1940s and 1950s, but it became apparent that a more general and more broadly based tax would be necessary to meet revenue needs. In 1961, Texas adopted a general sales tax on most items sold. At the same time, Texas, like most states, first drastically reduced its property taxes, and then abandoned them for exclusive use by local governments. Texas has adopted several types of sales taxes:

1. General sales taxes are broadly based taxes collected on the retail price of most items.

2. Selective sales taxes, also known as **excise taxes,** are levied on the sale, manufacture, or use of particular items, such as liquor, cigarettes, and gasoline. Because these taxes are often included in the items' purchase price, they are often **hidden taxes.**

3. Gross-receipts taxes are taxes on the total gross revenue (sales) of certain enterprises, such as utilities and insurance companies.

As shown in Figure 26–2, most state tax revenue in 2006–2007 came from various sales tax collections. The general sales tax (6.25 percent on retail sales of most items) yielded 26.3 percent of the state's revenues; motor fuels taxes, 4.8 percent; and motor vehicle sales and rental taxes, 4.4 percent. Once a major source of state revenue, *severance taxes* (production taxes on oil and natural gas) now account for only 2.5 percent. Texas also collects special taxes on a range of items and activities, such as tobacco, alcohol, registration of motor vehicles, hotel and motel occupancy, insurance company operations, and bingo games.

Most states, like Texas, rely heavily on sales and gross-receipts taxes, but few are as dependent on them as Texas. Texas is one of seven states without a personal

| **General Sales Tax**
A broad-based tax collected on the retail price of most items.

| **Selective Sales Tax, or Excise Tax**
A tax levied on specific items only.

| **Hidden Tax**
A tax that is reflected in higher prices of the goods and services sold.

| **Gross-Receipts Tax**
A tax on the gross revenues of certain enterprises.

income tax; and, excluding the corporate franchise tax, it is one of only four states without a corporate income tax. In fifteen states, income taxes account for the largest share of revenues.

State taxes remain low in Texas compared with those in other states. Whereas the average state collects 6.0 percent of its residents' incomes in taxes, Texas collects 4.5 percent. Only Colorado and New Hampshire collect a smaller percentage than Texas.

The Politics of Taxation

As with all other public policies, elected politicians in response to pressure from various interests design a state's tax policy. (An example of tax politics appears in this chapter's *Politics and Public School Finance* feature on the next page.) Tax policies are hotly debated, and these debates often refer to the "public interest," but in reality, taxes are evaluated according to the way particular taxes affect various groups in society.

In the battle over taxation, one of the most volatile issues is what should be taxed. The decision about *what* to tax is really a decision about *whom* to tax and how heavily to tax them. Thus, many people who have the power to influence the decision makers are likely to attempt to secure preferential tax status for their own group of taxpayers. What seems to motivate almost every group is the principle that the best tax is the one somebody else pays. In the following discussion, we examine what is taxed by the Texas government and how those choices affect various groups.

Broad-Based versus Narrow-Based Taxes. Not all taxes are equally effective in raising funds for the public till. **Tax rates** (the tax per unit on a given item or activity) may be raised or lowered, but simply raising the tax rate may not guarantee increased revenues. That is because tax rates affect the **tax base** (the object taxed). Excessive property taxes discourage construction and repair of buildings, for example. High income taxes can discourage general economic activity and individual initiative, undermining the tax base. High tax rates on a narrow base tend to destroy the base and thus make the tax ineffective as a source of revenue. To raise necessary revenue, then, a tax must not discourage too much of the activity that produces the revenue. Instead, most governments tax a wide variety of items and activities, having found that **broad-based taxes** (those paid by a large number of taxpayers)—such as taxes on property, general sales taxes, and income taxes—are most effective at raising revenue.

Regulatory Taxes. Taxes do more than simply pay for the services of government; they often serve as a tool for social or economic control. Rewarding approved behavior with lower taxation or punishing socially undesirable action with a higher tax can have a definite effect on conduct. Many federal tax loopholes (discussed in Chapter 16) are designed to reward particular economic choices, such as saving and investing. Because higher-income taxpayers have more discretionary income, they are financially better able to spend in ways favored by the federal tax structure. Low- and middle-income taxpayers must spend most of their after-tax income on consumption as they buy the essentials of life.

Most state **regulatory taxes** are designed to control isolated individual choices, especially those with moral overtones, and are sometimes called "sin taxes." The most prominent example of such state regulatory taxation is the "use" tax to discourage the consumption of such items as alcohol and tobacco. Texas has an excise tax (selective sales tax) on alcoholic beverages that ranges from $6.00 per barrel of beer to $2.40 per gallon of distilled liquor. Bars pay 5 cents per drink sold. Taxes on alcohol accounted for 1.0 percent of state revenues in 2006–2007. Cigarettes are taxed at $1.41 per pack (the eleventh highest rate among the fifty states), and other forms of tobacco are also taxed; these taxes constituted 0.8 percent of Texas's total revenue.

Tax Rate
The amount of tax per unit of taxable item or activity.

Tax Base
The object or activity taxed.

Broad-Based Tax
A tax designed to be paid by a large number of taxpayers.

Regulatory Tax
A tax imposed with the intent of exerting social or economic control by reducing taxes on approved behavior or imposing higher taxes on an undesirable activity.

POLITICS AND PUBLIC SCHOOL FINANCE | Players at the 2006 Special Legislative Session

BACKGROUND

By 2002, Texans were paying a larger share of their personal income in property taxes than residents of forty other states.* The Texas legislature added to the school tax burden by reducing the state's share of public school funding, forcing local school districts to raise local property taxes to finance an increasing portion of the cost of public education.

Many local school boards had little discretion in setting local property tax rates or spending their revenues because they were taxing at or near the maximum rate simply to meet state mandates. In effect, state law commanded local districts to tax near the maximum rate and determined how districts spent most of their revenues. In 2005, the Texas Supreme Court ruled that the state's system of public school finance amounted to a statewide property tax in violation of Article VIII, Section 1-e of the state constitution.†

THE PERRY PLAN

Anticipating the court ruling, Republican governor Rick Perry had appointed John Sharp, a Democrat and former state comptroller, to head a bipartisan tax-reform commission to study property tax reform. The Sharp Commission recommended that the state replace part of the local property tax with additional state funds to be financed by an increase in cigarette taxes, an enforcement provision to collect more motor vehicle sales taxes, and a new broad-based business tax to replace the loophole-ridden franchise tax. Governor Perry then called a special session to consider the Sharp Commission's recommendations.

PLAN SUPPORTERS

Under pressure to show leadership during his reelection campaign and facing a court-mandated June 2006 deadline to remedy the school finance system, the governor and his staff assembled an impressive coalition of interest groups and lobbyists. Businesses that paid the franchise tax would benefit from lower rates made possible by expanding business taxes to cover at least 50,000 businesses that had been exempt. Statewide, Texas businesses paid over 40 percent of school property taxes, and many were natural allies in the effort to reduce them.

Other groups endorsing the tax plan included the League of United Latin American Voters (LULAC) and the Texas Trial Lawyers Association, many of whose members would be exempted from the new business tax. The support of the pow-

*U.S. Census Bureau and U.S. Bureau of Economic Analysis data reported in Legislative Budget Board, *Fiscal Size-Up 2006–2007*, p. 43.

†*Neeley v. West Orange-Cove Independent School District,* 176 S.W.3d 746 (Tex. 2005).

erful Texas Medical Association was tentative until it won certain concessions relating to deductions and exemptions from the business tax for its members. Texans Investing in Healthy Living, a coalition including the American Heart Association and American Cancer Society, supported the proposal for higher tobacco taxes.

PLAN CRITICS

Democratic legislators criticized the plan because it was too regressive, giving tax relief to high-income property owners and not enough benefits to renters. They also joined other critics who argued that the plan lacked funds for teacher pay raises, tutoring, dropout prevention, educational enrichment, and equalization between rich and poor districts. Among these critics were various education advocacy groups and their lobbyists.

The state's most conservative Republican groups opposed any new taxes and argued that the state's surplus should be used entirely to finance property tax cuts. Miscellaneous additional groups also opposed the plan, and others sought to change it. Lobbyists for the tobacco industry fought the hike in cigarette taxes. The National Federation of Independent Business and the Texas Automobile Dealers Association feared paying the business tax because it is based on sales rather than profits.

THE RESULT

In the end, the legislature passed bills that increased cigarette taxes to $1.41 per pack and required vehicle buyers to pay the motor vehicle sales tax based on the actual value of the vehicle. The centerpiece of the new state tax plan was a 1 percent gross-receipts tax on corporations and limited partnerships after taking a deduction for either cost of goods or personnel. The tax rate for retailers, wholesalers, and restaurants was set at 0.5 percent. Sole proprietorships, general partnerships, and companies with under $300,000 in annual revenues were exempted.

Revenues from these state taxes are earmarked entirely for public schools and are expected to increase the state share of school operating costs from 38 percent to 50 percent. Most local school districts should be able to reduce their operational property tax rates by one-third when the plan is fully implemented.

FOR CRITICAL ANALYSIS

1. *Should public officials take into account how public policies will affect interest group members? What role do lobbyists play in presenting their groups' views and values to political leaders?*

2. *How does the saga of school finance changes illustrate the political processes of conflict, compromise, and coalition building?*

Texans continue to drink and smoke, so high state use taxes do not entirely prevent "sin," but they place a substantial share of the tax burden on the "sinner." Indeed, the regulatory intent of use taxes may be a rationalization. A large part of the motive behind such taxes may be to place the tax burden on others, since the most vocal advocates of alcohol and tobacco taxes are those who abstain. Proponents, however, argue that regulatory taxes have some effect on behavior; the small annual decline in cigarette sales in Texas may be partially attributed to their cost.

Benefits Received.   On the surface, nothing would seem fairer than taxation according to benefits received—let those who benefit from a public service pay for it. Americans have become accustomed to believing that this principle operates in the private sector of the economy and should be applied in the public sector as well.

An example of a **benefits-received tax** in Texas is a 20-cent-per-gallon tax on gasoline and diesel fuel. Three-fourths of the income from taxes on motor fuels is directed into the Texas highway trust fund. The amount of fuel a person uses, and the associated taxes, should represent the benefits that person obtains from highway building and maintenance.

Although not strictly a tax, tuition paid by students in state colleges and universities is based on the benefits-received principle. Most of the cost of public college education in Texas is paid out of state and local tax revenues, but an increasing share of the cost of higher education is paid by student tuitions on the presumption that a student should pay a larger share of the cost of the service from which he or she so greatly benefits. Likewise, revenues from hunting and fishing permits are used for wildlife management.

The benefits-received principle seems reasonable, but few government services are truly special services provided only for special groups. Although the student is a major beneficiary of state-supported higher education, for example, society also benefits from the skills that are added to the bank of human resources. Even the elderly widow who has never owned a car benefits from highways when she buys fresh tomatoes from the supermarket or goes to the hospital in the event of illness. Most government services, such as highways, schools, and law enforcement, take on the character of a public or collective good whose beneficiaries cannot be accurately determined.

Another reason behind government's providing a public service is to make that service available to all. Few people could afford to attend Texas's public colleges and universities, for example, if they had to pay the full cost of higher education.

Ability to Pay.   Most taxes are rationalized according to some measure of taxpayers' ability to pay them. The most common **ability-to-pay taxes** are levied on property, sales, and income. Property taxes are based on the premise that the more valuable people's property is, the wealthier they are, and hence the greater their ability to pay taxes. Sales taxes are based on the premise that the more a person buys, the greater the individual's purchasing power. Income taxes are based on the assumption that the more a person earns, the greater that person's ability to pay.

No base is completely adequate as a measure of a person's ability to pay. During Europe's feudal era, property reflected a person's wealth. With the coming of the commercial revolution, real wealth came to be measured in terms of cash funds rather than land. Nevertheless, the taxes on real estate remain, while more modern forms of ownership, such as stocks, bonds, and other securities, are seldom taxed.

Taxes based on funds (income or expenditure) are also an inadequate measure of true wealth. Income taxes reflect current taxable income and do not account for wealth accumulated in past years. Furthermore, exemptions allow the taxpayer to avoid taxes legally, even on current income. Taxes on consumption and spending (sales taxes) are an even less equitable measure of the ability to pay. Sales taxes measure wealth only as it is spent. Income saved or invested is not spent and so is not taxed. Since it is a general rule of economic behavior that the wealthier a person is,

| Benefits-Received Tax
A tax assessed according to the services received by the payers.

| Ability-to-Pay Tax
A tax apportioned according to taxpayers' financial capacity.

TABLE 26–1 | FEDERAL INCOME TAX RATES FOR SINGLE INDIVIDUALS, 2006

TAXABLE INCOME	TAX RATE
$0–7,550	10%
7,550–30,650	15
30,650–74,200	25
74,200–154,800	28
154,800–336,550	33
Over $336,550	35

Source: Internal Revenue Service.

the more the person saves or invests, sales taxes weigh disproportionately on the "have-nots" and "have-littles," who must spend the largest portion of their income on the necessities of life.

Tax Rates.   Most people would like to pay as little as possible in taxes, but it turns out that they pay quite a bit (though Texans pay less than most). The average working American works more than one-third of the year (from the first day of January to almost the end of April) to pay taxes to all levels of government—federal, state, and local.

Averages obscure the real effect of taxes on the taxpayer, however. The so-called loopholes in the federal income tax structure have been well publicized, but every tax—federal, state, and local—treats various taxpayers differently. What in the political world is used to justify the unequal burden of taxation?

Progressive Taxes.   *Progressive tax rates*, such as those used in the federal income tax system, increase as the base increases. Individuals at the very bottom of the financial totem pole have no taxable income and pay nothing, but as incomes increase, the rate increases stepwise from 10 percent to 35 percent. The higher rates apply only to *marginal* increments in income, however; for example, a single individual with $340,000 in taxable income pays a rate of 10 percent on the first $7,550, just as lower-income taxpayers do; a rate of 15 percent on taxable income above $7,550 and less than $30,650; and so forth, as shown in Table 26–1.

Liberals and other supporters of progressive taxation argue that persons with higher incomes can better afford to pay higher tax rates and that lower-income persons should be left with a larger share of their incomes to maintain the necessities of life. Lower-income persons also spend a larger share of their incomes on consumption, which is the largest driving force in the economy. Such arguments have not convinced Texans, who adopted a state constitutional amendment that forbids a state income tax unless voters approve. Even then, it can be used only for education and property tax relief.

Regressive Tax Rate
A tax rate that declines as the base increases; for example, sales taxes and consumption taxes. Regressive tax rates place more of a burden on low- and middle-income taxpayers than on wealthier ones.

Regressive Taxes.   Texas is characterized by **regressive tax rates,** which decline as the base increases. For example, the state general sales tax (6.25 percent, among the highest in the nation) is proportional to the value of sales, but because of patterns of consumption, the effective rate actually declines as a person's income increases. Table 26–2 shows that if a family's income increases, so does its general sales tax payment. That fact seems reasonable; we would expect purchases of taxable items to increase as income increases. But note that as income increases, an ever-smaller *percentage* of that income is used for taxable purchases. Presumably, more money is saved, invested, or spent on tax-exempt items. Thus, despite exemptions for certain essential items, the effective rate of the Texas general sales tax declines as family income increases; a working-class individual with an income of $35,000 pays an effective sales tax rate more than twice as high as one earning $190,000 annually. Similarly, the percentage of income paid in property and excise taxes declines as income increases.

Declining Marginal Propensity to Consume
The tendency, as income increases, for persons to devote a smaller proportion of their income to consumer spending and a larger proportion to savings or investments.

There is a simple explanation for the regressive quality in most state and local taxes: the **declining marginal propensity to consume.** As income increases, a person saves and invests more, thus spending a smaller percentage of that income on consumer items. Compare two smokers. One earns $20,000 per year and the other $200,000 per year. Does the smoker who earns $200,000 per year smoke ten times as much as the one who earns $20,000? Of course not! Let us assume that each smoker consumes one package of cigarettes a day; each therefore pays $514.65 a year in Texas tobacco taxes. For the low-income individual, tobacco taxes represent almost seven days' earnings, but the other smoker earned the income to pay tobacco taxes in only five hours and twenty-one minutes.

TABLE 26–2 | TEXAS GENERAL SALES TAX PAID IN DOLLARS AND AS A PERCENTAGE OF TAXABLE INCOME, 2005

TAXABLE INCOME	TEXAS GENERAL SALES TAX	PERCENTAGE OF TAXABLE INCOME
$ 10,000	$ 216	2.16%
25,000	377	1.51
35,000	484	1.38
45,000	540	1.20
55,000	610	1.11
65,000	674	1.04
75,000	738	0.98
85,000	794	0.93
95,000	849	0.89
110,000	923	0.83
130,000	1,025	0.79
150,000	1,115	0.74
170,000	1,206	0.71
190,000	1,289	0.68
1,000,000	1,713	0.17

Source: Internal Revenue Service, *Form 1040*, 2005, p. A-11.

Consumption of most items follows a similar pattern. The mansion represents a smaller share of income for the millionaire than a shack does for a poor person. Proportionately, the Rolls-Royce is less a burden to its owner than the old Chevrolet to its less affluent owner. Obviously, there are exceptions, but in general, appetites do not increase proportionately with income. Consequently, almost any tax on consumption will not reflect ability to pay. Yet all of Texas's state and local taxes are based on some form of consumption—property taxes, general sales taxes, gross-receipts taxes, or selective sales taxes.

Even business taxes may be regressive for individuals because of **tax shifting.** Businesses regard their tax burden as part of their operating cost, and much of that cost is shifted to customers in the form of higher prices. Thus, many business taxes become, in effect, "consumer" taxes—and, like other consumer taxes, regressive relative to income. Local property taxes are also regressive even when individuals rent their dwellings. When property taxes increase, property owners raise rents.

Taking into account all state and local taxes and tax shifting, Texas has the fifth most regressive tax structure among the fifty states. Data from the Texas comptroller's office published in 2005 indicate that those with the lowest fifth of household incomes paid an average of 14.2 percent of their income in total state and local taxes; the highest-income one-fifth of households paid 5.1 percent.

Conservatives and high-income groups who support regressive taxes argue that taxes on higher-income individuals should be kept low to allow them to save and invest to stimulate the economy—this is known as **supply-side economics.** They argue that applying higher rates to higher incomes is unfair and that sales and property taxes are easier to collect, harder to evade or avoid, and generally less burdensome than progressive income taxes.

| Tax Shifting
The practice by which businesses pass taxes to consumers in the form of higher prices.

| Supply-Side Economics
The theory that higher-income taxpayers should be taxed less because their savings and investments stimulate the economy.

Other Revenues

Besides taxes, as indicated earlier, Texas has several other sources of revenue. The federal government represents an important source of funds, and the state legislature can also borrow funds by issuing bonds, although borrowing is severely restricted. The remainder of the state's revenues comes from miscellaneous sources.

Federal Grants-in-Aid. Federal funds are provided for Texas state and local government programs. For the 2006–2007 period, Texas received about $46.7 billion in federal funds, which represents 35 percent of state revenues (see Figure 26–3). A large majority of the funds Texas spends for health and human services and around 40 percent of its expenditures for transportation originate as federal grants. Although there has been movement toward consolidating federal grant-in-aid programs, they are so numerous that it is only possible to generalize in discussing them.

The evolution of federal grants to state and local governments has a long and controversial history. Although some grants from the national government to the states began as early as 1785, the adoption of the income tax in 1913 drastically altered the financial relationship between the national and state governments by making possible extensive aid to state and local governments.

As discussed in Chapter 3, the Great Depression of the 1930s brought with it a series of financial problems more severe than any that state and local governments had previously experienced. Increased demands for state and local services when revenues were rapidly declining stimulated a long series of New Deal grant-in-aid programs, ranging from welfare to public health and unemployment insurance.

As discussed previously in Chapter 19, most of these early grant-in-aid programs were *categorical grants*. Under such aid programs, Congress appropriates funds for a specific purpose and sets up a formula for their distribution. Certain conditions are attached to these grant programs:

1. The receiving government agrees to match the federal funds with its own at a ratio fixed by law (between 10 and 90 percent of the cost of the program).
2. The receiving government administers the program. For example, federal funds are made available for Medicaid, but it is the state that actually pays client benefits.
3. The receiving government must meet minimum standards of federal law. For example, states are forbidden to spend federal funds in any way that promotes racial segregation.

Sometimes additional conditions are attached to categorical grants, such as regional planning and accounting requirements.

Today, most federal aid is in the form of *block grants* (see Chapter 19) specifying general purposes, such as job training or community development, but allowing the state or local government to determine precisely how the funds should be spent. Conditions may also be established for receipt of block grants, but state and local

FIGURE 26–3 | FEDERAL FUNDS AS A SHARE OF ALL TEXAS FUNDS, 2006–2007 BUDGET PERIOD

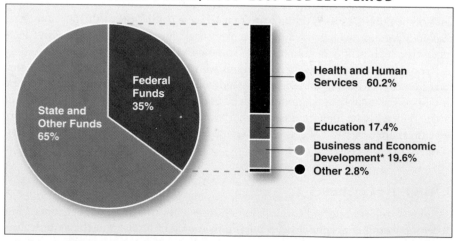

*Primarily highways.
Source: Legislative Budget Board, *Fiscal Size-Up, 2006–2007* (Austin: Legislative Budget Board, 2005), p. 29.

governments have greater administrative flexibility than with categorical grants. In recent years, federal transportation, welfare, and many other grants have been reformed to allow for significant devolution of power to the states through block grants.

Borrowing. Forty state constitutions or statutes require the legislature to pass a balanced budget. The Texas Constitution is more effective at limiting state borrowing than those of most other states. At the beginning of each legislative session, the comptroller of public accounts reports to the legislature the total amount of revenues expected from current taxes and other sources, and the legislature can in turn appropriate no more than this amount unless it enacts new tax laws. A few exceptions exist to this general limit: (1) the legislature, by a nearly impossible four-fifths vote, may borrow in emergencies, and (2) the 1876 constitution may be amended to provide for the issuance of bonds for specific programs. Such restrictions have been very effective; the state's bonded indebtedness is about 27 percent of the per capita debt of the average state.

State bonds are classified as (1) **general-obligation bonds** (to be repaid from general revenues), which have been used to finance prison construction, veterans' real estate programs, water development, and higher education, and (2) **revenue bonds**, to be repaid with the revenues from the service they finance, such as higher education bonds financed by tuition revenue.

Other Sources of Revenue. In addition to taxing, grants-in-aid, and borrowing, several miscellaneous sources provide revenue to the Texas government. The state receives a small share of its income from the lottery; various licenses, fines, and fees; dividends from investments; and the sale and leasing of public lands.

| Devolution
The attempt to enhance the power of state or local governments by substituting more flexible block grants instead of restrictive categorical grants in aid.

| General-Obligation Bond
A bond to be repaid from general taxes and other revenues; such bond issues usually must be approved by voters.

| Revenue Bond
A bond to be repaid with revenues from the project financed, such as utilities or sports stadiums.

Budgeting and Spending

Having discussed the various sources of state revenue, we now turn to the other end of the income stream—budgeting and spending. We begin by describing the budgetary process and then discuss spending policies.

The Budgetary Process

The budgetary process includes two basic steps. First, a budget plan must be formulated. Then the legislature must appropriate the funds necessary to implement the plan.

Budget Planning. Every state has developed some sort of central budgeting agency. Typically, such agencies are set up within the executive branch and are provided with a staff to analyze and evaluate budget requests before submitting a comprehensive budget to the legislature for its consideration. In some states, budget preparation is the joint responsibility of both the legislative and the executive branches.

Texas has established a dual system of budget preparation in which the legislative and executive branches prepare separate budgets. In 1949, Texas took its first serious step toward a budget-planning agency when it established the Legislative Budget Board (LBB), a legislative agency made up of the presiding officers of the Texas House and Senate plus four other members from each of the two houses. In 1951, a second (separate) budgeting agency was formed in the governor's office.

These two budgeting agencies engage in some joint activities. A full year before the legislature meets, they jointly prepare forms on which the state's operating agencies submit their budgetary requests. After these requests are submitted, joint hearings are held, but the LBB's staff and the governor's staff independently prepare budget proposals. Not surprisingly, these two proposed budgets differ considerably,

Incremental Budgeting
A budgeting practice in which an agency bases its budget requests on past appropriations plus increases to cover inflation and increased demand for services; process assumes that past appropriations justify current budgetary requests.

Zero-Based Budgeting
A budgeting practice in which existing programs are evaluated as if they were new programs rather than on the basis of past levels of funding.

Appropriations Process
The process by which a legislative body legally authorizes a government to spend specific sums of money to provide various programs and services.

Dedicated, or Earmarked, Funds
Revenues dedicated for a specific purpose by the constitution or by statute.

as each of the two branches, the legislative and the executive, has its own distinct perspectives, goals, and political considerations.

In preparing their budgetary requests, agencies have a strong tendency toward incremental budgeting—that is, they tend to base their current budget requests on past appropriations plus some additional amount. In the rush of the short 140-day session, the legislature cannot conscientiously evaluate billions of dollars in budget requests, so it reviews ongoing programs in light of past expenditures, whereas new spending programs are viewed more critically. This process inherently assumes that past appropriations reflect current needs. Reformers frequently advocate zero-based budgeting, which would instead evaluate existing programs as if they were new programs for which funding had to be justified.

Appropriations.   It is through the appropriations process that the legislature legally authorizes the state to spend money to provide its various programs and services. Appropriations bills follow the same steps as other legislation (described in Chapter 23), through standing committee consideration, floor action, conference committee compromise, final voting, and approval by the governor. The powerful House Appropriations and Senate Finance committees are the targets of particularly intense lobbying by special interest groups and state administrative agencies. In addition, during most of the legislative process, the recommendations of the LBB carry greater weight than those of the governor because they usually reflect the wishes of the legislature's powerful presiding officers.

Perhaps the governor's most effective influence in the appropriations process results from the item veto. Like forty-two other governors, the Texas chief executive can veto particular items of expenditure without vetoing the whole bill. Although all vetoes can be legally overridden by a two-thirds vote of the legislature, in practice item vetoes on appropriations bills are final. The legislature finishes its work on the appropriations bill so late in the session that it has usually gone home by the time the governor takes up the bill; obviously, such after-session vetoes are immune to an override attempt.

In spite of the importance of the appropriations process, the legislature's control over state expenditures is limited in several ways. Dedicated, or earmarked, funds prevent the legislature from systematically reviewing the state's expenditures. For example, three-fourths of revenues from motor fuel taxes are dedicated to the State Highway Fund and one-fourth to the Available School Fund. Earnings from state lands are automatically directed to the Permanent University Fund and the Permanent School Fund. Contributions to the Teacher Retirement Fund may be used only for their specified purpose. The Texas Constitution and state statutes automatically channel 45 percent of state revenues to specified purposes with little or no legislative involvement. Of course, federal grants, court orders, and other restrictions also limit the legislature as it adopts appropriations bills. Only one-sixth of the state's budget is discretionary funding (unaffected by federal, state, statutory, or court requirements).

Biennial legislative sessions themselves make it difficult to spend state funds rationally. It is impossible to predict with precision, say, how many students will enroll in a college for the upcoming semester. Nevertheless, the legislature is expected to predict the state's financial needs two years in advance based on how many students will enroll in all public colleges in the state as well as elementary and secondary schools, how many applicants will be found eligible for unemployment and welfare benefits, how many potholes will develop along state highways, how many criminals will be sentenced to state prison, how many patients will be admitted to state hospitals, and so on. Inevitably, some agencies will be overfunded, and others will have too little. Overfunded agencies always find ways to spend whatever money they have, while others literally run out of money during the two-year budget period.

The Politics of Spending

A wide variety of factors affects the level of state spending and complicates efforts toward rational budget planning. Nowhere is the dynamic nature of politics as evident as in public finance; nowhere is the conflict between competing economic interests more visible than in the budgetary process. Behind the large figures that represent the state's final budget are vigorous conflict, compromise, and coalition building. Most of society's programs are evaluated not only according to their merit but also in light of the competing demands of other programs and other economic interests. Government programs and problems, including highways, education, urban decay, poverty, crime, and the environment—in short, all the problems and challenges of a modern society—compete for a share of the public treasury.

Powerful political constituencies, interest groups, and their lobbyists join forces with state agencies to defend the programs that benefit them. This alliance between administrative agencies and interest groups brings great pressure to bear on the legislative process. Legislators themselves trade votes (a process called **logrolling**) to gain funding to benefit their districts or their political supporters.

No single decision better typifies the political character of a state than its budget decision. The whole pattern of spending is, in a sense, a shorthand description of which problems the state has decided to face and which challenges it has chosen to meet. The budget shows how much of which services the state will offer and to whom. Figure 26–4 shows how Texans spent their state revenues in the 2006–2007 budget period. The most costly service in Texas remains education. Public and higher education accounted for 39.6 percent of the state budget. Health and human services (including Medicaid and public assistance), in second place, accounted for 35.0 percent. Transportation, primarily highways, accounted for 10.9 percent. These three services consumed more than four-fifths of the state's budget, with a wide variety of miscellaneous services using up the remainder.

Both individuals and groups benefit from government services, and these benefits are the objects of much of the political activity in the state. The way state services affect various groups influences how those groups evaluate state programs. In the remainder of the chapter, we outline the state's most significant services and then explore some of the major political issues surrounding them.

| Logrolling
Trading votes among legislators, especially to fund local projects to benefit their constituents.

FIGURE 26–4 | STATE APPROPRIATIONS BY FUNCTION, 2006–2007 BUDGET PERIOD (IN BILLIONS OF DOLLARS)

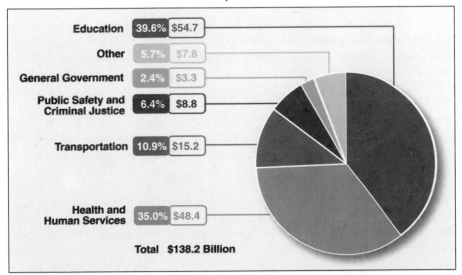

Education 39.6% $54.7
Other 5.7% $7.8
General Government 2.4% $3.3
Public Safety and Criminal Justice 6.4% $8.8
Transportation 10.9% $15.2
Health and Human Services 35.0% $48.4

Total $138.2 Billion

Source: Legislative Budget Board, *Fiscal Size-Up, 2006–2007* (Austin: Legislative Budget Board, 2005), pp. 9, 327.

Education

Public schools were accepted institutions in the North by the early nineteenth century, but they did not take root in the South (including Texas) until after the Civil War. In Texas, the constitution of 1876 provided that land be set aside to finance schools, but meaningful state support for public education started with a compulsory attendance law, enacted in 1915, and a constitutional amendment that provided for free textbooks in 1918. In 1949, the Gilmer-Aikin law increased state funding and established the Texas Education Agency (TEA), which carries out the state's educational program. Since that time, the most sweeping changes in education resulted when House Bill 72 passed in 1984 to establish state test standards for student performance and teacher competence. President George W. Bush later urged use of such "high-stakes" testing nationwide.

More recent educational reforms targeted unconstitutional financial inequities among school districts dependent on property tax and increased local control by allowing school districts flexibility in textbook selection. The state legislature authorized the State Board of Education (SBOE) to establish schools with special program charters. These schools are able to recruit students from across existing school district boundaries. There are now 296 such charter schools, free of most SBE rules and state legal requirements, such as minimum school days, maximum class size, and requirements to hire certified teachers. Some charter schools have used this flexibility to offer successfully creative approaches to education; others have produced results that are not so obviously improved.

Entire school districts may also exempt themselves from most state regulations by adopting a home-rule school district charter. Texas is the first state to allow such districts. Adoption of home-rule charters is difficult, however, requiring a majority vote in an election in which at least 25 percent of registered voters participate. Many state legislators now also favor *privatizing* schools by providing vouchers to help students to buy their education from private and religious organizations, as discussed in this chapter's opening *What If . . .* feature.

Elementary and Secondary Schools

Today, public elementary and secondary education has grown from an underfinanced local function into a major state-local partnership. The TEA administers approximately 24 percent of all state expenditures, helping local school districts educate the approximately 90 percent of Texas students who attend public elementary and secondary schools. Public-policy decisions affect the knowledge, attitudes, and earning potential of these 4.3 million students and the approximately 300,000 individuals who teach them.

Public School Administration. As in other states, public school administration in Texas has three basic aspects:

1. Substantial local control in a joint state-local partnership.
2. Emphasis on "professional" administration supervised by laypersons.
3. Independence from the general structure of government.

Next, we consider the relationship of state administration and local administration.

State Administration. The Texas Constitution, the legislature, and the State Board of Education have established the basic decision-making organizations and financial arrangements for public education in the state. The legislature approves the budget for the state's share of the cost of public education and sets certain standards, but it leaves most routine decision making to the TEA and local school districts.

The State Board of Education, which we discussed in Chapter 24, establishes general rules and guidelines for the TEA. The SBOE approves organizational plans, recommends a budget to the governor and the Legislative Budget Board, and implements funding formulas established by the legislature. It sets standards for operating public schools and requires management, cost-accounting, and financial reports from local districts. Moreover, the SBOE recommends a candidate for commissioner of education, who is appointed by the governor with the consent of the senate.

The commissioner serves as the state's principal executive officer for education; she or he is assigned a number of assistant and associate commissioners and has a professional staff. They carry out the regulations and policies established by the legislature and the SBOE concerning public school programs. As professionals, the commissioner and staff have enough experience to make recommendations to the SBOE and to influence substantially its decisions.

Local Administration.   Texas has 1,037 school districts (more than any other state), and these districts are the basic structure for local control. Voters in independent school districts elect seven or nine trustees (depending on the district's population) at large or from single-member electoral districts for either three- or four-year terms. These trustees set the district's tax rate and determine school policies within the guidelines established by the TEA. They approve the budget, contract for instructional supplies and construction, and hire and fire personnel. Their most important decision is the hiring of a professional superintendent, who is responsible for the executive or administrative functions of the school district.

Elected state and local school boards usually follow the recommendations of professional administrators (the commissioner and the superintendents). Most educational decisions are made independently of general government. Nevertheless, we should not conclude that this constitutes independence or that localization or "professionalism" keeps education free of politics. On the contrary, whenever important public decisions are made, political controversy and conflict arise.

The Politics of Public Education.   One of the most important decisions concerning public education is what education should be. Should it promote traditional views of society, reinforce the dominant political culture, and teach "acceptable" attitudes? Alternatively, should it teach students to be independent thinkers, capable of evaluating ideas for themselves? Because the Texas state educational system determines the curriculum, selects textbooks, and hires and fires teachers, it must answer these fundamental questions.

Curriculum.   The TEA determines most of the basic curriculum for Texas public schools. Some school districts supplement this basic curriculum with a variety of elective and specialized courses, but it is in the basic courses—history, civics, biology, and English—that a student is most likely to be exposed to issues that may fundamentally affect attitudes. How should a student be exposed to the theory of evolution? What about a course in sex education? In the social sciences, should the political system be pictured in terms of its ideals or as it actually operates, with all of its mistakes and weaknesses? How should the roles of women and minorities be presented? Should students who do not speak standard English be gradually taught English through bilingual education, or should they immediately be immersed in the core curriculum taught in English? The substance of education in Texas is important in other respects as well. Although a large proportion of public school students will never enroll in an institution of higher learning, much educational effort and testing have been directed toward college preparatory courses that provide graduates few, if any, usable job skills. Historically, vocational, agricultural, and home economics programs were viewed as "burial grounds" for pupils who had failed in the traditional academic programs. Educational decision makers have only

DID YOU KNOW . . .

That Texas students taking the Scholastic Aptitude Test (SAT) in 2005 ranked forty-ninth in average verbal scores and forty-sixth in math scores among the fifty states?

recently begun to recognize the need for highly skilled technical workers who possess other practical life skills.

Textbooks.   The SBOE selects a list of approved textbooks that the state will buy for public school courses. The selection process generates intense political battles between conservative organizations (such as the Texas Public Policy Foundation, Mel Gabler's Educational Research Analysts, and Texas Citizens for a Sound Economy) and liberal groups (such as the Texas Freedom Network). In general, the conservatives dominate the battle. Some publishers withdraw their text offerings, while others change the content of their texts to satisfy the SBOE, which controls the second largest textbook market in the nation. As a result, Texas's textbook decisions effectively determine the content of texts used in public schools in much of the nation.

Legally, the State Board of Education can determine only the accuracy of textbooks, but it has used this power to pressure publishers to submit texts that reflect the political and religious values of its members. One publisher eliminated references to "fossil fuels formed millions of years ago" from a science text because it conflicts with some interpretations of the time line in the Bible. Another eliminated sections that were perceived as too kind to Muslims because they asserted that Osama bin Laden's actions were inconsistent with commonly accepted Islamic teachings (even though this was the official policy view of the president and the U.S. government). An environmental science text was rejected because it favorably mentioned the Endangered Species Act and warned of the threat of global warming (even though, again, the conservative federal administration in power accepted both). Under recent pressure from religious conservatives, publishers submitted health textbooks that presented an abstinence-only approach to sex education, excluding essential information about how to prevent unwanted pregnancies and sexually transmitted diseases. A Texas government text was rejected because it included an article that asserted that religious conservatives influence the SBOE!

In general, the textbooks on the acceptable list defend the status quo and reflect the dominant values in Texas political culture. Although they now include material on the heritage of ethnic minorities in Texas, many politically controversial

State Board of Education members are shown at their desks with samples of health textbooks before a meeting of the board in 2004. Social conservatives and sex education advocates squared off at the final public hearing before the board adopted new health textbooks for Texas school students. A Texas Department of Public Safety officer stands in the background as people look at some of the books. (AP Photo/Harry Cabluck)

issues are avoided. In addition, budget restraints often prevent the purchase of text-books with recent copyrights and hence more contemporary information than older textbooks contain.

Faculties. A fifteen-member state board for educator certification establishes standards for qualification, conduct, and certification of public school teachers. Actual hiring of teachers is a local matter. Most districts do not follow a publicly announced policy of hiring or dismissing teachers because of their political view-points, but in many districts, teachers are carefully screened for their attitudes. Salary and working conditions are perpetual issues of dissatisfaction among teach-ers because they affect morale and recruitment, especially as the legislature cuts per capita public school funding. The student-teacher ratios in Texas schools remain similar to those in other states, but increasing public demands for accountability have added reporting and other paperwork to teachers' workloads beyond the stan-dard expectations for lesson planning, grading, and communicating with parents.

Expected income is certainly a factor when people choose their careers, and edu-cation simply does not rank favorably among the professions. Furthermore, Texas teachers' average salary of $41,009 in 2004–2005 ranked thirty-third among the fifty states (14 percent below the national average), according to the National Education Association. The TEA reported that one-third of beginning teachers leave the profession by their fifth year. The State Board of Educator Certification estimated there are 350,000 certified teachers who do not teach, and the board expects a teacher shortage of 50,000 by 2010.

Students. Public schools have changed considerably in recent years. The number of students attending Texas public schools has been increasing at a rate of over 2 percent per year, and that increase is expected to continue for the next decade. Students are also more ethnically diverse than in the past.

Scores on the Texas Assessment of Knowledge and Skills (TAKS) test measure student achievement. Student accountability programs limit *social promotion* (pro-motion to the next grade based on age rather than level of learning), and an exit test is used to determine whether a student receives a diploma. The "no pass, no play" rule forbids students from participating in extracurricular activities without obtaining a passing grade in academic subjects. Most high school students are required to take four years of math and science.

Despite these efforts, only 64 percent of eleventh graders met TAKS standards in 2006 (79 percent of whites, 52 percent of Hispanics, and 45 percent of African Americans passed). In 2005, fourth- and eighth-grade Texas students taking the National Assessment of Educational Progress ("The Nation's Report Card") scored close to the national average in math and reading. Texas ranks thirty-sixth in high school graduation rates.

Public School Finance. In 2004–2005, expenditures for public school operations in Texas were $7,142 per student, ranking Texas fortieth among the fifty states (17 percent below the national average). The actual distribution of these funds is so complex that it has been said that there are probably only four or five people in the state who fully understand Texas's system of school finance. Public school funding comes from three sources: federal, state, and local.

Federal grants increased for 2004–2005 to $6.9 billion. Most of the funds from federal grants are used for child nutrition and special needs, military, and low-income students.

State funding comes from a variety of sources. The Permanent School Fund was established in 1854 and invests receipts of rentals, sales, and mineral royalties from Texas's public lands. Only the interest and dividends from this permanent endow-ment may be spent. Earnings from the Permanent School Fund and one-fourth of the motor fuels tax make up the Available School Fund. Part of this fund is used for textbooks; the remainder is distributed to local school districts based on students in average daily attendance. Basing distribution of state funds on attendance focuses a school district's attention on truancy.

The Foundation School Program (FSP) accounts for the largest portion of state and local funding by far. The FSP is structured as a state-local partnership to bring some financial equality to local districts despite vast differences in local tax resources. State funds come from general revenues, a new broad-based business gross-receipts tax, and higher tobacco taxes.

Local funding comes from two sources: ad valorem property taxes and general-obligation bonds. Bonds are used to finance construction and other capital improvement projects. Property taxes are used to pay about half of the FSP's basic operating expenses, with the state paying for the remainder. The market value of property is determined by the county appraisal authority for all local governments within the county, and local district boards then set the property tax rate stated as an amount per $100.00 of property value.

Local school district trustees may set the property tax rate for maintenance and operations up to a maximum of $1.22 per $100.00 of property values in 2007. For 2008, the cap was lowered to $1.00 per $100.00 valuation. The state supplements local funds to ensure that each district has a $2,748 basic allotment per student. The state also guarantees that each additional cent in local tax must yield at least $31.95 per student.

In addition, to provide greater equality in local funding, the richer districts must reduce their taxable property per student to a ceiling of $319,500 by sharing directly with poorer districts or by sending money to the state for redistribution to other districts. Most wealthy districts simply send money to the state. Some local tax revenues are not subject to these "recapture" requirements. Districts may tax up to an additional 50 cents per $100 for construction and debt service and another 6 cents per $100 for educational enrichment.

Additional state funds are also available for smaller districts; for programs for the talented and gifted; for special vocational, compensatory, and bilingual education; for college readiness programs in high schools; and for a wide variety of other special programs and circumstances.

School Finance Inequities.   The current school finance system resulted from over two decades of struggle, litigation, and failed reform efforts. Because the old state funding system could not overcome significant inequalities resulting from heavy dependence on local property taxes, a lawsuit attacking the Texas system of educational finance was filed in federal court. Parents of several students in the Edgewood Independent School District in San Antonio charged that funding inequalities violated the Fourteenth Amendment to the U.S. Constitution, which guarantees that no state shall deny any person the equal protection of the laws. Ultimately, the United States Supreme Court declined to strike down Texas's system of school finance because it failed to find a fundamental U.S. constitutional right to equally funded public education.[1]

Later, the battle over inequality shifted to the state level. In 1987, as mentioned in earlier chapters, a state district court decided a different challenge to the funding system, *Edgewood v. Kirby*. The court based its decision on a variety of provisions in the Texas Constitution guaranteeing a suitable and efficient school system. Citing numerous disparities between wealthy and poor districts resulting from heavy reliance on local property taxes, the court found the funding system unconstitutional. In 1989, the Texas Supreme Court unanimously upheld the lower court decision.[2]

---

[1]*San Antonio Independent School District v. Rodriguez,* 411 U.S. 1 (1973).
[2]*Edgewood Independent School District v. Kirby,* 777 S.W.2d 391 (Tex. 1989).

After a series of aborted attempts and adverse court rulings, the legislature established the current system. Revenues per student now depend primarily on the tax rate, because the state guarantees that a particular local property tax rate will produce a specific amount of revenue or the state will make up the difference. The requirement that wealthier districts share their revenues with poorer districts outraged some parents and school officials, who describe the system as "socialistic" or a "Robin Hood" plan that interferes with local control and their right to educate their children.

Despite the changes, the West Orange-Cove Consolidated Independent School District still has $35,900 more revenues for a class of twenty students than does the Huntsville Independent School District. Table 26–3 shows that student TAKS test scores—and the factors sometimes thought to affect them—also continue to vary dramatically from district to district in Texas.

Higher Education

Like public schools, higher education is a major state service, accounting for 13 percent of state expenditures during the 2006–2007 budget period. Texas public institutions of higher education include thirty-five general academic institutions and universities, nine health-related institutions, three lower-division institutions, and one technical college system. Fifty public community colleges operate on more than seventy campuses.

Figure 26–5 on the following page shows that public institutions enroll almost 90 percent of all students in Texas higher education. The majority of students enroll in public community colleges where average tuition and fees cost about one-third as much as at public universities.

Administration of Colleges and Universities. The Texas Higher Education Coordinating Board was established to coordinate the complex system of higher education in the state. The governor, with the consent of the senate, appoints its eighteen members, and they serve for six-year terms. The Coordinating Board appoints the commissioner of higher education to supervise its staff. Together, the board and staff outline the role of each public college and university and determine future needs for programs, curricula, and physical plants.

Because Texas's colleges and universities were not established systematically, the Coordinating Board has difficulty making sense of how they all relate to one another. Politically powerful boards of regents compete to impose their views on higher education, as do other groups. Regents and trustees set basic policies for these

TABLE 26–3 | SELECTED TEXAS SCHOOL DISTRICT PROFILES

School	Enrollment	Percent Minority*	Students per Teacher	Average Teacher Experience (Years)	Percent Meeting TAKS Standard†	Revenue per Student‡
Houston I.S.D	208,454	91.2%	17.4	11.7	50%	$ 7,624
Dallas I.S.D.	157,743	94.2	15.4	12.3	49	8,384
Plano I.S.D.	52,113	40.3	13.9	9.8	84	8,701
Edgewood I.S.D.	12,571	98.7	19.1	11.2	44	8,664
Huntsville I.S.D.	6,634	50.1	15.8	11.9	58	7,552
Alamo Heights I.S.D.	4,374	32.6	15.9	14.9	81	8,617
West Orange-Cove I.S.D.	2,916	67.6	13.3	13.8	41	9,342
Wink-Loving I.S.D.	330	29.4	7.8	14.9	63	16,465
Statewide	**4,383,871**	**62.3**	**14.9**	**11.5**	**62**	**8,101**

*African American, Hispanic, Native American, and Pacific Islander.
†The Standard Accountability Indicator among all grades tested.
‡Actual revenues from all sources after equalization.
Source: Texas Education Agency, *2004–2005 Academic Excellence Indicator System, District Reports.*

FIGURE 26–5 | TEXAS HIGHER EDUCATION ENROLLMENTS, FALL 2004

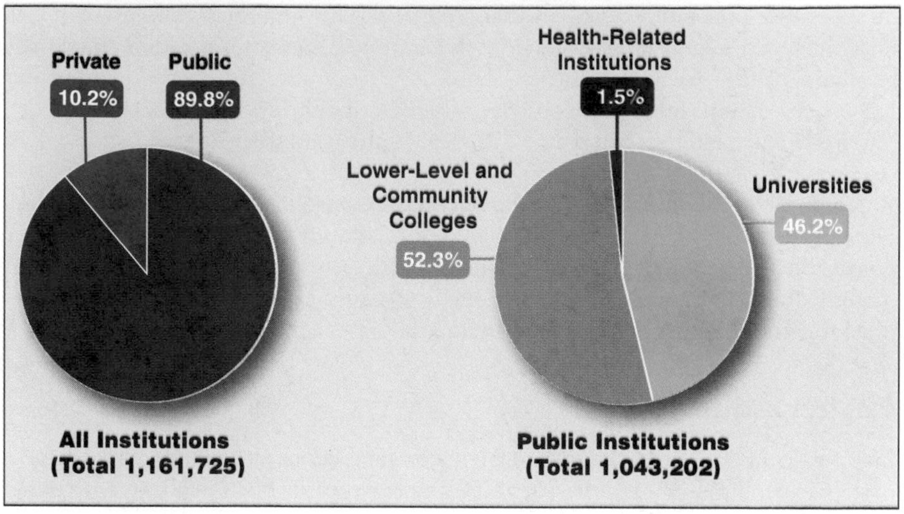

Private 10.2% **Public** 89.8%

All Institutions (Total 1,161,725)

Health-Related Institutions 1.5%

Lower-Level and Community Colleges 52.3%

Universities 46.2%

Public Institutions (Total 1,043,202)

Source: Texas Higher Education Coordinating Board.

institutions, within the limits of state law and the rules and guidelines established by the Coordinating Board.

Some boards of regents govern single-campus institutions. Others govern institutions located on several campuses:

- The University of Texas system includes the University of Texas at Austin (with the nation's second largest student population on a single campus) and other campuses located at Arlington, Brownsville, Dallas, El Paso, Permian Basin, San Antonio, and Tyler, as well as the University of Texas—Pan American and several medical and health units.
- The Texas A&M system has its main campus at College Station, with additional campuses at Corpus Christi, Commerce, Texarkana, Galveston, Kingsville, Prairie View A&M, Tarleton State, West Texas A&M, and Texas A&M International.
- The Texas State University system includes Angelo State, Sam Houston State, Texas State University at San Marcos, Sul Ross State, Sul Ross State—Rio Grande Valley, Lamar University, Lamar Institute of Technology, and Lamar State College in Orange and Port Arthur.
- The University of Houston has its main campus in Houston, as well as a downtown campus and campuses at Clear Lake and Victoria.

The administrative structure of senior colleges and universities may include systemwide administrators (chancellors), campus presidents, deans, and other officers. The Coordinating Board also generally supervises community colleges, which are authorized and financed largely by the state. Unlike four-year institutions (which are usually designed to attract students from larger regions of the state and nation as well as international students), community colleges are established by voters in one or more school districts primarily to serve area residents. They may be governed either by an independently elected board or by the trustees of a local public school district.

The traditional role of the two-year college, generally referred to in the past as a junior college, has been to offer academic courses to freshmen and sophomores who would later transfer to four-year colleges. Although most of their students are enrolled in transferable academic courses, two-year colleges have responded to the demands resulting from economic diversification by adopting a "community college" approach—adding adult, continuing, and special education courses as well as technical specialties. The curriculum, low cost, and geographic and financial accessibility of community colleges have resulted in increasing enrollments, especially in academic programs.

The Politics of Higher Education. It is difficult to measure objectively many of the benefits of higher education, such as personal satisfaction and contributions to society and the economy. Individual financial benefits, however, are very clear. High school graduates have an average annual income of $30,649; those with an associate's degree earn $37,480; college graduates have an average income of $62,320.[3]

In spite of its benefits, legislative bodies and boards of regents and trustees have often been critical in their evaluations of higher education and its results. Calls for faculty and student accountability have been frequent. Yet there are no generally agreed-on answers to the questions raised about higher education: What should its goals be? How should it measure success in achieving those goals? To whom should it be accountable? We examine some issues concerning higher education in the remainder of this section.

Faculty Issues. Salaries are a perpetual issue when Texas institutions of higher education recruit new faculty. Average full-time public college and university faculty salaries, for example, are still significantly below the national average.

Rationalizing their attempts as an effort to promote faculty accountability, college and university administrators have long sought to dilute job-protection guarantees for professors. State law requires governing boards to adopt procedures for periodic reevaluation of all tenured faculty. Faculties generally fear such policies as a threat to academic freedom and a tool for political repression by administrators.

Financial Issues. Financing higher education is a continuing issue. Like elementary and secondary schools, most colleges and universities in Texas must struggle with relatively small budgets. Meanwhile, increasing college enrollments and demands for specialized, high-cost programs are increasing at a time when prisons, health care, and other services are also placing more demands on state revenues. Revenues in turn are limited by the legislature's reluctance to increase taxes. Proposals to cope with financial pressures include closing institutions with smaller enrollments, reducing duplication, restricting student services, raising tuitions, and delaying construction plans or the implementation of new degree programs.

Student Retention. Related to financial issues is the issue of affordability. College and university boards have been raising tuitions, mandatory student fees, and housing costs. Table 26–4 on the following page shows that between 1999 and 2006, average tuition and fees at Texas public universities rose 96 percent, to $4,867. At community colleges, tuition and fees increased by 72 percent.[4] Financial accessibility of higher education is thus a growing concern.

High costs, lack of course availability, inadequate academic preparation, and personal factors all contribute to the problem of student retention. The University of Texas Board of Regents has been particularly concerned with the rate of student graduation. Table 26–5 on the next page shows the low rates of degree completion within four and six years at various University of Texas campuses. Retaining students

[3]U.S. Census Bureau, Current Population Reports, *2005 Annual Social and Economic Supplement*, Table PINC-03.
[4]Texas Higher Education Coordinating Board data cited in Carole Keeton Strayhorn, *Texas: Where We Stand* (Austin: Office of the Comptroller of Public Accounts, February 2006).

TABLE 26-4 | TEXAS RESIDENT TUITION AND FEES, 30 CREDIT HOURS

FISCAL YEAR	UNIVERSITIES	COMMUNITY COLLEGES
1999	$2,489	$ 865
2000	2,700	919
2001	2,654	841
2002	3,016	980
2003	3,441	1,120
2004	3,782	1,245
2005	4,332	1,453
2006	4,867	1,483

Source: Texas Higher Education Coordinating Board.

is also a significant issue at other institutions of higher learning, especially community colleges.

Inequalities.   Inequality in the distribution of limited public resources is also an issue. General legislative appropriations have been more generous for the University of Texas (UT) at Austin and Texas A&M University than for other colleges and universities. Furthermore, the state constitution earmarked more than two million acres of public land for the Permanent University Fund (PUF), now with an investment value of over $9 billion. Two-thirds of the earnings from the PUF go to the campuses of the University of Texas system, and one-third goes to Texas A&M University campuses. A long-awaited constitutional amendment now requires the legislature to establish a higher-education fund of $2 billion in permanent endowments for the benefit of state universities that do not participate in PUF funding. The legislature has been slow to provide this funding, however.

Affirmative Action.   Institutions of higher education have struggled with other inequities as well. One concerns efforts to recruit minority students to increase ethnic diversity and offer more services to underserved populations. Those efforts became especially difficult when the federal Fifth Circuit Court of Appeals ruled that race could not be considered in affirmative action admissions policies.[5] The Texas legislature responded by requiring that general college and university academic institutions automatically admit students from the top 10 percent of their high school graduating class regardless of test scores (as discussed in Chapter 23). This policy guaranteed that the top-ranking students in predominantly minority high schools

[5]*Hopwood v. Texas*, 84 F.3d 720 (5th Cir. 1996).

TABLE 26-5 | GRADUATION RATES OF UNDERGRADUATES AT THE UNIVERSITY OF TEXAS CAMPUSES

CAMPUS	FOUR YEARS	SIX YEARS
Arlington	14.5%	36.8%
Austin	41.3	70.1
Dallas	29.6	56.2
El Paso	4.5	25.6
Pan American	8.4	26.2
Permian Basin	15.5	29.5
San Antonio	6.1	27.6
Tyler	49.7	NA

Source: Texas Higher Education Coordinating Board, 2005.

would be able to attend a public university in Texas. Other states attempted to achieve diversity by considering low family income and other special nonracial obstacles that make it difficult for students to meet standard admission criteria.

The United States Supreme Court has begun to allow race to be considered in college admissions policies so long as specific point advantages are not assigned to minorities.[6] These decisions have sent most administrators scrambling to find acceptable affirmative action policies.

Health and Human Services

The second most costly category of state spending can be broadly classified as health and human services. This category encompasses public assistance, Medicaid for the poor, and a variety of other programs. In the 2006–2007 budget period, these programs cost $48.4 billion (35 percent of the state's total budget). About 60 percent of this funding originates as grants-in-aid from the federal government.

The Texas Health and Human Services Commission provides a variety of social services, including Temporary Assistance to Needy Families, Medicaid, and the Children's Health Insurance Program, as shown in Figure 26–6. The commission also coordinates planning, rulemaking, and budgeting among its four subsidiary social-service agencies:

[6]*Grutter v. Bollinger*, 539 U.S. 306 (2003); and *Gratz v. Bollinger*, 539 U.S. 234 (2003).

FIGURE 26–6 | TEXAS HEALTH AND HUMAN SERVICES AGENCIES

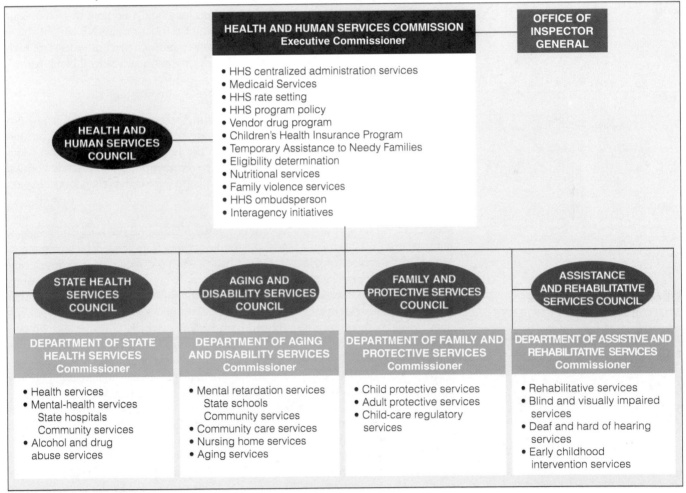

Source: Health and Human Services Commission.

the Department of Aging and Disability Services, the Department of Assistive and Rehabilitative Services, the Department of Family and Protective Services, and the Department of State Health Services. In general, social services can be categorized as income-support programs, health programs, or unemployment programs.

Income Support Programs

One important income-support program is Temporary Assistance to Needy Families (TANF), designed for children whose parents are incapable of providing for the children's basic needs. More than two-thirds of TANF recipients are children. Unless they are disabled or needed at home to care for very young children, adult TANF recipients are referred for employment counseling, assessment, and job placement.

The TANF-Basic program serves those who are deprived of support due to the absence or disability of one or both parents (whose income is at least 86 percent below the poverty level). TANF grants are also available for two-parent families in which the principal wage earner is unemployed and the family income does not exceed the criteria established for the basic program.

Federal and state regulations now place various limits on TANF benefits. Adult eligibility is usually limited to two years at a time, with a maximum five-year lifetime benefit. These welfare reforms were intended to force able-bodied individuals out of dependency and into productive work. Some federal funds are distributed as block grants to the states to allow them flexibility in developing support services, child care, job training and placement, and rehabilitation programs to help welfare recipients find work. Table 26–6 shows that these reforms have substantially reduced the number of TANF recipients in Texas.

In 2005, the maximum monthly TANF grant for a family of three was $223, considerably below the national average. Adjusting for inflation, TANF benefits have declined considerably over the years. Texas now spends 0.2 percent of its state budget for TANF, and 65.0 percent of this amount originates as a federal block grant.

Health Programs

Although opponents of government's assuming responsibility for public health describe it as "socialized medicine," health care has concerned public authorities since Moses imposed strict hygienic codes on the Jews during their biblical exodus from Egypt. In the United States, the federal government began to provide hospital care to the merchant marine in 1798. Today, health care is the second most expensive service Texas provides.

Medicaid.   Texas spends 18.7 percent of the state budget on the Medicaid program, but more than 60.0 percent of Medicaid funding comes from the federal government. Medicaid reimburses providers for most health services, including eyeglasses, prescription drugs, physicians' fees, laboratory and X-ray services, family planning, ambulance transportation, Medicare Part B premiums, and a wide variety of other medical expenses. Generally, these providers are in managed care (HMO-type) systems. *Medicaid* should not be confused with *Medicare*, which is available to all persons over age sixty-five, is financed by federal payroll taxes, and is administered by the U.S. Department of Health and Human Services. In contrast, only certain categories of individuals are eligible for the state-administered Medicaid program: (1) any persons eligible for TANF or Supplemental Security Income (SSI), a federal program that may be available to aged, blind, or disabled individuals; (2) low-income persons residing in institutions who qualify for SSI except for certain income requirements; (3) children up to nineteen years of age whose family financial status would qualify for TANF but who reside in families with two able-bodied parents; (4) pregnant women who would qualify for TANF but have no other children; (5) children ages six through eighteen who reside in families with income below the federal poverty

TABLE 26–6 | AVERAGE MONTHLY TANF RECIPIENTS

Year	TANF Recipients
2002	358,765
2003	367,893
2004	273,520
2005	224,284
2006*	228,427
2007*	232,171

*Estimated.
Source: Texas Department of Human Services.

level; (6) children under age six whose families' income is at or below 133 percent of the federal poverty level; (7) pregnant women and infants under one year of age who reside in families with income below 185 percent of the federal poverty level; (8) medically needy individuals whose income is not more than one-third higher than that allowed for TANF participation; and (9) Medicare beneficiaries whose incomes are no more than 135 percent of the federal poverty level.[7] Well over 90 percent of Medicaid patients are elderly persons, persons with disabilities, or children.

Other Health Programs. For low-income children who are not eligible for Medicaid, the Children's Health Insurance Program (CHIP) helps parents with incomes of less than 200 percent of the poverty level buy health insurance for their children. Despite these programs, one in five Texas children is uninsured.[8]

The state Department of Health Services licenses hospitals and provides personal health programs for special populations. The Women, Infants, and Children (WIC) program provides nutrition and health assistance for women who are pregnant, have just given birth, or are breastfeeding infants. In addition, the health department operates a lung and tuberculosis hospital in San Antonio and a general-services hospital in Harlingen. Because this department deals with communicable diseases, it is likely to be a center of attention in the event of an epidemic or a biological terrorist attack.

The Department of Health Services also operates general psychiatric hospitals and locally governed special or contract mental-health facilities and community centers. Most such problems, however, are treated privately or not at all. For individuals treated at public expense, Texas, like most states, provides treatment on a community, outpatient basis. Some 3 million Texans suffering from mental illness require mental-health services, but only 5 percent of them receive services from the state. Another half-million Texans are developmentally disabled, but only 30,000 of them receive direct state services.

Health-care delivery is becoming much more expensive, especially because the population is aging and because expensive but more effective new technology is being used. As a result, individual health-care costs are increasing more rapidly than general inflation, causing insurance premiums to rise and coverage to be reduced. State Medicaid and private insurance costs have mushroomed. Texas has more people without health insurance than most states, and many of them are treated by struggling county hospitals. There are limits to the resources a society can devote to health care, and such care is rationed by the market to those who can afford it and by the government to those lucky enough to qualify for a government program. Too often, rationing health care is the same as rationing life.

Unemployment Programs

As discussed previously in Chapter 16, with the Social Security Act of 1935, the U.S. Congress established a system of unemployment insurance that would become a partnership program between the states and the federal government. This act imposed a tax on covered employers to establish a nationwide system of unemployment insurance administered by the federal government. The act provided that most of this tax would be set aside in the states that adopted an acceptable state program. Thus, every state in the union was pressured to adopt a state system of unemployment insurance.

Today, every state has an unemployment insurance program. Benefits are financed from state taxes on employers, but some administrative costs are paid with federal funds. These programs are actually administered by the state. In Texas,

---

[7]"Texas Medicaid Program," Texas Health and Human Services Commission, available at www.hhsc.state.tx.us/medicaid/index.html.
[8]U.S. Census Bureau, *Current Population Survey*, 2003 and 2004.

| DID YOU KNOW . . .

That in a recent year Texas ranked forty-ninth among the fifty states in per capita spending (26 percent below the national average)? Texas's per capita expenditures for education ranked fortieth among the fifty states and were 14 percent below the national average; per capita expenditures for highways ranked forty-fourth (19 percent below the national average) and those for welfare ranked thirty-seventh (33 percent below the national average)?

unemployment insurance is administered by the Texas Workforce Commission (TWC), a three-member board appointed by the governor, with the consent of the senate, for six-year overlapping terms.

Under Texas's rather restrictive laws, a worker who loses his or her job may be able to collect a weekly benefit payment of from $54 to $336 for a maximum of twenty-six weeks. The payments are based on past earnings regardless of need or family size. A worker receiving benefits must register for job placement with the TWC. In addition, a worker is ineligible to receive benefits (at least for a time) if he or she voluntarily quit, was fired for cause, or was unemployed because of a labor dispute. Because the rate at which employers are taxed is based on claims made by former employees, employers have an interest in contesting employee claims.

Handling unemployment insurance claims is a minor part of the TWC's activities; its major functions are to provide a workforce for employers, gather employment statistics, enforce child-labor laws, and provide various special job-training and rehabilitation services. Able-bodied welfare recipients are referred to the TWC for training and child-care services. Regional workforce development boards plan one-stop career development centers in twenty-eight areas across the state.

Transportation

The third most costly service provided by the state of Texas is transportation. As we mentioned earlier, transportation (primarily highways) accounted for about 10.9 percent of expenditures in 2006–2007.

Highway Programs

In the early days of Texas history, road construction was primarily the responsibility of the county. Most Texas counties still maintain a property tax dedicated to the construction and maintenance of roads, and in rural areas, road building remains a major function of county government. The efforts are too small and too poorly financed, however, to provide the expensive, coordinated, statewide network of roads needed by highly mobile Texans in the modern world.

In contrast to county roads, state highways in Texas are better financed. In 1916, the national government encouraged state governments to assume the major responsibility for highway construction and maintenance. The 1916 Federal Aid Road Act made available federal funds to cover one-half of the construction costs for state highways. To become eligible for those funds, a state was required to establish an agency to develop a coordinated plan for the state highway system and to administer construction and maintenance programs. Texas responded by establishing the Texas Highway Department, now known as the Department of Transportation. The department is supervised by a five-member commission appointed by the governor, with the consent of the senate, for six-year overlapping terms. The commission appoints an executive director who oversees the department and supervises the work of regional district offices.

Newer federal aid programs and increased funding for existing ones have expanded the responsibilities of the Transportation Department. The earliest highway-building program was designed to provide only major highways along primary routes. Federal funding later became available for secondary roads, and Texas established the farm-to-market program to assume state maintenance of many county roads as the rural road network was paved, extended, and improved. Finally, beginning in 1956, Congress made funds available for 90 percent of the cost of constructing express, limited-access highways to connect major cities in the United States. Altogether, the state highway system today consists of 79,645 miles of highways (including 339 miles of park and recreation roads) and carries almost three-fourths of the state's motor vehicle traffic (see Table | 26–7).

Funding for the highway program is a joint federal-state responsibility. In the 2006–2007 period, the federal government, mostly from the federal gasoline tax, provided 47 percent of the Transportation Department's revenues. The federal government pays for 90 percent of the construction cost of interstate highways and 80 percent of the cost of other primary and secondary highways. This large federal contribution has allowed the national government to demand such restrictions as meeting clean-air standards and setting a minimum drinking age of twenty-one years as conditions for receiving federal aid.

State monies account for 53 percent of Transportation Department funding. The state highway fund is supported through a sales tax on lubricants, motor vehicle registration fees, and three-fourths of the 20-cent-per-gallon motor fuels tax. The majority of the Transportation Department's expenditures are for construction, and most of the remainder is for highway maintenance. The department also handles federal funding for mass public transportation, issues motor vehicle titles, and regulates commercial motor carriers.

The Politics of Transportation

The Good Roads and Transportation Association, a private organization supported by highway contractors and other groups, lobbied for the establishment of the state highway fund and for increases in motor fuel taxes and still attempts to guard the fund against those who would spend any part of it for other purposes. Despite the organization's efforts, per capita state highway funding in Texas is now among America's lowest.

Texans also remain unreceptive to alternatives. Automobile transportation is as close to the hearts of Texans as it is to other Americans: no other mode of transportation seems as convenient because no other is as individualized. Buses, trains, and airplanes cannot take individuals exactly where they want to go exactly when they want to go there. Only in New England, New York, Washington, D.C., and Chicago is mass transit a viable alternative to the personal vehicles that have become a way of life as well as a status symbol. The manufacture, maintenance, and fueling of automobiles have become dominant elements of the economy. Drive-through restaurants, drive-through banking facilities, and even drive-through churches have influenced people's habits. For the young, motor vehicles have influenced dating and mate selection. They have become a manner of personal expression as well; small efficient compacts, large luxurious sedans, SUVs, pickup trucks, and finely tuned sports cars express different personal images and self-concepts.

So dependent are Texans on their automobiles that they ignore the cost of using their vehicles to themselves individually and to society. Texas's annual highway death toll is close to four thousand, and thousands more are injured every year. The motor vehicle is also the single most important contributor to atmospheric pollution, a factor in global warming (the "greenhouse effect"), and a significant source of refuse that finds its way into junkyards and landfills. As the least efficient mode of transportation now available, the individual motor vehicle is in direct conflict

TABLE 26-7 | THE TEXAS HIGHWAY SYSTEM

Type of Roadway	Total Miles	Percentage of Traffic Accommodated
Interstate highways	9,953	26%
Farm-to-market roads	40,996	11
Federal and state highways	28,357	36

Note: Figures do not include more than 222,000 miles of city streets and county roads, which accommodate approximately one-third of traffic.
Source: Legislative Budget Board, *Fiscal Size-Up, 2006–2007* (Austin: Legislative Budget Board, 2005), pp. 339–340.

with the need to conserve energy and reduce our strategic dependence on foreign oil (a factor in terrorism and foreign wars).

Because of these problems, some people advocate increasing the investment of public funds in alternative means of transportation. With adequate financing, railroads could once again become rapid and comfortable. In many big cities, mass transportation provided by buses and trains could become an attractive alternative. Nevertheless, in some areas where significant investment has been made in mass transportation, the public has not responded with increased use. Given Texans' love affair with the automobile and their strong individualism, it seems doubtful that the state would seriously consider significant funding for any of these alternatives.

MAKING A DIFFERENCE | Becoming an Intelligent Taxpayer and Consumer of State Services

Texas students or their families pay local property taxes either directly, if they are homeowners, or indirectly as hidden taxes if they rent their dwellings. Texas has among the lowest *state* taxes in the nation partly because the state has pushed the cost of many services down to the *local* level. As a result, Texans pay among the highest local property tax rates in the country.

Why Should You Care?

Your local property taxes have been rising because property values have increased because of low mortgage interest rates and high demand for housing. You (or your family) may be among many local property taxpayers who have seen taxes grow much more rapidly than their incomes. You should realize, however, that you could have a direct impact on the ad valorem taxes you (or your family) pay.

What Can You Do?

Your local property taxes are based on the appraised value of your real estate. Local governments in your area use a central countywide appraisal district usually accessible online. It determines the value of your property.

You can protest the appraised value of your property with this appraisal authority. Be prepared with photos, specific measurements of

floor space and land area, and a list of any defects that might diminish the value of the property. How do you know what the appraised value of your property should be? You can research the appraised values of other comparable properties in your neighborhood; these values are a matter of public record and are available in the appraisal district of the county where you live.

You may be eligible for a homestead exemption if you live in a home you own. Such an exemption allows you to pay less in property taxes than you would otherwise. A special exemption is also available for the elderly. It is the taxpayer's responsibility to apply for these exemptions. To locate your county appraisal authority and to find the appraised value of any property, go to **www.txcountydata.com**.

Tips on Consuming State Services

- Much state and federal tuition assistance goes undistributed. Visit your school's financial aid office to determine whether you qualify for tuition help.
- A parent's failure to make child-support payments may force the other parent to apply for Temporary Assistance to Needy Families. If you

have this problem, call the attorney general's child-support enforcement office at the number listed in your local telephone directory.

- Those who witness child abuse or neglect should call Protective and Regulatory Services at (800) 252-5400.
- See if your family and friends are eligible for state social services by checking links at **www.hhsc.state.tx. us/about_hhsc/HHS_Agencies.html**.
- Before you buy a new vehicle, contact the Texas Department of Transportation, which maintains "lemon law" records at **www.dot. state.tx.us**.
- When you buy auto and home-owner's insurance, check with the Texas Department of Insurance, which publishes rates and numbers of customer complaints. Go to **www.tdi.state.tx.us/consumer/ index.html**.
- If you need emergency road assistance or wish to report drug trafficking, call the Department of Public Safety at (800) 525-5555.
- Apply for a job or unemployment compensation at the Texas Workforce Commission, **www.tdi. state.tx.us/consumer/index.html**.
- The most comprehensive Web site for state services is at **www.state. tx.us**.

Key Terms

ability-to-pay tax 825

appropriations process 830

benefits-received tax 825

broad-based tax 823

declining marginal propensity
to consume 826

dedicated, or earmarked,
funds 830

devolution 829

excise tax 822

general-obligation bond 829

general sales tax 822

gross-receipts tax 822

hidden tax 822

incremental budgeting 830

logrolling 831

regressive tax rate 826

regulatory tax 823

revenue bond 829

selective sales tax 822

supply-side economics 827

tax base 823

tax rate 823

tax shifting 827

zero-based budgeting 830

Chapter Summary

1 State tax rates are low in Texas compared with other states and are not rising as a percentage of personal income. Nevertheless, almost half of state revenues are raised through taxes. A substantial portion (more than one-third) comes from federal grants-in-aid, and miscellaneous sources account for the rest. State borrowing is limited.

2 Although political self-interest determines which kinds of taxes are used, taxing decisions may be rationalized as serving some regulatory purpose or reflecting benefits received or ability to pay.

3 Both narrow- and broad-based taxes are used in Texas. The largest single state tax is the general sales tax, which is regressive relative to income because it falls most heavily on middle- and lower-income people. Other state taxes, as well as the ad valorem tax employed by local governments, are also regressive in their effect. The federal income tax is somewhat progressive.

4 The Legislative Budget Board, the state legislature, and the governor become involved in state spending decisions. The process is political. Perhaps no other type of decision evokes more consistent and passionate political efforts from interest groups and administrative agencies.

5 Education, health and human services, and transportation are the major services that state government offers, together constituting more than four-fifths of the total cost of Texas's state government. These services have a significant effect on the way Texans live and even on the way they think. It is nearly impossible to evaluate them objectively because they affect varying groups so differently.

6 The educational system of Texas is generally decentralized and independent of the normal course of partisan politics. Its administrators and curricula are conservative, as is much of Texas politics. Compared with other states, per capita expenditures are about average. Texas has more public school students than many states, however, so per-student expenditures, like teacher salaries, are below average.

7 Health-care services are both publicly and privately financed in Texas, as in the rest of the nation, and they are plagued by a similar problem: the rising costs of providing better services to more people. A smaller proportion of residents are insured to cover these costs in Texas than in most other states, however.

8 In many ways, the Texas system of public welfare reflects the same values that are present in the state educational system. It too is poorly financed, and the public-assistance programs that the state has adopted were established only with the financial support of the national government. Few of these programs are designed to eliminate the root causes of poverty.

9 The highway system has consistently lost funding despite the efforts of the Good Roads and Transportation Association, and per capita spending for highways is less than in most other states. Texans refuse to consider increased spending for highways or alternative means of transportation.

10 Individuals' and groups' positions on these and virtually all public policies differ according to who benefits and who pays the cost for which public services. The process of allocating costs and benefits is the very essence of politics.

Selected Print and Media Resources

SUGGESTED READINGS

Blau, Joel, and Mimi Abramovitz. *The Dynamics of Social Welfare Policy.* New York: Oxford University Press, 2004. This work examines national social-welfare policy in the context of history, social change, and the economy.

Heller, Donald E., ed. *The States and Public Higher Education Policy: Affordability, Access, and Accountability.* Baltimore: Johns Hopkins University Press, 2001. In this series of essays, various authors explore some of the most serious issues states face in making decisions about higher education.

Legislative Budget Board. *Fiscal Size-Up, 2006–2007.* Austin: Legislative Budget Board, 2005. This state publication details state taxing and spending programs as well as recent developments in Texas public policy.

Strayhorn, Carole Keeton. *Tax Exemptions and Tax Incidence: A Report to the Governor and the 79th Texas Legislature.* Austin: Office of the Comptroller, 2005. This excellent analysis of major Texas taxes demonstrates who bears the burden of each tax and how business taxation ultimately falls on consumers.

MEDIA RESOURCES

The Battle over School Choice—This PBS *Frontline* video explores the heated debate over whether public school reform or privatization (including voucher plans) is a better choice.

The Merrow Report: In Schools We Trust—Americans rarely agree on what public education should do: Teach basics? Train workers?

Inculcate democratic values and tolerance? This PBS video explores varying views on public education.

NOW with Bill Moyers: Medicaid Mess—This PBS feature deals with the tough choices concerning Medicaid and also discusses the cultural values that divide America.

Tax Me If You Can—Produced by PBS *Frontline*, this video offers an inside look at how big corporations and wealthy individuals use tax shelters to avoid paying income taxes.

E·MOCRACY | Explore Public Policy in Texas

Taxing and spending policies generate much political controversy. The Internet makes it possible for various interest groups and individuals to publicize their views on these issues. At the same time, it makes available resources students can use to evaluate public policies and utilize state services.

Logging On

The key site for taxes and the budget is the Window on State Government of the Comptroller of Public Accounts at

www.window.state.tx.us

Scroll down to "Tax Rates" to see what the state taxes and how much. You can also research tax and budget issues in the comprehensive *Fiscal Size-Up* publication available at

www.lbb.state.tx.us

Special interest groups provide persuasive arguments for their views of taxation. The Texas Taxpayers and Research Association represents the conservative and business perspective on taxation. Go to

www.ttara.org

Click on "Documents" to examine the group's lobbying positions. For the lib-

eral and labor position, browse the Citizens for Tax Justice site at

www.ctj.org

The Center for Policy Alternatives presents public-policy analyses and trends for the fifty states at

www.stateaction.org

Click on "State Issues" to learn about vouchers, welfare reform, mental-health policies, and environmental and energy policies.

The Texas Education Agency is the key site for public education. Visit the TEA site at

www.tea.state.tx.us

To examine the complex funding of Texas public schools, go to

www.capitol.state.tx.us

Click on "Statutes" and then on "Education Code." Scroll to Chapters 41, 42, and 43.

Special interest groups have very different views about public school textbooks and curricula. For the conservative view, see a discussion of textbooks in "Research and Reports" at the Texas Public Policy Foundation site at

www.texaspolicy.com

For the liberal view, browse the Texas Freedom Network site at

http://www.tfn.org

To learn about the official process for textbook adoption, go to the Texas Education Agency site at

www.tea.state.tx.us/textbooks

For information about the financing of public education, visit the Legislative Budget Board Web site at

www.lbb.state.tx.us

and click on "Publications."

Online Review

At **www.politicalscience.wadsworth.com/schmidt12**, you will find a free Study Guide to this book. For each chapter, there are two online quizzes to help you master the material.

• The PoliPrep Self-Study Assessment provides a pretest for each major section of the chapter. PoliPrep then generates a customized study plan. After you complete the study plan, a posttest evaluates your progress.

• The Tutorial Quiz for each chapter provides questions on the chapter contents, including the features. The questions are organized to match the major sections of the chapter.

27 | Local Government

What If . . .
Mayors and City Council Members
in Texas Were Elected in Partisan Elections?

BACKGROUND

In partisan elections, candidates run under political party labels. In nonpartisan elections, however, there is no mention of party affiliation on the ballot. In Texas, all municipal elections are nonpartisan.

Nonpartisan elections are a product of the Progressive Era (1900–1917). In those days, party-based political "machines" run by "bosses" controlled large cities such as New York and Philadelphia. Party bosses doled out patronage (city jobs and contracts) to supporters in exchange for help at election time.

Reformers considered machine practices to be corrupt. They believed that the best-qualified individuals, not party loyalists, should fill municipal jobs. They argued that city contracts should be granted on the basis of competitive bidding, not party allegiance. The Progressive movement won various reforms designed to bring businesslike practices to city hall, including concepts such as the following, which we describe in greater detail later in this chapter:

- Creating the position of city manager (an appointed executive who is presumably less political than an elected mayor).
- Instituting a civil service system (under which government employees are hired on the basis of merit and cannot be required to participate in politics).
- Establishing nonpartisan elections.

WHAT IF MAYORS AND CITY COUNCIL MEMBERS IN TEXAS WERE ELECTED IN PARTISAN ELECTIONS?

Partisan elections are a fixture of state and national politics. Either Democrats or Republicans control the U.S. Congress and state legislatures. In Texas, candidates for county government positions run under party labels. Why not have partisan elections for mayoral and city council positions in Texas as well?

Political parties generate interest in political campaigns, and that translates into more people participating in elections. For that reason, voter turnout tends to be higher in partisan elections than in nonpartisan elections. If candidates for the mayor's position or a city council seat were to run as Democrats or Republicans, more people would vote in municipal elections.

A party label gives voters some information about what a candidate stands for and about the approach the candidate will take to solve government problems. In local elections, where party labels are absent, voters often rely on other factors when trying to distinguish among candidates, such as race and ethnicity. Basing votes on factors such as these can contribute to polarization in a community.

SAFEGUARDS AGAINST POLITICAL MACHINES

Some may fear that partisan elections would help launch a new era of local political party machines. That is unlikely to happen. The civil service system and competitive bidding practices for contracts are now standard features of Texas municipal government. The city-manager form of government has been widely adopted throughout the state. In other words, the characteristics of local government that date back to the Progressive Era are still largely in place in Texas.

In addition, political bosses did not have to contend with a variety of other restrictive measures passed in the second half of the twentieth century. Texas today has laws on ethics and campaign finance. Texas is covered by the national Voting Rights Act, which protects minority participation in politics. Many municipalities impose term limits on mayors and councilpersons. These laws would help to safeguard against boss-run political machines. In the contemporary political landscape, partisan elections in Texas cities might simply promote a more informed electorate and increase political participation at the local level.

FOR CRITICAL ANALYSIS

1. In nonpartisan elections, voters may pick out candidates who are locally prominent and who are more conservative than the voting public. For example, when Minnesota adopted partisan elections for state lawmakers in 1974, the majority party in the legislature immediately changed from Republican to Democrat. Given what happened in Minnesota, which political interests in Texas might favor partisan municipal elections, and which might oppose them?
2. How might partisan municipal elections influence local public policy?

The sheer number of local governments in Texas can challenge the interested citizen who wants to connect with local officials on a routine basis. (See Table 27–1 for a comparison of local governments in Texas and in the United States as a whole.) Anyone who lives in a metropolitan area is likely to be governed by several **special districts** (such as a hospital district, a metropolitan transit authority, and a municipal utility district), in addition to the two **general-purpose governments**—the municipal and county governments.

Information about local governments is available from a variety of print and electronic media. Adequately covering thousands of local governments is no small challenge, however. Political scientist Doris A. Graber has observed that "given the many active political units that require media attention, media reporting, of necessity, is highly selective and superficial."[1] The public cannot, moreover, depend on local political parties to provide information and generate interest about all local governments. In Texas, political parties do not nominate candidates below the county level, as we explained in the *What If . . .* feature at the beginning of this chapter.

In the following sections, we examine the various institutional features of cities, counties, and special districts. We also look at issues and trends in local government. Finally, given the growing interest in finding regional solutions to local problems, we discuss the role of councils of governments (COGs) at the local level.

| Special District

A local government that provides one or more services to one or more jurisdictions that are not provided by general-purpose governments.

| General-Purpose Government

A municipal or county government. In contrast to special districts, general-purpose governments provide a wide range of services.

| Municipalities

All local governments in Texas are bound by federal and state laws as well as the U.S. and Texas constitutions. The relationship between state and local governments follows from the fact that states, including Texas, have a *unitary* form of government. (We discussed unitary governments, as opposed to federal systems, in Chapter 3.) Municipalities—like counties, special districts, and school districts—are creatures of the state and have only as much power as the Texas Constitution and Texas legislature grant them. Texas has seen a marked increase in the number of municipalities in the state since the 1950s (see Table 27–2).

[1] Doris A. Graber, *Mass Media and American Politics*, 6th ed. (Washington, D.C.: Congressional Quarterly, 2001), p. 320.

TABLE 27–1 | U.S. AND TEXAS LOCAL GOVERNMENTS BY TYPE

	TOTAL	COUNTY	MUNICIPAL	TOWNSHIP	SCHOOL DISTRICT	SPECIAL DISTRICT
United States	87,849	3,034	19,431	16,506	13,522	35,356
Texas	4,784	254	1,196	–	1,089	2,245

Source: U.S. Census Bureau, Preliminary Report, *2002 Census of Governments*; and *2002 Census of Governments*, Vol. 1, No. 1. Available at **www.census.gov/prod/2003pubs/gc021x1.pdf**.

TABLE 27–2 | MUNICIPAL GOVERNMENTS IN TEXAS, 1952–2002

1952	1962	1972	1982	1992	1997	2002
738	866	981	1,121	1,171	1,177	1,196

Source: U.S. Census Bureau, *2002 Census of Governments*, Vol. 1, No. 1. Available at **www.census.gov/prod/2003pubs/gc021x1.pdf**.

General-Law and Home-Rule Cities

Texas cities are classified as either general-law or home-rule cities. According to the Texas Municipal League, the vast majority of Texas cities—about 75 percent—are general-law cities, and over five thousand unincorporated communities have no municipal government.

General-Law City
A city operating under general state laws that apply to all local government units of a similar type. In Texas, cities with a population of five thousand or less are (in most instances) general-law cities.

A **general-law city** is an incorporated community with a population of five thousand or less and is limited in the subject matter on which it may legislate. A city with a population of over five thousand may, by majority vote, become a **home-rule city**. This means it can adopt its own **charter** and structure its local government as it sees fit. Municipal home rule was established in 1912 by a state constitutional amendment. The Texas Constitution allows a home-rule city whose population has dropped to five thousand or less to retain its home-rule designation.

Home-Rule City
A city with the state-granted right to frame, adopt, and amend its own charter.

Charter
An organizing document for corporations or municipalities.

Direct Democracy at the Municipal Level.   In addition to enabling a city to establish its own charter and laws (also called *ordinances*), home rule permits local voters to impose their will directly on the city government through the **initiative**, the **referendum**, and the **recall**. According to the Texas Municipal League, most home-rule cities have all three provisions.

Initiative
A procedure by which voters can propose a law (or, in some states, a constitutional amendment); in Texas, limited to home-rule cities.

With the initiative power, after a campaign obtains signatures from a designated percentage of registered voters, it can force a sometimes-reluctant city council to place a proposed ordinance on the ballot. If the proposal passes by a majority vote, it becomes law. The following are examples of issues that have been resolved in Texas cities by popular vote as a result of the initiative power:

Referendum
An electoral device whereby legislative or constitutional measures are referred by the legislature to the voters for approval or disapproval; in Texas, limited to home-rule cities.

- Should a city increase the municipal minimum wage?
- Should a city impose a cap on the property tax rate?
- Should a city freeze the property tax exemption for seniors and people with disabilities?

Recall
A procedure allowing the people to vote to dismiss an elected official from office before his or her term has expired; in Texas, limited to home-rule cities.

Voters who wish to remove an existing ordinance can petition the council to hold a referendum election to determine whether the law should remain in effect. An example of an ordinance that was the subject of a referendum election is a smoking ban in Lubbock. In 2001, voters decided to retain the ban.

Finally, voters can, by petition, force the council to hold a recall election that would permit the people to remove the mayor or a member of the council. Texas attorney general Greg Abbott ruled that recalled members of a city council must step down once the election results are certified—even if that leaves the council without a quorum.[2]

The Limits of Home Rule.   While home-rule cities have wider latitude than general-law cities in their day-to-day operations, they still must contend with state limitations on their authority. For example, state law determines the specific dates on which municipal elections can be held. Voters are free to amend city charters, but the Texas Constitution permits cities to hold charter elections only every two years. In addition, an election establishing a metropolitan transit authority can be held only in cities that meet a population requirement determined by the Texas legislature.

Forms of Municipal Government

Council-Manager System
A municipal system featuring an elected city council and a city manager who is hired by the council. The council makes policy decisions, and the manager is responsible for the day-to-day operations of the city government.

There are three common forms of municipal government: the council-manager system, the mayor-council system, and the commission system.

The Council-Manager System.   In a **council-manager system** (see Figure 27–1), an elected city council makes laws and hires a professional manager who is respon-

---

[2] Texas Attorney General Opinion No. GA-0175 (2004).

sible for both executing council policies and managing the day-to-day operations of city government. The manager serves at the pleasure of the council.

The powers of the city manager come from the city charter and from the delegation of authority by the council through direct assignment and passage of ordinances. For example, the city manager is responsible for selecting key personnel and for submitting a proposed budget to the council for its approval. The city council will probably seek the manager's opinion on a wide variety of matters, including what tax rate the city should adopt, whether the city should call a bond election, and the feasibility of recommendations made by interest groups. But these issues are ultimately up to the council, and the city manager is expected to implement whatever decisions the council makes.

The Mayor's Role.   In a council-manager form of government, a mayor may be either selected by the council from among its members or independently elected by the voters. The mayor presides over council meetings, has limited or no veto power, and has, for the most part, only the same legislative authority as other members of the council. The salaries of the mayor and council members are minimal compared with that of the full-time city manager. (In some cities, the mayor and council are paid no salary at all.)

The Powers of the Mayor.   The mayor in a council-manager system does have important ceremonial powers, such as signing proclamations and issuing keys to the city to important dignitaries. While the office is institutionally weak, a high-profile mayor can wield considerable influence. In the 1980s, Henry Cisneros achieved national attention as mayor of San Antonio. In 1995, Dallas mayor Ron Kirk made history as the first African American elected to that position in the city's history. San Antonio and Dallas are the two largest Texas cities that use the council-manager system.

As noted earlier, council-manager government was initiated as part of a reform movement early in the twentieth century. Reformers were attempting to substitute "efficient and businesslike management" for the then-prevalent system of "boss rule," in which politics was the key consideration in every city hall decision. The principal criticism of the council-manager system is that the voters do not directly elect the chief executive officer of the city.

FIGURE 27–1 | COMMON FORMS OF MUNICIPAL GOVERNMENT

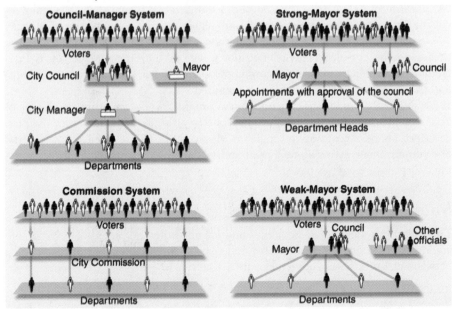

Strong-Mayor System
A form of municipal government in which substantial authority (such as authority over appointments and the budget) is lodged in the office of the mayor, who is elected in a citywide election.

The Mayor-Council System—Strong Mayor. Mayor-council systems take two common forms—the strong-mayor and weak-mayor forms—each with many variations. In the **strong-mayor system** (see Figure 27–1 on page 853), the mayor, who is chosen in a citywide election, is both the chief executive and the leader of the city council (a legislative position). The mayor makes appointments, prepares the budget, and is responsible for the management of city government. The mayor also sets the council agenda, proposes policy, and (in many cities) may veto council actions.

Critics of the strong-mayor system believe that it makes the office of mayor too powerful. Critics also believe that the system may become excessively politicized and will fail to distribute services to constituents fairly or efficiently. This system conjures up the image of urban machines of the 1800s. Mayors who led such machines appointed political cronies as department heads, hired campaign workers as city employees, and awarded contracts to supporters.

Although it was criticized by early-twentieth-century reformers, the strong-mayor form of government did not die out. It was often restructured, however, to include an elected city comptroller (or controller), thus preventing the mayor from having complete control of city finances. (Houston, for example, elects a city controller, who serves as the chief financial officer for the city.) Rules were also adopted to require that contracts be awarded to the lowest and best bidder.

Houston and Pasadena are the two largest Texas cities with a strong-mayor form of government. El Paso was the second largest city with such a system until 2004. That year, El Paso voters approved the establishment of the council-manager form of government, and a city manager was hired. In 2005 Dallas voters rejected two attempts to replace the city's council-manager system with a strong-mayor form of government.

Weak-Mayor System
A form of municipal government in which an elected mayor and city council, often along with other elected officers, share administrative responsibilities.

The Mayor-Council System—Weak Mayor. The **weak-mayor system** (see Figure 27–1 on page 853) lacks clear lines of authority because the mayor and council share administrative duties. Power, in effect, is decentralized. Under this system, voters may have difficulty determining who should be held accountable when problems and mismanagement occur. This type of government is not common in Texas, although it is used by a number of small cities.

Commission System
A system that allows the members of a city council to serve as heads of city departments.

The Commission System. The **commission system** (see Figure 27–1 on page 853) is another variety of municipal government found across the United States. In this system, voters elect one set of officials, who act as both executives and legislators. The commissioners, sitting together, are the municipal legislature, but each administers a city department individually. A manager or administrative assistant may be employed, but the ultimate administrative authority still remains with the elected commissioners.

Commissioners may possess technical knowledge about city government because they supervise city departments. Because power in the city bureaucracy is fragmented among separately elected commissioners, however, coordination is difficult, and the checks-and-balances system is impaired.

In Texas, home-rule cities are unlikely to use this form of government. A type of commission system is found in some general-law cities, but it differs from the plan described above. According to the Texas Municipal League, "In a general law city, one commissioner, acting alone, has no individual power; only the commission acting collectively, exercises power."[3]

Municipal Elections Systems

The election systems used by Texas municipalities have sparked a considerable amount of legal and political controversy. The debate has focused on the choice between at-large and single-member-district elections.

---

[3] *Handbook for Mayors and Councilmembers: General Law Cities* (Austin: Texas Municipal League, 2001), p. 9.

In 2005, then Dallas mayor Laura Miller proposed a strong-mayor proposition that she claimed would pull Dallas out of a rut and get the city moving. Voters did not approve the change. (AP Photo/Donna McWilliam)

At-large elections—citywide elections—usually take one of two forms. In the **pure at-large system,** all the voters elect all the members of the city council. The voters simply choose among all the candidates to fill the available council seats, and the winning candidates are those who receive the most votes. With the **at-large place system,** each candidate runs for a specific seat on the council (place 1, place 2, and so forth) and is elected by either a plurality or a majority of votes cast citywide for that particular seat. Variations of either system may require that a candidate live in a particular district of the city, but the candidates are still elected by all the voters in the city. In contrast, with **single-member districts,** each council member is elected from a particular district by the voters who live in that district.

At-Large Systems versus District Systems.   Supporters of at-large elections say that they promote the public interest because council members must take a citywide view of problems. They charge that council members elected from districts are focused on the needs of their districts rather than the interests of the community as a whole.

Critics of at-large elections maintain that the system allows a simple majority of voters to elect all council members (who typically come from the upper-income brackets and live in the higher-income areas of town). When a citywide majority elects all council members, the interests of racial, ethnic, and ideological minorities in the community are not represented at city hall. These critics charge that effective neighborhood representation serves the interest of the entire city and is more likely to occur when each district elects its own representative to the council.

Single-Member Districts and Minorities.   Although major Texas cities have usually resisted single-member districts, successful legal action by minority groups in the federal courts has forced them to abandon at-large elections. Several cities have instituted a mixed system in which a majority of the council members live in, and are elected from, single-member districts, while the mayor and a number of additional council members are elected at large. One study found that Mexican American candidates in Texas cities were more likely to win the district positions than the at-large seats in mixed systems.[4] Another investigation drew similar conclusions about African American candidates in the state but found that, for

At-Large Election
A citywide (or, in some states, countywide) election.

Pure At-Large System
An at-large election system in which all voters elect all the members of the city council, and candidates do not run for specific seats.

At-Large Place System
An at-large election system in which all voters elect all the members of the city council, and each candidate runs for a specific seat on the council.

Single-Member District
A district in which the voters elect a single member of a legislative body, who runs for election only in that district.

Mexican American candidates, "the pattern was less clear primarily because they were sharply underrepresented in both components."[5]

Another Alternative: Cumulative Voting. While the single-member-district system has been the primary means of increasing minority representation on city councils, some cities have adopted other methods of achieving this goal. One alternative system is cumulative voting (CV). Under this plan, city council members are elected in at-large elections. The number of votes a voter can cast corresponds to the number of seats on the council.

The key characteristic of CV is that the voter can cast more than one vote for a particular candidate. If, for example, there are five seats on the city council, a voter can cast all five votes for one candidate or can cast, say, three votes for one candidate and the remaining two votes for another candidate. Theoretically, members of a voting minority in the city could cast all their votes for a single candidate and increase the chances of that candidate's winning. Two political scientists have concluded, however, that "CV systems . . . guarantee no electoral outcomes. Minority voters must be mobilized and vote cohesively to take advantage of the opportunities CV provides."[6]

According to the organization FairVote–Center for Voting and Democracy, more than fifty local jurisdictions in Texas adopted cumulative voting in the 1990s. Most are school districts. In about 20 percent of the communities where cumulative voting is found, both the school board and the city council have adopted the method. The Amarillo Independent School District resolved a lawsuit by adopting cumulative voting and is the largest jurisdiction in the nation to use this election system.

| Cumulative Voting (CV)
An at-large election system in which voters can cast one or more votes for a single candidate. For example, a voter who can cast up to five votes in a city council election can cast all five votes for one candidate or spread the votes among several candidates.

Revenue Sources and Limitations

Sources and amounts of revenue vary greatly among Texas municipalities according to various factors, including the following:

- The size of the city's population.
- The amount and type of taxes the city is allowed and willing to levy.
- The total assessed value of taxable property within the city limits.
- The needs of the residents.

The local political culture determines expectations about appropriate standards of services and tolerable levels of taxation (see Table 27–3). External forces—such as a downturn in the national economy, the closing of a local military base, or federal and state mandates—also influence the economic climate of a community.

In Texas, state aid represents a considerably lower percentage of municipal revenue than is the norm in many other states. Thus, sales and property taxes are important sources of revenue for Texas cities.

[4]J. L. Polinard, Robert D. Wrinkle, Tomas Longoria, and Norman E. Binder, *Electoral Structure and Urban Policy: The Impact on Mexican-American Communities* (Armonk, N.Y.: M. E. Sharpe, 1994), p. 55.

[5]Robert Brischetto, David R. Richards, Chandler Davidson, and Bernard Grofman, "Texas," in *Quiet Revolution in the South: The Impact of the Voting Rights Act 1965–1990*, ed. Chandler Davidson and Bernard Grofman (Princeton, N.J.: Princeton University Press, 1994), p. 252.

[6]Robert R. Brischetto and Richard L. Engstrom, "Cumulative Voting and Latino Representation: Exit Surveys in Fifteen Texas Communities," *Social Science Quarterly* (December 1997).

TABLE 27–3 | PROPERTY TAXES LEVIED BY TEXAS LOCAL GOVERNMENTS IN 2003 (IN BILLIONS OF DOLLARS)

COUNTIES	CITIES	SPECIAL DISTRICTS	SCHOOL DISTRICTS	TOTAL
4.1	4.4	3.1	17.3	28.9

Source: Texas Comptroller of Public Accounts.

The Sales Tax. A 1 percent municipal sales tax was authorized by the legislature in 1968, and since then Texas cities have become heavily dependent on it. Although all taxes are affected by economic conditions, sales tax revenues vary more sharply during economic cycles of recession and recovery than do property tax revenues. In addition, the budgetary problems of state and national governments make their assistance to cities unreliable. Cities therefore need to build a reserve fund into their budgets to compensate for these somewhat inconsistent sources of revenues.

Property Taxes. Municipalities, school districts, and counties depend heavily on property taxes, in which the tax rate is a percentage of the assessed value of real estate. In a community with a low *tax base*, or total assessed value, the local government has a limited capacity to raise taxes from this source. Thus, a "poor" city must have a high tax rate to provide adequate services. Furthermore, any loss in assessed property values causes a decline in the city's tax base.

The property tax rate in general-law cities depends on the size of the city. The maximum property tax rate of a general-law city, however, is $1.50 per $100.00 of assessed value. Home-rule municipalities can set property tax rates as high as $2.50 per $100.00 of assessed value.

Limits on Property Taxes. Some Texas cities have taken measures to limit increases in property taxes. For example, the Corpus Christi city charter contains a property tax cap of $0.68 per $100.00 valuation. (The tax hikes that are tied to voter-approved bonds are not applied toward the cap.) In 2003, Texas voters approved Proposition 13, which allows cities, towns, counties, and junior college districts to freeze property taxes for people who are disabled or elderly. According to the Texas comptroller's office, by April 2004 nearly thirty local governments (mostly municipalities) had adopted the tax freeze; more adopted the measure in November of that year. Once the freeze is in place, neither the governing body nor the voters can repeal it.

Voters in non-school-district jurisdictions (cities, counties, and special districts) may petition for a rollback election to limit an increase in the property tax rate to no more than 8 percent, plus additional revenue to meet debt-service requirements. For school districts, an election to decide if a tax increase will stand is automatically held if the increase exceeds $0.06 per $100.00 of assessed valuation; no petition is

> **| DID YOU KNOW . . .**
> That according to the Legislative Budget Board, there are more than 3,700 local governments in Texas collecting the property tax?

| Sales Tax
A tax collected on the retail price of purchased items.

| Property Tax
A tax on the assessed value of real estate.

| Rollback Election
In Texas, an election that permits voters to lower a local property tax increase to 8 percent.

Seventy-one percent of Ameriquest Field in Arlington was financed with a city sales tax, and 29 percent was funded by the owners of the Texas Rangers baseball team. In all, taxpayers funded $135 million of the project that was completed in 1994. Who benefits from taxpayer-financed stadiums? (Photo Courtesy of the Texas Rangers)

| User Fee
A charge paid by an individual who receives a particular government service, such as water provision or garbage collection.

| Public Debt
Sums owed by governments.

necessary. According to the Texas comptroller's office, more than three hundred local governments (mostly school districts) have held rollback elections since 1982.

User Fees.   When citizens are charged for services received, the charges are called **user fees.** These fees are increasingly popular for two reasons: (1) citizens' opposition to higher taxes and (2) the notion that people should pay for what they actually use. User fees may be collected for city-provided electricity, water, sewage, and garbage collection, as well as for swimming pools, golf courses, and ambulance services. The Texas Municipal League has found that user fees bring in 21 percent of municipal revenue. Permits, business licenses, and inspection fees round out the usual sources of city revenue.

The advantage of heavy dependence on user fees is that the user of the service pays the expense for providing the service. This satisfies a basic sense of justice because the nonusers are not paying for services they do not consume. Obviously, however, if the fees rise too steeply, the poor may feel "priced out" of the service.

Borrowing.   Local governments use **public debt**—normally, bond issues that must be approved by the voters in a referendum—to fund infrastructure projects such as roads, buildings, and public facilities. The amount and use of the debt are determined by the same legal, political, economic, and cultural factors that determine the source and amount of tax revenues. The law in Texas explicitly limits the amount of long-term debt to a percentage of assessed valuation of property within the boundaries of the government. This restriction is intended to keep governments from falling into bankruptcy, as many did during the Great Depression of the 1930s.

Trends and Issues

A series of trends and issues are important in understanding the current circumstances of Texas municipalities. These include population changes, economic development issues, the problem of mandates from higher levels of government, annexation issues, and term limits for local officials.

Population Trends.   According to the 2000 census, some Texas cities grew much more rapidly than others in the 1990s. Plano, for example, saw a 72.5 percent change in population, while Corpus Christi grew by only 7.8 percent. Laredo grew by 43.7 percent while Lubbock's population increased by only 7.2 percent. A community's rate of growth can have a significant impact on the public-policy decisions made by local officials. Table 27–4 shows the populations of the fifteen largest counties and cities in Texas.

| Development Corporation Act
A state law that allows select Texas cities to raise the sales tax for economic development, subject to voter approval.

Economic Development.   The **Development Corporation Act** allows many Texas cities to adopt a sales tax for economic development projects, subject to voter approval. The adopting cities have either a 4A or 4B designation, and the classifications determine how the funds can be spent. According to the Texas attorney general's *Economic Development Handbook for Texas Cities,* 4A status is open only to cities that meet certain population standards, while all cities are eligible for the 4B designation.

Sales tax revenue based on 4A is used for projects related to industry and manufacturing and can be tied to a decrease in the property tax rate. The 4B designation is more expansive in scope, allowing cities to use revenue for a wide range of projects, including professional and amateur sports facilities, public park improvements, and affordable housing. Since 1989, over five hundred cities have approved a sales tax hike for economic development under one of the designations, and more than eighty have passed increases under both the 4A and 4B designations. The economic development sales tax is particularly popular with small jurisdictions. According to the Texas Economic Development Council, over half of the cities that have adopted the tax have a population of less than five thousand.

TABLE 27–4 | POPULATION OF THE LARGEST COUNTIES AND INCORPORATED CITIES IN TEXAS, 2003 AND 2000

GEOGRAPHIC AREA	POPULATION		PERCENTAGE INCREASE
	2003	**2000**	
COUNTY			
Harris	3,596,086	3,414,981	5.3%
Dallas	2,284,096	2,225,342	2.6
Tarrant	1,559,148	1,454,461	7.2
Bexar	1,471,644	1,397,817	5.3
Travis	857,204	819,844	4.6
El Paso	705,436	681,700	3.5
Hidalgo	635,540	573,923	0.7
Collin	597,147	500,055	9.4
Denton	510,795	438,811	6.4
Fort Bend	419,772	358,956	6.9
Cameron	363,092	336,784	7.8
Montgomery	344,700	297,531	9.4
Nueces	315,206	313,420	0.6
Williamson	303,587	254,968	9.1
Galveston	266,775	250,725	6.4
CITY			
Houston	2,009,690	1,958,258	2.6%
San Antonio	1,214,725	1,154,897	5.2
Dallas	1,208,318	1,190,334	1.5
Austin	672,011	660,413	1.8
Fort Worth	585,122	543,677	7.6
El Paso	584,113	565,212	3.3
Arlington	355,007	334,646	6.1
Corpus Christi	279,208	277,292	0.7
Plano	241,991	224,094	8.0
Garland	218,027	215,968	1.0
Lubbock	206,481	199,749	3.4
Laredo	197,488	178,842	0.4
Irving	194,455	191,876	1.3
Amarillo	178,612	173,879	2.7
Brownsville	156,178	140,748	1.0

Source: U.S. Census Bureau, *States and Puerto Rico Population Estimates by Age and Sex*, July 1, 2004. Available at **www.census.gov/popest/estimates.php**.

Government Mandates. Texas cities—like most cities in the nation—have seen both a decline in federal and state government dollars and an increase in the number of mandates imposed by these governments. A **mandate** is a law passed by Congress or a state legislature requiring a lower-level government to meet an obligation. Some notable examples of federal mandates are the Americans with Disabilities Act, the National Voter Registration Act (Motor Voter Act), the Help America Vote Act, and the No Child Left Behind Act. Supporters of mandates argue that they permit the federal and state governments to meet important needs in a uniform fashion. Critics charge that mandates—particularly those that are unfunded—impose a heavy financial burden on those governments required to fulfill the obligations.

In the late 1990s, the Texas legislature passed HB 66, which established the Unfunded Mandates Interagency Work Group. The state auditor, the state comptroller, the director of the Legislative Budget Board, a senator (selected by the lieutenant governor), and a representative (selected by the speaker) make up the group. Its charge is to keep a record of unfunded mandates that are passed by the legislature so that lawmakers have a sense of the impact of these mandates on other governments.

|Mandate
A requirement or standard imposed on one level of government by a higher level of government.

| **Annexation**
The act of bringing unincorporated areas under the jurisdiction of a city.

| **Extraterritorial Jurisdiction (ETJ)**
In Texas, a buffer area that extends beyond a city's limits. Cities can enforce some laws, such as zoning and building codes, in an ETJ.

| **Colonia**
In Texas, an unincorporated urban district along the U.S.-Mexican border. Colonias are often impoverished and are chiefly inhabited by Mexican Americans.

| **Term Limit**
A restriction on the number of times a person can be elected to a particular office.

Several types of unfunded mandates are exempt from the list, however, including those that are passed in compliance with the Texas Constitution, federal law, or a court order, as well as those that are established as a result of a popular election.

Annexation. Big cities in Texas have not suffered as much as many other U.S. cities from "white flight," urban decay, the evacuation of industry, and declining tax bases. Texas cities have escaped some of the worst of these problems because of the state's liberal **annexation** laws.

The Municipal Annexation Act establishes a buffer area, known as **extraterritorial jurisdiction (ETJ),** that extends from one-half mile to five miles beyond the city's limits, depending on the city's population. The city may enforce zoning and building codes in the outlying area, and new cities may not be incorporated within the ETJ. The law also gives home-rule cities the power to annex an area equal to 10 percent of their existing area each year without the consent of the inhabitants of the area to be annexed. With this protection and with long-range planning, Texas cities can avoid being boxed in by suburban "bedroom" cities.

One strategy involves annexing "fingers" of land outward from the existing city limits and placing the area between the fingers into the ETJ. The unincorporated areas within the ETJ may then be annexed as they become sufficiently populated to warrant it. Central cities that plan ahead are therefore free to extend their boundaries and recapture both the tax base and the population that may have "fled" the city. Increasingly, though, inhabitants of outlying areas are raising objections to the state's municipal annexation laws. These persons resent the fact that their jurisdictions can be annexed without their permission.

The Texas legislature passed a comprehensive annexation bill—the first in over three decades—in 1999. The measure requires cities to give notice of annexation plans three years in advance, participate in arbitration with areas to be annexed, and deliver services within two and a half years. (Exceptions to the last requirement can be triggered under certain circumstances.) Outlying areas face limits to what they can do if they want to avoid annexation.

A special annexation issue involves **colonias.** A colonia is an unincorporated urban district along the U.S.-Mexican border. They are typically severely impoverished and must contend with a multitude of problems, including substandard housing, unsanitary drinking water, and lack of proper sewage disposal. The Texas attorney general's office has identified more than 1,800 colonias in twenty-nine Texas counties, most of which lie along the U.S.-Mexico border.

These colonias are eligible for financial aid from the state. But what happens to the aid a colonia receives if it is annexed? In 1999, the Texas legislature passed a law that allows a colonia eligible for state aid to continue to receive it for five years after annexation.

Term Limits. Although the United States Supreme Court has ruled that **term limits** for members of the U.S. Congress are unconstitutional,[7] over 2,800 cities in the United States—including eight of the ten largest cities—have term-limit laws for local offices.[8] Proponents of term limits believe that city hall is best governed by new blood and fresh ideas and that limiting the number of terms council members may serve is the best way to achieve that goal. Opponents, though, worry that cities stand to lose experienced, effective council members.

According to the Texas Municipal League, term-limit laws have been approved by the voters in over sixty cities in the state, with the bulk of the adoptions occurring in the early 1990s. These laws are less than uniform. Some cities allow a per-

---

[7]*U.S. Term Limits v. Thornton,* 514 U.S. 779 (1995).
[8]Danielle Fagre, "Microcosm of the Movement: Local Term Limits in the United States," *U.S. Term Limits,* 1995. Available at **www.termlimits.org/Current_Info/microcosm**.

son who has served the maximum number of terms to run again after sitting out a term. In contrast, a San Antonio council member who has served for two terms can never run for that seat again, which amounts to a lifetime ban. In Austin, a council member is limited to two consecutive three-year terms, but that limit can be waived with a petition signed by 5 percent of the registered voters represented by the council member.

Attempts to weaken city term-limit laws through state laws or litigation have been unsuccessful. Voters also do not appear to be anxious to remove or modify the limits once they are in place. In 2000, voters in Austin rejected a proposition that would have repealed the city's term-limit law. Four years later, San Antonio voters said no to a ballot measure that would have permitted council members to serve beyond two terms.

Counties

Like the counties in most other states, Texas counties are established and structured by the state constitution and the legislature. The county serves as a general-purpose government and as an administrative arm of the state, carrying out the state's laws and collecting certain state taxes. Although the county is an arm of the state, state supervision is minimal.

County government is far less flexible than municipal government in its organization and functions. Texas counties do not have home rule. At one time, a constitutional provision authorized county home rule. The provision was so poorly written and so difficult to implement that no county in the state was able to use it to reorganize, and it was subsequently repealed.

Because counties cannot pass ordinances unless specifically authorized by the state, new state statutes or constitutional amendments are often necessary to allow a county to deal with contemporary problems. The needs of Harris County, with a population of 3,596,086 in 2003, are significantly different from those of Loving

The Red River courthouse in Clarksville was completed in 1885. It is one of the oldest surviving courthouses in Texas. (Photo Courtesy of Newman/Flickr.com)

County, which had only 62 inhabitants in that year. (We examine Loving County government in this chapter's *Politics and County Government* feature.) The demands placed on Montgomery County, which saw population growth of 9.4 percent in the three years from 2000 to 2003, are likely to be different from those placed on Jefferson County, which experienced a population decrease of 1.2 percent during the same period. Yet Texas law allows only modest variations in county governments to accommodate these differences. (Many state laws, however, are unique to specific counties because of their population or their location—a law pertaining to a coastal county, for example.)

Counties are also limited in their ability to tax their citizens. Counties can impose property taxes at a maximum rate of $0.80 per $100.00 of assessed valuation, but they have the power to collect additional taxes beyond this limit—if the voters approve—to cover long-term debt for infrastructure, such as courthouses, criminal justice buildings, farm-to-market roads, flood control, and county road and bridge maintenance.

Functions of Counties

County government is responsible for administering county, state, and national elections, but not those for municipalities, school districts, and other special districts. County government acts for the state in the following areas:

1. Securing rights-of-way for highways.
2. Providing law enforcement.
3. Registering births, deaths, and marriages.
4. Housing state district courts.
5. Registering motor vehicles.
6. Recording land titles and deeds.
7. Collecting some state taxes and fees.

Optional Powers. County government also has optional powers specifically authorized by state law, and these powers are found in various state codes. For example, according to the Local Government Code, a county government may undertake the following activities:

1. Establish and maintain libraries.
2. Operate and maintain parks.
3. Establish recreational and cultural facilities (such as auditoriums and convention centers).
4. Appoint a county historical commission.
5. Regulate sexually oriented businesses.

According to the Health and Safety Code, a county government has the authority to maintain a county hospital.

Intergovernment Cooperation. A county government may also enter into an agreement with another local government to provide a service or program. For example, the Local Government Code permits county-city partnerships to purchase and maintain parks, museums, and historic sites. The Interlocal Cooperation Act, a part of the code, authorizes various local governments, including counties, cities, and special districts, to contract with each other for the provision of various "administrative functions," such as tax assessment and collection and records management. The various governmen-

Citizens rally at the capitol in Austin in support of the Texas Library Association. Maintaining libraries is an optional power of counties. (Photo Courtesy of "dmatp"/Flickr.com)

POLITICS AND COUNTY GOVERNMENT | Loving County—Small Is Beautiful

Loving County, Texas, lies immediately south of southeastern New Mexico. No county in the United States has a smaller population than Loving. In 2000, the census put the number of inhabitants at sixty-seven. The census estimate for 2003 was sixty-two. These figures raise an obvious question: How do you run a county that has so few people? The answer appears to be, "Quite nicely, thank you."

THE ECONOMY OF LOVING COUNTY

Loving County contains a single unorganized town—the county seat of Mentone, which has a post office and a cafe but no gasoline station, grocery store, or cemetery. The county receives less than ten inches of rain a year and is virtually a desert. A handful of ranches manage to survive, but the county economy is actually based on oil and natural gas. Loving has more oil wells than people, and most of its adults work in the oil and gas industries. Another source of personal income in Loving is oil and gas royalties paid to landowners.

LOVING COUNTY GOVERNMENT

Loving County fills all the standard county offices established in Texas—twelve in total. It seems unlikely that many other jurisdictions in the world have such high percentages of their adult populations serving as elected officials. The Texas nepotism law, which prohibits patronage among relatives, is a significant problem for Loving, and officials must plan carefully to avoid violating it.

In 2003, the county collected $1,296,986 in property taxes (and spent only $215,184 on the roads). Loving therefore collected $20,919 in property taxes for every man, woman, and child in a county where the average yearly salary per job was $17,857 in 2002.

The Loving County courthouse in Mentone, Texas.
(Photo Courtesy of Drew/Vicious Circle)

How is this possible? The answer is the oil and gas wells, which make up 98 percent of the assessed valuation in the county. Loving residents are not taxing their own homes and businesses to maintain the county government—they are taxing the oil and gas industries to provide county residents with jobs as county officials. Indeed, Loving was not organized as a county until 1931, after oil and gas had been discovered. Before 1931, Loving was administered by neighboring Reeves County.

FOR CRITICAL ANALYSIS

If Loving were not organized as a county, what might happen to the county's population? Why?

---

tal units may also jointly provide "governmental functions and services," including police and fire protection, streets and roads, public health and welfare, and waste disposal.

Structure and Organization of Counties

County government consists of a number of independently elected officials (see Figure 27–2 on the next page). The county governing body, the **commissioners court**, consists of the **county judge** and four **county commissioners**. The commissioners court is not a judicial body but a legislature of limited authority that approves the budget for all operations of the county, sets the tax rate, and passes ordinances.

The commissioners court does not have direct control over the many elected department heads of county government, but it wields considerable influence

| **Commissioners Court**
In Texas, the policymaking body of a county. A commissioners court consists of a county judge (the presiding officer), who is elected in countywide elections, and four county commissioners elected from individual precincts.

| **County Judge**
In Texas, an official elected countywide to preside over the commissioners court and to try certain minor cases.

| **County Commissioner**
One of a group of officials elected to administer a county; in Texas, a member of the commissioners court who is elected from a district, or precinct.

FIGURE 27–2 | TEXAS COUNTY OFFICIALS ELECTED BY VOTERS

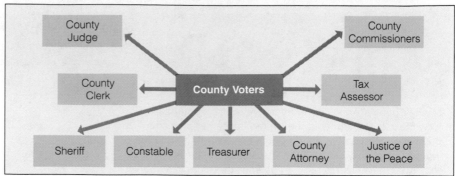

| Sheriff
The chief law enforcement officer of a county—in most states, an elected official. In Texas, the sheriff's budget must be approved by the commissioners court, which limits the sheriff's authority.

through its budgetary power. The county sheriff, for example, is responsible to county voters for enforcing the law and maintaining order and security in the county jail. The commissioners court, however, must provide the funds to build the jail and must approve its staff; authorize expenditures for each vehicle and its gas and repairs; and authorize deputies, clerks, and their salaries. The sheriff, therefore, is accountable not only to the voters but also to other elected county officials.

County Judges.   The county judge is elected for a four-year term from the county at large to preside over the commissioners court. According to the Texas comptroller's office, the powers of the county judge are found in over fifty provisions of the Local Government Code, as well as many other state codes. The Texas Association of Counties lists many powers held by Texas county judges, including the following:

1. Preparing the budget (a responsibility the county judge shares with the county clerk or auditor in counties with populations under 225,000).
2. Supervising election-related activities (calling elections, posting election notices, and receiving and canvassing election results).
3. Conducting hearings for beer and wine permits.
4. Performing marriage ceremonies.
5. Conducting hearings on state hospital admittance for people with mental illness and other mental disabilities.
6. Serving as the head of civil defense and disaster relief for the county.

Additionally, a county judge may have judicial authority, but the obligations in this area depend on the county.

The County Commissioners.   Four county commissioners make up the remaining membership of the court and are elected for four-year terms. Commissioners are elected in single-member districts (or precincts, as they are called in Texas). In 1968, the United States Supreme Court ruled that commissioner districts must be drawn on the basis of the one-person, one-vote principle.[9] During the next two decades, county governments faced many legal challenges because of malapportioned precincts. For example, between 1974 and 1984, the Mexican American Legal Defense and Educational Fund and the Southwest Voter Registration Education Project filed voting-rights lawsuits in over eighty counties.[10]

Commissioners are frequently called "road commissioners" because they are responsible for the county roads and bridges within their precincts (unless a county engineer has been hired to do that job). Each commissioner is given a certain

---

[9]*Avery v. Midland County,* 390 U.S. 474 (1968).
[10]David Montejano, *Anglos and Mexicans in the Making of Texas, 1836–1986* (Austin: University of Texas Press, 1987), p. 296.

Lupe Valdez was elected sheriff of Dallas County in 2004. With a relatively large budget and staff of deputies to assist them in enforcing state law throughout the county, sheriffs, next to county judges, are usually the most powerful county officers. (AP Photo/LM Otero)

amount of revenue and has almost total authority to determine how it will be spent on roads and bridges. Rural residents often consider building and maintenance of rural roads the primary responsibilities of the commissioners.

Law Enforcement Officers. Officers with law enforcement duties include the county sheriff and constables. The sheriff, next to the county judge, is usually the most powerful county officer because he or she has a relatively large budget and a staff of deputies to assist in enforcing state law throughout the county. The sheriff's department usually refrains from patrolling within the corporate limits of cities, the better to use scarce resources and avoid jurisdictional disputes with city police. The department also operates the county jail and delivers and executes court papers (such as court orders).

Constables are elected from the same precincts as justices of the peace and serve as process officers of that court. They are also general law enforcement officers. In metropolitan counties such as Harris and Montgomery, constables have many deputies and are the heads of important law enforcement agencies.

In some counties, the office of constable has remained unfilled for years. Because the office is provided for in the Texas Constitution, however, the only way to abolish it has been by constitutional amendment. In 2002, voters approved an amendment that allows a commissioners court to abolish a constable office that has been vacant for over seven years. An abolished office can be restored by the commissioners court or by voter approval.

County Financial Officers. Officials with financial duties include the tax assessor-collector, the treasurer, and the auditor. The tax assessor-collector is probably the most important of these. The office has the following responsibilities:

1. Collecting various county taxes and fees.
2. Collecting certain state taxes and fees, particularly motor vehicle registration fees (license plate fees) and the motor vehicle sales tax.
3. Registering voters.

The county treasurer is responsible for receiving, depositing, and disbursing funds. Some counties have done away with the treasurer's office. When a county wishes to do this, the commissioners court must petition the legislature for a constitutional

Constable
A law enforcement officer. In Texas, constables are elected at the county level and serve as process officers of justice of the peace courts.

Tax Assessor-Collector
In Texas, a county financial officer whose responsibilities include collecting county taxes or fees and registering voters.

County Treasurer
A county official who is responsible for receiving, depositing, and disbursing county funds.

amendment to allow its county's voters to eliminate the county treasurer's office. The most likely recipient of the treasurer's duties will be the auditor.

The county auditor reviews all county financial records and ensures that expenditures are made in accordance with law. Whereas other key county officials are elected, county auditors are appointed for two-year terms by district judges.

Clerical Officers.   Officials with clerical duties include county and district clerks. The county clerk serves as the county's chief record keeper and election officer. In some ways, the office parallels that of the Texas secretary of state. The county clerk has the following duties:

1. Serving as clerk for the county commissioners court.
2. Maintaining records for justices of the peace, for county courts, and for district courts in counties with populations of less than eight thousand.
3. Recording deeds, mortgages, wills, and contracts.
4. Issuing marriage licenses and maintaining certain records of births and deaths.
5. Serving on the county election board, certifying candidates running for county office, and carrying out other "housekeeping" functions in connection with elections, including preserving the results of state, county, and local elections.

In counties with populations of over eight thousand, the district clerk assumes the county clerk's role as record keeper for the district courts. (The county clerk continues to maintain records for the constitutional county court and any county courts-at-law in existence; these courts were discussed in Chapter 25.)

Legal Officers.   County attorneys and district attorneys perform a variety of functions. Some counties have only one of these officials—either a county or a district attorney. This official prosecutes all criminal cases, gives advisory opinions to county officials that define their authority, and represents the county in civil proceedings.

If a county has both a district attorney and a county attorney, the district attorney specializes in prosecuting cases in district court, while the county attorney handles lesser cases. District attorneys are neither subordinate to nor part of county government in Texas, but their office space and salaries are partly paid by the counties. County attorneys are wholly county officials.

Other Officials.   In some counties, commissioners courts or voters have created other executive officers. There may be five or more members of a county board of school trustees, a county superintendent of schools, a county surveyor, a county weigher, and even a county inspector of hides and animals. Counties may also authorize such appointive officers as the county election administrator, county health officer, county medical examiner, county agricultural agent, and home demonstration agent.

Issues and Trends

The institutional features of Texas county government date to the 1800s. The demands of modern society are placing an increasingly heavy burden on this level of government. Next, we review some frequent criticisms of county government that follow from outdated structures and discuss the measures counties can take to deal with contemporary problems.

Constitutional Rigidity.   The great mass of detailed and restrictive material in the Texas Constitution creates problems of rigidity and inflexibility, and additional controls are scattered throughout the civil statutes. The result is a collection of legal requirements that are applied equally to the four largest counties in the state—Harris,

County Auditor
In Texas, a county financial officer whose duties, depending on the population of the county, may include reviewing county financial records and (in large counties) serving as the chief budget officer.

County Clerk
The chief record keeper and elections officer of a county.

District Clerk
In Texas, the record keeper for the district court in a county with a population that exceeds eight thousand.

County Attorney
In Texas, a county legal officer who gives legal advice to the commissioners court, represents the county in court, and prosecutes crimes. If a county has both a county attorney and a district attorney, the latter prosecutes felony crimes.

District Attorney
An official who prosecutes felony cases.

Dallas, Tarrant, and Bexar—and to the scores of counties that have populations of less than twenty thousand. This standardized approach gives little consideration to the special needs of individual counties. Two political scientists have observed that the nation's "state legislatures have exercised virtually unlimited authority in prescribing the limits of county discretion."[11] This general observation clearly applies to Texas. Under the current system, change has to come from the state legislature.

The Long Ballot.   So many county officials are independently elected, and the operations of county government are so decentralized, that voters may find it difficult to monitor the many positions involved in county government. The current system of electing county officials is sometimes said to use a **long ballot,** because the ballot includes a long list of county offices to be filled. Reformers recommend a **short ballot** with fewer elected county officials. More officials would be appointed, and a county-manager system or an elected county executive would be established. Defenders of the long ballot counter that the direct election of public officials ensures that government will remain responsive to the needs and demands of the voters.

Unit Road System.   One reform that counties are permitted to undertake is to establish a **unit road system.** This system takes the day-to-day responsibility for roads away from individual county commissioners and concentrates it in the hands of a professional engineer who is responsible to the commissioners court. The voters may petition for an election to establish the unit road system, or commissioners may initiate the change themselves.

Supporters of this system maintain that it brings greater coordination and professionalism to the building of roads in rural areas. The current practice in most counties—dividing funds for roads and bridges among the four commissioners—is defended by those who believe these activities should remain the direct responsibility of elected officials.

The Civil Service System.   Students of government often criticize the use of the **spoils system** to hire employees. Under this system, political loyalty rather than competence may be the main factor in the recruitment and retention of government workers. A county worker's job security may depend on political allegiance to a particular official and on that official's reelection. When a new official is elected, there may be a substantial turnover of county employees.

Opponents of these practices propose a **civil service** system that bases employment and promotion on specific qualifications and performance. Because civil service systems also prohibit termination of employment except for proven cause, such systems offer job security, which allegedly attracts qualified personnel. Supporters of this system maintain that it encourages professionalism, increases efficiency, and allows uniform application of equal opportunity requirements.

In contrast, supporters of the spoils system point out that elected officials are responsible for their employees' performance and therefore should have the authority to hire and fire at will. They also argue that an elected official would be foolish to release competent employees simply because they had gained their experience under a predecessor. Finally, they argue that the civil service system provides so much job security that complacency and indifference to the public interest may result.

Eligibility for Civil Service Systems.   Texas counties with populations of 200,000 or more may establish a civil service system for county employees, while counties with populations of over 500,000 may also establish a civil service system for the sheriff's

Long Ballot
An election ballot listing many independently elected offices.

Short Ballot
An election ballot listing only a few independently elected offices.

Unit Road System
In Texas, a system that concentrates the day-to-day responsibilities of roads in the hands of a professional engineer rather than individual county commissioners. The engineer is ultimately responsible to the commissioners court.

Spoils System
The awarding of government jobs to political supporters and friends.

Civil Service
A collective term for the body of employees working for a government who have gained their position through a merit system.

---

[11]David R. Berman and Tanis J. Salant, "The Changing Role of Counties in the Intergovernment System," in *The American County: Frontiers of Knowledge,* ed. Donald C. Menzel (Tuscaloosa: University of Alabama Press, 1996), p. 24.

office. According to the Texas Association of Counties, a civil service system exists in half of the twenty counties that meet the eligibility requirement. All seven counties that can establish this system in their sheriff's department have done so.

Consolidation.   Students of county government point to **consolidation** as a means of reducing both the number of local governments and the duplication of government services. Consolidation can take a variety of forms, from merging the county and local governments within the county into a single government (a *metro government*) to having various local governments share the expenses of selected services.

There are two major obstacles to consolidation of governments. First, consolidation requires action on the part of the state legislature, followed by voter approval. Second, independently elected officials at the local level are likely to resist a move that would merge local responsibilities and reduce the number of political offices. Additionally, "public choice" theorists maintain that government fragmentation is preferable to a monopoly, that smaller governments are more responsive than larger ones, and that the current system forces governments to be competitive.[12]

City-county consolidation bills have failed to win passage in the Texas legislature in the past. It is probable that local governments will continue to make consolidation changes in a piecemeal fashion. For example, Texas has established a countywide appraisal authority for property taxes, and all local governments must accept its property appraisals.

Special Districts

Special districts are local governments that provide single or closely related services that are not provided by general-purpose county or municipal governments. (Although the more than one thousand independent school districts in Texas constitute a type of special-purpose government, other districts are the focus of this chapter. School districts were discussed in Chapter 26.) In a suburban area outside the city limits, for example, a special district may be established to provide water and sewer facilities for a housing development. This government unit will have the authority to borrow to build the system and may assess taxes and user fees on property owners and residents.

The number of special districts has grown considerably over the years, as shown in Table 27-5. In fact, special districts are the most numerous of all local governments in Texas (see Table 27-1 on page 851). According to the Census Bureau, two-thirds of the special districts in Texas provide a single service. The rest are classified as "multiple-function districts," and most of those provide municipal utilities (sewer and water). Examples of special districts in the state include the following:

- Airport authorities.
- Drainage districts.
- Hospital authorities.
- Municipal utility districts (MUDs).
- Navigation districts.
- Metropolitan transit authorities (MTAs—see Figure 27–3).
- River authorities.
- Rural fire-prevention districts.
- Noxious weed control districts.

Some individuals who serve on the governing boards of special districts are elected, while city councils and county commissioners appoint others. In some cases, council members and commissioners serve on these boards themselves.

[12]A thorough discussion of metropolitan fragmentation can be found in Virginia Gray and Peter Eisinger, *American States and Cities*, 2d ed. (New York: Addison-Wesley Educational Publishers, 1997), Chapter 11.

TABLE 27–5 | **SPECIAL DISTRICTS IN TEXAS, 1952–2002**

1952	1962	1972	1982	1992	2002
491	733	1,215	1,681	2,266	2,245

Source: U.S. Census Bureau, *2002 Census of Governments*, Vol. 1, No. 1.
Available at **www.census.gov/prod/2003pubs/gc021x1.pdf**.

Dependent Agencies

Special districts should not be confused with **dependent agencies.** The Bureau of the Census recognizes some government entities as dependent agencies rather than special districts because they are closely tied to general-purpose governments and do not have as much independence as special districts in budgeting and administration.

An example of a dependent agency is a crime control and prevention district, which is subject to voter approval and remains in existence for only a designated number of years unless the voters approve an extension. A crime control district (as it is sometimes called) also collects a voter-approved sales tax. This type of dependent agency has become increasingly popular since the 1990s, particularly in cities located in Tarrant County. Fort Worth became the first Texas city to approve such a district in 1995. In 2006 the Texas comptroller's office reported thirty-nine crime control districts in the state. More than 60 percent of the districts collect a one-half-cent sales tax, while most of the remaining districts rely on a one-fourth-cent tax.

Dependent Agency
A government entity that is closely linked to general-purpose governments. Dependent agencies do not have the independence of special districts.

FIGURE 27–3 | **CITIES AND COUNTIES SERVED BY PUBLIC TRANSPORTATION SYSTEMS (METROPOLITAN TRANSIT AUTHORITIES, OR MTAS)**

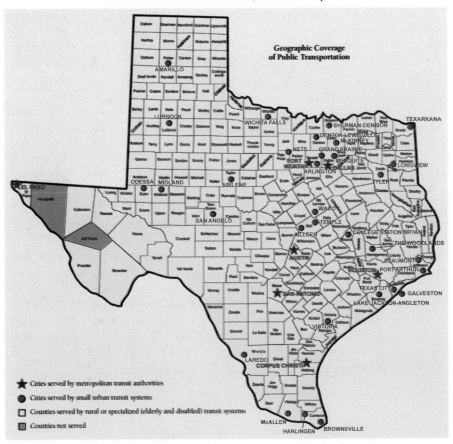

Source: Texas Department of Transportation.

Reasons for Using Special Districts

Having a service provided by a special district rather than a general-purpose government is appealing to many for a variety of reasons. A city or county may have limited revenue because of a downturn in the economy, the loss of a major industry, new unfunded mandates, or fewer federal dollars. The general-purpose government may have hit its sales tax ceiling (2 percent) as mandated by the state. Popular or political sentiment may be that city and county property taxes are already too high, and there may be a strong antitax organization in the community eager to make that point. Little or no support may exist for raising taxes or cutting other services to accommodate another service responsibility.

Furthermore, the service need in question may be unique to only a small area within a city or county. Why tax the entire jurisdiction? Alternatively, the demand for a service may extend beyond a single jurisdiction, calling for a special district that is multicity or multicounty in scope. For a host of reasons, a special district as an alternative revenue source can become an attractive option.

Issues and Trends

Special districts can be dissolved. According to the Local Government Code, a municipality can annex a special district. The municipality then takes ownership of the district's property and assets and assumes responsibility for the district's debts, liabilities, and services. The national trend, though, has clearly been toward an increase in the number of special districts, and this trend is also evident in Texas. (See again Table 27–5 on the previous page.) Some people believe that the growing number of special districts may be a problem.

"Hidden" Governments. Special districts are sometimes called "hidden" governments. For one thing, the actions of district officials and employees are less visible than if a county or city provided the services. In addition, when elections are held at times or places other than those for general elections, voter turnout is quite low.

Cost. Because special districts are often small, they may purchase in limited quantities at higher prices than larger governments. Additionally, if special districts have little or no authority to tax, they are forced to borrow by issuing revenue bonds, which are paid from fees collected for the service provided, rather than from general-obligation bonds, which are paid from tax revenue.

Because revenue bonds are less secure than general-obligation bonds, residents are forced to pay higher interest rates just to service the bonded indebtedness. Special districts may also have a lower bond rating than larger, general-function governments, which further increases their cost of borrowing.

A study of special districts in over three hundred U.S. metropolitan areas concluded that the special-purpose approach to governing is more costly than the general-purpose approach. Additionally, "social-welfare functions" (such as hospitals, housing, and welfare) tend to receive more revenue in metropolitan areas with fewer special districts. "Housekeeping functions" (including fire protection, natural resources, and police protection) and "development functions" (including airports, water, and highways) tend to receive more revenue in areas in which special districts are more prevalent.[13]

---

[13]Kathryn A. Foster, *The Political Economy of Special-Purpose Government* (Washington, D.C.: Georgetown University Press, 1997), pp. 221–224.

Councils of Governments

Councils of governments (COGs) represent an attempt by the state to encourage coordination of local government activities on a regional basis. The first COG in Texas was formed in 1966, and today there are twenty-four COGs encompassing all regions of Texas. Figure 27–4 shows the boundaries, populations, and Web site addresses of the twenty-four Texas COGs. According to the Texas Association of Regional Councils (TARC), more than two thousand governments in Texas belong to COGs. Most of the members are municipal and county governments.

A COG is not another government and has no jurisdiction over the various local governments within its borders. Rather, it is a voluntary grouping of governments that have not relinquished any of their self-government rights. COGs provide several significant services to their members, including regional planning, technical

| Council of Governments (COG)
A voluntary organization of counties, municipalities, and other authorities that seeks to coordinate responses to area-wide problems.

FIGURE 27–4 | COUNCILS OF GOVERNMENTS IN TEXAS

This map shows the comptroller's thirteen regions and the twenty-four corresponding regional governments. Regional governing bodies are shown with Web site addresses and the U.S. Census 2000 population. Texas's total population in 2000 was 20,851,820.

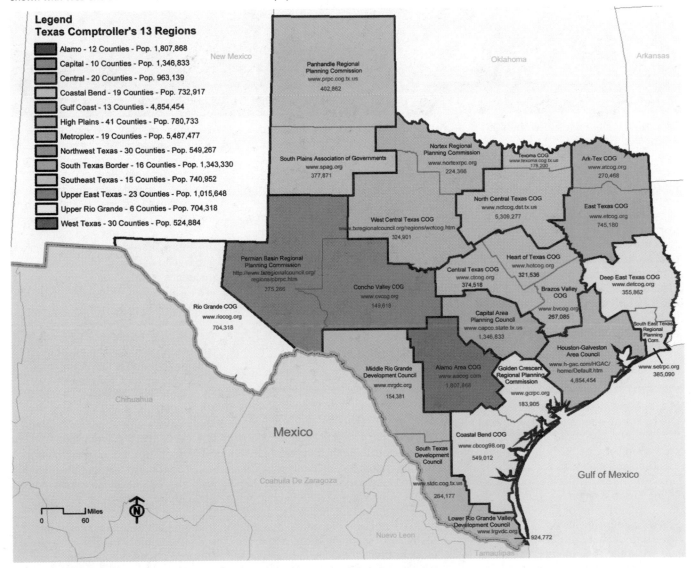

Legend
Texas Comptroller's 13 Regions

- Alamo - 12 Counties - Pop. 1,807,868
- Capital - 10 Counties - Pop. 1,346,833
- Central - 20 Counties - Pop. 963,139
- Coastal Bend - 19 Counties - Pop. 732,917
- Gulf Coast - 13 Counties - 4,854,454
- High Plains - 41 Counties - Pop. 780,733
- Metroplex - 19 Counties - Pop. 5,487,477
- Northwest Texas - 30 Counties - Pop. 549,267
- South Texas Border - 16 Counties - Pop. 1,343,330
- Southeast Texas - 15 Counties - Pop. 740,952
- Upper East Texas - 23 Counties - Pop. 1,015,648
- Upper Rio Grande - 6 Counties - Pop. 704,318
- West Texas - 30 Counties - Pop. 524,884

Sources: ESRI Data, Texas Comptroller, and U.S. Census Bureau's 2000 Population Statistics Disclaimer.
Note: Map data provided "as is" with no warranties of any kind. Colors have no specific representation other than cartographic display.

services, and help in applying for grants. When requested by member governments, COGs provide research into problem areas and organize and operate training facilities, such as police academies.

One of the major issues on the agenda of Texas COGs is homeland security. The Texas Association of Regional Councils is working with the Texas Engineering Extension Service and the governor's Texas homeland security coordinator to facilitate the implementation of the state's Homeland Security Project. The TARC Web site (**www.txregionalcouncil.org**) lists homeland security training workshops that were held at COGs throughout the state, including workshops entitled "Operational Weapons of Mass Destruction Response for Law Enforcement Train-the-Trainer," "Counterterrorism Training," "Multihazard Program for Schools," and "Radiation Safety Training."

By bringing local officials together, COGs provide a base for the exchange of ideas and knowledge. While COGs do not solve the problems facing local governments, they do encourage local officials to recognize the magnitude of these problems and cooperate in managing some of them.

MAKING A DIFFERENCE | Involvement at the Local Level

Like the laws handed down by the national and state governments, the policies made by cities, counties, and special districts have a major bearing on our lives. While we can correspond with elected officials and bureaucrats at every level of government in one fashion or another, the best chance of communicating with government officials in an immediate manner—and sometimes even face to face—is at the local level. In addition, we share a common bond with those who fill our local government offices: like us, they live in our community.

Why Should You Care?

Local government issues often give rise to strong differences of opinion in the community. Should a city council pass a smoking ban? Should it replace an at-large election system with single-member districts? Should it change from a city-manager to a strong-mayor form of government? Should a municipality and a county government share the expense of a jail, or should they maintain separate jail facilities? Should two neighboring

counties join forces to establish and fund a park? Should a metropolitan transit authority change bus routes or suspend service on holidays?

Elected and appointed officials may disagree on what to do about these matters, but unless they decide to take no action at all, they will cast votes or adopt policies that affect everyone in the community. Local government officials should, and often do, seek the views of the public. The public also has many other opportunities to express informed opinions.

What Can You Do?

You can take the following steps to influence local governments:

- **Observe and Learn about Local Government.** Organize a "city hall day" at your college or university. Hold panel discussions on key issues facing your community. Invite local elected officials (such as the mayor and members of the city council), appointed officials (such as the city manager, the city secretary, and the heads of various

city departments), and city hall reporters to serve on the panels.

Attend a city council meeting or a county commissioners court meeting. If your local cable system carries these meetings, watch them regularly.

Attend a court trial, and watch the county attorney or district attorney in action. If a constable maintains a "ride-along" program, ask if you can participate.

- **Get Your Message Out.** At a meeting of the city council, a special-district board, or the county commissioners court, sign up to speak about an issue that matters to you during the "public comments" part of the meeting.

Write a letter to the editor of a newspaper about a local issue that is important to you. Your letter could spark an exchange of ideas in your community. It might even lead local elected officials to take action.

- **Participate.** Participate in a local campaign. Candidates often need volunteers to help organize rallies and get-out-the-vote drives, stuff envelopes, work phone banks, and pass out campaign literature.

Key Terms

annexation 860	county attorney 866	general-law city 852	sales tax 857
at-large election 855	county auditor 866	general-purpose government 851	sheriff 864
at-large place system 855	county clerk 866		short ballot 867
charter 852	county commissioner 863	home-rule city 852	single-member district 855
civil service 867	county judge 863	initiative 852	special district 851
colonia 860	county treasurer 865	long ballot 867	spoils system 867
commission system 854	cumulative voting (CV) 856	mandate 859	strong-mayor system 854
commissioners court 863	dependent agency 869	property tax 857	tax assessor-collector 865
consolidation 868	Development Corporation Act 858	public debt 858	term limit 860
constable 865		pure at-large system 855	unit road system 867
council of governments (COG) 871	district attorney 866	recall 852	user fee 858
	district clerk 866	referendum 852	weak-mayor system 854
council-manager system 852	extraterritorial jurisdiction (ETJ) 860	rollback election 857	

Chapter Summary

1 Municipalities, counties, and special districts provide many services that have a direct impact on our daily lives. It is important, then, to examine these governments in both their historical and contemporary contexts.

2 The municipal reform movement of the early twentieth century had a major effect on Texas cities. Key features of the reform era—nonpartisan elections, the council-manager form of government, and at-large elections—are characteristic of many Texas cities. Some cities with Hispanic and African American populations have (often by court order) replaced at-large elections with single-member districts, modified election systems, or cumulative voting to enhance the chances that minority candidates can be elected to the city council.

3 The initiative, the referendum, recall elections, rollback elections, term-limit laws, and economic development sales tax elections offer voters the opportunity to exert direct influence over municipal government.

4 Texas county government is largely a product of the 1800s, yet the county is increasingly being called on to resolve problems once considered almost exclusively urban.

5 Local governments rely on a variety of revenue sources—property and sales taxes, user fees, public debt, and state and federal dollars—to provide services to the people.

6 Government is largely fragmented at the local level. While there can be friction between governments (for example, in the area of annexation), there can also be cooperation (such as interlocal agreements). Any significant changes in the structural relationship among cities, counties, and special districts, however, will probably be incremental rather than sweeping.

Selected Print and Media Resources

SUGGESTED READINGS

Bowler, Shaun, and Todd Andrew Donovan. *Demanding Choices: Opinion, Voting, and Direct Democracy.* Ann Arbor: University of Michigan Press, 1998. The authors give a comprehensive overview of the role the voter plays in referendums.

Grey, Lawrence. *How to Win a Local Election: A Complete Step-by-Step Guide.* New York: M. Evans & Co., 1999. A former Ohio appellate judge offers sound advice on the many aspects of running for local office.

Pelissero, John, ed. *Cities, Politics, and Policy: A Comparative Analysis.* Washington, D.C.: CQ Press, 2003. This book is a collection of articles focusing on major urban issues, including intergovernmental relations, political participation, race and ethnicity, power, decision making, economic development, urban service delivery, finance, and suburban and metropolitan government.

Riordon, William L. *Plunkitt of Tammany Hall: A Series of Very Plain Talks on Very Practical Politics.* Boston: Bedford/St. Martin's, 1994. This book offers the perspective of George Washington Plunkitt, a Tammany Hall ward boss, on why the political machine is preferable to political reform.

MEDIA RESOURCES

City Hall—A 1996 film that depicts a New York mayor (Al Pacino) and the corruption that can surface in big-city politics.

Lone Star—A 1996 murder mystery that depicts the interaction among the residents of a small South Texas border community.

E·MOCRACY | Dealing with Local Government Online

Individuals conduct only a tiny fraction—less than 1 percent—of their fund-related transactions with federal, state, and local governments over the Internet each year. This percentage should increase sharply over the next decade as more governments make it possible for citizens to pay fines, register automobiles, and more via the Internet.

The range of information we can access on the Internet is also growing and is certainly not limited to government resources. Now, the number of places where we can access that information is growing as well. Children are becoming more exposed to cyberspace as public schools add computers to their classroom tools. Community centers, public libraries, and other local organizations and entities often have computers that can be used by patrons who otherwise would not have access to the Internet. As a result of these innovations, standing in long lines at the post office to file taxes or at the employment office to apply for a job might one day be a thing of the past.

| Logging On

A useful source of information about local government in Texas is the U.S. Census Bureau's "People QuickFacts," which provides an abundance of data on all 254 Texas counties. Go to

**quickfacts.census.gov/qfd/
states/48000.html**

Enter the name of a county, and click on "Go."

Most major cities in Texas have their own Web sites. You can use these sites to compare different types of city government. Cities that use the council-manager system include Austin, Dallas, and San Antonio:

www.ci.austin.tx.us

www.dallascityhall.com

www.ci.sat.tx.us

Houston and Pasadena use the mayor-council system:

www.houstontx.gov

www.ci.pasadena.tx.us

For links to other Texas cities and to Texas counties, go to

www.state.tx.us

Click on "Cities" or "Counties."

Special districts can provide almost any kind of governmental service. A hospital district is one example. Information about hospital and other health-related districts can be found at the Texas comptroller's Web site:

**www.window.state.tx.us/
specialrpt/hcs/pg57.html**

Another example is a metropolitan transit authority (MTA). The Texas Department of Transportation provides information about MTAs in the state at

**www.dot.state.tx.us/services/
public_transportation/mta.htm**

Councils of governments are regional planning organizations that try to coordinate the activities of local governments in their regions. See the regions at

www.txregionalcouncil.org

| Online Review

At **www.politicalscience.wadsworth.com/
schmidt12**, you will find a free Study Guide to this book. For each chapter, there are two online quizzes to help you master the material.

• The PoliPrep Self-Study Assessment provides a pretest for each major section of the chapter. PoliPrep then generates a customized study plan. After you complete the study plan, a posttest evaluates your progress.

• The Tutorial Quiz for each chapter provides questions on the chapter contents, including the features. The questions are organized to match the major sections of the chapter.

In Congress, July 4, 1776

A Declaration by the Representatives of the United States of America, in General Congress assembled. When in the Course of human Events, it becomes necessary for one People to dissolve the Political Bands which have connected them with another, and to assume among the Powers of the Earth, the separate and equal Station to which the Laws of Nature and of Nature's God entitle them, a decent Respect to the Opinions of Mankind requires that they should declare the causes which impel them to the Separation.

We hold these Truths to be self-evident, that all Men are created equal, that they are endowed by their Creator with certain unalienable Rights, that among these are Life, Liberty, and the Pursuit of Happiness—That to secure these Rights, Governments are instituted among Men, deriving their just Powers from the Consent of the Governed, that whenever any Form of Government becomes destructive of these Ends, it is the Right of the People to alter or to abolish it, and to institute new Government, laying its Foundation on such Principles, and organizing its Powers in such Forms, as to them shall seem most likely to effect their Safety and Happiness. Prudence, indeed, will dictate that Governments long established should not be changed for light and transient Causes; and accordingly all Experience hath shewn, that Mankind are more disposed to suffer, while Evils are sufferable, than to right themselves by abolishing the Forms to which they are accustomed. But when a long Train of Abuses and Usurpations, pursuing invariably the same Object, evinces a Design to reduce them under absolute Despotism, it is their Right, it is their Duty, to throw off such Government, and to provide new Guards for their future Security. Such has been the patient Sufferance of these Colonies; and such is now the Necessity which constrains them to alter their former Systems of Government. The History of the present King of Great-Britain is a History of repeated Injuries and Usurpations, all having in direct Object the Establishment of an absolute Tyranny over these States. To prove this, let Facts be submitted to a candid World.

He has refused his Assent to Laws, the most wholesome and necessary for the public Good.

He has forbidden his Governors to pass Laws of immediate and pressing Importance, unless suspended in their Operation till his Assent should be obtained; and when so suspended, he has utterly neglected to attend to them.

He has refused to pass other Laws for the Accommodation of large Districts of People, unless those People would relinquish the Right of Representation in the Legislature, a Right inestimable to them, and formidable to Tyrants only.

He has called together Legislative Bodies at Places unusual, uncomfortable, and distant from the Depository of their Public Records, for the sole Purpose of fatiguing them into Compliance with his Measures.

He has dissolved Representative Houses repeatedly, for opposing with manly Firmness his Invasions on the Rights of the People.

He has refused for a long Time, after such Dissolutions, to cause others to be elected; whereby the Legislative Powers, incapable of Annihilation, have returned to the People at large for their exercise; the State remaining in the mean time exposed to all the Dangers of Invasion from without, and Convulsions within.

He has endeavoured to prevent the Population of these States; for that Purpose obstructing the Laws for Naturalization of Foreigners; refusing to pass others to encourage their Migrations hither, and raising the Conditions of new Appropriations of Lands.

He has obstructed the Administration of Justice, by refusing his Assent to Laws for establishing Judiciary Powers.

He has made Judges dependent on his Will alone, for the Tenure of their offices, and the Amount and payment of their Salaries.

He has erected a Multitude of new Offices, and sent hither Swarms of Officers to harass our People, and eat out their Substance.

He has kept among us, in Times of Peace, Standing Armies, without the consent of our Legislatures.

He has affected to render the Military independent of, and superior to the Civil Power.

He has combined with others to subject us to a Jurisdiction foreign to our Constitution, and unacknowledged by our Laws; giving his Assent to their Acts of pretended Legislation:

For quartering large Bodies of Armed Troops among us:

For protecting them, by a mock Trial, from Punishment for any Murders which they should commit on the Inhabitants of these States:

For cutting off our Trade with all Parts of the World:

For imposing Taxes on us without our Consent:

For depriving us, in many cases, of the Benefits of Trial by Jury:

For transporting us beyond Seas to be tried for pretended Offences:

For abolishing the free System of English Laws in a neighbouring Province, establishing therein an arbitrary Government, and enlarging its Boundaries, so as to render it at once an Example and fit Instrument for introducing the same absolute Rule into these Colonies:

For taking away our Charters, abolishing our most valuable Laws, and altering fundamentally the Forms of our Governments:

For suspending our own Legislatures, and declaring themselves invested with Power to legislate for us in all Cases whatsoever.

He has abdicated Government here, by declaring us out of his Protection and waging War against us.

He has plundered our Seas, ravaged our Coasts, burnt our towns, and destroyed the Lives of our People.

He is, at this Time, transporting large Armies of foreign Mercenaries to compleat the works of Death, Desolation, and Tyranny, already begun with circumstances of Cruelty and Perfidy, scarcely paralleled in the most barbarous Ages, and totally unworthy the Head of a civilized Nation.

He has constrained our fellow Citizens taken Captive on the high Seas to bear Arms against their Country, to become the Executioners of their Friends and Brethren, or to fall themselves by their Hands.

He has excited domestic Insurrections amongst us, and has endeavoured to bring on the Inhabitants of our Frontiers, the merciless Indian Savages, whose known Rule of Warfare, is an undistinguished Destruction, of all Ages, Sexes and Conditions.

In every state of these Oppressions we have Petitioned for Redress in the most humble Terms: Our repeated Petitions have been answered only by repeated Injury. A Prince, whose Character is thus marked by every act which may define a Tyrant, is unfit to be the Ruler of a free People.

Nor have we been wanting in Attentions to our British Brethren. We have warned them from Time to Time of Attempts by their Legislature to extend an unwarrantable Jurisdiction over us. We have reminded them of the Circumstances of our Emigration and Settlement here. We have appealed to their native Justice and Magnanimity, and we have conjured them by the Ties of our common Kindred to disavow these Usurpations, which, would inevitably interrupt our Connections and Correspondence. They too have been deaf to the Voice of Justice and of Consanguinity. We must, therefore, acquiesce in the Necessity, which denounces our Separation, and hold them, as we hold the rest of Mankind, Enemies in War, in Peace, Friends.

We, therefore, the Representatives of the UNITED STATES OF AMERICA, in General Congress Assembled, appealing to the Supreme Judge of the World for the Rectitude of our Intentions, do, in the Name, and by the Authority of the good People of these Colonies, solemnly Publish and Declare, That these United Colonies are, and of Right ought to be, Free and Independent States; that they are absolved from all Allegiance to the British Crown, and that all political Connection between them and the State of Great-Britain, is and ought to be totally dissolved; and that as Free and Independent States, they have full Power to levy War, conclude Peace, contract Alliances, establish Commerce, and to do all other Acts and Things which Independent States may of right do. And for the support of this declaration, with a firm Reliance on the Protection of divine Providence, we mutually pledge to each other our lives, our Fortunes, and our sacred Honor.

Many important court cases are discussed in references in footnotes throughout this book. Court decisions are recorded and published. When a court case is mentioned, the notation that is used to refer to, or to cite, the case denotes where the published decision can be found.

State courts of appeals decisions are usually published in two places, the state reports of that particular state and the more widely used *National Reporter System* published by West Publishing Company. Some states no longer publish their own reports. The *National Reporter System* divides the states into the following geographic areas: Atlantic (A. or A.2d, where *2d* refers to *Second Series*), South Eastern (S.E. or S.E.2d), South Western (S.W., S.W.2d, or S.W.3d), North Western (N.W. or N.W.2d), North Eastern (N.E. or N.E.2d), Southern (So. or So.2d), and Pacific (P., P.2d, or P.3d).

Federal trial court decisions are published unofficially in West's *Federal Supplement* (F.Supp. or F.Supp.2d), and opinions from the circuit courts of appeals are reported unofficially in West's *Federal Reporter* (F., F.2d, or F.3d). Opinions from the United States Supreme Court are reported in the *United States Reports* (U.S.), the *Lawyers' Edition of the Supreme Court Reports* (L.Ed. or L.Ed.2d), West's *Supreme Court Reporter* (S.Ct.), and other publications. The *United States Reports* is the official publication of United States Supreme Court decisions. It is published by the federal government. Many early decisions are missing from these volumes. The citations of the early volumes of the *United States Reports* include the names of the actual reporters, such as Dallas, Cranch, or Wheaton.

McCulloch v. Maryland, for example, is cited as 17 U.S. (4 Wheat.) 316. Only after 1874 did the present citation system, in which cases are cited based solely on their volume and page numbers in the *United States Reports*, come into being. The *Lawyers' Edition of the Supreme Court Reports* is an unofficial and more complete edition of Supreme Court decisions. West's *Supreme Court Reporter* is an unofficial edition of decisions dating from October 1882. These volumes contain headnotes and numerous brief editorial statements of the law involved in each case.

State courts of appeals decisions are cited by giving the name of the case; the volume, name, and page number of the state's official report (if the state publishes its own reports); the volume, unit, and page number of the *National Reporter*; and the volume, name, and page number of any other selected reporter. Federal court citations are also listed by giving the name of the case and the volume, name, and page number of the reports. In addition to the citation, this textbook lists the year of the decision in parentheses. Consider, for example, the case *Locke v. Davey*, 540 U.S. 712 (2004). The Supreme Court's decision of this case may be found in volume 540 of the *United States Reports* on page 712. The case was decided in 2004.

Today, many courts, including the United States Supreme Court, publish their opinions online. This makes it much easier for students to find and read cases, or summaries of cases, that have significant consequences for American government and politics. To access cases via the Internet, use the URLs given in the *Logging On* section at the end of Chapter 14.

In 1787, after the newly drafted U.S. Constitution was submitted to the thirteen states for ratification, a major political debate ensued between the Federalists (who favored ratification) and the Anti-Federalists (who opposed ratification). Anti-Federalists in New York were particularly critical of the Constitution, and in response to their objections, Federalists Alexander Hamilton, James Madison, and John Jay wrote a series of eighty-five essays in defense of the Constitution. The essays were published in New York newspapers and reprinted in other newspapers throughout the country.

For students of American government, the essays, collectively known as the Federalist Papers, are particularly important because they provide a glimpse of the founders' political philosophy and intentions in designing the Constitution—and, consequently, in shaping the American philosophy of government.

We have included in this appendix three of these essays: Federalist Papers No. 10, No. 51, and No. 78. Each essay has been annotated by the authors to indicate its importance in American political thought and to clarify the meaning of particular passages.

Federalist Paper No. 10

Federalist Paper No. 10, penned by James Madison, has often been singled out as a key document in American political thought. In this essay, Madison attacks the Anti-Federalists' fear that a republican form of government will inevitably give rise to "factions"—small political parties or groups united by a common interest—that will control the government. Factions will be harmful to the country because they will implement policies beneficial to their own interests but adverse to other people's rights and to the public good. In this essay, Madison attempts to lay to rest this fear by explaining how, in a large republic such as the United States, there will be so many different factions, held together by regional or local interests, that no single one of them will dominate national politics.

Madison opens his essay with a paragraph discussing how important it is to devise a plan of government that can control the "instability, injustice, and confusion" brought about by factions.

Among the numerous advantages promised by a well-constructed Union, none deserves to be more accurately developed than its tendency to break and control the violence of faction. The friend of popular governments never finds himself so much alarmed for their character and fate as when he contemplates their propensity to this dangerous vice. He will not fail, therefore, to set a due value on any plan which, without violating the principles to which he is attached, provides a proper cure for it. The instability, injustice, and confusion introduced into the public councils have, in truth, been the mortal diseases under which popular governments have everywhere perished, as they continue to be the favorite and fruitful topics from which the adversaries to liberty derive their most specious declamations. The valuable improvements made by the American constitutions on the popular models, both ancient and modern, cannot

certainly be too much admired; but it would be an unwarrantable partiality to contend that they have as effectually obviated the danger on this side, as was wished and expected. Complaints are everywhere heard from our most considerate and virtuous citizens, equally the friends of public and private faith and of public and personal liberty, that our governments are too unstable, that the public good is disregarded in the conflicts of rival parties, and that measures are too often decided, not according to the rules of justice and the rights of the minor party, but by the superior force of an interested and overbearing majority. However anxiously we may wish that these complaints had no foundation, the evidence of known facts will not permit us to deny that they are in some degree true. It will be found, indeed, on a candid review of our situation, that some of the distresses under which we labor have been erroneously charged on the operation of our governments; but it will be found, at the same time, that other causes will not alone account for many of our heaviest misfortunes; and, particularly, for that prevailing and increasing distrust of public engagements and alarm for private rights which are echoed from one end of the continent to the other. These must be chiefly, if not wholly, effects of the unsteadiness and injustice with which a factious spirit has tainted our public administration.

Madison now defines what he means by the term faction.

By a faction I understand a number of citizens, whether amounting to a majority or minority of the whole, who are united and actuated by some common impulse of passion, or of interest, adverse to the rights of other citizens, or the permanent and aggregate interests of the community.

Madison next contends that there are two methods by which the "mischiefs of faction" can be cured: by removing the causes of faction or by controlling their effects. In the following paragraphs, Madison explains how liberty itself nourishes factions. Therefore, to abolish factions would involve abolishing liberty—a cure "worse than the disease."

There are two methods of curing the mischiefs of faction: the one, by removing its causes; the other, by controlling its effects.

There are again two methods of removing the causes of faction: the one, by destroying the liberty which is essential to its existence; the other, by giving to every citizen the same opinions, the same passions, and the same interests.

It could never be more truly said than of the first remedy that it was worse than the disease. Liberty is to faction what air is to fire, an aliment without which it instantly expires. But it could not be a less folly to abolish liberty, which is essential to political life, because it nourishes faction than it would be to wish the annihilation of air, which is essential to animal life, because it imparts to fire its destructive agency.

The second expedient is as impracticable as the first would be unwise. As long as the reason of man continues fallible, and he is at liberty to exercise it, different opinions will be formed. As long as the connection subsists between his reason and his self-love, his opinions and his passions will have a reciprocal influence on each other; and the former will be objects to which the latter will attach themselves. The diversity in the faculties of men, from which the rights of property originate, is not less an insuperable obstacle to a uniformity of interests. The protection of these faculties is the first object of government. From the protection of different and unequal faculties of acquiring property, the possession of different degrees and kinds of property immediately results; and from the influence of these on the sentiments and views of the respective proprietors ensues a division of the society into different interests and parties.

The latent causes of faction are thus sown in the nature of man; and we see them everywhere brought into different degrees of activity, according to the different circumstances of civil society. A zeal for different opinions concerning religion, concerning government, and many other points, as well of speculation as of practice; an attachment to different leaders ambitiously contending for pre-eminence and power; or to persons of other descriptions whose fortunes have been interesting to the human passions, have, in turn, divided mankind into parties, inflamed them with mutual animosity, and rendered them much more disposed to vex and oppress each other than to co-operate for their common good. So strong is this propensity of mankind to fall into mutual animosities that where no substantial occasion presents itself the most frivolous and fanciful distinctions have been sufficient to kindle their unfriendly passions and excite their most violent conflicts. But the most common and durable source of factions has been the various and unequal distribution of property. Those who hold and those who are without property have ever formed distinct interests in society. Those who are creditors, and those who are debtors, fall under a like discrimination. A landed interest, a manufacturing interest, a mercantile interest, a moneyed interest, with many lesser interests, grow up of necessity in civilized nations, and divide them into different classes, actuated by different sentiments and views. The regulation of these various and interfering interests forms the principal task of modern legislation and involves the spirit of party and faction in the necessary and ordinary operations of government.

No man is allowed to be a judge in his own cause, because his interest would certainly bias his judgment, and, not improbably, corrupt his integrity. With equal, nay with greater reason, a body of men are unfit to be both judges and parties at the same time; yet what are many of the most important acts of legislation but so many judicial determinations, not indeed concerning the rights of single persons, but concerning the rights of large bodies of citizens? And what are the different classes of legislators but advocates and parties to the causes which they determine? Is a law proposed concerning private debts? It is a question to which the creditors are parties on one side and the debtors on the other. Justice ought to hold the balance between them. Yet the parties are, and must be, themselves the judges; and the most numerous party, or in other words, the most powerful faction must be expected to prevail. Shall domestic manufacturers be encouraged, and in what degree, by restrictions on foreign manufacturers? [These] are questions which would be differently decided by the landed and the manufacturing classes, and probably by neither with a sole regard to justice and the public good. The apportionment of taxes on the various descriptions of property is an act which seems to require the most exact impartiality; yet there is, perhaps, no legislative act in which greater opportunity and temptation are given to a predominant party to trample on the rules of jus-

tice. Every shilling with which they overburden the inferior number is a shilling saved to their own pockets.

It is in vain to say that enlightened statesmen will be able to adjust these clashing interests and render them all subservient to the public good. Enlightened statesmen will not always be at the helm. Nor, in many cases, can such an adjustment be made at all without taking into view indirect and remote considerations, which will rarely prevail over the immediate interest which one party may find in disregarding the rights of another or the good of the whole.

The inference to which we are brought is that the *causes* of faction cannot be removed and that relief is only to be sought in the means of controlling its *effects*.

Having concluded that "the causes of faction cannot be removed," Madison now looks in some detail at the other method by which factions can be cured—by controlling their effects. This is the heart of his essay. He begins by positing a significant question: How can you have self-government without risking the possibility that a ruling faction, particularly a majority faction, might tyrannize over the rights of others?

If a faction consists of less than a majority, relief is supplied by the republican principle, which enables the majority to defeat its sinister views by regular vote. It may clog the administration, it may convulse the society; but it will be unable to execute and mask its violence under the forms of the Constitution. When a majority is included in a faction, the form of popular government, on the other hand, enables it to sacrifice to its ruling passion or interest both the public good and the rights of other citizens. To secure the public good and private rights against the danger of such a faction, and at the same time to preserve the spirit and the form of popular government, is then the great object to which our inquiries are directed. Let me add that it is the great desideratum by which alone this form of government can be rescued from the opprobrium under which it has so long labored and be recommended to the esteem and adoption of mankind.

Madison now sets forth the idea that one way to control the effects of factions is to ensure that the majority is rendered incapable of acting in concert in order to "carry into effect schemes of oppression." He goes on to state that in a democracy, in which all citizens participate personally in government decision making, there is no way to prevent the majority from communicating with each other and, as a result, acting in concert.

By what means is this object attainable? Evidently by one of two only. Either the existence of the same passion or interest in a majority at the same time must be prevented, or the majority, having such coexistent passion or interest, must be rendered, by their number and local situation, unable to concert and carry into effect schemes of oppression. If the impulse and the opportunity be suffered to coincide, we well know that neither moral nor religious motives can be relied on as an adequate control. They are not found to be such on the injustice and violence of individuals, and lose their efficacy in proportion to the number combined together, that is, in proportion as their efficacy becomes needful.

From this view of the subject it may be concluded that a pure democracy, by which I mean a society consisting of a small number of citizens, who assemble and administer the government in person, can admit of no cure for the mischiefs of faction. A common passion or interest will, in almost every case, be felt by a majority of the whole; a communication and concert results from the form of government itself; and there is nothing to check the inducements to sacrifice the weaker party or an obnoxious individual. Hence it is that such democracies have ever been spectacles of turbulence and contention; have ever been found incompatible with personal security or the rights of property; and have in general been as short in their lives as they have been violent in their deaths. Theoretic politicians, who have patronized this species of government, have erroneously supposed that by reducing mankind to a perfect equality in their political rights, they would at the same time be perfectly equalized and assimilated in their possessions, their opinions, and their passions.

Madison now moves on to discuss the benefits of a republic with respect to controlling the effects of factions. He begins by defining a republic and then pointing out the "two great points of difference" between a republic and a democracy: a republic is governed by a small body of elected representatives, not by the people directly; and a republic can extend over a much larger territory and embrace more citizens than a democracy can.

A republic, by which I mean a government in which the scheme of representation takes place, opens a different prospect and promises the cure for which we are seeking. Let us examine the points in which it varies from pure democracy, and we shall comprehend both the nature of the cure and the efficacy which it must derive from the Union.

The two great points of difference between a democracy and a republic are: first, the delegation of the government, in the latter, to a small number of citizens elected by the rest; secondly, the greater number of citizens and greater sphere of country over which the latter may be extended.

In the following four paragraphs, Madison explains how in a republic, particularly a large republic, the delegation of authority to elected representatives will increase the likelihood that those who govern will be "fit" for their positions and that a proper balance will be achieved between local (factional) interests and national interests. Note how he stresses that the new federal Constitution, by dividing powers between state governments and the national government, provides a "happy combination in this respect."

The effect of the first difference is, on the one hand, to refine and enlarge the public views by passing them through the medium of a chosen body of citizens, whose wisdom may best discern the true interest of their country and whose patriotism and love of justice will be least likely to sacrifice it to temporary or partial considerations. Under such a regulation it may well happen that the public voice, pronounced by the representatives of the people, will be more consonant to the public good than if pronounced by the people themselves, convened for the purpose. On the other hand, the effect may be inverted. Men of factious tempers, of local prejudices, or of sinister designs, may, by intrigue, by corruption, or by other means, first obtain the suffrages, and then betray the interests of the people. The question resulting is, whether small or extensive republics are most favorable to the election of proper guardians of the public weal; and it is clearly decided in favor of the latter by two obvious considerations.

In the first place, it is to be remarked that however small the republic may be the representatives must be raised to a certain number in order to guard against the cabals of a few; and that however large it may be, they must be limited to a certain number in order to guard against the confusion of a multitude. Hence, the number of representatives in the two cases not being in proportion to that of the constituents, and being proportionally greater in the small republic, it

follows that if the proportion of fit characters be not less in the large than in the small republic, the former will present a greater option, and consequently a greater probability of a fit choice.

In the next place, as each representative will be chosen by a greater number of citizens in the large than in the small republic, it will be more difficult for unworthy candidates to practice with success the vicious arts by which elections are too often carried; and the suffrages of the people being more free, will be more likely to center on men who possess the most attractive merit and the most diffusive and established characters.

It must be confessed that in this, as in most other cases, there is a mean, on both sides of which inconveniencies will be found to lie. By enlarging too much the number of electors, you render the representative too little acquainted with all their local circumstances and lesser interests; as by reducing it too much, you render him unduly attached to these, and too little fit to comprehend and pursue great and national objects. The federal Constitution forms a happy combination in this respect; the great and aggregate interests being referred to the national, the local and particular to the State legislatures.

Madison now looks more closely at the other difference between a republic and a democracy—namely, that a republic can encompass a larger territory and more citizens than a democracy can. In the remaining paragraphs of his essay, Madison concludes that in a large republic, it will be difficult for factions to act in concert. Although a factious group—religious, political, economic, or otherwise—may control a local or regional government, it will have little chance of gathering a national following. This is because in a large republic, there will be numerous factions whose work will offset the work of any one particular faction ("sect"). As Madison phrases it, these numerous factions will "secure the national councils against any danger from that source."

The other point of difference is the greater number of citizens and extent of territory which may be brought within the compass of republican than of democratic government; and it is this circumstance principally which renders factious combinations less to be dreaded in the former than in the latter. The smaller the society, the fewer probably will be the distinct parties and interests composing it; the fewer the distinct parties and interests, the more frequently will a majority be found of the same party; and the smaller the number of individuals composing a majority, and the smaller the compass within which they are placed, the more easily will they concert and execute their plans of oppression. Extend the sphere and you take in a greater variety of parties and interests; you make it less probable that a majority of the whole will have a common motive to invade the rights of other citizens; or if such a common motive exists, it will be more difficult for all who feel it to discover their own strength and to act in unison with each other. Besides other impediments, it may be remarked that, where there is a consciousness of unjust or dishonorable purposes, communication is always checked by distrust in proportion to the number whose concurrence is necessary.

Hence, it clearly appears that the same advantage which a republic has over a democracy in controlling the effects of faction is enjoyed by a large over a small republic—is enjoyed by the Union over the States composing it. Does this advantage consist in the substitution of representatives whose enlightened views and virtuous sentiments render them superior to local prejudices and to schemes of injustice? It will not be denied that the representation of the Union will be most likely to possess these requisite endowments.

Does it consist in the greater security afforded by a greater variety of parties, against the event of any one party being able to outnumber and oppress the rest? In an equal degree does the increased variety of parties comprised within the Union increase this security. Does it, in fine, consist in the greater obstacles opposed to the concert and accomplishment of the secret wishes of an unjust and interested majority? Here again the extent of the Union gives it the most palpable advantage.

The influence of factious leaders may kindle a flame within their particular States but will be unable to spread a general conflagration through the other States. A religious sect may degenerate into a political faction in a part of the Confederacy; but the variety of sects dispersed over the entire face of it must secure the national councils against any danger from that source. A rage for paper money, for an abolition of debts, for an equal division of property, or for any other improper or wicked project, will be less apt to pervade the whole body of the Union than a particular member of it, in the same proportion as such a malady is more likely to taint a particular county or district than an entire State.

In the extent and proper structure of the Union, therefore, we behold a republican remedy for the diseases most incident to republican government. And according to the degree of pleasure and pride we feel in being republicans ought to be our zeal in cherishing the spirit and supporting the character of federalists.

Publius
(James Madison)

Federalist Paper No. 51

Federalist Paper No. 51, also authored by James Madison, is another classic in American political theory. Although the Federalists wanted a strong national government, they had not abandoned the traditional American view, particularly notable during the revolutionary era, that those holding powerful government positions could not be trusted to put national interests and the common good above their own personal interests. In this essay, Madison explains why the separation of the national government's powers into three branches—executive, legislative, and judicial—and a federal structure of government offer the best protection against tyranny.

To what expedient, then, shall we finally resort, for maintaining in practice the necessary partition of power among the several departments as laid down in the Constitution? The only answer that can be given is that as all these exterior provisions are found to be inadequate the defect must be supplied, by so contriving the interior structure of the government as that its several constituent parts may, by their mutual relations, be the means of keeping each other in their proper places. Without presuming to undertake a full development of this important idea I will hazard a few general observations which may perhaps place it in a clearer light, and enable us to form a more correct judgment of the principles and structure of the government planned by the convention.

In the next two paragraphs, Madison stresses that for the powers of the different branches (departments) of government to be truly separated, the personnel in one branch should not be dependent on another branch for their appointment or for the "emoluments" (compensation) attached to their offices.

In order to lay a due foundation for that separate and distinct exercise of the different powers of government, which to a certain extent is admitted on all hands to be essential to the preservation of liberty, it is evident that each department should have a will of its own; and consequently should be so constituted that the members of each should have as little agency as possible in the appointment of the members of the others. Were this principle rigorously adhered to, it would require that all the appointments for the supreme executive, legislative, and judiciary magistracies should be drawn from the same fountain of authority, the people, through channels having no communication whatever with one another. Perhaps such a plan of constructing the several departments would be less difficult in practice than it may in contemplation appear. Some difficulties, however, and some additional expense would attend the execution of it. Some deviations, therefore, from the principle must be admitted. In the constitution of the judiciary department in particular, it might be inexpedient to insist rigorously on the principle: first, because peculiar qualifications being essential in the members, the primary consideration ought to be to select that mode of choice which best secures these qualifications; second, because the permanent tenure by which the appointments are held in that department must soon destroy all sense of dependence on the authority conferring them.

It is equally evident that the members of each department should be as little dependent as possible on those of the others for the emoluments annexed to their offices. Were the executive magistrate, or the judges, not independent of the legislature in this particular, their independence in every other would be merely nominal.

In the following passages, which are among the most widely quoted of Madison's writings, he explains how the separation of the powers of government into three branches helps to counter the effects of personal ambition on government. The separation of powers allows personal motives to be linked to the constitutional rights of a branch of government. In effect, competing personal interests in each branch will help to keep the powers of the three government branches separate and, in so doing, will help to guard the public interest.

But the great security against a gradual concentration of the several powers in the same department consists in giving to those who administer each department the necessary constitutional means and personal motives to resist encroachments of the others. The provision for defense must in this, as in all other cases, be made commensurate to the danger of attack. Ambition must be made to counteract ambition. The interest of the man must be connected with the constitutional rights of the place. It may be a reflection on human nature that such devices should be necessary to control the abuses of government. But what is government itself but the greatest of all reflections on human nature? If men were angels, no government would be necessary. If angels were to govern men, neither external nor internal controls on government would be necessary. In framing a government which is to be administered by men over men, the great difficulty lies in this: you must first enable the government to control the governed; and in the next place oblige it to control itself. A dependence on the people is, no doubt, the primary control on the government; but experience has taught mankind the necessity of auxiliary precautions.

This policy of supplying, by opposite and rival interests, the defect of better motives, might be traced through the whole system of human affairs, private as well as public. We see it particularly displayed in all the subordinate distributions of power, where the constant aim is to divide and arrange the several offices in such a manner as that each may be a check on the other—that the private interest of every individual may be a sentinel over the public rights. These inventions of prudence cannot be less requisite in the distribution of the supreme powers of the State.

Madison now addresses the issue of equality between the branches of government. The legislature will necessarily predominate, but if the executive is given an "absolute negative" (absolute veto power) over legislative actions, this also could lead to an abuse of power. Madison concludes that the division of the legislature into two "branches" (parts, or chambers) will act as a check on the legislature's powers.

But it is not possible to give to each department an equal power of self-defense. In republican government, the legislative authority necessarily predominates. The remedy for this inconveniency is to divide the legislature into different branches; and to render them, by different modes of election and different principles of action, as little connected with each other as the nature of their common functions and their common dependence on the society will admit. It may even be necessary to guard against dangerous encroachments by still further precautions. As the weight of the legislative authority requires that it should be thus divided, the weakness of the executive may require, on the other hand, that it should be fortified. An absolute negative on the legislature appears, at first view, to be the natural defense with which the executive magistrate should be armed. But perhaps it would be neither altogether safe nor alone sufficient. On ordinary occasions it might not be exerted with the requisite firmness, and on extraordinary occasions it might be perfidiously abused. May not this defect of an absolute negative be supplied by some qualified connection between this weaker department and the weaker branch of the stronger department, by which the latter may be led to support the constitutional rights of the former, without being too much detached from the rights of its own department?

If the principles on which these observations are founded be just, as I persuade myself they are, and they be applied as a criterion to the several State constitutions, and to the federal Constitution, it will be found that if the latter does not perfectly correspond with them, the former are infinitely less able to bear such a test.

In the remainder of the essay, Madison discusses how a federal system of government, in which powers are divided between the states and the national government, offers "double security" against tyranny.

There are, moreover, two considerations particularly applicable to the federal system of America, which place that system in a very interesting point of view.

First. In a single republic, all the power surrendered by the people is submitted to the administration of a single government; and the usurpations are guarded against by a division of the government into distinct and separate departments. In the compound republic of America, the power surrendered by the people is first divided between two distinct governments, and then the portion allotted to each subdivided among distinct and separate departments. Hence a double security arises to the rights of the people. The different governments will control each other, at the same time that each will be controlled by itself.

Second. It is of great importance in a republic not only to guard the society against the oppression of its rulers, but to guard one part of society against the injustice of the other part. Different interests necessarily exist in different classes of citizens. If a majority be united by a common interest, the rights of the minority will be insecure. There are but two methods of providing against this evil: the one by creating a will in the community independent of the majority—that is, of the society itself; the other, by comprehending in the society so many separate descriptions of citizens as will render an unjust combination of a majority of the whole very improbable, if not impracticable. The first method prevails in all governments possessing an hereditary or self-appointed authority. This, at best, is but a precarious security; because a power independent of the society may as well espouse the unjust views of the major as the rightful interests of the minor party, and may possibly be turned against both parties. The second method will be exemplified in the federal republic of the United States. Whilst all authority in it will be derived from and dependent on the society, the society itself will be broken into so many parts, interests and classes of citizens, that the rights of individuals, or of the minority, will be in little danger from interested combinations of the majority.

In a free government the security for civil rights must be the same as that for religious rights. It consists in the one case in the multiplicity of interests, and in the other in the multiplicity of sects. The degree of security in both cases will depend on the number of interests and sects; and this may be presumed to depend on the extent of country and number of people comprehended under the same government. This view of the subject must particularly recommend a proper federal system to all the sincere and considerate friends of republican government, since it shows that in exact proportion as the territory of the Union may be formed into more circumscribed Confederacies, or States, oppressive combinations of a majority will be facilitated; the best security, under the republican forms, for the rights of every class of citizen, will be diminished; and consequently the stability and independence of some member of the government, the only other security, must be proportionally increased. Justice is the end of government. It is the end of civil society. It ever has been and ever will be pursued until it be obtained, or until liberty be lost in the pursuit. In a society under the forms of which the stronger faction can readily unite and oppress the weaker, anarchy may as truly be said to reign as in a state of nature, where the weaker individual is not secured against the violence of the stronger; and as, in the latter state, even the stronger individuals are prompted, by the uncertainty of their condition, to submit to a government which may protect the weak as well as themselves; so, in the former state, will the more powerful factions or parties be gradually induced, by a like motive, to wish for a government which will protect all parties, the weaker as well as the more powerful.

It can be little doubted that if the State of Rhode Island was separated from the Confederacy and left to itself, the insecurity of rights under the popular form of government within such narrow limits would be displayed by such reiterated oppressions of factious majorities that some power altogether independent of the people would soon be called for by the voice of the very factions whose misrule had proved the necessity of it. In the extended republic of the United States, and among the great variety of interests, parties, and sects which it embraces, a coalition of a majority of the whole society could seldom take place on any other principles than those of justice and the general good; whilst there being thus less danger to a minor from the will of a major party, there must be less pretext, also, to provide for the security of the former, by introducing into the government a will not dependent on the latter, or, in other words, a will independent of the society itself. It is no less certain than it is important, notwithstanding the contrary opinions which have been entertained, that the larger the society, provided it lie within a practicable sphere, the more duly capable it will be of self-government. And happily for the republican cause, the practicable sphere may be carried to a very great extent by a judicious modification and mixture of the *federal principle*.

Publius
(James Madison)

Federalist Paper No. 78

In this essay, Alexander Hamilton looks at the role of the judicial branch (the courts) in the new government fashioned by the Constitution's framers. The essay is historically significant because, among other things, it provides a basis for the courts' power of judicial review, which was not explicitly set forth in the Constitution (see Chapters 3 and 14).

After some brief introductory remarks, Hamilton explains why the founders decided that federal judges should be appointed and given lifetime tenure. Note how he describes the judiciary as the "weakest" and "least dangerous" branch of government. Because of this, claims Hamilton, "all possible care" is required to enable the judiciary to defend itself against attacks by the other two branches of government. Above all, the independence of the judicial branch should be secured, because if judicial powers were combined with legislative or executive powers, there would be no liberty.

We proceed now to an examination of the judiciary department of the proposed government.

In unfolding the defects of the existing Confederation, the utility and necessity of a federal judicature have been clearly pointed out. It is the less necessary to recapitulate the considerations there urged, as the propriety of the institution in the abstract is not disputed; the only questions which have been raised being relative to the manner of constituting it, and to its extent. To these points, therefore, our observations shall be confined.

The manner of constituting it seems to embrace these several objects: 1st. The mode of appointing the judges. 2d. The tenure by which they are to hold their places. 3d. The partition of the judiciary authority between different courts, and their relations to each other.

First. As to the mode of appointing the judges; this is the same with that of appointing the officers of the Union in general, and has been so fully discussed in the last two numbers, that nothing can be said here which would not be useless repetition.

Second. As to the tenure by which the judges are to hold their places; this chiefly concerns their duration in office; the provisions for their support; the precautions for their responsibility.

According to the plan of the convention, all judges who may be appointed by the United States are to hold their offices during good behavior; which is conformable to the most approved of the State constitutions and among the rest, to that of this State. Its propriety having been drawn into question by the adversaries of that plan, is no light symptom of the rage for objection, which disorders their imaginations and judgments. The standard of good behavior for the continuance in office of the judicial magistracy, is certainly one of the most valuable of the modern improvements in the practice of government. In a monarchy it is an excellent barrier to the despotism of the prince; in a republic it is a no less excellent barrier to the encroachments and oppressions of the representative body. And it is the best expedient which can be devised in any government, to secure a steady, upright, and impartial administration of the laws.

Whoever attentively considers the different departments of power must perceive, that, in a government in which they are separated from each other, the judiciary, from the nature of its functions, will always be the least dangerous to the political rights of the Constitution; because it will be least in a capacity to annoy or injure them. The Executive not only dispenses the honors, but holds the sword of the community. The legislature not only commands the purse, but prescribes the rules by which the duties and rights of every citizen are to be regulated. The judiciary, on the contrary, has no influence over either the sword or the purse; no direction either of the strength or of the wealth of the society; and can take no active resolution whatever. It may truly be said to have neither force nor will, but merely judgment; and must ultimately depend upon the aid of the executive arm even for the efficacy of its judgments.

This simple view of the matter suggests several important consequences. It proves incontestably, that the judiciary is beyond comparison the weakest of the three departments of power; that it can never attack with success either of the other two; and that all possible care is requisite to enable it to defend itself against their attacks. It equally proves, that though individual oppression may now and then proceed from the courts of justice, the general liberty of the people can never be endangered from that quarter; I mean so long as the judiciary remains truly distinct from both the legislature and the Executive. For I agree, that "there is no liberty, if the power of judging is not separated from the legislative and executive powers." And it proves, in the last place, that as liberty can have nothing to fear from the judiciary alone, but would have everything to fear from its union with either of the other departments; that as all the effects of such a union must ensue from a dependence of the former on the latter, notwithstanding a nominal and apparent separation; that as, from the natural feebleness of the judiciary, it is in continual jeopardy of being overpowered, awed, or influenced by its co-ordinate branches; and that as nothing can contribute so much to its firmness and independence as permanency in office, this quality may therefore be justly regarded as an indispensable ingredient in its constitution, and, in a great measure, as the citadel of the public justice and the public security.

Hamilton now stresses that the "complete independence of the courts" is essential in a limited government, because it is up to the courts to interpret the laws. Just as a federal court can decide which of two conflicting statutes should take priority, so can that court decide whether a statute conflicts with the Constitution. Essentially, Hamilton sets forth here the theory of judicial review—the power of the courts to decide whether actions of the other branches of government are (or are not) consistent with the Constitution. Hamilton points out that this "exercise of judicial discretion, in determining between two contradictory laws," does not mean that the judicial branch is superior to the legislative branch. Rather, it "supposes" that the power of the people (as declared in the Constitution) is superior to both the judiciary and the legislature.

The complete independence of the courts of justice is peculiarly essential in a limited Constitution. By a limited Constitution, I understand one which contains certain specified exceptions to the legislative authority; such, for instance, as that it shall pass no bills of attainder, no ex-post-facto laws, and the like. Limitations of this kind can be preserved in practice no other way than through the medium of courts of justice, whose duty it must be to declare all acts contrary to the manifest tenor of the Constitution void. Without this, all the reservations of particular rights or privileges would amount to nothing. Some perplexity respecting the rights of the courts to pronounce legislative acts void, because contrary to the Constitution, has arisen from an imagination that the doctrine would imply a superiority of the judiciary to the legislative power. It is urged that the authority which can declare the acts of another void, must necessarily be superior to the one whose acts may be declared void. As this doctrine is of great importance in all the American constitutions, a brief discussion of the ground on which it rests cannot be unacceptable.

There is no position which depends on clearer principles, than that every act of a delegated authority, contrary to the tenor of the commission under which it is exercised, is void. No legislative act, therefore, contrary to the Constitution, can be valid. To deny this, would be to affirm, that the deputy is greater than his principal; that the servant is above his master; that the representatives of the people are superior to the people themselves; that men acting by virtue of powers, may do not only what their powers do not authorize, but what they forbid.

If it be said that the legislative body are themselves the constitutional judges of their own powers, and that the construction they put upon them is conclusive upon the other departments, it may be answered, that this cannot be the natural presumption, where it is not to be collected from any particular provisions in the Constitution. It is not otherwise to be supposed, that the Constitution could intend to enable the representatives of the people to substitute their will to that of their constituents. It is far more rational to suppose, that the courts were designed to be an intermediate body between the people and the legislature, in order, among other things, to keep the latter within the limits assigned to their authority. The interpretation of the laws is the proper and peculiar province of the courts. A constitution is, in fact, and must be regarded by the judges, as a fundamental law. It therefore belongs to them to ascertain its meaning, as well as the meaning of any particular act proceeding from the legislative body. If there should happen to be an irreconcilable variance between the two, that which has the superior obligation and validity ought, of course, to be preferred; or, in other words, the Constitution ought to be preferred to the statute, the intention of the people to the intention of their agents.

Nor does this conclusion by any means suppose a superiority of the judicial to the legislative power. It only supposes that the power of the people is superior to both; and that where the will of the legislature, declared in its statutes, stands in opposition to that of the people, declared in the Constitution, the judges ought to be governed by the latter rather than the former. They ought to regulate their decisions by the fundamental laws, rather than by those which are not fundamental.

This exercise of judicial discretion, in determining between two contradictory laws, is exemplified in a familiar instance. It not uncommonly happens, that there are two statutes existing at one time, clashing in whole or in part with each other, and neither of them containing any repealing clause or expression. In such a case, it is the province of the courts to liquidate and fix their meaning and operation. So far as they can, by any fair construction, be reconciled to each other, reason and law conspire to dictate that this should be done; where this is impracticable, it becomes a matter of necessity to give effect to one, in exclusion of the other. The rule which has obtained in the courts for determining their relative validity is, that the last in order of time shall be preferred to the first. But this is a mere rule of construction, not derived from any positive law, but from the nature and reason of the thing. It is a rule not enjoined upon the courts by legislative provision, but adopted by themselves, as consonant to truth the propriety, for the direction of their conduct as interpreters of the law. They thought it reasonable, that between

the interfering acts of an equal authority, that which was the last indication of its will should have the preference.

But in regard to the interfering acts of a superior and subordinate authority, of an original and derivative power, the nature and reason of the thing indicate the converse of that rule as proper to be followed. They teach us that the prior act of a superior ought to be preferred to the subsequent act of an inferior and subordinate authority; and that accordingly, whenever a particular statute contravenes the Constitution, it will be the duty of the judicial tribunals to adhere to the latter and disregard the former.

It can be of no weight to say that the courts, on the pretense of a repugnancy, may substitute their own pleasure to the constitutional intentions of the legislature. This might as well happen in the case of two contradictory statutes; or it might as well happen in every adjudication upon any single statute. The courts must declare the sense of the law; and if they should be disposed to exercise will instead of judgment, the consequence would equally be the substitution of their pleasure to that of the legislative body. The observation, if it prove anything, would prove that there ought to be no judges distinct from that body.

If, then, the courts of justice are to be considered as the bulwarks of a limited Constitution against legislative encroachments, this consideration will afford a strong argument for the permanent tenure of judicial offices, since nothing will contribute so much as this to that independent spirit in the judges which must be essential to the faithful performance of so arduous a duty.

The independence of the judges is equally requisite to guard the Constitution and the rights of individuals from the effects of those ill humors, which the arts of designing men, or the influence of particular conjunctures, sometimes disseminate among the people themselves, and which, though they speedily give place to better information, and more deliberate reflection, have a tendency, in the meantime, to occasion dangerous innovations in the government, and serious oppressions of the minor party in the community. Though I trust the friends of the proposed Constitution will never concur with its enemies, in questioning that fundamental principle of republican government, which admits the right of the people to alter or abolish the established Constitution, whenever they find it inconsistent with their happiness, yet it is not to be inferred from this principle, that the representatives of the people, whenever a momentary inclination happens to lay hold of a majority of their constituents, incompatible with the provisions of the existing Constitution, would, on that account, be justifiable in a violation of those provisions; or that the courts would be under a greater obligation to connive at infractions in this shape, than when they had proceeded wholly from the cabals of the representative body. Until the people have, by some solemn and authoritative act, annulled or changed the established form, it is binding upon themselves collectively, as well as individually; and no presumption, or even knowledge, of their sentiments, can warrant their representatives in a departure from it, prior to such an act. But it is easy to see, that it would require an uncommon portion of fortitude in the judges to do their duty as faithful guardians of the Constitution, where legislative invasions of it had been instigated by the major voice of the community.

But it is not with a view to infractions of the Constitution only, that the independence of the judges may be an essential safeguard against the effects of occasional ill humors in the society. These sometimes extend no farther than to the injury of the private rights of particular classes of citizens, by unjust and partial laws. Here also the firmness of the judicial magistracy is of vast importance in mitigating the severity and confining the operation of such laws. It not only serves to moderate the immediate mischiefs of those which may have been passed, but it operates as a check upon the legislative body in passing them; who, perceiving that obstacles to the success of iniquitous intention are to be expected from the scruples of the courts, are in a manner compelled, by the very motives of the injustice they meditate, to qualify their attempts. This is a circumstance calculated to have more influence upon the character of our governments, than but few may be aware of. The benefits of the integrity and moderation of the judiciary have already been felt in more States than one; and though they may have displeased those whose sinister expectations they may have disappointed, they must have commanded the esteem and applause of all the virtuous and disinterested. Considerate men, of every description, ought to prize whatever will tend to beget or fortify that temper in the courts; as no man can be sure that he may not be tomorrow the victim of a spirit of injustice, by which he may be a gainer today. And every man must now feel, that the inevitable tendency of such a spirit is to sap the foundations of public and private confidence, and to introduce in its stead universal distrust and distress.

That inflexible and uniform adherence to the rights of the Constitution, and of individuals, which we perceive to be indispensable in the courts of justice, can certainly not be expected from judges who hold their offices by a temporary commission. Periodical appointments, however regulated, or by whomsoever made, would, in some way or other, be fatal to their necessary independence. If the power of making them was committed either to the Executive or legislature, there would be danger of an improper complaisance to the branch which possessed it; if to both, there would be an unwillingness to hazard the displeasure of either; if to the people, or to persons chosen by them for the special purpose, there would be too great a disposition to consult popularity, to justify a reliance that nothing would be consulted but the Constitution and the laws.

Hamilton points to yet another reason why lifetime tenure for federal judges will benefit the public: effective judgments rest on a knowledge of judicial precedents and the law, and such knowledge can only be obtained through experience on the bench. A "temporary duration of office," according to Hamilton, would "discourage individuals [of 'fit character'] from quitting a lucrative practice to serve on the bench" and ultimately would "throw the administration of justice into the hands of the less able, and less well qualified."

There is yet a further and a weightier reason for the permanency of the judicial offices, which is deducible from the nature of the qualifications they require. It has been frequently remarked, with great propriety, that a voluminous code of laws is one of the inconveniences necessarily connected with the advantages of a free government. To avoid an arbitrary discretion in the courts, it is indispensable that they should be bound down by strict rules and precedents, which serve to define and point out their duty in every particular case that comes before them; and it will readily be conceived from the variety of controversies which grow out of the folly and wickedness of mankind, that the records of those precedents must unavoidably swell to a very considerable bulk, and must demand long and laborious study to acquire a competent knowledge of them. Hence it is, that there can be but few men in the society who will have sufficient skill in the laws to qualify them for the stations of judges. And making the proper deductions for the ordinary depravity of human nature, the number must be still smaller of those who unite the requisite integrity with the requisite knowledge. These considerations apprise us, that the government can have no great option between fit character; and that a temporary duration in office, which would naturally discourage such characters from quitting a lucrative line of practice to accept a seat on the bench, would have a tendency to throw the administration of justice into hands less able, and less well qualified, to conduct it with utility and dignity. In the present circumstances of this country, and in those in which it is likely to be for a long time to come, the disadvantages on this score would be greater than they may at first sight appear; but it must be confessed, that they are far inferior to those which present themselves under other aspects of the subject.

Upon the whole, there can be no room to doubt that the convention acted wisely in copying from the models of those constitutions which have established good behavior as the tenure of their judicial offices, in point of duration; and that so far from being blamable on this account, their plan would have been inexcusably defective, if it had wanted this important feature of good government. The experience of Great Britain affords an illustrious comment on the excellence of the institution.

Publius
(Alexander Hamilton)

Chief Justices

Name	Years of Service	State App't from	Appointing President	Age at App't	Political Affiliation	Educational Background*
Fuller, Melville Weston	1888–1910	Illinois	Cleveland	55	Democrat	Bowdoin College; studied at Harvard Law School
White, Edward Douglass	1910–1921	Louisiana	Taft	65	Democrat	Mount St. Mary's College; Georgetown College (now University)
Taft, William Howard	1921–1930	Connecticut	Harding	64	Republican	Yale; Cincinnati Law School
Hughes, Charles Evans	1930–1941	New York	Hoover	68	Republican	Colgate University; Brown; Columbia Law School
Stone, Harlan Fiske	1941–1946	New York	Roosevelt, F.	69	Republican	Amherst College; Columbia
Vinson, Frederick Moore	1946–1953	Kentucky	Truman	56	Democrat	Centre College
Warren, Earl	1953–1969	California	Eisenhower	62	Republican	University of California, Berkeley
Burger, Warren Earl	1969–1986	Virginia	Nixon	62	Republican	University of Minnesota; St. Paul College of Law (Mitchell College)
Rehnquist, William Hubbs	1986–2005	Virginia	Reagan	62	Republican	Stanford; Harvard; Stanford University Law School
Roberts, John G., Jr.	2005–present	District of Columbia	G. W. Bush	50	Republican	Harvard; Harvard Law School

*Source: Educational background information derived from Elder Witt, *Guide to the U.S. Supreme Court*, 2d ed. (Washington, D.C.: Congressional Quarterly Press, Inc., 1990). Reprinted with the permission of the publisher.

Associate Justices

Name	Years of Service	State App't from	Appointing President	Age at App't	Political Affiliation	Educational Background*
Harlan, John Marshall	1877–1911	Kentucky	Hayes	61	Republican	Centre College; studied law at Transylvania University
Gray, Horace	1882–1902	Massachusetts	Arthur	54	Republican	Harvard College; Harvard Law School
Brewer, David Josiah	1890–1910	Kansas	Harrison	53	Republican	Wesleyan University; Yale; Albany Law School
Brown, Henry Billings	1891–1906	Michigan	Harrison	55	Republican	Yale; studied at Yale Law School and Harvard Law School
Shiras, George, Jr.	1892–1903	Pennsylvania	Harrison	61	Republican	Ohio University; Yale; studied law at Yale and privately
White, Edward Douglass	1894–1910	Louisiana	Cleveland	49	Democrat	Mount St. Mary's College; Georgetown College (now University)
Peckham, Rufus Wheeler	1896–1909	New York	Cleveland	58	Democrat	Read law in father's firm
McKenna, Joseph	1898–1925	California	McKinley	55	Republican	Benicia Collegiate Institute, Law Department
Holmes, Oliver Wendell, Jr.	1902–1932	Massachusetts	Roosevelt, T.	61	Republican	Harvard College; studied law at Harvard Law School

Name	Years of Service	State App't from	Appointing President	Age at App't	Political Affiliation	Educational Background*
Day, William Rufus	1903–1922	Ohio	Roosevelt, T.	54	Republican	University of Michigan; University of Michigan Law School
Moody, William Henry	1906–1910	Massachusetts	Roosevelt, T.	53	Republican	Harvard; Harvard Law School
Lurton, Horace Harmon	1910–1914	Tennessee	Taft	66	Democrat	University of Chicago; Cumberland Law School
Hughes, Charles Evans	1910–1916	New York	Taft	48	Republican	Colgate University; Brown University; Columbia Law School
Van Devanter, Willis	1911–1937	Wyoming	Taft	52	Republican	Indiana Asbury University; University of Cincinnati Law School
Lamar, Joseph Rucker	1911–1916	Georgia	Taft	54	Democrat	University of Georgia; Bethany College; Washington and Lee University
Pitney, Mahlon	1912–1922	New Jersey	Taft	54	Republican	College of New Jersey (Princeton); read law under father
McReynolds, James Clark	1914–1941	Tennessee	Wilson	52	Democrat	Vanderbilt University; University of Virginia
Brandeis, Louis Dembitz	1916–1939	Massachusetts	Wilson	60	Democrat	Harvard Law School
Clarke, John Hessin	1916–1922	Ohio	Wilson	59	Democrat	Western Reserve University; read law under father
Sutherland, George	1922–1938	Utah	Harding	60	Republican	Brigham Young Academy; one year at University of Michigan Law School
Butler, Pierce	1923–1939	Minnesota	Harding	57	Democrat	Carleton College
Sanford, Edward Terry	1923–1930	Tennessee	Harding	58	Republican	University of Tennessee; Harvard; Harvard Law School
Stone, Harlan Fiske	1925–1941	New York	Coolidge	53	Republican	Amherst College; Columbia University Law School
Roberts, Owen Josephus	1930–1945	Pennsylvania	Hoover	55	Republican	University of Pennsylvania; University of Pennsylvania Law School
Cardozo, Benjamin Nathan	1932–1938	New York	Hoover	62	Democrat	Columbia University; two years at Columbia Law School
Black, Hugo Lafayette	1937–1971	Alabama	Roosevelt, F.	51	Democrat	Birmingham Medical College; University of Alabama Law School
Reed, Stanley Forman	1938–1957	Kentucky	Roosevelt, F.	54	Democrat	Kentucky Wesleyan University; Foreman Yale; studied law at University of Virginia and Columbia University; University of Paris
Frankfurter, Felix	1939–1962	Massachusetts	Roosevelt, F.	57	Independent	College of the City of New York; Harvard Law School
Douglas, William Orville	1939–1975	Connecticut	Roosevelt, F.	41	Democrat	Whitman College; Columbia University Law School
Murphy, Frank	1940–1949	Michigan	Roosevelt, F.	50	Democrat	University of Michigan; Lincoln's Inn, London; Trinity College
Byrnes, James Francis	1941–1942	South Carolina	Roosevelt, F.	62	Democrat	Read law privately

(Continued)

Associate Justices (Continued)

Name	Years of Service	State App't from	Appointing President	Age at App't	Political Affiliation	Educational Background*
Jackson, Robert Houghwout	1941–1954	New York	Roosevelt, F.	49	Democrat	Albany Law School
Rutledge, Wiley Blount	1943–1949	Iowa	Roosevelt, F.	49	Democrat	University of Wisconsin; University of Colorado
Burton, Harold Hitz	1945–1958	Ohio	Truman	57	Republican	Bowdoin College; Harvard Law School
Clark, Thomas Campbell	1949–1967	Texas	Truman	50	Democrat	University of Texas
Minton, Sherman	1949–1956	Indiana	Truman	59	Democrat	Indiana University College of Law; Yale Law School
Harlan, John Marshall	1955–1971	New York	Eisenhower	56	Republican	Princeton; Oxford University; New York Law School
Brennan, William J., Jr.	1956–1990	New Jersey	Eisenhower	50	Democrat	University of Pennsylvania; Harvard Law School
Whittaker, Charles Evans	1957–1962	Missouri	Eisenhower	56	Republican	University of Kansas City Law School
Stewart, Potter	1958–1981	Ohio	Eisenhower	43	Republican	Yale; Yale Law School
White, Byron Raymond	1962–1993	Colorado	Kennedy	45	Democrat	University of Colorado; Oxford University; Yale Law School
Goldberg, Arthur Joseph	1962–1965	Illinois	Kennedy	54	Democrat	Northwestern University
Fortas, Abe	1965–1969	Tennessee	Johnson, L.	55	Democrat	Southwestern College; Yale Law School
Marshall, Thurgood	1967–1991	New York	Johnson, L.	59	Democrat	Lincoln University; Howard University Law School
Blackmun, Harry A.	1970–1994	Minnesota	Nixon	62	Republican	Harvard; Harvard Law School
Powell, Lewis F., Jr.	1972–1987	Virginia	Nixon	65	Democrat	Washington and Lee University; Washington and Lee University Law School; Harvard Law School
Rehnquist, William H.	1972–1986	Arizona	Nixon	48	Republican	Stanford; Harvard; Stanford University Law School
Stevens, John Paul	1975–present	Illinois	Ford	55	Republican	University of Colorado; Northwestern University Law School
O'Connor, Sandra Day	1981–2006	Arizona	Reagan	51	Republican	Stanford; Stanford University Law School
Scalia, Antonin	1986–present	Virginia	Reagan	50	Republican	Georgetown University; Harvard Law School
Kennedy, Anthony M.	1988–present	California	Reagan	52	Republican	Stanford; London School of Economics; Harvard Law School
Souter, David Hackett	1990–present	New Hampshire	G. H. W. Bush	51	Republican	Harvard; Oxford University
Thomas, Clarence	1991–present	District of Columbia	G. H. W. Bush	43	Republican	Holy Cross College; Yale Law School
Ginsburg, Ruth Bader	1993–present	District of Columbia	Clinton	60	Democrat	Cornell University; Columbia Law School
Breyer, Stephen G.	1994–present	Massachusetts	Clinton	55	Democrat	Stanford University; Oxford University; Harvard Law School
Alito, Samuel Anthony, Jr.	2006–present	District of Columbia	G. W. Bush	55	Republican	Princeton University; Yale Law School

Congress	Years	President	Majority Party in House	Majority Party in Senate
57th	1901–1903	McKinley/T. Roosevelt	Republican	Republican
58th	1903–1905	T. Roosevelt	Republican	Republican
59th	1905–1907	T. Roosevelt	Republican	Republican
60th	1907–1909	T. Roosevelt	Republican	Republican
61st	1909–1911	Taft	Republican	Republican
62d	1911–1913	Taft	Democratic	Republican
63d	1913–1915	Wilson	Democratic	Democratic
64th	1915–1917	Wilson	Democratic	Democratic
65th	1917–1919	Wilson	Democratic	Democratic
66th	1919–1921	Wilson	Republican	Republican
67th	1921–1923	Harding	Republican	Republican
68th	1923–1925	Harding/Coolidge	Republican	Republican
69th	1925–1927	Coolidge	Republican	Republican
70th	1927–1929	Coolidge	Republican	Republican
71st	1929–1931	Hoover	Republican	Republican
72d	1931–1933	Hoover	Democratic	Republican
73d	1933–1935	F. Roosevelt	Democratic	Democratic
74th	1935–1937	F. Roosevelt	Democratic	Democratic
75th	1937–1939	F. Roosevelt	Democratic	Democratic
76th	1939–1941	F. Roosevelt	Democratic	Democratic
77th	1941–1943	F. Roosevelt	Democratic	Democratic
78th	1943–1945	F. Roosevelt	Democratic	Democratic
79th	1945–1947	F. Roosevelt/Truman	Democratic	Democratic
80th	1947–1949	Truman	Republican	Democratic
81st	1949–1951	Truman	Democratic	Democratic
82d	1951–1953	Truman	Democratic	Democratic
83d	1953–1955	Eisenhower	Republican	Republican
84th	1955–1957	Eisenhower	Democratic	Democratic
85th	1957–1959	Eisenhower	Democratic	Democratic
86th	1959–1961	Eisenhower	Democratic	Democratic
87th	1961–1963	Kennedy	Democratic	Democratic
88th	1963–1965	Kennedy/Johnson	Democratic	Democratic
89th	1965–1967	Johnson	Democratic	Democratic
90th	1967–1969	Johnson	Democratic	Democratic
91st	1969–1971	Nixon	Democratic	Democratic
92d	1971–1973	Nixon	Democratic	Democratic
93d	1973–1975	Nixon/Ford	Democratic	Democratic
94th	1975–1977	Ford	Democratic	Democratic
95th	1977–1979	Carter	Democratic	Democratic
96th	1979–1981	Carter	Democratic	Democratic
97th	1981–1983	Reagan	Democratic	Republican
98th	1983–1985	Reagan	Democratic	Republican
99th	1985–1987	Reagan	Democratic	Republican
100th	1987–1989	Reagan	Democratic	Democratic
101st	1989–1991	G. H. W. Bush	Democratic	Democratic
102d	1991–1993	G. H. W. Bush	Democratic	Democratic
103d	1993–1995	Clinton	Democratic	Democratic
104th	1995–1997	Clinton	Republican	Republican
105th	1997–1999	Clinton	Republican	Republican
106th	1999–2001	Clinton	Republican	Republican
107th	2001–2003	G. W. Bush	Republican	Democratic
108th	2003–2005	G. W. Bush	Republican	Republican
109th	2005–2007	G. W. Bush	Republican	Republican
110th	2007–2009	G. W. Bush	Democratic	Democratic

Acid Rain: Lluvia Acida
Acquisitive Model: Modelo Adquisitivo
Actionable: Procesable, Enjuiciable
Action-Reaction Syndrome: Sídrome de Acción y Reacción
Actual Malice: Malicia Expresa
Administrative Agency: Agencia Administrativa
Advice and Consent: Consejo y Consentimiento
Affirm: Afirmar
Affirmative Action: Acción Afirmativa
Agenda Setting: Agenda Establecida
Aid to Families with Dependent Children (AFDC): Ayuda para Familias con Niños Dependientes
Amicus Curiae Brief: Tercer persona o grupo no involucrado en el caso, admitido en un juicio para hacer valer el intéres público o el de un grupo social importante.
Anarchy: Anarquía
Anti-Federalists: Anti-Federalistas
Appellate Court: Corte de Apelación
Appointment Power: Poder de Apuntamiento
Appropriation: Apropiación
Aristocracy: Aristocracia
Attentive Public: Público Atento
Australian Ballot: Voto Australiano
Authority: Autoridad
Authorization: Autorización

Bad-Tendency Rule: Regla de Tendencia-mala
"Beauty Contest": Concurso de Belleza
Bicameralism: Bicameralismo
Bicameral Legislature: Legislatura Bicameral
Bill of Rights: Declaración de Derechos
Blanket Primary: Primaria Comprensiva

Block Grants: Concesiones de Bloque
Bureaucracy: Burocracia
Busing: Transporte Público

Cabinet: Gabinete, Consejo de Ministros
Cabinet Department: Departamento del Gabinete
Cadre: El núcleo de activistas de partidos políticos encargados de cumplir las funciones importantes de los partidos políticos americanos.
Canvassing Board: Consejo encargado con la encuesta de una violación.
Capture: Captura, toma
Casework: Trabajo de Caso
Categorical Grants-in-Aid: Concesiones Categóricas de Ayuda
Caucus: Reunión de Dirigentes
Challenge: Reto
Checks and Balances: Chequeos y Equilibrio
Chief Diplomat: Jefe Diplomático
Chief Executive: Jefe Ejecutivo
Chief Legislator: Jefe Legislador
Chief of Staff: Jefe de Personal
Chief of State: Jefe de Estado
Civil Law: Derecho Civil
Civil Liberties: Libertades Civiles
Civil Rights: Derechos Civiles
Civil Service: Servicio Civil
Civil Service Commission: Comisión de Servicio Civil
Class-Action Suit: Demanda en representación de un grupo o clase.
Class Politics: Política de Clase
Clear and Present Danger Test: Prueba de Peligro Claro y Presente
Climate Control: Control de Clima
Closed Primary: Primaria Cerrada
Cloture: Cierre al voto
Coattail Effect: Effecto de Cola de Chaqueta
Cold War: Guerra Fría

Commander in Chief: Comandante en Jefe
Commerce Clause: Clausula de Comercio
Commercial Speech: Discurso Comercial
Common Law: Ley Común, Derecho Consuetudinario
Comparable Worth: Valor Comparable
Compliance: De acuerdo
Concurrent Majority: Mayoría Concurrente
Concurring Opinion: Opinión Concurrente
Confederal System: Sistema Confederal
Confederation: Confederación
Conference Committee: Comité de Conferencia
Consensus: Concenso
Consent of the People: Consentimiento de la Gente
Conservatism: Calidad de Conservador
Conservative Coalition: Coalición Conservadora
Consolidation: Consolidación
Constant Dollars: Dólares Constantes
Constitutional Initiative: Iniciativa Constitucional
Constitutional Power: Poder Constitucional
Containment: Contenimiento
Continuing Resolution: Resolució Contínua
Cooley's Rule: Régla de Cooley
Cooperative Federalism: Federalismo Cooperativo
Corrupt Practices Acts: Leyes Contra Acciones Corruptas
Council of Economic Advisers (CEA): Consejo de Asesores Económicos
Council of Government (COG): Consejo de Gobierno

County: Condado
Credentials Committee: Comité de Credenciales
Criminal Law: Ley Criminal

De Facto **Segregation:** Segregación de Hecho
De Jure **Segregation:** Segregación Cotidiana
Defamation of Character: Defamación de Carácter
Democracy: Democracia
Democratic Party: Partido Democratico
Dillon's Rule: Régla de Dillon
Diplomacy: Diplomácia
Direct Democracy: Democracia Directa
Direct Primary: Primaria Directa
Direct Technique: Técnica Directa
Discharge Petition: Petición de Descargo
Dissenting Opinion: Opinión Disidente
Divisive Opinion: Opinión Divisiva
Domestic Policy: Principio Político Doméstico
Dual Citizenship: Ciudadanía Dual
Dual Federalism: Federalismo Dual
Détente: No Spanish equivalent

Economic Aid: Ayuda Económica
Economic Regulation: Regulación Económica
Elastic Clause, or Necessary and Proper Clause: Cláusula Flexible o Cláusula Propia Necesaria
Elector: Elector
Electoral College: Colegio Electoral
Electronic Media: Media Electronica
Elite: Elite (el selecto)
Elite Theory: Teoría Elitista (de lo selecto)
Emergency Power: Poder de Emergencia
Enumerated Power: Poder Enumerado
Environmental Impact Statement (EIS): Afirmación de Impacto Ambiental
Equality: Igualdad
Equalization: Igualación

Equal Employment Opportunity Commission (EEOC): Comisión de Igualdad de Oportunidad en el Empleo
Era of Good Feeling: Era de Buen Sentimiento
Era of Personal Politics: Era de Política Personal
Establishment Clause: Cláusula de Establecimiento
Euthanasia: Eutanasia
Exclusionary Rule: Regla de Exclusión
Executive Agreement: Acuerdo Ejecutivo
Executive Budget: Presupuesto Ejecutivo
Executive Office of the President (EOP): Oficina Ejecutiva del Presidente
Executive Order: Orden Ejecutivo
Executive Privilege: Privilegio Ejecutivo
Expressed Power: Poder Expresado
Extradite: Entregar por Extradición

Faction: Facción
Fairness Doctrine: Doctrina de Justicia
Fall Review: Revision de Otoño
Federalists: Federalistas
Federal Mandate: Mandato Federal
Federal Open Market Committee (FOMC): Comité Federal de Libre Mercado
Federal Register: Registro Federal
Federal System: Sistema Federal
Fighting Words: Palabras de Provocación
Filibuster: Obstrucción de iniciativas de ley
Fireside Chat: Charla de Hogar
First Budget Resolution: Resolució Primera Presupuesta
First Continental Congress: Primér Congreso Continental
Fiscal Policy: Politico Fiscal
Fiscal Year (FY): Año Fiscal
Fluidity: Fluidez
Food Stamps: Estampillas para Comida
Foreign Policy: Politica Extranjera
Foreign Policy Process: Proceso de Politica Extranjera

Franking: Franqueando
Fraternity: Fraternidad
Free Exercise Clause: Cláusula de Ejercicio Libre
Full Faith and Credit Clause: Cláusula de Completa Fé y Crédito
Functional Consolidation: Consolidación Funcional

Gag Order: Orden de Silencio
Garbage Can Model: Modelo Bote de Basura
Gender Gap: Brecha de Género
General Law City: Regla General Urbana
General Sales Tax: Impuesto General de Ventas
Generational Effect: Efecto Generacional
Gerrymandering: División arbitraria de los distritos electorales con fines políticos.
Government: Gobierno
Government Corporation: Corporación Gubernamental
Government in the Sunshine Act: Gobierno en la acta: Luz del Sol
Grandfather Clause: Clausula del Abuelo
Grand Jury: Gran Jurado
Great Compromise: Grán Acuerdo de Negociación

Hatch Act (Political Activities Act): Acta Hatch (acta de actividades politicas)
Hecklers' Veto: Veto de Abuchamiento
Home Rule City: Regla Urbana
Horizontal Federalism: Federalismo Horizontal
Hyperpluralism: Hiperpluralismo

Ideologue: Ideólogo
Ideology: Ideología
Image Building: Construcción de Imágen
Impeachment: Acción Penal Contra un Funcionario Público
Inalienable Rights: Derechos Inalienables
Income Transfer: Transferencia de Ingresos
Incorporation Theory: Teoría de Incorporación

Independent: Independiente
Independent Candidate: Candidato Independiente
Independent Executive Agency: Agencia Ejecutiva Independiente
Independent Regulatory Agency: Agencia Regulatoria Independiente
Indirect Technique: Técnica Indirecta
Inherent Power: Poder Inherente
Initiative: Iniciativa
Injunction: Injunción, Prohibición Judicial
In-Kind Subsidy: Subsidio de Clase
Institution: Institución
Instructed Delegate: Delegado con Instrucciones
Intelligence Community: Comunidad de Inteligencia
Intensity: Intensidad
Interest Group: Grupo de Interés
Interposition: Interposición
Interstate Compact: Compacto Interestatal
Iron Curtain: Cortina de Acero
Iron Triangle: Triágulo de Acero
Isolationist Foreign Policy: Politica Extranjera de Aislamiento
Issue Voting: Voto Temático
Item Veto: Artículo de Veto

Jim Crow Laws: No Spanish equivalent.
Joint Committee: Comité Mancomunado
Judicial Activism: Activismo Judicial
Judicial Implementation: Implementacion Judicial
Judicial Restraint: Restricción Judicial
Judicial Review: Revisión Judicial
Jurisdiction: Jurisdicción
Justiciable Dispute: Disputa Judiciaria
Justiciable Question: Pregunta Justiciable

Keynesian Economics: Economía Keynesiana
Kitchen Cabinet: Gabinete de Cocina

Labor Movement: Movimiento Laboral

Latent Public Opinion: Opinión Pública Latente
Lawmaking: Hacedores de Ley
Legislative History: Historia Legislativa
Legislative Initiative: Iniciativa de legislación
Legislative Veto: Veto Legislativo
Legislature: Legislatura
Legitimacy: Legitimidad
Libel: Libelo, Difamación Escrita
Liberalism: Liberalismo
Liberty: Libertad
Limited Government: Gobierno Limitado
Line Organization: Organización de Linea
Literacy Test: Exámen de alfabetización
Litigate: Litigar
Lobbying: Cabildeo
Logrolling: Práctica legislativa que consiste en incluir en un mismo proyecto de ley temas de diversa ídole.
Loophole: Hueco Legal, Escapatoria

Madisonian Model: Modelo Madisónico
Majority: Mayoría
Majority Floor Leader: Líder Mayoritario de Piso
Majority Leader of the House: Líder Mayoritario de la Casa
Majority Opinion: Opinión Mayoritaria
Majority Rule: Regla de Mayoría
Managed News: Noticias Manipuladas
Mandatory Retirement: Retiro Mandatorio
Matching Funds: Fondos Combinados
Material Incentive: Incentivo Material
Media: Media
Media Access: Acceso de Media
Merit System: Sistema de Mérito
Military-Industrial Complex: Complejo Industriomilitar
Minority Floor Leader: Líder Minoritario de Piso
Minority Leader of the House: Líder Minorial del Cuerpo Legislativo

Monetary Policy: Politica Monetaria
Monopolistic Model: Modelo Monopólico
Monroe Doctrine: Doctrina Monroe
Moral Idealism: Idealismo Moral
Municipal Home Rule: Regla Municipal

Narrowcasting: Mensaje Dirigído
National Committee: Comité Nacional
National Convention: Convención Nacional
National Politics: Politica Nacional
National Security Council (NSC): Concilio de Seguridad Nacional
National Security Policy: Politica de Seguridad Nacional
Natural Aristocracy: Aristocracia Natural
Natural Rights: Derechos Naturales
Necessaries: Necesidades
Negative Constituents: Constituyentes Negativos
New England Town: Pueblo de Nueva Inglaterra
New Federalism: Federalismo Nuevo
Nullification: Nulidad, Anulación

Office-Block, or Massachusetts, Ballot: Cuadro-Oficina, o Massachusetts, Voto
Office of Management and Budget (OMB): Oficina de Administració y Presupuesto
Oligarchy: Oligarquía
Ombudsperson: Funcionario que representa al ciudadano ante el gobierno.
Open Primary: Primaria Abierta
Opinion: Opinión
Opinion Leader: Líder de Opinión
Opinion Poll: Encuesta, Conjunto de Opinión
Oral Arguments: Argumentos Orales
Oversight: Inadvertencia, Omisión

Paid-for Political Announcement: Anuncios Politicos Pagados
Pardon: Perdón
Party-Column, or Indiana, Ballot: Partido-Columna, o Indiana, Voto

Party Identification: Identificación de Partido

Party Identifier: Identificador de Partido

Party-in-Electorate: Partido Electoral

Party-in-Government: Partido en Gobierno

Party Organization: Organización de Partido

Party Platform: Plataforma de Partido

Patronage: Patrocinio

Peer Group: Grupo de Contemporáneos

Pendleton Act (Civil Service Reform Act): Acta Pendleton (Acta de Reforma al Servicio Civil)

Personal Attack Rule: Regla de Ataque Personal

Petit Jury: Jurado Ordinario

Pluralism: Pluralismo

Plurality: Pluralidad

Pocket Veto: Veto de Bolsillo

Police Power: Poder Policiaco

Policy Trade-offs: Intercambio de Politicas

Political Action Committee (PAC): Comité de Acción Política

Political Consultant: Consultante Político

Political Culture: Cultura Politica

Political Party: Partido Político

Political Question: Pregunta Politica

Political Realism: Realismo Político

Political Socialization: Socialización Politica

Political Tolerance: Tolerancia Política

Political Trust: Confianza Política

Politico: Político

Politics: Politica

Poll Tax: Impuesto sobre el sufragio

Poll Watcher: Observador de Encuesta

Popular Sovereignty: Soberanía Popular

Power: Poder

Precedent: Precedente

Preferred-Position Test: Prueba de Posición Preferida

Presidential Primary: Primaria Presidencial

President Pro Tempore: Presidente Provisoriamente

Press Secretary: Secretaría de Prensa

Prior Restraint: Restricción Anterior

Privileges and Immunities: Privilégios e Imunidades

Privitization, or Contracting Out: Privatización

Property: Propiedad

Property Tax: Impuesto de Propiedad

Public Agenda: Agenda Pública

Public Debt Financing: Financiamiento de Deuda Pública

Public Debt, or National Debt: Deuda Pública o Nacional

Public Interest: Interes Público

Public Opinion: Opinión Pública

Purposive Incentive: Incentivo de Propósito

Ratification: Ratificación

Rational Ignorance Effect: Effecto de Ignorancia Racional

Reapportionment: Redistribución

Recall: Suspender

Recognition Power: Poder de Reconocimiento

Recycling: Reciclaje

Redistricting: Redistrictificación

Referendum: Referédum

Registration: Registración

Regressive Tax: Impuestos Regresivos

Relevance: Pertinencia

Remand: Reenviar

Representation: Representación

Representative Assembly: Asamblea Representativa

Representative Democracy: Democracia Representativa

Reprieve: Trequa, Suspensión

Republic: República

Republican Party: Partido Republicano

Resulting Powers: Poderes Resultados

Reverse: Cambiarse a lo contrario

Reverse Discrimination: Discriminación Reversiva

Rule of Four: Regla de Cuatro

Rules Committee: Comité Regulador

Runoff Primary: Primaria Residual

Safe Seat: Asiento Seguro

Sampling Error: Error de Encuesta

Secession: Secesión

Second Budget Resolution: Resolución Segunda Presupuestal

Second Continental Congress: Segundo Congreso Continental

Sectional Politics: Política Seccional

Segregation: Segregación

Select Committee: Comité Selecto

Selectperson: Persona Selecta

Senatorial Courtesy: Cortesia Senatorial

Seniority System: Sistema Señiorial

Separate-but-Equal Doctrine: Separados pero iguales

Separation of Powers: Separación de Poderes

Service Sector: Sector de Servicio

Sexual Harassment: Acosamiento Sexual

Sex Discrimination: Discriminacion Sexual

Slander: Difamación Oral, Calumnia

Sliding-Scale Test: Prueba Escalonada

Social Movement: Movimiento Social

Social Security: Seguridad Social

Socioeconomic Status: Estado Socioeconómico

Solidary Incentive: Incentivo de Solideridad

Solid South: Súr Sólido

Sound Bite: Mordida de Sonido

Soviet Bloc: Bloque Soviético

Speaker of the House: Vocero de la Casa

Spin: Girar/Giro

Spin Doctor: Doctor en Giro

Spin-off Party: Partido Estático

Spoils System: Sistema de Despojos

Spring Review: Revisión de Primavera

Stability: Estabilidad

Standing Committee: Comité de Sostenimiento

Stare Decisis: El principio característico del ley comú por el cual los precedentes jurisprudenciales tienen fuerza obligatoria, no sólo entre las partes, sino tambien para casos sucesivos análogos.

State: Estado

State Central Committee: Comité Central del Estado

State of the Union Message: Mensaje Sobre el Estado de la Unión

Statutory Power: Poder Estatorial

Strategic Arms Limitation Treaty (SALT I): Tratado de Limitación de Armas Estratégicas

Subpoena: Orden de Testificación

Subsidy: Subsidio

Suffrage: Sufrágio

Sunset Legislation: Legislación Sunset

Superdelegate: Líder de partido o oficial elegido quien tiene el derecho de votar.

Supplemental Security Income (SSI): Ingresos de Seguridad Suplementaria

Supremacy Clause: Cláusula de Supremacia

Supremacy Doctrine: Doctrina de Supremacia

Symbolic Speech: Discurso Simbólico

Technical Assistance: Asistencia Técnica

Third Party: Tercer Partido

Third-Party Candidate: Candidato de Tercer Partido

Ticket Splitting: División de Boletos

Totalitarian Regime: Régimen Totalitario

Town Manager System: Sistema de Administrador Municipal

Town Meeting: Junta Municipal

Township: Municipio

Tracking Poll: Seguimiento de Encuesta

Trial Court: Tribunal de Primera

Truman Doctrine: Doctrina Truman

Trustee: Depositario

Twelfth Amendment: Doceava Enmienda

Twenty-fifth Amendment: Veinticincoava Enmienda

Two-Party System: Sistema de Dos Partidos

Unanimous Opinion: Opinión Unánime

Underground Economy: Economía Subterráea

Unicameral Legislature: Legislatura Unicameral

Unincorporated Area: Area no Incorporada

Unitary System: Sistema Unitario

Unit Rule: Regla de Unidad

Universal Suffrage: Sufragio Universal

U.S. Treasury Bond: Bono de la Tesoreria de E.U.A.

Veto Message: Comunicado de Veto

Voter Turnout: Renaimiento de Votantes

War Powers Act: Acta de Poderes de Guerra

Washington Community: Comunidad de Washington

Weberian Model: Modelo Weberiano

Whip: Látigo

Whistleblower: Privatización o Contratista

White House Office: Oficina de la Casa Blanca

White House Press Corps: Cuerpo de Prensa de la Casa Blanca

White Primary: Sufragio en Elección Primaria/Blancos Solamente

Writ of *Certiorari*: Prueba de certeza; orden emitida por el tribunal de apelaciones para que el tribunal inferior dé lugar a la apelación.

Writ of *Habeas Corpus*: Prueba de Evidencia Concreta

Writ of *Mandamus*: Un mandato por la corte para que un acto se lleve a cabo.

Yellow Journalism: Amarillismo Periodístico

Glossary

A

Access The ability to contact an official either in person or by telephone. Campaign contributions are often given in hopes of gaining access to elected officials.

Acquisitive Model A model of bureaucracy that views top level bureaucrats as seeking constantly to expand the size of their budgets and the staffs of their departments or agencies so as to gain greater power and influence in the public sector.

Acquitted Found not guilty.

Ad Hoc Committee A temporary committee.

Ad Valorem Tax A tax levied according to the value of what is being taxed, such as a property tax.

Adjutant General The principal staff officer of an army, who passes communications to the commanding general and distributes the general's orders to subordinates. In the example of the Texas National Guard and Texas State Guard, the "commanding general" is the governor. *Adjutant* comes from a Latin word meaning "helper."

Actual Malice In libel cases, either knowledge of a defamatory statement's falsity or a reckless disregard for the truth.

Administrative Agency A federal, state, or local government unit established to perform a specific function. Administrative agencies are created and authorized by legislative bodies to administer and enforce specific laws.

Administrative Law Rules and regulations written by administrators to implement laws. The effectiveness of a law is often determined by how the corresponding administrative law is written.

Adversary System A legal system in which parties to a legal action are opponents and are responsible for bringing the facts and law related to their case before the court.

Advice and Consent The power vested in the U.S. Senate by the Constitution (Article II, Section 2) to give its advice and consent to the president on treaties and presidential appointments.

Affirm To declare that a court ruling is valid and must stand.

Affirmative Action A policy in educational admissions or job hiring that gives special consideration or compensatory treatment to traditionally disadvantaged groups in an effort to overcome present effects of past discrimination.

Agenda Setting Determining which public-policy questions will be debated or considered.

Amicus Curiae Brief A brief (a document containing a legal argument supporting a desired outcome in a particular case) filed by a third party, or *amicus curiae* (Latin for "friend of the court"), who is not directly involved in the litigation but who has an interest in the outcome of the case.

Annexation The incorporation of a territory into a larger political unit, such as a country, state, county, or city.

Anti-Federalist An individual who opposed the ratification of the new Constitution in 1787. The Anti-Federalists were opposed to a strong central government.

Antitrust Legislation Legislation directed against economic monopolies.

Appellate Court A court having jurisdiction to review cases and issues that were originally tried in lower courts.

Appellate Jurisdiction The authority vested in an appellate court to review and revise the judicial actions of inferior courts.

Appointment Power The authority vested in the president to fill a government office or position. Positions filled by presidential appointment include those in the executive branch and the federal judiciary, commissioned officers in the armed forces, and members of the independent regulatory commissions.

Appropriation The passage, by Congress, of a spending bill, specifying the amount of authorized funds that actually will be allocated for an agency's use.

Aristocracy Rule by the "best"; in reality, rule by an upper class.

Arraignment The first act in a criminal proceeding, in which the defendant is brought before a court to hear the charges against him or her and to enter a plea of guilty or not guilty.

At-Large Election A citywide (or, in some states, countywide) election.

At-Large Place System An at-large election system in which all voters elect all the members of the city council and each candidate runs for a specific seat on the council.

Attentive Public That portion of the general public that pays attention to policy issues.

Attorney General's Opinion In Texas and other states, an interpretation of the state's constitution or laws by the state attorney general. Officials may request such opinions, and although the opinions are not legally binding, they are usually followed.

Australian Ballot A secret ballot prepared, distributed, and tabulated by government officials at public expense. Since 1888, all states have used the Australian ballot rather than an open, public ballot.

Authoritarianism A type of regime in which only the government itself is fully controlled by the ruler. Social and economic institutions exist that are not under the government's control. Contrast *totalitarianism*.

Authority The right and power of a government or other entity to enforce its decisions and compel obedience.

Authorization A formal declaration by a legislative committee that a certain amount of funding may be available to an agency. Some authorizations terminate in a year; others are renewable automatically without further congressional action.

Automatic, or Built-In, Stabilizers Certain federal programs that cause changes in national income during economic fluctuations without the action of Congress and the president. Examples are the federal income tax system and unemployment compensation.

B

Balance of Trade The difference between the value of a nation's exports of goods and its imports of goods.

"Beauty Contest" A presidential primary in which contending candidates compete for popular votes but the results have little or no impact on the selection of delegates to the national convention.

Bias An inclination or a preference that interferes with impartial judgment.

Bicameral Legislature A legislature made up of two chambers, or parts. The U.S. Congress, composed of the House of Representatives and the Senate, is a bicameral legislature.

Bicameralism The division of a legislature into two separate assemblies.

Bicultural Encompassing two cultures.

Binational Belonging to two nations.

Black Codes State laws passed after the Civil War that deprived freed slaves of rights and privileges.

Block Grant A federal grant that provides funds to a state or local government for some general functional area, such as criminal justice or mental health.

Blocking Bill In Texas, a bill placed early on the senate calendar that will never actually be considered. A rule—which can be suspended by a two-thirds vote—requires that the senate address bills in chronological order. The blocking bill ensures that a measure must win the vote of two-thirds of the senate even to be considered.

Blue-Ribbon Commission A commission composed of public personalities or authorities on the subject that is being considered. In Texas, such a commission may have both fact-finding and recommending authority.

Boards and Commissions In Texas, bodies consisting of three to eighteen members that supervise most state agencies.

Boycott A form of pressure or protest—an organized refusal to purchase a particular product or deal with a particular business.

Broad Construction A judicial philosophy that looks to the context and purpose of a law when making an interpretation.

Budget Deficit Government expenditures that exceed receipts.

Budgetary Power The power to propose a spending plan to the legislature. The governor of Texas has limited budgetary power because of the competing authority of the Legislative Budget Committee.

Burden of Proof In a court case, a party's duty to convince a judge or jury that the party's version of the facts is true. The standard of proof is higher in a criminal case than in a civil one.

Bureaucracy A large organization that is structured hierarchically to carry out specific functions.

Busing In the context of civil rights, the transportation of public school students from areas where they live to schools in other areas to eliminate school segregation based on residential patterns.

C

Cabinet An advisory group selected by the president to aid in decision making. The cabinet includes the heads of fifteen executive departments and others named by the president. Depending on the president, the cabinet may be highly influential or relatively insignificant in its advisory role.

Cabinet System At the state government level, a form of executive organization that allows the governor to appoint and remove top-level administrators, giving the governor more control over the administration.

Calendars Committee The committee in the Texas House of Representatives that assigns bills to the calendars for floor action. (The less-important Local and Consent Calendars Committee also performs this function.)

Capitalism An economic system characterized by the private ownership of wealth-creating assets and also by free markets and freedom of contract.

Capture The act of gaining direct or indirect control over agency personnel and decision makers by the industry that is being regulated.

Case Law The rules and principles announced in court decisions. Case law includes judicial interpretations of common law principles and doctrines as well as interpretations of constitutional law, statutory law, and administrative law.

Casework Personal work for constituents by members of Congress.

Categorical Grant A federal grant to a state or local government that must be used for a very specific program or project.

Caucus A closed meeting of party leaders to select party candidates or to decide on policy; also, a meeting of party members designed to select candidates and propose policies.

Chad A small fragment of paper produced by the punching of a data card, such as a punch-card ballot.

Change of Venue A change in the site of a trial.

Charter A document issued by a government that grants to a person, a group of persons, or a corporation the right to carry on one or more specific activities. A state government can grant a charter to a municipality.

Charter School A school authorized by a state that is free of various rules and regulations imposed by the state on public schools.

Checks and Balances A major principle of the American government system whereby each branch of the government exercises a check on the actions of the others.

Chief Diplomat The role of the president in recognizing foreign governments, making treaties, and making executive agreements.

Chief Executive The role of the president as head of the executive branch of the government.

Chief Legislator The role of the president in influencing the making of laws.

Chief of Staff The person who is named to direct the White House Office and advise the president.

Chief of State Nationally, the head of state—the president of the United States, for example. In Texas and other states, the governor—who serves as the symbol of the state and performs ceremonial duties—is the chief of state.

Civic Duty A citizen's understood obligation to register, to vote, to be knowledgeable, and to take action to make the community a better place.

Civil Disobedience A nonviolent, public refusal to obey allegedly unjust laws.

Civil Law The law regulating conduct between private persons over noncriminal matters. Under civil law, the government provides the forum for the settlement of disputes between private parties in such matters as contracts, domestic relations, and business relations.

Civil Liberties Those personal freedoms that are protected for all individuals and that generally deal with individual freedom. Civil liberties typically involve restraining the government's actions against individuals.

Civil Rights Generally, all rights rooted in the Fourteenth Amendment's guarantee of equal protection under the law.

Civil Service A collective term for the body of employees working for the government. Generally, the term is understood to apply to all those who gain government employment through a merit system.

Civil Service Commission The initial central personnel agency of the national government; created in 1883.

Class-Action Suit A lawsuit filed by an individual seeking damages for "all persons similarly situated."

Clear and Present Danger Test The test proposed by Justice Oliver Wendell Holmes for determining when government may restrict free speech. Restrictions are permissible, he argued, only when speech presents a "clear and present danger" to the public order.

Clemency Relief from criminal punishment granted by an executive. In Texas, the power of the governor to grant clemency is strictly limited.

Clientele Persons represented by a government agency or a politician.

Closed Primary A type of primary in which the voter is limited to choosing candidates of the party of which he or she is a member.

Cloture An action by which legislative debate is ended so that a floor vote must be taken.

Coattail Effect The influence of a popular candidate on the electoral success of other candidates on the same party ticket. The effect is increased by the party-column ballot, which encourages straight-ticket voting.

Cold War The ideological, political, and economic impasse that existed between the United States and the Soviet Union following World War II.

Colonia In Texas, an unincorporated urban district along the U.S.-Mexican border. Colonias are typically impoverished and are chiefly inhabited by Mexican Americans.

Commander in Chief The role of the president as supreme commander of the military forces of the United States and of the state National Guard units when they are called into federal service.

Commerce Clause The section of the Constitution in which Congress is given the power to regulate trade among the states and with foreign countries.

Commercial Speech Advertising statements, which increasingly have been given First Amendment protection.

Commission System A system that allows the members of a city council to serve as heads of city departments.

Commissioners Court In Texas, the policymaking body of a county. A commissioners court consists of a county judge (the presiding officer), who is elected in countywide elections, and four commissioners elected from individual precincts.

Committee of the Whole An entire legislative body (such as the Texas Senate) acting as a committee. The committee's purpose is to allow the body to relax its rules and thereby expedite legislation.

Common Law Judge-made law that originated in England from decisions shaped according to prevailing customs. Decisions were applied to similar situations and thus gradually became common to the nation.

Community Property Any property that a married couple has acquired during their marriage. In certain states, it is divided equally between them in the event of a divorce.

Communism A revolutionary variant of socialism that favors a partisan (and often totalitarian) dictatorship, government control of all enterprises, and the replacement of free markets by central planning.

Concurrent Powers Powers held jointly by the national and state governments.

Concurring Opinion A separate opinion prepared by a judge who supports the decision of the majority of the court but who wants to make or clarify a particular point or to voice disapproval of the grounds on which the decision was made.

Confederation A political system in which states or regional governments retain ultimate authority except for those powers they expressly delegate to a central government. A voluntary association of independent states, in which the member states agree to limited restraints on their freedom of action.

Conference Committee A special joint committee appointed to reconcile differences when bills pass the two chambers of Congress in different forms.

Conflict of Interest A situation that arises when a legislator, bureaucrat, executive official, or judge can make an official decision that results in a personal economic advantage. The result is a potential or real conflict between the personal interests of the officeholder and the general interests of the public.

Consensus General agreement among the citizenry on an issue.

Consent of the People The idea that governments and laws derive their legitimacy from the consent of the governed.

Conservatism A set of beliefs that includes a limited role for the national government in helping individuals, support for traditional values and lifestyles, and a cautious response to change.

Conservative Coalition An alliance of Republicans and southern Democrats in the House or the Senate to oppose liberal legislation and support conservative legislation.

Consolidation The union of two or more governmental units to form a single unit.

Constable A law enforcement officer. In Texas, constables are elected at the county level and serve as process officers of justice of the peace courts.

Constituent One of the people represented by a legislator or other elected or appointed official.

Constitutional Initiative An electoral device whereby citizens can propose a constitutional amendment through petitions signed by the required number of registered voters.

Constitutional Power A power vested in the president by Article II of the Constitution.

Consumer Price Index (CPI) A measure of the change in price over time of a specific group of goods and services used by the average household.

Containment A U.S. diplomatic policy adopted by the Truman administration to "build situations of strength" around the globe to contain Communist power within its existing boundaries.

Continuing Resolution A temporary law that Congress passes when an appropriations bill has not been decided by the beginning of the new fiscal year on October 1.

Cooley's Rule The view that cities should be able to govern themselves, presented in an 1871 Michigan decision by Judge Thomas Cooley.

Cooperative Federalism The theory that the states and the national government should cooperate in solving problems.

Co-optation The "capturing" of an agency by members of an interest group. In effect, governmental power comes to be exercised by a private interest.

Corrupt Practices Acts A series of acts passed by Congress in an attempt to limit and regulate the size and sources of contributions and expenditures in political campaigns.

Council of Governments (COG) A voluntary organization of counties, municipalities, and other authorities that seeks to coordinate responses to area-wide problems.

Council-Manager System A municipal system featuring an elected city council and a city manager who is hired by the council. The council makes policy decisions, and the manager is responsible for the day-to-day operations of the city government.

County The chief governmental unit set up by the state to administer state law and business at the local level. Counties are drawn up by area, rather than by rural or urban criteria.

County Attorney In Texas, a county legal officer who gives legal advice to the commissioners court, represents the county in court, and prosecutes crimes. If a county has both a county attorney and a district attorney, the latter prosecutes felony crimes.

County Auditor In Texas, a county financial officer whose duties, depending on the population of the county, may include reviewing county financial records and (in large counties) serving as the chief budget officer.

County Clerk The chief record keeper and elections officer of a county.

County Commissioner One of a group of officials elected to administer a county; in Texas, a member of the commissioners court who is elected from a district, or precinct.

County Courts-at-Law In Texas, county courts in addition to the constitutional county court. They are established by the legislature in all but the smallest Texas counties and may have criminal or civil jurisdiction. They form a level of courts superior to justice of the peace and municipal courts but inferior to district courts.

County Judge In Texas, an official elected countywide to preside over the commissioners court and to try certain minor cases.

County Treasurer A county official who is responsible for receiving, depositing, and disbursing. A county official who is responsible for receiving, depositing, and disbursing county funds.

Credentials Committee A committee used by political parties at their national conventions to determine which delegates may participate. The committee inspects the claim of each prospective delegate to be seated as a legitimate representative of his or her state.

Creole A descendant of European Spanish (or in some regions, French) immigrants to the Americas.

Criminal Law The law that defines crimes and provides punishment for violations. In criminal cases, the government is the prosecutor because crimes are against the public order.

Crossover Voting A circumstance in which members of one political party vote in the other party's primary to influence which nominee is selected by the other party.

Cumulative Voting An at-large election system in which voters can cast one or more votes for a single candidate. For example, a voter who can cast up to five votes in a city council election can cast all five votes for one candidate or spread the votes among several candidates.

Current Account Balance A wider concept than the balance of trade. The current account balance includes the balance of trade in services, unilateral transfers, and other items.

D

De Facto Segregation Racial segregation that occurs because of past social and economic conditions and residential patterns.

De Jure Segregation Racial segregation that occurs because of laws or administrative decisions by public agencies.

Deadwood In the context of state government, constitutional provisions made inoperative by conflicting federal constitutional or statutory law.

Dealignment A decline in party loyalties that reduces long-term party commitment.

Decentralization In American party politics, distribution of power to state and local party organizations rather than concentration of power in the national organization. In government, distribution of authority to local and regional governments rather than concentration of authority in a central government.

Defamation of Character Wrongfully hurting a person's good reputation. The law has imposed a general duty on all persons to refrain from making false, defamatory statements about others.

Defense Policy A subset of national security policy that generally refers to the set of policies that direct the scale and size of the U.S. armed forces.

Deferred Adjudication A procedure that allows a judge to postpone final sentencing in a criminal case; charges are dismissed if the defendant completes a satisfactory probationary period.

Democracy A system of government in which ultimate political authority is vested in the people. Derived from the Greek words *demos* ("the people") and *kratos* ("authority").

Democratic Party One of the two major American political parties that evolved out of the Republican Party of Thomas Jefferson.

Democratic Republic A republic in which representatives elected by the people make and enforce laws and policies.

Dependent Agency Government entities that are closely linked to general-purpose governments. They do not have the independence of special districts.

Détente A French word meaning a relaxation of tensions. The term characterizes U.S.-Soviet policy as it developed under President Richard Nixon and Secretary of State Henry Kissinger. Détente stressed direct cooperative dealings with Cold War rivals but avoided ideological accommodation.

Development Corporation Act A state law that allows select Texas cities to raise the sales tax for economic development, subject to voter approval.

Devolution The transfer of powers from a national or central government to a state or local government.

Dillon's Rule The narrowest possible interpretation of the legal status of local governments, outlined by Judge John F. Dillon, who in 1872 stated that a municipal corporation can exercise only those powers expressly granted by state law.

Diplomacy The total process by which states carry on political relations with each other; the settling of conflicts among nations by peaceful means.

Diplomatic Recognition The formal acknowledgment of a foreign government as legitimate.

Direct Democracy A system of government in which political decisions are made by the people directly, rather than by their elected representatives; probably possible only in small political communities.

Direct Primary An intra-party election in which the voters select the candidates who will run on a party's ticket in the subsequent general election. In Texas, nominees must win a majority of the votes, which often means there are primary runoff elections between the top two candidates.

Direct Technique An interest group activity that involves interaction with government officials to further the group's goals.

Directive Authority The power to issue binding orders to state agencies. This power is severely limited for the governor of Texas.

Discharge Petition A procedure by which a bill in the House of Representatives may be forced out of a committee (discharged) that has refused to report it for consideration by the House. The discharge petition must be signed by an absolute majority (218) of representatives and is used only on rare occasions.

Discretion An official's power to make decisions based on personal judgment rather than on the specific requirements of the law. The freedom to decide or make choices.

Dissenting Opinion A separate opinion in which a judge dissents from (disagrees with) the conclusion reached by the majority on the court and expounds his or her own views about the case.

District Attorney An official who prosecutes felony cases.

District Clerk In Texas, the record keeper for the district court in a county with a population that exceeds eight thousand.

Diversity of Citizenship A basis for federal court jurisdiction over a lawsuit that involves citizens of different states or (more rarely) citizens of a U.S. state and citizens or subjects of a foreign country. The amount in controversy must be at least $75,000 before a federal court can take jurisdiction in such cases.

Divided Government A situation in which one major political party controls the presidency and the other controls the chambers of Congress or in which one party controls a state governorship and the other controls the state legislature.

Divisive Opinion Public opinion that is polarized between two quite different positions.

Docket The schedule of court activity.

Domestic Policy Public plans or courses of action that concern internal issues of national importance, such as poverty, crime, and the environment.

Dominant Culture The values, customs, language, and ideals established by the group or groups in a society that traditionally have controlled politics and government institutions in that society.

Down-Ticket An elective position located "down-ticket" on the ballot.

Dual Federalism A system of government in which the states and the national government each remain supreme within their own spheres. The doctrine looks on nation and state as co-equal sovereign powers. It holds that acts of states within their reserved powers are legitimate limitations on the powers of the national government.

Due Process Established rules and principles for the administration of justice designed to safeguard the rights of the individual. The right to due process of law is provided by the U.S. Constitution and most state constitutions.

E

Earned-Income Tax Credit (EITC) Program A government program that helps low-income workers by giving back part or all of their Social Security taxes.

Economic Aid Assistance to other nations in the form of grants, loans, or credits to buy the assisting nation's products.

Elastic Clause, or Necessary and Proper Clause The clause in Article I, Section 8, that grants Congress the power to do whatever is necessary to execute its specifically delegated powers.

Election Judges Public officials who are responsible for enforcing election rules at polling places on Election Day.

Elective Accountability   A condition in which officials are directly accountable to the voters for their actions.

Elector   A person on the partisan slate that is selected early in the presidential election year according to state laws and the applicable political party apparatus to cast ballots for president and vice president. The number of electors in each state is equal to that state's number of representatives in both chambers of Congress.

Electoral College   A group of persons called electors selected by the voters in each state and Washington, D.C.; this group officially elects the president and vice president of the United States. The number of electors in each state is equal to the number of each state's representatives in both chambers of Congress. The Twenty-third Amendment to the Constitution permits Washington, D.C., to have as many electors as the smallest state.

Electronic Media   Communication channels that involve electronic transmissions, such as radio, television, and, to an increasing extent, the Internet.

Elite Theory   A perspective holding that society is ruled by a small number of people who exercise power in their self-interest.

Emergency Power   An inherent power exercised by the president during a period of national crisis, particularly in foreign affairs.

Enabling Act   Legislation that confers on appropriate officials the power to implement or enforce the law.

Enabling Legislation   A statute enacted by Congress that authorizes the creation of an administrative agency and specifies the name, purpose, composition, functions, and powers of the agency being created.

Enumerated Powers   Powers specifically granted to the national government by the Constitution. The first seventeen clauses of Article I, Section 8, specify most of the enumerated powers of Congress.

Environmental Impact Statement (EIS)   As a requirement mandated by the National Environmental Policy Act, a report that must show the costs and benefits of major federal actions that could significantly affect the quality of the environment.

Equality   The idea that all people are of equal worth.

Era of Good Feelings   The years from 1817 to 1825, when James Monroe was president and there was, in effect, no political opposition.

Establishment Clause   The part of the First Amendment prohibiting the establishment of a church officially supported by the national government. It is applied to questions of state and local government aid to religious organizations and schools, questions of the legality of allowing or requiring school prayers, and questions of the teaching of evolution versus fundamentalist theories of creation.

Evangelical   Having to do with a broad spectrum of Protestant Christianity that emphasizes salvation and traditional values. Evangelical voters are likely to support culturally conservative politics.

Ex Officio   Having a position by virtue of holding a particular office. For example, the lieutenant governor of Texas serves *ex officio* as the presiding officer of the Texas Senate.

Examining Trial   A relatively uncommon procedure that may be requested by felony defendants in Texas. In an examining trial, a justice of the peace reviews the facts and decides whether the case should go to criminal court.

Exclusionary Rule   A policy forbidding the admission at trial of illegally seized evidence.

Executive Agreement   An international agreement made by the president, without senatorial ratification, with the head of a foreign state.

Executive Budget   The budget prepared and submitted by the president to Congress.

Executive Office of the President (EOP)   An organization established by President Franklin D. Roosevelt by executive order under the Reorganization Act of 1939 to assist the president in carrying out major duties.

Executive Order   A rule or regulation issued by the president that has the effect of law. Executive orders can implement and give administrative effect to provisions in the Constitution, to treaties, and to statutes.

Executive Privilege   The right of executive officials to withhold information from or to refuse to appear before a legislative committee. Executive privilege is enjoyed by the president and by those executive officials accorded that right by the president.

Exports   Goods and services produced domestically for sale abroad.

Expressed Power   A constitutional or statutory power of the president that is expressly written into the Constitution or into statutory law.

Extraterritorial Jurisdiction (ETJ)   In Texas, a buffer area that extends beyond a city's limits. Cities can enforce some laws, such as zoning and building codes, in an ETJ.

F

Faction   A group or bloc in a legislature or political party acting together in pursuit of some special interest or position.

Fall Review   The time every year when, after receiving formal federal agency requests for funding for the next fiscal year, the Office of Management and Budget reviews the requests, makes changes, and submits its recommendations to the president.

Fascism   A twentieth-century ideology—often totalitarian—that exalts the national collective united behind an absolute ruler. Fascism rejects liberal individualism, values action over rational deliberation, and glorifies war.

FBI Index Crimes   A set of crimes reported by the FBI and commonly used as a way of measuring the overall crime rate. The index crimes are murder and non-negligent manslaughter, forcible rape, robbery, aggravated assault, burglary, theft, and motor vehicle theft.

Fed   The Federal Reserve System created by Congress in 1913 as the nation's central banking organization.

Federal Mandate   A requirement in federal legislation that forces states and municipalities to comply with certain rules.

Federal Open Market Committee   The most important body within the Federal Reserve System. The Federal Open Market Committee decides how monetary policy should be carried out by the Federal Reserve System.

Federal Question   A question that pertains to the U.S. Constitution, acts of Congress, or treaties. A federal question provides a basis for federal jurisdiction.

Federal Register   A publication of the executive branch of the U.S. government that prints executive orders, rules, and regulations.

Federal System   A system of government in which power is divided between a central government and regional, or subdivisional, governments. Each level must have some domain in which its policies are dominant and some genuine political or constitutional guarantee of its authority.

Federalist   The name given to one who was in favor of the adoption of the U.S. Constitution and the creation of a federal union with a strong central government.

Felony   A crime—such as arson, murder, rape, or robbery—that carries the most severe sanctions, usually ranging from one year in prison to death.

Feminism   The movement that supports political, economic, and social equality for women.

Filibuster   The use of unlimited debate as a delaying tactic to block a bill.

First Budget Resolution   A resolution passed by Congress in May that sets overall revenue and spending goals for the following fiscal year.

Fiscal Policy   The federal government's use of taxation and spending policies to affect overall business activity.

Fiscal Year (FY)   A twelve-month period that is used for bookkeeping, or accounting, purposes. Usually, the fiscal year does not coincide with the calendar year. For example, the federal government's fiscal year runs from October 1 through September 30.

Floor Leaders   Legislators who are responsible for getting party members to vote for or against particular legislation.

Focus Group   A small group of individuals who are led in discussion by a professional consultant to gather opinions on and responses to candidates and issues.

Food Stamps   Coupons issued by the federal government to low-income individuals to be used for the purchase of food.

Foreclosure   The legal process by which a lender takes possession of a mortgaged property when the borrower defaults on the loan.

Foreign Policy   A nation's external goals and the techniques and strategies used to achieve them.

Foreign Policy Process   The steps by which external goals are decided and acted on.

Formal Powers   Legal powers granted to the governor by constitution or statute. Powers of this type, when exercised by the U.S. president, are called expressed powers.

Fragmentation   In state government, a division of power among separately elected executive officials. A plural executive is a fragmented executive.

Franking   A policy that enables members of Congress to send material through the mail by substituting their facsimile signature (frank) for postage.

Free Exercise Clause   The provision of the First Amendment guaranteeing the free exercise of religion.

Free Rider Problem   The difficulty interest groups face in recruiting members when the benefits they achieve can be gained without joining the group.

Freedmen's Bureau   The Bureau of Refugees, Freedmen and Abandoned Lands was established in 1865 to aid refugees of the Civil War (including former slaves) and to administer confiscated property. Among other tasks, it sought to provide education to the former slaves. It was disbanded in 1872.

Front-Loading   The practice of moving presidential primary elections to the early part of the campaign, to maximize the impact of certain states or regions on the nomination.

Front-Runner   The presidential candidate who appears to be ahead at a given time in the primary season.

Full Employment   An arbitrary level of unemployment that corresponds to "normal" friction in the labor market. In 1986, a 6.5 percent rate of unemployment was considered full employment. Today, it is assumed to be around 5 percent.

Functional Consolidation   The cooperation of two or more units of local government in providing services to their inhabitants.

G

Gag Order   An order issued by a judge restricting the publication of news about a trial in progress or a pretrial hearing in order to protect the accused's right to a fair trial.

Gender Discrimination   Any practice, policy, or procedure that denies equality of treatment to an individual or to a group because of gender.

Gender Gap   A term most often used to describe the difference between the percentage of women who vote for a particular candidate and the percentage of men who vote for the candidate. The term came into use after the 1980 presidential elections.

General Jurisdiction Exists when a court's authority to hear cases is not significantly restricted. A court of general jurisdiction normally can hear a broad range of cases.

General-Law Charter City structure established by statute. Most smaller Texas cities choose among several available options allowed by the state legislature.

General-Law City A city operating under general state laws that apply to all local government units of a similar type. In Texas, cities with a population of five thousand or less are (in most instances) general-law cities.

General-Purpose Government A municipal or county government. In contrast to special districts, general-purpose governments provide a wide range of services.

General Sales Tax A tax levied as a proportion of the retail price of a commodity at the point of sale.

Generational Effect A long-lasting effect of events of a particular time on the political opinions or preferences of those who came of political age at that time.

Gerrymandering The drawing of legislative district boundary lines for the purpose of obtaining partisan or factional advantage. A district is said to be gerrymandered when its shape is manipulated by the dominant party in the state legislature to maximize electoral strength at the expense of the minority party.

Government The institution in which decisions are made that resolve conflicts or allocate benefits and privileges. It is unique because it has the ultimate authority within society.

Government Corporation An agency of government that administers a quasi-business enterprise. These corporations are used when activities are primarily commercial. They produce revenue for their continued existence, and they require greater flexibility than is permitted for departments and agencies.

Government in the Sunshine Act A law that requires all multiheaded federal agencies to conduct their business regularly in public session.

Grand Jury A jury that sits in pretrial proceedings to determine if sufficient evidence exists to try an individual and, therefore, approve an indictment.

Grandfather Clause A device used by southern states to exempt whites from state taxes and literacy laws originally intended to disenfranchise African Americans. It restricted voting to those who could prove their grandfathers had voted before 1867.

Grassroots The lowest organizational level of a political party.

Great Compromise The compromise between the New Jersey and the Virginia plans that created one chamber of Congress based on population and one chamber representing each state equally; also called the Connecticut Compromise.

Gross Domestic Product (GDP) The dollar value of all final goods and services produced in a one-year period.

Gross Public Debt The net public debt plus interagency borrowings within the government.

H

Hatch Act An act passed in 1939 that restricted the political activities of government employees. It also prohibited a political group from spending more than $3 million in any campaign and limited individual contributions to a committee to $5,000. The act was designed to control political influence buying.

Head of State In the United States, the role of the president as ceremonial head of the government.

Hispanic Someone who can claim a heritage from a Spanish-speaking country. The term is used only in the United States or other countries that receive immigrants—Spanish-speaking persons living in Spanish-speaking countries normally do not apply the term to themselves.

Home Rule The right of a local government to write a charter establishing any organizational structure or program that does not conflict with state law. In Texas, reserved for municipalities with populations over five thousand.

Home-Rule City A city with the state-granted right to frame, adopt, and amend its own charter.

House and Senate Journals The official public records of the actions of the two chambers of the Texas legislature. The two journals are issued daily during sessions.

I

Ideology A comprehensive set of beliefs about the nature of people and about the institutions and role of government.

Impeachment As authorized by Articles I and II of the Constitution, an action by the House of Representatives to accuse the president, vice president, or other civil officers of the United States of committing "Treason, Bribery, or other high Crimes and Misdemeanors."

Implementation The carrying out of laws by executive officials and the bureaucrats who work for them.

Import Quota A restriction imposed on the value or number of units of a particular good that can be brought into a country. Foreign suppliers are unable to sell more than the amount specified in the import quota.

Imports Goods and services produced outside a country but sold within its borders.

Incarceration Rate The number of persons held in jail or prison for every one hundred thousand persons in a particular population group.

Income Transfer A transfer of income from some individuals in the economy to other individuals. This is generally done by way of the government. It is a transfer in the sense that no current services are rendered by the recipients.

Incorporation Theory The view that most of the protections of the Bill of Rights apply to state governments through the Fourteenth Amendment's due process clause.

Incumbent The current holder of an office.

Independent A voter or candidate who does not identify with a political party.

Independent Executive Agency A federal agency that is not part of a cabinet department but reports directly to the president.

Independent Expenditures Unregulated political contributions from PACs, ideological organizations, and individuals. A group or an individual may spend funds on campaign advertising or other activities so long as those expenditures are not coordinated with those of any candidate.

Independent Regulatory Agency An agency outside the major executive departments charged with making and implementing rules and regulations to protect the public interest.

Independent School District A local government that operates a school system independent of general-purpose governments.

Indiana Ballot See *Party-Column Ballot.*

Indictment A formal accusation issued by a grand jury against a party charged with a crime when the jury determines that there is sufficient evidence to bring the accused to trial.

Indirect Appointive Power In Texas, the power of the governor to appoint supervisory boards (but not operational directors) for most state agencies. The supervisory boards and commissions usually appoint the actual head of most state agencies in Texas.

Indirect Technique A strategy employed by interest groups that uses third parties to influence government officials.

Inflation A sustained rise in the general price level of goods and services.

Informal Powers Powers not directly granted by law. The governor's informal powers may follow from powers granted by law but may also come from the governor's persuasive abilities, which are affected by the governor's personality, popularity, and political support.

Inherent Power A power of the president derived from the loosely worded statements in the Constitution that "the executive Power shall be vested in a President" and that the president should "take Care that the Laws be faithfully executed"; defined through practice rather than through constitutional or statutory law.

Initiative A procedure by which voters can propose a law (or, in some states, a constitutional amendment); in Texas, limited to home-rule cities.

In-Kind Subsidy A good or service—such as food stamps, housing, or medical care—provided by the government to low-income groups.

Institution An ongoing organization that performs certain functions for society.

Instructed Delegate A legislator who is an agent of the voters who elected him or her and who votes according to the views of constituents regardless of personal assessments.

Intelligence Community The government agencies that are involved in gathering information about the capabilities and intentions of foreign governments and that engage in covert activities to further U.S. foreign policy aims.

Interest Group An organized group of individuals sharing common objectives who actively attempt to influence policymakers.

Internationality Having family and/or business interests in two or more nations.

Interstate Compact An agreement between two or more states. Agreements on minor matters are made without congressional consent, but any compact that tends to increase the power of the contracting states relative to other states or relative to the national government generally requires the consent of Congress. Such compacts serve as a means by which states can solve regional problems.

Iron Curtain The term used to describe the division of Europe between the Soviet Union and the West; popularized by Winston Churchill in a speech portraying Europe as being divided by an iron curtain, with the nations of Eastern Europe behind the curtain and increasingly under Soviet control.

Iron Texas Star The Texas version of the iron triangle. A policymaking coalition that includes interest groups; the lieutenant governor and the speaker of the house; standing committees of the legislature; the governor; and administrators, boards, and commissions.

Iron Triangle The three-way alliance among legislators, bureaucrats, and interest groups to make or preserve policies that benefit their respective interests.

Isolationist Foreign Policy Abstaining from an active role in international affairs or alliances, which characterized U.S. foreign policy toward Europe during most of the 1800s.

Issue Advocacy Advertising Advertising paid for by interest groups that supports or opposes a candidate or candidate's position on an issue without mentioning voting or elections.

Issue Network A group of individuals or organizations—which may consist of legislators or legislative staff members, interest group leaders, bureaucrats, the media, scholars, and other experts—that supports a particular policy position on a given issue, such as one on the environment, taxation, or consumer safety.

Item Veto   The power to veto particular sections or items of an appropriations bill while signing the remainder of the bill into law. The governors of most states have this power.

J

Joint Committee   A legislative committee composed of members from both chambers of Congress.

Judicial Activism   A doctrine holding that the Supreme Court should take an active role in using its powers to check the activities of Congress, state legislatures, and administrative agencies when those government bodies exceed their authority.

Judicial Implementation   The way in which court decisions are translated into action.

Judicial Restraint   A doctrine holding that the Supreme Court should defer to the decisions made by the elected representatives of the people in the legislative and executive branches.

Judicial Review   The power of the Supreme Court or any court to declare unconstitutional federal or state laws and other acts of government.

Jurisdiction   The authority of a court to decide certain cases. Not all courts have the authority to decide all cases. Where a case arises and what its subject matter is are two jurisdictional factors.

Justiciable Question   A question that may be raised and reviewed in court.

K

Keynesian Economics   A school of economic thought, named after English economist John Maynard Keynes, that tends to favor active federal government policymaking to stabilize economy-wide fluctuations, usually by implementing discretionary fiscal policy.

Kitchen Cabinet   The informal advisers to the president.

Ku Klux Klan (KKK)   Any of several white supremacist organizations. The first klans were founded during the Reconstruction era following the Civil War.

L

La Réunion   A failed French socialist colony of the 1800s located within the city limits of modern Dallas. Its skilled and educated inhabitants benefited early Dallas.

Labor Movement   Generally, the full range of economic and political expression of working-class interests; politically, the organization of working-class interests.

Latent Interests   Public-policy interests that are not recognized or addressed by a group at a particular time.

Late-Train Contribution   A contribution given to a candidate in the period that begins after an election and ends thirty days before a regular legislative session.

Lawmaking   The process of deciding the legal rules that govern society. Such laws may regulate minor affairs or establish broad national policies.

Legislative Audit Committee   In Texas, a committee that performs audits of state agencies and departments for the legislature.

Legislative Budget Board   The primary budgeting entity for Texas state government.

Legislative Council   In Texas, a body that provides research support, information, and bill-drafting assistance to legislators.

Legislature   A governmental body primarily responsible for the making of laws.

Legitimacy   Popular acceptance of the right and power of a government or other entity to exercise authority.

Libel   A written defamation of a person's character, reputation, business, or property rights. To a limited degree, the First Amendment protects the press from libel actions.

Liberalism   A set of beliefs that includes the advocacy of positive government action to improve the welfare of individuals, support for civil rights, and tolerance for political and social change.

Libertarianism   A political ideology based on skepticism or opposition toward almost all government activities.

Liberty   The greatest freedom of individuals that is consistent with the freedom of other individuals in the society.

Limited Government   A form of government based on the principle that the powers of government should be clearly limited either through a written document or through wide public understanding; characterized by institutional checks to ensure that government serves the public rather than private interests.

Limited Jurisdiction   Exists when a court's authority to hear cases is restricted to certain types of claims, such as tax claims or bankruptcy petitions.

Line Organization   With respect to the federal government, an administrative unit that is directly accountable to the president.

Line-Item Veto   The power of an executive to veto individual lines or items within a piece of legislation without vetoing the entire bill.

Literacy Test   A test administered as a precondition for voting, often used to prevent African Americans from exercising their right to vote.

Litigate   To engage in a legal proceeding or seek relief in a court of law; to carry on a lawsuit.

Lobbyist   An organization or individual that attempts to influence the passage, defeat, or contents of legislation and the administrative decisions of government.

Long Ballot   An election ballot listing many independently elected offices.

Loophole   A legal method by which individuals and businesses are allowed to reduce the tax liabilities owed to the government.

Loose Monetary Policy   Monetary policy that makes credit inexpensive and abundant, possibly leading to inflation.

M

Madisonian Model   A structure of government proposed by James Madison in which the powers of the government are separated into three branches: executive, legislative, and judicial.

Majoritarianism   A political theory holding that in a democracy, the government ought to do what the majority of the people want.

Majority   (1) More than 50 percent; (2) Full age; the age at which a person is entitled by law to the right to manage her or his own affairs and to the full enjoyment of civil rights.

Majority Leader of the House   A legislative position held by an important party member in the House of Representatives. The majority leader is selected by the majority party in caucus or conference to foster cohesion among party members and to act as spokesperson for the majority party in the House.

Majority Opinion   A court opinion reflecting the views of the majority of the judges.

Majority Rule   A basic principle of democracy asserting that the greatest number of citizens in any political unit should select officials and determine policies.

Managed News   Information generated and distributed by the government in such a way as to give government interests priority over candor.

Mandate   A requirement or standard imposed on one level of government by a higher level of government.

Mandatory Retirement   Forced retirement when a person reaches a certain age.

Maquiladora   A factory in the Mexican border region that assembles goods imported duty-free into Mexico for export. In Spanish, it literally means "twin plant."

Mark Up   In legislation, to amend, change, or rewrite bills while they are in committee.

Massachusetts Ballot   See *Office-Block Ballot*.

Material Incentive   A reason or motive having to do with economic benefits or opportunities.

Media   The channels of mass communication.

Media Access   The public's right of access to the media. The Federal Communications Commission and the courts gradually have taken the stance that citizens do have a right to media access.

Medicaid   A joint state-federal program that provides medical care to the poor (including indigent elderly persons in nursing homes). The program is funded out of general government revenues.

Medicare   A federal health-insurance program that covers U.S. residents over the age of sixty-five. The costs are met by a tax on employment.

Merit System   The selection, retention, and promotion of government employees on the basis of competitive examinations.

Message Power   The ability of a governor (or a U.S. president) to focus the attention of the press, legislators, and citizens on legislative proposals that he or she considers important. The visibility of the office gives the chief executive instant public attention.

Mestizo   A person of both Spanish and American Indian lineage.

Metroplex   The greater Dallas–Fort Worth metropolitan area.

Military-Industrial Complex   The mutually beneficial relationship between the armed forces and defense contractors.

Minority Leader of the House   The party leader elected by the minority party in the House.

Misdemeanor   A lesser crime than a felony, punishable by a fine or imprisonment for up to one year.

Missouri Plan   A method of selecting judges that combines appointment and election. Under the plan, the state governor or another official selects judges from nominees chosen by a nonpartisan committee. After a year on the bench, the judges face a popular election to determine whether the public wishes them to remain in office.

Mistrial   A trial judged to be invalid because of fundamental error. When a mistrial is declared, the trial must start again, beginning with the selection of the jury.

Monetary Policy   The use of changes in the amount of money in circulation to alter credit markets, employment, and the rate of inflation.

Monopolistic Model   A model of bureaucracy that compares bureaucracies to monopolistic business firms. Lack of competition within a bureaucracy leads to inefficient and costly operations. Because bureaucracies are not penalized for inefficiency, there is no incentive to reduce costs or use resources more productively.

Monroe Doctrine   A policy statement included in President James Monroe's 1823 annual message to Congress, which set out three principles: (1) European nations should not establish new colonies in the Western Hemisphere, (2) European nations should not intervene in the affairs of independent nations of the Western Hemisphere, and (3) the United States would not interfere in the affairs of European nations.

Moral Idealism A philosophy that sees all nations as willing to cooperate and agree on moral standards for conduct.

Municipal Home Rule The power vested in a local unit of government to draft or change its own charter and to manage its own affairs.

N

Narrowcasting Broadcasting that is targeted to one small sector of the population.

National Committee A standing committee of a national political party established to direct and coordinate party activities during the four-year period between national party conventions.

National Convention The meeting held every four years by each major party to select presidential and vice-presidential candidates, to write a platform, to choose a national committee, and to conduct party business. In theory, the national convention is at the top of a hierarchy of party conventions (the local and state conventions are below it) that consider candidates and issues.

National Health Insurance A plan to provide universal health insurance under which the government provides basic health insurance to all citizens. In most such plans, the program is funded by taxes on wages or salaries.

National Security Council (NSC) A staff agency in the Executive Office of the President established by the National Security Act of 1947. The NSC advises the president on domestic and foreign matters involving national security.

National Security Policy Foreign and domestic policy designed to protect the independence and political and economic integrity of a nation; policy that is concerned with the safety and defense of the nation.

Natural Rights Rights held to be inherent in natural law, not dependent on governments. John Locke stated that natural law, being superior to human law, specifies certain rights of "life, liberty, and property." These rights, altered to become "life, liberty, and the pursuit of happiness," are asserted in the Declaration of Independence.

Necessaries In contract law, necessaries include whatever is reasonably necessary for suitable subsistence as measured by age, state, condition in life, and so on.

Necessary and Proper Clause See *Elastic Clause.*

Negative Campaigning A strategy in political campaigns of attacking the opposing candidate's issue positions or—especially—his or her character.

Negative Constituents Citizens who openly oppose government foreign policies.

Net Public Debt The accumulation of all past federal government deficits; the total amount owed by the federal government to individuals, businesses, and foreigners.

New England Town A governmental unit in the New England states that combines the roles of city and county in one unit.

No-Fault Plan An automobile insurance system mandated by some states (but not Texas) that allows an injured party to collect from the individual's own insurance company, regardless of who was at fault in the accident.

Normal Trade Relations (NTR) Status A status granted through an international treaty by which each member nation must treat other members at least as well as it treats the country that receives its most favorable treatment. This status was formerly known as *most-favored-nation* status.

North American Free Trade Agreement (NAFTA) A treaty between the United States, Mexico, and Canada that calls for the gradual removal of tariffs and other trade restrictions. NAFTA came into effect in 1994.

O

Office of Management and Budget (OMB) A division of the Executive Office of the President created by executive order in 1970 to replace the Bureau of the Budget. The OMB's main functions are to assist the president in preparing the annual budget, to clear and coordinate all departmental agency budgets, to help set fiscal policy, and to supervise the administration of the federal budget.

Office-Block, or Massachusetts, Ballot A form of general election ballot in which candidates for elective office are grouped together under the title of each office. It emphasizes voting for the office and the individual candidate, rather than for the party.

Ogallala Aquifer A major underground source of water for irrigation and human consumption in northern West Texas and the Texas Panhandle, as well as other states.

Ombudsperson An official who hears and investigates complaints by private individuals against public officials or agencies. The original word—*ombudsman*—is Swedish and means "commissioner."

Open Primary A type of primary in which any registered voter can choose among the candidates of either party (but may vote for candidates of only one party).

Open-Meetings Law A law that requires meetings of government decision-making bodies to be open to public scrutiny (with some exceptions).

Open-Records Law A law requiring that records of all government proceedings and decisions be available to the public.

Opinion The statement by a judge or a court of the decision reached in a case tried or argued before it. The opinion sets forth the law that applies to the case and details the legal reasoning on which the ruling was based.

Opinion Leader One who is able to influence the opinions of others because of position, expertise, or personality. Such leaders help to shape public opinion.

Opinion Poll A method of systematically questioning a small, selected sample of respondents who are deemed representative of the total population. Opinion polls are widely used by government, business, university scholars, political candidates, and voluntary groups to provide reasonably accurate data on public attitudes, beliefs, expectations, and behavior.

Oral Arguments The verbal arguments presented in person by attorneys to an appellate court. Each attorney presents reasons to the court why the court should rule in her or his client's favor.

Order A state of peace and security. Maintaining order by protecting members of society from violence and criminal activity is the oldest purpose of government.

Organic Law The superior law that establishes governing institutions and organizes their formal power relationship.

Oversight The responsibility Congress has for following up on laws it has enacted to ensure that they are being enforced and administered in the way Congress intended.

Original Jurisdiction The authority of a court to consider a case in the first instance; the power to try a case, as opposed to appellate jurisdiction, which involves the power to review cases decided by other courts.

P

Pairing In political redistricting, placing two incumbent officeholders from the same party in the same district. (Only one of these officeholders can be reelected.)

Pardon The granting of a release from the punishment or legal consequences of a crime; a pardon can be granted by the president before or after a conviction.

Parole Early release from prison under official supervision.

Participation Paradox The fact that people vote even though their individual votes rarely influence the outcome of an election.

Partisan Election An election between candidates who are nominated by their parties and whose party affiliation is designated on the ballot. In Texas, all state and county officials (including judges) are selected in this manner. Only municipal and some special district elections are nonpartisan in Texas.

Party Identification Linking oneself to a particular political party.

Party Identifier A person who identifies with a political party.

Party Organization The formal structure and leadership of a political party, including election committees; local, state, and national executives; and paid professional staff.

Party Platform A document drawn up by the platform committee at each national convention, outlining the policies, positions, and principles of the party; it is then submitted to the entire convention for approval.

Party-Column, or Indiana, Ballot A form of general election ballot in which candidates for elective office are arranged in columns under their respective party labels and symbols. It emphasizes voting for the party, rather than for the office or individual.

Party-in-Government All of the elected and appointed officials who identify with a political party.

Party-in-the-Electorate Those members of the general public who identify with a political party or who express a preference for one party over another.

Patronage Rewarding faithful party workers and followers with government employment and contracts.

Peer Group A group consisting of members sharing common social characteristics. These groups play an important part in the socialization process, helping to shape attitudes and beliefs.

Pendleton Act (Civil Service Reform Act) The law, as amended over the years, that remains the basic statute regulating federal employment personnel policies. It established the principle of employment on the basis of merit and created the Civil Service Commission to administer the personnel service.

Permanent School Fund In Texas, a fund that provides support to the public school system. Leases, rents, and royalties from designated public school land are deposited into the fund.

Personal Recognizance A defendant's personal promise to appear in court.

Picket-Fence Federalism A model of federalism in which specific programs and policies (depicted as vertical pickets in a picket fence) involve all levels of government—national, state, and local (depicted by the horizontal boards in a picket fence).

Pigeonhole The action by which a legislative committee tables a bill and then ignores it.

Plea Bargaining Negotiations that take place between the prosecution and the defense in a criminal case in which the defendant normally is offered a lighter sentence or other benefits in return for a guilty plea.

Pluralism A theory that views politics as a conflict among interest groups. Political decision making is characterized by bargaining and compromise.

Plurality The total votes cast for a candidate who receives more votes than any other candidate but not necessarily a majority. Most national, state, and local electoral laws provide for winning elections by a plurality vote.

Pocket Veto A special veto power exercised by the chief executive after a legislative body has adjourned. Bills not signed by the chief executive die after a specified period of time. If the legislature wishes to reconsider such a bill, it must be reintroduced in the following session. The governor of Texas does not have a pocket veto.

Point of Order A formal question to the chairperson about the legitimacy of a parliamentary process. A successful point of order can result in the postponement or defeat of legislation.

Police Power The authority to legislate for the protection of the health, morals, safety, and welfare of the people. In the United States, most police power is a reserved power of the states.

Political Action Committee (PAC) A committee set up by and representing a corporation, labor union, or special interest group. PACs raise and give campaign donations on behalf of the organizations or groups they represent. In Texas, they must report their income and expenditures to the Texas Ethics Commission.

Political Consultant A paid professional hired to devise a campaign strategy and manage a campaign. Image building is the crucial task of the political consultant.

Political Culture The collection of beliefs and attitudes toward government and the political process held by a community or nation.

Political Party A group of political activists who organize to win elections, operate the government, and determine public policy.

Political Question An issue that a court believes should be decided by the executive or legislative branch.

Political Realism A philosophy that sees each nation as acting principally in its own interest.

Political Socialization The process through which individuals learn a set of political attitudes and form opinions about social issues. The family and the educational system are two of the most important forces in the political socialization process.

Political Trust The degree to which individuals express trust in the government and political institutions, usually measured through a specific series of survey questions.

Politics The struggle or process to decide which members of society get certain benefits or privileges and which members of society are excluded from benefits or privileges; more specifically, the struggle over power or influence within organizations or informal groups that can grant benefits or privileges.

Poll Tax A special tax that must be paid as a qualification for voting. The Twenty-fourth Amendment to the Constitution outlawed the poll tax in national elections, and in 1966 the Supreme Court declared it unconstitutional in all elections.

Popular Sovereignty The concept that ultimate political authority is based on the will of the people.

Pragmatism The philosophy that ideas should be judged by their practical results rather than on an ideological basis. American political parties are usually pragmatic because they are typically more interested in winning elections than in taking clear stands on issues.

Precedent A court rule bearing on subsequent legal decisions in similar cases. Judges rely on precedents in deciding cases.

Presession Bargaining In Texas and other states, negotiation that lets the governor and legislative leaders reach compromises on particular bills before the beginning of the legislative session. This usually ensures the passage of the bills.

President Pro Tempore The temporary presiding officer of the Senate in the absence of the vice president.

Presidential Primary A statewide primary election of delegates to a political party's national convention to help a party determine its presidential nominee. Such delegates are either pledged to a particular candidate or unpledged.

Presiding Officers In Texas, the chief officers of the state senate and house. They are the lieutenant governor, who presides over the senate, and the speaker of the house.

Press Secretary The individual responsible for representing the White House before the media. The press secretary writes news releases, provides background information, sets up press conferences, and generally handles communication for the White House.

Pressure Group A term for an interest group that expresses its purpose of persuading government officials to follow a course of action desired by the members.

Prior Restraint Restraining an action before it has actually occurred. In relation to the press, prior restraint means censorship.

Privatization The replacement of government services with services provided by private firms.

Probation A sentencing alternative to imprisonment in which the court releases convicted defendants under supervision as long as certain conditions are observed.

Progressive Movement A political movement within both major parties in the early twentieth century. Progressives believed that the power of the government should be used to restrain the growing power of large corporations.

Progressive Tax A tax that rises in percentage terms as incomes rise.

Property Anything that is or may be subject to ownership. As conceived by the political philosopher John Locke, the right to property is a natural right superior to human law (laws made by government).

Property Tax A tax on the value of real estate. This tax is limited to state and local governments and is a particularly important source of revenue for local governments.

Prohibition Outlawing of the production, sale, and consumption of alcoholic beverages.

Public Agenda Issues that commonly are perceived by members of the political community as meriting public attention and governmental action. The media play an important role in setting the public agenda by focusing attention on certain topics.

Public Debt Funds owed by governments.

Public Figures Public officials, movie stars, and generally all persons who become known to the public because of their positions or activities.

Public Interest The best interests of the collective, overall community; the national good, rather than the narrow interests of a self-serving group.

Public Opinion The aggregate of individual attitudes or beliefs shared by some portion of the adult population. There is no one public opinion, because there are many different "publics."

Purposive Incentive A reason or motive having to do with ethical beliefs or ideological principles.

Punitive Damage Award A financial payment that may be awarded to a plaintiff in a civil case to punish the defendant and deter similar conduct in the future.

Pure At-Large System An at-large election system in which all voters elect all the members of the city council and candidates do not run for specific seats.

Q

Quorum The number of members of a legislative chamber or other body that must be present for the body to conduct business.

R

Ranchero Culture The traditions, beliefs, and practices of Creole ranch owners, who defined themselves in contrast to the part-Indian Mestizos.

Ranking Minority Members The senior members of the minority party on a legislative committee.

Ratification Formal approval.

Rational Ignorance Effect When people purposely and rationally decide not to become informed on an issue because they believe that their vote on the issue is not likely to be a deciding one; a lack of incentive to seek the necessary information to cast an intelligent vote.

Realignment A process in which a substantial group of voters switches party allegiance, producing a long-term change in the political landscape.

Reapportionment The allocation of seats in the House of Representatives to each state after each census.

Recall A procedure allowing the people to vote to dismiss an elected official from office before his or her term has expired; in Texas, limited to home-rule cities.

Recession Two or more successive quarters in which the economy shrinks instead of grows.

Redistricting The redrawing of the boundaries of the congressional districts within a state.

Reduction Veto The power of governors in some states (but not Texas) to reduce amounts in an appropriations bill without striking them out altogether.

Referendum An electoral device whereby legislative or constitutional measures are referred by the legislature to the voters for approval or disapproval; in Texas, limited to home-rule cities.

Registration The entry of a person's name onto the list of eligible voters for elections. To register, a person must meet certain legal requirements relating to age, citizenship, and residency.

Regressive Tax A tax that falls in percentage terms as incomes rise.

Regular Session A legislative session scheduled by the constitution. Texas regular sessions are biennial (once every two years) rather than annual as in most states and in Congress.

Remand To send a case back to the court that originally heard it.

Removal Power The power to dismiss government officials. In Texas, the governor can remove an official that he or she appointed only with the consent of two-thirds of the state senate.

Representation The function of members of Congress as elected officials in representing the views of their constituents.

Representative Assembly A legislature composed of individuals who represent the population.

Representative Democracy A form of government in which representatives elected by the people make and enforce laws and policies; may retain the monarchy in a ceremonial role.

Reprieve Postponing the execution of a sentence imposed by a court of law; usually done for humanitarian reasons or to await new evidence.

Republic A form of government in which sovereignty rests with the people, who elect agents to represent them in lawmaking and other decisions.

Republican Party One of the two major American political parties. It emerged in the 1850s as an antislavery party. It consisted of former northern Whigs and antislavery Democrats.

Reverse To annul or make void a court ruling on account of some error or irregularity.

Reverse Discrimination The charge that affirmative action programs requiring preferential treatment or quotas discriminate against those who do not have minority status.

Reverse-Income Effect A tendency for wealthier states or regions to favor the Democrats and for less wealthy states or regions to favor the Republicans. The effect appears paradoxical because it reverses traditional patterns of support.

Revolving Door The interchange of employees between the legislature, government agencies, and related private special interest groups.

Rollback Election In Texas, an election that permits voters to lower a local property tax increase to 8 percent.

Rule of Four A United States Supreme Court procedure according to which four justices must vote to hear a case in order for the case to come before the full Court.

Rules Committee A standing committee of the House of Representatives that provides special rules under which specific bills can be debated, amended, and considered by the House.

Rump Convention A meeting of members from a larger convention who secede and organize their own convention elsewhere.

Runoff Primary A second primary election that pits the two top vote-getters from the first primary against each other. Such an election is held in states like Texas when the winner of the first primary did not receive a majority of the votes.

S

Safe Seat A district that returns the legislator with 55 percent of the vote or more.

Sales Tax A tax collected on the retail price of purchased items.

Sampling Error The difference between sample results and the true result if the entire population had been interviewed.

Secession The separation of a territory from a larger political unit. Specifically, the secession of southern states from the Union in 1860 and 1861.

Second Budget Resolution A resolution passed by Congress in September that sets "binding" limits on taxes and spending for the next fiscal year beginning October 1.

Select Committee A temporary legislative committee established for a limited time period and for a special purpose.

Selectperson A member of the governing group of a town.

Senate Majority Leader The chief spokesperson of the majority party in the Senate, who directs the legislative program and party strategy.

Senate Minority Leader The party officer in the Senate who commands the minority party's opposition to the policies of the majority party and directs the legislative program and strategy of his or her party.

Senatorial Courtesy In regard to federal district court judgeship nominations, a Senate tradition allowing a senator to veto a judicial appointment in his or her state by indicating that the appointment is personally not acceptable. At that point, the Senate may reject the nomination, or the president may withdraw consideration of the nominee.

Seniority System A custom followed in both chambers of Congress specifying that the member of the majority party with the longest term of continuous service will be given preference when a committee chairperson (or a holder of another significant post) is selected.

Separate-but-Equal Doctrine The doctrine holding that segregation in schools and public accommodations does not imply that one race is superior to another, and that separate-but-equal facilities do not violate the equal protection clause.

Separation of Powers The principle of dividing governmental powers among the executive, the legislative, and the judicial branches of government.

Severance Tax A tax on raw materials (such as oil and natural gas) after they have been removed from their natural state.

Sexual Harassment Unwanted physical or verbal conduct or abuse of a sexual nature that interferes with a recipient's job performance, creates a hostile environment, or carries with it an implicit or explicit threat of adverse employment consequences.

Sheriff The chief law enforcement officer of a county—in most states, an elected official. In Texas, the sheriff's budget must be approved by the commissioners court, which limits the sheriff's authority.

Shivercrat A follower of Governor Allan Shivers of Texas (1949–1957). Shivercrats split their votes between conservative Democrats for state office and Republicans for the U.S. presidency.

Short Ballot An election ballot listing only a few independently elected offices.

Single-Member District A district in which the voters elect a single member of a legislative body, who runs for election only in that district.

Single-Payer Plan A plan under which one entity has a monopoly on issuing a particular type of insurance. Typically, the entity is the government, and the insurance is basic health coverage.

Slander The public uttering of a false statement that harms the good reputation of another. The statement must be made to, or within the hearing of, persons other than the defamed party.

Social Contract A voluntary agreement among individuals to secure their rights and welfare by creating a government and abiding by its rules.

Socialism A political ideology based on strong support for economic and social equality. Socialists traditionally envisioned a society in which large privately owned businesses were taken over by the government or by employee cooperatives.

Social Movement A movement that represents the demands of a large segment of the public for political, economic, or social change.

Socioeconomic Status The value assigned to a person due to occupation or income. An upper-class person, for example, has high socioeconomic status.

Soft Money Contributions that are given to parties or party committees to help fund general party activities and that do not come under federal limits on campaign contributions.

Solidary Incentive A reason or motive having to do with the desire to associate with others and to share with others a particular interest or hobby.

Sound Bite A brief, memorable comment that easily can be fit into news broadcasts.

Soviet Bloc The Eastern European countries that installed Communist regimes after World War II and were politically dominated by the Soviet Union.

Speaker of the House The presiding officer in the House of Representatives. The Speaker is always a member of the majority party and is the most powerful and influential member of the House.

Special District A local government that provides services to a jurisdiction that are not provided by general-purpose governments. Examples are municipal utility districts, hospital authorities, and transit authorities.

Special Session A legislative session that is not specifically scheduled by the state constitution or by statute. In Texas, a special session can only be called by the governor, who has complete authority to set the legislative agenda of the session. The legislature may consider nonlegislative subjects (such as impeachment) without the governor's consent.

Spin An interpretation of campaign events or election results that is most favorable to the candidate's campaign strategy.

Spin Doctor A political campaign adviser who tries to convince journalists of the truth of a particular interpretation of events.

Spindletop A major oil discovery in 1901 near Beaumont that began the industrialization of Texas.

Splinter Party A new party formed by a dissident faction within a major political party. Usually, splinter parties have emerged when a particular personality was at odds with the major party.

Spoils System The awarding of government jobs to political supporters and friends; generally associated with President Andrew Jackson.

Spring Review The time every year when the Office of Management and Budget requires federal agencies to review their programs, activities, and goals and submit their requests for funding for the next fiscal year.

Standing Committee A permanent legislative committee that considers bills within a certain subject area.

Stare Decisis To stand on decided cases; the judicial policy of following precedents established by past decisions.

State A group of people occupying a specific area and organized under one government; may be either a nation or a subunit of a nation.

Statute-Like Details Detailed state constitutional provisions characterized by the narrow scope usually found in statutory law.

Statutory Law Law passed by legislatures and eventually compiled in law codes.

State Central Committee The principal organized structure of each political party within each state. This committee is responsible for carrying out policy decisions of the party's state convention.

State of the Union Message An annual message to Congress in which the president proposes a legislative program. The message is addressed not only to Congress but also to the American people and to the world. It offers the opportunity to dramatize policies and objectives and to gain public support.

Statutory Power A power created through laws enacted by Congress.

Straight-Ticket Voting Voting exclusively for the candidates of one party.

Strategic Arms Limitation Treaty (SALT I) A treaty between the United States and the Soviet Union to stabilize the nuclear arms competition between the two countries. SALT I talks began in 1969, and agreements were signed on May 26, 1972.

Strict Construction A judicial philosophy that looks to the "letter of the law" when interpreting the Constitution or a particular statute.

Strong-Mayor System A form of municipal government in which substantial authority (such as authority over appointments and the budget) is lodged in the office of mayor, who is elected in a citywide election.

Subpoena A legal writ requiring a person's appearance in court to give testimony.

Subsidies Grants or special tax exemptions provided by the government to individuals or businesses in the private sector.

Suffrage The right to vote; the franchise.

Sunset Advisory Commission In Texas, a body that periodically evaluates most government agencies and departments. The commission may recommend the restructuring, abolition, or alteration of the jurisdiction of an agency.

Sunset Legislation A law requiring that an existing program be reviewed regularly for its effectiveness and be terminated unless specifically extended as a result of this review.

Superdelegate   A party leader or elected official who is given the right to vote at the party's national convention. Superdelegates are not elected at the state level.

Supplemental Security Income (SSI)   A federal program established to provide assistance to elderly persons and disabled persons.

Supremacy Clause   The constitutional provision that makes the Constitution and federal laws superior to all conflicting state and local laws.

Supremacy Doctrine   A doctrine that asserts the superiority of national law over state or regional laws. This principle is rooted in Article VI of the Constitution, which provides that the Constitution, the laws passed by the national government under its constitutional powers, and all treaties constitute the supreme law of the land.

Suspension of the Rule   Setting aside of the rules of a legislative body so that another set of rules can be used.

Swing Voters   Voters who frequently swing their support from one party to another.

Symbolic Speech   Nonverbal expression of beliefs, which is given substantial protection by the courts.

T

Table   In a legislature or similar body, to cease action on a particular measure. A motion to table is not debatable.

Tagging   In the Texas Senate, a rule that allows a senator to halt a standing committee's consideration of a bill for forty-eight hours.

Tariffs   Taxes on imports.

Tax Abatement   A reduction of or exemption from taxes (usually real estate taxes); typically granted by a local government in exchange for broader economic benefits such as employment for local residents.

Tax Assessor-Collector   In Texas, a county financial officer whose responsibilities include collecting county taxes or fees and registering voters.

Technical Assistance   The practice of sending experts with technical skills in such areas as agriculture, engineering, or business to aid other nations.

Temporary Assistance to Needy Families (TANF)   A state-administered program in which grants from the national government are given to the states, which use the funds to provide assistance to those eligible to receive welfare benefits. The TANF program was created by the Welfare Reform Act of 1996 and replaced the former AFDC program.

Tenant Farmer   A farmer who does not own the land that he or she farms but rents it from a landowner.

Term Limit   A restriction on the number of times a person can be elected to a particular office.

Texas Ethics Commission   A constitutionally authorized body that has the power to investigate ethics violations and to penalize violators of Texas ethics laws.

Texas Register   A publication that contains all official notices of the Texas state government and some notices of regional bodies. It is found in all university libraries and large municipal libraries in Texas.

The Calendar   In the Texas legislature, the schedule that serves as a conduit for legislation between the committees and the primary legislative body.

The Floor   The place where a legislative body debates, amends, votes on, enacts, and defeats proposed legislation; the entire house or senate acting as a whole.

The Lobby   Collectively, the most politically and economically powerful special interest groups in Texas.

The Valley (of the Rio Grande)   An area along the Texas side of the Rio Grande known for its production of citrus fruits.

Third Party   A political party other than the two major political parties (Republican and Democratic). Sometimes, third parties are composed of dissatisfied groups that have split from the major parties. They act as indicators of political trends and as safety valves for dissident groups.

Threat to Veto   An informal power by which a state governor (or the U.S. president) threatens to veto legislation so as to affect the content of the legislation while it is still in the legislature.

Ticket Splitting   Voting for candidates of two or more parties for different offices. For example, a voter splits her ticket if she votes for a Republican presidential candidate and for a Democratic congressional candidate.

Tidelands   An area that extends three leagues (about ten miles) off the Texas coast. The tidelands controversy developed when offshore oil was discovered and the federal government contended that the jurisdiction of Texas extended only three miles out from the coast.

Tight Monetary Policy   Monetary policy that makes credit expensive in an effort to slow the economy.

Tipping   A phenomenon that occurs when a group that is growing in population becomes large enough to change the political balance in a district, state, or country.

Tort Reform   In civil law, a tort is a wrong or injury (other than a breach of contract). Tort reform is an effort to limit liability in tort cases.

Totalitarian Regime   A form of government that controls all aspects of the political and social life of a nation. All power resides with the government. The citizens have no power to choose the leadership or policies of the country.

Town Manager System   A form of city government in which voters elect three selectpersons, who then appoint a professional town manager, who in turn appoints other officials.

Town Meeting   The governing authority of a New England town. Qualified voters may participate in the election of officers and in the passage of legislation.

Township   A rural unit of government based on federal land surveys of the American frontier in the 1780s. Townships have declined significantly in importance.

Tracking Poll   A poll taken for the candidate on a nearly daily basis as election day approaches.

Trial Court   The court in which most cases begin and in which questions of fact are examined.

Truman Doctrine   The policy adopted by President Harry Truman in 1947 to halt Communist expansion in southeastern Europe.

Trustee   In regard to a legislator, one who acts according to her or his conscience and the broad interests of the entire society.

Twelfth Amendment   An amendment to the Constitution adopted in 1804 that specifies the separate election of the president and vice president by the electoral college.

Twenty-fifth Amendment   An amendment to the Constitution adopted in 1967 that establishes procedures for filling vacancies in the two top executive offices and that makes provisions for situations involving presidential disability.

Two-Party System   A political system in which only two parties have a reasonable chance of winning.

U

U.S. Treasury Bond   Evidence of debt issued by the federal government; similar to corporate bonds but issued by the U.S. Treasury.

Umbrella Organization   An organization created by interest groups to promote common goals. A number of interest groups may choose this mechanism to coordinate their efforts to influence government when they share the same policy goals. The umbrella organization may be temporary or permanent.

Unanimous Opinion   A court opinion or determination on which all judges agree.

Unemployment   The inability of those who are in the labor force to find a job; the total number of those in the labor force actively looking for a job, but unable to find one.

Unfunded Mandate   A requirement imposed on a lower level of government by a higher level of government. The requirement is not accompanied by the funds to pay for the resulting expenses.

Unicameral Legislature   A legislature with only one legislative body, as compared with a bicameral (two-house) legislature, such as the U.S. Congress. Nebraska is the only state in the Union with a unicameral legislature.

Unincorporated Area   An area not located within the boundary of a municipality.

Unit Road System   In Texas, a system that concentrates the day-to-day responsibilities of roads in the hands of a professional engineer rather than individual county commissioners. The engineer is ultimately responsible to the commissioners court.

Unit Rule   A rule by which all of a state's electoral votes are cast for the presidential candidate receiving a plurality of the popular vote in that state.

Unitary System   A centralized governmental system in which local or subdivisional governments exercise only those powers given to them by the central government.

Universal Suffrage   The right of all adults to vote for their representatives.

User Fee   A charge paid by an individual who receives a particular government service, such as water provision or garbage collection.

User-Benefit Theory   The principle that the people who benefit from certain types of governmental services should also be the ones to pay the costs for those services.

V

Victimless Crime   A crime in which there does not appear to be a victim; a consensual crime. (Alternatively, the person breaking the law may be considered the primary victim.) Examples often cited include prostitution, gambling, and illegal drug possession.

Veto Message   The president's formal explanation of a veto when legislation is returned to Congress.

Vote-Eligible Population (VEP)   The total number of persons actually eligible to cast a ballot, excluding noncitizens, felons, and other ineligible persons but including citizens who are temporarily abroad (and who may vote absentee).

Voter Turnout   The percentage of citizens taking part in the election process; the number of eligible voters that actually "turn out" on Election Day to cast their ballots.

Voting-Age Population (VAP)   The total number of persons in the United States or a state who are eighteen years of age or older, regardless of citizenship, military status, felony conviction, or mental state.

Voucher   In educational policy, a state grant to the parents of a school-age child that can be used to pay for private school tuition.

W

Weak-Mayor System   A form of municipal government in which an elected mayor and city council, often along with other elected officers, share administrative responsibilities.

Wage and Price Controls   Government-imposed controls on the maximum prices that may be charged for specific goods and services, plus controls on permissible wage increases.

War Powers Resolution   A law passed in 1973 spelling out the conditions under which the president can commit troops without congressional approval.

Washington Community   Individuals regularly involved with politics in Washington, D.C.

Watergate Break-In   The 1972 illegal entry into the Democratic National Committee offices by participants in President Richard Nixon's reelection campaign.

Weberian Model   A model of bureaucracy developed by the German sociologist Max Weber, who viewed bureaucracies as rational, hierarchical organizations in which power flows from the top downward and decisions are based on logical reasoning and data analysis.

Whig Party   A major party in the United States during the first half of the 1800s, formally established in 1836. The Whig Party was dominated by anti-Jackson elements and represented a variety of regional interests. It fell apart as a national party in the early 1850s.

Whip   A member of Congress who aids the majority or minority leader of the House or the Senate.

Whistleblower   An insider who brings to public attention gross governmental inefficiency or an illegal action.

White House Office   The personal office of the president, which tends to presidential political needs and manages the media.

White House Press Corps   A group of reporters assigned full time to cover the presidency.

White Primary   A state primary election that restricts voting to whites only; outlawed by the Supreme Court in 1944.

Winter Garden   An area of South Texas known for its vegetable production.

Writ of *Certiorari*   An order issued by a higher court to a lower court to send up the record of a case for review. It is the principal vehicle for United States Supreme Court review.

Writ of *Habeas Corpus*   An order that requires a jailer to bring a person before a court or judge and explain why the person is being held. *Haebeas corpus* is Latin and literally means "you have the body."

Writ of Information   In criminal law, a formal accusation filed by a prosecutor against a party charged with a crime. It is an alternative to an indictment and does not involve a grand jury.

Y

Yellow Journalism   A term for sensationalistic, irresponsible journalism. Reputedly, the term is an allusion to the cartoon "The Yellow Kid" in the old *New York World*, a newspaper especially noted for its sensationalism.

Index

CHAPTER-OPENING PHOTO CREDITS

CHAPTER 1   AP Photo/Haraz N. Ghanbari

CHAPTER 2   Independence National Historical Park Photo

CHAPTER 3   AP Photo/M. Spencer Green

CHAPTER 4   AP Photo/Dale Sparks

CHAPTER 5   Image by © Raymond Gehman/Corbis

CHAPTER 6   AP Photo/Chad Rachman

CHAPTER 7   AP Photo/Rick Bowmer

CHAPTER 8   AP Photo/Evan Vucci

CHAPTER 9   AP Photo/Ron Edmonds

CHAPTER 10   AP Photo/Paplo Martinez Monsivais

CHAPTER 11   AP Photo/Charles Dhrapak

CHAPTER 12   U.S. Air Force Photo by Airman 1st Class Jason P. Robertson

CHAPTER 13   NASA Photo

CHAPTER 14   U.S. Supreme Court Photo by Jonathan Hutson

CHAPTER 15   U.S. Customs and Border Protection Photo by James Tourtellotte

CHAPTER 16   AP Photo/Ron Edmonds

CHAPTER 17   Department of Defense Photo by Spc. Danielle Howard, U.S. Army

CHAPTER 18   Photo Courtesy of Texas Historic Commission

CHAPTER 19   AP Photo

CHAPTER 20   AP Photo/Kelly West

CHAPTER 21   Image by © Mike Segar/Reuters/Corbis

CHAPTER 22   AP Photo/Paplo Martinez Monsivais

CHAPTER 23   AP Photo/Harry Cabluck/File

CHAPTER 24   AP Photo/Harry Cabluck

CHAPTER 25   AP Photo/Harry Cabluck

CHAPTER 26   AP Photo/Jack Plunkett

CHAPTER 27   Photo Courtesy of Flickr/Seth Gaines

The United States of America

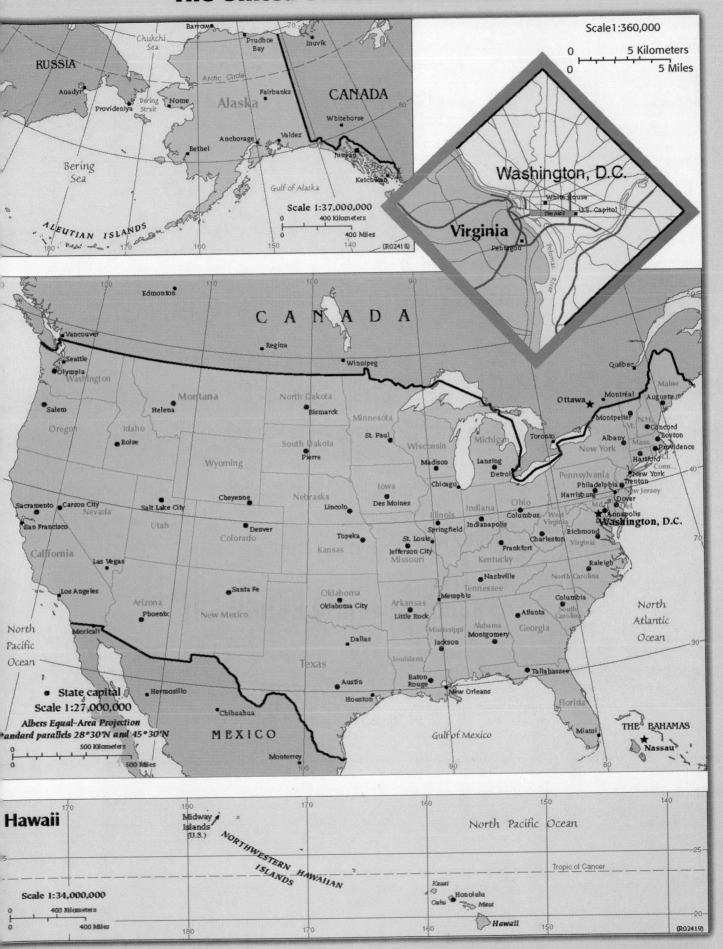

Scale 1:360,000

0 5 Kilometers
0 5 Miles

Washington, D.C.

White House
The Mall
U.S. Capitol

Virginia

Pentagon

Potomac River

RUSSIA

Chukchi Sea

Barrow
Prudhoe Bay
Inuvik

Arctic Circle

Alaska

CANADA

Fairbanks

70
60

Anadyr
Providenlya
Bering Strait
Nome

Whitehorse

Bering Sea

Bethel

Anchorage
Valdez
Juneau

Gulf of Alaska

Ketchikan

ALEUTIAN ISLANDS

Scale 1:37,000,000
0 400 Kilometers
0 400 Miles

(R02418)

180 170 160 150 140

CANADA

Edmonton

120 110 100 90

Vancouver
Seattle
Olympia
Washington

Regina

Winnipeg

Québec

Maine

Ottawa Montréal Augusta

Salem
Oregon

Montana

North Dakota

Minnesota

Toronto

Montpelier
N.H.
Concord Boston
Mass. Providence
R.I.

Helena

Bismarck

St. Paul

Wisconsin

Michigan

Lansing

Detroit

Albany
New York
Hartford
Conn.

Boise
Idaho

South Dakota

Pierre

Madison

Chicago

Pennsylvania
Harrisburg

New York
Trenton
Philadelphia
New Jersey
Dover
Del.

Wyoming

Iowa

Des Moines

Illinois Indiana Ohio

Columbus

40

Sacramento
Carson City
Nevada

Salt Lake City

Cheyenne

Nebraska

Lincoln

Indianapolis

West Virginia

Maryland
Annapolis
Washington, D.C.

San Francisco

Utah

Denver

Colorado

Topeka

St. Louis

Springfield

Charleston

Richmond

Virginia

70

California

Las Vegas

Kansas

Jefferson City
Missouri

Frankfort

Kentucky

Raleigh
North Carolina

Los Angeles

Santa Fe

Nashville
Tennessee

Arizona
Phoenix

New Mexico

Oklahoma
Oklahoma City

Arkansas
Little Rock

Memphis

Columbia
South Carolina

North Atlantic Ocean

Mexicali

Dallas

Mississippi
Alabama
Montgomery
Georgia

Atlanta

North Pacific Ocean

• **State capital**
Scale 1:27,000,000

Albers Equal-Area Projection
standard parallels 28°30'N and 45°30'N

500 Kilometers
500 Miles

Hermosillo

Texas

Austin

Louisiana

Jackson

Baton Rouge
New Orleans

Tallahassee

Florida

Houston

Chihuahua

MEXICO

Monterrey

Gulf of Mexico

Miami

THE BAHAMAS

Nassau

30

100 90 80

Hawaii

170 180 170 160 150 140

Midway Islands (U.S.)

North Pacific Ocean

NORTHWESTERN HAWAIIAN ISLANDS

25

Tropic of Cancer

Scale 1:34,000,000

400 Kilometers
400 Miles

Kauai
Oahu Honolulu
Maui

Hawaii

20

(R02419)

180 170 160 150

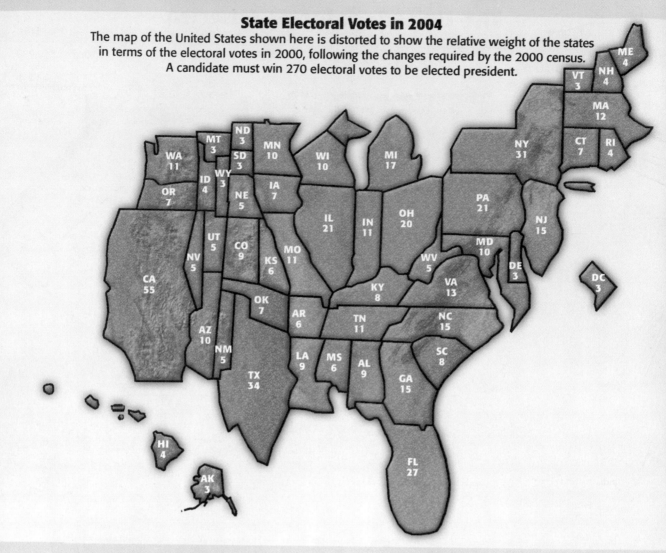

State Electoral Votes in 2004

The map of the United States shown here is distorted to show the relative weight of the states in terms of the electoral votes in 2000, following the changes required by the 2000 census. A candidate must win 270 electoral votes to be elected president.

2004 Presidential Election Results

George W. Bush won 286 electoral votes

John F. Kerry won 252 electoral votes

Six Flags of Texas—A Texas Timeline

Six different flags have flown over Texas during eight changes of sovereignty. The accepted sequence of these flags follows:

SPAIN	FRANCE	MEXICO	REPUBLIC OF TEXAS	CONFEDERATE STATES	UNITED STATES
685; 1690–1821	1685–1690	1821–1836	1836–1845	1861–1865	1845–1861; 1865 to present

PINEDA'S SHIP

1519—Spanish explorer Alonso Alvarez de Pineda, who charted the coast of the Gulf of Mexico, led the first European expedition to Texas.

de CORONADO

1540–1542—In a fruitless search for a "city of gold," Spanish conquistador Francisco Vásquez de Coronado explored New Mexico and visited the Texas Panhandle and Kansas.

MISSIONARIES

1629—Responding to a vision reported by Jumano Indians, Spanish missionaries from New Mexico traveled to an area near modern San Angelo. They returned for six months in 1631 to establish the first (albeit temporary) Spanish mission in Texas.

MISSION

1681–1682—The first permanent Spanish mission in Texas was founded at Ysleta, within the city limits of modern El Paso. Residents consisted of Spanish missionaries and Christian Indians who fled from New Mexico following the Pueblo Revolt by Indians in that region. The first mission, a wood structure, was replaced by an adobe building in 1692. The current church dates to 1851.

FORT ST. LOUIS

April 1689—Alonso de Leon, sent to confront the French, discovered the ruins of Fort St. Louis. De Leon founded a series of missions, but these were soon destroyed by the Indians.

THE ALAMO

1731—Sixteen families from the Canary Islands established the Villa of San Fernando de Bexar, a precursor of modern San Antonio and the first civil jurisdiction in Texas. The villa was adjacent to the mission San Antonio de Valero, founded in 1718. In 1758, the mission completed a church building later known as the Alamo.

IBARVO

1779—Colonists led by Antonio Gil Ibarvo settled an abandoned mission at Nacogdoches, the first town in East Texas.

ADAMS

1826—President John Quincy Adams offered to buy Texas for one million dollars. Mexico rejected the offer.

April 1836—At the Battle of San Jacinto, Texan forces under Sam Houston routed the Mexican army. The battle was decisive and led to the independence of Texas.

HOUSTON

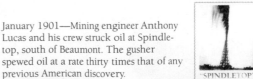
TEXAS CONFEDERATE FLAG

March 1861—By a vote of the Succession Convention, Texas joined the Confederate States of America. Texas governor Sam Houston resigned in protest.

-1520-
-1530-
-1540-
-1550-
-1560-
-1570-
-1580-
-1590-
-1600-
-1610-
-1620-
-1630-
-1640-
-1650-
-1660-
-1670-
-1680-
-1690-
-1700-
-1710-
-1720-
-1730-
-1740-
-1750-
-1760-
-1770-
-1780-
-1790-
-1800-
-1810-
-1820-
-1830-
-1840-
-1850-
-1860-
-1870-
-1880-
-1890-
-1900-

November 1528—Álvar Núñez Cabeza de Vaca of Spain was shipwrecked, probably at Galveston Island. He explored Texas and other parts of the Southwest for six years before returning to Mexico.

de VACA

1542—Hernando de Soto, the first European to document the Mississippi, died on the banks of that river in Arkansas. De Soto had led a disaster-prone expedition across the South from the Carolinas to Texas. His men fled, but it took them a year to return to Mexico through Texas.

de SOTO

April 1598—En route to New Mexico, Juan de Oñate stopped at El Paso, which he named. (Later that year, de Oñate founded the first permanent Spanish settlement in New Mexico.) At El Paso, de Oñate held a thanksgiving ceremony and feast with friendly local Indians and claimed the watershed of the Rio Grande for Spain.

de ONATE

February 1685—The French explorer Rene Robert Cavelier, Sieur de La Salle landed at Matagorda Bay after attempting to locate the mouth of the Mississippi. His colonists built Fort St. Louis, and he claimed the land for France. La Salle was later murdered by one of his men, and in 1688 the settlement was destroyed by Indians.

LA SALLE

1716–1717—In these years, Spain finally succeeded in founding missions in East Texas, thus establishing Spain's claim to the area against the French. Antonio Margil de Jesus, shown here preaching, became the leader of the missions. Unlike de Leon, who had oppressed the Indians, Father Margil was well regarded.

MARGIL

1821—Spain reconfirmed a grant of colonization rights to Stephen F. Austin. (The grant was initially made to Austin's father, who died). Austin's colony was located on the Brazos and Colorado rivers and initially consisted of 297 Anglo families.

STEPHEN F. AUSTIN

March 6, 1836—At the Alamo, fighters for Texan independence were overwhelmed by the Mexican army. Almost all of the defenders died.

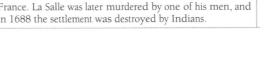
BATTLE OF THE ALAMO

December 1845—The U.S. Congress passed a joint resolution admitting Texas into the Union as the 28th state. President James K. Polk signed the resolution.

POLK

January 1901—Mining engineer Anthony Lucas and his crew struck oil at Spindletop, south of Beaumont. The gusher spewed oil at a rate thirty times that of any previous American discovery.

"SPINDLETOP"

The Governors of Texas

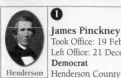
❶ James Pinckney Henderson
Took Office: 19 February 1846
Left Office: 21 December 1847
Democrat
Henderson — Henderson County

❷ George T. Wood
Took Office: 21 December 1847
Left Office: 21 December 1849
Democrat
Wood — Wood County

❸ Peter Hansborough Bell
Took Office: 21 December 1849
Left Office: 23 November 1853
Democrat
Bell — Bell County

❹ J. W. Henderson
Took Office: 23 November 1853
Left Office: 21 December 1853
Democrat
J.W. Henderson

❺ Elisha M. Pease
Took Office: 21 December 1853
Left Office: 21 December 1857
Unionist
Pease

❻ Hardin R. Runnels
Took Office: 21 December 1857
Left Office: 21 December 1859
Democrat
Runnels

❼ Sam Houston
Took Office: 21 December 1859
Left Office: 16 March 1861
Democrat
Houston — Houston County

❽ Edward Clark
Took Office: 16 March 1861
Left Office: 7 November 1861
Democrat
Clark

❾ Francis R. Lubbock
Took Office: 7 November 1861
Left Office: 5 November 1863
Democrat
Lubbock

❿ Pendleton Murrah
Took Office: 5 November 1863
Left Office: June 1865
Democrat
Murrah

❿ Fletcher Stockdale
Took Office: June 1865
Left Office: 19 June 1865
Democrat
Stockdale

⓫ Andrew J. Hamilton
Took Office: 19 June 1865
Left Office: 9 August 1866
Democrat
Hamilton

⓬ James W. Throckmorton
Took Office: 9 August 1866
Left Office: 8 August 1867
Democrat
Throckmorton

⓭ Elisha M. Pease
Took Office: 8 August 1867
Left Office: 30 September 1869
Republican
Pease

⓮ Edmund J. Davis
Took Office: 8 January 1870
Left Office: 15 January 1874
Republican
Davis

⓯ Richard Coke
Took Office: 15 January 1874
Left Office: 1 December 1876
Democrat
Coke — Coke County

⓰ Richard B. Hubbard
Took Office: 1 December 1876
Left Office: 21 January 1879
Democrat
Hubbard

⓱ Oran M. Roberts
Took Office: 21 January 1879
Left Office: 16 January 1883
Democrat
Roberts

⓲ John Ireland
Took Office: 16 January 1883
Left Office: 18 January 1887
Democrat
Ireland

⓳ Lawrence Sullivan Ross
Took Office: 18 January 1887
Left Office: 20 January 1891
Democrat
Ross

⓴ James Stephen Hogg
Took Office: 20 January 1891
Left Office: 15 January 1895
Democrat
Hogg

㉑ Charles A. Culberson
Took Office: 15 January 1895
Left Office: 17 January 1899
Democrat
Culberson

㉒ Joseph D. Sayers
Took Office: 17 January 1899
Left Office: 20 January 1903
Democrat
Sayers

㉓ S.W.T. Lanham
Took Office: 20 January 1903
Left Office: 15 January 1907
Democrat
Lanham

㉔ Thomas Mitchell Campbell
Took Office: 15 January 1907
Left Office: 17 January 1911
Democrat
Campbell

㉕ Oscar Branch Colquitt
Took Office: 17 January 1911
Left Office: 19 January 1915
Democrat
Colquitt

㉖ James E. Ferguson
Took Office: 19 January 1915
Left Office: 25 August 1917
Democrat
Ferguson

㉗ William Pettus Hobby Sr.
Took Office: 25 August 1917
Left Office: 18 January 1921
Democrat
Hobby

㉘ Pat Morris Neff
Took Office: 18 January 1921
Left Office: 20 January 1925
Democrat
Neff

㉙ Miriam A. Ferguson
Took Office: 20 January 1925
Left Office: 17 January 1927
Democrat
M. Ferguson

㉚ Dan Moody
Took Office: 17 January 1927
Left Office: 20 January 1931
Democrat
Moody

㉛ Ross S. Sterling
Took Office: 20 January 1931
Left Office: 17 January 1933
Democrat
Sterling

㉜ Miriam A. Ferguson
Took Office: 17 January 1933
Left Office: 15 January 1935
Democrat
M. Ferguson

㉝ James V. Allred
Took Office: 15 January 1935
Left Office: 17 January 1939
Democrat
Allred

㉞ W. Lee O'Daniel
Took Office: 17 January 1939
Left Office: 4 August 1941
Democrat
O'Daniel

㉟ Coke R. Stevenson
Took Office: 4 August 1941
Left Office: 21 January 1947
Democrat
Stevenson

㊱ Beauford H. Jester
Took Office: 21 January 1947
Left Office: 11 July 1949
Democrat
Jester

㊲ Allan Shivers
Took Office: 11 July 1949
Left Office: 15 January 19
Democrat
Shivers

㊳ Price Daniel
Took Office: 15 January 1
Left Office: 15 January 19
Democrat
Daniel

㊴ John B. Connally Jr.
Took Office: 15 January 1
Left Office: 15 January 19
Democrat
Connally

㊵ Preston Smith
Took Office: 21 January 1
Left Office: 16 January 19
Democrat
Smith

㊶ Dolph Briscoe
Took Office: 16 January 1
Left Office: 16 January 19
Democrat
Briscoe

㊷ William P. Clements
Took Office: 16 January 1
Left Office: 18 January 19
Republican
Clements

㊸ Mark White
Took Office: 18 January 1
Left Office: 20 January 19
Democrat
White

㊹ William P. Clements
Took Office: 20 January 1
Left Office: 15 January 19
Republican
Clements

㊺ Ann Richards
Took Office: 15 January 1
Left Office: 17 January 19
Democrat
Richards

㊻ George W. Bush
Took Office: 17 January 1
Left Office: 21 December
Republican
Bush

㊼ J. Richard Perry
Took Office: 21 Decembe
Presently Serving in Offic
Republican
Perry